Memory Babe

Memory Babe:
A CRITICAL BIOGRAPHY OF
JACK KEROUAC

GERALD NICOSIA

A FRED JORDAN BOOK

GROVE PRESS, INC./NEW YORK

Copyright © 1983 by Gerald Nicosia

First Evergreen Edition 1984

Library of Congress Cataloging in Publication Data

Nicosia, Gerald
  Memory babe.
  "A Fred Jordan book."
  Bibliography: p. 700.
  Includes index.
  1. Kerouac, Jack, 1922–1969.   2. Authors, American—20th century—Biography.
3. Bohemianism—United States—Biography.   I. Title.
PS3521.E735Z79   1983   813'.54   82-24212
ISBN 0-394-62243-X

Manufactured in the United States of America

GROVE PRESS, INC., 196 West Houston Street, New York, N.Y., 10014

To John Jacob and Carl Macki

POETS WITH HEART

THE AUTHOR IS GRATEFUL to the following publishers and literary agents for permission to reprint from previously copyrighted materials:

Corinth Books, for excerpts from THE SCRIPTURE OF THE GOLDEN ETERNITY by Jack Kerouac, copyright © 1960 by Jack Kerouac.

Coward, McCann & Geoghegan, Inc., for excerpts from VANITY OF DULUOZ by Jack Kerouac, copyright © 1968 by Jack Kerouac; and for excerpts from DESOLATION ANGELS by Jack Kerouac, copyright © 1965 by Jack Kerouac.

Elsevier-Dutton Publishing Co., Inc., for excerpts from NOTHING MORE TO DECLARE by John Clellon Holmes, copyright © 1967 by John Clellon Holmes.

Farrar, Straus & Giroux, Inc., for excerpts from VISIONS OF GERARD by Jack Kerouac, copyright © 1963 by Jack Kerouac.

Grove Press, Inc., for excerpts from the following works by Jack Kerouac: THE SUBTERRANEANS, copyright © 1958 by Jack Kerouac; DOCTOR SAX, copyright © 1959 by Jack Kerouac; MEXICO CITY BLUES, copyright © 1959 by Jack Kerouac; LONESOME TRAVELER, copyright © 1960 by Jack Kerouac; SATORI IN PARIS, copyright © 1966 by Jack Kerouac; PIC, copyright © 1971 by the Estate of Jack Kerouac.

Harcourt Brace Jovanovich, Inc., for excerpts from THE TOWN AND THE CITY by Jack Kerouac, copyright © 1950 by Jack Kerouac, renewed 1978 by Stella S. Kerouac.

McGraw-Hill Book Company, for excerpts from VISIONS OF CODY by Jack Kerouac, copyright © 1972 by the Estate of Jack Kerouac.

Penguin Books Ltd., for excerpts from FAUST/PART ONE, translated by Philip Wayne, Penguin Classics, pages 24, 66, and 67, copyright © 1949 by the Estate of Philip Wayne, and for excerpts from FAUST/PART TWO, translated by Philip Wayne, Penguin Classics, pages 171, 219, 258, 270, copyright © 1959 by the Estate of Philip Wayne.

The Sterling Lord Agency, Inc., for excerpts from the following works by Jack Kerouac: MAGGIE CASSIDY, copyright © 1959 by Jack Kerouac; TRISTESSA, copyright © 1960 by Jack Kerouac; BIG SUR, copyright © 1962 by Jack Kerouac; OLD ANGEL MIDNIGHT, copyright © 1959 by Jack Kerouac.

Viking Penguin Inc., for excerpts from ON THE ROAD by Jack Kerouac, copyright © 1957 by Jack Kerouac; and for excerpts from THE DHARMA BUMS by Jack Kerouac, copyright © 1958 by Jack Kerouac.

Grateful acknowledgment is made to the following institutions for permission to use and quote from material in their holdings:

Letters of Neal Cassady, Allen Ginsberg, and Carl Solomon, and Jack Kerouac's "On the Road Journal," on deposit at The Humanities Research Center, The University of Texas at Austin; letters of Carl Solomon and William S. Burroughs on deposit in the Jack Kerouac Papers, Rare Book and Manuscript Library, Columbia University; letters of Gregory Corso, Peter Orlovsky, and Jack Kerouac on deposit in the Allen Ginsberg Papers, Rare Book and Manuscript Library, Columbia University; interview with Jack Kerouac and the original manuscript of The Town and the City, on deposit at the Northport-East Northport Public Library, Northport, New York; letters of Jack Kerouac on deposit at Reed College, Portland, Oregon; letters of Jack Kerouac on deposit at the University of California, Davis; letters of Jack Kerouac to Malcolm Cowley on deposit at Newberry Library, Chicago; letters of Jack Kerouac to Lawrence Ferlinghetti on deposit at University of California, Berkeley.

Contents

Acknowledgments

Prologue: Americans Twice Over   15

B O O K O N E 1 9 2 2 – 1 9 4 6

ONE: The Trademark of a Breton   21

TWO: The Ruins of Pearl Harbor   58

THREE: The Sound of New York   93

FOUR: Wolfeans and Black Priests   131

B O O K T W O 1 9 4 7 – 1 9 5 5

FIVE: Metamorphosis   183

SIX: Slow Boat to China   234

SEVEN: The Sponsors of Waste   286

EIGHT: More Day to Dawn   334

NINE: The Footsteps of the Bard   388

TEN: Double Vision   452

B O O K T H R E E 1 9 5 6 – 1 9 6 9

ELEVEN: Clowns in a Circus of Power   513

TWELVE: "The Obsessive Violence of Rimbaud" and "The Raveled Nerve-Ends of Huysmans"   556

THIRTEEN: The Ghosts of Northport   619

FOURTEEN: Jack's Last Tape   656

Epilogue	698
Books by *Jack Kerouac*	699
Sources and Notes	700
Index	745

Acknowledgments

It is almost a cliché by now for biographers to begin by saying, "This book could not have been written without the help of . . ." In my own case that cliché is doubly true since not only did I receive vital information from the people named below, but also, in many cases, essential financial aid in the form of room and board, transportation, the use of a telephone, and a variety of other services that I could not have afforded on my own.

Above all, I do not wish to rank the importance of various contributions; sometimes a half hour's conversation provided a key to some obscure facet of Kerouac's life that I could not have gathered from days of conversation with anyone else. Yet I feel obligated to mention my special debts to certain people, who cared for my personal as well as professional needs, and who became to me—far above just "sources of information"—all that one could wish of a best friend. Stanley Twardowicz, whom Kerouac called "the most compassionate man I ever met," has been, I say with some pride, a father to me from the first day I set foot in New York. Tony Sampas and Father Armand Morissette guided me through the highly fortified social frontiers of Lowell. The nuns of St. Jean Baptiste cooked me a breakfast one morning the equal of which I have never eaten before or since. Joseph Chaput and Carolyn Cassady have both hosted me for extensive periods. John Montgomery drove me up a couple of mountains in his unsprung truck. Thomas Livornese gave me fare for a cab at three in the morning, rather than letting me risk the New York subway. Gregory Corso spent a long night in North Beach teaching me "what it's all about." Allen Ginsberg trusted me with complete access to his enormous and invaluable archives at Columbia University. While I was laid up with a broken arm in the spring of 1980, Carolyn Cassady transcribed a mountain of tapes; without her monumental labor, this book might still be a-writing. And during the final redaction of the text, I was served nobly by the critical intelligence of my editor, Fred Jordan.

The following people have all contributed to the accuracy and the richness of this text, through interviews and correspondence, letters and documents which they provided, and, in some cases, editorial advice. But, of course, for all inaccuracies I myself must be held solely accountable. My most heartfelt thanks to:

Victor Alberts, Bill Alexander, Donald Allen, David Amram, Cliff Anderson, Alan Ansen, Harold Anton, George J. Apostolos, Ken Arndt, Ed Balchowsky, Amiri Baraka, Barbara (waitress in The Cosmo), Richard Barnetz, Robert Beauchamp, Nadine Beauchamp, Henry Beaulieu, Jr., Julian Beaulieu, Victor-Lévy Beaulieu, Annette Beauregard, Manny Bello, Jacques Beckwith, Lois Sorrells Beckwith, Ted Berrigan, Wilfred Bertrand, Nell Blaine, Jay Blaise, Paul Blake, Jr., Tammy Blake, Albert Blazon, Stanley Bocko, Paul Bourgeois, Ray Bremser, Justin Brierly, Paul Brouillette, Beverly Burford, Robert Burford, Shirley Burke, William S. Burroughs, William Burroughs, Jr., George Butterick, Marie Cantlon, Clayton Carlson, Lucien Carr, Carolyn Cassady, Paul Carroll, Ernest Cate, Anthony Chaput, Joseph Chaput, Armand Charbonneau, Dr. Ann Charters, Hal Chase, Chino (patron of Nicky's), Odysseus "Duke" Chiungos, Robert Christianson, Jim Christy, Andy Clausen, Bernice Lemire Clay, Marshall Clements, George Constantinides, Gregory Corso, Malcolm Cowley, Robert Creeley, James Curtis, James Cudworth, William Dabilis, Jorge Davila, Norman Davis, Brian Dean, John Delamus, Emil Descheneaux, Cornelius Desmond, Dr. Dan DeSole, Elzear Dionne, Peter Dizoglio, Lillian Dodson, Robert Donlin, James Dowling, Fred Drescher, James Droney, Robert Duncan, Paul Dunnigan, Steve Eastham, Rambling Jack Elliot, Helen Elliott, Arthur Louis Eno, Frank Feminella, Lawrence Ferlinghetti, Huck Finneral, Barbara Forst, Miles Forst, Clare Mullen Foye, Raymond Foye, Robert Frank, William Frankel, Armand Gauthier, Al Gelpi, William Georges, Arthur Gervais, Barry Gifford, Thomas Gill, Allen Ginsberg, Victor Gioscia, Albert "Pancho" Gonzales, Stanley Gould, Max Gordon, Leo Grenier, Walter Gutman, Howard Hart, Bobbie Louise Hawkins, LuAnne Henderson, Al Hinkle, Helen Hinkle, John Clellon Holmes, Shirley Holmes, Hugh (former bartender at Nicky's), Armand Houde, Peter Houde, Herbert Huncke, Byron Hunt, Charles Jarvis, Ted Joans, Fred Jordan, Joyce Glassman Johnson, Matsumi Kanemitsu, Bob Kaufman, Eileen Kaufman, Alfred Kazin, Doris Kerouac, Frankie Edith Parker Kerouac, Jan Kerouac, Georgia Kingsland, John Kingsland, William Koumantzelis, Seymour Krim, Joanne Kyger, Philip Lamantia, James Laughlin, Robert Lax, Dr. Timothy Leary, Alene Lee, Lawrence Lee, Henri Lenoir, Chris Lerner, Nathan Lerner, Alfred Leslie, Thomas Livornese, Thea Snyder Lowry, Thomas Machado, John Mahoney, Maurice Mailhaut, David Markson, Michael McClure, Locke McCorkle, Fred McDarrah, Gregory McDonald, Mike McGrady, George McGuane, Robert McLeod, Dennis McNally, Duncan McNaughton, Ray McNulty, Jacky Gibson Mercer, Rita Mercier, Jack Micheline, Robert Miller, George Montgomery, John Montgomery, James Ryan Morris, Fr. Armand Morissette, Howard Moss, Dody James Müller, Dr. Cornelius Murphy, Mary McCarron Murphy, George Murray, Leo Nadeau, George Nelson, Luther Nichols, Manual Nobriga, Phyllis Nobriga, Joseph Nolan, Harold Norse, James O'Dea, Joanne O'Dea, George O'Maera, Peter Orlovsky, Reginald Ouellette, Roger Ouellette, Dr. Thomas Parkinson, Virginia Mayhew Patel, Leo Parla, Jay Pendergast, Pete (the bartender at Gunther's), Pierre (former bartender at The Three Copper Men), Fernanda Pivano, George Poirier, Dianne Randall, Kenneth Rexroth, Albert "Skippy" Roberge, Arthur Roberge, Joan Roberts, Barney Rosset, Adolph Rothman, Beatrice Kerouac Rouleau, Charles Ruiter, Elmer Rynne, Albert Saijo, Roland Salvas, Demosthenes "Sam" Samaras, Anthony Sampas (Jack Kerouac's brother-in-law), Anthony Sampas (Jack Kerouac's nephew), Helen Sampas, John Sampas, Mary Sampas, Nick Sampas, Ed Sanders, Victor Sawyer, Aram Saroyan, Marina Sampas Schell, Peter Schell, Joseph Scianni, William Shotwell, Philip Singer, Lawrence Smith, Gary Snyder, Carl Solomon, Joseph Sorota, Ray St. Louis, Ed Stringham, Joan Stuart, Mary Sweeney, Joseph Sullivan, Jr., James Taylor, John Tatsios, Allan Temko, Bill Tomson, Peter Tsapatsaris, Steve Tsotakos, Stanley Twardowicz, Janine Pommy Vega, Lucia Hacker Vernarelli, Joseph Voyer, Phoebe Ferris Voyer, Peter Vugaropolis, Gerard Wagner, Helen Weaver, Brom Weber, Philip Whalen, Ed White, Ted Wilentz, Victor Wong, Georgia Zamanakas, and Nick Zamanakas.

I also wish to express grateful appreciation to The National Society of Arts and Letters for a grant that subsidized much of this research; and to the following institutions and their personnel for access to various archives of pertinent material, and for permission to use their material in the writing of this biography:

The Northport Public Library; The Rare Book and Manuscript Library, Columbia University; The Humanities Research Center, The University of Texas at Austin; The University of California, Davis; The University of California, Berkeley; Newberry Library, Chicago; Reed College.

Loving thanks to my unflagging patron, my mother, Sylvia Fremer Nicosia, *aka* San.

My deepest debt is to the spirit of Jack Kerouac.
Hallelujah!

G.N.
San Francisco
December, 1980

Milton! thou shouldst be living at this hour:
England hath need of thee
—WILLIAM WORDSWORTH

Whoso would be a man, must be a nonconformist.
—RALPH WALDO EMERSON

PROLOGUE:
Americans Twice Over

By the turn of the century the United States was well on its way to becoming the most powerful nation in the world. It used many other countries but it didn't need any one of them. Immigrants from all over southern and eastern Europe were hustled through Ellis Island to stock the factories of New York and Chicago. Another group poured south across the Canadian border. Among their ancestors had been many of the original explorers of North America. They had once owned almost half the continent; now they didn't own even the province in which they lived: Quebec. They were French-Canadians, derogatorily called "Canucks"; and though they came through no port of entry, they were enlisted just as quickly as other "foreigners" into the mills of New England.

Yet it must have been a wondrous journey from the stony bluffs of the St. Lawrence to the broad, gently rolling meadows of Vermont and New Hampshire, to the lush river valleys of Massachusetts. The splendor of that new land fired a determination in the Canucks that made the miserly New Englanders fear them worse than the emancipated slaves. Indeed they became *les blancs nègres*; epithets such as "white niggers" and "dumb Frenchmen" were used to obscure the real threat posed by these strong, handsome Franco-Americans, heir to as much European culture as the Puritans, and native to American soil for almost as many generations. Not even seventy-two hours a week of underpaid mill work could keep these people in their place. They were so "demented" they often had families of over a dozen kids, so that the ones lost from disease and lint-filled lungs were always more than replaced. To this day the politics of many New England cities has been geared toward blinding this great block of immigrants to its own strength.

In truth, however, the French-Canadians helped keep themselves subservient. They collaborated in maintaining their ghettos by calling them parishes, using the Catholic Church to preserve their language and to educate their children about the evils of a Protestant world. Although clannishness proved their weakness, it was also their strength. Having lived in British Canada as virtual exiles from an alien commerce and government, the French-Canadians had become reconciled to their insignificance in the mainstream of history.

They had turned inward, to the comforts of the home, to the warmth of comradeship, to the glory of their own imagination. Like the Irish under England, they had been "buggered into art."

Not only into art, but into craftiness. Some of them became exceedingly shrewd, learning how to make a nickel from the barest prospect and to make that nickel go further than another's dollar. Others duped themselves with such delusions of grandeur that they became literally mad. In between, in every French-Canadian tenement town, there were more than a normal share of halfwits, oddballs, and maniacs. Whether skilled workers or gossipy cranks, they were people with a dream. The failure to realize it in Canada made them cling to it twice as tightly in the United States, where "life, liberty, and the pursuit of happiness" were the functions of every main street. The promise of the United States to these Americans twice over was no less than the actual rebirth of joy.

BOOK ONE

1922–1946

Jack Kerouac, 1942.

ONE
The Trademark of
a Breton

1.

In his last years Jack Kerouac often argued with skeptics about the necessity of believing in spirit. Once, after failing to convince artist Stanley Twardowicz, Jack said, "I'm going back to Canada" and left Stan's studio. When he got home, a few blocks away in Northport, Long Island, he returned to the long-unfinished novel about his Canadian ancestors. And though he would never finish it—nor even get back to Canada for a few more years—he had proved a point. It was the point he had spent his life proving: that the past is the root of the future, and that a man cannot live without the continuity of both. The novel was to be called *Memory Babe*.

He was a man for whom nothing was secure, not even his name. He had been baptized Jean Louis Kirouac, son of Leo Kéroack and Gabrielle L'Evesque. In the rectory of the poor unfinished St. Louis de France Church in Centralville, the nicest French section of Lowell, Massachusetts, his name meant so little that even a priest could carelessly misspell it. All his life, in fact, people misspelled and often deliberately mispronounced his name. It made him so angry he determined to trace his ancestry with the minute curiosity of a lover—for he had the great virtue of self-love—and fix it on the sensitized plate of art so that it would be remembered forever.

He wrote that he remembered the day of his birth. Five-thirty in the afternoon, March 12, 1922, he knew (as his mother later confirmed) that the melting ice and rocks of the Merrimack River shone with the same red light that entered his beaded and lace-curtained bedroom at 9 Lupine Road, amid a row of single-family "cottages" to which every French-Canadian tenement dweller aspired.

It was among his less extravagant claims. He declared that Kerouac was "the oldest Irish name on earth," that Isolde was a Kerouac kidnapped by the Cornishman Tristan, who killed her fiancé, Morold, to prove his love. He even remembered how on "early mornings in spring when the robins sing in the mist" he had had to strap on gear and headdress "to meet the monsters of Brittany," whither his Cornish ancestors, the Kernuaks, had migrated. According to family legend, in France they became the Lebris de Kerouacs, who fought in the royalist uprising in the *Vendée*. Earlier, his "old close uncles" told him, the Baron François Louis Alexandre Lebris de Kerouac had gone to Quebec to help Montcalm fight Wolfe for the valley of the St. Lawrence. Although the French lost, he was supposedly granted one hundred miles along Rivière du Loup, where he met an Iroquois princess, whom he married, then deserted. Having returned to France the Baron was commanded by his father to act honorably, so he crossed the sea again and took his Iroquois wife north, hunting and trapping. His six or seven sons begat families of their own, called *les tucsons*, "the tough ones," who either headed north to found new Iroquois nations, or south to New England to work in the mills, start little businesses (candy stores and print shops), and eventually even try "being big writers in New York."

Among his father's maternal ancestors Jack found the explorer Bernier; and through his mother's Norman folks, the Lévesques, he claimed relation to Napoleon Bonaparte! To friends he suggested he might be a great great-grandson or grandnephew of Pope Pius VI, who reigned during Napoleon's conquest of Italy, as well as a reincarnation of the English thief Robert Horton, hanged in 1750. Toward the end of his life he was tracing his Cornish ancestors back to Persia, among whose warrior caste lived the Buddha.

Though he would concede much of this lore to be only "generally true," there was a greater truth in the fact—for which his own writing served as documentation—that he remembered everything he heard, as though the mere phenomenality of words were sacred. Moreover, that lore was reinforced by the actual heroics of a family that never ceased to believe in its own worth.

In the nineteenth century the Kirouack family were potato farmers in the small villages outlying the city of Rivière du Loup. One of them, Jean-Baptiste Kirouack, having become a gaffer carpenter, married Clémentine Bernier. Soon after the birth of their son Joseph Alcide Léon Kirouack, on August 5, 1889, the family moved to Nashua—in French pronounced Nashué—New Hampshire.

There Jean-Baptiste built his own balloon-frame wooden house. Blasphemous as Lear, he cursed at thunderstorms swinging his kerosene lantern: "Go ahead, go, if you're more powerful than I am strike me and put out the light!" Greedy women got an even worse lambasting, and the only thing he would soften to was the "whiskey blanc" he made himself with potato peels. That drink, known in Russia as vodka, finally killed him. But his balloon-frame house stood throughout the lifetimes of his seven children.

The family had their share of troubles. One daughter was a cripple, another went mad and threw knives at people, a third, as Jack later claimed, was "enamoured of male companionship." Like the crippled daughter, two of the sons were sterile. Another son, Joe, suffered from severe asthma. But the family was grateful for the good life in the United States, where they no longer had to live on potato-peel soup. For a year Jean-Baptiste's lumber business prospered enough for him to send his son Leo (as Joseph Alcide Léon was called) to a private school in Rhode Island. Probably through the mother's influence, the rest of the sons went to parochial school, and one daughter to a nunnery. But Jean-Baptiste's high spirits and free-thinking ways infected them all.

Leo, who grew into a powerful, stocky young man, was a fine athlete and a gay blade. Darkly handsome, he knew how to strut in his pink suspenders to catch the eyes of strawberry blondes, and how to win their hearts with a barbershop quartet and buttered popcorn, beating off bullies *à la* Frank Merriwell. He had a way with words as well, writing for the French weekly newspaper, *L'Impartial*, where he was also learning the trade of printer.

In the larger city of Lowell, Massachusetts, fourteen miles south, there had been a French newspaper called *L'Etoile*, established in the 1880's. After going bankrupt about 1910, *L'Etoile* was bought out by Louis Biron, owner of *L'Impartial*. By 1912 Leo Kéroack (as he now spelled his name) had become typesetter, reporter, writer, and translator—for *L'Impartial* borrowed articles in English from the morning papers. Leo's many talents suited him ideally for helping *L'Etoile* get back on its feet, so Biron transferred him to Lowell. Like all good bachelors of the day, Leo went to live with family, his sister Mrs. Vaillancourt, on Ennell Street in Centralville.

At *L'Etoile* Leo made friends with a young man called "Scoopy" Dionne, who was impressed with Leo's skill both as a reporter and an advertising solicitor. After work they played baseball on the school grounds, where Scoopy found Leo driven to excel. Perhaps it was homesickness, but in any case Leo returned to Nashua to look for a wife. Black-haired and blue-eyed, Gabrielle Lévesque refused to be led into the dark beyond the street. She was an orphan who had worked since girlhood in a shoeshop. Patiently she waited to find a man who would build his life around her. Although at times deeply rueful, she was no less "the girl that married dear old dad": affectionate, simple, and sensible. Later Leo would tell his children he had married his first *real* girl.

Their marriage took place on October 25, 1915. At twenty-six, Leo had thoughts of making his fortune in California, where two of his friends had already gone. Instead he simply brought his wife back to Lowell, where he had steady work at *L'Etoile*. In 1916 their first child, son Francis Gerard, was born. Soon after that, Leo made use of his business contacts to start selling insurance for Metropolitan Life. Two years later, Gabrielle gave him a daughter, Caroline, called Ti Nin or "Little Nin." In 1922, with exceeding difficulty, she bore her last child, Jean-Louis (named after Leo's father and after both her father, Louis Lévesque, and her mother, Josephine Jean), called Ti

Jean. Not until years later, when he began to encounter non-French people, would Ti Jean become "Jackie" or simply "Jack."

Leo began to see that he had little chance to rise at *L'Etoile*. When Biron put out a special anniversary issue, three times as large as the normal paper, Leo worked night and day canvassing enough ads to fill it. At the end of the week he found the usual $25 in his pay envelope. Angrily accosting Biron, he demanded, "No increase in pay? No bonus? Not even any compliments?" Somber-looking Biron replied, "If you want a compliment instead of money, I'll write you a beautiful compliment, but you won't be able to cash it anywhere."

Always resourceful, Leo decided to make money from his enthusiasm for movies and burlesque. Lowell's dozen theaters needed programs printed weekly, and advertisers were always glad to buy space on such programs. To provide these, Leo opened a small print shop on Market Street, the Spotlight Print. With it he was also able to print a small paper, the *Spotlight,* featuring digests of local theatrical productions—witty critiques that he enjoyed doing, and which many people in Lowell remembered with pleasure years afterward. About the same time, through his friendship with a spastic employee, Charley Connors, an insider at City Hall, Leo began contributing political columns to Connors' own paper, the *Focus.*

As Leo prospered, there were moves in 1925 to 35 Burnaby Street and in 1926 to 34 Beaulieu Street. But large houses in better neighborhoods could not alleviate the gloom caused by Gerard's rheumatic fever, from which he suffered for two years, and his death in 1926 left a deep wound in them all.

Gerard's illness may have started the first fights between Gabrielle and Leo, which grew increasingly bitter toward the end of their married life. A devout Catholic, Gabrielle looked to her religion for solace. To Leo, there was no solace anywhere. It should not be taken that Gabrielle was a slave to the Church. She had once refused to apologize to some nuns for a certain remark; rather than do so, she accepted the penance of kneeling on raw rice. Yet even in her independence she abided by the Church's rules. She not only attended church on all required days, but would go to pray or light candles every day of the week. Leo was not about to serve what he saw as a money-making enterprise. Not only did he refuse to attend Mass; but when Gabrielle asked a priest to come and speak with him, he told the priest to "get lost" right in front of the neighbors. In a French-Canadian neighborhood at that time, such an act was shocking.

Within the community there was dissatisfaction enough with the Church. The priests were calling union organizers "Bolshevists" and advising their mill-working parishioners that man was meant to live by the sweat of his brow, and the more hours they worked, the less time they would have to sin. At home, after the Sunday sermon, many French-Canadian workers were muttering about the priest: "That sonofabitch is not working two hours a week—the hell with him!" Lowell, like the rest of industrial America, was being swept by a new demand for rewards in this world as well as in the next. But to take a stand in public on such issues required great courage.

2.

Courage was the one trait Leo and Gabrielle shared. Friends and relatives marveled at her composure in the face of her oldest son's impending death. She went about household chores and the extra duties of nursing Gerard with boundless energy and cheerfulness, and enough optimism left over to buoy her husband and children too.

Household life revolved around the invalid, who spent most of his pain-racked hours in bed. Although Jackie was a strong, chubby child—whom Leo would fondly call "Ti Pousse" for his fat thumbs— he spent little time playing outdoors and made no friends in the neighborhood. Instead, Jackie attached himself with fierce devotion to his older brother. Because they were so different but always together, neighbors thought of them as "bread and butter." Black-haired and ruddy, Jackie was a little "spitfire" who scared the neighborhood children away. Tall and frail, sandy-haired and pale, Gerard was both gentle and outgoing. Gerard loved to pull his wagon through the neighborhood, and sometimes he ran from sheer exuberance, though the doctor had warned against it. While Gerard won friends, Jackie kept in the background. Eventually Gerard's friends had to come to the house to visit him in bed. Then Jackie would get very angry and complain to their mother that Gerard was being taken away from him. Siding with Jackie, Gabrielle usually asked the other children to leave, telling them, "Gerard belongs to Jackie."

Gerard was an extraordinary child. His drawings amazed everyone. He had doubtless been taught to draw by Leo, who created his own artwork for the advertisements he printed. In addition, Gerard had a great love for animals. In the back yard he kept a pet rabbit; on the porch roof just below his bedroom window, he sprinkled crumbs for the birds; he even took a hurt mouse from a trap and nursed it back to health. When their cat ate the mouse, he gently lectured the cat on the immorality of eating one's neighbors!

As he approached death, Gerard grew increasingly tranquil. He would feed hungry neighbor children, and explain the importance of kindness to four-year-old Jackie as if Jackie were his mental equal. In the eyes of both his mother and the nuns who taught him, Gerard was progressing into martyred sainthood.

Among the French-Canadians there was a tradition of child saints. At that time the most famous was Marie-Rose Ferron, the "stigmatised woman of Woonsocket." Born in Quebec in 1902, from the age of three she had a special devotion for St. Anthony of Padua. The Child Jesus also appeared to her with a cross, showed her his wounds, and left their marks on her invalid body. In 1925 she went to Providence, Rhode Island, to take upon herself the punishment for a group of excommunicated French Catholics known as the Sentinel-ists, people who had fought to keep control of the upper-grade parochial schools, which had been wrested from them by the Anglo-Saxon bishop of Providence. Marie-Rose offered her power of speech, eyes, mind, and "all that I hold dear" if it would be of use to God in converting the apostates, and most of them did return to the Church. But most significantly for Gerard, she had stated that "death is only a passage that leads to life," an insight she had had as her family made the passage from Quebec to the United States. Gerard may have heard the story from his mother; certainly the teachings Jack later attributed to Gerard have a similar ring. If Gabrielle repeated the story to Jack as he got older, Marie-Rose and Gerard may have tended to blur together in his mind.

Even before he could talk, Ti Jean was forced to take instruction from his brother. More damaging still to Ti Jean's self-confidence must have been his mother's continual references to Gerard's superiority. And the burden of a saint in the family is augmented by the saint's departure. Gerard taught Ti Jean saintliness almost like Jesus handing over the keys of the Kingdom to his chosen disciple. On Sunday afternoons he would lead Ti Jean by the hand around the Stations of the Cross outside the Franco-American Orphanage on Pawtucket Street, explaining their significance. Just across the way stood the somber brick Archambault Funeral Home, where Gerard would soon be laid out. If in life Gerard was Jackie's best friend, in death he would become Jackie's sternest critic, for his goodness would be remembered as an inhuman absolute.

Even before Gerard was gone, Jackie was hallucinating "visions"; and almost all had to do with the next world, or at any rate with a better world than this. In his novel *Visions of Gerard*, Jack recalled a sort of fairy-tale scene, in which he was being wheeled out of a shoe shop in the rain as a little old man walked off toward some "Pure Land." Although that term is Buddhistic and must have been acquired many years after the event, the experience was probably real. He was to cherish a vision of his mother's brown bathrobe enfolding him, floating him off the ground and warming him back to life as a gray sawdust-smelling mist forced its way into the house. Their house on Beaulieu Street was built over an ancient cemetery; when the house rattled and plaster cracked and dolls fell from the shelf, Gerard would claim it was the work of the ghosts. On Farmland

Road, above their house on Lupine, was an old stone mansion that he called a castle; after Gerard's death, across from their second-floor flat on Hildreth and Lilley, there was another deserted old house that he was sure was haunted, and one may imagine who was now among the ghosts. Soon after Gerard died, Jackie began having visions of swarms of white dots, the kind Gerard had seen with eyes clenched in pain, which obliterated his vision of the "real world." In the church at Gerard's funeral, overwhelmed by "choirs of children song," Jackie had a "swarm vision" combined with the "Pure Land" vision that served as a kind of climax to his childhood.[1]

At age four Jack was thrust into his brother's role as spiritual center of the family. Even that early he must have sensed his awful specialness. His parents began to worry over his health. When his father would come home from work and find Jackie sitting by himself on the porch, the little boy's gloominess would make him want to cry. His mother tried taking him to New York, to Coney Island and the Roxy, but years later Jack only remembered feeling buried in the subway's "black air of the night." Although she constantly encouraged him to be active, even hanging the rhyme "Jack be Nimble, Jack be Quick!" on his bedroom wall, her attention embarrassed him. For the rest of his life he was troubled by the fact that she had bathed him until he was already capable of an erection.

When Jack first heard of Gerard's death, thinking it some special good news, he gleefully ran to tell his father, who gently reprimanded him. That may well have been the beginning of Jack's guilt over Gerard's death, a guilt which grew all his life. At the St. Louis de France Parochial School in Centralville, the black-garbed nuns, who had filed reverently past Gerard's bier, disciplined Jack with beatings he never forgot. The love and respect he had for such religious teachers made the hurt all the more puzzling.

The mystery of real people was nothing compared to the other mysteries with which the Church confronted him. In the auditorium of the school he saw a movie in which the statue of Ste. Thérèse turned its head. The small basement church was full of dark niches, and when the nuns told him of a ball of lightning that had hovered inside their room during a thunderstorm, Jack reports in *Doctor Sax* that he not only believed them but "understood mysticism at once." The world was full of powerful forces that were no less deadly for being invisible. Human life, as Jack watched it, must have seemed beset with painful and sometimes deadly surprises.

To begin with, there was much illness in the Kerouac family. Debilitated from asthma, Uncle Joe was forced to give up his grocery store; Leo had begun to suffer from rheumatism while Gerard was dying, and later was badly disabled with asthma too; Ti Nin had appendicitis. Even when they were all well, however, Jack must have been distraught over the fierce quarrels between his parents.

Leo had grown stout—at five foot seven he now weighed about two hundred forty pounds—and hotheaded as well. He chain-smoked Old Golds all day, and after work he went for a "little nip," which he defined as "a pint or so of good Schenley's or better some nice Canadian Club." From the tragedy at home he sought refuge in boisterous companionship. Through his contacts with theater managers he got to know many famous vaudevillians, including W. C. Fields. He managed a baseball team at the C.M.A.C., a Catholic sportsmen's organization. Puffing on a cigar he would swagger down the street in his bowler, looking for people just to talk to (though he might try to sell an insurance policy as well). And he began seeking out poker games, where the hope of a big win could make him forget all the bigger losses. When he consistently lost at poker, he turned to the race track, and began to lose even larger stakes.

Toward the end of Leo's life, Gabrielle told him that she was grateful he had always paid the rent and kept food on the table. But in the late twenties and early thirties there were plenty of fireworks in the Kerouac household: Leo exploding at his own stupidity, and Gabrielle at the wanton destruction of her family's security. Leo had one of the most active printing businesses in Lowell, yet he brought home barely enough money to pay their bills. In addition to printing for the theaters, he did job printing for the mills and shoeshops, and he even had a contract from one of the largest advertising agencies in Boston, Dowd & Ostreicher. His friends tried to discourage him from throwing away most of his earnings on horses, but he was not a man who could be talked out of anything.

For a while that indomitable will made him seem infinitely strong to his children, like a grownup Gerard. Morever, his fiery temper was balanced by a lovable warmth. Silly things his children said could break his heart, and big things like the country "going to the dogs" would make him lose his temper; but much of the time he just lived from moment to moment with the wondering, winking glee of a child. In the happy times, Gabrielle would share in his mirth. They would tell jokes together, or sing together while she played the piano. Their house was known throughout the neighborhood for its frequent, noisy card games and parties. The Kerouacs helped organize a social set of seven couples, "The Jolly Fourteen," that gathered from house to house in Centralville.

At the height of Leo's prosperity he bought a new Buick, but for a long time he couldn't learn how to drive it—so he hired one of his workers at the printing plant, Armand Gauthier, as his chauffeur. Every Sunday they would go for a drive in the country, and once the whole family even went up to Montreal. Yet the shadow of Leo's weakness was beginning to darken their gaiety—like the reminder that, even in taking his family for a ride, he couldn't manage on his own. All the more reason for Jack to want to live independent of everyone, and the only place he could do that was in the world of his imagination.

When his parents fought, Jack went out to the back yard and watched through steamy windows as the neighbor families ate dinner, thinking they were ghosts eating ghost food and he was a ghost too; then he looked up at the darkening sky full of stars and wondered where the universe ended. That habit of looking to the sky for solace, when all on earth failed him, persisted throughout his life. Gerard had failed him by leaving when Jack needed him most, and now Jack must be Gerard. In a similar way his mother made Jack feel he must be what his father ought to—and *could*—have been. Although Jack's sister was his regular playmate for a few years after Gerard died, he gradually came to live much like an only child. During the day he would play whole baseball games or run horse races simply with marbles, recording their results in his own newspapers; or he would act out his own "movies" to Victrola music and then write and illustrate them in notebooks. Leo printed some of these cartoon stories in his printshop. At age eleven one of Jack's stories became so long he called it a novel. In fantasy Jack was champion at the very same tasks his father had botched in the real world.[2]

But for every thrill, fantasy exacts a price in terror. In the dark, without the actual presence of his parents to comfort him, the real world came near to crumbling away. He saw his own plaster statue of Ste. Thérèse turn its head. Jesus or the Virgin Mary shook his bed; and in between times, "French or Catholic or Family Ghosts . . . swarmed in corners and open closet doors." His mother's black-lacquered cross with a Jesus figurine that glowed in the dark tormented him like a vampire that awoke at night. If his bedroom door stood slightly ajar, or worse, if a black coat was hung on it, he would envision a bogeyman watching him and start to cry. The night alone could terrify him with its black suggestion of death and mourning.

At the back of all these fears was a nightmare he had throughout his life: the night of Gerard's death, he and his sister in an upstairs bedroom listening to all the "weeping, yelling, and arguing" of the relatives who had come to their house for the wake; the terror and anger at senseless waste caused by their cousins setting off all their Fourth of July firecrackers outside—like an orgy of cruelty, the uncovering, beneath civilized decorum, of the fact of mortality. With the certain knowledge that they would all die, despite the ragings and groanings of a clan united against the dark night, came the constant fear that either or both of his parents would die. Because of it he refused for years to sleep by himself, insisted on crawling in between his mother and Nin.

Not until he was almost ten and his family had moved from Centralville—with funerals all around, always a wreath on some door—to the livelier if poorer neighborhood of Pawtucketville, did Jack begin to control his terror.

3.

But there were good times even in Centralville. Since their father printed programs for the Royal Theatre, Jack and Nin got free passes. From 1927 on, they went to see as many movies as they pleased. And though the movies themselves added to Jack's store of romantic fantasies, the act of going to the theater—mixing with the crowd in the balcony and evading the old usher with a hook instead of a hand—gave him confidence in dealing with the outside world. Another contact with that world was the boxing gym his father opened around 1930. Armand Gauthier, Leo's Sunday chauffeur, had proved his great strength by accidentally wrenching the arm off one of Leo's printing presses, a feat that earned him the nickname "Grosbras." For a while Leo had great fun placing bets on Armand as an arm-wrestler. Since Armand looked so mild-mannered, people would gladly bet against him. Invariably Armand would slam down his opponent's arm, and Leo would rake in the money. Eventually Leo got the idea to manage Armand as a professional wrestler.

At the gym to watch him practice, Jack found his first hero: an incredibly strong man who was yet soft-spoken and immensely kind. When Armand came over for dinner, Jack and Nin would both hang from his flexed biceps; later, when his father began to promote wrestling matches, Jack got to follow Armand and Leo around New England, even up to Montreal. Armand was equally engaging for his mortal passions, like avenging himself on wrestlers who spat in his face, and flirting with Jack's female cousins. He was Jack's first guide into areas beyond the ken of Gerard. Soon Jack began his own arm-wrestling career as "the Masked Marvel."

Behind the little hill with the Cross, at the end of the Stations of the Cross, Jack found the parochial-school boys playing with their "dingdongs." [3] He tried playing with his own, and when the priest found out he made Jack say a whole rosary plus ten *Notre Pères* and ten *Salut Maries* as penance. Another time, when Jack told him he had been peeking at another boy's penis at the urinals, the priest gave an equally harsh penance—after first asking, "How big was it?" Of these early ties between religion and sex, Jack would write, "The Church carried me from one Savior to another"—meaning, probably, that sin made him conscious of his responsibility to other people, of his really belonging to society.

Often Jack's cousin Beatrice Rouleau, who wanted to be a professional pianist, would come to the house and play for Gabrielle. Jack would listen raptly, but when Gabrielle suggested he take lessons he refused because it would be too "sissy." Beatrice found Jack a "different" sort of child, obviously an introvert, who at age nine was already spending many hours reading. But behind his quiet presence she glimpsed real brilliance.

The curriculum at St. Louis school was demanding. In the morning, after the morning prayer in English, Jack studied English grammar, spelling, geography, American history, and arithmetic. In the afternoon all the classes were in French: French spelling and grammar, Canadian history, catechism, and holy history, which included both Biblical stories and the history of the Church. Like Beatrice, his fourth-grade teacher found him exceptional. In geography and history he paid especially close attention to her. At first she thought he was Polish because *Kerouac* was different from other French names. Then one Saturday she heard her name mentioned on the radio, and later discovered Jack had been on a children's quiz program. Afterward they spent more time together, though he was still extremely shy. His gentleness impressed her too.

As Jack began to shine, Leo sank further into self-abasement. In 1931 he went to see his old friend Scoopy Dionne. For several years Scoopy had done well in business, and though he had lost a great deal in the stock market crash of 1929, he still owned the largest meat market in Centralville. Leo explained that his printing business would improve if he could move to larger and more convenient quarters. He asked Scoopy for $3,000 to move his shop from Market Street to the Industrial Complex at 95 Bridge Street, next to the old Massachusetts Textile Mills. Scoopy had no reservations about making him the loan. Not only did Leo have plenty of equipment—a duplex printing press, a linotype, and a Hoffman job printing press—but he had also proved to Scoopy that he was expert at every aspect of printing. Moreover, to this day Scoopy says Leo "could write better than his son."

But the new print shop did not help Leo's financial situation. The next year, 1932, the family moved to Pawtucketville, which was a step down socially, although Pawtucketville was still a nicer area than the real tenement neighborhood of "Little Canada," with its multiple-family block buildings packed into the loop of land just across the Merrimack River.

In Pawtucketville began the "beautiful childhood" Jack later wrote about. In the fifth grade at St. Joseph's Parochial School, Jack was soon one of the top scholars. Only two boys had a higher grade-point average. One of them was Arthur Louis Eno, son of a local judge, who looked so much like Gerard that Jack, as he later recalled, immediately "fell in love." Jack would pray at his brother's picture or at the crucifix in church for Arthur to love him in return, or simply to give him his hand and say, "Ti Jean, you're nice!" Jack even wrote him love poems. As a result, Arthur's father sometimes drove them out to his farm, where they played cowboys and Indians on the compost heap. Unfortunately, the next year, St. Joseph's School notified the Kerouacs that they lived outside the official zone, and that Jack would have to matriculate at Bartlett Junior High School. Angrily Jack's father claimed that it was Judge Eno who had ousted Jack because Jack was challenging Arthur for top scholastic honors. In any case, Jack had learned so well under the Marist Brothers that he was jumped immediately to the seventh grade in public school.

For the first time in his life Jack had to learn every subject in English, which had scarcely been used at St. Joseph's School. At eighteen Jack would still be speaking "halting" English, and now at age eleven he had so much trouble with this second language that some of his teachers thought him slow-witted. But his friends knew better. During classes Jack would draw sketches of his various classmates, often adding written sketches underneath, and pass them to friends like his football buddy Demosthenes "Sam" Samaras for amusement. On the way home from school he often carried a spiral notebook, describing the people and places he passed, which he would also show to his friends.

Jack's homeroom and English teacher, Miss Dinneen, grew fond of him for his extreme neatness and politeness. But the person who most keenly recognized Jack's intelligence was the Bartlett School librarian, Miss Mansfield. She had organized a "Scribblers' Club," which met after school, and one day Jack's new Greek friend, Sebastian Sampas, brought him along. When Jack first showed her a story, "The Cop on the Beat," it was so good she doubted he had actually written it. After he convinced her that the story was his own, she read it to the group, and to her classes, as a brilliant example of descriptive writing. For years afterward she was one of his strongest champions in Lowell, positive he had real talent for a literary career. Because he was enrolled in the commercial course rather than the college course, he could not take Miss Mansfield's English class. Nevertheless, Miss Dinneen's methods—encouraging the students to use "vivid words," and making them "see, hear, smell, taste, and feel what they described"—kept Jack's writing on the right track. Miss Dinneen found his themes so brilliant that she often talked about them with Miss Mansfield. Years later she remarked of Jack: "He probably should have been the teacher, and I the willing pupil."

There was certainly enough drama around him to serve as material. At home he would hear of his father's latest adventures at the race track, for the old man was always trying out new betting systems. At the print shop Jack listened to the boisterous conversations of the workers, and watched his father's actual heroics, like punching a client who had cheated him or throwing out a Greek patriarch who haggled too long over price. Already a speed typist, Jack would sit at the machine on his father's desk and type for hours. Many more hours were spent on long walks with his mother and aunt, listening to their gossip and his mother's long stories about Montreal and New Hampshire. Indeed the Kerouac family was beginning to lead the sort of exciting life that produced fresh stories every day. One time Leo won a racehorse in a claiming race at Rockingham, then lost it a few weeks later. Another time the mayor of Lawrence gave the Kerouacs a horse, and Jack and all the neighborhood kids took turns riding it, till it ran away.

Jack was finding a great deal of intellectual excitement these days too, since he now had access to a fine library. At Bartlett he had become close friends with a very bright boy a little younger than himself. John MacDonald had amassed and catalogued books ranging from the Greek philosophers through Shakespeare to the novels of James Joyce and D. H. Lawrence. He and Jack spent time at each other's houses and took long walks together.

Despite this spectrum of opportunities and Jack's zest to explore them, he was far from secure. The sight of a man with a watermelon suffering a heart attack on the Moody Street Bridge, along with the cry of an axe-wielding neighbor having a seizure the same night, sent Jack trembling back into his mother's bed. One summer his parents went to Canada, leaving Jack at the house of a friend, Leo Nadeau, for a couple of months. Though Jack entertained the family with tricks and jokes during the day, almost every night he cried himself to sleep, telling Leo how much he wanted to be back with his parents, how much he loved both of them.

For many hours Jack would work alone at his cartoons, and the neighbor children were amazed both at the skill with which he drew characters and the new technique he had developed: if you flipped the pages of his comic book, the characters seemed to move as if they were alive. Jack's imagination was fired by two of the Houde Brothers, Mike and Pete, who had gotten so excited by comics like *The Shadow* and *The Green Hornet* that they roved the neighborhood at night with capes, hiding in trees and scaring pedestrians, sometimes by blowing fire from their mouths. To the terrorized inhabitants they were known as the "moon men," and for a while Jack joined them as a "moon man" himself. He even became adept at squirting out a mouthful of kerosene and then quickly igniting it. Soon he began to practice scaring people on his own. Wearing a gunny sack for a cape, and his father's old slouch hat, Jack would burst out of the dark or from behind trees with a sinister *Mwee! hee! hee! ha! ha!* Starting with the Shadow character, he improvised a range of personalities—though it is hard to say just when he gave them definite names: "Count Condu" for the vampire, "Dr. Sax" for the rather clownish, vaudevillian detective, etc. In the shack behind the Houdes' house he would sometimes perform these routines for hours, successfully entertaining kids who were themselves clever actors.

When Jack moved to Pawtucketville he already had one friend: Michel Fournier, son of one of the couples in The Jolly Fourteen. Mrs. Fournier had worked with his mother at the St. Louis Paroisse bazaars. Jack and Mike would take turns sleeping over at each other's homes, and in bed there was some sex-play too. Unlike Jack, Mike did not know about "mystery" and so was not afraid of the dark. Neither were the new friends Jack was making all over Pawtucketville. They were too involved in endless competitive sports.

Watching baseball at the nearby field of the Textile Institute, Jack was awed by the self-assurance of a young man who pitched with graceful control. Joseph Henry "Scotty" Beaulieu looked older than Jack but was about the same age, and they soon became buddies. The coincidence of his surname with the name of the street where Jack had lived in fear seemed a sign that his life would not be all black. Through Scotty Jack met Freddy Bertrand, a handsome, free-spoken, girl-crazy kid, who had been an orphan for years until his father returned to reunite the family. Roland "Salvey" Salvas, a lanky comedian and "spitting champion," and George J. Apostolos, a "tragic" Greek (at least as Jack saw him) with a widowed mother, completed their gang. Although Jack thought of them, especially "G.J." and Freddy, as opposite types, they all participated in the struggles and celebrations of a working-class neighborhood. When he was with them, life was action—whipping through double plays, breaking their old track records, smoking two cigarettes at a time, masturbating in marathon sessions with Omar, the local halfwit—and he "didn't give a shit about no Doctor Sax."

Jack had another friend who was never part of the group, a boy of English ancestry named Billy Chandler. Billy was a lonely dreamer and a talented cartoonist himself, who encouraged Jack to draw by saying that a cartoonist could "sit around the green jungles of Guatemala" rather than spending his life doing dirty work in the noisy mills of Lowell. When they passed through those mill-yards Jack thought with horror of his mother now toiling in a mill. The "possible difference" that Billy's encouragement offered was very exciting; it was the chance to control one's own life rather than being dominated by circumstances, a difference art could provide.

4.

The Shadow magazine had now become more important to Jack than even to the Houde Brothers. From the brown gloom of DesJardins's candy store—where the old man was reputed to seduce little children in the back room—Jack would carry the magazine to his upstairs bedroom. Alone in bed with candy and cat, he would follow the adventures of that avenger of evil as intently as if they were sequels to the life of Gerard. Gerard too had been a cartoonist, in fact had been Jack's first drawing instructor. When Jack began to draw his own Shadow comic strip, he was following Gerard in a new way. It was a way better suited to his nature than a fanatic asceticism. Now he could live bodily in the world while expressing his spirit in the fight for good, the correcting of the world's miseries. The nighttime shadows that for years had terrorized him could now be transformed into the very symbol of justice.

At first the Lamont Cranston character blended with Jack's other fantasy figures, such as Count Condu and Doctor Sax. But gradually Sax emerged as his true hero, a silent figure who hovered in the background of war games on the nearby sandbank and kept watch on the follies and secret vices of the gang. Whereas Lamont Cranston wielded a .45 and made short work of mowing down his gangland enemies, Sax evolved—perhaps through association with harmless neighborhood pranksters like the Houdes—into a nonviolent student of evil, rather than its mortal enemy. Sax became Jack's "personal angel, private shadow, secret lover," [4] and he learned to manipulate him to suit his needs.

In Pawtucketville Jack was trying for a new life, and to begin with he wanted to become a great athlete as well as just an ordinary guy. But the tragedy that dogged his family dogged him too: his first acquaintance there, Ninip Houde, was dragged under the wheels of a milk wagon; his foot got infected, and he died. Not only did the accident leave Jack with a lifelong horror of wheels, it added another ghost to the pack already on his heels, and G.J. didn't help by telling him that Ninip's ghost was haunting the little park across from his house on Phebe Avenue. To fight his urge to cry, Jack identified with Sax, "a mad fool of power" whose knowledge of death amounted almost to a challenge, and who feared nothing let alone mere darkness. The impersonation was complete when Jack, wearing his sister's cloak, began prowling the neighborhood at night as the "Silver Tin Can." Tossing a tin can through someone's open window, he would laugh like the Shadow; or else he would quietly steal things just as an experiment—bathing trunks, a vaulting pole, a wagon—storing them all in his cellar with the intent to return them eventually. One day he even speculated with terrified Billy, who had been one of his victims, as to who the "Silver Tin Can" might be! The point was that he was now the master of crime. Understanding the simple frauds behind most "evil," he had less reason to fear it.

Jack soon learned the cost of dabbling in crime. Since G.J. was the only Greek in the area, Jack's mother angrily accused *him* of being the "Silver Tin Can." Shifting guiltily from foot to foot, Jack was too frightened of her to confess. But afterward his sister reported the missing cape; and when Mrs. Chandler pointed the finger at him, Jack finally admitted his misdeeds. Gabrielle ordered him to stop reading "them damned thrilling magazines." Although he certainly didn't stop, he carried his investigations into areas that would bring pride, not shame, to his family.

There were many other problems at home. Though a working woman, Gabrielle still kept her house clean and prettily decorated, cooked huge meals, and tried to make life cheerful. Always she pretended to believe that things would get better. Whereas Leo accepted the imminence of Gerard's death, Gabrielle had spoken of his recovery until the very end; and then, for one of the few times in her life, had become hysterical. During those last months, perhaps due to the strain of suppressing her fear, most of her teeth had fallen out. But now even her amazing self-reliance could not hide the deterioration of their situation. Leo was groping for new ways of making money to replace what he spent at the race track, but every new scheme seemed just to involve more loss. All his life Jack kept grim memories of those repeated failures, like a rainy trip to the race track in Providence, Rhode Island, around Thanksgiving, 1934 (described in *Dr. Sax*), where they found "no Turkeys in the fog, no Roger Williams"; or seeing a hopeful teenage boxer leaving his father's gym, hurrying to catch the bus for a match in some strange town, where he would probably just get his nose broken for a few bucks.

Leo began managing the bowling lanes at the Pawtucketville Social Club, where Jack enjoyed many sociable hours shooting pool. He was also something of a legend around there for his interest in the old men, whom he would spend hours questioning and listening to. But another house move in 1935—to 35 Sarah Avenue—seems to indicate further problems with bills. The *coup de grâce* was struck by the flood of 1936, which came just a few days after Jack's fourteenth birthday.

Heavy rains falling on deep-piled snow, with the ground still frozen, had swelled the Merrimack into an Amazon. The entire Rosemont Terrace district of Lowell was inundated. In some parts of Centralville the water rose thirteen feet above street level. Upriver in Nashua the flood waters had swept up thousands of telephone poles from the creosoting plant, and by the time they reached Lowell they were flying along like battering rams to explode anything in their path. The Kerouac house on Sarah was on high ground, but Leo's shop on Bridge Street was a few feet below street level and got touched by the tip end of the flood. He did not suffer very much damage, but with his precarious finances it was enough to put him out of business. He had no insurance. When his creditors demanded payment, which would bankrupt him, he put his business into receivership and made an assignment to pay off fifty percent of all his debts. Although Scoopy Dionne was not one of the creditors harrying him, Leo brought him a note for $1,500, which he promised to make good as soon as possible.

For the rest of his life Leo maintained that his business had been taken from him for political reasons. Ever since he had been asked to run for mayor around 1930—and had declined, saying it would be too hard to throw all the crooks out of Lowell—he claimed he represented a threat to those crooks he knew too much about. But he might just have been a victim of ordinary business greed, since one of his creditors, Edmund Dastous, was a tough entrepreneur who demanded a profit from everything he turned his hand to.

Some respite came when Leo got the contract to print a newspaper, the *Billerica News.* But not long afterward a fresh crisis began brewing in the family, one that had nothing to do with money. Caroline had annnounced that she was going to marry Charlie Morissette, a great big, very funny man several years older than herself, a man with little prospect of making a good living. Gabrielle was so incensed she rushed to the priest to try and stop the marriage. But the priest told her she had no right to interfere. On May 30, 1937, just after her eighteenth birthday, Caroline was wed despite Gabrielle's predictions of a quick disaster. Jackie was now the only one remaining on whom Gabrielle could pin her hopes.

She could no longer pin them on Leo. At the Social Club he would buy drinks for everyone, telling them that life was sweet and God was good, all the while getting drunk himself. Suddenly he would begin to cry, but such jags turned quickly to drunken laughter, only to shift again into mournfulness; finally friends would carry him home, where his wife would give him a sedative. The horror, he told Jack, was in seeing himself a fool and yet knowing there was no sense in it, knowing he had done his best, yet that his best was not good enough. Jack was shocked to see a man so big and strong lie moaning in torment, not only helpless as a baby but unable to care for life anymore.

His father's cynicism was bound to drive young Jack still deeper into himself. If, in later life, he sometimes refused to grow up, it was with a real knowledge of what adulthood entailed. In addition, Leo bequeathed to his son a social animosity, a feeling that the civilized world was arranged for the exploitation of poor minorities like the Canucks, and this sense of injustice led to a rebelliousness against the standing order. Not that Leo Kerouac ever became a criminal, but he never lost the dream of leaving wife and family to wander the country fancy-free. With the right gambling system, he told Jack, he could travel from race track to race track, making a good living without ever having to work.

Gabrielle didn't like such talk, and she repeatedly had to bring

Leo to his feet, even if it meant insulting him about his failures. But eventually she saw that she would have to enhance her children's opportunities by herself. She got a job as a skiver in a shoeshop, cutting shoe leather to size, and with her enormous energy she was often able to finish a day's allotment in about three hours. With her money stashed in her corset, she would return home to fix her children goodies like hot chocolate and walnut fudge. She spent plenty of money on them too; in 1936 she took Jack on a trip to Brooklyn to visit her stepmother. She assured her children that she wouldn't abandon them even when they grew up: she would always be there to help them as though they were still her babies.

After Caroline left home, Gabrielle continued to shower such treats on Jack, while reminding him of what she had done for both of them. Yet even as a child he had discovered the trap of such dependence. At age eight he had run away from home with Mike Fournier. But every step of the eight-mile hike to Pelham, New Hampshire, Jack had felt guilty over betraying his family and the shelter they provided. In a panic he wanted to return to Lowell, but he could not remember the way. And in a very real sense—as real as a nightmare that foreshadows reality—he never did get home again. The security was no longer there, or rather he simply knew that it had been only an illusion fostered by his mother. His loyalty to that illusion helped develop two conflicting traits in the boy who, on the one hand, sought to be best in everything, an excellent student and athletic champion, and, on the other, was embittered by the cold and callous way to success, who withdrew from what he saw as stupid and aimless competition. Jack could fight fiercely to win a game, a race, or a girl's love, but he was more often the shy intellectual who would keep to himself in school and blush when some strange girl would smile his way.

Every personality is fragmented somewhere, and in Jack's case the faults were caused by too much love and too much fear. The artwork he kept producing reflected the reality of his life. Even his Shadow-Sax romances were just a luridly tinted version of his actual childhood, which had taken place in the shadow of Gerard, and later his mother, both of whom he had tagged after.

Day and night he slipped away to roam fields and riverbanks by himself. When he spoke to other children, it was often just to lecture them against cruelty to animals; he was known as an eccentric for protecting squirrels from getting stoned and snakes from getting fried in a can. In his room he wrote diaries and little novels. With two decks of special cards he had created himself, Jack could play a whole season of baseball in solitude; and with his marbles he invented an indoor horse-racing game, whose results he reported in his own newspaper. All the statistics of these imaginary games and races he noted down carefully in red ink, and then memorized, as he memorized real sports statistics from the newspaper and facts from books. In this escapism his mother was his conspirator, insisting that Jackie be left alone and bringing snacks to his room, until finally she called, *"Ti Jean, c'est le temps pour soupe!"* and he would have to come to supper.

There were things his mother could not protect him from. Going to school every day he had to cross the Moody Street Bridge, where he had seen the man with the watermelon die of a heart attack, and from which one of his cousins had once tried to commit suicide. There had been an actual suicide there too, which he had read about. For the rest of his life that bridge was a source of terror to him. As a child he couldn't help picturing himself lying on the jagged rocks far below. And he had nightmares of the Merrimack foaming into white horses while the wooden planks fell out and he hovered above on the beams, watching the "armies" of destruction. Some of the other boys used to climb on those beams, but Jack himself never dared.

5.

One of the things his mother fortunately couldn't protect him from was his friends. She didn't like most of them. G.J. was suspect as a Greek, and Leo added that he was a "sex fiend." Scotty Beaulieu was fatherless and poor; both Jack's parents, though especially his mother, preferred him to be with boys whose parents had influence and who would likely become important themselves. Yet it was the ordinary ones who really helped Jack turn his weaknesses into strengths.

They let him teach them how to play his private games, and Scotty even helped him tally the averages. They praised his feats of memory, giving him the nickname "Memory Babe," which he was proud of all his life. They made fun of his fears until finally he joined in their laughter.

One Saturday night they were all sitting on their favorite stoop on the corner of Riverside and Moody, teasing the neighborhood drunk, Luxey Smith. Luxey responded as usual: "The hell with you kids!" This night, Jack suggested they help get the drunk man home. Always worried about the helpless, he thought Luxey was so drunk he was bound to get hurt. On the way to his shack Luxey spooked them with a tale of caves underneath the Lowell Technical Institute that were filled with "Chinamen"! Through the tangle of trees and uncut grass they carried Luxey inside. There were cobwebs all over. Freddy and Jack went to lay him on the couch. Suddenly there was a crash, Luxey screamed, and they all ran out. Jack refused to leave, worrying that they had killed Luxey by letting him roll off onto the wood floor. In a gesture he had learned from the movies, G.J. belted Jack in the face, yelling, "Snap out of it!" But for days Jack scanned the obituaries. When Luxey finally showed up drunk again, zigzagging down the street, G.J. teased Jack for his concern by nicknaming him "Zagg." The name pleased Jack so much he began doing zigzagging imitations of Luxey, and the gang remembered him as "Zagg" for the rest of their lives.

Just northwest of Pawtucketville was the farmland of Dracut. Pete Houde and a friend had built a playground there known as "Dracut Tigers Field." At baseball Jack proved a spectacular outfielder, a skillful catcher, and a long-ball slugger, though he had trouble hitting curve balls. But football was his forte. By his midteens he was the best player there and every team wanted him, for it was almost impossible to win against him. He developed a rugged style of blocking by butting his opponents in the stomach, thirty years before headfirst tackles came into fashion in professional football. For years he had been improving his speed as a track runner, timing himself on the cinder track at the Textile Institute with a timing device he had built from a phonograph turntable. Though he was only about five foot eight, he had big thighs that drove his legs like pistons, and he had been building his body with an Olympic exercise program and using high-energy foods. Once he got around the end with the football, few could catch him. Those who did were likely to see stars! Many players who hit Jack just bounced off, and if he went down for a second, he would bounce back up and keep running. Scotty said the only way to tackle Jack was to grab him around the neck.

He became the team captain. Despite his aggressive playing, he insisted that their object was good sportsmanship. Whenever a fight would start, he would be the first to break it up, reminding the sore losers that they were just there "to have fun." Jack often got mad himself, but he kept his anger secret until he found a clever way to get revenge unnoticed. In the little park between Sarah and Moody there was a huge oak, from which the Houde Brothers had hung a board and a five-pound coffee can for basketball. As they played after dark one night, Bob Rondeau struck Jack deliberately. From then on Bob found himself getting jabbed by Jack's elbow and ass, though he always contrived to make the blows seem accidental. On the way home, Jack asked if G.J. and Scotty had seen this or that detail of the episode, wanting his friends to appreciate his sly response.

It was not that Jack carried more grudges than the average person, he simply got picked on a good deal more. G.J. enjoyed kicking him in the balls and then hiding behind Bob Morissette, the brother of his gigantic brother-in-law. Called "Iddyboy," Bob liked to shake his arms like a gorilla, and he would do anything G.J. told him. When G.J. would sic him on Jack, Jack would beg for mercy. Later, of course, Jack might hide in G.J.'s hallway to pay him back. But one day, in a sandlot football game, Jack's vengeance went too far. Under cover of a mass of bodies, an older boy named Carrufel punched him in the nose. A few days later Jack tackled him so hard that Carrufel was carried off the field unconscious—with Jack's father on the sideline cheering.

To those who were fair to him, there was no more devoted and helpful friend than Jack Kerouac. Scotty wanted to become a great pitcher like the Dean brothers, and he was upset when the Lowell Recreation Department set up a W.P.A. baseball league but excluded Pawtucketville. There were to be teams from every playground in the city, and Pawtucketville had no real playground. Jack helped Scotty write a letter to the director describing their team and explaining how much they wanted to play, so that eventually the Pawtucketville team was allowed to enter.

Jack and Scotty became co-managers of the team, and together they kept careful records of their players' performance. Practice was held at the Dracut Tigers Field, where the game normally ended when the ball landed in cow dung, and then they would all go for a swim at the "ledge," a quarry where they could dive from huge boulders into deep water. They played six or seven practice games before the W.P.A. league started its season in June. From then on, the team met at Jack's home—now the fourth floor of the Textile Lunch building on Moody Street—before each game. In spite of their enthusiasm, their record the first year was one win, ten losses. Jack had the highest batting average and led in home runs, but he also had the most strikeouts; he would hit the ball a mile or not at all.

That fall, 1936, playing the baseball card game together in Jack's room, he and Scotty planned changes that would make their team number one. When their paper work got boring, they would turn on the radio to "The 920 Club." Jack was crazy about drummers Buddy Rich and Gene Krupa, and he set up three different-sized suitcases by his bed, to drum on in time with the music. Scotty was surprised that Jack's mother, unlike Freddy's, would never tell them to quiet down.

Next summer, 1937, in the first game of the season, Jack hit the ball so hard it struck halfway up the wall of a mill building over 250 feet away; but the ball bounced right back to the centerfielder, and he was held to a double. Jack and Scotty brooded over their two-to-one loss. Fortunately, when any member of the gang took something too seriously, there would always be another to relieve the situation with comedy. Being a lefty, G.J. asked to pitch in the next game, boasting a secret windup, wherein he would lift his leg so high the batters would not see the ball. As it turned out, he either walked or

balked with every batter, and at the end of the first inning their
opponents were winning five to nothing. At the moment Scotty and
Jack were furious. Scotty slammed a home run so far it got stuck in a
tree beyond the field. After they won the game, however, and went
to celebrate at the Chair City Ice Cream Shop, they kidded G.J.
about his "performance," and for a long time it served to remind
them they loved each other even more than baseball.

It turned out to be a great season. Jack was belting doubles,
triples, and homers in almost every game; and in the celebrations
after victories he got into the habit of eating hot fudge sundaes. They
almost won the championship. In the game with South Common,
losing four to three, with two out in the ninth and Jack on third,
Ernie Noval came to bat. Since Ernie couldn't hit, Scotty coached
Jack to steal home. Seeing Jack's big lead-off, the catcher threw to
third, but the ball sailed over the third baseman's head. Jack dashed
in to the plate, where the catcher tagged him out. He still had the
ball and had merely thrown a potato! Jack and Scotty were so naive
they accepted the defeat. Only later did Jack check on the rules,
discovering that the potato was illegal and resolving that the following year they would stand for no more dirty tricks.

The ball season had brought them all closer together, and Jack's
junior year of high school they frequently cut classes to meet at
Freddy's house, across the street from Jack's on Moody. Freddy had
quit school and now stayed home to watch his two brothers and
sister while his mother and father worked. Listening to the radio by
himself, to bands like Wayne King and André Baruch, Jack had already learned to pick out the individual instruments; he was now a
connoisseur of singers too. With "The 920 Club" on the radio, they
would take turns puffing on Freddy's cigarettes as they listened to
the Eberle Brothers and Helen O'Connell, and when Cab Calloway
sang "Jumpin' Jive" they would go crazy. One day Jack ran into the
other room to find Salvey, yelling, "Come on, you've got to hear this
new Italian kid! He's the greatest!" It was Sinatra.

The only hitch was that Jack's mother might find them, and then
there would be hell to pay. Soon, however, the Bertrand family
moved to Moody Street across the bridge, a location safe enough
that they could plan hooky days in advance.

During the football season, the gang would sometimes watch the
Lowell Textile team play, and afterwards organize their own games
nearby. When they lacked a football they simply stuffed a stocking
with rags and tied it at both ends. There was plenty of horseplay,
with Jack having fun murdering G.J. or getting some fresh revenge
on Bob Rondeau. Sometimes Iddyboy would join them, and it took
four or five guys to pull him down, as many as it took to pull down
Jack.

Jack made good use of these scrub games. He worked out new

plays and practiced them to perfection for Lowell High games. Unfortunately, he was kept with the jayvees most of his junior year; when he was finally moved to the varsity team, he didn't start in any games and was barely used. Jack's father insisted that politics was involved, since he had made many enemies with remarks about the corruption in "Stinktown on the Merrimack." Leo also told Jack that some of the fathers were paying the coach to play their sons, an assertion which seemed true in at least one case, that of a millionaire's son with no talent. As if to roust Coach Keady, Leo would show up to cheer Jack at practice sessions.

Keady was a rough old buck who wouldn't listen to anyone. Once he found eleven players that worked well together, he never thought of interchanging them with others. When the team went on the road, he never took more than fifteen players. The assistant coach, "Fritz" Drescher, was upset about Keady's not giving all the kids an equal chance to play, but not even Drescher dared confront Keady on the issue. On top of everything, Keady had two other jobs, one of which was college coaching, and he wasn't too concerned with the problems of Lowell High. But Keady may have been saving Jack, since a high school coach's reputation was made by the players he sent on to college, and he may not have wanted Jack to get hurt at this early stage. In the fall of his junior year Jack was still only fifteen.

Such new examples of life's unfairness started Jack brooding again. He was trying harder than ever to succeed in the outside world. After the football season, he competed in track and proved one of the fastest runners on the thirty-five-yard hurdles and the thirty-yard dash, though he tired on long races like the three hundred. That winter he played basketball with the Y.M.C.A. team, since he was too short for the Lowell High team. His teammates were struck with his seriousness. Even in earlier years, in sandlot games, his sober expression had earned him nicknames like "little Christ" and "Dejesus." But now his behavior was even stranger. Walking home from football practice with his good friend Duke Chiungos, Jack would sometimes go for miles without speaking a word. When he finally started to talk, the pent-up words would pour out in a nonstop monologue. Still, Jack would not talk about his personal problems. Of the troubles then rending the family, even the gang members caught no more than a few hints. Like his mother, he found it painful to talk about family matters with outsiders. Jack's father spoke his mind more freely, which made the boys like him, and he seemed glad to have them there to listen.

At least the gang provided sympathy, even though Jack was reluctant to trust in it. In high school he had none of them around him, since G.J was taking only business classes and Scotty had dropped two years behind. Consequently Jack kept so much to himself that many kids disliked him, taking his reticence for arrogance; the more charitable simply thought of him as an oddball. In classes, however, he would frequently question the teacher until he understood a subject thoroughly. He often made the honor roll too.

Roger Ouellette, one of Gerard's old friends, was in a couple of Jack's classes. Remembering the sullen little boy who used to be jealous of his presence, Roger was surprised when Jack came over one day and asked him, "You remember the old days?" When Roger said yes, Jack asked shyly, "You remember my brother Gerry?" When Roger said yes again, Jack said he wanted to get together soon to talk about him, but somehow he never found time.

There were many reasons for him to feel like a misfit. One day, while still on the jayvee football team, he had gone into the locker room earlier than usual to shower. It was an unwritten tradition that the varsity players got to shower first. A few of them, including star athlete Henry Mazur, were still in there. Jack innocently slipped in, only to have the bigger Mazur bodily toss him out. It was an uncalled-for insult that rankled all his life. But even Jack's close friends weren't always sympathetic with the kind of life he led. At home he sometimes talked for hours about his "race horses," the marbles that sped across his bedroom floor when the "starting gate," a ruler, was quickly lifted. Each one had its own name and an elaborate history, and to the gang it seemed Jack hardly realized they were still just marbles. One day G.J. picked up all forty or fifty glassies and scattered them outside, ending the career of "Man o' War" and all Jack's other favorites.

Undaunted, Jack decided to see if real horse racing was worth his while. On an expedition to the Boston Public Library, he, G.J., and Scotty examined old newspapers for the racing reports over a full year. They tried various systems of betting—picking a favorite horse, then if he lost, doubling the bet on the next horse, etc. When they checked the actual results of the races, they had lost money every time. After five hours of marking down horses and bets, Jack concluded that the track could not be beaten and decided he would never try.

6.

The flood of 1936 had completely destroyed Scoopy Dionne's meat market. After two years of trying and failing to get loans, Dionne declared bankruptcy early in 1938. When his lawyer asked about his assets, he mentioned the $1,500 note from Leo Kerouac, though Dionne had never expected to collect on it, and even doubted whether Leo had actually registered it at City Hall. As it turned out, the note had been registered. Since his lawyer did not include it on the declaration of bankruptcy, Dionne almost went to jail for concealing assets. Though present in the courtroom, Leo Kerouac, fearing that anything he might say would result in a fatal encumbrance on his print shop, made no explanation in Dionne's defense. The lost money Dionne could forgive, but for a long time he felt bitter about Leo's moral cowardice.

Leo's worst fears were realized anyway. The trustees of Dionne's bankruptcy pressured Leo for the $1,500. As a result, Leo's own creditors forced him to sell out his equipment to the *Billerica News*. After many years of owning his own business he now had to seek employment at other shops. For a while he worked at the Owl Print Shop, but they couldn't keep him long, and he bounced from job to job for over a year until he was hired on a steady basis by Sullivan Printers. There, because of his dark skin and bushy black hair, he was considered a "decent good hardworking industrious Indian" and admitted to the union. The bosses thought him a "nice guy," though among themselves they called him a "Hudson's Bay seal." [5]

By early 1938 Jack was beginning to make a name for himself as a track star, but his own integrity made him no more popular than his father's shiftiness. It wasn't the fact of his being stronger and smarter than others that was separating him from community, friends, and even his own parents, it was his sense of loyalty to what was unique in himself. In the close-knit world of Lowell, writing your own rules—which was equivalent to considering yourself better than others—was a much worse sin than ordinary drinking and whoring. Perhaps people sensed that he was not going to remain small-town, that he was too honest and thoughtful to live by manners and moralities he had not tested firsthand.

His parents, of course, wanted him to succeed, but by their own definition of success, which was to gather more wealth and esteem than one's neighbors. They told Jack he should spend less time with his friends and more time with bright, respected young men like Jim O'Dea and Jim Cudworth. Both were honored athletes who might help Jack in his sports career; and to be Irish in Lowell meant doors opened a lot more quickly. Disturbed by his parents' mercenary values, Jack told G.J. what they had said and promised he would never heed their advice.

In bad need of someone to talk to, Jack went to the rectory of St. Jean Baptiste, the church of his boyhood. He hadn't attended Mass since he was fourteen—with the excuse that his father had warned him away from Father O'Connell, who listened to jazz! Jack laid his newest problem before the young priest on duty.

Father Armand Morissette was a native Lowellian who knew Jack's parents and his Uncle Joe but had seen Jack only once or twice. He was, in addition, a man who had had his own problems reconciling his conscience with Church dogma. Nevertheless, it surprised him to hear this teenage football and track star, handsome as an actor, complain that everybody was laughing at him because he wanted to be a writer. "I'm not laughing," Father Morissette told him. "But it's a rough life, you know."

Jack complained that most people said writers were "sissies," and that they told him, "Work like everybody else! Don't be a bum!"

"You're from a poor family; you'll have to try for a scholarship," Father Morissette said as gently as possible. He was aware of the delicate personality that ambition could easily derange. Though Jack's sincerity and strong will made the priest believe he would succeed, he foresaw a long string of disappointments. He told Jack that the best place to go was New York. Encouraged, Jack made up his mind to switch from the commercial course, which he had been in for the past three years at Lowell High, to the college course.

Lowell would soon enough respect the Kerouac determination. That spring Jack and Scotty advertised in the sports pages for new baseball players; they found several, including "Skippy" Roberge, who would later play in the major leagues. This year they lined up two W.P.A. teams, one for the junior and one for the senior leagues. With the added incentive of a trip to a Red Sox game for the winners, Jack and Scotty hit ten home runs apiece, with Jack batting .385 and Scotty only ten points less. In the game with South Common, the "potato team," they produced a surprise of their own: one of their new players, Leon Montaigne. Unknown in the league, Montaigne struck out most of South Common's batters, and he even hit the double that gave them a two-point lead. For the first time Pawtucketville was champion of the junior league. Once again, Chair City Ice Cream did a splendid business.

In the senior league they lost the title by one game. But they still got a trip; they were bussed into Boston to see the Red Sox beat the St. Louis Browns nine to five. On the way back, they were all exuberant with a sense of work well done, feeling they had proved a point about never giving up.

That fall Jack was being talked about as the next football hero of Lowell High. Scotty was still only a sophomore, and the baseball coach was anxious to get him on the team next spring, which would require Scotty to make better grades than in the past. Since Jack and Scotty both felt they had something going for them, they played hooky much less. In fact, Scotty almost made the honor roll, but in November they transferred him to the industrial course and his grades dipped. Jack encouraged Scotty to talk with one teacher, whose grading system seemed unfair, but the talk did no good. When the coaches discovered that Scotty turned eighteen in December, they realized he was ineligible for the team anyway. Scotty dropped out to work for the W.P.A., digging sewer trenches for the city.

Jack had his own troubles that fall. Coach Keady still didn't put him in the starting lineup, and Jack only started in the first game because the other "scat back," Pete Kouchalakos, had injured his ankle. In that game Jack made five of the seven first downs and two touchdowns that were called back, averaged ten yards a try, and made a twenty yard run almost to the goal line, after which the quarterback appointed himself to carry the ball over. The second game, Kouchalakos, whose ankle had healed, was started instead of Jack. Allowed to play only the last two minutes, Jack made two first downs anyway (twelve and thirteen yards apiece). The third game he was only sent in during the second half, ran back a punt sixty-four yards for a touchdown, then scored two more touchdowns of twenty-five yards apiece, averaging over twenty yards for each time he carried the ball. When he still was not started in the fourth game, the kids in the stands began chanting, "We want Kerouac!" He was put in for the last minute and made no gain. For the one quarter that the coach used him in the fifth game, he scored three touchdowns.

Jack's father believed that his own unpopularity was holding Jack back. Leo had recently punched a wrestler in the mouth after a fixed match, and he was making sharper cracks about the inefficiency of Lowell's city government. Leo also blamed the long-standing preference for Irish players over French, though the previous coach had been more flagrant in that respect than Keady. He did have a number of excellent backs to choose from that year, and his first choice was always final, but Keady had not spent much time choosing. He was busy working at the dog track in Boston in the evenings, and he would often leave practice sessions early, forcing Drescher to lie that he was still in the darkened stands.

Drescher liked Jack immensely. He had never seen a boy who wanted so badly, and tried so hard, to be a first-stringer. If Jack made a mistake during a game, he would sit on the bench brooding about it until long after everyone else had gone home, so that Drescher finally had to shoo him out of the locker room. Jack liked the way Drescher would pat him on the back when he did something well, the first sign of appreciation he had ever received from a coach.

One of the things Keady held against Jack was that he was a little slow in grasping instructions. When Drescher told him this, Jack explained that he still had some difficulty with English. In class too, on tests, he often didn't do as well as he could have because it took so long to read through all the questions. Drescher suggested he study the dictionary. The next time they met, Jack recited a list of new vocabulary words he had memorized, a practice he kept up the rest of the school year.

The game in which Jack scored three touchdowns had been against Lowell's Catholic high school, Keith Academy. On the sidelines was a Keith alumnus, Elmer Rynne. In high school Rynne had played varsity football, and later he quarterbacked for the Laurier Club's semipro team. At twenty-seven, he already owned Lull & Hartford, the oldest sporting goods store in the country, and as a freelance sports reporter, he had his eye on Jack. In the early thirties, through sports reportage for *L'Etoile*, Leo had come to know Rynne. During the game Leo approached him to ask if he could help Jack's career. Just at that moment Jack caught the ball on a kickoff and ran it back for a touchdown. Later, Rynne called up his friend Eddie Donohue at Lawrence, who was a good friend of Ralph Hewitt, assistant athletic director of Columbia University.

There was a good deal of confusion as to how to use Jack, which may have contributed to his not being played consistently. Keady's son "Baron," an assistant coach, was so impressed with Jack's blocking that he wanted to use him as an end. But Keady himself thought him too small for that position. In those days it was common to keep a fast, light runner in reserve as a "situation back," who could be put in when the ball had been moved close enough to the opposing goal line. Since Jack filled the bill as situation back, Keady perhaps found it superfluous to use him otherwise.

Then, too, Jack had some genuine weaknesses as a player. Even if Keady instructed him to hesitate before running, he usually took off as soon as he got the ball. He fumbled frequently, and Keady was forever hollering at him to hold the ball with two hands, though Jack maintained he couldn't dart and weave as fast without one hand free for balance. He wasn't skilled at punting, either, but in that department he was learning from his Polish friend Joe Sorota.

One day Jack found another Polish buddy being beaten up by a much bigger guy, who seemed about to kill him. Ferociously Jack rushed in and punched the assailant into submission. It was the only time anyone had seen Jack use his strength to hurt another. Similarly surprised by the intensity of his affection, Sorota asked, "What nationality is 'Kerouac' anyway? Greek?"

"I'm Dutch," Jack said with a smile, but did not elaborate.

However unusual, the name Kerouac was becoming pretty well known even beyond Lowell. Sportswriters in Boston were impressed with his figures, even if he was "the twelfth man on the Lowell High School Eleven." [6] Frank Leahy and the other Boston College coaches, who would soon transfer to Notre Dame, were already scouting him. Yet Lowell didn't play him in the next game against Malden, which resulted in a scoreless tie. In the game after that, against Lynn Classical, Jack played only long enough to drop a crucial touchdown pass. Lynn won six to nothing. Every night for a week afterward, Jack stayed on the practice field with a friend until well after dark, to practice catching passes. When Drescher told him he didn't have to go through such an ordeal, Jack said he was making sure that goof would never happen again.

The next game was played in New Britain, Connecticut. The whole team fooled around in hotel suites the night before, and some even sneaked off to a dance. Jack didn't take part in the ensuing twenty-to-nothing Lowell defeat.

After that fiasco the regulars were resting, and Jack was put in with a bunch of second-string kids to thrash through what he called the "raining mud" of Nashua, New Hampshire, his parents' hometown. Although Lowell lost nineteen to thirteen, Jack advanced 130 out of 149 total yards for Lowell, including a sixty-yard run and a fifteen-yard touchdown run after receiving a pass. Lou Little, the head coach of Columbia and a pal of Keady's at the Boston dog track, was very interested. So were scouts from Duke University, and Frank Leahy decided he wanted Jack at all costs. But Jack was bitter that he hadn't gotten a Turkish bath at the Rex Hotel, like the resting "heroes," and rumors were flying that somebody had planned a loss at Nashua to raise the odds on the upcoming Thanksgiving game.

Like his father, Jack felt he was a better man than the world gave him credit for, and he was determined to finally get that credit. He frequently stopped into Frank Sargent's office at the *Courier-Citizen* to make sure he was getting sufficient coverage, and the sportswriters were amused at how badly he wanted to see his name in lights. Others, however, were beginning to find this "very forward kid" [7] repugnant. Ironically, every step toward prominence increased Jack's alienation.

His bitterness was more than professional. He confided to Sorota that in the two days he had spent in Connecticut he had met and fallen in love with a beautiful girl—and they had planned to marry! Though he wrote her many letters, she never answered.

There was only one other French-Canadian on the varsity team, Julian Beaulieu. On the bus rides to games they would always sit together, and he was the only teammate with whom Jack spent many hours conversing. Many of their talks centered on religion and the inadequacies Jack found in the Catholic Church. On one trip, around this time, he asserted that if he were God he would change a great many things: "This is how I'd do it," etc. Finally he concluded, "I *am* God, and if I don't die by the time I'm thirty-three, I'll kill myself."

In the big Thanksgiving game Jack was not put in until the second half. Though they stayed in Lowell for their Thanksgiving dinner, G.J., Scotty, and Freddy got together at Freddy's house to listen to the game on the radio. It seemed to Scotty that Jack was "getting the end of the stick." When he was finally put in, he did them proud.

The game was played before an audience of fourteen thousand shivering spectators. A bone-chilling wind was cutting across the field, which was too soft for much fancy running, and in the first half the evenly matched teams had made only slight advances, with no score. Five minutes before the end of the third quarter, Lowell got its first break. On a fourth down the Lawrence kicker went back into his end zone to kick. The ball shot straight up and bounced in and out of the end zone, an automatic safety, giving Lowell a two-to-nothing margin.

The next Lawrence kick was run back to Lawrence's twenty-eight yard line by Chuck Ruiter. From there Jack and quarterback Chris Zoukis took turns advancing the ball to the fourteen. On the next play, Zoukis tossed a flat pass which Jack, running hard, was barely able to snag at his knees. Off balance and beset by tacklers, he fought his way nine yards to the goal line and just barely tumbled over. The next day his father was angry that the paper described Zoukis's pass as "beautiful." But he could not have been more angry than Pete Kouchalakos, the back Jack had replaced. There was no further scoring for the rest of the game, and back in the locker room, with everyone else jubilant over Lowell's victory, Kouchalakos smashed down his helmet, knowing Jack and not he had emerged the hero.

Frank Leahy came to Thanksgiving dinner at the Kerouac's home, and a few days later Lou Little's men were sniffing Jack out with promises of a good job for his father. Jack had dreamed of college from age twelve, when he'd seen a movie of Bing Crosby serenading a coed in the moonlight outside the frat house. That movie had actually impelled him to start playing football. Now his dream of college seemed as real as all those points he had chalked up —both of which would end, as he punned in *Vanity of Duluoz,* in the "morgue."

7.

In his schoolwork Jack was getting A's and B's. Once a week he cut classes to study on his own in the Lowell Public Library, reading Goethe and Hugo, showing off to himself that he could absorb things like William Penn's *Maxims*, methodically examining the Harvard Classics, and getting truly excited over H. G. Wells' *Outline of History* and the classic Eleventh Edition of the *Encyclopedia Britannica*. At one point he read all the books on chess; until he had mastered the game, he would neither attend classes nor even play ball with his friends. Usually after the library he would go to "study" the movies at the Rialto Theatre. Then, especially during snowstorms, he would hike in the Dracut woods.

Jack considered his English teacher, Joe Pyne, the best teacher he ever had. Aside from his reputation as a lush, Pyne was known as one of the least scholarly teachers in the school, but he was also remembered as extremely gentle and sweet. Pyne took an interest in Jack and helped him to appreciate Emily Dickinson and other American poets. On his other teachers Jack made little impression. Raymond Sullivan, the high-school principal, knew Jack because he was a star athlete, but whenever he approached Jack about his interests and plans, Jack seemed evasive and anxious to escape.

A couple of hobos from Lowell had become rather famous for traveling across country and back, and Jack told his friend Albert Blazon he could wish no better life for himself. In school he still barely talked, seldom smiled, and almost never laughed, but now many students were feeling curiosity if not actual good will toward him. Friends, like his teammate Charlie Ruiter, found him no person to play jokes on. Ruiter felt genuinely sorry for this hero who had to wear the same sports jacket (when he was not wearing his varsity sweater) every day for three years in a row. But when there was a short-story contest in the literary magazine, he couldn't help being amused by how badly Jack wished to win. Submitting a story plagiarized from *Liberty*, Ruiter beat out Jack's piece. Jack told Ruiter angrily, "You didn't write that!"

There were many girls now who had crushes on Jack, but he ignored them as though they didn't exist. In study hall, cheerleader Mary McCarron would excitedly receive notes from Jack—always to find, to her disappointment, that they were from another boy and Jack was merely passing them along.

Jack wanted a girlfriend badly, but she was a Hollywood dream creature, and he had no idea how to find her. With the gang he listened to romantic songs like Glenn Miller's "Moonlight Serenade" and "Sunrise Serenade." One Saturday night they went to the Rex Ballroom. "Deep Purple," a favorite of Jack's, was playing, but none of them knew how to dance; all night long they stood watching, with no idea where to start. At the Rex the following Saturday, Jack, Scotty, and G.J. spotted two short young men, both with curly red hair, who because they could jitterbug managed to get all the girls. Jack and his friends decided they had better introduce themselves. It turned out one "Red" was Irish, Ray McNulty, and the other French, Ray St. Louis. McNulty and St. Louis were glad to share their expertise. Every week from then on, the gang would show up at the Rex for lessons, and one "Red" or the other would take them into a corner or up to the balcony. Now that the football season was over, Jack didn't worry about playing hooky, so they began to meet at Freddy's again and would practice their dancing there too.

Even after much practice Jack and Scotty were still too shy to ask a girl to dance. Although hardly shy, G.J. was too cynical to worry much about girls; he would dismiss the vanity of all such striving with remarks like: "It's a cruel, lousy, goddamn world with its cold winters and having to work goddamn hard to live in this crazy world." But something in the glamorous, carefree lifestyle of McNulty and St. Louis had caught Jack's fancy, and he began to spend time with them. McNulty and St. Louis had both been to black jazz clubs in Boston and knew how to talk jive. Both had used marijuana and benzedrine. In Lowell their occupations were tamer— they would find a party, crash it, and quickly win over the girls with their dancing. Jack was so fascinated he tried to imitate all their moves. Yet even when St. Louis "gave" Jack some of his extra girls, he danced so awkwardly and acted so tongue-tied he got nowhere. To McNulty and St. Louis it was a lark to have this football hero always on their trail. Crossing the Moody Street Bridge one day, McNulty looked back over his shoulder and laughed, "You know, Jack, you really *are* the Shadow!"

McNulty and St. Louis were two friends Jack did not bring home.

New Year's Eve, 1938, there was a big dance at the Rex, and Jack resolved he was going to find a steady girl. He already had great plans for conquering life and could no longer be delayed by his fears. G.J., however, wasn't impressed with any of Jack's plans, and told him he'd just end up as "honorary chairman of the burper's convention of general farts in the motors division of the superintendents of Wall Street."

His hair grown long, St. Louis raved about seeing Gene Krupa in Boston. McNulty wore a button-down lounge lapel and looked both sad and glamorous. St. Louis had a slim, pretty brunette he wanted Jack to meet. When Jack lagged, St. Louis had to virtually push him into her arms. Her name was Mary Carney, and after they danced she took turns dancing with all the gang, relaxing them with her easy conversation until they had confidence for other girls. Jack didn't seem particularly impressed with her. In many respects she was timid and almost plain, and she certainly wasn't intellectual. But he liked her maternal quality.

Within a few weeks they were seeing a lot of each other. Her father and brothers were railroadmen, and they lived in a big old wood house with a sprawling, tree-shaded porch along the Concord River in South Lowell. Although it was midwinter, Jack would hike several miles each way just to spend a few hours talking with her in her living room. She was the one who had to kiss him first.

His shyness over, they would contrive to meet alone for prolonged necking, unable because of mutual fears and guilts to go any further. In the dark, subterranean church of Ste. Jeanne d'Arc, where he had had his first Communion, Jack went to pray for her love. But the next time they met and he tried to get beyond her lips, she refused.

Mary had no interest in the things Jack wanted, the life of a famous writer, money and popularity. She simply wanted a hard-working husband with whom to raise a family in Lowell. Although

Jack was always a perfect gentleman, kind and considerate, she quickly realized he was leery of marriage. When she began seeing other boys between dates with Jack, he grew furious and called her a tease.

The situation was complicated by his simultaneous romance with a tall, chic redhead named Peggy Coffey. Although not quite beautiful, Peggy was a baton twirler and band singer, and moved in a much more fashionable social set than Mary. Furthermore, she made no bones about her sex appeal and was rather amused at Jack's bashfulness. At a sports banquet in the fall, she had pulled him onto the dance floor and made him talk about kissing; when Jack failed to make a move after several long afternoons of talk, Peggy had kissed *him*. He would have had little trouble getting her to do more, but he was upset by the fact that she liked many other boys too. All the same, Jack's classier friends, like Jim O'Dea, thought Peggy above comparison with Mary. Because of Mary's tall, thin build, they called her "Stretch." O'Dea couldn't imagine why Jack would want to throw over a sophisticated, bubbly girl like Peggy for such a "plain jane."

Torn between Peggy and Mary, Jack's imagination worked overtime. In Kerouac's novel *Maggie Cassidy*, we learn that Mary lived near the slow, dark Concord River, among trees in the quiet outskirts of town. Peggy's house was near the broad, frothing Merrimack, the highway, the big bridge, the carnival and football field just across from the factories. Mary with her "railroad family" tradition would demand he keep his roots in Lowell; Peggy with her dreams of singing in a big band was pushing him toward the world. Thus far in his life the magnets had always come in pairs, yanking him in opposite directions. Just as his grandparents had been caught between Canada and the U.S.A., and their grandparents between France and Canada, and their distant forefathers between Cornwall and France, so the descendent of them all vacillated between the known and the new world.

Peggy's kisses came with no strings attached; Mary's were limited "like Napoleon brandy," with the threat that soon there would be no more unless she and Jack became engaged. When he prayed for help with his love troubles, as Jack recorded in *Maggie Cassidy*, he heard only silence, from which he deduced that God didn't get mixed up in the affairs of the world. With such logic he was setting a trap for himself: once he had gone into the world he could do anything, because he would already have left God behind—but he would never get free of the attendant guilt. Even without the world's help, he had a genius for dilemmas. But the world was helping. On the one side were all those Glenn Miller and Tommy Dorsey songs sighing that love was the answer; on the other was his mother telling him to forget girls and lead a decent life, warning that he would later regret such a waste of time. Jack was forced into the non sequitur that love had to end with his youth, and was stung by the imperative to act quickly or never at all.

Yet he couldn't bring himself to any decisive action. The school magazine, *The Review*, wondered why Jack and Peggy were staring into each other's eyes so often without getting anywhere; it requested someone to properly "introduce" them. Peggy seemed to care for Jack, and as he repeatedly dated, then drifted away from her throughout the school year, the gossip column kept asking that someone help this "swell couple" to "get started" or "fix them up again." With Mary, Jack was just as reluctant to commit himself. Though he would blame her for keeping him away, and for hurting him with her many other flirtations, on certain occasions he deliberately avoided her. It almost seemed he was using Peggy to make Mary jealous. Mary's jealousy would buy him time; or if she got angry enough to break up, that would solve his problem.

Peggy was the girl he talked about to people he wanted to impress, friends who were themselves popular. Some, like football hero Duke Chiungos, had never seen him so emotionally involved before. But Mary was the girl Jack contemplated marrying, hence the one his mother objected to. After several years at the skiving machine she wanted Jack to move up in the world and pressed for him to go to Columbia University in New York, so she could get a taste of the big city too. Seeing that Mary would tie him down, she warned him not to get serious.

To G.J., Jack almost never mentioned Peggy, but he gushed over Mary for six months straight, until G.J. got sick of hearing about her and worried that Jack would get hurt. Mary seemed too different from Jack to ever understand him. Mainly, G.J. felt that Jack got too intensely involved with whatever girl he happened to be with at the moment. In that sense, every girl was the wrong one, because Jack wanted someone that his world could revolve around, someone who could pull together all his helter-skelter motions. In a nice way G.J. tried to get Jack to see that Mary might be just an adolescent crush; he said, "You grab a butterfly, you kill it." When that didn't work, G.J. told him to screw women and leave them. Unconvinced, Jack went to Salvey, who reminded him that love was religious and that marriage would at least get Mary into bed.

Most of the girls Jack saw in high school were either plotting or waiting and dreaming; the former seemed catty, the latter he thought would die a "high school death" at sixteen. Avoiding both, Jack played hooky twice a week. But he began feeling guilty for stringing along Mary while his heart kept returning to Peggy.

Peggy had a new boyfriend, but she told Jack she would be singing their song, "Heart and Soul," at a local show. Hopelessly confused, Jack prayed to his mother's phosphorescent crucifix that he might suffer like Christ and so be saved. His prayers were answered by his falling in love with Mary—for real.

Because she had not gotten beyond junior high school, Mary shied away from his high-school world. He would soon be the highest scorer on the track team, and it hurt him not to have her watching at practice or cheering him at the meets. But Peggy often showed up, joking about watching his legs and kidding with Leo, who really liked her. Yet, almost against his will, Jack began stealing away from his other friends to phone Mary. He even broke a date to bowl with his father, just home from working out of town, to run over and see her, knowing she was mad that he had been seeing Peggy, that she would want him all for herself or not at all. When he got to Mary she kissed him and clung to him, told him she was his and needed him and loved him and he was a fool for not realizing it.

He decided he wanted to marry her. She told him he was too young, he had no trade, and she reminded him of his career. When he shrugged off that dream, she suggested he become a brakeman, they could live in a little house by the tracks and have babies. He told her that was just what he wanted, grabbing her. She slapped his face and said he hadn't heard her. They wrestled for hours, until finally she insisted he go. After he meekly agreed, she warned him to stay away from Peggy. Then, in tears, she said she would never love anyone so much again, but she got confused about which day she was supposed to see him, as if she had other rendezvous.

At a surprise birthday party thrown by his sister and her husband, in March, Mary piqued him by her participation in kissing games with all the other boys. G.J. took him aside and told him to stop getting worked up. This time his language was harsher. He thought Jack and Mary "didn't belong on the same planet, let alone the same city." Her dream was of a little cottage, a husband working eight-to-five, and a family; G.J. knew "that wasn't Zagg at all." Yet Mary seemed to think life with her, in Lowell, would make Jack happiest. When Jack kept asking, "What should I do?" G.J. told him.

As if to salvage something out of the confusion, Jack called Leon Lamoureaux, the *Courier-Citizen*'s photographer, to make sure they carried shots of his party!

Then Jack found that Mary had another serious boyfriend, a boxer with a roadster. As if he could not compete himself, Jack asked his baseball buddy, Jim Cudworth, who had met Mary at the birthday party, to date her. He even encouraged Jim to take her to the prom. But when Jim accepted the offer, Jack was terribly jealous.

One night Mary simply sent Jack away. She needed time to think, uncertain if she really ought to get married so young. Jack's mother told him to put off seeing her until spring or summer. He began to think of himself as torn between Mary and Magdalene. The choice appeared to be between virginity—marrying his first real love—and prostitution, the continuous pursuit of new loves, cheapening the value of each.

As he was to do all his life at such impasses, Jack surrendered to the moment. When he was with each of them the joy of romance was foremost in his mind; alone, he would return to the bitter troubles he couldn't share, building walls to keep others out. By summertime he was no longer the important boy in either girl's life.

8.

But it was imperative to decide soon on a college. At night, as he recalled in an early draft of *The Town and the City*, he watched the lights stretching across the countryside, wanting to see everything everywhere. From the movies Jack knew New York *was* the world, like Johnson's London. With visions of the waterfront, Central Park, Don Ameche on Fifth Avenue, and Hedy Lamarr on his arm at the Ritz, it was easy enough to agree with his mother that Columbia University was the best place to learn to be an insurance executive. Quite frankly she told him to leave Mary, and as a bribe used her shoeshop savings to buy him a new sports jacket, ties, and shirts, so he would look fashionable in New York.

His father, on the other hand, wanted Jack to sign with Boston College; the coach there, Leahy, planned to take Jack with him to Notre Dame. Leo disliked Lou Little of Columbia, whose real name was Luigi Piccolo. He thought him a social fake, a snob who kissed the feet of the upper classes. In Leo's eyes, Little was merely recruiting Jack as a "ringer" to win prestige for his rich-boy team; in effect, hiring Jack with a scholarship. And Little's promise of a good job for Leo, as part of the deal, seemed no more than a gesture of contempt. The offer had been made through an intermediary, as though Little couldn't take direct notice of someone so far beneath him.

Jack too had a few misgivings about Columbia, especially about their insistence that he go first to a prep school, Horace Mann, for a year. He knew he was bright and felt he wasn't being directed to Horace Mann so much to correct deficiencies in his education as to varnish him with a little "culture," although at seventeen he was actually rather young to play college ball. The very word "prep" seemed to show the class snobbishness of Columbia, a gibe at his working-class background and lack of sophistication. But Jack also knew he would never get sophisticated in Newton Heights, Massachusetts, much less in South Bend, Indiana. And there was no doubt about the quality education Columbia could provide.

Leo was now working at Sullivan Printers, which handled all the jobwork for Boston College, a Catholic school. Leahy pressured the Sullivan Brothers, and they in turn pressured Leo, offering him a promotion if Jack signed with Leahy and hinting that if Jack went elsewhere he would be fired. Undeterred, Gabrielle made arrangements for Jack to stay with her stepmother in Brooklyn while he attended Horace Mann. Soon afterward, Leo had to go on the road to find work.

With Jack's father out of town much of the time and his mother totally indulgent, he drifted in a kind of corrupt paradise. He still spent time with the gang, walking to Kearney Square for hot fudge sundaes at the B.C. soda fountain, or discussing books with G.J., the group's one reader. Eventually Scotty saved enough money from his W.P.A. salary to buy a 1930 two-door Chevy coach, and for the first time they were on wheels. But Jack's main garden of pleasure was Shedd Park.

With his track teammate Steve Eastham, Jack joined the Shedd Park gang. During the day they "hunted beaver"; every night, with binoculars, they watched a blonde lady undress before an open window. The gang was led by a couple of wild kids who started raiding the outdoor ice boxes on Fort Hill, just behind the park. The people who lived on Fort Hill were wealthy; in summer they kept great reserves of food in outdoor sheds. Jack, who was always hungry now, helped himself along with the others. At last they went too far, stealing many bottles of expensive liquor, though they hardly intended to drink it and hid most of it in the woods. But the police were called in; and whether or not Jack was questioned, he seems to have spent the rest of the summer quietly.

Ralph Furey of Columbia wanted Jack to come down early so they could make definite plans for his future, and Gabrielle wanted to go along to see him settled in safely at her stepmother's. But the Kerouacs were now so poor they lacked even the bus fare to New York. Jack went to see Elmer Rynne, who arranged for them to get a ride with the Lowell Trucking Company. But a week beforehand, the owner called Rynne to say his insurance wouldn't cover passengers. When Jack asked Rynne for the bus fare, Rynne took the money from the cash register of Lull & Hartford. As he left the store Jack kept turning around and waving, a broad smile on his face.

Still, just before Jack's departure, G.J. sensed he didn't really want to leave Lowell. His parents tried to dispel his fears with arguments like: "Never mind today, let's think about tomorrow." But to G.J. it seemed they were asking too much of him. From some need of their own, they were making him over into someone he wasn't.

Yet, in the last analysis, his parents were hardly culpable in sending him to college; it was Jack's own decision to get on the bus to New York. Sometimes none of the choices open to us is the one we really want to take, and so we have to take a second or third choice, and the courage with which we take it is a pretty good measure of our character. "The trademark of a Breton is stubborn," Kerouac later wrote in a song, but *stubborn* is just a modest man's word for brave.

TWO
The Ruins of
Pearl Harbor

1.

During 1938 and early 1939 much of the Western world struggled to ignore the thundering horsemen of the Nazi apocalypse. On Jack's birthday, March 12, 1938, German Panzers rolled into Austria; in September, Chamberlain signed away the Czech Sudetenland to Hitler's Third Reich for "peace in our time," and on March 15, 1939, the Germans invaded the rest of truncated Czechoslovakia. On September 1, the Wehrmacht marched into Poland, and Germany's Führer had become the most successful attention-getter since Genghis Khan.

In such times, well might a sensitive and intelligent young man begin to question the nature of success. All the more poignant was this self-examination for the young Jack Kerouac, faced with his own personal vision of horror—poverty, the disintegration of his family, his father's breakdown, and his own failure to be the popular hero he had always imagined himself. With his sister married and his mother in the shoe factory, the Kerouac household was empty and quiet. Boredom was just the beginning of his malaise. Listening to the dripping faucets in their tenement flat he would ask himself over and over how he could take care of himself, what work he was good for, and what goals he should pursue in life. The fact that he couldn't make sense of either the cruelty outside or the bitterness within him steadily weakened his will to go on living. There is good evidence that he had serious thoughts of suicide.[8] In place of solutions, as he wrote in *Vanity of Duluoz*, he found "blackness everywhere."

Some parts of that blackness had a tinge more color, like the finely wrought despondencies of his literary and movie heroes such as Jean Valjean, Prince Andrey Bolkonsky, Anna Karenina, Greta Garbo, Byron, Tristan, and Hedda Gabler. The summer after his last year in high school Jack had found a similar distracting kaleidoscope in the crafty antics of his new juvenile criminal friends. But the ultimate rainbow of false hopes hovered garishly over the wealth at Horace Mann Prep School. The world's explosion in September 1939 revealed nothing but black death under a splendid pageant of national banners. So too did Jack find, beneath the colorful pennants of college glory, that he was really fighting for his life.

The shock of discovering the universal competition for survival may explain the great creativity—both in actual journal and story writing, and in real-life explorations—of Jack's first year in New York. In later years he would possess more sophisticated techniques of expression, but seldom would there be a greater rush of energy. Starting in the fall of 1939, it gushed for several years until it left him high and dry among the "most evil and intelligent" group of supermen ever to haunt the Columbia University campus.[9]

Gabrielle loved the clean halls and ivy-covered granite walls of Horace Mann, and felt that now "Jackie" (as she still called him) was where he should be, among people who could help him rise in the world. With her son an insurance executive, she could shop at the Fifth Avenue department stores, eat in fancy restaurants, relax at the Ziegfeld follies and Jack Dempsey fights! The first night at his step-grandmother's house in Brooklyn Jack lay sleepless, tantalized by similar ghostly visions of the American Dream. He was haunted because New York was in many ways just a larger Lowell, with its own ethnic groups—Jews and Italians in place of the Greeks and French—vying for the prizes, although the prizes loomed so much vaster that he almost shrank from them in awe. But with the possibility of becoming a "journalistic champion" on a New York paper, he might seriously contemplate a penthouse with fireplace and the Gershwins for neighbors, a wardrobe of dinner jackets, topcoats, and white scarves, and a gorgeous movie-queen wife like Gene Tierney. To realize that his dreams might come true sent him reeling, he later wrote, like a marble in a bowling alley that opened into infinite night. He was hopelessly lost. And yet gambling for stakes bigger than he could afford to lose was no small thrill.

As Jack and his mother strolled around the Horace Mann grounds, set on a high bluff overlooking upper Manhattan, he wondered about the strange country he would discover there. He realized he hadn't even begun to examine his own life—not only his relations with people, but the complex growth of his mind and the sense of himself as an artist that he had developed by reading books like *Lust for Life*, about Van Gogh and Gauguin.

At his step-grandmother's house he began keeping a journal, and he planned his studies with the design of acquiring universal knowledge. His "Uncle" Pete Adamakis, his step-grandmother's husband, was his co-conspirator in the realms of forbidden learning, handing Jack one of Jules Romain's novels from his vast library in the cellar.

But Jack's academic enthusiasm was quickly fretted.

Every school day he had to travel two and a half hours by subway, from Brooklyn to Van Cortlandt Park. After a full day of classes he would have to spend hours at football practice, then take another long subway ride home, where he barely had time to eat before going to bed. His only study time was on the subway, but he soon found his textbooks less interesting than the faces around him. On his second school day he played hooky, and got off the subway at Times Square to watch the junkies and whores mingling with thousands of other working people, an assortment he had never imagined in Lowell. He went to see an Alice Faye movie at the Paramount, then to the Apollo Theatre for French movies—Jean Gabin in *The Lower Depths* and Louis Jouvet in *Bizarre, Bizarre,* then across the street for Errol Flynn and Miriam Hopkins in *Virginia City.* Times Square held so much potential learning—from the outdoor lunch counters through which funneled enough species of humanity to satiate a Lautrec, to the New York Public Library, two blocks away, housing books even his Uncle Pete lacked—that for the rest of his life Jack was haunted by it as a symbol of all America: at night the red glare of the neons hovered in the little patch of sky above the tall buildings, sealing off the area like a giant room. That crowded chamber was in the heart of the city that was itself the very heart of the land of promises.

Pursuing those promises Jack worked diligently. Not only did he have a scholarship to maintain, but he felt guilty over his father's being fired from Sullivan Printers because he hadn't gone to Boston College. Despite his jaunts around the city he kept up a .92 average, and the work wasn't all drudgery. Jack's history teacher might have been a bore who tried to explain the Trojan War in terms of economic factors, but his English teacher continued the survey of great literature begun by his high school mentor Joe Pyne. In math, Professor Gilmore would keep their wits awake by tossing out a number series that might be no more "mathematical" than the express stops on the Seventh Avenue subway. The French professor, more sympathetic than Jack expected, asked him to read aloud passages of prose in his Canuck *patois,* to let the other students get the proper accent!

If Jack did not understand all the forces that blew him about, he always reacted to them brilliantly. He hardly knew the reason for many of the tasks he had to learn—how to determine the specific gravity of a metal, or plot out the laws of acceleration, or use logarithms—but he exulted in the mastery of all. Moreover, while absorbing this broadside of "college preparation," he was using duty to serve his own curiosity: reading classic French authors in the original texts, discussing classical music and European history, and inquiring into a diversity of religions. Such subjects had interested him since childhood, but he had never before had the time or guidance to explore them in depth.

In football too Jack pushed far beyond his old limits. He finally had a coach who would play him in every game. The coach even let him pass and punt, and with a little practice Jack was kicking perfect spirals, sometimes sixty-five yards. The coach had plenty of tricky plays to teach them too. Led by a quarterback as powerful and strategy-minded as Billy Quinn, their team was bound to take the New York City high-school championship. There were many other powerful players too—Italians, Germans, even another French-Canadian, "ringers" like himself. But it was almost always Jack who made the headlines.

Not yet a well-coordinated team, Horace Mann lost its first game and no one expected they would beat St. John's Prep School in their second. Jack tackled St. John's' potential touchdown runner so hard that he terrified Columbia's assistant freshman coach, who almost got knocked over himself as Jack and his victim tumbled through the crowd at the sidelines. No one was hurt. Horace Mann won six to nothing, an upset which made sports fans all over the city take notice.

On Armistice Day Jack's father came down to watch him play against Garden City, Long Island. Horace Mann won twenty-seven to nothing, but the victory was spoiled for Jack by his having knocked a Garden City player unconscious with one of his headfirst tackles. It reminded him of the time in Lowell, in a sandlot game, when he had done the same thing to a boy named Carrufel. But that time Jack had been seeking justice—Carrufel had secretly punched him in the mouth. This time Garden City player had done nothing to deserve getting his brain bashed. The accident left Jack with still another guilt about his football heroics.

The game helped repay the debt he owed his father, though, because Leo had a great time joking with the other players in the locker room and doing the town with his champion son. He and Jack went to Jack Delaney's steak house on Sheridan Square in Greenwich Village. Satisfied that Jack was progressing in his studies and was well taken care of at the Adamakis's, Leo returned home confident that Jack would make the grade at Columbia the following year. After the game against St. John's Prep, Lou Little had come over to chat with Jack, telling him how much he liked his work. Leo's own future must have seemed brighter now too, since Little would be obliged to fulfill his promise of a "good job."

The last game of the season was against Tome, a Maryland team. Catching a punt on his own twenty-eight yard line, Jack cut and veered all the way for a touchdown, the only score in the game. Later he made a sixty-five-yard run; he also kicked a surprise fifty-five-yard punt that rolled almost to the Tome goal line, and he even completed a forward pass to Quinn for a first down. Not only was the Horace Mann victory another great upset, but Jack's name was plastered across sports sections from New York to Lowell. *The New York Times* extolled his virtues, the *Herald Tribune* called his touchdown sprint "the highlight of the game." He was rated one of the best backs ever to play for Horace Mann. Three years in a row Horace Mann had been unable to score a point against Tome, which was undefeated everywhere. If Jack could crack their defense, there was probably no football machine in the country that could stop him. Ralph Furey, Columbia's freshman coach, as well as two of Little's scouts, had been on the sidelines.

That night as one newspaper put it, "the name of Kerouac was law in the dormitories." Jack planned to bring a couple of his fellow students home with him for Thanksgiving, to impress his old friends and his parents. If Leo and Gabrielle were proud of his familiar football prowess, they must have been virtually incredulous about his new friends, who were the cream of New York society.

Ninety-six percent of the students at Horace Mann were Jewish, most from wealthy families. In Lowell Jack had known neither Jews nor the wealthy Anglo-Saxon and Irish citizens who lived in the exclusive suburb of Chelmsford. As a result, he had only a limited understanding of class distinctions. He knew the working class as he knew what it meant to be rich, but he hardly suspected that the difference between middle and upper-middle class, or between rich and very rich, could determine a city boy's whole future. To Jack, the glittering buildings of New York were already a dream come true. The friendship of other brilliant young men conferred a casual power. That they arrived each morning by limousine, bringing chicken and turkey sandwiches for lunch, while he came by subway with peanut butter and jelly or plain butter sandwiches, seemed no obstacle to friendship, especially since they gladly shared what they had for the warmth of his company.

Because he was fascinated by the lives of these rich Jews, the differences, rather than keeping him apart from them, served as a magnet to hold him tight against the periphery of their world of glamor and luxury. He was overwhelmed at eating dinner off expensive china and drinking wine from crystal goblets. For their part, these young plutocrats, often frail and stilted, enjoyed the combination of Jack's strength and vigor with his bright wit. For a while the apparent equality of the exchange blinded him to how they were often using him for amusement. Feeding the culturally deprived athlete, they would watch him struggle to remember his Emily Post manners (taught him by his sister) the way some people watch to see how a polar bear will pick up a marshmallow. And yet they couldn't prevent him from getting an even greater kick, as a voyeur among voyeurs.

With several of the more easygoing boys Jack did develop a mutual respect. Pete Gordon, son of a Wall Street financier, would sometimes bring Jack home on weekends. Though his father patronized Jack (as the butler brought in his grapefruit) by comparing him to various ancient Greeks, they agreed on the motto *"mens sana in corpore sano,"* a healthy mind in a healthy body. (Jack later suggested the old man garbled the quote, saying *"mens sana et mens corpora."*) More importantly, Pete himself had a genuine desire to help Jack develop as a writer, encouraging him to read Hemingway so he would have a better prose stylist to imitate than Sir Arthur Conan Doyle, Jack's then favorite. Pete also showed him around, and took him to avant-garde movies and to hear Dixieland jazz.

Jack was also accepted into the rollicking bosom of a clique of jokers, among them Eddy Gilbert, Burt Stollmack, Morty Maxwell, and Dick Sheresky, who hipped his naïveté to their fast humor. They often used double-talk and word play, larding their speech with the grotesquely apt names of odd-looking students. Soon Jack could drop the names of Rudo Globus, Merrill Garfinkel, or Shel Blumenkrantz as nonchalantly as the best of them. No one, however, could crack their dull days open like Eddy Gilbert.

Just the sight of Eddy coming down the hall, or even the mention of his name, would send the others into convulsions. Curly-haired and wry-faced, Eddy was known as "the Horace Mannikin." As the scion of a wealthy Long Island family, he had found very early that he could be anything he wanted, and he never tired of sampling the options. His extravagant high jinks were, to Jack, just the embodiment of a boundless American optimism, which they shared, and which was the strongest bond between them. Stultified by the poverty of Lowell, Jack's optimism had developed much less obstreperously than Eddy's. But if and when it was properly nourished, he would gladly caper madly like this carefree boy genius.

On the chess team together, Eddy and Jack could only beat their opponents if they refrained from looking at each other—otherwise they would burst out laughing. If most of Jack's rich friends were fascinated by his good looks and body power, Eddy was one of the few to appreciate a mind as receptive as his own. Frequently on weekends he would invite Jack to stay at his parents' house in Flushing, and Jack never forgot the splendor of Eddy's room. The fancy curtains, the tennis racket on the wall, the brass-handled dresser full of clean socks and shirts, and the closet full of tennis shoes and golden shoe trees left him breathless.

Eddy's father was a lumber dealer who carried hundred dollar bills in his wallet, and he delighted in giving Jack his first sight of one. Eddy himself reminded Jack of their social difference by paying him two dollars apiece for English term papers (though Jack sold these to many other rich kids too, as well as doing them for free for the football ringers). At any rate, Eddy sometimes traded with Jack by doing his math, and in a sense it was a joke because the teachers knew what they were doing and gave them each seventy minus on such swaps. But for all their kidding, and for all Eddy's sincere affection, there was no hiding the screened porch, the obsequious maid, the smell of bacon and eggs cooking downstairs when they awoke on Sunday morning, or, at night, the Fitzgeraldian "moonlight on the lawn." As Jack was getting swept up in this sea of sensitivity, he was also finding that the only way he could survive was as an observer on someone else's ship. His classmates were planning on becoming great restaurateurs, realtors, department store tycoons, scientists, and (like Eddy) financial wizards. The only form of wizardry Jack could afford was the Balzacian magic of making all but his eyes disappear.

No wonder he was writing Mary Carney about his homesickness, about how discouraged he had grown, and how much he wanted to see her again. In turn she, G.J., Scotty, and Freddy had been writing how much they missed him too, how strange they found his being gone from Lowell. Jack hoped he could have the best of both worlds. On Thanksgiving vacation he introduced Lowell to two of his society friends, Pete Gordon and Bob Olsted, bringing everyone together like a master of ceremonies, as though he could create one happy family from all the different people in his life. How different could they be if they were all his friends? To see, he would pit one against another, then stand back to watch the interplay. At the sight of these mad New Yorkers Salvey gleefully broke a huge windowpane on Moody Street, but when Jack bounced them off G.J., the reaction was more subtle.

Jack had yelled, "G.J.! G.J.! Wait'll you see these guys!" Then to Pete and Bob he said, "Wait'll you guys see this guy!" Pete and Bob found nothing exceptional about G.J., who was as quick-minded as they were, but a lot more humble. Bob offered to show G.J. how to shave without missing a puff on a cigarette. After Bob finished the demonstration, G.J. asked, "Could you do it again? I didn't quite see how you did it." Bob lathered up and performed again. Then G.J. said, "Run through it once more, so I can see it from another angle." Still another time G.J. made him do it so Jack could "take notes"— and Bob finally cut himself!

But while they struggled to find something in common, Jack snuck off to see Mary. They fell into each other's arms and pledged their love anew, promising to meet again at Christmas. There was no time to find out how each had changed, no way to make further plans, but they couldn't deny their mutual need.

It was a triumphant Thanksgiving at the Kerouacs'. The *Lowell Sun* printed a long article about Jack's return, enumerating his achievements and announcing his definite berth on the Columbia freshman team the next fall. Jack had even secured a position with the *World-Telegram* to cover the Horace Mann basketball games, and he proudly told the *Sun* reporter he had "had this type of work in mind since his high school days." At seventeen Jack had, incredibly, put foundations under all his dreams. A year before he wouldn't have dared confront his parents with the truth about his wanting to be a writer. Now his career seemed so safe and the direction of his life so clear that he no longer feared displeasing anyone in the pursuit of his ambitions.

He didn't know the world itself would jolt him loose from that smugness. The first jolt came from as far away as Africa.

2.

Lowell's Merrimack Hotel, across from the railroad depot, had a mirrored ballroom where jazz dance bands were featured every weekend. Whether or not Jack had ever gone there, his exposure to jazz was probably minimal. Real jazz was not on the radio or in any of the fashionable clubs of the East during the thirties, but flourished in "open" cities like Kansas City and Chicago. In New York the fast driving tempo, innovative rhythms, and improvisation that made jazz "hot" could be heard mostly in Harlem, where many musicians lived hand-to-mouth on the shared proceeds from after-hours sessions in the poorest cellar bars. Black men had no reason to welcome visitors from the race that had put them in such places.

After escaping the Nazi blitz, however, a young Jew with a taste for jive wasn't about to worry over dirty looks. Besides, although Seymour Wyse's father had sent him to America for safety, Seymour knew better than his famous chemist dad that America was for fun. In math class at Horace Mann, Seymour was called "Nutso." This class comedian's best audience was Jack Kerouac. Jack admired the cool way Seymour would slouch in his fancy sports coat, like a hepcat, when he failed to answer the professor's questions. After the football season, Jack followed him to Harlem hot spots like the Savoy, Minton's, and the Apollo Theater to see the original hepcats and hear what made them groove.

Until then, Jack had thought the best band in New York was Muggsy Spanier's, a small Dixieland group still sizzling with the Chicago style. But Spanier, a white ex–sandlot baseball player from Chicago's Austin High School, had nothing on the Count. From the moment Jack heard Count Basie's Big Swing Machine, powered by soloists like Lester "Prez" Young, Herschel Evans, Harry "Sweets" Edison, Buck Clayton, and Dicky Wells, he lost his taste for smoothie imitations. In its commercial white form the vehicle of black culture had become national necking music or, worse, the background for tea dances at the Plaza. The very qualities that made swing popular—chord progressions usually limited to triads and seventh chords, simple syncopations, melodies bound to the phrase structure of dance music—restricted its expressiveness as an art form.

The Count had learned his style in Kansas City, where swing had grown directly out of the blues. Commercial swing had an exciting, razzle-dazzle quality, but Kansas City swing still showed feeling.

There was a tremendous drive to the Kansas City style, too, which resulted from piling riff on riff far beyond the normal expectations of swing music. Kansas City swing had a solid, slap-stick beat. Basie's band had the strongest rhythm section in the country, yet its beat—like the whispering brushes of drummer Jo Jones—was always felt more than heard, and there was room for much individual creativity. The great innovator Lester "Prez" Young, who had turned the exuberance of swing to a new "cool" intensity, became one of Jack's greatest heroes. In 1939 and 1940, the intuitive logic that would explode swing with shifting accents and harsh asymmetries was just seeping into the work of Prez, Dizzy Gillespie, Charlie "Bird" Parker, and Thelonius Monk. Jack, choosing Basie's band to teach him the tricks of spontaneous sound, must have foreseen early the force of that still unnamed brainchild: bop.

One of Jack's first reactions to Harlem jazz was to start a music column in *The Horace Mann Record*. There, with the help of Wyse and future songwriter Donald Wolf among others, Jack instructed his classmates that they ought to be paying attention to solo improvisation in jazz, rather than the blasting brass of most swing bands. After interviewing the Count, Jack wrote: "Basie's swing arrangements are not blaring, but they contain more drive, more power, and more thrill than the loudest gang of corn artists can acquire by blowing their horns apart." He also examined the way the various band members worked together to preserve each player's peculiarities of style, and he stressed the soloists' perfect control of their instruments, which permitted intelligent innovation.

Another classmate, Albert Avakian, was the brother of George Avakian, a jazz critic. George sent the Horace Mann library a set of Chicago-style jazz albums he had produced himself, and Jack and Albert reviewed them in detail in the *Record*. The powerful drive of these Chicago musicians amazed Jack, as did the spectrum of feeling they managed to convey. Albert brought Jack home to hear his own collection, among which were old recordings of Bix Beiderbecke, the self-destructive alcoholic cornetist whose clean melodic lines and subtle improvisations had strongly influenced Prez.

With Mort Maxwell Jack went to the Paramount Theatre to interview Glenn Miller, though by this time Jack was more impressed with Miller's saying "shit" than with his rather tame swing. Still, Jack loved the frenzied joy Miller induced in his audience. Sometimes he would sit in the front row at Jimmy Lunceford's performances, feeling a similar ecstasy as that big band overwhelmed his senses. Yet he already had a discerning ear, and among his other musical favorites were Duke Ellington, Harry James, Artie Shaw, and Frank Sinatra.

That winter Jack had plenty of leisure, since he was too short for the basketball team and Horace Mann didn't sponsor indoor track. It was a time rife with new pleasures. Just the sound of jazz had a vast impact on him, opening his mind to a range of feelings long stifled in Lowell, and making him realize that with enough technical virtuosity and imaginative daring an artist could express every nuance of his emotions. But the new world to which jazz introduced Jack also woke him to the reality of black men's humanity, something of a discovery in 1940 for a boy from a lily-white New England town. Hanging out in Harlem he was now getting to know many of the musicians and learning their private kicks. Here he smoked his first marijuana, recently made illegal, and probably tried benzedrine as well. And though he had lost his virginity in December with a red-haired prostitute in midtown Manhattan, he soon acquired a taste for the black prostitutes in the jazz scene uptown.

At the same time he was also expanding his forays into high society. Dick Sheresky brought Jack to his penthouse to meet his sister Jacky. In Yonkers he went skating with Bob Olsted's sister. David Rhodes let him stay at his Park Avenue apartment. Joe Kennedy (not the famous one) accepted him into a wealthy Irish group that included William F. Buckley, Jr. Dean Charles Tellinghast even introduced his son to Jack. With Mort Maxwell Jack had wild adventures he would never have dared in Lowell, like reaching into the subway to knock men's hats off just as the train started. There were drinks at the Plaza, concerts at Carnegie Hall, strolls through the World's Fair, drives to Yale, candlelight dates, and smooching in the dark of plush living rooms. Jack, like the Biblical dog under the table, fed on the scraps of others' good fortune.

Mentally he was active too. The Brooklyn of Whitman fascinated him (he didn't yet know Thomas Wolfe), and he would take long walks by himself, often crossing the Brooklyn Bridge. He also did some solitary explorations in the Village, hanging around jazz clubs like Nick's. His meditations were clarifying and deepening his world view, as can be seen by the two short stories he wrote for *The Horace Mann Quarterly*.

The first story, "The Brothers," published in 1939, was a murder mystery solved by a detective whose persistent inductive reasoning is nothing short of boring. The only interesting thing about "The Brothers"—aside from the fact that it shows how studiously Jack had absorbed all the conventions of the genre—is the setting. The story both begins and ends with reference to the homey comforts of an aunt's house in a little town called Pelham. Pelham, New Hampshire, was the town to which Jack had run away as a child, and his own aunts lived in similar small New Hampshire towns. The detectives have learned to track crime in the big city, but the source of their unfailing righteousness seems to lie in a love for simple things like "Aunt Hilary's squash pie." The fact that this particular murder does take place in the small town, and is committed by one brother upon another, heightens the sense of the "brotherly love" proper to a family by showing the base materialism of the brute who betrays it.

The second story, "Une Veille de Noel," published in 1940, contains much more variation, probably one of the first influences of jazz in his writing (though he could have learned variation from football too). In fact, "Une Veille de Noel" fails as a story because it is almost all variation, but that is the really remarkable thing about it. We get snatches of many of Kerouac's later literary fortes: a native American symbolism, figured here in the glow of red neon on snowswept city streets; a casual, yet deep recognition of human frailty in the great preacher who "liked to sleep too much all his life—ruined his brilliant career"; a precise attention to physical details in the "Spanish music" on the radio and "the moist circle formed by the bottom of his glass"; and the deadpan surrealistic slapstick of an angel stopping in his local bar to say "Merry Christmas."

Although "Une Veille de Noel" has the sort of surprise, moralistic ending of an O. Henry short story, its theme is much more profound. This theme would become central to all of Kerouac's later writings: that the universe is microcosmically present in the smallest frames, such as a poor man's kitchen, a young boy's window, or, as here, a barroom isolated from the outside world by a blizzard. Jack might have found the theme in Emily Dickinson, Walt Whitman, or any number of other writers; a few years later he would find it elaborated in Blake. But in "Une Veille de Noel" he treats it with freshness and the sort of piercing honesty one finds in Stephen Crane, who also had a penchant for gathering various American types in one place, so that their interaction becomes a paradigm of American society. There is also a conscious parody of Hemingway, melding "A Clean, Well-Lighted Place" and "The Gambler, the Nun, and the Radio" into a tender satire of American loneliness— Kerouac once referred to the story as "The Counterman, the Drunkard, and the Collegian."

Tone is usually one of the last things a writer develops, so it should be no surprise that the young Kerouac had trouble knowing whether he was writing a serious religious parable, a cute takeoff on "The Emperor's New Clothes," or a joke at the expense of drunkards, who may be used to seeing pink elephants but get a little shook when they see an actual angel. But that he had the courage to put an actual angel into a short story—Wolfe had been condemned as sentimental for just his marble ones—shows that the eighteen-year-old Kerouac was already staking off highly original territory. The description of the angel with deep brown eyes and bloodless white skin suggests a resurrected Christ, an even bolder revision of things sacred. The story supposedly caused something of a sensation at Horace Mann.

3.

During Christmas vacation Jack saw Mary again. His experience with whores, which he had hinted about in letters to her, only made her think him primed for marriage. She worried more about his society friends, for there seemed no way she could fit into his life alongside them. Although he wanted to marry her, his mother insisted that his studies must come first; Gabrielle suggested he simply take her to a dance instead! Working out of town now, his father wasn't around to offer advice. Jack and Mary had another tearful good-bye, and reluctantly he left her to her many other boy friends in Lowell.

By the time he invited her to his spring prom, Mary was steadily dating Jimmy Taylor, the boxer with the roadster. Since he had an "inside track," Jimmy didn't fear Jack's competition. Mary made it clear to everyone, including Jack, that she wanted no part of New York. In fact, she wouldn't even have attended the prom had he not insisted on it.

When she came to New York, Jack let Peter Gordon lend her his ritzy roof. That was the beginning of the end since in Mary's eyes sophisticated Peter was simply "fast." Though she had grown into a slender Clara Bow type of beauty who flustered the boys at the Commodore Ballroom, her best pink gown lagged sadly behind the Lord & Taylor formals worn by the powdered and bejeweled society girls at the prom. With a rose in her hair she was as beloved to Jack as ever, but he was no longer the same to her. Wearing white tie and tails given him by Burt Stollmack's uncle, and with his face beet red from a sun lamp, he hardly seemed the shy Canuck kid who would be happy working on the railroad, raising kids in a cottage. When she heard some rich girl sneering over her "homemade dress," Mary burst into tears.

Their whole evening was wrecked, as well as whatever chance they had for a lifetime together. She told him she would never marry him if he lived in New York. Lowell held the only security she knew, and she prophesied that it would be Jack's only security too, that his rich friends would forget him when the wind shifted. If he stayed in New York, she warned, he would burn himself out like a moth in a locomotive firebox; and pointedly she asked what the towers of Manhattan could be to him compared to her love. Neither that night nor the next two days they spent together could he come up with an answer to keep her from returning to Lowell hurt and disillusioned.[10] A few years later, discussing the event with Allan Temko, a Columbia friend, Jack would see it as a major turning point in his life.

For the rest of his life, both in his writing and in conversation, Jack would assert that his love for Mary was of an intensity never to be repeated. Every few years he returned to Lowell to tell her that she was the one love of his life, and their parting would be repeated, each time with increasing brusqueness and bitterness, as his lifestyle grew increasingly distant from any she could have desired.

He was caught in a dilemma that would impale many spirits stronger than himself, for a new sexual freedom was already driving permanent wedges in families across the nation. The Depression was ending; people suddenly had money to play again, with nothing to stop them but fear of the consequences of "sin," and how could those consequences be any worse than the economic purgation they had already been through? For Jack the dilemma was even worse because, as a writer, the freedom to experience life was essential.

The values his parents had given him—to get married and raise a family, and to get an education and better himself in the big city— had proved to be at odds. The fact that he couldn't do both at the same time kept him alternating between domesticity with his family and the public life of a writer (making money and "the scene"). His was an aggravated case of the disease peculiar to his age: a splitting of the old morality into two separate codes, honor and expediency. You were now successful or you were good, but seldom both. In short, there was no Pure Land in the modern world. The Pure Land was the past, and only to that could you look for stability. The newborn writer had his theme cut out for him.

In Jack's personal life that split was a good deal more destructive. From time to time the demands of the world would become so egregious he would simply quit, leave success and popularity as he had left Mary, and drift around the country, frustrated by the fact that every act was only a halfway measure, born of a failure of his original purpose. As guilt from that failure mounted, he would lapse into the self-flagellation he called *beat*. And in his writing the self-flagellation generated a double-edged irony that sliced life open to its core.

His sense of irony helped him through the humiliation of his graduation from Horace Mann. Lacking money to buy a white suit, he was condemned to wait behind the gym until the ceremonies were over. He spurned the "pomp and circumstance" by lying in the grass reading Walt Whitman, a start toward his understanding the painful triumph of the common man in America.

That summer, 1940, his parents were living on Gershom Avenue. Though now very poor, they didn't ask him to get a job, for it seemed more important that he should continue the studies that had already brought him honor. He read voraciously, pinning new vocabulary words all over his bedroom wall, and kept a philosophical journal, with comments about the "marvelousness of perfect nothingness" in the empty sky, and about the sense of eternity he got from killing a moth that crawled across his page. The stories he wrote were based on Hemingway, but Thoreau and Thomas Hardy fascinated him too. What most influenced him, however, was a biography of Jack London. That rugged adventurer, who went after stories like other men do big game, living and recording his life at the same time, gave Jack the model for his own literary career. It wasn't hard to identify with London, for Jack himself had reached a point where work and play merged and fun was the most serious thing in his life. Jack's happiness even seemed to influence his father. Despite having lost his job managing the Pawtucketville Social Club, Leo spent much time bowling and shooting pool there that summer, whooping it up with his old friend Mike Fournier, Sr., so that the whole neighborhood could hear.

One day Jack heard someone calling his name out on the street. Looking down from the high front porch he recognized Sebastian "Sammy" Sampas, the boy who had introduced him to Miss Mansfield's literary club at Bartlett Junior High. Sammy had felt tenderly toward Jack ever since Jack had rescued him from a beating by several older kids during a "war" between the Irish and the Greeks. Though the same age, Sammy had been a year behind Jack in school. The flood had literally washed the Sampas family out of Rosemont Terrace, and sent them packing to the Highlands, which was why Jack hadn't seen Sammy for a few years. When Jack asked him why he had decided to visit, Sammy replied that he had been watching Jack for a long time and had discovered their similar interests.

Sammy wanted to be an actor and a poet. Unlike Jack he wasn't shy about his artistic inclinations, but would occasionally jump up on café tables to declaim Byron and Shelley. Having heard of Jack's pretensions to being "Baron Jean-Louis Lebris de Kerouac," Sammy announced that he was really Sampas Sampatacacus, the "Prince of Crete." Sammy's best friend was John Koumantzelis, another Lowell High track star, who used to accompany Jack on his wanderings around Boston after meets. Sammy was also close friends with John MacDonald, the kid at Bartlett with the big library, whose literary ambition was now as great as Jack's. In fact, Sammy was at the center of a circle of Lowell intellectuals that included Cornelius "Connie" Murphy, a whiz at physics, George Constantinides, who would later work for the CIA, Ed Tully, another aspiring writer, and Jim O'Dea, who would be considered as a Vice-Presidential running mate by John F. Kennedy. They called themselves "the young Prometheans," for they were dedicated to using their brains and power for the betterment of mankind, and it didn't take long for an idealist like Jack to join them.

Jack, Sammy, and John Koumantzelis formed a strikingly handsome trio, but Jack and John were the chief girl hunters, since Sammy still had an ethereal notion of love born from his passion for all of humanity. Because of his flamboyant gestures—bursting into tears over the inevitable death of all beauty, and posturing with a cigarette holder and his father's black overcoat worn as a cape— some people considered Sam effeminate. When Jack's father heard that he would soon be studying drama at Emerson College in Boston, he asked if Sam intended to be another Greta Garbo. At times Sam would even serenade Jack with romantic songs. But it would be a mistake to consider their relationship gay; thus far Jack's only sexual experiences had been with hookers in New York and Sam considered sex outside of marriage immoral. Whatever their respective sexual orientations, they developed profound affection and respect for each other. Their friendship had a very practical basis. Sammy, like every other artist in America, wanted to be understood. And Jack, he sensed correctly, loved the world enough to want to understand it.

Sammy quickly infected Jack with his passion for William Saroyan. Here was a writer who wrote with tender humor about small-town people, a writer who found the simplest actions of every-day life worthy of investigation, and who most often tempered his judgments with sympathy. The fact that Jack's father considered Saroyan an idiot—feeling Saroyan had no sense of the tragedy of a life like Leo's—only increased Leo's belief that Sammy was a bad influence on Jack. Jack, however, was no longer paying much attention to his father's prejudices. When Sammy recommended Thomas Wolfe, Jack took his suggestion and made one of the greatest discoveries of his artistic life.

Sammy himself had mixed feelings about Wolfe. He thought Jack should rather concentrate on Byron, who showed more social responsibility. But Wolfe's sincere love of America, and his gigantic effort to create an idiom that could fully express the beauty of America, captured Jack's heart. To the end of his life Jack would tell people that he preferred Wolfe even to such other favorites as Melville and Whitman, whose voices he found essentially European. He never stopped reading Wolfe with amazement and delight. By this time G.J. had become as much a literary influence on Jack as Sammy. While Jack was gone from Lowell they had kept up a voluminous correspondence, full of poetry as well as bawdy wit. Like Jack, G.J. "flipped" when he read Wolfe. Jack and G.J. would copy out favorite passages to read to each other. Another of G.J.'s favorite authors was de Maupassant, whom he recommended to Jack.

Only a small part of Jack's discoveries that summer were literary. He spent most of his time with his old friends. At the Rialto Theatre they made friends with two ushers, George Dastou and a Polish kid called "Beansey." Soon G.J. got a part-time job there, and on Saturday nights he would let in a group of girls for free, as long as they promised to meet the guys afterward. Often enough they ended up walking home by themselves down Moody Street, which was lined with taverns and dives; among servicemen it was known as "the tail of two cities." At Barrett's Café Jack had his first beer.

Bob Crosby was one of their favorites on "The 920 Club." When they heard he was coming to Canobie Lake Park, they all saved their money to see him. Bob and Ray Eberle sang that evening too. Afterward, they were so excited they returned to Barrett's for three large beers apiece. When they started feeling sick, they headed for the ice cream parlor on Bridge Street to get something to eat. On the way they grabbed people in the street to proclaim that everybody was God. At the ice cream parlor Jack disappeared, and they found him outside, leaning over the railing above the canal, throwing up.

"What the hell did you do?" G.J. asked Jack. Jack told him he had drunk some tomato juice, which he had always been recommending to them for hangovers.

"Pretty good stuff, heh?" asked G.J.

"Yeah, it sure flies," Jack said in a sickly voice.

Soon to be married, Freddy spent little time with them. Jack introduced Sammy as a new member, but there were obstacles to his acceptance. When Sammy and Jack talked literature, the conversation went over the heads of Scotty and Salvey; nor did those two care for Sammy's poetry recitals. Even G.J. found that Jack and Sammy related "on a higher level." Moreover, there was a long-standing feud between G.J.'s and Sammy's families, because a Sampatacacus had killed an Apostolakos (as the surname was originally spelled) in a coffeehouse on Market Street. G.J. himself held no grudge, though, and he and Sammy usually enjoyed each other's company.

Still, G.J. used to enjoy puncturing Sammy's pretensions. Sammy advertised his resemblance to Victor Mature, and although quite tall, he would walk on the inside of the sidewalk to look even taller. One night G.J. let them all into the Rialto after hours, and Sammy put on a one-man performance of Shakespeare. He really enjoyed capering around the stage, declaiming over all their heads, but he was so awkward he fell off. Grabbing Sam by the head, G.J. yelled, "Stay away from him! His back might be broken! I'll apply first aid!" and then twisted Sam's neck hard.

Jack kept promising to show the guys New York, but no one had money for the trip. George Dastou and Beansey, the ushers at the Rialto, told them there was no need to go that far since a girl called "Dirty Marilyn" would take care of them all after the double feature. And as promised, she did.

She hid in the ladies' room until the audience had left; when she came out all the guys took turns fucking her behind the stage. One night Dastou and Beansey told the gang they would have to fuck her in Scotty's car, since they could no longer use the theater. In the first car there were four guys, who took so long that Jack, G.J., and Scotty got sick of waiting. Jack said it was crazy to sit there watching. Although not bashful with the gang, Jack was embarrassed about sex in front of others. When they got home, he said he was amazed that a woman could like sex enough to take on two carloads of men.

Most of their activities that summer were a lot more wholesome. They formed a basketball team, the "Five Aces," to play at the Boys Club. Freddy and Salvey were the only tall members, and on one occasion G.J. fouled out before he even touched the ball. Their team ended up in last place, though they joked that they had the strongest team in the league since they were "holding the others up."

Jack wanted to keep in shape for football in the fall. At Dracut Tigers Field they would practice double plays, or just take turns whacking the ball till they made ten outs apiece—Jack bare-chested, by now burned quite brown. Sometimes he would bring his timing device over to the cinder track at the Textile Institute, and make them all run till they couldn't stand up. Other times they just went for relaxing swims at Pine Brook, where one of the Marist brothers who had taught Jack would swim in his shorts. One hot day Jack's father came and took a flying leap into the brook, but there had been a long dry spell and the fat man flopped painfully into three feet of water. It was one of the first occasions when Jack, as he later told Allen Ginsberg, felt a mature sympathy for his father, a realization of the old man's spent strength and lost dreams.

Jack had a wealth of simple pleasures. He and G.J. went to the C.M.A.C. to watch wrestling. Imitating the wrestler Eddie Fouché, G.J. would try to pin Jack, earning the nickname "Fouch," though Jack always came out on top. Some days Jack went to the Rialto to watch G.J. put up letters on the marquee. As G.J. removed the name of the old feature, he would say, "Hey, Zagg, that's show biz!" and Jack would grin in delight. Sometimes Jack gathered an audience of two or three vagrants from the diner next door. If G.J. hammed it up too long, Dastou, the manager, would come out to hurry him up.

Toward the end of the summer Frank Leahy of Boston College asked Jack to come for a tryout. He went, and the Boston backfield coach told Leahy Jack was the best halfback he had ever seen. Jack was also tempted by the fact that the Boston coaches would let him run straight downfield, whereas Little would force him to learn his KT–79 reverse play, which—in Jack's view—entailed a lot of wasted effort. But he steadfastly refused Boston's offers.

When G.J. started working in a mill afternoons and evenings, Jack offered to walk him and his girl to the mill, so she wouldn't have to walk home alone. Appreciating Jack's generosity, G.J. agreed—soon to find that the girl was no longer his, but Jack's! When he found another girl Jack pulled the same trick, but G.J. was glad to see him finally overcoming his shyness.

The sight of G.J. going to work in a dirty red-brick mill must have made Jack realize they could not prolong childhood forever. Many of the mills were now empty, because to avoid paying union wages over half the mill owners had moved their operations down South. Lowellians felt lucky just to land one of the waning mill jobs, but Jack repeatedly asserted that he would rather do anything than become a "mill rat."

And yet he had never felt more desolate about having to leave Lowell. At the last minute he wanted to give up his scholarship to Columbia. He even talked about living in the woods like Thoreau, until his parents set him straight about the value of a college education. The only problem was that they again lacked the fare to New York. This time Jack approached the Nadeau brothers, who were about to drive down to the World's Fair. Leo wanted to go too, to talk to Lou Little about the job he had never gotten. The Nadeau brothers agreed, as long as Leo would chip in for gas. Because they were also taking another friend, Emil Descheneaux, Jack and his father had to ride in the rumble seat of their little Rockne. Practical jokers, the Nadeau brothers gave Leo the roughest ride of his life— but Leo got even by not paying a cent for gas!

Leo and Jack went to the World's Fair and ate in some nice restaurants, but there was a gloom over all their celebrations. With France fallen, London under blitz, and Russia fast slipping down the Nazi drain, the world was hardly concerned about college football. Moreover, Lou Little showed no personal interest in them, leaving Jack's instruction to freshman coach Ralph Furey, and not granting Leo an interview. When Leo said good-bye, exhorting Jack to make his family proud, there were tears in the old man's eyes.

4.

Jack's room in Hartley Hall was full of cockroaches and had a depressing view of Amsterdam Avenue. He managed to switch to Livingston Hall, from which he could see the frieze of the new Columbia library, engraved with the names of the world's greatest writers. Gazing out at "Goethe . . . Voltaire . . . Shakespeare . . . Molière . . . Dante," his radio tuned to the classical music of WQXR, Jack sat in the glow of his reading lamp, puffing on a pipe and sighing to himself that he had finally become a collegian.

Though scrimmage under the lights at Baker Field was exciting, Jack especially loved the Manor House, the old training house under big trees, which felt haunted. But his football career turned out to be more literally haunted, as he again faced exclusion from the starting lineup. This time the injustice was greater than at Lowell High, because Columbia's freshman team was the poorest Jack had ever played on. And, as he himself admitted, when no one encouraged him he was apt to get lazy. Out on the practice field till dark every evening, his eyes began to stray across the Harlem River to the bright lights that gave more certain promise of adventure.

College was harder work than he had supposed. He had to read the *Iliad,* the *Odyssey,* John Stuart Mill, Aeschylus, Plato, and Horace within a few weeks. There were four hours of football practice each weekday, and to pay for his meals he had to wash dishes in the cafeteria. Dean Hawkes did invite Jack to his house for dinner, along with three other boys, and showed them his dinosaur egg. It was one of the few official kindnesses Jack ever received from Columbia.

The first game of the season, against Rutgers, Jack wasn't put in until the second half. Columbia lost eighteen to seven, though the school newspaper said Jack was probably the best back on the field. A few days later Little came down to Baker Field to watch Jack run. He brought his backfield coach, Cliff Battles, once a great football player himself and a boyhood hero of Jack's. Battles liked Jack enough to see that he was started in the second game, against St. Benedict's Prep School.

With Little, Ralph Furey, Battles, and the coach of the Army team on the sidelines, Jack ran back the kickoff ninety yards, just missing a touchdown. A few plays later, after he caught a punt, he tried to wrest free from a couple of tacklers and cracked his right tibia. The trainer told him it was just a sprain. The next few days at practice, Jack kept complaining about the pain, but Little insisted he run it off. After a week Jack finally got them to take X-rays; then they put his leg in a cast, and he was out of action the rest of the season.

Fortunately his leg hadn't been seriously injured by running on the fractured bone, but his morale had been dampened by Little's taunts. Previously, Leo had suggested that Little was ignoring Jack because the coach favored Italian players. Now Jack began to think that Little distrusted him for his continuing flirtations with Leahy at Boston College. The previous winter Jack had been taken to dinner by Bill Sullivan, the owner of Sullivan Printers. On another occasion Frank Leahy himself had taken Jack to a play on Times Square, and when Jack had gone downstairs to the washroom, he had seen Ralph Furey watching him. Now Jack felt a definite malice in Little, as Little threatened to keep him from running altogether the second year by making him a guard.

Jack liked the leisure his injury gave him. Every night he would relax by the fireplace in the Lion's Den restaurant, eating filet mignon and hot fudge sundaes. He finally had time to read all his assigned books, and all of Thomas Wolfe as well, which made such a powerful impression on him that he wrote G.J.—now in the Civilian Conservation Corps in Colorado —letters "like books," describing his reactions to Wolfe's literary discovery of America. Many years later, in *Vanity of Duluoz,* Jack credited Wolfe with awakening him to the idea of America as a poem, rather than just a place to work and struggle in. Wolfe renewed Jack's desire to travel through America, which had first been stirred by the rail-riding hobos of the Depression.

He also spent more time than ever on Times Square, seeing movies he would remember all his life: French films with Louis Jouvet and Jean Gabin, the sensitive antihero who was one of his male ideals; Basil Rathbone as Sherlock Holmes; epic romances like *Union Pacific*, with Barbara Stanwyck and Joel McCrea; and, perhaps most memorably, Harry Bauer as Georg Friedrich Handel, who made Jack cry as he knelt to pray for inspiration. Sometimes he would take the subway in the other direction, to Harlem, and wander the streets in continual amazement at the life of black people.

In the Lion's Den Jack got interested in a Welsh girl named Vicki Williams, though he never got up courage to do more than watch her dance. Instead of making friends, he would retire to his room to write long Wolfean stories and continue the journal he had begun at his aunt's house in Brooklyn.

In most of his studies Jack got good grades, including an A in French. His only problem subject was chemistry, for which a black friend, Jimmy Thomas, helped him study. Jack had become so popular as the injured football hero, hobbling around campus on his crutches, that someone started a campaign to get him elected vice-president of next year's sophomore class. His old friends from Horace Mann frequently visited him, and he spent a lot of time with Joe Kennedy and William F. Buckley, Jr.

That winter and spring, Jack reported sports for the college paper and wrote term papers for his friends. He joined the Phi Gamma Delta fraternity, where with tears in his eyes he would drink beer and listen to Glenn Miller and Frank Sinatra records full blast. There was an endless supply of great books in the Columbia library, and on campus he kept making new friends. With some of them he would go to the West End Bar. Outside, men pissed on the sidewalk; inside he talked football with the huge bartender, Johnny Glassman, who had a great liking for him.

Among his new friends there were none with whom he could have serious literary or philosophical conversations. On one occasion, which troubled him all his life, he joined a few other football players in beating up a homosexual violinist in the Village. A few years later, he would refer to all these friends as a "bunch of jerks." The spiritual void they left could only be filled by long, solitary walks across the Brooklyn Bridge, retracing the steps of Wolfe. Drawn away from his studies by those lonely pilgrimages, he would usually end up in Bowery hasheries to write what he had seen.

By the time spring training began, Jack's leg was completely healed, and his campaign for vice-president perhaps indicated to Little that his halfback planned to stay at Columbia. In any case, Little became friendlier. The newspapers reported that he might make Jack a starter with the Columbia varsity the following fall, quite an honor for a sophomore, even if the new military draft was beginning to thin college ranks. The only rub was that Little, having relegated Jack to the wingback position, preferred to save him as a climax runner, meaning Jack would probably see action as infrequently as he had at Lowell High School. Little hinted, however, that whether or not Jack would start every game depended on his gaining polish as a passer and kicker. Since until now Jack had been able to accomplish everything he had set his mind to, this ultimatum didn't seem very threatening.

That May Leo came down to visit Jack again, just in time to learn that his son had been elected vice-president of the sophomore class. Their joy was clouded by Jack's failing chemistry. The chemistry professor told him he would have to make up the course at home during the summer or lose his scholarship.

That summer Jack did everything but study chemistry. He had met a girl from a college in North Adams, who was working at a wealthy retirement hotel in Manchester, Vermont. She wanted Jack to visit her there, only she asked that he bring dates for her three girlfriends too. Since Freddy had gotten married, and Salvey was working out of town, Jack brought G.J., Scotty, and Sammy to meet them.

When they got to the inn, they were all on their best behavior. As the girls weren't to get off work for a few hours, they suggested meeting later at a drugstore in town. Outside on the porch G.J. looked at all the old millionaires "rocking their lives away," watching the sunset without even any water around, and it reminded him of a graveyard.

"Jesus Christ, Zagg!" G.J. said, "let's get outa this place!"

To kill time they began driving around town, and finally headed for the swimming hole, a local quarry. On the way they stopped for a pint of whisky, and then all of them got drunk except Sam, who didn't drink. Jack dove down twenty feet and stayed there until Sam, thinking he was drowning, dove after him. Jack emerged laughing. Then, to show them how strong he was, he tried to wrap one young tree around another—not once, but twice around!

Back at the drugstore the girls hadn't arrived. Jack ordered a ginger ale, Scotty a root beer, and G.J. a Coke. Theatrical as ever, Sammy said, "I'll have a fresh fruit sundae, *and I do mean fresh fruit!*" They all laughed and said he could recite poetry to the girls. G.J. bragged that he was going to "make" his girl. Finally most of them got so sick they had to go lie down in the car. G.J. and Jack staggered over to the hotel and sat down on the porch. Rocking among the old people, they started discussing their "stocks and bonds," though they didn't fool anybody. Eventually they were all so drunk that all they could do was lamely apologize to the girls that the date would have to be called off.

Jack never got over the shock in those girls' eyes at the transformation wrought in three hours! All the way home, resting on Sammy's lap, Jack brooded over his ruined love. Over and over he asked, "Why did we do it?" even though G.J. kept telling him, "Christ! We didn't do nothin'!" At the sight of Jack's misery, Sammy started to cry.

On the way home Sam and Jack fell asleep, and G.J. relieved Scotty at the wheel, but as they came down the mountains, he started to doze too. Scotty managed to stop the car just before they plowed through a road sign and plunged down seventy-five feet. A year before, also in Vermont, Jack had had a serious crack-up; the impact of these accidents was something he never recovered from. Years later, writing to Ed White, he blamed the fear of crashing for his failure to learn to drive properly.

That summer Sammy and Jack were reading Dos Passos' *U.S.A.* trilogy and *Manhattan Transfer,* and Joyce's *A Portrait of the Artist as a Young Man.* But even more impressive than Sammy's literacy was his perpetual sadness. His response to human suffering was to practice "the arts of kindness," and he told his friends that of them all, Jack was the one who would someday become a great writer.

He and Jack hitchhiked to Boston several times, to see movies or just lounge in Boston Common watching the people. Sometimes Sammy would make soapbox speeches about the benefits of communism, in his eyes equivalent to the Brotherhood of Man. Jack also hitchhiked to Boston with Billy Chandler, with the vague notion of getting on a merchant ship.

On the Fourth of July, Jack, G.J., and Scotty went to a burlesque show at the Old Howard in Boston, their first. After the show there was a long line to the bathroom.

"Are they going to the head or are they playing with themselves?" Jack complained.

"We'll soon find out!" G.J. said, laughing.

Playing the man about town, Jack led the others to a bar on Scollay Square, where he claimed they would find "plenty of snatch." The bar was filled with sailors and Marines. There were sailors from the French Navy too, but the *patois* Jack and Scotty spoke was almost unintelligible to the French sailors, as was their Parisian French to the boys. Although they hung around for several hours drinking beer, the "snatch" never materialized. Jack said, "Let's try hotels—all you do is contact the elevator man." All night they tried and failed to find a whore, and finally went home disappointed.

Sometimes they visited Sam at Emerson College, where he was studying acting. Then they would walk together all over Boston, Jack studying the architecture of old buildings and lecturing about different kinds of windows. South Station was Jack's favorite spot in

Boston, both for its historical atmosphere and the endless flow of people he could observe there.

In Boston Jack and G.J. revived their childhood glee with practical jokes. One day they entered the lobby of the Fox and Hound, an exclusive gentlemen's club, and peeped in at a room full of distinguished, cigar-smoking, proper Bostonians in pinstripe suits, sunk down in overstuffed leather chairs. To look older, G.J. had worn an old felt hat, now blocked and cleaned, that he had found at Pine Brook. Although Jack wanted to get in as much as G.J., he was timid. Striding up to the man at the desk, G.J. asked, "Pardon me, is Mr. Cranston in? Lamont Cranston? Will you page him for us, please?" In a minute they heard the loudspeakers announce: "Mr. Lamont Cranston in the lobby, please!" Looking at each other, Jack and G.J. burst out laughing, then hurried out to the nearest soda fountain to celebrate their coup.

With only eleven cents between them, G.J. encouraged Jack to have his favorite hot fudge sundae, and ordered a soda for himself, saying, "Don't worry, Zagg. I'm gonna make a phone call, and when I get back there'll be no problem." Jack was always the willing butt of G.J.'s practical jokes; curiosity to see how they would turn out overcame his prudence. When G.J. got to the phone booth he sidestepped right out the door and took off, leaving Jack to settle the bill.

That summer they spent a lot more time in the barrooms of Lowell: the Hi-Ball, the Hofbrau, the Crystal, and the Pioneer Club. The last became their favorite since it was quiet and had private booths where they could talk for hours. Jack and G.J. had been seeing a lot of David Niven movies, and Jack was awed by Niven's suavity. Always the first to debunk Jack's romantic illusions, G.J. said, "David Niven's got nothing. I can smoke a cigarette, balance a teacup, read a book, and make a point with my hands all at the same time!" When Jack expressed disbelief, G.J. ordered a beer and a saucer—which served as Niven's "teacup"—and balanced them in his lap. Then he picked up a place mat, which he pretended to "read." Jack reminded him he still had to make a gesture. G.J. said, "Look, you've got to come a little closer to get the full impact of this!" As Jack leaned over him, G.J. threw the beer in his face and ran out, leaving him with the shattered glass and screaming owner. Once again, Jack had to pay.

Jack was G.J.'s best buddy; and when he asked himself why he did such mean things, he could only answer that it was fun getting reactions from a guy as "impressionable" as Jack. But after the incident at the Pioneer Club, Jack's reaction was to hunt for G.J. for two days, vowing to kill him for real this time. When Jack finally found him, G.J. rationalized: "I failed! I thought I could do it, Zagg, but something distracted me!" To his surprise, Jack accepted the explanation, and their friendship resumed strong as ever.

Sometimes they would have philosophical discussions, but more often G.J. would just say things off the top of his head, for the amusement of seeing Jack swallow them. Always interested in words, Jack would seize on certain phrases of G.J.'s and say, "Oh, my God! That's just beautiful!" At the Pioneer Club, tired of Jack's enthusiasm, G.J. pounded on the table and said, *"This* is God!" Jack whipped out his notebook and said, "Hey! I'm gonna write that down!"

5.

Jack's sense of humor enabled G.J. to overlook his occasional pomposity. But Sammy and the intellectuals around him were harder for G.J. to take. Sometimes Jack's friends and Sammy's would meet at the Pioneer Club, and then Jack would be caught in the middle. G.J. and Scotty were bored listening to Sammy and Connie Murphy talking about books and poetry. Though in Scotty's entire life he never read any books other than Jack's, until the day he died he remembered the name of "Saroyam." Trying to satisfy everyone, Jack simultaneously talked literature with the intellectuals and sports with the others. At some point the conflict went beyond just serious pursuits versus having fun, and G.J. and Sam had a heated quarrel. After that, Jack saw his two groups of friends separately.

G.J. enrolled in a commercial college. With Fred married, Salvey working out of town, and Scotty still working for the W.P.A., it was natural Jack would begin spending more time with Sammy. But the great attraction between Sammy and Jack cannot be explained so simply. At that point each was the perfect complement to the other's frustrated life.

In contrast to Jack, Sam had come from a large family, he had six brothers and three sisters. Although Sam's mother was even more "foreign" than Jack's—Mrs. Sampas never learned to speak English, while Jack's mother spoke English with a strong French accent—the Sampases were more determined than the Kerouacs to break out of their ethnic rut. After the flood they had moved into an almost exclusively Irish section of the Lowell Highlands. At first they were shunned by their new neighbors, but eventually the family's good will and gentle behavior endeared them to everyone. There was a cultural force at work too, for while the French continued to raise their children to accept factory work and the begetting of more children as the highest goals in life, Greek parents impressed upon their children the importance of a college education. (In their encouragement of Jack to go to college, Leo and Gabrielle were extremely atypical of the French community.) Sammy's older brother Charlie had graduated from Boston College in 1933, with a degree in journalism, and was now a prominent columnist on the *Lowell Sun.*

When Charlie came home from college he had brought with him two truckloads of books, which his young brother Sebastian lost no time devouring.

The Sampas family knew much tragedy. The father had killed a man in a gambling quarrel and was imprisoned for several years. They had learned meekness and kindness in response to the shame, and their darkened, ramshackle house became like a temple of humility in the neighborhood.

One of the critical experiences in Sammy's life had occurred when he was twelve. He fell in love with a girl in his class in the Bartlett school. Despite his barrage of fervent love poems, she hardly seemed to notice him. When Sam went to the teacher to complain that he was "shattered," the teacher told him that he must simply accept the girl's lack of interest. A tall and good-looking boy, Sam demanded some reason for her coldness. Finally the teacher told him that the girl was Irish, and her family was prejudiced against Greeks. For days he declaimed, in his histrionic way: "Can you imagine *that?* That I will *never, never* have this love reciprocated!" Regardless of the theatrics, the blow was real. Years later he would tell friends it was one of the most brutal revelations of his life.

A year later he experienced another trauma. Sam had been chosen to recite a poem at an eighth-grade assembly. His overly dramatic gestures elicited hootings from his classmates, and someone wisecracked about the "sissy poet." Midway through the poem Sam forgot the lines and started to cry. Later, however, he adopted a defiant stance, refusing to hide anything. Another thing in Sam's favor was the Greek community itself, which honored its artistic tradition and was much more receptive to the pursuit of "culture" than the French community. French intellectuals were largely restricted to the clergy. In those days few of the French children even went to high school; and college, other than a seminary, was as unimaginable as the career of a poet.

At the time Jack and Sam became close, it was unusual for Greeks, Irishmen, and Frenchmen to form friendships outside their particular nationality. Of course Sam had grown up near Jack and they had belonged to the literary club at Bartlett together. In high school his older sister Stella had had a crush on Jack and sometimes carried *his* books as they walked home. But Sam had reached across the Irish boundary too, which was a good deal more formidable. This summer he spent considerable time with the brightest Irish boys in Lowell: Jim O'Dea, Connie Murphy, Ed Tully, George Murray, and John MacDonald. Sam's criteria for friendships were human and rational.

Another amazing thing about Sam's group was the diverse characters of its members. Murphy and Murray were interested in science and technology. O'Dea and Constantinides were politically inclined. Tully, MacDonald, and Kerouac were the chief *literateurs*. But Sam touched something in all of them; he was the drawing card that brought them all together.

Naturally there were frequent clashes. A student at Boston College, Murphy couldn't relax with any homework undone. One night after watching the show at the Laurier Club—one of their favorite hangouts, along with the less glamorous saloons of Moody Street—Jack, Sammy, and Ed Tully dragged Murphy over to the Monument Café for an all-night gab session. To Jack and Sammy, staying up all night was one of the great experiences in life. They fed each other's enthusiasms as they fed the jukebox with change, to watch endless "soundies," miniature movies that accompanied the music. By morning Murphy was so weary and disgusted he took a cab home, vowing never to waste his time so "idiotically" again. Besides, Murphy thought Jack had too great a penchant for loafing. He felt Jack something of a "pretender," too, since Jack seemed to like the glory of being a writer better than the daily grind of writing. And Murphy didn't really consider writing work anyway, since he often did it in his spare time, for amusement, while continuing to support his widowed mother and family. Nor did he care for Jack's occasionally coming up short when it was time to pay for drinks. George Constantinides was chafed by Jack's arrogance, by his he-man swagger. Actually Constantinides was so brilliant and serious that Jack folded in front of him and put on that cocky façade to cover up. Admittedly Constantinides was a bit jealous of Jack's reputation as a great athlete and ladies' man, but he felt justified in complaining to Sam about Jack's lack of humility.[11]

Sammy's diplomacy was superb. He told George, "You should know Jack the way I know him. Jack has great questions about religion—he's moving away from his religious upbringing and French-Canadian values." When Jack was with the whole group he rarely talked about serious matters; in fact, he seemed uncomfortable discussing his literary ambitions. But Sam claimed that Jack was "completely different" when they were alone together, that Jack was a "much more sensitive person than meets the eyes." He told George that he and Jack had long, deep talks about life and art, in which Jack poured out all his hopes and fears.

George believed Sam because he knew that Sam's great warmth and capacity for encouragement could draw out the best in anyone. Sam would spend long periods alone with each of them, and they would each reveal themselves more completely to him than to anyone else, simply because each was able to be more himself in Sam's presence. And Sam took a genuine interest in their plans; he studied up on their particular areas of interest so he could discuss them more intelligently. He had even pried open John Koumantzelis, who was more withdrawn than Jack. On the long walks John and Sammy took together, John finally talked about himself, confiding feelings "more profound" than anyone suspected. Sammy claimed to know the real John, just as he knew "another Jack." [12]

Sam lectured them that they had been brought up in an environment where one had to grasp for beauty: it wouldn't be handed to them; they would have to search for it. He arranged the practical details of their quest like an impresario. To the others Sam admitted that Jack had far more literary talent than himself, and in heart-to-heart talks with Jack he stressed that Jack must concentrate on his writing more than he had in the past. Above all, he saw that Jack needed the recognition and support of his peers, which he was too shy to seek out by himself. Sammy was intrigued by the "Round Table" at the Hotel Algonquin, where Alexander Woollcott and his literary friends assembled to stimulate and encourage one another. Consequently, he devised the notion of literary evenings at the Eight Ball Café, where the "Friends of Sam" would gather to write together, then discuss their writings afterward.

The Eight Ball Café was on Suffolk Street, right alongside the canal. During the day a bookie operation was conducted in the barroom upstairs, but after the track closed for the day the management let Sammy's group occupy the booths for hours on end. In the evenings, half a dozen of them would go up there, each into his own cubbyhole, and write a story. After they were done, they would read one another's stories and offer criticism—though each writer, except for Sammy, uniformly thought his story the best! Sammy always lauded Jack's as the outstanding performance. The others were pretty hard on Jack, complaining that he wrote just like he spoke, spewing out a wild flow of words.

One time Jack produced a story about a gray-bearded old man in flowing white robes, preaching on Times Square about the redemption of souls. Over and over the "prophet" spoke of the danger of men "losing their immortal souls." Although there was no plot and the only development the suggestion that the old man was the Second Messiah, Jack was very proud of it. He was angry when Connie Murphy and George Dastou called it a failure. A bit more sympathetic, George Murray told Jack it was "interesting," whereupon Jack offered it to him as a gift! Murray replied, "Gee, Jack, you ought to keep things like this for yourself." [13]

Jack was so quiet about his own life that peripheral members of the group like Murray didn't know that he had already seen Times Square, and so they thought he was just inventing the descriptions of places he would like to see. To a large extent, Jack's writing at this period was fantasy. Jim O'Dea found him continually creating far-fetched adventures set in faraway places. The only realistic story Jack wrote was about a train ride beginning at the Lowell depot, but even that owed more to *Of Time and the River* than to his observation of his native locale. Murray and Jack got along very well because they had both read many books by Jack London; when they got together, London was usually the subject of their conversation. Jack was fascinated by the drunken collapse of London's career, those tragic, unproductive final years when London would burst into barrooms vaunting, "I'm *Jack London!*" to people who could at best pity the ruined hulk of the once dynamic author-adventurer. One day at the Eight Ball Café they all raised glasses of beer and vowed what they would achieve in life. Sammy would be a great actor, and Jack pledged to become "the world's greatest writer."

In some respects Jack was preferred to Sammy as a companion. Most of the group members liked what Murray termed Jack's "ready smile" and affable nature, his quick response to jokes and his own witty conversation, though he would often dominate conversations without ever speaking directly about himself. Nevertheless, he consistently provided fun for a live wire like Murray as well as intellectual stimulation for a hard-nosed student like Murphy. With Sammy, on the other hand, their nerves were put to the test. He was beloved for his great heart—he was the kind of man who would literally give people the shirt off his back—but a few beers, as O'Dea recalled, would cause Sammy to "gyrate and emote," scream, or recite Shakespeare at the top of his lungs. In Jack the group found a more ordinary and hence "real" guy.

The one thing they all shared was a love of popular music. Sinatra was their idol; they also listened every night to "The Chesterfield Hour," which featured among others the Andrews Sisters, Jimmy and Tommy Dorsey, Glenn Miller, and Artie Shaw. Often they would go to the record store across from City Hall to listen to new records for free. John MacDonald had a tremendous collection of 78's, as well as Red Label opera records. Of big bands the group favored Artie Shaw's; Sammy would walk the streets singing "Begin the Beguine." The group had other simple good times too, going to picnics and dancing—Sam was a fine dancer—at Canobie Lake and Lakeview.

In Sam's view, sex wasn't one of those simple pleasures. Since Jack didn't share his extreme idealism in this regard, they clashed. Peggy Coffey had dropped back into Jack's life and soon Jack was spending more time with her than with the guys or at his writing. Many evenings they just sprawled on the grass singing pop tunes, but it was no secret they were going to bed too (often at Jack's house while both his parents worked). Sammy told Jack he should do the honorable thing: marry her. To Jim O'Dea Jack had once mentioned wanting to marry Peggy, but he now showed absolutely no inclination toward marriage. Sammy began lecturing the others about the immorality of Jack's actions, perhaps hoping their unified pressure might make Jack capitulate. But the group members found Sammy's moral ardor merely the occasion for a practical joke.

One afternoon Sam stated that he knew Jack and Peggy were alone together. The others got the idea of telephoning Jack every few minutes to interrupt his lovemaking. Each time they would say they were calling "just to see what's going on," and Jack would bellow, "For God's sake, leave me alone!"

Sammy was less angry than disappointed that Jack could defy the code of chivalry he himself upheld. To Sammy it was clear that Peggy was simply at Jack's beck and call—he would drop her when it suited him and return to her when he felt sufficient lust. It was beyond Sammy's understanding how a man of Jack's deep sentiment could behave so cruelly. In any case, Sammy's classifications of human behavior were not realistic. He loved to tell the story of Prometheus's altruistic sacrifice to bring humanity fire. The tale never ceased to make him cry, but it was also to him the great symbol that should guide their lives. One who didn't follow Prometheus was a "cad." Forced to classify Jack that way, Sammy must have felt all the more gloomy about mankind's future. Frequently he recited the opening of Shelley's poem *Adonais*: "I weep for Adonais—he is dead!" It didn't take much interpretation to see that he was lamenting the death of the Jack he loved, the "real Jack" he thought he knew so well.

6.

The group members never heard Jack talk about religion; nor would he accompany practicing Catholics like O'Dea to Confession or Mass. But far from renouncing Catholicism, Jack was getting deeply involved in his own private theological debate.

Once again he went to see the liberal priest, Father "Spike" Morissette. He told Spike that he loved to sense the mysterious, to tremble; to him such feelings were an experience of God. He found mystery everywhere, not just in church. Jack felt that in many ways Catholicism enslaved people, for instance, by telling the poor to accept suffering because they would have their reward in heaven. Advancing himself in the world and getting some of the pleasures denied his parents seemed a legitimate pursuit. "Christ is joy," he told the priest, "not damnation. That's why He cursed the fucking Pharisees." Jack's own experience of Christianity was a longing to fly out into endless space, though he confessed that in such total liberation he feared the loss of identity. But Spike was impressed with the strong identity Jack already possessed and ironically, while Jack left as troubled as before, the priest gained from him support for his own iconoclasm. Father Morissette later declared that Jack Kerouac had been the chief influence in his own life, giving him the courage to unfetter his own identity.[14]

However Jack might have been floundering spiritually, he was actually leading a rather simple and wholesome life. He played baseball with O'Dea, and would often join him for supper at O'Dea's aunt's house. He and O'Dea double-dated, Jack always bringing Peggy. Although still not much of a dancer, Jack was so handsome and well-known that plenty of girls wanted to meet him, and O'Dea marveled that he never tried to date anyone else. Most of the time they just went to the movies, then parked on Pawtucket Boulevard to neck. Sometimes Jack stayed over at O'Dea's, where they'd sit up all night drinking beer and talking more about literature than life. Jack talked little about girls, more about baseball, but mostly about his absolute dedication to becoming a writer. He made it clear to Jim that football was strictly a means to an end, saying he had chosen Columbia not for its football team but rather for an Ivy League education.

O'Dea worried that Jack wouldn't be able to handle that Ivy League world. Jack didn't seem as brilliant as the others, and he always appeared more comfortable in the Pawtucketville gang than with people as literate as himself. It amazed O'Dea that someone who could enjoy the Saturday morning gang bangs at the Rialto would also enjoy following Sammy through the aisles of the Lowell library or having refined discussions with Miss Mansfield, now the elder stateswoman of Lowell's intelligentsia. O'Dea was glad Jack had Sammy to guide him. Only Sammy had enough warmth and enthusiasm to open vistas for Jack that couldn't be seen from the Rialto Theatre or the playing field.

In many ways Sammy *was* Stephen Dedalus, the hero of *A Portrait of the Artist as a Young Man*. That novel excited the whole group with its portrayal of the creative individual's struggle against society. For a while Jack, along with the others, tried writing like Joyce. Eventually most of them settled for imitating Dos Passos, whose style seemed a compromise between Joyce's extreme discipline and Wolfe's verbal abandon. Although Jack admitted Wolfe's flaws, Wolfe remained his literary god. But he also admired the satiric naturalism of Ivan Bunin's *The Gentleman from San Francisco*. Bunin's sharp eye for detail and his acid wit served a very modern sensibility; his novella about the prosperous American businessman who goes to Europe "for two whole years . . . solely for the sake of pleasure," [15] only to die the first month in Capri, probed the hollowness of materialism. It was O'Dea who introduced Jack to Bunin. Sammy's concern with the world's ills tended to be more ponderous (he had grieved when Stalin signed a pact with Hitler), far less tongue-in-cheek. He showed Jack *The Decline of the West* by Spengler, one of his brother Charlie's books. Its long, rhythmic, yet intricately precise sentences, constructed by translator Charles Atkinson, later became a strong influence on Jack's own style.

During the summer Jack's father, now an itinerant linotypist, had been working all over Massachusetts and Connecticut. When Leo found a steady job in New Haven, he decided to set up a new home there. Caught up in his romantic dreams, Jack felt only a slight nostalgia about losing his childhood base in Lowell. While Gabrielle and Jack's cousin Beatrice cast their fortunes with tea leaves in the kitchen, he sat on the porch, gazing at the stars and wondering where his own life might lead. He daydreamed of becoming the world's greatest athlete, actor, and writer. Much later in his life he saw that daydream as the crux from which his life veered in an entirely new direction. After a summer of relentless self-improvement, he suddenly realized—like Gray in the "Elegy in a Country Churchyard"—that all ambitions end in the grave. In other words, he had nothing better to do than enjoy life, because all his achievements could give him no more lasting happiness than he had always known from moment to moment.[16]

The cutting-free from Lowell betokened the spiritual cutting-free inside him. Either way it was far from a joyous experience. Leo had rented them an apartment in a black neighborhood, but Gabrielle refused to live there. Before they finally got settled in a new place, a cottage by the ocean, Jack's cat was lost, their possessions disordered, and all of them thoroughly disoriented.

Riding in the moving van, Leo, Gabrielle, and Jack had been nipping at a bottle of whisky. By the time they got to the cottage, in a driving rainstorm, Jack's agitation sent him out on a long swim in the lashing waves of Long Island Sound. Watching from the cottage, his parents feared he would drown. The next day, in sunshine, Jack swam out a full mile, past where they could even see him. When he once again returned safely, they told him to quit those dangerous stunts and start thinking about the serious studies ahead. Columbia was permitting him to take chemistry over again. If he would just concentrate on that difficult subject, his education should proceed smoothly.

Dick Sheresky and Burt Stollmack drove Jack down to Columbia. Since he was already a day late, he went directly to practice at Baker Field, getting a chill reception from both his fellow players and Little. But there were plenty of old friends around the campus to make him feel welcome, including a huge, merrily mad Frenchman named Henri Cru.

Jack had first met Cru at Horace Mann, where he used to sell daggers to the younger kids. Raised in Paris, he spoke French eloquently, and somewhere he had acquired a penchant for elegant naval uniforms larded with "scrambled eggs," which set off his dark good looks. This giant dandy had a great sense of humor perfectly complemented by Jack's, for while Cru could laugh at Jack's "peasanty" ways (a favorite Kerouac word), Jack had a humorous appreciation of Cru's princely vanity. More importantly, they responded to each other's basic, childlike kindness and decency and to their mutual *joie de vivre*. To both of them New York was an immense playground, and they gladly became children again the better to enjoy it. Jack would bang on Cru's door, shouting, "Kerouac!" and Cru would greet him screaming that Jack must be crazy. Their friendship grew out of a joint willingness to take whatever part would most tickle the other's fancy.

Cru's mother lived in an apartment building on 116th Street, near the Columbia campus. One day, in the elevator, Cru met a nineteen-year-old girl from Grosse Pointe, Michigan, who was living there with her grandmother. Frankie Edith Parker had come to New York ostensibly to study art, but basically she wanted the exciting life only a big city could offer. Grosse Pointe was an extraordinarily conservative suburb of Detroit, peopled mostly with stodgy, stultified millionaires. Raised in a wealthy family herself, Frankie had decided early on that what she really wanted was something money couldn't buy, at least not in Grosse Pointe: a continuous supply of stimulating companions and unusual experiences. She had proved so wild that sending her to school in New York relieved her parents of a major source of embarrassment.

Dressed in his naval uniform, replete with officer's hat and gold braid, Cru looked to Frankie as glamorous as a French movie star, and they both fell in love. They even made vague plans to marry, but both had other sweethearts and neither took the promise too seriously. When Jack came to town, Cru told her, "I have a wonderful buddy I want you to meet." Jack arrived wearing an old sweater, looking like a bum beside the peacock Cru. The problem he had talking to Frankie's deaf grandmother just increased his shyness. Frankie was further amused at how impressed Jack was with their plush apartment. Uncomfortable there, he asked Frankie and Cru to join him at a nearby delicatessen.

A hot dog covered with sauerkraut was a new experience for Frankie, and she ordered and ate six in a row! Later Jack would declare that from that moment he was in love with her. As Henri sat stiff and pompous, Frankie talked and ate and talked and ate, and Jack gaped in admiration at her total spontaneity. Unfortunately, she was less than struck with Jack. He lacked Cru's perfect manners, his eyes seemed prone to brood, he didn't laugh heartily like Cru; at most he gave an occasional wicked chuckle. On the other hand, Frankie was flattered by Jack's attention to her beauty, and she did feel some attraction to him.

When Jack asked her to come watch him practice at Baker Field, she agreed. Soon he was coming to visit her in her grandmother's apartment as well, and as Frankie warmed to him, he confided to her his general unhappiness at Columbia and his particular hatred for Lou Little.

Although Columbia had a good team that year, the coming war threatened to break it up. Already their quarterback Len Will had joined the Marines. The worst blow for Jack was Little's decision to use senior backs Adam Spiegel and Hugh McIlhennan in the starting lineup. Once again Little jeered at Jack's build, saying he was too small to be a back, and that he had the big legs of a lineman rather than a runner. When he outright insulted Jack in front of the others by saying Jack wasn't good enough to run the KT-79 reverse deception, Jack realized that Little had no intention of making him a regular, this year or next. It seemed clear that he was trying to get Jack out of the way so he could develop his favorite, Paul Governali, as a star back.

Yet, considering that an education was Jack's primary goal at Columbia, he might well have humored Little. Frankie was surprised at the passion Little had wrought in him. In one breath Jack would complain that Little wouldn't try any of the plays he had devised, and in the next breath he would assert that football was barbaric and that he wasn't at all proud of playing it well. She sympathized with his hatred of violence, but football practice hardly seemed an exorbitant price for a good education. When he used the latest tiff with Little as an excuse for quitting college, she turned her romantic thoughts elsewhere.

7.

Leaving Frankie and Columbia behind, Jack got on a bus bound South. His ticket took him only as far as Washington, D.C., but it was adventure enough on which to start his new career, and it probably strengthened the independence he needed when he returned to face his father in New Haven. But when Leo heard that Little had refused to start Jack in the opening game, he sympathized with Jack's bitterness.

Jack got a job in a local tire factory but quit after only half a day's work. Suddenly Leo's pent-up anger erupted. He told Jack to get out and earn his own living and stop burdening them. As Leo saw it, they had made great sacrifices for his college education, and now he had willfully thrown it away. With bravado Jack declared he was going to become a great writer, which Leo thought impossible for a Canuck. Determined to prove his father wrong Jack left for Hartford, where his old friend Mike Fournier had found him a job as a gas-station attendant. Once separated from his father his anger changed to guilt, and he felt as if "he had slashed his father's eyes for no reason." [17]

In a cockroachy room on Main Street in Hartford, using a rented Underwood typewriter, Jack wrote his first full-length book, a collection of short stories called *Atop an Underwood*. He later described them as "in the Saroyan-Hemingway-Wolfe style." With almost no money for meals until he got his first check, he literally fainted from hunger at work one day. His fellow mechanic Dick Wakefield took him home, where Dick's mother stuffed Jack with food and Dick himself loaned him two dollars. Throughout October and early November, 1941, Jack spent most of his free time alone writing, though once he picked up a girl in a lunchroom, and another time Dick found girls for both of them. When G.J. telephoned, proposing Scotty drive all three of them to New York, Jack jumped at the chance to get away.

The next morning Scotty and G.J. picked up Jack at the Atlantic filling station, and from there Jack directed them to his parents' cottage in New Haven. After Gabrielle fixed them a big breakfast, they drove straight to New York. Scotty had no idea that Jack had quit college. G.J. felt that Jack's parents had been pushing him too hard, and that a respite might do him good. Since neither Scotty nor G.J. had ever pressured Jack with great expectations, he could relax with them. Besides, far from giving the impression that his academic life was over, Jack asked them to drop him off at Livingston Hall on the Columbia campus.

After touring the World's Fair, Scotty and G.J. rejoined him and they went to a Chinese restaurant, the aquarium, and to Staten Island on the ferry, with Jack instructing them to look back at the New York skyline, exactly as they had seen it in so many movies. Back in Manhattan Jack took them to Madison Square Garden, where Gene Krupa was playing, and after a ride to Harlem on the subway, to a restaurant on Ninth Avenue where Bunny Berigan was scheduled to play. If all the names failed to overwhelm his guests, Jack knew they would be polished off by the seven-course dinner, something they hadn't known existed. But when the chicken arrived tied with strings, Jack was as baffled as the others and attempted to attack it with a butter knife. The waiter intervened, telling him he couldn't do that. Jack replied, "That's OK, Mac, I've got a strong arm."

Having bought a bottle of rum, Jack led them to the Burlesque Showhouse on Ninth Avenue, and asked the usher for first-row balcony seats. On stage thirty girls turned around to remove their bras, then turned full face to the audience. As G.J.'s and Scotty's eyes bulged, Jack said nonchalantly, "This is routine." Between the nudity and the rum they were all getting horny, but again Jack assured them, "I know just the place, because I've been there before."

At the All America Hotel, he took them upstairs to meet "Lucille." Jack had her first, then G.J., and finally Scotty, whom she asked, "Are you from Oklahoma too?"

Boasting that in New York the bars were open to four A.M., Jack kept them walking the streets until almost dawn. As G.J. and Scotty reminisced about the fun they had had their second year in the W.P.A. league, Jack's gaiety rapidly faded. He began to talk about how he had run into the same problem at Columbia as at Lowell High, saying he would never be given a chance to prove himself. It was so unusual for Jack to talk about his troubles that Scotty remembered that sudden unburdening for the rest of his life. Eventually Scotty became so sick from drinking that G.J. had to drive them back to New Haven.

In a few days Jack had to confront another set of memories from Lowell, as Sammy Sampas arrived to share his lonely Thanksgiving. More than usual Sammy felt the sadness of life, but Jack assured him he was doing what he thought best, pledging that his future success as a writer would justify his apparent failure at the moment. Nevertheless, they seemed to gain little comfort in each other's company.[18]

Jack spent two more weeks laboring at his short stories. His reprieve came in the form of a telephone call from his father, announcing that he had a new job back in Lowell. Riding home in the back of the moving truck, Jack cried tears of joy. Leo had rented a house on Crawford Street in Pawtucketville, not far from their old home at the Textile Lunch. But with G.J. now working out of state, the old gang had ceased to exist. To add to Jack's gloom—as he immersed himself in Dostoyevsky's study of madness, *Notes from Underground*—came a premonition that the whole world was about to change drastically for the worse.

He started a new journal, but it didn't dispel his restlessness. In midnight walks past the brick mills Jack felt the full weight of his failure, realizing what few, miserable alternatives attended his loss of the glamor of New York. Postponing the search for a job, he hung around cafés and saw movies. After seeing *Citizen Kane* one Sunday night, he rushed out of the theater, anxious to begin writing a movie script as poetic as Orson Welles'. On the way home a newsboy accosted him with the headline: "Japs Bomb Pearl Harbor!"

The ruins of Pearl Harbor lay all about him in Lowell. Jack must have realized there and then that the hometown he knew was lost, that the only way to keep it was to turn his back, to fight the riptide by ignoring every sign of change. But he was no man to lie to himself and all his instincts were to flow with events, to learn by observing his own drift. He would follow America to annihilation if that were its destiny, for how else should an American end?

Realizing the imminence of a final break with Lowell, Jack was in no haste to consummate it. No music is sweeter—so said Shakespeare—than that with a "dying fall," and for Jack there was now nothing more important in the world to do than enjoy being home.

THREE
The Sound of New York

1.

Jack's friends thought it funny that he showed little interest in the war. Almost indifferently he signed up to become a cadet in the naval air force V-12 program. As it would take a few months before the Navy called him for an examination, he went to see Tom Costello, the owner of the *Lowell Sun,* for a job on the delivery trucks. Remembering Jack's football heroics, Costello immediately made Jack a sports reporter.

Leo occasionally did typesetting for the *Sun,* and he was proud to be able to set his own son's stories. He conceded that Jack might have a prosperous future as a journalist. The job suited Jack because he could usually finish his reports by noon, and then he could spend the rest of the day typing a novel he had just begun, entitled *Vanity of Duluoz.* Seeing Jack tied to his typewriter from morning to evening, the senior sportswriter, George McGuane, praised the young man's diligence. But when McGuane discovered that Jack was doing his own work on company time, he thought him a "faker." As if to redeem himself, Jack tried to show McGuane his ability to "dream up stories," which made McGuane think him even more of an "oddball." [19] Undoubtedly Jack was putting much more effort into his fiction than his news stories, which were mediocre. In any case, he was hardly being given signal recognition—his byline was misprinted: "Jack Korouac"! The other employees in the newsroom found Jack silent and withdrawn.

With Sammy's group, however, Jack shared the excitement of discovering *Ulysses.* Sammy, John MacDonald, Jim O'Dea, and Jack made a careful study of Molly Bloom's soliloquy, and Jack was amazed at the discipline that had gone into producing the illusion of stream of consciousness. They all tried to imitate that carefully crafted babble, and Jack was especially proud when John MacDonald told him his efforts had "power" and "promise."

The first three months of 1942 Jack lived with a sort of fairyland detachment. He was free to try out whatever sort of life best suited him, with nothing of real consequence compared to the war he must soon help fight. While his parents slept he would stay awake in the kitchen, reading *Ulysses,* Goethe's *Faust,* and the Book of Job, until daybreak. With only two hours' sleep, he would put in a full workday at the *Sun,* then head for the Y.M.C.A. to exercise with punching bags, swim, play basketball, and run the three hundred. After the "Y" he would spend hours studying in the Lowell library, taking elaborate notes on H. G. Wells' *Outline of History* and looking up puzzling or interesting references in his favorite Eleventh Edition of the *Encyclopedia Britannica.* Taking a quick break for supper at home, Jack would return for a "second round" in his projected conquest of all earthly knowledge. After the library closed at nine P.M., he would meet Sammy for a beer or a hot fudge sundae and more long, soulful talks.

He was seeing Peggy Coffey again, but mainly as the passive recipient of her love, for he had grown restless and was looking for fresh romance. When Sammy discovered that Jack was dropping Peggy, he rebuked him again.

Jack was feeling increasingly antagonistic toward Sammy's sadness. To Jack, life was finding excitement; and there were never enough activities to work off all his nervous energy. Although as sensitive as Sam, Jack had no desire to moon poetically over the tragedy of life. Rather, his instinct was to outrun it, to lose it in the oblivion of spent energy, while searching for new and possibly more hopeful experiences. At the "Y" Jack met a kid three years younger than himself, Billy Dabilis, who embodied this philosophy of action. With Billy's Dummer Street gang, the "Arrows," Jack played all night.

The Arrows consisted mainly of Greeks, none intellectual but all intelligently curious. Among them was one Jew, Mike Marmer, who wanted to become a playwright. In all-night cafés like the Plaza on Kearney Square, he and Jack had long discussions about writing and Jack continually talked about his plans to travel around the country to meet many different kinds of people. Most of the gang complained that Jack was "talking riddles" or "talking ragtime." [20] In any case, they all liked his charisma and enthusiasm.

On Saturday nights Jack would go with Billy and a saxophone player, Tommy Sakallarios, to hear the big bands at the Commodore. Like Red St. Louis, Billy would gather a pack of girls with his fancy dancing. Jack had more fun talking with the musicians and singers on the bandstand or backstage. He was intrigued by their way of life and questioned them about the places they had seen and the people they had met on the road. He would also ask where they had come from and what they thought about life. Surprised by his sympathy, the band members often spoke openly with him. One of the musicians Jack talked to there was Gene Krupa.

Friday nights, at the Catholic Youth Organization dances, Jack ran afoul of the nuns. Failing to understand his excited talk about

what life should be, the nuns decided he was "dangerous" and kept a
close eye on him. Jack would annoy them too by whipping off his tie
as soon as he got into the crowd. When the chaperones chided him
about it, he complained that he didn't like to be "tied up": "It's
choking my life away!" What really worried them was his interest in
the band members. In those days for a girl to date a musician was
morally equivalent to joining a whorehouse, and a young man who
associated with bands was—to put it mildly—joining the forces of
corruption.

The atmosphere was looser at the "coed dances" at the Y.M.C.A.
on Wednesday nights; a guy could at least escort a girl home without
the nuns taking down his name, address, and their minute-by-minute
itinerary. At the "Y," girls under eighteen would dance from eight to
eleven; then they would be replaced by the older ladies of twenty-
one or so, who had just got off the second shift at the mills. Many of
these women had husbands in the Service and were as restless at
night as the guys who had yet to join up. Jack never had much
success with either set of women. As soon as they heard him talk
about traveling, they got scared off, assuming he wanted them to
leave town with him!

Jack and Billy would stay until the very end of the dances. As
Billy had a car, Jack would often ride with him to take girls home,
but seldom wanted to go home himself. He preferred to take long
walks. Occasionally Billy and some of the others would accompany
him, if they were in a mood to hear Jack's nonstop monologue. Eventually Jack would end up in the all-night cafés. Having little money,
he would make his own "tomato soup" with a bottle of catsup, salt
and pepper, and a cup of hot water; or he would pick up the scraps
others had left. He seemed able to cover the whole city in a single
night, asking a million questions of everybody he met; or else he just
entertained himself with the jukebox or sat in a corner reading.
Come dawn, he would sometimes hop onto the back of one of the
horse-drawn wagons at the Olympia Bakery and help himself to a
crust of bread dipped in the cream at the top of a milk bottle. People
got the impression he would do anything to stay awake.

On Sundays Jack occasionally accompanied the Greek boys to
the Holy Trinity Greek Orthodox Church, whose Byzantine gold
dome he loved, and afterward hung around the Greek coffeehouses
on "Charlie's corners," at the intersection of Suffolk Street and the
canal. In those coffeehouses the old Greek patriarchs would spend
hours sipping their wine or *ouzo*, playing cards, and smoking hashish
from traditional pipes. Many had communist leanings and were
known as *Bolsheviki*. Like a little kid Jack sat at their feet, talking to
them and listening.

He was spending more time with the Greeks than with the
French, and began to ridicule Canuck provincialism. Parodying the

broken English of an old Frenchman, Jack would say, "Hey! Up de street de parade's comin' down!" Sometimes in a French store he'd tell the clerk, "I'll have two of those and another one," forcing the clerk to say, "You wan *t'ree?*"—a word no Frenchman cared to pronounce. But he was just as scornful of his Greek friends when he saw them living in a rut. He scoffed: "All you guys do is get up, go to work, go back home, hang around the coffeehouse, go to church, go down to the coffeehouse, have your spinach pie, go out at night looking for girls, and come back to the coffeehouse again!" If one of them finally snagged a girl, he would bring her to the coffeehouse to parade her before his friends. But to Jack the most pitiful symbol of their boredom was the game of "picky," in which they would make their way round and round the block whacking one stick with another. Yet it was apparent that Jack needed *them* to ease his own boredom. Whenever they had to go home for family meals, from which he was excluded, he would plead with them to stay.

By March the itch to move got the better of him. Instead of interviewing the baseball coach at Lowell Textile Institute, he sat in his room, staring at the wall. When his father asked why he wasn't working, he vaguely suggested he might return to Columbia. Leo was sure Columbia wouldn't want Jack back; as he saw it, Jack was merely looking for an excuse to return to "Pew York." At that point Jack exploded too, accusing his father of wanting to keep him in Lowell forever. Leo rejoined that his once sweet, innocent little boy had become a "punk." When Gabrielle took Jack's side, Leo turned on her too. With the fresh guilt of having helped fragment his already riven family, Jack bought a bus ticket to Washington, D.C., where George Apostolos was working.

In his hotel room George awoke one night blinded by a flashlight, a .45 pistol pointed in his face. When he heard the voice that accused him of "squealing," he yelled, "Go ahead, you son of a bitch, pull the trigger," grateful his old "Shadow" had traveled so far to honor him with another practical joke. Although G.J. already had a roommate, a construction worker named Dutton, he made room for Jack too. Dutton got Jack a job on the construction crew at the Pentagon.

But Jack didn't like Dutton, a real southerner, who tried to run down black men with his car on the way to work. Then it seemed no one was really working much anyway. The sheet metal worker who was to apprentice Jack was drunk every day and often disappeared for hours at a time. Many men spent the day sleeping in "holes" amidst the construction material. The first day Jack slept with the slackers. The next day he preferred to wander around the construction site listening to the black men sing. In the following days he sometimes ditched work to explore the city. He was beginning to drink heavily, and to drink whiskey and gin instead of just beer.

Walking down Pennsylvania Avenue he reached into his back pocket for a nip of gin with which to salute the flag, and from his torn construction pants his cock waved out at the capitol. He thought it a great joke.

In the evenings he would go out with G.J. looking for girls. Since it was wartime, and his inhibitions were loosened by drinking, he was able to find someone for sex almost every night. G.J. was astonished at the changes in Jack since they were in Lowell. Jack had rarely drunk hard liquor, and he had never had a casual attitude toward girls. Now he switched girls as carelessly as he quit jobs. No longer determined to master every activity he undertook, Jack abruptly traded his construction job for work as a short-order cook and soda jerk in a diner.

In the diner a girl named Jeannie from Macon, Georgia, caught his attention with a deck of pornographic playing cards, then invited him to move in with her. She had other boyfriends, but Jack didn't care, especially since her principal lover had only one arm. Telling the story to G.J., Jack joked that he only had to walk her poodle every day and she would support him in style. Jack even brought G.J. to meet his rival, to let him appreciate the spectacle of a one-armed cab driver. G.J. was leading a pretty wild life himself at that point. But in later years, as he thought over that interlude in Washington, D.C., he realized it was the first time he had felt Jack was being driven by some powerful fear. It seemed as if Jack knew he was going to die in a short time and was trying to cram everything into a few years.[21]

2.

In Jack's words, it was "slavering thoughts" of Peggy Coffey that brought him back to Lowell.[22] But once there he found a bevy of new girls, such as Pauline Beland, and Peggy was again just a standby. Sammy's group was largely dispersed. Once in a while he and Jack would hitchhike to Boston to see Connie Murphy, and stay over at Connie's sister's house. To Connie, Jack seemed as sociable and devoid of pretense as ever. But back at the Eight Ball Café George Murray was surprised to see that Jack now drank whiskey most of the time and had become a connoisseur of mixed drinks.

Many nights Jack sought out Billy Dabilis, this time hitchhiking clear across Massachusetts to Springfield just for a cup of coffee, or to Hyannisport on the Cape to watch the Kennedys sitting on their front porch in tennis shoes, reading Alexis de Tocqueville and John Adams. Jack confessed to Billy that he had great difficulty sleeping;

and as Billy suffered from insomnia too, he was always ready to take off anywhere at Jack's request. One day Billy set out to fetch a loaf of bread for his mother and ended up spending two weeks with Jack at Weir's Beach in Laconia, New Hampshire. Jack told him, "The most important thing for your mind is to be active . . . get a job, any kind of odd job." They worked as dishwashers. Jack hung around the boats, and in the evenings there was dancing at Irwin's Pier. No longer shy, Jack liked to meet the vacationers, and would ask where they came from and how they lived. Billy noticed he had more success with girls now too. But sometimes, as in the past, he would disappear for three or four hours. In any case, after the dances Jack would find somewhere else to go. It seemed to Billy that he was staying up twenty-four hours a day, day after day.

Back in Lowell Jack haunted the all-night cafés again. Billy got a job washing dishes at the Ideal Restaurant, and Jack would stop by to help out in exchange for a meal. Afterward, he would sit in the corner, feeding the jukebox and reading or making notes. Again he talked about getting away from Lowell and boasted of the excitement in New York. "You can't imagine the life out there. It's different every day, every hour, every minute." Sometimes he and Billy washed dishes and peeled potatoes at the Dutch Tea Room to get money for dances. Tired of borrowing from his mother, Jack told Billy that he wanted to be his own person, which meant he would have to support himself.

With Billy he went to get work at a carnival, enthusiastic about the chance to see the country. But after they helped set up the tents, the owner refused to pay them. Renting a bike for a dime proved a cheap way for Jack to travel, and he also began collecting discarded trolley passes to use riding out to Lakeview, where there was a dance hall and amusement park. When he couldn't get a pass, he posed as a worker, wearing dungarees and carrying a lunch pail, so that people would more willingly give him a ride. The summer crowd at Lakeview provided more characters for Jack to "interview." Once he went with Billy to a Greek picnic, but there he was closely scrutinized—Greek picnics being places where marriages were arranged, and he still a Canuck outsider. All the same, it was fresh "material" for him to study.[23]

He rode with Billy taking soldiers to and from Fort Devvons. To get gas, he showed Billy how to puncture gas tanks and then plug them, so that they could take a quart from each car until they had enough—marking plugged cars for future use. Glassy-eyed, Jack talked steadily through the night, but he didn't seem to be drinking. Billy surmised he was using benzedrine, especially since, in Boston, he spoke familiarly with all kinds of fast characters. Later, too, Jack showed the moodiness of "benny drag."

Nevertheless, part of his moodiness was due, as always, to being misunderstood. He was always stressing that he saw a different way of life, which others failed to see. He took many more solitary walks and spent hours atop the little hill on Cardinal O'Connell Parkway, reading—as usual, with a pencil in his hand—or idly tossing his jackknife.

He told Billy, "You aren't ever going to be anything in this world unless you do what you want to do, when you want to do it—don't plan anything, just go out and do it." George Apostolos had helped get Ray McNulty into the merchant marine, and he told McNulty it would be a good idea for Jack to ship out too, since he was worried about Jack's recent use of drugs. Jack liked the idea and asked O'Dea to join the merchant marine with him. In mid-June they went to Boston and got ordinary seamen's papers. Twenty-nine days in a row they hitchhiked to the National Maritime Union in Arlington Heights without getting assigned to a ship. A few times Sammy came along too, but he wasn't even able to get shipping papers. The thirtieth day Jack went by himself. Tired of waiting for a ship, he enlisted in the marines and went to Scollay Square to get drunk. The next day, advised by a seaman, he went back to the N.M.U. Hall. A scullion's job was available on the S.S. *Dorchester*. Forgetting his obligation to the marines, Jack signed on.

Sammy was desolate that he couldn't sail with Jack, but Jack told him he really wanted to be by himself for a few months. That night he drank until he passed out under the toilet bowl in the Scollay Square Café. The next morning, after washing himself in the bay, he set sail for Murmansk. It was the deadliest run in the merchant marine; the German submarines picked off dozens of ships each month.

The *Dorchester* was taking a construction crew to Greenland, but it also carried a large powder magazine. Recording his adventures in a journal, like Jack London, Jack claimed he didn't fear death. In letters to O'Dea, too, Jack stressed that he loved the freedom of the open sea, and that the danger didn't frighten him. The challenge of the foggy, iceberg-ridden North Atlantic stirred his seafaring Breton instincts. Yet the two torpedo attacks during the voyage left their mark. A few months later, back in Lowell, Jack held out trembling hands to his boyhood friend Leo Nadeau and blamed the merchant marine for making him think about death. Having learned the truth of "here today, gone tomorrow," he told Leo, he had decided to spend his money and have fun.

Neither bawdy nor boisterous enough to suit the other sailors, Jack made few friends. The crew continually teased him about his lack of mechanical knowledge. Knife fights among them made him uneasy. The huge black cook, Old Glory, did like Jack; he was a blues singer, whose world view accorded perfectly with Jack's: "Everybody's puttin' down a hype." They both believed that the killing on both sides was madness, that war was a lie perpetrated on the masses for the benefit of a favored few. Jack later wrote that the roots of his pacifism lay in the realization, during a submarine attack on the *Dorchester,* that most men who die in war have no real desire to harm one another.[24]

One morning he was astonished to see the enormous cliffs of a Greenland fjord. As Eskimos approached the ship in kayaks, his fellow sailors pelted them with oranges and Jack felt outraged at this gratuitous insult to their hospitality. Conscious of his own Indian blood, Jack knew these people had as rich a culture and perhaps more courage than the white men who came to exploit them and their land.

After the ship anchored, an Eskimo in his kayak drew near and began talking to Jack in his Eskimo language. Then he performed the trick of shooting under the hull of the ship, emerging wet and smiling on the other side. Seeing he wanted to trade, Jack handed his Horace Mann football sweater out the porthole, and the Eskimo handed him a homemade harpoon with a steel head. Jack wrote to Jim O'Dea that this incident was the high point of his trip.

It was a long process unloading all the supplies and machines needed to build an air base. To pass the time, Jack went to watch movies on a Coast Guard cutter. Still bored, he and another crewman, Duke Ford, went ashore pretending they wanted to eat in the construction crew's mess hall, when they really planned to go mountain climbing. With no equipment they actualy climbed a four thousand foot peak, naming it Mount Ford-Kerouac. On the way down Jack accidentally started an avalanche and just barely missed getting thrown down with it.

On board the *Dorchester* was a twenty-nine-year-old communist from Greenwich Village, Pat Reel, who had fought for the Loyalists in Spain and, at home, organized labor unions. He lectured Jack on communism, and Jack in turn showed Mike his diary, whose ideologically unsuitable portions Mike deleted.

Before they started homeward, they learned that their sister ship, the S.S. *Chatham,* had been torpedoed and sunk off Belle Isle Strait. An October tempest was raging in the Atlantic, and without the weight of her cargo the *Dorchester* was tossed like a cork. Jack led some men upstairs to the construction workers' old bunks and started a pillow fight; then, braving the storm, he practiced football runs on the deck. When the ship docked in Sydney, Nova Scotia, he was kept from going ashore as punishment for his unapproved mountain-climbing expedition. But with no one else on the ship, he went up to the captain's bridge and called his own bumboat to go ashore, where the entire crew was getting drunk.

This time he was AWOL for real, and almost with every step he got into deeper trouble. He helped push a shack into the harbor, then got drunk in the dance halls and clubs, and finally began break-

ing into houses in the company of other sailors and two Indian prostitutes. After sleeping in a miner's home, he went downtown and got
so drunk he couldn't remember where he was or even the name of
his ship. Only the voice of Dinah Shore on the U.S.O. Club's radio
made him remember his home in America, and he daydreamed of
New York and blondes. Outside again, stumbling through an alley,
he was arrested by the Canadian Shore Patrol; but after they locked
him in a barracks, he crawled out through the window and began
playing baseball with the Canadian navy. Then he sauntered downtown for more drinks, and finally called for another bumboat to take
him back to the *Dorchester*. It turned out that there were two more
stragglers still ashore. The only punishment Jack received was to be
docked two days' pay, and to have his name misspelled on the notice
of reprimand.

In late October, 1942, the *Dorchester* sailed into New York harbor, continuing on into Long Island Sound, up the Cape Cod Canal
and into Boston Harbor. On deck Jack was paid his $470 by G.J.,
now serving in the Coast Guard, and as he came down the gangplank
he saw Sammy waiting for him. Jack displayed his harpoon, and they
rode back to Lowell together.[25]

At home Jack found a telegram from Lou Little offering him his
last chance to return to the Columbia football team. Excited about
the prospect of going back to New York, Jack took Sammy out to
celebrate. In front of Connie Murphy, Jack pulled out his wad of
money and, inviting Sammy to join him in New York, handed
Sammy train fare. Connie almost fell over in shock, since he had
never before witnessed Jack lend anyone a nickel.

The next day Jack and his father took a train to New York. On its
very next voyage the *Dorchester* was sunk. Over a thousand lives
were lost, including Jack's friend Glory.

At Columbia Jack was back to washing dishes, scrimmaging all
afternoon, and reading works like *Hamlet* in three days. Little told
him that since he now weighed only 155 pounds, he would have to
be a back and not a guard. But when Jack mentioned the long over-
due job for his father, Little hardly responded.

The old Columbia regulars had almost all gone to war, and the
new team was young and inexperienced. Once again Little set about
teaching Jack the KT-79 fake. On the sidelines the Army coach and
the Brown coach asked to see "Keroach," as Little called Jack. Jack
performed the play perfectly.

Four days later Sammy came down from Lowell. Though Jack
was supposed to be writing papers on *King Lear* and *Macbeth*, he let
Sammy take him on long walks to the Brooklyn Bridge. They even
visited the apartment where Wolfe had written *Of Time and the
River*. Then Jack took Sammy to Harlem to show him his new passion, jazz.

Sammy was appalled at how heavily Jack was drinking, but that was only the beginning of his disillusionment. Jack began taking benzedrine and smoking marijuana, which absolutely horrified Sam. Dragging Sam from club to club, Jack picked up a string of whores, pimps, and assorted street characters. When Sam pleaded with him to return to the campus, Jack declared that a writer must "experience life in all its phases," and accused Sam of not being courageous enough to explore life as Wolfe had done. Sam claimed he wasn't looking down upon Jack's new friends, but that he was very uncomfortable among them and had no taste for "carousing."

That night a riot started, and Sammy was forced to seek shelter with Jack in a tenement, as the riot continued throughout the next day. In Sam's eyes, Jack seemed to go mad with drink and drugs; he later reported witnessing Jack's participation in endless rounds of sex with both men and women. The things Jack did disgusted Sam as unthinkably "kinky." [26]

When Sam returned to Lowell he had a long talk with George Constantinides about Jack. Sam was afraid that in the pursuit of new experiences Jack would destroy his talent. However interesting these particular facets of life, Sam felt that the lifestyle necessary to "study" them would prevent Jack from producing serious literature. Finally Sam admitted his personal biases. Although an iconoclast himself, he could see no beauty in this sort of rebellion.

Back at Columbia, Jack had to deal with his father's expectations, which were a good deal more practical. Having patronized prostitutes in Lowell, Leo scarcely worried about his son's commerce with them. The old man merely wanted a secure job. Eventually Jack managed to get Leo an interview with Little, who refused to keep his old promise. Calling Little a wop, Leo told Jack that if the coach didn't use him in the upcoming game against Army, Jack should come home.

The game against Army was especially important to Jack because one of the Army players was his "great enemy" Henry Mazur,[27] who as a senior on the Lowell High team had thrown fifteen-year-old Jack out of the showers. Jack wanted to get revenge by tackling Mazur headfirst as he had tackled Carrufel on the sandlot. But all game he sat on the bench, asking, "Now, coach?" while Little just looked away or said, "You lost too much weight while at sea."

The following Monday, Jack decided he would rather remain in his room listening to Beethoven's Fifth Symphony than go to football practice. Later he wandered over to Mort Lippmann's dormitory room to hear Lippmann play jazz piano like Mel Powell. Next he drifted in to see Jack Fitzgerald, a fiery would-be writer and jazz aficionado. After returning his chemistry equipment, Jack headed for Frankie Edith Parker's grandmother's apartment.

As soon as he had returned to Columbia he had looked up Frankie—whom he was now calling "Edie"—but by this time she had lost interest in him. The Columbia area was flooded with V-12 naval cadets, and Edie was dating quite a number of them simultaneously. Every day Jack would watch her walk down Amsterdam Avenue, where she always fed a raggedy, gray horse that pulled a trash cart. Desolate, he wrote her a love letter praising her tenderness toward animals, a feeling he shared, and describing an imaginary walk they might take through a forest. At the end, he stated that in the "deepest, darkest, dankest woods" she should lift a stone, and there she would find his heart. From the moment she read the letter, she was in love with him.

While her deaf grandmother slept in the other room, Jack and Edie made love on the living-room couch. Then they went down to the West End Bar, where Edie laughed at the Columbia linemen pissing on the sidewalk. But when Jack told her he was going home to await induction into the V-12 program, she was furious. There was no need for him to worry about being drafted, since athletic departments worked overtime finding deferments for good athletes. Edie accused him of thinking only of himself, of not really caring about her. Leaving her in tears, Jack packed his belongings and took the train to Lowell.

3.

It was December 1942. The call from the navy came quickly; but, sick with German measles, Jack had to ask them to wait two weeks. Confined to his room, tended by his mother, he listened to Shostakovich's Fifth Symphony and hand-printed a second novel, called *The Sea Is My Brother.* The prose was imitation Melville, long, bombastic sentences filled with romantic and poetic appreciations of the sea. Jack later called it "a crock as literature."

When he was finally examined by the naval air force in Boston, he failed the physical because of a deviated septum, and he had difficulty computing altitudes as well. Excluded from officer training, he was assigned to the regular navy boot camp at Newport, Rhode Island.

In the barracks Jack was bored listening to eighteen-year-olds talk about their girlfriends, and he found marching and drilling even duller. Guard duty and garbage-can duty were bother enough, but regulations were anathema to him. He could see no good reason why he couldn't smoke before breakfast. And he had trouble remembering to call officers "sir"—he told the navy dentist, "Hey, doc, don't hurt me!" and was reprimanded for not addressing a lieutenant properly.

Having appraised his high intelligence and athletic ability, the navy decided to train him as a ranger or commando. They told him he would perform missions like swimming ashore at night to murder enemy guards and demolish installations, etc. The idea was revolting to him. He wrote to Jim O'Dea that he wanted no part of the navy and that he would find some way to return to the freedom of the merchants. O'Dea replied avuncularly that "these people are for serious" and that Jack had better consider his actions carefully. In his next letter, Jack detailed his plan to begin reporting headaches every day, which he would follow up with silly behavior. He boasted: "I'm crazy as a fox—watch and see!"

When the commanding officer caught him smoking one morning, he slapped the cigarette out of Jack's mouth, and Jack belted him. It seems he was not immediately arrested, but there was talk about a court of inquiry. Soon afterward, he laid down his rifle on the drill field and walked by himself to the naval library. He was reading and taking notes when the military police arrested him. Jack told them he was a field marshall. When they reminded him he was in line for the submarine service, he told them he had claustrophobia, adding, "I ain't a frogman, I'm just a frog."

The officer in charge told Jack that he would have to be examined by psychiatrists. If they found him sane, he would be court-martialed. Jack was taken by ambulance to the base hospital. After giving him a physical examination, the psychiatrists began poring over his novel, *The Sea Is My Brother.*

A naval intelligence officer came to question him. The officer claimed Jack had the highest IQ in the history of Newport Naval Base, which made the navy suspect he was "an officer in the American Communist Party." [28] Jack told him that the only thing he believed in was "absolute personal freedom at all times." To the doctors Jack explained: "It's not that I *will not* accept discipline, it's that I *cannot.* I'm not a warrior, I'm a scholar."

While the doctors pondered how to handle his case, Jack was locked in with a hairy madman known as "Roncho the Modmo" and several other patients, including a manic-depressive from West Virginia and a French boy from Massachusetts, who languished by the window singing "Shine on Harvest Moon." Although Jack harmonized with him, the kid said only a few words to him and never spoke again. There was at least one other intelligent, witty man there, a six-foot-five former Louisiana State football player named William Holmes Hubbard, nicknamed "Big Slim." Big Slim's only weakness was a penchant for punching people with his huge fists, but fortunately he took an immediate liking to Jack.

While teaching Jack how to cheat at blackjack, Slim described his own merchant marine adventures and his scrapes with the law. His language, a mixture of dialects from Louisiana cracker to Wild

West cowboy, fascinated Jack. Jack picked up expressions from him, like "That ain't no Harvard lie," that he used for the rest of his life. But it was Big Slim's freewheeling personality that affected Jack most. He had worked at a variety of jobs all across the country, ranging from oil worker in the East Texas oil fields to tug worker in New York harbor. The story Jack liked best was how he had decided to become a hobo. As a child, Slim had seen a hobo politely ask his mother for a piece of the pie cooling on a windowsill, and his mother had given it. From that time on he had known he could wander the country and always have his needs taken care of.

At five every morning Slim would pick up Jack's mattress to roust him out of bed, and they would have breakfast together. Slim told Jack they should hide their butter knives; with these they could break the locks and hop freights to Butte, Montana, to meet another hobo buddy, Mississippi Gene.

Initially Jack had felt frightened in the hospital, imagining he saw through his fellow patients' heads. Thanks to Slim's camaraderie, he gained the courage to begin examining the parameters of madness. Sitting with even the worst patients, Jack would listen and learn. One guy had tried to commit suicide by shooting himself in the head, only to find that the bullet had gone completely through without killing him. Jack asked how he felt, and the guy replied, "Blaahhhh! It don't bother me." Soon Jack got his sense of humor back. When actors Leonid Kinsky and Akim Tamiroff came to visit the ward, he actually entertained them with his old trick of "talking ragtime" (as people in Lowell described his intellectual double-talk).

The psychiatrists didn't believe Jack was crazy. When they asked if he was a pacifist, he replied that he wasn't, but merely "indifferent to war." It looked like he might be court-martialed.

His father came down to see if he were really insane, but finding Jack as sharp as ever, Leo laughed savagely and praised him for finally fighting back. Jack had always been a little too shy, he said, and it pleased him that he was finally waking up. After raging against the admirals, Roosevelt and "his ugly wife," and the "Marxist Communist Jews" who allegedly had started the war as part of a plot, Leo told Jack he was doing the right thing and took the train back to Lowell.

Having already enlisted in the Army Medical Corps, Sammy got a brief leave to visit Jack. Still cherishing his melioristic faith, Sammy was appalled to find Jack in this "house of suffering." [29] He wondered what good Jack could do there, and left bewildered.

Jack did manage to forestall court-martial by getting himself classified Section Eight. The front of the hospital was at right angles to the drill field where they staged a review of the recruit battalion every Saturday morning. As the recruits stood at attention, the admiral and any visiting brass would parade down the front of the battalion. One Saturday morning Jack dashed out of the hospital stark naked and ran the length of the battalion front, yelling, "Geronimo!" Diagnosing Jack's malady as *dementia praecox*, the doctors sent him to the naval hospital at Bethesda, Maryland. They found his butter knife; and when a search turned up Slim's butter knife, he was shipped to Bethesda too.

This time Jack found himself in a ward where the inmates howled like coyotes. But he was developing a new confidence, so that when the psychiatrist (whom Kerouac identified only as "Dr. Rosenberg" in his private character key to the *Duluoz Legend*) probed him with hackneyed questions he continually responded with fresh tricks of wordplay. When the doctor asked who Jack really thought he was, he answered meekly, like Oliver Twist: "I, sir?" And when the doctor wanted him to elaborate his assertion that he was Samuel Johnson, he turned the doctor in a circle: "A man of letters is a man of independence"! Finally, seeing the psychiatrist would just keep pouncing on his witticisms as signs of illness, Jack again stated simply that he was incapable of submitting to discipline. His diagnosis was changed to "schizoid personality" with "angel tendencies" (an early epithet for unrealistic self-aggrandizement), and the navy offered him an honorable discharge for "indifferent character."

In May 1942, waiting for his discharge, Jack lounged around Washington, D.C., getting drunk or gazing westward from the asylum window, wondering if he had made the wrong choice in leaving the navy, if somehow he might have betrayed his youthful dream of being a "real American Man." [30]

After making him sign a form stating that he could never file for a bonus or a pension, and taking back all his government-issue clothing, the navy gave him fifteen dollars to buy himself civilian clothes. In his new shirt and slacks he spent a few evenings strolling around Bethesda, with the lilacs in bloom and an occasional Wave on his arm. Then it was another train ride home.

Home was now an apartment over a drugstore in Ozone Park, Long Island. Divorced from Charlie Morissette, Jack's sister Nin had enlisted in the Women's Army Corps. His parents had figured they would see more of both their children by living close to New York. They had lugged down all their belongings, even their $5 piano, because it wouldn't be home without Gabrielle playing and singing her French-Canadian ditties. It being wartime, they both found jobs, she making Army shoes in a Brooklyn factory and Leo working as a linotypist in the city. They lived cheaply, and for the first time in years were putting money in the bank. Saturday nights they went to theaters and restaurants in Manhattan, in a kind of second courtship. Gabrielle was so happy she sometimes gave Leo permission to bet on the horses.

For Jack, however, there was more thrashing in his bed at night contemplating horrors of cosmic loss—the rapid slipping-away of everything dear to him.[31] Remembering his axiom that the most important thing for the mind is to be active, he went down to the N.M.U. Hall and signed on the S.S. *George Weems.* Before he sailed he went to see Edie, who was spending the summer in Asbury Park, New Jersey, with her grandmother. All her girl friends there were jealous. Even her grandmother was coming to like Jack, finding him gentle and polite, even if his clothes were still shabby. Making him wear earrings, Edie took Jack to the beach as her gypsy. They made love. Finally he told her he was shipping out in a week, but he promised that on his return he would join her and her friend Joan in an apartment in New York. She called him a rat but told him she loved him anyway.

From her house on the Atlantic coast, Edie watched a luxury liner run aground and burn, and the vision recurred in many nightmares, where the burning ship had become Jack's own. But during the four months of his absence her fear for his life changed to anger at being abandoned. She eventually became so callous she duplicated his original love letter to her, and sold copies for $1 apiece to V-12's who wanted to use it for their own seductions. It was actually such a good letter it earned her $50.

While still in Ozone Park, Jack had a surprise visit from Big Slim. He, Jack, and Leo went to the race track in Jamaica. After losing their money they started drinking, took a train to Penn Station and began hitting the nearby saloons. After a while Leo had to quit from exhaustion, and Jack and Slim went on drinking themselves senseless through the night. In the morning Jack left Slim staggering in front of the Seamen's Union.

In late June, 1943, Jack set sail as an ordinary seaman on the *George Weems,* which was carrying five-hundred-pound bombs to Liverpool. Before they sailed he had taken a dive off the poop deck into the harbor, angering the boatswain, who later ridiculed him for reading so much in his bunk. But Jack thrilled to be an adventurer again, and even the threat of the gargantuan German battleship *Bismarck* couldn't prevent him from savoring the wild sights and sounds of his dawn watches on the bow.

Using the purser's typewriter, he worked on *The Sea Is My Brother.* But, as he read Galsworthy's *Forsyte Saga,* he conceived the idea of writing a series of novels that would connect as "one grand tale," representing the "legend" of his life.[32]

On watch one evening he spotted a mine, saving the ship from destruction. Still the first mate criticized his performance, and even complained that Jack didn't make good coffee. His malevolence was like that of Melville's old and scarred villain Claggart toward the innocent, young and handsome seaman Billy Budd. During a bad squall, with the ship pitching severely, the first mate sent him up to the crow's nest. Jack was just barely able to hang onto the ladder.

Later the members of the deck crew held a union meeting, denouncing the first mate for what looked like attempted murder. But during another storm the first mate ordered Jack to jump from the ship into the lifeboats, which were suspended four feet outside the hull. He was to bail them, though they contained hardly any water. Once again Jack accomplished the feat. When he overslept fifteen minutes, the mate sniggeringly called him "Sleeping Beauty" (normally he called him Keroach, as Little had). At the next seamen's union meeting, the first mate was denounced again.

One morning their ship was attacked by German submarines. Knowing that if a torpedo did hit them—with all their dynamite— they would be blown to smithereens, Jack simply rolled over in his bunk and went back to sleep. His experience in the mental hospital had left him with a sense of helplessness and an acceptance of death.

When the ship entered the Irish Sea, with early morning sunshine clearing the mist to reveal green meadows with cows and thatched huts, Jack began to cry. Besides his enthusiasm over James Joyce's country, he revered Ireland as the true ancestral home of the Kerouacs, as he had often been told the story of their migrations from Ireland to Cornwall to Brittany.

Their captain was a sober man but it seemed that at the sight of Liverpool he had finally gotten drunk, for instead of touching at the dock, the ship rammed and demolished it. Fortunately the rotten wooden wharf gave way, or part of Liverpool would have vanished.

The first two days Jack worked on the ship, so that he could have two consecutive days free in England. Imitating the Lancashire accents of the longshoremen, and studying the old seadogs on neighboring ships, he realized that someday he might really be a great writer like Conrad or Melville. No longer "fooling around with poetry," as he was to call it later, Jack would get down to the serious business of recording what he had witnessed.

For his leave he dressed in a black leather jacket, khaki shirt, black tie, and—shades of Henri Cru!—a visored hat with phony gold braid. After a brief stop at the U.S.O. club, he took a train to London. It was now early September, and the green countryside recalled the romance of the English movies he loved. In London he was dazzled exploring all the places he had heard or read about. He went to a Tschaikowsky concert at the Royal Albert Hall. When an air raid began, the audience demanded that the concert continue.

Then he and a couple of soldiers made their way through the blacked-out city to Piccadilly Circus, where they got drunk and found prostitutes. In the morning, after observing life in an English inn, Jack returned to the Piccadilly bars for more beer. Because the prostitute had taken most of his money he had to go to the American shipping office to borrow some. On the way an old Englishman with homburg and umbrella tapped him on the shoulder, asking, "I say, which way to Threadneedle Street?" Years later Jack claimed that experience presented him with the quintessence of England.

Back in Liverpool he found another prostitute and engaged her right against a monument. He had to make his way to the ship through another blackout, but he was more afraid of the English ruffians than of the German bombs. England had lived up to his romantic notions of its grand history and culture, but he had also been impressed with the poverty of its inhabitants: the pubs closed for lack of beer, people reputedly eating sausage made with sawdust and storing coal in their bathtubs. On his last morning in Liverpool that vision of "beatness," as he later called it, prompted him to conceive of "the Duluoz Legend." Sitting at the typewriter in the purser's office, he suddenly foresaw as his life's work the creation of "a contemporary history record." The style wouldn't matter as much as fidelity to the events and thoughts that registered on his consciousness.[33]

4.

On its return trip through the stormy North Atlantic, the *Weems* was again attacked by submarines. Jack hardly talked, except to reassure the second cook that there was "no place to go." But the moment he saw the Manhattan skyline he was filled with joy, and with his pay envelope in hand, as well as a beer from the Brooklyn pier, he amazed the whole crew with his wild talk.

He immediately took the subway to Columbia to see Edie. Wet from the cold October rain, he climbed the five flights of stairs to her new apartment at 421 West 118th Street, where she lived with Joan Vollmer Adams. Edie was radiant with love. After she fixed him their favorite snack of cold asparagus with mayonnaise and ripe olives, they pulled down the shades and went to bed.

In Ozone Park Jack found both his parents in high spirits. Since they wanted to meet Edie he brought her out, and they all had beers in the German tavern on Liberty Avenue and Cross Bay Boulevard. Gabrielle developed a good rapport with Edie, who was as simple and fun-loving at heart as Gabrielle herself. All the same, Gabrielle was distressed to learn that Jack planned on moving in with Edie, and got no comfort from his promise to return home periodically. As Jack reported to Edie, it grieved her to see him "living in sin."

Gabrielle was worried about Leo too. He constantly complained about having to work nights, about the coldness of people in the streets and subways, and the terrible loneliness he had known ever since leaving New England. Much fatter than before, bald and always sweating, Leo hardly looked like the stalwart businessman who had briskly walked the streets of Lowell, hailing old friends. He reminded Edie of a miserable character she had seen in a movie about the garment district.[34]

It was a relief for Jack and Edie to return to the city. Her family disapproved of her living on her own, fearing just such a liaison as she was about to inaugurate. As Kerouac related in *The Town and the City*, they discussed the "issue" of living together. From some book she had picked up the phrase "horrible bourgeois world," and it was this chimera she sought to avoid at all costs. Though she still felt the weight of her Grosse Pointe training, which specified that all her activities should be directed toward settling down and rearing children, she was braced in her decision to live with Jack by the example of her girlfriends, who were also enjoying sexual and social freedom. For his part, Jack quickly overcame the guilt he felt at hurting his mother by thoughts of the adventures he would have with this affectionate and "aggressively alive" girl.[35] He wondered that he could ever have desired some slinky movie star in a clinging gown, lounging in a penthouse, when it was so much more fun to live with a childlike gleeful girl in a plain apartment decorated by hand and furnished with love. To a "cornball" like Jack they were Frankie and Johnnie, the star-crossed lovers of romantic ballad,[36] and they set about pursuing their destiny at a fevered pitch.

Edie's roommate, Joan, was a brilliant young Barnard graduate from upstate New York, a beautiful woman whose contempt for flattery developed into a protective gloss of sophistication and cynicism, which in her case was later hardened by a bad marriage. She spent hours reading in the bathtub, and she had to have every edition of every New York newspaper every day. She recognized at once that Jack was a genuinely gifted writer, and his social awkwardness moved her to mother him.

Jack was writing stories and articles for magazines, using his merchant-marine experience and other adventures for material. He had become such a speed typist that the carriage bell on his typewriter would ring like an alarm clock. Since he typed all night, it was hard for Edie to sleep; she complained, reminding him she had to get up early for her art classes. But she was actually falling ever more deeply in love with him. Although Jack got depressed as his magazine stories were consistently rejected, his poverty caused no problem in their household. If Edie used up her month's allowance in two days, she had only to write home that she was starving. When the fresh reserve of cash arrived, they would likely spend it all on beer and other makings for a party—and then she would merely write home again! In the meantime she could always go around the corner to her grandmother for a loan.

With a sixth floor walk-up apartment, they didn't have to worry about her grandmother paying a surprise visit. And it was a good thing, since their apartment was usually filled with an assortment of raffish characters. Joan had friends like Dicky, a Broadway street person, and Alex, an old artist from Greenwich Village, who painted murals in bars in exchange for drinks. Joan was courted by an elegant Columbia student named John Kingsland, who sought to emulate Oscar Wilde. Edie's sister Charlotte sometimes visited with her friends Bill Sweeten and Bill Maxey, seamen who later shipped with Jack. Edie's girlfriends from Asbury Park often dropped by. Many of them flirted with Jack and sometimes he would take one of them to bed, which incensed Edie and provoked her to continue dating V-12's.

Yet the magnetism between them was so great even infidelity couldn't diminish their love. For one thing, they both spent a large part of their waking hours eating. Sometimes Jack would just lie around the apartment all day while Edie prepared an endless succession of dishes. The huge breakfasts she cooked became his favorite meals and they also often ate at expensive restaurants, especially lobster houses. Later, after movies or just long strolls, they usually stopped at Bickford's cafeteria for corned beef hash with an egg on a muffin. To tease her, Jack would ask, "Are you still hungry?"—alluding to the day she ate six hot dogs in a row. Once, watching her eat, he declared, "You invoke Mephisto." She ate the way she lived, and he told her it was her uninhibited passion he loved.

They enjoyed sex together, but it was far from Jack's consuming interest. Their intimacy was more like that of brother and sister, springing from virtually identical temperaments. They both possessed a boundless vitality. Both loved to travel and explore the unknown. Both were exceptionally open-hearted and tolerant. Both could create excitement from the dullest situation. If there were nothing else to do they would play word games, making puns and inventing funny names like "Carlotta Cranberry" for their friends. Bed was just another place for games and storytelling, and Jack's lovemaking involved his playing roles like Dr. Sax and the Shadow. It was a place where he showed her great tenderness beyond just touching, and as they lay in each other's arms, he would tell her of his brother, Gerard, and the sadness left in him by Gerard's death.

Aside from his obsession with writing, Jack's greatest passion was music. He played classical music on the radio until it drove Edie crazy. Beethoven was one of his favorite composers as well as a personal hero, and he also liked Bach and Debussy. But it was jazz they both liked best. Their song, naturally, was Billie Holiday's "I Cover the Waterfront," and they would go to hear her on 52nd Street as well as in little clubs up in Harlem. Uptown Lady Day would sit at the tables with customers, and Jack and Edie ofte' talked with her. They also went to famous places like Minton's a the Cotton Club. Often Seymour Wyse accompanied them; as they walked along he and Jack would riff together and Seymour, with his flawless ear, would correct Jack whenever he missed a note. Sometimes a piano player Jack had met at Columbia would come too. With Edie's sister Charlotte and Henri Cru along, their night might turn into a moveable musical party. They would walk the streets in Harlem and Morningside Heights until dawn. Through Seymour, whose brother was an editor of *Downbeat* magazine, Jack and Edie got to know Lester Young, Billy Eckstine, and many other musicians. Jack would ask Prez to play "On the Sunny Side of the Street," and then sing along to it—it was one of his favorite songs.

The bebop revolution was underway. The previous fall, at the Three Deuces on 52nd Street, Jack and Seymour had heard Charlie Parker and Dizzy Gillespie "playing a goofy new sound." [37] Although Jack knew they were serious musicians, he didn't care for this early bop, and now, in late 1943, he still wasn't listening much to Bird and Diz, but he had already heard another bop pioneer, Slam Stewart. Listening to Stewart's solos, Jack would get so caught up he would start playing an invisible bass and scat along at the same time. He had an ear for originality. He often took Edie to hear the virtuoso pianist Art Tatum, who played spectacular chord variations with breathtaking speed; they also listened to Leadbelly's country blues and work songs. Jack was always interested in different dialects, but, thanks to Wolfe, he was especially curious about the South and often talked with Edie of wanting to see it.

They spent almost as much time at the movies as listening to jazz. It was common for them to go to three separate movie houses along 42nd Street and see three movies at each one. Jack loved French movies because he loved to hear French spoken (as he loved to speak it). Naturally he had to see every movie with Jean Gabin, whose French sounded much better to him than the guttural "Arabic" pronunciation of Parisians. *Fantasia* so entranced him that he went back to see it at the Thalia fifteen times. Humphrey Bogart was another of his heroes. Wearing Edie's father's brown felt hat, Jack did the best Bogart imitation she had ever seen.

For variety Jack and Edie sometimes spent an evening on a round of parties. They had become friends with Burl Ives, then just a folk singer living on Washington Square. He would invite them to his house for his special salad and rollicking singalongs. At one cocktail party in the Village Jack met Ernest Hemingway. After addressing him as "Papa," Jack proved too tongue-tied to make much of an impression on his former idol.

James T. Farrell was living near Edie's apartment, and Jack sometimes met him in the nearby Gold Rail restaurant, where they had "serious discussions" about writing and life.[38] Especially marvelous to Jack was the fact that Farrell was managing to raise a family while remaining a prolific writer. Charlotte was now in college in Washington, D.C. When she came to visit Edie and Jack, she had so much fun she failed to write her English term paper. Jack wrote the paper for her, discussing Farrell's novel *My Days of Anger*. He thought it a good book "primarily because of its frankness," but he complained that it was difficult to read because "there is no definite plot." The paper turned out too good for Charlotte to submit as her own.

John Garfield's parents lived next door to Jack's in Ozone Park. Garfield paid their rent but never came to visit them, which Jack deplored, although he was always praising Garfield's acting.

Jack's and Edie's home away from home was the West End Bar, where the owner, Nate, would give them credit for food. Since Jack adored anyone who did things with exuberance, he loved Johnny, the bartender. Johnny was the only man Jack knew who could, from a standing position, jump completely over the bar. Although he disliked the physical violence of football, Jack loved to invent new plays on paper, and he often sat alone at the West End working on them. Intrigued by the combination of mathematics with intuition, Jack would also sit for hours "doping out" the horses, making imaginary bets which he later showed to Edie to prove his skill as a gambler. He had no intention of going to the track but rather played such mental games for relaxation.

More often the West End was Jack's social center. He drank and talked literature with Jack Fitzgerald, the Columbia student and writer. Fitzgerald and his friend Duncan Purcell, who was in love with Joan, were both from Poughkeepsie. "Uncle Dunc" and "Fitz" shared Jack's small-town infatuation with the big city, and all three sometimes enhanced their wonder with prodigious drinking. When the whole group was drunk at the West End one night, the discussion turned to Fitzgerald's perpetual lack of a girl, all the more strange because he was good-looking. To prove his virility Fitzgerald picked up "West End Mary," a notorious barfly, and took her back to Edie's apartment, where she inexplicably had to take off nine dresses before they could make love. Fitzgerald's haplessness endeared him to Jack.

Gradually Edie was educating Jack to be less gauche himself. Explaining that with his dark complexion he should wear white and black, navy blue, or gray, she used her own money to outfit him with a new wardrobe. One thing she didn't have to teach him was cleanliness. He took baths and showers all day, was forever washing his hands, and took meticulous care of his teeth. What maddened Edie was his obsession with the toothbrush—after knocking out the drops of water, he dried it on a towel! Jack's good manners made a favorable impression on her tycoon father. Separated from Edie's mother, Mr. Parker was often in New York, and several times he took them to dinner. Edie's sister thought Jack "adorable," and by now he had endeared himself to her grandmother too. Marriage seemed in order. But whenever she brought up the subject Jack procrastinated, saying he was too poor. If she reminded him of her trust fund, he would promise: "OK, we'll get married sometime." One time she tried to get him to be more definite, and he exploded that she thought marriage was "like a love story in the ladies' magazines," that she'd have to learn to stop "fooling around" first.[39]

5.

Although Edie sometimes regretted Jack's lack of commitment, she enjoyed dating different men. Her V-12's still drifted into their apartment, and she was making new friends in her art class, which was taught by George Grosz. Late in 1943 she became interested in the slender, blond, very handsome young man who had happened in to watch her sketching. The student, Lucien Carr, had irresistibly devilish, slanting green eyes. While Jack was staying on Long Island with his parents, Edie invited Lucien to the apartment. Raised in affluence in St. Louis, and having passed through a dozen prep schools and colleges on his way to Columbia, Lucien was as sophisticated as the Grosse Pointers with whom she grew up. When Jack showed up on the weekend, he acted aloof toward this new, formidable rival.

Lucien loved Edie's "hell for leather" attitude, but he was two years younger and had his eye on other girls, including a bright Barnard student named Céline Young. No longer so threatened by Lucien, Jack began to appreciate his brilliant mind. He was even more struck by Lucien's casual derring-do. Lucien was a master of gratuitous acts, like flinging a plate of food over his shoulder, in a restaurant, on an impulse of displeasure. One day Jack heard gunshots in the alley below, and in from the fire escape bounded Lucien, claiming he was being pursued. In fact, Lucien had actually been chased cross-country by a homosexual who was obsessed with him.

Wherever Lucien went, his beauty and grace drew stares, especially love-looks from women. Many men resented Lucien simply because he could get away with wearing red shirts and red bandannas, or because he could out-argue them in a bar. Writing to Allen (September 6, 1945), Jack expressed his own anger against the "bloodless fish" who were always "snarling out of the corners of their mouths" at Lucien, and Jack was always moved to defend him. But most of Jack's high jinks with Lucien were childishly innocent.

Lucien liked to sing. His repertoire comprised bawdy songs, folk songs, even communist work songs, and Jack would sing with him. One night Lucien told Jack to get in a barrel, and he rolled Jack down the sidewalks of upper Broadway. Another night, in a heavy rain, they flopped in a gutter, singing and pouring black ink on each other's heads. Jack admired Lucien's abandon, but Lucien appreciated Jack's warmth; he was amazed at how "each person who came along was someone for Kerouac to love." In addition, Jack and Lucien embodied each other's concept of the romantic hero. The stocky Breton with blue eyes and coal black hair possessed an earthy magnetism Carr lacked; the winsome, gracile Scotch aristocrat seemed a "blond Tyrone Power" to Jack. Since Jack was already more of an observer than a doer, Lucien became a prime target of his curiosity. Frequently Jack found himself wondering where Lucien was at the moment and would hurry off to find him.[40]

At the apartment Lucien would say, "Let's have a party!" and Edie would ask, "What kind of party?" and Lucien would say something like, "Let's have an artichoke party!" In that case, they would go to the store and buy up all the artichokes. After Lucien fixed his special hollandaise sauce, they would set out little plates in a circle, put the pot of sauce in the middle, and start passing the food and beer. Lucien always had a fresh batch of risqué songs to teach them. When the apartment got too smoky and messy, they would head down to the West End for further drinking. Nobody but Joan ever bothered to clean up. Seeing Jack drunk, Edie would be amazed at how loud and rowdy he became. Sober, he was far from outgoing. The transformation reminded her of *Dr. Jekyll and Mr. Hyde*. It also made her realize that all his talk about Doctor Sax and the Shadow related to different selves within Jack, selves he usually kept hidden.[41]

Edie's other friends were more interested in politics than was Jack. After the closing of most of Columbia's fraternities (possibly, according to Edie, because of "problems with Communists"), some of her friends began attending Communist "fifth-column" meetings. A few times Edie and Jack went with them. Jack was mainly interested in meeting different types of people. When they asked him to sign up, he declared: "Ah, no! No cards for me! Leave me alone!" To Edie, a bunch of multimillionaires gathered in a Park Avenue penthouse to discuss the plight of poor workers seemed ridiculous. Nevertheless, they both enjoyed meeting the "radical" world, and getting a few free meals to boot!

Thanks to Lucien, they also met a seventeen-year-old would-be labor leader named Allen Ginsberg. With horn-rimmed glasses and protruding ears, Allen timidly entered the apartment one afternoon looking for the "romantic seaman who writes poem books," as Lucien had described Jack. What Allen saw was a big, tough-looking jock lounging in an armchair, wolfing down a huge breakfast. Disconcerted, Allen said, "Discretion is the better part of valor!" and Jack replied, "Aw, come off it!"

As they sat staring at each other, Allen was impressed with Jack's self-assurance, but he also divined the sensitivity underneath. Jack meanwhile assayed Allen's shallowness.[42] On the surface Allen was everything Jack despised—a skinny Jewish intellectual homosexual. But Jack's heart opened to anyone who showed real feeling or who spoke honestly of his experiences. After a while he amazed Allen by suggesting they take a walk together. As they walked, Allen reminisced about his childhood, recalling his sense of "ghost presence" in the tall, shadowy hedges near a church and a funeral home on the street where he grew up, in Paterson, New Jersey. At age ten or twelve, as he passed those hedges on his way home from the movies, he would feel overwhelmed by the loneliness of the universe. It seemed strange to be walking in the midst of space, and even stranger to contemplate the infinity of that space. He would ask himself, "Where does the universe end? And how could it end?" Because of Jack's receptiveness, Allen talked about his experiences as he actually remembered them; for the first time, he realized, he was talking from his "native mind" rather than mouthing clichés from books or maxims—like "discretion is the better part of valor"—taught him by his father. But even greater was Allen's surprise to hear Jack say, "Gee, I have thoughts like that all the time." Jack began to tell Allen about his own childhood questions, the nights he had stood alone in the backyard gazing at the stars and pondering the same unanswerables.

In the following weeks Allen and Jack took several walks together, continuing their philosophical conversations. It turned out Allen had been rooming just across from Lucien in the Union Theological Seminary, since dormitory rooms at Columbia had been preempted by the V-12's. Hearing Brahms' Trio No. 1 coming from across the hall, Allen had gone to meet his cultivated neighbor. The door was opened by an "angelic-looking kid," blond and pale, and Allen fell in love. Now, walking with Jack, Allen described his nostalgia on leaving the seminary. As he had carried out his belongings, he had begun saying, "Good-bye, door, good-bye, hall, good-bye, stair number one, good-bye, stair number two," and so on down seven flights of stairs. Jack told Allen that he also said wistful good-byes to the places he left, and Jack wondered if other people shared their consciousness of how transitory life is. The tale of this incident revealed the similarity of their natures, both raked by enormous tides of love and tender concern. From that day on, there was an indestructible bond between them.

Since Allen was four years younger than Jack and Edie, he often got in the way like a kid hanging around grown-ups. Because of student curfew he couldn't follow them up to Harlem, and Jack got tired of his sitting around their apartment listening all the time. A poet himself, Allen admired Jack as a mature writer, but it was apparent that he had fallen in love with Jack as well. To get rid of him, according to Edie, she and Jack would send him out for cigarettes or on other errands.

At this point Allen realized his homosexuality but feared to divulge it, lest it bring him shame and rejection. But there were many other gay men around the apartment who tried to seduce Jack. As Edie saw it, Jack's passivity and reluctance to hurt made gay men feel that he accepted them. But others, like John Kingsland, found Jack's leanings definitely bisexual. In any case, Jack didn't feel threatened by gays; and, in his general tolerance, soon came to accept homosexuality as just another interesting lifestyle.

Lucien Carr was having more serious problems as an object of homosexual attention. When he was fourteen years old, in St. Louis, his physical education instructor, David Kammerer, had fallen in love with him. Kammerer's family was well-to-do, and he later attained further social prominence as an English instructor at Washington University. But by the time Lucien was nineteen, Kammerer had sacrificed his teaching career and all self-respect to abandon himself to his hopeless passion. To escape him, Lucien had changed schools every year; but wherever he went, Kammerer followed. Working in New York as a janitor, Kammerer trailed Lucien all over the Columbia campus and even barged into Edie's apartment a few times. Tall, red-bearded, he raced in and out, hardly speaking except to ask Lucien's whereabouts. Jack felt something strange about him, as if, though outwardly strong, he were a secret cripple.

Jack's problems were less dramatic but equally serious. He was uncomfortable being supported by Edie. Even after he found work as a telephone operator in a local hotel and as a script synopsizer for Columbia Pictures, there were still obstacles to their getting married. They often had dinner with his family, usually at their favorite German restaurant, Luchow's. Though outwardly convivial, the gatherings had undertones of tension. Nin was doubtless preoccupied with her personal problems, but Edie found her rather cold. Gabrielle was concerned about the immoral life to which Edie had led Jack, and she wrote Edie frequent letters about the necessity of Jack getting married to remain a good Catholic. At the same time Gabrielle complained to Jack that Edie used foul language (Edie always said exactly what she felt) and that she was too wild to make him a faithful wife. In the last analysis, however, Gabrielle would assent to any arrangement "Jackie" wanted. As for Leo, he insulted Edie as he did everyone, flinging back his own hurt at the world. He told Jack Edie was a "slut" and predicted she would turn him into a "bum." [43]

To Jack, home still meant warmth and his mother's good cooking, but the actual domestic life there was ravaged by his father's bitterness. Repeated loss of jobs, and his intense loneliness in New York, had hardened Leo to where he no longer felt for others but remained imprisoned in self-pity. Communication between father and son had dwindled, on Jack's side to explanations about the need to gather material for his writing, and on Leo's to complaints about the injustices he had suffered.

Leo insisted that he had always "done right," and that it was society, and especially the government, that had wronged him. Besides castigating the liberal Democrats, he now blamed the "aliens" —meaning Jews—for his financial ruin. He also criticized the Jews for making other people fight "their" war against Hitler—an issue that was sensitive for Jack too, since he had already lost many good friends, including John Koumantzelis, on the European front. Although Jack may have begun to absorb his father's anti-Semitism he had no inclination to practice it in daily life, as Leo did. Once, when a rabbi got in Leo's way, Leo knocked him in the gutter. Listening to his father's diatribes Jack silently smoked cigarette after cigarette, as though that nervous habit had become the last bond between them. Jack's relations with his mother were no longer as happy as before, either. After Leo lashed at her, she would sometimes hurt Jack in an irrational attempt to get back at her husband, lamenting that Jack hadn't become the good son Gerard would have been. And yet the anger of both his parents came largely from their frustrated love and tenderness. While he was away from home, they would both sit by the window for hours watching for him to come walking up Cross Bay Boulevard and waving to them, as he always did.

6.

Jack's life in Manhattan came to be a great relief from the gloom of Ozone Park. He was getting a glamorous reputation around Columbia, which brought a steady stream of people to the apartment. In the company of Kammerer, a tall thin St. Louis aristocrat named William Burroughs came to ask Jack for advice about getting into the merchant marine. Burroughs, a friend of Lucien's too, immediately interested Jack with his seersucker jacket and funny "English lord" mannerisms, like blowing out of his nose to ease his sinuses. Jack quickly realized that Burroughs, like Kammerer, had come to talk about Lucien but he also saw that there was a great intellect beneath this genteel façade.

Having heard abut Burroughs' explorations of underworld life, including extensive experiments with drugs, Jack was surprised to find him such a plain-looking fellow, bespectacled, with emotionless blue eyes and thin, sandy hair. The irony of his appearance was heightened by the casual way he mentioned his past jobs as bartender in Newark and exterminator in Chicago. But Jack's interest in him was most strongly sparked by a suspicion that Burroughs had really come to "dig" a "seaman type." Fresh from a shower, with only pants on, Jack felt as if Burroughs were digging his body too.[44] It amused him to be studied as a type of anything, since he had already probed the complexity of his own and others' personalities, but he sympathized with the curiosity that led Burroughs all over the city in his peculiar anthropological studies.

Born in 1914, Burroughs had done graduate work in ethnology and archeology at Harvard in the 1930s, and had studied medicine at the University of Vienna. Later, on his own, he had made himself an authority on the street life in a number of cities. But his investigations, into whatever lower depths, never lost their intellectual foundation. In the fields that interested him—such as psychology, history, and literature—he read greedily, always seeking new theories and individualistic expression. Burroughs had already done some writing himself, including a collaboration at Harvard on a story entitled "Twilight's Last Gleaming." An utterly cynical, dryly witty satire of the sinking of the *Titanic*, it made Jack realize that this "St. Louis clique" comprised "the most evil and intelligent" men he had yet met. Though he wanted to learn more about them, they were bored with his idealism; his only saving grace in their eyes was his Canuck skepticism.

One night Burroughs suggested that Jack wear his merchant seaman uniform so that he would have an easier time seducing women, and Jack replied that he wouldn't do such a "finkish" thing. Although Burroughs rejoined, "It's a finkish world," he began to develop a strong respect for Jack's honesty and integrity.

In Burroughs' apartment in the Village, Jack sat frowning as Lucien amused himself biting shards out of his beer glass, a stunt Kammerer tried painfully to imitate. Then Burroughs offered them a tray of razor blades and lightbulbs. Beneath that calculated madness Jack perceived a fierce, unrestrained pursuit of experience, a feat he admired but had never quite been able to manage himself. Listening to Burroughs' "marvelous" tales, Jack shuddered to find such an intelligent appreciation of the ugly and dreary aspects of city life.

Burroughs' grandfather had founded the Burroughs Office Machine Company, though his parents had sold off all their stock before the Depression and currently operated an antique shop. Every month they sent Bill $200 for living expenses. Despite their modest wealth, to Jack the Burroughs family seemed like tycoons; he was always in awe of people—and Lucien was another—who were detached from the mundane financial worries by which he himself was bedeviled. One day, seeing a hole in Burroughs' suit coat, Lucien and

Kammerer began ripping the coat apart to make decorations for the chandeliers and bookcases. The poor boy from Lowell was both frightened and fascinated by such wanton destruction.

Jack's rich friends were a taunt to his father. When he brought Lucien to meet Leo, Leo resented having to buy a drink for a "millionaire's son." Later Leo told Jack that Lucien was a "mischievous young punk" [45] who would get Jack in trouble, and Leo warned Jack away from Burroughs too. But his father's tired cynicism could hardly oppose the magic of Rimbaud, Lautréamont, Baudelaire, Apollinaire, Rilke, and Nietzsche, whose works Jack was learning about from Lucien, Kammerer, and Burroughs.

Burroughs especially had wonderful wisdom to share. When Allen first met him, in Kammerer's apartment in the Village, Lucien was describing a fight in which someone had bitten off part of someone else's ear. Coolly Burroughs pronounced: "In the words of the immortal bard, ' 'Tis too starved an argument for my sword.' " It was the first time Allen had heard Shakespeare quoted intelligently, and he was amazed that Burroughs' fund of wisdom immediately yielded such an apt comment. The range and depth of Burroughs' reading drew respect from both Jack and Allen.

They were all leading thoroughly intellectual lives, and every day were stimulated by the discovery of some new truth. The period of discovering the power in books is usually full of hope—especially for young people—but there was a certain negative bias in the books Jack and his friends were reading. The works that excited them were almost all critical of conventional ethics. The greatest moral revolutionary they read was Rimbaud, from whom Lucien had derived the concept of a "New Vision." Rimbaud's imperative to be "absolutely modern" required viewing the world without preconceptions, but in Jack's eyes the complete abandonment of one's past was a dangerous act of self-hate. Jack felt that Lucien had lost faith in human kindness and hence had sought a "post-human post-intelligence," a "post-soul."

From Rimbaud they also acquired the concept of "seasons": epochs when they would all go through a similar development. This was certainly one of the most self-analytical periods for all of them. Jack too was seeking a "New Vision," but he preferred to search for the "ultimate" through art. In works like *Finnegans Wake, Ulysses,* and *The Magic Mountain,* Jack claimed, "new vision" sprang from the imaginative arrangement of "humankind materials." [46] The intense involvement of Jack and his friends in real affairs didn't lessen their spiritual curiosity. Baudelaire's cry, *"Plonger au fond du gouffre, ciel ou enfer, qu'importe?"* (To plunge to the bottom of the gulf, heaven or hell, what does it matter?), assured them that the most sordid activities could bear spiritual fruit if perceived with sufficient openness. That is, awareness justified even the most terrible things it saw.

To develop their awareness, they had to find new things to see. Burroughs solved this problem by invading realms previously forbidden to him, like Eighth Avenue bars that served as marketplaces for guns, drugs, and flesh. Frequently he wandered around in some costume just to get people's reactions. Although Burroughs does not now recall it, Edie and her sister Charlotte recall Bill dressed as both a priest and a cowboy; and in the latter outfit, he allegedly entertained them with tales of his "life out West." Lucien Carr concurred with this recollection of the Parker sisters, saying, "It was very easy for Bill to make himself look like a priest just by turning his collar around." But Jack was impressed simply by Burroughs' Brooks Brothers suits; he talked about them so much that Edie suggested he get one himself. In cold weather, Burroughs' ensemble included a Chesterfield coat and homburg hat. Charlotte thought Burroughs looked like an undertaker, but Edie thought he was usually playing Sherlock Holmes. In any case, Edie was sure he was always playing some part. The key to his character seemed to lie in various movies which had impressed him so greatly he had chosen to live them out himself.

Jack didn't have to look so far for adventure; he had it every minute living with Edie. In early 1944 they rode the crest of their romance. He called her "Birdnote," and from her joy drew courage to shock the world of stuffy respectability. Lowell was one of his chief targets in the war against dullness. When G.J. came to visit him in New York, Jack arranged for one of Edie's girlfriends to answer the door in her birthday suit; behind her, Jack stood draped only in a towel. George Murray and Connie Murphy found him working as a bouncer in a bar in Greenwich Village, but Jack explained that his lumberjack shirt and tough look were just show. Instead of bouncing troublemakers, he offered them a drink! Later, he took his two old friends to Edie's apartment for a big party. The daring girls who wore jeans, T-shirts, and no bras astounded Murray, but he was repelled by what he saw as the amorality of Jack's new environment. When the apartment got too crowded, someone yelled, "The cops are coming!" Finding no cops outside, Jack took George and Connie to a nearby bar to continue drinking, and with laughter and jokes put Murray at ease, as he always had. But Murphy regretted that Jack was surrendering to his old irresponsibility.

In his correspondence with Jim O'Dea, now in the marines, Jack described his pleasures and wild sensations on marijuana. O'Dea sensed that he was supposed to be shocked, but he only felt, "So what?" In those days Harry Anslinger was warning people that behind every axe murderer was a joint, and O'Dea figured the warnings of such a fanatic were exaggerated. Yet O'Dea worried that Jack had lost his head like a kid in a candy shop, where at least some of the candies were poisons. The way Jack evoked his ecstasy at hearing Thelonius Monk in the Village and Eddie Condon on 52nd Street, he

sounded like a delirious sailor glad to drown in the siren song of jazz
and not at all like Jack London setting out for robust adventures. But
what puzzled O'Dea most were the repeated reports of Jack's
homosexuality.

Nothing O'Dea remembered about Jack could place him in bed
with another man. Jack had seemed more affectionate than most of
the group members—he liked to hug and put his arms around his
friends—but that was normal behavior for a Frenchman. All that
Lowell knew about homosexuals was that they were strange and to
be laughed at, and neither stereotype fit Jack. There was actually
only one known homosexual in Lowell. "Tommy O.," a professional
pool player, was called "the queer," and everybody joked about him.
An older man, he was never known to have sexual relations with
anyone. The female impersonator Manny Dyers, who played at the
Laurier Club, was suspected of being homosexual, but he had "established his bona fidus" as a man by running back and forth through
the Lincoln Rangers football team. Jack knew both Tommy O. and
Manny, but so did almost everybody else in Lowell.[47]

Jack had told Connie Murphy that his first homosexual experiences had taken place in the merchant marine. Jack said that many
of the crewmen had sex with one another because they were driven
by sexual need, and he found that deplorable. What he regretted
most was being exposed to that way of life, because although it
wasn't his "cup of tea," he had been "thirsty" and learned to drink
it. The confession seemed particularly anguished, as if Jack needed
to unburden himself of something shameful, and to affirm that he
was normal. In between voyages, during the war years, Jack went to
bed with numerous girls (in a bragging mood years later, he reckoned 250 such conquests[48]). But he was occasionally having sex with
men in the city, too, though probably only as the passive recipient of
fellatio.

Whatever his sexual makeup, Jack very definitely wanted to get
married. Several times he brought Edie to Lowell to let his friends
meet his prospective wife. Along the way, on bus or train, Jack
would point out some little cottage all by itself as the place he would
like them to live. He especially loved to see the lights of such a
cottage on a rainy night. But Edie suspected this domestic side to
Jack was more romantic than real; he alway seemed to prefer looking in from outside to actually being in there with the responsibilities of a family. In plain terms, she didn't find him "good marriage-
able material." [49] Although he offered her no security, she throve on
the excitement of being with him. Looking at the sunrise after talking with him all night—on subjects ranging from Greek mythology to
his lordly ancestry—she never failed to be astonished at how fast he
made time pass.

In Lowell Jack showed her all the scenes of his childhood, including the Franco-American Orphanage with its Stations of the Cross, and Pawtucket Street, which he called "the street of death" because all the nineteenth-century mill owners' mansions along it had been turned into funeral parlors. Among them was Archambault's Funeral Home, where Gerard had been laid out. Until then Edie had never been in New England, and her first impression of Lowell was of a fishing village without the water. Neither the shallow, rocky Merrimack nor the narrow Concord offered many watery vistas. Lowell's canals, which served the mills, had caused the city to be called "the Venice of the West," but in reality they were hardly noticeable. All the same, Edie was enchanted with the rows of little houses, as well as her first lobster sandwiches.

Jack took her to meet John MacDonald and showed her his large library, explaining how John had been the first person to interest him in poetry. Fondly Jack described the long walks they used to take together along the Merrimack, reciting poetry; then she, Jack, and John went for such a walk. Jack regretted that she couldn't meet Sammy, who was now serving overseas. Unlike most of his rough-and-tumble boyhood friends, he told her, Sammy and John had been two "soft and gentle" influences on his life.[50]

Jack arranged for Edie to stay with G.J.'s girlfriend Lorraine. That night the four of them went to a roadhouse, where Edie got so drunk she wandered outside and collapsed under G.J.'s car. Unable to find her, the others were about to drive away, when Jack spotted her and pulled her out, saving her life.

Recently married, Scotty had been in training with the Hartford Bees, a minor-league baseball team, but like Jack he was being ignored by coaches. G.J. brought Jack to see him. Scotty's wife fixed them baked beans on their old cast-iron stove; and as Jack relished the dinner, he told Scotty he looked forward to being married himself.

To G.J. Jack revealed how wealthy Edie's father was, and asked if he thought she would make him a good wife. G.J. replied unenthusiastically, "Yeah, Zagg, sure." Jack tried to pump G.J. for more specific impressions. Sensing that Jack merely wanted his own opinion fortified, G.J. told him, "You don't need my permission." Like a lawyer Jack kept haranguing his witness: "Based on your experience, would you say. . . ?" Finally G.J. exploded: "Zagg, you're gonna do what you want to do, OK? So do it!" But Jack kept pleading that he needed an honest opinion. Knowing what he wanted to hear, G.J. said, "OK, Jack, I like her."

Jack impressed G.J. as a man on the run, running futilely, as though he'd gotten caught on some kind of treadmill in New York. It seemed as if he had come back to Lowell because it was the one place he could stop running. Jack spoke of having lost his chance at Columbia. He told G.J. he would have done all right in college if his parents had let him alone. Little might have liked him, he said, if his father hadn't told Little how to coach.

Jack was in a conciliatory mood, and one breach he mended was that between George and Sammy. He showed George a letter Sammy had written from Italy, in which Sammy said he'd come to realize that G.J. was "a good kid."

7.

Back in New York, Jack received a voice recording from Sammy. On it he recited the opening of Shelley's *Adonais*: "I weep for Adonais— he is dead! . . ." The most striking part of the record was the long valediction, in which Sammy's stammering voice grew fainter and fainter: "So long, Jack old boy . . . take it easy, please . . . good-bye . . . take care of yourself now . . . farewell . . . I guess . . . 'bye . . . so long . . . good-bye, old man." In early March, 1944, Jack learned that Sammy had been wounded at Anzio and had died a few days later in a North African hospital. The shock sent him reeling away from the past and forced him to grope for meaning in the present.

He and Edie went to Grosse Pointe, Michigan, to visit her mother and father, who were now divorced. On her father's yacht on Lake St. Clair, they made love under the red Hudson's Bay blankets. Jack listened to the old magnate's tales of sailing with mannequins' legs stuck out the portholes, to shock his staid neighbors. Jack reveled at the parties given by the wild young socialites of Grosse Pointe, happy to hear their confident cries of "There's a beer in the refrigerator waiting for me!" At the same time the immense wealth of Edie's friends bewildered him. He had never learned to drive a car—except in reverse gear, for parking—while these people, if they did not collect cars as a hobby, generally owned at least one car for every day of the week. Henry Ford and Dick Fruehoff (of Fruehoff trucks) were nearby neighbors. Inevitably several of Edie's rich girlfriends flirted with the handsome writer, and Jack landed in bed with one. His "adventuresomeness" disappointed her, though she had made no commitment to spend her life with him.

When they returned to New York, Jack lost himself in the world of bop. By now bop was jazz's biggest bombshell, and he studied its explosion with the man who recorded it, Jerry Newman, to whom he had been introduced by Seymour Wyse. A balding, cherubic young Jew, Newman had for years been taking his recording apparatus to Harlem clubs. Jack liked him immediately. Newman's sense of humor was much like his: as a practical joke, he would later suggest Gillespie name one of his arrangements "Kerouac" (Dizzy didn't know Jack, but he liked the sound of the name better than

"Ginsberg," which Newman had also suggested). Moreover, Jack approved of Newman's brand of pleasure-seeking: he always had a supply of marijuana, in drinking he surpassed even Jack, and he drank absinthe with wormwood, a drink Jack had only read about in the lives of Rimbaud and other nineteenth-century alcoholic artists. At Newman's record store in Greenwich Village, Jack listened to the records Newman produced, as well as to private recordings of bop performances few other white men had heard.

Jack's preeminent interest was the revolution in the sound of jazz saxophone in the styles of Prez, Bird, Coleman Hawkins, Illinois Jacquet, and others. The saxophone had begun to talk with a human voice, with the rhythms and phrasings of black speech. In effect, the soloist discarded the melody of the song he was playing and improvised a completely new melody more consonant with his whims of the moment and the workings of the instrument. The bop saxophonist's flight along a variable-noted line had to stop only when he ran out of breath. The possibilities of new sound were infinite, and the only limitation the physical stamina of the performer. Bird sometimes extemporized for hours until his audience lost all sense of time and place.

Though bop was a heart-cry, it could only be played by musicians with great technical virtuosity. With Wyse's help, Jack learned the intricacies of that achievement. The result was that he developed his own "bop ear" for the unique sounds inside his head. It would take him several more years before he would learn how to play that personal music—i.e., get it on paper—so that others could hear it too.

Many of bop's innovators were extremely tormented men and died early deaths. In this case, the energy to explore the inexhaustible reaches of soul seems to have come, in large part, from equally inexhaustible stores of anguish. A similar dynamic was apparently operating in the young Kerouac's relentless pursuit of a totally expressive fiction. Though he would get shouting and giggling drunk on liquor, and spiritually high on music, pot, and various drugs, Jack was far from happy. One of the things Edie loved about him was his beautiful, sad blue eyes, which always looked about to cry. She was continually amazed by the depth of tragedy they reflected. Sometimes she laughed at how he seemed to like being unhappy, but she also felt frustrated by his acceptance of misery, as if it were his lot by birth. At twenty-two he already acted like an old man. In that respect she preferred Lucien to Jack, since Lucien never seemed worried about anything. Although she sympathized with the part of Jack that still grieved for Gerard, she wished he would learn to joke and laugh like other people and she wearied of the evil chuckle he cultivated in place of real mirth. When he did laugh, he sounded like the Shadow, the Green Hornet, or one of his characters.

Jack and his friends had a habit of speaking about people and situations in terms of literary archetypes. They would have "Dostoyevskian confrontations," endure horrors out of Kafka, and see friends reenacting scenes from novels. Lucien was a golden-haloed "child of the rainbow" like Rimbaud; his girlfriend Céline was the aloof temptress Clavdia of *The Magic Mountain.* Jack began to call Edie "Nastassya," after the sensitive courtesan in Dostoyevsky's *The Idiot,* whose infidelity drives Prince Myshkin irretrievably mad.

Jack's restiveness was nearly driving Edie mad. To discourage him from abandoning her again, she revealed to him the consequences of his last sea voyage on the S.S. *George Weems.* While he was at sea, she had discovered she was pregnant, hiding the fact from her grandmother till she was almost four months along. When her grandmother finally learned of the situation, she insisted Edie have an abortion. Convinced that Jack was an irresponsible sailor, Edie's grandmother took her away and made the arrangements. At that stage in her pregnancy, the abortion was very difficult. Afterward Edie learned that the fetus would have been a son. Hearing the story, Jack became furious.

He told her he would have wanted the child very much. She said she wouldn't have acquiesced to the abortion if he had written from overseas assuring her of his return. It seemed to her that he was interested chiefly in a reproduction of himself, and that he had scarcely considered the difficulties of raising a child. But Jack pointed out that the child would have been more than adequately provided for by her trust fund. Nothing she said could assuage his anger.

In May 1944, Jack got on a bus for New Orleans. Failing to get a ship there, he went on a drunken binge, then wrote to his mother and Edie for money to return to New York. On the way back he stopped in Asheville, North Carolina, to get drunk with Thomas Wolfe's older brother, and his trail of carousing led through Raleigh and Washington, D.C.; but when he finally got back to the apartment on 118th Street Edie welcomed him as warmly as ever.

Jack often quoted Wolfe's title *You Can't Go Home Again,* but he was always eager to return to a domestic routine. He got a cat, called Kitkat, and Edie got a dog, called Woofit. They had more fun with word games, and began discussing each other's dreams. Duncan Purcell, who was studying psychology, instructed them in Freudian dream interpretation. In Purcell's view, Jack's way of sleeping on his stomach with one arm raised above his head, represented a desire to return to the womb. Edie said she wanted to crawl inside *Jack* and hide there. Basically Jack was interested in dreams as a means of fortune-telling and as a source of other mysteries. Although he acknowledged his oedipal complex he never saw fit to worry about it, and Edie felt he was actually growing away from his mother's influence, no longer an apron-stringed boy.

She too was becoming more independent from her family by working as a fork-lift operator at the port of embarcation for the Liberty Ships. Working nights, she once saw a ship get sunk a few hours after she loaded it, and she was thankful Jack was safe at home, typing. In the daytime he began teaching her literature. He gave her a reading list, which included the new Saroyan novel he loved, *The Human Comedy.*

The fact that Edie showed little inclination to marry Jack, however, convinced his parents that he was involved with the wrong woman. Leo and Gabrielle both wrote to Nin of their worry that he was throwing away the best years of his life. Nin, in turn, wrote Jack (in July 1944) like a Dutch uncle, censuring him for living with Edie and for thinking he was different from other people:

> You're not being my own sweet brother who was fine, dignified and on his way-up to a bright future. That kind of living is for other people Jack dear, but not for *us.* We may be poor and haven't always had the best but we must always have family pride for Gabe and Leo. They brought us up to have high moral standards and it's our duty to see that we keep them through life . . . Go home darling, and try to make our folks' last years as pleasant as can be. You can still have your Escapades, without hurting them. . . .

8.

That summer, a new unrest was fomented by David Kammerer's obsession with Lucien Carr. Each rebuff from Lucien increased Kammerer's determination to have him as a lover, and Kammerer's actions grew more reckless. Excluded from a MacDougal Street party where Lucien was, Kammerer climbed the marquee of the bar downstairs and popped in through a window. One night he climbed the fire escape of Warren Hall, Lucien's dormitory, so that he could sneak in and leer for half an hour at his sleeping idol. Kammerer's persistent failures left him vindictive. Once, finding neither Lucien nor anyone else at Edie's apartment, he tried to hang Kitkat, who was saved just in time by Burroughs. The act smacked of vengeance, since Kammerer was jealous that Lucien was spending so much time with Jack and Edie. Lucien decided he had better leave New York. When Jack heard about Lucien's desire to ship to Europe, he wanted to join him.

After the invasion of France, Jack and Lucien thought of getting on a supply ship, then jumping ship at the first French port. With Jack speaking Breton, and Lucien acting as his deaf-mute brother, they would make their way to Paris. The happy vision of living as a vagabond poet made Jack forget his obligation to Edie. He and Lucien were about to sign on a ship in Brooklyn, but the departing crewmen warned them that the chief mate was a "fascist." Caught eating roast beef and drinking milk from the ship's galley, Jack and Lucien found just how fierce that chief mate could be—and what was worse, the big brute resembled Kammerer! When the mate refused to let them make a trial run up to Albany before signing on, Jack and Lucien quit the ship.

Lucien appreciated Jack's complete lack of malice. Even in barrooms Jack never used his muscles to prove his manhood, and in fights he only defended himself. When someone insulted him, he would get a "funny mad look," after which he usually told Lucien, "Let's get out of here!" [51] Lucien felt he could trust Jack completely.

Early one morning in the middle of August 1944, Lucien woke Edie and Jack with the words: "I just got rid of the old man." Edie had no idea what Lucien meant, and Jack told her to go out and get them some breakfast. While she was gone, Lucien told Jack how he had been forced to kill Kammerer the night before, in Morningside Park, where Kammerer had tried to rape him. In self-defense Lucien had stabbed Kammerer with his Boy Scout knife and then, in fear of the consequences, had weighted Kammerer's body and dumped it in the Hudson River. Although Lucien had already seen Burroughs, who recommended that he turn himself in, Lucien wanted Jack to help him dispose of the knife and Kammerer's glasses. The night before, Jack had told Kammerer he could find Lucien in the West End Bar; as a result, Jack felt some guilt himself. Jack accompanied Lucien while he dropped the knife down a sewer grate; then, in Morningside Park, he drew the attention of passers-by by pretending to urinate, while Lucien buried Kammerer's glasses.

After they walked around Harlem, Lucien got some money from his psychiatrist, and he and Jack went downtown to a movie; later they dawdled in the Museum of Modern Art. Finally Lucien headed for his aunt's, where he would contact the family lawyer.

Too nervous to stay in the apartment, Jack took Edie out to four movies. For a few more hours they just wandered along Broadway, stopping for chocolates and killing time, and Edie wondered why Jack didn't want to go into the West End. Back at the apartment, Jack told her what had happened. Before they could figure how to escape, two policemen broke down the door, and one of them yelled, "Is this a dope den?" Edie was terrified. Jack tried to act nonchalant, but the policemen told him he was being arrested as a material witness, since he had failed to report a homicide of which he had knowledge. Just as the police were leading them out, John Kingsland walked in the door. To keep him out of trouble, Jack and Edie pretended not to know him.

At the precinct house Edie was released but Jack detained. If a murder charge should be brought against Lucien, Jack would be tried as an accessory after the fact for helping Lucien dispose of the weapon; however, if Lucien were only guilty of manslaughter, Jack would probably be cleared. Since one of the questions in the case was whether or not Lucien was a homosexual, the police began interrogating his friends. Jack maintained they were both heterosexual, and the police seemed to believe him.

The newspapers played up the killing, focusing on the "pale," "intellectual-looking" college student; and Lucien didn't help quell publicity by carrying a copy of Yeats' *A Vision* to his arraignment in Homicide Court. Paradoxically, though Lucien was in much more trouble than Jack, Jack envied Lucien for the special treatment he was receiving. The officials approached Lucien respectfully, as though he were some sort of hero, while they shunted Jack around like an anonymous minor hoodlum. The detectives were paying a lot more attention to the two beautiful girls, Edie and Céline, whom they had called in for questioning. Then Jack's sense of inferiority turned to rampant paranoia, and he even suspected Allen Ginsberg of trying to promote his own literary career during his interrogation by the District Attorney. But the worst blow to Jack's pride was his father's refusal to put up $100 for bail. After telling Jack he had disgraced the Kerouac name, Leo hung up the phone.

Jack was further sickened by being taken to the morgue to identify the blue and bloated body of Kammerer. Later two Mafia killers, Ernest "The Hawk" Ruppolo and Willie Gallo, came to Jack's cell hoping to uncover some lurid details. Jack had to answer the same questions to a steady stream of misfits for the next few days.

Jack turned to Edie for bail money, but her inheritance from her grandfather had not yet gone through probate. Her family's lawyer would only dispense the money if she and Jack were married. Jack agreed to the condition. On August 22, he was led out of the jail by a plainclothesman, who served as his best man. Edie and Céline, her maid of honor, met them at City Hall. After the wedding the plainclothesman bought them all drinks and then escorted Jack back to his cell for a lonely honeymoon.

Before the bail money arrived, Jack's parents came to visit him in jail. Puzzled by his marriage they nonetheless forgave his mistakes, feeling he had been victimized by his friends, and they wished him and Edie well.

Soon after Jack got out on bail, he and Edie packed up their belongings and pets and took a train to Grosse Pointe. The train ride was arduous, since it was still wartime and all seats had been taken by the military. Now on her own, Edie's mother didn't have as much money as before, but room was made for them in the flat where Edie's mother and sister lived. Until then Jack had never thought much about the difference in his and Edie's backgrounds.

Now, dependent on the charity of a strange family, he began to chafe. He quipped sarcastically, "My mother works in a shoe company, and your mother owns one." Her family also owned hotels, shipyards, and—shades of Lowell—textile plants. Suddenly freed of material worries, he wondered if he would have anything to write about, complaining: "There's no tragedy in Grosse Pointe." But when he actually arrived there, in a chauffeured Packard limousine, he saw that the tragedy would be his own life. The huge manorial homes reminded him of the former mill owners' mansions on Pawtucket Street in Lowell, and he yelled, "You're nothing but a bunch of old funeral parlors! A bunch of lousy funeral parlors for dead people!"

In time he would find jumping clubs and live friends in Grosse Pointe too, but as he had once felt the pain of breaking away from Lowell, he now felt the vacuum left by the loss of New York. Life there had been filled with hope, like a joyous jazz solo, but the solo had ended and a death knell had ushered in the prospect of playing duet.

The only certainty was that Jack would keep making music with the only sounds he knew how to make: words. Even as he relinquished the hope of settling down as a family man—for he told Edie he would stay in Grosse Pointe only long enough to pay back the $100—he renewed his old vow of becoming a great writer.

What was to make him a great writer was his ability to break free from almost every traditional American value he had been bred to accept—to break free enough, at least, to view himself as the crippled product of those values, and as such typical of millions of very neurotic midcentury Americans. The world he was about to leave forever was imaged perfectly in Grosse Pointe, whose silent elegance could not hide its tense fear of the coming crash of all those empires built by ruthless individualism, the crash of all that had made America both great and monstrous.

FOUR
Wolfeans and Black Priests

1.

With its chandeliers, fine furniture, lace tablecloths, china, silver service, and bell for the butler, the apartment at 1407 Somerset in Grosse Pointe seemed the lap of luxury for Jack Kerouac, although it felt a trifle cramped to the Parkers when the new arrival spent hours on the toilet reading Shakespeare and the Bible. Fortunately, all three women—mother and two daughters—loved Jack. Edith's mother wished he might dress a little better, but then Edie preferred old clothes herself—that is, when she wasn't out riding in her jodhpurs. Edie's mother was also pleased with Jack's patriotism. Not to be outdone, Edie joined the war effort by working as a riveter at the Chrysler plant. Jack's job was considerably easier. The Fruehoff family had installed him as an inspector of ball bearings in their trailer factory. After a few minutes of work around midnight, Jack sat by himself, reading and taking notes until eight in the morning.

And every day he went to the public library. He was making a systematic study of literary criticism, as well as expanding his acquaintance with great books. During the day he wrote voluminously, beginning a new novel and keeping a diary besides. Charlotte tried reading the novel, hand-printed on his favorite yellow tablet paper, but she got lost among a multitude of characters. The novel was about his childhood, and she was struck by his remarkable memory.

Jack's many hours in seclusion began to vex Edie, who was eager for a social life. Edie scarcely read and though she wanted to learn about books to please him, she was usually busy finding ways to have a good time. Still shy, Jack avoided her crowds of friends; he preferred to sit in a corner talking to Charlotte. He told Charlotte about his "inferiority complex" [52] at Horace Mann—where, he felt, the rich kids had sought his friendship merely as a trophy, a football player they could display like an exotic animal to the delicate sensibilities of high society. Now, having shed his glamor, he was sure they would never open the door to him. He was also bitter about being excluded from the graduation ceremony because he lacked the proper accoutrements. It seemed to him that most of Edie's friends were similarly shallow, that they judged him not on his intellectual accomplishments but on the clothes he wore and the car he never learned to drive. Seeing her friends arrive in chauffeured limousines was an affront to which he never grew inured. That some of those limousines brought Edie new boyfriends just added salt to the wound.

Of course Jack and Edie both understood that their marriage had occurred solely for the convenience of getting Jack out of jail, and neither of them felt any more monogamous for having signed a piece of paper. Marriage made no difference in their behavior. Yet they still loved each other, and each longed for a more fulfilling relationship. Jack again dreamed of raising a healthy, butter-fed country family; Edie wished his eyes would not stray so often to her girlfriends.

Failing to find any intellectuals in Grosse Pointe, Jack settled for drinking companions at the Rustic Cabin bar. The yachting set could hardly make him forget his friends in New York, but he realized he would miss his friends just as much if he returned there since a great dispersal had taken place after Lucien's arrest. Lucien, having pled guilty to manslaughter, was now in the Elmira State Reformatory; Burroughs, out on bail as a material witness, had rejoined his family in St. Louis. Other visitors to the apartment had vanished before suspicion could point their way. Besides, the dullness of Edie's friends was somewhat alleviated by the flippant way she dealt with them, for the honesty of her wit was something he admired very much.

Jack made few concessions to Grosse Pointe etiquette. To her friends' mansions he wore his old black leather jacket and lumber-jack boots, and he was never without a five-o'clock shadow. When people asked his profession, he replied, "Artist." Even Edie's mother had a hard time conceiving of him as an author, which in her experience was a dignified, rather sedate sort of person, like Pearl Buck. Unable to satisfy anyone, Jack simply slept a lot. Also he often talked of resuming his travels, to gather fresh material with which to break his growing writer's block.

In early October, 1944, after paying back the bail money, Jack told Edie he would return to New York. At that point Edie was resigned to a separation. If anyone felt bad it was Jack, who seemed disappointed she didn't try harder to keep him in Grosse Pointe. Farewells were always hard on him anyway. Mr. Parker arranged a truck ride for him to New York.

When Jack didn't write Edie for two months afterward, however, she was disturbed enough by his callousness to write his mother about it, and Gabrielle's reply was remarkably shrewd and compassionate. "I don't mind telling you dear Jack is quite irresponsible[,] he never worked before I mean at a real job," Gabrielle confided, warning Edie that "he'll need your help in more ways than one if he's to be a success. Writing is a long grind before it gets profitable."

But Gabrielle also promised that their marriage would work if Edie had sufficient faith and patience in him, and she predicted that with a good woman behind him, her son would "go far someday in his writing." She even invited Edie to live with her until Jack returned. Nevertheless, Gabrielle was probably also using Edie to maneuver Jack back into her own life. A few weeks after his marriage, she had begun inflicting guilt on Jack with letters that told of her disappointment at finding herself and Leo alone in New York, since, she stressed, they had moved there "just to enjoy all this with you."

As soon as Jack got back to New York, he signed on the S.S. *Robert Treat Paine.* Because of the shortage of seamen, he was designated an acting able-bodied seaman, although he knew little about the operation of a ship. Spotting his ineptitude, the huge bosun immediately began to taunt him, calling him "Handsome" in front of the other crewmen.

Before the ship sailed, Jack returned to Columbia to look up Allen and Céline. Allen's friend John Hollander had already written a Dostoyevskian story about the "murder" in the *Columbia Spectator,* and Hollander congratulated Jack on finally becoming a "Wolfean" writer. Jack was gloomy enough thinking of the long hand-printed novel he had lost in a taxicab, and he felt even worse being photographed as a criminal celebrity in the Columbia bookstore. When Céline began flirting with him, Jack looked to her for some comfort in sex, only to find she was just teasing.

In the West End Bar, when Jack began to get serious about taking her to bed, Céline turned her attention to two naval officers. Since Jack was with Allen and another poet, Grover Smith, the naval officers decided Céline was being molested by "queers" and threatened to beat up Jack and his friends. After practicing his punches in the washroom, Jack led the officers outside to fight. The two of them got the best of him and Allen stepped in to help but was quickly brushed aside. When they started banging Jack's head against the pavement, Johnny the bartender stopped the fight. Jack spent the night in Warren Hall, a dormitory, crying in Céline's arms.

When his ship finally sailed for Norfolk, Virginia, Jack felt reborn. Entering Norfolk harbor he was even permitted to take the helm. But after they docked, the bosun warned him that he planned to teach him some rough lessons on the ensuing voyage to Naples. Moreover, the bosun persisted in calling Jack "Pretty Boy" and "Baby Face." Knowing he couldn't repulse a 230-pound homosexual, Jack jumped ship. With his duffel bag stuffed under his jacket, he slipped along the docks like the Shadow; but hopping a bus in town, he confronted the bosun and his cohort, the ship's carpenter. Only by persuading them the duffel bag belonged to a friend was Jack able to get away. That night in town, he met his old Lowell buddy Jimmy Cudworth. The next day he caught a bus to New York.

As a result of the incident in Norfolk, the merchant marine re-

jected Jack's job applications for a year, and he was never to free
himself completely from the stigma of having been blacklisted in
wartime.

In New York he got a room on the sixth floor of Warren Hall.
Though still distracted by Céline, he settled into a serious literary
apprenticeship. His family didn't know he was in the city, and the
only person he saw regularly was Allen, who shared his literary
monomania. One of the first things Jack and Allen did together that
fall was to pay a "formal visit" [53] to Burroughs, to learn the bases of
his mystery and power. Burroughs lectured them on semantics,
pointing out that words are not identical with the things they represent, stressing the difficulty of getting at things themselves, the *a
priori* "facts" [54] that existed previous to the mind's conceptualiza-
tion. Before they left, Burroughs lent them about a dozen books—
including Kafka's *The Castle,* Korzybski's *Science and Sanity,* Hart
Crane's *Collected Poems,* Rimbaud's *Collected Poems,* Cocteau's
Opium, Yeats' *A Vision,* Spengler's *Decline of the West,* and works
by Céline and Blake. He also showed them some Mayan codices and
discussed the eighteenth-century Italian philosopher Vico. All these
sources contain imaginative schemata for ordering civilization.
Vico's circular theory of history, for example, had served as the philosophical framework of *Finnegans Wake.* Tremendously ambitious,
rational and intuitive compasses of human culture, these works
sprang from the confidence that mind could conquer matter, and
they must have inspired as much optimism in the novitiates as the
serene analytical eye of Burroughs himself.

Jack spent a few months reading those works, as well as Lautréamont, Koestler, Huxley, Wells, Nietzsche, Freud, Aeschylus,
Goethe, and many other poets, novelists, playwrights, philosophers,
and psychologists. At the same time he made elaborate notes, attempting to synthesize the ideas he encountered in literature, painting, and music. Besides following the development of bop, he was
attempting to analyze the works of classical composers like Beethoven, Shostakovich, Stravinsky, and Schoenberg. On his wall hung a
card reading "The Blood of the Poet" (the title of a Cocteau film,
partly written in his own blood), and he wrote by candlelight, later
burning the pages to prove that he wrote from a pure artistic motive
rather than for money or fame.

Jack defined his mission as "self ultimacy," which included the
creation of a new "artistic morality." [55] This new morality justified
his search for fresh experience, as long as those experiences didn't
directly harm other people. Practical as ever, Bill Burroughs saw
that Jack was doing some harm to himself by his intense seclusion,
and so he took Jack out to dinner and movies or to his Riverside
Drive apartment for an occasional shot of morphine. Jack began
submitting his latest writings for Bill's learned opinion; though less

than enthusiastic, Bill would pronounce them "good." Burroughs continued to help Jack appreciate Shakespeare and other classic writers like Pope, while also exposing Jack to lesser-known but equally powerful innovators like Pierre Louÿs. Besides their teacher-pupil relationship, a deep friendship was growing between Bill and Jack, based largely on their mutual loneliness and need for encouragement.

Just before Christmas 1944, Jack received word from Edie's father that she had been seriously injured in an auto accident. He returned to Grosse Pointe and trudged through a blizzard to the Parkers' house. The sight of a wreath on the door—which in Lowell signified a death in the family—caused him to faint in the snow at her doorstep. The wreath turned out to be just a Christmas decoration; Edie, given fifty-two stitches after crashing through a windshield, was on the road to recovery. Jack borrowed $100 from her mother to get to New Orleans, where he planned to ship out. Failing to get a ship, Jack returned to New York and began writing his "life's wife" (as he now called Edie) to join him. She came, and they both moved into the new 115th Street apartment of her former roommate Joan Adams.

2.

A communal family formed in this five-bedroom apartment. Joan now had a baby girl, Julie. To help pay the rent she welcomed other boarders. Since Joan was so witty, Jack and Allen decided to introduce her to Burroughs. She appreciated Bill's humor, and when he quickly moved in it was the start of a genuine romance. Another boarder was Vicki Russell, a friend of Huncke's. A six-foot redhead, Vicki had been a "gun moll" [56] and currently worked as a hooker; she knew more about drugs than any of them. Allen began spending time at the apartment too. The final member of their menage was Hal Chase, a Columbia anthropology student. Blond and brilliant, Hal became a replacement for Lucien. Although he was physically stronger than Lucien and more aggressive with women, he was also prone to withdraw into solitude. Jack responded warmly to that shyness in Hal, who had grown up in Denver, a town as provincial as Lowell. But Hal's small town was in the West, which, to Jack, lent him an overawing majesty. Jack never doubted that the West was the real America.

Life in the apartment was far from wholesome Hollywood Americana. Everybody took turns in everybody else's bed, and sometimes six of them would sprawl on one bed. They were using marijuana, morphine, and benzedrine. Vicki taught them how to remove the benzedrine-soaked paper strips from benzedrine inhalers, which were sold over the counter in drugstores. Swallowing one or two strips would get you high, more would make you "sweat and suffer." [57] The first time Jack tried it Vicki gave him an overdose, causing him to lose several pounds in three days. Edie tried benzedrine too but it only made her sick, and she soon gave it up. In the Angler Bar on Eighth Avenue and 42nd Street, Burroughs was making friends with professional thieves, who stashed their guns and stolen property in the apartment. One of the thieves, Phil White, was in the habit of killing liquor-store owners, though Jack only learned that fact after White had hanged himself in the Tombs. Bill apprenticed himself to subway "lush workers," muggers who victimized drunks. He introduced many of these vicious characters to Jack, who found them repellent. Sick with benzedrine depression much of the time, Jack wandered through the city in a daze of hallucinations.

There were good times too. Although Burroughs spent a large portion of his income on narcotics he still managed to live well, and he often took Jack and Edie out to dinner. As they explored Chinatown together, Burroughs regaled them with exotic tales, telling of decadent old Chinese who savored their dinner while being fellated by a boy who knelt between their legs. Bill thought Edie's appetite so marvelous he suggested some restaurant place her in the window as an advertisement. Sometimes Burroughs took them to more dangerous places like the White Rose bar in midtown. There they would meet Bill's friend Herbert Huncke, a Times Square hustler and junkie, and Huncke would introduce them to characters ranging from petty thieves to real gangsters. The criminal milieu gave Burroughs another stage on which to perform, but the action there was deadly real. One night a gangster named Lucky fell in love with Edie and when some guy at the bar said hello to her, Lucky stabbed him! After that, Edie refused to mingle with Huncke's hoodlum friends.

Nevertheless, Jack continued to spend a lot of time with Burroughs, following him to his seedy haunts as well as to the University Club for dinner. Burroughs became his teacher in "very complicated matters" as well as his guide through "the nether ways of the city." Years later, describing this episode in his life, Jack would compare himself to one of Balzac's provincials observing "the big evil city" in the company of "daemons," and even to Balzac himself exploring the underworld of Paris. He maintained he was "studying everything," [58] and certainly many of the underworld characters found him exceptionally sensitive to their lives. Huncke was struck by how Jack's eyes flashed in all directions, taking in everything at once. Burroughs never let the law stand in the way of his research, and among his many actual crimes was the attempted robbery of a Turkish bath. Though he had been arrested a few times, he hardly seemed worried about his future. Jack was envious of the privilege conferred by Burroughs' money. Despite his father's condemnation of that whole crowd, Jack couldn't resist the chance to gain so many new experiences without "paying" for them himself. On Burroughs' tab he could purchase the whole city, from top to bottom.

There were some things they all simply took for the asking, such as sex. There were bills to be paid there too, though, even if deferred. When Joan's husband Paul Adams returned from the war, he discovered Joan and the rest of them together on one bed, high on benzedrine. Paul couldn't believe that this was what he had "fought for," and he and Joan were soon divorced.

Jack later blamed the war for claiming a sizable stock of his own childhood faith. Part of his "emotional bankruptcy" was due simply to the large number of close friends he had lost in the war: Billy Chandler, the cartoonist, Jimmy "Chief" Scondras, a Lowell High football star who had helped teach Jack how to play, John Koumantzelis, Sam Sampas. Moreover, the survivors who replaced these "great guys" seemed to be living by an entirely different code. In the cold glare of postwar selfishness, Jack scarcely recognized the characters of his youth, those staunch optimists of the thirties, men like his own father, pursuing a communal prosperity just around the corner.

Leo Kerouac had hit his final run of bad luck. He had contracted cancer of the spleen, and sat at home all day while Gabrielle supported him with her work in the shoe factory. The disease caused his abdomen to swell with fluid, which had to be drained by a doctor every two weeks. The horror of Leo's suffering increased Jack's despair over life in general, as well as adding to his stock of guilt. Leo was outraged at the flabby, pale wreck Jack had become, at all the dreams for his son's glory that Jack had let die. Leo still insisted that a man "should make the best" of his troubles,[59] and he attributed Jack's shiftlessness to the bad influence of Burroughs and Ginsberg. They would destroy Jack, he prophesied. Not only did Leo feel a strong repugnance toward their sexual inversion, but in Allen's case he was repelled by his nervously aggressive manner. Leo warned Jack not to let them look in his writing notebooks, lest they steal anything of worth. Most of the time, however, Leo was dubious about Jack's own ability to succeed as a writer. Jack's romantic melancholy seemed merely unproductive self-pity. When Jack said he admired Tschaikowsky's spontaneous bouts of tears, Leo accused him of worshiping distant, glamorous misery while spurning his own father's common troubles. Once again, the excitement in Manhattan was a refuge for Jack against the gloom, and now doom, at home.

Jack and Allen would read Hart Crane to each other and walk to the Brooklyn Bridge to study its epic proportions in the new light of Crane's architectonic, shimmering prosody. Allen was beginning to write a great deal of poetry and was already respected on campus as a promising young poet; he brought a circle of young intellectual writers into contact with the apartment group. With Burroughs there the atmosphere was already suffused with rationalism. Burroughs was undergoing depth analysis, and his analyst had chosen to probe his many alternate personalities. Beneath the top layer, the distinguished scion of St. Louis aristocracy, there was a nervous, possibly lesbian English governess. Farther down, the doctor found an old Southern sharecropper sitting on the banks of the Mississippi, catching catfish. Altogether Burroughs seemed to contain seven or eight separate characters. The last was a silent, starving, skull-headed Chinese, on the banks of the muddy Yangtze—a man with no words, no ideals, and no beliefs: Burroughs' ultimate persona. He made use of his new knowledge to help analyze Allen and Jack; they each spent an hour every day on the living-room couch, free-associating in Burroughs' presence.

Most of their psychologizing was a lot more informal. They often put on charades, Burroughs as well as the others acting out various archetypal personalities. Chase had already been typed by Allen as a "child of the rainbow," like Lucien, and with his Indian's hawk nose and good physique he was a natural for the role of "the brash, innocent, mountaineering Denver boy," showing off his "state-fair fresh manners." [60] Jack used the charades to try out various American character types he had observed. In addition, they held all-night discussions, in which each person bared his soul to all the others. If they didn't always solve one another's problems, they at least made significant progress in understanding those problems. They also infused one another with the energy to keep on seeking answers.

Edie no longer had a big allowance, and she and Jack often lived on the tidbits of food provided by Fifth Avenue bars. But mainly she worried about Jack's new desperate look. To take care of him, she went to work as a cigarette girl at the Zanzibar, "21," and other nightclubs. At four in the morning she would return to the apartment, usually to find Jack and the others too strung out on drugs to be much company. As Edie's alienation from them increased, the ordered if somewhat monotonous life in Grosse Pointe began to appear more attractive.

Jack was still doing a considerable amount of writing, though discarding a large portion of it as unworthy. He had to work himself up into the mood to write. With the shades pulled down he would pace about nervously, listen to the radio, take benzedrine, smoke, drink coffee or beer, and finally sit down at his typewriter. He typed rapidly, turning out page after page; then, just as impetuously, he might stop and after glancing through the typed pages crumple and fling them into the waste basket. Sometimes it was necessary to recast a scene a dozen or more times before he got it just as he wanted it.

He was still working on *The Sea Is My Brother*. For a long time he had felt severed from Columbia. The only professor with whom he had gotten along well was Mark Van Doren. In his Shakespeare course Van Doren had given Jack an A, of which Jack was lastingly proud. But now Allen helped reconnect Jack with the English faculty. He took *The Sea Is My Brother* to Raymond Weaver, the Columbia literature professor who had rediscovered Herman Melville.

Having traveled in Japan, Weaver questioned students like a Zen master; he was thoroughly conversant with mystical philosophies too. After reading the novel he gave Jack a reading list, which included Melville's *Pierre*, Plotinus, and the Egyptian Gnostics. It was the first time Allen had heard the word *Gnostic*. Both he and Jack were excited to discover this Western counterpart to Eastern Buddhism (having read a little about Buddhism in Spengler). Posing a system of as many worlds as there are brains, Gnosticism awakened them to a primitive concept of "emptiness," a theme that later became central to both Kerouac and Ginsberg.

Since his trip on the S.S. *George Weems*, when he had read *The Forsyte Saga*, the majority of Jack's writings were autobiographical. Significantly, on May 1, 1945, the day the world got news of Hitler's death, he conceived the notion of a novel that would contrast his life in a small New England community with the exciting dissolution he had found in New York. Although the novel would follow Jack into his new environment, its true hero would be Lowell, which he renamed Galloway. The old moral values of Lowell had been proved right by might, but the victory, at least in the eyes of the young, was belied by the murderous world the war had left behind. Sensing the momentary nature of this old American fighting glory, Jack realized the theme of his own life, and decided to write a book that would immortalize both. At first he called the novel simply "Galloway."

It is hard to determine the exact point at which Jack began steadily writing "Galloway." In *Vanity of Duluoz* he states that he began *The Town and the City*, as "Galloway" was later retitled, early in 1946, but remarks in his letters suggest he was already seriously committed to the novel by mid-1945.

Though he was developing confidence and steadiness in the practice of his trade, his personality was suffering from severe stresses. One night, in the spring of 1945, he went to Allen's dormitory room at Columbia to discuss a conversation he had just had with Burroughs. Bill had told Jack, "The trouble with you is you're just tied to your mother's apron strings." Bill saw Jack going in a wide circle around his mother, and he predicted that as Jack got older the circle would keep getting smaller. The insight had chilled Jack, and he spent several hours telling Allen just how tightly he was "tied" to his mother,[61] how he had internalized so many of her ideas about life. Until then, Allen had simply regarded Jack as just another guy who spent time with his family, when he needed rest or a livelihood, and

Jack's confession surprised him as much as it drew him closer to his flawed hero.

By the time they finished talking, it was one o'clock in the morning. Still very much in love with Jack, Allen eagerly offered him his bed. Six months earlier, Jack's tolerance had moved Allen to emerge from the "closet." He had admitted: "Jack, you know I love you, and I want to sleep with you, and I really like men." At that time, Jack had replied, "Oooooh, no!" This evening, after their long talk, Allen ended up sleeping on a pallet on the floor, and they both primly remained in their underwear. They even left the door open to the adjoining room, occupied by Allen's roommate Bill Lancaster. Lancaster knew that Allen had sex problems and had recommended Allen to the Karen Horney League, of which his mother was chairwoman.

3.

Allen's maladjustment at Columbia was more than sexual. To begin with, he dressed a little Chaplinesque, appearing rather ragged and unshaven. A naive factory-town boy, he was out of his depth in this sea of Ivy League snobbery. Some of his *faux pas* were serious enough for Dean McKnight to call his father. For instance, Allen had started a novel based on Columbia life that touched on the matter of homosexuality, and most of the characters were easily recognizable. McKnight felt the publication of such a novel would be scandalous and ordered Allen to desist from completing it. On another occasion Mr. Ginsberg was summoned because Allen had been caught drinking beer in the West End Bar until three in the morning, in the company of rowdy and undesirable companions like Jack. After Jack's arrest as a material witness to the slaying of David Kammerer, Columbia had officially designated Jack "an unwholesome influence on the students," [63] banning him from the campus.

A scholarship student, Allen well knew the tenuousness of his stay at Columbia, and felt profound guilt each time the Dean humiliated his father. Yet he had a knack for getting himself back in trouble almost as soon as his father ceased weeping over McKnight's latest threat of expulsion. Each time Allen goofed, he felt more fear that he would end up in a madhouse as his mother had. Of course, it may well have been the fear of madness that was driving Allen to test the limits of sanity—trying to find the edge of the cliff before he actually fell off.

In any case, on the day of Jack's visit to Hamilton Hall, Allen had retaliated in a rather bizarre way against the Irish cleaning woman who never washed his windows. In the dirty film on the window he had done some obscene finger paintings, to which he appended the captions: "Butler has no balls" and "Fuck the Jews." Although Allen was aroused against the cleaning woman's seeming anti-Semitism—and despite his temptation, as editor of the *Columbia Jester,* to get another laugh—his prank was intended primarily to hasten the cleaning of his windows. But instead the cleaning woman reported the incident to the Director of Student-Faculty Relations, Dean Fermin, who happened to have been one of Jack's football coaches. Fermin and Jack had gotten along well on the football field; but after Jack's involvement in the Carr homicide with its overtones of homosexuality, Fermin saw him as a bad investment, regretting the disgrace Jack had brought, if only by implication, to Columbia sports.

As Jack and Allen lay separately like innocent lambs, sleeping off their poetic night, Dean Fermin entered the dormitory room without knocking. Jack sprang out of Allen's bed and ran into the other room, jumping into Lancaster's bed (Lancaster was in class) and pulling the covers over his head.

Fermin ordered Allen to clean the window, which he did. Allen wanted to plead, "We didn't do anything!" but thought it more prudent not to bring up the subject. Actually Allen wasn't sure if he had done anything, since he was still a virgin. As it turned out, the university avoided broaching the question of Allen's homosexuality, concentrating their wrath on his indecent exposure of glass. The only official acknowledgment of Jack's stay was a $2.63 "overnight guest" fine levied against Allen, though McKnight doubtless alluded to Allen's irregular roommate when he huffed, "Mr. Ginsberg, I hope you realize the enormity of what you have done." Allen was asked to withdraw from Columbia pending a psychologist's verdict that he was mature and fit for study. The penalty probably would have been stiffer had Allen's father not been a distinguished teacher and poet. Certainly Jack could have done little to improve Allen's case, but Allen was angry that Jack had "run home to mother." [64]

For Allen the experience became one of the cornerstones of his new hip consciousness. He had just begun reading Céline's *Journey to the End of the Night* and was struck by the World War I soldier's stark realization on the battlefield that the world had gone completely mad. According to Céline, the only way to safety lay in dissociating oneself from the rest of humanity and becoming "invisible." Trapped in McKnight's office Allen had a similar awakening to the insanity of those in power, a revelation he would later connect with Céline's belief that society was bound to destroy itself, that there would be premature pain and death for everyone, that no one would get out alive.

Being banned from the campus had hurt Jack deeply, and now he must have felt considerable anguish at having again proved himself "an unwholesome influence." In addition, the experience must have

added to his private guilt over his homosexual feelings. By this time
he was beyond the influence of Roman Catholic strictures about sex,
and he was capable of enjoying sex with both men and women. He
even joked with Hal Chase about various gay crushes, like his romantic feelings toward John Kingsland. Within a year after the debacle
in Hamilton Hall, Jack would go to bed with Allen a couple of times.
At the same time he insisted, like Céline, that gay sex was "not in my
line." [65]

In early September, 1945, Jack wrote Allen that he was annoyed
by the illusion everyone had that he was "torn in two by all this,"
referring ambiguously to both the split between gays and straights
and between criminals and respectable people among his friends. In
this letter Jack tried to resolve the problem of his possible homosexuality. To his "waking nature," he wrote, the physical aspects of gay
sex were disgusting; and though the desire for it might exist in his
subconscious, there was no way of determining that for sure. He
concluded that he must "Drive on!" and dissolve his "neurosis" in
"the white fire of action." Yet the whole letter has the ring of an
apology, and his guilt is never far below the surface. He claims that
he only suffers when he is "caught" doing something wrong by "el-
ders" or people who will punish him. For example, he says he never
worried about starting a serious forest fire in Massachusetts when he
was a boy, because no one knew he had done it. In perhaps his
greatest act of whistling in the dark, Jack asserted that he was no
Puritan and never had to answer to himself. But, in fact, the subject
that provoked four single-spaced typed pages of rationalization
about the "mystery" of his character was an episode of homosexual
behavior. At a drunken party with Burroughs and several gay
friends, Jack had participated in the various kicks, including sexual
ones, and had felt so much remorse about it the next day that he
broke off a subsequent engagement with Burroughs.

One truth did emerge from the self-appraisal in that letter: Jack's
declaration that his art was more important to him than anything.
The variety of his troubles in the outside world didn't approach the
complexity of his inner life, and it was this inner life, he told Allen,
that he cherished most of all. The greatest problem for him to resolve, he stated, was to find an "art-method" capable of unleashing
the inner life. He felt that once he found such a method, the ambiguities in his character would be resolved as well; that is, in making the
workings of his mind clear to others, he would come to dominate the
mystery others saw in him and could manipulate that mystery to his
own uses. He even reveled in the fact that Allen saw a "strange
madness long growing" in him, and that Lucien had declared, "You
never seem to give yourself away completely." The more estranged
others were from him, the more time he would have for his solitary
labors in the "cave" of art.

Jack's obsession with art was actually making him rather inhuman. The tone of that whole letter is snide, overweening. It is the letter of a young man who, well aware of his immense mental superiority, has suddenly realized that he also has a knowledge of the world sophisticated enough to make others notice him. He condescends to his friends and those who have helped him, stating that Lucien's "New Vision" will prove useless without a method to express it; accusing Professor Lionel Trilling of foolishness, because Trilling felt Jack and Allen were playing "High Priests of Art"; reproaching Allen's lack of "essential character, of the kind I respect." How far Jack had come from the universal kindness preached by Gerard and Sammy is evident by the pleasure he now takes in deception. Connie Murphy had written from Germany, inquiring about Jack's involvement in the Carr homicide case. Jack wrote Allen that he planned to "spread it on thick" so that he could "worm" his way back into the confidence of one of Murphy's friends.

The other side of the coin is that Jack had good claim to be proud of his accomplishments. In the summer of 1945 he was reading a great range of poetry and prose, and writing three novels simultaneously. One of the most influential authors he encountered was Stendhal, especially in *The Red and the Black.* For a young man who had thus far built almost his whole literary career out of his hegira from Lowell, it was natural to respond deeply to a novel whose hero was also trying to escape an inescapable small town. "For Julian," wrote Stendhal, "achieving success meant first of all leaving Verrières." At this period Jack was also perusing as much of Céline as he could find. Céline's temperament, outwardly blustering and inwardly tender, was very similar to both Jack's and Jack's father's, an expression of that frustrated rage Jack would later specify as typically Breton. As for Jack's own writing, one novel was certainly *The Town and the City* (in the reference to Murphy, Jack calls him "one of the Galloway Prometheans"). Another novel, which he was coauthoring with Burroughs, was called alternately, *And the Hippos Were Boiled in Their Tanks,* or, *I Wish I Were You.* It was a Dashiell Hammett style murder mystery about Lucien and Kammerer.

The title, *And the Hippos Were Boiled in Their Tanks,* came from a news broadcast Bill had once heard. The announcer concluded his news roundup with a story about a fire at the St. Louis zoo; suddenly, his civic pride went out of control and his voice cracked hysterically as he read: ". . . and the hippos were boiled in their tanks!" The futility of such grandiose emotions struck Burroughs, who had a propensity for satire. Jerry Newman collected recordings of such unintentionally funny or lewd radio broadcasts, and in Newman's studio Bill and Jack especially enjoyed listening to a drunken BBC newscaster, who said things like, "Princess Margaret spent a wonderful weekend inside her parents at Balmoral Castle." In such slips Burroughs saw that one's private and unconscious thoughts are always capable of breaking through the veneer of proper manners. That insight was the impetus for his "routines," the short, one-actor dramas he would perform for his friends. *The Hippos,* however, probably owed more to the decadent French Symbolist poets than to a Swiftian savage humor (which emerged in Burroughs' own novels).

Of the three novels Jack referred to in a letter to Allen, August 23, 1945, the third is moot. It could have been a continuation of *The Sea Is My Brother* or *Vanity of Duluoz,* or the separate version of the Carr homicide that he had begun with Allen. Allen and Jack were continually making notes for new stories out of the people and events in their lives, and they had even given each other fictional names: Jack was "Ducasse" (the real surname of the French pre-Surrealist Lautréamont) and Allen was "Bleistein." Allen and Jack also handled many of the same themes. The bleak picture of modern life in Allen's short story "A Version of the Apocalypse" found its way into the description of Times Square in *The Town and the City.* In Spengler's *Decline of the West* both of them had read the prophecy of current civilization's ineluctable demise. But Allen added something new to Jack's vision of decay, a happy foil to Jack's sense of hopelessness: the concept of the "angel," a being who is elevated spiritually as he is degraded in body. The revelation of the junkies and prostitutes of Times Square as a host of angels profoundly affected Jack's writing for the rest of his life.

In a letter to Allen, September 6, 1945, Jack admitted that with him and Bill he was prone to discuss "disease and loss and death." But by the summer of 1945 both men had less influence on Jack simply because they were often removed from his sphere of activities. After vacating his room in Hamilton Hall, Allen had lived full time in the communal apartment on 115th Street. But within a couple of months, counselors pressured him into joining the maritime service; in July 1945, he entered basic training at Sheepshead Bay. Burroughs tried enrolling there too, but was dissatisfied with the way they treated him and managed to get discharged in a few days. After that, he began moving around the city frequently, though Jack remained in contact with him through the University Club, where Bill received his family's checks. The only male friend Jack still saw on a daily basis was Hal Chase, whose views and lifestyle were almost diametrically opposed to Bill's and Allen's and whose conversation, rather than being the voice of despair, was like a breeze of hope from pioneer America.

Bill and Allen were interested in Hal as a type of "cowpuncher," but to Jack, Hal was in fact a "hero of the snowy West." The key word was *West,* for as Jack saw it, to have grown up in that vast land couldn't help but make a person larger than normal human size. Jack told Hal that what he loved about America was its bigness. Physically Hal was no bigger than Jack, but he did possess extraordinary qualities. In Jack's words, Hal was "sixteen steps ahead" of everyone (Lucien had been only "six steps ahead"). Hal spent hours every day reading, and he read much faster than Jack. In addition to taking anthropology and archeology courses, Hal had made an intensive study of philosophy. He had found Spengler on his own, and had written a long paper comparing the philosophical concepts of time: time as an organic function (Spengler) versus time as a continuum (Bergson). Unlike Burroughs, Hal dismissed the organic theory.

While Jack admired his scholarship, he was in awe of Hal's ability to charm women. Hal was known as a "cocksman," and bragged of the variety of sexual acts he had performed with women, including making love in a mirrored room. Although Edie disliked his narcissism, Hal had no trouble making conquests in their group. For a while even the reserved Céline thawed to him. But the greatest bond between Jack and Hal was a perennial romantic hopefulness, a two-fisted grappling with obstacles that was practiced in Lowell's slums as well as the Queen City of the Plains. Hal, more than anyone since Sammy, was like a brother to Jack.

4.

Hal had been directed to Columbia by a powerful Denver lawyer and high-school counselor named Justin Brierly. Wealthy, ambitious, and talented, Brierly had an iron in almost every fire in Denver—he was, for example, one of the chief backers of the Central City Opera festival, which drew many tourists each summer. Consequently, he was one of Columbia University's most powerful alumni. He had even been designated a representative of the Columbia faculty. Brierly had a natural interest in bright, attractive young men, but that interest was directed toward no sordid exploitation of them. Rather, he cared enough about the promising boys he discovered to get them started in distinguished, remunerative careers. By the mid-forties, he had sent so many first-rate students to Columbia that Denver had acquired a distinct and formidable presence on that New York City campus. Even the head of the Columbia *Spectator* was one of his protégés.

Whenever Brierly was in New York he looked up his favorite students, and Hal Chase was one of them. Brierly tolerated what he called Chase's "eccentricity" because he had never found anyone else so extremely bright. Eventually he tracked Hal down to the communal apartment. Hal introduced him to Jack, who impressed Brierly favorably with his intelligence and good looks, and because he seemed to want to take care of Hal. But what Brierly found most outstanding was the energy Jack poured into his writing. Watching him type a hundred words a minute, Brierly was reminded of Thomas Wolfe knocking off literature "by the pound," and all his life he remembered the sight of Jack pounding furiously at his typewriter, in a self-absorbed trance. Even allowing for the corrections of twenty-twenty hindsight, it seems Brierly did get some inkling of the technique Ginsberg would later label "spontaneous bop prosody."

In any case, Jack reminded Brierly of a tremendously vital—if somewhat wild—nineteen-year-old hipster, who had gotten in trouble with the law in Denver. Raised by a drunken, bummish father in the Larimer Street slums, Neal Cassady had compensated for his deprivation by taking pleasure in fast cars and sex. Beginning at age fourteen, he stole some five hundred cars before his ardor was quelled by several stretches in reform school. His sex life, begun even earlier (he claimed at age nine), is past accounting; but his friends considered him the greatest cocksman in Denver. Always in need of money, Neal learned to shoot pool and to work a variety of confidence games; for a while he was even a hustler.[66] In October 1941, at the house of his uncle, Brierly had encountered Neal descending the staircase, in the nude. Though of average size Neal had a muscular body, wavy light brown hair, and piercing blue eyes. It didn't take long for Brierly to recognize his intelligence. That same day, Brierly began a long series of attempts to rehabilitate him.

Jack had heard of Neal's exploits from Hal even before meeting Brierly. Hal had described Neal as "one of the world's greatest lovers," a talent Jack admired even more than simple sexual prowess. Sometimes Hal was bothered by Neal's "goofiness"—he related the time Neal had brought him up to a mountain cabin in a stolen car, and then spent two days shuttling different girls up there and back— but Jack just delighted in such stories. What really amazed him, however, was that this consummate car thief and womanizer spent hours studying by himself in the Denver library, reading such philosophers as Kant, Schopenhauer, Nietzsche, and Santayana, and such writers as Shakespeare, Dumas, Dostoyevsky, and Proust. When Brierly came to New York, he let Jack read the letters Neal had written him from the reformatory, and Jack was bowled over by the intellectual subtlety of this kid who had hardly known the inside of a schoolroom.

Wishing to enter Columbia, Neal frequently wrote to Hal, and Hal showed the letters to Jack. In Hal's view, Neal was the perfect "antihero" for Jack to write about. Despite Neal's many attempts to write, Hal didn't think Neal likely to produce serious literature, and his reading always seemed at least partly phony to Hal. It was clear that he read to impress people, and that he generated an enthusiasm for books because it induced people to do nice things for him. By contrast, Hal was certain Jack's enthusiasm for books was genuine.

Hal loved to hear Jack talk. Often Jack described places in the city he had seen on his walks, dazzling Hal with his virtuoso command of English. Hal was impressed with his love of the language, his enthusiasm for putting words together just to hear their sound even if they didn't always make sense. Hal thought Jack the first writer since Joyce to pay such exquisite attention to the sound of language. Indeed, they used to read aloud random pages of *Finnegans Wake* to each other, just to appreciate the verbal pyrotechnics and sleight-of-tongue, since they understood little of Joyce's meaning. Jack confessed that for content he still preferred Joyce's *Portrait of the Artist,* but he liked the *idea* of a book like *Finnegans Wake.* His own freshness with the language was due, Jack thought, to having learned English as a second language. Comparing himself to Joseph Conrad, he said he had been fortunate to be able to listen to the sound of English before he attached any significance to the individual words. At its best, Jack felt English had a coolness like the dialogues in Cocteau's movies, a detachment that let the speaker stand back and view himself while talking or writing.

Jack discussed his writing method with Hal. He said he would first think out a scene, making a few notes to set up the characters and the action. Then he would occupy himself with any medium— radio, movies, etc.—to keep from directly thinking about what he must write. When the scene finally "gelled" for him, he would rush to type it out before he lost it, typing so fast that Hal, like Edie, thought he was listening to an alarm clock. It seemed to work best for him to set up a scene in the morning, since the inspiration usually hit him at night. But often, even after long gestation, the resulting work failed to satisfy him, and he would throw away what he had typed and start his "meditation" all over. The long waits were for him the most frustrating part of writing, and he complained that he sometimes never got a scene out the way he wanted it. The problem, he said, was to find just the *one word* that would tie the composition together satisfyingly, like a tonic note in music. For each scene his task was to intuit that key word, which was the hardest part, and then to "get back to the tonic" just as he brought the scene to completion.[67] Such was Jack's integrity that he never shirked the struggle to find that one word, though had he done so he might have completed his works much sooner.

At one point he tried to write drunk like Wolfe, standing up and scrawling a few words to the page, but he failed to produce anything worthwhile. At other times he would type spontaneous descriptions of people and places, amazing everyone with his speed and facility, but he told Hal he didn't consider such pieces "great literature." Jack wanted to drink life in big drafts, like Wolfe, and he knew that he was capable of creating huge novels that provided panoramas of the whole of America. Hal agreed. He had never met anyone more talented with words. Jack's gift seemed to exceed even Allen's or Bill's, and Hal was forever telling people how great a writer Jack would become.

Hal was equally impressed with Jack's manner of reading. During the several years he was close to him, Hal saw Jack reading only about half a dozen books. Jack read very slowly, and would reread each major scene of a novel until he understood its dynamics perfectly. He always sought to determine whether a scene was dramatically right or wrong at its particular place in the novel, and he wouldn't move on until he was satisfied his judgment was as good or better than the novelist's. *The Brothers Karamazov*, which Hal lent him, took Jack seven months to finish. His selection of books was very deliberate; he always chose those that would help him with his current writing.

His visual sense also amazed Hal. As they walked around the city, Jack demonstrated his eye for detail and color. Color especially affected him, and he and Hal discussed the significance of individual colors, the feelings produced by each, and the way colors combined to produce mood. Jack talked about the effect of both color and sound on a child raised in the Catholic Church.

Cutting his classes, Hal joined Jack on walks all over the city. To get going they would chew a strip or two from benzedrine inhalers (wrapped in chewing gum), and with occasional strips to renew their energy and enthusiasm, they sometimes managed to go four or five days without sleep. At the end of such a marathon, totally exhausted, they would listen to bop, and they would hear the music in a way they felt it could never be heard otherwise. They thought that this pushing the body and mind to the furthest limit attuned them to the essence of bop.

There were drawbacks to taking benzedrine from inhalers, since the strips contained other chemicals too. Joan, who used more than any of them, had hideous sores all over her body. Those long bouts with the inhalers always left Jack in a deep depression, though he claimed such brooding was good for a writer, leading to useful introspection. There was never any doubt that they were exploring states of consciousness. Jack said drugs would help him understand people and, most importantly, himself.

Jack and Hal were always thinking about the future. Whatever they did in the present didn't matter as long as they emerged from it wiser and more capable. Whereas Allen seemed interested in different states of consciousness for their own sake, Jack continually talked about how he would use his drug experiences as a writer. Similarly, Bill and Allen had become a part of the underworld, hanging out with Times Square criminals, in a way that was impossible for Jack, who wanted only to observe.

Both Jack and Hal had some interest in the criminal as a political figure, a revolutionary opposed to an unjust society. After the war the country seemed to have grown suddenly mean, cruel, dominated by an overgrown military filled with warmongers who immediately wanted to encounter Russia. A figure like Herbert Huncke, the Times Square junkie, was attractive because he affirmed human needs and feelings in the face of an inhuman establishment. All of them in that apartment, like so many other young people, felt themselves misfits. They were products of the Depression, raised on an idealism that had died along with basic decency in the ovens of Auschwitz, in the bomb rubble of London, Dresden, Cologne, and, above all, Hiroshima and Nagasaki. As the country bent wearily, with brute indifference, toward the Cold War of the 1950s, these young people groped hopelessly in a world in which they simply did not know how to live.

In such a world it was to be expected that bright, questioning persons would turn to nihilism, but Jack and Hal were only half-hearted nihilists. They were interested in the nihilist position, interested to see how it was articulated by philosophers like Nietzsche. But in reality the existing social order seemed too solid to overturn. The huge, mightily armed government was impossible to deny, or at any rate denial seemed incapable of stopping its atrocities. As a consequence, the theories of Nietzsche and Spengler did not seem realistic to them. At best they were useful to point out signs of decay and dissolution—the existence of such works being a sign in itself.

In *Thus Spake Zarathustra,* Jack picked out the occasional sharp insights into human nature. He especially liked the thumbnail sketch, "Of the Pale Criminal," which limned a character like Raskolnikov's, but in many less pages than *Crime and Punishment.* The wisdom preserved in such literature seemed marvelous to Hal and Jack, and they spent long nights discussing how a certain writer might have come up with various striking insights. Such insights appeared to originate in that quality called genius. They didn't believe in the Nietzschean superman, however. Even in works of pure philosophy Jack remained conscious of the language itself, intrigued by the way a philosopher would use words to convey thoughts.

Because Jack had studied less than Hal, he often seemed naïve. Hal thought both Jack and Allen lacked a sense of history. As they walked around the city, Jack would speak of New York as eternal, as though it would always be there just because they could still sit in a café where Wolfe had eaten or visit some place where he had lived. Hal tried to remind them that although those buildings had stood for fifty years there had been no trace of them a thousand years earlier, and would probably be no trace of them a thousand years hence. But in the whole group it seemed only Hal and John Kingsland possessed a historical perspective.

One night, listening to jazz, Jack and Hal discussed the word *kicks,* a word on every hipster's tongue. To Jack, "getting kicks" referred to the immediate gratification of desires, a concept which fascinated him. What amused Hal was how hard Jack tried to have kicks—so hard that he never really had them. In the same way he would try to be cool with women and couldn't. Women liked Jack, were attracted to his looks, but he could never quite get to them. Instead he always asked for one of Hal's girls, or if Hal was gone, he might make a play for one. A few times Hal got upset with Jack's laying claim to his girls, but most of the time he was sympathetic with this strange but serious sexual problem Jack admitted: he could only make a girl whom his friend had made first.

In fact Jack and Hal often discussed sex. Though Jack talked about having a sexual problem, it wasn't something he worried a great deal about. He simply felt he was burdened with a romantic shyness and a sense of sex as "very important" from his upbringing in the thirties. He had also never been able to overcome his great sense of physical modesty, perhaps the result of his mother's taboo on any reference to sex in the home. For years he had washed his own handkerchiefs so that his mother wouldn't find evidence of his masturbation, and he had been mortified once when she had questioned why they were always wet (but there was no other way around her belief that any sex under her roof, other than marital sex, was a sinful contamination of her pure household). Jack had also experienced some sexual failures with women, but once again he attributed the problem to the inhibitions of his early training. Jack didn't see his sexual susceptibility to men as the cause of his problem with women. When he spoke of his "infatuation" with John Kingsland, it was with humorous detachment, observing how Kingsland was himself infatuated with Columbia professor Raymond Weaver. Moreover, Jack claimed his indulgence in bisexuality was like his experience with drugs, something he would later use in his writing. His plan for the future, he told Hal, was to marry some "fantastic" woman. She was an essential part of the dream of success, riches, and material splendor fostered by his mother.[68]

As Hal saw it, everyone in that apartment was a little too obsessed with sex and especially with homosexuality. Of course they all laughed about Allen's attempted seductions—he was always pressuring Hal and Jack—but Hal sensed a certain morbidity in their constant sexual self-analysis. For one thing, there was a false ring to Allen's sudden declaration one day that he had "decided to become homosexual," as though he had affected the pose as an aid to some new spiritual exploration, or as an interesting addition to his career. Certainly Allen wasn't naturally effeminate and had no gay mannerisms. Hal was actually rather annoyed with the game Allen seemed to be playing of "Let's find your hidden homosexuality." A good part of their group psychoanalysis was concerned with the "homosexual sickness." For Hal's part, it seemed a waste of time to be continually dredging up memories of their childhood sexual experiences. Jack was always talking about the time he had had an erection while his mother was bathing him; he claimed he often dreamed about this traumatic event. To Hal it seemed silly, nothing that should have given a healthy person any worry.

Of all of them, Burroughs seemed the one most enmeshed in roles. But when he attempted to act out the various personae revealed in the course of his depth analysis—while doing the "Georgia cracker sadistic slavedriver," for example, he would even speak in dialect—he always seemed false, pathetic, and funny. The fact that he was so unsuccessful in his roles endeared him to Jack and Hal. They thought him a great comic genius, though he didn't seem to realize it (at times, though, they glimpsed enough method in his folly to suspect he did). Jack found Burroughs very similar to his father. Both men tried pitifully hard to succeed and yet repeatedly failed; both wanted badly to be loved and, instead, usually had to settle for contempt. Later, in his writing, Jack would lump his father, Bill, and W. C. Fields in a triumvirate of bumbling American resilience. In any case, there was hardly anything funnier for them than watching Burroughs recline on a sofa, attempting to project an air of perfect calm, and looking totally nervous and ill at ease!

Undoubtedly much good derived from their constant sharing of experiences. It's a safe bet that few groups of people in American history, up to that time, had ever communicated so totally with one another. They would stay up all night verbalizing their feelings, often describing little adventures of the day and analyzing how they had reacted. As in a modern encounter session, the group provided sympathy while encouraging the speaker's complete honesty. Occasionally Burroughs would inject some psychological jargon—such as the distinction between sadistic and masochistic—but most of the time they just relied on common sense, as when Joan talked Jack out of the idea of romancing her. In truth, most of them were better adjusted to their problems at that point than at any subsequent time. Edie, for example, was always torn between her bohemian inclinations and her Grosse Pointe ideals. She also suffered as a not especially gifted, unambitious playgirl in an apartment full of committed artistic geniuses. Yet she lived with more independence then than she would be able to do for many years afterward. Edie credited the group with teaching her to understand herself. In her case, at least, there was no need for drink or drugs as long as she had the others' sincere concern.

For a while they all went to the same bars, continually bumped into one another on the street, and had endless "Dostoyevskian confrontations" [69] in which each would inquire about the state of the other's soul, as though they were running a kind of spiritual news service. They laughed about how difficult it was to ever be alone. There were roughly ten people in their group, and each always had an idea of the whereabouts and latest activities of all the rest, since like slices of one pie they all touched the common center of the apartment. Hal Chase recalled that "you could dip into the set at any point and stay with it for days on end."

5.

Within the group, each was pursuing his own goals independent of the others. This summer Jack tried writing "potable magazine love stories" (as he referred to them in a card to Allen, August 10, 1945), which were rejected like all his others. In August, still ineligible for a merchant marine assignment, he went to work as a busboy at a summer camp. After a few days he left, complaining that he had to clean latrines and that the Jewish guests didn't tip enough. But getting a living was not as great a source of fragmentation as getting laid. Jack disregarded any loyalty he might have felt toward Jack Fitzgerald when he felt like sleeping with Fitzgerald's girlfriend Eileen; and when he made a play for Céline, it was an affront to both Hal, her new boyfriend, and to Edie, her girlfriend.

Actually Jack was coming to ignore Edie completely. With Burroughs he explored Turkish baths and the "vast field of poppies" on Times Square. When he had "exhausted the possibilities" of Bill's instruction, he was more prone to isolate himself, practicing a "Thomas Wolfish fiery rejection and romantic disapproval," [70] than to try patching up old liaisons. The decay of her teeth from poor diet was the last straw for Edie. Tired of docilely serving her errant husband, she quit her cigarette concession and without even packing went to live with her grandmother in Asbury Park.

For a short time Jack got his job back at Columbia Pictures. When he bumped into Céline one day, he took her to the West End for drinks with a group of their friends and talked about staging a party when he got paid, which would give him an occasion to see Edie again. Céline said Edie would probably come only if he personally sent her an invitation. Pride getting the better of him, Jack indignantly refused to write her, since he claimed she never answered his letters. In truth, he had never been able to admit that he needed her. But with a few beers he unbent a little. He agreed to at least telephone her. He said he would still be living with her if he had had more money, but he simply couldn't bear being totally dependent on her. Then he began talking about going to college in Los Angeles in order to be near Hollywood. As a rich script writer, he speculated, he would be able to meet his "ideal woman"—a submissive, seductive, black-haired, blue-eyed beauty. Angrily Céline broke in: "For God's sake, Jack, do you think you'll ever find another woman who understands you as well as Edie? You're a pretty moody guy and you'll never find another girl who can put up with your moods the way Edie can." Jack sat up, looking surprised, as if it were the first time that idea had ever crossed his mind.[71]

But before he could reach her, Edie's best friend spirited her back to Grosse Pointe.

Though Hal Chase remained physically in the apartment, he found himself drifting away mentally. Because of the long periods he spent studying, he had often avoided their rounds of partying. Also of late, when he did find himself at parties, he suffered from terror seizures, which forced him to leave. Besides his general dislike of crowds, he had begun to feel intense pain about wasting his time and energy. Moreover, he grew reluctant to share in their use of drugs, and avoided their communal sex, blaming his "fear of paresis."

Joan was slipping into a solitary hole too, but not by her own decision; hers was the locked hell of a benzedrine addict. The sight of her limping down Eighth Avenue to Whelan's drugstore, lost in a "Benzedrine psychosis," [72] haunted Jack for years as a cameo of the diseased loneliness of Times Square and of all the rootless exiles in the city.

As strange as her life had become, it was not startling to all the other deviant denizens of the apartment. As part of his study of detective fiction, Burroughs mingled with all sorts of hard-boiled Broadway characters; while they wandered through the apartment, he played with his own collection of guns. Huncke and other junkies often stopped in, and there were always needles lying around, along with various drugs and stashes of stolen goods. The dangerous atmosphere was relieved somewhat by the comical visits of a mellow old coat thief named Bill Garver. In a cafeteria like Horn and Hardart's, Garver would hang up his shabby overcoat, then have some coffee while he watched other men hang up nice overcoats, noting where each man sat. Garver would leave wearing a Brooks Brothers or some other valuable coat, which he could pawn for $20. By stealing two or three coats a day, he was able to support his heroin habit. Burroughs himself was occasionally forced to forge prescriptions to satisfy his own growing habit.

Whether it was all the benzedrine she took, or just a naturally delicate auditory sense, Joan could hear people talking across the street. The others thought of her as an uncanny owl, but she claimed such hypersensitivity was natural to a mother—she had to hear her baby, Julie. In any case, she began to worry about the conversations she overheard between an old husband and wife in the apartment below them. This couple had become aware of the wild scene upstairs. They were sick of the raucous all-night conversations, and the old lady called Joan a whore. Their suspicions were also aroused by the lack of patriotism in her cynical comments about the stupidity of the new haberdasher President, Truman. Worse, they had an inkling that Joan's guests were "dope fiends." Eventually they began to discuss whether they should call the police.

During this same period, the old couple had big fights over sex, evidently hating each other as much as they did their neighbors. As their quarrels grew angrier, the rest of the apartment dwellers grew worried too. As soon as any of them came in, they would ask Joan, "What's going on downstairs now?" Joan reported the pair's long conversations in meticulous detail. After five months, the soap opera culminated when Joan reported the husband chasing his wife with a kitchen knife. Joan told the others they had to prevent her murder, and Jack and Allen volunteered. They rushed downstairs and knocked furiously on the door, until they realized nobody was home. Joan had been having exquisitely complex auditory hallucinations. When Jack and Allen explained that she had merely been listening to empty ghosts, she proceeded to analyze in equal complexity the nature of such auditory hallucinations.

There were times when Jack made as little sense to Allen as Joan. Jack was always talking about "visions"—he seemed to have them almost every day—and Allen puzzled over what he meant by the term. Allen remembered Prince Myshkin's mystical auras just before his epileptic fits, in *The Idiot*. But, although Jack often referred to himself as Myshkin, he seemed to be talking about more common perceptions of the world. Sitting at home, he would suddenly become aware of his family moving around him; or coming into the city, he would see all of them cramped in the apartment and envision them as "a bunch of Dostoyevskian creeps," cut off from the countryside and "conspiring" together because they lacked a real family. Eventually Allen realized that, by *vision,* Jack was referring to a special sort of visual "take," a sudden intuitive understanding of things triggered by some momentary sight. The fruit of such moments was an acute sensation of space, a panoramic awareness of the infinite universe surrounding him.[73]

There were other, more practical differences between Allen and Jack; and between Allen and Bill, on one side, and Jack and Hal on the other. The fundamental split was between "queer" and "straight" sexuality, and between the respective attitudes toward life engendered by those two lifestyles. Whatever Jack's homosexual experience—and he certainly had sex with men far less regularly than with women—he fought all his life against the label *queer*. It wasn't just a matter of defending his masculinity; for when drunk he often boasted of the men who had "blown" him, invited other men to do so, or challenged men to let him fuck them. But he believed in man's role as the head of the family, as the ruggedly honest, stoically suffering breadwinner who "took no shit from anyone," the role personified by his father, as well as countless film heroes from Jean Gabin to Gary Cooper. The "queer" stance—sniffling, sardonic, dissembling—seemed the very opposite of this.[74] Having grown up in the West, with its manly men, womanly women, and plain-speaking ways, Hal was even more repulsed by the gay culture of New York than Jack.

To both Hal and Jack, the issue at stake was much larger than whom you went to bed with; it was a question of the destiny of America and the quality of American life. Allen would speak disparagingly of America as dense, stupid, and unconscious. Jack liked the fact that so much of America was unconscious, because he was the same himself; in fact, he wrote out of that unconsciousness. Jack identified with America insofar as they both contained a great many paradoxes; and, as he saw it, it was important *not* to try to resolve them all. The liberal-radical quest to "find the answers" would get one irretrievably lost. Jack's way, like that of pioneer America, was to *live the answers*.

Hal and Jack were interested in Rimbaud and Baudelaire, with their delicate tracings of the convolutions of decadence, but they did not love them as they loved the great raw strength of Wolfe. Jack was, of course, always interested in French authors, and he liked their simple human insights—like the bittersweet satisfaction of the speaker in *Les Fleurs du Mal* when he hears the gurgling stomach of an old whore who once drove him mad. But Allen, Bill, and Lucien seemed to have swallowed Rimbaud and Baudelaire whole. Allen had recently written a long prize-winning poem, "The Last Voyage," modeled on the "Voyage" section of *Les Fleurs du Mal*. What really disturbed Hal and Jack, however, was that these others, including the late Kammerer, had affected literary roles instead of living life honestly. The tragedy of Kammerer's death seemed at least partly due to their conscious acting-out of the Verlaine-Rimbaud scenario of unrequited gay love and violent retribution.

One night in the fall of 1945, all of them on benzedrine, Jack got in bed with Bill, and Hal in bed with Allen—all in the same room. At some point, despite their physical intimacy and camaraderie, Hal suddenly conceived of Jack and himself as vastly different from the other two. Disregarding their geographical origins, Hal saw Allen and Bill as men of the East—city men, sophisticated, looking eastward to the culture of Europe. Rooted in America, Jack and Hal faced West, longing for the solitude and individual freedom of the wilderness. At that moment Hal had his first premonition of the tragedy likely to befall Jack. He realized that Allen and Bill would easily learn to handle the social demands of fame, should it come, but that Jack would never be able to live the life of a famous writer.

As they lay in bed, Hal elaborated the difference between the "Wolfeans" (himself and Jack) and the "non-Wolfeans" (Bill and Allen). The Wolfeans were heterosexual all-American boys, dewy-eyed believers in America's great future. The non-Wolfeans—alternately called Baudelaireans, and later rechristened Black Priests by Jack—were "sinister European fairy Jew Communists," who didn't believe in a wide open, lyrical America. The Baudelaireans tried to seduce the American boys from their innocent faith just as they lusted after their healthy bodies. Allen not only thought the distinction rather funny but actually got very upset, as though Hal were judging him inferior, or practicing a subtle anti-Semitism. In the first place, Allen really loved Jack and would have preferred to be sleeping with him; and here he was in bed with somebody whom he didn't love, and who was an unsympathetic "Wolfean" to boot! Additionally, Allen did sense a deficiency in his own knowledge of America. Whereas Hal and Jack had both traveled considerably about the continent, Allen hadn't been farther south than Washington, D.C., farther north than the Bronx, or farther west than Newark. Since Burroughs had already crisscrossed Europe, Allen felt outranked by him too. Sensing big cellophane curtains between all of them, Allen protested, "It's not fair to be divided like this!" Nevertheless, with the passing years, Hal came to regard that night's discussion as "a good piece of work."

The distinction became a kind of inside joke. They turned it into a drama, which they performed together. Wearing his father's straw hat, Jack played the wealthy but innocent "American in Paris." Bill wore a wig and a skirt as the "lesbian countess," who would bring Jack to the "well-groomed Hungarian," played by Allen. The Hungarian preyed upon guileless Wolfean Americans by selling them forged artistic masterworks, and the lesbian countess was his shill. Their apartment transformed into the Hungarian's "atelier," Allen would say, "Yes, young man, you vant some culture, and I understand that you vant to buy some art vorks that I have brought from Hungary when I had to flee Hitler. . . ." From there they would embark on long improvisations, elaborating the character roles that later became archetypal in both Kerouac's and Burroughs' fiction. The routine itself would become one of Burroughs' major literary techniques, allowing him to quickly introduce and remove what might be termed floating characters, like Dr. Benway in *Naked Lunch*. These routines also gave birth to the fast-paced scenes of black comedy in that novel, like the "talking asshole" and "blue movie" vignettes, which through subtle variation became powerful motifs.

6.

Jack and Allen were very close in one respect: they shared a special kind of idealism. Even Edie, who had come to dislike Allen as one of the people who had separated her from Jack, wrote Allen that "of all the people at Columbia you are beyond a doubt the truest one to your ideals. . . ." This idealism was neither facile nor over-optimistic; it was the hard-won faith of men who had suffered and survived many more hardships than most people their age. Such uncompromising joy, sweetened by the very intensity of the struggle to achieve it, was glimpsed by Rimbaud in *A Season in Hell*:

> When shall we go beyond the mountains and the shores, to greet the birth of new toil, of new wisdom, the flight of tyrants, of demons, the end of superstition, to adore—the first to adore!—Christmas on the earth.
>
> The song of the heavens, the marching of peoples! Slaves, let us not curse life.

But whereas Rimbaud had failed to integrate his poignant visionary moments into an enduring "unity of being" (to use Allen's phrase), Allen and Jack resolved to attain "Supreme Reality." Slogans like "God is dead" had sickened them all by depriving life of any semblance of meaning. To go on living, it was essential to believe that one could—as Jack would later put it—"see God's face." Such was the ultimate goal of their "New Vision." Where they went looking for it was not churches or monasteries but places like Times Square and the Angler Bar.

There is no understanding these incipient "Beats," at this point in their lives, without referring to their overwhelming sense of the holiness of the street—which is to say, the holiness of every spot of ground trod by man. Holy is the only way to describe their feeling that Times Square was a single giant room. Studying the intricate copper and stonework on the cornices and tops of the buildings, Jack and Allen had been drawn to look at the open sky above. For both of them, the sight of the city (and earth) "hanging in space" triggered a sudden mystic awareness of time's passage within eternity, of the perishable world within a permanent void. At night the sky over Times Square had an apocalyptic glow, due to the reflection of red neons from the smog. The projection of this garish Technicolor ceiling over the simple starry heavens of their childhood made them feel—as acutely as a bodily pain—that their world was dying. The last days forecast in the Bible were no longer just dreamy prophecy but an actual source of daily anguish, as well as hope for the world that would follow.

That "panoramic awareness" of themselves in space became a philosophical and artistic touchstone for both Jack and Allen. They were awestruck by "this handiwork of intelligence in every direction" and amazed to perceive, beyond the fine masonry of New York, the supernal masonry of the universe. That revelation put the first serious crack in their provincial consciousness; they were no longer just Americans, with a particular tradition to live up to, but ghosts in the living room of space, forced to admit the superfluousness of all human culture and of their own existence too. The message of those flashing red neons was of the emptiness beyond the roof of their lives, of their undeniable mortality. They were tiny mites passing through a vanishing kingdom who discovered themselves made of the same vanishing substance. It was at this time that Jack and Allen began addressing each other as ghosts, with greetings like: "What've you got to say tonight, old phantom?" or "What solid speech have you got?" [75] The impact of that ghostliness was so strong that Jack would later use it effectively in one of the climactic scenes in *On the Road*, when Ed Dunkel sees a ghost on Times Square and goes out hunting it.

It might seem that a vision of the universe as absolutely empty must have been terribly depressing to these young men; but the actual result was quite the contrary. To begin with, the shared vision deepened the sympathy between them. Moreover, there is a great exultancy to the realization that all one's troubles are illusory. That feeling of miraculous relief is at the heart of what is called "the religious experience," and may indeed be the closest approximation to pure ecstasy man knows. But above all this vision of emptiness cleared away the rubble of past philosophies, moralities, and es-thetics, so that Jack and Allen could begin to experience the world in a completely fresh manner. They suddenly felt themselves com-pletely alive—an event which, according to Thoreau, is among the rarest in human history—and saw life all around them. About this time, Jack and Allen had almost simultaneous visions of a certain building on 34th Street as the hulk of a living giant. That weird coincidence was followed by a series of parallel mystical experiences between the two of them that continued as long as Jack lived.

Jack felt that Allen was very much like Sammy, just as concerned with ideas, just as interested in people's "souls." At times he lost patience with the "complicated emotional intrigues" Allen got in-volved in, and he sometimes worried that Allen's subtle intellec-tuality verged on madness; but he never tired of hearing him discuss the endless stream of new people he met, for Allen observed things that "the regular man never did notice as he hurried by with his lunchpail." [76] It is important to remember that Sammy too saw as-pects of people that others couldn't see. When Jack finally got Allen admitted to his home in Ozone Park—through his mother's wall of disapproval—one of the first things he did was to play for Allen the record Sammy had mailed him from overseas. Jack told Allen that Sammy had been the person most sympathetic to him as a poet. His memory of Sammy was of a Shelley-like, lost, innocent poet, for whom he would always have a great love.

Jack's father was also reminded of Sammy when he met Allen,

but only because they were both "screwballs." Leo considered Sammy to have been harmless and good-hearted, but he found Allen lacking in both qualities. Almost immediately Allen had picked an argument with the old man about communism, declaring that he was a "Russian" (actually a Russian Jew) and that Americans could no longer live because they were too "repressed." Leo had never heard anyone talk so fast in his whole life. Allen impressed him with his learning—though much of what he said was Marxist dogma about religion being "the opiate of the people"—and Leo was certainly sympathetic to many of Allen's criticisms of the Catholic Church. What really upset Leo was Allen's scorn for people who believed in the old-time personal God. As Leo saw it, people had a right to believe in anything they wanted to, and that right was the basis of America, what Americans had died to keep.

On the subject of government, Leo found Allen maniacally simplistic. Allen insisted that Americans were all capitalists on the one hand and slaves on the other, that the only solution was for the government to control commerce. Leo replied that, in that case, they would all be slaves. Finding Allen suddenly agreeing with him, or at least interested in this new idea, Leo thought him more of a maniac. He told Allen, "OK, sonny, when the big day comes you take over and we'll do anything you say, we've got nothing else to do. Then you and your partners can live all you want, you can run up and down the street throwing flowers around and you can kick over all the ashcans you want, we won't stop you from living, we won't repress you!" Leo laughed at this "perfect nut," but he was uneasy with him too.[77]

One day Jack, Allen, Hal Chase, and Leo all went for a walk in Ozone Park. Jack and Allen led, while Hal walked slowly behind with Leo. Watching Allen's nervous, awkward stride as he darted between them, Leo dubbed Allen "the cockroach." [78] The nickname hinted at Leo's real fear of Allen as a scavenger who would live off Jack's talent, at the same time soiling Jack with the filth of the gutter Leo had struggled all his life to lift Jack out of.

Jack's parents got along with Hal much better than with Allen. Hal was the sort of clean-cut, dedicated worker with whom they preferred Jack to associate. Gabrielle treated Hal well and in their long talks showed him the merry, zestful side of her that Jack loved. Her tremendous energy impressed him as much as her boundless devotion to Jack's happiness. The only aspect of her character Hal found disagreeable was her ambition for wealth, which she foisted on Jack. She wasn't happy with his being a writer. Although she respected the profession of writing, it seemed a long shot to her goal. Since she made Jack believe he ought to be rich and famous, he felt pain and despair because he wasn't; nor was he consoled by Hal's counsel that "the carrot isn't worth the effort." Jack's love for his father left him vulnerable in a different way. Although they frequently fought, Jack immensely admired his father's strength. His father was his masculine ideal, and it troubled Jack that he hadn't yet been able to live up to him. Paradoxically, however, Hal seemed to sense more sympathy between Leo and Jack than between Jack and his mother.

Leo was as critical as ever of the "bunch of dope fiends and crooks" that were Jack's friends. He said he had expected Jack to turn out a "bum" the day four-year-old Jack had run up to him gleefully announcing Gerard's death. Although Leo deplored Jack's wasting money on drinking, it was chiefly the "dope" he objected to. It even struck Hal that Jack was drinking so heavily to fit into his father's and Lowell's world. Leo rejected most of Jack's friends not so much because they were Jews as because they were "misfits," men who didn't work or "produce." Jack's drinking was a way of making himself familiar and acceptable again to his father.[79]

In November 1945, Jack began spending much more time at home. His father was critically ill and needed Jack to care for him. Benzedrine was neccessary to counter Jack's extreme depression, and with or without it he spent hours brooding over the sources of his anguish.

His letters at this period took on a singular brilliance of self-analysis. Sitting in the "cursed kitchen," where his father got his stomach drained every two weeks, Jack wrote to Allen of the great sympathy he felt toward him, acknowledging their "common madness" and suggesting they lay aside their respective masks: Jack's of "dislike" for Allen, Allen's of "masochism." Through their endless posings they had acquired an "unrelieved heaviness of personality." Having encumbered themselves with all sorts of intellectual labels, they no longer thought change possible and so made no effort to move. Although Bill was the "grandest mirror" in which Jack could judge his own character, he saw that it was futile to maintain a stubborn opposition to Bill, which merely prevented his own growth. He saw Bill and himself fighting an "interminable duel," firing the same shots at each other, with the same facial expressions, in a frozen dawn—as though they were the puppets of a "mad bore." Jack and Allen, Bill and Hal, Hal and Céline, Joan and Bill, and Jack and Edie all seemed to be involved in such duels.

In this particular letter Jack went on to examine what he considered Hal's "sham." He asserted that the dichotomy between Wolfeans and non-Wolfeans simply hid Hal's fear of experiencing life. He realized that he too loved to play such intellectual games, getting tangled in their "compulsive falsehoods" while enjoying "the charming pathos of such techniques per se." Compared to Hal, Allen seemed to be largely free of such shams and confusions. Jack decided he would follow Allen's path, using his new insights to climb up to "the next level and proceed from there." Most of his writing until then seemed spoiled by the same proclivity for "cunning concealment," and henceforth he intended to write "of what I really know, and don't or didn't want to know."

In the comprehension of anyone, and especially of a writer, one has to take confessions at considerably less than face value. Since writers command one of the finest media for propaganda, they are capable of, if not actually prone to, a perpetual whistling in the dark. Jack did indeed embark upon ever vaster voyages in the sea of human experience. But whether motivated to know life, or merely to escape it by courting death (or whether pursuing life and death at the same time), is hard to say.

He had always seemed strong enough to handle the amount of drinking he did, which was about average in their group, but one day Hal found him passed out in an Eighth Avenue bar. After he carried Jack home and forced him to wake up, he learned that Jack had taken Nembutals and beer, a combination that can be fatal.

Just before Christmas Jack, Allen, and Hal spent five days and nights on benzedrine, roaming the city. On the last night, though they were all enervated, Jack insisted they hike to the Brooklyn Bridge. When they got there they were hassled by a couple of policemen, with whom Jack got into a heated argument. Finally they headed back, but when Allen flagged, Jack lifted him onto his back and carried him almost a mile to the Seventh Avenue subway. Along the way Allen sang Bach's *Toccata and Fugue in D Minor,* and by the time they got to the subway he was rested enough to take off with Hal to listen to more music. But Jack, on the verge of collapsing, headed home.

7.

Immediately afterward, Jack became seriously ill and had to be taken to Queens General Hospital. The Veterans Administration provided for his medical expenses, but the diagnosis of thrombophlebitis was far from comforting. The disease—in Jack's case brought on probably by a combination of overexertion and excessive benzedrine use—caused blood clotting in the legs. If one of the clots were to work its way to the heart, he would quickly die. With his legs wrapped in hot compresses and propped up on pillows, he lay for weeks as the doctors speculated about the need for surgery. A group of young patients in the hospital serenaded him, and he used the time to continue reading *The Brothers Karamazov,* as well as Djuna Barnes' *Nightwood.* But his most significant experience there was the realization that his life could be cut short at any moment.

However confident he might be of his talent, he now had to face the fact that he was gambling the whole of it against time, and time had just stacked the deck.

Jack's vision of death in the hospital was not limited to his own mortality; for the first time he saw clearly that all life bore the same burden of imminent dissolution. When he described his "new vision" of death inherent in life many years later in *Vanity of Duluoz,* he used the imagery of the sixteenth-century English poets: nature typified by the bud that blooms only to wither. The power of that vision was not in its originality, but it may be a necessary vision to anyone bent on doing serious work. Norman Mailer made a plausible case that writers don't write honestly, out of their full strength, until they realize that every line they produce—like anyone's daily work—is a temporary hedge against death. For Jack this realization was combined with a Spenglerian view of the inevitable darkness closing over all civilizations, a cosmic phenomenon which narrow-sighted "city intellectuals" tried to grasp in terms of jargon like "existentialism," "hipsterism," and "bourgeois decadence." [80] The idea that grew out of this amalgam of philosophies, poesies, and self-pity was one of the most seminal ever to come to Jack. He saw city dwellers living in ignorance because they were cut off from the fundamental knowledge of life and death stored in folk traditions, which were preserved in the country and small towns.

When he returned home, partially well, it was with a new and stronger dedication to becoming a writer. For a whole year he had been working on the novel about Lucien and Kammerer, *And the Hippos Were Boiled in Their Tanks.* While living at home in Ozone Park, he had been writing alternate chapters, which he later integrated with the chapters produced by Burroughs. Now, in early 1946, Jack quickly concluded *The Hippos,* which came to about two hundred pages.

The first work in which he attempted to embody his new insight was a story about his stay in the hospital, a self-consciously spooky imitation of *Nightwood* that read like a bad parody. When John Kingsland laughed at it—as he had laughed at Jack's poem about Burroughs, "A Remembrance of Walking Past the Hotel Wilson" (beginning: "Here once the kindly dope fiend lived")—Jack was mortified that Kingsland couldn't tell when he was writing seriously.

Soon Jack began to concentrate on the novel he had been calling "Galloway." Influenced by Spengler, as well as the fierce crosscurrents between his home and friends, he retitled the novel *The Town and the City.* It was to be a "huge novel explaining everything to everybody."

He had plenty of time to write it, since he had to stay near his father all the while his mother was at work, watching for the emergency that loomed ever nearer. When the doctor drained Leo's stomach, Leo groaned and wept softly, and the courage with which he faced death left Jack feeling miserable at his own weakness to face life. The old man spent all day sitting in his bathrobe, a blanket over his knees. His shrunken chest and hollow eyes terrified Jack, confronting him with the fact that this man was the source of whatever strength he had once had. The phrase "God is dead" now took on an even more horrible meaning, as Jack realized that the last person he could trust to care for him was leaving him for good.[81]

Hal noticed that the sympathy between Jack and Leo had grown even stronger now that Jack was sick too. Jack seemed oddly pleased to have discovered his own "mortal flaw" in the phlebitis, since in at least one way he was now more like his father. But his concern for his father's suffering went far beyond this father-son rivalry. One day, as Leo tried to stand up on his numb legs, he collapsed on the floor. That moment Jack's heart was torn—as he wrote years later to Carolyn Cassady—by a surge of compassion.

Now that Jack was completely receptive to the lessons his father had to teach, Leo chose to bequeath him the belief that all the effort of a lifetime came to absolutely nothing—an utterly black pessimism, studded with the warnings of hysterical bigotry. One of the last things his father said to him was, "Beware of the niggers and the Jews."

In early spring, Jack spent a whole night walking the streets, unable to sleep. The next morning he had an argument with his father over how to brew coffee. Then the doctor (whom Jack always referred to pointedly as Jewish) came to drain him, and shortly afterward Leo died in Jack's arms. His last words were, "Take care of your mother whatever you do. Promise me." Jack promised, and looked down at all the ink on his father's hands.

For the first time in months he telephoned Edie, who was in Grosse Pointe, and told her how shaken he was.

Leo's body was taken to Nashua, New Hampshire, for burial beside Gerard. Among his father's relatives, Jack experienced a return to the roots he had just begun to write about. At the wake he observed the old ladies in black saying rosaries before his father's casket, and all the other solemn rituals of friends and relatives come to pay their last respects. But it was the setting itself that moved Jack most, the small frame houses, the big families, the family dinners, even a pet collie that he remembered from his youth. Having returned to a place where he was known, where he belonged, he was at last able to view New York with some objectivity. Contrasted with these earthy folk, who handled matters of life and death so simply and practically, city people seemed unreal, uselessly morbid. Jack felt as though he had committed "some needless and atrocious folly" by attempting to live in two conflicting worlds, and for the first time he saw how seriously torn he was between them.

At the funeral he noted the difference between his mother's and father's relatives. While the Lévesques were gentle, quiet, and dignified, the Kerouacs were nervous and blustering, freely venting their anger and sorrow. Jack wasn't pleased when his Uncle Ernest Kerouac said that Jack was as "ambitious and proud and crazy" as Leo, but his identification with his father was now fixed irrevocably, and would grow stronger with each passing year.

After the funeral Jack spent a short time in Lowell. A photo of him at this time shows him reading a book, smoking, looking dazed and abstracted, as though he had just fallen off a cliff and survived, and realized life didn't matter anyway: the picture of a man with a deeply suppressed hurt. He didn't see many of his old friends, but he did seek out Charlie Sampas, Sammy's older brother, the columnist on the *Lowell Sun*. In the old days Jack and Sammy would sometimes ask Charlie for fatherly advice. Now, sitting with him in a tavern on Moody Street, Jack confessed his literary ambitions. Charlie advised him to stay out of Lowell, saying that Jack could get the necessary perspective on his native town only by leaving it, as Joyce had exiled himself from Dublin.

Back in Ozone Park, while Gabrielle cleaned house, Jack turned religiously to the composition of *The Town and the City*. Now, more than ever, writing was a sacred act for him, an adoration and lamentation over his dead brother and dead father and the clean, gentle world he had sacrificed for the hollow prize of experiencing "all of life." In the notebooks in which he recorded the novel's progress he often wrote hymns and prayers, and he said a prayer each day before starting to write. Intending to pour all his sins and sufferings into the book, he hoped that when it was finished he would be "redeemed." [82]

By redemption he might have meant some sort of spiritual cleansing. He certainly wished to be understood, if not commended, by the rest of his family. Perhaps he even had a vague notion that the basic problems of his life would be solved by the fame and money a successful book could bring.

A best-seller can hardly alter the writer's personality, however, and what Jack's close friends saw in him was a very deeply troubled, withdrawn, not-so-young man. At twenty-four he was still having great difficulty sustaining relationships with women. Several times he seemed to be seriously interested in someone, only to break off the affair by running home to his mother and his writing. Hal and Jack discussed Jack's fear of "giving himself away." [83] Jack seemed to have a tremendous sexual insecurity and admitted a repugnance for the orgasmic response itself. In the giving of semen to a woman he felt as if he were losing part of himself. As far as Hal could see, Jack's problem was not ambivalence about whether he preferred men or women, but simply a lack of continuity in his sexual experience. As a result, his sexuality was almost infantile.

Jack seemed to think that his problem with women would be taken care of when he found the right woman to take care of him. He and Hal often saw French movies on Times Square and then ate in an underground French restaurant on 50th Street. At the cash register stood an old, wizened Frenchwoman, who looked a little like Gabrielle. Jack told Hal that the French always put the woman in charge of money, because a woman's place was in managing the practical affairs of life.

Jack missed Edie very much and was forever telling his friends how great she was. But their life together was past, as now even the communal apartment was being abandoned. When Jack returned to pack his belongings, he met her sister Charlotte, who had come to collect Edie's things. Jack looked well and told her he was earning a little money as a night clerk and elevator operator in one of the campus hotels. Taller than Jack, she laughed when he called her "Little Sister," as of old, and she invited him to come with her to see her grandmother. Jack had been visiting the old woman regularly, but this time she was angry at him. It had become apparent that he and Edie were headed for divorce, and to people of her social standing *divorce* was a bad word. The fault, as she saw it, was with Jack for making no effort to keep the marriage together.

Without a woman, Jack was occupying his free time almost exclusively with jazz, and with one of his most congenial companions, Jack Fitzgerald. In many ways Jack felt closer to Fitzgerald than to any of the other people around Columbia. Fitzgerald had reluctantly entered the family tile business in order to support a family, but he still found time to write. He was working on a novel about his experiences in the Battle of the Bulge, and Jack considered him one of the three or four really gifted young writers he knew. On the surface a rowdy joker, Fitzgerald was as compassionate as Jack, as hurt by the pain of others. And like Jack, he tried to drown that hurt with very heavy drinking.

One day Fitzgerald read Jack and Hal a story about a "black cat" chasing a "white chick," who repeatedly teased and eluded him. The characters represented the two hands of a pianist during a jazz composition. Jack liked the story very much, and felt that Fitzgerald had found a perfect metaphor for the spontaneity of jazz. It was ironic that Jack should appreciate that quality, since—in Hal's view—he was virtually incapable of spontaneous behavior. Jack seemed uneasy in almost any social interaction, at least when sober. And even with the loosening effect of drink, he could only take being with people for a few days; then he had to withdraw, to be alone to think. Since Hal was going through a similar phase due to his urgent need to get down to work, he became the perfect companion for Jack's philosophical moments.

As 1946 wore on, Jack worked steadily at *The Town and the City*. As the page count grew, he began to realize that he was creating a

serious novel, one that could bring him recognition throughout the
United States, rather than just among a coterie of ten people. That is
a frightening realization for any twenty-four-year-old, let alone one
of Jack's introspective propensity. He and Hal discussed the nature
of publicity. To Jack, one's picture in the papers was simply "notoriety," something he didn't desire. What he wanted was "fame" in the
sense that Shakespeare and Stendhal possessed it, a recognition that
would endure through the ages, even though it might not come in his
own lifetime. Yet he also expressed the belief that he would become
famous young.

He and Hal went to see the movie *Morning Glory*, starring Kath-
arine Hepburn, the story of a stand-in who, given the chance to
perform one night, wins instant acclaim, and quickly gains many
friends who abandon her just as quickly when her success fades. This
superficial fame was what Jack dreaded most. He and Hal talked
about the way fans would tear off pieces of a star's clothing—like
Maenads tearing apart a handsome youth and coming away with bits
of his hair or skin—while they stupidly thought they had captured
the substance of the person. It was a prophetic discussion for the
man who would later be idolized as the King of the Beats.

8.

If we can believe Jack's later account of the matter in a letter to Carl
Solomon, he was already causing something of a ruckus among publishers and agents with his novel *And the Hippos Were Boiled in
Their Tanks*. Lucien had gotten wind of the novel's existence and
asked Jack to "bury it under a floorboard," but Bill and Jack were
circulating it as the work of one "Seward Lewis," a pseudonym
composed of their respective middle names. Their sensational treatment of the "murder" shocked publishers to a degree that none
dared accept it.

Jack was also getting something of a reputation around the Columbia campus. Although he was still officially unwelcome, he was
spending a good deal of time there and in the West End Bar. By the
summer of 1946 large numbers of veterans were drifting back from
the war, and many were using their GI benefits to attend colleges
they couldn't have afforded before. With his unusual interest in new
people, Jack was there to meet them. Around Columbia he wasn't
known as a writer primarily—in fact, Johnny the bartender refused
to believe he was a writer at all—but rather as a warm, friendly guy
who would enjoy whatever you happened to be enjoying. For many
of these new students, uneasy their first time in the chill atmosphere
of the Ivy League, Jack served as a gentle guide and mentor.

One such student was Tom Livornese, a shy Sicilian-American from Queens, three years younger than Jack. While in the service on Guam, Tom had played piano in a jazz band with Joe Burkhardt, who had been an arranger for Dizzie Gillespie and for the Boyd Raeburn band in Chicago. Chicago had become the fountainhead of new jazz sounds, with bebop developing alongside the progressive jazz of new bands like Raeburn's. Burkhardt had additional ties to mainstream jazz, since he had studied under Duke Ellington and Billy Strayhorn. Tom was also a close friend of Chubby Jackson, whose five-piece band was then playing in New York. Although Tom was enrolled in a premed curriculum at Columbia, he was taking his elective courses in music. Yet, despite his extensive technical knowledge of jazz, he never approached it from the outside, as a pedant, but always with the intuitive feeling of a musician.

Tom and Jack took an instantaneous liking to each other, and they soon began spending at least one day a week together listening to jazz. In contrast to the rigid polarity of the postwar period—the harsh lines drawn between Left and Right, for example—jazz had never seen a greater variety of forms providing beneficial stimulation to one another. There coexisted in harmony: swing, "classic" jazz, bebop—under the new banner of "hard" or "funky" bop—progressive or "cool" jazz, and Afro-Cuban rhythms. Much of the innovation was heard in small groups like Bill Harris' and Flip Phillips'; it was to these that Jack and Tom most often listened, and they naturally spent a great deal of time with Chubby Jackson's group.

The roles of teacher and learner were often exchanged, because Jack was always discovering new jazz talents on his own. The most important new sound Jack introduced to Tom was that of Lenny Tristano, the blind pianist. Tristano's complex chord progressions, people joked, made that other blind pianist, Art Tatum, "take a second look." Tristano's music alternated restlessly between tension and relaxation and kept the listener continuously off balance with asymmetric phrases and constantly shifting accents.

It is important to remember that Jack's own response to music was largely intuitive. Up to this point he had had little formal training in music, and yet he was instinctively able to pick out the best musicians of his day, often while they still worked in obscurity. What Tom offered Jack was an insight into the meaning of music as it is expressed through structure, while Jack made Tom aware of the sociological significance of jazz.

Tom had an interest in law (he eventually became a lawyer), and he knew a good deal about the continuing struggle of black people for their civil rights. For example, he had read about the famous *Plessy versus Ferguson* case in 1896, in which the Supreme Court of the United States had decided that the races could be kept separate as long as they were provided with equal facilities. But Tom "never thought Plessy existed or didn't exist" when he was playing with other musicians. Then Jack came along and said, "For God's sake, you got a chance to work here with guys and do things that are just beyond comprehension in other places." [84] After all his years as a musician, Tom suddenly realized that music is a language common enough so that you can forget all the alleged differences between the people who produce it, and just give in and enjoy it. Moreover, Jack made him see that such an open approach to life could be moved into other areas, that it was a key to the opening of society itself. To Tom, that insight indicated a remarkable maturity on Jack's part—a revelation all the more remarkable because maturity was one of the last things with which people ever credited Jack.

Jack encouraged Tom in his musical career by assuring him of the importance of the independent creative work he could do there, however small his contribution. But Jack also needed moral support, in order to remain "out there in an enormous swim." [85] Tom, as well as many others, sensed that Jack was walking around like a wounded animal, in desperate need of some sheltering, some protection, until his hurts turned into scars. At the same time he dreaded too much protection, because his vulnerability was the index to his sensitivity, and to cut down the one would inevitably reduce the other. What Jack needed were friends who would support him uncritically, but who also knew when to warn him against going too far.

Among those who read the riot act to Jack, there were few whose company he enjoyed more than Allan Temko's. They had been introduced by Jack Fitzgerald a couple of years earlier, while Allan was still in the navy, but didn't become close until 1946, when Allan, an aspiring writer, resumed his studies at Columbia. In all-night literary discussions Jack would talk on and on about the greatness of Wolfe, and Allan liked to hear him even though he considered Wolfe's works "kid stuff." [86] His own favorite writer was Hemingway. To Jack it seemed that Allan even talked in Hemingway dialogue, and when they were together Jack himself would start talking like a Hemingway character. Eventually they'd both put on the Hemingway act as a running joke, which Allan took as good-naturedly as Jack did Allan's sarcasm about Wolfe.

Allan liked Jack alone, but he didn't like Jack with his friends. Soon after they met, Jack introduced Allan to Burroughs, whom Allan found brilliant but "reptilian." (When another person made the same remark, Burroughs responded: "What's he got against reptiles?") Having read accounts of the Carr homicide, Allan was convinced that Lucien was a spoiled rich kid who had murdered someone simply because he was certain he could get away with it. Burroughs seemed another "mad aristocrat" quite as capable of cold-blooded murder. Allan had trouble understanding Jack's interest in these "loathsome" people, and reproached him for pursuing the pleasures of a voyeur. Conceding that Jack was extremely sensitive, Allan nevertheless concluded that he lacked sufficient intelligence to see through his "brilliant but destructive friends."

Allan was also repelled by the way Jack's friends, including Ginsberg, seemed to hate women. He felt that Jack had a great fear of women that sometimes turned into hatred. Educated women seemed to devastate Jack, and he only seemed able to get along with women who were susceptible to his sexual magnetism, or else women at a hopeless social disadvantage. Telling of his affair with Mary Carney, Jack asserted that she was the one girl he had really loved. Yet the story centered more on the people who had hurt her, like the "rich Jewish girls" who had sneered at her dress, than on Mary herself.

Edie had once asked Allan if she should marry Jack, and he had replied, "If you love each other, why not?" Edie rejoined, "You know where I come from and where he came from." Allan had recommended she marry Jack, even though he felt she was "one of the self-destructive people," and even though "she didn't seem to understand all of the problems she was getting into"—one of which, in Allan's eyes, was Jack's "sublimated homosexuality." At the time, having just begun to know Jack, Allan was still confident Jack could work out his problems.

With the passing years that confidence waned, as Allan came to know the circumstances of Jack's daily life. Allan's family lived in Richmond Hill, not far from Ozone Park, and he spent a lot of time at Jack's home. Jack's mother seemed to have "a lot of character and grit," and Allan liked her. She liked him, but "for the wrong reasons." Because he was respectable and could help Jack's career, she treated him well. By the same token, she would be rude to anyone who might cost Jack money, including the women he dated. As Allan saw it, Jack was not conventionally homosexual, but rather had succumbed to the fears of his parents. "Old Americans," [87] they had been scared by everything new, including the foreign (non-French-Canadian) women who might exploit Jack. But most of all they feared corporate America, which was now so powerful it exploited everyone and, conspiring with government, stood above the law. Whereas Ginsberg's brilliant parents had given Allen an intellectual framework with which to begin tackling such huge problems, Jack's parents had showed him no tool but their own anger.

Ginsberg, Temko, and most of Jack's other friends were also well-provided with the comforts of life, while Jack barely had the necessities. He didn't even own one decent suit, and he was perpetually hungry. Temko's mother had to feed Jack great quantities of food whenever he came to their home.

But Jack's poverty gave him a common-sense approach to the basic problems of life, which Allan liked. In the same way, it was his

sincere enthusiasm for Wolfe that made Allan stay up all night listening to Jack's home-grown theories, even though Allan found others like Hal Chase better qualified to discuss literary techniques. And
whereas Hal had been able to turn on and off his zest for life, almost
as if with a spigot, Jack's zest was irrepressible. Allan loved to walk
with him along the railroad line in Ozone Park, to hear him imitating the sounds of the engines chugging or letting off steam, or just
whooping at the sight of them. He even liked to watch Jack's hurried
workingman's stride, head down, hands in pockets, and to hear him
tell about the mill workers in Lowell who walked the same way.

There was a rare tolerance in Jack that also distinguished him
from the others. Hal more or less shunned Allan's company, irritated
by his tough-guy pose and reluctant to be pumped—as Allan had a
way of doing—for information about the West. Hal was fond of analyzing people; for example, he classed Allan as "very different" from
Jack, though he believed they shared some similar traits. Jack was
one of the last people to judge anyone, and he was capable of enjoying almost every person for exactly what he was, no more, no less.

The summer of 1946 Hal was back in Denver, but he and Jack
corresponded regularly. To convince his friends that Jack was a great
writer, Hal showed them his letters. One person who read them was
Neal Cassady. Married to a sixteen-year-old dark-blond beauty
named LuAnne, Neal was nevertheless entangled with other women
and working a variety of jobs to care for all of them. Whether or not
Jack's letters served as an impetus, Neal decided he wanted to enter
Columbia in the upcoming fall term.

Although Hal considered him something less than a genius, he
felt Neal would have no trouble handling the coursework. Since Neal
had a high-school equivalency diploma, the only obstacle to his admission was his lack of college test scores. When Hal returned to
New York, he persuaded three professors to admit Neal to their
classes if he passed a special oral examination, and set up appoint-
ments for Neal to take those examinations before the term started.
Hal was anxious for Jack to meet Neal, since he believed him to be
just the sort of character Jack needed to write about. But Neal never
arrived. The professors felt snubbed, and they made it clear to Hal
that they weren't interested in giving this ingrate a second chance.

Another of Hal's friends, also a protégé of Brierly, did arrive that
fall. Recently discharged from the navy, Ed White was returning to
Columbia to finish his bachelor's degree. In Denver he had read
Hal's letters from Jack, and he was looking forward to meeting this
freewheeling writer. He had heard tales of their "existentialist" life
in the communal apartment, and the figures of Kerouac and Ginsberg seemed to be doing the sorts of things he wanted to do himself.
Thus far Ed had always been restrained by decorum, but he hoped to
learn a few artistic tricks.

Although Ed wasn't one of the "mad ones" (the phrase Kerouac used in *On the Road* to describe friends like Neal) who fascinated Jack, they immediately related to each other in a number of areas. Ed was genuinely interested in literature, painting, and architecture, and he could talk about those subjects with more finesse than anyone Jack had yet met. He also shared Jack's passion for jazz. Jack began taking him around to the small clubs in Harlem to hear the musicians he had discovered, one of whom was the as-yet-unacclaimed Mel Tormé. Like Tom, Ed was enthralled by Jack's divining rod for genius, and by the magic that made everyone Jack knew part of a single charmed circle. Jack's friends almost seemed carefully chosen to please one another, each with a particular complementary talent, and Jack would proudly share them as if they were prized Christmas presents. He let Ed and Tom see Burroughs make his sinister entrance out of the night, and brought them to hear Jack Fitzgerald talk a blue streak. Ed and Tom were suitably enchanted.

Ed's respectability, courtesy, and polished manners made a hit with Gabrielle, and Ed became a frequent guest in their home. At that time Jack was in the habit of taking his mother's large teakettle, which she called a "bom," down to the local tavern to be filled with beer. After splitting a "bom," he and Ed would walk the streets of Ozone Park, quietly talking. Although Ed wasn't given to the sort of soul baring that Jack had indulged in with members of the apartment, he appealed very strongly to Jack with his rare combination of sophistication and decency. This year Ed and Hal were sharing a top floor garret in Livingston Hall, and Jack often met them there. For the first time Jack was comfortable on campus and had "a true Columbia feeling." [88] Since Hal was sick of the aimlessness of past years, Ed replaced him as Jack's sidekick on those all-day-and-all-night walks. One thing Hal and Jack agreed upon: Ed was "the most just man" either of them had ever met.

Although Hal's friends liked Ed—as they liked Jack, and didn't like Temko—Ed never became a part of any real group around Columbia. He was always a bit reserved, always more an observer than a doer. Of course when Jack was sober he was much the same. But drunk Jack was now indisputably a performer, which was in fact one of the sources of dispute between him and Hal. Hal felt Jack was selling out his integrity by performing, that he was pandering his talents for approval and love when he should be putting them to serious work. But Jack was also capable of coming alive without the stimulation of drink if he were with people he cared about and could trust. When he and Allen got together, the allusions flew hot and fast. Ed was amazed at the literary interpretations they continually placed on life—saying, "This is like in Kafka," or, "This is like Rimbaud"—which were always interesting and usually apt.

One of Jack's favorite ways of making things happen was to bring together two people with strong personalities who had never met each other before. At the resulting mental duel Jack would be an attentive spectator, savoring every nuance of emotion, both to grat-ify his own slapstick sense of humor and to store the experience for future literary use. He knew that somebody might get hurt a little bit, but at the same time such confrontations were part of the ego game of life, which he desperately wanted to promote.

After two years at Elmira State Reformatory Lucien had been paroled and was again in New York. Meeting him, Ed thought Lu-cien a "mental wizard" much like Hal. Predictably, Jack decided to bring about a confrontation between Lucien and Hal. Jack was in the habit of recounting Carr's homicide in lurid detail for his friends, and so he gave Hal a thorough briefing about Lucien prior to their encounter. As Jack told the story, Kammerer was an intelligent and fairly likable fellow who had simply wanted to die, and hence his death had been no tragedy. Though Jack didn't exactly approve of Lucien's deed, he had helped him out of loyalty, and even had a touch of admiration for the panache with which this "smart-assed, vital rich kid," as he called him, had brought it off—the flair of his walking in, the morning after, and saying, "I got rid of the old man" (though according to Jack it was Burroughs who had always been telling Lucien to get rid of him). There was a part of Jack that didn't feel everything was right in America, even though he loved it and wanted to conserve its old-time values. It was that dissatisfied side of Jack that responded so strongly to Lucien.

At this point, however, Hal could hardly have been less inclined to intellectual competition with anyone, and the notoriety that still attached to Lucien made him even more leery of getting involved. For his part, Lucien was concerned to stay out of trouble so as not to violate his parole, and he keenly wanted to settle down into some kind of normal life. Nothing would have made Lucien happier than for people to simply forget his youthful misdeed—which, thanks largely to Jack, they never did—and he wasn't at all anxious to dis-play his flamboyance. The meeting between Hal and Lucien was uneventful, except that Hal again noticed how very different from Jack were the friends he chose. Whatever Jack was looking for in this particular confrontation certainly didn't materialize, but that didn't discourage him from continuing the search. If it was fireworks he wanted, he wouldn't have to look much further.

9.

For months Hal had been telling everyone about this "unbelievable crazy quixotic man," and Neal Cassady, as though he already knew he was the star, didn't disappoint them with his entrance.

In early December, 1946, LuAnne took Neal away from his Denver girlfriends by getting him to move in with her aunt in Sidney, Nebraska. Neal got a job in a gas station and she worked as a maid, but within a few days he got the itch to go to New York. For traveling expenses LuAnne stole three hundred dollars from her aunt's strongbox, and Neal helped himself to her uncle's car. After they drove through a blizzard the car stopped dead in North Platte, Nebraska, and they made the rest of the journey by bus. But as soon as LuAnne stepped off the bus she wanted to get another one going home. Neal ran after her; they fought and made up. Then, holding onto a meager satchel of clothes, volumes of Shakespeare and Proust, and his teenage wife, twenty-year-old Neal Cassady strode out of the Greyhound Bus Station on 50th Street and into the wonderland of Times Square.

Hungry, they went first to Hector's cafeteria, where the enormous, shining array of foods—such as they had literally never seen before—dazzled them into forgetting they had only thirty-five dollars left. After sampling a variety of pastries, they went back out to stare at Times Square. Neal was brimming with excitement and ambition, telling LuAnne all his dreams and hopes for their future—how he would study at Columbia and become a writer. But she was paying no more attention to his words than he was himself.

They spent three hours gawking at the huge billboards: the Camel sign with the man blowing smoke rings, the black washerwoman bending over a tub from which suds tumbled out, the gigantic neon comic strip of Fritz the Cat. Neal was always magnanimous with women, and he treated LuAnne to whatever delicacies she fancied. Together they sipped their first orangeade.

Reality first laid its chill hand on them when they went to find a hotel room. Every place they tried, the desk clerks, disbelieving they were actually married, refused to let them in. Finally, at the St. George Hotel, Neal rented a room for himself and sneaked LuAnne up to it an hour later. It was a small room with a single bed, and a little window overlooking an alley. To most people it would have been the worst possible impression of New York, but to them it was beautiful.

The next morning they rode up to Columbia and found Hal and Ed in Livingston Hall. Hal was still mad at Neal for wasting his chance to get admitted to Columbia, but the whirlwind of activity that accompanied Neal's arrival anywhere swept Hal up too, and he began sending word to all his friends to come meet the *enfant terrible*. In the West End, Hal and Neal bumped into Allen Ginsberg. In those days Allen was prepared to fall in love with almost anyone at first sight, and Neal could have enamored Allen were Allen blindfolded. Beyond Neal's enormous erotic attraction, Allen was ecstatic to find—at last!—a mind as quick as his own. Back at Livingston Hall, he and Neal slid into rapid-fire talk that lasted for hours.

Ed was less than enthusiastic about Neal's descent on them. He had met Neal in Denver but had never gotten along well with him. Even though he already knew some of the grisly details of Neal's childhood—the lack of support, material or spiritual, from either of his parents, the endless agonies of where to go, what to do—Ed found it hard to sympathize with anyone so patently parasitic. To Ed, Neal's insecurity didn't excuse his selfish use of other people. That Neal had attached himself to Allen was even less of an attraction for Ed. He considered Allen a tag-along, to whom he was in the habit of saying, "Beat it, kid!"

Allan Temko came for a look, found Neal good-looking and thought LuAnne an "idiot." Other than that, Temko had no use for a "sponger" and "criminal" like Neal. From what Temko had heard about Neal's exploitation of women and the myriad loves he had left behind, as well from the way Neal seemed to be dragging along LuAnne as a sexual convenience, Temko concluded that Neal hated women as much as Ginsberg and Burroughs. In addition, he felt Neal shared the ruthlessness of Burroughs, and he decided to have as little as possible to do with either of them.

When Tom Livornese arrived, Neal began talking to this dark, curly-haired Sicilian as if he himself were "the Great White Father that had come here from the West, to con everyone in town." Having been halfway around the world, Tom was hardly pleased to be treated like "a little city Italian kid"; and what was worse, Neal was using "an astronomic con of the worst sort," which even a real "little city Italian kid" could see through. From the start, Tom felt a psychopathic quality about Neal, which later encounters confirmed. At the same time Tom sensed a tragedy about him too, as though Neal were likely to die in prison from some great con game that didn't quite come off. Nonetheless, Tom saw that he had promise, that he was bright, even if he hadn't yet learned suitable ways to present his intelligence. More importantly, he responded to Neal as "a very interesting human being." [89]

By this time a few more of Hal's friends had stopped in, and most of them, including Tom, were interested in LuAnne. With her heavy ringlets of russet hair, smoky blue eyes, and pinup body, LuAnne stirred more than a friendly curiosity. She was the sort of marvelous hometown girl they would have liked to snare for themselves. Yet they felt less envy toward Neal than admiration that he had managed to attach himself to this beautiful girl. LuAnne's glory reflected on Neal, as though she were an extension of himself.

By the time Jack walked in, the room was filled with men, but LuAnne noticed him right away, and Neal was immediately aware of her interest. Allen had just been telling Neal about Jack and hurried to introduce them. Automatically Neal had become tremendously jealous of Jack—of his male power and beauty—but simultaneously Jack appealed to him for the same reasons. After Jack got into the conversation, Neal couldn't help being drawn to him. As far as LuAnne could see, Jack was experiencing the same mixture of attraction and repulsion toward Neal. Neal was not as "pretty" as Jack,[90] but he was holding everyone's interest through sheer will, an act of bravado Jack could never match. On the other hand, Jack saw that Neal really didn't know what he was saying, that he was using big words and intellectual phrases in a crass effort to impress them.

Hal too was upset with the way Neal was trying to ingratiate himself, and he felt that on this occasion Neal was being particularly obnoxious in the role of Uriah Heep. Of course Hal tolerated Neal's oiliness because he understood that it was a product of his underprivileged background. Lacking money, degrees, or any other tickets to society, Neal had to get by on his wits alone. That was a trait Jack admired greatly, and it didn't take long for him to see what Neal was really doing.

All the same, that meeting between Jack and Neal wasn't wholly successful. Jack didn't even choose to mention it in *On the Road*, the first complete book he wrote about Neal. After so much suspense Neal's actual arrival seemed anticlimactic, not because Neal was a disappointment, but because, except for Allen, none of them basically liked him! Even a true friend like Hal wasn't pleased with the caricatured personality Neal had become in New York.

Allen, naturally, couldn't get enough of Neal. He already wanted to carry their nonstop, eyeball-to-eyeball dialogue into eternity, if possible, and the first stop was taking Neal and LuAnne to see the movie *The Testament of Dr. Mabuse*. After a day and a half of restaurants and movies, Neal was out of money. The second night they managed to catch some sleep on the couches in the lobby of Livingston Hall, but it was difficult to explain LuAnne's presence there, since she wasn't permitted to enter any of the boys' rooms (she had been sneaked up earlier). The next day, Allen talked his cousin into letting Neal and LuAnne stay in his cold water flat in Spanish Harlem.

A few days later Jack came with Hal and Ed to see Neal again. Neal answered the door in the nude; behind him LuAnne jumped off the couch and disappeared. Standing unself-consciously in the doorway, Neal asked them to wait outside for a minute until he was "through." It was Jack's first glimpse of the "Nietzschean hero" Hal had been telling him about, the love god whom women adored: half slender-hipped cowboy like Gene Autry, half Greek athletic champion, with a sex organ big enough for both.[91]

This time Jack stayed with Neal until dawn, drinking beer and talking. He was intrigued by how intently Neal listened to him, with his head down, bobbing and nodding like a boxer taking instructions, punctuating everything Jack said with a "Yes" or "That's right." Neal was in almost constant motion; he even flapped his arms when he talked. Neal and Jack must have been surprised to discover how much they had in common. Both had been raised Catholics, and both had left the Church because it had seemed to exclude joy. Both had largely educated themselves by reading, often in public libraries. Both had played a variety of sports in youth; both were exceptionally fast runners, and both excelled at football. Playing college football had always been a dream of Neal's—he had once hitchhiked halfway across country just to see Notre Dame play. That Jack had already starred in college football greatly increased Neal's respect for him, but it also excited his jealousy. They arm-wrestled to test each other's strength. Each of them felt inferior in the other's presence; and, sadly, neither realized how much the other really liked him.

That night a friendship began to grow between Jack and LuAnne. She had been feeling terribly inadequate around all those sophisticated superminds, and Jack was the first one to treat her as an equal. Besides showing a sincere interest in what she had to say, he never talked down to her. Two things about him surprised her. When she had first met him with the large group in Hal's room, he had seemed very quiet and too shy to even speak to her. In the Harlem flat, however, when they were on a one-to-one basis, he talked as freely as if she were an old friend. But the second surprising thing was that Jack seemed totally oblivious of her sexual interest in him. By this time, in her own words, she "adored" him, but he treated her "like one of the fellows." That is not to say LuAnne was planning an affair with Jack, but merely that she had never before met a man that handsome who didn't use his sexual attraction to manipulate women. Jack not only didn't use it, he seemed unaware that he had any at all. He even talked about how "all the other fellows could do better" than he did.

A few years later, when Jack wrote the final version of *On the Road,* he began the novel with an accurate rendering of that scene in the Harlem flat—except that in the printed text, for the sake of propriety, Neal was dressed in a pair of shorts before he opened the door to a new season in Jack's life.

In reality, that season was quite slow in coming around, much slower than Neal himself. Neal and LuAnne couldn't stay long with Allen's cousin. Although Tom Livornese usually commuted to Columbia from his home in Lynbrook, he had rented a tiny apartment on 103rd Street, for convenience. Hal prevailed on Tom to let Neal and LuAnne move into his "linen closet." Later Tom regretted the arrangement, but only because everyone in contact with the visitors developed crab lice (one of the less literary influences of Neal Cassady). Before Tom could evict them, they moved out on their own.

All the guys were busy studying except Jack, who always seemed, in LuAnne's phrase, "like he was at odd ends." Since Neal had nothing pressing to do either, he and Jack began seeing more of each other. To get money to live, Neal sent LuAnne to work.

She found a job in a bakery. Impatient for her paycheck, Neal told her to steal some money from the cash register. The first day on the job she attempted the theft and was caught. Fortunately the woman in charge didn't call the police; she simply fired LuAnne, who was dazed, and put her on a bus for Columbia. After getting off the bus, LuAnne wandered, lost, in a snowstorm until dark, when one of Hal's friends found her. When she told the story to Neal, she burst into tears at having disappointed him, and for several weeks had terrifying hallucinations of leaving her body, which would plunge her into a hysteria that lasted for hours. Although Neal held her and comforted her, there seemed no way to prevent the hallucinations from returning. Finally, having gotten a job parking cars, he moved her into a small apartment in Bayonne, New Jersey.

For a short time LuAnne was happy with her domestic life, sewing curtains, decorating, and cooking supper for Neal, who returned to her regularly after work. But one evening, without any forethought, she told him that the police had been there looking for him. They hadn't had a fight; there was no reason for her to fabricate such a story. Neal naturally believed her. She herself never understood why she lied to him, unless moved by some instinct of self-preservation she couldn't name. In any case, even as the words were leaving her lips, she foresaw the panic they would precipitate in Neal. The fifteen months he had spent in reform schools had imbued him with such a horror of confinement that had she tried to confess, he would never have believed her. He grabbed his essential belongings, leaving her to pack the rest, and rushed for the bus station. She met him with his trunk in Jersey City, they slept in a parked car, and he got on a bus for Hartford.

After three days of hiding out in the Berkshires Neal returned to New York, convinced of LuAnne's deception. But by that time, with money chipped in by his friends, she had already boarded a bus for Denver.

For the next couple of months Neal stayed on in New York, working at the parking lot. He still wanted very much to get a formal education and to become a writer, and according to Hal, if anyone could teach him, it was Jack. One night he appeared at Jack's door in Ozone Park, saying he had come to learn how to write. Jack knew he mainly needed a place to stay, but wanting to learn more about him, he took him in for a few days, although Gabrielle thought Neal a madman, or at best a bum.

For years Jack had more or less treasured the notion of his own madness. It gave a unique stamp to his character, like a trademark that confirmed his identity. He now began to see Neal's particular madness, and to sympathize with his reluctance to compromise. Jack discovered that many beliefs he had held in secret—like the holiness of sex, and the essential oneness of sex and love—were openly acknowledged by Neal, even practiced by him like a creed. More than anything else Jack admired, and was envious of, Neal's confidence in dealing with a world hostile to his values. Similarly Neal was as humiliated as he was awed by Jack's ability to sit down and write for several hours at a stretch—something Neal rarely had the concentration to achieve. Each was for the other a visible example of what he would like to be but couldn't. Inevitably, the progress of their friendship was slowed by a great deal of mutual frustration.

One night Jack took Neal into the city to meet his old friend Vicki, and at her place Neal met Allen too. From that night on Allen took Neal under his amorous wing, trading instruction in literature for Neal's affection, and Jack saw little of him before Neal returned to Denver in early March 1947.

There can be little doubt Jack already thought of Neal as some kind of hero. They all did, at least all of them who visited him at the parking lot. Tom Livornese, though a good driver himself, watched in terror and then amazement as Neal parked his Buick in one smooth, snaking movement from zero to forty to zero again. Jack was even more impressed by such stunts. But besides his physical courage, Neal possessed an extraordinary warmth, and with him Jack was able to have that eyeball-to-eyeball communion he had lost when Joan's apartment broke up. But for some reason he didn't go out of his way to see Neal, though he came into the city fairly often to attend parties with Ed and to hear jazz with Tom. Neal may have been an even madder jazz devotee, yet Jack never brought him along on their weekly excursions to the clubs; in those two months Tom never heard Jack mention Neal once. Possibly Jack wanted to keep his relationship with Neal separate from the others, but it's a better guess that all that Neal had really done this time around—and it was enough—was to plant a seed. He let Jack glimpse a possible solution to the value split that Hal had termed the division between Wolfeans and Baudelaireans, or Black Priests. Jack saw Neal as the only one capable of unifying them simply because he was both. Although not exactly a defrocked priest, Neal was a fallen choir boy, which theologically speaking is the same thing. Jack, once a choir boy too, hadn't fallen nearly as far. For the sake of his survival scam, Neal had sold out everything Americans were supposed to cherish. But that con itself—as any W. C. Fields fan knows—couldn't be more American. Besides, all artists deal in illusions. Neal permanently changed the direction of Jack's writing by showing him that a man could both be an artist—if only a con artist—and live in the world at the same time.

BOOK TWO

1947–1955

Jack Kerouac and Neal Cassady, 1952.

FIVE
Metamorphosis

1.

On his way back to Denver, Neal wrote Jack a stammering, half-illiterate letter that might as well have been a masterpiece. What Jack called "The Great Sex Letter" narrated Neal's two attempts to seduce women on the Greyhound bus—the first a failure, the second a success. Scrawled drunkenly in a bar almost immediately after the adventure, Neal's letter was full of false starts, crossouts, misspellings, and solecisms. Its sentence structure was as conventional as any grade school child's, its vocabulary slightly better, and its only interesting feature the freedom (for 1947) with which Neal used common but literarily taboo words like *blow, bang* , and *screw*. Yet at the end of the letter he announced that he had been trying to produce "a continuous chain of undisciplined thought." And like no one else in Neal's life, except maybe Allen Ginsberg, Jack took him at his word.

Jack had planned to go West as early as the summer of 1945, but had quit his summer job before saving enough money. Later, listening to Hal's stories, he wanted to see Denver. When he made friends with Ed White, he promised to visit both Ed and Hal out there. That Denver was the current home of Neal Cassady cinched it for Jack as the creative capital of America.

In the spring of 1947 Jack met another Denverite, a tall, pretty blonde named Beverly Burford, a girlfriend of Ed's. After Ed wrote her about Jack and sent her a photo of him in football uniform, she and Jack began to correspond. A pilot in the Civil Air Patrol, Beverly joined the Air Transport Command and was sent to New York. When she met Jack she realized that the photo had been a private joke of Ed's, that far from being just a rugged athlete, Jack was gentle and sensitive and a dedicated writer. On occasion he'd get wildly drunk, but often they'd sit up all night over just one bottle of wine. Whatever romance they felt was subsidiary to her attachment to Ed. She and Jack became companions.

Upper middle class and clean-cut, Beverly was a perfect friend for Jack to invite to the house, though he took the precaution of introducing her to his mother as "a friend of Ed's." Gabrielle loved her; Beverly was delighted with Gabrielle's hospitality and warmth and also impressed with her adoration for Jack. Quite untypically, Gabrielle encouraged her to stay over at their apartment, which Beverly often did.

Compared to this girl who literally flew around the country as she pleased, Jack could hardly consider himself a free-roving Jack London. The freedom of the West in the Denverites dwarfed his own independence, pushing him to really break loose.

That spring when he heard Nat King Cole singing the Bobby Troup song "Get Your Kicks on Route 66," seeing America seemed the greatest kick of all. But he was stuck in Ozone Park on his exhausting trek through *The Town and the City*, now halfway done at about six hundred pages. It seemed everyone was moving except himself. One night he and Tom Livornese were talking with Chubby Jackson, and Chubby caught Jack's Western fever. Chubby said he would disband his group and take off for Chicago, where he had been offered a job writing for a children's television program. That a man could so easily switch from jazz in New York to children's TV in Chicago astounded Jack. American life seemed marvelously fluid and frighteningly rootless.

At the same time he was growing more conscious of his past. Eddie Gilbert held a Horace Mann class reunion at his estate near Manhasset. Once again Jack played softball and drank toasts to Rudo Globus, Malc Bersohn, Marty Beller, and all the silly, sad human names that left them "rolling under the table in stitches" (as he described the event much later for *Life* magazine). It was the last time he saw most of his Horace Mann classmates, but he was already delving even further into his past. *The Town and the City* explored his relationship with his father. When Tom Livornese visited, Jack often brought out the newspapers and posters Leo had printed—he had saved them all—and they would spend hours studying the exquisite craftsmanship. Jack's strongest feeling toward his father seemed a sense of regret that Leo couldn't see the serious work his son was now doing.

Showing this family history was Jack's way of bringing Tom and himself closer; Hal, Ed, and Beverly were the only others admitted at this time to his home life. Yet he needed to share his experiences, especially his joy and wonderment at the pageant of life, which he observed as exuberantly as if he were the first man to discover it. Frequently Jack called his friends' attention to treasures he thought they might otherwise have overlooked, and would repeat a piece of written or spoken language until people finally *listened* to it. If someone protested that he had already heard it, Jack would tell him to "hear *more*." He extended this sort of guidance in all areas of the arts, and there was really little egotism involved in it. To Jack an artist was someone practiced in finding beauty, and he wanted to lend his professional competence to people he cared about. The point was that these perceptions were of too great a value to belong only to himself.

Although Jack was by now proficient in discussing the technical aspects of jazz, the sort of musical awareness he fostered in Tom was usually of a much more elemental nature. He would ask Tom to sing with him and pay attention to the meaning of the lyrics. For example, one of Jack's favorite songs was "Oh What a Beautiful Morning!" from the musical *Oklahoma!* Tom liked the melody, but Jack told him to concentrate on the line, "Oh, the sounds of the earth are like music." To Jack there were always images attached to words, and he wanted other people to look for them too.

Jack also loved scat singing, in which a vocalist accompanies a jazz solo, or creates his own by using his voice as an instrument. The scat singer mouths nonsense syllables (or sometimes provocatively suggestive ones) just for the sounds they convey. In the late forties scat singers like King Pleasure fit lyrics to solos by Parker and Gillespie, and Jack and Tom listened to many of these records. At Birdland they would often scat together.

Jack had always been available to discuss someone's latest problems or artistic theories, but there was no one with whom he could discuss his own severe difficulties with *The Town and the City*. Despite his "reverent, mad feelings" toward the book, he couldn't write it with the freedom he wanted and generally wrote less than 1,500 words at a sitting.

That spring Hal Chase graduated early from Columbia and returned to Denver. Ed White still had a year to study for his B.A., but he too planned to summer in Denver as did Allan Temko.

Allen Ginsberg was already somewhat removed from Jack's orbit, having felt the previous year that Jack was avoiding him. Allen had joined a very brilliant and sophisticated group of Columbia students. Almost all English majors, they were led by a well-to-do, married, would-be poet named Gene Pippin. Pippin and his friends were ambitious and professional. Initially they didn't attract Jack, who sensed their snobbishness and probably felt miffed at their intellectualism. When Allen recommended Jack read Christopher Marlowe, Jack replied that Marlowe stank "to herring," the sort of hasty put-down that always betrayed defensiveness about his inadequacy.

As 1947 wore on, Allen made plans to follow Neal to Denver and, when Justin Brierly came to New York, wangled an invitation and a job offer with the Central City Opera festival. Knowing he could at least stay alive in Denver while courting Neal, Allen took off in May, planning to stop en route to visit Bill and Joan Burroughs on their farm in Texas.

Lucien Carr had recently been promoted to a responsible position at United Press International and could hardly spend all night carousing. With a growing writer's block, there was little to keep Jack in New York and good reason to get to Denver, for he and Neal had been corresponding regularly. Amazed by Jack's extravagant praise of "The Great Sex Letter," Neal insisted "it was just the setting down of a continuous chain of thought reaction," something for which he felt he had to apologize, pleading that he'd been drunk and high when he wrote it. But it was exactly that spontaneity that interested Jack. Writing by free association had been done extensively by Proust, as well as many of the Romantic poets, including Wordsworth and Coleridge, and its roots went back to the lyrical poets of Greece and Rome. Despite such precedents, Jack thought he detected something new and natively American in Neal's "scribbling."

The very word *scribbling* was important to Jack. He and Neal threw it at each other—Jack encouraging Neal to scribble more, and Neal complying with the scornful disclaimer that scribbling was the easiest thing for him to do, too easy to consider it serious writing. Neal thought Jack far more capable than himself of "just dashing off an extemporaneous letter." Neal was extremely conscious of the inadequacies of language. Not only did his mind's flow outstrip the train of words he put on paper, so that what he was writing always lagged far behind what he wanted to say at the moment, but he knew as well as any philosopher that words cannot capture the actual tortuosities of thought and feeling. With words one imitates reality, and imitation is a lie, a con, a new reality substituted for the old one: "The process of writing forces you into a form and therefore, you just say things rather than feel them." He advised Jack to avoid the futility of trying to direct that process: "To play safe force yourself to think and then write rather than think what to write about and what to say as you write."

Neal wrote like he talked, supposedly on six separate levels. Each time a new idea occurred, he would abandon his present line of thought to follow the new thread, which inevitably split off in several new directions, and those digressions would beget fresh ones. Although his tale might never get told, his mind would be unraveled to extraordinary depths.

The peculiar thing about Neal's method was its humility. As he wrote, he kept apologizing for not saying what he meant. If Neal was conscious of the infinite potential of his mind at any single moment, he was also aware of its ability to take off instantly on an unforeseen course.

There was no suggestion in Proust that recalling the past was an impossible quest. The truly American feature of Neal's writing was the boundless self-wonder of it—the way it kept gaping at itself and rubbing its eyes and saying "I'll be damned!" Thus the paradox of Jack's perceiving Neal as a quintessential American writer, while Neal himself claimed he was "incapable of being concerned with America and all it means at the moment." It was natural for such writing to come from a man like Cassady. Few individuals have been more a mystery to themselves—or more misunderstood by others. In his letters to Jack that spring, Neal recounted his unreasonable, futile pursuit of LuAnne, as well as the fruits of such madness: lost jobs, flights from the police, desperate shifts for shelter and food (like stealing the change off newsstands). How Jack must have admired the simple honesty of Neal's saying: "I've been fighting all sorts of negative things"—something he himself could scarcely admit. Moreover, Jack was grateful both for Neal's open-hearted encouragement of his writing and for the offer to help him get set up in Denver.

But aside from his lack of money, Jack had family obligations. His sister Nin had remarried. Her new husband was a government missile technician, Paul Blake, and they were living in the deep South. At the end of June, 1947, Jack accompanied his mother on a two-week visit to their house. He wrote friends that he had a great time observing the blacks in "niggertown" and listening to his brother-in-law's laconic southern wit, and he and Paul even went down to Georgia to see the alligators in Okefenokee swamp.[92]

Back in New York in mid-July, Jack was still restless. Then Henri Cru hit town after having wandered the globe as a merchant seaman. He brought Jack some good marijuana from Panama and in a few days left for San Francisco, to line up a job for himself as chief electrician on another ship. When he offered to get Jack hired on the same ship as an assistant electrician, Jack jumped at the chance. His mother thought a trip would do him good.

Rather than borrow money from her, Jack decided to hitchhike part of the way in order to meet people, to talk with as well as see America. For months he had been reading histories of the West, and now he began to study road maps. With his romantic sense of quest, he picked out one long red line, Route 6, that led from Cape Cod to Los Angeles. It reminded him of the pioneer trails, and he planned to follow it all the way to Denver.

2.

Before he left, Jack sent out letters to announce his arrival, which show how greatly he had already compartmentalized his friends. In a card to Ed White, he stressed his desire to see both him and Hal, and asked Ed to look for Hal, who was reportedly hiding out in the mountains. Almost as an afterthought, he mentioned: "If Neal is in Denver, maybe you could tell him I'm passing through also?" But in a letter to Bill Burroughs, mailed at the same time, Jack stated that it was Allen and "Neal, particularly," whom he wanted to contact there. He wrote to Bill thinking Allen and Neal might be together on Bill's farm, but Allen had gone straight to Denver, so Bill forwarded the letter. In it, Jack complained about losing track of Neal, and tailored the letter to appeal to Bill's proclivities, mentioning black women in the South chasing one another with meat cleavers, and a shootout in the local black church during services.

Jack left Ozone Park on July 17, 1947, aiming to arrive in Denver between July 22 and July 24. After taking the Seventh Avenue subway to the end of the line at 242nd Street, he rode trolleys to the northern city limit of Yonkers. From there he hitchhiked north along the east bank of the Hudson River until he reached Bear Mountain Bridge, where Route 6 came in from Connecticut. There was almost no traffic on Route 6, and as it started pouring rain, Jack found himself stranded in the upstate wilderness. He finally got a ride to Newburgh and then took a bus back to New York. Disgusted with his failure to get started, he used most of his money to buy a bus ticket to Chicago.

When he got to Chicago in the early morning, he checked into the Y.M.C.A. and spent the whole day sleeping. That night he explored the hot spots on North Clark and South Halsted and went to hear bop in the Loop. He even walked through Skid Row on Madison Street with a squad car at his heels. Feeling the sameness of this city with the other cities he had known, he had a vision of himself as simply enacting, in his own way, the frantic search for an unknown goal that had already uprooted so many members of his generation.

He now had a definite sense of his mission to find something, *anything*. The next afternoon he set out by bus to bypass the heavy traffic around Chicago, and got off in Joliet, where a truck ride took him a few miles west to the intersection of Route 6 and Route 66. There he was picked up by a middle-aged woman, who asked him to drive her car to Davenport, Iowa. When they got to the Mississippi, it was a hazy afternoon and the river was shallow, but the sight overwhelmed him. Crossing it made him acutely conscious that he was now in the West, but even more strongly it made him feel that both East and West were just sections of one nation, with a long history of migrations of many peoples.

Jack always balanced his sense of the basic American unity with his feel for the important regional differences on which that massive strength was founded. As he walked around Davenport, Iowa, he was keenly attuned to the Midwest smells, the different feel of the sun. Yet he also noted that men went to work here just like anywhere, and even wore the same kinds of hats as they drove home.

He got a ride to the prairie at the edge of town, but was stranded when night set in and had to come back into Davenport. There he caught a bus to the city limits and got off near some gas stations, where he was picked up by a truck that took him to Iowa City. The first driver signaled to another truck to stop for Jack, the second driver took him nearly to Des Moines, and he hitched the rest of the way into the city with a couple of boys from the University of Iowa.

Exhausted, and turned away at the Y.M.C.A., he had to stay in a gloomy hotel by the railroad tracks.

The next morning, waking in an old hard bed, Jack had one of the strangest sensations in his life. Home was now so far behind that he didn't know who he was [93]; he was no longer Jack Kerouac the mill-town athlete, but some new Jack Kerouac, a seeker of America like London and Wolfe—but with two world wars and a sexual revolution complicating his identity. To find out who this new Jack Kerouac was would be the purpose of his life as a writer.

Traveling, Jack's sense of himself as an American couldn't have been stronger, and appropriately, he nourished himself the whole way on apple pie and ice cream. After a big portion of this, and after ogling the farm girls, he got a couple of short rides to Adel, Iowa. There he met another hitchhiker, a thirty-year-old Irish drunk from New York, who seemed to be on the run. The Irishman suggested they hitch together, but they only got as far as Stuart, Iowa. At an old saloon Jack bought the Irishman some beers, just to watch him get happy and excited, but then they spent all night and the early morning trying in vain to get a ride. Since the Irishman reminded Jack of his brother-in-law, he offered to buy bus tickets for both of them to Omaha.

In Omaha, Jack saw his first cowboy in boots and ten-gallon hat, but except for his outfit the man looked no different than the beat Times Square characters like Herbert Huncke. On a ride to Grand Island, Nebraska, listening to an old rancher talk about men who rode the rails during the Depression, Jack noted that his own life was falling in with another American tradition, that of the man who moves on out of necessity, when living conditions in one place become unbearable or when the land itself can no longer support life. The rancher told him about the great dustclouds that choked the Great Plains during the thirties. Jack's generation was fleeing a different cloud, made of atomic particles and shaped like a mushroom— a cloud so powerful that even the *threat* of it was stifling.

In one Nebraska town, while the rancher got a tire fixed, Jack and the Irishman went into a diner. An old farmer came in laughing and jabbering about how hungry he was, and Jack was enchanted. In the man's raw, easy laughter he heard the true sound of the West.

A couple more rides took Jack and the Irishman to Shelton, Nebraska, where, passed by a stream of farmers and suspicious tourists, they stood soaking in a cold rain. Jack lent the Irishman a worn plaid wool shirt. When an old man stopped and said he could only take one rider, the Irishman jumped in. Soon Jack got a hundred-mile ride to Gothenburg.

From Gothenburg he had a wild ride all the way to Cheyenne, Wyoming, with two brothers who were taking a flatbed truck to Los Angeles, where they would buy farm machinery to sell in Minnesota.

Along the way they picked up any hitchhikers who dared to ride on the open platform behind the cab. They drove fast over bumpy roads and enjoyed scaring the bums they were helping, but to Jack the lift was pure exhilaration. Passing a bottle of whiskey back and forth, sharing cigarettes, singing country songs, Jack learned as much as he could about the various riders. One hobo, "Montana Slim," who reminded him of Big Slim Hubbard from the naval psychiatric hospital, knew all the ways a man could stay alive without working steadily, and he advised the others how to follow a harvest northward all summer.

It was Wild West Week in Cheyenne. With Montana Slim Jack explored the saloons, repelled by the fat, bourgeois couples dressed as cowboys and cowgirls, some of whom even fired blank pistols. It seemed to him as though the West were reduced to caricaturing its traditions with tawdry costumes and gimmicks. Drinking, he spent five of the seven dollars he had left, then tried to pick up a Mexican waitress, but her boyfriend intervened. Later he bought drinks for two sullen girls, one a blonde he wanted to take to bed, but she wanted to go to New York and wasn't about to get involved with a guy going the other way. Jack spent the night sleeping in the bus station.

In the morning he awoke with two dollars and a headache, but leaving the station recovered at once, dazzled by his first sight of the snow-capped Rocky Mountains. Hitching along the highway closest to the mountains, he got a ride to Longmont, Colorado, where he experienced another epiphany—a sudden appreciation of the vastness of the land stretching before him. In *On the Road,* Jack used that scene to present one of the book's mantras: "Wow!"

A businessman then took him all the way to Denver. Jack asked to be let off at Larimer Street, amid the rundown buildings where Neal had been raised. But there was no immediate way to find Neal, so he reached Hal Chase, who was working at the Denver Art Museum.

Hal had been leading a new quiet life, working on the great Indian collection amassed by Eric Douglas, a self-educated anthropologist and poet, and much of the time he lived in the mountains, digging for relics. He showed Jack some of Denver's historic places: the gold-domed capitol, Union Station, the Windsor Hotel, a sooty monument to the opulence of bonanza days, where Neal and his father had lived for many years. No longer friendly with Neal, Hal didn't know his whereabouts and he had broken off with Allen Ginsberg too.

That afternoon Jack slept at Hal's house. Later Hal contacted Ed White, who had a whole house at his disposal, since his parents were gone for the summer. Allan Temko was already living with Ed, and Jack could have his own room there too.

3.

As soon as Jack moved in, he sensed a conspiracy. Allan Temko had become a dandy, wearing a silk dressing gown while he wrote Hemingway-style short stories. Neither Allan nor Ed wanted anything to do with Neal and Allen Ginsberg and socialized only with Beverly Burford and her brother Bob, and Hal when he was around. Meanwhile Ginsberg, who was working in May's department store and living in a basement apartment on Grant Street, played host to Neal and Neal's old gang. This mélange was further complicated by Neal's two women: LuAnne and a blond University of Denver graduate student, Carolyn Robinson.

Jack had no money, but everybody wanted a share of his energy to boost their own fun, and there was fun to be had all over Denver that summer. Even Temko, full of Hemingwayan disdain for America's imitative culture, was having a ball observing Western types and courting Ed's sister Jeanie. Temko liked Jack because he felt Jack lacked the phony sophistication of most self-styled artists. But Jack was unenthused over Temko's tales of drinking wine in the Basque country of France and Temko lacked Jack's interest in the names of the railroads, like "Great Northern" and "Rock Island Line," that he had read on boxcars. There was no doubt in anyone's mind, however, that Jack was as serious a writer as Temko. All summer Jack carried a notebook and would stop to write in it on any street corner.

Both Beverly and Bob Burford, who lived a few blocks from Ed, loved to hear Jack read aloud sections of prose from his notebooks. He wrote no stories but simply descriptions of the people and places he had seen, yet the writing was suffused with his sense of adventure and of the promise of life. Some of it was overwritten, loaded with allusions to Shakespeare and Beethoven, and purple phrases like "wan dementia" and "gloomy darkness." Yet he made the stars, "greensward," and dew of Denver seem much more real than before to these natives.

Bob had been Ed's friend from boyhood. Although his wealthy family had educated his artistic taste, he played many sports and had recently been working in the Steamboat Springs coal mines. Temko and Jack were the first two writers he met, and he was struck immediately by the difference between them. Temko seemed to approach the West like de Tocqueville visiting America and he seemed to be declaring himself a writer principally for the satisfaction *he* got from it; whereas Jack spoke of his vocation as a writer as a means of giving satisfaction to *others*. In practical ways Jack was always aiding people with his writing skill. Because Bob was having trouble with a girl he liked, Jack composed a love letter for him. As soon as she got the letter, she phoned Bob and was his girl for the rest of the summer.

T-shirted, handsome, his blue eyes shining under his black thatch, Jack was the picture of health and seemed astonishingly strong. He played football and helped slug a church softball team to victory. After the games he and Ed's group would go out to drink in jazz clubs like the Rossonian and Club 39 in Five Points, Denver's black section. Although they all drank heavily, they would recover quickly the next day.

Bev Burford found Jack's drinking just another aspect of his childishness. She thought he tipped up a bottle as if he were looking for something inside it, a key to himself perhaps, and his failure to discover anything pushed him on to the next. In a similar way he sought Neal, as if their identities might be tied together. One day he got a call from Allen, who told him about Neal's simultaneous love affairs with the two women and himself. Neal was on a tight schedule among those three lovers and his job. That night Allen led Jack to Carolyn Robinson's apartment, then ducked into the alley to hide. Neal opened the door nude, while a beautiful blonde watched Jack from the bed. After introducing Carolyn to his "old buddy Jack," Neal left her there with the promise to return in two hours.

Since she had fallen in love with Neal, Carolyn had been courageously expanding her horizons. Raised in Nashville by a prosperous, proper Midwest family and educated at Bennington, she had been prepared to marry a conventional gentleman. By a clever impersonation Neal appeared to fit that bill, and even had she harbored any doubts, love was the guiding factor in her life. She let him have his way with her, trusting that somehow she could turn him into a tender, faithful lover. She knew that he was still married to LuAnne, but he assured her that he was trying to get a divorce. As for Allen, she knew little more than that he was a good friend of Neal's, a Columbia student and poet who would help Neal in his own academic and writing career.

Neal had actually arranged for Allen to spend several nights sleeping in Carolyn's hotel room while Neal was also there, and all three of them often went out to cafés together. Allen's loud talk, exuberant gestures, and occasional singing to himself would draw looks that embarrassed her. Other than those few foibles, she held nothing against him, not even the fact that he and Neal got their kicks in certain questionable ways, such as swallowing those paper strips from benzedrine inhalers. She tried benzedrine with them once, with mixed results.

After Jack and Neal left Carolyn's apartment, Allen joined them and began trying to talk Neal out of visiting two nurse sisters. That summer Allen had been struggling to win Neal's heart by luring him into soul-baring, philosophical discussions. Working his own sort of con, Neal was learning as much as he could from Allen while giving him a modicum of sexual satisfaction. Although Neal found some enjoyment in almost any kind of sexuality, he only had eyes for women, and loving Allen had come to be something of a chore. While Allen complained, and got new inspiration for the book of poems he was writing, *Denver Doldrums,* Neal led Jack to the nurses' house.

Bob Burford joined them there for a gay, drunken party, from which Neal vanished for an hour to keep his rendezvous with Carolyn. Around dawn they took off for Ed White's apartment, but Allan Temko tried to keep them out. Jack told him, "Get back in your closet or I'll bust ya!" Although Temko shut himself in his room, Jack and the others decided to hit the bars for fresh kicks.

The brief affair Jack had with one of the nurses was only a minor joy of Denver. He was clearly having the time of his life. He talked madly of his love for Thomas Wolfe and listened while Temko talked of Hemingway and Twain. Both men were caught up in hunting for the artistic gold that would bring them fame and fortune, and they spurred each other's ambition.

Except for Hal Chase, none of the Denverites understood what Jack saw in Neal. Jack would usually meet Neal at Peterson's Pool Hall, where, he thought, Neal strutted in native grandeur among the awestruck pool sharks of the West. By way of offering a great thrill, Jack invited Bob Burford along, which made Bob laugh. Bob knew of pool hustlers in Denver who played for $1,000 a game, while the boys at Peterson's played for $1, just to pay for the time at the table.

Of course Bob realized that the interplay of such different characters was of great interest to a writer. At one extreme was short, stocky Temko with his seersucker suits and little bow ties; at the other was tallish, slender Allen Ginsberg, running around Denver in just swimming trunks—a shocking sight in 1947. Once Allen even wore a dress shirt and bow tie with the swimming trunks. In T-shirt and jeans Neal was not quite as outlandish but still was shabby compared to the Burfords and Whites. In the middle was Jack, loose and natural, but still dignified, enjoying the fun of all these confrontations.

Although Ginsberg seems to have been mocking Temko, Allen told Jack he wasn't concerned with Temko's friends except for Hal. More and more Allen was coming to see himself, Jack, and Neal as a key creative triangle, and devoting himself to their mutual development. Those who didn't recognize this unique triangle of genius met the scorn of Allen's "deadly eyes," as Jack called them, but Allen claimed he had no special vanity about his supposed power to mesmerize or dominate others. In fact, he admitted his propensity for getting in trouble and complained of having to drag around the "weary load" of his "queerness." [94]

Allen never felt real anger toward others. For people's ignorance he had only compassion, and the only character traits that distressed him were insincerity and a lack of seriousness. In Neal he could forgive anything because Neal seemed to understand mankind's essential unity, the unity of John Donne's "No man is an island." Acting on that knowledge, Neal was forever trying to create bridges between people, which to Allen seemed the most angelic activity possible. He also felt that he and Neal could accomplish this bridging more effectively together, by combining Allen's brilliant and intuitive mind with Neal's open-hearted gregariousness. According to Jack, they were *all* angels, "fallen angels," who hurt one another because they were all "locked in themselves," in their private sorrows. Allen accepted Jack's notion that there were "fallen angels" full of secret love, who loved him even if they didn't show it—but he had trouble seeing such wings on Temko and Burford. In contrast, Jack seemed more compassionate than usual. Previously he had regarded Allen's endless loving and giving as somewhat unmanly, and felt he sacrificed the virtues of dignity, individuality, and solitariness and "traded his soul for love." But in Denver that summer, Jack "redeemed himself" in Allen's eyes by the "sweet" way he accepted Allen's unqualified love for Neal.

The ten days Jack spent in Denver were a turning-point, at which he switched allegiance from his bourgeois professional friends to the group he later called "beat," of which Allen and Neal were charter members. Seeing how Ed, Bob, and Temko scorned Neal, Jack must have realized how readily they would have scorned *him* too, had he lacked the charm and prestige of his writing, since his background was closer to Neal's than to theirs. Ginsberg was considered déclassé because of his sexual inversion, yet, like Jack, he was tentatively accepted in the fashionable group because his literary efforts were formidable. In Allen's view, he and Jack were both "nouveau riche," that is, their acceptance into nice society was too recent and too contingent on future accomplishments for either of them to ever feel comfortable there.

Allen told Jack that Hal's striving toward a "mature and businesslike level" was simply a retreat from his own social insecurity. The issue of "maturity" was irrelevant to their friendship, and hence a spurious reason for severing it. Allen knew well enough the importance of "labor on earth or settling down," and he felt Hal's withdrawal to be an act that would leave him unhappy for the rest of his life, like some fatally disappointed F. Scott Fitzgerald character. A critical decision in the formation of the Beat Generation was Allen's opting for joy over gloom. Rejecting the roles of "a sad Sebastian or a sad prophetic Jew" in which Jack had cast him, Allen reaffirmed his pledge at eighteen to become a "Great Lover." [95] And Jack, suddenly, was with him all the way.

How natural then for Jack to turn to Neal too. While Ed, Bob, and Temko had girlfriends Neal had loves; he was capable of feeling enormous raptures over a particular girl and he retained the ideal of monogamy as the most honorable path for a man, even if he never practiced it. That summer he couldn't stop extolling the virtues of Carolyn. As if he didn't want Jack to see how he was already defiling his new love, Neal never once brought Jack to see LuAnne, though she and Neal were having frequent trysts. It was Carolyn Neal introduced to Jack as his wife-to-be. This sophisticated, highly intelligent woman was his pride and joy, the kind of woman he'd always felt he should marry.

Carolyn found Jack better-looking than Neal and was attracted to his warm, gentle nature. But she and Jack both respected her duty to be faithful to Neal and tried to act their respective parts as his fiancée and good buddy. Several times Jack visited her at the university, where she was studying drama, and after her rehearsals they shyly explored each other's backgrounds, and their common acquaintance with New England. Carolyn was intrigued by this dark, romantic stranger and his clever observations, and fascinated by the nickel notebook in which he kept jotting down his momentary impressions. Neal also had a way of throwing Jack and Carolyn together that made it hard for them to remain mere acquaintances.

One night the three of them went to a tavern, and Neal repeatedly left Jack and Carolyn to play the juke box and gab with other patrons, then would come back to report his discoveries and rap with Jack. Carolyn delighted in watching their crazy facial expressions and wild gestures, and listening to their goofy chuckles and giggles. It seemed Jack and Neal were actually mimicking each other, driving each other to ever greater pitches of silly joy. But Neal wouldn't dance with her, and while he was gone, Jack asked her to dance.

Beneath Jack's tenderness Carolyn felt the great tension of his need for her, and she was frightened by her response. He whispered in her ear, "It's too bad . . . Neal saw you first."

But there was no time for Jack to dwell on lost chances. Temko, the Whites, and the Burfords were taking a jaunt to Central City for the opera festival, where Bob had been offered the use of a large abandoned Victorian house. In the nineteenth century, Central City had been one of the richest silver mining towns in the country, and had even built its own opera house, which had recently been refurbished. Bob's old house was in such bad shape that, even with the help of numerous chorus boys and girls, it took a whole day's work to make livable. This sort of expedition into American history was right up Jack's alley.

Talking like a character in Hemingway, sneering at the phony "bastards" who came to spoil every historic place and artistic occasion, Jack spoofed Temko's cynicism as well as the fools who produced it.

Then Jack dashed off to be a guest at the afternoon performance of *Fidelio*, with Beverly on his arm. As the baritone rose from the dungeon crying, "What gloom!" Jack felt like crying too, so overwhelmed was he by the power of Beethoven's art, which had caught up to the exact present feeling in his life. But, as always, Jack's gloom was really joy felt too intensely, for he was always too easily submerged in the depth of his own emotion. Later, when Justin Brierly wanted to introduce him to the cast, he ducked away before getting tied down with formality.

Jack was learning to improvise his life much as he had learned to improvise literature. He, Bob, and Ed rushed over to the opera stars' apartment to get cleaned up, using the stars' electric shavers and fancy colognes and singing in the shower so the neighbors would think they were stars too. Next they hit some of the old saloons, and Jack drank beer to get higher than he already was from the two-mile altitude. The player pianos were fixed to play various arias. Members of the chorus came in and started singing. Jack talked a blue streak about the great writer he was going to become. While Bob admired Jack's drive, he also began to worry a little about him, as though with his literary monomania Jack were building a powerful trap that might someday cripple him or limit his chances for happiness.

Later there was an all-night party. Gambling was legal in Central City during the opera season, and Bob arranged for a casino to be set up in the house. Between forays to the bars, they played roulette and craps by candlelight, sang, danced, and drank. In one bar Jack met Brierly, who wanted to introduce him to a famous tenor. Just as Jack was about to flee, Bob punched an Argentinian tourist, and they and Ed escaped together. Later Temko joined them as they returned to the same bar, where Bob proceeded to throw a highball in the tenor's face. Again they fled, and this time ended up in a bar where the local miners were just arriving for breakfast. These workmen had no use for a bunch of drunken punks and asked them to leave. In protest, Bob and Jack shoved a few chairs around, but they avoided starting a fistfight and left.

The next day they returned to Denver, and Jack was sorry to learn that he had missed seeing Neal and Allen in Central City the previous night. To Bob it was ridiculous that Jack should be so concerned about Neal; it seemed Jack was trying to make himself a colorful character in Neal's image and that because Jack wasn't as naturally aggressive and flamboyant, he was always straining to fit the part. Jack was still an onlooker with Neal too, and seeing how Neal had turned Carolyn's head had put him in even greater awe of his prowess with women. Burford and his friends were much less impressed with Neal as a lady's man simply because of their difference in class; they weren't about to envy a man who seemed to belong in a penny arcade, and whose mistresses were—in their eyes— "gangbangs" or unpaid whores.

Before saying good-bye to Ed White's group, Jack had further discussions with Temko about Hemingway, and they wished each other luck. Temko showed them all a story he had written about a man from New York, like himself, who came to Denver and stayed at the Brown Palace Hotel. At the end of the story, looking out from his window at the sun setting over the mountains, he realized that the sun didn't really set in Denver, that he had to go on, farther west to California. Burford thought the story awful, and for the first time realized Jack might actually have a chance; although Temko and Jack both talked brilliantly, Jack had come much closer to getting his wit on paper. At the time, Jack spared Temko his literary criticism, but years later, still remembering the inadvertent humor of Temko's ending, Jack slipped a parody of it into *On the Road.*

With the quip "Our revels now are ended," Jack left Ed's and headed out to find Neal and Allen, who were nowhere around. For a couple of days he wandered the Larimer Street area hunting for Neal's lost father, and at last found Allen and Neal and got to know Neal's friends a little. They were brawny, six-foot-six Al Hinkle, who followed Neal around like a puppy, Jimmy Holmes, a shy, stooped pool hustler, and handsome, athletic Bill Tomson, Neal's rival as leader—though Bill could never match Neal's mad freedom, the total letting-go that made him so thrillingly unpredictable.

4.

After wiring his mother for $50, Jack bought a bus ticket to San Francisco. He phoned Neal, who said he and Allen might join Jack out there, but when the bus left, the only friend present to wave good-bye was Ed White.

Bob and Ed had described the spectacular sight of the Great Divide at Steamboat Springs, but on the bus Jack crossed it in Creston, Wyoming, at midnight and saw almost nothing. At dawn he eagerly scrutinized Salt Lake City, Neal's birthplace, but saw nothing there as remarkable as Neal. Coming down from the Sierra Nevada into the warm, coastal air of California, he felt anew his romance with the West, and just before dawn he glimpsed the lights of San Francisco across the bay. But then from sheer exhaustion he fell asleep and didn't awake until the bus jounced into the station at Market and Fourth Streets. In the foggy dawn he wandered the streets outside the station, crazy with love for this magical city on the tip of the American frontier. Now all he had read by and about Jack London was as real as the pavement under his feet.

It was August 10, 1947, and he was two weeks late for his scheduled meeting with Henri Cru. He hurried across the Golden Gate

Bridge to Marin City, only to find that their jobs on the merchant ship had never materialized. Instead, Cru was working as a security guard in a barracks for overseas construction workers. He was living in a shack with a beautiful woman, who was clearly using him for maintenance and good times. With a temperament much like that of the writer Céline, Cru derived an ironic merriment from human depravity—the worse things got, the more he laughed, and bit his lip at the same time. Jack's lack of a remunerative career and his compulsive wandering drew him ever closer to Cru, who had a heart to match Jack's and was just as sensitive to suffering. By this time they were like brothers in misery.

They were probably the happiest unhappy people in the world, though, since Cru had more schemes for reaching fame and fortune than Jack, and all of them nuttier. Jack simply planned to be another Thomas Wolfe, but Cru envisioned him as a glamorous Hollywood scriptwriter. Cru claimed he had a friend whose father was a famous director, so Jack spent his first six days in the shack writing a forty-thousand-word screenplay about New York. Jack wrote to Ed White that he had never worked so intensely, though later he thought the story "too sad," and Cru never succeeded in interesting the director in it. At the time, however, Jack imagined himself returning to Denver in a Buick convertible with a case of Scotch.

He and Henri still wanted to ship out, only now they were searching for an around-the-world passenger ship on which Jack could serve as yeoman. In the meantime Jack applied for a guard job with Cru's firm, Morrisson and Knudsen, and was surprised to be hired. Henri equipped him with a .32 automatic pistol. Having befriended so many criminals, Jack felt strange being a cop, but it seemed like a good way to make some money, much of which he could save by living cheaply at Cru's. Unless he went to sea, he planned to be back in New York by November.

On weekends he often went to San Francisco. One day he, Henri, and Henri's girl rowed out to an abandoned freighter anchored in the bay, where they had a picnic and the girl frolicked in the nude. Jack wanted her but she wanted money, and Henri wanted Jack to keep his hands off. By himself Jack walked all over the city, exploring the bars and looking for girls, but he only succeeded in attracting a few homosexuals, and was revolted by them. In an ugly mood, he joined a bunch of red-necks who were beating up some longhair.[96]

When Al Hinkle came to San Francisco, he and Jack went out to hear jazz. Listening to a "great unknown Tristano," Jack thought of Tom Livornese. The pianist played "Louise" with two or three fingers, doing intricate yet simple combinations without straying far from the melody, and Jack wished he could discuss the technique with Tom. He missed the sophistication of New York.

Neal and Allen were now living on Bill Burroughs' farm in New

Waverly, Texas. In the spring of 1946, Bill had been arrested for forging prescriptions. With a serious heroin habit, he was desperate; reluctantly he let Joan contact his psychiatrist, who contacted his parents. The judge let him off with a suspended sentence on the condition he return to them in St. Louis. They agreed to set him up again provided he stay away from New York. In the meantime several of Joan's friends had been arrested for theft—with the goods stored in her apartment—and she herself was arrested while in a benzedrine psychosis and confined in Bellevue. As soon as she was released, Bill took her and her daughter Julie down to Texas, and they bought a ninety-nine-acre farm in the bayou country just north of Houston, where Bill proceeded to raise marijuana. Though they were not legally married Joan began calling herself Mrs. Burroughs, and she soon gave birth to a son, whom they named William Burroughs, Jr. Bill's old Harvard friend, Kells Elvins, lived nearby, and when Bill needed more companionship, he sent bus fare to Herbert Huncke. With Neal and Allen there too, their ramshackle farmhouse hosted a new communal family.

Jack wrote to Allen that he longed to "make contact" with him and Neal, and Allen wrote back reassuring Jack that "the contact is there," that he could always depend on their friendship. Neal wrote Jack a few letters too, stating that he was Jack's "loving brother" and asking Jack to forgive his withdrawn condition: "Don't think . . . I'm not sincere with you or that I enjoy your sadness." He also explained (though not in detail) that Allen's sexual interest in him was putting a strain on them both. Burroughs planned to return to New York at the end of September to sell his marijuana, and Neal was to drive Bill's jeep. Jack wrote that he wanted to come along. With elaborate apologies Neal answered that, though Bill missed Jack too, there just wouldn't be room.

Jack also wrote Ed White, who was returning to Columbia, that he should stop in Michigan and see Edie. Jack wanted to know what she thought about his current activities, and what her own life was like now, but he admitted that Edie was a "stormy" enigma he would probably never comprehend, and that he was drawn to her against his will. It was Ed himself that he was most looking forward to seeing again. He told Ed, "I think we're trying to outdo each other in honesty." Jack felt Ed's father had been an "old American type" much like his own; that he and Ed both came from "honest American families," whose rapid extinction had been lamented by Leo Kerouac. Jack promised to be back in New York in time for the Penn-Columbia football game.

In late September, 1947, Jack quit his guard job. Before leaving San Francisco, he accompanied Henri and his girl to a dinner with Henri's stepfather and his new wife. Jack was supposed to help Henri make a good impression on his stepfather, a distinguished

European doctor, but instead Jack got drunk; and then to top things off Allan Temko appeared, drunken and unshaven, and insisted on joining them. Temko practiced his unsubtle satire on Henri's stepfather. Henri was furious. The next day Jack avoided him by climbing the surrounding hills. The following morning, while Henri and the girl were still asleep, Jack went to Oakland and hitched a ride south.

With only two rides he made Bakersfield, four hundred miles south, but as night set in the cars streaming toward Los Angeles ignored him. By midnight he was freezing, and walked to the bus station to buy a ticket to L.A. There he fell in love at first sight with a beautiful, tiny Mexican girl. When she showed up on his bus he sat across from her, started a conversation, moved to her seat, and stayed with her for a couple of weeks.

He had crossed a great divide in his own life. Until that point all his crazy deeds, even taking drugs, were things a Lowell boy might do—however much he'd be censured for them. But a white boy from Lowell didn't live with a brown-skinned Mexican. The girl's name was Bea Franco, and from the night they met they planned to hitchhike to New York—on Route 66—and make a home together, though Jack must have known that his plans would lead him away from her eventually.

Bea Franco introduced him to a beater world than he had known even on Times Square or Larimer Street in Denver, a world of absolute poverty where no one could be trusted and everyone had to be. That first night with Bea in Los Angeles he was terrified that she was a prostitute setting him up to be robbed by her pimp. She in turn thought *he* was a pimp. After sweet lovemaking they were more certain of each other's gentle intentions, but suspicions continued to trouble them. To Bea, Jack seemed like a college boy traveling the country for excitement—hardly a marriage prospect for a Mexican migrant worker. Jack learned she had been married and had a son, who was currently staying with relatives. Wary of the double responsibility she might place upon him, he took care not to let her discover just what assets, financial and otherwise, he had.

In a very ruthless way he was just having an experience. They strolled down South Main Street, stopped at hot-dog and chili joints, listened to bop in bars, tried and failed to get jobs at drive-ins and diners, and eventually went to the black part of town, where Bea retrieved some clothes from a friend. Later, after she borrowed $5 from her sister, she and Jack embarked on the improbable task of hitchhiking to New York. They spent several hours getting nowhere, and finally Jack rented another room for the night. The next day they took a bus back to Bakersfield, where Bea said they could get work picking grapes. Jack followed just to see what would become of her—for his own salvation was only as far away as the nearest Western

Union office, from which he could always wire his mother for money to get home.

Finding no jobs in Bakersfield, they got drunk and hitched to her hometown, Selma. They drank more with Bea's brother and his friend, who also had designs on her. Jack felt like a character in *Of Mice and Men*, but he was seeing people and places he could never have imagined. Outside town Jack rented a tent for himself, Bea, and her seven-year-old son. Picking cotton at three dollars per hundred pounds he was barely able to buy their daily food. At the end of a week he couldn't pay the rent, and they returned to Selma, where he wired his mother for $50 and then waited in hiding while Bea went to her parents' shack and, after an argument, was accepted back. That night she and Jack slept in a truck. The next day she arranged for him to stay in a neighbor's barn, while she picked grapes to support them. After one more night, Jack collected the money from his mother and hitched to Hollywood.

At Columbia Pictures he picked up his rejected movie script. His money bought him a bus ticket as far as Pittsburgh. Before leaving, he wandered Hollywood and made ten salami sandwiches to last the trip.

It was late October, and Jack studied the vagaries of the American continent as his bus swooped up through the Southwest to St. Louis. There, at midday, he walked along the Mississippi, watching the great logs of Montana roll down to the Gulf, past the rotting hulks of steamboats beached in mud. Back on the bus he began necking with a girl from Columbus, Ohio, who bought him some meals. They agreed to meet in New York. When Jack got off in Pittsburgh, his sandwiches were gone and he had a dime in his pocket.

In the rainy night he hitched to Harrisburg, Pennsylvania. As he walked the forested cliffs of the Susquehanna, he was accosted by a little old hobo with a weatherbeaten cardboard satchel, who insisted on leading him to the "bridge." The man jabbered endlessly about meals he had mooched at Red Cross offices and retirement homes. Claiming he was bound for Canada, he seemed to be going in circles around the entire Appalachian wilderness, and Jack's suspicion was confirmed when a driver picked Jack up and told him that the old man—"the Ghost of the Susquehanna" as Jack called him in later novels—had led him in exactly the wrong direction. After several months of wandering, Jack must have found the old man an ominous reminder of what *he* could easily become, were it not for the clean bed, good meals, and ordered life his mother held in wait.

The ride took him back to Harrisburg, where he slept in the railroad station until the station masters threw him out in the morning. His next hitch was with a salesman who believed in starvation diets, and who offered only bread-and-butter sandwiches though

Jack explained that he was actually starving. Still he was overjoyed to be carried all the way back to the city.

On Times Square he panhandled a quarter for transportation to Ozone Park. Seeing how thin he'd become, his mother stuffed him with food. That night he couldn't sleep thinking about the work ahead, the wild stories he had to tell. During the next seven months he wrote the last six hundred pages of *The Town and the City*.

While Jack was in California, Neal had driven Burroughs and Huncke to New York with their load of marijuana. Burroughs didn't stay long and Huncke soon got arrested. Neal stayed at Jack's home as long as he could, then headed for San Francisco to join Carolyn and missed Jack by two days. After suffering a romantic disappointment with Neal in Houston, Allen Ginsberg had hired onto a ship bound for Dakar, Senegal, but he would be back in New York in a couple of weeks. In the meantime the Chase-White-Livornese team was back at Columbia drawing new people into their intellectual vortex, and former Columbia students like Jack Fitzgerald were still part of the scene.

5.

Although Jack himself was soon drawn into the swirl of New York, he didn't lose touch with Neal. Neal was now living with Carolyn, and, at least in the beginning, felt he could be content with her alone (though he did worry about her middle-class Bennington background). In this new relaxed environment Neal was able to return to his writing, and he began recording daily thoughts as well as attempting "to recall all my past life." He believed that his unusual success was due to "having escaped the fixation on my need to write," so that he could put aside all his conceptions about what he should write and just start saying *something*. It seemed to him that the greater a writer's drive and intensity, the more his outlook tended to narrow, and he worried that Jack was suffering from such a block: "But really now, Jack, are you healthy?" Just as Jack often pretended to be rough and surly to hide his enormous sense of humor, Neal felt Jack had become overly mannered in his writing as a reaction to the mad talk he preferred.

For the next few months their letters were filled with a discussion of their writing problems. Despite his hard work in a gas station, Neal was leading a vigorous intellectual life, reading Joyce and Spengler and hearing Mann lecture on Nietzsche. Though early in their acquaintance Neal had acknowledged a difference in their personalities, he now dwelled on "the obvious similarity of our basic natures," which he saw in a "preoccupation with our ages" and a "mutual over-balanced, and semi-confused, method of logic." More and more Neal used the expression "blood brothers" to symbolize their special relationship. Contingent on that blood brotherhood was the assumption that Jack's creativity flowed in the same complex, obstreperous lines as Neal's; hence any method that worked for Neal would work for Jack. No longer merely seeking advice, Neal now proffered it freely to Jack. Moreover, as Neal explained, "most [advisors] are negative, but I'm positive." Almost offhandedly, in a letter dated January 7, 1948, he wrote words of great later impact:

> I have always held that when one writes one should forget all rules, literary style, and other such pretensions as large words, lordly clauses and other phrases as such, i.e.—rolling the words around in the mouth as one would wine and proper or not putting them down because they sound so good. Rather, I think, one should write, as nearly as possible, as if he were the first person on earth and was humbly and sincerely putting on paper that which he saw and experienced, loved and lost; what his passing thoughts were and his sorrows and desires; and these things should be said with careful avoidance of common phrases, trite usage of hackneyed words and the like. One must combine Wolfe and Flaubert—and Dickens.
>
> Art is good when it springs from necessity. This kind of origin is the guarantee of its value; there is no other.

Just at the point he and Jack had developed such a fine creative rapport, Neal's letters abruptly stopped, and didn't resume until six months later. Neal had hinted at the cause. LuAnne had come to San Francisco at the beginning of December, and after agreeing to get their marriage annulled, they were seeing each other regularly. At first Neal merely spoke of the "interesting problem" of "keeping Lu and Carolyn seperated [sic]." It was an exciting game: "I am with both of them at different hours of the same day, daily, I must be on my toes to keep Carolyn from knowing." In the last letter to Jack before his silence, Neal mentioned "the considerable tension both LuAnne and Carolyn are causing in me," which resulted in psychosomatic asthma and hives. But Jack still had no inkling of the demon LuAnne was soon to become to Neal. During the six-month silence, he assumed Neal was in prison.

After his return to New York, Jack spent much of his time buried in his room, writing. Only when he needed a break, after significant progress in the novel, did he come into Manhattan looking for his friends. They were impressed with his expanded horizons, with the cosmic view developed by his travels.

Often Jack talked of Goethe's *Faust* and the way Spengler had used Faust to typify "Western Man's" endless reaching into space.

To Jack, Spengler had found the essence of the western soul in Faust's craving for infinity. Jack had a wondering appreciation of technological achievements, but he had no interest in technical knowledge. Hal, who was very interested in science, found this paradox strange, and thought it even stranger that Jack's aversion to mechanics extended to the arts. For example, though Jack usually reacted strongly to paintings, he would never attempt to learn painterly techniques. His paradoxes were themselves endless. Despite his worldliness, he never thought in terms of changing the world, as Allen Ginsberg did. Hal felt that the root of most of those paradoxes was in Jack's small-town background, and that it was this fidelity to his heritage that made him original as an artist. Although Jack was a classicist in the sense that he had respectfully absorbed earlier literary traditions, he was also belligerently anti-intellectual. Long before it was fashionable, he spoke of baseball and football as fit subjects for literature, revealing an innocence that Hal, for one, found refreshing.

When it came to dealing with people and seeking their love, however, that innocence left him vulnerable. Money and fame seemed closer to him than ever before, but he told Hal that he didn't want a woman to love him for his money or for anything he did, he wanted to be loved for himself. Hal felt he was perhaps a bit too proud in his assertion that he didn't need to earn anyone's love.

Once, while Hal and his girlfriend Ginger were visiting in Ozone Park, Ginger left a nude picture of herself in Jack's dresser. Jack was more than sexually provoked, he was profoundly disturbed that his friend's lover could break several codes of honor at once. Jack wasn't an easy man for women to entice, but Ginger knew that by upsetting him she could count on his coming to her, if only to find out how she could do such a thing. Hal was busy with his graduate work much of the time, and she sought a flirtation with Jack for diversion, and perhaps to make Hal jealous. Her trick worked. Jack went up to her room several times while Hal was away. When their affair broke up, Jack was hurt, but during the next year, as he and Hal drifted apart, Jack began to blame himself for "seducing" Ginger. He felt he had "criticized" Hal by taking his woman, and had intentionally "shriveled" Hal's "soul." Although Neal comforted Jack that Hal's pride probably needed shrinking, the eventual loss of Hal's friendship became for Jack one of the most "horrifying" experiences of 1948.[97]

Ginger was just one of Jack's numerous false starts. Ed White felt that Jack was handicapped by his Catholic and French-Canadian attitudes: Jack would sometimes say that women were either like the Virgin Mary—pure, self-sacrificing like his mother, to be adored but not touched—or they were whores. But there was also a deep warmth and physical need in him that reached out to women, setting up a countercurrent to his misogyny. Sensing his confusion, women found it easy to "work" him, and many did.

There were also practical matters making romance difficult for Jack. He had almost no spending money, he liked to write at night and sleep during the day, his schedule was too erratic for any woman to depend on him. Even when he was with a woman, he would often withdraw into periods of silence, and act as if he didn't know what was happening. Close friends like Ed White understood that Jack was really listening to everybody and remembering everything. Sometimes, to make his observation less conspicuous, he would put his head down and let his eyelids droop, as though he were sinking into a drunken stupor. Such behavior wasn't calculated to win a woman's heart. Then, too, he believed conversations with women were less serious than those with men, and there were many times when a woman got angry because he simply wasn't paying attention to what she said.

Still, many women fell in love with Jack, not only for his good looks but for the compassion that underlay his eccentric mien. Women who had suffered a great deal were most apt to realize that sympathy and to love him for it. Vicki Russell from Grosse Pointe had big pictures of three men on her wall, captioned respectively: "The Head," "The Hand," and "The Heart." Pianist George Handy was The Hand; Charlie Parker was The Head; Jack was The Heart. In the picture Jack was wearing his merchant marine uniform, and Ginsberg said he looked romantic. When Jack repeated the remark someone else said, "No, you just look bewildered." Because he spent so much time just sitting and listening, rarely talking, many people thought him unintelligent, and he was frequently treated like a fool.

One of the things that genuinely bewildered Jack was his relationship with the Catholic Church. Many of the people around him saw postwar life as absurd and reacted against that absurdity by trying to create their own meaningful, individualistic lifestyles. Someone like Burroughs was closer to being a practicing existentialist than Jack, who was never easy operating without a sense of moral purpose. But Jack had read enough precursors of existentialism like Kafka and Céline to appreciate its power as a literary movement, and eventually his literary enthusiasm began effecting changes in his attitudes toward life. With Ed and Hal, he had long discussions about whether or not he should leave the Church, seeing that as one of his major problems. Since Hal had never had such a problem, he and Jack were drawn closer by mutual curiosity. Jack told them about Father Spike, the wisecracking freethinking priest from Lowell, and talked of writing a story about him.

Spike's detachment was something Jack admired greatly but could never manage himself. The second half of *The Town and the City* dealt with the prostitutes, drug users, and assorted criminals of

206 · M E M O R Y B A B E

Times Square, and already Jack felt guilty about the embarrassment
it would cause his mother and sister to read such stories under his
name. Striving harder than ever to be a dutiful son, he accompanied
his mother to North Carolina at Christmastime, 1947, so they could
celebrate the holidays with his sister and brother-in-law. He returned to New York in time for a New Year's Eve party with Ed
White.

Although Jack was still groping for the proper path, 1948 was the
year the direction signs were finally in a language he could read.
Previously his alienated intellectual friends had comprised a small
group. But in 1948 so many young people were "hip" to the folly of
ordinary law-abiding submission that a new word came into general
usage: *hipster.*

Amid this deluge of hipsters nobody could decide exactly what a
hipster was, and the term inspired a controversy that only died down
a decade later, when it was eclipsed by the problem of defining
"beats" or "beatniks." In Norman Mailer's 1957 essay, "The White
Negro," he painted the hipster as a heroic criminal who lived violently rather than conform because, in a totalitarian society, violence
was the only avenue of self-expression. Like the black, the hipster
knew he couldn't trust society to choose what was good for him, so
he had to determine goodness for himself through his own feelings.
Mailer's hipster lived only in the present and—in the shadow of an
atomic apocalypse—preferred to act rather than waste time thinking
about right and wrong.

Kerouac objected very strongly to this emphasis on the hipster's
psychopathic and murderous instincts, on his delinquent, selfish, and
self-destructive conduct. "Hip," wrote Mailer, "is the affirmation of
the barbarian." Hip to Jack was the quintessence of holy, the furthest refinement in a civilized understanding of life. It meant showing the utmost kindness and consideration to one's fellow sufferers in
a world becoming progressively more flawed. Mailer might see a
hustler and thief like Huncke as someone who escaped complicity in
great social crimes like war and genocide by immersing himself in
his own private crimes born of honest passion and need. Jack, on the
other hand, found Huncke honorable because Huncke had learned
the truth of universal suffering and actually lived his belief in the
brotherhood of man.

As early as 1948 this sort of ideological split had divided hipsters
into "cool" and "hot." The cool hipster talked and moved as little as
possible, conserving energy for the few kicks he managed to find.
The hot hipster found kicks everywhere and expended energy as
though he had the resources of the sun. Distinctly a hot hipster, Jack
rushed from pad to pad to "make it" with everybody, from bar to
bar to keep his vitality flowing, and from jazz joint to jazz joint to
scream with the most "wild bawling jazz," like that of Willis Jackson, Lucky Thompson, and Chubby Jackson.[98]

The hipsters were so sharp they could spot each other on the street, and Jack often walked the streets in a group, making new friends along the way. Bop joints were the hipster's hometown. In the fall of 1947, Charlie Parker had returned to New York from California, where he'd gone crazy on drugs and spent several months "relaxin' at Camarillo" [99] State Hospital. Fully recuperated, Bird was now hitting his stride, blowing choruses with such speed and deftness that professional musicians gasped and audiences "flipped." The Royal Roost, a chicken shack on Broadway, was turned into a jazz club, and the disc jockey "Symphony Sid" Torin broadcast live from there, as well as from other famous clubs like Bop City and Birdland. Whether alone working or with friends, Jack was almost always tuned in to Sid's all-night show. Birdland had been named for Parker and, like the Roost, frequently hosted the new Charlie Parker Quintet—a gathering of five superlative musicians, including Miles Davis, whose technical brilliance had cáptivated Jack years before, when Davis had been an unknown trumpeter sitting in on sessions in the Village.

By now Bird was certainly Jack's favorite jazzman. Like a brother to Jack in temperament, Bird could in the space of a day go from sullen broodings to drunken gaiety or the giddiness of a junk high—from withdrawn silence to the heights of lyrical communication on his horn. Bird made enemies as fast as he made friends, he was notoriously undependable and as liable to be fired as to get a raise, but almost everybody who met him remembered him with undying love—and awe at the shooting star they'd been privileged to glimpse. One of the highlights of 1948 for Jack was seeing him strolling down Eighth Avenue with Babs Gonzales and a beautiful girl— the greatest jazz musician of the day, digging life with the openness of a child, or of Jack himself.

With Ed and Tom, Jack went to 52nd Street to hear the many small groups recently come from Chicago. Lee Konitz and Al Cohn were two of his new favorite saxophonists, and he "discovered" vocalists Mel Tormé and Sarah Vaughan. At Ben Jonson's, an after-hours place in Harlem, the music was only on a jukebox, but Jack liked the atmosphere and enjoyed talking with the musicians who dropped in. He and Tom pursued musicians throughout the city, and they even got invited into Mel Tormé's apartment in the Hotel Sutton. Tormé seemed interested in their talk and in the writings they showed him.

At Columbia Tom was taking a course in twentieth-century music under the famous professor and short-story writer Douglas Moore. Once, when Ed and Jack wanted to go out, Tom complained that he had a paper to write. Asking what Tom wanted to say, Jack sat at the typewriter and pounded out a paper in fifteen minutes, a case for the historical significance of bop. Moore gave the paper a D. Undaunted, Jack and Tom developed their arguments further and resubmitted the paper, which then received a B. Picking up the gauntlet again, they gave the paper a final working-over and got an A.

Jack's spontaneous writing amazed Ed and Tom because it was something no serious writer at that time would try. Many people scorned Jack for the method, as though it showed his lack of skill, but Ed and Tom realized its challenge as an experiment. Anxious to try all literary forms, Jack even wrote the lyric for a tune Tom composed, and whenever Tom visited him at home, he would bring out stacks of manuscripts and read them aloud. There were rolls of paper he had filled with writing, and he talked about plans to try using toilet paper. For a writer of twenty-six Jack's output was vast.

He explained how stories and novelettes would keep springing from his major works. If he had an idea to go off in a particular direction he went that way, even if the result had little relation to the original. He showed Ed and Tom a story called "Orpheus Emerged," the end product of about fourteen successive spinoffs, each one a story in its own right. It was important for him to explore every possible direction in which the major work could go before he decided which way it *should* go. Such an approach allowed him to create a balanced structure in the big work, but it required enormous amounts of time and concentration, even from a speed typist like himself. Hence it was necessary for him to spend most of his work sessions actually writing or making notes. He could afford little time for introspection, although he often examined his subjects intellectually in the journals he kept during the writing of every novel. Such was the breadth of Jack's vision that his preponderant task was to lay it down step by step, foot by foot; he could get to the refinements later. Gabrielle was forever telling Tom: "How hard my Jackie works! He's here for hours and he works and he types and he types and he works!"

But he still found time to help his friends. When Ed had to cancel out of taking Tom's younger sister Maria to a high-school dance, Jack agreed to take his place. The suit Ed lent him didn't fit, and as usual Jack couldn't get his tie knotted properly. It was impossible to get Jack to look right in anything except a lumberjack shirt and blue jeans, but Ed was one of the few who didn't patronize him for his provincialism—in fact, Ed saw those quirks as part of the complexity of Jack's character. Tom, however, flew into a rage when Jack arrived dusty and bedraggled just before the dance. Even the flowers he had brought for Maria were wilted. After Jack confessed that he had walked the entire eleven miles from Ozone Park to Tom's house in Queens, Tom hollered that he could have picked him up in his car. Still calm, Jack explained that this was the first chance he had had in four years "to walk the Sunrise"—meaning the Sunrise Highway.

He had so much fun with Maria that he double-dated with her and Tom a few more times. But he was already far beyond her high-school world, and there were obstacles in his own nature to deepening the attachment. Among the many chivalric codes he lived by was one that said you mustn't hurt your friend's sister. By now it was clear to Tom that Jack was "too heavy, too serious, too drunk, too involved with his own life, to ever be able to carry on a relationship other than the most casual with a woman." And yet Jack's peculiar tragedy was that he didn't want a light, expedient relationship, he wanted emotional involvement, or at least something shared, before sex. Because such commitment would interfere with more important goals, he often avoided women altogether. Besides, in his mother he already had an almost perfect camp follower. Although she couldn't satisfy his sexual needs, she supported him economically and emotionally while demanding nothing—at least openly—in return.

6.

Jack began making trips back to Lowell, and the only friend he took with him was Hal Chase. Denver had reminded Jack so much of Lowell that Jack assumed Hal would understand his love for his hometown. He introduced Hal to his boyhood friends, and they had a good time talking sports together. When Jack and his friends tried to sing like Sinatra and act like Italian gangsters, Hal laughed sympathetically. He was repelled, though, when they seriously discussed living in Hollywood, having been fed notions of glamor from Charlie Sampas' celebrity gossip column in the Lowell *Sun*. In vain Hal tried to tell them that life there would be as horribly superficial as in Las Vegas.

Jack also brought Hal to meet Mike Fournier, now a farmer with five children. Although Jack thought Mike "the simplest, best guy in the world," Hal complained privately that Mike "could be a little more sensitive." Jack retorted angrily that *sensitive* was a "fancy campus word," and that such a discrimination was as irrelevant now as when he and Mike were eleven-year-old pals.[100]

Though conscious in his own way of Lowell's limitations, Jack at least stood on sure ground there. Back in New York he watched with some awe, but mostly Canuck skepticism, as Allen Ginsberg metamorphosed into a visionary poet and literary prophet. Allen had returned from Africa too late to register for the fall session at Columbia, but he quickly renewed old friendships there, displaying a mysterious self-possession—like a man who, having been to the ends of the earth and accepted every humiliation, was ready for something really new.

Late in 1947 Allen had begun having visions, though Jack thought he was merely "flipping." The visions culminated in May of 1948, when Allen was living in Harlem. Lying in his room, after reading Blake and masturbating, he heard Blake's voice reciting the poem, "Ah Sun-Flower." Three similar visions occurred during the next few weeks. At this time Allen was also posing as Dostoyevsky's "underground man" and inciting "confrontations" among his many disparate friends. He "wanted to live in a big tragedy-comedy Dostoyevskian universe . . . where everybody was involved in seeking God and all the heroes were holy idiots." Naturally Jack imagined Allen might be reporting visions to stir a mystical sensibility in everyone else.

He also felt Allen might be using visions to disguise simple sexual longings, and he referred to Allen's furtive lusting as "obnoxious." To counter such puritanism in Jack, Allen wrote him, "If you want to know my true nature, I am at the moment one of those people who goes around showing his cock to juvenile delinquents." Piquing Jack further, Allen declared that his latest vision was just "rubbish, just a big fantasy . . . I really knew it while I was telling you, though I only realized it fully later. . . . If you think that's my major virtue, a vision, o no." And yet, to keep Jack off balance, Allen insisted that the vision "had elements of nature in it." [101]

In 1948 Allen returned to Columbia to finish work on his B.A. Inspired by his visions, he was also writing a great deal of poetry. He added "Dakar Doldrums" to his *Book of Doldrums*, and began working on several long, complex poems exploring his own "madness." Also, asked to contribute to a chain novel written by some homosexual friends, he returned to the novel he had started years before about his early experiences at Columbia. Although his father objected to the barbarous characters, Allen refused to portray life dishonestly, and he accused his father of evading a true esthetic judgment of the work.[102] Obviously Jack and Burroughs had had a strong influence in directing Allen toward a greater realism.

The literary relationship between Jack and Allen at this period greatly affected the works of both writers for years to come. So much sharing of ideas and imagery took place between them that later they were often unable to remember just who had first conceived of a certain subject or phrase. Jack claimed he had dreamed of a Shrouded Stranger pursuing him across the desert, but Allen may have been the first to actually use the phrase "Shrouded Stranger." [103] *The Town and the City* and Allen's poetry of the late forties are both woven with motifs like light in darkness, rainy nights, rivers, stars, and ghosts. Words like *light, dark, night, star, vision, dream, angel, haunted, mad, sad, gone,* etc., are repeated by both authors until they take on the power of litany. In fact, by mid-1948 Allen and Jack had arrived at an identical literary goal, which Allen

expressed as "an exhaustive, massive vision of life (american, wherever I am)." It was one of the rare occasions in literature where two
authors drew freely on each other's imagination, each confident that
the other's originality would preclude plagiarism.

Allen and Jack were rapidly gaining respect for each other's
work. At a time when Ginsberg was considered just another academic poet, Jack was touting Allen's genius to everyone he met. For
a long time Allen had simply imagined *The Town and the City* to be
another book of poetic impressions like *The Sea Is My Brother*. But
early in 1948 Jack let him read the nearly finished manuscript, and
Allen was overwhelmed by the power and scope of it. *The Town and
the City* seemed the purest combination of poetry and prose he had
ever read. The long sentences were full of symphonic repetitions and
balances, and Kerouac was playing with vowel sounds like a musician joyfully inventing chords. The novel was also a great American
Bildungsroman—indeed Jack acknowledged the influence of Wolfe,
Proust, and Mann—but it also synthesized ideas from writers as divergent as Céline, Gide, Sherwood Anderson, and Thoreau. Jack
explained that he had separated different aspects of his own personality into several main characters. What impressed Allen most
was the ripeness of Kerouac's world-view: the articulation of space
and time consciousness, the themes of loneliness, loss, and death.

When Allen finished reading *The Town and the City* he actually
cried, and then wrote a sonnet. Determined to help Jack get it published, he began carrying partial copies of it around the city, sometimes virtually forcing people to read it. Allen had taken his own
Book of Doldrums to Mark Van Doren at Columbia. At the end of
April, 1948, as *The Town and the City* neared completion at 380,000
words, Allen suggested Jack show it to Van Doren too, since his
recommendation could help overcome publishers' fears of bringing
out such a big book by an unknown author. Jack had talked to Van
Doren about *The Town and the City* when he was just beginning it.
He agreed to submit the manuscript to him now because Van Doren
was the only professor at Columbia who had spoken to him with
humility. Jack told Allen that what he wanted most was paternal
approval. Van Doren, being a "moral man . . . my kind of favorite
man," was the sort of replacement father Jack needed badly.

Allen had become his replacement brother. Besides helping Jack
in the roles of literary critic and agent, he did an even more important service by breaking open many of Jack's remaining provincial
attitudes. Allen had developed the concept of "bringing the monster
to your door." He would act out whatever character was most frightening or repugnant to the person he was with. Since one of Jack's
bugbears was homosexuality, Allen would inform him of all the supposedly straight men he had gone to bed with. Allen also enjoyed
mocking Jack's sacred cows. Signing one letter "Sebastian," Allen

told Jack he would meet him "carrying a volume of Saroyan in my hair." [105]

Jack also feared madness, and it was Allen who forced him to see that what seemed unreal was "the only thing, the inevitable—the *one*. There is no evasion of it. . . ." In some sense Jack's writing of *The Town and the City* was an attempt to return to an old-fashioned, pre-World-War-II sanity that acknowledged boundaries and limitations, while Allen with his pursuit of hallucinations wanted to break through all conventions, to plunge into pure experience. When Jack tended to withdraw from the daring experiments of the past few years, Allen beckoned him back into the unknown stretches of mind that Jack had glimpsed through madness and the use of drugs. To arrive at new knowledge, Allen realized, they would have to "destroy their present lives"; but Jack was still far less willing than he to hasten the apocalypse.

At times communication between them was strained, but it never failed critically. After writing Jack a refined, placid letter inviting him to the Seder at the Ginsberg household, Allen met him in the subway and asked Jack to beat him up! Jack patiently rebuked him. Later Allen apologized, admitting he sometimes tried to make a "superior virtue of individuality" out of his sickness.

For months neither Allen nor Jack had heard from Neal. Jack was planning to go to Denver in June and hoped to see him, if he wasn't in jail. In April Allen got a letter from Neal revealing that he had married Carolyn in San Francisco on April 1. To get his marriage with LuAnne annulled he'd had to make two separate trips to Denver, which he did both times in two days flat. On the first trip he'd nearly frozen to death when his car broke down on Donner Pass. Later it came out that Neal had been living erratically for several months and had even attempted suicide. After learning that Carolyn was pregnant, he had continued to vacillate between her and LuAnne, and was having sexual relations with numerous other women besides. Under the stress of trying to satisfy all of them, he had developed into a borderline psychotic. Nevertheless, after marrying Carolyn, Neal settled into something like a domestic routine and began working steadily on the railroad. Jack and Allen were happy for him, if a little disappointed that they could no longer include him in plans to careen around the country.

In early spring Bill Burroughs visited New York, and during his brief stay he, Jack, and Allen "rushed and roared" around town. After Burroughs left, Jack and Allen focused their human studies on several other mad characters. Huncke was back on the scene, stealing anything he could get his hands on to support his drug habit, and simultaneously keeping a journal to record his states of mind. But when Huncke moved in with a young thief and his girl, he asked Allen to stop bothering him. To allay his loneliness, Allen began haunting homosexual bars in the Village, on Times Square, and 72nd Street. He also frequented the Pokerino, the Times Square penny arcade about which he wrote the story "A Version of the Apocalypse," and which Jack described in *The Town and the City* as the "Nickle-O."

Allen and Jack had both been spending a lot of time with a group of Columbia intellectuals, who all lived in a tenement at 45th Street and 10th Avenue. The first one to move into the building was Gene Pippin: those who joined him were almost all English majors setting out to be teachers and poets, with the exception of John Hohnsbeen, an art student. Occupying five or six apartments, the Columbia group comprised Pippin and his wife Mary, Hohnsbeen, Billy Lieberman, Russell Durgin, Leo Natanson and his wife Phoebe, and a few others like Ginsberg and Bill Frankel who visited there often. All between twenty-one and twenty-five, they were extremely bright and deeply concerned with cultural history.

All of them had great respect for Allen's literary judgment, which was conventionally avant-garde. Yvor Winters and William Carlos Williams were two of the group's literary masters; though Allen hadn't yet read Winters, he had already made the acquaintance of Williams, who lived in Rutherford, New Jersey, near his hometown. Guided by Williams' dictum that "the life is in the details," Allen would eventually ride out the end of the New Criticism and begin training himself to write with a precise eye and ear. Since he had already read a great deal of modern poetry, and had spent years sorting out his thoughts about literature, he commanded attention when he spoke professionally. On Allen's word the others in the Columbia group accepted Jack as a promising writer, even though they saw almost none of the virtues Allen ascribed to *The Town and the City*. But the mere fact that Jack had written a thousand-page novel was respected as an important achievement.

Everyone had great personal affection for Allen, who was waiflike and always searching so hard. Jack, on the other hand, stood out for his health, sanity, and vigor; the Columbia people were drawn to him just because a football player was such a curious being in their midst. Later he impressed them with his broad reading and his ability to converse about art, although in areas like opera and painting he did a lot more listening than talking. It was clear to everyone that Jack wanted an education, and his enthusiasm and openness were much respected.

A practicing poet, Pippin became quite close to Jack, and both he and Allen helped initiate Jack into the complexities of modern poetry. Pippin also introduced Jack to various people in the arts he probably wouldn't have met otherwise, like Jacob Bean, who would later become curator of prints and drawings at the Metropolitan Museum. Bean had gone to Harvard and belonged to an intellectual group that included Howard Moss, a poet and editor at *The New Yorker*. This latter group had strong ties to still another social circle, which revolved around a young Harvard Law School graduate named Bill Cannastra. Pippin himself was related to Cannastra in the sense that Pippin's wife Mary was the sister of Cannastra's lover "Bruce Shotwell." ° Since Cannastra was continually throwing huge all-night parties, it was inevitable he and Jack would meet.

7.

On the surface Jack and Bill were quite different. About the only trait they seemed to share, besides a high IQ, was an exceptional physical beauty. But Jack was shy and awkward, Bill outgoing and extremely graceful. Jack looked to the future, Bill sought oblivion. While Jack struggled to build his career, Bill willfully threw his down the drain.

Cannastra's wealthy aristocratic mother had brought her machinist husband over from Italy. She had great expectations for her two sons but couldn't bear her own frustrated ambition, and so attempted (and failed) to commit suicide by swallowing lye. The pattern of near-suicide was set for her younger son, Bill, who kept brushing against death until it finally snagged him. He seized any opportunity to put himself in danger. His special delight was dodging nimbly through traffic, and many times he actually got knocked down. One night in the middle of a rainstorm he dove into a lake and refused to answer his friends' calls, pretending he had drowned. At his parties he initiated a variety of grisly death games, such as walking barefoot across broken glass or seeing who could keep his head the longest in an unlit turned-on gas oven. Combined with his extraordinary charm and substantial intellectual gifts, Bill's self-destructiveness made him all the more alluring. People always wanted to save him. The more love they showered on him, the more cruelty he returned. Sometimes it was aimed at others, like his attempt to set fire to a friend who had passed out, but more often directed toward himself.

Raised in Schenectady, New York, Cannastra had been overwhelmed by the affluence and elegance of Harvard. His shock had been greater than Jack's at Horace Mann, for whereas Jack merely visited among the rich, Cannastra was immediately accepted into chichi circles for which he had little training and too much inclination. He quickly made friends with W. H. Auden, and through Au-

° In this and two other instances the quotation marks indicate the use of a pseudonym in order to protect the privacy of the person involved.

den met the many glamorous European writers then congregated at Harvard. The irony was that Bill's brilliance and charm carried him to success in endeavors where he would have preferred to fail. Drunk and totally unprepared, he passed his bar examination. Yet in his heart he wanted to be an artist, not a lawyer. To please his parents he began practicing law in New York, but after repeatedly showing up for work late and often drunk, he was fired. He had a brief stint at Random House, serving as an advisor in the compilation of their new dictionary, and he was immensely proud when one of his definitions was included in the final product. Mainly, however, he just turned to cultivating his love of opera and painting. He also made a few feeble attempts to write, which he wanted badly to do, but for which he could never manage sufficient concentration.

Jack and Bill took an immediate, powerful liking to each other. Like Jack, Bill seemed "different" from most people. Both of them lacked any sort of hostility or pettiness. Although Bill was far more capable of violence than Jack, Jack felt Bill was the victim of his own tender heart, and so, curiously, like his lost brother, Gerard.

The parties Bill gave in his loft at 125 W. 21st Street were attended by artists and intellectuals from all over the city. Many of these people, like Frankel, Durgin, and the young writers Ed Stringham and Alan Harrington, knew Jack from Columbia circles so that he had a ready-made place in Cannastra's group. Some of Bill's close friends, though, found Jack a little too self-important. Bill's lover Lucia Vernarelli was disturbed by the worship being tendered Jack, and she was disgusted by the way he would sometimes speak as if he were casting pearls to swine. Doubtless Jack wouldn't have been so warmly welcomed in the group had it not been for the great affection and respect Bill felt for him.

Although Bill's friends generally surpassed him in every way except perhaps looks, he was indisputably their leader. Most of his guests were more talented, either painted, played, sang, or wrote better; most were more sensitive, and almost all had more money. But none had the power to fascinate an audience instantly and at will as Cannastra could. At his parties there always came a point— the point everyone waited for—when he would pull off some unimaginably reckless feat, when he would either scare his guests witless or flabbergast them by trespassing some sacred boundary. In fact, one of the most striking things about Bill was that he acknowledged no boundaries at all.

He was definitely a voyeur. He had peepholes in his bathroom, and he liked to climb over roofs, slide down drainpipes, etc., just to get a peek into other people's dwellings. But a more subtle, almost philosophical voyeurism fueled his flamboyance. By acting outrageously he could pierce his friends' defenses, and by watching their reactions he could gauge their true characters. Cannastra was as much a student of human nature as Jack, and like Jack he would risk almost anything for a deeper insight.

Bill risked his life almost daily. His favorite stunts included climbing up the front of a building, walking around the upper ledges, and jumping over airshafts; despite his agility he came several times within a hair's breadth of falling. Yet some grace seemed to uphold him, just as it always protected him from the people he angered with his social breaches. One night at a "jungle party" (his parties all had themes) Bill dressed as a palm tree, wearing only a jock strap and an enormous headdress. Later in the evening his girlfriend Lucia went down to a nearby bar with Ed Stringham. Lucia was facing the door when her mouth suddenly dropped open, and Stringham turned to see Cannastra entering the bar in his tree costume. Ed and Lucia expected the local bullies to tear Bill apart, but somehow everyone was so dumbfounded by the simple way he came looking for his friends that no one touched him.

When Jack and Bill first became friends Jack was still very raw, still wide open to the possibilities of life, and Bill was far more self-controlled than he would be a couple of years later. The Cannastra of 1948 was not the frantic, explosive man of 1950, who drank himself beyond all human feeling so that he could once and for all put paid to his humanity. The Bill to whom Jack responded so warmly was someone high on life and always getting higher. For his part, Bill found Jack one of the few people who would follow him to any extreme of terror or ecstasy. Whereas Bill might shock or amaze the others, he actually involved Jack. One night, for example, at that "special moment," Bill announced that he was going to run around the block naked, and Jack offered to join him. Since it was totally black outside, those who watched from the windows couldn't tell if the two were really naked. In fact, Jack later admitted he'd kept his shorts on. But what impressed the onlookers was that someone of Jack's dignity would attempt to match Cannastra's madness. There were always a few clowns who joined Cannastra for laughs. One in particular, a law student named "Bob Stern," mimicked Cannastra in everything, even his stupendous drinking. All Stern lacked was Cannastra's taste and discrimination and charisma, but because he lacked them he was of no importance to most of the people in the group. By contrast, almost everyone there cared about Jack, and they worried that he so readily accepted Cannastra's challenges.

Jack knew what he was doing. He always had a nose for potential teachers, and Cannastra had already served up a veritable banquet of food for thought. To begin with, there was always music playing in Cannastra's loft. Bill had memorized the librettos of numerous operas in several foreign languages and often sang along to the records. He also had a huge collection of traditional jazz and blues records. Just as with opera, his guests listened intently and spent hours analyzing every aspect of the music. Cannastra and his friends, including Jack, often attended traditional jazz concerts at Stuyvesant Hall and other spots on the East Side. The music of older jazz musicians like Bunk Johnson and George Lewis had been overlooked for many years after their early "race records," sold primarily in black communities. But now, for the first time, these artists were performing in New York for white connoisseurs and sophisticates who would never have heard them in backwoods Louisiana or Mississippi. That kind of cultural shock was something Cannastra had spent his life promoting, so it was no wonder he loved it.

John Hammond had organized these concerts to insure that many of America's older jazz musicians wouldn't die in anonymity. Though in their sixties or past, most had played only at dances. Seizing the chance to hear them in concert, the audiences listened religiously. Hipsters like Jack then carried that reverence for "traditional" jazz over to bop. More than ever before, he was listening hard to music as music, and learning the links between bop and earlier forms. What he loved about bop was its direct release from the musician's heart. "Traditional" jazz was more formal, although these concerts were all improvised in the sense that there were no written notes, and it was closely linked to blues, another kind of music Jack adored.

Performances of blues were rare in New York, but everyone in Cannastra's group bent an ear to his old race records, to hear in this music the roots of jazz. They listened to almost all forms of country music too, especially Bluegrass, which in New York was then called "plucking music" or "truckstop jukebox music." Jack shared their enthusiasm for it, and like the others he often danced to its driving rhythms. In one year they wore out twenty copies of "The Beatty Steel Blues," a straight instrumental, steel-guitar piece that later influenced rock-'n'-rollers like Elvis Presley. Although Bluegrass lacked the intricacy and revolutionary qualities of bop, it generated a fierce excitement just as bop did, and for that reason it was equally important to them. The folk singer Rambling Jack Elliot, a friend of Cannastra's, introduced the group to the classic Depression ballads of Woody Guthrie.

Jack was already writing a large amount of poetry. Ginsberg insisted that he and Jack together were exploring an aspect of poetic meter that had long been ignored: the natural flow of breath, as it is broken up by pauses between breaths. Undoubtedly Jack was getting educated in this area from the traditional blues singers, especially blues "shouters."

Jack's conception of poetry was also affected by the content of traditional blues. Blues singers memorialized in song every place they went and everything they did. In their world, you hadn't been anywhere, or done anything, unless you sang a blues about it. A prime example from that period was Lonnie Johnson's song, "From 20 to 44," a favorite of Ginsberg's.[106] Ages 20 and 44 marked the lower and upper limits of the new military draft, and Johnson's song began: "From 18 to 35 it didn't cross my mind/But now that they say 20 to 44/It looks like everybody's gotta go. . . ." Johnson was simply making music out of his response to the Selective Service Act. Another classic example is the "Kansas City Blues," a direct statement of the singer's reaction to that city: "Well I been to Kansas City/Girls and everything are really all right." If Jack's literary version of the blues was usually more reflective, his poems retained the occasional quality of those songs, born from the wish to celebrate even simple experiences by sharing them. Since the blues reported how someone felt at a particular moment, they could be happy as well as sad. For Jack, they served as the perfect vehicle to express— as the bop musician did in pure sound—his immediate, ongoing response to the world.

However stimulating Cannastra's passion for music, the most important thing about him—for Jack—was the enormous variety of people he knew. Many of the people Jack met through him became lifelong friends, and almost all left a lasting impression.

Some of Cannastra's friends were established writers, like Paul Goodman; others were involved in publishing, like Moss and Frankel, an editor at Random House. There were also aspiring writers, and Frankel was continually asked to read manuscripts. He recalls that out of all the people in that group, Jack Kerouac made the least demands on him. In fact, Jack was so self-effacing that for many months Frankel thought his surname was "Carroway"! This modesty was all the more striking since his genius was endlessly extolled by Ginsberg, who acted as though his main mission in life were to explicate Kerouac's writing. Since Allen was actually rather sedentary and scholarly, he succeeded well in translating the hard-living drive of Jack's writing into terms the academics could comprehend. It was Allen who finally handed Frankel *The Town and the City*. Although the novel was too conventional to interest most of the people in that group, Frankel liked the book greatly. Nevertheless, he saw no sign in it that Jack was capable of any significant innovation. He felt that Jack would either go on to write a dozen or so long novels like *The Town and the City*, or else stop writing. He was to be happily disappointed.

Howard Moss loved Cannastra for the way he remained untouched by the usual American idea of material success, and Moss found a similar purity in Kerouac. Bill and Jack were what those like Moss wanted to be but could never manage. Once Moss went with Jack to Smiles Bar in the Village, and when Jack started smoking marijuana he became frightened. To let Howard try it without risking arrest, Jack went into the men's room and blew some smoke out through the louvers.

Someone even further removed from Jack's world was Edwin Denby, who had written several books on dance and was dance critic for *The New York Herald Tribune*. A neighbor of Cannastra's, Denby was worshiped by the group, since theatrical dancing and ballet were as momentous to them as music. Despite Jack's lack of interest in that kind of dance, he was moved by the others' respect for Denby.

At times Jack struck sparks off those who wielded authority in his field. One of the literary mandarins of the group, Alan Ansen was an intimate of W. H. Auden, who with his lover Chester Kallman were frequently at Bill's loft. Although Ansen was in love with Bill, he hardly relished the exotic, rather un-American atmosphere in which Bill throve. When people asked Ansen what his politics were, he'd answer "Whig" and mean it. He was also deeply involved in "culture culture," concerned about the ultimate refinements of opera and the nature of Gongorism, the kind of esoteric subjects Jack abhorred. Kerouac's claims as a writer meant nothing to Alan. Seeing Jack tongue-tied and withdrawn into corners much of the time, he decided Jack was a "pretender" and lost no time conveying that judgment to the others.[107]

As a rule, Jack was able to get along with people of any social or cultural stratum. He became close friends with Bill's lover Bruce Shotwell, a mathematician who had made contributions to algebra and topology. Bruce behaved like Jack in that he would work seriously for long stretches and then indulge in episodes of wild violence with Cannastra. But regardless of people's temperament, Jack was attracted to anyone who lived or worked with gusto.

Often, on the spur of the moment, Cannastra would say, "Let's go down the block and talk to people." One day he led Jack, Ginsberg, and Frankel to the nearby loft of Nell Blaine, a painter who sometimes hosted Cannastra's parties when his own loft was in shambles. At Nell Blaine's they met Larry Rivers. Later to make a name as a painter, Rivers then thought of himself primarily as a musician. Though he and Jack were only slightly acquainted, they engaged in a colloquy about music. At that time they were both leading lives for which they hadn't been prepared by their upbringing, and both were seeking a discipline to work in. So eagerly were they talking that when Cannastra suddenly stepped out the window and began making his way around the outside of the building, Jack and Larry never once looked away from each other.

Through Nell Blaine Jack met a number of painters, including Jane Freilicher and the man who would later direct *Pull My Daisy*, Alfred Leslie. Leslie, in turn, knew Willem de Kooning and de Kooning's friends, who hung out at the Cedar Tavern on 8th Street and University Place, which Jack also began to frequent at this time. Although he had very little liking for modern art, he became drinking buddies with several of the most famous abstract-expressionist painters, such as de Kooning, Franz Kline, and Jackson Pollock. De

Kooning was in the habit of lending his paintings to any friend with an available wall. Bill Hardy, whose parties Jack often attended, had a huge loft literally crammed from floor to ceiling with magnificent de Koonings.

Although almost everyone Cannastra knew was connected to the arts, they comprised an extraordinay diversity of personalities. Larry Rivers and Nell Blaine had developed habits of hard work over years of devoted application. At the other extreme were those who were often out of control, like Cannastra himself, someone completely free of any rational relation to the world. By comparing the disciplined artists with those like Cannastra, Jack could see the options.

There was a big gay contingent in Cannastra's group. Cannastra himself went to bed with men and women with equal frequency, and the social climate at his parties encouraged bisexuality. Although Jack already had many homosexual friends, these were the first gay people he knew who were really comfortable with their sexual identity. Because this milieu was an extension of the bohemian life he had embraced after dropping out of Columbia, it was very accessible to him; but the experiences he had at Cannastra's loft were so fresh and different that they widened him much further.

Cannastra was continually prodding people with identity games. On a simple level, for example, when he gave a dinner there was always—largely improvised and very strange—some type of food they could all share: one enormous pancake, a tremendous amount of salad mixed in a fire bucket, etc. Some people thought these things just frivolous, but Bill knew that partaking food together, as in the Christian ritual of "breaking bread," creates a bond between people. Or he would sometimes make people aware of their own peculiarities. At one party Jack attended, each person was handed a Chinese black silk jacket upon entering. The jackets were loose and baggy and somehow fitted everyone, so that they all looked alike. Yet because of this the real differences between them—the way they talked, sat, walked, etc.—became all the more obvious.

Under Cannastra's bombardment, the inhibitions that had bound Jack for years began to loosen. Practically every gathering at the loft was planned to end as a sexual occasion. As much as these orgies gratified Cannnastra's voyeurism, there was probably a deeper motivation involved, for a large part of Cannastra's life was a struggle to feel less like an outsider, to blend in with everyone else and relax. As Oscar Wilde pointed out, it's a terrible burden to be beautiful, intelligent, or somehow special, and Cannastra was all three. At any rate, after getting thoroughly drunk, people climbed on top of one another on the beds, everyone groping everyone else. Actual sex acts when they occurred were virtually meaningless. Many of the gay men made plays for Jack, and some of their plays were successful.[108] Still, he always had to be very, very drunk to participate in homosexual encounters. At various times he and Bill also "collaborated" in bed with a couple of women. Nevertheless, Jack's sexual expression remained sporadic. Among all those people he stood out for the degree of his isolation. He was neither married like Pippin and Frankel nor did he have any long love affairs as Cannastra had, nor did he even seem to fantasize much about sex, as Allen was always doing and telling about.

There was always a sense of Jack's frustration, of the anger boiling just under the surface, that left him lonely in a room filled with no matter how many friends. He couldn't help being shy but he was mad at his own shyness, and to compensate, when drunk, he'd often become aggressive, questioning what people had said, defending his own position more forcefully than he needed to. He had a way of bursting into a room and demanding that everybody come alive, fast. It was a rather engaging style, and there were times when it was needed and actually worked. But because he was drinking so heavily much of the time, he maintained this manner even when most people simply wanted to talk. He practiced his boisterousness on occasions that didn't at all justify it, and as a consequence often fell flat on his face. Just as often, afterward, he would disappear from the group for a long period. Restlessness was his most pronounced characteristic. Even when he was most with them, they all expected that he would soon be gone again. He didn't seem capable of settling anywhere. But that, of course, was part of his fascination too.

8.

The Town and the City was finished the first week of May, 1948. After packing it off to Scribner's, Thomas Wolfe's publisher, Jack wrote to Neal expressing his gratitude: "*You,* more than anyone else, can be said to be the biggest pitchfork that got me howling and screaming across the pea-patch towards my inevitable duties. It's that wonderful Nealish creativeness that did it."

Free for the first time in three years, Jack wandered the streets, fell in love with an eighteen-year-old girl at the roller rink, and pursued her for four days until she jilted him because he didn't have a job. Then he went to a party thrown by Tony Manocchio, Lucien Carr's friend, and for the first time he worried that Lucien drank too much. The next morning, as he and Tony helped Lucien get to an Air Lines bus, Tony told Lucien, "Jack's girl is sweet and beautiful but dumb." Lucien replied, "Everybody in the world is sweet and beautiful but dumb." Jack liked the remark so much he later slipped it into a revision of *The Town and the City.*

Toward the end of May, Nin gave birth to a premature baby boy.

Jack and his mother rushed to North Carolina to care for her and the household. While he was down there, he had another brief, futile infatuation with a nurse. By the time he got back, Ed had graduated from Columbia, and both he and Hal had left for Denver. Jack was impressed that Ed had been elected to Phi Beta Kappa. For several weeks prior to his finals Ed had been drinking and carousing, and he had only crammed during the last weekend beforehand. The feat confirmed Jack's notion that a genius could spontaneously achieve what ordinary people had to labor toward for years.

Scribner's rejected *The Town and the City*, but Jack's spirits were not at all dampened. Someone told him that the editors there hadn't even read it because it was so messy.

The summer of 1948 Jack was like the Green Hornet, seen everywhere in New York, met by everyone, but really known by very few. He talked with Alec Wilder, Sarah Vaughan's arranger. He argued with composer David Diamond about the music of Lenny Tristano, and thought Diamond "a very snotty guy" because he got mad when Jack spilled a bottle of wine in his piano. Allan Temko stopped in town on his way from San Francisco to Paris, telling Jack he wanted to "view America from a distance" and that he would find out more about America by talking to Europeans. To Jack that was "demon logic." Europe interested Jack only as the place his people had *come from*, not as a source of new truths. All the same, they had a good time talking Hemingway dialogue and discussing their favorite funny guys.

Beverly Burford had arranged a good job for Jack in Denver, but though he wanted to get moving again he felt he should stay in New York to await acceptance of the book. After revising and retyping over four hundred pages, he sent the manuscript to Albert Erskine at Random House in early July.

He was still lonesome for a romance, and even tried looking up Ginger, Hal's old girlfriend. At six in the morning he barged into her apartment carrying a quart of milk and announced that he was "taking over." When she seemed offended, he told her that he was "no Siegfried" and didn't care to die in a lover's arms. Quoting from *The Town and the City*, he said that if she rejected him he would simply go back to looking at "doorways and women's legs." In despair he took off his clothes and sauntered into her shower. A few days later he finally succeeded in seducing a redheaded girl he had met at a party. Unfortunately she was rather frigid and wanted to jump off the roof. Their love was hopeless because she was on her way to Paris and, besides, she was swept off her feet by Huncke the morning after. Jack made a date to meet her under the Arc de Triomphe.

Nowadays he was quoting from *The Town and the City* all the time, especially in letters to friends, because he was so proud of the prose. His confidence in the book was bolstered by the many writers, like Alan Harrington and Ed Stringham, who had already expressed great admiration for it. Publishing contacts seemed to be springing up all over New York; even Lucien's girlfriend Barbara offered to submit the novel to her uncle, an editor at Macmillan. But Jack's pleasure came simply from the realization that "a book written is written *forever*" and that his claim to artistry had been "nailed to the wall."

Amid the whirl of new faces that summer, Jack met the man who was to become his second blood brother. Ed Stringham and Alan Harrington were literary intellectuals, a class of people Jack respected but never aspired to join, whose lifestyle was far removed from the debauchery he needed for inspiration. Although he wasn't bored by *them*, he would have been bored had he tried to live as they did. For their part, Stringham and Harrington found Jack's literary background deficient. His reading seemed wide but spotty; he was forever quoting Wolfe, Melville, and Céline. Moreover, his attempts to seem literate were pitifully jejune—like the post card he sent Stringham, which read: *"C'est toujours un voyage au bout de la nuit."* Stringham had left Wolfe behind in high school. Yet Jack's appreciation of the power and vitality of Wolfe made them all admit Wolfe's genius anew. Neither Stringham nor Harrington doubted that Jack had more talent than they did. Stringham thought the descriptions of football in *The Town and the City* "astounding," for he had never before encountered such scenes in serious literature. Stringham and Harrington conveyed their enthusiasm for this new writer to their mutual friend, a deeply read, intellectual writer named John Clellon Holmes.

Russell Durgin of the Columbia group now had an apartment in Spanish Harlem. On the hot Fourth of July weekend he gave a party to which Ginsberg, Kerouac, and Harrington were invited, and Harrington brought along Holmes. While they were still on the street, Harrington said, "There's Kerouac." All Holmes saw was a group of dark, handsome men buying beer in a grocery store. None of them looked like "the author of a novel, weighing twenty pounds in the hand, that was being seriously touted to publishers" by people Holmes respected. Kerouac, it turned out, was the one who looked like the "tee-shirted younger brother of the others." When Holmes took a minute to talk with him, he was surprised at the tender shyness of Jack's eyes, and by the way Jack stayed attuned to everything happening on the street.

At the party Holmes met Ginsberg for the first time too. Allen was setting off firecrackers in ashtrays to liven things up, and talking eagerly and intimately even with people he didn't know. Jack was much more unobtrusive. But the curious thing about both Allen and Jack was that each kept talking about the other. Knowing that Holmes was a writer who might have publishing connections, Allen immediately asked Holmes to read *The Town and the City*. Far less businesslike, Jack apologized for Allen's antics, assuring Holmes that Allen was "a big poet . . . all involved with visions and apocalypses." Of the two, Ginsberg seemed more knowledgeable in a literary way; but, inexplicably, Jack was the one with whom Holmes identified.

Kerouac and Holmes became friends almost overnight. All sorts of coincidences seemed to tie their lives together. They both had the same birthday, though Holmes was four years younger. Both were from New England. The night after the great flood of 1936, Holmes had prowled along one of the tributaries of the Merrimack while Jack walked along the Merrimack itself. Beyond such curiosities was the deep sympathy of men bound to the same profession, and beyond that a mysterious affinity of natures, a sort of effortless ability to anticipate each other's reactions.

At first Holmes was impressed by Jack's powerful presence, and by the open way he registered emotions. Different from all the other writers he knew, Jack wasn't in the least competitive or secretive about his work. What interested Jack in Holmes was his "avidity." Though Holmes used too many ponderous expressions like "come to terms with," he also refused "to let life slip out of his hands." Moreover, like Ginsberg, Holmes seemed to be striving for a "love-belief,"and Jack felt that John was even nearer to it than Allen, that John was "by nature . . . actually *in* it." [109] When Jack learned about the severe migraine headaches John had had while serving in a naval hospital during the war, he empathized still more fully with him, remembering his own alienation in the naval psychiatric ward.

Reading *The Town and the City* in the notebooks in which it had originally been written, Holmes was carried away by the expansive, rushing flow of the book—a veritable literary Mississippi. And as a creator of avant-garde allegorical fiction, he was relieved to find Kerouac no threat in that direction. Soon Holmes would feel such devotion to Jack that any literary rivalry would seem insignificant, but at this early stage of their acquaintance the fact that they worked in different areas undoubtedly made it easier for John to relate to an overpowering genius like Kerouac. As Holmes put it in *Nothing More to Declare*, Kerouac was about as easy to ignore as Niagara Falls: "You always felt the strong pull of his special view of the world." Jack needed no such assurance to open *his* heart to Holmes. Two months after they met, Jack handed Holmes the private journals he had kept during the writing of *The Town and the City*, the journals in which he dutifully recorded his progress, agonized over his failures, and, like a taunting coach, roused himself from slumps.

Jack often stayed at Holmes' apartment, and he spent many hours discussing literature with the trio of Holmes, Ed Stringham, and Alan Harrington. Ed had known Jack the longest. Allen Ginsberg had introduced them one night in the West End Bar, when Jack had been carrying his enormous manuscript around like some medieval writer in search of a patron. Since Ed considered Allen a bad romantic poet, he had initially been suspicious of Jack, who acted as if the world were his oyster. As Allen explained it, Jack had been a great football player and was now a great novelist. After Ed read *The Town and the City*, Jack's self-confidence seemed justified. If anything, Ed was surprised at the thirst for praise that underlay Jack's bravado. "Do you really think this is good?" he would ask of a piece of his writing, obviously knowing it was good but pleased to hear someone confirm it.

No one knew then how much Jack needed encouragement. Ranged with Cannastra, Jack seemed the least likely person in the world to destroy himself. Yet sometimes Ed and the others glimpsed his dark side, and there was always an element of distrust in their relationship with him. When they discussed books Jack didn't know, he would become silent and subdued, and if they criticized his own manuscript, he would sulk. Feeling excluded, he would tend to drink more heavily than usual, and once drunk he would get belligerently anti-intellectual.

Although everyone in those Cannastra-Columbia circles drank heavily, no one, except perhaps Bill himself, drank like Jack. He never seemed to get seriously ill from drinking, as Bill often did, and it amazed people that he could drink that much and still write regularly. But then they had become writers in a much different way than Jack, and whatever mysteries attended his genius were assumed to be part of his metamorphosis from football player into novelist.

In any case, one character weakness in Jack was only too apparent to them: that strange mixture of misogyny and naïveté about women. Jack would denounce his current girlfriend whenever she wasn't around. Even more pathetically, he was always describing his ideal woman—a combination of "earth mother," "cute chick," and several other impossible antinomies.[110] Introduced to the young literary agent Rae Everitt, Jack immediately stared at her with brooding sexual interest, much to the chagrin of John, Ed, and Alan. Later, Alan scolded Jack, saying he simply ought to ask Rae out, but Jack insisted that he "worked subtle." More often Jack just made a plain fool of himself with women. One night at the West End, drunk, he and one of Cannastra's friends, another former football player, decided to prove their virility by picking up "Rhoda Pagoda." This notorious whore followed them to a nearby apartment, but when she learned they had no money she refused to perform. Back at the bar she ridiculed them, and they were humiliated. In his journal Holmes noted that Jack could only deal with women if they were married or if he were drunk. In the first case, there could be no risk to his ego; in the second, ego no longer mattered.

But in literary matters Holmes' encouragement was crucial. At a point when Jack might have been tempted to shelve *The Town and the City*, Holmes offered praise and brotherly suggestions, motivating Jack to keep on with revisions. On September 9, 1948, he completed another version of the novel with a new ending, though still not the ending that he finally used. Holmes, however, was less able to promote the book than Ed Stringham, who worked for *Publishers Weekly* and had many contacts at the *Columbia Review*. Stringham recommended the book to several people, including David Diamond, who was a friend of Alfred Kazin.

A distinguished critic, Kazin was then teaching literature at the New School for Social Research. The fact that Kazin might soon be reading his book may well have influenced Jack to enroll at the New School. He also knew that Holmes would attend classes there that fall. In addition, there was the incentive of a $75-per-month stipend that he would receive as a student, through his GI benefits. Jack signed up for a course in world literature with Tartak, a course in myth with Slochower, and a creative-writing course with Brom Weber.

9.

In the meantime Allen was immersed in a study of Cézanne, and let Jack read a paper he'd written. The visions of those paintings literally dizzied Jack as he wandered drunkenly through Manhattan with Tom Livornese. Suddenly he saw "everything in its true contour and light." As in the past, they walked the city through the night and into the next day, then called up Lucien to infuse fresh blood into the expedition. They woke him up with Tristano records, and then went out drinking, with Jack paying special attention to the different types of light, so that even the smoky green of a glass of pernod seemed something Cézanne had painted. Later Lucien said he was sorry Jack couldn't earn a living within the system, as he was doing at U.P.I., but Jack understood that Lucien was merely saddened by his own failure to pursue the artistic dreams he'd had at Columbia.

In Washington Square, helping a girl who had fallen rollerskating, Jack and Lucien discussed pain and joy. Lucien described the hopes he had nurtured in the reformatory and claimed that after his abasement there life grew more joyous all the time. It struck Jack that Lucien had found the key to a happy life, as Burroughs had, in disregarding all of society's expectations, in just accepting the turns of fortune as they came. But Lucien felt Jack still worried about what others thought of him. Reluctant to admit to such worry, Jack said he knew that people all loved one another deep down. He proposed that people sometimes felt confused because if they felt love constantly they would soon cease to perceive it, that love was like the color green, which could only be seen by contrast with other colors.

When Jack related this theory to Allen in a letter, Allen replied that Jack was trying to hide his feelings. According to Allen, "The only reality is green, love . . . it is just the whole point of life not to be self conscious. . . ." Allen felt Jack was holding back love so that he could maintain a rational, discriminative view of life and keep himself safely separate from others. Allen reminded Jack that Jack had once asked him to stop peering into his soul. What Jack feared, it seemed, was that someone might discover his "feelings of gibbering idiocy"—while in Allen's view it was just that area, "the doubt in the back of the head," that was most important to investigate. Fear of seeing in oneself what others really see there is natural but must be overcome. As Allen recalled: "I was frightened as a kid by the transfiguration scene in Jekyll and Hyde. That is because it recalled my true self to me. So miraculous and unbelievable is this true self, is life, that it seems like an image of horror. Once we accept that horror we see that it was all a fit, that horror was the birth pains, the pangs of recognition of self deception, and we are in love, in green." His advice to Jack was thus to "go mad, what you think now is mad is really love and sane."

Jack felt Allen was "getting ugly" and for a brief time avoided seeing him. With startling honesty Allen then wrote Jack that he (Allen) had gone mad from too much suffering, and that he was like a man who had committed suicide but lived through it to see his friends weeping for him. But he also reminded Jack that he had been "calling to people to save me, and no one put out his hand. . . ." [111] A cry like that was something Jack couldn't ignore.

Yet he himself could barely stay afloat in the storm of uncertainties engulfing him that fall, and before he could reach out to Allen he needed someone to lift him from his own gloom. Jack's latest love affair had ended disastrously. A seventeen-year-old beauty named Jinny Baker had given every sign of liking him, but when he responded with too much affection she showered him with contempt. He'd met her at Lucien's and had alternately badgered and fawned on her, and she had alternately teased and rejected him, until they ended up hating each other. The real pain of it was that Jack still loved her too. Coming at a time when he was depleted both physically and spiritually, even a minor heartbreak was enough to tip Jack into an abyss of madness. Holmes was very worried about him. Lucien sought to wangle a job for him at U.P.I., but Jack spurned employment there as beneath his dignity, preferring to live like "silent sorrowful Sam Johnson."

At the New School he encountered fresh antagonism. There were a few bright spots, like Alfred Kazin's classes on *Moby Dick*. Kazin

228 · M E M O R Y   B A B E

and Jack got along very well. In Tartak's course Jack enjoyed reading *War and Peace,* but the angry literary arguments seemed silly. Professor Slochower was a worse pedant, and Jack aimed to deflate his reverence for mythology in a term paper, stating that "Myth is nothing but concept built on a particular which is never repeated." Such "concept" was what Neal called "prevision"—and to Jack's mind it interfered with the joy of living moment by moment. But whereas his dispute with Slochower was purely ideological, Jack felt a personal animosity in his creative writing teacher, Brom Weber.

Friction had been building as Jack listened to Weber criticize his idols Wolfe and Céline. Only four years older, Weber tried to act professorially aloof and objective, an attitude which also repelled Jack. Yet, although submissions were voluntary (there were no grades in the course), Jack brought Weber several parts of *The Town and the City.* While he waited for Weber's reaction, he made an appointment to see David Diamond.

At first Jack and Diamond had gotten along well, despite the wine in the piano. Small and prematurely bald, Diamond was attracted to the vigor of soldiers and sailors. Naturally he found Jack appealing. Gays quickly sensed Jack's sexual ambiguity, and despite his denunciations of effeminacy as a "defacing" of manhood, he was pleased when homosexuals admired him. He himself often spoke about his ideal of male beauty, which was embodied in Lucien Carr. Moreover, Jack's bitterness toward women was something with which homosexuals could sympathize.

Nevertheless, some bad feeling had recently developed between him and Diamond. One evening, at the latter's house, Jack had encountered a friend of David Kammerer, who praised Kammerer's character and condemned Lucien. Jack grew vehement in Lucien's defense, arguing that Kammerer typified the worst sort of "queer." Perhaps defensively, Diamond had sided with Kammerer's friend.

Now, when Jack came to see him, Diamond said he was shocked at his excessive drinking and partying, and his habit of late-night phone calls. In the Village, Diamond had heard that Jack was a "dope addict," that he acted like a "maniac" at parties, and that he baited and beat up homosexuals. Diamond insisted that Jack would never become a great artist if he continued this way. Jack's attitude and opinions also shocked him, and Diamond warned that he had no use for people who lacked a "mature sense of values." [112] Writers like Céline, Diamond averred, were better off dead for the sake of culture and progress. But Jack couldn't even claim kinship with such real creative artists, since—in Diamond's view—*The Town and the City* was merely a prodigious feat of memory, a Wolfean symphony conducted by a precocious kid. He called Jack "childish" and "enervating," and angered him even more by "castigating Jesus." Diamond said he couldn't afford to risk his reputation by associating with people like him—which Jack took as an insult to his family—and banished Jack from his company forever. Then he consoled Jack for the loss of his friendship and (if we can accept Jack's journal as fact) demanded that he go to bed with him! (In his journal Jack later complained that Diamond had insulted his taste as well as his manhood.) After deciding that it would be wrong to clout a composer of beautiful music, Jack quietly left.

In a black mood Jack went to Lucien's and (as recorded in his *On the Road* Journal) heard Lucien telling the tale of a mass murderer in Tacoma. Once Jack had wondered if Lucien ever felt sorry about killing Kammerer, but now Jack began to think murder might be a joyous occasion. Half mad, he hurried to Bickford's cafeteria on Times Square and wrote a story called "Confession of Three Murders." So strongly did he imagine having murdered three people that when his mind drifted from his writing he actually felt a terrifying guilt. Struggling against alienation, he walked to the Roxy Hotel to see Huncke, then just stared at the building and turned back. He spent the night at Tony Manocchio's and when he awoke the next morning was again overcome by the feeling of having murdered David Diamond, as well as two others. But thanks to Tony's refreshing sweetness, he soon felt well enough to attend Brom Weber's class that afternoon.

It was the day Weber chose to deal with *The Town and the City*. Students' works were criticized by the whole class, with Weber leading the discussion. He found Jack's novel incoherent in places and much too imitative of Wolfe. A few months earlier, when Ginsberg had gently suggested that Jack might be using Wolfe more as a vehicle than a master, Jack had felt his intelligence insulted. Now, hearing the same charge from a stranger and a member of the establishment, he was hurt to the quick. Even more devastating was Weber's assessment that the novel as a whole was a failure, and that at best Jack might save a few parts of it.

After class, Jack told Weber that Wolfe was his model in life as well as in writing. Weber replied that Wolfe's fiction was at times incoherent and unfocused, though he liked Wolfe's exuberance just as he liked Jack's. But in Jack's view a true writer was a medium, and anything that came out of him was therefore satisfactory literature. He even talked about writing automatically on rolls of paper. Weber felt that since Jack had voluntarily turned in parts of his novel, he must have realized it needed some editing, and he explained that he was trying to approach Jack's work as a potential editor. Editing, however, was beneath Jack's consideration—he said he had a whole trunk full of manuscripts "that some lesser being would have to put in order." It seemed Jack had simply brought the manuscript to receive praise, and Weber's adverse criticism had struck him as a personal rejection. But Weber didn't want to play lay analyst. He simply told Jack that the writer and the work were two separate things. Jack left, unable to express his anger face to face.

At home, in his journal, he excoriated both Diamond and Weber, asserting that critics were not makers like himself but merely destroyers. He felt that if he let himself believe what they had said, he would be forced to kill himself. Remembering Diamond's remark about Céline, he was even convinced that what such criticizers wanted was for him to die.

Certainly the publishers were giving him no cause to be cheerful. For two months Little, Brown had been considering *The Town and the City*; finally in early December they rejected the book, saying it was too long and too risky to edit. Remarkably, Jack still didn't lose faith in his ability to write. In fact, he wrote in his journal that *The Town and the City* would someday be hailed as a great book. What disturbed him was that the long wait for recognition might damage his personality and will to create. The wound Diamond and Weber had inflicted was salted by the publisher Putnam's rejecting one of his short stories as "immature." John Holmes, in an argument, had also hinted at Jack's immaturity, though Jack found Holmes tender and admitted the argument had resulted from his own derisiveness.

The person most able to sympathize with Jack was Ginsberg, since he was currently having similar trouble adjusting. As he approached graduation from Columbia, Allen began looking for a job and discovered with horror that he had "no angle to offer keen-eyed employers." Rebuffed everywhere, from department store to newspaper office, he wandered the city gloomy and "haunted by Bickford's dishwashing machine."

At the next session of Weber's class, Allen rose dramatically beside Jack and declared, "Mark Van Doren is the ideal teacher!" Allen proceeded to tell how Van Doren embraced his students' psyches, and loved *them* as well as their works. Jack seconded everything Allen said. The class, which contained such future novelists as Mario Puzo and George Mandel, began "vibrating." [113] For the next four hours they engaged in the closest thing to a revival meeting Weber had ever experienced.

Jack and Allen argued that their work was less important than *they* were, and that the most valuable thing Weber could provide was concern for them as persons. Weber replied that teachers and editors weren't in the business of dispensing love. Allen rejoined that their writing was a manifestation of their personalities, and that it was as necessary to love one as the other. Many of the students protested that a writer didn't need to be loved and that they weren't coming to class to express a *self*. They mouthed the precepts of the New Criticism, dominant in the late forties and early fifties, which stated that the work is primary in the reader-writer relationship. Weber added that Jack was taking criticism unprofessionally, that it should be accepted at an intellectual rather than emotional level. "But everything is emotional," Jack objected, and Allen followed up with a lot of lush mystical language. At last Jack stated flatly that he didn't believe in criticism of any kind because his writing was "a prayer to God." Then he and Allen claimed to be modern-day saints. Some of the others laughed, but the room kept vibrating.

Carrying the discussion to the purpose of literature, Allen and Jack reacted against the absolutism and omniscient attitude then prevalent in the academic establishment. They ridiculed the pseudo-scientific attempt to make definitive judgments about every piece of writing. Weber agreed that such judgments were always "nonab-solute," [114] but he maintained the necessity of judging the work apart from the writer. As an example, Weber cited Céline, whose anti-Semitism disaccorded with the humanity and compassion of his works.

Allen and Jack began giggling and spoofing about God and Shakespeare and the fact that writers were usually "morally mo-ronic." Several weeks later, in a letter to Weber, Jack reflected that he and Allen had acted so irreverently from "terrified depths"; for Jack, who had always "believed in morality," was leery of the new amoral climate that seemed to be sweeping the country. But in class that day, he asserted that an artist naturally believes in what he says, though like anyone else the artist may keep fluctuating to his last day. It was worse than pompous, he felt, to disbelieve in Tolstoy's moral fervor or the "heavy earnestness" of Wolfe.

In the letter to Weber, Jack clarified his argument, proposing that "perhaps nothing is true but everything is real." He speculated that all life as well as art might be a mental creation: "even a big lie . . . which we make; all a myth like the Divine Comedy." The act of creating life, he thought, might be just like the myths people make about their friends; and he equated these myths with the American preoccupation with *"the light,"* which he discounted as perhaps no more than "the silly mist in our eyes when we're happy and rushing down steps together somewhere, anywhere." In conclusion, he told Weber that the only thing he liked about Céline was when Céline wrote about "the end of the night," when he showed compassion for "someone going beyond the streetlamp into the dark. . . ." The rest of Céline was "poppycock," he felt, compared with Céline's pro-found sense of the tenuousness of human life.

To the end of the class, Jack seemed determined to make Weber "love" him. Just as doggedly Allen fought at his side. Since Weber refused to soften, Jack grew very distressed. Weber was sorry, but he hoped the humiliation might be salutary—at least as far as exposing Jack to the reality of the literary life, where scarcely anyone de-ferred to a writer's individuality.

Outside the New School Allen told Jack, "You really work for your money!" Jack replied, "What money?" His GI checks had been held up for two months.

In later discussions with Weber, Jack explained that because Western culture was inhibited, his primary concern was with "finding himself as a writer" [116] rather than with putting his writing in perspective. In any case, his talk lacked a real intellectual basis, and Wolfe remained the center of all his literary references. Yet Weber never doubted that Jack was a tenacious and dedicated writer, and that if he would accept the discipline of a good editor (who could offer the incentive of a monetary advance) he could surely produce an important work. To help Jack's writing get serious consideration, Weber asked Kazin to present *The Town and the City* to Harcourt Brace, for whom Kazin served as a literary scout. Because Weber recommended so few of his students' manuscripts, Kazin was prepared to give it careful attention. Unfortunately, Jack thought he was getting a chill reception from Kazin, since he was forced to leave the manuscript with a doorman at his house. When he got home, he noted in his journal that he was more discouraged than he had ever been, and he believed he would have to write off his work on the novel as "the years of a madman."

Professionally Jack was beginning to mingle with some of the most powerful people in the arts, but privately he was still very much the simple, lonely boy from Lowell. One day on the subway he bumped into George Murray, whom he'd known in Sam Sampas' group. Jack's eyes lit up, and with surprising warmth he asked George over for Sunday dinner in Ozone Park. When Connie Murphy contacted him, Jack invited him to dinner too. Meeting Jack's mother for the first time, Connie was surprised to learn she still supported him by working in a shoe factory. Already a physicist, Murphy was unimpressed when Jack showed him piles of typed pages and reams of yellow paper covered with hand-printing, and he advised Jack to go out and make something of his life. Since Jack pleaded that writing was important to him, Murphy demanded, "Why can't you work all day and write at night?" But all he got for an answer was a lot of "weird" talk about how the world had changed. "The fellas around here are strange," Jack said. "They don't play ball anymore." [117]

At the New School Jack was attending Eugene O'Neill's lectures. After one lecture, Jack and a Tibetan friend met a frustrated young Japanese poet named Matsumi Kanemitsu. All three went out for drinks, and Kanemitsu judged Jack a "real square." He seemed excessively serious and self-conscious and a utopian to boot. Mostly he talked about how much he wanted to be a great writer.

In his journal Jack acknowledged that he was sick. Not only was he suffering from bouts of actual nausea, but he was also having frequent "paranoiac attacks." Sometimes he was frightened at the amount of anger seething in him, though it never quite burst out as Allen's did. While Allen had taken to hurling wineglasses, and other defiant gestures—"savage" acts that appalled a scholar like Alan Harrington—Jack would merely walk off his mean moods, imagining that he was shooting at cars that bore down on him or choking people that passed him on the street. After reading Melville's "Bartleby the Scrivener," he recognized himself as "a catatonic case, a depressive," much like Bartleby. Even at sixteen, he noted in his journal, he had "preferred not to" work. What bothered him now, though, was the fact that after three years of work he had earned nothing and was still a "loafer" in his mother's house.

Even more disturbing was the realization that the people who were supposed to be "the bearers of the torch against commercialism"—like Diamond, Weber, and the publisher Putnam, who had recently told Jack to "grow up and go to work"—were the very ones who discouraged artists. His book had been a gift to the world; the most brutal spectacle of his life had been to watch the literary forum dismember it and judge "the poor simplicities" of his heart. With memories of a good man like his father, and dreams of an affectionate and just race modeled after his own family, Jack could hardly believe people could be so ugly. If he were going to be treated like Kafka's Gregor, he resolved not to languish in his room but to break out and "devour" his enemies.[118]

SIX
Slow Boat to China

1.

Much of Jack's mounting rage in the fall of 1948 was channeled into two new novels, which he worked on concurrently. One was the story of his boyhood Shadow fantasies. Based on a recent dream about such a figure, it was called *Doctor Sax; the Myth of the Rainy Night.* The other novel, *On the Road,* was intended to be complementary; while *Doctor Sax* treated the supernatural, *On the Road* was a naturalistic story of a modern Western hero based on Neal Cassady. *On the Road* would pick up where *The Town and the City* left off. In the last scene of the latter novel, the hero, Peter Martin, has begun hitchhiking across America. In fact, Jack planned to make all three novels part of the great many "intertwined" books he had envisioned years before as the *Duluoz Legend.* But in his early conception *On the Road* was far less autobiographical than the version published ten years later, and the hero Warren Beauchamp, growing up on a ranch in California, had a much more prosperous background than Neal's. By contrast, the narrator, Ray Smith, was to be, not a brilliant writer like Kerouac, but a shadowy, if nattily dressed, hipster. Still, much like Jack with Neal, Smith followed Beauchamp with unconscious devotion.

Jack was now able to write with much greater freedom than in *The Town and the City.* With ease he averaged over 1,500 words per day for the month of November. Most of the writing was of *On the Road,* which he judged "a powerful and singularly gloomy book . . . but good." He felt he had finally learned to make prose sound beautiful without the "heaviness" that had marred *The Town and the City.*[119]

He may also have learned a lighter touch from Lewis Carroll, who was then one of his favorite authors. White had sent Jack a roundel from *Alice in Wonderland,* with the instruction that he should apply his friends' names to the various roles. Jack did so, even trying Jesus in the place of the protagonist, and the result "tore his guts out." But in effect it was a breakthrough into a more relaxed vision of life; since, like Dostoyevsky, he now realized that "we're all alike and all doing the same thing," that everyone's madness stemmed from the same attempt to be sane.

He was also letting off steam by spending weekends in Pough-keepsie with Jack Fitzgerald. "Fitz" was one of the few people with whom he could relax completely, since nothing was sacrosanct to him. Seeing how lonely and sex-starved Jack was, Fitz fixed him up, with a high-school girl. Jack and Fitz made up myths about their dead fathers, "George Martin" (of *The Town and the City*) and "Old Mad Murphy" (of Fitzgerald's novel), which helped Jack release some of his remaining guilt. They pictured their fathers in heaven, sitting on clouds, watching them "much as Melville's father might have looked down on Herman when he wandered around Liverpool trying to decipher his father's outdated map & guide-book." The two old men swore and spat and got so tired of watching the earth they decided to get drunk; but knowing how difficult it would be for their sons to be fathers (Fitzgerald already had a child), the old men kept on trying to guide them.

Fitzgerald shared with friends his great love for his family, just as he continually made people feel the baby kicking inside his wife. Feeling poured out of Fitzgerald in torrents. Some nights he would get up on a bandstand and improvise chorus after chorus of blues, and Jack would often get up and sing with him.

Jack also began to have surprising success with women. He started steadily dating a married woman named Pauline. Separated from a roughneck truck driver, she was raising their baby by working as a model for the artist Alan Wood-Thomas. Some of Jack's friends felt she was just using him to make her husband jealous, but on Jack's side, at least, the passion was genuine. Tall, blond, sloe-eyed, and "Lombardian," she seemed as naïve as Edie but less bitter. Her string of bad breaks reminded Jack of Neal. Although deeply moved by her suffering, he was reluctant to interfere in a marriage. At the same time he was seeing another very beautiful but "less spiritual" girl, Adele Morales, a kind of "educated Bea Franco," [120] who liked to wear black Persian slacks and wanted Jack as a friend.

As a matter of fact, the original Bea Franco kept writing Jack from Fresno, asking to see him again in love letters that both warmed his heart and broke it, since he didn't know what to tell her. His thoughts were definitely running to marriage and children. He wrote in his journal that he wanted to be surrounded by a wife and a flock of youngsters, for whom he would sing all day, leading them to "ecstasy." Technically he was still married to Edie, though they had agreed to give each other a divorce on request. Lack of money, he wrote, was the only thing keeping him from remarrying. But he was thinking in more practical terms now. Even were his mother to accept a Mexican daughter-in-law, Bea Franco would never be able to negotiate the artistic and intellectual circles he was passing through.

For a while Jack imagined Adele to be the sort of warm, sexy girl with whom he could relax. After his debacles with Diamond and

Weber he took her to an Italian dinner with Tony Manocchio, and she comforted him so much that he gave her parts of his novel to read. The next night, however, she talked about being psycho-analyzed. Since Jack was contemptuous of people who depended on psychoanalysis, they had a long argument. He followed her home to Brooklyn, they kissed in her hall, and she went in alone. He returned to Manhattan to sleep at Holmes' apartment.

There was already a strong attraction between Jack and Holmes' wife, Marian. But at this stage Jack and John were much too anxious to please one another for either to openly notice it. Moreover, they were watching each other intently—two observant novelists creating a vacuum between them by the opposing pulls of their curiosity—and it embarrassed Jack that Holmes was gaining far more knowl-edge of him than he was of Holmes. Sensing John peeking over his shoulder, he began hedging a little. Jack was never one to act on a woman's flirtations anyway; at most he would let a woman have her way with him—that is, practically force her to rape him (as he claimed Shakespeare had been raped by Anne Hathaway!). Holmes was amazed by this backwardness.

Rae Everitt came to Holmes' apartment and started making eyes at Jack. Holmes kept expecting Jack to make a move, but Jack never made it. That night Jack, John, Marian, Rae, and Bar-bara Bowles went to the Wood-Thomases, where they encountered Pauline. Neighbors and children dropped in, and they all sang, danced, and told jokes for hours. Jack was delighted. Pauline appeared to him as "perhaps the finest woman" he would ever know,[121] and he realized he was in love with her and wanted to marry her. Yet his sexual desire suddenly focused on Rae, and he tried to take her to Ginsberg's apartment nearby. Rae ran home, leaving Jack to grumble that Ed Stringham was right about his al-ways ending up with "stupid neurotic women."

Briefly Jack resumed his romance with Adele, though by now Allen was "conspiring" against it. She and Jack kissed in Shine's Bar & Grille till both were dizzy, and Jack was sure he felt "the most tremendous love sensations" since Mary Carney, whom Adele even resembled. In her hall in Brooklyn they kissed again, and stared into each other's eyes, but once more they parted before getting to bed. Frustrated, Jack knew he loved her "in the eyes of God" and won-dered why a man and woman couldn't just have sex "without pre-liminaries." His ideal love relationship, he confided in his journal, would take place in the "Forest of Arden"—a phrase from Shake-speare.

He and Allen had once had a long discussion about Rosalind's line in As You Like It: "Well, this is the Forest of Arden." They speculated as to how the actor was meant to pronounce it, for it seemed fraught with metaphysical significance. Jack and Allen felt that Shakespeare was using the Forest of Arden as a metaphor for man's existence in space and eternity, and the line "Well, this is the Forest of Arden" seemed to express man's wonder at finding himself surrounded by ineffable mysteries. Frequently Jack and Allen would parody the line, saying, "So this is Manhattan" or "So this is Jack Kerouac," etc., to express their sense of the poignance of each moment within the drama of their own lives. As Jack explained the phrase "Forest of Arden" to Holmes, it seemed to represent the unity of mankind: "dense masses of people going about all their ways of being." For Jack it also came to have a specific sexual meaning. The Forest of Arden was a place where swains loved lasses, and it just happened "as among deers and does in God's creation." [122]

For the past few months he had been halfheartedly searching for a job. He went down to the waterfront, but a longshoreman's story about the undependability of such work depressed him still further. Learning that Neal would soon get laid off from the railroad, he proposed they go to sea. For months they had played with the idea of buying a ranch or farm together, and as seamen they would be able to save money toward that goal. Since Burroughs was doing well with his Texas farm, Jack began to think farm life might ideally suit a writer. If need be, he would hitch to the West Coast. Finally, in early December, he received a check for $160 from the Veterans Administration, which eased the financial pressure on him and his mother. He was able to help her with the rent, buy Christmas presents, and still put enough aside for his trip to California.

With a bulge in his pocket the world seemed so much brighter Jack felt he had been a fool to ever worry. Remembering all the times in galley, jail, and sickbed when he had simply gazed at the sky for sustenance, full of trust and love, he resolved to "die, give up, go mad, and begin to be happy again."

One night he got drunk with about twenty friends and invited them all out to his home. Everyone tried to dissuade him, but he insisted that they had to see his mother. Always worried about her, he wanted to include her in the revelry. Finally he promised, "My mother will cook us marvelous steaks." At ten P.M. a score of dead drunk people crashed into the Ozone Park apartment. His mother started arguing with him, impelling them all back to Manhattan. Ed Stringham, who was along, understood that it was part of Kerouac's Jack London fantasy. Jack had explained to Ed that when he became a famous writer he wanted to live as London had. He would have a beautiful house, hold a continuous party, and play host to everybody he liked, offering them an assortment of beautiful women and lots of good food and drink. That way he could always keep his friends around him. To Ed it seemed Jack had acquired the rather meretricious goal of becoming "a big-scale Cannastra."

Another night, after the West End closed, he led a large group up to an after-hours club in Harlem. At times like this, at his best, Jack was great fun to drink with, to just be with. He knew the password to get in, and they listened to jazz, drank, and danced until dawn. Since Ed seemed interested (which was essential), Jack told him the whole story of Doctor Sax. It was one of the most striking performances Ed had ever witnessed. Everyone watched the sunrise, and Jack was euphoric to behold blacks and whites together, all having the best possible time. Even when some man made a pass at him, it didn't break the charm. Jack said gently, "No, I'm not interested," and they all left in peace.

Nevertheless, some of Jack's kicks seemed dull to Stringham and Harrington. His and Allen's "ritual" of going to the Royal Roost and rocking back and forth all evening seeme⌐ silly to them [123]; and they didn't care to smoke grass, since it didn't enhance *their* appreciation of the music. Allen, especially, was too "manic" and "frantically nervous" for Ed. After Allen stood on his head on Ed's couch, Ed wrote Allen that he would rather not see him anymore. By contrast, Stringham and Harrington never found Jack intolerable, but they did worry that their friend John Holmes was overwhelmed by Jack's energy and charisma. It distressed them to see John trying to bridge the gap between himself and Jack in "an almost servile way." [124]

Whatever their motivations, Jack and John were developing a special and productive relationship. Jack deplored the divisiveness within the artistic community. Because so many intellectuals were rejecting him, he appreciated acceptance from Holmes all the more. Holmes had rock-hard values, which Jack greatly admired, and his work ethic was no less strong than Jack's own. When he told Jack that he wanted "honesty and safety and knowledge," Jack realized that they were shooting for the same goals. Jack too was on guard against delusions and believed their mission as writers was to achieve a "complete honesty," for that seemed the only answer to the immense problems of conscience and belief facing their generation. What distinguished Holmes from Jack's "old Carr-Burroughs-Adams-Ginsberg crowd," who also probed for self-knowledge, was that he tried his best "to be humanly good." As a result, Jack didn't feel "cold and lost" with John and his wife as he did among those others.[125]

Yet one man like Holmes wasn't enough to enliven the sterility of New York's intelligentsia, the parties where people jumped from subject to subject "like kingfishers." Besides, John and Jack were scarcely in perfect harmony themselves. Still rankled by John's charge of immaturity, Jack wrote Allen that Holmes was a "weasel." Increasingly he looked to Allen and Neal for sympathy.

2.

During his struggle against depression in the fall of 1948, Jack gained strength from his continuing correspondence with Neal, although few of his friends could see why he should be influenced by Neal at all. In fact, writing to Ed White, Jack even apologized for referring to Neal along with Ed, Tom, and Fitzgerald as one of the "finest boys in the world." The secret may be that only people who had read Neal's letters—or talked with him for hours on end, like Allen— knew the extent of his awareness. Outsiders saw a psychopath who seemed to use people with abandon. Some insiders (like Carolyn) saw an immensely intelligent man condemned to know all the intricacies and furthest ramifications of his weakness without the slightest ability to end it. Allen, however, found Neal remarkable chiefly for his willingness to share his strength with others. If Neal went overboard in anything, according to Allen, it was in the excess of his desire to be kind and give of himself. Whatever aid he coaxed from Allen could hardly compare with the value of his love, for as Allen remarked years later, "I needed affection much more than he did."

In mid-June, 1948, Jack had received his first letter from Neal in six months. In that letter he had chronicled his "tortures": simultaneous involvement with LuAnne and Carolyn, unemployment, an attempt to shoot himself, and manic pursuit of kicks. The reason he was finally able to write about them was that he had found a slight measure of peace living as Carolyn's husband and working on the railroad. Regardless, he still felt "lost," realizing that any equilibrium was temporary amid the tremendous explosions of his pleasure drive. But with his very lostness he challenged the world, and most especially Jack, to formulate "a new morality, philosophy, & psychology" that could accommodate a man like him.

From June through November he wrote Jack regularly, reaffirming the fact that they were "blood brothers" [126] and suggesting ways that they could help each other in both living and writing. Gradually a plan evolved for them to buy a ranch or farm together, on which their two families would live communally. At first it was just an amusing idea, which Neal made the subject of some rather funny jokes. "Your mother (Bless her) & Carolyn (Bless her) are exactly alike," he wrote Jack. In a later letter Neal got carried away describing his fantasy of a "Shakespearean house," which would house a score of people, including G.J. Apostolos, Jim Holmes, Burroughs, and Huncke! But soon the simple value of the idea began to sink in: "Carolyn, like most of us, wishes a gurantee [*sic*] as to the outcome of most undertakings, particularly this one. I have always known of no such gurantee . . . So what if it doesn't come off well. So what if the household is destroyed . . . must one always build a house and then have to go down the road apiece to see his friend and share his life?" In their exceptional broadmindedness Neal and Jack were already working out solutions to problems that would monopolize much of the energy of the generation after them.

Neal's writing was definitely improving, and at times he even showed off, in one instance tantalizing Jack with a passage that sounded like the description of a sexual act, but turned out to be an account of his reactions listening to jazz. But his ambition kept outdistancing his accomplishments. Reading Neal's letter of July 23, Jack must have been reminded of his own teenage fantasies. Neal wrote: "I will write a symphony, a play, a novel, a motion picture. I shall play and lead the orchestra, act in and direct the play, write the critique to my novel, be the director, cameraman and hero of the picture. Thats all me. Me and Leonardo . . . I am starting Sax lessons in Sept. . . . Psychoanalysis follows in Oct." In a later letter he told Jack: "You present, (Just as you told me you once wanted) a perfect all-American growth—(as did Balzac or Voltaire a all-French growth)—to me." Coming from an all-American like Neal, that was quite a compliment. Furthermore, because they were so much alike, Neal asserted, they could "unite to each other & be full of contradictions—rights & wrongs, up & down . . . & still expect each other to understand."

He goaded Jack: "Put up your dukes (like us brothers will do) 'en gard'—take your stance & defend yourself. (Please)." Jack understood that Neal was asking him to bare his real feelings, to "dissolve the hypocrite's agreement" people make with society to speak and act in unreal ways. Telling and showing all seemed the way that everybody should live, for, naked, Jack agreed, everyone would "become same and sane." In his view, this sort of "unveiling for each other" and "confession of daydreams" was what made people love one another and made life worth living. When Neal suggested it was time he and Jack go "into action as one," Jack knew that Neal intended a sort of love crusade, and he was eager to get moving.

The practical details of their quest were still to be arranged. On September 7, Carolyn had given birth to a daughter, Cathleen JoAnne. For a long time she had planned to go to Hollywood to try to get work as a costume designer. When she decided to stay home with her family, Neal's railroad job remained their last hope for saving a lot of money in a short time, to buy a ranch with Jack. Neal was even prepared to send Jack the money to come West, so that he could work on the railroad too. But on November 2, Californians voted to repeal the "full-crew" law, permitting the railroads to lay off surplus personnel during slack seasons. Since Neal had been hired only a few months before, his work would be cut off by January 1.

More than ever, Jack and Neal needed to see each other. When, after prodigious bouts of promiscuous sex, Neal finally came to admit that no woman could satisfy him, he naturally looked to the "kick of inward pleasure" [127] that came from sharing experiences with Jack. More of an observer, more of a loner, Jack knew that "inward kick" better than Neal. But he worried that Neal seemed to be burying himself in his work, and giving up writing to plunge into strictly nonverbal kicks like sex and music. Neal's letters were filled with superficial concerns. One of the reasons Jack suggested they go to sea together was to jar him from this "blank period." [128]

December was hectic with new ventures. At the opening night of Tom Livornese's jazz trio, Jack basked in his old friend's new glory. Learning that Ed White and Bob Burford were going to Paris the next year, Jack got an urge to join them. He visited the French Cultural Office and applied to the Sorbonne, though he had no idea how to come up with boat fare. Preparing for every contingency, he signed up for another session at the New School. Meanwhile his sister, her husband, and their baby were about to move in with Jack and Gabrielle in Ozone Park. To Jack it seemed like a good idea, since he could then go to either California or France without feeling guilty about leaving his mother alone. Actually Gabrielle was encouraging him to get some new experiences—she told him a writer shouldn't stagnate at home—but she preferred that he travel with "that fine, decent Ed White and his pals" rather than Neal. [129] In any case, Jack would first have to accompany her to North Carolina for the holidays, and to pick up Nin's belongings.

He was seeing a lot of Pauline, certain now that he was in love. Wanting to marry her as soon as possible, he even considered work in a gas station, though the idea made him shudder. In a letter to Allen, Jack wrote that he had become a "Factualist" like Burroughs, who had coined the term to refer to his method of dealing with all mental data—including perceptions of material objects, fantasies, dreams, and visions—as different levels of fact. But Jack meant by it only his acceptance of the fact that he would die. He had finally come to realize that in all man's struggles, "nothing can be lost, nothing can be saved." As a result, he was reconciled to earning a living in whatever way necessary, and to limiting his love to one woman. The main thing, he saw, was just to live practically, to get through life without complaining about the privileges one lacked. "My whole theory now," he said, "is that I have no theory."

Just before he left for North Carolina, he had a minor blowup with Allen. It began with Allen screaming over the telephone like a "queer." Jack hung up, but Allen mailed him a "smutty picture" of naked men on a beach. Not only did it frighten Gabrielle (who read his mail), but its homosexual insinuation put Jack on the defensive. He wrote Allen that he saw women as beautiful goddesses, whom he always wanted to "lay"; and though he saw men as equally beautiful gods, he merely wanted to put his arm around them "as we walk somewhere." Mostly he was angry at both Allen and Burroughs—he even said he hated them—beause they had always ridiculed his vision of the divinity in man. What Jack liked about Hal was that he still walked around with a godlike sense of himself, just as Jack had when he was a football player. He maintained that he and Hal happily accepted their flesh, while Allen and Bill leered at each other, still bound by rational concepts of evil. Now it was Jack's turn to demand that Allen "give up, go mad, for once." [130]

Allen's apparent challenge to accept his homosexuality hit home, and it took Jack two long letters to work out his response to it. Jack stressed his intention to marry and raise children, protesting a bit too much that he loved "everything about little children." He even suggested that Allen's homosexuality sprang from a hatred of everyone: women, children, and most of all men. He was sure Allen must hate both him and Neal for refusing to be his lovers. He felt he had slipped into the false position of trying to act and think like Allen, and that such pretense of total amity had led to the hysteria of Allen's demanding Jack beat him up in the subway. Jack claimed he (Jack) had been more honest in the early days of their friendship, when he had glared at Allen and called him names.

Mixed in with the hysterical outbursts at Allen are statements of his deep love for him. Jack says he's glad Allen sent him the picture. The two men staring at the sea represent Allen and himself; that sort of silent, ascetic nakedness is the ideal relationship between them. (A few months earlier, however, Allen had written Jack that he wanted to touch people because he believed love should be conveyed in action.) Caught in a tangle of ambivalences, Jack states that he believes in shelter from the cold, good food, drinks, accessible women, the interplay of the sexes, casual talk, tales, books, and the joyful world of Dickens. Then he admits he is being "honest-dishonest." He takes a sentence about people sheltering themselves from the "cold-warmth" and breaks apart the phrases in the manner of Williams until finally it consists of one-word lines meaningless in themselves.

In the last analysis, Jack thinks it might be better to say nothing, or just to make sounds like animals. But he is glad that he and Allen can be so "old-brotherish" as to attack each other honestly, and he admires Allen for taking "this shit" [131] the way no one else would. Having become aware of their hypocrisy toward each other, they could move on to deeper perceptions. As a result, Jack felt a new philosophical excitement running between himself and Allen.

A day later, on December 15, Neal called from San Francisco: he had bought a new 1949 Hudson and was about to leave for New York. He would pick up Jack, drive him back to San Francisco, and then they would go down to Arizona, where jobs were available on the railroad. Al Hinkle was also coming East, but neither of them had much money, and as an additional problem Neal had to figure how to support Carolyn while he was gone. Jack offered to send him fifty dollars, though it turned out he was only able to send ten. He told Neal to meet him in Rocky Mount, North Carolina, at his sister's house.

It occurred to him that Neal might have stolen the car, especially since he called a second time to ask that the money be sent to him in another name and at a different address. Jack also suspected Neal might be escaping creditors or even abandoning Carolyn. But the tremendous excitement over being able to see him again eclipsed all Jack's worries about the future. Nor did he consider the grisly scene that might be occurring between husband and wife in San Francisco. To buy the Hudson Neal had used all their savings. Worse, the realization that Neal could abandon her with a three-month-old baby drove Carolyn to the verge of hysteria.

All Jack could think about was getting Allen to arrange a big New Year's Eve party. He put aside his gloomy journal, skipped his last classes with Brom Weber, and left for North Carolina.

3.

Neal and Al Hinkle had been laid off the railroad the first week of December 1948. After several months of domesticity, Neal was again profoundly restless. Al, who could live awhile off his unemployment compensation, was spoiling for an adventure too. In a way Jack was just Neal's excuse to get back on the road, though in his defense it should be said that Al pressured him to go to New York, and that he was reluctant to leave Carolyn. Neal had just enough money for the down payment on the car, which had a radio but no heater. Needing extra money, Al asked his girlfriend Helen to come along. She insisted he marry her first, so he did. Shortly after they started, Neal began smoking pot in the car, which seriously upset her. When she ran out of money in Tucson, Neal and Al left her there, although Al did give her his railroad pass, good all the way to New Orleans, and told her they'd pick her up there in a week. In a travel bureau in San Francisco they had enlisted another rider, a sailor bound for Kansas, who only discovered en route that Neal was taking him there via the Southwest. In New Mexico the sailor got another surprise when Neal turned the car north to Denver.

By now LuAnne was engaged to be married again, to a seaman currently at sea, but when Neal invited her to New York she joyfully accepted. This time, however, she wasn't the naïve little girl who had let Neal dump her in a room in New Jersey. She was merely coming along for kicks, and she intended to have as much fun as he. If she felt like going to bed with someone else, she would—a condition to which Neal assented. His only stipulation was that she couldn't sleep with Al Hinkle. It seemed Neal was a bit jealous of Al, who was six foot six and handsome. But Al found Neal's jealousy rather strange, since for years he had revered Neal.

The sailor abandoned ship in Denver, and with good reason. It was fifteen below zero, and Neal's heaterless California car turned into a meat freezer, with the three of them huddled together for dear life. As they went south, the weather improved only slightly. They had to drive with the windows down to keep the windshield from frosting over. On one icy stretch of road the car skidded into a ditch and had to be pulled out by a farmer with two horses. The trip became a grueling test of endurance. With almost no money left for food or gas they tried picking up hitchhikers, but few of those had anything to contribute. Finally they found an old wino who promised to stake them if Neal would drive him home—two hundred miles out of their way. When they got to his room, all they found was a pile of rotten potatoes under the sink; LuAnne fried them while Neal dragged the wino around town searching for somebody to lend them money. Returning empty-handed, he joined the others in devouring the potatoes. Then, for the first time in Al's and LuAnne's experience, they saw Neal moved to violence by someone other than a woman he loved (for he and LuAnne often fought physically). He hit the wino, and they left. The rest of the way to North Carolina Neal helped himself at gas pumps, running the meter back to zero before the attendant came around.

On Christmas Eve, the muddy maroon Hudson pulled up in front of the Blakes' little house in Rocky Mount. Jack scarcely recognized Neal, who was unshaven and wore a pair of gas-station coveralls. LuAnne wore a pair of Neal's coveralls too, and all of them looked exceedingly dirty. Jack immediately invited them in. While Al and LuAnne waited in the car for a few minutes, Neal rushed in without embarrassment, for he always took people at their word. LuAnne was impressed at how warmly Jack welcomed them. Not at all ashamed in front of his bewildered relatives, Jack offered his guests the Christmas turkey with full trimmings. Neal lit into the goodies, while again Al and LuAnne trailed hesitantly. From Neal's description, LuAnne had been led to expect that Jack's mother was an ogre, but she was soon pleasantly surprised.

Neal won Gabrielle's favor by offering to move Nin's furniture to New York. With the first load he drove Jack, Al, and LuAnne to Ozone Park. They got there frozen but happy together in their misery. After settling Al and LuAnne in the apartment, Jack returned with Neal to Rocky Mount for his mother and the rest of the furniture. Along the way they got high on marijuana, picked up hitchhikers, and gabbed nonstop. On the second trip Neal got a speeding ticket, and Gabrielle had to pay the fine. Back in New York Jack was amazed to discover that he and Neal had covered two thousand miles in three days.

While they were gone, Hinkle had pawned his railroad watch and LuAnne had pawned her diamond engagement ring. They had also washed their clothes and hung them all over the apartment.

When Jack's mother arrived, LuAnne ran around trying to gather them up, but Gabrielle graciously told her not to fuss. In fact, she made them all feel very welcome.

Jack showed them his recent writing. He had already sketched out the complete story of *Doctor Sax; the Myth of the Rainy Night*. It began with the Vampire, in the form of a bat, flying from Rumania to Lowell in a soft nighttime rain. At the door of Jack's boyhood "castle," the bat changed into a man in a black cloak, a kind of Burroughs-figure. After he knocked, the castle door was opened by a female vampire with circles under her eyes, and the Burroughs vampire said, "My dear, you look lovelier than ever." Alongside these supernatural events, he would work in the 1936 flood and the antics of himself and his friends playing the Shadow. The significance of the rainy night, Jack explained, was that on such nights "the world is softened and somehow connected together forever." The other novel, *On the Road*, was naturally of more interest to them. He told them he had invented much of the story, and for background had used Neal's recollections of Ed Uhl's ranch, where he had worked on probation from reform school.

During the few days they stayed at the apartment, Jack was often working on both books. All of them were impressed and Neal, especially, admired Jack's ability to sit at the typewriter for several hours at a stretch, for to him such solitary labor was unbearable.

Although Jack throve on his friends' belief in him, he couldn't keep them in Ozone Park, since Nin and her family would soon be moving in. Manhattan would be a more convenient location for them anyway, and they could all have more fun away from his mother's watch. They began searching for a friend in Manhattan who could lodge the three of them. The only person immediately available was Ed Stringham, who put them up for a night and fed them frankfurters.

To Ed it was clear that Jack was fascinated with Neal's way of handling women. Jack was also playing straight man to get Neal to display his wit, and it was embarrassing to see him in such a subservient role. When Ed saw Neal in action, he was terrified. They all hopped in the Hudson and rushed down to 42nd Street to find Huncke, then rushed back up to the Royal Roost. Soon Ed learned that he was safe in Neal's hands, at least while they were attached to a steering wheel. But he was still distressed by the way Neal worked on people to get whatever he could from them. One of the things Ed liked about Jack was that he wasn't at all an operator. Luckily for Neal, Allen Ginsberg was more than happy to be used, and when they found him the next day he let the whole crew move into his apartment on York Avenue.

Allen was now working nights at Associated Press and writing long Blakean poems. Many years of failing to be loved, of failing to be respectable like his father, of worrying over his mother in the mental hospital, had bequeathed him a gentle dignity and a weary skepticism. He asked the purpose of Neal's flight across the country, and as usual Neal's only answer was to dash off somewhere else. Yet no matter how settled Allen became, he was always ready to keep up with the madness of someone he loved. So when Neal and the others moved in, he took time off from his job and just grooved with them a while, as curious as Jack to see where the kicks would end.

A big New Year's Eve party was held at the basement apartment of Herb Benjamin. There were three bands playing, and in the crush of people were Columbia students, uptown women in furs, and artists and teaheads of all description. Jack brought Pauline, who was upset by his new wildness in the presence of Neal. Actually Jack was troubled about their relationship, wondering if she would ever divorce her husband and worried that even if she did, she could never understand his restless lifestyle. Neal told Jack he would fix things up. As a result, Jack got drunk faster than usual, letting Neal take Pauline aside for a good talk, which turned out so good that she followed him out to the Hudson for a more private conference.

For the first time Jack got really angry at Neal. Cocky from all the booze he tried to drag LuAnne to bed, but he came on so strong and acted so gauche that she was repelled. Jack told her how he planned to rebuke Neal, but by the time Neal returned, he was too high to recall any grudge. He and Neal raced around the city picking up more people.

Back at the party Neal encountered Lucien. There was a natural rivalry between them, since they were both conscious of being Jack's heroes, Neal the Western and Lucien the Eastern. Neal was envious that Jack had already written a novel about Lucien (*The Hippos*), and that Jack attached so much mythological significance to the killing of Kammerer. Granting that Lucien might once have been a "child of the rainbow," Neal claimed he was now just a rather conventional coward, trying to make a go in the commercial world and "living in the illusion of the past." [132] Arbitrating between them, Jack said that Neal was his "brother," while Lucien was his "laird." With his Breton ancestry Jack felt a kinship with other Celts, like Irish Neal and Scotch Lucien. But he felt a special closeness to Lucien, since he believed the surname *Carr* derived from the same Celtic root, *ker* (house), that occurred in his own surname. Whereas he and Neal were merely "blood brothers," Jack liked to think that he and Lucien actually shared royal ancestors. Though Lucien had little use for Jack's crazy friends, and less for Jack's sophistry, he indulged Jack from a deep affection, knowing his desperate need to find people to receive his tenderness.

In the early morning of New Year's Day, 1949, they ended up at Holmes' apartment amid a coalition of revelers fragmented from other parties. Neal brought in a man and woman who had opium to smoke and then as the pipe started going around, he disappeared again. Left alone together, getting mellow on the opium, Jack and LuAnne felt a resurgence of their long-deferred romance, but once again Jack was reluctant to just grapple her. Instead he asked her to dance, and they began swirling and leaping around the room. Several times Jack even tossed her in the air and caught her. The intimacy between them that had begun developing during LuAnne's first visit to New York suddenly blossomed. Through that dance they compensated for their mutual sense of inadequacy, of being out of place amid people to whom kicks came easy. As they danced together, their confidence soared, and they didn't care who was watching.

In the days to come, both Neal and LuAnne tried to persuade Jack to forget Pauline. Neither of them thought her his type. She seemed giggly, demanding, and hopelessly square (she thought people who smoked pot were addicts). Besides, Neal warned, Jack was liable to be killed by her vengeful husband. But his loyalty to her was unshakable, and Neal and LuAnne were amazed to see their old timid Jack so willing to take chances.

Part of his new self-assurance came from the feeling that he would soon get a break in his literary career. Alfred Kazin was now reading *The Town and the City*. Although Jack considered Kazin's recommendation his "last chance" to get the novel published,[133] he no longer doubted that he would go on writing. Besides, he was confident that Kazin would like the book. And even if he didn't, Jack believed what Neal had told him: "Everything's always all right. And that's *it*."

It was their term for the meaning and happiness most people spent a lifetime seeking, but which was available to anyone who just stayed in touch with his own consciousness. One could only find *it* by coasting from moment to moment with the flux of mind. *It* represented the dissolution of time and the immediate experience of immortality. Neal's philosophy suited Jack perfectly, since Jack had decided to forget the pressures of earning a living and family responsibilities and just involve himself in living. He wanted to spend some time meeting people, seeing places, doing things. In a few weeks he and Neal would head down to New Orleans to ship out, and if they didn't succeed at that, they would move on to San Francisco. Now, while Neal met people and pursued adventures all over town, Jack and LuAnne had long talks, and she was surprised that for the first time he really seemed happy.

Al Hinkle was in the habit of disappearing for a few days, just to walk around the city by himself. During one of his absences, Jack took Neal and LuAnne to visit Alan Ansen in Woodmere, Long Island. Ansen met them at the train station and as soon as Neal saw him, he knew Ansen had *it* too. Ansen was huge, homely, and un-abashedly effeminate. As they walked through this quiet, wealthy town, he kept swishing and screaming. He lived in a mansion with his aristocratic aunt, who detested all his wild friends. Needless to say, she was flabbergasted at the sight of Jack's motley crew. But Neal rushed right in, yelling, "How do you do? Lovely house!" When she took Ansen aside and tried to protest, he told her, "Go fuck yourself!" They fought awhile, then Ansen told the others not to worry about the "old bag" because he "ran the place."

Upstairs, Jack browsed bedazzled among Ansen's thousands of rare books, while Neal and LuAnne rummaged through his thousands of records and tapes. They put on a Verdi opera, and Alan acted it out in torn pajamas, with him singing soprano and LuAnne bass! When they all got terribly drunk, Neal and LuAnne got into a bitter fight and started wrestling; he knocked her down, but a second later was on his knees, kissing her, and to LuAnne it felt like they were in a scene from the movies. Finally Neal went to bed with Alan, and she and Jack took a bath together. By this time Neal was practically pushing Jack into her arms, with the assurance that the harder he pushed, the guiltier Jack would feel. By instigating an affair between them, Neal pratically guaranteed that they would never get seriously involved, and at the same time he prevented LuAnne from straying to men who were more dangerous competition.

Ansen returned with them to Ginsberg's apartment, bringing a couple of sailors he had picked up. Ginsberg was disgusted with such camp. His apartment was tiny, and he was liable to be overwhelmed by the brouhahas Ansen engineered.[134]

Despite the crazy arrangement, Allen persisted in his semi-straight life. Al Hinkle slept on the couch, and Neal and LuAnne slept on Ginsberg's cot. When Allen came home from work at six in the morning, he somehow managed to climb in with them. He would put his head on one of Neal's shoulders, while LuAnne had her head on the other. Neal was sharing his attention with all of them, even if he couldn't satisfy Allen's specific demand for sex. LuAnne, Neal, and Allen (in that order) had slept as a threesome almost two years before in Denver, and on those occasions too, the only sex had occurred between Neal and LuAnne. In a sense Allen was another token man he tossed to LuAnne, to appease her demand for sexual variety. Nevertheless, she accepted the routine with alacrity, placating Allen by cleaning house and cooking her famous spaghetti—in a dishpan! To help pay expenses, she even got a job in the drugstore at Radio City.

To get to work at seven in the morning she had to retire early, while the others stayed up all night drinking and getting high. Ed Stringham thought it disgraceful that a woman should have to support an apartment full of men (Jack was hanging around practically full time now too). There were parties every night, and one night LuAnne herself resented missing the fun. She smoked pot, took benzedrine, and drank until it was time to go to work. Seeing how stoned she was, everybody rode down to Radio City with her and tried to sober her up in a coffee shop. The coffee didn't work, and she lost the job.

She and Neal also stayed with the Holmeses for a couple of weeks. Holmes had heard Jack raving about this cowboy genius and was anxious to get to know Neal. Learning Neal's new whereabouts, people from all over the city descended on the apartment. It baffled LuAnne how John could go on writing amid such distraction. His wife Marian worked every day to support the household, and they seemed to have an ideal relationship. All the more was LuAnne confounded to see Marian flirting with Jack right under John's nose. But with Marian Jack behaved as he was prone to do with women; he retreated shyly, half disbelieving her attraction to him, and half flustered that he should be chased by his best friend's wife.

4.

Jack had reason to feel shame at home too. After Nin, Paul, and Paul, Jr., moved in, the family complained that Jack was spending too little time with them, so he agreed to join them in the spring on a communal farm in New Jersey, growing alfalfa. But in the meantime, he suggested he could help them most by going to sea with Neal and saving some money. He sincerely wanted to repent for the many years he had wasted "goofing off." [135] Even after receiving his letter of acceptance from the Sorbonne, he maintained his resolve to stay with his family (after returning from sea) for at least another six months. He wrote Ed White that he would love to explore Paris with him, and that he even contemplated going to China afterward. But he explained that, just as he had learned he couldn't "screw every woman in the world" (one of Wolfe's desires), so he knew he had to make choices about what to accomplish. Right now his books and family were high priority.

Still, as much as he loved his family, being with them caused him intense pain. The little baby, Paul, splashed in a tub on the same spot where, two years before, his father's ravaged belly had been tapped just before he died. Watching life grow out of death filled Jack with "savageness." But at this point he was obsessed with the freedom of the will, and he determined to curb his anger and turn toward "sweeter things, sweeter intentions, sweeter thoughts, greater life." The power of choice gave him the joyfulness, he imagined, of a bird wheeling in the sky, free to dive where it wished. For himelf he chose neither exile nor perpetual kicks, but rather marriage, domesticity, and "the babies of my own flesh." [136]

In mid-January, marriage and settling down were no longer just a remote possibility, when he learned that Alfred Kazin had recommended his novel to Robert Giroux at Harcourt Brace. Jack made arrangements to complete his courses at the New School. He even wrote Brom Weber apologizing for having missed his last classes, and trying to patch up their misunderstanding. Yet, despite the encouragement, he could never quite get his own life in focus with Neal nearby.

Jack liked nothing better than to watch Neal wow a potpourri of intellectuals, socialites, and hotshots, perhaps because he had impressed so few of them himself. Neal picked up a rich woman from the Upper East Side, who for a while paid all his bills. Lean, dressed all in black, with a huge hat, this "Spider Woman" looked weirdly out of place in a dirty room full of beer cans. Jack tried to enhance Neal in her eyes, boasting, "You think I'm a great writer? This guy's a much greater writer than I am!" When she asked to see something Neal had written, Jack was in a fix until one of Neal's letters was procured. He insisted Neal read it aloud. Although she didn't understand a word of it, she was enchanted with his presentation. Neal was certainly a much better actor than Jack. Anyway, as far as they were concerned the words didn't matter, since life could never be reproduced exactly in language. In their writing they tried to generate the sort of ecstasy they felt listening to jazz, and the important thing to Jack was that Neal always managed to convey his *experience.*

Jack promoted Neal as a myth figure, just as Allen had done for Jack; in effect, Jack and Neal's relationship became a mirror image of the intense, almost priestly bond between Jack and Allen. Ginsberg exercised an enormous authority over Jack, who would listen to his advice over the more knowledgeable word of Holmes, Harrington, and Stringham, because Allen was the only type of intellectual he could trust: one who valued feeling above reason. Still, Stringham and his friends had the persistent feeling that Allen was trying to control Jack. Their continual recourse to mysticism especially irritated Stringham and Harrington. Even Holmes, who accepted Jack (at least) as a literary prophet, was often fuddled by the mystical gobbledygook Jack and Allen spoke together. In his journal, John noted that Jack and Allen seemed to have their own private language, full of symbols so arcane and all-embracing—like the "Forest of Arden"—as to be virtually meaningless. What puzzled him more was that Jack insisted Allen's poetry was "real imaginative . . . really great" even though Jack admitted he couldn't understand it! Admiring the power of Allen's imagery, Jack was prepared to defend him even when he shrieked childish nonsense. Allen's "death like hold on Jack" worried Holmes,[137] but Jack rejoiced in the fact that someone should think so much like him that he could abjure his individuality. What Jack longed for (he wrote Holmes) was "the eventual world-wide melling of minds," and his rapport with Allen seemed a big step in that direction.

Jack's admiration for Neal was of a different order. Despite Neal's considerable intellect, what overwhelmed Jack, distorting his literary judgment, was Neal's personality. He realized that Neal was conning everyone, but he also saw that Neal often felt guilty. If Neal's blarney paid off, it made him feel even worse. Although Neal had originally learned to con as a matter of sheer survival, his continued deceptions were more often a response to loneliness. That he had the courage to go on conning, aware of the utter hopelessness of ever assuaging that loneliness, was to Jack a wonderfully heroic feat, a sort of yoga, or penance for dragging his misery through the world.

Neal met Cannastra, who admired him although the two never got to know each other well. Like Jack, Neal was someone who would follow Bill into all his private abysses. There was also a *nostalgie de la boue* among Cannastra's friends. When they wanted to go to some bar besides their standard, the San Remo, they would either pick a high-camp place like Tony's Trueville or, far more often, the most proletarian bar available. They were drawn to places like the Belgica, a Basque tavern, where they all pretended to speak Basque. Neal fit perfectly into the drinking, campy side of the Cannastra group. Merely another specimen to be observed, he wasn't important the way Jack was. Jack and Allen tried in vain to explain what they saw in Neal, but his life was just too remote from the group's concerns. That kind of class difference cut through the whole scene, so that even one's college—Cannastra's Harvard versus Stern's New York University, for example—affected how one was accepted.

Neal and Jack had some of their best times by themselves. High on marijuana, the two of them went to hear George Shearing at Birdland. Neal's shouts of "Yes! Yes! Yes!" seemed to drive Shearing to ever more rapid and complex bursts of chords. Yet Neal compared the blind pianist to God; Shearing was self-contained in his own perfection, even if conscious and perhaps glad of the world's appreciation. When "God" left the stage, there was nothing to do but return to the "rainy night." [138] Neal's simple profundity in the midst of such frantic kicks was a major source of inspiration for *On the Road*.

Jack was having memorable talks with many others too. After LuAnne told him her life story, they discussed love, fantasizing about the "Slow Boat to China," the title of a popular song, which eventually became the name of Neal's Hudson. With Allen, as with Neal, Jack discussed "Everything." Solemn as a *vates* in his silk bathrobe, Allen predicted the "days of wrath" soon to befall them all. In the West End, he asked Neal and Jack, "How did we get here, angels?" Jack replied, "This life is our last chance to be honest . . . really the Last Chance Saloon." [139] But it was through Al Hinkle that Jack got his greatest new insight.

During his walks around the city, Hinkle had seen several visions, including his own ghost dogging him on Times Square, and he described these visions and many earlier ones to Jack. In his youth Hinkle had been a seaman, and Jack was amazed to hear him referring to angels as simply as he talked of the sea, girls, and other experiences. Life was all one to him, the rational and the mad, and he enjoyed every minute. It struck Jack that he had "foreseen" Hinkle when he created the character of Ray Smith in *On the Road*. Hinkle confirmed his suspicion that the new American hipsters, the "furtives," had gone beyond simple flesh kicks and were now concerned with God and holy Visions.

Visions' capital V and the noun *furtive* had both originated with Jack. In the fall of 1948, he and John Holmes had had many discussions about their generation. Tantalized by concise epithets like "Lost Generation" and "Existentialism," Holmes had been prodding Jack to characterize their own attitude. In *Nothing More to Declare*, Holmes recalled Jack's seminal insight into the new consciousness:

> . . . one evening as he described the way the young hipsters of Times Square walked down the street—watchful, cat-like, inquisitive, close to the buildings, *in* the street but not *of* it—I interrupted him to say that I thought we *all* walked like that, but what was the peculiar quality of mind behind it?
>
> "It's a sort of furtiveness," he said. "Like we were a generation of furtives. You know, with an inner knowledge there's no use flaunting on that level, the level of the 'public,' a kind of beatness—I mean, being right down to it, to ourselves, because we all *really* know where we are—and a weariness with all the forms, all the conventions of the world. . . . It's something like that. So I guess you might say we're a *beat* generation," and he laughed a conspiratorial, the-Shadow-knows kind of laugh at his own words and at the look on my face.

At one of the parties while Neal was in town, Jack elaborated his definition of the Beat Generation. He told Hinkle that he had also intended the connotation of *upbeat*. For the first time in years he believed man's future was secure. If the present generation was beat, he said, it was soon to be *beatific*. In fact, he used the expression "beatific generation"—an occurrence, had it been documented, which would have disproved the charge years later that *beatific* was an irrelevant afterthought to *beat*. *Beatific* had implications for his writing too. Understanding that the strength of his generation lay in a kind of ascetic renunciation, Jack achieved a "creative insouciance." After he ceased worrying about the fate of *The Town and the City,* he realized its creation had been "inevitable," just as his future works would also be inevitable. He was overcome with joy to discover that his life's work was simply to "love God and . . . write it." [140]

Out of suffering he was forging an idealism far greater, and yet more realistic and resilient, than the ambitious dreams of his youth. As he had once planned to triumph personally over all obstacles and hardships, he now envisioned the salvation of his entire generation. Holmes shared Jack's optimism, and together they predicted that "all America's picking up, changing, becoming sweeter, no more wars, sweet presidents. . . ." *Picking up* was a pun on the term for using drugs to get high, and certainly an honest pleasure-seeking was to be part of the coming American Shangri-La. But the real key to tranquility would be found in a gentle tolerance toward all one's neighbors, even the so-called criminals like Neal, who if treated with sufficient kindness would turn out to be merely backward saints. As Jack and Holmes envisioned him, the great American of the future would be "the hitchhiking Negro saint"—an apotheosis of the Americans currently most despised. It was the beat-down Americans who put the most effort into the search for love, and speaking of that quest Holmes said, "Something will come of it," a catch-phrase Jack used all his life to refer to their 1948 optimism.

Coming after these talks with Holmes, his immersion in "honky-tonk nights" profoundly altered his conception of *On the Road.* He planned to retitle the novel "The Hipsters" or "The Gone Ones" or "The Furtives," and to make it a study of "the Hunkies and the Neals and the LuAnnes." And yet, as he noted in his journal, Neal's arrival in New York didn't strengthen his naturalistic intentions for *On the Road* so much as it enlarged his "supernatural Godly intentions" for *Doctor Sax.*[141]

Emboldened by Neal, Jack wrote to Brom Weber (in the letter cited earlier), explaining the basis of his literary mysticism and reworking a Nietzschean aphorism: "Perhaps nothing is true but everything is real." He also prophesied that their divergent ideas would prove to be "as the dawdlings of seagulls when the great ship is sinking (OR arriving.)—with its big freight of meaningful decision." In the same rhapsodic mood, he began deluging Alfred Kazin with letters about Doctor Sax, written on yellow paper and simply "crazy" in Kazin's eyes.

Kazin wasn't the only one to whom Jack had become incomprehensible. Exhausted from revels with Neal and others, he frequently broke his promises to meet Pauline. She was horrified by his irresponsibility and by her own credulity in planning to marry him. To stir him to some definite action, she replied with frenzied sarcasm and recriminations. She hoped he would go to hell, she wrote, so that the devil would keep him on his feet with a pitchfork, as punishment for his taking her to bed so often! She also threatened to have her husband beat him up. Jack felt he could handle her husband in a fight, but he was profoundly disturbed by the charges she brought against his character. "My husband isn't a bastard like the likes of you," she wrote."You couldn't even polish his shoes. The pity of it all is this, that I can't get you to go out and work. I'd make you work so damn hard the sweat would fall from your brow like the rain you keep talking about. That's the only thing that will save you. Work, Manual Labor. I suggest that you try writing about real people like us and not jerks like Doctor Sax and his rainy nights. Don't ever call yourself a religious writer again, you don't know your ass from a hole in the ground about religion. You brought me down to your level but that won't be for long."

To prove he wasn't affected by the letter, Jack showed it to all his friends. Neal joked about her summoning God as a witness against him. According to Neal, most "pieces" just complained about their men screwing around or not doing the dishes.[142] To Neal a woman was scarcely more than her anatomy, but Jack's swagger masked a great deal of guilt. Pauline felt that Jack's passive acceptance of their breakup, his failure to even try to defend himself, showed his essential lack of character. Although he concluded she was a "whore," what embittered him most was the realization that "We're all whores." In his journal he worried about his growing "loutishness," which even Lucien had remarked. After rationalizing that his loutishness was a character mask to be used literarily, he confessed in anguish that at one time he "would have considered becoming an imbecile and going out to shine her husband's bloody shoes." Now such prostration was "too much" for him; he concluded that it was "too late."

Jack was caught in a bind—too late for Pauline and too soon for LuAnne. One night at Allen's, Neal suggested Jack and LuAnne climb into bed with him. To begin with, Jack was uneasy because it was his father's deathbed, which he had given to Allen. Then, despite the pleasure of stroking LuAnne (sunk in the sag between them), Jack found himself unable to actually make love under Neal's scrutiny. He asked Neal to leave the room and when he was gone, told LuAnne they should postpone romantic involvement until they reached San Francisco and Neal returned to Carolyn. In his journal Jack claimed he really didn't care whether he had an affair with LuAnne. In truth, he still cared too much about everything.

Although Pauline discredited Jack's spiritual aims, he was now writing intensely religious poems in his journal. In one he dealt with the powerful conflict between his desire to serve God and his desire to see the world, which was the "city of God." On the one hand, he felt he should stay in the home where God had "appointed" him to write, on the other he knew that it was only on "the streets of God" that he would find the things he wanted to write about. In this poem, he resolves to see "what I will never see again" even though the result be God's anger. Despite his assuming the persona of Lucifer, the poem ends with Jack lying in a pool of red light in his own room, having passed through death to live again: a resurrected Christ. That tension between angelic and diabolic nature would animate much of his best writing; indeed it would be one of the chief sources of energy for the Beat Generation.

5.

Jack intended to stay in New York only long enough to finish his classes at the New School and to hear Harcourt Brace's verdict on his novel. He let his hair grow long, left most of his letters unanswered, and neglected Adele as he had Pauline. His new maxim was "Mystic makes no mud," by which he meant that an impulsive "boppish" way of life let him see his own intentions more clearly than "the narrow 'white light' of our surface rationality." [143] When the others momentarily changed their plan to go to New Orleans, deciding instead to stay in Allen's apartment, he helped assemble the necessary accoutrements: heater, phonographs, wire recorder, and pot. That plan was rejected in favor of another to go to sea, which was replaced in turn by some other whim. Always Jack followed placidly, no longer worried where it would get him, just glad to be going. As a concession to his mother, though, he did get a haircut.

Carolyn wrote from San Francisco asking money to buy a couch, and Jack sent eighteen dollars (with the slight regret that he could have used the money for new shirts). He was convinced there were no problems he couldn't solve with some equally off-handed gesture. Still, the uncertainty of his future left a "knot" in his stomach. There were too many options he couldn't write off. He was once again deeply satisfied by the domesticity in Ozone Park, but he was still intrigued by the prospect of studying at the Sorbonne and exploring Paris with Ed White. Traveling with Neal was far from the most attractive choice. Neal had begun beating LuAnne again, and at a bop club he took two dollars from Lucien's wallet. If the hip side of Jack was interested in such "savagery," his older moral side was both shocked and disappointed. He considered simply going to sea by himself.

Neal's "sweet lunacy" appealed to only one of his many moods. Often he preferred the quiet company of his brother-in-law Paul;

they'd go looking for jobs together, or spend an evening watching a John Wayne movie. Jack admired this big, plainspoken, hard-working southerner as much as he did the "high cats" of Times Square. He himself still had an enormous capacity for hard work—a greater capacity for it, perhaps, than any of his friends (excepting John Holmes). In one week he wrote term papers on Satanism, Whitman, Dreiser and Lewis, and Tolstoy.

Throughout this whole period of vacillation, he retained the conviction that he was a "man of destiny." In his journal he wrote that he was being punished by God for some unspecified crime. His punishment, however, would be to "learn all" and to "labor great books"! One of the forces driving him was guilt over having disappointed his father. Fortunately his father had displayed as much benevolence as wrath, leaving Jack with a strong sense that everyone's needs would eventually be met. His optimism was daily being confirmed, as he saw his mother serenely giving all she had to her family, saw lonely Allen Ginsberg attracting an ever larger coterie of friends, saw Neal finding love without having to con for it. At the same time, however, Jack felt that his own destiny was to be a martyr to his joys: to "burn." In giving light to the world, it seemed, his own life must necessarily be consumed in pain and strife—he could gain no permanent satisfaction. Searching his desires, he realized that he was frightened of the lonely peace of heaven. It was only the struggle to get there for which he lived. Thoughts of suicide teased him with a final solution to this paradox, but he bluffed that he could endure any outrage, including the publishers' continued delay in accepting his book.

He and Neal were both looking for an excuse to get moving. Ed White and Bob Burford were due in New York in early February, since they would be sailing for Europe on the *Queen Mary*, and Jack even contemplated driving to Denver with Neal to pick them up. In the meantime, Burroughs called from New Orleans to complain that Helen Hinkle had moved in with him. Penniless, she was determined to wait for Al's return. Besides being a burden, she was also probably an embarrassment to Burroughs, who was then occupied with making underworld connections to satisfy his heroin habit. Jack and Neal agreed to deliver Al Hinkle as soon as possible. For traveling expenses Hinkle sold his leather jacket, and Jack withdrew from the bank the few dollars left from his GI benefits.

On the evening of January 19, 1949, Jack, Neal, LuAnne, and Al set out through the Lincoln Tunnel into New Jersey. Jack and Neal were both tremendously excited to be traveling West together. For all of them the trip was a fantasy come true, and like a little kid set free Jack was willing to try anything, even driving the car for a stretch. They arrived in Washington, D.C., on the day of Harry Truman's inauguration, and saw a display of military firepower that could have quickly ignited the Cold War.

In Virginia Al took the wheel and passed a stopped school bus, which was on the other side of a divided highway. Probably because of their California plates, they were stopped by the police. At the courthouse the police grew interested in LuAnne, who was eighteen but looked much younger. She also had an ounce of pot in her underwear. The police questioned them separately. When they asked LuAnne what she was doing, she told them she was Neal's wife. When they questioned Neal, he said he was returning to his wife in California. After lengthy explanations, the police decided to let them go with a stiff fine. Already enraged by the interruption to the trip, Neal became frantic at the thought of losing most of his gas money. To keep him from exploding, Hinkle volunteered to serve time in jail in lieu of paying the fine. Neal quickly accepted Al's offer, but the police insisted Neal pay the twenty-five dollars under threat of bringing more serious charges against him.

They were forced to pick up hitchhikers. A Jewish boy said he could get some money from any Jewish jewelry store. He went into the first store they saw, and Jack followed him to watch his routine. Explaining that he was a "good Jewish boy," he asked for five dollars to keep from having to steal, and to everyone's amazement he got it. With the money the group bought cheese, bread, and potato chips to last the rest of the way to New Orleans.

At night Neal began pulling his old trick of coasting silently into gas stations, then putting in the gas himself and running back the meter after every few dollars' worth in case the attendant woke up. By daybreak they were passing the northern tip of Florida, and though they were nearly broke they were having a high time, with Jack and Neal banging on the dashboard to the rhythm of the radio. Figuring they had enough money to split two orders of hotcakes they stopped at a diner. The owner's employees had all failed to show up for the morning rush. Hinkle offered him their services washing dishes and waiting on customers, and in exchange the owner fed them all the hotcakes they could eat. Later they sold their spare tire for a tank of gas.

That night, as they drove through the bayou country approaching New Orleans, they listened on the radio to mystery stories. LuAnne nestled between Jack and Neal like a frightened child. To frighten her more, Jack related the killing of David Kammerer. With his arm tightly around her he described every minute detail, vividly demonstrating the stabbing, while Neal giggled like a conspirator at her torture.

When they heard New Orleans jazz on the radio, and smelled the Mississippi River and the teeming city, they went wild with joy. On the ferry to Algiers Neal leaned over the railing, danced on the bridge, and looked ready to fly into space. But the sight of Burroughs' place quickly quenched their zeal. The house was rickety, the grass high as a fence, and the actual fence and outbuildings already collapsed. Bill wasn't there, and Joan greeted them spirit-lessly.

When Bill got home he welcomed Jack, though he disliked having his house invaded by Jack's starving fellow travelers. Bill was especially angry with Neal, who seemed to be leading Jack and the others on costly, fatiguing, and totally futile flights across the country. Bill and Jack immediately began having long talks together, while Al and Helen struck up their first real romance, Neal and LuAnne devoured what little food was around, Joan ate benzedrine strips, and the children wandered where they pleased.

Bill and Joan had both changed a great deal since Jack had last seen them. Having been arrested for drunken driving in Texas, Bill had felt the need to keep on the move like a fugitive. He was embittered, moreover, by the growing government bureaucracy, which seemed to have no other *raison d'être* than to persecute loners and individualists like himself. Now he was on his way to fresh legal troubles as he scoured New Orleans for a steady heroin supply. A lot of the fire had gone out of him. He had never spent much time in bars, but now he was opposed to going to any bar with Jack. He spent all day in his chair in the corner, with the shades drawn, reading a book or newspaper or nodding out. Sometimes he set up Joan's benzedrine inhalers across the room and cracked them open with his pellet gun. Mostly he just talked about his favorite columnist, the fanatically conservative Westbrook Pegler, and extolled the virtues of prefabricated Lustron houses. His only further amusement was to take string and tie up his many cats, then untie them, and start all over.

If Jack was disappointed in Bill's listlessness, he was shocked by Joan's diseased appearance and psychotic behavior. For the past four years she had been using benzedrine constantly, and she now consumed from three to ten tubes of paper per day. In the fall of 1947 she had again been forcibly hospitalized in Bellevue on suspicion of insanity, and had secured a rapid release only because her husband was a member of the University Club. All the while she had been growing gaunt and hard-faced and a recent case of polio had left her with a limp, further caricaturing her beauty. She puttered about the house and yard day and night, seldom talking except to answer some remark made by Bill—for she could still hear at phenomenal distances—or to take over the conversation when he tired. Her devotion to him was as fierce as her concern for her children, but the hot poker in her flesh distracted her from a calm consideration of their needs, forced her to concentrate on her one overwhelming need for more drugs. In search of some useful task, she often ended up by a big tree in the yard, raking off the thousands of lizards, which climbed right back on. Bill himself would occasionally take a potshot at them.

Having spent years with Neal, LuAnne and Al were not particularly impressed by the strangeness of the household. None of them was even aware that Bill was on the needle, especially since he continually lectured them about the evils of heroin: "A little pot's OK," he'd say, "but stay away from the hard stuff!"

What struck LuAnne most strongly in New Orleans was Jack's sudden loss of exuberance. She suspected he was being influenced by Bill. Neal had gone into a big song and dance to borrow some money from Bill, which he refused to lend. Neal's victims usually knew they were being conned and enjoyed it, because he expended so much effort that it was more like they were paying for the show. But Burroughs had already seen the show in Texas and New York and didn't care to pay for it again. That Jack's old teacher saw the clichés at the heart of Neal's routine of pleading and promising might have upset him. Another cause of Jack's disillusionment was probably his discovery that Neal intended to live with LuAnne again after they got to California, for he was now telling LuAnne he would set her up in a house in Watsonville, at the other end of the railroad line from San Francisco, dividing his free time between her and Carolyn. There was no way Jack could ever make a pass at her as long as Neal was in the picture. He would never overstep the strict code he applied to friendship, any more than he would dare compete with Neal.

Jack's feeling for LuAnne ran deep. One afternoon in New Orleans, Bill and Neal took off together. Left alone, Jack and LuAnne went to a park and smoked pot. He pointed out an endless succession of things he saw in the clouds, encouraging her to do the same, saying that God had told Noah to look for His covenant in the clouds. Years later the beautiful memory of that afternoon would take on a tragic significance for her.

Al Hinkle's marriage to Helen had been more or less of a joke, but he now began to respect her intelligence. Although Burroughs eventually offered to let them both stay, Al preferred to get a job and set up housekeeping with her in New Orleans. When Jack's next GI check arrived, he, Neal, and LuAnne took off by themselves through the Southwest.

As they crossed the Texas desert, it was so hot Neal suggested they all undress. Jack and LuAnne were both reluctant, but Neal never lost a chance to display his pretty body, and the others followed his example. Glimpsing the three striking nudes squished together in the front seat, passing truck drivers nearly swerved off the road. At some Indian ruins Neal led them on a naked romp among the stone blocks and broken statues. As another car neared, Jack and LuAnne ran back to the Hudson while Neal simply posed as a statue.

With Neal's approval Jack grew expert at stealing bread and cheese from sleepy supermarkets. In El Paso, Texas, they realized they would need more money for gas to San Francisco. After vainly searching for riders at share-the-ride places and the bus station, Neal considered pimping for LuAnne, but she was unenthused. A Mexican boy offered to arrange a connection for some pot, but he wanted Neal to help him mug someone afterward. Although Jack was hesitant about meeting the boy in a dark alley, Neal talked him into it. Seeing how LuAnne admired Neal's courage, Jack doubted she would ever keep their secret agreement to live together in San Francisco or New York.

At the wheel as they coasted down the mountains into Benson, Arizona, Jack got another dollar for gas by pawning a watch given him by his brother-in-law. When a policeman demanded to see his driver's license Jack pointed to Neal, sleeping beside LuAnne in the back seat, and the officer ordered Neal to come out with his hands up. After Neal produced sufficient documents the policeman released them, but his official pettiness reminded Jack of why he preferred the humanity of an antihero to that of the automatons of law and order.

He directed Neal to Tucson, Arizona, so they could borrow some money from Alan Harrington. They found Alan seated in the desert, typing at a little table next to an adobe house, where he lived with his wife. He took them to his mother's large hacienda nearby. A wealthy woman, she patronized the arts and kept a young bearded would-be writer in residence. They spent the day and evening boozing and basking in the luxuries there. It was terribly hot, and when the young writer kissed LuAnne, Neal flew into a jealous rage. While Neal and the writer argued, Jack and LuAnne did their crazy Nijinsky-ish dancing to the expensive stereo. Jack had planned to stay for a couple of days, but Neal insisted they leave.

Five dollars from Alan fueled them to Bakersfield, California, where an Okie hitchhiker got them $3 from his family. In the late afternoon they came through the Oakland foothills to see San Francisco shining whitely against a golden sunset and the first balloons of Pacific potato-patch fog. The city of "secret Chinatown chop sueys" and pink neon cocktail bar signs never failed to thrill Jack. But without any preliminaries Neal asked him and LuAnne where they wanted to be dropped off. Gaping at each other, they were suddenly aware that they had nowhere to go. Finally LuAnne said, "O'Farrell Street," and Neal replied, "Fine, fine, that's great, that Blackstone Hotel. . . ."

6.

Aiming for a homecoming dinner with Carolyn, Neal set their suitcases on the sidewalk and said he'd call them soon. As he drove away, Jack turned in a daze to LuAnne and asked, "You got any money?" He and LuAnne hadn't a penny between them. LuAnne had never seen a man look so lost. Jack waited for her to take the initiative, and finally she went to talk with the proprietor of the hotel, whom she knew and who agreed to let them stay there for a few days on credit. Then LuAnne took Jack to her girlfriend's for a meal.

Both of them were utterly confused. Against her better judgment LuAnne had allowed herself to get involved with Neal again; and now, as always, he had deeply hurt her without even seeming to realize it. But she at least had known what to expect, whereas Jack had been caught completely off guard. In their hotel room that first night, he cried in her arms. They stayed in the room for three days straight, talking their hearts out and making love. But LuAnne needed a man to lean on, and he wanted to lean on her. Without any real foundation they planned an idyllic future as husband and wife, then awoke every morning to the questions of where to eat and would the manager throw them out? Weary of waiting for Jack to act, she went to borrow money from some seamen, friends of her fiancé, who hadn't yet returned from sea. She also went out with her girlfriend's boss, who owned a night club, hoping he might hire her too. In his furious paranoia Jack assumed she had turned to prostitution.

LuAnne found she could no longer reach him. Without the supercharger of Neal behind them he ignored her. To be with Neal he had given all his money and thrown aside all his other interests, and now he wondered how he had been deluded into making such a hopeless trip. He wandered the streets, full of guilt over having betrayed his hard-working mother and her comfortable home, glaring into restaurant windows and imagining himself the bummish reincarnation of an eighteenth-century thief. Even when Neal returned a week later to bring him to his house, Jack couldn't muster any more faith in him. His sympathy was stirred, though, when he saw how hard Neal was trying to make his marriage work, for he had landed a job selling cookware. In any case, he was still ready to join Neal for kicks, like listening to Slim Gaillard and pursuing musicians and women all over town. But when his mother forwarded another GI check, he was glad of the chance to leave.

He and Neal had been seeing LuAnne regularly. On Jack's last night there, they took her to a black jazz club in Oakland, to hear a tenor player who was a friend of Neal's. In Denver they had often spent whole nights in Five Points, the black section, without encountering any hostility, but at this club in Oakland, a black man pulled the chair out from under LuAnne. As Jack looked around wildly to find the culprit, the tension and hate surged against them more forcefully than the music, although Neal, bopping about at the foot of the bandstand, was oblivious. Jack and LuAnne nervously waited for him to return. In the meantime she had to go to the ladies' room, where three women cornered her, and only permitted her to leave after she convinced them she was a whore. She and Jack finally talked Neal into leaving, though he thought they were crazy. As they headed for the door, the crowd blocked and buffeted them. Outside, Jack told LuAnne he had thought that any minute he'd get a knife in the ribs.

The next day at the bus station he and LuAnne parted with a few tears, agreeing that they should settle their separate lives before trying to live together. He had to learn the fate of *The Town and the City,* she had to decide if she would actually marry her fiancé. But Jack's mind was more on the adventure of fresh travels than on failed romances. Stumping the ticket agent, he requested to get to New York via the Pacific Northwest. With ten home-made sandwiches he rode north through a blizzard all the way to Seattle, then cut east past the Dalles, through Idaho to Butte, Montana, where he spent a night in the saloons and was deeply moved by an old blackjack dealer who reminded him of his father and W. C. Fields. The next day he rolled through the Dakota Badlands, down through Minnesota and Wisconsin to Chicago, and finally stopped again for a day in Detroit to see Edie. Her mother was remarried, to another millionaire, an heir of the Berry Paint Company, and they all lived in a brownstone mansion on Lake Shore Drive in Grosse Pointe. Jack was fascinated by the castlelike tower that held Edie's room. She was studying "floralculture," and he suggested she return to college in New York. They made vague plans to try living together again, but she was now completely dependent on her family, and Jack had less than ever to offer her in the way of security.

Although seeing Edie always left him with a special glow, the most important product of the whole cross-continental trip was a detailed travel journal, in which he had recorded fresh characters and landscapes that would give verisimilitude to *On the Road.*

He got home the second week of February, in the middle of the night, and devoured all the eggs and bacon in the house. The next day he registered at the New School. Learning that Ed White and Bob Burford were about to sail for Europe, he walked all the way to the dock to see them off. Another Denverite, Frank "Buck" Jeffries, was going with them; although this was the first time they met, Jack took a shine to Buck's fun-loving spirit. Aboard the *Queen Mary* that night there was a big party, whose guests included Ginsberg, Ed Stringham, Tom Livornese, Hal Chase, Ginger, and Lucien. Jack spent the night getting drunk on champagne in their cabin, which was located far down and amidships. Wanting Jack's companionship in Paris, Burford tried to keep him from hearing the announcement for guests to go ashore. Finally Bob openly tempted him with visions of "big blasts" together. Although Jack toyed with the idea of stowing away, he finally declared that he had important work to finish in New York. It was after midnight, and they barely got him off the ship in time. He promised to visit them in Paris.

Back in Ozone Park he found *Doctor Sax* rapidly taking shape in his mind—as "a description of darkness"—and he hurried to get it on paper. At the same time he was occupied with a full load of courses at the New School.

In the style of T. S. Eliot he wrote a painstaking critical essay called "The Minimization of Thomas Wolfe in His Own Time." His chief aim was to distinguish between the "intellectual" and the "metaphysical" mind, and to insist on the latter's superior power and beauty. As an example, he supposed the two different minds considering "a man musing on eternity." The intellectual mind would merely label this phenomenon as "wonderingly thinking"; whereas a metaphysical "genius" like Shakespeare would coin the phrase "dumbly mulling," whose meaning was conveyed less by the definition of the words than by their very sound, the lag and drone of the assonance and alliteration. In literature the intellectual mind produced prose; the metaphysical mind, poetry. As a novelist, his preference for the metaphysical approach meant he was staking out one of the most difficult territories: prose-poetry. It would force him to thunder cosmic wisdom, like a Goethe or Melville, or to make a gibbering fool of himself—which all lords of language did on occasion. Jack acknowledged that Wolfe was not often "metaphysically sharp," but he felt that at his best Wolfe could sound inimitable metaphysical music, in lines like "Great boats are blowing in the gulfs of night." To Jack it was important that a writer be accurate in tone as well as diction, and that he strive for "the furthest possible reach of an idea, or image, the most basic, simple, possible way of evoking this feeling on the edge of relative meaning. . . ."

In the first few months of 1949, his journal grew increasingly philosophical and religious. Preoccupied as always with the problem of will, he concluded that man's free will existed in his ignorance of God's foreordained plan. He hypothesized the origin of language in man's complaint to God over human misery. Though such complaint was both ignorant and fruitless, it often produced "song" of great beauty. To the psychoanalytic charge that his love of God was a death-instinct, he responded that neurosis theory was itself a manifestation of anxiety. He felt that man could know no absolute truth, only degrees of light. At present Jack himself had to make do with a few "tapers burning in my wilderness." The source of light was the eye of God, toward which he was irresistibly drawn.

Although he drew courage from the idea that he was approaching "direct feelings with God," his personal life grew desperate. Assuming that *The Town and the City* was too big and dull to sell, he cast about for a "lovely girl" who could share his "understanding of eternity." Happily married he could go on to write *Doctor Sax,* which he now considered a necessary preparation for *On the Road.* As for getting a living, he supposed he could "steal fruit" from some-body else's garden. The mask of Satan was always just a bluff with him, as he continued to worry about his mother having to work on her feet all day. Ahead he saw death for both of them, the "jump to spacelessness"; and though he claimed to find comfort in the thought of melting into the universe, he feared to find not an Easter Resur-rection or Paradise but only "wrathful lights." He admitted that his gloom came chiefly from his loneliness.

The drinking binges he went on to relieve that loneliness made him feel worse. He and Lucien discussed the absurdity of life, and the "silly" poses most people maintained as a futile defense against failure and death. Despite the universal folly, Lucien claimed it was possible to stand "on solid ground." But Jack felt that even someone like Lucien who noticed the absurdity was silly. One night Jack brought George Murray and Connie Murphy to a wild party—with Holmes, Stringham, even "Rhoda Pagoda"—and watched his two Lowell friends keep their feet "on solid ground" all evening. Murray and Murphy were contemptuous of all the agonized frenzy, while those who flaunted their despair were bored by such stoics. Adele Morales, who was at the party too, shared the Lowellites' disgust at the "sick society" she saw there. Still, Jack preferred the company of people who let their hearts show, who knew that the point of life was to live. They were more "metaphysical," hence more "interest-ing." The people with their feet on the ground committed the most serious error by refusing to admit their own silliness. Instead of ac-cepting a party just as it was, they moped and fretted, keeping them-selves forever "on the outer peripheries of life's swirl," just as the confirmed drunks did. Jack resolved to participate in neither form of escape. He would remain "in the calm center, in the arc of the Eye." But the eye itself was never really calm; it was continually filled with visions of God and Shrouded Angels in Hooded Trees, as he recorded in the numerous poems he was now composing.

At any rate, he found himself diametrically opposed to the cere-bral snobbism Henry James espoused in *Daisy Miller* through the words of Mrs. Costello: "You may be very sure she thinks of nothing. She goes on from day to day, hour to hour, as they did in the Golden Age. I can imagine nothing more vulgar." It was Jack's ambition to be able to cease thinking, which would mean an end to writing too, and he hoped to reach that stage of perfect meditation by the age of thirty-five.

By late March, 1949, his writing was as confused as his relations with friends and lovers. He couldn't decide which novel to complete first, *Doctor Sax* or *On the Road,* and vacillated between them almost daily. On the one hand, he saw *Doctor Sax* as the poem capping *The*

Town and the City; on the other, he worried that its theme was too frivolous, and that the whole idea of the book might be "loony." Too discouraged to continue with it, he tried to restructure *On the Road*, which had reached an impasse due to his failure to get a clear picture of its heroes. Thus far he couldn't even decide who was to be the hero: the narrator Ray Smith, based on himself; or Ray "Red" Moultrie, the character based on Neal. To get around this dilemma he decided to reduce Ray Smith to a purely receptive observer: "the hero's Panza, the hero's Boswell, the hero's Pip." Smith, as Kerouac now conceived of him, would be most like Pip in *Moby Dick*, an idiotic boy, too soft and saintly to survive in ordinary society.

Smith roams the country with the hero Red Moultrie, a man of vast experiences, who has worked a variety of jobs and spent three years in prison. Like Jack, Moultrie was to have been a college student and a successful but unrewarded athlete (a minor-league outfielder); he would end up ranging the country and the world as a truck driver and seaman, vainly searching for some way to use his strength and brilliance. Moultrie's experience robbing safes, however, was more akin to Neal's career as a car thief, and Moultrie's lengthy stay in prison paralleled Neal's youth in reformatories more nearly than Jack's two weeks in jail as a material witness. But Moultrie was also to be compounded of the many witty outcasts and vagabonds Jack had met in his own travels, including Big Slim Hubbard from the navy psycho ward. Moreover, he was to be "an artist of life" like Burroughs, a man who had milked "spiritual merit" from a dreary existence. In his spiritual dimension Moultrie owed a debt to Melville's Confidence Man as well as to Bunyan's Pilgrim. Kerouac actually conceived of the story as a religious allegory: a disinherited man seeking, in Bunyan's words, "an inheritance incorruptible, undefiled, and that fadeth not away." [144]

Anxious to write more fully about Neal, Jack muddled the plot by introducing the character of Vern Pomeroy. Pomeroy's father is a Texas hobo who worked on the Moultrie ranch in California, where Vern grew up with Red. Searching the West for his father, Pomeroy runs across Moultrie, who is trying to recover the land he should rightfully have inherited. With "Smitty" tagging along, Pomeroy and Moultrie set out together to find both their fathers. As if Jack were not already satisfied to have given the reader double vision, he then proceeded to link this new plot to that of *The Town and the City*. It turns out Moultrie had met Joe Martin while hitchhiking in 1941, and through Joe he had met Paul Hathaway, Liz Martin, and Buddy Fredericks. After getting out of prison, Moultrie met Junky (Huncke), Levinsky (Ginsberg), and Dennison (Burroughs), and even managed to glimpse Peter Martin once. By this time Liz (originally based on Peggy Coffey) had come to resemble Vicki Russell. In Denver Moultrie happens to know characters based on Hal Chase, Ed

White, Bob Burford, and all their friends. To season this hodge-podge, Pomeroy drags in a LuAnne character, and Big Slim himself appears!

Clearly Kerouac was still struggling, as he had in *The Town and the City*, to work a multitude of socially and geographically separated characters into a single narrative line. The huge novels of Dickens, Dostoyevsky, and other nineteenth-century masters were peopled with hundreds of characters and managed to chronicle diverse segments of society. But such novels were meant to be read in installments in periodicals or at leisure over a long period, in an era when there were few other diversions as relatively inexpensive. Moreover, the plot of such novels was assumed to be highly contrived for the sake of long-term continuity, and the readers practiced as great a suspension of disbelief as the audience watching Henry V conquer France on the floorboards of the Globe Theatre. Striving for a far greater realism, a psychological as well as social one, twentieth-century novelists were being forced to discard linear fiction and to develop new forms that more accurately reflected the actual workings of the mind. The greatest challenge fell upon those who wanted to treat an old-fashioned panorama of society with this subtler, subjective realism, to explore the mechanism of perception as it encountered a panoply of people and places. The most successful innovators along this line had been Proust and Joyce, both of whom Kerouac studied in detail.

Emerging from the heap of improbabilities in *On the Road* was a strangely apt identification of Jack and Neal. Almost with a will of their own, the characters of Moultrie and Pomeroy verged toward each other, threatening to merge into a single Bible-reading, visionary ex-convict, not a hardened criminal, but an "accomplice," a reluctant exile from a politically betrayed America, which offered no more frontiers for a fresh start. Yet Jack wanted to keep the characters separate, to have Moultrie and Pomeroy represent, respectively, the upper and lower classes, which had both lost out after the war. Still unable to get a sure grasp on his hero(es), it was no wonder he turned hastily back to *Doctor Sax* for the relief of fantasy.

Already ten thousand words into *Doctor Sax*, he had come to think of it more as a poem, in which the organization must be extremely tight and no word wasted. He decided that the total length should not exceed sixty thousand words; it would read more like a novella. He realized that to finish either of his novels he must get his nose back to the grindstone, and so he devised a new writing schedule. Starting on March 25, he would try to produce five thousand words per week, finishing the novel by May 31. The schedule was slower than the one to which he had held himself while completing *The Town and the City*, but he felt that with "poetry" it was essential to write more deliberately. Under the best of circumstances he probably couldn't have completed *Doctor Sax* so soon; but there is no doubt he was on his way to substantial breakthroughs in both novels when, a few days after starting his new discipline, the walls of commercial publishing tumbled down on his head and knocked him out of kilter for the next two years.

7.

It all started with a visit to Mark Van Doren. Jack told him a Chinese parable that ended with the imperative "Do what you will when you think of it, at once." Van Doren immediately telephoned Harcourt Brace to recommend *The Town and the City*. The next day, March 29, 1949, Jack received a letter from editor Robert Giroux, accepting the book and offering him a $1,000 advance. Just turned twenty-seven years old and about to be an author under contract, Jack was ecstatic. In his journal he wrote a page-long prayer of thanks to God, printing over the letters a second time to make them stand out. To Ed White he wrote in praise of Giroux, who seemed to have read the book with great sensitivity.

The advance would redeem his pledge to care for his mother and dispel at last his "cloud of inferiority complex." The first order of business was to get his family set up on a homestead out West; then he would join Ed and the others in Paris. Among the joys Jack anticipated was to sit in some Parisian park in a red dusk, watching the children play and exchanging intelligent commentary with Ed, although he wouldn't mind a jaunt down to the Riviera to inspect the "women in diaper suits." Meanwhile, since there was a Hollywood clause in his contract, Jack naïvely imagined he might be called to write the screenplay for his novel, or even to co-star in the movie with Lana Turner! He signed the letter to Ed "Bet-A-Thousand Kerouac." [145]

What he was betting was his whole life on the gamble that he could endure the stresses of a public artist and successfully promote his genius to the world. At first it seemed he actually throve on the glamor and attention. He envisioned long, productive evenings in Giroux's office, he and his editor in their "good Arrow" shirt sleeves, working on revisions of the book. Gulping coffee (sometimes spiked) from cartons and gazing out at the glowing big-city night, it would be easy to imagine himself a Hollywood scriptwriter or a partner in some famous song-writing team. But there were forebodings too. To a neighbor, Jack compared the sale of his novel with his first trip to a whorehouse. On each occasion he was both thrilled and chilled by the certainty of finally getting what he'd always wanted, and "getting it but good." Each conquest was procured at the expense of considerable nausea, for whenever he entered his own dream world he had to confront the "abyss" of self that had created it. Still, he hoped that once he had crossed to the "other side" he would gain a new perspective.[146]

That perspective came sooner than he expected, as he suddenly found himself separated from two of his closest friends by the barrier of human law. Jack had always respected Ginsberg and Burroughs for that "spirit of revelation" that led them endlessly toward new frontiers of knowledge, but within the space of two weeks both were arrested, charged with serious crimes.

In mid-April, city narcotics agents found heroin in Burroughs' automobile. A subsequent search of his house turned up a cache of firearms. Since Bill already had one narcotics arrest (in New York), there was a chance he might get sent to the state penitentiary. The agents also found letters from Allen requesting marijuana. If agents were to search Allen's apartment, he would be in deep trouble himself. In February, a starved and sick Huncke had come to Allen for sanctuary, and after he recuperated he began using the apartment as a drop-off for stolen goods. Huncke and his friends Vicki Russell and Little Jack Melody filled the place with $10,000 worth of booty from a detective's home. Worse, any cop stumbling in would also find Allen's numerous journals and bundles of letters, which would implicate him in a variety of drug and sexual offenses.

Although he had become too passive to control Huncke, Allen could at least remove his share of the incriminating material. Allen rode with Vicki and Huncke in Little Jack Melody's stolen car to transport his archives to his brother's house. When Little Jack entered a one-way street the wrong way a police cruiser pursued them. Little Jack panicked, swerving around and almost knocking down an officer. Then he led the police on a wild chase until the car overturned, casting Allen's interior life into a heap of evidence, which was swiftly confiscated. Vicki and Little Jack were arrested; Huncke and Allen managed to escape. Allen's glasses had been broken, and he stumbled blindly through "the wilderness of Long Island." When he finally reached his apartment, he found Huncke apathetically sweeping the floor, oblivious to the piles of loot. Allen's address was all over the scattered documents, and the police soon came to deliver him, as he told Jack, to "the wrath of God." [147]

Unlike Jack's father, Louis Ginsberg quickly put up the $2,500 bail for his son. Since Huncke, Vicki, and Little Jack all had long criminal records, Allen could contend that he was merely a disturbed youth who had been naively misled. It seemed likely that he would get off without any criminal conviction, if he submitted to psychiatric care. Yet Jack was stunned by the disgrace of such a serious scholar and artist, especially coming on the heels of Bill's downfall.

To Jack, jail seemed the ugly but logical outcome of their years of living in "furtive, imaginary hideouts." He felt that they had had no real need to live outside the law. Besides, by playing at cops and robbers they were endangering a host of friends; he himself might be questioned because he'd left his radio in Allen's apartment. Repulsed by the Times Square world of "compulsive lawbreaking" and paranoia, Jack vowed to work earnestly on his books. The "criminal revolution" sweeping the country seemed dumb,[148] and Jack wanted to keep as far from it as possible. Even if society was hateful, it was self-defeating to defy it and get enmeshed in its laws, just for the sake of displaying righteous indignation. In his view, society couldn't be wrong, only the individual soul. The more society was goaded, the more it would *exist*, given body and energy by the very people who feared it. Like Thoreau before him, Jack believed the only way to oppose evil was to ignore it. Already deep into explorations of subjectivity, he was convinced that everything the mind perceived or conceived came from inside. Hence it should be as easy for a person to live in joy as sorrow; one had but to choose. Allen alone was excluded from Jack's condemnation, for Jack thought him too kind-hearted to act vindictively toward anyone.

Jack's new life would have its best chance out West. With the book advance he planned to move his mother and his sister's family to Colorado. There he hoped to find the loyal, homespun woman who would help him run a wheat farm and populate the state. It was a major turning-point in Jack's life. He concluded that his youth had ended, and he was eager to shoulder the responsibilities of manhood. Recalling his favorite song from *South Pacific*, he gloried in the lines "I'm as corny as Kansas in August, I'm as normal as blueberry pie" as depicting the kind of person he wanted most to be. There was no question that he was going to continue writing books on his wheat farm, since he blithely assumed he could handle both trades as efficiently as he was now plying the single one of literature.

After evenings with Giroux, revising *The Town and the City*, Jack returned home to write *On the Road* until dawn. So confident was he now of his literary ability that he quit the New School to devote full time to his fiction.

On the Road was swiftly gaining depth and complexity. He began to see it as an allegory about the betrayal of America. Reading American history, he fastened on 1848 as the year America lost its collective good sense and carefree heart. In 1848 several wagon trains had been bound West, men with their families, furniture, and tools. When gold was discovered at Sutter's Mill in early 1849, many of them unhitched their horses from the wagons, abandoned their families, and raced blindly to some miserable fate. As Jack saw it: "All the gravity and glee and wonder of their lives and their loves was forgotten for mere gold." One hundred years later, like the com-

pletion of a cycle, Neal Cassady had abandoned his family in California and raced East for the fool's gold of glitter and kicks. Neal's
madness seemed only an exacerbated case of the same materialistic
malady destroying America, where, as Jack wrote in his journal, the
cupboard was often emptied "for the sake of some golden automobile," which merely spun in traffic circles. Again like Thoreau, Kerouac questioned the haste of his neighbors. He wondered where they
were bound, and suspected they were missing the real joys of life,
things as simple as "a tree, with birds in it." Jack extended the
metaphor to describe the liberal intellectuals, who sought flashy,
rationalistic solutions to eternal mysteries. For Jack the entire twentieth century was a massive gold strike, distracting almost everyone
from the pursuit of truth. Some of the "old wagons" were still rolling, though, and among them was his family, bound for honest labor
in Colorado.

Jack certainly enjoyed material comforts as much as any American, but he knew that neither riches nor poverty could affect the
essential quality of his life. He affirmed what had been written by
John Keats, another "old wagon," in 1819: "However I should like to
enjoy what the competences of life procure, I am in no wise dashed
at a different prospect, I have spent too many thoughtful days and
moralized through too many nights for that." Furthermore, Keats
assured Jack that "old wagons" didn't have to plod through life, for
Keats' poetry had blazed with intense sensuality, with a "heathen"
lust for his beloved Fanny Brawne.[149]

In *On the Road* he was trying to create a character who would
typify this "old wagon" sensibility. He now planned to base the hero,
Red Moultrie, largely on himself. Like Jack, Red would have betrayed many of his boyhood ideals. The young Red admired from
afar a great beauty, a combination of Mary Carney and Peggy Coffey, who later became a famous jazz singer. Leaving his native valley
(of the South Platte near Denver), Red married "a Mexican Bea,"
then lost her through several years of frantic travels and a long
stretch in jail. In the meantime the girl singer would have gone to
Paris and returned to the valley. The plot would center around Red's
return to the valley to retrieve both his first love and some fragments
of his lost purpose.

Above all, the novel was to embody a precise American realism.
Jack's journal notes would provide an intimate sense of the road and
the cities along it: New York, Chicago, New Orleans, Denver, Butte,
and San Franisco. The novel would literally become a study of place.
Besides carnies and other people of the road, its characters would
include the cities themselves and actual slices of American terrain:
the San Joaquin Valley, the Dalles, Battle Mountain, Lookout Pass;
the Mississippi, Susquehanna, and South Platte Rivers; and whole
states like Texas, Iowa, Arizona, and Nevada. The "rockbound

spine" of *On the Road* would be the rocky surface of America, connected by roads and rivers with towns whose quiddity sounded in their very names: Rocky Mount, Opelousas, Truckee, Salome, Laramie, Longmount, Algiers, Big Timber. This design sprang naturally from the Galloway-New York axis of *The Town and the City,* just as Jack conceived of *On the Road*'s plot as a more ambitious sequel to the earlier novel's story. Nevertheless, *On the Road* would be distinguished by a much higher fidelity to his own experience. He planned to include the "American in Paris" theme only if he got to see Paris himself. Not even Red's criminal past would be invented, for Jack intended to use details of a safe robbery committed by Joan Adams' friend Whitey.

On the Road would also be unified by a structure of interwoven symbolisms. Jack made a note in his journal to "get *seasons* straight"; and in fact he was to mark change with the cycle of the seasons—like Thoreau and so many other American writers—in almost all his novels from this time on. In *On the Road* seasons would be associated with regions. For example, Red would come to New York City, the South, and New Orleans in spring; Iowa, Nebraska, Denver, Nevada, and San Francisco in summer; Chicago, the San Joaquin Valley, St. Louis, and Indiana in fall; and Butte, North Dakota, Portland, and Idaho in winter. Jack also sketched out a highly original weather symbolism. The hope and promise of spring, of a young America, would be imaged in rainy nights, chill windy nights, and cool mornings. Summer's passion, representing the nation's maturity, would be reflected from a hot sun—walking in the road, sleeping in the field— and in the "soft" nights—swimming, watching little-league baseball. San Francisco and summer set up a unique equation in Jack's mind. Fall, the decline of man and country, would be conveyed in strong winds whipping under streetlights, carrying off leaves and dry husks, and in sunsets. America's winter (death before new life) would be expressed in a season of freezing cold, "icy star-nights," and blizzards. The seasons were also to be carefully matched to an itinerary of Red's "travails."

A consistent color symbolism also signaled shifts in meaning and mood. As Jack's first memory was of his mother's brown bathrobe, Red's first memory was of the brown mountainside near the family ranch, set against the clear, cold blue of the morning sky (to make Red's memories even more specific, Jack planned to use details from his recurring cliff dreams). Red's very name suggests his fiery spirit, for Kerouac uses the color—as it is employed in many religious and occult symbolisms—to represent passion, human activity, and the life force behind these. Blue, in his iconology, also has the conventional meanings of purity, tranquillity, eternity, and cosmic indifference. Brown, gray, and yellow all commonly signify the mortal world, time and decay; but he uses those colors in a more positive way,

272 · M E M O R Y   B A B E

emphasizing the warmth and tenderness of life, especially of the family, even as it is passing away.

Without a doubt, the most ambitious symbolism in *On the Road* belonged to its religious allegory. The most basic correspondence was between Red's attempt to recover his inheritance and modern man's search for a meaningful place in some cosmic scheme. The valley from which Red enters the world, and to which he returns, symbolized humility and its "spirit of revelation." The choice of such symbols was suggested by Bunyan's *Pilgrim's Progress*, the influence of which can also be seen in the attention Jack paid to the "states of Red's soul." He intended them to mirror America's rise and fall, but they also commented on man's lot, in the tradition of Shakespeare's "Seven Ages of Man." The five stages Jack listed in his journal were: 1) the purity of Red's early road life, meeting the Ghost of the Susquehanna, and going to jail; 2) the "miserable indifference and haschisch [sic] of Vern" (Neal) and their later road life together; 3) the confusion and "unhinged" enthusiasm of winning $40,000 in Butte; 4) the effort to regain purity and live rationally; 5) repentance and the return of joy. Already intrigued with the possibility of inverting time, Jack noted that the sequence of the stages could be changed.

Utilizing a hero who has just been released from prison, he was able to focus on life as a series of discrete moments. As Red travels West, he feels like a man just returned from the dead. Every moment counts. Whether joyous or depressed, he reacts to everything along the road with the same "saintly intensity." Pursuing pure experience, he is—from Kerouac's viewpoint—actually in a mystical trance; and his travels anywhere constitute a holy pilgrimage. While in jail Red has learned to pray, and out on the road he actually sees God's face, which imparts the message: "Forgive everything!" [150]

Hitchhiking, Red is often stranded and endures endless horrors, which always change in time to a graver sorrow, until he finally accepts the mortification of the traveling life, seeing it as the "travailing-life." The climactic scene occurs in Benson, Arizona, where Red (like Jack and Neal before him) is hassled by the police. It is just after sunrise, and Red stares into space, realizing that it would be as superfluous to rage against the injustice of man as to rejoice over the beauty of nature. Conscious that both are just there, Red attains a perfect stoicism very close to the Taoist practice of *wu-wei* (nonassertion) and the passive receptiveness of many schools of Buddhism. Indeed Spengler had equated Buddhism with stoicism in *The Decline of the West*, a work whose influence on Jack steadily increased. The very notion of cycles in human consciousness—a development from passive to active personality and back again—is basic to Spengler's organic theory of the growth and death of civilizations. Of course Yeats' *A Vision*, another book important to Jack, also proposed that the various human character types fit neatly into a circle, ending where they began.

What is most compelling about Jack's particular ontological design is its finely balanced weave of symbols and motifs. He does not merely speculate about existence, but he always seeks out the exact *thing* that will bespeak each idea, letting the images rather than mere words interact on the reader. He is even capable of taking stock symbols from the oldest mythologies and making them talk in a modern voice. For instance, *stars* are a prime symbol throughout most of his novels, and they usually retain their traditional significance of high hopes or ideals. But in Kerouac's universe—as in Einstein's or Heisenberg's—those very symbols of permanence are always in motion, always waxing or waning, embodying all the contradictions and mysteries of the theory of relativity or the uncertainty principle. In his notes for *On the Road*, he remarks that when Red stops to look at the sky, it will introduce the " 'mixing-of-the-men-with-stars' theme," thus anticipating the space age by over a decade.

When tradition had no apt symbol for his thought Jack was capable of inventing one, and his coinages were often striking enough to become part of the cultural heritage. While *stars* represented human hope, which always returned, Jack needed an equally potent symbol to express human loss, the inevitable failure of health, wealth, wisdom, and life itself. That symbol had already been added to his repertoire in 1948 and was just waiting to be used. For Jack, *beat* was not only an adjective but a noun; it summoned up the picture of someone "not only poor, but homeless—without the consolations of the poor family man." The beat was the man who wandered under the stars and could only look up at them, wishing he could fly, and by so doing actually flying a little bit, flying high enough eventually to know the stars were only a dream anyway. Even "wino-hoboes" were on pilgrimages because they too sought the impossible—sometimes just the money for a supper. In the symbol of *beat* Jack realized he had the perfect mixture of blues and "mystic signification" to roll *On the Road* out of his head and into the arteries of current American life.

8.

On the Road didn't get far because it ran out of fuel, and that fuel was Jack's certainty about his future. From day to day he wavered between fearing fame and longing for worldly success. All the "darkness" and "solitary affright" that had gone into the writing of *The Town and the City* (and which he hoped would be indicated by a black binding) was replaced by his stark terror at facing Harcourt Brace's publicity campaign. Just posing for a professional photographer required courage, but his real dread was of having to lie to the world on behalf of "John Kerouac," the name on the title page. He already realized that he would be expected to impersonate a sober, suave, and totally virtuous author, and that to do so he would have to become a complete stranger to himself. In a letter to Ed White, Jack prophesied his literary future. He saw himself "staggering drunkenly into the Ladies Literary Circle of Des Moines and puking over the lectern."

On the other hand, if David O. Selznick bought movie rights to the novel, as Giroux hinted might happen, he planned to hustle off to Hollywood to help write the scenario. Once in the door, he could embark on a long Hollywood career of turning classic books into classic movies. Writing was still enough of a joy for him that he wanted to convert the world to his kind of artistic enthusiasm. His own works, like *Doctor Sax* (now under revision), would have high priority for scenarization, but he also envisioned movie versions of almost all his favorite books. The possibilities were virtually endless, and in his journal he listed just the first to come to mind: *Look Homeward, Angel; Of Time and the River; Benito Cereno; Heart of Darkness; Nigger of the Narcissus; Passage to India; The Castle; The Sorrows of Young Werther; Journey to the End of the Night; The Brothers Karamazov; Roughing It;* and "a really great *Huckleberry Finn.*" His most important criterion was that movies be based on "*real* things," truths about the human condition, even if in the guise of fiction.

He also planned to write scripts that would present the lives of great men—Thoreau, for example—with complete accuracy. Jack decried sensationalized film biographies. The lives of great men, he believed, were "neither pretentious nor dull." Since people appreciated the men themselves, it shouldn't be necessary to portray them pretentiously or larger than life. Jack conceived a series of such realistic screen lives. But his most challenging concept was a new kind of Western, one true to history, and without the "silly heroes" that audiences no longer believed in. Rather than black-clad villains and white-suited heroes chasing each other across studio lots, Jack thought it would be far more interesting to see a historical reenactment of the life of Bat Masterson, say, taking place in an exact simulation of 1880 Denver. It was not a mere realism at which he was aiming, but "something like a *deepening* of the facts that appear on the face of reality—that is, actuality."

If Jack's reach exceeded his immediate grasp, it was because he was afraid of demanding too little of himself. Basking rather complacently in the prospect of luxury and myriad women, he was chastened to read an entry in one of his old notebooks. In 1946, with far more wisdom than he seemed to have at present, he had written: "Money is only a step in the drama of Faustian becoming." The entry reminded him that the big money he had been hunting for years was but a means to an end, and that the big questions of direction and procedure had yet to be decided.

Yet he had no idea how to deal with even the small problems produced by living with money. He knew he needed to dress well but had only the vaguest idea of how one accomplished such a thing. With Tom Livornese's guidance, he went on a shopping spree at Howard's. He chose a pearl gray flannel suit for daily wear, and since he was "hell bent for a little fun," a wine sports jacket with contrasting slacks. Tom explained how he could mix the wine jacket with the pearl pants to create a third ensemble, which they completed with a pearl shirt and wine tie. All told, Jack spent several hundred dollars, but for once he didn't worry about money. Owning three separate outfits was a heady new experience, and he wore them so often around New York that thirty years later his friends still recalled them vividly. Tom even came to feel that helping to pick out those clothes was one of the most significant things he did for Jack.

A few months later Jack was photographed for the book jacket wearing suit and tie, his first and last official portrait with neck-button closed. In those days he still meticulously slicked his hair, and in the jacket photo, a quarter profile, his eyes are slightly downcast, as though he were musing on some profound problem. The image conveyed the way he wanted to write. Tom Livornese was certain that "Jack felt heavy, enormously weighted" with his intense emotions, and one of Jack's deepest fears was that he was not a balanced talent. Unlike Wolfe, who chiefly bemoaned man's fate, he wanted to be a "calming, mature influence on the waters of American letters." But to do so, he realized, he would have to put himself on a little bit, just as he sometimes acted out different roles to shock or amuse others.

The root of Jack's dilemma as an artist was that he detested deception, especially dishonesty to oneself. Bored one Sunday, he played the record " 'Gaitor Tail," featuring Willie Jackson on tenor saxophone with Cootie Williams' group. The wild sound hit him like straight whiskey and "pulled him out of his shoes." At that moment all the music critics in the world couldn't make him deny what he felt, and in his journal he raved for almost a page about the joys connected with this "crazy jazz," cheering, "If it's going to be anything, let it go all out like *Willie Jackson* does!" Then, as if in apology for having lost his equanimity, he added the postscript: "Since in any case my Sundays are so quiet."

His ambivalence also showed in a term paper he had been writing before he quit the New School. Surveying the various schools of philosophy throughout history, he attempted to relate the beliefs of each age to the social customs and living conditions then prevalent. The thesis of the paper, as in Spengler, was that no philosophy, religion, or morality outlasted the particular environment that produced it. Philosophies came and went in cycles; and the mid-twentieth century seemed to be returning to the Renaissance view of Socinus, a rationalist who denied that Jesus was divine and that man was naturally sinful. Amid such moral relativism the only sensible position to Jack was "Do what thou wilt." In his notes for the essay, he explained that what he resented about liberal intellectuals was their "demand that everyone comply with the rules set down as to how to think and what to do." Although he might be thought a "reactionary," what he really wanted was for everyone to mind his own business. And yet he still longed for "progress" and believed men ought to work hard to better the world. In a letter to Ed White he formulated the paradox: "There is no need to care, but care is man's only need." Clearly his heart rejected the isolation and anarchy preached by his mind. The only resolution he could imagine was for everyone to work separately, in solitude ("no talk" he wrote in his journal), toward a worldwide utopia.[151] That position was very close to Thoreau's, but its lameness was aptly illustrated in Jack's own family, and by the personal problems that continued to plague him.

Though Jack and his brother-in-law were good buddies and frequently played baseball and football together, Paul was less than eager to ply his electronics trade in the wilds of Colorado. Much to Jack's chagrin, even his mother predicted the communal farm's speedy demise (and her hunches were usually right). In addition, Jack learned that his independence took its toll among his friends. He had conjured up visions of a new Denver romance with Beverly Burford, only to find that she didn't answer his letters. Then one day he picked up a *Denver Post* and saw her picture above a marriage announcement. It had been natural for him to avoid people for long periods when he needed to work; but friends, especially women, lost patience with his unpredictability.

Hal Chase was one of the people alienated by Jack's selfish ways. Knowing he could always return to his "workaday lonely room" in Ozone Park, Jack had often barged into Hal's dormitory when he felt like getting drunk, oblivious to Hal's pleas that he couldn't work among so many distractions. Now he wanted to reconcile with Hal, not only because they would soon be neighbors, but because he felt somehow unprotected without the friendship of this serious, honest man.

As an excuse to see him, Jack planned to ask Hal for help in finding accommodations in Denver. He visited Hal's new apartment several times but failed to find him home. Finally, in response to a letter from Jack, Hal wrote that he "dreaded meeting any of the old crowd." He had vowed that he "would not revert to the aimlessness of '45 and '46" and was currently "hanging on by the teeth." Nevertheless, in mid-May, Jack persuaded Hal to take another trip with him to Lowell. At a hotel off Scollay Square, Jack awoke in the middle of the night, distraught to find himself back in Boston. Looking down at his lap he discovered Hal's hand giving him an erection. Hal was asleep, but Jack ran terrified into the bathroom. The next night ended even more disastrously in a police station in Lowell. Exhausted after several hours in the cooler, they were released in the morning and collapsed in a hotel room, where Jack began having extraordinary daydreams that were like visions.

He imagined that there were two very distinct orders of men. He and Ed White belonged to the "Judas" category. "Tanned by the sun, muscular, taut, tense, full of fleshly torsions and understandable lusts," Jack wrote, they were men whose joys and sufferings showed plainly in their sweat, their frown or laugh. Hal and Lucien, on the other hand, were represented by the frail hand, cool brow, and smug, mournful eyes of Jesus. The Judas-men were always sending out feelers to the world, worried what others might think of them, and wincing for fear of being rejected. The Jesus-men realized that no one is ever really unwanted or alone, but they hated themselves because with all their knowledge they were incapable of simple feeling.

When Jack explained his theory to Hal, Hal was hurt, thinking he had dreamed it up as a means to sever their friendship, and suddenly Jack realized that Hal had hit upon an even more important truth. Lucien had always seemed "six steps ahead of all of us," but Hal was clearly "ten steps ahead of Lucien." Moreover, Jack was amazed by the way Hal fought against this division, defending Jack against his own theory with the pity he always felt for the helpless. Using his "hypnotic will," he forced Jack to retract his conclusions, proving to Jack what an essentially good man Hal was. All the greater then was Jack's horror to discover that lonely demon in himself, that impulse toward fragmentation, which would keep Hal and him from any long-term, productive relationship.

Before leaving for Colorado Jack also went up to Poughkeepsie to visit Jack Fitzgerald. With Duncan Purcell they disposed of thirty quarts of beer in one weekend. Between frantic trips to bars for more booze and to the Tulip Street whorehouses, Jack tried to explain that "life on earth was actually heaven itself," that everyone was an angel "with wings," and that when they died they would all be "buried in heaven forever." Fitzgerald missed Jack's point, insisting, "I like people who are conscious of the gigantic sadness of the whole mad thing . . . the dumb bastards." With a similar bitterness Fitzgerald predicted, "Someday everybody in the world will refuse to go to work on Monday morning and then the whole mad, gigantically sad

thing will change . . . into God knows what, the dumb bastards."
Jack felt frustrated at the lack of real communication between them,
especially since he knew Fitz displayed a lot more humor and compassion in the novel he was writing about his father, "Mighty Mike
and Mad Murphy." Doubtless Jack felt some guilt too for harrying
Fitz's wife Jeanne, who had two small children to care for, and for
encouraging Fitz to stay home from work himself.

While at their house Jack had a dream both beautiful and terrifying. Dozens of friends, lovers, and relatives trooped into various
front parlors in a red afternoon. At the center of a great argument,
Jack not only tried to "pacify everybody, but to make a separate
peace with each individual." At one point he stole a baseball bat
from a store, impressing everyone with his daring, only to learn later
that his mother had secretly paid for it. The dream left him with an
overwhelming feeling of his own falseness. Confessing this "sense of
loneliness and terror" to Fitz and Jeanne, he was somewhat reassured to hear them say they had nightmares almost identical to his.
He left Poughkeepsie with the conviction that everyone's ills could
be cured by frequent, thorough confessions. But at home he realized
how much had been left unsaid, how "alone and foolish" he remained. Relating all of this in a letter to Ed White, May 12, 1949, he
confessed that he found it easier to speak his heart in letters, although even those were often incoherent, composed of "dreamtalk."
It seemed that only a lifetime of "explaining it all" in books would
"get that mad cark out of my heart (and the reader's heart)."

In the same letter to Ed White, he declared that lonely nights
and the "perspiring vision" of his "morbid nature" were paying off
in artistic breakthroughs. His most frequently recurring nightmare
concerned the "Shrouded Stranger." On April 12, he'd had a long
discussion with Ginsberg regarding the origin of this figure. Jack
related a dream of his, from many years before, of Jerusalem and
Arabia. While other men struggled diligently across the desert to the
Protective City, he wandered about looking for the soft repose of an
oasis. Gradually he became aware that he was being pursued by a
"Hooded Wayfarer Without a Name," who carried a stave and
trailed a "shroud of dust." No matter how he hurried, the stranger
continued to gain on him. Knowing he could never make the Protective City in time, he hid in a house beside the road to waylay the
Stranger with a rifle, which turned into a rubber toy as the Stranger
drew nearer. The Protective City was just over the hill, but Jack was
stuck in the house, awaiting his doom. Fascinated with the dream,
Ginsberg prodded him to identify the Stranger. Jack thought it was
merely his own self wearing a shroud.

That night, April 12, during an eclipse of the moon, he awoke
from a dream of the Shrouded Stranger, then slipped into a visionary
trance. The house in Ozone Park suddenly became the weird house

he had dreamed of many times, "with many meanings and existences, like a great well-placed word in a line of poetry or prose." From Cross Bay Boulevard the house was transported to the edge of the world, and through its open windows he was able to reach out to all things. Down the street stretched continents, and up the street, strange cities. Crowds rushed through the rainy night, shouting—the familiar faces of men and women flashing through the city lights. Even Jesus passed by. At that moment the whole universe was present with Jack, and he was one with it.

For weeks he puzzled over the meaning of that vision. Finally he decided it was a parable of man's life. Man passed from the hell of darkness before birth into "the LIGHT of earth, which, for merely being LIGHT, is heaven." The development of a soul on earth was merely the successive visions of an eye peeking out of the darkness. Jack felt that in his trance after the dream of the Shrouded Stranger he had glimpsed another world, a world men could see before being given the "light of life." Each world was but a different sort of dream, and in each we rearranged "the memories of other dreams, other existences, like file-cards."

The interpretation of that vision had crucial implications for Jack's art. To realize that such mysteries weren't "exotic or esoteric, but merely the thing we all feel" inspired him to try to universalize his notions. He knew that such experiences couldn't be communicated logically, or in any kind of dialectic; rather, he would have to find a way of rearranging the elements of life into some sort of pattern that would suggest their link with infinity, their interconnectedness in a cosmic web. Speaking for himself, the writer would then give meaning to everyone's life. "How ironic it is," Jack wrote to Ed White, "that the critics will say I don't realize what I'm saying . . . altho it's true, of course," meaning that his art would reach perfection as he recorded a completely unconscious, unaltered flow of the visions passing through him.

In a letter to Ed White, May 12, 1949, Jack made what is perhaps the most important single statement of his literary theory. He wrote that he believed "the truth" could not be stated in any formula, but that it existed only in the movement *"from moment to moment* [italics mine] incomprehensible, ungraspable, but terribly clear." Its rush across his brain forced him to hustle "to catch the fresh dream, the fresh thought," as though he were "a fisherman of the deep, with old, partially useful nets." He also compared himself to a man attempting to pan for gold with a little thimble. It was not his job to try to determine what was true, he wrote, because "any formula would give a picture of false clearness, like glass reflecting a reflection only." Since the first reflection was "the clarity itself," any further attempt to clarify it through the "glass" of a formula would be false, an inevitable warping of the original configuration of the light. Thus he preferred to show "the fire itself," whose secret lay in its particular glimmer and hue. Nor would it satisfy him to simply create a fiction based on theories about this process; instead, he preferred to "dance on the edges of relative knowledge," as he felt Shakespeare and other great writers had, making of literature a sort of rueful yet funny mockery of human limitations.

Not until 1951 would Kerouac produce a draft of *On the Road* containing verbal configurations of the "moment" that approximated his experience in the Shrouded Stranger trance. The scenes of *On the Road* he was presently writing narrated Red's life in prison and were filled with memories of childhood—groups gathered around the magic of a Saturday night radio mystery program, for example—that would later find their way into *Doctor Sax*. As always, the loose ends of Jack's life, threatening to unravel to madness or death, continually called his attention away from his work.

9.

The move to Denver seemed his last hope for a reintegrated existence. To support himself and his mother until his royalties started, he would seek a sportswriting job on the *Post*, since Buck Jeffries' father was on the staff. He also imagined Denver would yield him plenty of willing women, and that his future kids would grow up happy and healthy there. Most importantly, he hoped to find in Denver a "Carlylean, earnest gravity" similar to the workaday attitude of Lowell. That earnestness, he wrote Ed, was the only thing in life he feared to lose.

No city could have filled Jack's tall order, but, in any case, he himself floundered over what sort of salvation he should seek. In an earlier letter he had written Ed that he was going to Denver to "retire." When he arrived there by himself in late May, he was farther removed from the world than he'd expected. The only old friend he could locate was Justin Brierly. Struck by Jack's determination to make a "new life," Justin helped install him in a small house in Westwood, a suburb in the hills west of Denver. After setting aside money for rent and food, Jack was so poor he had to borrow blankets from Justin. The trouble and expense didn't count, though, next to the joy he felt at finally taking his mother out of the shoe shop. Unfortunately, when she did come to Denver, she was far from happy. Although Nin and Paul had moved with her they soon went to work, and already Paul spoke of returning to the good fishing in North Carolina. Jack himself left Gabrielle alone much of the time. With no one familiar to talk to, she felt as forlorn as if stranded in a foreign country. Worse, she was afraid to live so close to the mountains, and since it was a wet spring she worried that her house would be assaulted by rivers of mud. Almost from the start it was clear that Jack's plan had flopped, that his dream of a life in the country would have to be postponed, but he still aimed to milk the West for a few new experiences.

The mountain meadows filled with sunflowers and butterflies reminded him of a Rubens, and he spent many afternoons painting them in his mind. He also hitchhiked into Denver to sit around Neal's Larimer Street poolhalls and went to twenty-cent movies that embodied "the Myth of the Gray West." It amazed him to hear the natives continually mentioning movie cowboy Roy Rogers, his wife, Dale Evans, and his horse, Trigger, just as New York intellectuals referred their sensibility to Dostoeyvsky and Whittaker Chambers. A middle-aged Okie woman with a couple of young children took a liking to Jack; and as they explored the hills on horseback she swore like a man, pleasing him immensely. He even rode his horse in a ring in a local rodeo.

Justin Brierly took Jack to a party for Lucius Beebe, who repelled Jack with his melancholy search for "the last remaining best things." The other members of Denver society Jack met there seemed just as shallow. Getting drunk, he told dirty stories and made a fool of himself. Another night, in the company of one of his "talented" boys, Justin drove Jack around Denver, pointing a spotlight into dark houses to comment cynically upon the provincial furnishings. As always, Jack enjoyed Justin's combination of refined irony and bourgeois zest. Nicknamed "Dancingmaster Death" by Ginsberg, Brierly seemed like a character created jointly by André Gide and Sinclair Lewis. But when Justin wanted him to play the big writer, Jack balked. Repeating Lucien's judgment, Jack claimed he was merely "the Queen of the May," which to him meant only someone fated for glory among a host of equally deserving candidates. But Justin and his boy thought Jack was making a tasteless gay joke. They wanted to show him the castles of mining barons and explain the ways of wealth, while Jack merely wanted to talk about Neal and his friends. Since it was so much trouble to explain himself to people like Justin, Jack preferred to walk the roads by himself. Writing to Holmes, he said he had decided to return to "the Rattling Trucks, where I don't have to explain anything, and where nothing is explained, only real."

In July, Harcourt Brace editor Robert Giroux came to Denver to help Jack with revisions of *The Town and the City*. Giroux was also interested in seeing *On the Road*, for which Jack hoped Giroux might swing an advance. Giroux's literary credentials were impeccable. A friend of luminaries like T. S. Eliot, Stephen Spender, and Robert Lowell, he had pilgrimaged to many of the greatest writers of his day, visiting Ezra Pound in the madhouse and Thomas Merton in his monastery. After riding with Brierly to the Central City Opera festival, Jack and Giroux hitchhiked in the mountains, and editor and author developed a rare intimacy. The fact that Giroux was a "big businessman" [152] and an acquaintance of the Rockefellers pleased Jack too, especially since his mother predicted Giroux would make him rich. (As a French Catholic, he had quickly gained her heart.) Soon Jack was chummily recommending he read the works of Allen Ginsberg and Alan Harrington.

Before leaving Denver, Giroux promised he would take Jack to operas and shows in New York, and they even planned to meet in Rome in the spring. Yet Jack harbored doubts about Giroux's sensitivity. Among his many changes in *The Town and the City*, Giroux had condensed a child's words from, "I see you . . . peekaboo!" to just, "I see you." Horrified, Jack asked him if he knew what he had done, and Giroux replied, "Of course," seemingly unaware that he had mutilated an exact transcription of American speech.

Dissatisfaction with the editorial process was just a minor part of Jack's discontent that summer. Although he wasn't then completely aware of his own feelings, he later reproached himself for succumbing to the flattery of both Brierly and Giroux. Pridefully he had taught Giroux about "the road," playfully he had served as a paid stud for an old maid friend of Brierly's. But while reaping the rewards of a successful author he had unwittingly become a performer, and hence had ceased to be his own man. Failing to find any immediate source for his bitterness, he flung a wrathful arrow all the way back to New York in the form of a poison pen letter to Brom Weber, his erstwhile professor at the New School. Claiming that Weber's criticism had left him too depressed to write well, Jack charged Weber with depriving American literature of several months of his work!

Besides being misdirected, the accusation against Weber had no basis in fact. Kerouac was actually on the verge of a major prose innovation, and wouldn't come this close to it again until April 1951, when he finally pressed on to capture a modern American idiom in *On the Road*. Now, in late June, 1949, Jack wrote to Holmes setting out his literary theory in precise detail. Jack credited G.J. Apostolos with teaching him style and tone. He related an incident in which he and G.J. had arranged a boxing match for Iddyboy Morissette. As Iddyboy's trainers and seconds, Jack and G.J. outfitted themselves with striped shirts, derby hats, cigars, sponges, and pails, and George even learned to imitate a warning buzzer. Before the first round, G.J. sounded a "Ba-a-a-a-a-a!" that lasted twenty seconds, but the round itself only lasted a second as Iddyboy kayoed his opponent with one punch. Although their elaborate preparations had served no practical purpose, Jack was struck by the beauty of such enthusiasm and gratuitous effort.

Rereading the serious passages in *The Town and the City*, Jack happily discovered that same "Ba-a-a-a-a-a" sound, especially in the chapter about "rainy nights." It was as if, despite the narrator's sense of his own falsehood, he realized the genuine worth in speaking passionately about anything. "The main thing," Jack explained to Holmes, "is that I took the trouble to say it all." Ginsberg had expressed the same sentiment in the refrain to one of his poems: "Anyway it happened"—which Jack liked as much as he did Huncke's snide lament: "Oh mother I can't dance." The fact that Huncke complained with such wit showed that he *could* "dance" and that he enjoyed doing so, even though he had reasons for remaining a misfit.

The reason people were clever, Jack felt, was to keep from saying what they really meant. Because people always hid their deepest wisdom, one could only know a person's soul by listening for the nuances of humor in his voice. In Ginsberg, for example, he heard that crazy laugh of self-deprecation when Allen talked about Blake's "Visions of Beulaaaaah"—the same muted madness that sounded in Boccaccio's *Decameron* and Rabelais' *Crazy-Book*, in the speeches of Shakespeare's servants and fools, and in the first chapter of Céline's *Death on the Installment Plan*, where the narrator screams at the view from beneath his mother's skirts. Jack didn't contest the need for "serious hidden invocations," which Ginsberg said he put in his poetry; rather, he felt one should be selective about that seriousness. To Holmes, Jack proposed: "Death is about the only serious thing, because it puts an end to all the unseriousness anyhow, and it's too late to laugh . . . the dividing line between seriousness and unseriousness is almost unknown, and is where our best knowledges take flower." That dividing line, if only he could find it, would lead *On the Road* from the banality of a Western adventure story into new meaning. And he was finding it, he believed; he was beginning to hear that crazy sound again.

But with his family gone and his home no more than empty rooms, he preferred to hear some reassuring, friendly voices. He managed to contact Hal, who was in the hills, but they were only able to meet briefly a couple of times. At first he agreed to join Hal's excavating team, but then, after stating that Denver was too wild and primitive for his mother, he said no more about archeological expeditions, and Hal naturally assumed he would return to New York with her. When Hal made no further effort to see him, Jack felt snubbed, and blamed Ginger for plotting to keep them apart. Writing to Ginsberg, Jack raged that Ginger was "stark gone" and that Hal must be "dead" to let her manipulate him. But not all of the friction between them was due to misunderstanding. When Jack mentioned that he was dissatisfied with the editing of *The Town and the City*, Hal told him, "Then go somewhere else—don't put up with it." He was disappointed to hear Jack defend the hack marketing of his book as necessary, while Jack was angry that Hal should be so insensitive to his basic needs.

Although Jack felt a strong desire to return to New York, his closest friends there were either gone or inaccessible. Burroughs had moved to Pharr, Texas, to await his trial on drug charges in New Orleans. Holmes and Lucien were immersed in their respective literary and journalistic careers. Huncke was in jail. Ginsberg was sequestered in the Columbia Psychiatric Institute. To avoid indictment by the grand jury investigating Little Jack Melody's activities, Allen had placed himself under psychiatric observation. He was now dutifully following the counsel of his father, his lawyer, his doctors, and his professors Mark Van Doren and Lionel and Diana Trilling. Burroughs thought Allen must really be crazy to submit to such "old women," and he advised Allen to face the criminal charges instead. The only law Allen had actually broken was that against receiving stolen goods, and the authorities would have a hard time proving he had had any knowledge of what the others were doing.

Nevertheless, Allen seemed to be almost enjoying himself in the "bughouse," garnering all sorts of new experiences for future literary use, as well as making unusual friends. The most interesting and intelligent patient he met there was a big, homely, young Jewish surrealist named Carl Solomon. The first day, waiting to be assigned a bed, Allen mischievously began to recount his mystical experiences to the plain-looking fat fellow beside him. With a glint of conspiratorial glee, Solomon replied, "Oh well, you're nowhere—first wait awhile and you'll meet some of the other repentant mystics." Taken aback, Allen retreated into pedantry, declaring, "I'm Myshkin [Dostoyevsky's holy idiot]." Not to be outshone, Solomon rejoined, "I'm Kirilov," alluding to the nihilist character in *The Possessed*, who had tired of all beliefs and could find value in nothing but suicide.

During the next few months in the mental hospital, Allen became good friends with Carl, who entertained him with surrealist antics and witty tales of his European travels. Carl also introduced him to several important French authors, including Jean Genet, Henri Michaux, and Antonin Artaud, and he related his electrifying meeting with Artaud in Paris. Solomon's biting irony—"There are no intellectuals in madhouses" was one of his more quotable lines— helped give Allen a saner perspective on his own disordered but hardly sick life. Having left the Bronx to live as a homosexual in Greenwich Village, Solomon had presented himself at the hospital on his twenty-first birthday, demanding a lobotomy (the most expedient alternative to suicide he could imagine). Better than any doctor he could teach Allen the price of nonconformity, and unlike most members of the medical profession, he knew it was worth the price.

Despite his amusement, Allen well knew the dangers of living in a totalitarian establishment, "where the Doctors are in control and have the means to persuade even the most recalcitrant." Jack, who remembered his own terror in the navy nuthouse, worried that Allen might go mad for real from pretending to be so. He felt that Allen had always flirted with madness in an attempt to justify his mother's illness, and to spite what Allen had called his father's "sober but hateful sanity." Although he approved of Allen's loyalty to his mother, he now chided Allen for wasting his time and talent in such an isolated place. Jack, for one, greatly missed Allen's sympathetic companionship.

Out of loneliness certainly, and perhaps as a recourse to normalcy, he resumed corresponding with Edie. They contemplated studying together in Italy after he got the second installment of his advance, due around Christmas, though they would have to live cheaply until he received his first royalties in October 1950. He was confident *The Town and the City* would eventually provide a comfortable life for him in Paris, from which he could explore Europe at leisure. As for Edie, he confessed to Allen that he wanted to live with her again primarily for sex. From her latest communications—"I love to drink coffee with people in the morning," she wrote—Jack gathered she had become simply "a sad, straight woman," who could never understand his furors with people like Neal. Indeed Neal was the person he wanted most to see. Twice Jack had written him, inquiring about the possibility of his mother working in a San Francisco shoe shop, and threatening to go to China if his confusion wasn't soon resolved. But Neal failed to respond.

SEVEN
The Sponsors
of Waste

1.

Torn between visiting Bill in Texas, joining Edie in Detroit, working
as a miner or fry cook in Butte, Montana, or returning directly to
New York, Jack finally received the long letter Neal had taken almost a month to write. Dated successively July 4, July 16, July 17,
and July 23, the letter told of the unimaginable string of misfortunes
Neal had endured since early February, when he had broken his
thumb attempting to punch LuAnne. Permanently in love with her,
he had been tortured watching her pass from man to man, and finally
he had attempted to beat her into submission, but his fist missed her
forehead and struck the wall instead. As a result, he succeeded only
in crippling his left hand, his writing and throwing hand. Set in a
cast with a traction pin, the thumb had got infected, probably from
washing Cathy's diapers since Neal performed the domestic chores
while Carolyn worked—and it was later reinjured from excessive use
when he went to work as a tire recapper. Once chronic osteomyelitis
set in, there was no alternative but to amputate the tip of the thumb.

In the meantime, while he was recuperating from that operation,
Neal learned that LuAnne's new husband was scouring San Francisco for him, bent on revenge. With his lengthy criminal record,
Neal worried that even if he hurt the man in self-defense he would
get sent to San Quentin. To add to his misery, his nose collapsed at
the site of an old operation, he developed a cyst on his leg, his feet
began troubling him, the penicillin he was taking for the infection
produced an allergic reaction, which had to be combatted with another medicine, and the thumb gave him so much pain he had to
take codeine too. And then Carolyn just happened to get pregnant.
Through it all, Neal had retained his vitality—running the household,
providing some income when well enough, and even resuming work
on his autobiography. Yet he was slowly being engulfed by a depression that had nothing to do with his situation or physical condition.
That depression had been the chief cause of his delay in answering
Jack, although he refused to admit it, and instead made excuses
about having to burn outdated letters, about Jack's disconnected
telephone, and about his own continuing inability to express his true
feelings.

While he congratulated Jack upon the acceptance of his book, he bitterly noted the rift between them, which had been widened by Jack's success. The arrest of Burroughs, Huncke, and Allen served to make Neal all the more aware of the clash in every man's life between constructive and destructive forces. He had come to believe that there were two basic groups of men: those in whom the positive forces predominated, who steadily developed their talents and achieved ever higher goals, and those who spent their entire lives struggling against negativity. Contrasted with an achiever like Jack, he now saw himself among the born losers, men like Huncke who had been beaten down so long they could no longer believe in a happy destiny. "Even thru your period in the nuthouse with Big Slim, your part in Lucien's business, etc.," he wrote Jack, "your deep anchor has been this involvement with writing, which, unerringly threw you into the other camp. The camp of involvement had your mother, father, and other factors. To be blunt, you were never in jail so many goddamn times you had nightmares of future arrests. You were never actually obsessed with the year-by-year more-and-more apparent fact that you couldn't escape the law's stranglehold."

One interesting sidelight from that letter is the revelation of how little Neal and Jack still knew about each other. Neal recommends Jack "try five-points in Denver for bop, the Rossonian hotel. . . ," places to which Jack had been introduced years before by Ed White and which were already his old hangouts.

On the heels of Neal's first letter, which would have sent Jack anywhere but San Francisco, came a second letter in which he literally begged Jack to visit him. Jack might well have distrusted the unlimited good will Neal suddenly extended—the promises of "music, talk . . . bop, mad nigger joints . . . beer, cigars and smutty jokes, nights of crazy happenings. . . ." But—as he later wrote in *On the Road*—everything had fallen apart inside him; outside of his literary productions, his past life was an almost total failure, and there was nothing more to fear in even the maddest life.

Crossing the Colorado-Utah border in a drive-away car, Jack saw a vision of God in the clouds, pointing a finger that betokened approval of his new path. At two in the morning he knocked on the door of Neal's crooked little house at 29 Russell Street, amid the old frame houses of Russian Hill, and as usual Neal greeted him naked. Immediately they began talking a mile a minute in the kitchen, while upstairs their declamations were punctuated by Carolyn's sobs. When Neal went upstairs to console her, Jack heard her screaming, "You're a liar!"

What Carolyn resented most was not the frenzy Jack stimulated in Neal, but rather the fact that when they were together they usually ignored her completely. For a week they rushed around town, mostly seeking pot connections, and even the night they attempted to cater to her by taking her along was a dismal failure—in her view, since they still didn't talk to *her*. One night they brought home Henri Cru. Seeing her bathing Cathy, Cru exclaimed, "What a charming domestic scene!" Carolyn burst into tears, hurt and indignant that things weren't as Henri pictured them. The next morning, when Jack and Neal returned, she threw them both out.

On the street Neal was a sorry sight, unshaven, dressed in torn, sagging pants and T-shirt, carrying a seabag and tied-together cardboard suitcase, and somehow holding his big white-bandaged thumb above everything, as if to test the wind. Since the Hudson had been repossessed, he didn't even have a car. But he no longer seemed to worry, as he once had, about how he would survive. Although he "cared about everything in principle," he would accept whatever shifts the world put him to. He had entered completely into what Jack and Allen called his "blank period." He still talked rapidly and insisted Jack "dig everything," [153] but he jumped erratically from subject to subject, and often lapsed into long silences. Out of pity Jack offered to pay his way to New York, and even to Italy when he got his next check from the publisher. Suddenly Neal looked at him in a new way, for the first time convinced that Jack really cared about him.

Neal's Denver buddy Bill Tomson was then living in San Francisco, and he chauffeured them around in search of a place to stay. Neal thought of Helen Hinkle, who was living alone since Al had left her again, and whose friend Lorraine had a car. Although Helen was none too fond of Neal—she blamed him for infecting Al with the wandering bug—she did like Jack a great deal. She rebuked Neal for leaving Carolyn, but took them in anyway primarily because she thought he would soon return home. To help him let off some steam, she agreed to go out on the town with them.

Lorraine's clunker barely made it to the first jazz club, where Neal toked and sweated away the evening. After he and Jack went to Oakland with some blacks for more pot, Helen and Lorraine rejoined them at Jackson's Nook, an after-hours club. At dawn they perfunctorily asked the girls to sleep with them; when they declined, Neal took Jack to a friend's hotel room. After a few hours' sleep, they found a drive-away car bound for Denver, then returned to Helen's to collect their bags. She was shocked to discover that Neal really was abandoning his family. Claiming that the bandage made his hand useless, he asked Helen to write his farewell note, assuring Carolyn he would never return to force her "to start all over." Since he could as well have asked Jack to perform that distasteful task, Helen felt as though he were trying to make her a partner in the crime. In any case, she did his bidding and afterward went to Carolyn's to apologize for having written the note, only to learn that it was all Neal had left. This time, in contrast to his past jaunts, he had vanished without so much as a phone call.

Riding to Sacramento Neal and Jack discussed the bop they had heard the night before. Neal asserted that the alto saxophonist had had *it,* and Jack pressed him for a definition. The closest Neal could come (as recorded in *On the Road,* p. 170) was to say that *it* began when Time stopped, an event that could be precipitated by a musician's "filling empty space with the substance of our lives, confessions of his bellybottom strain, remembrance of ideas, rehashes of old blowing . . . with such infinite feeling soul-exploratory for the tune of the moment that everybody knows it's not the tune that counts but *it.*"

Getting beyond mere abstractions, Neal and Jack finally began to talk about themselves. They related every incident and fantasy of their respective childhoods, no matter how shameful or pitiful, and with great joy they discovered that they had shared many experiences. For example, riding in cars as children, they had both imagined themselves holding a giant scythe that mowed down trees, telephone poles, and even (in Neal's case) mountains; such coincidences seemed to reveal an underlying psychic unity that bound them—and by implication, all men—together. Talking more and more heatedly, they actually began to rock the car, scaring their fellow riders, a couple of tourists. When the driver complained, Neal launched a tirade against people who worried for nothing, mimicking their timid talk.

That night, in a hotel room in Sacramento, Neal hustled the driver, a homosexual, into bed. Their violent intercourse kept Jack cloistered in the toilet. Neal was annoyed that the man failed to pay him. Taking the wheel the next day, he raced furiously all the way to the Utah salt flats, engineering near head-on collisions that terrified everyone but Jack, who had learned to trust him implicitly so long as he was in motion. The glowing lights of Salt Lake City mocked Neal with memories of his desolate birth there, but it was in Denver, city of his early troubles with the law, that his frustration finally exploded.

They had planned to relax a few days in Denver and look for Neal's hobo father, but they did neither. The tension of the past 1,200 miles at top speed over mountains and across desert had left them dazed and vaguely angry at each other. Standing together at urinals, Jack misunderstood Neal's advice to take care of his kidneys; he felt Neal was patronizing him because he was four years older. When he hollered that he was no "old fag," Neal rushed outside to cry. Although Jack later apologized, the fragility of their friendship had been amply demonstrated. More disturbing was Neal's meeting with his older half brother Jack Daly, who had cared for him when they were young. Daly asked Neal to sign a paper renouncing any claim he and his father might have on his (and Daly's) mother's family. Feeling exiled again in this city that had cheated him of a childhood, Neal sought to make connections in the only way he knew, by just taking what he wanted.

At the Okie woman's house Neal had eyes for her fourteen-year-old daughter; in response to Jack's dissuasion, he smashed one of the girl's favorite records. The woman herself drew Neal's wrath because she refused to buy a $100 car for him. Later, at a carnival, he vainly pursued a lovely nine-year-old Mexican girl. The next day he persisted in his attempts to seduce a teenage neighbor until the girl's mother came after him with a shotgun. To prove he could still get things done, he spent a whole night stealing cars, one after another, and finally collapsed in the Okie's bed, leaving a detective's car outside her door. Horrified by visions of prison, Jack forced Neal to wake up and move the car, which broke down only a half mile away. In the morning, together with a couple of Jesuit college students, they contracted to drive a Cadillac limousine to Chicago. Having bolstered his manhood with a waitress who liked big machines, Neal took Jack across the Great Plains on the wildest ride of his life.

He booted the Caddy to 110 miles an hour, unrolling his past on the eastward road. Their first stop—after sliding into a ditch and demolishing a fender—was Ed Uhl's ranch near Sterling, Colorado. Uhl had befriended Neal when he worked on the ranch as part of his probation from reform school, and now Neal determined to impress him with his new eminence as chauffeur to one of the world's richest men: Jack! Uhl looked worried, knowing Neal's tall tales covered even taller crimes. Even while his wife fed them delicious home-made peach ice cream, Neal and Jack chafed at being a hundred miles from nowhere, and as soon as politeness permitted, they bolted for the Caddy. A night later they would be in Chicago.

The eighteen hours between Uhl's ranch and Chicago were an important "period" in Jack's life. Watching the white line of the highway, following that thread as it bound together a continent like a modern, more efficient river, he listened to more of Neal's history. In Des Moines they barely dented a black man's bumper; later they were stopped by police because he'd reported that their Cadillac was stolen. Several hours later in mid-Illinois Neal very nearly killed them passing—at 110—a line of cars on a two-lane bridge in the teeth of an oncoming semitrailer. Cognizant at last of the razor's edge Neal kept between himself and death, Jack recoiled in terror from the prospect of a shared extinction. But as Aram Saroyan has pointed out (in an unpublished essay, "The Driver: Reflections on Jack Kerouac"), the trip's impact on Jack came from more than the daring adventures and his new insights into Neal. Neal's split-second decisions taught Jack a *style* of dealing with reality, which, however dangerous, achieved increments in consciousness beyond what other men could gain from the same experience.

The secret, of course, was that Neal lived faster than any man

Jack had ever known. Ginsberg, Holmes, and most of his intellectual friends *considered* problems; Neal dealt with them instantaneously because he knew the consequences of delay (especially at 110 miles an hour) could be worse than intuition's occasional gaffe. Something died in Jack that trip. The young Jack, who had composed Wolfean sentences to prove he was smarter than the world that had rejected him, now rejected his smugness, threw away his smartness, and answered the urgencies of both life and art with the sense of the moment. He would put himself on the line, as vulnerable in his lines of prose as Neal on that line of highway.

In Chicago they spent a night listening to young bop musicians, who were already building on the work of architects like Lester Young, Charlie Parker, and Miles Davis. At Neets O'Day's club they encountered George Shearing again, and after "God" showered them with new chords, the other musicians reached toward even subtler harmonies. Jack thrilled to realize: "There's always more, a little further—it never ends." Until nine in the morning he and Neal chased musicians and girls around the city, then returned the Cadillac, all bashed in and barely running, to the owner's mechanic—and never heard a word about it.

After taking a bus to Detroit, they tramped several miles to Grosse Pointe and camped, ragged and grimy, inside the iron pickets of Edie's stepfather's mansion. When neighbors called the police to roust them, they went to an all-night moviehouse and dozed to the drone of Peter Lorre and the twangs of singing cowboy Eddy Dean. The next day they met Edie, who bubbled with pleasure to see the only man who had ever been her friend as well as lover. After lodging them at her girlfriend's, Edie pawned a typewriter to give Jack spending money.

For a week Jack and Neal cruised in luxury cars to a succession of lavish parties. Edie even got them admitted to the Grosse Pointe Country Club, where they feasted on the fat of Fords and Duponts, flaunting their chinos and T-shirts on canopied patios. One midnight, with Neal at the wheel of some Motown battleship, all three of them glided down the sandy trail of the golf course, beneath hundred-foot elms and oaks, through which filtered that "moonlight on the lawn" Jack had been seeking since youth. In fact, he'd suddenly recouped all the losses of the past five years. Again he had an affectionate, devoted wife, a home, and the means to live in style—if he wanted them. And he could scarcely explain to himself why he didn't.

A couple of years later, in *Visions of Cody,* he wrote simply that he and Edie "were no longer on the same team." It was plainer than ever that Grosse Pointe was where she belonged, even if she had been happier in New York's bohemia. Now, with so much dirt in his ears that he looked like a bum, Jack was actually frisked on the street there. Moreover, any future home of his would have to accept Neal

Cassady too, and Grosse Pointe was clearly no such place. For the first time since childhood, Neal had been too subdued even to flirt with any of the women around him. Edie tried to fix him up with the plutocratic girl at whose house he and Jack stayed. But while Jack entranced their hostess by playing the piano for hours, Neal only caught her attention when he ended a party by flushing his shorts down the toilet and clogging the pipes.

Before Jack left town, he and Edie agreed it was time to dissolve their marriage legally. She called her father, who contacted his lawyer Ernest Sneed. To save the trouble of a trial in New York, where the only ground for divorce was adultery, Sneed finagled an annulment.

Jack and Neal rode to New York with a man taking a new Chrysler. It was already late August when they tasted the Apple in the airwaves of Symphony Sid. Times Square was under reconstruction, the city charged with fall excitement. Still they foresaw a bleak winter. Lacking money, Jack broke his promise to take Neal to Italy, and Gabrielle refused to let Neal stay with her more than a few days. After leaving Denver, she had rented a small apartment at 94-21 134th Street in Richmond Hill, not far from their old home in Ozone Park. The night they arrived in Queens, Jack and Neal walked the streets meditatively, as they had never done before, and vowed to be friends forever.

2.

Their detachment didn't last long. At a party a few nights later Neal met Diana Hansen, a statuesque brunette who yearned for the love of a cowboy. Since Neal dreamed of conquering a New York model, he moved into her apartment. He got a job parking cars, and after work went to hear bop at Birdland as often as he could afford it. But mostly he just lounged at home in a silk robe, sipping beer, smoking pot, listening to records, holding court before her friends, or talking with Jack and Allen. Although Neal usually wasn't satisfied with just one woman, New York kept him too intimidated to woo many others. And neither his wife nor his mistress gave him any peace. Carolyn requested child support for their year-old daughter Cathy, and on January 26, 1950, she presented him with a new responsibility named Jamie: a second baby girl. In the meantime Diana prodded Neal to marry her, and when she got pregnant in February insisted Neal divorce Carolyn, who balked at a final break. However unreliable, Neal was the only husband Carolyn wanted, and she had never stopped loving him.

In New York, Jack immediately plunged into fresh rounds of

parties, at which he was lionized as a soon-to-be-famous novelist. He started dating a "cool chick" named Reva, who advised him to "try a few marriages before your own." "With alimony?" Jack replied.[154] In early October, 1949, Holmes gave a big party in his Lexington Avenue apartment to welcome Ed White home from Europe. Released for the weekend from the Psychiatric Institute, Ginsberg was there, along with Jack Fitzgerald and Tom Livornese. Reva bored everyone telling how she played with the Cleveland Indians whenever they came to town. Drunk, Jack gathered everyone around the typewriter to compose a round-robin dramatic poem. The idea was for each of them to create verse speeches that could later be read into Tom's wire recorder.

Weary of writing in solitude, Jack loved projects in which everyone could participate, and he especially liked to see people pooling their talents just as jazz musicians in a band stimulated one another. Spontaneity increased when one person's impulses bounced freely off another's; hence music served as a chief metaphor for the type of creativity he sought. "With bop behind, we go ahead," was one of the lines he contributed. Their poem was even structured musically, tied together with chorales, as well as choruses from "When You're Smilin'," one of Jack's favorite songs. In the poem he and Allen tried to top each other's linguistic extravagance:

ALLEN: Let us all join our loving voices in the Paen of our paradise, in the peroration of our plums, in the apotheosus of our pollens, the plucking of our apollos, the arising of our Ariadnes, the arking of our floodlit Phantasmakos, the larking of our wreathed, robin-hallowed, lark realmed, eagle eyried, creole orisoned hummingbird halowed, nightingale renowned coronation.

JACK: Thus did Blook in the bushes bleak his doom-ed eyes raise to the Firmament of the Archangels Trumpeting The Day of the Bedevilled and Misbegotten Heretical Beelzeburs And Fallen Souls Who in their Mires of the Foundations Did their Large Emboldened Eyes raise Defiant and Thunder-Loving to the High Arcades in Arcanums of Air of God Himself Begat. Oh Blook, Oh Blook, Oh Blook—so may your Hyperion Sorrows all Sea-Sunk and Unimaginable Descend. Amen.

Such verbal competitions—"dirty dozens" Ginsberg called them—were to become an important aspect of Beat literature. The interesting thing is how the individuality of each writer survives within the competition. Ginsberg's earthy cry for unity remains distinct from Jack's spiritual lament and his prayer for redemption. The respective titles each gave the poem reflect this instinct to preserve the source of their art, even after it has been mingled with others':

Allen called the poem "Wire to the Crack of Doom," Jack titled it "Blook's Way"—Blook being the imaginary bleak spook who inhabits the very real world of his boyhood in *Doctor Sax*.

The poem turned out to be the most successful effort of the evening. Deep in his cups, Fitzgerald began describing how people around the world shit in different ways and in different places, and the others chimed in with recollections from their military experience. Not even John's "little pistol" of a wife could crack the lethargy that brought the party to a maudlin end. Sitting in a circle, they struggled to say things bright enough to entertain one another; and, failing, just made noises like apes and gestures like animals. Depressed by the stupidity of their sodden condition, they accepted it as the only alternative to the even more unbearable human condition at the end of America's most tragic decade.

In early November, Allan Temko returned to New York with his recently finished novel. Privately Jack criticized Temko's resurrection of the tough-guy Hemingway hero, remarking to Ed White that "the modern hero is more like Charles Chaplin." But rejoicing at the "radiant and sincere heart" that shone out of all Temko's writing, Jack gladly acted as "big favor guy" by recommending the novel to Robert Giroux. Unfortunately Temko satirized a couple of Giroux's sacred cows: the Catholic Church and "cool logical conservatism." [155] He also complained to Giroux about Columbia intellectuals who rode to school on the subway with pastrami sandwiches in their briefcases. It turned out Giroux had been one himself. The novel was rejected.

The further revisions of *The Town and the City* Giroux requested were not finished until November 18. His extensive cuts had removed many scenes Jack considered essential, though Jack himself now admitted that the book was flawed with "grave imitations of Wolfe." In any case, he prefaced the book with a short poem depicting Giroux as a morning star of kindness in his dark life. Because of company policy, the poem was later reduced to a simple dedication.

As 1949 drew to a close, Jack saw his dream of publication becoming reality. He liked the bleak landscape on the book jacket, though he worried that the photo on the back made him look like a "faggot." When he heard that the galleys would soon be read in Hollywood, he asked Ed White to join him on a trip to Paris. He even expected to return a year later with a French wife: "naïve, one I can teach."

No sooner revived, Jack's enthusiasm was palled by the attrition of his friends. Burroughs jumped bail from the drug charges in New Orleans and fled to Mexico. Jack Fitzgerald, despite his talent, would probably never finish his novel about Mad Murphy because he couldn't stop opening beer bottles. Most disappointing to Jack was the new callousness in Neal. Cops in Brooklyn caught him smoking a joint, but faced with a whole gang, Diana, Jack, Ginsberg, Temko, and Fitzgerald, they weren't sure whom to arrest. Panicking, Neal said the stuff belonged to Fitz, but added, as they slapped Fitz around, that they should be lenient because he was a "queer." Neal's jailbird logic worked to the extent that no one was charged with possession, but Jack felt betrayed and refused to see him at all for several weeks. In fact, the incident so disturbed Jack that, as he wrote to Ed White, he contemplated "shutting up for a year or two . . . winding a shroud around and just watching and listening." [156]

At the same time, he felt a revulsion against the verbal excesses in his past writing. Frightened by piles of old books in used-book shops, he resolved to make every word count, and "the lesser the better." He also wanted to get beyond the "adolescent naturalism" that communicated solely through grammar, variations of person and tense: "he said," "I say," etc. He sought a form "somewhere between the drama and the Cervantes-novel," similar to Joyce's "Walpurgis Nacht," [157] the Nighttown scene in *Ulysses* and the Saturday night tavern scene in *Finnegans Wake*. Other models for this interplay of plot and intimate monologue were Melville's *Moby Dick* and *The Confidence Man*. But Jack bridled at the excessive obscurity and ambiguity in Joyce and the later Melville (especially in a work like *Pierre*). The secret of a great work, he thought, was a clarity and simplicity that spoke to everyone, an ideal Shakespeare had achieved.

Facing the unknown world of success as a professional author, Jack ended the year lamenting to Ed White that he'd lost his carefree youth via jail and a premature marriage. Giroux had fond memories of his own college days, and he showed Jack his Columbia Alumni magazine, which contained cheerful pictures of Justin Brierly with Eisenhower, as well as Ike helping Coach Ralph Furey break ground at Baker Field. Jack's only comfortable haunt at Columbia, the old Manor House, was being torn down to make way for a sleek new training house. Adding to his sense of nostalgia *manqué*, he read Thomas Merton's autobiography, *The Seven Story Mountain*. Merton's intense experience at Columbia made Jack rue his own "ragged tattered madness on its periphery," and revived the bitter memory of 1945, when he had been barred from the campus by Dean McKnight. The honorary degree that Giroux forecast for him could scarcely replace a campus life. Above all, Jack was grateful to Ed and Hal for the few happy months he'd shared in their garret in Livingston Hall.

Walking the waterfront in January 1950, Jack foresaw "cracks . . . opening in the ground." A whore and an old man with a lunchcart looked like angels, and he suddenly thought that life *is* heaven despite its load of suffering. Besieged by visions of devils too, he felt ever closer to Allen Ginsberg, and praised him as "a great man always." At the parties thrown by Bill Cannastra and Walter Adams, an old Columbia friend, Jack watched for "the blinding flash of white light" of an Archangel heralding a new decade of prophecy. They seemed on the verge of a new world, in which angels and devils could mingle peacefully with "Satyrs and Whatnots and Spooks" and all other creatures of the mind. A world, Jack wanted, where he didn't have to say good-bye to anyone.

Now that he was to be published in England by the same house that had published Goldsmith and Johnson, "the milltown corner-cowboy" took his place beside those reserved eighteenth-century gentlemen, who had spurned corners and "rowdyism" in favor of tearoom talk. Humorously Jack noted that the neoclassical intellectual community had been all male just like the present one, with the one difference that Johnson's confreres hadn't been confined to "fruits, nuts, & cherries." [158] Yet the problem he had dealing with the preponderance of gay men in the arts explained only a part of his continuing alienation. A serious rift still existed between him and members of the academic establishment like Mark Van Doren. At Giroux's request, Van Doren wrote a blurb for the jacket of *The Town and the City,* declaring Kerouac "wiser than Thomas Wolfe." An insult to Jack's literary theory, the blurb seemed to prove to Jack that Wolfe was wiser than Van Doren! Drunk and walking down Bleecker Street one night with John Holmes, Jack mimicked Van Doren's way of talking. Out of the mist appeared Van Doren himself, walking toward them and pretending not to recognize him. As they passed, Jack saw (or imagined) that Van Doren was carrying the letter to Harcourt Brace containing his official critical comment.

Far from upset, Jack reveled in the mystery of such coincidences. He wrote Ed White that he had overcome his depression by "sheer manic activity" and "an immersion in the world itself." Having accepted that "there are as many moods & truths as people," he managed to get along well with everyone. Tom Livornese and Allan Temko frequently came over to talk and walk, and Jack's home was pleasanter since his mother was so happy about his successful career. With Ginsberg soon to be released from the hospital, the "literary life" in New York couldn't have been rosier. But Jack's thoughts turned restlessly westward. Partly he was afraid of the autographing parties being organized by Harcourt Brace, and partly he wanted to explore new towns and territory: the Colorado mining camps around Cripple Creek and Leadville, northwest and central Wyoming, Tucson, Arizona, and Mexico City. Perhaps the main reason for such a trip, though, was to see Ed White and relive some of the simple good times that had marked his first trip West in the summer of 1947. Frank Jeffries and Bev Burford were back in Denver now too. Even the news that Hal Chase was "incurably married" to Ginger didn't disturb Jack. Marriage, an old-fashioned settling down, seemed the right goal for all of them.

At one of his big parties, Walter Adams told Jack that the most important criterion among them was, Who can beat up whom? He and Jack arm-wrestled, breaking a table, and Jack won—whereupon Adams pronounced Jack a good novelist. Later, Adams tried to arrange fights between Jack and Neal, and Jack and Lucien, to determine his hierarchy of values, but then he stumbled into a girl in a corner and forgot about muscles. Drunk on beer, Jack imagined him talking gibberish to a mad girl lost on the moors. At midnight bottles started breaking, and "the sword of the Archangel flashed." [159] Jack saw before him a panorama of the fifties, which sent him fleeing to his mother's kitchen, to sober up on eggs and a letter from Ed White. When Adams staged his next bash, Jack stayed home to work.

Conversations with Temko worried him too. Temko's quest for recognition, which mirrored his own, came to seem the greatest obstacle to serious work. Work, Jack realized now, was "just ragged and sad, and not at all like fame and fortune." However foolish Temko was for blaming his bitterness on "America," an abstraction, Jack couldn't condemn him because he saw the same folly in himself. In fact, his sympathy for Temko extended to everyone, as far as each person suffered the same plight of "mortality & feeblest understanding & death." In despair he wrote to Ed that the only answer he knew was the "bom," though Livornese's "aristocratic liberality of good wishes" seemed a workable compromise. Knowledge mostly served to hurt and impede, Jack thought, and like Burroughs he preferred to deal with "facts." Facts were simply momentary perceptions or insights, subject to the law of relativity, and "equally 'true' from any vantage they operate."

3.

The publication date of *The Town and the City* had been advanced to March 2. Jack was still enrolled at the New School, mainly to collect his GI benefit checks, which paid the rent. For the next term he asked a friend to register in his place, so that he could head west early in the spring.

His latest obsession was to find a flood that he could describe in his novel-in-progress. *On the Road* had blurred into *Doctor Sax*. Indeed that lack of independent structure would plague all his novels, although, as with great chroniclers like Balzac and Proust, the complex linkage eventually became a source of strength. A new main character in *On the Road* was a young alcoholic newspaperman, cynical like Lucien, who drove around the country searching for great floods that drowned the depravity of cities. In any case, Kerouac's subjects were coming clear: rainy nights, hitchhiking, rivers, floods, states, towns, black music, freights, the plains, and hobos. The whole book was to be like a hobo's song, and Jack composed his own campfire ditty to state its theme: "Home in Missoula, home in Truckee, home in Opelousas, but ain't no home for me. Home in old Medora, home in Wounded Knee, home in Ogallala, home I'll never be, home I'll never be." Slightly condensed, the song would serve as one of the pivotal points in the final version of *On the Road*.

Holmes and Kerouac were busily exchanging literary ideas. Like Jack, John had been strongly affected by Neal's lifelong joy ride. In his notes for a narrative called "The Afternoon of a Tenor-man," Holmes tried to define what Neal sought—and what bop musicians seemed to seek in almost the same way—as "the Kirillovian [*sic*] moment of immersion in the It." The allusion was to Dostoyevsky's character Kirilov, who craved a single meaningful moment, and finally traded his life for one in the act of suicide. Holmes and Kerouac were both attempting to deal with the post-war community of writers, artists, musicians, jazz buffs, junkies, and street people, who shared (in Holmes' words) "precious connections as though life were a continual emergency situation, and they allies in a common cause." In addition, they both tapped the reservoir of "visions" that attend lives of spiritual torment; but Jack's mystical temperament always gave him an edge in understanding the visionary experience, as distinct from merely reporting it.

Yet at this point Holmes may have realized more fully than Kerouac the stakes riding on jazz and jazzlike art. Writing to Jack on February 3, 1950, he expressed the cosmic potentiality of the tenor player's odyssey as "the trek of the American across his wastes. On all sides lie the dangers of the journey: police, temerity, wildness, spiritual impoverishment. Ahead lies what? Some intoxicative moment of fruition, some undefinable phrase or note or tone that will be hit, will be hit, will be hit! . . . All he knows is that something speaks within him and he has been bestowed with the mechanics of prophecy. The tenor-man swings on and on in a vaccuum [*sic*]. He is thoroughly self-indulgent, but he threatens at any moment to save the rest of us with his earnest efforts at grace." Five years later that theme would be elaborated beautifully by Kerouac in the last few choruses of *Mexico City Blues*, which invoke Charlie Parker to "lay the bane off me, and every body."

On the other hand, Jack was closer to the source of street wisdom than Holmes. In Poughkeepsie with Jack Fitzgerald, he met a handsome, bisexual mulatto named Cleophus, who preached like Allen, gesticulated like Neal, and drank like both Jacks. Barely literate, Cleo zealously performed his "mission in life," which was to gladden men and children and to spread the Gospel. With a combination of theological subtlety and hip sensibility, he told Jack that he wanted to "dig everybody" and would thereby "save" them! He and Jack discussed the possibility that the Second Coming would be televised, so that all the world could witness it. Strangely, Cleo suggested that the Second Coming would occur at 17th Street and Eighth Avenue, on the same corner where, in 1947, Jack and Allen had first conceived of New York as the Forest of Arden. Finding such a funky, self-made prophet proved to Jack that America was full of great unknown people working good *invisibly.*

Like Cleophus, he and Allen had risen from the streets; and they would as surely influence America, Jack believed, as the working men who ate ham on rye and drank beer in the White Rose bars every noon. A very wealthy man named John Kelly had recently written Jack offering him financial help and even room in his mansion. Inspired by Cleophus, Jack wrote back an angry letter calling down a Biblical curse on Kelly and the small fraction of America that read *Time* and *Fortune.* However, America was still a greater country than Soviet Russia, he felt, because America comprised millions of strong-willed individuals who would suffer "ragged pilgrymages," if necesary, to avoid the degradation of concentration camps and slave labor. And he felt the American masses had no false pride, despite the patriotic rodomontade of a few powerful men like Kelly, and despite the false advertising of shoddy products such men foisted on the public. When working men went wrong, it was usually because they tried to imitate the prideful rich, at least that was how Jack explained the cruelty of Neal. There would be no contentment in America, he warned, until everyone, the rich included, admitted that money could make no man a whit happier.

One night at Fitzgerald's, Jack awoke to a room full of ghosts, literally haunted by the spiritual decline of America, the grasping materialism and coldness and distrust of one's neighbors (for this was the time when the fearsome "communists" conjured by Senator Joe McCarthy began driving out the harmless Halloween spooks of the Depression). Not until he found a light did he breathe easily, but come dawn he suffered fresh horrors contemplating his personal failures: the loss of Edie and other good women, the deterioration of his body (getting fat, out of condition, and sick from drink), even the dishonesty that persisted in his writing. He remembered what Fitz had told him: "When a man stops overflowing, his soul dies and he dies and the country dies," and renewed his resolution to lead a spiritual revolution in America. He would give the nation "a true optimism based on the facts," demonstrating the power of his moral vision in both the strength of his writing and the vigor of his life. Someday he would offer his gifts in the political arena too. To begin with, he would rebuild the family base from which his original strength had sprung. Having turned down a job in Hollywood, no longer his ideal town, he planned to get a newspaper job in San Francisco, rent a modest place near downtown, and redouble his efforts to find a wife. To Allen he wrote of his longing "to be a father in the flesh."

As publication neared, Jack began dating a beautiful blonde named Grace. After receiving a telegram that Tom Livornese was killed in a car crash, he rushed to his house, only to find that the telegram had been a ruse and Livornese so alive that he stole Grace! Jack would have been desolate had he not rebounded directly into a new romance with a beautiful "honey-brunette" named Sara Yokeley, a coworker of Lucien's at U.P.I.

Once again he was engulfed in a swirl of activity. He met celebrities he'd once idolized, like Artie Shaw, and became drinking buddies with his English publisher, Frank Morley of Eyre & Spottiswoode. He began seeing Neal again, for even though Neal might be a "fatheaded prick" and "bastard," he was undeniably Jack's blood brother: a man who got wild when he got high. Together they rode in a taxi to the opera with a couple of gay editors, who fawned for sexual favors as though Jack and Neal were rough trade out for a buck.

The name *Kerouac* splashed into print. Brierly submitted an article about Jack to the Denver *Post,* and Allan Temko wrote a full-page appreciation of his work for the Rocky Mount (North Carolina) *Herald.* Gabe was angry that Temko assumed Jack's sleeves had been too short in prep school—for she'd spent plenty of money to outfit him sharply—but Jack liked Temko's notion that Jack had "discovered the sad myth of American status."

The Town and the City was released on March 2, 1950. Jack proudly bore copies to both friends and skeptics, "to prove he was a writer after all." The book even redeemed him in the eyes of the West End's bartender, Johnny, who had grown dubious about Jack's association with people like Ginsberg and Carr. Harcourt Brace, however, saved its fanfare for Thomas Merton, whose latest work they had released concurrently with Jack's. Moreover, Giroux was not present to help promote *The Town and the City*—a dereliction Jack never forgave him—because he had gone to Rome for the jubilee of the Pope.

Adding to Jack's woes, even the novel's good reviews, like the one by Charles Poore in *The New York Times,* praising "the depth and breadth of his vision," stressed his debt to Thomas Wolfe. Then there were the bad reviews like Hugh Downey's in the Lowell *Sun.* Offended by gibes at Lowell and its inhabitants, specifically by the portrait of the Greek gays outside the local Y.M.C.A., and by George Martin's (Leo Kerouac's) reference to Lowell as "the stinkingest stinking town," Downey ignored the book's literary merits and chided Jack for his subject matter and "cheap style." His reproach extended, by implication, even to Jack's parents:

> It is an unpleasant story, however, with language often pro-
> fane and vulgar. Through the whole story there is excessive
> drinking, and many of the characters, especially in New York,
> are women of easy virtue, dope fiends, or Greenwich Village
> queers. The book lacks any strong characters, and conse-
> quently the story never hits on all cylinders. Readers will
> have a feeling of pity for most members of the family, with
> special regard for the parents who were not strong enough to
> wield the proper influence over their children.

Nevertheless, another member of the *Sun* staff, James Droney, wrote a tribute to Jack for having honored Lowell by preserving it in serious literature. Later Droney engineered the serialization of selections from the novel in the *Sun*, with accompanying photo layouts matching Jack's fictional descriptions with the actual people and places that had inspired them.

The reviews didn't bother Jack as much as the endless distractions built into the publishing process. Autographing books turned out to be rather pleasant, but he fretted over a thousand other errands like cashing checks and paying bills, picking out new clothes, seeing people and more people. Through it all he drank too much, and yearned for the times he had hurried to the city "eagerly in search of a few simple pleasures, to relax off lonely work." Still, he didn't shirk but endured the world almost stoically, knowing he would have to meet a variety of people in order to "gauge the focus of the culture." His goal was to reach a full spectrum of the public with books "half-way between the 'precious and the trashy' . . . the esoteric and the popular." Envisioning himself as Christ meeting Pilate, he believed he would have to pass beyond the veil of concern for anything in the world. Emerging with perfect indifference, he would then be able to speak his thoughts exactly as they came to him.

Jack thought of the world in a New Testament sense, as "the place where men do *not* what they wish, or their hearts tell them, but what they think they ought to, and feel told to do." At the same time he suffered from the desire to be a "great man." As he confessed to Ed White, his writing had developed from his boyhood quest to create orderly worlds in his room, born of his need to make life a game with fair rules. Yet even his ambition could be reconciled with the solitary path he preferred, for Jack believed his excellence would shine of its own accord, that he didn't need any "connections." The really great man, he asserted, was someone like Blake, or

Carlyle's heroes, or even Christ, who spent most of his lifetime in silence. What really doomed Jack's asceticism was that he couldn't stop caring about the people he knew.

Back in Lowell for an autographing party at the Bon Marché department store, there were tears in his eyes as tall, comic-faced Roland Salvas strode toward him grinning, and they hugged like bears cavorting after a long winter. When Father Spike Morissette popped in, Jack said, "I told you so!" Happy reunion dinners followed with Charley Sampas, Louis Eno, and Jim O'Dea at the Blue Moon Café, and with G.J. and his old Pawtucketville friends at the Speare House. But there were disquieting moments too. Elmer Rynne had brought his wife into the Bon Marché to meet Jack, and Jack had run over to embrace him. Describing how Elmer had arranged for him to go to Columbia, and even given him the busfare to get there, Jack told Mrs. Rynne, "I feel so sorry I didn't put your husband in my book." Rynne scowled, then answered Jack's puzzlement: "All I need is to be one of your fornicators and masturbators."

Although Jack was interviewed on the radio, Lowell's basic response was to ignore him. One night at Jim Droney's Pub on Broadway, an old favorite hangout, he gathered an armful of empty Harvard Ale bottles, restoppered them, and slipped them into the Franklin stove. People figured he was just stoking the fire, but a few minutes later the room erupted like Pearl Harbor, and Jack laughed madly at the commotion he'd finally caused.

4.

The real satisfaction Jack got from the novel came from the sensitive response of close friends. Ginsberg had been quick to see the correspondence between the three main brothers in *The Town and the City*—Joe, Francis, and Peter—and their respective counterparts in *The Brothers Karamazov*: Dmitri, Ivan, and Alyosha. Joe, like Dmitri the eldest, is a soldier and vagabond, proud of his body, drawn strongly to women, living and suffering almost exclusively in the flesh. At the other extreme, both middle brothers, Ivan and Francis, have a highly developed intellect; both are dignified, secretive, secretly proud, and tormented by their own tortuous logic. The most admirable brother in both books is the youngest. Alyosha is the Myshkin-like saint carried to his furthest limits, the most perfect human being imaginable. A man whose love and selflessness were unmistakable beacons, Alyosha was "the one man in the world whom you might leave alone without a penny, in the centre of an unknown town of a million inhabitants, and he would not come to harm, he would not die of cold and hunger, for he would be fed and sheltered at once." Though no saint, Peter, like Alyosha, is a solitary dreamer who idealizes women and romance, pursues truth rather than money, and never condemns anyone. Moreover, both Alyosha and Peter have an earthiness that lends them an admirable humility, but which troubles them with its accompanying sensuality. They represent that deeply confused nature Dostoyevsky images as an angel with an insect inside him.

Ed White pleased Jack by noting how Francis differed from Ivan. Fact is that Jack had filled in the broad character outlines borrowed from Dostoyevsky with a detailed observation of the people around him, and of his own nature. Tall, skinny, sullen Francis owed as much to Burroughs' physiognomy as to Bill's ice-pick intellect and icy character. Francis (who bears Gerard Kerouac's real first name) also shares many of Jack's own traits, as do the other brothers. Early in the novel's composition, Jack told Allen that he was splitting his mind into discrete parts and embodying each part in a different person. There are many tip-offs in the text itself to Jack's pervasive presence. For example, Francis had a twin brother Julian, who died in childhood like Gerard (and did the name *Julian* come from Jack's single French-Canadian pal on the football team?). Like Jack, Francis is fascinated by New York and falls into the freethinking web of Greenwich Village, where he is dissected and eaten alive by far more practiced iconoclasts. Indeed there was a saying about Jack that he was just a Columbia football player who had gotten lost in the Minettas, the street and lane in the Village where he had first encountered New York's intellectual crowd.

Other friends had sat for the brothers' portraits too, sometimes unknowingly. Kerouac based a good portion of Joe's story on the antics of his Lowell buddy Mike Fournier. Still, Joe's passion for driving is patently Neal's, and his all-American innocent wonder is shaded with the attitudes and actions of Neal, Jack, and Hal Chase.

The Town and the City also reveals a strong influence from Saroyan, not only in its humanitarianism and reverence for humble things, but in its specific interpretation of the postwar sensibility. In *The Human Comedy,* a young wanderer speaks with the identical voice—lost, beat, nihilistic—of Kerouac's Times Square crew: "The whole world's gone crazy. I can't live the kind of life I want to live and I don't feel like living any other kind. It's not money that I want or need. I know I could get a job, especially now. But I don't like the people you've got to get a job from." Not only is the ceaseless movement of soldiers during wartime a motif of uprootedness in both books, but certain scenes in Kerouac's story seem to have been lifted directly from *The Human Comedy.* Depicting the anonymous tenderness between soldiers far from home, in his chapter "On the Train," Saroyan sounds the exact note of defiant innocence (or "innocence under pressure," to paraphrase Hemingway) struck by Kerouac as he describes nighttime in the Union Station in Denver, with Joe passing around a fifth of whiskey and Patricia minding babies for the soldiers' wives.

From Wolfe he got a different sound, the irresistible squeal of joy in the flesh. One of Jack's favorite passages in Wolfe concerned those moments when Eugene Gant was so overwhelmed by springtime fire in his blood that he'd yelp: "Eeeeeee!!!" That this ponderous elephant of a man would suddenly wriggle with intestinal glee tickled Jack's sense of the absurd, and the ingenuousness of that cry became his central reference point in Wolfe's universe. *Glee* may be the most overused word in *The Town and the City*, but the redundancy reflects particularly an American excess of feeling.

Overwriting had become an American tradition, from Twain's tall tales to Dreiser's tableaus clogged with minutiae. But Twain in the end could no longer tell the difference between the banality of truth and the even more bathetic lies he loved, and he continued to lie because the truth was hard to take straight. Dreiser never shirked sordid sights, but his prose was clumsy and unmusical. The prose of Thomas Wolfe, a more recent panoramist, flowed with vowel harmonies, and elemental rhythms like the wash of the sea or the clack of a railroad train, but his focus was blurred.

In *Of Time and the River*, describing a "cosmic moment" similar to those Kerouac experienced, Wolfe wrote: "Day passed into night, night merged into day again like the unbroken weaving of a magic web, and he stayed on week after week, plunged in a strange and legendary spell of time that seemed suspended and detached from the world of measurable event, fixed in unmoving moment, unsilent silence, changeless change." To express such profound feeling Wolfe resorted to a heap of abstractions, couched in language pretty to the ear. The young Kerouac was already a master of alliteration and assonance, yet unlike Wolfe his epiphanies about timelessness are consistently presented through a series of precise perceptions. When Kerouac renders a moment, the reader knows the exact time, place, and other details of the narrator's situation. He had a musical ear like Wolfe, a painterly eye like Dreiser, and the perspective of a humorist like Twain. Of course one must also reckon with the influence of William Carlos Williams, for half of the literary art of both Ginsberg and Kerouac came out of Williams' maxim: "No ideas but in things," or as Kerouac translated it: "Details are the life of the novel."

One of the most memorable moments in *The Town and the City* occurs during a Thanksgiving football game. Like a camera zooming from long-distance to close-up shots and back again, Kerouac repeatedly shifts the reader's view from Peter running with the ball to vistas of the stadium under gray November clouds. Even as Peter makes his climactic dash across the goal line we are simultaneously aware of him as the bruised, staggering, larger-than-life hero and as the tiny dark figure seen from the stands high above, on a field that itself vanishes to an infinitesimal dot as the seeing eye retires into the vastness of space. Discussing the origin of this zoom technique, Jack told Allen he had been strongly affected by the end of the movie *Children of Paradise,* where the hero pursues his lover through a carnival crowd, unsure whether he's going to meet her or lose her. Suddenly the camera draws back from his part of the crowd, so that he's lost in a sea of anonymous faces. Then the camera pans back to view the whole street filled with people. Pulling back farther, it scans the fairgrounds through which the street passes and then finally pulls back again, and the audience looks out from atop some cathedral and sees not only the fairgrounds and the street, but the entire city and the mountains beyond. Although *Children of Paradise* gave Kerouac a specific approach to what he called "panoramic consciousness," it was a concept with which he and Ginsberg had long been familiar and which they'd studied, for example, in the paintings of Brueghel.

In the football scene, Kerouac employs a similar fade-out technique with sound, as he describes the thud of bodies, the band's blare, and the crowd's roar all dissolving in the wind, diminished finally to "one vast whispering sigh" rising skyward. There is actually an exceptional attention to sound in the novel. Kerouac is continually noting those sounds one just barely hears—the dripping of eaves, the echo of far thunder, the voices on the breeze from across the river. This subtle appreciation augments his consciousness of space. In fact, almost all his senses are attuned to immensity. Whether watching "broken clouds fleeing across the ragged heavens," smelling rank birch that suggests "mud that's dark and moist," or bathing in waves of "misty March air," Kerouac's characters are always being informed of their own insignificance, their lostness in a void of swarming sensations.

People were always impressed by Kerouac's special love of sound, which was obvious just from the way Jack talked. He pronounced his consonants very distinctly, and rolled his vowels—especially *o*'s and *u*'s—sensuously over his large lower lip, making them hum and whine and moan. His articulation would have served a tragedian well, but in *The Town and the City* the lush language obstructs the flow of the story. Ginsberg felt that the prose mimicked melancholy strings, a music Kerouac associated with time and remembrance, not only from the violins that signaled the end of most movie melodramas, but from the "eternal" quality of classical works like Brahms' Cello Quintet. The practical result of his literary fiddling, however, is that three adjectives are often used where one would do: "his fiery, colorful, violent antics," "a slow, senile, wondrous trembling," etc.

Repetition becomes the very essence of his style. Certain words—*glee, wonder, sad, lost, rain, dark, night, dream, vision, light* (to name just a few)—are chanted throughout the novel like litanies or mantras. Kerouac is probably not being consciously Roman Catholic or Hindu, but the method does have a basis in religion. The Latin chants of the old Catholic Mass awed even those who understood not a word of them, and perhaps those who understood them least, like little children, were inspired most of all. Sounds that are repeatedly associated with a specific occasion, mood, or circumstance take on a significance whose power increases in proportion to the hearer's inability to interpret their meaning. Introducing Latin prayers into foreign cultures where only the reason for speaking the words was known, and not their actual translation, the Catholic Church developed a simple and effective technique to convey the presence of mystery. To the same end, Kerouac uses a single word in so many contexts that one can no longer say exactly what it means. For example, there is no easy definition of the word *rain* in any Kerouac novel. One has to approach it on numerous levels, for it is always the real wetting rain as well as the allegorical rain of spirit, but the essential ambiguity can never be resolved, in fact is the thing at which Kerouac (like his mentor Melville) was aiming.

Repetition in English literature goes back to the popular (or folk) ballads, which began to be composed around the year 1200. Such ballads were communicated orally, and repetition of key words and lines made them easier to remember. In some ballads, like "Lord Randall," the same line recurs in every stanza; in others, like "Edward," one line is repeated *within* each stanza. Similarly, in *The Town and the City*, Kerouac repeats whole sentences or clauses at the beginning and end of certain passages, and sometimes even within one paragraph: "What does the sudden sight of the town all desolate and rain-blurred there, its lonely lights haloing in darkness, its empty streets, its houses brooding under trees, what does the sight of the town rain-drowned and silent do to him?" Such repetitions work well in a ballad, which is a short poem meant to be sung to a simple tune. Told in quatrains with four stresses to the line, the ballad's story must be trimmed to the bones. By contrast, such repetitions in a thousand-page novel grow unbearably tedious.

Fortunately Kerouac's extraordinary ear gave rhythm to even his wordiest prose. For example, a sentence from the heavily-embroidered opening description of spring in Galloway can be scanned as follows:

Oň the stréet thĕ sággiňg sňowbaňk, thĕ rúnniňg gúttĕr,
thĕ nóisў tháw, thĕ lўrĭcăl néwneš everўwhére.

The alternation of anapests and iambs makes the line trip quickly like a dancer falling forward over his own feet, and finally catching his balance on the last step, the strongly accented vowel sound. The line, like almost every one Kerouac ever wrote, is meant to be read aloud, and read fast. The elongated, r-colored vowel at the end lets the breath out in a powerful rush, granting a pause before the reader soft-shoes through the next sentence. Kerouac's affinity for such complex rhythms may be traceable at least in part to his love for Poe. A combination of anapestic and iambic meter gives the hypnotic quality to such masterpieces as "Ulalume" and "Annabelle Lee," two of his favorite poems, which he often quoted aloud to his friends (and rolled "my darling—my darling" as no one else could, says Ginsberg). Kerouac also told friends that he considered Poe one of the great prose stylists, perhaps because Poe observed slight distinction between poetry and prose, as did Kerouac himself. A notion of all writing as enchantment, as ritual expression of inner vision, was common to both of them.

Of note is the absence of bop rhythm in *The Town and the City*. Not until *Visions of Cody* did Kerouac master sentences based on phrases like *"bebop a-rebop"* and *"oo bop sh'bam a-kloogle mop."* Bebop phrases often end with a long-short pattern, which cannot be strictly represented in poetics by either an iamb or a dactyl, since "long" and "short" refer to the length of time a note is held. While the length of syllables is of prime importance in classical prosody, it has customarily been ignored in English verse. Perhaps the closest literary equivalent to bop's continually shifting accents is Williams' concept of "variable measure." In any case, scat singing, based in black speech, builds excitement through a teasing delay of completion. In the phrase "salt peanuts," the essential concluding note—*nuts*—slips in like a squiggle of sound after the ridiculously prolonged screech of *pea*. In like manner, those sentences for which Kerouac became famous, and which changed the sound of American prose, comprised a series of clipped clauses pushing frenziedly toward abrupt conclusion and release of meaning in a final strongly accented short syllable, exploding usually with a consonantal stop—*mop!*

If Kerouac had written that sentence about springtime a few years later, he would doubtless have cut it to something like: "On the street sagging snowbank running gutter noisy thaw," and then tied it to several other streamlined statements with the tension of expectation: when is this sentence going to be finished? Too often critics have complained about his never learning to revise his work. The point they miss is that a writer can learn to cut words in his head before he puts pen to paper. Even if Kerouac had never "blotted a line" (and he blotted plenty, as will be shown later), he could have written well just through his impeccable sense of composition. Whether putting together sounds or images, he quickly sensed when some part was out of balance with the rest. By the second half of *The*

Town and the City he knew that a ballad style wasn't going to work.

Most readers of *The Town and the City* prefer the final third of the book, the "New York" (and especially the "Times Square") sections. The reasons advanced for this preference are usually that Kerouac's eye grew sharper describing subject matter more stimulating to his imagination, or that in these sections he had developed more of a jazz style. The truth is that his eye was sharp throughout the whole book but his ear simply became more attentive to ordinary speech. Recording large swaths of Ginsberg's, Huncke's, and Burroughs' actual dialogue could have expedited this process, as well as making him more aware of the spare syntax of the modern American street. Hustlers, criminals, and junkies had to say what they wanted in as few words as possible and none dared reveal more than was necessary. Yet by their laconic speech and cagey silences they revealed what they most wished to hide. A woman hearing Burroughs' wry wit remarked him a combination of Will Rogers and Baron Corvo, and she wasn't far from wrong. All of which is to explain how Kerouac came to avoid repetition in the second half of *The Town and the City*: he learned he could tell a story better by considering what to omit as well as what to leave in.

Nevertheless, by thinking of the novel in sections, readers have too often missed the fact that it is a carefully contrived whole. Kerouac was disappointed that people overlooked the parallel incidents that connect the lives of the Martin children. For example, the conversation between the three brothers during the father's funeral, about "slaps in the face," recalls the slap in the face Francis had given Peter when they were kids. Furthermore, even Jack's friends failed to realize that he intended the father, George Martin, to be the "greatest hero" of the book. Jack wrote Ed White that the father represented "care" and "concern." [160] His death makes the story a tragedy both on the personal level, as a loss to his family, and on the universal, as a loss to mankind.

Conventionally structured, the novel is divided into five major parts, like a five-act Shakespearean tragedy, a form that is traceable to Seneca. The first part ends on the success of Peter's football career. The second ends with the failure of the father's printing business. But Kerouac makes a point that the family emerges equally strong from both experiences, that happiness is generated just by the family's closeness, regardless of whether they share triumphs or troubles.

Weather always provides important motifs in Kerouac, and Part 2 is bound together by a kind of dialectic between good and bad weather. Early on, Francis lectures Peter against being lulled by the sunny joys of daytime, lest he forget that the day turns into "a cold night . . . that's icy blackness. The one you can't live in . . . your winter night . . . all merciless and hopeless, the one that kills you in the end, the one that has no consideration of any human pith or earthly significance except to destroy all of us completely." At the end of Part 2, as a counterpoint, George Martin is comforted by his daughter Ruth, who helps pay the family's debts by working beside him at another printing firm. Ruth's compassion gives the old man "evidence that the sun shone on the earth even through all the error, misery, and madness. . . ."

Part 3 ends in total confusion, with the family suffering a much more serious loss as it is scattered geographically by World War II. Having embraced the national cause of fighting foreign enemies, the family members have lost the most important purpose of their lives, which—according to Kerouac—is their duty to take care of one another.

Part 4 ends with two deaths. The young Rimbaud figure, Kenny Wood, drives his homosexual admirer, Waldo Meister, to suicide. Shortly afterward, Peter gets back a letter sent to his poet friend, Alex Panos, stationed in Italy; it is stamped: "ADDRESSEE REPORTED DECEASED." The world of the novel has been plunged into moral chaos. There is an overwhelming sense of universal guilt, of characters having participated through carelessness in crimes against the human family. Neither Kenny nor Peter are actually guilty of murder, but both have failed to "keep faith" and to "remember" the bonds between all men,[161] which was Alex's dying pledge. In his own strange way Waldo Meister had also kept faith by refusing to surrender his passion for Kenny, or to accept some tepid compromise in its place. Granted that Alex and Waldo stand at opposite poles of integrity: Alex has an altruistic love for all men, while Waldo has a selfish love for one man. Yet there is a black irony in the fact that the two characters who hold to their path are the first to die. It is as though Kerouac were asking the same questions as Job: "Wherefore do the wicked live, become old, yea, are mighty in power?" Through their fanatical purity Alex and Waldo both sacrificed themselves, thereby losing all chance of doing further good in the world. Peter's greatest virtue is his flexibility. However adulterated his ideals, he is free to go on. By charting a precarious course of moral relativity, he keeps open the possibility of doing *some* good in the future—seizing the occasions for it that arise from moment to moment.

Part 5, the shortest section, ends with a double death too. The deaths of George Martin and his son Charlie are anticlimactic, merely confirming the dark view of the universe already enunciated. Regarding death as the ultimate human tragedy, Kerouac aligns himself with both the classical and Elizabethan dramatic traditions. But at the same time he explores the very modern concept of tragedy as failure to communicate; indeed he was one of the first writers to examine the generation gap between parent and child. The long conversations between Peter and George Martin are meticulous records of two people totally refusing to recognize the premises of each other's argument. As such, Peter and his father become not only respective types of youth versus old age, but also representatives of the twentieth century.

Near the very end of the novel Kerouac betokens man's frustrated communication with a letter from Charlie to his father. Bulldozer operators on Okinawa turn up Charlie's body and find the letter in his pocket, a few days after George Martin's death. Worthy of Beckett is that symbol of the futility of language: an unsent letter from the dead to the dead. That scene is the true end of the novel. All the rest—the father's burial and the beginning of Peter's life "on the road"—is just a link to the novels with which Kerouac planned to continue the saga of his own life.

His primary method of tying the five parts of the novel together is through a subtle interweaving of motifs. Mocking Hemingway's assertion that "all American literature comes from one book by Mark Twain, *Huckleberry Finn*," Kerouac wrote his first biographer, Bernice Lemire, in 1961, that he had situated the Martin house on the Merrimack "for the sake of River Fiction." He was also amused that Canadian critic Warren Tallman said the presence of the river "satisfied all the demands of Thirties Fiction." But to some extent Kerouac did lard *The Town and the City* with hokey and hackneyed symbols like rivers, stars and trees swishing in the moonlight. Yet he also introduced several new motifs into American fiction, and it is at least partly upon these that his claim as a major novelist rests.

As Seymour Krim suggested, Kerouac may have been the first novelist to make us see "the neon rainbow in the oil slick." He was certainly the first novelist to capture the lonely, unmoved emptiness of America's red brick factories, as well as the bitter loneliness of spent passion hidden by "the red brick wall behind the red neons" of cheap hotels. In *The Town and the City*, however, he is just beginning to study the spectrum of "red brick" and "neon." These two motifs remain subsidiary to at least four others, which might be categorized, in order of ascending importance, as 1) reflected light, 2) rainy nights, 3) slanting red (or afternoon) light, 4) light shining in darkness.

Kerouac's *oeuvre* was to become one vast exploration of subjectivity, and in *The Town and the City* he begins to examine the way reality is perceived as a rainbow body of light, reflected and refracted so many times that the percipient is prevented from tracing its origin. He doesn't just appreciate illusion for its prettiness, but catalogues it as a basis for his phenomenology with the alertness and wariness of a Hindu contemplating Maya. There is also a kind of Proustian nostalgia mixed in with his reverence for the mystery of light. Kerouac argues for the finality of reality as it passes before our eyes, that it won't come back, and that its evanescent goldenness is spared only in memory and art.

A favorite Kerouac image of reflected light is "the river gleaming in starlight," which occurs in *The Town and the City* and many of his later books. Starlight is bent initially passing through the earth's atmosphere; reflected from the moving surface of the river, it is completely severed from its source. Self-born, emerging unpredictably from lightless places, this reflected light proclaims an irrational but undeniable beauty; often its mystery is connected with the beauty of love, as when Kerouac writes of starlight or moonlight reflected from a lover's eyes. To him, the fact that what we call reality is known from indirect and (in a sense) self-created light makes this "reality" no different from what we call "dreams." Already in *The Town and the City* we find Kerouac referring to man's sleeping and waking life as indistinguishable. Asleep or awake, man faces the mystery of light, and one dream, even if it is called reality, is no more substantial than another.

Nevertheless, the fact that man continually reads meaning into empty things suggests that emptiness itself may betray the working of spirit, that the void may be alive, and thus is born the concept of ghosts. Kerouac writes of Peter in *The Town and the City:* "Something complete, and wise, and brutal too, had dreamed this world into existence, this world in which he wandered haunted." The theme of ghosts would come to obsess him for the rest of his life.

Another major motif of the novel, the "rainy night," had also occupied him for a number of years. Edie recalls that he preferred making love to her on rainy nights, when he would also be inspired to tell her long mystery stories. Writing to John Holmes, May 1, 1950, Kerouac asserted that "life is drenched in spirit; it rains spirit; we would *suffer* were it *not so.*" The night itself was always one of his fascinations, a time when people throw off the inhibitions of daytime morality, the restrictions of the workaday world, and come alive with the excitement that is, for Kerouac, man's most precious inheritance from God. At the same time the night encourages excesses of passion, breeding the anger, greed, and lust that are man's least angelic traits. From both Céline and Djuna Barnes, Kerouac learned about using the night as a symbol of man's ambivalent condition, his limbo between redemption and damnation. (The famous line in *On the Road* about "the night, what it does to you" is actually a close paraphrase of one from Barnes' *Nightwood*: "the night does something to a person's identity, even when asleep.") But the rainy night is pure Kerouac. In *The Town and the City*, it is a time when the characters can directly contact all that is greater than they, and are united in both a physical and spiritual sense with the rest of the universe. By the same token, the rainy night is overwhelmingly sad, because it brings the realization that such union is only temporary, that the fate of man's consciousness is to remain essentially separate. Of Peter, Kerouac writes: "He stood on the sidewalk, looked at the rain, and wondered: What is this rain falling on our houses and on our heads in this world, what is this rain?"

The slanting red light of afternoon sun also stirs wonder in man. Kerouac may have learned to express this motif from an Emily Dickinson poem:

> There's a certain slant of light
> On winter afternoons,
> That oppresses, like the weight
> Of cathedral tunes.
>
> Heavenly hurt it gives us;
> We can find no scar,
> But internal difference
> Where the meanings are.
>
> None may teach it anything,
> 'Tis the seal, despair—
> An imperial affliction
> Sent us of the air.
>
> When it comes, the landscape listens,
> Shadows hold their breath;
> When it goes, 'tis like the distance
> On the look of death.

In Kerouac's work, such a slant of light almost always ushers in a moment of pure being, when time and space seem to dissolve, and one feels a harmony of thought and sense that is immortal, though it doesn't last. This paradox of changelessness within change—or vice versa, since words can scarcely approximate the experience—has been known by mystics of many different religions. The Buddhists term such transcendence of self a "cosmic moment." Kerouac's special gift is to use the red slant of light to ground mysteries in an earthly setting and simultaneously to reveal the cosmic nature of things mundane. Thus he writes: "In the slanting afternoon light, by the basement window that faced the pavement, old George Martin sat dying"; earlier, George "saw Manhattan itself towering across the river in the great red light of the world's afternoon."

The motif of light shining in darkness has roots in mysticism too. In virtually every religion light has been used to symbolize God, the life force (spirit), wisdom, goodness, etc. The very word "enlightenment" is a metaphor given semantic status. The western world's most impressive images of spiritual light were bequeathed by Christianity:

Then spake Jesus again unto them, saying, I am the light of the world: he that followeth me shall not walk in darkness, but shall have the light of life. (John 8:12)

For God, who commanded the light to shine out of darkness, hath shined in our hearts, to give the light of the knowledge of the glory of God in the face of Jesus Christ. (II Corinthians 4:6)

. . . ye do well that ye take heed, as unto a light that shineth in a dark place, until the day dawn, and the day star arise in your hearts. (II Peter 1:19)

In the first few centuries of the Christian era, the Manichaean sect interpreted human life as a war between light and darkness, seeing the soul as a light trapped within the darkness of the body. Manichaeism was, in part, an outgrowth of Gnosticism, and Kerouac probably encountered Manichaean doctrines in the Gnostic texts given him by Columbia professor Raymond Weaver in 1942. In any case, his 1943–44 notebooks are filled with poems developing a conception of life as "A moment of light/Whose root grows/ In the darkness." Undoubtedly his imagery of light-in-darkness derived from multiple sources. Goethe's *Faust,* for one, must have contributed strongly to his sense of man's life as passage from darkness to light, for that is the goal of Faust's marriage to Helen, and the union of Germany and Greece. In Goethe, as in Kerouac, the light is continually threatened by the encroachment of darkness, personified in *Faust* by Mephistopheles.

For Kerouac, light-in-darkness usually suggests home, warmth, and shelter, often beyond the wanderer's reach like "lamplight burning in a shack across the American darkness, the American prairie darkness." In *The Town and the City,* he elaborates the motif of light-in-darkness more than any other, so that it is almost impossible to convey the range of its development without quoting half the book. Combined with the motif of reflected light, light-in-darkness creates an impression of holiness and majesty: "The very sheen of starlight on the glossy snows, the little red and blue and green lights in the windows of homes, the icicles hanging from eaves—all these things, in the silence of mystery and prophecy fulfilled, were the altar flickers and divine meanings that had to come every year at Christmas." Kerouac often combines light-in-darkness with other motifs too, forming mosaics that express very complex ideas with relatively simple word pictures. For example, light-in-darkness comes to represent the flame of love, and even the flow of consciousness itself: "The whole world was raining, but they were together in the warm sweet atmosphere of themselves, in the faint light their eyes made in the darkness. . . ." Light-in-darkness is often specifically identified with the power of women to give and sustain life: "This woman had turned on the light . . . brewed some coffee, put out the plates, opened some cans and heated a supper . . . and now, as they [the men] came in lonely and dark and bewildered, she sat them down, kissed them with delighted understanding, brought the food steaming to them and bade them live, love, and abide in the earth. . . ."

The apotheosis of light-in-darkness is the city, especially New York, a place where man need never face the darkness. It is tempting to connect Kerouac's attitude here with the Hemingway story, "A Clean, Well-Lighted Place," though Wolfe too discussed Edison's immense influence on modern life. In fact, one passage in *The Town and the City* closely parallels a passage in *Of Time and the River*. Riding at night on a train bound north, Eugene Gant is struck by the glaring bulbs of a small-town square and movie theater, to which most of the inhabitants have been drawn like moths. Using many of the same words and phrases—*blaze, explode, hard white light, Great White Way*—Kerouac describes Peter's entry into New York by bus: ". . . they began to see a sea of heads weaving underneath lights unlike the lights they had already seen. These lights were a blazing daytime in themselves, a magical universe of lights sparkling and throbbing with the intensity of a flash explosion. They were white like the hard white light of a blowtorch, they were the Great White Way itself."

The threat that light-in-darkness will eventually be overwhelmed by the darkness, like the threat that the rainy night will eventually become a never-ending Deluge, limns the tenuousness of human life, and suggests the courage with which man must daily face annihilation. In the concluding paragraphs of *The Town and the City,* the dangers before Peter, and his will to challenge them, are expressed in a medley of several major motifs (and with a debt to Dos Passos, whose *U.S.A.* trilogy ends with the young rambler Vag thumbing a ride):

He was on the road again, traveling the continent westward, going off to further and further years, alone by the waters of life, alone, looking towards the lights of the river's cape, towards tapers burning warmly in the towns, looking down along the shore in remembrance of the dearness of his father and of all life.

The heat-lightning glowed softly in the dark, and crowded treetop shores and wandering waters showed through shrouds of rain. . . .

He put up the collar of his jacket, and bowed his head, and hurried along.

Besides motifs, the use of color serves to unify the novel. Kerouac's color associations are quite traditional. Red, which predominates, signifies human activity and passion, though Kerouac adds the nuance of a post-mortem, of actions viewed after the fact, when their futility or decadence can be fully known. There is a peculiar desolation, for example, associated with the red neon of his bars and roadhouses. Gold is consistently used to suggest perfection, especially that which is heavenly or eternal: "From the open door of the church warm golden light swarmed out on the snow." For Kerouac, gold tends to summon a certain irony, though, since he is always aware of the false (fool's) gold that is usually mistaken for the real thing—hence the "gold-flecked shade" and bells ringing in the "golden light" of the prep-school campus, where Peter basks in false security among self-absorbed wealthy friends. Blue is a much less ambiguous index of heavenly purity. Brown, a particular favorite, denotes the homespun side of life—simplicity, warmth, and humility—as in "old brown wicker chairs," the "brown leather jacket" of the tomboy Liz, and the "great powerful brown hands" of a drunken but pious workman.

In later novels Kerouac would invent funny names for his characters, which captured the essence of those people in a word or two, but the flippancy of the names also allowed the reader to participate in the sort of name game Kerouac actually used to play with his first wife. You match your intelligence against his, he comes up with the most outlandish moniker he can imagine, and you try to intuit the secret relevance. The riddles are sometimes a dead giveaway—like "Irwin Garden" for the Jewish utopian Irwin Allen Ginsberg (a name Allen himself made up). But just the continuity of the game throughout a number of novels serves as a unifying device. Although the game has already begun in *The Town and the City*, Kerouac is playing it here merely with himself and his close friends. The average reader would not know that "Martin," the fictional name of the Kerouac family, was the name of the street in Rosemont Terrace on which the Sampas family had once lived (as well as the actual surname of certain Kerouac relatives); or that "Jeepo," the gorilla-man Francis meets in the navy nuthouse, shared the nickname of one of the wild nurses Jack met in Denver; or that the namesake of "Tooey Warner," the brutal motorcycle cop in the novel, was Tooey Snyder of Grosse Pointe, Edie's new beau.

Little has been written about Kerouac's sense of humor, but it was a prominent feature of his personality and provided a definite tongue-in-cheek tone to much of his writing. A Kerouac novel is held together by its voice as much as by anything else. Describing how Peter is shocked to see his sister dancing so close to another boy, he writes: "He decides that life is more exciting than he supposed it was allowed." The remark, says Ginsberg, is "completely Kerouac."

What it conveys is that innocent wonder so sincere it could laugh at itself without being false, a kind heart whose sarcasm fell equally upon target and speaker.

Years after *The Town and the City* was published, Kerouac would disclaim it as too traditional a piece of fiction. "And nothing," he wrote Bernice Lemire, "could be worse than fiction after Proust & Joyce." But in several respects the novel actually verges toward the nonlinear.

His handling of space and time is very modern. Any clock—even the clock of an atom's vibratory frequency—slows down as it approaches the speed of light. No event can be situated without four coordinates, referring to three directions in space and the fourth dimension of time—but, according to the special theory of relativity, that fourth coordinate, *when*, has no absolute meaning. In his general relativity theory, Einstein went on to assert that the relationship between time and space is influenced by matter and its motion. The size and mass of an object is itself dependent on the object's speed—any body of matter accelerated to the speed of light would theoretically have infinite mass. Furthermore, space is deformed by moving material bodies. A ray of light, some scientists say, will eventually return to its source, following the shortest possible route, which will be a curved rather than a straight line. Though all of these assertions rest on complicated mathematical formulas, which no layman can prove or disprove, still their impact on the artistic minds of this century has been paramount. At least partly from the relativity theories, Kerouac derived his notion that all space and all time can be collapsed in an instant—the cosmic moment—through memory or prophetic vision.

The Town and the City abounds in both "space collapses" and "time collapses." The mechanism by which they are generally triggered is association. No new claim is made for Kerouac here, since Proust spent two thousand pages delineating structures of association, which had already been deeply probed by seventeenth- and eighteenth-century philosophers like Locke, Hartley, and Bishop Berkeley.

At its most vapid, Kerouac's space collapse becomes nothing more than a geographical catalogue, as when he describes Peter's feeling in Times Square: "It was the same as Scollay Square in Boston, or the Loop in Chicago, or Canal Street in New Orleans, or Curtis Street in Denver, or West Twelfth in Kansas City, or Market Street in San Francisco, or South Main Street in Los Angeles." But even in *The Town and the City* the space collapses give promise of something more philosophical, projecting a sense of all men joined together in a single place, for which the "Forest of Arden" or the "vast room of Times Square" are just metaphorical labels easily exchanged. What impels the experience is man's need to reach out to everything beyond his immediate grasp (Spengler's "Faustian quest"), to bring the far near: "There were dim lights burning far off on the highway, on the river. There were lights even beyond those, stretching miles off in the night; he [Joe] wanted to go there, to see what was there. There were lights like that stretching across the country, across all states and cities and places, and things happening everywhere even now."

While the space collapse implies conquest of material worlds, the time collapse, Kerouac's forte, is much more ethereal and often mystical. Even simple memories spark profound insight into time's illusion. Alone and homesick in the Chicago railyards, George Martin thinks:

> "Why, I remember seeing something like this years ago in New Hampshire. It was my uncle Bob, what did he call himself?—a railroad 'boomer'—and they used to have card games in a caboose just like this one, I remember the night now, it was that night the circus came to Lacoshua and Uncle Bob played poker with the circus men. I was watching from outside. Why, I must have been ten years old then—"
>
> And suddenly he was wrung with a great confused desire to live forever.
>
> . . . What had he done, where had he gone, why was it that he could not live again, and live forever, and do all the things he had forgotten to do. And why were all the things that he himself had done so confused, so especial and finished. . . .

Near the end of his life, Jack asked a friend, Billy Koumantzelis: "From the time you are born, even if you remember the very first day, to thirty seconds before you die—what's in between?" Billy waited; Jack answered: "Nothing." Although the same answer had been given by Goethe's Mephistopheles, Jack felt that logic could never solve that riddle. Rather, tantalized by the power of words to suggest more than they say, he kept restating the problem in poetic terms. The time collapse brings together the points of birth and death, showing that man's life is the passage of a phantom, or the "vapour, that appeareth for a little time, and then vanisheth away" (James 4:14). At the end of *The Town and the City* Kerouac creates such a mood as Marguerite Martin follows her husband's coffin:

> She had been an orphan, lonely in the world, and then George Martin had found her and married her, and they had lived a lifetime together, and now she was a widow, the mother of grave young people silent at her side. They passed the church beneath the trees, and later the dark house where she was born, and then the places where she had played as a little girl, the place where the circus had come to town with

Sitting Bull and Buffalo Bill long ago, the park where she had first seen Martin, the fields where they had strolled under forlorn moons, and then the countryside, the old cemetery under brooding shaggy pines, in the hills, where he was to be buried forever.

Both space collapse and time collapse are often prominent features of the cosmic moment. In Saroyan's *The Daring Young Man on the Flying Trapeze,* Kerouac had first encountered the concept of life as a sequence of extraordinary moments. By the time he came to write *Visions of Cody,* he had learned to structure fiction through the natural succession of such moments. They occur spontaneously when the narrator is surrounded by a harmony of sense perceptions, or are catalyzed by a certain memory, which releases a flood of associations. In *The Town and the City,* he already displays a good grasp of the psychological mechanism involved in such moments, which characteristically begin with a particular sight that stirs his imagination, and tend to end abruptly with some jarring sound:

> Then, as the sun came up in full brilliant array far off over the hills, fanning light all over the sky and gilding little dawn-clouds that were regimented beautifully overhead, the boys fell silent, in awe, and stood on two little hills watching, Panos and Campbell on one hill, and Peter alone on another, all of them brooding and reflective. It was a strange little moment of meditation in the deep stillness of the morning, with only the sound of a farmer's horse neighing faintly far away and clip-clopping on a road, and someone whistling far away, and a barndoor closing.

In *The Town and the City,* Kerouac is just beginning to test his ability to dispense with plot; and like a swimmer afraid to get beyond his depth, he doesn't let the tide of moments carry him very far from the shoreline of traditional linear form. The moments appear erratically and at times even obstruct the progress of the story:

> The race was at a mile and a sixteenth. Just as the horses were being led in the stalls, the sun suddenly reappeared through a gap in the clouds and everything was hushed and ruddy with fading light, a coolness and freshness spread in the air, the rainwater dripped from the grandstand roof and twinkled in the puddles. To Mickey it was like the last day of the world, the late afternoon of time and destiny, the sad glowing reddish light that he always remembered from his childhood as the companion of hushed and muted wonder.

The Town and the City is the apprentice work of a major novelist, flawed by an imitative and verbose style, and confused with a welter of tentative approaches, but nonetheless notable for the highly consistent symbolism Kerouac develops to deal with troubling questions like loss, sickness, and death.

5.

When Giroux got back from Rome, he dressed Jack in a tuxedo and took him on a circuit of operas and cocktail parties. Jack's best time was meeting Carl Sandburg, who hugged him and said, "Ah! Jack! You're just like me. I used to hitchhike through Illinois, Indiana. I was a hobo." Bad times were much more frequent. At parties Jack was repeatedly ridiculed by slick New York types, who, finding him incapable of defending himself, took advantage of him in every conceivable way. One night the librettist John La Touche made a pass at him and when Jack got angry he was chided for making an unpleasant scene. These hand-shaking tours were so draining that every few days he would need to retire to his mother's in Richmond Hill.

On the town, Jack bumped into Hal Chase, who noticed that Jack constantly wore the "nowhere grin" that indicated he was doing something he knew he shouldn't be. Hal warned him that the "easy handout" would have to be paid for later.[162] Although Jack was suspicious of it too, he said he wanted to get what he could. Then, handing Hal a copy of the novel, he tried so hard to do a spontaneous dedication that it took him half an hour to find something to write. Distressed to see him acting such a fool, just to please, Hal told him he didn't have to perform to be a successful writer, but Jack didn't seem convinced.

In early April, 1950, he was stunned to learn that his novel had virtually ceased selling. Worse, Harcourt Brace was no longer advertising it, and the paltry royalties already accumulated were not even sufficient to repay his advance. He had been counting on a large royalty check in October to bail him out; now he realized that his $300 in the bank might have to carry him for a year. He wrote his Denver friends that his trip west would have to be postponed. At its best, the prospect of hitting the road had never been pleasant, he explained, and without money it was even more "raw and chilly and dark." But he vowed to see them soon even if he had to appear as a "ragged apparition."

Jack began to feel that Giroux was partly responsible for the book's commercial failure, not only because he had been absent during publication, but also because he had tampered with the style and deleted many important passages. In later years he would claim that Giroux "threw away half of the manuscript," and that he "took the girls out." [163] Giroux did delete scenes involving Ruth, Liz, and Elena, a character based on Bea Franco. But the manuscript now available in the Northport, New York, Public Library seems no more than twenty-five percent longer than the printed version. It is true that some of the characterizations were flattened by Giroux's editing. A few examples of what he expunged are long sections in which Francis contemplates suicide, Joe romps with his "two-hundred-pound sweetie," and George Martin derides the effeminacy of Alex Panos. Jack was scarcely comforted by Giroux's statements about "the dignity of the laurel wreath," though he found some solace in Giroux's prediction that the book would sell in the future.

Recalling his disappointment in Denver the past spring, Jack realized that even if his piddling wishes weren't satisfied, his soul continued to find sources of joy. He thought it still possible for him "to live each moment *bombarded by grace,* as was meant." [164] His art and life had reached a striking harmony.

His romance with the "honey-brunette" had turned into a love affair bound straight for the altar. Her name was Sara Yokeley, and she was an editor at U.P.I. Not just "an old woman at the hearth" was she, he boasted to friends, but a woman who could talk about "the whole world of current facts." On Easter they went to St. Patrick's Cathedral to cover the parade together. Although they shared an interest in writing, the most important factor in Jack's decision to propose marriage was her domesticity—her willingness to provide the peace and homey comforts that enabled him to work. When he was lonely she accompanied him to Bop City, Dodger games, and French restaurants. During the day, while she worked, he wandered down Broadway to the Hudson River; sometimes he wrote in cafeterias, but usually he returned to her apartment to labor over the novel he was now calling "Gone on the Road." When she got home, she'd cook him a big supper, fix him a few highballs, play cards with him, and be "my last sweetheart, my first love." Never had he dreamed so "fine" a woman would even look his way, and he hardly dared believe she really cared about him—especially since she also seemed to care about Lucien Carr.

Lucien had been her previous lover, and for a couple of weeks he tried to win her back, succeeding so well that Jack took to calling him "the blond assassin." Finally Jack threatened to break off relations with both of them unless they stopped seeing each other. Lucien cut Jack to the quick by telling him, "You'd be awful easy to forget," but Sara let Jack move in again, for a brief time. Neal helped cheer him, telling Jack, "Think what it means to realize you're not really worried." Word came of royalties from the English publisher, and from the Lowell *Sun* for serialization rights; in addition, Twentieth Century teased him with prospects of a career in Hollywood. Jack and Sara planned to go to Paris in the fall of 1950 or the winter of 1951, perhaps on their honeymoon. But Lucien kept "haunting" her,[165] and her receptiveness to him made Jack so uneasy he wanted to get away to Denver. Once while they were visiting the Holmeses, Marian took Sara's wallet and accidentally pulled out a picture of Lucien under Jack's picture. Marian said, "Oops!", which only made it harder for Jack and Sara to face the sadness of their mutual uncertainty.

Still lacking travel money, Jack asked Justin Brierly to help him squeeze some publicity funds out of Harcourt Brace. The gimmick was for Justin to write the publisher, complaining that *The Town and the City* was dying an unnatural death, and offering to organize an autograph party. When Giroux showed Brierly's letter to his bosses, they dispensed $120 for Jack's plane fare to Denver. He bought a bus ticket instead and pocketed the difference.

Jack had been planning to go on from Denver to his Hollywood job and if that failed, to work in the Climax or Leadville or Butte mines, or the East Texas oil fields; failing these, he would spend the rest of the summer with Burroughs in Mexico City. Before leaving New York, however, he eased his financial worries by selling a story to the avant-garde magazine *Neurotica*, published by Holmes' friend Jay Landesman. *Neurotica* would also publish the roundelay "Pull My Daisy" composed jointly by Jack and Allen a year earlier.

Jack said good-bye to Neal in the railyards near his home. As Neal walked away he kept turning back to wave again, gave the highball, ran around in a circle, made crazy signs. In later years Jack performed the same way for people he didn't want to leave.

Arriving in Denver at the end of May, Jack was met by Ed White and Frank Jeffries, who could drain carafes of wine like water and leap spectacularly over parked cars. Dejected about a failed acting career in London, and hedged in by his father's respectability, Jeffries revived in Jack's company, for he sensed that Jack loved his craziness. Since Ed's parents were out of town for the summer, Jack stayed with him, and for a few days they loafed in bars with Jeffries and Beverly Burford, or spent quiet times together discussing literature. Jack showed him the manuscript of *Doctor Sax* and talked about another story he planned to write about two black boys hitchhiking together cross country. Later Jack moved into a basement apartment Beverly had fixed for him, and a round of parties began.

Upon reaching Denver Jack had felt grateful for the company of old friends, and, as always, awed and humbled by the western landscape. But his mood quickly darkened. In the jazz clubs at Five Points many girls were initially smitten with him, but he made short work of alienating them all. Sometimes he would openly discourage a flirtation, but more often he'd be in the midst of a lively conversation when a deep, swamping wave of gloom would suddenly propel him into hours of brooding, in which any lover would founder. It was

Beverly's special gift to shatter any wall behind which a person might isolate himself. She made no romantic demands on Jack, just drank and laughed with him, and reacted as spontaneously as he did. As a result, she was one of the few women with whom he felt at ease.

The fate of *The Town and the City* preoccupied him; he was clearly disappointed that the novel had brought him so little recognition. Not that he thought himself the only genius relegated to obscurity. Inscribing a copy of Denton Welch's *Maiden Voyage* to Brierly, he lamented that none of the 15th Street book dealers would buy it even though Welch was the literary predecessor of the much touted Capote. For the autographing party at Daniel's and Fisher's department store Beverly made Jack don his flannel suit, and he mustered some of his old dignity. But his polish wore off fast when Neal burst in wearing a grubby T-shirt and jeans. Although Brierly was angry, Jack just basked in the brightness Neal brought to any room.

Having bought a car and made another marathon drive straight from New York, Neal now proposed taking Jack along to Mexico, where he was on his way to get a quick divorce from Carolyn. With Neal's agreement, Carolyn had already instituted divorce proceedings in California, and an interlocutory decree had just been granted. But Diana was about to give birth to Neal's child, and he felt the urgency of marrying her to legitimize it. Of course he was also seeking a chance to leave both Diana and New York, nor can one discount the lure of Mexican marijuana. In any case, his sudden arrival on June 2 drastically changed the dynamics of Jack's stay in Denver. Previously Beverly had been keeping Jack incommunicado, or so thought Al and Helen Hinkle, who failed to get through to him. Earlier that day Neal and Bill Tomson had besieged Beverly's house and Jack had come out on the porch like a lost sheep to renounce the heresy of genteel kicks.

After the autographing, Al Hinkle's sister gave a party for Jack. Neal whirled in like a dervish, with Jack trailing shyly, both of them stoned out of their heads. They'd obviously been to Elitch's Gardens—literally or metaphorically. The amusement park where hipsters smoked pot on the lawn, "Elitch's Gardens" became Jack's friends' code word for pot, and to smoke it was to "elitch." Despite the fact that Al's brother-in-law, a policeman, knew they were high, Neal proceeded to make one of his big passes at Al's sister. The move might not have been entirely self-destructive, however, since, according to Al, Neal didn't know how to relate at an afternoon buffet and cocktail party. His idea was that at any social event he should take somebody to bed—and since he was an outsider here, the person he'd naturally choose was the hostess. Al's sister not only rebuffed him, but told Al he was "the devil incarnate."

After the party most of the guests migrated to the Windsor

Hotel, once the plush pride of Gold Rush days with diamond dust in the mirrors and a floor paved with silver dollars, but now just another flophouse. Neal and his father had stayed there and the memories were too much for him; although he usually abstained from liquor he got obstreperously drunk. Jack and a few others wrote a postcard to Allen Ginsberg. Neal's squib read: "Dearest Allen—It's watermelon time again. From the 'queen city' of the plains." That was no innocent joke but the expression of Neal's real bitterness at again playing "white nigger." Jack had no love for the role either—though he at least had the consolation of being "honored" in it, while Neal was merely tolerated. Both he and Neal went into the men's room to punch an inch-thick door, and both ended up cracking a finger. Then Neal took off while Jack went to other parties; they were reunited in a car with Ed, Frank, Al, and the pool hustler Jim Holmes—bound for Mexican Town and Five Points, and winding up in Beverly's basement. Having discovered that Jeffries was as mad as he was, Neal invited him to Mexico.

Jack wanted Ed to come too, but he declined. Being around Neal tired him, and he was even more irritated by the way Jack became someone "quite different" to impress Neal and his friends.[166] On the one hand, Jack cherished Ed's stability and reliability; their friendship endured a lifetime. On the other, Jack was capable of poking fun at anyone's timid ways, even Ed's. In *On the Road*, describing his departure from Denver with Neal and Frank, Jack has "Tim Grey" (whose very name is a caricature of Ed) stand by a washline, waving in the sunset. The scene was also a gibe at Temko's famous story about the tenderfoot at the Brown Palace Hotel.

Jack was fascinated by the descent through Texas, from the crackerbox towns and buffalo grass of the Panhandle to the billowing heat and sinister all-night lunchrooms of Laredo; and once across the border into Nuevo Laredo another new world appeared. Before the border inspection, he had made Neal discard his pot seeds, but the guards let everybody through with a cheerful wave. The three of them headed for a café—when suddenly Neal froze, seeing a cop bearing down on them—but he had only come to stare.

At dawn, bowling toward Monterrey over the desert once traversed by fleeing desperados, they sighted the jagged peaks of the Sierra Madre, source of Humphrey Bogart's elusive treasure in the movie Jack loved. So entranced was he that he forgot his fear of driving and took the wheel for several hours. When they hit Victoria, the treasure couldn't have come easier. A Mexican boy named Gregorio rolled them huge "bombers" of potent marijuana and led them to a whorehouse full of twelve-year-old girls. All afternoon Jack, Neal, and Frank danced the mambo and took turns with the girls. Outside, cops gaped through the windows, waiting for their twenty-four-cent rake-off.

That evening they crossed into the jungle at the Tropic of Cancer. In El Limón Neal slept on the sandy shoulder of the road, Frank lay in the back seat of the car, and Jack sprawled on the roof. Devoured by swarms of mosquitoes, and harassed by the sound of wild horses trotting around like ghosts, they nevertheless awoke with an even greater thirst for adventure. Deeper into the jungle the towns had Mayan names, and they parked and exchanged gifts with the natives. Crossing the steep Mesa Central Range they reached plains Jack thought "biblical," with Arab-like shepherds and sheepfolds. Another climb brought them to Mexico City, a mile and a half up. "A city of *muchachas*," they got girls there for a dollar apiece, and after sex regained their strength on filet mignon, also a dollar.

Soon they found Burroughs, living with Joan and the two children on Cerrada de Medellin. Mexico also catered to *his* fantasies, which ran to guns and dope. They rented a cheap two-bedroom apartment next door. For a week the three roamed the city, stopping at every joint that had a jukebox and girls, and staying high. One night a cop even showed them some better back-street places.

Frank enrolled in writing and acting courses at Mexico City College. Neal claimed he got his divorce from Carolyn. Jack, who had come there for good times, found himself stricken with dysentery and abandoned at the same time. Loaded with a Prince Albert can of grass, Neal took off for New York to marry Diana after filching a few dollars from Jack's and Frank's wallets. To the surprise of Ed White, who deplored such a breach of friendship, Jack later said he accepted the theft because it was so true to Neal's character.

6.

Jack had had another reason for coming to Mexico: to let the new novel, *On the Road,* simmer for a few months. That purpose was served better than he could have imagined by his access to a steady supply of marijuana. He smoked it constantly, bringing to light a stream of subconscious subjects. As one example, he became obsessed with the image of a rose, on a rainy night, traveling down the river to the sea. That image would later fit centrally in the symbology of both *On the Road* and *Doctor Sax.* At this point, in fact, Jack was trying to amalgamate the two manuscripts into one novel. He refused to finish *On the Road* unless he could find some way of making it communicate the "incommunicable." As he wrote Ed White, he wanted "to work in revelations, not just spin silly tales for money. I want to fish as deep as possible into my own subconscious in the belief that once that far down, everyone will understand because they are the same that far down." Often before going to sleep he read from the Bible, and the words struck him with the force of fresh prophecy.

The constant use of marijuana made him like a man waking from a nightmare—when, half asleep, he considers what he's dreamed, and it all seems weirdly real. Sweating, pencil in hand, Jack recorded the visions of those "dim regions" with the attention of a scientist. He conceived of himself as Céline, making a "journey to the end of the night" with the certainty of finally reaching light.

The chief danger of such a voyage was that it might end in another world. Writing to Holmes, Jack declared himself ready for just that consequence. Since it was an "evil world" they lived in, he wrote, the Light of spirit was often hidden by darkness and had to be sought out. Once that Light was found, however, it would "not be a defense against this world but an entryway into the next"; and, ironically, that next world was habitable not by men, but only by ghosts. Hence Jack found "no hope in this world for any of us except temporary glimpses of the Light and the transient bliss of such moments." Believing that death would surely end even this minimal triumph, he declared the earth an "odious and oppressive place" that had reft him of his former optimism.

All Jack's life, he believed, subconscious thoughts in the French language kept taking him back to "childhood revelations of the world." Now at last he was able to begin erecting a novelistic form in which to interpret this process. The new hero he conceived was a French-Canadian well versed in the English language and culture. The hero's companion would be a "pure" French-Canadian, whom the hero calls "Cousin," which among the country folk in Quebec literally means "my kind." The two would travel together like Don Quixote and Sancho Panza, and the cousin would continually reprimand the hero for his "English silliness." Jack wanted to portray the conflict between the unrelieved gravity of the true, clannish Canuck and the romantic hopefulness of a Canuck like himself who had set out to conquer the Anglo-American world. This conflict could be enlivened, he wrote Ed, by a technique in which "every moment of life, every scene, is fraught with a prophecy of the next moment, and this is indicated by signs and hints that everybody knows it's so."

Jack knew he would have to get back to New York to execute this new work—and several more he had planned, including a Civil War novel—because marijuana kept him from writing clear sentences. His chief production that summer was some involuted, jabberwockyish fairy tales. He longed to be sober again, in an old sweater in his cold Richmond Hill room, for he was ready to discredit the "2,000 American novels . . . published every year repeating the same old formulas that have failed and failed and failed." Mexico was playing strange tricks with his memory, so that at times he imagined he was back in Lowell, and then, upon contemplation, attained a state of mind completely outside of time and place.

To get this experience into literature, he realized, would require a spiritual as well as technical breakthrough. His point of departure was the fact that while wandering high through Mexico City, many of the streets and places, and even the special quality of a certain afternoon, seemed identical to places and times he had known as a boy in Lowell. The strange congruity of human experience in spheres as divergent as Lowell and Mexico City made him hope for the revelation of some meaning pertinent not only to his own future but to that of all men. In his writing, therefore, he set about to record each real event in his life, in order that others might gain hope from "what happened there, never to change, forever fixed and existant, with all its messages and hints of what may yet happen *on that level* and finally on all levels possibly." Premising that his "subconscious gropings" were the same as everyone else's around the globe, he foresaw his works heralding "a great world religion based on the hopes and images of childhood and made into form in the rational vigor of adulthood."

Any attempt to understand Kerouac's approach to writing must take into account his deeply religious temperament. A framework larger than tone, style, and point-of-view must be used to comprehend the work of writers—like Blake, Whitman, Yeats—who are also prophets. Similarly, with Kerouac, one must keep in mind that every day that summer in Mexico City he prayed—sometimes on his knees—to be an angel, to have a vision. Only after that occurred would there be something worth reflecting in the "fiery glass" of his writing. What he wanted was nothing so dramatic as the Star of the Nativity in Handel's window, which had inspired the *Messiah*, but some humble sight more like the dark room in Rouault's painting *Out of the Depths Have I Cried to Thee O Lord*, or even the faces of people he loved, transfigured by the rainy night. Those faces would have to be American, because it was only America he loved, regardless of the "universal light" he sought there.

The paradox of going to Mexico to find America was common to many Beat writers. Burroughs told Jack and Frank that he found more "early American spirit" south of the border—as seen in low taxes, protection from legal problems for a small pay-off, and the cheapness of junk (which had once been legal in the United States). He was then working on his novel *Junkie*, and contemplated buying a house and settling in Mexico permanently.

On one level Bill was the enterprising individualist preaching laissez faire because it permitted him the most profits; on another he was a highly eccentric egomaniac who resented any restriction society might put on his schemes and kicks, however dangerous to himself or others. There was a good deal of paranoia in both Bill and Jack. Now in Mexico Bill speculated about a "super-drug" that would turn people into insects, and thereby turned his own mind to insect thoughts. With Jack babbling about "seventeen angels in the sidewalk," Joan, herself deep in benzedrine psychosis, didn't know what to make of either of them.

In Mexico City to visit Jeffries, Justin Brierly pegged Burroughs as "the essence of decadence." Although he admitted that Bill was probably "the brightest of all of them," he wouldn't cross the courtyard to visit him despite Jack's pleas that he and Bill ought to be friends.

It was a bullfight that made Jack decide to leave Mexico. He was so moved by the bull's noble death in the face of the ignoble cruelty of his killers, that he was ready to walk all the way back to New York to protest man's bestiality. To Holmes he wrote that his old hero Hemingway was a fool, and that "a bull dies too big a death for the cowards in the seats."

As he walked home from the bullring, high, Jack passed an ancient Indian village of stone huts on a brown stream that looked to him like the Ganges. Feeling God's presence, he was drawn to a pile of orange bricks and sat down. Images swirled about him, then one emerged above the others: "the Great Walking Saint of On the Road." This was a man who, as a penance, spent his life walking around America, "digging" everyone and everything, redeeming ignorance, squalor, and suffering by his unqualified love. The involuntary pilgrim, kept on the move by the unlivableness of every place he goes, and made holy by his inability to see sin, was the role Kerouac forecast for his own old age, but it was also the first literary persona he created worthy of Neal Cassady, whose vital presence found the rest of the country terribly wanting. At last Jack felt ready to go home, and he was almost ready to write *On the Road*.

His most pressing need was for a wife. The security of a steady love life would aid immeasurably in writing about all those grueling, loveless journeys. The problem was finding the right woman. He was dead broke, and his elaborate plans for traveling to Havana, Paris, London, Quebec, Maine, and Lowell had to be scrapped. Instead he hitchhiked to New York in late July, and arrived "savaged" and "burned down" (according to Holmes), and to recuperate drove with John and Lucien to Cape Cod. There he met and began an affair with a girl named Nancy, but after three weeks he returned to New York for fear she would hurt him as Sara had. Having made him jealous with another lover, Nancy confirmed his view that most women want to see men fight, and he feared that "the woman who will hate violence and love tenderness" might be just a phantom.

Writing to Ed White, Jack worried that he had been humiliated by too many women to ever fall in love again, and went on to say he might return to Mexico, become a bongo drummer, and marry a native girl. He could live in a hut on the edge of town and raise his own pot; all day he'd lie in bed with his wife, and at night he'd play with a native band at some prosperous whorehouse. While on Cape Cod, he had asked one of Cannastra's friends, Helen Parker, to accompany him to Mexico for just such a life, but with two sons and numerous fiancés, she declined. Besides, she was currently being sparked by Allen Ginsberg, whom she'd had the honor of deflowering.

The psychiatrists had convinced Allen that he would never be mentally healthy until he "went straight," so after surveying all the girls he knew, he had written Helen that she was his choice. Soon he was also regularly bedding a girl named Dusty. His new position on the *New Jersey Labor Herald* was an additional step toward a regular, mundane life.

Jack felt a peculiar loneliness, as well, since for the first time in a year he didn't have Neal's company readily available. From Mexico City Neal had driven as far as Louisiana, where his car had finally conked out; he had flown from there to New York. For three weeks he stayed with Diana, smoking pot and arguing with her every evening about their future. As Allen saw it, Neal and Diana could have gone on living together indefinitely if she hadn't tried to capture him "with authority and ritual." Getting pregnant had been her "trick," which Neal had "let pass ambiguously." Now, having lost his parking-lot job, he was "shuddery and nervous" facing the prospect of a new wife and child to support. When a telegram came from the Southern Pacific asking him to return to work in San Francisco, he accepted the offer, though he promised to come back to her when he got laid off, and he married her as planned. On July 10, two hours after the ceremony making Diana Hansen his third wife, Neal used his railroad pass to board a streamliner for Kansas City and points West. After brief stops to see his brother Jim in Missouri and Ed White in Denver, he showed up on Carolyn's doorstep at 29 Russell Street. It took a few months of finagling and cajoling, but he finally resumed his second marriage just where he'd left off—complete with deceptions, pledges to reform, and broken hearts all around.

For Jack, August 1950 was made even grimmer by the disintegration of world peace. He had never been one to worry much about political disputes. Earlier, in April, when Senator Joseph McCarthy had launched into his purge of "communists" in the State Department, Jack had declared in the tradition of Thoreau: "A *good* man should not be a *public* man, unless he longs to be stoned." He also contended that a strong president like Lincoln would have brushed McCarthy aside. But that summer, political blunders nearly led to international suicide. On June 24, great numbers of North Korean troops equipped with Russian tanks had crossed the 38th parallel into South Korea; on June 27, President Truman had pledged American arms for the defense of the South Korean republic against the communist invaders; and on June 30, Truman committed American troops to the fight. The undeclared Korean War had begun, and during the whole month of July the American forces reeled south-ward under massive, highly mechanized attacks. The casualties were staggering. Even the most patriotic Americans were questioning our presence in Korea, and pacifists like Kerouac were aghast. On August 1, he wrote to Jim Sampas, Sammy's brother, who was of draftable age, that their only recourse was "to believe in Guardian Angels," because if the war wasn't over shortly, "it will be time to say good-bye all around."

On August 6, thanks to reinforcements from the United Nations forces, the retreat ended; but the daily combat grew fiercer, with each side opposing the other with ever more powerful weapons. On August 13, Ginsberg wrote to Jack: "You once promised me years ago that if you really thought we would someday be at fight with Russia you would have a change of life, give up, go mad, drop dead, stop writing, and become a new lost Kerouac. Well, what have you been waiting for?"

By the end of August he had stopped waiting. Stimulated both by Neal's absence and by the letters Neal continued to write him about his adventures, Jack began work on an entirely new book, which would tell of the good hard times they had known as children, of their Depression boyhood that was like Eden compared to the Gehenna of modern warfare. The book began with a long piece about the day Neal met his three closest friends in Peterson's Poolhall in Denver. Neal had treated similar subjects in long, symmetrical, Proustian sentences in his unfinished autobiography (published posthumously as *The First Third*), and Jack's style was a sympathetic parody.

The writing was different from any Jack had done before, and it was going very slowly. He was peeling back layer after layer of memory, trying to set forth his full stock of mental pictures of Neal—his "visions" of Neal—to find how and when the two of them had begun keeping tabs on each other in such a tender way, as if he were trying to answer the questions: When did Neal first appear? In whose mind is this drama? The book was just another form of the "love check" he and Neal and Allen were continually making on one another.[167] One particular passage climaxed with an enormously protracted cosmic moment centered on a football field in Denver, with the red afternoon sun fixing Neal and all his friends in perfect youthful glory. One of the best pieces of writing Kerouac ever did, it was eventually incorporated into *Visions of Cody*.

By November Jack wrote Neal that he was confident his new work was greater than any he'd done before. After two months of smoking pot and brooding alone in his room in Richmond Hill, he had emerged with a vast, stoic strength. As Allen described him, Jack seemed "more settled in reality, more sober . . . like a post 20's survivor, F. Scott Fitzgerald after the party of ego was over." There had been some pretty bad times, to be sure. To Jim Sampas he had complained that his four years of work on *The Town and the City* were wasted. The descriptions of *"la vie en douleur"* he sent Ed White sounded precariously close to suicide notes. Despite plenty of female company—Beverly Burford had stopped in New York on her way to Germany, and there was a woman named Reanna around— Jack said he felt "inappropriate for life." Although he concluded that God had put man in "this pit of night" to test his endurance, he himself was already almost too weary to care about the outcome.

He wrote a story called "A Good Heart," which opened with a woman standing on a dark bridge with her shoes in her hand, staring at the waters below. Accosted by a simple-hearted mute, she tried to drive him away, but he persisted in his silent pleas that she shouldn't jump. Finally realizing she couldn't jump as long as he watched her, she let him lead her to his home. Although the story ended rather mawkishly, with the mute teaching her to accept his love and live as he did, Jack was proud to have composed "a good, Christian story." The unstated theme, of course, was that helping the woman had given *the mute* a reason to go on living.

Jack too was committed to caring for his friends. Secluded in the trainmen's dormitory in Watsonville, lost in the "inner-inner land" of endless toking, masturbating to sheer exhaustion, Neal tried to figure how he might tie at least one of the many women he'd lost— LuAnne, or Carolyn, or Diana, or even his first love, Agnes Miller— into a love knot that would hold. But none of his come-ons worked and he even managed to embitter complaisant Diana when she came to San Francisco to visit him in October. His relationships remained as fragmentary as the book he kept trying to write. Jack was his only good angel, without Allen's sexual angle or Carolyn's emotional in- volvement. Through their correspondence Jack steadily encouraged his artistic creativity, advising him to seek a way of "living to defeat death." The comradely feelings of one so brilliant and sensitive as Jack also went a long way toward bolstering Neal's morale, and they outdid each other planning travels together: a jaunt to Lowell (whenever Neal got back to New York), an annual spring trip to Mexico, side trips to Cuba and South America.

Fired from his newspaper job, jilted by Helen, and struggling to write a novel about Huncke, Allen too received bounteous sympathy and counsel from Jack. But neither Jack's best efforts nor anyone else's could save the most deeply wounded of them all, Bill Can- nastra.

7.

During the previous two years Bill's drinking had gotten completely out of control. He'd guzzle liquor so fast that the transformation from gentle scholar to cruel prankster was, according to Howard Moss, like the swoosh when you light a gas stove. As his disappointment with himself intensified, and as his desperation increased, his stunts became ever more reckless. He was caught on a spiral to death, and everyone saw it. Lovers who truly cared for him forced themselves to break away from him, because they could no longer bear the throes of his prolonged suicide. Their desertion, in turn, hastened his flight into oblivion. By the summer of 1950, this "Great Angel" with "such beauty in his face" (as he'd been called by Allen) was leading an incredibly squalid and lonely life.

Bereft of most close friends, Bill sought any sort of company he could get, and what he ended up with generally were people who wanted to be entertained. He was surrounded by parasites who enjoyed moralizing about him, even while they got their kicks watching him break down the old morality. Analyzing Bill's dilemma, his Harvard friend John Snow wrote Allen: "Cannastra continues to be kept on the condition that he remains beautifully sad and intelligently desperate. This inevitably defeats those who really want to save him . . . Tony H— saved him the way a cat saves a mouse to destroy at his leisure. My own feelings on the subject are that if Cannastra were either dumber or less handsome there would be no problem. The prospect of so much beauty and intelligence going to waste is so attractive to less beautiful and intelligent people that they are willing to sponsor it."

But one of his companions that fall was a very pretty, twenty-year-old woman from upstate New York, Joan Haverty, whom he'd met on Cape Cod two years earlier. Rebelling against a strict mother, she had come to New York to live on her own. Although she was bright and interested in the arts, she was too shy to mingle in the usual bohemian circles. Bill became both her teacher and playmate, and remained tender with her even when he stopped being so with others, because he respected her innocence. Dressed as a sailor, Joan would climb fire escapes with him to peep into strangers' apartments, and later they'd discuss the pathetic way most people lived. Bill and Joan only became lovers "accidentally," for his sexual orientation was turning more and more toward men—and, besides, he was morally troubled just by the existence of his sexual nature. Often he recommended she replace him with a more rugged, conventionally masculine man.

The critical blow to Bill's self-esteem was a "Dear John" letter from the woman he had been engaged to marry. Shortly after this rejection, Joan found him very drunk, hoarsely singing his favorite song by the Ink Spots, in staccato phrases: "For all . . . we know . . . we may . . . never meet again."

On the night of October 12, Cannastra and some friends had left a party and were bound for his place by subway. Just as the train was pulling out of the Bleecker Street station, someone spoke of their friend, a black barmaid named Winnie, and Bill made as if to climb out the window, as if going back to see her. Some say he lost his balance and called for friends to pull him back in. Others say he meant to jump clear to the platform, and if left to himself might have made it, but his friends mistakenly restrained him. In any case, his head cracked against a pillar in the tunnel and he was pulled out and dragged under the train. The debate over Cannastra's death—was it accidental or planned?—went on for years. The only certain thing was that it marked the end of an era for his friends. He was their sacrificial lamb. Afterward, in the words of Bill Frankel, "everyone made a pretty-near final decision about what they wanted to do with the rest of their lives. Most of them tried to make friendships—some sexual, some not—so deep that they'd stand up for a lifetime."

After Bill's death, Joan moved into his loft to preserve it. On the evening of Friday, November 3, she was making hot chocolate for a quondam lover named Herb, a rather pedantic graduate student more than ten years her senior. Someone began hollering down on the street. When she went to the window he identified himself as Kerouac, and since the name sounded familiar, she threw down the keys, and marveled at how quickly he covered the distance to catch them. When he appeared upstairs with his neatly pressed clothes and carefully combed hair, she assumed he must belong to somebody. To her surprise he asked if she belonged to Herb. Herb answered, "Nope!"

Jack had been coming into the city once a week to see Reanna. His spirits were high, perhaps *because* he'd learned just how bad off he was: Harcourt Brace had sent him a statement declaring his book $665 in the red. Having nothing left to lose, he broke off with Giroux and signed up with the William Morris Agency. He realized that his ultimate success or failure depended solely on himself—on the strength of his work and character—and he would no longer defer to anyone's expectations. He was burning bridges at a frightful rate. Beverly had gotten miffed because he'd walked out of her *bon voyage* party to smoke pot, but he wasn't about to dissemble virtues he lacked, even for friends. Like Neal, who was already scheming to come east at Christmas to see his new infant son, Jack would let the world learn to love his faults, for they at least were genuine.

Bound for a party at Lucien's loft, which was right next to Cannastra's, Jack got sidetracked by Joan's hot chocolate. In return, he offered her a copy of *The Town and the City*. He also invited her to come with him to Lucien's, suggesting they make a surprise entrance from the fire escape. Since she was still wearing her skirt from work, Herb told her to change into jeans, to forestall any Peeping Toms below. Jack objected: "You look nice in your skirt!" Joan felt flattered.

That night Jack slept at Lucien's, and in the morning Joan invited him over for breakfast. Later, on their way to a movie, she was intrigued by the stories he invented about the people and places they passed. But the next night, when he came around again to propose marriage, she was still some ways from being in love with him. Why she said yes a few days later is something Joan herself never quite determined.

For one thing, she needed a reason to stay in New York, to avoid returning to her mother in Albany. For another Jack seemed like the ideal, strong husband Bill had prescribed for her. Most importantly, however, he was someone who could admire her, even if the domestic, submissive woman who charmed him lived only in his head. Herb, by contrast, had regarded her merely as a naive, funny country girl.

For his part, Jack was satisfied that Joan, unlike Reanna, would be nice to his mother. Moreover, even if Joan was an inch taller than he, she was certainly his type: a slender brunette "waif of a girl"— neat and eager, with a "classy way of coming on" despite her shyness.

They applied for the license on Tuesday, November 14. To prove he was no longer married to Edie, Jack telephoned her father's lawyer Ernest J. Sneed in North Carolina and Sneed confirmed that he had filed for an annulment. Waiting for this information, the City Clerk's office stayed open a few minutes past closing, so that when Jack and Joan returned on Friday to be married, they failed to satisfy the requirement of a seventy-two-hour waiting period. The Clerk's office wouldn't reopen until Monday, but Jack insisted they had to be married that day, because the beer keg had already been installed in Cannastra's loft and the reception was underway. Hence he led her to his relative, Judge Vincent Lupiano, who married them with Allen and Lucien standing as best men.

Walking back to the loft, Joan's feelings were vague. She sensed that they "had made a commitment to the marriage but not to each other." Jack, meanwhile, was amazingly chipper.

"Tomorrow we'll get my desk moved up to the loft!" he announced. "That's the next line of business!"

He had no idea the sponsors of waste were about to do a job on him.

EIGHT
More Day to Dawn

1.

Greeted by two hundred strangers in the 21st Street loft, Joan Haverty Kerouac felt as if she were at a play, and that the marriage would be over when the people went home. Everyone got drunk but the gaiety was largely forced, especially since Jack himself seemed to be struggling desperately to get the party off the ground. Few of the people there knew one another. The irony of reveling again in Cannastra's old loft lent tragic overtones to the affair, which in itself was squalid and dreary. The toilet clogged, the beer keg overflowed, a platter of sausages fell behind the refrigerator, a coffeepot flew out the window.

Not only was the marriage strangely impromptu, but Jack's friends found Joan unsympathetic and "not with it." [168] Jack declared that he had taken a romantic plunge, and he didn't introduce his bride as someone who would be part of any of their groups. Ginsberg and Ed Stringham agreed that he was headed for disaster. Holmes kept repeating, "I *believe* in you, Jack and Joan!" until Joan herself wondered, "Don't you know this is a joke?" Frankel and his Columbia friends marveled that Jack should be entering into a simple, conventional love marriage. The few married people in the Columbia group were pairs of students or pairs of professional people, like Frankel and his wife, who both worked in publishing. Jack's marriage seemed as unique to them as everything else about him, and his uniqueness was a trait they admired. But they also saw the toll it took on him, as his happiness that night was clearly just an act, a way he knew he should be feeling. The Columbia people thought the marriage too meaningless to last more than a few months; they foresaw it doomed, even under the best circumstances, by Jack's restlessness.

Later that night Jack collapsed on the bed, and after Joan helped him undress he passed out. The next morning, when he asked if he'd made her happy, she replied, "Beyond my wildest dreams." He immediately wrote Neal that Joan had been "impregnated on the 18th."

Despite his jokes about having had a "private Second Coming,"

Jack took the marriage very seriously. In the past year, several real apocalypses had shown him the need for a stable home, and Joan seemed to embody the "great Grace" for which he'd prayed. His original plan was for both of them to go to Mexico in May or June. Beforehand, he would apply for Fullbright and Guggenheim fellowships, but would live with "lint-pockets" if necessary until the acceptance of his next book. In late December, getting word that Neal would be in New York by February 8 (his twenty-fifth birthday), Jack decided he and Joan should accompany Neal back to the Coast. En route they could stop in Denver to get Neal's father out of jail; then in San Francisco they would settle next door to each other. They dreamed of raising large families together—Neal envisioned them "tossing the little wigglies over the backyard fence"—and hoped to spur each other's creativity. Jack especially looked forward to doing voice studies on Neal's new tape recorder.

Joan worked evenings in a department store during the Christmas rush. Lonely in the loft, Jack insisted they join his mother in Richmond Hill. Just before Christmas, Tom Livornese helped them move, and Gabrielle was so jubilant to have Jack home she fixed them all pancakes at two in the morning. Jack too was overjoyed to be wolfing food again in his mother's kitchen, which he said was "ever the source of life" for him.

Before attempting to finish *On the Road*, he studied various English prose styles. Although he ably imitated the paragraph-long, complex sentences, freighted with innumerable dependent clauses, of seventeenth-century masters like Swift, he concluded that such a style would prevent his saying anything to the point about the modern age. He envisioned a modern sentence made of Proustian parentheses transformed into clauses, but had trouble putting the idea into practice.

At bottom he was still bothered by a sense of dishonesty, especially since his friends seemed to be leading much more open lives than he. Even a con man like Neal never disguised his desires for sex, drugs, "eyeball kicks," etc., and acted always from an honest emotion, whether love or anger at lovelessness. Late in October, Lucien was hassled for sleeping in a church. Incensed, he yelled, "The last sanctuary!" at the police, until they dislocated his arm. Jack greatly respected such old-fashioned courage of one's convictions, and he was all the more disturbed by Lucien's description of him as a crooked French storekeeper. According to Lucien, Jack was trying to peddle a bag of beans with one rotten bean hidden at the bottom. Or sometimes he referred to Jack as a trickster who always kept one trick a secret. What he meant was that Jack could never be quite sincere because his eye was always on the main chance of becoming a great writer. As Jack admitted to Ed White, he would strive to write even his last mortal confession in a pleasing style.

The only way out of such self-conscious art, he felt, lay along the lines of modern musical composition, as in the work of Bartók and Schönberg. Jack wanted to discover "the basic tones of existence" as they were embodied in both characters and the human character generically. With those tones he would organize variations as in jazz, using his "knowledge of the 'IT' of feeling." Such writing would comprise large amounts of dialogue, and the endless talk would be structured by the classic jazz pattern of "18 bars, bridge, and take-out 8 bars." If one character got to really "blowing," Jack would let him keep taking further "choruses" until all his emotions were spent. By bringing different combinations of characters together in discussions, he could achieve the effect of instruments responding to one another in a band. As he explained the technique to Ed White: "When No. 1 talks to No. 2 and No. 3, it is not the same as No. 1 talking to No. 2 alone, or 2 and 3 discussing 1, or all three silent together, or 3 alone in his eternity." When all the characters fell into a silence, the author's voice would take over as a "choral hymn" or "oratorio." [169]

This complicated form derived from Jack's perception of the small number of character types any writer has to work with. He was looking to expand literature beyond the limited range of possible plot situations, just as bop musicians had broken free of the repertoire of swing melodies by reaching for a broader harmonic spread. What is often missed—and Jack discussed this fact with Tom Livornese—is that bop derives its interesting quality not so much from its immediate conception as from its larger musical base. Quite simply, a bop composition has more tones available to it to build from. Creating an equivalent to bop in writing depended upon the author's ability to find new ways of looking at old things. Jack now had a form for this literary music—what he called "Organized Variations on a Theme on Existence"—but he lacked the content: the "tones" themselves.

He asked Ed White and other friends what kind of book they would like to see him write. Although it was essential for him to know what was happening in the world and especially in America, he claimed he could only know what his friends let him know. The most valuable thing anyone could give him was their heartfelt vision of what he could do, and he sought earnestly to know "what does a guy like me have to offer in the way of a book to a world in its present state?" As before, it was Neal Cassady who finally gave him a clear answer.

On December 30, 1950, Jack received a 23,000-word typewritten letter from Neal, which Jack pronounced "the greatest story" he'd ever read by an American writer. In the letter, Neal poured out his heart about a girl, hotel rooms, crying and cocksucking, attempts at suicide, poolrooms, hospitals, jails, and the tragic and farcical events of Christmas Eve 1945, in Denver. The story concerned chiefly a girl who had tried to commit suicide because she thought she wasn't good enough for Neal (who was then a bum on Glenarm Street), so disturbing him that he "spread her legs and stared into her soul with wonder." A moment later she tried to jump out the window. Remembering her with nostalgia, Neal concluded that she was "saved because and only because she thought she wasn't good enough" for him. Yet the subject of the story was, most remarkably, the development of Neal's "soul."

Jack was astonished that Neal had found a way to write about intensely real things like miscarriages and dwarfish cabdrivers, which were too sordid, grisly, or improbable for most literature. These were things he himself hadn't yet learned how to organize into a single narrative, though he considered them the most important things to tell about. Jack thought Neal's letter a "novelette" that "outmatches Celine, Wolfe; matches Dostoyevsky in its highest moments; has all of Joyce at its command. . . ." No writer before had made him know so completely the thoughts of a young homeless man in jail, or made him feel so deeply a motherless man's vast need for women or a jailbird's haunting fear of arrest. Above all, he was mortified by the humility with which Neal produced such a masterpiece, for Neal didn't even consider himself a writer, whereas Jack truly believed him "a much greater writer than I am."

Though Jack doubted that either Brierly or Giroux would acknowledge Neal's genius, he saw the letter as a watershed in literary history, marking the start of an "American Renaissance." Not only did Neal now "belong to the world," but Jack predicted a wave of American writers would follow in his footsteps. Outcasts and madmen, rising "from the streets and the land with a language," would give the nation "a vision all their own, eloquent, confessional, sublime, and pure."

But just as his admiration for Neal was increasing, a painful sense of being rejected by Neal began to grow in him. Fed by misunderstanding on both sides, that hurt came to cloud their friendship for the rest of their lives. Because Neal had never spoken a word in praise of *The Town and the City*, Jack concluded that he had found it worthless. When he'd pushed him to make some comment about it, Neal had said, "You're the kind of writer who'll go on forever!" Jack interpreted this as an insult. For months Jack had been growing defensive about his ability to write, especially since a rumor started circulating around New York that "Jack Kerouac's friends love him but not his book." That fall, as Neal came to demonstrate his own literary power in the succession of long letters culminating in the novelette, Jack found himself "so haunted by his complete influence" that he could scarcely mention Neal's name, and often blocked it from his thoughts. Not without bitterness he now proclaimed Neal, rather than himself, "the one" [170]—the man who would knock American letters on its collective, professorial ass.

But proclaim him Jack did, as the "new American colossus," and carried the letter to all his friends. Surprised that Holmes and Alan Harrington weren't impressed, he assured Neal that he'd keep working to get it published; he planned next to try his own English publisher, Frank Morley. He even took pains to explain to Neal what made his letter great. As confession, Jack thought it ranked with Dostoyevsky's *Notes from Underground.* Neal's style had the "muscular rush" of Joyce, Céline, Dostoyevsky, and Proust; and because his narrative was "kickwriting," an account of his "mad joys," it sustained excitement better than works of those other writers. Dreiser and Wolfe seemed dull beside him. "Melville," Jack asserted, "was never truer." Hemingway was flushed from the cover of his "sparse and halting" sentences, and Fitzgerald's subjects appeared as "sweetly unnecessary" as Neal's were "painfully necessary."

Due to the loss of the original "Joan Anderson letter" (as it was dubbed after its main character), it is impossible to evaluate Jack's judgments about it. The surviving fragment, published in *The First Third,* reveals badly overwritten, hyperbolic prose, although Neal sometimes rises to precise, poetic statements like "To have seen a specter isn't everything, and there are deathmasks piled, one atop the other, clear to heaven." The story is even more gravely flawed by patent self-deceptions, as when Neal blames his loss of Joan on the fact that one afternoon he drank too many beers. What is important, however, is that Neal doesn't shirk description of any activity he participated in, day and night, over a period of several days. At one point, relating a sexual encounter, he notes that a great many of his scenes occur in bathrooms; but he refuses to alter or apologize for that fact, explaining that he writes "just the incidents exactly as they occurred." That single statement gave Jack the permission he needed to make actual reality—unadorned and unbowdlerized—his subject. Three decades and powers of freedom later, many critics fail to realize the impact of Neal's dictum that *you could write about life without changing anything.* Certainly there had been nonfiction novels as early as the nineteenth century, prime examples being Twain's *Roughing It* and *Innocents Abroad.* But, as Aaron Latham pointed out, it would be difficult to imagine *In Cold Blood* (1965), *The Electric Kool-Aid Acid Test* (1968), and the ensuing avalanche of "New Journalism" had Jack Kerouac not learned from Neal Cassady that fiction doesn't have to be false.

2.

At first Jack's wife and mother got along well. In fact, they kept each other company watching television on the nights he visited his friends in Manhattan. Denying Joan permission to join him, Jerry Newman, and Seymour Wyse on a walk along the docks, Jack told her, "You might get hurt!" Clowning and playfulness were his male prerogatives. Women, he made it clear, were meant to stay home with the dishes.

For all that, and for all her severe mental problems, Joan was learning to love Jack. She saw much good in him, much sensitivity, and the fact that he wanted to care for his mother just enhanced his "nice-boy" image. He was, besides, her "Angel Bunny," who amused her when she got too serious. Once, when all his boyish charm failed to draw a smile, he stood on his head on a busy sidewalk. His suit jacket fell down over his head, all his change and keys fell out of his pockets, and Joan laughed. Jack also told her endless stories, but she wished he would take a little interest in what she had to say. If she tried to describe any of her experiences, he cruelly shushed her, till finally she snapped, "Oh! I thought we were having a *conversation.*" "No, we're not!" Jack corrected. Another time she started to argue with Jack about Truman, and he was outraged that she dared to oppose him. To make a point, she set down her steam iron on Seymour Wyse's pants, which she'd been pegging, and accidentally burned a hole through them. Henceforth she knew better than to have an opinion on anything.

Gabrielle felt it was her mission in life to care for Jack, and Joan's duty to learn from her. Joan was peeved to hear she didn't make potato salad or even slice a hot dog properly, that she missed a little dust under the back leg of the bed, that there'd be bugs because she left the dishes unwashed overnight. No matter what she was doing, Gabe suggested Joan could do better at it. Jack gave Joan no support, since he too thought she should learn to do things his mother's way. It didn't take long to put Joan's nose out of joint, and the deep-seated rebelliousness that Jack had never suspected came to the fore. Once when she got home from work, close to midnight, Jack asked her to bake him a spice cake right then. Since she had to get up early the next morning, she refused, whereupon Jack shouted, "You should never deny your son anything!" Realizing his slip, he apologized: "You make a husband grouchy when you deny him things." Later, lying in bed, Joan heard Gabe consoling him, and soon she smelled spice cake baking.

Jack wanted to sleep in his old room, through which Gabe had to pass to get to her room. Every morning Gabe would extend a dripping cold glass over Joan to announce: "Jack-kie! Your juice!" Every night at the supper table Joan would have to listen to Gabe complaining about the "foreigners" taking over America; among those foreigners she counted Allen Ginsberg and anybody whose parents had not been born in either the United States or Canada. In addition, Gabe continually voiced her fear that the communists were about to poison the water supply. Alone with Joan, she would extol Jack's

340 · M E M O R Y   B A B E

genius. Gabe had been very impressed by the refrigerator and television Jack had bought her with his advance from *The Town and the City,* and she was also pleased that her son had written a "religious novel."

However glad that Gabe accepted her as a member of the family, Joan balked at being a child again in another woman's home. She had to turn over her paycheck, and Gabe doled out their busfare and lunch money. Especially irritating was the fact that Gabe and Jack spoke French together most of the time. Joan knew they often talked about her because she heard them referring to "La Belle." Nevertheless Joan actually had a better friendship with Gabe than with Jack, because he didn't want to be friends with a woman. Joan planned to move out, hoping to break up the mother-son rapport that excluded her, but if necessary she'd return to living on her own again rather than remain a husbandless wife.

Jack forbade discussion of their leaving. Totally frustrated, Joan stayed in bed for three days, eating nothing. Finally Gabe came in with a bowl of chicken soup, warning Joan she had to eat to stay alive. Joan said she preferred to die. Gabe said, "You eat first!" After Gabe spoon-fed her the soup, Joan went out to find a new job and an apartment. The day the movers came she was at work; she had given them instructions to take only her things, unless Jack specifically told them he wanted to come too. During her break she went to the apartment and found him on the sidewalk, seated, slippers in hand, atop his precious rolltop desk (a gift from Nin and Paul). Jack and Joan started living in the apartment at 454 West 20th Street in mid-January, 1951.

Originally Neal had promised to bring them a railroad pass so they could both ride free most of the way to San Francisco. He had even invited them to live in his attic, offering Jack the use of his typewriter, tape recorder, alto saxophone, and car. On January 8, Neal had written that he couldn't get the pass, and that they should save up for a truck. A week or so after Jack and Joan moved into the 20th Street apartment, Neal appeared prematurely. Broke and unusually quiet, he had come to see his new son, Neal Cassady III, and to explain to Diana why he had chosen to make his permanent home with Carolyn. Diana threw him out after one night, and a few days later he prepared to return to San Francisco, still urging Jack and Joan to follow as soon as they had the means.

The night Neal was leaving he stopped to see Jack, who was bound for a Duke Ellington concert with Joan and Henri Cru and his girl. Earlier Joan had been disgusted watching Jack lap up pink-shirted Cru's *suavité* and take instructions from Henri about "the details of clothing." [171] Cru had even rented a limousine for the occasion. When Neal asked for a ride to Penn Station, Henri snapped, "Absolutely not!" Shivering in his thin coat, Neal looked so much more real to Joan than Cru that she despised Jack for ignoring his request. As they drove away, Neal began running up the street, a heroic contrast to Jack's servile passivity.

Joan worked as a waitress at Stouffer's and resented Jack's lying in bed all morning. She didn't think much of *The Town and the City,* and she felt that his artist's life was at least partly a product of his mother's having spoiled him. Joan was appalled, for example, to find that he didn't even know what size socks or shirt he wore, since his mother had always bought them. As a result of Joan's grumbling, he got a part-time job synopsizing scripts for Twentieth Century-Fox.

In February Neal pleaded with Jack to hurry to San Francisco, because he was tormented by loneliness and nightmares. But the train pass he wangled would only take Jack as far as Atlanta, Georgia. In a second letter, Neal enclosed another autobiographical fragment that he'd composed about the time of the "Joan letter." Fresh material would not come. Due partly to his heavy use of marijuana and hashish, Neal was slipping into another "blank period," the worst ever. It sometimes took him twenty minutes to formulate a sentence. In any case, there was a positive aspect to this blankness, since he was once again applying much of his energy to his familial duties. Jack didn't hear from him again until April 1, when he sent a postcard saying that he still loved Jack but that he could no longer write more than a paragraph. He had run out of pot, and continuing wrangles between Carolyn and Diana (by letter and phone) left him sick to his stomach with sorrow.

Early 1951 was a time of sober reassessment for Jack too. He now conceded that he had been "over-enthusiastic" about Neal's abilities as a writer. Though he still believed Neal a "saint," [172] with a sensibility as deep as Dostoyevsky's, he felt Neal lacked the ability to work. Significantly, Jack spent the first few months of his marriage figuring ways to insure a tranquil work life for himself. His mother was leaving New York to move in with his sister in North Carolina. Either Mexico or Peru seemed the likeliest spot for him and Joan to settle, both for the cheapness of living and the societies he wanted to study. Even if he didn't get a Guggenheim fellowship, he hoped an advance for *On the Road* would permit them to move by fall. As soon as he had money enough, he would buy a house down there, and raise his children away from the "greedy" United States.

Friends like Helen Parker, who knew Jack's wilder days, were astonished to find him placidly ensconced in the domestic life, writing at his rolltop desk while Joan sat quietly in her corner sewing. Jack also described to Joan his vision of their living in a cabin in the hills, where his greatest pleasure would be to sit in a rocking chair in front of the woodstove, his feet propped on the oven door. They visited the Fitzgeralds in Poughkeepsie, and seeing Jean in a housedress and bobby sox, with her hair in rollers, he told Joan: "That's the kind of woman I've always liked, a real homey type." Another time Joan showed him a cartoon of an old lady in bathrobe and slippers ladling dinner for an old guy in his undershirt, hunched at the kitchen table under a naked light bulb. "Is this what you'd like your home life to be?" she mocked, and Jack replied grinning, "Yeah! That's it! You can just about smell cabbage cooking on the stove."

After a few months Joan still hadn't gotten pregnant. Worried that ordinary intercourse wouldn't work for them, they abstained from sex for long periods to allow Jack to accumulate sperm, and after intercourse Joan would stand on her head to facilitate fertilization.

Married or not, Jack maintained his devotion to the double standard. When Joan went up to Albany to visit her mother, he asked Lucien to find him a girl. Lucien took him to meet his new girlfriend, Helen Elliott, a Barnard freshman, and she fixed Jack up with another Barnard student, Joan Eisner. At the West End Bar, Columbia undergraduates cheered Jack and Lucien as though they were celebrities. Both girls were in especial awe of Jack, since Lucien had introduced him as "the great football hero Jack Kerouac." The four of them decided they'd hit every bar from 116th Street to 96th Street, and accomplished the feat. Terribly drunk, Jack led Joan Eisner to a friend's house, where he melted what was left of her proper façade with a collection of pornographic pictures.

It would be a mistake to think that by 1951 Jack was already some sort of sexual "free-swinger," as the concept developed in the 1970's. Contrary to Jack's scandalous reputation, Helen Elliott found that he was actually more reserved and conventional than Carr, Ginsberg, or any of the others in that circle. Despite the pride Jack took in his physical strength, he remained extraordinarily shy throughout his life.

In early March, 1951, John Holmes brought Jack the completed manuscript of his novel, which was to be published a year later as *Go*. The characters were based on John and his wife, Jack, and many of their mutual acquaintances, including Neal, LuAnne, Cannastra, Ginsberg, and Huncke. Jack gently advised John how to improve the book, praising much of it, although he found his own portrait in "Gene Pasternak" unrealistic. The title Holmes was using for the book, "The Beat Generation," had been coined by Jack, who suggested he modify it to "The Beat Ones." Jack was also a little upset that Holmes had transcribed much of their real conversation directly from his journals into the novel. Although Jack admitted that the "stageless prose play" was a "perfectly legitimate" artistic form, and although he himself would later employ large chunks of recorded dialogue in his own novels, the presence of his verbatim speeches in *Go* doubtless contributed to his later accusing Holmes of plagiarism.

He and John also had a long discussion about Jack's problems with *On the Road.* Jack told how he had been struggling to create plausible backgrounds and family situations for his characters, and how he finally had to admit that he couldn't catch the thing about it that he wanted that way. "I'm going to forget all that horseshit," he concluded. "I'm just going to write it as it happened." Lately Joan had been asking him, "What did you and Neal really do?" and he decided to write the novel as if he were answering her questions.

Embarking on this new version, much truer to his original experience, Jack was initially stymied by his inability to sustain a free flow of words. Specifically, he was distracted by the need to keep putting fresh pages into his typewriter. In early April, he got the idea of taping together Cannastra's twenty-foot strips of Japanese drawing paper to form a roll that could be fed continuously through his typewriter. Since he liked to have Joan sleeping near him while he worked, he set up a screen around his desk to protect her from the light. For the next twenty days he typed almost nonstop. He slept rarely. When Joan returned from her job, she provided him with a steady supply of coffee and pea soup. He was sweating so badly that he went through dozens of T-shirts a day, wringing them out and hanging them all over the apartment. By April 9, he had written thirty-four thousand words, by April 20, eighty-six thousand, nearly finishing the novel. The whole manuscript was a single paragraph with no commas and few periods. Toward the end, he worked at Lucien's nearby loft, and became furious when Lucien's dog chewed up the last few feet of the roll. But nothing could diminish his ecstasy at having helped initiate "a new trend in American literature." [173] He had finally found his own literary road.

3.

Both trail and superhighway, *On the Road* led from *Moby Dick* and *Huckleberry Finn* into the twenty-first century—from outer to inner space. Ahab in *Moby Dick* searched for the purveyors of cosmic evil, while Huck Finn looked for a good society, all the while chronicling the ubiquitous social ills he found. Both heroes searched for something outside themselves. By contrast, the heroes of *On the Road,* Dean Moriarty (Neal) and Sal Paradise (Jack), no matter how far they travel in the external world, are ceaselessly penetrating deeper into their own souls. They are constantly aware that their travel, by the excitement and curiosity it generates, is a means to understanding themselves. Travel to them is a conscious philosophical method by which they test the store of hand-me-down truisms. Moreover, as a potent imaginative symbol, travel is a philosopher's stone that turns every experience into a spiritual lesson.

Kerouac's approach to the journey is much closer to the Whitman of "Song of the Open Road." Whitman's persona travels just to learn that he doesn't need to: "Henceforth I ask not good-fortune,/ I myself am good-fortune." The road simply reflects back the self, and it is a finer mirror even than the poet's own language: "You express me better than I can express myself. . . ." What the traveler learns about himself is the greatest marvel he encounters: "I am larger, better than I thought,/ I did not know I held so much goodness." Above all, Whitman insists that learning is an experiential process: "Wisdom cannot be pass'd from one having it to another not having it,/ Wisdom is of the soul, is not susceptible of proof, is its own proof,/ . . . Now I re-examine philosophies and religions,/ They may prove well in the lecture-rooms, yet not prove at all under the spacious clouds and along the landscape and flowing currents."

The motto of Whitman's persona could just as well have been spoken by Dean Moriarty or Sal Paradise: "I and mine do not convince by arguments, similes, rhymes,/ We convince by our presence." For Whitman, as for Kerouac, travel is a statement of personal optimism; it affirms both a willingness to attempt the impossible and a belief that every limit may be transcended: "To see nothing anywhere but what you may reach it and pass it,/ To conceive no time, however distant, but what you may reach it and pass it. . . ." The road in both Kerouac and Whitman leads finally to a universal extension of love. As an invitation away from selfishness, the road is its own reward, its own reason for being: "Camerado, I give you my hand!/ I give you my love more precious than money,/ I give you myself before preaching or law;/ Will you give me yourself? will you come travel with me?/ Shall we stick by each other as long as we live?"

Kerouac's Cadillac limousine covers much the same territory as Whitman's horse-trolley. Yet On the Road has often been attacked for being outside any recognizable American literary tradition, even though in the use of an idiomatic American diction Kerouac follows, among others, Twain, Jack London, James Farrell, and John Dos Passos. To a far greater extent than Nelson Algren, Kerouac makes the lingo of the jazz and drug subcultures part of his actual prose, as distinct from its use in dialogue. As a study of the privations, despairs, and frenzies of proletarian life, On the Road holds its own with Dos Passos' U.S.A. trilogy, and it is certainly more concise than Dos Passos. Kerouac's antiheroes learned a lot of their tricks from Jack London's outlaws. London's persona in The Road prefers running to fighting, advises living in the present moment, and rejects society's values while rigorously upholding his own private moral code. While the tramp may have no legal or social authority, he has, according to London, the power of witnessing injustice and telling about it, and thus he may serve as one of the most powerful forces for change. Like Kerouac, London believed that the best stories were improvised, and as an example of the method he cited the hobo who is forced to make up credible tales while begging: "The successful hobo must be an artist. He must create spontaneously and instantaneously—and not upon a theme selected from the plentitude of his own imagination, but upon the theme he reads in the face of the person who opens the door. . . ."

Doubtless as a tip-off to their influence, Kerouac employs many distinctive words and epithets of London and Dos Passos, such as the use of "bo" for *hobo*, "Chi" for *Chicago*, and "yare" for *yes*. Not only do London and Dos Passos make frequent use of the phrase "on the road," but both refer to bumming across country as "beating one's way," a fact that casts new light on the origin of the term "Beat Generation," especially since Kerouac spoke of "beating his way" in letters. London devotes a long section to the way a hobo adopts a road name, and Kerouac shows that he has learned the lesson with characters like "Louisiana Slim" and "Mississippi Gene." Many of Kerouac's allusions to his predecessors are simply playful, as when he names a pool shark "Tommy Snark"—the *Snark* being the ketch on which London sailed across the Pacific.

The influence of Wolfe is still very evident too. Wolfe's Faustian hero seeks to devour the earth; Kerouac's equally hungry travelers, being slightly more patriotic, find banquet enough in the American continent. Whereas Wolfe painted the panorama of America from a train window, Kerouac captured even more sweeping vistas from car and bus. There is also in Wolfe, as in Kerouac, a sense of the preciousness of things perceived but once, never to be recaptured in the same configuration. Timelessness is evoked by both writers through their awareness, even as the moment passes, that they will later remember it. Everything is seen with a double vision, for as they observe their present life they simultaneously regard it from the perspective of the future. From the flashing visions in Eugene Gant's train window in *Of Time and the River*, Wolfe defined the paradox of evanescence that was to stamp every work of Kerouac as well: ". . . all the strange and bitter miracle of life—how, why, or in what way, he does not know—is in that instant greeting and farewell; for once seen, and lost the moment that he sees it, it is his forever and he can never forget it."

What is important is that Kerouac, while following all of these traditions, provided his own highly modern synthesis. He saw in Neal Cassady a man undertaking the vision quest, that testing ritual present in every culture, and he interpreted what Neal sought as the body of America and the individualistic characteristics of the souls in America, and articulated these discoveries in terms clear enough for others to learn from them.

Through the spiritualization of their own lives, Sal Paradise and

Dean Moriarty respiritualize America. What they find are things Cold War America never even knew to look for:

> And just for a moment I had reached the point of ecstasy that I always wanted to reach, which was the complete step across chronological time into timeless shadows, and wonderment in the bleakness of the mortal realm, and the sensation of death kicking at my heels to move on, with a phantom dogging its own heels, and myself hurrying to a plank where all the angels dove off and flew into the holy void of uncreated emptiness, the potent and inconceivable radiancies shining in bright Mind Essence, innumerable lotus-lands falling open in the magic mothswarm of heaven.

These are heady kicks, to be sure, but *On the Road* is a tightly unified novel. The recurrence of cosmic moments, like the one quoted above, is a chief organizing factor. Much more deeply than in *The Town and the City*, Kerouac explores the stimuli that produce such moments. Although the impetus may be any unusual physical condition such as sickness, exhaustion, or excessive hunger, the explosion of cosmic awareness is most often generated by physical ecstasy, whether in listening to jazz or making love. When music and orgasm combine, as in one of the concluding scenes in a Mexican whorehouse, the visionary moment scintillates. Yet Kerouac can narrate the event with the detachment of double-entendre:

> "More Mambo Jambo," "Chattanooga de Mambo," "Mambo Numero Ocho"—all these tremendous numbers resounded and flared in the golden, mysterious afternoon like the sounds you expect to hear on the last day of the world and the Second Coming. The trumpets seemed so loud I thought they could hear them clear out in the desert, where the trumpets had originated anyway. The drums were mad. The mambo beat is the conga beat from Congo, the river of Africa and the world; it's really the world beat. ° ° ° The final trumpet choruses that came with drum climaxes on conga and bongo drums, on the great mad Chattanooga record, froze Dean in his tracks for a moment till he shuddered and sweated; then when the trumpets bit the drowsy air with their quivering echoes, like a cavern's or a cave's, his eyes grew large and round as though seeing the devil, and he closed them tight. I myself was shaken like a puppet by it; I heard the trumpets flail the light I had seen and trembled in my boots.

This serious humor pervades the novel. It exists, for example, in Kerouac's name game. "Sal Paradise" derived from Jack's misreading of the words "sad paradise" in one of Ginsberg's poems, but the inference of a "sallow" or decayed paradise is still plain. "Dean

347 · *More Day to Dawn*

Moriarty" is an academic step higher than Professor Moriarty, Sherlock Holmes' favorite villain. If Professor Moriarty was Holmes' most nefarious opponent, Moriarty's great intelligence and energy also stimulated Holmes to his most brilliant feats of crime detection. There is also a pun on the fact that Neal was the greatest "opponent" of John Clellon Holmes, who like Sherlock would have been insufferably bored without "Moriarty's" challenge to his stiff morality.

Kerouac never lets us forget that his characters are on a religious quest. Although he uses standard liturgical terminology, we soon find that he is making associative leaps into realms beyond any denominational church. "The road to heaven" begins on the strip of concrete between Denver and San Francisco, heaven turns out to be located in Mexico, and God appears onstage in the persons of George Shearing, Slim Gaillard, and Dean himself. Dean is variously represented as God, the devil, Christ, an angel, a saint, a prophet. Sal himself becomes a Christ figure. A Mexican girl along the road is the Virgin Mother. Far from being irreverent, Kerouac is demolishing the hidebound belief that holy mysteries are the sole property of a priest or pastor, and is returning religion to the mass of people. In several places he openly jeers at conventional religion, as when he refers to two Jesuit students who "had nothing on their bird-beans except a lot of ill-understood Aquinas for stuffing for their pepper."

On the Road is a paean to the brotherhood of man, which is established through a complex set of identifications, the basis of which is Sal's acceptance of Neal as his brother. Together they participate in "the fall," wrestle with their respective angels, discover the invisible forces that bind them like telephone wires to the world that seems to reject them, and finally—sleeping on a Mexican road, buried in a swarming mass of insects—become one with the earth itself. The whole point of this metamorphosis is not merely that the characters are enriched by strengthening their ties with humanity, but that like Christ they have sacrificed their selfhood for the benefit of all. Sal is instructed by the Walking Prophet to "go moan for man." Called "Zacatecan Jack," the Prophet is an alter ego of the narrator (as well as of Dean), and the instruction becomes the controlling mantra of the book. Like the best postmodernist fiction, *On the Road* provides its own excuse for being; how and why the novel is written becomes the novel's very subject.

The religious quest finds itself symbolized in a network of overlapping motifs. One central image is a rose flowing downriver to the sea on a rainy night; its native American variants include "the Montana log" rolling by "in the black river of the night." Kerouac uses these tokens of vanishing radiance and power (drawing on such Blake poems as "The Sick Rose" and "The Tyger") to suggest the magic of spirit. Stars too serve as a symbol of intangible purity and unattainable aspiration, but as they revolve away from us they are also revolving toward us, keeping us always in hopeful expectation of their return. It is the *motion* of stars Kerouac stresses, from the marvelous double-image of "fabulous yellow roman candles exploding like spiders across the stars" at the start of the book, to the evening star "shedding her sparkler dims on the prairie" at the conclusion. Like *star*, many other words recur with the frequency of a litany: *beat, vision, dream, night, lost, gone, sad, ghost* (most of which are key words for Wolfe too). The thrust of all these symbolisms is to establish the cyclical nature of what men designate "truth" or "the absolute," etc. To this end Kerouac also uses many time collapses and images of light springing from darkness, and pays close attention to the passage of the seasons. The story begins and ends in winter. The book completes one cycle in the life of the narrator, since at the opening he has just lost one wife, and at the close he has finally found another.

Any attempt to merely enumerate themes would not do *On the Road* justice, for the book operates on many levels. It also provides a comprehensive social criticism of post–World War II America. This criticism ranges from a mild satire of greed: "Everybody in America is a natural-born thief "—to a serious concern with conformism: "Everybody's doing what they think they're supposed to do"—to a horror at the increasing violence, repression of healthy pleasure, and militaristic mania: "A bomb had come that could crack all our bridges and roads and reduce them to jumbles. . . ." Furthermore, Kerouac is able to capture the new state of mind that derives directly from the frenetic pace of modern American life. The poignancy of *On the Road* lies in its sense of accelerated doom, as every joy terminates almost immediately in desperation.

4.

The first person to whom Jack brought the 120-foot roll manuscript of *On the Road* was John Holmes. Jack had used the real names of the people he was writing about, just as Holmes had in *Go*. One of the problems they had discussing this new *On the Road* was due to the fact that Holmes had dealt with many of the same events in his own novel and had come to a different, generally more moralistic, understanding of them. As well as his travels with Neal, Jack had included long sections about their adventures in New York and San Francisco. Holmes felt that the latter were extraneous to the novel, which was about being adrift in America, and rushing from coast to coast. Jack, however, felt that Holmes was laying claim to the New York material.

In any case, Holmes saw a great many admirable things in *On the Road*. He was impressed that Jack had turned his shyness to account by fashioning a narrator who was a "shambler after people," a follower rather than leader, just like he was. Sal Paradise stands as a link between the old and new realities. His passivity and curiosity become the pivot of the book; his receptiveness to new experience provides a way into it for more conventional people. The whole vision of the book is Sal's, not Dean's, and Holmes marveled at the complex matrix by which Jack had made his own cerebral, literary sensibility serve the voluble, experiential sensibility of Neal.

Jack also showed *On the Road* to Allen, who liked its youthful freshness. Jack admitted that he didn't know how to end it, though, because he was afraid to prophesy a fate for Neal that might not come true.

But Jack's jubilance fell dead in the offices of Harcourt Brace. Ceremoniously unrolling *On the Road* across Giroux's carpet, Jack prepared to exult with his old editor over this hard-earned triumph. Disconcerted instead, Giroux remarked that it would be impossible to revise such a manuscript. After denouncing him as a "crass idiot," Jack returned to Joan in a mood she describes as "hurt but prideful." He boasted that his work was so great he had no need of Harcourt Brace.

Holmes took *On the Road* to his own agent, Rae Everitt of MCA Management. When Rae said the novel needed "lots of revision," Jack grew confused and depressed, especially since good friends like Lucien were also clamoring for him to give the book a more conventional form. To sympathetic Ed Stringham, he bitterly cursed all the "slick, cynical sophisticates" of publishing, behind whose cool praise he detected a cruel laughter. He confessed that he had expected to take New York by storm with *On the Road*. Instead of recognition for his accomplishments, all he had gained from fashionable literary society was a reputation as a buffoon. The more they needled him, the more he played the role of the "rough lumberjack genius" as a defense. Laughing out of the wrong side of his mouth, he told Stringham, "Well, I'm just a dumb Canuck." And he began to resort more to his sole other defense: drink.

Also at this time his relationship with Joan was deteriorating rapidly. She needed a man strong enough to curb her own willfulness, and kind enough to make cooperation a pleasure. What she got was a husband too selfish to even share his cigarettes with her, and so impulsive that his leadership brought their household to ruin. In May, they went to see Helen Parker and her new beau off to Mexico. Jack insisted Joan keep buying them rounds of drinks, even though she was spending the grocery money. On the way home he spotted a vegetable stand and started yelling that he had to have "spring's first asparagus," oblivious to the fact that her purse was empty. When she finally made him realize there was no way he could get his asparagus, he turned abruptly away in a deep sulk.

From the start Jack had been so possessive of Joan that he even begrudged sharing their loft with Cannastra's ghost, or so she felt, for when she would use some speech mannerism she'd picked up from Bill, he would immediately reprimand her: "Be yourself—don't mimic!" It's possible, of course, that Jack was just guarding his own memories of Cannastra.

A more disturbing episode involved Cannastra's buddy Bob Stern. One night when Jack and Joan were still living in the loft, Stern had stood under their window calling for Bill, though he knew Bill was dead. Finally, figuring he was drunk, Joan let him come up and fixed a place for him to sleep. Jack angrily plunked down at his desk, tossing things around and giving her horrible dark looks over his shoulder.

The first summer Joan had come to Cape Cod, Stern had arranged a little party on Bill's fishing boat, during which he made love to Joan while the crew secretly looked on. Bill had made sure that all his friends on the Cape knew of the stunt, and there's a good chance Jack eventually learned of it.

During the spring that he and Joan were living on West 20th Street, Jack chanced to meet Stern one day just as he was leaving the house. On an errand to Twentieth Century Pictures, Jack was dressed in suit and tie. Stern made some offhand remark about Joan, which Jack interpreted as an innuendo that his wife was promiscuous. He demanded that Stern show respect, whereupon Stern taunted: "Are you kidding? I love Joan more than you do." Furious, Jack stepped toward him, but Stern pulled out a knife and swiftly cut Jack's tie off just below the knot. Jack returned to Joan looking like a little boy who'd lost his toy to a bully, and he was even further mortified when the story got to be a joke among their friends.

Joan had her own just cause for jealousy. Discussing her sexual problems with Marian Holmes, she was shocked when Marian responded knowingly: "That's because Jack's a minuteman!" Jack's affair with Marian may have antedated his vows to Joan, but Joan soon discovered that he had a few current thrills as well: returning home from another visit to her mother's, Joan was accosted by the irate landlady, who complained that her husband had been playing house with a girl from Barnard.

During one of Joan's rampages Jack told Seymour Wyse that her behavior baffled him and his English friend replied: "The problem, Jack, is you're not bringin' 'ome the bycon." Jack himself declared that their marriage had failed because she wasn't a Catholic. The one thing he really couldn't forgive her, however, was the critical wound she dealt his pride.

He'd taken to living away from their apartment a good deal of

the time, sleeping mostly at Lucien's. One night he returned unexpectedly to find Joan consoling herself with the company of a guy
who worked in the restaurant with her. The pain of her "infidelity"
was such that for years Jack told friends he would never remarry so
that no woman could hurt him like that again.

In early June, Joan told him that she might be pregnant. His first
reaction was anger mixed with fear. Her eyes were on the prominent
vein that ran from his forehead past the corner of his eye, which was
throbbing violently as it always did in times of crisis. Hoping she was
mistaken, he sent her to his sister's doctor for an examination. When
the doctor confirmed her pregnancy, Jack was up in arms. He told
her: "Of course I want children, but not now!" Stressing that his new
book would be difficult to sell, he pleaded his inability to support a
child. The solution he proposed had already been tried successfully
by Lucien's girlfriend: a trip to a certain doctor in Chicago. Abortion was unthinkable to Joan, and when he insisted on it, she told
him to get out, and he did. He went to Lucien's for a week or so, and
then to his mother in Kinston, North Carolina.

While he was still at Lucien's, Joan telephoned Gabrielle, intending to tell her the whole story of their separation. As soon as Gabe
heard that Jack had left, she asked if he had hurt her. "Because if
Jackie ever hurt you," she asserted, "I never forgive him." Joan realized that Gabe would never let Jack walk out on a pregnant wife,
and that if she knew Joan were pregnant she would force him to
return to her. To spare both Jack and his mother further misery, Joan
assured Gabe that the breakup wasn't anybody's fault in particular,
and omitted mentioning her pregnancy. A short time afterward, she
returned to her mother in Albany.

When Jack first returned to his mother, he too denied the possibility that Joan might be pregnant. A few months later, when she
filed for a warrant from the Domestic Relations Court, to compel
Jack to pay for her prenatal care, he had to devise a story to cover
his first lie. So he told his mother that Joan had been unfaithful to
him and that there was no way the child could be his own.

Neal had sent a telegram inviting Jack to San Francisco, and
Lucien had asked him to come to Mexico with himself and Allen, but
North Carolina proved the best haven. That summer in Mexico City,
Joan's benzedrine psychosis was pushing her to the verge of suicide,
and she often drove 100 miles an hour over unpaved roads. As Jack
later wrote to Neal, if he had been in Mexico with them, his own
gloom might have so deepened that he would either have killed himself or ended up with a drug habit.

By contrast Kinston, North Carolina, was a domestic paradise.
Nin's son Paul was now three years old, and Gabe loved to coddle
him: cooking him treats, singing and playing piano for him, telling
him stories just as she had done for little Jackie. It was at this time

that she became known as "Mémère," which is a French-Canadian child's version of *grand-mère*, grandmother.

Jack needed more than mothering. Almost as soon as he arrived in Kinston, he fell victim to the worst attack of phlebitis he'd had in years. This bout of the illness may well have been psychogenic. *Visions of Cody* includes a letter Jack wrote to Neal shortly after leaving Joan, and in the letter he links his recurring thoughts of death with his terrible guilt: "I feel like I've done wrong, to myself the most wrong, I'm throwing away something that I can't even find in the incredible clutter of my being but it's going out with the refuse en masse, buried in the middle of it. . . ." There is no doubt that in abandoning his wife and unborn child, Jack was going against something important in himself. He believed in families and children, and to deny himself the experience of those things was perhaps a greater cruelty than any he inflicted on his wife and future daughter.

The first two weeks in July, he had to sit with his leg propped up on a chair. It was a time of great soul-searching, from which he emerged with a strengthened commitment to his literary vocation. When Ginsberg wrote that he had gotten a job with *Newsweek*, Jack chided him for "having lost contact with the stars." Having worked as a reporter, Jack had found that it was too easy to live shielded from the world by a desk and a telephone, and he encouraged Allen to stop seeking easy solutions to the deep problems of living as an artist.

Ginsberg had also conveyed to Jack many of Rae Everitt's suggested changes in *On the Road*. Retyped on regular bond, the roll had been turned into a 450-page manuscript, and Rae wanted it cut to 300. Her central objection was that Jack had built a whole novel around characters whom *she* found unsympathetic, and she wished Jack would "get on to other material." Nevertheless, she thought the jazz scenes the best in American literature, and declared the whole book worth publishing just for their sake. Most importantly, both Rae and Allen asked Jack to provide a fuller character study of Neal.

Jack wrestled with the paradox that while his vision of America was probably "unwritable," the expression of his love for America was essential to his sense of purpose as a writer. Reading *The Friend of the Family*, he was impressed more than ever with Dostoyevsky's deep understanding of character. On the one hand, he wanted to write so honestly of the heart that when he died men would mourn the loss of his purity just as they had mourned for Dostoyevsky and Carlyle.[174] On the other hand, he realized that he couldn't help digressing from character to a "lyric-alto knowing of this land." As he wrote to Holmes, the dichotomy between the Wolfean and Dostoyevskian points of view was so fundamental to his nature that it could be traced "down to the cradle, and further." The challenge in his writing was to develop a "deep form" that would permit the confluence of these two streams of thought.

From England, Seymour Wyse heartened Jack with his verdict that *On the Road* "really swings"; and that no matter how hard to sell, the book proved Jack was "in an entirely new groove now." Still, on the level of practicality, Jack agreed wholeheartedly with Allen's and Rae's suggestions. But the problem, as he saw it, was that while they were on the "straight narrow easy roads" of business, he was on Blake's "crooked road of prophecy." In revising *On the Road* he attempted to find a middle path.

The manuscript had already been divided into five "books," and Jack planned to remove most of the non-Neal material from the first two. Such cuts would have included the "Mexican girl" section as well as the scenes with Henri Cru in Marin City and San Francisco, all of which would be saved for a future novel called "California Nights." By way of replacement, he would expand the story of Neal's early days in Denver. He was already writing many such insertions that attempted to "plumb Neal's depths." At the same time, he envisioned another book to render the "perfect" Neal, in which he would surround Neal with imaginary characters like the Imbecile, the Walking Saint, and Pictorial Review Jackson. An orphaned black boy from North Carolina, the character of "Pic" had been haunting Jack for a couple of years, and he evidently did a little writing about him that summer. Yet, if the present *On the Road* were false from the point of view of art, it was the version truest to reality, and so he couldn't dismiss it out of hand. Besides, as he wrote to Holmes, *On the Road*—even as it now stood—was a good deal less false than *The Town and the City*.

Among Jack's burgeoning plans was a novel about jazz called "Horn." By contrast with the "spontaneous unartified too-pure too-raw criticizable 'Road,' " he intended to give "Horn" a formal structure. To this end, he was putting himself through a crash course of novelists who were meticulous craftsmen: Hawthorne, Flaubert, Henry James, Gorky, Faulkner, D. H. Lawrence, Proust (*Cities of the Plain*). *Madame Bovary* seemed "excellent"; *The Ambassadors* Jack thought utterly worthless because it lacked exaggeration; Gorky didn't come up to Dostoyevsky; and in *The Rainbow* D. H. Lawrence appeared to have the same problem as he himself: "he thinks he knows too much." His reading comprised nonfiction prose too— Blake's *Marriage of Heaven and Hell*, Melville's *The Encantadas*, Whitman's *Specimen Days*—as well as an assortment of modern poetic stylists: Whitman, Dickinson, Hart Crane, Sandburg, Yeats, and St.-John Perse (whose *Anabase* Jack translated himself).

Part of his renewed dedication to writing was a serious vow of poverty. He would continue his creative labors, he wrote Holmes, even if he never had an extra dollar until the day he died. Another obligation he assumed was to further the work of the fellow writers in whom he believed. Currently he and Allen were both trying to interest publishers in Burroughs' novel *Junky*. After rejections from

Jason Epstein and Louis Simpson, Allen had submitted it to his friend Carl Solomon, who was now working as an editor for Ace Books, owned by his uncle A. A. Wyn. When Jack submitted a copy to New Directions, James Laughlin evinced interest but asked for certain changes. Carrying on these dealings by mail, Allen and Jack were frustrated by Bill's sudden departure for Panama and Ecuador with "a pretty boy from school." Of late in Mexico Bill had repeatedly run afoul of the law. The government refused to grant him citizenship or even a permit to work or to invest his money; consequently it was financially impossible for him to remain there. His plan was to establish a new base in South America and then to send for Joan and the children. In the meantime she'd lost contact with him, and was unable to find the alternate drafts of *Junky* that Jack and Allen needed to serve as his agents.

Another crucial decision Jack made in North Carolina was to accept Neal's offer of a place to live in exchange for instruction in writing. Neal described how he and Carolyn had fixed up their attic at 29 Russell Street just for him. There was a bed on the floor, a three foot–by–four foot sheet of plywood for a desk, a huge dictionary, a typewriter, paper, Dexedrine, marijuana, bongo drums, a radio, and—most alluringly—a tape recorder, which Jack sought to use for "experiments in new narrative techniques." A C-melody saxophone was to be Neal's next acquisition, and with a friend to give them cheap lessons, it would be the perfect chance for Jack to realize his own dream of becoming a jazz musician. Moreover, since the Southern Pacific was recruiting new employees, he could immediately start earning $400 or more a month. The only hitch was that to be assured of a job he ought to arrive by the middle of August. Neal wrote:

> You going to write another book huh? I'm trying to write one, right? You love me, don't you? I love you, don't I? If we're so allfired good, then think of the funny times historians of future will have in digging up period in last half of 51 when K lived with C, much like Gaugin and Van Gooh, or Niethche and Wagner, or anybody and how, during this time of hard work and reorientation C. learned while K. perfected his art and how under the tutoring of the young master K., C. ironed out much of his word difficulties and in the magnificent attic K did his best work. . . .

Not the least attractive part of the bargain was Neal's promise to take Jack to Little Harlem to hear some of the wildest spontaneous jazz in America, which would provide material for his projected novel "Horn." Although Carolyn was pregnant with their third child, Neal assured Jack that this time she would welcome him and might even—after giving birth—participate in a few orgies. In any case, as far as Jack was concerned, Neal could give him infinitely more than he could give Neal.

Originally Jack planned to ride with Lucien to Mexico City and back to Laredo, then make it on his own the rest of the way to San Francisco. Lucien was leaving New York on August 7. But unexpectedly, Jack was laid up for an entire month; a few days after he returned to New York, he was stricken with another attack of phlebitis worse than the first. Lucien had to leave without him. Neal's next letter, boasting of the homey bliss at 29 Russell Street and promising frolics at the "gonest whorehouses in Watsonville," found Jack in a Kingsbridge V.A. Hospital sickbed.

5.

Jack's doctors warned that he would have to stop smoking altogether, take blood-thinning pills, and guard his health carefully. Greatly increased was the risk of a blood clot reaching his heart, lungs, or brain, where it would spell instant death. Despite the gloomy prognosis, his spirits were exceptionally high during the month he spent in the hospital. He read *The Brothers Karamazov* again, and began completely rewriting *On the Road* by hand. When he was stumped by a certain passage, he would translate it into *joual* (Canuck French) and then retranslate it into English, thereby obtaining the most direct possible syntax and the simplest natural rhythms.

When he got out, he convalesced at his mother's new apartment in Richmond Hill. She had moved back into their old building at 94-31 134th Street, but they now lived downstairs and had to contend with noisy neighbors overhead. The new place was also smaller than their old one and so uncomfortable that Jack suddenly felt the prison walls of his poverty. Meanwhile Carolyn joined Neal in encouraging him to stay with them. Despite psychoanalytic therapy, Neal was slipping still deeper into his "blankness," and she hoped Jack's presense would interest him again in something besides whores and pot.

The events of September 7, 1951, in Mexico City shook Neal, Jack, and everyone who knew Bill and Joan Burroughs. Shortly after Bill returned there, he and Joan hosted an all-night party. Drunk, Joan set a shot glass on her head and challenged Bill to shoot it off. With his .38 caliber pistol, Bill took careful aim and put a hole through her forehead. The newspapers labeled the incident a "William Tell" killing. Bill later found that the sights on the pistol were defective. Regardless, he was arrested for homicide, and once again the freewheeling group to which he belonged learned the price of testing limits.

Two days later, Carolyn presented Neal with a son, whom they named after Neal's two best friends: John Allen Cassady. His initials spelled JAC. The healthy domesticity of their household must have contrasted sharply in Jack's mind with the fatal decadence of the Burroughses. But Jack was still too weak to travel West to see him.

Back from the Valley of no imaginary Shadow, Jack found simple pleasures like watching the World Series profoundly satisfying. When Bobby Thomson's home run won the National League pennant for the Giants, he rejoiced and wrote poems announcing that "it is possible for the human spirit to win after all!" Another exhilarating event that fall was the return of Ed White to Columbia. Although Ed's decision to study architecture excited Jack's curiosity—he reminded Ed that architecture was Faust's last dream— Jack was elated just to regain the company of this gentle scholar.

Jack continued to revise *On the Road*. Sensing a need for some perspective on the plethora of action, he created short inserts that served as guideposts. One of the most famous lines in the book was such an insert: "the only people for me are the mad ones, the ones who are mad to live, mad to talk, mad to be saved, desirous of everything at the same time, the ones who never yawn or say a commonplace thing, but burn, burn, burn. . . ." Allen was pleased with the revision, as was Lucien, who now thought the novel "like Faulkner."

Jack was frequently drawn into New York by his many friends. The trio of Ed White, Tom Livornese, and Jack Fitzgerald was reunited; Tom's sister Maria and Hal Chase's wife Ginger were on the scene; Allen Ginsberg was living at the Mills Hotel on Bleecker Street; Alan Ansen, John Kingsland, and much of Cannastra's old group still hung out together; Lucien, John Holmes, and Jerry Newman were throwing weekly parties. Jack began an affair with Allen's girlfriend Dusty, who was simultaneously involved with several other men, and Jerry Newman occasionally provided him with a whore. Newman now had his own music store in the Village, where Jack could hear his fill of jazz tapes and records, including those bearing Newman's own Esoteric label. For the first time in years he found himself rushing breathlessly around the city in continuous expectation of fresh delight, and very seldom was he disappointed. As a typical caper, John Kingsland recalls Jack and Allen bursting drunkenly into his apartment to gush over Stephen Spender's autobiography *World Within World*. After writing a long inscription to Kingsland in the book, they handed it to him and went their merry way.

There were quiet, serious times too. Often Jack would meet Ed White for supper. On October 25—a day that had special significance to Jack, since it was his parents' anniversary and also Nin's birthday—he and Ed were in a Chinese restaurant on 124th Street.

Ed had been carrying little architectural notebooks around the city, sketching buildings, and he suggested Jack try sketching with words in his own notebooks. According to Ed, it was possible to sketch from memory as well as from the world at hand. As a literary technique the trick would be to make words correspond like pencil strokes to what the mind perceived. That night Jack stopped in front of a bakery window and filled his first notebook with word sketches. During the next couple of months he spent many days wandering the city alone, sketching everything in sight until he actually lost consciousness that he was writing. In the evenings he would come to Ed's room to read aloud what he had written.

But as the fall wore on, his tranquility gave way to an increasing franticness. With *On the Road* stalled at MCA, he worried as to how he could earn a living, yet he spurned Carl Solomon's offer of a $250 advance on the novel as insultingly low. Actually Ace Books was quite interested in acquiring Kerouac's work, and they were even prepared to splurge much of their advertising budget on him, but as a small paperback house they couldn't pay much before publication. Unfortunately, Solomon was exactly the wrong person to deal with Jack. He still engaged people with manic intensity if not outright hysteria, and his sense of humor ran to a deep black surrealist irony, the very antithesis of Jack's childlike reverence for life. Jack hardly appreciated being lectured about "the problem of The Brilliant Young Punk's Second Book." Worse, Solomon kidded him that in the publishing business "writers are trade and editors are aunties," and he tried to overcome Jack's stodginess by taunting that *The Town and the City* bespoke "a repressed homosexuality." To Jack those were fighting words. He called Solomon an incompetent lunatic, a greedy Jew, and a homosexual, and threatened to break his glasses! [175]

From Albany Joan threatened to take legal action to force Jack to support her during her pregnancy. Hardly vindictive, she was simply caught in the bind of being dependent upon the domineering mother she had been trying to escape, and her mother wasn't anxious to assume the burden of a new child. When Jack procrastinated, as usual, Joan wrote him charging that he was a writer only by virtue of egotism and nerve, and that all his writing amounted to was a refusal to be like normal people. She vowed not only to pursue him ceaselessly for alimony but to take steps to see that he didn't write any more. This attack on his art was soon given teeth by a warrant from the Domestic Relations Court. For four weeks Jack sent her five dollars a week for her prenatal care, in the meantime seeking the cheapest way to get to Neal's attic. Unlike most of his New York friends, who were already tiring of his drunken pranks, Neal still offered Jack an unconditional welcome.

Henri Cru was about to ship on the S.S. *President Harding*, a merchantman bound round the world, stopping at San Francisco, Japan, Hong Kong, the Philippines, Malaysia, and returning to New York via the Suez Canal. The promise of cavorting with Cru intrigued Jack as much as the romance of such a voyage. Wearing his old white seaman's cap, Jack went to the National Maritime Union Hall to try to sign on.

On the way home he stopped at Allen's new apartment on 15th Street, where he met a dark, wavy-haired, funny Italian poet named Gregory Corso. Twenty-one, Corso had been released a year before from Clinton Prison, where as one of the youngest inmates he had served three years for robbery. He had been sent to prison rather than a reformatory because the authorities feared his genius. He had devised a team plan in which the actual robbers in bank or store would keep in contact with a sentry outside through walkie-talkies. In prison, an older inmate gave him several novels, as well as a dictionary, and soon Corso was frequenting the library to check out works like *Les Misérables* and histories of classical Greece. In no time, literature became his consuming passion, and he began writing poetry. On the printed page he entered the rich, heroic world of his fantasies, in sharp contrast to the life he had known. His mother had abandoned him as an infant, and in childhood he had seen his father only sporadically. Ten different foster families had shown him only gangster-ridden streets in poor Italian neighborhoods, as in Greenwich Village and the Bronx.

Shortly after his release from prison, Corso was talking with an artist friend in the Pony Stable, a lesbian bar in the Village. A tallish, skinny guy with weird dark eyes behind thick glasses joined them; Corso figured he was a homosexual on the make. When they spoke of poetry, Corso pulled out a sheaf of his latest poems, and the newcomer thought they were terrific. He introduced himself as Allen Ginsberg, explained that he wrote poetry himself, and took Corso to meet Mark Van Doren. Later, Corso told Allen how every night for a month he had watched the silhouette of "this chick across the street fucking this guy." Allen suggested they go together and knock on her door. When they got there, Allen was stunned by the bizarre coincidence. He told Corso, "I'm the guy who's doing the fucking!" [176] The girl was Dusty.

Jack warmed instantly to the tender heart that shone through Corso's rough clowning. Corso liked Jack for his energy, his goodness, his good looks, and his manliness. They didn't get a chance to know each other better, however, because Jack felt the urgency of getting out of New York to escape Joan's demands.

Although he had been offered a job by the Marine Cooks and Stewards Union on a ship bound for France, he declined it to be able to sail with Cru. Since all positions on the *President Harding* were filled, he decided to follow the ship to its next port, San Pedro,

California, where a friendly union agent might be able to help him get on. With money borrowed from Cru and Rae Everitt, he took a bus to San Francisco. He arrived on Tuesday, December 18 and called Al Hinkle, but Neal came to pick him up. It was suppertime, and Jack apologized for disrupting his home life, but Neal dismissed his worries, saying, "I always like to see a guy do anything he wants." As they walked arm in arm through the rail yards, Neal shared his last joint with Jack to reassure him that they were really brothers.

Neal got him four days' work in the railroad baggage department; but of the $40 he made, ten was blown in Little Harlem and later, at a party with some black prostitutes. Carolyn exploded over their debauchery, but by this time she'd learned that throwing Neal out was not the answer. Rather, she fed them a wonderful dinner featuring her mother's hickory-smoked ham.

Jack had a bad cold when Neal put him in the caboose of the Zipper, the express freight train to Los Angeles. Jack claimed he was Neal's brother and so was allowed to ride free. In L.A. he holed up in a hotel until he felt better; then, waiting for the *President Harding*, he roamed Skid Row, filling more notebooks with his "sketching."

The new technique worked very well, for it permitted him to make the process of writing into the subject of his writing. For years Jack had been intrigued, not so much with *what* he was describing, as with *how* and *why* he was scribbling at all. He didn't write to know the world, but to know *his visions* of the world, to examine the various stages of his awareness of things. On the simplest level, he was trying to find the mental components that added up to a writer's personality. "Sketching" put the writer at the very center of the composition. Plot and theme were reduced to the passage of perceptions across his sensorium. Thus, the focus of the writing was narrowed to a single, sharply delimited point of view: this particular writer's peephole into reality. Nevertheless the technique also granted an incredible freedom, since there was no longer any reason to exclude from one's writing any detail that came to mind.

Conventional modes of composition had forced the writer to ignore much of what he really thought. Lifting the censorship of the conscious self, Kerouac opened the door to the unconscious, by all accounts the mind's richest storehouse. Three decades later, postmodernists would claim to be exploring new approaches to the novel that Kerouac had already developed in 1951. For—according to at least one definition—postmodernists "write a fiction that is more and more about itself and its processes, less and less about objective reality and life in the world." Yet unlike most of his successors, Kerouac took his subjective visions with a grain of salt. After a frenzied catalogue of sordid sights at a Los Angeles penny arcade, for example, he laughs at his own frenzy, restoring a note of sanity, by turning himself into just another of the objects he describes: "Now a Negro family comes to Playland from hotsun street— Now I'm being swept away by a broom!"

After the *President Harding* arrived, Cru treated Jack to a few gala days in Hollywood and Santa Monica, the climax a Christmas dinner aboard ship. But Jack still failed to get a job due to his lack of seniority, and also perhaps to his record of having jumped ship.

Back in San Francisco he resumed living in the Cassadys' attic. His first night there it rained heavily; he stayed up alone, telling the entire tale of *Doctor Sax* into Neal's tape recorder.

It was impossible to get hired as a brakeman in January, so he accepted work as a baggage handler and yard clerk. The daily grind increased his admiration for Neal. Jack told Carolyn that he wished he could be husband, father, worker, and fun-lover all at once, the way Neal was. Since the financial failure of *The Town and the City*, his mother and sister had renewed their complaints about his refusal to adopt a regular work routine. In his sister's judgment he had become a bum, and however much it pained him to be thought one, he now admitted to Carolyn that Nin was probably right. Although he stuck to the railroad work for several months, he did so mainly to save up enough money to live in Mexico, where he could write free from the distraction of earning a living. In addition, the job enabled him to learn about his hero's working life. But the crucial realization forced upon Jack during this period was that he could never be a reliable breadwinner, a jolt whose shock waves reverberated to the end of his life.

He had always considered himself an ordinary, square guy like his father, even though Leo's lifestyle was poles apart from his. And much as he still wanted children, he had to accept the fact that he wasn't the businessman and authoritarian figure he thought a father should be. The Cassady children permitted him to enjoy the benefits of fatherhood without the concomitant responsibilities. Cathy, 3, and Jamie, almost 2, were continually regaled with Jack's elaborate tales. With so much of a child still in him, he was a natural hit with them. Baby John he avoided only because he feared to hurt or drop him.

Jack's long accumulated loneliness flowed out in torrents of conversation. He reviled his wife, talked about his writing, read aloud sections of his new version of *On the Road,* and recounted his daydreams and actual dreams. Carolyn had the impression that he longed to bring Neal into his private dream-world. Jack found the task especially difficult because the blank wall in Neal grew steadily. Much of Jack's misery derived from the solitude necessary to dream and write, and each time he rediscovered that necessity he would grow more desperate to bounce his fantasies and writings off someone. Living so much in his own head he'd keep popping out like a groundhog to test the temper of other flesh and blood—and when the weather proved forbidding he'd often withdraw for weeks at a time. No matter how often he came out, though, he couldn't escape the fact that home was on the inside of that hole. The dilemma that impaled him, as it does so many artists, was that he couldn't bear living alone.

When he failed to get any sort of response from Neal, or when Neal was at work, Jack confided in Carolyn. Up to this point she scarcely knew him, and what she had known had been rather frightening. At times, especially when Neal left her with the excuse that he had to see Jack, she had thought of him as Neal's "devil." If she objected, Neal would say that Jack came first, that he'd made promises to Jack—until she always felt like asking if he hadn't made promises to her too. Publication of *The Town and the City* had naturally increased her respect for Jack's talent and seriousness, and by now she could see that his influence was, if anything, to channel Neal's energy toward constructive ends. Hence she was more than willing to listen when Jack lamented about the latest misunderstanding between himself and Carl Solomon or about the stupidity of publishers in general, asking with typical Kerouacian naïveté: "Why don't they realize I'm good?"

The physical attraction between Jack and Carolyn put a terrible strain on their fumbling attempts at friendship. The code of honor they both lived by put them off-limits to each other, and they scrupulously avoided the slightest word or action that could be interpreted as flirtation. The tension between them was heightened by the fact that Jack had to pass through Neal and Carolyn's bedroom to get to his attic or to come down to the bathroom. He was so physically modest, moreover, that it embarrassed him if *anyone* knew he was going to the bathroom, and his awkwardness embarrassed the others. By February 8, Carolyn's malaise began to manifest itself in physical symptoms. Absent all day, Jack failed to help celebrate Neal's birthday. As the hours passed without his return, the left half of Carolyn's face grew numb. A doctor diagnosed her illness as Bell's palsy, which sometimes has an emotional genesis.

Around midnight the phone rang, and Neal answered it. He told her that Jack was in jail, and that he had to go bail him out. The next morning the two of them returned with two black prostitutes and apologies. Getting wiser, Carolyn politely asked the women to leave. Returning with Neal the next evening, Jack was so penitent he stayed in the attic for twenty-four hours, peeing out the window when he had to, and didn't come down until Carolyn went to the doctor's office. When she returned, she found a second inscription added to her copy of *The Town and the City*: "With deepest apologies I can offer for the fiasco, the foolish tragic Saturday of Neal's birthday all because I got drunk. Please forgive me, Carolyn, it'll never happen again."

Shortly afterward, the railroad called Neal down to San Luis

Obispo for two weeks. Carolyn's palsy forced her to wear a patch over the eye she couldn't close, and to hook her lip in place with a paper clip and rubber band. She could neither ignore Jack's presence nor admit the way she felt about him. It was impossible for her to gain even a humorous release, although the situation verged on farce when a local liquor store owner asked why she was buying beer when her husband (meaning Jack) liked sweet wine. In leaving for San Luis Obispo, Neal did his best to light the fuse of this volatile situation. He advised Jack and Carolyn: "Well, you know what they say . . . 'My best pal and my best gal.' Have a ball kiddies, so long."

The two weeks Neal was gone Jack did his best to duck Carolyn. She could hardly get him to eat dinner with her. They were both tortured, she because Neal seemed to be treating her like a whore, Jack because Neal was suggesting he make love to a woman as "untouchable" as his mother. When Neal came back, she asked him if he had made that treacherous remark because he was afraid such a thing would happen anyway and didn't want to look like a fool, or because he really wanted it to happen. Neal replied, "I thought it would've been kind of nice." That answer was the cruelest thing Neal ever said to her. It told her that there wasn't one convention Neal wouldn't tear down or turn inside out, and that she would have to endure new emotional cataclysms as long as they were married.

If these were the variables, she resolved to change the equation between the three of them so that her side didn't always come out zero. *Okay, Neal dear,* she thought, *let's try it your way.*[177]

6.

The next evening that Neal was away, Carolyn seduced Jack. It was merely a problem of overcoming his moral block to sleeping with his best friend's wife. This she did by fixing him a candlelit supper, his favorite: pizza, salad, and wine. She wore perfume, played soft romantic music, and made him sit beside her on the couch. In short, after she'd done everything possible to convince him that *she* was instigating the affair, he let down his guard and became her lover. The critical factor was his assurance that he wasn't hurting her. With Neal he had no such worry, since Neal had always encouraged him to enjoy his women, and had asked to share Jack's women as well. If Jack had any guilt about his adultery, it was probably only regarding the Cassady children. Concern for their belief in the purity of their mother was doubtless the reason he never wrote about his erotic episodes with her.

The danger for Jack was that he fell more deeply in love with Carolyn than she with him. Although he sometimes put up his familiar safety barriers—for example, telling her that blondes weren't really his type—he also praised her old-fashioned femininity. He said she was the only woman he could talk to and not be interrupted, and he appreciated the meek way she catered to his whims. Even though he would never have tried to take her away from Neal, he talked about how he would like to marry her. The reason he even let himself think this was that he knew Neal wasn't a proper husband. With his numerous mistresses and whores, Neal was breaking the codes of honor and loyalty himself, and Jack felt he could have made her happier because he would have been more faithful. Carolyn pretended to share his enthusiasm about getting married, but aside from the fact that Neal was the only man she really wanted, she knew that life would be worse married to Jack. It was clear she would be "just his mother." At least Neal respected her right to have opinions and feelings, but with Jack there was the constant strain of having to follow *his* moods, so as to know how to please him. That much effort wasn't worth her trouble for Jack alone. In her view, "he was not that exciting as a man, and he certainly wasn't in bed." Their relationship was on a road leading nowhere, because she sought a sexually aggressive lover, and for Jack it was virtually impossible to be that way with any woman but a prostitute.

Neal seemed pleased that they had accepted his offer. He actually became more attentive to her now that he had some sort of challenge to meet. An element of sadism was present in all Neal's lovemaking—at least with women—to the extent that he had to "conquer" them. If a woman was passive like Carolyn, he would search out a few likely rivals and bring them to her himself. As long as Neal came out the better man he was content to keep playing the game. At least in the beginning, Jack and Carolyn tacitly agreed to play by his rules. When Neal wanted to be with Carolyn, Jack would stay upstairs working or else go out, and he never approached her when Neal was at home.

Amongst the three of them there commenced a period of great warmth and openness. For Carolyn it was now possible to participate in some of the fun Jack and Neal used to have by themselves. At home, playing the radio, Jack and Neal reading aloud to each other from Proust or Spengler or their works-in-progress, they'd all get into discussions of music and literature. Some nights they each took several parts in a Shakespearean play and acted the whole thing out, the men vying to outdo each other's histrionics in order to impress her. At a nearby tennis court they would again compete for her attention, making up for their lack of skill with displays of power and agility. If Neal was too tired to join them, Carolyn and Jack would walk by themselves to Aquatic Park or Chinatown, and in a little Chinese restaurant off St. Francis Park they'd feast on won ton soup and fried rice.

This living arrangement benefited Jack's writing in two ways. Besides boosting his morale, to get him over the depression of splitting up with Joan, it enabled him to study his chief hero in depth. Living under the same roof, as if they were indeed the brothers they always claimed to be, Neal found it easier to tell Jack about many of the painful and shameful experiences he had heretofore obscured.

They'd get high on wine or pot, Jack would turn on the tape recorder, and they'd talk. Their free-associative, confessional style owed as much to the communal group on 115th Street (whose methodology Neal had absorbed through Jack and Allen) as to the general psychoanalytical climate born of the prodigious insecurity in post–World War II America. Sometimes, to loosen Neal further, Jack would bring home a couple of seamen friends to join in the dialogue. To stimulate discussion they'd play records or make their own music with a recorder, wooden flute, harmonica, maracas, bongos, or any available pots, pans, and oatmeal cartons (which Jack loved to drum on). When it proved impossible to avoid a certain tense awareness of the turning tape reels, Jack used that self-consciousness to further his exploration of mind process: the way we perceive and pierce through illusion. After each night's talk, Jack would carefully transcribe the tape, and then read aloud portions of the transcription at their next session, so that they could comment on their own misapprehensions and verbal dodges. Being at once actor and spectator, they obtained extraordinary new perspectives on the ungraspability of their own lives.

Jack was at one of those magical points in a writer's life when everything he does, and everything that happens to him, feeds directly into the book he's writing. Walking on Russian Hill one night, he discovered a movie crew filming Joan Crawford in *Sudden Fear*. After rushing home for his notebook, he spent hours sketching the crowd, the cops, the neighbors, the technicians, and the tired actress repeating her performance a dozen times under klieg lights glaring through the fog. Jack was so excited he stayed up all night typing the piece, which he called "Joan Crawford in the Fog," and in the morning he read it to Neal and Carolyn. Sensing that not what he had seen but *the way he had seen it* was connected to Neal, Jack slipped the scene into the mushrooming manuscript of *On the Road*. Later he would universalize the character of Joan Crawford with the name "Joan Rawshanks."

Frequenting the Marine Cooks and Stewards Union Hall in hopes of getting a ship, Jack made friends with two seamen, Charley Mew and Al Sublette. Four-foot-ten Charley was a reliable connection for pot, but on the tapes, unfortunately, his greatest service is as a foil for Jack and Neal's conversation. Charley's trite, repetitious remarks about jazz and sex show how much more deeply Jack and Neal are probing the same matters. Sublette, a mulatto hipster with a fine musical ear, became much closer to Jack. From him, Jack gained an insider's knowledge of the hybrid San Francisco jazz scene.

In the space of a few miles, one was able to observe two very different, spontaneous, and noncommercial forms of black music. Bop abounded in the Fillmore district, which had become a very sophisticated black neighborhood. At Fillmore clubs like Jackson's Nook, connoisseurs listened to the music with a kind of sporting detachment. By contrast, Little Harlem was a much smaller community—just a few blocks—of much poorer, working-class blacks, located just south of Skid Row and the Southern Pacific Station at Third and Townsend, and Jack often walked there after work. It contained a bar also named Little Harlem, whose clientèle consisted almost exclusively of people from the neighborhood. Packed, the bar held maybe a hundred people, but on weekends it was one of the wildest rhythm-and-blues places around. But whereas in the Fillmore clubs people came to hear "jazz with brains," [178] and to think about what they heard, the customers at Little Harlem wanted to drink, fight, dance, wail, and jazz (that is, *fuck*) away all the cares of their workaday life, and the place was filled with prostitutes in bathrobes, vomiting drunks, and musicians come from day-labor jobs. Between Little Harlem and the Fillmore Jack had at his disposal a sort of living anthropological record of the past fifty years of black music in America: the development from blues to bop.

During this period, Jack even touched base with his first jazz experiences. Meeting Billie Holiday in a club, he talked to her—he proudly wrote Holmes—"with her dog in my arms."

The history of jazz was to provide one of the chief frameworks by which Kerouac measured the stature of his American hero in the new version of *On the Road.* This book, which he was still attempting to conjoin with the roll manuscript he'd typed in April, eventually became a separate work, *Visions of Cody.* (For clarity I generally refer to it as *Visions of Cody* from this point on, although Jack didn't distinguish between the two books until at least May, 1952. The hero, still in transition, was now called Dean Pomeray. In May, he would refer to the new novel as *Visions of Neal.*) Jack already conceived of *Visions of Cody* as a combination of *Ulysses* and *Finnegans Wake*—*Ulysses* in the sense of a colloquy of voices from literature and the street, and *Finnegans Wake* in that the hero would be a representative of mankind. That H. C. Earwicker and Cody Pomeray were separated by the Atlantic Ocean and a quarter century, and that Kerouac had heard few non-American voices, were not weaknesses but strengths. But however much he may have wanted to imitate Joyce, the patterns Joyce set down would in no way fit "the unbelievable huge bulge" of life in a place like Little Harlem. Joyce's shopkeepers were enfeebled by the weight of too many crumbled civilizations; the Americans Kerouac knew weren't yet housebroken to their first civilization. Unquestionably Joyce did bequeath to Kerouac the desire to fit his own society into a universal human history, and since America lacked the great ancient kings and mythological leaders of Ireland, he seized upon the jazz world as the richest, most imaginative source of American folk tradition.

In early 1952, Kerouac ran across a friend from New York, another admirer of jazz, the surrealist poet Philip Lamantia. Born in San Francisco in 1927, Lamantia had left home at fifteen, moved to New York, helped edit the surrealist magazine *View*, and become involved with the crowd of hipsters in the Village, where he had met Jack in the late forties. In New York, they had both made the rounds from Birdland and Bop City to the nearby Latin dance halls, where one could hear Caribbean mambo and Afro-Cuban rhythms like those of conga drummer Chano Pozo—an important refeeding of jazz through its African roots. Now in San Francisco they continued their discussion of the significance of jazz to their generation.

A Sicilian Catholic whose mind had outstripped his environment since childhood, Lamantia was a solitary questioner and quester much like Jack. For Lamantia, as for Kerouac, the "beat" attitude was the only means of spiritual survival after the atom-bomb apocalypse. Along with Hiroshima had been annihilated all of the previous generation's hopes for a socialist utopia, indeed for any political solution to human misery. Seeking to transcend a world of unrelievable horror, Lamantia took the same route as Kerouac in attempting to sacralize the mundane. In the jazz milieu they found people who abjured conventional society in a rebellion that wasn't in the least political. It was based on a dialectical relationship between the way these people were living—their frantic outward pursuit of kicks—and the tremendous inwardness generated in them by way of compensation. The wilder the action, the deeper the meditation that followed it. In the same way, being beat led to an enthusiasm for whatever lay beyond fatigue. Listening to jazz was a way of crossing such boundaries into new worlds, where the magic of the unexpected converted you like a miracle. Or, in Lamantia's words: "There were ways in which, as one sat listening to Bird in 1948 or to completely unknown people in Little Harlem, one actually was elevated to the stars!" [179]

For Lamantia, drug-taking was a sacrament, a form of Communion just as jazz was. In Mexico he had learned how to eat peyote, and one night at Neal's house he initiated Neal and Jack. At first Jack was frightened, because Lamantia's friend John Hoffman had recently died in Mexico, allegedly of an overdose of peyote. But Lamantia convinced him that at worst he would have to endure a few hours of nausea from the cactus buttons, which would then reward him with "technicolor visions." The first time Jack took peyote he had a powerful revelation of how it felt to die. The second time he took it, with Lamantia and several others in a house in Berkeley, he slept on the floor for twelve hours—a strange reaction, as everyone else was totally alert. Jack claimed he had hallucinated music, and soon afterward he made startling progress, by his own account, in learning to play Neal's C-melody saxophone. At this time he also began doing a great deal of artwork, using Carolyn's pastels.

The visit to Lamantia provoked the first antagonism between Jack and Neal. Lamantia was living with a wealthy friend, and the plush surroundings had brought out all of Neal's Okie inferiority. Worse, Lamantia acted like a decadent, defrocked priest, and he and his friends spoke of their drug experiences in arcane language. Neal—who, for all that may be said against him, was the world's own democrat—countered their esotericism with stories of working on the railroad. On the way home, Jack rebuked him for talking like a peasant at a gathering of nobles. The next night, when Jack asked Neal to drive him to Lamantia's again, Neal refused.

Carolyn effected a reconciliation by talking Neal into buying Jack a Chinese dinner. But hostility kept breaking out afresh. Neal would complain about Jack's insufficient contribution for groceries, and Jack would be unable to explain his own feelings in the face of Neal's blank expression. Other times, when Jack tried to communicate some excitement, Neal would mutter, "Yeah, yeah." Yet Neal's blasé attitude bothered Jack less than his exclusive, overwhelming concern with money, which was anathema to Jack. He also felt Carolyn was partly accountable for Neal's materialism. To pay for "things they never use," and to save up for a trip to see her parents in Tennessee, Neal had to work seven days a week, recapping tires when he wasn't on duty as a brakeman. Of course, when Jack complained against her in a letter to Allen, he typically ignored the fact that Neal's new car and steady supply of pot cost something too.

7.

All in all, Jack was happier living with the Cassadys than he had been in years. The privacy and security of their attic, equipped with his favorite, all-encompassing Eleventh Edition of the *Encyclopedia Britannica*, permitted him to write with a freedom and range he had never attempted before. And more than ever before, even his friends failed to understand where his writing was going.

His correspondence with Carl Solomon grew into a tragic comedy of errors. On December 27, 1951, Jack wrote to Carl recommending that Ace Books consider Neal's novel-in-progress. While promoting Neal's literary career, Jack also indicated that he preferred to let Neal write about himself, a hint that his own novel-in-progress was shifting to a more autobiographical subject. Since Jack was supposedly revising *On the Road,* Carl was startled to read that he had suddenly begun writing about the "downtown redbrick neon in Lowell." Nevertheless, Solomon agreed to read Neal's manuscript, and he also persuaded his uncle to accept *On the Road* on the terms presented by Rae Everitt. Rae had asked for an advance of $1,000, $250 to be paid immediately, and $100 a month thereafter to sustain Jack while he undertook further revisions.

At the end of January, 1952, Carl sent Jack news of the book's acceptance. Jack's response knocked him for a loop. First, he announced that he intended to finish *On the Road* by his birthday, March 12. Second, he assured Carl that the novel wouldn't need any more revision. Third, he requested that the remaining $750 of the advance be applied toward a second novel, *Doctor Sax,* which he would commence writing as soon as he finished *On the Road.* Fourth, he insisted that he deal only with Solomon, not with the owner Wyn. To bring Jack back to a sense of the reality of publishing, Solomon showered him with his peculiar brand of jesting insults. He accused Jack of "work-shirking tactics" and a neurotic fear of criticism. He reproached his weakness in wanting Neal to write the "road" book for him. He not only denied Jack's claim to being a great writer, but asserted that in refusing to use his talents fully Jack was "killing Cannastra and Joan Burroughs and John Hoffman—even while such people help to kill you." He also chided Jack for using drugs and acting like a tough guy, and advised that "the hip-bohemian-criminal-poetic conformism is a brotherhood of useless agony. . . ." Most damagingly, Solomon censured his pride in posing as a spoiled prince, and urged Jack to remember "that a writer is now a laborer like any other, that he must present *work* for payment. . . ." He said there would be no point in Wyn's doling out $100 each month if Jack didn't need the money to work on *On the Road,* and suggested he plan to "spend up to 2 years re-moulding" the book. Carl also warned that Jack had a reputation for being irresponsible with publishers' money, since he was still in debt to Harcourt Brace.

At this most inopportune moment, Rae Everitt quit MCA, leaving rash Jack to deal with Ace by himself. He clung to his demand that *On the Road* be published just as he submitted it. Solomon then made the major tactical blunder of trying to get around Jack's willfulness by currying favor with Neal. He persisted in asking for Neal's manuscript, and after it was sent he wrote to Neal comparing Jack and him as writers. Although Solomon acknowledged Jack's "technical (i.e. conventional) ability," he speculated that Jack wouldn't find a way out of his "confused tangle of literary forms" until he solved his "personality problem." By contrast, Solomon credited Neal with "clear vision, vital content, grasp of character. . . ." Perceiving that Neal's basic problem was a lack of technical skill, Carl advised him to study popular contemporary stylists like Mickey Spillane, as well as to take a creative writing course. At the end of the letter, Carl planted a barb with which to tear Jack from his smug solidarity with Neal, realizing that until Jack's psychological dependence on Neal was severed, he would never need to grapple with many of the blocks that were limiting his creativity. "Don't listen to Kerouac, he knows nothing. He tries to confuse everybody," Carl taunted, knowing Jack would be reading over Neal's shoulder. "He is using your life as an excuse to brag."

Incensed, Jack tried to get Allen on his side by ridiculing Carl's recommendation that Neal read Mickey Spillane: "What does he think our boy is, an idiot?" Jack also started beleaguering Allen with arguments in favor of "spontaneity" in writing, a subject of which all of his friends would get an earful for the next several years. His current reason for resisting changes was less theoretical than emotional; he wrote Holmes that he didn't want *On the Road* cut down "to sissy size," as he believed *The Town and the City* had been.

Allen, however, realized that Solomon was struggling to get the more conservative people at Ace Books just to take Kerouac, Cassady, and Burroughs seriously. Unlike Jack, Allen was also aware of Carl's personal problems, such as the breakup of his marriage, which were threatening to upset his precarious mental equilibrium. Hence Allen suggested that Jack agree to spend a year revising *On the Road*, and that he throw a little sand in Wyn's eyes regarding the great innovations he had made in the structure of the novel. Nevertheless, Allen had his own doubts concerning this new quirk about spontaneity. "All I wonder," he wrote Jack, "is if you're trying to escape (as I always do) the sweat of patient integration & structuring which you slaved over on T. & C." As an added incentive to accepting Wyn's terms, Allen said that MCA had evidently given up trying to place *On the Road*; inquiring there on Jack's behalf, he had learned that the manuscript was buried "on the bottom of a dusty closet."

From all directions Jack was blistered by rejections, and by the irony of all his friends making spectacular progress toward their goals. Allen had brought *On the Road* to former Columbia student Louis Simpson at Bobbs Merrill, but Simpson saw no merit in it; and Scribner's, to which it had been submitted by Rae Everitt, turned it down flat. By cruel coincidence, Scribner's accepted John Holmes' novel *Go* at about the same time. Allen too seemed on the verge of a commercial breakthrough, for William Carlos Williams was so impressed with his new book of poems, *Empty Mirror,* that he was prepared to recommend it to New Directions or Random House. To top off these astonishing reversals of fate, Lucien Carr crowned his advancement at U.P.I. with what seemed the perfect marriage to lovely Francesca Von Hartz.

Jack rarely envied other people's success. Although still smarting over the loss of Sara, he continued to praise Lucien as one of the "vast geniuses" who had shaped his thought. He gave Allen much valuable advice about his poems, and told him not to worry about borrowing phrases from him since he had often borrowed from Allen. He also continued plugging Bill's novel *Junky* to New Directions and Ace, and was genuinely thrilled when Ace finally accepted it.

It was only toward Holmes that Jack felt some resentment, because it seemed that Holmes had gained recognition by riding the wagon that only he and a few close friends were driving. What piqued him was merely that Holmes should benefit from a movement whose true direction he seemed ignorant of. A certain erotic tension cannot be discounted either in understanding Jack's unusual jealousy of Holmes. One of the poems Allen sent Jack was his "River Street Blues," in which he spells out his sexual relationship with Neal. Jack's annotation to this poem reads: "Holmes trying to ride this bandwagon triumvirate or 4-way angel-ball/ Allen Neal Lucien Jack/ Poor misleaded John." It would be naive to overlook the particular order of those names. They clearly comprise two "couples," if only in a Whitmanic "adhesive" sense. When Holmes wrote about that group of people, Jack felt as if he were making time with his friends—and to him jealousy was justified in love, if not in work.

In any case, he still extended Holmes the courtesy of allowing him to use the title *Go*, which overlapped with the title of one of Jack's short stories, "Go, Go, Go." Even more remarkable was his continuing concern for John's personal welfare. When he learned that John and Marian had separated he was dismayed, and exhorted Holmes to try to save the marriage. It hurt him to think of John and Marian losing the many "sweetnesses" they had cultivated for seven years,[180] and he didn't want to see John plunge into the feverish loneliness in which he himself was engulfed.

To his troubles was added the new worry of being hounded for money by Joan. On February 16, 1952, she had given birth to a daughter, Janet Michelle Kerouac. With investigators from the Brooklyn Uniform Support of Dependents and Abandonment Bureau scouring New York for him, Jack worried he would never be able to live with his mother openly again.

Despite this enormous pressure he worked steadily on *Visions of Cody*, occasionally using Carolyn's typewriter but mostly writing in pencil as he listened to Pat Henry's bop radio program from midnight to six AM. He finished the book exactly on his thirtieth birthday. Anxious that this in-depth treatment of Neal be published with the dignity of a hardback, Jack offered to let Ace do a shorter paperback of *On the Road*, based on an excerpt from the original roll manuscript, as well as a paperback of the novel about Lucien and Kammerer that he had co-authored with Burroughs in 1945, *And the*

Hippos Were Boiled in Their Tanks. When Wyn declined to make any blind commitments, however, Jack calmly agreed to let them handle *On the Road* as they saw fit. They sent him a contract, and he signed it. Although the $250 advance must have come like a sigh of relief, it could in no way match the satisfaction of having reached his "peak maturity." For he felt that he'd created a work that wouldn't be appreciated for twenty years but which was, as he wrote Allen, "the first modern novel."

8.

Visions of Cody was consciously created as a nonlinear novel. In the late fifties, when James McLaughlin agreed to publish a limited edition of selections from it, Kerouac prefaced the volume with a statement about the place of *Visions of Cody* in his much larger work, *The Duluoz Legend.* "Instead of just a horizontal account of travels on the road," he wrote, "I wanted a vertical, metaphysical study of Cody's character and its relationship to the general 'America.'" He added that the book "was based on my belief in the goodness of the hero and his position as an archetypal American Man."

When he had retyped the roll manuscript of *On the Road*, he had divided it conventionally into five major parts, based on the stages of Sal's friendship with Dean. The division of *Visions of Cody* is far more complex and far more integral to the themes of the work.

The first part relates the narrator's psychological preparation to meet the hero. Jack Duluoz is in New York, continually thinking about Cody Pomeray, and he finally writes Cody a letter announcing his decision to visit him in San Francisco. Told in a mixture of first and third persons, Parts 1 and 2 utilize many of the "sketches" Kerouac did in the fall of 1951.

The second part recounts both Cody's youth in Denver and the narrator's journey to join him in San Francisco. A tie is established between the narrator and his subject by revealing the heritage of American memories they share. Jack and Cody both grew up—gained their awareness of life—in poor, red-brick cities. They are depicted as two homeless, restless men, bound to keep moving (a paradox that energizes much of Kerouac's writing) as an expiation for some sort of universal guilt. When they manage to escape the road, through marriage for example, they must endure even worse torments. But the identification between Jack and Cody, which will grow stronger as the book progresses, counters this negative field of pain with the positive force of brotherhood.

The third part comprises transcriptions from the actual tapes Kerouac made with Cassady and some of their friends. The tapes introduce an intricate dovetailing of Cody's consciousness with Jack's. Telling each other their stories, the two main characters pool their perceptions and insights. Since they can now draw upon the same joint stock of knowledge and wisdom, they effectively become one mind.

The transcriptions stand as a series of mirrors turned toward one another, and the mind of Jack and Cody lies somewhere among them. The illusion begins with the fact that the tapes were initially meant to provide material for a prologue to Cody's novel. But all the way through, it is clear that Jack is seeking information about Cody for his own book. At one point he even reads aloud several sentences he's written, to test Cody's reaction, but when Cody begins to praise them Jack informs him that he has merely been parodying Dostoyevsky's *Notes from Underground.* At other points, Jack reads aloud portions of earlier transcriptions so that the characters can comment on their own speech, a device similar to the "play within the play" employed by Shakespeare. As they discuss their description of some scene, the characters occasionally reenact that scene—for example, playing Billie Holiday records as they examine their past night's recollections of "Huck" listening to Billie Holiday on "Bull's" farm in Texas. Further dislocations occur when a voice recorded earlier—such as "Evelyn" reading from *Hamlet*—accidentally obtrudes upon Cody and Jack's conversation. The dislocation may also be caused by the machine accidentally shutting off, or implemented by one of the characters, who stops it to step offstage. The purpose of all this sleight-of-word is to call objective, linear reality into question. At times that reality dissolves altogether:

CODY. *(to Jack)* Can't get it [a roach]? Ooh man, it's flaming

JACK. Oh . . . there was nothing there

CODY. No, there's nothing there . . . was a little flame . . . one little nothing that was there was going but you couldn't feel of it because it was so . . . small

Thus far in the book Kerouac's principal technique has been parody. In the last and most complex part, "Imitation of the Tape," he parodies everything that has gone before, not just in the book but in his life. For him, parody is no mere put-down, it is one of the highest art forms. After the first parody in Part 4, he demands: "don't you know I'm serious?"

The "Imitation" begins appropriately with the heading "COMPOSITION . . . . by Jackie Duluoz . . . . . 6B," for Kerouac is bent on taking us back to the origins of his writerly self. The remainder of the book contains hundreds of separate parodies, most of which are themselves many-layered. For example, the first in this section is ostensibly of a Western novel, such as those Kerouac read in adolescence. But we immediately recognize other voices. The line "Main Street . . . the one with the red bricks" is Kerouac ridiculing his tendency to get heavy-handed with symbolism. Much of the stammering and backtracking, of course, derives from Neal's sound: ". . . that I was standin in front of when—but you introduced (ain't that right?) me to them two suckers from Edmonton or somethin— yeh, that's right (just when you said that you reminded me . . .)." Kerouac even parodies his own weakness for parodying—for example, echoing mimicries from his earlier works.

As just a sampling, in the first twenty-five pages of the "Imitation" one can pick out parodies of Leo Kerouac's movie column in the *Spotlight*; of the opening paragraph of *The Town and the City*; of *On the Road* and voices in it such as the Mexican girl's and Remi Boncoeur's; of Shakespeare, Dickens, Yeats, Twain, Gertrude Stein, Hemingway, and Steinbeck; of Jesus Christ, Sherlock Holmes, W. C. Fields, Milton Berle, and Billie Holiday. Kerouac imitates the preceding tape transcriptions too, even to the point of breaking off words in the middle the way a speaker does: "you shrivel away like a pru—"

He has discovered that there are a multitude of voices in his head apart from his own, for *they* (whatever they are) are somehow speaking to *him*: "Hear me daddy, waitin for you all day long," calls one. The idea has been just to listen to those voices. But after twenty-five pages, the "Imitation" comes to an abrupt halt, choked by its own profusion. Once he succeeds in tapping his unconscious, it starts to flow too fast. Since the torrent can't all get out at once, it wells up, producing a tension that stanches its own flow. In Joycean compounds he explains: "doublewords ringing in my head nowlike i was goingtoburst my oldtop. . . ."

The basic problem is that Kerouac the writer can't help becoming conscious of his own act of listening and recording; and once he realizes what he's doing, he begins to direct the flow rather than simply follow it. He has to remind himself repeatedly to "go ahead and forget what you were saying, if you can't remember, crack go ahead, head, creak, crack, crack your head. . . ." Sometimes the sheer force of the flow breaks through again, but the difficulty of verbalizing unconscious imagery always acts as a brake: "fyou don't wash out an dkwhekek dhowowh but now I lost it again. . . ." Another hindrance is the conscious mind, which refuses to be given short shrift, and insists on having its own say: "you've got to explain yourself clearly or not at all." In the "Imitation," the raging battle between the writer's conscious and unconscious tears some sentences limb from limb, and at times you can even hear the cry of pain: "she is the foun(dloli) (Obscure in meaning), but nevertheless as a printer's son I feel obliged to say that this twaddle—shee—this twaddle— Sheee, plea, sir, plea, chiny towh, town, tow, how, ow, ow, wo, ow. . . ." Although the attempt to sustain the flow is doomed to fail, the process is not in vain. Miraculous visions have come to light, and Jack compares his awe to that of Cody and his first wife sweeping across the continent in car or bus: "well weredo we return to the trickof the d no we missed again and but now, ah, ahem, cunt, hm, look, ah, country, Joanna."

The first section of the "Imitation" is followed by the sketch "Joan Rawshanks in the Fog." Hollywood provides Kerouac with the perfect model for the triumph of illusion. The observor-narrator behind the cameras not only sees how reality can be manipulated, but also realizes how easily we can be tricked into accepting a single vision as the only truth. The deceptive "fotografter" is "just fiddling with his lightbulbs and put-up arrangements of tripods and subsidiary lights (with a cat standing next to him again wielding those strange riddled cardboards they use for estimating the inch-ounch of light they want, though how can anybody in a movie audience get to detect that when the picture finally flashes on the screen;). . . ." What Kerouac seeks is the meaning beneath the manifold visions: "what was your real tear, Joan, your real sorrows. . . ." Yet there is no way the narrator can verify his "dark suspicion" about what is actually going on. Since he knows nothing more solid than the vision, he is forced to play with shadows. The limitation on knowledge is one of the book's main themes, which Kerouac states near the very beginning: "I know now that paranoia is the vision of what's happening and psychosis is the hallucinated vision of what's happening, that paranoia is reality, that paranoia is the content of things, that paranoia's never satisfied."

In "Joan Rawshanks in the Fog," Kerouac carries his symbolism of the "moment" a step further than in previous works. Moviemaking teaches that only those things count that take place while the shutter of the camera is open. Whatever occurs in front of a rolling camera is fixed; it is a "take"; everything else is lost. Kerouac thus equates the events preserved on film in a "take" with the perceptions preserved in memory during a moment. The movies reveal a new, disheartening aspect of the moment. The multiplicity of takes ("there were three takes of every area of the action") belies the importance of any single one. Which one will be used and which others rejected is a matter of chance, of the particular concatenation of details that happen to be caught. The take, like the visionary moment, communicates no absolute truth. Each take, each vision, is simply and only itself:

> . . . now there's only the great silence of the great moment of Hollywood, the actual TAKE (how many producers got high on Take do you think?) just as in a bullfight, when the moment comes for the matador to stick his sword into the bull and kill it . . . it surprises you that the actual kill is a distant,

vague, almost dull flat happening like when Lou Gehrig [*sic*] actually did connect for a home run and the sharp flap of the bat on ball seems disappointing even though Gehrig hits another home run next time up, this one loud and clout in its sound, the actual moment, the central kill, the riddled middle idea, the thing, the Take, the actual juice suction of the camera catching a vastly planned action, the moment when we all know that the camera is germinating, a thing is being born whether we planned it right or not . . . the exact actual moment of the Take is when silence falls. . . .

Paradoxically, by showing reality up for a cheat, the movies have taught us the value of dreaming: "it isn't that Hollywood has won us with its dreams, it has only enhanced our own wild dreams. . . ." Aging, baggy-faced Joan Rawshanks inspires Jack to rhapsodize his own Song of Solomon, even if he cannot resist turning that too into a parody: "Your eyes are like the star of midnight, your lips are like the blood of a sacrifice by moonlight; your shoulders are like the yieldings of elephants in the flesh, as they mill and stamp, and moo and turn. . . ." The love he feels is as genuine as any, and he is willing to fight for her, but his weapon will be imagination: "Ruby, Mary, ruby mary, filthy bloody mary, you'll an old hag be? not without I don't have something to do about it. . . ." Imagination can coax back her beauty even if it cannot restore her youth:

> Poor doll, I know your juicy hole . . . don't die so; baby doll, your lips are cold, you don't stay high with me; if you could stay high with me forever, and together we'd lay in the pool of myself wrapped in your self, why, Andean princess, I'd lay you . . . if you die I die.
> Well and what could Clementina reply to that?

Art can't be gainsaid, any more than a woman can stop Jack from loving her; but the mind's victory is a cold one, and in a sense inhuman. The last line quoted above contains a double entendre, for it also refers to the fact that "Clementina" might be too weak to reply at all, if not already dead.

The next section of the "Imitation" presents the full range of Jack's visions of Cody, ordered not by sequence in time but by the mind's own train of association. The one in which he sees Cody as a member of the Three Stooges is rich in the details of American boyhood and is Kerouac at his best—sharp-witted, immensely informed, and thoroughly light-hearted. And it is not just a showpiece, but functions thematically as part of the novel's subjectivism: "Cody . . . thought of the Three Stooges, suddenly realizing—that life is strange and the Three Stooges exist—that in 10,000 years—that . . . all the goofs he felt in him were justified in the outside world and he had nothing to reproach himself for. . . ."

Continually hearing Neal read aloud from Proust and the Charles Atkinson translation of Spengler, influences which Kerouac acknowledges in the novel itself, aided him in expanding his sentences with more balanced rhythms and a periodic structure. He still scats mouthfuls of syllables just for the effect of the sound, but now the scattings tend to fall into larger, better defined movements of thought, and flow together toward the moment of revelation.

In this next-to-the-last section of the "Imitation," Kerouac examines all the ways that he and Neal love each other, including the sexual attraction between them. Like husband and wife, Jack and Cody become "one flesh," and freely exchange roles:

JACK. It was the same way when we had that dream about driving up the hill in the whiteness and you fell out of the car—

CODY. We had a dream?

JACK. Oh pardon my hard-on, I had a dream

CODY. Know full well that I'll never succumb to your advances

JACK. It was only your manly built, your beautiful eyes that attracted me so fair, on the cobblestones there

CODY. Don't think you can hang around here and make passes at ME

JACK. Tut, tut, nary a thought; I told the Judge I was a confidence man

Although Jack and Cody still speak and respond to each other, as in the exchange above, they also begin to speak directly to the audience, as oblivious of each other's presence as Shakespearean soliloquists of their fellow characters. At times both Jack and Cody slip into a stream-of-consciousness monologue straight out of *Ulysses*. Of course Kerouac is parodying Joyce too, just as Joyce parodied all his fellow English writers in the "Oxen of the Sun" section of *Ulysses*. Nor does Kerouac fail to remind us of his debt to Joyce with suitably punning allusions, such as "Bloom let the soap melt in his backpocket he was so hot" or

JACK. Yes—fit for desert nights, I'd say it was fit for rugs in loverooms

CODY. Blooms, blooms—but we'll turn off this tape

Like Joyce, and later Beckett, Kerouac uses the monologue to indicate the ultimate isolation of mind. Even if Cody is Jack's brother, he can never be more to Jack than a series of memories, as is Kerouac's real brother Gerard. At this point in the book, he employs a time collapse, identifying Neal with Gerard: "Cody is the brother I lost." That line, and its variations, are repeated for several pages like a litany, which resonates with the theme stated within the first few pages: "I accept lostness forever." Since his intent is to explore the subject of friendship and love to its furthest limits, he has finally arrived at the bitter end, which is the inevitable parting of friends and lovers, if not by the exigencies of life, then by death.

The narrator does everything he can not to lose Cody. He writes like him (echoing Neal's "Joan Anderson" letter): "Brew Moore whom I have seen like a ghost on the sidewalk . . ." He presses on, recording every memorable experience with Cody up to the very present, and so we get his account of the debacle on Neal's birthday, and of his peyote visions with Neal. But as the life of the writer catches up with the exact moment of the writing, he realizes this tack can take him no farther. He has been "a great rememberer redeeming life from darkness," in the manner of old storyteller Shakespeare, from whose 97th Sonnet he quotes: "What freezings have I felt; what dark days seen; what old December's bareness—everywhere." But time is of the essence, and it has run out. He has told all his tales of Cody. He tries to bluff optimism, quoting Neal and Ginsberg and alluding to Blake, but it is all empty words: "EVERYTHING'S ALL RIGHT; dead eyes see, are not blind. Roses riot everywhere. Sunflowers, Ah! I love you. Abstraction. You think? See rain. Comes afloat. Fell." In the words of Yeats, "the center cannot hold." The narrator writes a poem, mimicking "a young idealist," but well he knows that won't carry him much further. He racks his brain for any memories he might have missed; he seeks fertility in word-play; he even contemplates writing in French, by hand, or composing an ode:

> THINGS HAVE A DECEIVING LOOK OF PEACEFULNESS, THE BEAST
> is actually ready to leap—lookout—yet what about those
> French dreams last spring?—what, sweet hype? can't write?—
> find no machine to relabate your fond furlures; furloors,
> veleours, or velours, we know that in French, in print *a main*
> we cannot fail—
>   O Telegraph Hill!

When, a few lines later, words do fail, he tries "an ABSTRACT drawing." Finally he must face the task he has been avoiding: "The thing to do is put the quietus on the road." The linear story must be exploded from within, the concept of order annihilated: "The telling of the voyages again, for the very beginning; that is, immediately after this. The Voyages are told each in one breath, as is your own, to foreshadow that or this rearshadows *that, one!*" That is to say, the last section of the book will lead back into the beginning just as the last words of *Finnegans Wake* connect with the opening sentence, completing a circle. The meaning of that *"one!"* is, specifically, that a writer cannot avoid the order imposed by the pages of a book. Something must come first, something second, and so on. But that *"one!"*—first spoken by Big Slim—has also been established on several occasions as an agent of parody. It is the wink of the confidence man who would let us in on his secret, and that secret is the primal ambiguity of man's condition. The question might be expressed, paraphrasing schoolboy metaphysics, as: Which came first, the voyage or the telling?

Visions of Cody concludes with a superficially linear account of all Jack's trips and adventures with Cody since their first meeting in New York. But Kerouac has already prepared us to realize that re-telling a story is never a matter of simple repetition. That was the point of the long segment of tape transcriptions in Part 3, as well as the presentation of Neal's poolhall days in Part 2, which now calls for closer inspection.

The scene of Neal's arrival in Peterson's Pool Hall, opening Part 2, was the original piece of writing, the core, around which *Visions of Cody* developed. That scene itself parodied Chapter One of Neal's *The First Third*, as one may see by comparing their respective opening lines:

> For a long time I held a unique position. Among the hundreds of isolated creatures who haunted the streets of lower downtown Denver, there was not one so young as myself. (*The First Third*)

> Around the poolhalls of Denver during World War II a strange looking boy began to be noticeable to the characters who frequented the places afternoon and night and even to the casual visitors . . . a boy called Cody Pomeray, the son of a Larimer Street wino. (*Visions of Cody*)

The scene as first written ended with Cody's victorious tackle of "Earl Johnson" on the high-school football field. As Kerouac began to expand this piece, which was highly romantic, he followed Neal's heroics with an objective description of the discovery of an aborted fetus in a prairie. But Kerouac's emotions immediately intruded into the catalogue of facts; he began to vent his horror at the procreative function of women. Bringing himself up short, he then segues into another objective description of a night drive across the Western plains. But since he is writing about a Saturday-night expedition to meet girls, he can't help waxing lyrical. Once more he catches himself, declaring: "But I'll start again." Like reversing a film, he brings his characters back a few paces and lets them meet the girls all over, this time trying to concentrate on concrete details. Within a few lines he's back to his old subjective extravagance. The pattern for Part 2 is set.

Objective reality doesn't exist for Kerouac. When he tries to describe it, he realizes that he is deceiving himself, merely mouthing someone else's clichés or misconceptions. His own voice speaks only in the outpouring of imagination. Paradoxically, however, a certain objectivity can be achieved by reviewing one subjective vision through the lens of another, and this is the high function of parody. Later in Part 2, reveling in lewd fantasies about a woman in a pornographic picture, Kerouac suddenly senses he has lost his focus on the subject. The distance of parody quickly restores a clear perspective: "the exact nipple will tell us more than Ruth's entire life story, 'Around the beauty parlors of Brooklyn during World War II a strange energetic young lady began to be noticeable to the characters who frequented the places afternoon and night and even to the casual visitors. . . .' "

As Part 2 progresses, such self-parodies get more ambitious, until eventually Kerouac is retelling whole scenes. A Saturday night when Cody wears his first suit, and gets a flirtatious look from a classy woman, is retold detail for detail but at a faster pace. Kerouac achieves this speeding-up, which was of course a favorite trick of early motion pictures, through an assortment of devices including tense shifts and elliptical phrasing. For example, where in the first telling Cody yells, "Watson watch that new Caddy beat the light now!", in the second telling Cody yells, "Damn, damn, look at that Cadillac beat the light!" (In the first, the event is about to happen; in the second, it is already happening.) As an example of condensation that accelerates the action, compare:

> . . . a beautiful girl fixing on him from her casual one-leg-forward position by the weighing machine waiting for the bus a cold arrogant look of sensuality done with misty eyes and something suggestive, impatient, almost too personal to understand, astonishing him in the realization that he was wearing a suit for the first time in his life and this was the first official sex-appeal look from a regular high-heeled downtown socialite honey. . . . [first telling]

> . . . a bus-waiting girl, (again), legs akimbo, watching him suddenly with that snaky sexy lovelike look. . . . [second telling]

The speedup comments on the way good times seem to pass faster each time they're repeated. By the same token, it suggests the multiplicity of "levels" that exist within the same reality. In *Visions of Cody*, *level* and *layer* become two of Kerouac's new key words. One of the reasons he sees Cody as a hero is because of his cosmic attunement; he describes Cody as "so singing in his soul now that he had to talk on several levels to express himself. . . ."

The rationale for the apparently linear conclusion of Part 4 is given analogically by Cody in a speech to Joanna:

"Well now, Joanna, what we've got to do is sweep the floor and then scramble up those eggs and have a breakfast, we'll never crystallize in our plans or come to any rockbottom pure realization, decision, whichever, or nothin without perfect action and knowledge not only philosophical and on an emotional plane but pragmatic and simple."

By now, though, we know that Cody's desire for an orderly life is unfulfillable. As the narrator runs once more through his exploits with Cody, he realizes that each retelling is an additional loss, a fresh scrap tossed to "the dogs of eternity" as life slips away. Like a painter repainting the same scenes in darker shades, Kerouac's tone is suffused with pathos:

> . . . we [Cody, Jack, and Joanna] sent each other out of the room to do it alone, one by one, and were frightened by the darkness in the house, in fact the creaking mystery, philosophical void, the missing of the point, the obvious sadness of having to die never having known something about everything and ourselves we're dying by the hour to know and act upon immediately. . . .

Linearity is literally a dead end, and to abolish it he has somehow to circumvent death. Death, according to linear Hemingway, was the end of all true stories. By contrast, in the last section of *Visions of Cody*, Kerouac announces: "I'm writing this book *because* we're all going to die [italics mine]." For Kerouac, if the writer can't find a way out—that is, if he's merely adding to our knowledge of destruction—there's no point to his writing.

His way out lies, first, through a complete identification of Cody with America. The thread of American history has wound through every section of the book. In the early description of the poolhall, for example, we learned that Cody is following in the footsteps of such Curtis Street habitués as the Pensacola Kid, Willie Hoppe, Bat Masterson, Babe Ruth, Jelly Roll Morton, and Theodore Dreiser. Allusions to the Civil War abound throughout, and in the last section Cody is twice identified with a Civil War soldier. Significantly, he is pictured as a hapless Rebel, bereft of his homeland: "the Civil War soldier in the old photo who stands by a pile of lumber in a drizzle, waiting for arrest. . . ." Cody has also personified such American figures as a cowboy, a "hanging judge," an "Oklahoma posseman pursuer," an "Assistant D.A.," Clark Gable, W. C. Fields, and Franklin D. Roosevelt. As the book ends, he even becomes one with the American continent: "Denver began to imitate L.A. and spread for miles—and Cody spread all the way to California."

In the final pages, the strongest identification is between Cody and Lester Young. Just as Joyce incarnated legendary heroes in his modern protagonists Leopold Bloom and H. C. Earwicker, so does

Kerouac stand Cody in the shoes of one of the founders of modern jazz. To Kerouac, jazz is America's most vital tradition, and no one had a more graceful command of all its idioms than "the President of saxophone players." Like Bird, Prez had perfect control of his horn and could play in any key. But, above all, Prez had the gift of simplicity; he was more listenable than Parker. Where Parker typified the moody genius, Lester was more the regular guy who worked hard but kept his sense of humor, at least until it was sapped by drug addiction. Even then, in his last years of terrible suffering and failing powers, he still blew cool and easy. All of those qualities are implied when Cody says, "I, much like him [Lester], incline and do fall"—and when "Lionel" (Seymour Wyse) tells Jack: "America's real mad . . . Lester my boy Lester . . . And guys like Cody."

We are also asked to believe that Cody's development has been influenced by the development of jazz: "Lester blows all Kansas City to ecstasy and now Americans from coast to coast go mad, and fall by, and everybody's picking up—what? This had no effect on Cody?" Cody's blank period is a logical corollary of the advent of "cold jazz." Cody was forced to "come down" just as Lester had to lower his horn because of his weary, drooping posture. Here is where Kerouac's associationism triumphs over linear logic, for it flashes to him that America comes down too, in her greatest river, the Mississippi:

> Lester is just like the river, the river starts in near Butte, Montana in frozen snow caps (Three Forks) and meanders on down across states and entire territorial areas of dun bleak land with hawthorn crackling in the sleet, picks up rivers at Bismark, Omaha and St. Louis just north, another at Kay-ro, another in Arkansas, Tennessee, comes deluging on New Orleans with muddy news from the land and a roar of subterranean excitement that is like the vibration of the entire land sucked of its gut in mad midnight, fevered, hot, the big mudhole rank clawpole old frogular pawed-soul titanic Mississippi from the North, full of wires, cold wood and horn.

Since Cody = Lester, and Lester = America, Cody is reinforced in his position as representative American man. (And for the notion that the hero must be representative we can also look back to Kerouac's hero Thomas Carlyle.) While he is identifying Cody with America, Kerouac also ties him to the rest of humanity. Cody becomes a modern prototype of Everyman, the hero of medieval morality plays. As such, he is both male and female, and embodies good as well as evil. Jack calls Cody "a devil, an old witch, even an old bitch," and his "greatest enemy" as well as his "brother." He fills Cody's balloon with titles until it pops: "he's nothing but an empty minded, vacant, bourgeois Irish proletarian would-be Proust tire recapper—a nothing." Since Cody is everything, he is also nothing, for the universe is empty: "Cody talking, stern boned in a fixity pose, solid rock, the canny Scot, old Yeats, a future Dostoyevsky of inflexible tragic convictions and irritabilities. Some generation. Some nigger. And that big void over the beloved bending head of the earth." It is significant that Cody is identified with writers—"some nigger" another mocking gibe at Hemingway (in *To Have and Have Not*)— since the narrator depends on Cody to save *him* too.

We already know that Jack = Cody, so Jack too is flowing with the American river. He has also established himself as the cosmic writer, identifying himself throughout the book with worldwide literary greats from Poe, Melville, Whitman, Dreiser, Wolfe, and Dos Passos to Shakespeare, Joyce, Céline, and Genet. These identifications are often subtle. For example, passing through Pittsburgh the narrator has a vision of the "Ward Morehouse office buildings" from the *U.S.A.* trilogy; at another point his hero, merging with two of Joyce's characters (man and woman), becomes "Buck Mulligan O'Garty." Jack's future as a writer is one of the book's major subjects, as is his own mortality. The narrator continually reminds us that he is about to turn thirty, which he sees as the midpoint of his life, and that his writing if it is to be an accurate reflection of his mind must somehow take that fact into account. "Don't go down the hill of the other side of your life (30) for nothing," Jack tells himself. Once again Kerouac wrestles with a modernistic and postmodernistic problem, the attempt to unify subject matter with technique.

The approaching death of Jack and Cody is viewed within the context of a dying America. America lives only in those who believe in her, so that she and her champions pass away together. Jack titles an imaginary essay: "Beyond Cody There are only Thieves." Later he elaborates his thesis that a nation exists only by virtue of love. When love is lost, either by outright hatred or just fear of contact, i.e., selfishness and vanity, community dissolves:

> The sins of America are precisely that the streets . . . are empty where their houses are, there's no sense of neighborhood anymore . . . beyond this old honesty there can only be thieves. What is it now, that a well-dressed man who is a plumber in the Plumber's Union by day, and a beat-dressed man who is a retired barber meet on the street and think of each other wrong, as the law, or panhandler, or some such cubbyhole identification, worse than that, things like homosexual, or dopefiend, or dope pusher, or mugger, or even Communist and look away from each other's eyes . . . Looking at a man in the eye is now queer.

Yet the individual American is not to blame that America has not fulfilled its promise. The forces of destruction are inherent in life itself:

America is what laid on Cody Pomeray's soul the onus and the stigma—that in the form of a big plainclothesman beat the shit out of him in a backroom till he talked about something which isn't even important any more . . . It has evil roads behind gas tanks where murderous dogs snarl from behind wire fences and cruisers suddenly leap out like get-away cars but from a crime more secret, more baneful than words can tell— It is where Cody Pomeray learned that people aren't good, they want to be bad—where he learned they want to cringe and beat, and snarl is the name of their love-making—

Moby Dick, killed by the crew of a Scandinavian whaler in February 1952, "had to die." [181] Relating this actual newspaper item, Kerouac reminds us that even in its glorious youth America's philosophers prophesied corruption and betrayal. The America that is dying is the vigorous wildness of Thoreau's Walden woods, but Thoreau would be the last person to be surprised that nature had been devastated. Had he seen the White Whale, "Thoreau would have said 'Humph' and predicted the harpoon cannon and turned away." With a similar shrug Kerouac awaits the atom bomb:

The Indians with hands outstretched expect us three galoots goofing in an old V-8 to come over and give them dollars; they don't know we discovered the atom bomb yet, they only vaguely heard about it. We'll give it to them, alright. . . .

Tragedy is real, but only so long as it is contemplated as tragic. By now, Kerouac has exposed the layers of illusion that constitute our universe. What we see, or know, is absolutely dependent on our perspective at the time of seeing, or knowing. Since the universe, from atoms to galaxies, is perpetually moving, those perspectives keep shifting. Eventually everything, *even the conception of loss,* is lost in endless space—just as, at the end of Part 2, the jobless and loveless narrator suddenly dissolves in a cosmic fade-out:

Sitting on a stool facing blinding open door—parking lot beyond little porch of concrete—post—then brown fields, wire fences, oil cranes, blue haze, telegraph wires, shapeless black steels, hills, trees, houses, Pacific Sky over Pedro and then ocean.

The capacity of mind to subsume loss is the basis of Cody's optimism when he tells Jack that *"everything* [is] *always all right,"* and of Jack's optimism when he asserts that "I not only accept loss forever, I am made of loss—I am made of Cody, too." The life cycle of a man is like the life cycle of a nation (a Spenglerian idea). Death is inevitable for both, but it cannot end the process of living and dying.

Consciousness returns to its sources; everything man knows comes and goes in cycles. That precise observation was made a few thousand years ago by Solomon in Ecclesiastes (and picked up by Hemingway, who never seemed to understand it): "One generation passeth away, and another generation cometh: but the earth abideth forever." Kerouac changes only one term. After Einstein, we know the earth is destructible. Kerouac would say: "Mind abideth forever." It is certainly a basic religious insight. Kerouac's achievement in *Visions of Cody* is to create a text that doesn't just utter this truth but somehow reflects it.

What more perfect hero for such a book than Cody, who teaches circularity by traveling from place to place and woman to woman in endless cycles. As in *On the Road,* Kerouac again uses images of light-in-darkness to suggest rebirth. In *Visions of Cody* this symbolism becomes more sophisticated, permitting whole themes to be developed just by variations and combinations of such imagery. For example, he shows that it is light-in-darkness that makes space visible, much as Milton described it in hell. But for Kerouac light-in-darkness is also the measure of space:

> . . . house, clearing, watertank, tracks, lamp, and a few further indications of a townlet beyond the road's lamp—in one hollow misty carrousel of wild black space horses so close to one another that the only time you could see between them was when a faroff light indicated it, a railroad switch light or a roadlamp or an airport tower in the other county or the topmost glimmer of an antenna in a Cheyenne or whatever radio station.

And more clearly than before, he equates darkness with death, that we should grasp how significant it is, how hopeful of immortality, that light still shines at all. Light it is that creates "excitements in the huge dark of America, umalum, umalum," he writes, alluding to Poe's light of resurrection ("Ulalume"). Light is precious even if it be only the ghostly radiance that illuminates our sleep:

> In the loneliness of my life, my father dead, my brother dead, my mother faraway, my sister and my wife far away, nothing here but my own tragic hands that once were guarded by a world, a sweet attention, that now are left to guide and disappear their own way into the common dark of all our death, sleeping in me raw bed, alone and stupid: with just this one pride and consolation: my heart broke in the general despair and opened up inwards to the Lord, I made a supplication in this dream.

The imagery of light-in-darkness is more cogent in *Visions of Cody* than in *On the Road* because in the new book Kerouac spends much more time examining the manner in which we perceive light.

Early in Part 1, he describes a scene in a Manhattan cafeteria at night. There is a huge plate-glass window through which the narrator can see the street outside, and in the reflections of which he can also see the interior of the cafeteria. Additionally, there is a mirrored column inside the cafeteria, and the shiny fender of a car parked on the street, which multiply the reflections. Kerouac reports every image and reflected image and re-reflected image until he has woven a web so hallucinatory that it defies definition in terms of conventional reality. The narrator has, in effect, removed himself from ordinary time and place, from the props by which we assuage what Gore Vidal termed "our universal strangeness." Where he is left is anyone's guess, but it is surely a world closer to the equations of nuclear physics than to the fireside of Charles Dickens. The poet Robert Duncan, reading this scene in manuscript in 1954, was struck by Kerouac's extraordinary ability to sustain a 1500-word narrative in which the only exterior action, besides the passing of pedestrians, is the flashing of a neon light.

It is in *Visions of Cody* that he sharpens the imagery of red brick and red neon to such a degree that they can communicate fine nuances of meaning and emotion. The base of this symbology is the image of a red brick hotel wall catching the glint of a red neon sign, which for Kerouac suggests the intangible beauty and intimacy we always imagine on the inside of any world from which we are excluded, as if that hotel wall were being seen by some vagrant like Cody's father, too poor to rent a room. The real emotional content of the image, though, comes from the realization (of one who has already been on the inside) that the magic is not there—at least not for longer than it takes to climax with a pickup—that it must be somewhere else. It is, in short, the image of man's insatiable longing and his invariable disappointment. As such, it ties in with another important symbolism in *Visions of Cody*: the search for "the center of Saturday night," which of course exists nowhere but in the mind that created the notion. Both "the center of Saturday night" and "the redbrick wall behind red neons" suggest, on a deeper level, the elusive objective reality the narrator pursues. What is exceptional is Kerouac's ability to keep our attention focused on red brick and red neon as real things in a real world while they simultaneously operate on a variety of symbolic levels.

Space and time collapses in *Visions of Cody* enable Kerouac to reduce eons of earthly life into one crowded arena, like the giant room of Times Square, and then to blast it all with the worm of mortality, to devour it with the speed of light:

The trip proceeded, like the unrolling of a mighty thread of accomplished-moments, accomplished-ments, I want to go now, you better go now, wow, that girl, how I'd love to have her sitting on my lap, saying "I want to go now," softly, meaning I want to fuck, let's start, she's learned all the tenderness of the new generation, the hip generation, the modern generation, the generation that ten thousand years from now will lie in ruins beneath the decays of worn fossil, like oil under the cabbage leaves of old Carboniferous, if not Carbonomnivorous or better Carbonitis, the Dinosaurs rolled their own roaches in an ugh, ploppy sea, with Mormon fishtails rising slick and viney from the wet pluck and muck of mires, dismal, dawn, dumbdawn of reptiles.

The last few paragraphs of the novel integrate almost all its motifs and themes. The page-long coda begins at dawn and ends at sunset. Upon this simple time collapse is superimposed another of greater expanse: the summary of Cody's life from childhood to grave. Jack is watching Cody going to work in the morning, and the narrator's observations illustrate the timeless cycles that have given the book its structure: "the dew is on the road again and as forever. . . ." The religious quest for the absolute has been nothing more than a deathwatch on phenomena, and it dissolves in a cosmic fade-out: "the light of an automobile reflecting from the shiny silverpaint of a sidewalk tank this very instant, as silent . . . as a bird crossing the dawn in search of the mountain cross and the sea beyond the city at the end of the land."

The most exalted image of light-in-darkness, the stars, is now combined with several other motifs. As in *On the Road*, the stars betoken the return of all we lost: "make me a vow: promise my star of pity still burns for me." The most inspiring star, the morning star, is identified with Charlie Parker: "the morning-star lips in that pale woodshed sky. . . ." (To *lip* is the musician's term for putting his mouth to the mouthpiece of an instrument. The allusion is to Parker practicing as a boy in his mother's woodshed, and was quite clear while *On the Road* and *Visions of Cody* were still one work-in-progress, for Parker's history had been told in the Chicago jazz scenes in the roll manuscript.) Having connected stars with jazz, Kerouac proceeds to reveal them both as manifestations of procreative energy. Not only are stars alive—a thesis already implicit in *On the Road*, where they are usually in motion—but they *jazz* in the original sense, which was what went on in the rooms behind and above where the music was played: "she [the morning-star] shudders and shits sparks of light and waterfalls of droop and moistly hugens up a cunt for cocks of eyes crowing across the fences of Golden Southern America in her Dawn."

The last two sentences in the book acknowledge death, but it is only a death like the sun setting. The hero smiles because he knows that it proves no finality. Day is merely dawning somewhere else. Cody, America, Man, is on an endless journey to God: *"a Dios"*:

Adios, you who watched the sun go down, at the rail, by my side, smiling—
Adios, King.

It is perhaps the most confident ending in American literature since the "Conclusion" of *Walden,* with which it bears comparison. Thoreau wrote:

> I do not say that John or Jonathan will realize all this; but such is the character of that morrow which mere lapse of time can never make to dawn. The light which puts out our eyes is darkness to us. Only that day dawns to which we are awake. There is more day to dawn. The sun is but a morning star.

To have reinterpreted Thoreau's sensibility in twentieth-century terms was an incredible achievement, but during Kerouac's lifetime no publisher would bring out *Visions of Cody* in its entirety, chiefly because of what they took to be its sloppy form. Ginsberg, when he first read the manuscript, believed it "a holy mess." And strange as it may seem—after Studs Terkel and oral biographies and the interview as high art—what most of these people objected to was the presence in the manuscript of literal transcriptions of taped conversation. Neither before nor after the book was finally published did anyone think to *praise* Kerouac for this novelistic innovation. Rather, he was roundly condemned for having padded his novel with a cheap substitute for honest prose, as though he were just too lazy to do his necessary work as a writer.

When Kerouac fit the transcriptions into his manuscript, there undoubtedly occurred as much (or little) editing and selection as when any novelist takes a conversation recorded in his journal and incorporates it into a work of art—a common occurrence. Moreover, in his case, there was the added artistry of directing the conversations as they took place.

Ginsberg is nonetheless correct in pointing out that the transcriptions have a special value relative to the particular themes of the work: "The *art* lies in the consciousness of doing the thing, in the attention to the happening, in the sacramentalization of everyday reality. . . ." The care with which Kerouac transcribes the tapes and fashions a book to encompass them is part of the artistic process that *Visions of Cody* attempts to analyze. Not by accident does "The Tape" section end with the radio voice of a Preacher (Solomon?!), declaring: "I HEEEEEEEEEEEEEEEEEEERD!" In this regard, the reader should also note Jack's later complementary claim: "I have seen. . . ." The pivoting of the book between subjective illusions of sight and sound provides still another framework to make *Visions of Cody* one of the best-organized works in American literature perhaps, again, since *Walden.*

NINE
The Footsteps of the Bard

1.

Despite Allen's involvement in Jack's and Neal's literary affairs, he felt left out of their new intimacy. When misunderstandings developed between Jack and Neal, Allen was gratified to serve as counselor. He addressed his letters to both, and tried to restore the openness they'd had in the beginning. He also foresaw Jack's troubled future:

> If you [Neal] feel guilty about Jack . . . about you're rift with him, I mean—it's several reasons caused: primarily, I think Jack's flip, which makes it impossible for him to sympathize with others day to day—no that is'nt right—he just, I mean, demands that you agree with his ideas about how bad everybody is to him . . . He will remember telling me he hoped NY would blow up, so I came under his curse—I mean . . . I just felt intimidated then and could'nt protest the violence of his rage, though in a strange way I admired it. On the other hand Neal on account of your T [pot] & present long suffering silence as you have yourself observed you can't communicate, reassure, chitchat, joke with, talk serious with, etc., apparently, so it makes it hard on your guest.
>   . . . apparently a new world of reality or non-innocence is dawning on Jack, he is going into a great and classic new phase (like melville after Pierre) of self realism and shrinking of the world-ego, and must have much of great interest or secret hopes and disappointments and new resolves of great serious future import to settle.

Allen also undertook to straighten out Jack's legal difficulties with Joan. His brother, Eugene Brooks, a lawyer, contributed his services without charge. Jack's fear of going to jail and his hatred of Joan were intensifying because of the daily harassment of his mother and friends. According to Joan, one of the investigators from the D.A.'s office had fallen in love with her, and so was prosecuting the case with unwonted enthusiasm. On the pretext of hunting for Jack he escorted her all around town, and on one occasion even burst in on Lucien in bed with his wife. Hence Jack wasn't just being para-noiac in assuming he would have to run for the rest of his life, or else abandon his career, which required a certain amount of public exposure.

He finished retyping the new *On the Road* (*Visions of Cody*) in early April, 1952. Solomon asked him to delay sending it for a few weeks because he was in the midst of his own wage-and-hour nego-tiations with Wyn. In the meantime Jack asked Allen to return the twenty-three-page scene of Neal on the football field, of which he didn't have a copy.

Burroughs had been suggesting Jack join him in Mexico. He was then out on bail awaiting disposition of his own case. Since Neal was driving his family to Tennessee, Jack decided to ride with them as far as Nogales, Arizona. In Mexico he intended to sketch Bill as the subject for his next book, to be called "Down." He warned Allen not to divulge his plan lest Bill become "self-conscious and uninterest-ing." He also announced that his goal was to write three master-pieces in one year, as Shakespeare nearly did in two separate periods—*Henry V, Julius Caesar,* and *Hamlet* during 1598–1600; and *Othello, King Lear,* and *Macbeth* during 1604–1606.[182]

Jack wanted to get back to New York to see his mother, but he supposed it would be safer—given the problem with Joan—to spend a few months traveling through South America with Burroughs. If Bill were expelled from Mexico as a "pernicious foreigner," which seemed likely, he planned to get a farm in Panama and search Ec-uador for yage vines, a natural hallucinogen. Tempted by the pros-pect of unlimited pot again, Jack tried to get excited about these adventures. But when he contemplated the "equator, jungles, disease . . . rotten martinis rotting," he felt instead like a criminal bound for his just punishment.[183]

Nevertheless he left San Francisco with the Cassadys in late April, 1952. For the trip Neal replaced the back seat of his station wagon with a mattress. The girls rode up front with him, and Jack, Carolyn, and the baby sat on the mattress. While Jack and Carolyn were tormented by romantic longings, Neal couldn't decide what to feel. The night they drove through Arizona, Carolyn sat between the men. For a few hours their old rapport returned, as Neal lectured them about the stars and Jack stroked Carolyn's head resting on his shoulder. But in the morning, rather than stopping for a picnic as he'd promised, Neal hustled Jack to the border. At Jack's insistence they all had a beer in a Mexican café, but Neal declined to spend an hour driving around Nogales (in Sonora). He seemed sad and hostile as Jack stood by the wire fence waving good-bye. Carolyn thought Jack looked forlorn.

The bus ride to Mexico City took him back to prehistoric Amer-ica. Beside him twenty-five-year-old hepcat Enrique was carrying a stash of pot in his radio-repair gadget, and when Jack talked about peyote they immediately became friends. In the back of the bus, Jack drank mescal and sang bop tunes and the Mexicans taught him their songs. In Culiacán, Enrique led him to a stick hut, where a group of Indians tested his sincerity. After he correctly identified a pellet of opium, they judged him an authentic pleasure-seeker—after first thinking he might be a policeman from L.A. The host sprinkled opium in several marijuana cigars, and by the second drag Jack was high. A few more and he was easily speaking Spanish with them. Remembering his own Indian great-great-grandmother, he agreed when the host said, "The earth is ours." The next day they got him over his shakes with pepper soup, and after overcharging him for two ounces of pot, sent some cops to take most of it back.

That afternoon, on the beach at Mazatlán with Enrique, Jack experienced one of his "great rippling moments." He realized that "the Indian, the Mexican, is great, straight, simple and perfect." The next day in Mexico City, he ditched Enrique and went to Bill's alone. No revelation ever made Jack a whit less selfish.

He found Bill looking like a mad scholar, surrounded by a litter of pages comprising his new novel. It was about being "queer," and Jack suggested he call it just that. There was a new purity about Bill that touched him deeply. Bill missed Joan immensely, their children had been sent away, and his boyfriend had left him too. Like Jack, his life was tragically empty of anything but kicks and art.

They were getting plenty of both. Almost as soon as Jack arrived, he began a new "fellaheen south of the border book." On the bus trip he had met the peasant people he'd read about in Spengler, the "fellaheen," who fascinated him by their ability to survive from one civilization to the next without becoming part of any. The fellaheen were masters of adaptation, and from them he hoped to learn how to endure his own keenly felt oppression. Into this "book about Indians" Jack imagined he could fit Bill as "the last of the American giants." He also planned a massive Civil War novel on the order of *War and Peace*, with characters based on Lucien Carr, Melville, and Whitman. At the same time he was busily revising *Visions of Cody*. When he and Bill weren't working, they shot morphine or went to Turkish baths together, though sometimes Jack went to a prostitute by himself.

Like women, pot was of more interest to Jack than Bill. If Bill had a lot of company, Jack would smoke in the toilet, writing in pencil in his notebook. It was getting risky to smoke pot in Mexico City anyway, since the cops were using that as an excuse to arrest Americans. Still delicately poised above prison, Bill hardly relished having his apartment reek with the fumes of Jack's "three bombs a day."[184] But he couldn't help feeling tender toward Jack, who had washed up from a shipwrecked life with ten dollars and a pair of holey shoes. And when he read *Visions of Cody*, he was astounded by Jack's development as a writer.

They spent gentle days together. They went to the ballet. In the mountains with Bill's connection, Dave Tercerero, and his woman, they went to a fiesta, bathed in streams, hiked, practiced shooting (which had less to do with violence than with respecting each other's competence), and observed the biblical landscape. They made elaborate plans to float down the Amazon together on a raft, to lure Gore Vidal to Guatemala (to satisfy Bill's crush), to visit Tangier and Rome. When Allen wrote that he felt like a "mediocre sterile failure" and planned to reenter analysis, Jack replied that he would be better off joining them on their travels away from North America. Allen, however, worried that Jack was lost in exile, "going deeper into night."

Certainly he had lost a sense of himself as part of a community, but his professional sense of direction was scarcely ever lost. On May 17, he mailed the manuscript of *Visions of Cody* to Solomon. Since he had only a few dollars left, he sent it by the cheapest postal rate, and for three weeks sweated out news of its arrival. The football scene had finally caught up with him, via San Francisco, and he'd sent it back to Ginsberg. Allen foresaw trouble at Ace, since Solomon was already talking about revisions, so Jack asked Allen to read the manuscript before the editors got to it, the better to defend it against their criticisms. He greatly appreciated the work Allen was doing for him. When Allen chanced to remark that he would let someone else carry out a certain errand because he wasn't getting paid for this work, Jack insisted he begin taking a ten percent commission. That settled, he launched directly into a new novel.

2.

At last Jack felt capable of writing *Doctor Sax*. Fantasy had now become a feasible subject, because sketching had given him the means to "blow on a vision." [185] The breakthrough into a nonlinear form in *Visions of Cody* had allayed his worry about writing private myths; also the direction of his whole literary endeavor had shifted. The novelist James Park Sloan remarked that once a writer has written a nonlinear novel he can never again write a linear one, implying that in order to write a nonlinear novel one's sensibility must undergo a change so drastic that it is irreversible. This conclusion is borne out by Jack's letters of the period when he was beginning *Doctor Sax*, where his literary concerns appear exclusively nonlinear.

He wrote Allen that he was now writing what he heard in his head, seeking sound above meaning, sometimes against his better judgment—but with the assurance that Shakespeare often seemed to do the same, in lines like "greasy Joan doth keel the pot; and birds sit brooding in the snow. . . ." [186] To Holmes he explained: "what I am beginning to discover now is something beyond the novel and beyond the arbitrary confines of the story . . . into the realms of revealed Picture . . . *wild form*, man, *wild form*. Wild form's the only form that holds what I have to say—my mind is exploding to say something about every image and every memory . . . in narrowing circles around the core of my last writing."

"Nonlinear" didn't mean "nonstructured." Kerouac had a definite form in mind before writing each book. He envisioned *Doctor Sax* as "Faust Part Three." Spengler had interpreted the Faust legend—chiefly as seen through Goethe, who wrote *Faust, Parts One and Two*—as a mirror of Western man's belief in the "endlessness of the soul." Goethe had actually predicted the space age in Mephistopheles' taunt to Faust: "Towards the moon you hovered dreaming,/Perhaps your quest would take you there?" Faust will do anything, even conspire in a murder, as long as the devil feeds his insatiable appetite. In Kerouac's view, the century and a half since Goethe wrote *Faust* had seen the culmination of the bargain, the complete loss of Western man's soul. He intended *Doctor Sax* to herald a reverse trend. As much an enemy of evil as Lamont Cranston, Kerouac's hero would fight against Satanism and "call Faust a bastard." Still, there was enough ambivalence in the conception of Sax to give the character room to grow. While Sax "doesn't buy" the self-indulgence preached by the Marquis de Sade or Ernest Dowson, he *is* "a Faustian hero" in his quest for knowledge.[187] In that sense, he is also modeled on William Burroughs, as well as on Jack himself.

There are numerous similarities between *Faust* and much of Kerouac's work. In many ways his heroes find themselves just as torn between earth and heaven as Goethe's; they vacillate between experiencing life and retreating from it. In fact, both Kerouac and Goethe explore the related split between self and society, between the need to belong somewhere—to a family, community, and country—and the need to wander.

To represent these dichotomies Kerouac uses many of Goethe's own motifs. *Faust, Part Two* develops a dialectic between light and dark, with the angels proclaiming the joy of dawn, for example, while the devil extols the riches of darkness. Specific images from *Faust* recur in *Doctor Sax*: stars "glitter mirrored" in water; darkness as a "shroud"; sleep (or dream) as a "husk" which we shed by waking; roses as a blessing, a heavenly visitation to earth. The rose symbol especially is in common usage throughout Western literature, but in English verse it usually typifies fleshly love, and is a standard metaphor for the vulva. For Kerouac, as for Goethe, the rose is predominantly a symbol of angelic—pure, nonsexual—love.

Goethe also employed the technique of time collapse to call the phenomenal world into question. For example, in *Faust, Part Two*, the spirit of Helen, raised from the dead, looks on the palace she knew in childhood, before she was kidnapped to Troy. The complete change in the terms of her presence there produces a dissolution of objective reality. Like Kerouac's narrators, she is suddenly aware of being her own ghost: "Was all this me? Is still? And ever shall I be/ The phantom scare of them that lay proud cities waste?" Later Faust, hearing the church bell chime for death as it does for birth, shudders to realize that "mortal life" is "an empty dream." For both Kerouac and Goethe, death, as the suspension of time, reveals the illusoriness of the things that pass through it. The very fact that time is collapsible denies the absolute nature of existence.

Despite the entrance of the devil and his magic, *Faust, Part One* deals mainly with the real world of medieval Germany. *Part Two* concentrates on the realm of the supernatural and mythological. In *Doctor Sax* Kerouac attempts to synthesize the two worlds—reconciling "things corruptible" with their function as a "parable" (to use Goethe's terms).

If John Barth is correct in assuming that the true postmodernist writer has "one foot in fantasy, one in objective reality," then *Doctor Sax* was the first postmodernist novel in America.

It was also the most visually oriented book Kerouac had yet written. In the opening paragraph four layers of reality are superimposed: the physical world, a dream of the physical world, an artistic representation of the physical world in a dream, and an artistic representation of the dream representation of the physical world! These four levels are integrated via overlapping images, the material (so to speak) of which they are all composed:

> The other night I had a dream that I was sitting on the sidewalk on Moody Street, Pawtucketville, Lowell, Mass., with a pencil and paper in my hand saying to myself "Describe the wrinkly tar of this sidewalk, also the iron pickets of Textile Institute, or the doorway where Lousy and you and G.J.'s always sittin and dont stop to think of words when you do stop, just stop to think of the picture better—and let your mind off yourself in this work."

The method of stopping to clarify an image is used by many painters. If, as Kerouac states at the outset, "memory and dream are mingled in this mad universe," then all rational attempts to analyze such a chaos must be doomed. His painterly approach is thus integral to the theme presented in *Doctor Sax*. Painters do not try to capture reality by reflecting upon it, but rather immerse themselves in the immediacy of application, of putting pigment to canvas. In a similar way, the significance of *Doctor Sax* seeps out through Kerouac's intuitive arrangement of images. It is as valid for him to mix images drawn from reality, memory, and dream as for a painter to mix colors.

Doctor Sax is narrated in the first person, but during the course of the novel the reader is actually addressed by a number of different voices. For clarification the persona, Jackie Duluoz, who tells us his stories, will be referred to as "Jackie" or "the narrator." The man who is writing the novel, whose voice sometimes speaks over or through the persona, or directly to the reader in a theatrical aside, will be referred to as "the author" or "Kerouac."

In Book One of *Doctor Sax*, "Ghosts of the Pawtucketville Night," the narrator, Jackie Duluoz, explains the circumstances that led to his being haunted as a child. *Mystery* is one of the key words in this book. Since a mystery is simply something one doesn't understand, it is a natural circumstance in childhood. Quite realistically, Kerouac doesn't distinguish between the mysteries that children invent—such as the secret lives of imaginary beings—and real events and conditions they are too young to comprehend, like birth, sexual attraction, old age, and death. Thus in Kerouac's narrative real and imaginary characters populate the same time and space.

Indeed the child has the advantage over adults in this regard, for he operates with a unified sensibility and meets the world on his own creative terms. The child's dreaming is a way of meeting challenges, unlike the adult who compartmentalizes dreaming into the least important eight hours of his day. In *Doctor Sax* dreaming is equated with art, and the artist is identified with the perpetual child or, even more pertinently, with the child's fantasy. Doctor Sax, we learn, "looked a little like Carl Sandburg." Sax, of course, is also the name of an important instrument in the creation of modern jazz, so that the novel operates simultaneously as an allegory of the healing and invigorating powers of art. Jackie's friend Dicky Hampshire, a skilled cartoonist, boasts that as an artist he won't have to work in the mills but can live as he pleases.

Essentially *Doctor Sax* is a book about growing up; Kerouac later dubbed it a "puberty myth." Book One establishes the narrator's basic problem, which is change, and death as the most dreadful change of all. Horrified by his brother Gerard's death Jackie moves to Pawtucketville, where his new friends involve him in many exciting activities. But death intrudes again on his innocent happiness. A young friend, Zap Plouffe, is run over by a wagon. (The real "Zap," Ninip Houde, was actually seventeen when he died, not a "poor little boy," as Kerouac described him.) Jackie's father and a friend nearly drown. Neighbors die all around him. The Catholic Church insists he pay death his respects:

A kid across the street from Joe's died, we heard wailing; another kid in a street between Joe's and mine, died—rain, flowers—the smell of flowers—an old Legionnaire died, in blue gold horrors of cloth and velvet and insignias and paper-wreaths and the cadaverous death of satin pillows—Oh yoi yoi I hate that—my whole death and Sax is wound in satin coffins . . . they buried little boys in them . . . what a thing to gape at—AND THROUGH ROTTING SATIN.

I gave up the church to ease my horrors—too much candlelight, too much wax—

The escape back to life begins with the discovery of sex. Here we find Kerouac making yet another pun on "Doctor Sax," for this time it is sex that promises to cure his growing pains. Jackie and his friend Joe forget the scary sounds of night by playing with their "ding dongs." [188] Later, he and his friends relieve the boredom of summer evenings and rainy afternoons by having a "juvenile homosexual ball" or watching Zaza the idiot masturbate over and over. Not so dumb is this idiot, for he knows sex is the only alternative to death. One of the boys says of Zaza: "He'd rather jerk off than die." In short order, they all follow his example: "Later we simply forgot dark Saxes and hung ourselves on the kick of sex and adolescent lacerated love . . . where everafter the fellows disappear. . . ." The key discovery of Book One is that sex and all other "solutions" just lead back again to loss and death. Even the purest love, such as Jackie has for Ernie Malo, who resembles Gerard, forges no permanent bond. He accidentally hurts Ernie while they play, and soon Ernie becomes an unlovable "sour Yankee" anyway.[189]

The word *accident* is used repeatedly to describe even Jackie's conscious misdeeds, for though he seeks mischief he doesn't actually want to make anyone suffer and is often puzzled when suffering results from his waywardness:

I threw a piece of slate skimming in the air and accidentally caught Cy at the throat . . . Cy cried and bled into my mother's kitchen with that wound . . . my mother coaxes him to stop crying, bandages him, slate so neat and deadly everybody's mad at me . . . Bert Desjardins said "You should not do that."—Nobody could understand it was an accident.

Often, too, we cause pain through sheer ignorance. Stealing his friend Dicky's prize possessions, Jackie is amused by his terror, unaware that such betrayal will eventually make Dicky cry. As Jackie doesn't know why he hurts others, he also doesn't understand why others do harmful things to him. Punched in the face by a kid he hardly knows, he staggers home to his mother, wanting "to ask her why? why should he hit me?" Like Melville in *Billy Budd*, Kerouac inquires into "the mystery of iniquity," and like Dostoyevsky he finds only "universal guilt." Appropriately, biblical imagery of the Fall and the Flood—sin and retribution—contributute to the thematic development of *Doctor Sax*.

For Kerouac it makes no difference whether you lose your life or a childhood toy; the inevitability of loss is the principal tragedy. To recognize that man cannot escape loss is the fatal step from childhood to maturity, but that recognition is also a necessary preparation for the hardships ahead. Jackie comes of age when he loses the ball-bearing with which he plays his fanciful racing and baseball games. Kerouac describes the event in language redolent of Adam eating from the Tree of Knowledge of Good and Evil, and subsequently getting kicked out of the Garden:

> . . . there was something mysterious and shrouded and foreboding about this event which put an end to childish play—it made my eyes tired—"Wake up now Jack—face the awful world of black without your aeroplane balloons in your hand."—Behind the thudding apples of my ground, and his fence that shivers so, and winter on the pale horizon of autumn all hoary with his own news in a bigmitt cartoon editorial about storing up coal for the winter (Depression Themes, now it's atom-bomb bins in the cellar communist dope ring)—a huge goof to grow sick in your papers—behind winter my star sings, zings, I'm alright in my father's house. But doom came like a shot, when it did, like the foreboding said, and like is implied in the laugh of Doctor Sax as he glides among the muds where my ballbearing was lost. . . .

A child cannot ignore change. Growing up is also a process of losing one's illusions. At the conclusion of Book One, Jackie looks back on the childhood he's left:

> Little booble-face laughs, plays in the street, knows no different—Yet my father warned me for years, it's a dirty snaky deal with a fancy name—called L-I-F-E—more likely H-Y-P-E . . . How rotten the walls of life do get—how collapsed the tendon beam . . .

The pun on tendon-tenon neatly combines man's eventual loss of both body and property. But the greatest loss to the child is denoted by the word *hype*, for he has lost his sense of the world's reality. As he learns that life is made of no lasting substance, he finds himself dwelling among ghosts on a hollow globe, which offers no foundation for his own existence.

Throughout Book One, Kerouac has used his full range of techniques to illuminate the subjective nature of reality. In *Doctor Sax* time and space collapses become especially important because they permit Kerouac to speak without the limit of any single point of view. Already in *Visions of Cody* he was beginning to collapse the events in the story to the very moment of writing. In *Doctor Sax*, it is standard procedure for the narrator to draw upon the experiences of his whole life and of universal history, while supposedly telling about his childhood. In the past, critics spoke of "flashbacks" and "flash-forwards," but Kerouac's use of time and space collapses is more subtle and less awkward. Dependent upon emotion, the story flows through a train of memories and associations that is naturally outside time and place: "I saw my brother in a satin coffin, he was nine, he lay with the stillness of my former wife in her sleep. . . ." In addition, *Doctor Sax* is rife with the motifs that have by now become Kerouac's stock in trade: the slanting red sun of afternoon, red brick and red neon, light-in-darkness, rainy nights, roses, and rivers.

Kerouac shows his command of the idiom of Hollywood horror and violence in the thirties. He recreates a panoply of chichi villains ranging from the vampire Count Condu—as suave and glib as the various movie Draculas (and Kerouac had seen them all starting with *Nosferatu*), as primly dedicated as Eric Von Stroheim's prison commandant in *La Grande Illusion*—to La Contessa de Franziano, whose saccharine speech echoes any number of cinema seductresses: "Why Count . . . how you *do* manage to be vivacious before evening blood. . . ."

The trick, as every moviegoer knows, is to make the villains as extravagant, and hence as lovable, as the heroes. What we seek in movie stars, according to Quentin Crisp, is not morality but style. Sax is an engaging character not because he is the good guy, bent on foiling the Count and the Snake, at which he is notably unsuccessful anyway. What fascinates us in Sax is his dogged consistency. Based partially on W. C. Fields, Sax ignores his own ineptness and takes on the world by sheer force of personality. This Hollywood triumph lies at the core of *Doctor Sax*. The outcome of the stories—of Jackie and his friends, and of Jackie and Sax—matters less than their power to enchant us, to hold our interest. Asleep or awake, we persist in interpreting the visions that pass before us, as though consciousness merely translated between imagery and thought. It is the validity of these interpretations, these conceptions or fantasies, that Kerouac would test in *Doctor Sax*.

In Book Two, "A Gloomy Bookmovie," the narrator sees art as a means of carrying on his childhood game of imagining private worlds:

> I have a scheme to build bridges in the snow and let the gutter hollow canyons under . . . in the backyard of springtime baseball mud, I in the winter dig great steep Wall Streets in the snow and cut along giving them Alaskan names and avenues which is a game I'd still like to play—

Again we find Kerouac employing a form organic to the narrative, for he divides Book Two into cinematic "scenes" just as in childhood he allotted certain periods during each day to different activities. He intimates that we create our lives the way a director creates a movie. Our lives contain only those things we put in them. One of the marbles in Jackie's racing game is named Time Supply, and after describing it he remarks parenthetically, "no one else will ever name them." The very name of the marble reveals the crucial function of imagination. Time is the product of our fantasies, which "supply" it by filling the void with nameable, countable things.

Void is another key word in *Doctor Sax*. It signifies the primeval blankness, the screen on which are projected the mind's movies. What is ordinarily called the real world is also part of the void, which includes everything but the vision we momentarily hold in focus: "I dream of it [his desk] now on rainy nights turned almost vegetable by the open window, luridly green, as a tomato, as the rain falls in the block-hollow void outside all dank, adrip and dark. . . ." Because the moment, the explosion of insight and harmony, occurs in the void, it is always disconnected from the rest of our experience. And since we can understand nothing beyond it—indeed do not even understand the moment, simply perceive it—the closest we can come to true communication with another is when a moment is triggered in someone else by the same occasion that triggers it in us. Even so, such "telepathy" leaves two people no closer together, for by the conclusion of the moment both minds are lost again in the void:

> *"Il commence a tombez de la neige,"* someone is shouting in the background, coming in from the door ("Snow's startin to fall")—my father and I stand in that immobile instant communicating telepathic thought-paralysis, suspended in the void together, understanding something that's always already happened, wondering where we *were* now, joint reveries in a dumb stun in the cellar of men and smoke. . . . [italics mine]

At the end of Book Two, Kerouac reveals why the "bookmovie" is necessarily "gloomy." States the narrator: "In the fall of 1934 we took a grim voyage south in the rain to Rhode Island to see Time Supply win the Narragansett Special . . . a grim voyage, through exciting cities of great neons, Providence, the mist at the dim walls of great hotels, no Turkeys in the raw fog, no Roger Williams. . . ." The narrator's disillusion with America suggests that what is haunting him (and us) is the phantom suggestion that there is meaning to life. We learn that our lives should fall into a set of patterns, for example the heroic mold of our American forebears. We seem to sense patterns in the recurrence of certain experiences: *"I had seen it before,"* emphasizes the narrator, at the sight of a strange inn on the road. In the very last "scene," his mother is called to his father's social club to mend a tear in the pool-table cloth. There, far from the maternal, domestic lady she appeared at home in the opening "scenes," she now resembles a "great poolshark." On closer inspection, however, she reveals "the same sweet grave face you first saw in the window. . . ." But these patterns are always refractory; they refuse to yield their significance. At most they provide us with the realization of our mutual human ignorance, which is the sole content of those moments of telepathic insight.

Yet, if they give no answer, visions do confirm the existence of a question. They are proof of an ongoing mystery, the one irreducible fact we can hope to grasp. Mystery is where it's at, even if we don't know what "it" is. Though it cannot be solved, mystery can still be observed. With that in mind, the narrator announces: "I'm going on into the Shade."

Book Three, "More Ghosts," probes further into the alleged difference between fantasy and reality. If two such distinct poles could be identified, man's life could perhaps be located somewhere between them. In his racing game, the narrator tries to duplicate the conditions of real life. He chips his marbles so that they "go through processes of prime and decay like real horses." In that way he plans to create a destiny for each of them. Instead he ends up breaking too many and has to quit, and besides, boredom leads his mind to other concerns. Despite his playing God, the real world outside his window remains as mysterious as ever: "on the Boott Mills the great silent light shrouded the redbrick in a maze of haze sorrow, something mute but about to speak lurked in the sight of these silent glowing mills. . . ." The intuitive glimmers that come to him are nothing more than "the masturbatory surging triumph of the knowledge of reality," that is, a knowledge he has created within himself, and so unrelated to the mystery without.

The narrator begins to recount another time he played with fate, years earlier, by using his two hands to enact the drama of a Little Man pursued by a Great Bird. But one memory interrupts another, and suddenly the narrator is back in his thirteen-year-old present. At this point the author makes an editorial intrusion to inform us: "The very skeletal of the tale's beginning—" It is the Fourth of July Carnival, and the narrator tries to imitate the fireworks by a wild, zigzagging stream of language. But the moment is unfocused, characters wander in and out. "Beef," the neighbor he has started to describe, is suddenly an old man, and the narrator discovers he has nothing to say about him: "Beef is going into Eternity at his end without me—"

The narrative immediately dislocates to the Castle with its cast of fantasy characters. But the subject matter now has less to do with Jackie's childhood experiences, such as movies he's seen, and more with the author's own adult life outside the realm of the novel's twin plots.

Parodying John Holmes' 1949 verdict on hipsterism—"Something will come of it"—Count Condu says, "Of course that doesn't indicate that anything is going to come of these attempts." The Count's coffin has "Spenglerian metamorphosed scravenings on the lid." A new character is introduced, "our good friend Amadeus Baroque," who is a caricature of Alan Ansen. Amadeus Baroque—the name signifies something like "lover of the baroque God," or perhaps "to love God baroquely"—is an arty, affected homosexual who lounges in white silk pajamas and plays recherché records like an album of "Edith Piaf dying." The identification with Ansen is completed by the mention that Baroque has just completed litigation over "his mother's estate," for Ansen's wealthy aunt had also recently died, leaving him her estate in Woodmere. The discussion about the Dovist movement is a parody of current opinions about hipsters. Says the pragmatic Condu: "Dovists are after all mere lovers of—no different than the Brownings of other Romes, groaners of other gabbles. . . ." The Dovists also represent the Beat writers, like Kerouac and Ginsberg, who prophesy a shower of angelic blessings upon the horrors of their age. A Dovist poetic manifesto reads like much of the poetry Kerouac and Ginsberg were then writing: "On the Day, clouds of Seminal Gray Doves shall issue forth from the Snake's Mouth and it shall collapse in a prophetic Camp, they will rejoice and cry in the Golden Air, ' 'Twas but a husk of doves!' " The relegation of people into different factions smacks of Burroughs' cosmology, for Bill spoke of himself as part of a group of Factualists, who were opposed to other groups. From Kerouac's letters of this period, we know he was spending many hours listening to Bill. The character of Blook (bleak + spook) comes not from Jackie's childhood but from the author Kerouac's literary gambols years later—he appears, for example, in the play Kerouac composed jointly with Ginsberg, Holmes, Livornese, and White in 1949. The "peanut butter twigs" in Blook's hair were put there by surrealism, not a juvenile prank. The "stately lion" who descends into the cellar walked off the pages of Blake, whose work Kerouac was perusing as he wrote Doctor Sax.

The "skeletal of the tale" is something far different from plot. Within Book Three, the boy's simple fantasies, based on his limited experience, open into a hallucinated vision and allegory of the author's own life. To be sure, Kerouac's appropriation of his child-narrator's fantasies was implicit from the start. But the early Castle scenes at least bore some resemblance to what a child like Jackie might dream. In Book Three Kerouac cuts the last tie with any reality other than that in his head while he writes. Jackie's fantasy of Doctor Sax becomes as much Kerouac's literary property as is his own life. Both are melted down by the heat of his mature imagination, to be poured into a mold—the novel—which will at last reveal the truth they hide.

This remolding of experience is accomplished by reviewing it from new perspectives or with refined perception. In Doctor Sax,

Kerouac continually turns the "picture" upside down—a technique which will be developed further in future books—to show that the same "things" can have entirely different configurations: "seeing the Eagle was like suddenly realizing that the world was upside down and the bottom of the world was gold." The sophistication obtains chiefly from his ability to discover and emphasize motifs and to formulate them into coherent symbolisms. The same motifs and symbols pervade both plots, the realistic story and the fantasy, helping to unify them.

Color symbolism interpenetrates among the others. Brown, gray, and yellow are associated with the home, with nourishment and comfort (such as his mother's brown bathrobe), but also with mortal decay. Red is associated with business, social activities, and power (red brick mills, Jackie's red living room, Doctor Sax's laboratory). Green is associated with creativity, vigor, and the continuity of life (Jackie's desk, the pool table at the social club, the kitchen clock). White is the color of mystery (clouds; ghosts; the white sand of the sandbank where Doctor Sax first appeared). Blue and black when referring to darkness also signify mystery. Blue by itself reflects purity, and may suggest ethereal joy, but as the color of the sky or void it usually typifies qualities inhuman and austere ("the sky is piercingly heartbreakingly blue"). Black and purple express death, both its terror and the Church's morbid obsession with portraying it (Jackie's "phosphorescent Christ on a black-lacquered Cross"). Rose as a combination of white and red is a holy color, but one of sweetness rather than blinding light, the color of mediation between heaven and earth.

Most of these colors were used symbolically in Kerouac's earlier works too, but in *Doctor Sax* he makes prominent use of gold, a color that will take on increasing importance in future books. As a symbol of wealth, gold represents life's plentitude of visions: "Nights of 1922 when I was born, in the glittering unbelievable World of Gold and Rich Darkness of the Lowell of my prime father. . . ." Because gold is also a symbol of permanence, it suggests that those visions spring from an eternal fertility. Should each vision be of infinitesimal duration, the process of vision-making is still immortal. Gold thus becomes a symbol of ultimate spiritual hope.

Although Kerouac's attention to colors in *Doctor Sax* may have been influenced by his heavy use of marijuana while writing it, the technicolor vividness is highly appropriate to the novel's pictorial and cinematic structure. At the end of Book Three the full spectrum blazes from a montage of all his symbols of mystery, in one huge, baffling cosmic moment.

The moment begins in Jackie's waking dream about the alley where his father has a print shop. That alley is near the Keith's Theatre and the square with its red-neoned candy store. But Jackie's gay times there—going to shows, reading the funnies, drinking ice cream sodas—are darkened by sadder memories of rainy afternoons. His ambivalence is mirrored perfectly in the Marx Brothers movie *Animal Crackers*, which he saw at the Keith's: "Harpo . . . in a dark and unbelievably Doctor Sax garden where . . . God-Like the rain and sunshine just mixed for a Cosmic Joke by Chico 'Don't go out that door, it's raining—try this one'—tweet tweet birds—'see?' " Kerouac stages his own magical scene, where art mingles with life as the Marx Brothers and W. C. Fields walk the same alley as his father, a scene all the more eerie because none of the events are imaginary. Art does enter life, and affect it, just as life enters the work of art. At that wondrous point where they touch, the sorrow of life is redeemed. The past is not lost as long as it is available through memory and preserved in the tapestry of art. The act of summoning the past gives the narrator "inconceivable joy." No longer "a smalltown businessman in a smalltown," his mortal father now stands fixed in relation to the universe: "a man in a straw hat hurrying in a redbrick alley of Eternity."

The catch is that art is just another mirror of a reality inseparable from dream. As his father disappears into the printing plant, the narrator laments: "there's no telling what it is I really see in that dream—into the future really. Dreams are where participants in a drama recognize one another's death—there is no illusion of life in this Dream—" The only thing we know about these visions of life is that they end, that the void engulfs them, a "brown tragedy" against which the narrator fights desperately. In the final paragraph he musters a striking cavalcade of symbols, of all his known ways into the mystery of death:

W. C. Fields boards the "destiny train," which takes everyone to the same destination *à la* Wolfe. Night shadows red brick. Lamplight illuminates lonely windows. The winds of "winter night" howl under the Moody Street Bridge (established earlier in the novel as a symbol of death). Stars (true light) and moon (reflected light) shine down on the misty river, on both real ghosts and people merely shrouded in sleep. But as the ghosts of Jackie's father and W. C. Fields go their merry way, Sax grins—a taunt at the narrator's incomprehension. All his symbols are equally empty ghosts. Nothing remains for his own comfort in "the night of the cross eyed cat," this world of flawed vision. The art for which he had such high hopes is disparaged as "old musty records in the City Hall—an old, old book in the library files, with prints of Indians"—a laugh indeed to think such things could change the tenor of our existence.

The point is that symbols, however colorful, are ultimately meaningless until the central mystery of death can be explained. In Book Four, "The Night the Man With the Watermelon Died," the narrator is strolling across the Moody Street Bridge with his mother, gabbing happily "about the mysteries of life," when the man in front of them falls dead of a heart attack. Following the dead man's eyes, the narrator sees "the moon on shiny froth and rocks. . . ." That insubstantial vision reflecting in the eyes of a dead man, says the author, "is the long eternity we have been seeking." Since life cannot be grasped, there is no way to keep from losing it. Book Four chronicles the narrator's growing fear that he or his parents will die.

The color brown serves Kerouac well to show that death is an integral part of life, and vice versa. For while brown is the color of decay, it also betokens regeneration. It is, after all, the color of the earth, from whose compost of death springs new life. After the narrator recovers from the flu, and from his depression, by lying abed with his mother (Mother Earth?), his "resurrection" is imaged in brown: "There were Saturday mornings when a muddy brown pool was joyous to the test of squatting kids . . . as dewy and mornlike as brown mud water can get—with its reflected brown taffy clouds—"

Indeed the narrator begins to learn to welcome death, for the sake of the return to life it implies. But he doesn't want them separately. "Mell, river rose, mell," he apostrophizes. The rose, for all its suggestion of divine beauty, is also the classic symbol of mortal corruption. The narrator wants the universe to guarantee the flow of beauty, of life. Rereading Blake's poem "The Sick Rose," Kerouac felt Blake was foolish to dwell upon the death of roses, when all life and all material things go to destruction too. As he wrote to Ginsberg, modern man knows that Blake's "worm" is really the atom, which carries the law of dissolution within itself. By Einstein's equation, not just roses but all matter can vanish in a flash. The atom bomb becomes an increasingly important symbol in Kerouac's works of the fifties, as it became an increasingly greater threat to all human life. In *Doctor Sax*, the narrator says the loss of his ballbearing "turned my world upside down like the Atombomb." Despite the universal tendency toward annihilation (entropy), what is important to Kerouac is that roses do exist. The presence of a rose—if only for a little while—shows heaven's "grace."[190]

Kerouac's view of art in *Doctor Sax* shows a similar ambiguity. Art as an attempt to preserve the impermanent is doomed to fail; yet the momentary spell cast by art makes failure, as it makes time and loss, irrelevant. It is the spell, the sudden illumination, Kerouac celebrates as he explains how Jackie Duluoz (temporarily transformed into Amadeus Baroque) came to be the author of a book called *Doctor Sax*. Parodying Hawthorne's discovery of the Scarlet Letter and its history, which led him to write *The Scarlet Letter*, Kerouac describes Jackie's first encounter with the story of Doctor Sax in terms that suggest both the Fall and salvation:

One night long ago, in the thirties, in the height of the Depression a young man who was walking home . . . to a wretched furnished room over the Textile Lunch . . . saw a curlicueing yellow sheaf of papers sliding in the coldmoon January wind . . . What would anybody do seeing this thing, it was though it talked and begged to be picked up the way it sidled to him like a scorpion . . . he picked it up with his fingertips, he stooped to pluck it in his bearish coat, he saw it had writing on it . . . DOCTOR SAX . . . he briefly had time to read that ghoulish title, and undertucked the eerie manuscript which he'd plucked from tenemental coldnorth night of desolation like the Lamb is plucked from the black hills by the Grace of the Lord, and went home with it.

The "story within the story" frame reinforces Kerouac's concept of reality as mirror facing mirror. The recreation of the original manuscript of "Doctor Sax" allows him to parody his own mystification, adding yet another level of perception to the novel. In addition, he seizes the opportunity to parody the syllogistic, linear prose of his day:

Emilia St. Claire was a woman of whimsy; in this she was a tyrant, indeed a lovable tyrant. She could afford to be a tyrant for she was rich.

Parody and fantasy are products of the same vitality, which rearranges images of reality. Kerouac sees that power of mind as the lifegiving force. In Book Four, reading *The Shadow Magazine* helps the narrator overcome his horror at having seen the man die on the bridge: "death vanished into fantasies of life. . . ." Soon, however, the barbaric slaughter depicted in the movie *Trader Horn* renewed his fear of death. Because the knowledge of death continually dissatisfies us with life, Sax takes it upon himself to protect people from that knowledge. At the end of Book Four he declares: "these mortality rates—the children, the brown shroud of night—*meet* that I protect them from horrors they can not know. . . ." Sax embodies the will in man to interfere with natural process, to direct the cosmos, and as such he is the type of the artist. His foremost task is to abolish time. Sax's target, the Snake, which advances steadily toward humanity at an inch per hour, is like a giant clock.

That Sax's labors are superfluous is the point of the novel. While he makes a special trip to Mexico to do "special research on the culture of the eagle and the snake," the narrator merely looks into his mind's eye and observes events that took place thousands of years before: "on the windy top of the Pyramid of the Sun, just now, as I looked up from my chores . . . I saw the tiny movement and drowsy flutter of the priest up there cutting out some victim's heart. . . ." The image of an eagle holding a serpent, which originated in Aztec folklore and eventually became the national emblem of Mexico, lends even more significance to *Doctor Sax* since the serpent

Quetzalcoatl is regarded as both the destroyer of earth and the messiah of enlightenment. In a similar way, instead of struggling with dualisms, Kerouac unites them in the play of images. It is not correct to say that time doesn't exist in his works; rather, it exists as an infinity of levels that can be transcended in a moment, though not necessarily at will. What evolves in the novel, then, is a dialectic between the author and his hero over the issue of control. Their respective positions don't matter, but the pull back and forth creates a novel, a monument—like those stone snakes and eagles in Mexico—to the marvels of man's vision.

In Book Five, "The Flood," the narrator confronts natural "evil"—the harm that is wrought by forces outside man's control. Kerouac uses the flooding of the Merrimack River to reinforce the conception that life and death are part of one process, one flow. Throughout Book Five he refers to the Merrimack generically as the River, and both "River" and "Flood" are consistently capitalized to denote their universality. The narrator repeatedly remarks the river's brown color, since "brown" is by now Kerouac's code word for what Coleridge called "Life-in-Death." The shoreline battered by the raging river is called a "headstone" and a "bier of rock." The Life-in-Death theme is further emphasized by the fact that Sax lives underground in a "bier-shaped house," i.e., a grave. In this manner, he comes to represent Everyman, for all men live in their own grave, to the extent that they are aware of their imminent death.

The force that drives the flood is not alien to the narrator; on the contrary, it charges him with excitement too, and makes him crave a similar release: " 'Oh rose of the north, come down!' my soul I cried to the river—" The narrator is more than a vicarious participant in the river's orgy of fulfillment, for his sexual nature is now revealed as one with the cyclic rise and fall of the river. The river has developed just as Jackie has; Kerouac explicitly refers to its growth from an "infant childly phase." The river's ripe sexuality is betokened by the rose tossed into it by a "lover boy," who had originally intended the rose for his girl. The river is referred to as "swollen," like an engorged penis; above the river the clouds are "penetrated" by a shaft of light. Kerouac is reminding us that death is begotten in the same act that begets life. Earlier Jackie had told how his dog Beauty died the night he first masturbated, jesting with serious intent: "Beauty dies the night I discover sex, they wonder why I'm mad—" The personification of the river implies an organic flux in the universe itself. This sort of cosmic time collapse recalls Spengler's treatment of whole cultures as if they were organisms, with their future growth and decay genetically fixed at the moment of conception. Similarly Kerouac views man's consciousness as the rising and ebbing of visions. The essence of both life and the river is a pulse that precludes permanence.

The narrator sees the flood "as an evil monster bent on devouring everyone—for no special reason." But he also realizes that it does good by cleansing the earth of an oppressive civilization: "the demonic river—it's eating away everything that ever hated us—trees, houses, communities are capitulating." While the narrator is distressed by this paradox, Kerouac discerns that the confusion arises from a limited conception of reality. In the midst of Book Five, he makes a rather awkward editorial intrusion in order to present some poems explaining the problem.

"The Poems of the Night" and "The Song of the Myth of the Rainy Night" are Kerouac at his height of romantic bombast, when he is trying to write poetry somewhere between the seasoned gloom of Melville and the pithy allegories of Blake. Unfortunately he lacks both Melville's zingy wit and Blake's light touch. Nevertheless the poems are central to the novel, if only because they draw together its several themes, and preach acceptance, based on the relativity of all our perceptions: "Flaws in Heaven/Are no Pain." Do-gooders and evil-doers are united in the dance of life like islands in a sea: "Doctor Sax and Beelzabadoes the whirling polka/Gallipagos." The flood is merely "Liquid heaven in her drip," a sort of cosmic menstruation. The alternation between rain and evaporation typifies all other life cycles, including man's waking and sleeping: "Rain sleeps when the rain is over." Once again Kerouac quotes from the Dovists' verse (which possibly he is parodying): "Snake's not real,/'Twas a husk of doves." Those lines become the litany or mantra of the novel. Bringing images of light and darkness together, he insists that a unified sensibility can distinguish neither:

> The rain is really milk
> The night is really white
> The Shroud is really seen
> By the white eyes of the light

The final poem calls to readers to awake from the dream of reality with all its apparent dualities, by apprehending the source of both noumena and phenomena in the universal movie projector:

> Mix with the bone melt!
> Lute with the cry!
> So doth the rain blow down
> From all heaven's fantasy.

At the end of Book Five, Kerouac attributes the misery of modern America to its materialistic clinging to illusions. For all its progress, America is worse off than "primitive" societies, for it no longer knows why it is suffering and seeks reasons that are just further illusions. America's decline began with

. . . something hopeless, gray, dreary, nineteen-thirty-ish, lostish . . . Void of sweaty sticky clothes and dawg despair—something that can't possibly come back again in America and history, the gloom of the unaccomplished mudheap civilization when it gets caught with its pants down from a source it long lost contact with—City Hall golf politicians and clerks who also played golf complained that the river had drowned all the fairways and tees, these knickers types were disgruntled by natural phenomena.

Book Six, "The Castle," follows Jackie Duluoz's final steps to manhood. The narrator now seeks answers to life's mysteries in library books rather than movies. His growing cleverness is mimicked in a prose that cleverly mocks other writers. Parodying *For Whom the Bell Tolls*, Kerouac gibes at rationalistic Hemingway: "This was an afternoon of such bliss that the earth moved—actually moved, I knew why soon enough—Satan was beneath the rock and loam hungry to devour me. . . ." No such simpleton is Doctor Sax, but he too is an artist. We learn that Sax is an actor as well as a writer. It is his humorous interest in life that distinguishes him from the deadly serious, crime-solving Shadow of radio and comic book. Jackie has also chosen the path of art, and that is what makes the bond between Sax and himself:

And he [Sax] pulled out a mask of W. C. Fields with David Copperfield Mr. Swiggins hat and put it over the black part where his face was under the slouch hat. I gaped,—When I'd first heard the rustle of the bushes I thought it was The Shadow.
At that moment I knew that Doctor Sax was my friend.

The freedom of art, as opposed to the categories and restrictions of society, makes for a silly, Marx Brothers, nobody-gets-hurt slapstick. Jackie and Sax keep bumping and tripping, and for a moment Jackie becomes Groucho: "I'm gliding behind him slanted and leering. . . ." Doctor Sax camps, doing a Shadow laugh in a Canuck accent: "Moo-hoo-hoo-ha-ha-ha"! A local Canuck, who just made love with his girl "in a dirty barn in the Dracut Woods," somehow manages to kiss her good-bye "on a windy hill." During much of Book Six, the pain of life gets lost in all the fun. As a matter of fact, it was the section of the book Kerouac most enjoyed reading aloud.
Nevertheless the clowns say serious things. As Jackie and Sax peer into Gene Plouffe's bedroom window at night, seeing him engrossed in a *Star Western* story, Sax delivers his own version of "The Seven Ages of Man." But whereas Jacques in *As You Like It* teaches a stoical attitude toward growing old, Sax delivers a eulogy over the

loss of youth: "you'll never be as happy as you are now in your quiltish innocent book-devouring boyhood immortal night."

Book Six also sees the conclusion of Sax's attempts to destroy evil. Seeking unity, he is on the right track but his method is mistaken, for he simply plans to eliminate one half of the duality of good and evil: "Tonight," he says, "we make the worms unite in one pot of destruction." He is actually seeking to reverse the Fall, to return man permanently to the Edenic innocence of youth. But when Sax repudiates the sort of compassion taught by *On the Road*'s Walking Saint, even the narrator knows he has gotten too fanatical, and in effect joined the fiends he's fighting against:

> "Into that innocent land go as you are now, naked, when you go into the destruction of world snakes. Leery-head may moan, go ahead and do your groan, Leda and the Swan may moan, go a lone groan, listen to your *own* self—it ain't got nothin to do with what's around you, it's what you do inside at the controls of that locomotive crashing through life—"
>
> "Doctor Sax!" I cried "I don't understand what you're saying! You're mad! You're mad and I'm mad!"
>
> "Hee hee hee ha ya," he gaggled gispled, "this is the Moan victory."

All the same, Sax's madness is like the sound and fury of Groucho or Moe of the Three Stooges or W.C. in a tizzy, and it bespeaks as much inner gentleness as all the goofy clowning of a Saturday night in America. Kerouac specifies that the climactic events do take place on a Saturday night, a motif linking *Doctor Sax* to *Visions of Cody*. The variation consists in the fact that in *Visions of Cody* the protagonists seek the center of Saturday night, while in *Doctor Sax* they seek the source of evil, an interesting comment on Kerouac's lingering Puritanism. Yet above all Saturday night for Kerouac is movieland, so it's no surprise that Sax's lab looks like something out of Walt Disney, sporting a glowing red forge and a four-foot-high black cat. The Castle—replete with trapdoors, snakes, giant spiders and scorpions, and "a long file of gnomes pointing spears alternately at us and then at themselves in a little ceremony"—is unmistakably the Wicked Witch's castle in *The Wizard of Oz*, a film Kerouac saw just before he wrote the concluding scene to *Doctor Sax*. The relation to Kafka's Castle is evident too in the dreamy way Kerouac takes for granted his characters' non-sequiturs of speech and action.

As in *Visions of Cody*, the parodies run rampant as Kerouac builds toward climax. Jackie sounds like Huck Finn: "There were a thousand interesting things to notice." Sax instructing Jackie sounds like a blend of Captain Ahab and the doctor in *Nightwood*: "the shores of oceans will crash, in Southern Latitude climes, and the bark will plow thou hoary antique sea with a vast funebreal consonant splowsh of bow-foams—you're in on no mean squabble [with] the butcher's devil." The black cat talks like a "black cat" in a jazz club: "Oooh—Ah-man!", and he is at home in "The Blue Era" Doctor Sax creates by popping a blue balloon. The most pertinent parody is of the biblical end of the world. Sax's chemical jars are labeled in Hebrew, at the Castle people are whispering that it is "the last night," the Wizard plans to lead the Snake to Hebron.

From the Castle's parapet Jackie and Sax stare down into the eyes of the Snake. Sax tells Jackie: "The face of Satan stares you back, a huge and mookish thing, fool!" Sax's words are wiser than he is, for of course it is one's own face that is mirrored in another's eyes. Later the narrator has a clear realization—and this is the key to his gaining maturity—that the illusion of evil is within himself: "I looked down to face my horror, my tormentor, my mad-face demon mirror of myself." Mere knowledge cannot save the narrator, however, as he succumbs to his own Poeish helplessness: "I found myself looking into IT, I found myself compelled to fall." Man's guilt, such as it is, is as remote and unavoidable as Original Sin. According to the Wizard, the Snake's path—read: the birth of illusion—was "foreordained." Not surprisingly, when Sax dumps his blue potion ("blue"=jazz=art) on the Snake, it rises anyway. And the Snake radiates the color of life: "out came the great mountainous snake head slowly seeping from the earth like a gigantic worm coming out of an apple, but with great licking green tongue spitting fires. . . ."

It is the dawn of Easter Sunday. Doctor Sax suddenly looks like an ordinary man, like Bill Burroughs! The Snake is carried away by the Great Bird, a creature that originated in one of Jackie's earlier fantasies.

For Kerouac, man's salvation lies in the infinite levels of reality, symbolized by "the infinite number of levels in the Castle," where people on one level have no idea of what's going on elsewhere. Since all illusions are equally true and equally false, no single illusion can predominate or exclude any of the others. As Kerouac interprets the Resurrection of Christ, it is a parable of the inevitable fading of all illusions, including those of evil, sin, and suffering. Like the two Marys come to look for Christ's body, Kerouac reports of the Snake: "And I tell you I looked as long as I could and it was gone—absolutely gone."

Sax tacks a moral on the tale: "The Universe disposes of its own evil!" But the power of the ending is in a series of unifying images. While the Serpent soars with the Bird of Paradise, the Church announces Easter with "ding dong bells." Throughout the novel, "ding dong" was Kerouac's euphemism for *penis*, and the double entendre here conjoins the joy of body and spirit. In the last few lines of the novel, the narrator puts a rose in his hair, the rose itself a symbol merging carnal and spiritual beauty. But as he passes the Grotto with the Stations of the Cross, Jackie sees the French-Canadian women crawling on their knees, trying to do the same things with their prayers that Sax essayed with his potion: forfend evil, control the universe. So Jackie puts another rose in his hair in a final burlesque of dualism—two that equal one. He hastens to add, "By God," to show that it isn't disrespect he means, but a celebration of life in its original purity. That is the "home" to which he is returning. The way there can only be pictured, not explained, for while logic creates separations, the vision is always of one piece.

Significantly, Kerouac appends: "Written in Mexico City, Tenochtitlán, 1952/Ancient Capital of Azteca." The ancient Aztec capital, site of the modern city, was founded when the wandering tribe saw the prophesied sign of an eagle bearing aloft a serpent.

One would slight the magic quality of *Doctor Sax* not to mention the extraordinary range of the language itself. The novel contains a rich mixture of modern American idioms, traditional Yankeeisms, and Shakespearean grandiloquence, of neologisms and puns, even multilingual puns such as "alkalis of Hebron." There is also a healthy measure of self-parody, as when Kerouac recreates a *Star Western* story with the breathless race of dependent clauses that is the hallmark of his own prose: "Pete Vaquero Kid riding up a dry arroyo in the mesquite desolations of a flat table near Needle, the road to Needle angling off like a wriggly snake thru the brush humps of the desert below, suddenly 'Crack-Ow' a bullet pinged in the rock and Pete leveled with the dust in a flap of brushbeaten chaps and spur-jingles, lay still as a lizard in the sun."

The parody is all the funnier because Kerouac really had learned to write the fastest prose in American literature until that time. Not only do his jazz rhythms speed the pace, but his meanings are compacted with every device from the simple ellipsis common to American speech to poetic structures like synecdoche. In a few lines, for example, he can conjure a whole tenement neighborhood: "pots rattling in kitchens, complaints of an elder sister in the yard becoming a chant, which the littler ones accept, some with cat meows and sometimes actual cats to join in from their posts along the house and garbage cans—wrangles, African chatters at murky circles—moans of repliers, little coughs, mother-moans, pretty soon too late, go in and play no more. . . ." Add to these skills a virtuoso handling of alliteration, assonance, and other sound effects and it becomes clear why he told Lucien Carr a few years later, upon the publication of *Doctor Sax:* "It's the greatest book I ever wrote, or that I will write."

3.

Writing solely in pencil in his little notebooks, Jack finished *Doctor Sax* in two months, May and June of 1952. In little over one year he had produced three major works.

Pleasure came as easy for him now as work. A group of American hipsters and jazz musicians had descended on Mexico City. "Wig." a bass player whom Jack had known in San Francisco, connected with Burroughs for drugs and soon Jack was getting high with them and listening to Wig's record collection. They also gave him peyote, but after two trips he decided to quit because of stomach sickness. The teenage Indian prostitutes on Organo Street Jack seldom refused, since they cost from twelve to thirty-six cents apiece and caused him no distress other than a little guilt.

It wasn't guilt he suffered from but rather alienation. He felt betrayed and abandoned by all his friends. He had written to Neal and Carolyn twice and received no answer, and though the letters had merely failed to reach the Cassadys as they traveled between Tennessee and California, Jack's paranoia counter began clicking. He wrote Holmes that he "was never happier than in Frisco this past winter," but he had also been disturbed there by the "jealousy-kick" he felt growing in Neal. Before leaving he had told LuAnne that he didn't want to live in the Cassady household any more because Neal turned the *ménage à trois* into "a tempest in a teapot," just as he had with Jack and her. In a letter to Neal and Carolyn, he suggested they all try living together in Mexico for a while, but he also mentioned that he would travel a lot to places like Bangkok, Siam, and Butte, Montana! Returning to San Francisco to work on the railroad would be his "last resort."

To get out of his self-created obligation to Carolyn, Jack wrote her that he could never be a successful provider because he knew no practical trades as Neal did. He also explained that he would need what money he could make as a seaman to take care of his mother. He wanted to buy Mémère a trailer to put in his sister's back yard in North Carolina, which would serve as his home base too. In his usual passive posture, he agreed to accept whatever terms of love Neal and Carolyn might choose to offer him, but he expected no happiness. "I accept loss and death, and if you offer me some of your life I'm very grateful," he wrote, addressing both of them, "but I know that nothing will come of it, of life, but death. . . . Eternity is the only thing on my mind permanently. . . ."

New Orleans was the nearest port from which he could ship out, but he didn't even have six dollars for the second-class bus to get out of Mexico, so he could start hitchhiking. Because his mother wanted him to join the family in North Carolina for the Fourth of July, he decided to try shipping out from New York instead; also it was easier to get the M.C.S. Union jobs there. When the ten dollars Mémère sent him got stolen, he reluctantly wrote Neal asking for a loan of $20. Neal never sent it.

As Jack waited, his letter crossed with a letter from Carolyn that made him feel even worse. She described a family trip to Chinatown that had ended with Jamie spilling wonton soup on the seat of the car. The cozy domesticity she painted filled him with feelings of "doom." Reacting to her letter, Jack wrote Holmes that their family represented life to him, while for himself he saw nothing ahead but death. At thirty and still broke, Jack despaired to find that "my wife hates me and is trying to have me jailed, I have a daughter I'll never see, my old mother after all this time and work and worry and hopes is STILL working her ass off in a shoe shop. . . ." In great pain, he lamented that "nothing in life seems to want me or even remembers me."

Holmes had always been a stabilizing influence on him, but a serious misunderstanding threatened their friendship. Jack's feelings about the imminent publication of *Go* had been a volatile mixture of good will and jealousy—the latter fed by anger over his portrait in the novel, which seemed to imply that he had seduced Marian. The explosion came when Jack thought Holmes was about to steal material from him.

On May 28, Holmes wrote Jack that he was beginning work on the jazz novel he'd first sketched out in early 1950, "The Afternoon of a Tenor-Man." His conception of the book had become much more ambitious. Stretching the time span to include a night in the clubs, he planned to base characters on all the jazz stars of the time. Each would also represent a certain nineteenth-century American writer. The Charlie Parker figure would typify the brash, obsessed brilliance of Melville; the Billie Holiday figure would suggest a damned Emily Dickenson, and so forth. The novel would also contain supernumeraries like Jerry Newman, Seymour Wyse, Jack, and John. Holmes' thesis, however, was unchanged from the early notes he had sent Jack; it was "that jazz musicians most perfectly epitomize the sorry, and often fabulous, condition of the artist in America."

Holmes seemed to be treading on ground Jack had staked out for a proposed novel called "Hold Your Horn High" (which he now thought to call "Blow Baby Blow"). Jack felt John was breaking an agreement he had made to let Jack do the history of jazz. More disturbing was Holmes' intention to use a story about Billie and Lester that Jack had told him. Still, Jack thought it possible for both of them to do jazz novels, as long as Holmes dealt chiefly with jazz as a social phenomenon, leaving Jack the spiritual aspects: the "mystery" of "jazz characters" interacting, and the evolution from joyous to cool.[191] The problem, Jack explained in a letter to Holmes, was that plot ideas were what interested publishers; and if John took away one of his best plots, he'd be taking money out of Jack's pocket.

On June 9, Holmes sent Jack a copy of what he'd written, promising: "I will do nothing, agent, magazine, or mss. wise, with this until I hear from you." He was wounded by Jack's insults, such as the comment that John's literary comparisons were "slapped-on." Jack had also hinted at his ingratitude, mentioning a scene of New Year's Eve, 1948, that he had left out of *On the Road* because John had covered that "territory" in *Go*. What hurt John most, though, was that Jack could believe him capable of such disloyalty. John reaffirmed his respect for Jack's talent and dedication: "I have always thought you were born to write great, big novels and give back to American literature what it lost thru the hung-up Hemingways. . . ." In conclusion, he recommended Jack stop worrying about plagiarism and get on with writing his *Comédie Humaine* about "the generation of hip kids": "You're the only guy I know who could do it and never run out of something terrific to put in a book, even after the thirtieth one."

Holmes' letter effected a tenuous reconciliation. Jack agreed to swap subjects: "so you give me the Hip Generation idea, which I already had partially in mind as a super T & C with homegrounds in Kansas and bop brothers etc., and accept from me the jazz book idea." Nevertheless, his reply betrays an undercurrent of hostility. A large part of the friction came from John's failure to understand the difficult innovations Jack was undertaking. John himself wasn't interested in developing new novelistic forms, and he only saw that Jack's writing seemed to be getting "clogged"[192] with technical problems: "stop beating your head against those stones down there . . . much that you say about forms, and truth, and the 'arbitrary confines of a story' is the standard back-chat at the Remo every night." No wonder that Jack, in turn, gave Holmes left-handed compliments—such as the suggestion that Holmes had finally reached the place where Jack was four years before. Jack further remarked that Holmes' story seemed "exactly what I was on my way to do with Ray Smith Red Moultrie On the Road." By contrast, what Jack was now doing, he boasted, was "a general lassooing of the meaning in heaven and in the air kind of hallucinated, clairvoyant type trance yeats prose which I call modern prose now. . . ."

Jack's bitterness also emerged in a caricature of Holmes in *Doctor Sax*. Referring to the night in 1936 when they both walked along flooded rivers, Jack describes Holmes as a sissy with perfume in his hair and a shimmying walk. He calls this character "Eugene Pasternak," the name Holmes gave him in *Go*. The high water mark of Jack's paranoia came on June 23, when he wrote Carolyn that "Holmes has started publishing jazz stories THAT I MYSELF TOLD HIM, imagine the gall." Such was Kerouac's Canuck defensiveness that he could actually talk himself into believing that his worst fears had come to pass, while with the rational half of his mind he knew full well that most of his fears were unfounded.

Proof that Jack still trusted Holmes is in the letters Jack continued to write him, confiding his most intimate hopes and sorrows. Indeed it was to Holmes that Jack revealed the source of his madness. Asserting that he still believed in the existence of his own talent, Jack confessed that the creation of "lyric epic novels" could never overcome his feeling of "doom and despair on all sides waiting for everybody and especially for me who am so alone." He claimed that the effort he had expended writing three full-length novels since March 1951, combined with the icy reception given all of them, had left him "the loneliest writer in America."

The full force of Jack's hate was toward the publishing industry. Having finally received the *Visions of Cody* manuscript, Solomon and Ginsberg concurred that it was unpublishable and that Jack could do better. Although Allen sensed its greatness, he believed Jack "was not experimenting and exploring in new deep form, he was purposely just screwing around as if anything he did no matter what he did, was O.K." He and Solomon also completely ignored Jack's detailed accounts of his progress on *Doctor Sax*, and Jack felt they were infected with the bourgeois ethic of publishers. In his letter to Holmes, Jack predicted that the only way he could get such books published would be to die, so that the book jackets could read "published posthumously," guaranteeing a good sale. Giroux, the one editor he had thought his friend, seemed as blind as the rest: "Giroux not only feels that I am irresponsible and 'uncooperative' but also that if I could write a great book still I wouldn't do it out of sheer irresponsible spite and no-goodness." Jack saw only two alternatives for himself. Either he could let people steal his ideas and "die in disgrace, poverty, and loneliness," he told Holmes, "like Wilhelm Reich"; or, as he wrote to Carolyn, he could go to New York and commence punching editors in the nose.

His surliness and self-pity made him a poor house guest, and during June his relationship with Burroughs also deteriorated. Bill got a little tired of hearing him complain about the injustices done him. Jack had also grown rather hypochondriacal, worrying that he might get sick from "dirty food" and lamenting the lack of good American sanitation. The basic problem, though, was that Jack hadn't a cent left and was letting Bill support him. Bill himself was burdened with legal fees and the high cost of bail. Since Jack was virtually starving—down from 170 to 158 pounds—he felt justified in eating any food in the house. When Burroughs began hiding his half of the food, Jack thought Bill had "joined the sinister forces working against him." [193] These neurotic fears suited Bill just fine. He even began describing the boa constrictors, malaria, and murderous tribes of the Ecuadorian jungle, to discourage Jack from joining him on the projected expedition.[194]

Jack had to get out. Despite Neal's assurance that Jack could make $2,000 by Christmas if he'd return to work on the railroad, he chose to go home to his sister and mother. His only fear, he wrote Allen, was that he would end up being crazy, or a bum, or "an old slob, a fart in the middle of an autograph party." To forestall any of those ends, he sought "my Hut," the detachment of a self-reliant literary hermit, like Thoreau. He borrowed $20 from Bill with the promise to repay it as soon as he got a job, and left Mexico City on July 3, bound for Rocky Mount, North Carolina. His destination a secret because of Joan, he wrote Neal and Carolyn that he was going to live in a valley with the Indians.

Around mid-July, he made a brief trip from Rocky Mount to New York. Even in the depths of his gloom he never imagined the icy reception he would receive there. Allen told him that the new *On the Road* was "imperfect," and seemed to consider it "an undigested mass of images and references." Solomon smugly rejected the novel on the grounds that it wouldn't be acceptable on most book stands. *Doctor Sax* drew Carl's sneering insults. More than ever Jack felt like a peasant, a Lil Abner among slick, pitiless Jewish businessmen, and he recalled his humiliation by "the millionaire Jews of Horace Mann." At Harcourt Brace he got a different sort of jolt when he learned that two different sets of lawyers had hunted him there— Joan's investigators had been joined by his first wife's attorneys. Edie, however, merely wanted to have their marriage invalidated by the Catholic Church so that she could remarry a Catholic. Perhaps the cruelest blow came from his own mother, who was still living in Richmond Hill. Hearing of his obstinate refusal to cooperate with editors, Mémère declared that Jack's 1939 Vermont car crash must have damaged his brain.

About the only person in New York Jack really enjoyed seeing again was Gregory Corso. Although Jack got a little irritated with Corso's ostentatious talk of "Tannhäuser chariots," he sympathized with Gregory's poor background and Italian simplicity.

Sexually Corso was interested exclusively in girls, but he would occasionally let gay men like Allen have their pleasure with him. What disenchanted Corso with Allen—though it never disturbed the higher, poetic level of their friendship—was that Allen talked freely about his sexual experiences with his men friends. Reviewing the situation twenty-five years later, Corso explained: "Allen's got that kind of brain—he likes to open up the brain and find out why this person is this way. He figures it's allowable because he so checks himself out . . . he says he's homosexual . . . he lays his heart bare; therefore others should be laid bare." [195] The result, whether Allen planned it or not, was that he gained a certain control over those who were close to him. Corso also claims Allen would sometimes manipulate friends into bed on the pretext of making them good poets. He resented Allen posing as "Grandma Ginsie," and Allen's gossip struck him as worse than an imposition; to one raised in the closemouthed Italian tradition, "finking" on a friend was something you did only at gunpoint, if at all. By contrast, Jack pleased Corso with his shyness and Catholic reserve about such matters. He and Jack were both uncomfortable being sex objects to other men, and they commiserated with each other over having to barter their sexuality for artistic recognition.

By the end of July, Jack had returned to his sister's house in Rocky Mount. From a letter he wrote to Allen, it would appear Wyn was reconsidering *Visions of Cody.* He got a temporary job that paid well, and applied for work on the local railroad. But home had none of the welcome he'd expected, and he felt like the proverbial prophet without honor especially in his own family. His sister lacked sympathy for his problems and seemed to think his current lifestyle "queer"; her continual talk about money worries seemed like a hint for him to get going. Jack was anxious for a real home like he'd had with the Cassadys.

He had given Neal's name as a reference for the railroad job. In late August, when Neal got wind of Jack's whereabouts, he wrote urging him to return to California immediately in order to get hired as a brakeman on the Southern Pacific. The S.P. was hiring brakemen through mid-September, and although they wouldn't accept men thirty years old or over as trainees, Neal assured Jack that Al Hinkle's uncle, a head conductor, could get the railroad to make an exception for him. Neal and his family had moved into an eight-room house in San Jose, and once again he offered Jack a place to live, this time openly baiting the hook with the promise to share Carolyn. When Jack decided to take Neal's advice, his mother was furious. Mémère wrote him: "So you want to roam and leave—well, *don't you dare do anything that will dishonor your father's name.*" She was especially upset that he would rejoin his black friends there—she'd undoubtedly heard him talking about Al Sublette—and she sent him a clipping about rape in the subway with her own caption: "There's your damned niggers!"

Neal sent Jack some old railroad passes and a Trainmen's Brotherhood button, with instructions in how to talk his way into free train rides, but Jack was too shy to pull off such scams and preferred to hitch. Leaving Rocky Mount with five dollars, he promised to send Nin and Paul presents from China. "Never mind presents from China," Nin replied, "just mail me fifty dollars room and board for the month of August."

The last of his glory from *The Town and the City* seemed to wash out in the drenching rain on the road west. Eating out of cans, sleeping on railroad platforms, he spent a day getting over the Smokies, but then his luck changed when a kid in an Olds 88 convertible took him to Kansas City. Justin Brierly wired him money to get to Denver, where he was cared for by Ed White and Beverly Burford, and for a whole day sketched locales known to Neal. On September 2, Neal wired him $25 for bus fare, but he held onto the money and hitched to California. In San Francisco he caught the Zipper to San Jose, where he was met by Neal and Carolyn in their Model A Ford. Neal and Jack pounded each other on the back. Since Neal was on his way to work, Carolyn provided the rest of the welcome in the back seat of the Model A.

Once again, Jack could hardly get his fill of playing with the Cassady children—sitting them on his knees, telling them stories, taking them for walks. Jack's love for Carolyn blossomed now too, and they had their most tender times together: late-night dinners and lovemaking while Neal was away, with Carolyn slipping back into her own bed lest the children discover her with Jack. He and Neal got on well again too. They took turns reading into the tape recorder—Neal trying to do Proust's sentences in one breath and Jack doing *Doctor Sax* in a Fieldsian accent, to a chorus of encouraging "yeah's" from Neal. The three of them performed more Shakespearean plays together, and fooled around at the tennis court of the high school next door. Jack and Neal planned to watch football games there, even if Neal's enthusiasm ran more to the "young stuff in filmy sheer no underclothes dresses." [196]

Jack balked at beginning his student trips on the railroad, but Neal prodded him to it; and when Jack proved awkward and slow to learn, Neal coached him. But Jack was hampered by his fear of the wheels, and he was always so preoccupied with his writing that Carolyn thought it a miracle he didn't get run over. Neal was a highly efficient brakeman, and it irritated him that his "brother" couldn't keep up. To get Jack to improve he began to razz him about his clumsiness. Although Jack laughed at such criticism he was deeply hurt by it too, and ashamed that he couldn't be a sharp worker like Neal. Still, however proud Jack was when he finally became a "genu-wine brakie," the railroad meant only a source of material for his writing, and a source of income.

The real misery of railroad work for Jack was the complete lack of tenderness in his earthy, burly co-workers. Trainmen gave everybody a nickname, and once you accepted it and laughed with them, they'd take care of you for life. But Jack could never bear teasing, and he got sore every time they called him "Caraway Seed." Marking him for a dreamer they tended to leave him alone, making him feel more of an exile.

His dislike of the railroad left him all the more dependent on Carolyn's sympathetic ear, and Neal again envied their closeness. As always, Neal wanted to get in on the act, and one night he tried to promote a three-way ball, but Jack guiltily reverted to his old role of observer, and was incapable of functioning sexually. In any case, Neal's jealousy continued to grow, especially since Jack had stopped helping him sneak away to his girlfriends and good times in San Francisco. They began to take out their frustrations on each other.

Neal wisecracked about Jack's position in the family. He still supported Jack's writing—that, in fact, was the only constant of their twenty-year relationship—but he no longer wanted to talk about literature, which hurt Jack precisely because Neal had been the one person who would always give his ideas a sensitive and impartial hearing. Now, as soon as Jack mentioned writing, Neal changed the subject to money or work or bills. After a row about groceries, Jack bought a hot plate to cook in his own room.

They all realized the current situation had to end, and Jack thought the solution might be for Carolyn to have "one husband at a time." [197] He suggested she spend several months with him in Mexico, after the railroad began winter layoffs. At first Carolyn was shocked at the idea of leaving her children, but Jack convinced her that she needed a vacation. Moreover, she assumed he knew how far they could go without angering Neal. Indeed the minute Neal heard the plan he endorsed it.

But the truth was that Jack's proposal to Carolyn, and her acceptance, was more than Neal could handle. His strategy had backfired. He always believed in pushing his men friends and his women together under the assumption that they wouldn't be capable of real infidelity as long as he was overseeing it. He also took great pride in his superior "capacity" to satisfy women—he believed that once a woman had slept with him she wouldn't want to have sex with anyone else.[198] Carolyn's romance with Jack bewildered him, and, worse, left him feeling martyred.

One night, as Neal related to Al Hinkle, he was so upset to find Jack and Carolyn in bed that he berated Jack for stealing his wife. The next morning, Jack asked Neal to drive him to Skid Row in San Francisco, and not a word passed between them all the way there.

4.

Neal made it clear that he was glad to be rid of "bumbling Jack," who was such a disappointment to him. Yet Carolyn knew he was feeling a little guilty about hurting Jack, and Neal himself wrote to Allen about their troubles, doubtless hoping Allen could again act as intermediary. Jack too leaned toward forgiveness almost from the moment he left. And both tacitly understood that going to Skid Row was actually a way for Jack to get closer to Neal, in the sense of returning to Neal's origins.[199]

In early October, 1952, Jack moved into the Cameo Hotel near Third and Howard Streets. Not only did he choose to live among bums, he now identified with them; when Carolyn came to visit him there he carried a poorboy of Tokay wine around all day, even though he seldom drank from it. She was terrified to be in such a place and distraught to think of Jack *living* there, but the trappings of bums were now his security blanket, and the poorboy a kind of baby bottle. Jack believed he could never present the "dignified front" of author, as Thomas Wolfe had, that he could only be accepted among the "Indians" or "hoboes"—whom he saw as one nation of the heart.[200] Darkly he speculated, in a letter to Holmes, that were it not for his mother and the job on the railroad, people would instantly recognize him as a bum.

The irony dogging Jack's friendship with John now turned up in the form of a $20,000 paperback contract from Bantam Books for *Go*. When John received his first installment of $9,000 he immediately thought of Jack, who had told stories of eating grass in Mexico during the previous summer. Actually Jack was now earning $600 a month, but John sent him $50 in case he was still broke. Jack thanked him for the money, promising to add it to his "winter-writing stake." He also apologized for his nasty remarks about *Go* and his later accusations. Among all his friends, Jack wrote, only Holmes had shown himself "humane" and "a goodhearted fellow." To prove his point, Jack indulged—as he rarely did—in belittling his other friends. He called Burroughs "a vacuous old fool." He called Neal "a real asshole" with "the soul of a baboon," and regretted that Neal had conned him "like a yokel into listening to his crap & believing in his kind of franticness & silly sexfiend ideas." He claimed that Allen's kindliness covered secret hate.

Allen caught a blast for the letter he had written criticizing *Visions of Cody*. Trying to steer Jack back to a more conventionally plotted novel, he stated that there was nothing in this new work that he didn't already know about Neal. What Jack hated most was disingenuousness, and he couldn't believe that Allen and Carl with all their sophisticated appreciation of Genet and the surrealists couldn't see his own technical breakthroughs. He smelled jealousy and greed, felt used by "parasites," and saw himself the aging, soon-to-be-supplanted minion of a group of homosexuals. His scorching reply to Allen cited grievances against almost all his friends including Lucien, whom he charged with making him cry over Sara just to feed his own ego. Threatening to beat up Allen if they should meet again, Jack enjoined him to leave him alone forever.

Remembering what Hal Chase had told him about an artist's need to choose between integrity and commercial success, Jack decided to get tough. At MCA, his manuscripts had been passed along to Phyllis Jackson, Holmes' agent, and Jack asked Holmes to give her a list of instructions. To avoid having to revise his spontaneous works, he suggested she try to sell reprint rights to *The Town and the City*. He told Holmes he didn't care if *Doctor Sax* didn't get published until 1975, but was confident it would be accepted sooner because of its "science fiction" ending.[201]

Writing in his little notebooks in his hotel or in the rail yards—

where the other employees thought he was jotting his work record, since they all kept notebooks for that purpose—Jack began a new novel about the "hip generation." He projected a book as large as *The Town and the City*, which would contain a new fictional family based on friends like Lucien, Bill, and Neal. But in spite of his intention to write a topical novel, his mind kept reverting to the warmth of family and early friends, the Lowell womb that charged all his later experiences with memories of a paradise lost. Living on Skid Row, he was thinking now of the cheap hotel rooms he and his parents had occupied after leaving Lowell. He remembered the way his father would say "Perk up, Jackie, *pauvre* Jackie, we won't always be poor and abandoned," and the way his mother would cheerfully set out cold little suppers and say, *"Oui,* and look, here's the bread, the ham, the butter, the coffee, the little cups, we've got everything we need." Working on the Southern Pacific, he wondered if he might not have been happier marrying Mary Carney and going to work with her father and brothers on the Boston and Maine Railroad.

Some critics have tried to divide Kerouac's oeuvre systematically into "Beat" and "Lowell" novels, but in fact the strength of *The Duluoz Legend* and the integrity of its vision of America obtain from the fact that Jack was never capable of making such a distinction. Unconsciously, for the most part, he was defining the *Legend's* central theme—which might be termed "the loss of life as it is lived"— through the very intensity and urgency of his drive to get it down. The theme had strong ironic implications for his life as well as his art, and doubtless developed out of his need to bring the two into some kind of viable balance. His art became a means to help him survive. The more he lived, the more he would lose, and hence the more he would have to write about.

There was no more reason to restrain his excesses, to hold anything in reserve. He opened the floodgates to the energy boiling inside him, confident that whatever shape it came out in would be *the* form he wanted for his art. Some days he worked on the railroad twenty-four hours straight. The time he wasn't working or writing he walked the streets, talked with bums, and got drunk in his favorite bar at Third and Howard. Even in bed he could scarcely afford to sleep when there was so much life to be known. He'd lie awake listening to jazz on the radio, sipping his Tokay, and thinking thoughts like: "Some lost song is beating in my soul, that I have not sung, and cannot sing—the star of my fame and pity rides high and lonesome in this California night—" [202]

Jack was seldom late for work. To allow himself the maximum amount of sleep, he adhered to a strict schedule for making breakfast and getting to the station, cutting his margins so close that once, as he arrived, his train was already pulling out. He tried sprinting after it, failed to catch it, and instead caught hell from the conductor. He should have returned to the crew dispatcher, who could have put him on a faster train to Bayshore, where his local made its first stop. But Jack took a professional pride in doing things the hard way.

His goal was to "live life close to the bone," as Thoreau termed it; and a large part of his program, like Thoreau's, was to live as cheaply as possible. When he was in Watsonville, at the other end of the "chain-gang run," he'd often save the nominal cost of the trainmen's dorm by sleeping in the caboose or among the hoboes in the Pajaro River bottom. For meals on the job he'd stop in grocery stores for cheese and crackers. In his hotel room he usually cooked his own breakfast, and he even stinted on equipment, struggling to make his toast on a wire looped over the hotplate. Breakfast at home cost him only thirty-six cents, though once in a while he'd splurge on a sixty-cent breakfast at the Public Restaurant—where everything but the beefstew was edible, so long as you didn't get too nauseated watching the bums puke. To keep his total living expenses below $17 a week—and he often kept them down to $13—Jack would endure any suffering. When he lost his railroad gloves he forced himself to bare-hand cold steel for weeks until he found two mismatched gloves other men had lost.

Hardship he was built to endure, but the emotional cost of independence was higher than he'd reckoned. One day he told Al Hinkle that he expected to die young like Thomas Wolfe, adding that Neal would die young too. Hinkle scoffed: "You just can't face the prospect of anybody getting middle-aged." Jack objected that he could very well imagine Ginsberg and Burroughs living to a ripe old age. He insisted that he had a "vision" of his own existence being cut short, and that such a fate was inevitable. But his stoicism went to pieces when they started talking about their parents. Jack related how he'd gotten the spirit of adventure from his father, how much he wanted to emulate him, and how he often wondered if he were living up to his example. Then he started to cry.

Violence was sometimes just beneath the surface of his gaiety. At an after-hours place with Hinkle, Jack smuggled in his own bottle, and they stayed for several hours listening to an Italian quartet. Seated right in front of the sax player, Jack kept leading him and at the same time swigging steadily from the bottle. When the musicians went on their break at four-thirty, the sax player came over and after a few words punched Jack in the nose. Very drunk, Jack swung back and missed, and he and Al were both thrown out. Jack decided to wait for the musicians, and he wanted Al to help him beat them up, because in his view the attack had been unprovoked. Since there had been only a handful of customers in the club, Al suggested that the musicians might have been mad that he and Jack had spent only fifty cents there. Still dumbfounded, Jack complained, "Yeah, but I was really groovin' with him on that saxophone!" Al finally talked him into leaving, although Jack continued to anguish that he could be so misunderstood.

Jack's suppressed aggression kept the feud with Neal simmering. He wanted to assert his right to Carolyn's love, but he always felt he had to back away from Neal; and so although he continued to visit her, they mostly just drank wine together and showed affection. His sexual advances to her lessened, and since she wasn't interested in him sexually she didn't encourage him. Unable to be a tough guy himself, Jack deprecated Neal's "familiar American pseudo-virility of workingmen and basketball players"; [203] but the fact that Neal could fill those shoes and he couldn't increased his frustration and gloom. At the house in San Jose Carolyn once watched Jack brooding for hours, thinking he was musing over some literary problem. Finally he asked her to perform a certain sexual service, because that alone could cheer him up. She refused.[204]

It seemed like the final breakdown in communication when Neal hung up the phone on him; but not long afterward, when Jack was sleeping on the couch in the trainmen's lounge in San Jose, he was waked by Neal's laughter. "*There* you are, buddy! Come on, now, come on, now, no words, come on, now," Neal said,[205] and began to talk him into moving back. It was early November, and Jack must have been glad to get out of San Francisco's cold, rainy season. Still misanthropic at the house, he softened a little when Neal enthusiastically read portions of *Visions of Cody* into the tape recorder.

He made peace with Allen too. For weeks he had been repenting his angry letter, and the balance tipped toward apology when he received Allen's intelligent appreciation of *Doctor Sax*. But Jack split the humble pie, reminding Allen that the power of their works had derived originally from love and not the "paraphernalia of criticism." He chided Allen for viewing literature like a political reformer searching for needed improvements, and explained that such preconceptions would keep him from contacting what was fresh in his writing: the sounds and images turned up by the cutting edge of his "Pre-Literary" mind. The whole point of Jack's current writing method was to rediscover the way he had thought before he "learned the words the litterateurs [*sic*] use to describe what they're doing." [206]

Put simply, Jack's methodology was broader than the conventional criticism with which Allen had tried to compass it. To awaken him to this fact, Jack cited a couple of the new areas of experience that he was bringing into his art. One was the voice of early childhood, which was easier for him to isolate than for most, since for him it always spoke in French. Another was the realm of accident. He had permitted accident to influence the composition of *Doctor Sax*, for example, by ending a chapter whenever Burroughs would interrupt him. Before the breakthroughs of abstract expressionist painting, such lapses of conscious craft were considered irresponsible artistry, although Joyce had already incorporated chance fragments of conversation into *Finnegans Wake*. De Kooning, Kline, Pollock, and their confreres showed accident to be one of the directest routes into an artist's unconscious.

Now that the first shock waves of rejection were quieting down, Jack was also able to put aside his remaining quibbles with Holmes. He wrote Allen that he respected the sincerity of *Go*, the more so in comparison with the works of celebrated authors like Truman Capote. Holmes' article "This Is the Beat Generation," published in *The New York Times* on November 16, made Jack feel even more kindly toward him.

Use of the phrase "beat generation" in *Go* had piqued *Times* editor Gilbert Millstein to ask Holmes for an article defining it. Not only did Holmes credit Kerouac with the epithet, but he showed a more sophisticated understanding of the dynamics of beatness than Jack had previously allowed. Asserting that "the problem of modern life is essentially a spiritual problem," Holmes grasped the Spenglerian concept of a "Second Religiousness," which allegedly overtakes all late civilizations. His existential bias, to which Jack was indifferent, had taken a turn toward the faith and vulnerability Jack and Allen had first found on Times Square, in the community of thieves, hustlers, prostitutes, and junkies. Jack kidded John about trying to include the "Young Republicans" in this coterie. But Jack can only have agreed whole-heartedly when Holmes saw the Beat Generation as life-affirming rather than life-evading or life-denying: "They drink to 'come down' or to 'get high,' not to illustrate anything. Their excursions into drugs or promiscuity come out of curiosity, not disillusionment."

One of the article's benefits to Jack was a letter from an admirer in Lowell. Stella Sampas, Sammy's younger sister, wrote how pleased she was that the literary world wasn't entirely ignoring him, who had so much to give "us poor mortals."

5.

That fall Jack began a long impressionistic account of his life on the railroad, "Wine in the Railroad Earth" (later published as *October in the Railroad Earth*). He didn't yet think of it as a separate piece but rather as part of the epic novel of his own life, which for lack of a real title he was calling "the Duluoz Life." His idea was to have one large central novel, identifying the places and people in his private history. Further books could then be "dense spates from this Duluoz World, such as *Dr Sax* already is, & *Road* of Neal visions."

In "The Railroad Earth," he already permitted himself a good measure of denseness. He had learned from Proust that once the nature of the writer's consciousness is established, he is then free to simply perceive, and need not analyze or evaluate. "The Railroad Earth" marks another watershed, in that he no longer felt the need to set up characters and situations, as he had done to some degree in all his previous novels. This piece is actually a novella that fuses stream-of-consciousness and old-fashioned storytelling. It is full of incidents, but the incidents have no causal ties to any world other than that in the writer's mind.

In terms of the actual prose, Kerouac makes no effort to end a sentence where it "should" end grammatically, logically, or by any other standard. As long as his mind continues to run on, so does the sentence. He is pushing English syntax beyond the bugbear of "run-on sentence" to see how far a thought can actually go before miring in unintelligibility. Carried by the natural rhythms of thought and speech, and the mind's capacity to mock the rhythm of what it thinks about—driven mostly, in this case, by the staccato beat of freight trains—some of Kerouac's sentences roll on for a whole page. Unquestionably he demands one's sharpest attention to follow them to their conclusion, but the diligent reader is almost always rewarded with an unexpected increment of meaning that no series of simple sentences could have provided. These spontaneous bursts of thought unfold like a flower from the bud of some very condensed idea, in petal after petal organized by their structural necessity to a single image. Amid such complex sentences Kerouac salts little talky repetitions, ballad-like refrains, so that if the prose doesn't make book sense, it always makes talk sense: "nobody knew or far from cared who I was . . ."; or, "But and then at that time also I lay in my room. . . ." His perfect ear for idiom allows him to trim his sentences to the barest bones and still communicate: "the old men are not yet sitting with Sunday morn papers because still asleep. . . ." Read aloud, or listened to as if read aloud, the piece becomes one of his easiest to understand.

"The Railroad Earth" also coheres thematically. It is an affirmation of life in the face of death, a threnody for the concept of threnody: "O his father was dead and O his mother was dead and O his sister was dead and O his whereabout was dead was dead." The Wolfean train of death never stops, and so for Kerouac death itself becomes a symbol of life. As the train passes a man and woman making love between rows of grapevines, it becomes one with the land it rides over, with natural fertility. At the end of the novella, the image of death dissolves (with the help of a few puns) in the revitalizing image of sexual union:

> Jose is making her electricities mix and interrun with his and the whole earth charged with juices turns up the organo [the street of prostitutes in Mexico City] to the flower, the unfold-

ment, the stars bend to it, the whole world's coming as the
big engine booms and balls by with the madman of the white
cap California in there flossing and wow there's just no end to
all this wine—

A few pages earlier a vagrant youth disdained railroad life, telling the narrator: "Ah well I don't like going up and down the same
rail, if you ask me goin to sea is the real life. . . ." The narrator
replied: "What you talking about man it's great and you're moving
all the time. . . ." The youth's mistake is not to see that all life is
moving "up and down," that cycles are endless and no less delightful
for being repetitious. The "wine" of the concluding sentence is a
symbol of the delight that ignores death.

All the more remarkable that Jack should have produced such a
work at a time when death was constantly on his mind. His phlebitis
had flared up again, so that it was a relief when the railroad laid him
off in early December. He planned to recuperate in Mexico and was
about to bus down, but Neal insisted on driving him. Besides the
adventure, Neal wanted to replenish his pot supply. To get Carolyn
to approve the trip, Neal offered to let her join Jack later on for her
"vacation." Carolyn agreed to the bargain for the leverage it gave
her over Neal, but by this time she no longer wanted to live even
half her life with Jack.

On the way to Mexico City Neal let Jack drive, then hollered
that he was ruining the clutch, and Jack sulked. Neal stayed in Mexico City only long enough to get his pot, and a few days after his
departure Burroughs skipped bail, which had become exorbitant.
Although for months Bill had seethed over Jack's failure to repay the
twenty dollars, they now had a compassionate farewell. Having lost
his wife, children (who were in the custody of their grandparents),
and patrimony, Burroughs had little to take with him besides a few
daggers, his drugs, Joan's spices, his son's shoe, his daughter's school
case, and photos of Huncke, Lucien, and Allen. Jack felt he would
never see Bill again. The Mexican government's crackdown on drug
use was also driving out their mutual friends Dave Tercerero, a
pusher, and Bill Garver, the old overcoat thief and junkie who'd
come there from New York "to cultivate a habit." Quite alone, Jack
bought pottery to brighten his rooftop apartment, and wrote Carolyn that he was ready to show her a good time.

Neal was in agony awaiting Carolyn's decision to leave him.
Quitting the game, she told Neal she would stay home, but she didn't
have the heart to tell Jack. Neal was still vindictive enough to keep
Jack's last $30 paycheck, and Jack was all the angrier for knowing
why: before leaving San Jose, he had warned Neal that he wouldn't
pay for any of the gas, since Neal had instigated the car trip.

Just after Neal left Mexico, Jack wrote a complete novelette in
French in five days. It was about Neal and himself as kids meeting in

Chinatown with their fathers, and all of them ending up in a bedroom with "Uncle Bull Balloon" (the W. C. Fields–Burroughs character), a French-Canadian rake, and some sexy blondes. Jack thought
of it as the "solution" to the multiple *On the Road* plots. Afterward,
he resumed work on the large novel, "the Duluoz Life." He also sent
Holmes some new thoughts about the Beat Generation, suggesting
that a more apt title might be the "sex generation," because theirs
was the first generation to live in fear of sex rather than simply in
search of it. Kids growing up in the thirties, he asserted, were bombarded with slogans like "sex appeal" and "free love," and to their
first frustrated expectations were later added Reichian worries about
orgasm and "especially homosexual anxieties."

With Christmas approaching and no sign of Carolyn, Jack grew
unbearably lonely. He hitchhiked back to New York, mailing her an
apology for "running off." [207] But that she was very much on his
mind is evident from the new novel he began as soon as he got home,
what he called his "first Proustian love story." It was the tale of his
teenage love for Mary Carney, and it was Proustian in the way it
dissected the infinite delusions that constitute love's enchantment.
Sharing Proust's solipsism, Kerouac set out to show that love is always frustrated because one's emotions are essentially unknowable
to any other. At first untitled, the story was simply called "Mary
Carney"; a few months later he began to refer to it as "Love is
Sixteen, Mary Cassidy."

Supported and nurtured by his mother, Jack did three months of
steady writing in Richmond Hill. In addition to "Mary Cassidy," he
worked on the railroad sketch and translated the French novelette.
His chief comfort was marijuana mixed with hashish, which he
smoked in his pipe twice a day. Afternoons he'd relax listening to
Allen's radio, hoping to get Lester Young or Vivaldi; evenings he'd
watch TV and drink beer. For reading he had the complete works of
Genet in French, also borrowed from Allen.

The few times he went into New York were hectic and unsatisfy-
ing. He dropped into Ed White's apartment unannounced, and
struck up a friendship with Ed's roommate Jorge Davila, another
Columbia architectural student. A twenty-one-year-old Puerto Rican, Davila found Jack "real strange." Jack was always pulling out
his tiny notebooks to read things he'd just written, most of which
sounded "disjointed." His actions were "completely unpredictable."
One day he brought some pot and took Jorge down to Riverside
Drive to teach him to smoke, then suggested they go "smoke up" the
Columbia bookstore. He wasn't drinking very much, and he avoided
the hard liquor that Jorge and Ed often guzzled. But when they rode
the subway he slugged from a little bottle of cheap red wine in a
brown paper bag.

He was bursting with news of his latest book and with all the stories he wanted to put down, and although Jorge sympathized with this great need to share his writing, he couldn't respond to much of it because he didn't know the people Jack was writing about. With Ed, Jack would spend hours discussing their crazy friends; Jorge was forever hearing the names Cassady, Carr, and Burroughs. Of Bill Cannastra, another favorite topic, Jack said, "He was a saint." By contrast, he predicted his own life would end "not with a bang but a whimper." [208]

Jack had plenty of girls but no serious love affairs, since he was determined that no woman ever "own" him again. The women he saw, like Hal's ex-wife, Ginger, now a folksinger in the Village, and Dusty, were safe because of their promiscuity. With Dusty he had additional insurance, as he joked to Jorge, because she liked girls. His wife Joan, however, was purely "bad news." Jack spoke grimly of his need to keep running from her. To avoid paying child support, he was still receiving mail under aliases and at other addresses.

He bumped into his old Lowell friend Connie Murphy, who was now a health physicist, and invited him to Richmond Hill, where Jack proudly read him selections from *Visions of Cody*. But Murphy, who liked plotted novels, thought it carelessly written. By now all their mutual friends were well into careers and families. Mentioning his own daughter, Janet, Jack said he didn't feel obligated to support her because her mother had talked him into the marriage against his better judgment. To Connie, writing seemed just a means of dodging the responsibilities of real life. Once again, he advised Jack to get a "manly" job: "You get to your last and you work."

Jack would have liked to get railroad work, but his legs were still inflamed. In any case, it began to appear that he might indeed earn a living from his writing. Thanks to Allen, John, and John's agent, Phyllis Jackson, Viking Press was now considering *On the Road*, *Doctor Sax*, and the in-progress manuscript of "Mary Cassidy." Critic Malcolm Cowley, an editorial advisor to Viking, was much taken with *On the Road* and recommended they publish it. Regardless, the owner of Viking was offended by the book. Rumor had it that he vowed never to let Viking publish it in his lifetime.

Cowley asked Jack to lunch. Jack's first bad impression of him as a "pedantic Vermont professor" was reinforced when Cowley stared at him as though he were some literary sideshow. Although he was even more offended when Cowley suggested he take the fantasy out of *Doctor Sax* and peddle it as a realistic story of boyhood in Massachusetts, he was dazzled by Cowley's prediction that the book would earn him $50,000. When Jack snapped that Viking would publish *Doctor Sax* as is if he were Faulkner, Cowley replied that they would even publish it at a loss if Jack had another book that would make a gain. For a while Viking seemed to think "Mary Cassidy" might fill the bill, and they offered Jack $250 for an option on it. By March 20,

1953, Viking was considering an advance of $1,250 for "Mary Cassidy," and they told Jack that Bantam Books was dickering for paperback rights. But a week or two later Jack was so embittered— perhaps by what he felt were false promises—that he left Phyllis Jackson's office muttering that he didn't want to be published by anyone.

In February, he had a tiff with both Allen and John. As John's fortune increased, so did Jack's animosity toward him. On top of the $20,000 for *Go*, there was a false rumor abroad that John was about to receive an $80,000 inheritance. Part of Jack reveled vicariously in John's success—the Holmes who was eating in expensive restaurants and "chasing and hailing cabs with his coat flapping" was someone Jack wanted to emulate. When John bought a fourteen-room colonial house in Old Saybrook, Connecticut, Jack's envy nearly got the better of him. Four years younger, Holmes already had all Jack could have wished of success: a home in New England full of antique furniture and surrounded by big trees, "sea fens," and a sinking cemetery. The best Jack could now see for himself was a trailer among the Mexicans in Milpitas, California, where he and his mother could live unhounded by detectives, and where he could support her by working on the Southern Pacific. One night in mid-February, John and his new girlfriend Shirley were to meet Jack at Birdland. He told Jack they'd arrive late because he had to counsel a conscientious objector in Brooklyn beforehand, but then they got lost in Brooklyn and didn't get to the club until after Jack had left. Jack felt stood up and ignored John's note of apology.

About the same time, Ace Books was preparing to publish the novel *Junky* by Burroughs, who was using the pseudonym William Lee. For publicity in David Dempsey's column in *The New York Times*, Allen wrote a blurb linking Kerouac and Holmes as fellow Beat Generation experts who applauded the novel. But Jack had been growing disenchanted with Allen's bourgeois pretensions; Allen had a respectable job in market research and seemed "fat-faced and ugly." As though he had nearly exhausted Allen's intellect, Jack told him, "I want to see you and talk to you four times a year," and egged on by his mother's paranoia, accused Allen of exposing him to prosecution merely to "bruit" his name "for book trade reasons." He also wrote Allen that he didn't want his name associated with either "habit forming drugs" or Holmes.

The charges he brought against Holmes were crueler and more unjust. In a sour-grapes mood because Gilbert Millstein of the *Times* had rejected his essay "The History of Bop," Jack wrote John that he wanted to dissociate himself from "beatness." Not only had John's "Beat Generation" article soiled his "proud family name," but, claimed Jack, because of it even his agent now thought he was a "dope addict." Since Burroughs and Holmes were making money

while hiding behind their respective cloaks of anonymity and journalistic disinterest, Jack wondered why *he* should become an open
target for nothing. He also felt as if credit had come too late, since
his prophecies of the Beat Generation had been blue-penciled out of
The Town and the City, which would have been hailed as a more
important novel had they been left in. Ironically, Holmes was cap-
italizing on the notion of a generation that was already in decline,
for in Jack's view the youth of 1953 were "sleek beasts and mid-
dleclass subterraneans." As always, his deepest hostility was rooted
in his sense of kinship with the exploited people. "You're a man of
inherited wealth and I'm from the working class," he wrote Holmes,
denying John's seriousness as he insinuated that John had sent him
that $50 merely to play a Dostoyevskian game, pitting his own pride
against Jack's shame. Determined to bloody their friendship, Jack
claimed he and John had been brought together by "a connection of
only the most specious N.Y. kind." In a letter, Holmes asked him to
reconsider his attack in the light of common sense, but Jack didn't
reply. Reverting to older allegiances, Jack did send Allen a quote
praising *Junky.* Still anxious to see Jack recognized, Allen warned
him not to let Wyn know that MCA was submitting his novels to
Viking, since he had not yet fulfilled his contract to deliver an acceptable manuscript to Wyn. But all Jack could think of now was
becoming a self-sufficient laborer and a decent provider for his
mother. When he thought he might get a substantial sum for "Mary
Cassidy," he planned to buy a farm in Quebec. After that hope
collapsed in March, still longing for the comfort of his mythical
homeland, he decided to seek work on the Canadian National Pacific
Railroad. At the same time he was realistic enough to let Neal and
Carolyn know that he would probably return to the Southern
Pacific.

The strength that he managed to pull out of three months of
chaotic living resulted largely from the completion of another major
work, the novel that eventually came to be known as *Maggie
Cassidy.*

6.

Though *Maggie Cassidy* was a teenage love story it wasn't a "bit of
juvenilia," as John Ciardi later called it. It couldn't have been written any sooner in Kerouac's development than it was, for its essence
is a distant love affair looked at through the binoculars of disillusion.

Maggie Cassidy contains little more than the twisted skeleton of
a linear narrative. Its warps include time inversions—for example,
describing a kiss, then explaining how it came about—time col-

lapses—such as mentioning the start of a love affair, then shifting immediately to its conclusion as the boy dies overseas in the war— and extensive intermissions in the action for exploded moments, which are now cut perfectly to paragraph size. The flow of the narrative comes very close to being a chain of moments.

The first paragraph is a paradigm of the whole book. It sets the time as New Year's Eve, 1938, with a group of adolescent boys heading for their first big dance. Suspense is created by one boy's singing, "Jack o diamonds, you'll be my downfall," and the third-person authorial voice noting that he didn't know the downfall part of it yet. Ironically the narrator refers to the singer's "brokendoll neck," implying that he is already broken, even though he hasn't yet experienced the break. Capping the paragraph the narrator suddenly locates himself far in the future, looking backward: "It was the New Year 1939, before the war, before everyone knew the intention of the world toward America." Time is set going in two directions at once. The boys are on the verge of a new year and a new life, but the future consciousness of one of them (as we will soon find out that the narrator is among those boys) sees them blundering toward a destiny already as irrevocable as the past. Past and future collide in the present, producing a stasis which is the moment. Even the structure of the last sentence, with its short phrases and two lumbering *before*'s, forces the reader to slow his thought.

As the boys walk to the dance and begin to meet girls, there are hints of a second, almost supernatural, vision accompanying them— as though an angel were hovering overhead, seeing them simultaneously as real earthlings with ordinary goals and worries, and as ghosts already beyond even the memory of strife. Describing Jack Duluoz's tenement house, the narrator says:

> The back stairs were so dim, dusty, strange, as if loose-plastered, some day he would remember them in rueful dreams of rust and loss . . . dreams when G.J.'s shadow would fall across a piece of broken leg like pottery in the street, like modern paintings in their keen screaming lostness. . . . No idea in 1939 that the world would turn mad.

Not only has another time shift been slipped under the reader's foundering feet, but two new perspectives have been introduced: a "dream" or "shadow" consciousness, which is the primary religious consciousness, and the artistic consciousness.

Eventually Kerouac would merge those two viewpoints. But even here there is a hint that the many perspectives are all part of a single sensibility. Modern art screams over the loss of that unified awareness, just as religion has always dealt with the initial loss of innocence (in the West sin, in the East illusion) and the final loss of ignorance (Western redemption, Eastern knowledge of the One

Mind). That Kerouac is again echoing Wolfe with the word *lost* just adds another step to the staircase by which he climbs free of his own experience and of the limits of autobiographical fiction.

Each of the boys has his own dream of the future—Scotty thinking he'll get a car next summer, G.J. that he'll seduce his business teacher. But the narrator's point is that they never dream of what actually comes to pass. The point of view shifts abruptly to the first person: "Never dreaming, was I, poor Jack Duluoz, that the soul is dead." The awareness of death is an awakening to other levels of reality—in fact, Jack's father later talks about feeling alive and dead at the same time, claiming that as the source of his depth; it is as close as Kerouac ever comes to specifying the first cause of the moment. The narrator himself asserts that "love is the heritage, and cousin to death." We have but one life and one love, because both life and love exist by virtue of the void that marks their beginning and end. Man's will to change that situation is perpetually stymied; his "only word," spoken into that same void, is "choked forever."

Although Kerouac presents his love affair with Mary Carney realistically (she later claimed it was three-fourths accurate), the ultimate failure of Jack Duluoz to win Maggie functions allegorically as well. Early in the book she is associated with halos, starlight and moonlight, doves, flowers, and nakedness—images of fragility and evanescence. The enormous number of references to reflected light, from starlight on the river to moonlight in a garbage pail, reinforce the sense of life's tenuousness. Once again Kerouac equates light-in-darkness with human life. This time his emphasis is even closer to that of Wolfe, who used the proliferation of electric light in America as a metaphor for civilization's losing battle to illuminate the unknown.

When Kerouac describes Maggie's old wooden house, haunted by the hooting and rumbling and red glare of trains crossing the nearby railroad bridge, the echoes of Wolfe are unmistakable. And as in Wolfe, seasons bespeak the mysterious repetitions of time. Jumping from January to July, the first-person narrator describes "the fireflies, the moths, the bugs of New England" and many other cyclic features of life in that place, moving month by month back to the beginning of winter, the frozen river and snow-filled ruts in the street, where the story began. Wolfe too was impressed by the dreamlike nature of reality, but he preferred to think of man's life as a real spurt of flame in the darkness of space, whereas to Kerouac life is just another vision in the darkness of the mind:

> And at night the river flows, it bears pale stars on the holy water, some sink like veils, some show like fish, the great moon that once was rose now high like a blazing milk flails its white reflection vertical and deep in the dark surgey mass wall river's grinding bed push. As in a sad dream, under the

streetlamp, by pocky unpaved holes in dirt, the father James Cassidy comes home with lunchpail and lantern, limping, red-faced, and turns in for supper and sleep.

After returning to a winter setting, Kerouac begins describing the actions of summertime; he spins the wheels of the seasons back and forth, playing with the reader's time sense to awaken him to the timelessness of human experience. Kerouac's method is to break down every fixed conception in order to perceive conceptionless Reality. Through freely burgeoning metaphor, the piling up of ridiculously incongruous images, he emphasizes the arbitrariness of all comparison:

> Ice skaters, Swedes, Irish girls, yellers and singers—they throng on the white ice beneath the crinkly stars that have no altar moon, no voice, but down heavy tragic space make halyards of Heaven on in deep, to where the figures amassed by scientists cream in a cold mass; the veil of Heaven on tiaras and diadems of a great Eternity Brunette called night.

Nevertheless, certain symbols have thematic significance. Crowns and halos accentuate the purity of Maggie's virginity, which itself typifies the moment unborn and still unspoiled. The brevity of Jack's opportunity to win her love is signaled by every train whistling past her house; her father and brother even work for the railroad. Love is tied to time, hence the narrator associates his other girlfriend, Pauline Cole, with the high school clock. Love is "cousin to death" because the things we love die. Likewise the moment— because it is "weighted down in the middle with unbelievable freights," i.e., because it inheres *in things*—cannot be other than transitory.

By tense shifts from the past of the story's occurrence to the present of writing it, and by derangements in syntax, Kerouac attempts to mirror the process by which the mind is broken out of its ruts of learning to experience freshly its true nature. The moment is often triggered by disorientation. Startled, you forget *who* you are and *where* you are, and for a second or two you simply *are*. Such an experience is the narrator's first kiss with Maggie:

> . . . a moment's penetration of sweet lip flesh, a moment's drowned in thinking and kissing in it . . . I didn't know really who was kissing me for the very first instant . . . she descended to me from the upper dark where I'd thought only cold could be . . . the little hungry scent of perspiration warm in her flesh like preciousness.

Rimbaud had insisted that insight into reality could be gained only by deranging the senses, Pound by making everything new. Certainly Kerouac's phrases are seldom clichés—who would have expected "warm in her flesh like preciousness" instead of "warm and precious"? But he suggests that you needn't go out of your way to achieve "derangement," for the "excesses" of Rimbaud can't compare with the twentieth-century technology of destruction; but his main point is that any artificial derangement is superfluous, that there is a natural and perpetual derangement from the forces of life. He presents that derangement as the essential mechanism of consciousness, the occasion for all deep insight and enduring memory.

Plot is subordinate to the accumulation of moments, which are memory's store of wisdom. "I'll sing later—the story of Maggie," he writes, proceeding first to the moral, which is that we are all one. To God or to the One Mind, all sufferers are the same, futilely grasping at illusions:

> Ah life, God—we won't find them any more the Nova Scotias of flowers! No more saved afternoons! The shadows, the ancestors, they've all walked in the dust of 1900 seeking the new toys of the twentieth century just as Céline says—but it's still love has found us out, and in the stalls was nothing, eyes of drunken wolves was all. Ask the guys at war.

The narrator finds prototypes of sorrow everywhere: Jesus, a poor Mexican worker, Dante, Maggie, and even the crescent moon with "head bent." All-inclusive, his vision cannot be other than God's. But that vision which is, also is not—it is "nothing, just the consciousness that God awaits us." The desire for anything more produces "cries, frights, despairs—the ambiguities! the terrors!" The price of clinging to life is to "die in pain."

When the narrator sleeps, the pain ceases, because he is immersed in "the darkness and the death of *no time*." But upon awakening he is again caught up in the world's phantasmagoria. With the memory of Maggie his pain returns, as it always will so long as his consciousness remains tied to the cycles of time. Their love in fact proceeds by the seasons. Jack's love for Maggie grows ardent in winter, just as the cold fires his body with a rush of blood. Maggie's love for him dissolves, as the earth does, in the spring thaw. Significantly, two of the early titles for *Maggie Cassidy* were "Springtime Mary" and "Springtime Sixteen."

"Redbrick" here symbolizes the world of illusion that traps men—like the mills of Lowell—because they can't "see through" it. The colors of youth (rose and purple), of life (red and green), and of decay (yellow, brown, and gray) represent different aspects of illusion.

The most important color in the novel is gold. The key to the novel is given when the narrator describes his guilt at abandoning his father to see Maggie, even though she would rather he didn't come. He laments: "always the dross and dirty loss spine ribbing down life's poor gold and it so short and sweet." Throughout the book Kerouac plays on the two types of gold. One is the "dross," the metal gold used as the standard for money, which is essentially the same as fool's gold, a symbol for the falseness of material reality. It stands for the deception of sensual pleasure, of women seen as "gold sexpots." The second type is the gold of "home lights" and sunsets and memories (in contrast to the mortal brown of old photographs), the permanence earned by accepting impermanence. The second gold redeems the life we expend seeking the first. It shines with the true light we see by—not the "brown dumb street lamp" but "the actual light that actually upon her [Maggie] was bestowing and around her bathing, mote by mote made rare gold, dear magic . . . the commotion hysterical light of wonder." Such inner light "aureates" the world with the warmth of fantasy; it perdures in the timelessness of vision. Contrasted with it is reflected light, cold and lifeless, a prisoner of time. Beneath the Moody Street Bridge the narrator sees "the tiny milky rivulets of icy Time gurgling in the rockjags, the reflection of starry paradises in profound black pools," the funereal color recalling the people who (we learn elsewhere in the *Legend*) have killed themselves off that bridge.

Some people are lost like those lights that perish in blackness. There is a nice counterpoint in the novel between selfish passions, like Maggie's jealous love, and the self-sacrificing kindness of the narrator's mother and his friends. In that respect the book is a paean to human endurance. Kerouac sees mankind in a world like a Northern shack: "the blizzard cold seeped but the stove held out, the old man stoked it, stocked it and kicked it, he knew how to make a fire like he knew how to eat." Like Jack London, Kerouac believes the secret of life is knowing how to build a fire, but his sparks are struck not from Darwin or Nietzsche but from the heart.

And yet he is conscious in all his writings of the universe around him, of man's life moving in ever widening circles to infinity. Jack on his way home from school is also traversing inner and outer galaxies:

> In winter darkness, the Baghdad Arabian keenblue deepness of the piercing lovely January winter's dusk—it used to tear my heart out, one stabbing soft star was in the middle of the magicalest blue, throbbing like love—I saw Maggie's black hair in this night— In the shelves of Orion her eye shades, borrowed, gleamed a dark and proud vellum somber power brooding rich bracelets of the moon rose from our snow. . . .

The very act of recording the moment alters and extends it like dropping a stone from a rowboat and then pursuing the ripples as your oars make fresh ones. Kerouac once told John Holmes that he divided his life story into the numerous books of *The Duluoz Legend* because he couldn't fit the whole thing into one mold. But it is possible to see the episodic nature of the saga as another mirror, on a much greater scale, of the infinite ripples of existence.

Because the narrator wants to possess his "prime, youngjoy days, riches of sixteen," he ends up with the "dross and dirty loss." By trying to seize one ripple, he loses sight of the instantaneous outflow of all, and what he sought dissolves in his grasp—the way the two girls, Maggie and Pauline, though they both love him, draw away when he seeks to control them. A metaphor for this selfish love is provided by the mills near Maggie's house, which "enlist" the flow of the Concord River. Women are kin to rivers in their rippling moods, we are told. Jack tries to enlist Maggie's flow; but the closer he gets to her, riding toward her house, the grimmer he grows. Magic is as elusive as the moment that engenders it; and as if endowed with a Midas touch in reverse, Jack finds that gold in his hand is always merely lead. Similarly, his father ponders the problem that while one's life may be filled with riches there's no one to whom you can bequeath them; if gold is owned by Someone, we don't know whom.

The central symbolism of true and false gold resonates with several other symbolisms. Roses become Maggie's special symbol; they are the symbol of virgin saints but also the medieval metaphor for female sexuality, and the still more treacherous figure of mutability for the Elizabethans. This ambiguity is heightened by Kerouac's identifying Maggie with the fecundity and danger of spring: "the first green bedsprings of turf" but also "the drowning of idiots which we've come to expect of our spring now." Not only is the narrator's love a kind of moonshine, but women also raise the moon (create phantom children) from the well of their womb: "I'd want to rip her mouth out and murder her, sudden interior welling-up of tenderness profound, paining, dark, forming milky frown on forehead, raising moons by the conjuration-fingers up from the bottom of the well which is the womb, nature, black sod, time, death, birth."

The novel revolves around the strengthening and weakening of Jack's will to resist her "self-satisfied womanly idiocy-flesh," which is Maggie's sensual nature, the part of her concerned with time: the days he'll see her, the date he'll marry her. By concentration he can temporarily overcome time, as when he wins the track race by intuiting the exact second the gun will go off and getting the jump a fraction beforehand. Time is also partly defeated by the act of waking up to each new day—over and over the narrator describes his high resolves for a fresh start as he leaps out of bed in the morning. But his life is tied to "the sad finished-up streets of human time" the way his heart is tied to Maggie. Within the dream of love, misunderstandings are a still more elusive foxfire. Jack dreams of marriage, but his idea of being Maggie's husband is based only on his own pleasure, and so is doomed to disappoint them both.

The only permanent escape from time is through a realization of one's universal existence. In terms of human relationships this means performing deeds for others rather than oneself, as when Jack pretends he doesn't know about his surprise birthday party in order to delight Iddyboy, who helped plan it. For Kerouac acting, in the sense of giving oneself roles, is a major metaphor for the projection of cosmic vision essential to all of man's nobler conduct, such as hoping, believing, and showing kindness. (Iddyboy's firm belief that a man lives in the moon makes him a purely Kerouacian hero.) Jack's failure to identify with Maggie's needs leaves him loving a "ghost." Based on time, love fades into a ghost too, since time decrees change: "Everything went on as usual in the city itself—except that it was always changing, like me. . . ." Indeed change and our reactions to it are all that is eternal: "the chagrin of the reddy dusk up on Paddy McGillicuddy's street in the Acre up on the hill was mighty the same every time—and something eternal brooded in the sad red chimneys of the mills. . . ." The saddest part of growing up—and this is what *Maggie Cassidy* is ultimately about, for it isn't love that makes a boy a man so much as the loss of it—is that adults tend to become even more obsessed with their dreams when their world opens up, as Jack finds by leaving Maggie to go to prep school in New York. For the world itself is lost "like a marble ball rolling down eternity in a bowling alley opening out into darkness. . . ."

No place for love there. Although Jack and Maggie's romance revives briefly during the "winter cold" of the Thanksgiving and Christmas holidays, it once again fails to survive the growth cycle of spring. By this time his gold crucifix has "darkened"; and in the "gray dark Sainte Jeanne d'Arc basement" church, where he used to pray for Maggie's love, he now fantasizes raping the "honey-colored girl" in front of him. From the pure gold of spiritual love he has come down to the basest sensuality, and this counterfeit love is symbolized fittingly by the gaudy gold paint on the invitation to the equally garish Horace Mann prom, which he sends to Maggie. At that prom the rich society girls will show up Maggie's best pink dress with their Lord & Taylor gowns; hurt to the quick she will leave Jack for good, leaving him with "the Glitter Isle of dark New York America" and its "corpse ridden" Hudson River. Like the hotel barbershop, where he had gone to be groomed to please her, and had found only "empty mirrors along the backs of empty barber chairs," he has lost "the spilling molten hot gold of real life."

She had offered to let him marry her if they lived in Lowell, where with a rosary in her hand she would remind him of the holiness of life (roses perish, but the spirituality of prayer does not), and the snowflakes, those symbols of perishable earthly beauty, would come again and again to their roof. Since he rejects the proposition of changing *with* her, memory is the only salvation she offers him. "Remember what you were like, where your house, what your life," she advises, "you'll die without knowing what happened to my face, my love, my youth." But Jack in his bedazzlement embraces the novel sensations of city life, ensuring his loss of her. Christ warned against gaining the world but losing one's soul, and Kerouac reinterprets that theme darkly in regard to his own artistic achievement. As Jack Duluoz's vision broadens, his hold on reality diminishes. One pays for cosmic consciousness with the inevitable loss of one's "soul," one's individuality.

Jack's insatiable greed for experience sends him ravening. Three years later, when winter has come again, he returns to Lowell cocksure that he can finally seduce Maggie and get what he never could before, the pleasure of sex without the lifetime commitment of marriage. But the garage where he works is a symbol of his current imprisonment in illusion; leaving it to pick her up he "wore the wild look of a man emancipated into the redbrick heap of night from some bank jail."

He's had all sorts of travels, women, and education in and out of college, and the long catalog of his Faustian achievements is almost a parody of Wolfe's jadedness. Wolfe's heroes tried to possess the world and failed, collapsing in weariness and despair. Kerouac's hero feels that he has conquered the world, but in fact has only gotten further from the truth. The real accomplishment is the distance Kerouac has come from his former worship of Wolfe. In *The Town and the City*, the romantic tyro (Peter Martin) who sets out to see the world might have been carrying *Of Time and the River* as a Baedeker. At the end of *Maggie Cassidy*, the narration shifts abruptly back to an objective third-person point of view. Kerouac thus demonstrates that though his persona has run amok, consumed by lust, the artist has been weaned of his attachments and is now in control of his past.

Without asking permission Jack takes a Buick from the parking garage to impress Maggie; in a similar way he attempts to palm off his brutal scheme to have sex with her, in effect to rape her, as a rebirth of his love. But from his voice she can tell that he's changed. When she sees him she says he looks "cold hearted." To con her he says she'll "always look the same—good," but she sees he hasn't even looked. Taking her back to the garage he attempts intercourse in the car, but he's already drunk and can't get past her girdle. The scene could have been merely farcical, but the novel's multilayered structure makes that "thick rubber girdle" function remarkably well as a symbol of the reality that resists the narrator's every attempt to penetrate it.

At the period of writing *Maggie Cassidy*, *The Confidence Man* was one of Kerouac's favorite novels. The parallels between the two works are striking. In *The Confidence Man*, Melville finally concedes the utter elusiveness of reality, which he'd tracked through the labyrinths of several earlier novels. Elaborating endless dualities, Melville comes to only a tentative conclusion: "Something further may

follow of this Masquerade." That is to say, life is an unfinished equation between good and evil. At the end of the novel, the confidence
man, who may be the devil, poses as an old man who may be God.
His last act is to extinguish a lamp adorned with designs representing
both the Old and New Testaments.

Like *The Confidence Man, Maggie Cassidy* ends in darkness: "She
laughed in his face, he slammed the door shut, put out lights, drove
her home, drove the car back skittering crazily in the slush, sick,
cursing." The slush recalls the "melting" of his pure intentions those
previous springs. Earlier in the evening he had seen the "warm lights
of her house" but refused to go in; instead he had forced her outside
under the "dull streetlamps" so he could "swoon the wine of the
moon" again.

There is no explanation for the coexistence of the dualities in the
world (the illusions of light and dark, good and evil, etc.) and the
gold of holiness (the timeless beauty of life and spirit). Kerouac's
thesis seems to be that no conscious resolution is possible; at most
one can will oneself to be sensitive to moments when they occur.
Seeking evil—like Jack's planned seduction—is no more fruitful than
the pursuit of a delusory snowlike purity, as all his unanswered
prayers attest.

Loving and lusting, affection and cruelty, leave a man equally
deluded. The singing of "Jack o diamonds" at the beginning and end
of the book ties together the search for love and the quest to conquer: both are chancy. The book begins and ends with a detached
narrator seeing himself lost in a snowstorm at night. The change is
only from one illusion to another: where before he was attracted to
the "white" of Maggie's shy virginity, he is now drawn to the black
"hole of night." Her "sweetness" is hidden by the girdle the way the
true gold is hidden by the illusions of black and white and the diversity of colors in between. It is noteworthy that in the last two chapters black and white predominate, whereas the earlier chapters were
marked by a rainbow assortment of hues. Gold results from a unique
amalgam of all the primary colors; as constituents of the moment,
colors stand for the richness of perception. Black and white in their
stark opposition typify the relentless cycles of time.

Jack's refusal to go into her house, at the end, can be taken as a
renunciation of the colors that were prominent early in their romance. They met in a ballroom full of colored lights; their song was
"Deep Purple"; their ideal house was red outside, green inside, filled
with red chairs and baby cribs (red and green being the two principal tints of gold). The garage he takes her to is a deromanticized
h me, a utilitarian workplace and gloomy "prison" where the colors
of imagination are absent. As he leaves to pick her up the snow
thickens; the word *emancipated* has to be ironic. Even her street
"sits pale" before his blasé eyes. He is "interested in the dangers of

real life confronting"; but ironically, in spurning the gold of the moment he loses even the "wine" of sensual pleasure.

Throughout the novel Jack finds that joy is spontaneous and can't be prepared for—like Maggie's joy when he comes to see her on a different than usual night, or his own joy at his "surprise" birthday party, where the real surprise is how much Maggie actually cares for him. The moment is unpredictable and ephemeral, boiling gold that can't be procured but must come as a present, as Paul said Christian grace is given. But the everyday world, if somewhat more in our control, is also unpredictable and resistant to our wishes. In short, neither reality nor the imagination can be depended upon to satisfy us. Never realizing this, Jack remains trapped in dualism, perhaps the plainest symbol of which is his dilemma over whether to choose Pauline or Maggie. The book ends where it begins, Jack's sense of progress the grandest illusion of all.

In one of the key scenes of the book, after the surprise birthday party, Jack and Maggie stand at a taxi shelter in a blizzard, discussing their future, while the old men in an all-night diner across the street watch them through steamed-up windows. The old "tomcats" in the diner seem jovial and raucous to Jack, when in reality they are "ghosts," strangers to one another and fugitives, like his father, from their own loneliness. Equally deluded, the old men see Maggie and Jack as eager lovers, though at that very moment their love is foundering in the cross currents of their respective jealousies and ambitions. Only after joining his father and the other habitués in the diner does outsider Jack sense the void on both sides of the glass, disguised as a world by the tricks of steam and snow. The same structure—of phantoms seen from the outside looking in, from the inside looking out, and again from the outside looking in—characterizes the whole novel, and provides Kerouac's final commentary on the pervasiveness of illusion.

7.

From Montreal, which was depressing and unfriendly, Jack hurried on to California and was rehired as a brakeman with the Southern Pacific. Perhaps to keep out of Neal and Carolyn's way, he accepted an assignment in San Luis Obispo, 250 miles south of San Francisco. He took a hotel room there, but planned to move into the mountains as soon as he taught himself sufficient survival skills like "fishing and making Indian acorn mush and hunting." Actually he was so lonely even in the city that he wrote to Dusty proposing she become his "life mate." She passed the letter around as a joke.

In late May, 1953, Jack moved to San Jose to work on Conductor

Plomteau's local, though Al Hinkle warned him against it. Plomteau could get two crews' worth of work done in six hours, and anybody on his train "had to keep one foot in the air at all times." Nevertheless, Jack was confident that he could get in his good graces by speaking French with him. Saturdays Plomteau pushed his men the hardest, since the railroad assured everyone a full day's pay even if the work could be done in a few hours. All thumbs and two left feet, Jack ran afoul of Plomteau the first Saturday, started to talk French, and was ordered to sit outside the caboose for the rest of the day—to keep out of the way. Humiliated, he resigned, having worked little more than a month.

On April 10, Neal had been knocked off a boxcar and broke his ankle and foot. With him home and on crutches, this was no time for Jack to resume his affair with Carolyn. Besides, New York beckoned him with fresh hopes for his literary career. Cowley had been non-plused by his disappearance, for Viking was genuinely interested in negotiating for some of his works. When Wyn rejected *Maggie Cassidy*, Allen again stepped in as unofficial agent to keep Jack's manuscripts circulating, but Jack nixed his plan to submit excerpts to anthologies like *New World Writing* and *The Best American Short Stories*. An "architectural creation and symphony" like *Doctor Sax* ought to be "published nobly," Jack wrote him. Allen replied that both *Doctor Sax* and *Maggie Cassidy* could be published "reasonably soon."

As Neal wanted Jack to live with him and Carolyn, and Jack insisted on living in Skid Row San Francisco, relations between them grew strained again. Neal feared Jack was heading for a "fatal dissatisfaction" and warned him against "jumping off the deep end." Feeling more rejected, Jack seemingly did just that by signing on the S.S. *William Carruth*, bound for Alabama, New York, and Korea. Although his job as waiter in the officers' saloon was "very easy and cool," Jack got in trouble for his surliness. Nights he'd lie on deck on a cot, drinking and studying the stars with the aid of the chief mate's charts. When the ship docked in Mobile in late June, he got drunk with a prostitute and was caught strolling half-undressed with her down Main Street when he should have been working. Facing reprimand, he agreed to quit when the ship reached New Orleans. On the way, Jack lay on his deck cot, drunk again, watching a lightning storm. In New Orleans he added his $300 pay to the $300 he'd saved from the railroad, and headed for New York.

When he arrived back in Richmond Hill in July, his literary situation was better than he'd expected. Since Wyn had rejected three of his manuscripts, he was now free of his contract with Ace Books. According to Allen, the only thing delaying acceptance of the novels was the fact that his agents thought he didn't care to publish them. Jack hastily signed power-of-attorney forms giving Allen the authority to convince publishers he did. At Viking, Cowley was inspiring enthusiasm for the original *On the Road*, so that by early August Jack was confident of receiving a $1,500 advance on it.

He was restless to travel to places like Samarkand and Ulan Bator, but too poor to do much more than stay home with his mother and write. He continued work on "Wine in the Railroad Earth," and began revising *On the Road* as Cowley requested. Since his prose was getting "deeper and more obscure," he realized he wouldn't be able to earn a living from it for several years; again he thought of establishing a home in Mexico. Seriously concerned about his drinking, he practiced temperance for a month. His regimen also included abstinence from pot, which was easier to observe because he'd thrown his whole store of it overboard from the *Carruth* in a fit of fear. Meanwhile, he was reading Reich's *The Function of the Orgasm*. Positing that most mental and physical maladies are attributable to the electrical disturbance caused by insufficient or inadequate orgasms, Reich believed no person could be happy or fully productive without a full sex life. The book impressed him more than anything he had read since *Ulysses* in 1942, and he once more added a woman to the picture of his future.

Her incarnation wasn't hard to find. Jack was already familiar with the San Remo bar, where Village hipsters mingled with cruising homosexuals, both of whom performed outrageously for tourists on weekends. Allen introduced him to another Village bar, Fugazzi's, which harbored the coolest hipsters; dubbed "subterraneans" by Allen, they included Gerd Stern, Bill Keck, Anton Rosenberg, Mason Hoffenberg, Stanley Gould, and Peter Van Metre. Jack was fascinated with the subterraneans for their modernity, for their embodiment of the new era of "cold jazz" and "cold peace," [209] like the lingering truce in Korea. With Gould, who shared his love for jazz, Jack would sit in Minetta Lane, scatting. Basically, however, he was uneasy among them, and he saw nothing admirable in Gould's boast that he'd never worked in his life. Some of the subterraneans used hard drugs, in the one way of which Jack disapproved, as an escape from struggle and feeling. The chief reason for the mutual scorn between the subterraneans and Jack was that he was "hot." In Fugazzi's, while Jack was excitedly telling Gregory Corso a story, one cool hipster observed to another: "Dig that aggression." Yet Jack was to have his most intense love affair with a bright, well-educated black woman who tomboyed with them. Since she prefers to remain anonymous, she will be referred to as Mardou Fox.

Small, café-au-lait, with a classically beautiful profile, Mardou could match steps with the subterraneans intellectually. Her striking appearance and poise gave her the air of being one of their "chicks" —which is how Jack perceived her.

Mardou was exceptional both for her willingness to mingle with white men, to teach and learn from them, and for the respect she commanded as their equal. Though Jack saw her as their victim she never felt herself to be so, and in fact was pursuing her own goals.

Much like Jack, she found herself more an observer than a participant in the subterranean scene; but where the unresponsiveness of junkies merely irritated Jack, it occasionally menaced her precarious mental balance. She was then undergoing psychoanalysis. One night, visiting Gould in his apartment, she had taken a pill from him and had become terrified by the strangeness of her situation there. She fled in panic.

For a brief time she became a close friend of Allen, which was more a matter of deep reciprocal affection than of sexual attraction, for Allen was now well on the road back to homosexual orientation. The night she first met Jack, at a party, she was struck as favorably by his Hawaiian shirt (bought for travels in the Orient) as by his dark good looks. She especially liked his warmth. He was drawn to her sultry beauty and low, sophisticated, yet tenderly lisping voice. Allen subsequently arranged to have Jack meet her at his apartment. Dressed in an even fancier blue silk shirt and pressed slacks, Jack accompanied them to the Open Door to hear Charlie Parker; then Allen left Mardou and Jack to amuse themselves. After more drinking and jazz, he rode home with her on the bus to Paradise Alley, a tenement on the Lower East Side.

A few days later, sitting on his lap, she felt Jack's sympathy so strongly that she told him about her breakdown. Without realizing it, she was playing to his weakest suit. He loved her less for her vulnerability than for the honesty and clarity with which she confessed it. He thought her the most intelligent woman he had known since Joan Adams, and her life story moved him with the same "idealistic pathos" that he had found in Sebastian, Lucien, Allen, and Hal Chase. In fact, Jack wrote Ed White that he loved her "not only as a 'woman,' but as a 'man.' " He also claimed he was ready to go to work on the New York railroads to support her—but as his Negro mistress, à la Baudelaire, rather than as his wife. Jack's ideal life, as he sketched it for Ed, would consist of running with his railroad lantern "from Ma's house of big meals and wine and TV to Sweetheart's house of sex balls wine tea bop talk loveinvolvement."

One night, in John Holmes' apartment, John discovered them sitting on the floor—she in her slip—talking and laughing. Whenever John saw them together, Jack's thoughtfulness and openness with her were extraordinary. With no other woman had he seen Jack capable of expressing such intensity. Partly what disarmed Jack was her ability to reach out and hug him, kiss him, or even laugh at him. But John also felt Jack's fascination for someone—one of the very few people—as raw as himself. Also on the verge of cracking up, Jack sought the raft of (in Holmes' words) "a child of the night adrift on a flood."

Mardou liked *The Town and the City,* and was convinced he was a serious writer. She appreciated his physical modesty too—he got upset at one party where several women undressed—being very shy herself. Her love for jazz and her skill at scatting complex chords with him created another special tie; but in truth they shared precious little on which to build a long-term relationship. At times he stereotyped her—for example, though they both liked classical music, he discussed only jazz with her. Then there was the fundamental problem that he usually didn't care to hear anything a woman had to say. While her interest in psychology ran to Gestalt, perspective boxes, etc., Jack harped on Reich.

She wondered about his need to go home to his mother all the time, but she realized he had nowhere else to stay and was much more disturbed by his insecurity. Driving Jack from bar to apartment to bar was his constant fear that people no longer liked him. Above all, he worried about what people thought of him as a writer. The more he doubted himself the more he drank, and the more was he scoffed at by those he wanted to impress. Mardou didn't enjoy being dragged all over New York, and she thought it criminal the way Jack would try to pull Lucien away from his wife and their baby—as he heedlessly pulled others away from inviolable obligations—just to have a friendly audience or someone to pat his back. And she felt that the way he played up to homosexuals, and anyone else he thought could boost his career, seemed pitiful.

Perhaps the saddest spectacle was his desire to please the subterraneans. Most of them, especially the junkies, preferred bought kicks to Jack's dreams. Gould traveled around the country making dope connections and giving young girls their first taste of illicit goodies. Mardou thought both Jack and Allen foolish to call such men "angels" and "saints." Gould himself was offended by Jack's suggestion that being a hipster was a religious vocation. Mardou was also disappointed when Jack went back to wearing dungarees, for she felt that when he was trying to look young and defiant, he only looked silly. It distressed her to see him making such a critical blunder by choosing the wild life rather than the dignified path of a professional writer. Sometimes Jack had his own moments of regret, and confessed that he felt like an old man and that he was tired of the hipsters fooling around like kids.

Their actual romance lasted only the month of August. Lucien thought that had she been white Jack would probably have married her. To Ed White, Jack ascribed their breakup to her refusal to trust him. He explained that he had envisioned them living together in a cottage in the woods or in Mexico, with Mardou caring for her helpless mystical husband like Blake's wife—only Mardou evidently didn't think Jack's madness as harmless as Blake's. In truth, marriage was one of the last things on her mind; her most urgent quest was for a quiet life.

Jack connected his breakup with Mardou with a dream of Hal and Ginger, who were now living separated in New York. In the dream, he got $1,000 from his publisher and was also offered a job selling books in a company car. Instead, he took off for Mexico by bus. On the bus were Hal and Ginger with three children. The children were neglected while Ginger played guitar and sang (as she did in real life in the Village) and Hal displayed his sexual arousal to all the ladies. When one of the children started vomiting and neither Hal nor Ginger noticed, Jack got so angry he decided to return to New York to accept the book-selling job and "take care of my children if any with concern." But it was too late—if he cashed in his ticket he wouldn't have enough money to live on once he got back. As the dream ended, Jack felt doomed to lead his "drearily repetitious" life.[210]

Burroughs had arrived in New York from Columbia in mid-August, bringing with him several suitcases of dried *yage*, a psychedelic vine, and was lionized by the subterraneans. Now, while a surfeit of new people called for Jack's attention, he was irresistibly drawn back into the orbit of Bill and Allen, who were working together on an epistolary book, *The Yage Letters*. It was not just a question of Jack's no longer having time for Mardou but of his needing to be loved by Allen and Bill and the masculine artistic world of which they were a part. In the San Remo one night Bill finally got his chance to meet Gore Vidal, but before he could get to first base, Jack himself started flirting with Vidal. Despite Mardou's pleas for Jack to come home with her, he sent her home alone, promising to follow in a couple of hours. After kissing Vidal's hand, and showering the most abject flattery on his writing, Jack talked him into going to bed. But at Vidal's room in the Chelsea Hotel, Jack proved impotent. The next morning he asked Vidal for a dollar, as though he were indeed rough trade, the image Burroughs had accused him of projecting. A few nights later, to Mardou's increasing distaste, Jack went into a similar act with a blond "faun boy," [211] though he claimed he only wanted to entertain Bill and Allen.

To this situation was added the dynamite of Gregory Corso, who was now living more or less with Allen in his new apartment on East 7th Street. Making $45 a week as a copyboy at the New York *World Telegram*, Allen was already theoretically committed to supporting penniless poets, but Corso's cause was sweetened by his boyish charm and sex appeal. That Allen should have fallen for Gregory was the last thing Bill Burroughs wanted, because in the intimacy of all-night talk sessions, routines, and occasional sex, Bill discovered himself in love with Allen. As Bill chopped *yage* vines, his looks made Gregory's blood run cold. Mardou's apartment seemed the perfect haven for Gregory, and Jack's jealousy a much smaller risk than Bill's machete.

In Corso's behalf, it should be noted that he and Jack were at this point far from bosom friends. Clowning and kidding, Gregory thrust himself upon twenty-two-year-old Mardou, who was having enough trouble understanding Jack's thirty-one-year-old gloom. After heavy drinking with her and Jack at the Remo and Fugazzi's, Gregory asked if he could spend the night with them at her place, and she agreed. On the way he grabbed an empty pushcart and gave them a ride. They ended up at Allen's instead, where in the morning Jack and Allen got in a big fight over the fact that the stolen pushcart parked outside was jeopardizing Allen's security. Jack in his outraged pride, flinging down his key to Allen's apartment, began to seem a greater liability to Mardou's peace of mind than sly, mischiefmaking Gregory.

She felt that Jack was pushing her off on Gregory, especially since he'd told everyone about a dream he'd had in which Gregory went to bed with her. Yet when she and Gregory started wrestling in the back of novelist William Gaddis' car, Jack was incensed; then when she chose to go with Jack rather than stay home while Gregory was there, Jack repaid her with a night of sullen drinking at Alan Ansen's. Jack admitted to himself that he wanted to get out of the relationship, which was threatening his "white man's life" and his peaceful working arrangement at his mother's. As for his "white man's life," [212] it was mostly a fantasy of himself living like Faulkner on a homestead in the Deep South, discussing literature with some genteel doctor over a bottle of Old Granddad. The need Jack felt for his mother's approval—which was the real basis of his sense of obligation to her—was a much bigger obstacle to permanent involvement with Mardou. Knowing it would alienate her, Jack continued to abandon her in the middle of the night, on one occasion jumping out of the cab that was taking them home and hailing another cab to go meet Lucien. A few days later, when she told Jack she had slept with Gregory, he stormed and sulked over the fact that she had betrayed him.

8.

Mardou's final rejection of Jack came in early October. Shortly after, he went home and in three days and nights of speed typing on benzedrine produced a novel about their affair called *The Subterraneans*. The last two lines of the novel summarize the theory underlying all his art: "And I go home having lost her love./ And write this book."

More strongly than in his previous novels, Kerouac stresses the writer's role as "recording angel." Up to this time he has emphasized what man loses by living, but in *The Subterraneans* occurs his first unqualified assertion that art can transform loss to gain. His method is to show that life is the same everywhere, and then to reveal how the mind through its paranoias, dreams, and fantasies creates the variations that make it beautiful. *Sad* is one of the book's key words; according to Kerouac's aesthetic, being sad is closing oneself to the possibility of variation. When the narrator fears to lose Mardou, even birds look bleak. The answer to life's sadness is to accept change, and to restore and enhance the past imaginatively. This insight is given by Mardou in a letter to the narrator: "I am full of strange feelings, reliving and refashioning many old things."

The dissonance between the artistic bravado of *The Subterraneans* and the unrelieved pain of Kerouac's own life manifests in a voice both strikingly innocent and ignorant, like the prophecy of a blind oracle. One of the qualities in Kerouac's writing is just this sense of its being the other half of his life, the unlived life that might have been. In the words of John Clellon Holmes:

> The Jack role in *The Subterraneans* never seems to realize that he'd rather have the love than write about it. He [Kerouac] experienced most of his life to write about it, but there's something so poignant about that, because he isn't saying that living's better than writing; but he's saying, "I wish I could have had it and even not written about it" or "written about it much later"—that it was broken off, that it left severed ganglia, and that the only way to come to terms with it was to write about it. The only way to lose her was to write about it.

The power of *The Subterraneans* derives from Kerouac's finally having a literary theory that complemented his own incapacity to live as detachedly as he wanted to write. It now seemed to him that writing was a form of sexual expression; and that the more feeling it released (like Reich's postulated electrical discharge during orgasm), the more satisfactory the experience for both writer and reader. Where Reich saw civilization's restrictions on orgasm as debilitating to every aspect of man's life and thought, Kerouac saw the critical and academic restrictions on prose form as ruinous to both the writer and his work. The very essence of this new literary method was engagement, concern for the material written about, a coming together of mind and subject. To Ed White, Kerouac explained that he was trying "to swirl my brain from commonplace expression into seas of English. . . ." The next step in English literature, he believed, would have to be "because no other where to go the bio electric flow like orgasm from center of mind and jewel point of interest in memory or vision therein outward like coming to the object of love in one wild impulse surge electric language. . . ." He declared his belief that no writing mattered unless it contained this orgasmic intensity, and he speculated that "the way to come in writing is to *blow*, to use bop phrases excitedly beyond stringencies of sentence into as I say seas of English. . . ." In his estimation, rules and punctuation were secondary to sounds, rhythms, and the "electrical fury" of the writer himself, who should ideally be in tune with the electromagnetic "cosmic energy" postulated as fundamental by both Einstein and Reich. As an example, Jack instructed Ed not to start writing about the history of the Denver City Council but rather to "start writing about that fascinating little red bud on the bleak bush in front of the City and County Bldg or something you understand or bums in bottoms or jewel of personal colloquial interest. . . ."

As Warren Tallman was the first to point out, in the essay "Kerouac's Sound," the sense of a book like *The Subterraneans* is communicated by the very structure and sound of the sentences. Their composition is boplike; they usually convey a single thought or action, interspersed with shifts or side-trips (to use Tallman's terms) away from the narrative line. Among the major variations that expand the sentences, Tallman cites the narrator's self-analysis and the author's commentary on the "circumstances under which the sentence is being written." Additionally, the whole novel contains a running record of the process of its composition. The self-conscious novel dates back to the mid-eighteenth century, when Laurence Sterne founded the genre with *Tristram Shandy*; Sterne even used dashes, as Kerouac does, to mark the points of his endless digressions. But once again Kerouac makes the form comment on the novel's subject. The truth of nonlinear perception actually becomes the "moral" of his love story. Writes Tallman: "The narrative line follows the brief love-affair between Percepied [the narrator] and Mardou while the improvised details move, as the title would suggest, down into the clutter of their lives among the guilts and shames which come up from the subterranean depths to steal their love from them. The truth is in the improvisations."

Many of the sentences run on for a page or more, and they are not just longer versions of the standard English sentence. Certainly the innovation in Kerouac's language will not be fully appreciated until his syntax is subjected to the analysis of structural or transformational grammar. But a few simple observations are in order here. The standard English sentence has a subject doing something, sometimes to an object, or having something done to it. One or more additional sequences of subject-and-predicate may be joined to the first, either in an independent relationship (with *and*, *but*, etc.) or in a dependent relationship (with *if*, *while*, etc.). Kerouac's sentences are conventional in that they seldom lack a complete subject and predicate. The difference is that other clauses seem to grow out from within the main clause, or from inside one another, *rather than merely being added on.* Although Kerouac sometimes cheats by using dashes to keep a sentence from ending, he often succeeds in creating an organic whole in which thought begets thought, phrase generates phrase:

> I was coming down the street with Larry O'Hara drinking buddy of mine from all the times in San Francisco in my long and nervous and mad careers I've gotten drunk and in fact cadged drinks off friends with such "genial" regularity no-boby really cared to notice or announce that I am developing or was developing, in my youth, such bad freeloading habits though of course they did notice but liked me and as Sam said "Everybody comes to you for your gasoline boy, that's some filling station you got there" or say words to that effect—old Larry O'Hara always nice to me, a crazy Irish young business-man of San Francisco with Balzacian backroom in his book-store where they'd smoke tea and talk of the old days of the great Basie band or the days of the great Chu Berry—of whom more anon since she got involved with him too as she had to get involved with everyone because of knowing me who am nervous and many leveled and not in the least one-souled—not a piece of my pain has showed yet—or suffering—Angels, bear with me—I'm not even looking at the page but straight ahead into the sadglint of my wallroom and at a Sarah Vaughan Gerry Mulligan Radio KROW show on the desk in the form of a radio, in other words, they were sitting on the fender of a car in front of the Black Mask bar on Montgomery Street, Julian Alexander the Christlike unshaved thin youth-ful quiet strange almost as you or as Adam might say apoc-alyptic angel or saint of the subterraneans, certainly star (now), and she, Mardou Fox, whose face when I first saw it in Dante's bar around the corner made me think, "By God, I've got to get involved with that little woman" and maybe too because she was Negro.

Thematically *The Subterraneans* is a further exploration of the dreamlike nature of reality, the reality of dreams. *In* and its varia-tions—*inside, inkept, inward*—are key words too. Kerouac is pre-pared to admit that "gaiety, horror, the eventual H bomb" are all subjective phenomena, the product of random moods. He develops the idea that everything exists at the same time, and that the mind picks its experiences and feelings out of a grab bag of simultaneity. The discovery of this truth saves Mardou from the madness of her alienation, which had led to her wandering the streets naked; she says, "I understood all my moves as one obligation after another to communicate to whoever not accidentally but by *arrangement* was placed before me, communicate and exchange this news, the vibra-tion and the new meaning that I had, about everything happening to everyone all the time everywhere and for them not to worry. . . ." The insight comes to her on Easter, one of Kerouac's favorite symbols for the transcendence of mundane reality.

The mystery lies in the appearance of an arrangement, an order, to what the mind chooses to perceive. This order is emphasized by numerous correspondences throughout the novel. For example, at the moment of enlightenment Mardou has a vision of her father's face; at the end, when the narrator is reconciled to losing her, he has a vision of his mother's face.

Questioning the mind's control over reality, Kerouac examines man's ability to make his dreams come true. In the long sentence quoted above, from the opening of the novel, the narrator asserts that his affair with Mardou grew out of a wish born when he first saw her. Later in the novel, Mardou berates the narrator for letting his dreams fade: "But we should really break up, we've never done anything together, we were going to Mexico, and then you were going to get a job and we'd live together, then remember the loft idea, all big phantasms that like haven't worked out because you haven't pushed them from your mind out into the open world, haven't acted on them. . . ." The central irony of the book is that the narrator realizes his most fearful dream. After dreaming that Yuri (Gregory) makes love to Mardou right in front of him, the narrator dwells on the dream until Yuri finally does just that, as though they were actors taking their parts in a play.

The narrator's name is Leo Percepied. "Leo" was Kerouac's father's name, and "Percepied" is French for "pierced foot." Oedipus of Greek legend had his feet pierced as a child and derived his name indirectly from that fact, "Oedipus" being Greek for "swollen foot," the condition caused by his injury. While punning on *percipient,* one who perceives, Kerouac identifies Leo with Oedipus on a number of levels.

One of Leo's problems is that he has replaced his father in his mother's affections, and has in turn accepted her as his "wife"; he has the classic Oedipal complex. His affair with Mardou takes on significance in light of Kerouac's new interest in Reich, since Reich believed the Oedipal complex could be rendered harmless once one's damned-up sexual energy found a normal outlet. Metaphysically Leo and Oedipus suffer the same dilemma. Told by the Delphic Oracle that he will kill his father and murder his mother, Oedipus moves to another city to frustrate the prophecy, thereby facilitating its fulfillment. Seeking to evade his prophetic dream of losing Mardou, Leo precipitates the event. At the end of *Oedipus Rex,* horrified to realize that "those calamities we inflict on ourselves are those which cause the most pain," Oedipus stabs out his eyes. At the end of *The Subterraneans* Leo merely goes on to new visions—of his mother's loving face, and of Yuri as a "Funny Angel."

Imagining himself in a newsreel with Mardou, the narrator suddenly realizes that what is seen is only in the eye of the beholder. The anguish in his life is purely his own creation:

> ... both of us actually hysterically smiling and as tho nothing had happened at all and in fact like happy unconcerned people you see in newsreels busy going down the street to their chores and where-go's and we're in the same rainy newsreel mystery sad but inside of us (as must then be so inside the puppet filmdolls of screen) the great tumescent turbulent turmoil alliterative as a hammer on the brain bone bag and balls, bang I'm sorry I was ever born. . . .

That *The Subterraneans* ends less tragically than *Oedipus Rex* is due to the narrator's acceptance of his own strange vision [213] rather than rejecting it, as Oedipus does, to keep from seeing horrors. Yuri is an angel because, knowing that both dream and reality are tricks of imagination, he harmonizes with universal laws by becoming a jester himself; and the narrator has clearly learned an artistic lesson from him:

> ... but I continue the daydream and I look into his [Yuri's] eyes and I see suddenly the glare of a jester angel who made his presence on earth all a joke and I realize that this too with Mardou was a joke and I think, "Funny Angel, elevated amongst the subterraneans."

The lesson is that there is no need to make one's dreams real, as Leo had done earlier, while driven by paranoia to test the reality of his dream of Mardou's infidelity. Reality itself is a series of shadows, like the frames of a newsreel into which we dream meanings. Reality is sound *heard* as opposed to the infinite potentiality of sound. Tuning into dreams, like listening to bop, replaces the dull repetitions of reality with richer, rarer patterns. Significantly, Leo and Mardou enjoy telling each other their dreams. Mixed together, dream and reality produce the harsh static that marks the breakup of their affair. Yet both dream and reality are music—part of the same song: reality the melody and dream the variations.

The Subterraneans is rooted in dualistic philosophy, as can be seen just by the attention Kerouac pays to the division between black and white. The novel's insistence that mind authors the world is nonetheless a very Eastern concept and many of Kerouac's key words—*void, dream, mind, essence*—are common to Asian religions. Beginning with *On the Road,* and quite strongly by *Maggie Cassidy,* Kerouac's quest for a unified vision suggests the specific influence of Buddhist doctrine.

In the spring of 1953, Allen Ginsberg had begun an intensive study of Chinese and Japanese art, literature, and religion, and he began to communicate his new enthusiasm to his friends almost immediately. In Kerouac's own hand we have testimony that by the end of 1953 he too was a "big Buddhist" who "stayed home and read Asvhaghosha." There is some evidence that he was at least familiar with the story of Buddha's life as early as 1951.[214] He would have acquired some knowledge of Buddhism simply from Spengler's *Decline of the West*, and Thoreau's *Walden* familiarized him with a number of Indian and Chinese religious texts. But not until Kerouac's personal archives are released will scholars be able to determine how directly Eastern thought influenced these early novels.

Of Kerouac's creation of three major works in the period from October 1952, to October 1953, there is no question. *October in the Railroad Earth, Maggie Cassidy,* and *The Subterraneans* constituted a second *annus mirabilis*; back to back with the previous year's three masterworks, they represented an explosion of creativity unmatched in American literature since Melville, and filled the footsteps of the Immortal Bard.

TEN
Double Vision

1.

Shortly after writing *The Subterraneans* Jack brought the manuscript to Mardou as though it were a present. Having read only small parts of *On the Road*, because of the difficulty of the unpunctuated sentences, she hadn't realized how thoroughly autobiographical his fiction had become. Moreover, she had never suspected he might write about her, because she believed that "people wouldn't do that to their friends." [215] The manuscript, full of the most intimate details of their sex life, was a cruel shock. Concentrating on her anatomy while sparing his own, he had described what she felt were their ugliest encounters, for they had had many good times in bed. She was also upset by the ridiculous speeches he had put in her mouth, especially the one about how "the woman is the essence." She had once told him about a book she had been reading on phallic symbolism, while in the novel he credited her with formulating a theory about male "erections." [216]

At least part of the rancor between them grew out of her misunderstanding of the nature of his art—indeed at this stage virtually no one did understand it. Rather than putting words in her mouth, his intention was to let all the characters speak through him, because that was the way he actually heard them. The moment in *The Subterraneans* had evolved into an inspired monologue: the point of transformation, where incoming sound becomes one's own thought.

In response to Mardou's fright, he told her that she could destroy the manuscript, allegedly his only copy. However angry, she was reluctant to destroy an author's work (though later she guessed that the version he'd given her, typed on thin yellow bond, was not the first draft). To prevent her having to leave the Village, as she planned, Jack agreed to transpose the story from New York to San Francisco and to make the black heroine white.

On the Road was now so near publication that Jack thought his only worries were avoiding lawsuits with Neal and A. A. Wyn. Since Wyn still had some claim on a novel called *On the Road*, Jack thought to avert the problem by changing the title of the original scroll novel to "Heroes of the Hip Generation." As for Neal's possible libel case (a phantasm conjured mainly by Viking's paranoia), Jack would have to take his chances. From what the editors at Viking were saying, publication of the novel would be worth any risk. At Cowley's request, several editors had written evaluations of *On the Road*, and the consensus was that it was a "classic of our times." The editors felt that Kerouac's prose needed only "the lightly touching pencil," since its "lavish, reckless" quality well suited his material; but they did request that some of the cross-country trips be cut or condensed.

Exactly what transpired at Viking in the fall of 1953 may never be known, but the outcome of some closed-door meetings profoundly altered the direction of Jack's life. Cowley had contacted Arabelle Porter at *New World Writing* to recommend she publish an excerpt from *On the Road*, and this time Jack was ready to cooperate. On occasion he still acted rather hysterically—for instance, sending Cowley a denunciation of Gore Vidal and the homosexuals in literature—but Cowley was too broadminded to let Jack's temperament affect his judgment of the work. Possibly Jack's new agent, Stanley Colbert of Lord & Colbert, could have pushed harder. Or perhaps, as Holmes believes, the owner of Viking was categorically opposed to publishing the novel. In any case, by the end of the year the momentum there toward accepting it was spent.

That fall Jack was stimulated by a greatly widening circle of new acquaintances as well as a deepening of old friendships. Allen, Bill, and he shared pleasures and ideas intensified by the knowledge that they would soon be parting for months or years. Addicted to dolophine (methadone), Bill needed to live cheaply and with minimum interference from authorities; the only place left to do so seemed Africa. To clear his head of commerce, Allen planned to travel through Mexico, California, and Europe. Restless again, Jack wanted to go to Paris; but without money he saw California or the Southwest (where he could work on the railroad) as likelier destinations.

Questioned by Allen and Bill about his new writing methods, he produced a concise set of directions, "The Essentials of Spontaneous Prose." Kerouac had little gift for intellectualizing literature; an earlier attempt to explain the innovations of his own work, "Belief & Technique for Modern Prose," was a list of catchy phrases like "You're a Genius all the time." The most important statements in the "Essentials" had to do with the "undisturbed flow from the mind" from a "jewel center of interest," the notion of writing as Reichian release that Jack had articulated for Ed White. He tied this theory to Dostoyevsky's confessional method in *Notes from Underground* and William Carlos Williams' attempt to write with the "measured pauses" of speech. Kerouac's suggestion that the dash be used to separate breath phrasings was based on idiosyncrasy and not wholly practicable. His one real advance beyond Williams was the apprehension that rhythm develops within the thought process rather than being created by thought. Albeit the distinction is subtle, Kerouac really was moving toward a more spontaneous literary form, one in which errors, malapropisms, babble, and all forms of verbal stumbling fit into a grander context. The act of self-expression appears as the mind's ultimate product, just as the act of excretion completes all the other bodily processes, ending one cycle to begin another: "No pause to think of proper word but the infantile pileup of scatological buildup words till satisfaction is gained, which will turn out to be a great appending rhythm to a thought and be in accordance with Great Law of timing."

At the Cedar Tavern on 8th Street and University Place, Jack mingled with a group of artists who painted the way he wrote. They were abstract-expressionist painters, and the Cedar was the hangout of some of the greatest among them—like Jackson Pollock, Willem de Kooning, and Franz Kline. Pollock developed the concept of Action Painting, in which the form of the work was not preconceived, but flowed out of the painter's spontaneous muscular gestures. Pollock's major breakthrough had come with the discovery of drip painting, whereby he let paint fall onto the canvas from a brush or a punctured can. Drip painting exploded the rigid lines of representational art the way bop fractured the melodic lines of conventional jazz. Bop had been foreshadowed by the "inventor of jazz," Jelly Roll Morton, who said, "Write the music so that there are breaks, and then you can do good things in the breaks." In the modern revolutions in both jazz and painting, the "good things" admitted into the work comprised the whole realm of suppressed desire and feeling. With bop musicians and abstract-expressionist painters, Kerouac shared a great distrust of conscious design. When he wrote "Craft *is* craft," he meant that the attempt to impose form on an art work is the worst form of deception, self-deception, in which the artist has lost touch with his inner being, from which the deepest impulses of his art spring.

Pollock, Kline, and de Kooning were men like Kerouac for whom the physical life was preeminent, the strength and vigor of one's body a measure of the power of one's art. A big, burly man, Pollock was quiet when sober, but drunk he'd start pounding the bar for double Jack Danielses and pushing his weight around. When a new painter would try to join their group, he would challenge: "You wanta box?" If the neophyte put up his fists, Pollock would commend him: "You got guts!" and buy him a drink.[217] With almost all the habitués of the Cedar the ability to drink was the final touchstone of both man and artist.

De Kooning and Kline became lifelong buddies to Jack. Mutual friends of Kline and Kerouac were struck by the great similarity of their personalities. Both drank with a sober determination to release some terrible hidden fury that could never escape; instead, what came out was always the same sentimental, sloppy sadness. Both turned their infinite maladjustments into a compelling charm that made it almost impossible to hate them. Their self-destructiveness was like a saint's burden that one couldn't help pity—if not admire— them for carrying. Pollock, who was also bound for early death, knew Jack less well than the others, though Village artist Harold Anton recalls Jack once helping to calm him when he had started screaming—as he often did—at the incomprehensible stupidity of someone bothering him. All three painters had come through the Depression in poverty and obscurity and were dazzled by the lime-light into which they were suddenly thrust; worse, they discovered that the hunger for attention was more insatiable than the thirst for booze. Their anguish was virtually identical to that of Jack, who was also beginning to drink prodigiously to avoid being a serious man in a frivolous world.

Part of the foolishness around Jack was just the high jinks of youth, and though "silliness" bothered the grave, beleaguered Ca-nuck in him, the youthful world was always the one he chose to move in. He loved Gregory for the exuberance with which he ex-plored the delights of his newfound freedom, and for the dogged clownishness of a kid bent on exasperating complacent grownups: for instance, trying to sell Allen and Bill a suitcase full of stolen *crème de menthe!* Jack loved the modern young women on the Vil-lage scene and was especially intrigued by the "Three Graces": Iris Brodie, Sherry Martinelli, and a woman known as the "silent Ma-donna," who went on a seventy-two-hour talking jag and talked her way into and out of Bellevue. Wearing granny dresses and junkshop jewelry, her hair in a bun, the painter Sherry Martinelli visited Ezra Pound in St. Elizabeth's Hospital and became his mistress. Short-haired, masculine-clothed Iris Brodie was another gifted painter, whose canvases of delicate Klee-like mustard brown ships etched on a mustard brown ocean were not properly prepared or preserved. All three women used speed and heroin; and in the case of Iris, the rapid deterioration of her canvases signified some delicate thing in her soul that was also disintegrating.

If Jack was always hurt by the spectacle of childhood ground against the whetstone of maturity, he also learned strength from it. What demeaned and tormented him were the ignorant adults who made him play the clown to gain their love. At this point, few be-sides Allen and Bill realized what a great writer he had become. John Kingsland thought him still the jejune, humorless disciple of Djuna Barnes, as he had seen him in early 1946, when Jack couldn't distinguish between imitation and parody. Kingsland sincerely be-lieved that Jack hadn't read more than two books since getting out of high school. Of course at the parties at which Kingsland saw him,

Jack mostly just tagged along and watched; and though he might stand on his head to be noticed, he'd never talk literature. At most he'd turn his learning into a kind of game, which only he knew about. One night at Al Leslie's studio, which Helen Parker was sub-letting, Jack refused to argue with George Wickstrom about the rationalist versus the nonrationalist traditions; instead, he shouted "Buddha Buddha" whenever Wickstrom mentioned the name of some writer. No one suspected that he had already read the *Life of Buddha* and several other Eastern scriptures. Alan Ansen found Jack amusing, but screamed over the "tedium" of *Visions of Cody* and in fact used to enjoy patronizing Jack as "just a little boy who wants to be a novelist."

But then, Jack was a sex object to Ansen, as he was to many men in that world. Ansen talked Jack into going to bed with him at Kingsland's, and Kingsland remembers that Jack yielded to the blandishments of numerous others. Not that anyone ever dared treat him as gay, but gay men tended to prey on his fear of women. Jack's concern that he had small genitals was a subject of their camp, as was his fumbling sexual identity. When he spoke of the boys in the San Remo as "angels," they joked, it was with the same intent as Cocteau or Genet toward their source of inspiration.[218]

Helen Parker, lover and friend of many writers, sensed the depth in Jack that most people missed; she was always scolding Ansen and the others: "You don't understand him!" At Helen's, Jack met the singing cowboy and protégé of Woody Guthrie, Rambling Jack Elliot. Jack told him, "I like the language of bums," whereupon Rambling Jack pulled out his guitar and started playing Woody Guthrie songs. Reciprocating the treat, Jack spent three consecutive nights reading aloud the entire manuscript of *On the Road* to him. There were a number of others in New York who had ears for Jack's genius, such as Beverly Burford, who'd recently moved there, and Ed White, back for his final year at Columbia. But no matter how affable and voluble Jack would be at their parties—dancing and reading from his notebooks—friends like Jorge Davila sensed his repressed hostility. It never reached the stage of fist-fighting, yet Jack often antagonized people by the way he spoke: gritting his teeth and biting off his words. His use of dolophine and barbiturates at this time bespoke the same desire to obliterate something that wouldn't go away from him. Dragging after him like Marley's chains were all his betrayed dreams.

2.

He needed to warm himself by the family fires of the Cassady household. Still mending from his accident, Neal had been writing both

Jack and Allen to visit him, promising them good jobs in a parking lot as well as free room and board. With poorly masked bitterness, Jack wrote Carolyn that he no longer cared about publishing contracts, and projected a Thoreau-like existence for himself, in which his primary concern would be growing his own food. More realistically, he hoped to return to his old cycle of working several months on the railroad, followed by an equal period of writing in Mexico.

In late December Allen left on a journey to Florida, Cuba, Mexico, and San Francisco, where he planned to rendezvous with Jack. Having failed to crack New York publishing, he encouraged Jack to believe they could get their start on the West Coast. If need be, Allen promised to publish Jack's books himself.[219] For travel money, Jack worked the Christmas rush in the Post Office; but during the entire month of January 1954, he debated with himself whether or not to go. The deciding factor was a warmly welcoming letter from Carolyn, which pleased his mother. The knowledge that Jack had such concerned friends in California convinced Mémère that she and Jack ought to make their permanent home there. She suggested Jack go first and get his job back on the railroad while she saved a stake in New York. Securing his mother's happiness "among the palm trees of Santa Clara Valley" preceded all Jack's personal plans.

On January 27, Jack began a slow and harrowing trip hitching West. From L.A. he rode the Zipper two hundred miles freezing in the night wind off the ocean, and in Watsonville he literally ate grass. His reunion with the Cassadys around mid-February was largely a disappointment. Neal and Carolyn seemed obsessed with two subjects, both of which irked Jack. The first was their legal case against the railroad, which they were suing for damages because of Neal's accident. They expected to collect several thousand dollars and were continually talking about the new house they would be able to buy. The second was Edgar Cayce and his theories about reincarnation and karma. The last thing Jack wanted to hear from Neal was secondhand lectures on Atlantis, akashic records, and Gurdieff and Ouspensky. Jack's former "hero of the snowy West" now appeared like "Billy Graham in a suit." [220] The idea of karma was especially repugnant to Jack, who was weary of one life and didn't want to come back for a few hundred more. He believed Cayce's teachings about the immortality of one's personality appealed only to people still locked into egotism, exactly the delusion from which Jack was trying to free himself.

At the San Jose library he found Dwight Goddard's *A Buddhist Bible*, a formidable collection of Buddhist and Taoist writings from a variety of traditions and periods. At the root of Jack's sudden fascination with Buddhism may well have been an identification with the historic Buddha, Siddhartha Gautama. Born of a noble house, raised in luxury, Gautama renounced his wealth and royal privileges at the age of twenty-nine, to wander among the poor and suffering and so learn the true terms of earthly life. The descendant of a baron, Jack always thought of himself as an aristocrat; and if he never knew ease, yet he was always coddled by a mother who would give anything in her power to keep him hers. In addition, Jack felt he had renounced the privilege of his genius to share the simple sorrows and joys of the fellaheen. Curiously, when Jack retold the life of the Buddha to the *Paris Review* interviewers in 1967, he claimed that Gautama was *thirty-one* when he made his renunciation—Jack's own age when plunging into the Buddhist life.

The texts most influential on him were the *Diamond Sutra*, the *Surangama Sutra*, the *Lankavatara Scripture*, the *Tao-Teh-King*, and the *Sutra Spoken by the Sixth Patriarch*. Already in Ashvaghosha Jack had been struck by the profundity of the first two Noble Truths— "All Life is Sorrowful" and "The Cause of Suffering is Ignorant Desire"—as well as by the counsel to "repose beyond fate." During his first meditation (as described in his "Last Word" column in *Escapade*, October, 1959) he had seen "golden swarms of nothing, the true thing, the thus-ness of Creation." Without questioning the validity of his spiritual experience, it is possible to suggest that Jack then needed to believe all his afflictions an "imaginary concatenation of mind." For one in relentless misery it was useful to believe that happiness is empty; for one permanently deprived, that "there's nothing to yearn after." The *Diamond Sutra* served to exorcise the worst of his fears (he later claimed that it cured him even of his horror of falling under train wheels). Endlessly he quoted its injunction (from the translation in *A Buddhist Bible*, New York: E. P. Dutton, 1966, pp. 106-107) to discard all "arbitrary conceptions" about either the existence or nonexistence of phenomena, one's own selfhood, other selves, living beings, and a Universal Self.

The texts in the *Buddhist Bible* represented mainly Mahayana thought, which was a later development as Buddhism spread northward from India. The original Hinayana Buddhism taught the means to individual enlightenment by the solitary *arhat* (disciple), whereas Mahayana stressed that the salvation of one being was imperfect as long as there remained other beings to be saved. Mahayana appealed to the peculiar combination of selfishness and compassion in Jack's character, for in Mahayana the enlightened one was both a Tathagata and a Bodhisattva. The Tathagata simply passed through the world without any attachments: "The true Tathagata is never coming from anywhere, nor is he going anywhere." It would be hard to find a more apt description for a man who had left two wives, a daughter, numerous lovers and friends, and several careers as though they were just way stations on the road to his final dissolution. On the other hand, the Bodhisattva, who refused personal salvation that he might first save all sentient beings, practiced the same universal charity Jack had learned from his brother, Gerard. Indeed Jack later told his fellow Buddhist Gary Snyder that Buddhism was greater than Catholicism insofar as its compassion reached everywhere, far beyond just a certain parish or mission. In Snyder's view, the vast scope of Mahayana matched Jack's own big-heartedness.

Taoism, older and more naturalistic, spoke to the self-reliant, pragmatic Yankee, the Jack who wanted to live by his own hands like Thoreau, who loved Shakespeare's image of the happy man "seeking the food he eats, and pleased with what he gets." He found in the Tao both a worthy goal and a means of getting there:

> Oh for this one rare occurrence
> Gladly would I give ten thousand pieces of gold!
> A hat is on my head, a bundle on my back,
> And my staff, the refreshing breeze and the full moon.

There were no Japanese texts in the *Buddhist Bible,* but the *Sutra Spoken by the Sixth Patriarch* was one of the major statements of Chinese Ch'an Buddhism, which in Japan became Zen. Ch'an was a search for the essentials of the Dharma (universal law), and a simplification of ritual. Making little use of the vast body of sutras, Ch'an taught a "more direct and immediate realization of Reality." The followers of Ch'an didn't abandon the practice of Dhyana, quiet meditation, but they saw no harm in leading active lives. They believed that Prajna, transcendental wisdom, came in an instantaneous flash, what was later known in Japan as satori. For Hui-neng, all the teachings of the Buddha could be reduced to a self-realization of Mind-essence, which was Ultimate Reality. Hui-neng's insight that "from the beginning not a thing was" supported Jack's own prior assumption that daily life was a form of dream.

Zen never interested Jack as much as Indian and Chinese Buddhism, despite the affinities between his writing method and Zen dialogues and Koans. The Zen master uses words to show the futility of saying anything meaningful, much as Kerouac retreats from meaning into the direct communication of rhythm and harmonies of sound. Observing minute detail, while recognizing the illusiveness of all appearance, is a paradox in both Zen and Kerouac. Perhaps the reason Jack shied away from Zen was that it tends to be atheistic, whereas the original Buddhism was agnostic, and he never lost his need for a personal God, even though he could never accept any God that could create a world of suffering. Zen's greatest impact on his writing came through the haiku, a three-line, seventeen-syllable poem that creates a mental jump via the juxtaposition of highly clear images. After assimilating the haikus of such masters as Basho, Issa, and Shiki, Jack produced a large volume of haiku that contemporary Zen poets have judged among the best in English.

By March 1954, Allen still hadn't arrived in San Jose. Engrossed in the Mayan ruins and early culture of Chiapas, Mexico, his letters took weeks to reach the U.S., and he had Jack and Neal worried he was dead. That worry was the only thing still holding them together; soon after they learned that Allen was working on the *finca* of a woman archeologist, Jack returned to his favorite flophouse, the Cameo, in Skid Row San Francisco. Although for a few weeks Jack and Neal had gotten high together on benny and beer, their new intellectual arguments over Cayce versus Buddha soon degenerated into old gripes about who would pay for pork chops and how to fairly divide a pound of pot. Disturbed by Neal's increasing coldness, Jack was shocked (as he wrote to Allen) to see him knock his daughter Cathy clear across the room. But as he later admitted to Carolyn, his real reason for leaving was his own self-lacerating guilt: "it isn't that I'd soured on you, but that I thought you and Neal had soured on me after my lapses into impatience and irascibility. . . ." Jack's self-hate was evident too in his destruction of his *Doctor Sax* tape, which he erased to record the children singing ditties.

In San Francisco he spent a couple of weeks indulging in booze and drugs, and listening to jazz with Al Sublette. Sublette was grappling with his own emotional problems and so no help to Jack's morbid mood, and their rapport was further fretted by Jack's disdain for Al's favorite pastime, women. Buddhist scriptures generally recommend temperance in all sensual activities, to help break the mind's bondage to illusion. *Moderation* was not in Jack's vocabulary, but he seized the notion that women are temptresses as a rationalization for his perennially troubled relations with them. Swearing off sex, and bored with everyone, he stayed in his hotel room to write a series of seventy-nine poems called *San Francisco Blues*.

San Francisco Blues was the first piece in what would eventually become a massive *Book of Blues*, comprising poetic responses to such places as Mexico City, MacDougal Street, Berkeley, Orlando, and Washington, D.C. Judging by the testimonials that have come from major American poets like Charles Olson, Robert Duncan, Robert Creeley, Allen Ginsberg, Gregory Corso, Bob Kaufman, Philip Lamantia, Phil Whalen, Gary Snyder, and Michael McClure, and by its decisive influence on a whole new generation of American poets, Kerouac's *Blues* is one of the most important poetic works in the second half of the twentieth century. Such diverse poets as Duncan and Lamantia have credited him with creating one of the best literary equivalents of musical blues.

Regarding his poems as "choruses," Kerouac limited each one to the size of a page in his little notebooks, "like the form of a set number of bars in a jazz blues chorus." The principal connection to jazz was that "the form is determined by time, and by the musician's [i.e., poet's] spontaneous phrasing & harmonizing with the beat of the time as it waves on by in measured choruses." Also as in jazz, it was at the poet's discretion whether to carry an idea from one chorus into the next or to begin a new idea with each chorus. In place of conventional devices like meter and stanza, Kerouac adopted the discipline of "non stop ad libbing." Rhythm was essential, but rather than the limited number of traditional, regular beats he employed "the rhythm of how you decide to 'rush' yr statement." [221]

It may seem that Kerouac is confusing blues with bop, but actually he is perceiving their consanguinity. The day Charlie Parker died, he lamented that "many of the young guys coming up didn't know or had forgotten their foundation—the blues." Blues, Parker affirmed, was "the basis of jazz." Above all, what makes Kerouac's poems blues is that their diction and structure are dictated directly by his feelings. If he sings of childhood his phrasing will be as simple as his memories, and when his mind jumps to the implications of childish innocence, the poem jumps too:

> Little boys are angels
> Crying in the street
> Wear funny hats
> Wait for green lights
> Carry bust out tubes
> Around their necks

Little boys have been known to hang many things around their necks, but "bust out tubes" is clearly a child's description of Benzedrine inhalers, Jack's personal means of "busting out" of his confined youth. The image is quintessentially surrealistic because it satisfies an unconscious reality, however "unrealistic" in terms of our daily experience. (That the blues and surrealism spring from identical impulses has been demonstrated by Paul Garon in *Blues and the Poetic Spirit*.) The final turning of the poem follows the poet's sudden revulsion against childhood:

> And roam the railyards
> Of the great cities
> Looking for locomotives
> Full of shit.

The great latitude Kerouac gives himself in these poems can and occasionally does admit bathos. But unquestionably he has the power to move in the context of the language as it's being written just as a blues singer will be leaving his baby in one breath and going back to her in the next, as his mood shifts. At his best Kerouac can also laugh and cry almost within the same line, run the gamut from love to lust just as those passions move through us—in a single pulse.

He can exaggerate and get to the heart of the matter at once, because his likes and dislikes are the only truth he acknowledges:

> I came a wearyin
> From eastern hills;
> Yonder Nabathaque recessit
> The eastward to Aurora rolls,
> Somewhere West of Idalia
> Or east of Klamath Falls,
> One—Lost a black haired
>   Woman with thin feet
> And red bag hangin
> Who usta walk
>   Down Arapahoe Street
> In Denver
>   And make all the
>   cabbies cry
> And drugstore ponies
> Eating pool ° in Remsac's
> Sob, to see so lovely
> All the Time
> And all so Tight
> And young.

3.

In late April, 1954, Jack returned to his mother's home in Richmond Hill, convinced that only a monastic life studying and practicing Buddhism would keep him from suicide. "Assured" by Buddha that life was a dream, he renounced all activity, including sex and writing, except for "who-cares-anyhow" drunken binges. In his new-found tranquillity he set about to counsel all his friends to give up their worldly ambitions and passions. When Allen stopped writing for a time, and Bill began writing from Tangier, instructing Jack to find Allen before he deliquesced in a Mexican prison, Jack accused Allen of "trying to make people worry" and dismissed Bill's letters as the "hysterical worryings of junkey." Jack wrote Carolyn that it sufficed to communicate his concern for Allen in "telepathic messages."

For all his talk of "do nothing," Jack actually worked very hard that spring. He got a job on the Dock Railway on the Brooklyn waterfront, but had to quit after a couple of weeks because of an-

---

° Pun on *poule*, French for "chicken" and also "whore," and its English homonym, which is the boys' other favorite pastime.

other attack of phlebitis. But neither that nor Little, Brown's rejection of "The Beat Generation" (the original *On the Road*) slowed his literary productivity, although he was discouraged that most of his manuscripts were "unread & dusting" at his agent's; and he waited on tenterhooks for word from E. P. Dutton, which had "The Beat Generation," and from *New World Writing*, which had four excerpts from the novel. Meanwhile, he was continuously adding to "Some of the Dharma," begun in February as digests and interpretations of his Buddhist reading. It was rapidly taking on the proportions of a major work, as he expanded it with his own translations of Buddhist texts from the French, comparisons of Buddhism and Catholicism, original religious parables, poems, and reflections on his life. He was also typing up his *Book of Dreams,* a journal of his actual dreams, recorded hastily as soon as he awoke in order to capture the "bemused and mystified" logic of dreams in equally hazy, fragmentary prose. He even began his first science fiction story, "cityCityCITY."

"cityCityCITY" was conceived in a dream about an overpopulated future society, in which the government has computerized knowledge and life-and-death control of all its citizens. As Dennis McNally pointed out, the story evolved into an allegory of America in the fifties, and specifically of the "Commie hunting" being conducted that spring by Senator Joseph McCarthy. Having charged the Secretary of the Army and other high-level military officials with sheltering Communists, McCarthy initiated a Senate investigation, whose hearings were televised nationally. The Army-McCarthy clash ended with the Senator's humiliating defeat, as he finally overstepped both professional and common decency by slurring the reputation of a young lawyer who had nothing to do with the case. Like McCarthy, the character G-92 in "cityCityCITY" unconscionably destroys innocent people to prosecute personal vendettas and to win favor for himself.

The detached perspective in Jack's writing was lacking in his own life. Burroughs, writing him about his own great need for love, worried that Jack's Buddhism was a retreat from feeling and suffering, which he thought necessary steps in working out the meaning of life. Especially for a writer Bill saw grave danger in "cutting one's input." But far from withdrawing from society, Jack was actually martyring himself to it. He needed attention more than he ever had, and he would get it even at the cost of betraying his most cherished ideals. At a party at Bev Burford's, he and Jack Fitzgerald spent all night trying to upstage each other with outrageous words and deeds. "When they drop the atom bomb, I'll roll with the punch," said Fitz, who quickly got the better of the contest with his gift of gab and good timing. He and Kerouac kept going out to bars for respite and then returning for fresh tilts at each other, and by four A.M. they were both blind drunk. To everyone's astonishment, Jack suddenly began defending Senator McCarthy with "his own special logic that you couldn't make heads or tails of." [222] Fitz, however, still managed to one-up him by coming back into the room nude from the waist down.

Jack often managed to talk himself into believing things of which no one else could have convinced him. But the fact that in future years he became a staunch supporter of McCarthy may have been due to more than just its initial shock value. For as the senator himself came under fierce criticism, which eventually led to his fatal heart attack, he appealed to the sympathy Jack could withhold from no one in trouble or pain.[223]

The gentle kindness in Jack was still recognizable to those who elicited it. For a couple of years he had been corresponding with Robert Lax, an editor of *New Story* magazine in Paris. Bob Burford, also an editor of the magazine, had put them in touch, and though Jack was miffed at *New Story* for rejecting his stories, he was drawn to Lax, a Catholic convert and close friend of the Trappist monk and writer Thomas Merton. In letters Jack had always emphasized the "beat down, beat up or all-tired-out" aspect of the Beat Generation, but when he actually met Lax in New York that spring, almost all they talked about was religion. When Jack spoke of his admiration for Merton's life as a monk, Lax offered to get him admitted—as a guest—to the L'Eau Vive monastery at Soissy sur Seine. The idea of a literary retreat there excited Jack immensely. Yet philosophically he had reached his furthest divergence from Christianity. For the first time his friends heard him attacking Christ as egomaniacal and excessively political. He went so far as to suggest that if Christ had studied a little Buddhism, Christianity wouldn't be "the dualistic greed-and-sorrow Monster that it is."

The pattern of reaching toward the world and then withdrawing from it was to dominate the rest of his life. Jack's love for Mardou flared again as he peeked through the window of Riker's restaurant while she waited on tables. They took a few walks hand in hand, but he'd usually run off to get drunk with an unstable junkie girl and two black sisters whom he shared with Rambling Jack Elliot. Having made some of the changes in *The Subterraneans* Mardou requested, Jack brought her the manuscript for further suggestions. A few weeks later he returned to demand it back. Since her new boyfriend was there she didn't want to open the door, and when Jack threatened to force his way in, her friend threw the manuscript at him. The only further change she made in it was to delete too many *man*'s.

By early July Jack was tired of New York. He had been running around with a hundred friends such as Lucien, Holmes, Corso, Ansen, Jerry Newman, Henri Cru, Ed White, Jorge Davila, Stanley Gould, and saxophonist Brue Moore. Literary setbacks were trying his Buddhist equanimity, and the unkindest cut came from Mark

Van Doren. More than any other person, it was Van Doren to whom Jack felt he owed his literary career. Years before recommending *The Town and the City* to Giroux, Van Doren had singled Jack out of his class as the student with the deepest appreciation of Shakespeare. As Jack told Victor Gioscia, until he met Van Doren he had had little idea of how he might actually become a writer. Van Doren had not only given him a sense of literature's vast potential, he had also told him outright "You should write!"—convincing Jack that the goal was within his reach. In June, he had brought Van Doren *Doctor Sax* and *San Francisco Blues.* When he returned for the manuscripts, he found a note from Van Doren saying that *Doctor Sax* was "quite a work but I don't know where to place it" and that it was "monotonous and probably without meaning in the end." Of *San Francisco Blues* Van Doren said nothing.

In May Jack had written Carolyn that he would probably never return to California, but by July he was eager to return and even wanted his railroad job back. The difference was that Allen, having finally arrived at Neal's, planned to set up a permanent base in San Francisco. Whatever distrust Jack had harbored toward Allen had been completely melted by the five thousand-word "masterpiece" letter Allen had sent him about life in the Chiapas jungles. He proffered Jack a host of new ideas, and Jack was anxious to begin a new season with him. All he could afford, however, was a ten-day junket to his sister's in Rocky Mount.

When he got back he learned that Cowley's recommendation had carried the day at *New World Writing*, which had accepted his piece "Jazz of the Beat Generation," an amalgam of passages from *On the Road* and *Visions of Cody.* Cowley next sought to place "The Mexican Girl" piece. In his new book *The Literary Situation*, due out in October, Cowley cited Kerouac as the most authentic chronicler of the Beat Generation. Meanwhile Allen had met poet Kenneth Rexroth, a middle-aged Chicago poet transplanted to San Francisco, where he held a salon for anarchists and maverick writers. Beloved as a "hip square" and general sponsor of talent, Rexroth had already read Burroughs' *Junkie* with considerable interest, and he agreed to look at some of Kerouac's manuscripts with an eye to recommending them to New Directions, the publishing company for whom he worked as reader.

With Joan pressing her suit for child support, it seemed Jack would have to publish future works under a pseudonym. In any case, his chief route of escape from her lay in heavy drinking, which precipitated another bout of phlebitis; when the doctors tested his blood they warned him that he was killing himself. Jack once more vowed temperance, though he claimed he wasn't afraid of death but only wanted to be a "good tao bum." To prove his point he also took an oath of chastity. He wrote Burroughs that henceforth he would limit his sexual activity to masturbation. Bill replied that Jack was "sidestepping the issue without even approaching the solution." Sex was a good kick, Bill advised, and Jack would be better off if he simply avoided women. Bill warned that Buddhism frequently serves as a sort of "psychic junk." He believed it could offer no answer to Western problems because it was based on an alien experience. What Tibetan adept, he asked, could know the *facts* of a glaring, impersonal New York cafeteria at night? American Buddhists were simply trying to sit on sidelines that didn't exist. Bill insisted that when a man removes "love from his being in order to avoid suffering" he commits a crime as despicable as castration.

Through August Jack continued to work on "cityCityCITY," as well as yet another "On the Road," though growing steadily more "disgusted with life." At the end of the month he wrote Carolyn that he'd never been more miserable and that he was writing himself to death. The complexities of the new Cassady love triangle helped decide Jack against going to California. Horrified to discover Neal naked in Allen's bed, receiving a blow job from Allen, Carolyn asked Allen to leave. That shock was as nothing compared to the one she felt soon after when Neal went for psychiatric testing and was diagnosed as "pre-psychotic" and prone to sexual sadism. Jack advised her that Neal needed love more than most people, and reminded her that she had thrown *him* out too in 1949.

He wrote Neal a separate letter, to the Southern Pacific yard office, so Carolyn wouldn't see it. It was one of the most tender letters Jack ever sent anyone, man or woman. Having been diagnosed "schizoid" himself, he knew the trauma of self-doubt Neal must be going through, and he reassured him that madness was often the world's interpretation of artistic genius. Neal had ceased work on his autobiography, *The First Third*, because Carolyn, along with Edgar Cayce's followers, condemned writing about sex as sinful. Jack's letter was also a *cri de coeur* for his literary mentor not to abandon him, and he affirmed his belief in the holiness of Neal's regard for sex. He offered to do anything to get Neal writing again, even type his handwritten pages if he dare not use the typewriter at home, and he pledged to send Neal long letters and excerpts from his current writings. And, as Jack almost never did, he begged forgiveness from his "blood brother" for the barriers he could not help building against his friends.

Jack was caught in an even tougher dilemma as confidant to each of another pair of lovers: Bill and Allen. During the several months when Allen had stopped writing him, Bill had discovered just how badly he was "hooked on him." 224 Allen had been one of the few people able to receive Bill's love on an intellectual as well as physical level. Bill now realized that his routines had been developed as a means of releasing his pent-up love, and he seriously doubted that he could live without Allen. Wary of letting Bill become too dependent on him, Allen wrote him that he was interested in living with a woman, which scared Bill more. Although Jack sympathized with Allen's fear of Bill's new strangeness, he also felt that Bill and Allen ought to confront each other with "1947 confessions & honesty." He advised Bill to visit Allen, telling the "white lie" that Allen secretly wanted to be with Bill.[225] Temporarily angry at Jack's meddling, Allen nonetheless invited Bill to San Francisco. Bill arrived in New York in mid-September.

Bill stayed at the St. George Hotel in Brooklyn for a few weeks. Jack would come around with a half gallon of wine to discuss Buddhism with him and Ansen, who was about to leave for Venice. Ignoring Jack's lectures, Bill tried to get him to act as go-between in his love for Allen, and was consequently disappointed by Jack's feeble power of deception. As always, Jack was more interested in helping Bill with his writing than with what he called (in a letter to Allen cited above, October 26, 1954) the "concupiscences of homosexuals." When Bob Burford arrived in New York in late September, Jack gave him a copy of *Junkie*, asking him to try to get it translated into French. The book "smelled of whatever Burroughs was shooting at the time," and Burford thought the prose equally strong. But while Bob was "knocked out" by Bill's writing, he thought the man himself "evil." [226] The tension between Bob and Bill increased because Bob was having an affair with Ginger, who was repulsed by Bill's prolonged silences, ascetic face, Bulldog Drummond trenchcoat, and habit of lighting matches with an air pistol.

Ginger was no longer comfortable around Jack either. Raging against her apparent lustfulness, Jack began to cry over the fact that "birth is the cause of all sorrow." [227] Bob was disturbed to see how morose Jack grew from drinking. They were having a good time watching the World Series in a bar, when suddenly Jack lost all interest and began "just going through the motions" of getting drunker and drunker. As the evening progressed, Bob discovered that Jack was unwelcome among many of his former friends; door after door was slammed in their faces.

Jack complained that his agent, Sterling Lord, wasn't acting fast enough. The August 21 issue of the *Saturday Review* had carried an excerpt from Cowley's new book that mentioned Jack favorably. Jack thought *The Subterraneans* could tap the growing interest in the Beat Generation. Bob agreed, though he was even more impressed by *Visions of Cody*. As a representative of *New Story*, backed by such name writers as Sartre, Saroyan, Richard Wright, and Tennessee Williams, Burford went to Lord to convince him that Jack's works merited being pushed harder. Burford offered to take "The Beat Generation" to Knopf, as well as to seek out a French publisher for *The Town and the City*. Lord, however, asked Burford not to interfere, and as a concession offered to seek a French edition of *The Subterraneans*. "The Beat Generation" was still at Dutton.

Bob began getting late-night phone calls from Jack, who in his insomniac loneliness just wanted to talk. Before Bob left New York, he gave a big party in the apartment where he was staying, which belonged to photographer Jacques Lowe. At the party he introduced Jack to James Baldwin, but Jack disliked Baldwin's gayness, and Baldwin offended him by criticizing Burroughs. In the morning Bob saw a sobering sight, one he tried for years to forget. Sprawled on Lowe's new couch, Jack was slobbering and vomiting, too sick to even rise.[228]

After Allen wrote Bill a formal letter of rejection, Bill returned to Tangier. With his $120 pay for "Jazz of the Beat Generation," Jack had $300 saved. In October he went to Lowell with the vague idea of looking for a "shack." Principally he wanted to check some facts for a new nonfiction portrait of Lowell called "Book of Memory." Taking a room by the train depot, he wandered his boyhood streets as former neighbors stared at his garish clothes. He himself was afraid to approach people because he lacked a decent overcoat.

But he went to see Mary Carney at her old house, and she let him in to watch television and talked about her new boyfriend. Later, meeting G.J., Jack declared he was in love with her and would sweep her off her feet again. Although G.J. begged him not to go back to her, Jack insisted he had to, only he hadn't the courage to call her. When G.J. phoned in Jack's behalf, she agreed to another visit. Fortified by booze, and accompanied by G.J. and George Dastou, Jack waded into an armed camp on her porch. Mary was surrounded by her boyfriend, parents, and countless relatives, all silently and rigidly united in their resolve to keep him out of the house. G.J. tried to break the ice with a few pleasantries, but nothing could induce any of the Carneys even to ask Jack to sit down. Mumbling, he finally came out with some remark that went over everyone's heads; and on the way back, he was tortured by the realization that whatever was left between Mary and himself wasn't worth a half-hour of conversation. For two days he drank and agonized, until G.J. could no longer bear to be with him and passed him along to Scotty. Still more disturbing was G.J.'s sense that one lifetime was no longer enough for Jack, that he had to break some new record for the number of lives he could crowd into the next two or three years.

Before leaving Lowell, Jack went to the basement church of Ste. Jeanne d'Arc, and in the shadows of dusk saw the statue of the Virgin Mary turn its head. In his later rewriting of Beat history, he would cite that moment as the point when *beat* began to signify *beatific*. Actually, apart from Al Hinkle's even earlier memories, Jack had written to Allen in August explaining the beatitude of beat life, and the word *beatific* had been used in *The Subterraneans*, written in 1953.

4.

When he returned to New York Jack decided he would earn enough money to buy a panel truck and go into the desert for three months, for his "first complete solitude & Samadhi [contemplation]." Eventually, though, he wanted to move to San Francisco, where a new group seemed to be forming around Allen Ginsberg.

At the Cassadys' house in San Jose some tension had developed between Allen and Neal because of Allen's intense sexual desire, but now that Allen was living with a girlfriend in San Francisco, he and Neal resumed their old camaraderie—only at a pace so frantic Allen could scarcely enjoy it. Neal was more than glad to visit him in San Francisco as an excuse to stay away from Carolyn, with whom his marital discord was escalating. Though Neal was a concerned father, and a good provider for the family, he and Carolyn were not making it sexually—for Neal a major hiatus. Late that fall a painter friend of Allen's, Robert LaVigne, provided both Allen and Neal with their ideal lover, and in the same manner. Peter Orlovsky, a visionary junior college student just out of the army, and Natalie Jackson, a hauntingly lovely, tormented young woman, had both sat for nude portraits by LaVigne. Failing to become deeply involved with his girlfriend Sheila, Allen took a vow with Peter that each would care for the other's body and soul; indeed they became lifelong companions. Until her suicide a year later, Natalie served as Neal's de facto wife, satisfying his sexual needs more successfully than any other woman. On weekends and before or after work he returned home to visit Carolyn and to play with the kids.

Living at Al Sublette's North Beach hotel, the Marconi, among sockless mystic mental patients like Peter du Peru, Allen once again bridged the gap between the world of street kicks and literary academia, which in this case was bastioned in Berkeley. The central link in Ginsberg's chain of creativity was the brotherly circle of San Francisco poets. Around the corner from the Marconi was City Lights Bookstore, run by Lawrence Ferlinghetti, a Sorbonne-educated disciple of Charlie Chaplin, an orphan, seaman, and highly original poet with deep roots in both American and French literature. The surrealist Lamantia was back in his hometown, and he and Allen renewed their acquaintance. Through Rexroth, Ferlinghetti, Lamantia, and Gene Pippin (the Columbia poet now studying at Berkeley), Allen came in contact with poets Robert Duncan, Chris MacClaine, and Gerd Stern, experimental filmmaker Jordan Belson, and Tibetan Buddhist scholar Leonard Hall.

Allen was now making good money at the market research firm of Towne-Oller, and he fantasized about producing a movie with Belson using Neal, Bill, and Jack as actors. He thought of making Neal the hero of a love murder *à la* Dreiser's *An American Tragedy*, or doing a sort of Buddhist science fiction piece about "Burroughs on

Earth" in a future lifetime, or possibly even filming *Doctor Sax*. Intrigued by the title "Burroughs on Earth," Jack suggested they make a film about themselves as they actually were—Burroughs in a felt hat looking over his shoulder on a cable car, Neal working on the railroad, himself drinking wine with the bums of Howard Street. Jack also conceived of filming the actors and crew unawares, to capture their spontaneous antics and discussions so that the movie would also reveal the process by which it was made. His greatest enthusiasm was for a movie about the life of Buddha, a script of which he sketched out in a letter to Allen. At the same time he warned Allen against exploiting Buddhist knowledge for artistic glory. Naked sages living in caves like Milarepa, he reminded, were concerned with "matters *not* of esthetic interest and *not* abstract intellectual but crucial bone-simple elucidations of the Law of Creation."

Jack's biggest complaint was that none of his friends seemed to grasp the desperateness of his own situation. Burroughs, for example, had left for Florida without repaying the thirty dollars he'd borrowed, money Jack needed for a winter coat.[229] But Jack was no easy person to help. Jerry Newman, who had a fancy new studio, offered to pay him to arrange a recording session with Allen Eager. The deal ruptured when Jack called Newman an "old Jew" and heaved a garbage can at his head.

Jack's Buddhist studies continued in full force during the fall of 1954, but he was far from serene as publishers again built up and then dashed his hopes. He dutifully followed everyone's suggestions, retyping "The Beat Generation" to incorporate new revisions for Knopf. Determined "to stop the machine and go into the Bright Room forever," he resolved to give up drinking and "all non-disciple friendships," eat one meal a day, and write about nothing but Buddhism.[230] For the present he achieved only the last goal, however, as he frequently came through the city "on a tear." Lucien scoffed that Jack merely thought Buddha was the Pope.[231]

But his compassion was still much in evidence. Gregory Corso had met a wealthy seventeen-year-old girl named Hope Savage, who promised to take him to Harvard. As a child in her Southern hometown she had read classics of European romantic and decadent literature. Soon she was writing her own poetry; and dressed in a cloak and boots she set out to protect local animals from hunters. Assuming she was insane her parents sent her to an asylum, where she was given eighteen electroshock treatments. She was left with the permanent sense that something had been taken away from her, and she never wrote poetry again. She was also sexually frigid. Gregory in his zest for pleasure kept trying to get her into bed, but Jack was moved to protect the child in her and encouraged Gregory to be gentle.

In December 1954, by Jack's own account, he reached "the

lowest, beatest ebb" of his life thus far. He could not overcome his dependence on alcohol, benzedrine, goofballs, and cigarettes, even though such sensual indulgence precluded the perfect Samadhi he sought through frequent meditation—and might well end all spiritual effort with a fatal blood clot. To make matters worse, he was arrested for nonsupport of his daughter Janet. Plotting to "go away forever to Tibet," he went so far as to put rights to *The Town and the City* in his mother's name. For, as he advised himself in "Some of the Dharma," to be a Bodhisattva he would have to pursue his goal regardless of what happened along the way, and above all he must avoid fame. In a prophetic statement he described the two alternatives of the wise man: "Being famous, he will be hounded to his death; being a nonentity, no one will want to use him." [232]

In Domestic Relations Court in mid-January, Jack seemed like a pitiable "nonentity" to his wife Joan. Prepared to be sent to prison, he had brought along *A Buddhist Bible,* his Buddhist notes, and a new novel called "The Long Night of Life." His lawyer, Allen's brother Eugene Brooks, presented the judge with a doctor's statement that Jack was unfit for work because of his phlebitis, which convinced the judge to suspend the case for a year. The paternity test Jack had requested was also deferred, but his relief was mitigated by the disquieting discovery that he did indeed have a daughter. When Joan showed him photos of Janet he kept repeating, "Not my kid," but writing to Allen shortly afterward Jack admitted that he was struck by the girl's physical resemblance to him.

Jack's last refuge was his original family. His sister and her husband were about to build a house in Rocky Mount, which was to be home for Jack and his mother too. Jack's and Mémère's trip to North Carolina for the holidays seemed the start of a new era of family unity. They had a wild New Year's Eve party, where Jack danced with Nin and together they taught her son "Lil Paul" to dance, and at midnight Jack, costumed as Father Time, made Lil Paul run through the house in a diaper!

Back in New York in January 1955, he learned that Knopf had rejected "The Beat Generation" for its "looseness of structure," and Little, Brown had rejected *The Subterraneans* because of its Beat Generation content, though editor Seymour Lawrence had called it "beautiful." Despite Jack's telling himself that nothing was real, he suffered from loneliness even during his practice of Dhyana (sitting meditation). The wine and benny he took for solace increased his leg pains, which in turn made it harder for him to sit. It seemed he really needed isolation in the desert to clear his head, after which he hoped to join Allen and Neal in San Francisco.

But he had no money, and his folks needed him in Rocky Mount. The plan was for Mémère to move south permanently in July; until then, Jack would stay with Nin and Paul, caring for Lil Paul and

doing odd jobs. Change was always manna for Jack. Arriving in
Rocky Mount in late February, he exulted in his midnight meditations in the piney woods. He also delighted in his six-year-old
nephew. They played hide-and-seek and other games Jack invented;
at night in Paul's dark bedroom Jack would switch on a flashlight
under his chin, silhouetting his head as he exploded with a Shadow
laugh. "Uncle Jack" was a great storyteller as well. He told Paul,
"Now you're at an age that you should start reading," stressed that
reading would open the door to wonders of knowledge, and after
giving Paul a collection of works by Mark Twain, spent many nights
helping him read *Huckleberry Finn*. They had fun with sports too.
Jack and Paul, Sr., would often toss a football around, and Jack
promised to teach Lil Paul to play. One day, practicing tackling, he
threw Paul into the air and failed to catch him, so that he landed on
his head. Paul recalls that Jack continued to apologize for the accident until the end of his life.

Still, neither meditation, nor his nephew, nor news that Kenneth
Rexroth had recommended Cowley show his works to Edmund Wil-
son, could alleviate what Jack saw as his greatest problem: boredom.
He kicked himself for walking out on Cowley in April 1953, at the
very moment when Viking seemed likely to accept *On the Road*.
Had he forced the issue then, he reasoned, by now he might have
money to travel to Africa and the Orient as he wished. Out of that
ferment of boredom and regret poured two new works: "Bowery
Blues" poems, and a Buddhist handbook called alternately "Wake
Up" or "Buddha Tells Us." He also finished the story "cityCity-
CITY," and began planning a novel called "Visions of Bill." At this
time was born the apparent megalomania that made Jack so obnoxious in his later years even to many friends. He wrote Allen,
for example, that he intended "to be the greatest writer in the
world." [233] Originating far from vanity, such remarks betrayed a little man who wanted to be big.[234]

Increasingly his meditations turned into night-long musings over
a pitcher of his special moonshine punch. In his letters he became a
champion of whistling in the dark, claiming that he was "completely
happy" in anonymity, and that he expected no rewards from
his literary career since both the career and he were "imaginary
blossoms." In April, Dutton's rejection of "The Beat Generation"
plunged him into self-pity. His sense of martyrdom was fed by
Giroux, who had asked *not* to see any of Jack's spontaneous prose
books and then, after inquiring about "Buddha Tells Us," suddenly
lost interest in that too. Most maddening was the silence of Sterling
Lord. When Jack wrote asking that Lord either signal his desire to
keep marketing the manuscripts or else return them, Lord still failed
to reply. Jack determined to confront them both in New York in
June.

Not even the appearance in April of *New World Writing* with

"Jazz of the Beat Generation," his first publication in five years, helped restore his equilibrium. He was drunk so much of the time that he fluffed his job delivering television sets for his brother-in-law's repair business, and Paul and Nin's anger was the least of his worries. The fear of committing suicide drove him to retrieve his old lusts in a last-ditch effort to find something worth living for. "A girl's ass is the same as nothing," he rationalized, and practicing discipline the same as riot. Since the essence of his Buddhism was "nothing means nothing," he saw no reason to add privation to his intense torment, in the name of an enlightenment that—as he understood it—didn't exist. To Carolyn, he explained: "My Buddhism has deprived me of what was left of patience and fortitude in the Sangsara world of troubles; so, tho I was warned not to make a half-hold on ascetism, like grasping a blade of grass the wrong way, I got cut." [235]

Perhaps because Mémère was worried about Jack, she moved to Rocky Mount in April. Retired from the shoe factory, she invested her savings in Paul's business and pulled her weight as housekeeper. Jack had a private work space on the screened-in back porch, but with summer coming so were the bugs, and even his big Thoreauvian vegetable garden wasn't much fun to tend. The problem was where to go. On his recent sojourn in New York to pick up his mother, he'd been mortified by the ridicule of the subterraneans. San Francisco terrified him with the prospect of ceaseless drunken binges. In addition, he was ashamed to let Neal and Neal's children see him in his besotted despair, since he set so poor an example of the Buddhist life he'd preached to them the previous spring. Carolyn scared him most of all, because he still loved and desired her. Even though he dismissed his celibacy as unnecessary, he felt great guilt about the wrong he'd already done Neal by traducing his wife's virtue. Furthermore, Jack believed that all love affairs ended in a "miserable conditional mess." Again he came to the conclusion that a man like himself was bound to live alone in the desert or the woods. But what desert? What woods?

Writing had become so painful that he considered going to Tangier to collaborate on his next book with Bill, and sent Bill "cityCityCITY" to give him an idea of the type of work they might both find interesting. Recently cured of his heroin addiction, Bill was channeling his slim energies into a new novel, which eventually became *Naked Lunch*.[236] Bill saw that Jack's story was barely the seed of a novel, since he had failed to provide any specific characterizations. Nevertheless, his reply was sympathetic, and Jack admired the perseverance Bill showed in pursuing his original vein of material—sadism, perverted sex, totalitarian control systems, etc.—regardless of its unsaleability. In fact, Bill was now working in poverty comparable to Jack's, since his sole income was still just a small monthly check from home.

Jack saw the salvation of himself, Bill, and Allen in their brotherhood. Though they were excluded from the mainstream of publishing by their forbidden subject matter and unconventional expression, they had one advantage over popular writers: the loyalty of a few compatriots who would unquestionably champion them when the chips were down. In a tender letter to Allen, Jack vouched his unconditional support of his work and prophesied that "in a hundred years from now or earlier, Ginsberg will be the name, like Einstein in Science, that the Jews will bring up when they claim pride in Poetry." For his part, Allen was busily advocating Jack's works to West Coast literary luminaries, and at the same time distributing samples of them to his East Coast contacts like William Carlos Williams.

When Jack telephoned Lord to inquire about prospects for his Buddhist handbook, Lord's reply was "Is it any good?" Jack was so angry he considered dropping Lord and making his sister his agent instead. What really peeved him was that Lord had told him not to depend on Cowley, although Cowley was the only person in years who had done him any tangible good. Learning that Cowley had been angered by his publishing the jazz story under the pseudonym "Jean-Louis," after he'd gone to the trouble of publicly praising "John Kerouac," Jack sent Cowley a cringing apology.

In New York in June, he went on a drinking binge that aggrevated his phlebitis, resulting in a lump on his ankle the size of a baseball, and then explained to Cowley that it was his phlebitis that prevented him from supporting himself with a regular job. In light of Jack's childish pleas that he would jump off a bridge if his novels weren't published soon, Cowley displayed remarkable compassion and understanding toward him. If Dodd, Mead rejected "The Beat Generation," Cowley offered to push it again at Viking, this time aided by the enthusiasm of a new editor, Keith Jennison. In addition, Cowley conceived of several ways to get Jack living money in the meantime. He helped him apply for a $300 grant from the National Institute of Arts & Letters, and submitted more excerpts from the novels to various publications. It was like "a lamp suddenly being lit in the darkness" [237] when—all at once—*The Paris Review* accepted "The Mexican Girl," approval of the grant appeared imminent, and on his own Jack sold "cityCityCITY" to his poet friend David Burnett for *The New American Reader.* Since none of those resources materialized immediately, he was grateful for the $25 sent by Allen, who longed to have him in San Francisco.

Jack was disappointed that neither Cowley, Giroux, nor Lord was interested in "Buddha Tells Us," though Lord did send it to Harvard University Press. Giroux redeemed himself somewhat by declaring *Doctor Sax* "magnificent," despite his inability to sell it to Harcourt Brace. In any case, getting drunk in the Village with Cowley, being wined and dined by an editor from Dodd, Mead, helping

Corso edit poems for a new collection, recommending Ginsberg and Burroughs to publishers, and discussing books among other writers, Jack's morale took a manic leap. He began framing huge new works and completed another set of poems, "MacDougal Street Blues." Once again he thought of his writing as a mission, and in particular he aimed to wake America out of its current "middle-of-the-road" materialistic mediocrity. Deep in their cups, Jack and a friend drafted a message to the President: "Dear Eisenhower, We love you.——You're the great big white father. We'd like to fuck you."

For the first time Jack lived in the Village, staying with Lucien and other friends and sampling kicks like a kid in a candy store. He met old and new hipsters in the Riviera Bar where Henri Cru worked as bouncer, got high with Stanley Gould, conducted his own jam session on the waterfront at dawn. He also basked in the coming fame of his friends. Gregory, especially, was making a splash in the press and among publishers after his triumph at Harvard, where friends had published his first book, *The Vestal Lady on Brattle,* and produced his play, *This Hungup Age.* Jack was glad of Corso's success, believing his verbal madness as deft as that of Joyce and Christopher Smart.

In this swirl of celebrity, sex was everywhere for the asking—one hipster even arranged for Jack to become the gigolo of a beautiful French woman. Having accepted the Mahayana truth that Nirvana and Sangsara are one, i.e., that spiritual liberation and fleshly involvement manifest the same essence, Jack was ready to indulge. Yet now that he'd gone almost a year without intercourse he hesitated to take that final step back to his old world, which would necessitate the admission, so frightening, that it was not too late to begin a responsible life.

A life responsible to more than his career, that is, for he was continually seeking to master new areas of his trade. In the Village he read Ezra Pound's *Cantos,* but his initial enthusiasm for the freedom of the poetry soon dissolved in his disgust for Pound's pretentious diction and imitation of classical rhythms. Allen had come under Pound's influence a few months earlier. In May, he persuaded Towne-Oller to replace him with a computer; after a few months of collecting unemployment compensation and writing a lot of poetry, including *Howl,* he decided to enroll for a Master's Degree in English at the University of California, Berkeley. Back in Rocky Mount in July, Jack wrote advising him not to study Greek and Latin prosody, as he had planned, but rather to learn Sanskrit and begin translating Sutras. Mastering older poetic forms was "child's play," Jack asserted, compared to the task of writing an American poetry with a "Buddhist base," which was the only fresh and true direction he saw for it.

He got his own good advice from Cowley, who was chiefly responsible for getting him back on an even keel. Cowley stressed the need for literature to communicate, and Jack agreed to "try to control my *curve* and get it over the plate." The biggest obstacle to Viking's acceptance of *On the Road* was the risk of libel suits, since many of the characters were such accurate reproductions of real people. Cowley planned to circumvent that worry by writing a preface to the novel indicating its high seriousness. He also continued to circulate the manuscript among editors there. One of them, Evelyn Levine, summarized her evaluation of it as follows: "(1) The novel must be and will be published eventually. (2) Jack Kerouac is a fresh, new (and fascinating) talent. (3) The manuscript still needs a lot of work. (4) The novel must be published even if it is a literary and financial failure."

Such respect was not accorded Jack in his home. His sister and her husband resented his perpetual meditations and urged him to do some salaried work. The fact that he was practicing a "pagan" religion also nettled them, and at one point Nin accused him of playing God. "What, are ya jealous?" he snapped. Nin's nagging convinced him that women were murderously greedy; mimicking Burroughs, he wrote Allen that just the sight of a woman made him sick.

5.

With his heart set on a "thatched hut in Lowell," his imagination aimed toward the Orient, and San Francisco his planned destination, Jack hitchhiked to Texas, then detoured to Mexico City, arriving in early August. His alleged purpose was to obtain cheap penicillin for his phlebitis, but he partook liberally of marijuana and morphine too. Bill Garver was back on Orizaba Street, and Jack rented the rooftop apartment above him. Jack's new motto was "Conscious continual compassion and ordinary contentedness . . . simple kicks." Garver provided the opportunity for both. He shared his drugs with Jack, and in return Jack listened to his interminable lectures on history and literature and did him domestic favors like emptying his urine bucket. Mixing morphine with booze made Jack sick, and he got dysentery too. Worst of all, he was bored again and "inconceivably sad" as he sought vainly for some purpose in his moves. He forced himself to keep away from prostitutes but he couldn't help falling in love with Garver's connection, an Indian woman named Esperanza, who was the widow of Burroughs' former connection Dave Tercerero.

Esperanza was a junkie and worked as a prostitute as often as necessary to support her habit. Though there is no question that Jack sincerely cared for her, Gregory Corso, who saw them together a year later, felt their relationship also resembled that of a college boy trying to reform the first nice woman he meets in a brothel. Jack claimed she was beautiful; Gregory reports that her looks were wrecked by years of dissipation. Besides, Jack wrote Holmes that he really didn't like women much anymore. What he fell in love with, doubtless, was her suffering, which was greater than that of any person he knew. She lived in a filthy shack full of chickens, animals, and Catholic icons and was scorned by everyone, including her pimp El Negro. For all practical purposes, Jack's "romance" with her never existed, because she was never Esperanza Tercerero to him but rather Billie Holiday or a "Genet hero" or the Virgin Mary.[238] The tragedy of his love for her lay in that very blindness to the abyss between them. He never understood, for example, why she wouldn't accept his offer to support her so she wouldn't have to work the streets.

The story Jack wrote about Esperanza that August, "Trembling and Chaste," became Part One of the novel *Tristessa.* In some ways *Tristessa* is a more emphatically Buddhist replay of *The Subterraneans,* and so lacks some of the vitality of the earlier novel. Yet "Trembling and Chaste" is an affecting story of someone with absolutely nothing to live for, someone living merely toward the end of avoiding pain. Furthermore, Kerouac develops several perspectives by which one can appreciate the tension of such a life; in this case the dramatic tension of the story is Tristessa's own pain.

The narrative is stretched taut between the antipodes of Buddhism and Catholicism, between the subjective depreciation of life and the objective desire for it: "It's the old question of 'Yes life's not real' but you see a beautiful woman or something you can't get away from wanting because it is there in front of you." The book's central metaphor is rain, which appears in the first sentence, where Jack Duluoz is riding in a cab with Tristessa on a rainy Saturday night—a typical Kerouacian melding of motifs, which emphasizes the elusiveness of all desire, not just that for love. Later he specifies Saturday night as a microcosm of man's lifelong disappointment: "born to die, the man, so he plies the needle of Saturday Night every night is Saturday night and goes wild to wait, what else can he do. . . ." Rain continues to fall in varying intensity throughout "Trembling and Chaste." In Tristessa's house it merely "drizzles" in through the kitchen roof. When Jack leaves her, "it starts raining harder." As Part One ends, so does the rain: "Diminished is the drizzle that broke my calm." Kerouac is trading on a symbolism that goes back at least as far as Shakespeare's *King Lear,* whose Fool declares: "the rain it raineth every day." But Kerouac's rain has a peculiar power of resolving—that is, re-dissolving—all the other dichotomies that sustain the tension of the story: light and dark, "pain and loveliness," etc. The flux of that rain is the one absolute of life, as man's surest utterance is a question: "Art there, Lord Star?" [239]

Tristessa is a love story between the narrator and all Creation. Kerouac eulogizes the flow of love (and light) into the universal void, a flow to which man contributes, thereby redeeming all his agonizing mysteries: "Since beginningless time and into the never-ending future, men have loved women without telling them, and the Lord has loved them without telling, and the void is not the void because there's nothing to be empty of." The key word of the novel is *golden*, which signifies the purity of man's dreams, sublime even when they are of flesh: "I watch the final sad bar-doors, where flashes of women golden shining lace behinds I can see. . . ." What is golden about women's behinds is the eternal quality of the vision that embodies them. Mortality itself is a permanent facet of that vision: "the Dove . . . waits in her golden corner of the world waiting for perfect purity of death. . . ." Man is blessed because he reaches for the unreachable "Pure Land" or "white light" (Mahayana and Tantric epithets, respectively, for nirvana), and that "Pure Land" and "white light" is just the peace he makes with his inability to possess such absolutes:

> Worked hard for my father in the Pure Land, was strong and true, went to the city to see Tathagata [Buddha], leveled the ground for his feet, saw bumps everywhere and leveled the ground, he passed by and saw me and said, "First level your own mind, and then the earth will be level, even unto Mount Sumeru." . . .

Significantly, the story in Part One progresses from Saturday to Sunday. Sunday, the Christian Sabbath, betokens God's mercy to man—the grace man earns, in a sense, by giving up. On Sunday, Tristessa comes to teach Jack to "rest beyond heaven": "She points to the sky again, 'If my friend dont pay me back,' looking at me straight, 'my Lord pay me back—*more.*' "

Part Two of *Tristessa* was written a year later. It begins with a negation of the last statement in Part One: "Dimish'd never is the drizzle that broke no calm. . . ." The technique is quintessentially Buddhist, for by showing that the opposite of any statement is also true, one suggests a meaning beyond words. In the very next paragraph Kerouac returns to his Judeo-Christian framework, questioning God like Job: "O Lord, why have you done this to your angel-selves, this blight life, this ugh raggedy crap scene full of puke and thieves and dying?" That vacillation between Eastern and Western religion becomes itself a sort of Zen paradox, an insoluble Koan. Just as the Zen master answers with a concrete fact when the disciple asks a general question, and with a generality when he asks something specific, so Kerouac gives Eastern answers to Western questions, and vice versa.

Through his sexual weakness for women Jack is identified with Adam. Jack's ideal world, the "Garden of Arden, full of lovers and louts" who are "devoted to helping others all day long," is a hip Eden. The flaw in this world, however, comes not from disobedience to any law but rather from the attempt to delineate laws at all. The love between Tristessa and Jack waxes and wanes from moment to moment: "I keep staring at her, suddenly we love each other. . . ." At the end, admitting the impossibility of living with her, the narrator nevertheless praises the love-inspiring magic of "reality." Reversing Shakespeare, whose Hamlet wished his flesh would melt into a dew, Kerouac's hero welcomes the unity of body and soul: "But O the grace of some bones, that milt a little flesh hang-on, like Tristessa, and makes a woman." As the flesh is just a secretion of universal beauty, so is existence a kind of evanescent ooze on some God's bones—the point being that man's flesh and God's bones are inseparable. Man's questions are the flesh asking why it exists, when it doesn't have the means to answer itself; it can only *be*, its existence dependent at every moment on the "grace" of those bones. Love is invaluable because it is a glimpse—all we ever get—of that oneness: "A movie by God, showing us him—him,—and us showing him,—him which is us—for how can there be two, not-one?" The double-talk of that conclusion simply underlines the futility of trying to express unity in discriminative language.

Like *The Subterraneans*, *Tristessa* ends where it begins, at the point where art merges with life, with the narrator sitting down to write the book: "I'll write long sad tales about people in the legend of my life——" But this time Kerouac suggests that the reader participates in the unity of the artist with his work: "This part is my part of the movie, let's hear yours/ Solo." Love or no love, we all play the same singular, solitary music.

Part of the impetus to begin *Tristessa* was the good news that the National Institute of Arts and Letters was about to dispatch Jack's grant money. It also got him working on his railroad piece again (which he planned to expand into a novel called "Brakeman on the Railroad"), as well as on a record of his meditations called "Book of Ecstasies." He wrote Cowley that he rejoiced to believe again in his future as an American writer, and now could set to work in earnest filling in the gaps in *The Duluoz Legend*, which would require a life's work. The next priority was a novel about Gerard, which would cover Jack's first four years. As a renewed dedication to the holiness of his profession, he returned to his youthful ritual of writing by candlelight.

Jack's Buddhist studies confirmed that spontaneity was the only teacher of higher laws. His prose method was vindicated by the *Surangama Sutra,* in which the Buddha advised: "If you are now desirous of more perfectly understanding Supreme Enlightenment and the enlightening nature of pure Mind-Essence, you must learn to answer questions spontaneously with no recourse to discriminating thinking." Spontaneity also took on added importance as Jack began to see honesty as the highest goal in writing. The distinction between poetry and prose merely clouded the issue. As he wrote to Cowley (alluding, perhaps, to Dr. Williams), it was clear that honesty was one of the requirements for both prose and verse, and hence that "what a man most wishes to hide, revise, and un-say, is precisely what Literature is waiting and bleeding for—Every doctor knows, every prophet knows the convulsion of truth." Even if the writer had to yap like a wild man, Jack deemed it of the utmost importance to "get said what is only irrecoverably said once in time the way it comes, for time is of the essence."

No fanatic about spontaneity, Kerouac understood that certain types of writing require revision. In his own critical and philosophical pieces, he always took care to select the most accurate words. But the kind of poetry Allen was attempting, for instance, impressionistic epiphanies of America, seemed worthless to Jack unless illumined by the writer's heartfelt emotion burning at the moment of composition. When Allen sent him a long new poem addressed to Carl Solomon, which Jack entitled *Howl*, he was stirred by the power of the long, breath-measured, seriocomic lines, and he worried that Allen would invalidate his testimony against American madness with the "secondary emendations" Allen thought necessary.

It was to teach Ginsberg about spontaneous poetry that Jack sat down with coffee and a joint on his tiny rooftop for a few hours every morning, penciling little blues poems in his notebooks. Ginsberg had been making a big deal out of the fact that he and his Berkeley friends were *poets*, as though their work required more refined techniques than those Jack used for prose. "I'm an epic-poem writer," Jack later boasted to Allen. "I write poems a thousand feet long!" He also demonstrated that what he meant by spontaneity was not identical to speed. Several of these new blues "choruses" were written at the carefully measured rate of one line per hour—the way Christopher Smart wrote one line a day on his poem *Jubilate Agno*, to record his changing outlook while confined in an asylum. As Jack's notebooks filled with a highly unified series of poems, he began mailing copies of some of them to Allen in Berkeley. During August and the first half of September 1955, he composed 244 choruses, completing his greatest book of poems, *Mexico City Blues*.

Mexico City Blues is a Buddhist book that finally talks itself back to a Christian love of life. Engagement in life is called forth by the poet's delight in beauty, as a result of which the book becomes a dialectic between Buddhism and aestheticism, with the poet finally placing his vote in favor of the hand-racking "labor of nada" [240] that is his own writing: the inward-voyaging struggle of art. Early in the book the poet spurns his writing as ineffectual, and laments his restless mind's need to keep seeking answers. Finally there is a glorification of this self-exploratory instinct as the only way to "lay the bane off" life, to deal with suffering, which doesn't go away with the poet's Buddhist enlightenment. "If that's all you have to offer," Kerouac says figuratively to Buddhism, "then it would be better to commit suicide." It is art as the guardian of life that earns the poet's allegiance.

Kerouac's specific innovation in *Mexico City Blues* was in freeing himself from all artificial measure and, as Ginsberg says, "going out into the mind itself to find the shape" of the poem. Judging much free verse lax and dull, Kerouac invented a ditty, an elastic musical form to accommodate the organic growth of his thought. The parameters of that form, apart from the size of a notebook page, lay in the style itself, the requirements of rhythm and melody set by the poet's ear. Such a form was by no means easy to adhere to, for it demanded the poet's fluid command of assonance, alliteration, pitch, pauses, etc., so that every thought as it was uttered could find a music sufficient to carry it smoothly to conclusion. The cessation of either thought or music brought the poem to an end, because the cardinal requirement of this poetry was that the two flow together. Thus the abrupt ending of the 11th Chorus, a poem that is nothing more than a statement about its failure to get started, and as such represents a paradigm of Kerouac's technique:

> Brown wrote a book called
> The White and the Black
>
> Narcotic City
> switchin on
>
> Anger Falls—
> (musician stops,
> brooding on bandstand)

One can, if one wishes, "explicate" such a poem. "Brown" is Jack Kerouac, a white man who wishes he were black and is caught halfway between. He wrote a book called *The Town and the City*, which was about the meeting of his boyhood white world and the black jazz and drug subcultures of New York, and which was influenced by Stendhal's *The Red and the Black*. But the title "The White and the Black" also demeans the novel as a set of meaningless chicken scratches. The author "switches" from Western discrimination to the logic-obliterating experience of kicks, as the meter switches from iambic to trochaic, then breaks off. The source of the writer's "anger," however, is only marginally important to the poem; more important is the way the process of writing the poem has become the poem's subject.

Several of the poems were written in Garver's apartment, and

Kerouac often transcribed the old man's words directly into his text, not as a cute trick but because Garver's talk impinged on his consciousness to the extent that their two minds momentarily followed the same track. Kerouac is intent on getting every shift of the poet into the poem. Even his abandoning the poem must be recorded; if not in metaphor, as in the 11th Chorus, then with a literal account of the poet's frustration, as at the end of the 36th Chorus: "(ripping of paper indicates/ helplessness anyway)." Neither is the mind's extravagance to be curbed, even if it means extending the poem beyond the poet's knowledge into his ignorance:

> into underground caves
> where worshippers
> like Ignatius Loyola
> and the Hearer & Answerer
> of Prayer, Samantabhadra,
> what's his Indian name,
> preside
>   (48th Chorus)

Indeed the poet's very mistakes are essential to the poem, because to excise them means to falsify the train of thought that formed in the poet's mind during the time of composition. Ginsberg comments on this process as seen in the 97th Chorus: "The racing ahead of the mind in associations when it stumbles with a word on the tip of the tongue is included in the poem and becomes an organic part of the poem, and at the same time provides a rhythmic rush forward that is exquisite like a peroration in Shakespeare, arriving finally at the emphatic 'Neppy Tune.' " Ginsberg also points out that the strong accent at the end of the line has roots not only in bop but in Cassady's Okie speech, Carr's tough-Irishman speech, and Kerouac's own Massachusetts Canuck dialect. The resulting vigor is the antithesis of the old poetic "dying fall":

> Then all's wet underneath, to Eclipse
> (Ivan the Heaven Sea-Ice King, Euclid,
> Bloody Be Jupiter, Nucleus,
> Nuclid, What's-His-Name—the sea
> The sea-drang Scholar with mermaids,
> Bloody blasted dadflap thorn it
> —Neppy Tune—)
> All's wet clear to Neptune's Seat.
>   (97th Chorus)

Permeating the book is Kerouac's awareness that much of what occurs in the mind is ineffable, a conception both Gnostic and Tantric, but which may just have been native to his meditative nature, traceable all the way back to his broodings over his brother's death. One of the key words in *Mexico City Blues* is *empty*, and one of Kerouac's means of conveying emptiness is to show each thought-form as a "balloon" lost in space, an idea he and Allen got from the balloon-enclosed dialogue in comic strips. Specifically, Kerouac attempts to render *the gap in consciousness between thought-forms* with as much fidelity as he notes the thoughts themselves. The physical separation of choruses, and the layout of words on each page, help to achieve this effect. At times that gap is actually audible, as when one hears static on the radio. In the 110th Chorus, his attention to the mind's lonely vigil recalls Hemingway's treatment of man's addiction to consciousness—his need to stop the gaps—in the story "The Gambler, the Nun, and the Radio":

> Afternoons as a kid I'd listen
> to radio programs for to see
> the scratch between announcements
> Knowing the invalid is glad
> only because he's mad
> enough to appreciate every
> little thing that blazons there
> in the swarmstorm of his eye

The physiological counterpart of mental blanks is the pause between breaths. That pause is itself suggestive of the stasis in life we know as death, which as always is the central mystery Kerouac seeks to confront:

> the feeling of in and out
> your feeling of being alive
> is the feeling of in & out
> your feeling of being dead
> unalive
>
> When it comes you wont
> sneeze no more, Gesundheit.
> It wont happen, is what
> is—
> And
> it aint happenin now
>
> Smile & think deeply
> (158th Chorus)

It is Kerouac's honesty that generates the debate between Buddhism and what might be termed aesthetic Christianity. While philosophically the poet admits the correctness of Buddhism, he knows full well that as an artist his method is exuberance, not tranquility. Far from escaping the "burning house," the artist lights the fire:

> F. Scott Fitzgerald, the Alamoan
> Huckster Crockett Hero
> Who burned his Wife Down
> and tore up the 95 Devils
> with crashes of laughter
> and breaking of glass
> (30th Chorus)

The poet too is a holy man, a "Singer of Religion" and a "Convulsive writer of Poems/ And dialog for Saints" (31st), but one beset by doubts: "Contemplating suicide" (79th). His work, like the writings of Christian saints, is "a big structure of Confession" (87th). He thereby adds to illusion: "He hugens to re-double/ the image, in words" (100th). The Buddhists, however, perceive that creation itself is an illusion:

> One never dies
> One's never born
> So sing the optimists
> Of holy old religion
> trying to assuage
> (102nd)

Indeed the poet is bent on proving to himself that the world he celebrates does not exist. He realizes that what we call light is an illusion, because it is perceived after it has passed away:

> Light is Late
> yes
> because
>
> it happens after you realize it
> You dont see light
> Until sensation of seeing light
> Is registered in perception
> (107th)

Viewing ideas as a form of light, the poet deduces that consciousness is another after-the-fact phantom:

> You dont conceive of darkness
> Till you've been late with light
> When you learned difference
> Between equal poles abright
> with Arbitrary ideas
> (107th)

The sum of this logic is that there is no reason to rejoice or grieve, since nothing ever happens: "everything is perfect,/ Because it is empty" (113th).

Yet for Kerouac no knowledge can replace experience:

> But I get tired
> Of waiting in pain
> In a situation
> Where I ain't sure.
>   (130th)

Love recurs ceaselessly; and though it is a source of pain, it is also the genesis of his art. Like Matthew Arnold in "Dover Beach," he embraces the anonymous force that keeps drawing him back into the world, despite life's horror:

> Crashing interruptions
>   So I'm with you
>   happy once again
>   and singing all my blues
>   in tune with you
>   with you
>   (171st)

The crisis in *Mexico City Blues* occurs in Choruses 194–197. Although the poet is pledged to teach the "secrets of the Buddha Mountain," he is caught up like everyone else in an imaginary race, and the teachings he himself receives are from equally frantic participants:

> Flagged by Dominos of Bodhi °
> And Oil men Ragged Hero
>   Mechanic Sariputran ° °
> Minnesinging Gurus, on we rave.
>   (194th)

Imprisoned by Buddhism, feeling still escapes, and emerges beautiful because it is human. Likewise poetry is a vital explosion no philosophy can smother:

> The songs that erupt
> Are gist of the poesy,
> Come by themselves, hark
> Stark as prisoners in a cave
> Let out to sunlight, ragged
> And beautiful when you look close
> And see underneath the beards
> the holy blue eyes of humanity
> And brown
>   (195th)

° Bodhi = wisdom
° ° Sariputra = one of Buddha's chief disciples

Although man listens appreciatively while

> The stars on high sing
> songs of their own, in motion
> that doesnt move, real,
> Unreal, singsong, spheres:—
> (195th)

what he craves is a more personal, immediate sensation of truth, the
ecstasy of one soul speaking to another, the blast of Gabriel's horn:

> But human poetries
>   With God as their design
>   Sing with another law
>   Of spheres & ensigns
>
> And rip me a blues
> Son, blow me a bop,
> Let me hear 'bout heaven
> In Brass Fluglemop
> (195)

"So I write about heaven," Kerouac begins the 196th Chorus.
Blowing his own version of bop, he rejects the alternative of simply
waiting for death. He cares about his fellows and wants to save them,
even if all he can do is teach them their own insubstantiality:
"Wanta bring everyone/ Straight to the dream" (196th). But since
enlightenment is ungraspable, man can't be permanently saved:

> If you only could hold
>   what you know
> As you know it forever,
>   instead-a
> Moving from griefy to griefy,
>   lament to lament,
>
> Groan, and have to come out
>   and smile once again
>   (196th)

The flaw Kerouac sees in Buddhism is that even its promised liberation—"A hospital for the sick,/ Lying high in crystal"—is something
that must be sought. Tainted with the imperfection of all human
effort, it is as unrealistic as other utopias:

> Here I go rowin
> Thru Innifree
> Looking for Nirvana
>   Inside me
>   (196th)

Striving is the one aspect of the human condition that cannot be altered by Buddhism; for it simply teaches us a new want:

> I got the woozes
> Said the wrong thing
> Want gold want gold
> Gold of eternity
> > (209th)

And:

> *Poor!* I wish I was free
> of that slaving meat wheel
> and safe in heaven dead
> > (211th)

The 197th Chorus marks a major turning away from Buddhism. In his mind the poet can't find "Italy" (47th), let alone nirvana, but it is nonetheless the place where wilder ideas than either originate:

> Inside, Inside Me,
> I'se free
> Free as the bee
> Inside he.
> > Lord have a mercy
> > on Hallelujah Town
> I got to stomp my foot
> And say, whee
> > (197th)

Continuing in the dialect and repetitious phrasing of a black Gospel enthusiast, Kerouac rejects Buddhism in favor of the sensual riot that makes one forget the need for solutions:

> > hey dad, now oan,
> > from now oan,
> > I dont want
> > cant wanta
> > wont wanta
> > > hear about it
> > not in my Oakland
> > Saloon, not in my bar
> > Not in my brokenglass
> > Not in my jar

It is not existence in the abstract he would know, anyway, but life with warmth and a finger-snapping beat:

> Blue, black, race, grace,
> > face,
> I love ye.
> > (197th)

In the very next Chorus, Kerouac is back to his Buddhist paradoxes: "Nirvana aint inside me/ cause there aint no me" (198th). But he can't convince himself to forget his pleasures; something inside keeps calling for action:

> suck my lamppole, raise the bane,
>   hang the traitor
>   inside my brain
>   (213th)

Bored with Buddhism—"Fuck, I'm tired of this imagery" (216th-A)—Kerouac ends up again welcoming the sweet "delusion" of art [241]:

> Praised be man, he is existing in milk
>   and living in lillies—
> And his violin music takes place in milk
>   and creamy emptiness
>   (228th)

The philosophical argument of the book has come full circle. Its resolution requires a fresh perspective, outside the poet's own tautologies. In short, the book needs a hero, whose example can break the deadlock between Buddhist detachment and Christian (or artistic) involvement. That hero is Charlie Parker.

Parker was much on Jack's mind since he had died on Jack's 33rd birthday, March 12, 1955; and that summer in New York, Albert Avakian had showed him a photo of Bird looking strikingly beautiful in his coffin. The three penultimate Choruses in *Mexico City Blues* present with similar stark clarity the profile of an artist in whom resided the power—if not to save—then at least to spare multitudes from the pain in daily living.

The 239th Chorus begins by identifying Charlie Parker with Buddha. Bird was a calm sage, whose musical mastery inspired confidence like the pronouncement "All is well" by a joyful hermit. Bird laughed in the face of death. But unlike Buddha, he did not eschew passion and conflict. He took up the challenge of those who taunted him at jam sessions:

> . . . Charley burst
> His lungs to reach the speed
> Of what the speedsters wanted
> And what they wanted
> Was His Eternal Slowdown.
>   (239th)

Kerouac's point is that Parker's music reflected a profound knowledge of life, and served in its own way to banish ignorance. As a great musician Parker was "a great creator of forms/ That ultimately find expression/ In mores and what have you" (239th).

The basic method of art is deception, the antithesis of Buddhism's attempt to show truth in clear light. Unlike Buddhism, art makes no claim to "extinguish" suffering. But the delightful deceit of art, like the cheerful assurance of the Catholic Church, makes existence a good deal more bearable. No Buddhist saint who works transcendental miracles without lifting a finger, Parker is clearly a Christian saint insofar as his work is to make the earth more livable. Bird

> . . . wailed his little saxophone,
> The alto, with piercing clear
> > lament
> In perfect tune & shining harmony,
> Toot—as listeners reacted
> Without showing it, and began talking
> And soon the whole joint is rocking
> And everybody talking and Charley
> > Parker
> Whistling them on to the brink of eternity
> With his Irish St Patrick
> > patootle stick,
> And like the holy piss we blop
> And we plop in the waters of
> > slaughter
> > (240th)

Parker the artist is the supreme confidence man, who can make us believe life something other than we know it: "And how sweet a story it is/ When you hear Charley Parker tell it . . ." (241st). He cannot change our life—"Anyhow, made no difference"—but he can "devise" [242] a better world that we may possibly implement. In any case, the freshness of his inspiration is like a prayer that gives us hope of what salvation might be like: "Charley Parker, lay the bane/ off me, and every body" (241st).

The final, 242nd Chorus begins with an account of the "Diamond Samadhi," the experience of hearing the hush of soundlessness, which is supposed to illustrate the Buddhist truth that existence is mind-created. With sufficient material comforts and no worries, it would be easy to make the inner voyage to hear one's own music. But, as the poet now realizes, the knowledge that death will eventually cut short that voyage robs it of joy:

> The sound in your mind
> > is the first sound
> > > that you could sing
>
> If you were singing
> > at a cash register
> > > with nothing on yr mind—

> But when that grim reaper
> comes to lay you
> look out my lady

The poet would prefer suicide to waiting in pitiful pride for a humiliating, senseless death before his fellow men (John O'Twill being the well-tailored man of dumb propriety):

> T'were better to get rid o
> John O'Twill, then ° sit a-mortying
> In this Half Eternity with nobody
> To save the old man being hanged
> In my closet for nothing
> And everybody watches
> When the act is done—

But there is still one more alternative, and that is to assume the role of Charlie Parker and assert by sheer will that all is well, guarding humanity from the killing face of nothingness:

> Stop the murder and the suicide!
> All's well!
> I am the Guard

Despite the fact that Allen Ginsberg sees *Mexico City Blues* as evidence of Kerouac's intelligent understanding of Buddhism, it seems likely that the book marked the start of his emergence from Buddhist influence. When Gary Snyder met Kerouac a month later, he was convinced that Kerouac would be asking for Catholic last rites on his deathbed. As further evidence of the basic religious orientation of *Mexico City Blues,* one should consider that after it was published in 1959 Kerouac consistently autographed copies of the book by placing a cross under his signature, a practice he didn't normally use for his other books.

Whichever way the pendulum of criticism finally swings on this point, there are ample grounds to support the contention of poet Michael McClure that *Mexico City Blues* is "the finest long religious poem of the twentieth century."

6.

September 9, 1955, Jack left Mexico City with his bag stuffed with manuscripts, codeine, benzedrine, and pot. Saving the travel money Allen had sent him, he took a bus only as far as El Paso, then hitched to Los Angeles and rode the Zipper to Santa Barbara. On the train

---

° To make sense of this stanza, one must read *then* as a solecism for *than.*

he was heartened by a little bum who taught him a prayer to Saint Teresa. It seemed a good omen, since Teresa had vowed to shower the earth with roses—a special symbol to Jack. More importantly, the bum confirmed his belief that hobos lead a holy life, for Jack himself now planned to live as a *bhikku*, a wandering Buddhist monk.

After cooking and sleeping on the beach, under the stars, he got a ride all the way to San Francisco in a Mercury convertible, driven by a gorgeous blonde in a strapless bathing suit! In the rose-covered cottage at 1624 Milvia Street in Berkeley, he found Allen plotting poetry readings with a group of West Coast poets on their way to staging the San Francisco Poetry Renaissance. Jack had never felt greater love for Allen, nor greater need of his companionship, and they spent day and night talking, reading each other their latest works, and enjoying the intellectual-artistic community of which Allen was now a respected member. Neal came around often with Natalie, talking endlessly about Jesus and about Natalie's sure-fire system of betting the third-choice horse double-or-nothing in every race. Jack enjoyed going to the racetrack with them because it reminded him of trips to Rockingham with his father, though he himself would never place a bet. The excitement kept him drinking almost nonstop.

In late September, Allen brought him to one of Rexroth's literary soirées. Several poets were there, including two former students from Reed College in Portland, Gary Snyder and Philip Whalen. Snyder had been studying Buddhism since the late forties and was now learning Japanese at Berkeley and composing a thesis, *Myths and Texts*, based on American Indian lore. Raised in rural Oregon, Snyder and Whalen were familiar with wilderness life. Both had worked as fire lookouts in the High Cascades in Washington, a job from which Whalen had returned to San Francisco just a few weeks earlier. When a discussion of Buddhism began, Jack mentioned the *Pure Land Sutra* he'd been reading, and was startled to hear intelligent comments on it. "Why, there are other people here who have read these texts!" he exclaimed. Rexroth, in the first of his many snide put-downs of Jack, retorted, "Everybody in San Francisco is a Buddhist, Kerouac! Didn't you know that?"

Both Snyder and Whalen had read Jack's jazz story in *New World Writing*. Snyder had been impressed by the energy and evocativeness of the piece, and Whalen by its remarkable combination of Joycean voice with traditional American subjects. Discussing the story in a radio broadcast in May, Rexroth had ranked Jack with Céline and Genet. From their first meeting, however, they rubbed each other wrong. Immensely learned, Rexroth wanted to be respected as the arbiter of West Coast letters, and his weekly gatherings were aimed at reinforcing his authority. In part, his interest in helping young writers was based on the plaudits he derived from "discovering" them; according to Robert Creeley, Rexroth liked to consider himself "the authority that gave us reality." While holding court, he sometimes got carried away with the powers of his own rhetoric. When he claimed, for example, that he had had every woman in California, his guests were expected to show not amusement but admiration. The kind of storytelling Jack loved was Neal's eager fantasizing; Neal could speculate brilliantly about how beautiful life might be "if. . . ." By contrast, Jack scorned Rexroth's egocentric "blabbing." Chafed by this disrespect, Rexroth may also have felt the need to demean Jack because the others thought so highly of his ability; Rexroth was always edgy of anyone who seemed to be moving too close to his eminence. At any rate, by the spring of 1956, when he wrote his essay "Disengagement: The Art of the Beat Generation" for *New World Writing* No. 11, he spoke of Kerouac as being "in his small way the peer of Céline . . . or Beckett."

Soon after that night, Jack and Allen visited Gary in Berkeley, and Jack and Gary quickly struck up a friendship. Jack, who had been searching for a mentor since the death of Gerard, came as near finding one in Gary as he ever did. Eight years younger than Jack, Gary had achieved Emersonian self-reliance through disciplined work, and though he delighted in physical pleasures, unlike Neal he never let the pursuit of pleasure distract him from his serious goals. Gary was capable of living and working in the woodland hut that for Jack remained a lifelong dream. But hearing Jack read aloud from *October in the Railroad Earth*, he realized that Jack had a great deal to teach him about writing. And coming from such different backgrounds, they had a lot to learn from each other about America.

Allen and Gary were working with Rexroth to stage a poetry reading at the Six Gallery in San Francisco in early October. On the strength of *Mexico City Blues* and his recently composed *Berkeley Blues*, Jack was already an admired poet. Despite the urging of friends, he refused to read his works in public, though he liked to read them to a small group. The night of the reading, he and Allen met Gary and Phil Whalen at the Key Terminal in San Francisco. Whalen recalls that Jack was "jumpy," and so anxious not to feel like a stranger that he immediately told Phil, "You remind me of a guy I used to play baseball with in Lowell." At the gallery, the reading was deferred until Jack returned with a gallon of red wine. Then, much to Rexroth's annoyance, he began to yell "Go!", to moan, gurgle, and beat out the rhythms of the poetry on his jug (what Rexroth execrated as "fourth-dimensional counterpoint"). But all the other poets, including Philip Lamantia and Michael McClure, appreciated Jack's encouragement. The reading of *Howl* (though second to last) was the grand finale. By the end, Allen had the audience wildly stomping and chanting with him. Rexroth declared that Allen that night had begun a revolution in American poetry "from bridge to bridge," and within a year the prophecy was fulfilled. The day after the reading, Lawrence Ferlinghetti asked to publish *Howl* in the "Pocket Poets Series" of his City Lights press. For Jack it was a secret triumph. Alluding to his breakthrough in *Howl*, Ginsberg wrote: "Kerouac invented and initiated my practice of speech-flow prosody."

At the reading Jack met his former girlfriend Jinny Baker, and in the next few weeks had an affair with her, breaking his year-long celibacy. At Snyder's cottage there were intimate "orgies," where Gary taught his friends Oriental positions and a little philosophy; viewing sex as a "simple physical twitch" as well as "a gracious generous gift . . . to be shared," he doubtless helped relax Jack's inhibitions about it. In Gary's view, Jack's relations with women were hampered by Catholic guilt and anguish: "He operated from aversions and sharp senses of right and wrong." Jack frequently talked against both women and sex, and what was even more classically Catholic, he seemed to enjoy the repentance after sex as much as he reveled in the wickedness of the act itself. Gary also noticed that any time Jack was with a woman very long he'd begin to look constrained. Physically he was having trouble making love to Jinny too, so it was no surprise when soon they drifted apart.

He was in deep trouble, and he knew it. When Allen wanted to introduce him to a hipster named Bob Donlin, Jack begged off, saying he already knew too many people. Every new person usually became an additional drinking partner, and Donlin proved no exception; yet Jack liked his blue-eyed, dark-haired good looks and his Boston Irish Catholic wit. Donlin remembers that Jack didn't think himself good-looking and was convinced that his body was oddly proportioned, his neck too long and his legs too short. Both Donlin and Whalen recall Jack returning from numerous dates with women that had ended abruptly because he was too drunk or disinterested to make it in bed. To redeem himself, he attempted to pass the women along to some other man. He discussed his alcoholism with Bob, admitting that he could no longer deal with people when he was sober. To Phil he explained that on the one hand he wanted a woman who would give him sex and let him rove, and on the other he needed a stable wife who would care for Mémère after he was dead.

In tandem with his growing misogyny was a rage against homosexuals. Jack talked incessantly about all the "big old fags" he knew, doing devastating nasal imitations while claiming that "the whole question's boring to me." At the same time he betrayed more than a little fascination with the elegance of "high-teacup queens," [243] and he enjoyed being fawned on by the "gay poets" (real and would-be) who hung around Allen.[244]

The gallon jug of wine, his steadiest companion, left him frighteningly gloomy. At the house of Berkeley professor Thomas Parkinson, Jack swung his jug over the head of Parkinson's four-year-old daughter, and the six-foot-six scholar tossed him out. How much Jack had changed can be gauged by the shock of Allan Temko, who with his wife visited Allen's cottage one night. Having settled down to a respectable professorial life, Temko was appalled to find Jack and Allen surrounded by what he thought to be male hustlers, and told Jack such characters revolted him. Jack replied, "They're interesting if you get to know them." Temko's wife thought Jack "an absurd mug, a savage," and Temko himself felt Jack actually brought out the most vicious instincts in the company, if only because he was such a receptive audience.[245]

Still, Jack really cared about how people should live and though he accepted experimentation, he was concerned about the danger of hurting others. The idea of living religion was important to him, and where Buddhism diverged from common sense he repudiated it. He saw red, for example, when Gary told the story of Ummon coming upon two monks who were fighting over a cat. Grabbing a butcher knife, Ummon asked the monks to say a word of Zen fast, and when they failed he chopped the cat in half. "Anybody who would cut a kitty in half is just rotten!" Jack protested. Another time he and Gary argued over whether it was permissible to kill a harmful creature such as a rattlesnake. Gary tried to explain that sometimes "mindlessly not killing something is crueler than mindfully killing it," but Jack clung to the orthodox Buddhist view that all life must be spared. Gary felt that he refused to accept suffering as the basic condition of the universe, and that he was still using Buddhism as an escape. Indeed it may be that Buddhism merely protected Jack like the leather wrapper in which he carried his *Buddhist Bible*—that it served the same practical instinct.

Buddhism was one of the few subjects he didn't care to discuss with Gary. Although Jack had a quick grasp of the literary strength of Buddhist writings, and a certain intuitive grasp of their meaning, his thinking remained theistic. In that respect, he was more nearly Hindu than Buddhist. Gary felt that all Jack really got out of Mahayana was its universal compassion and its sense of the vastness of space and time: the kotis (myriads) of chilicosms (galaxies) and kalpas (eons). According to Gary, the concept-reducing, theism-reducing cutting edge of Mahayana metaphysics never touched him. Allen Ginsberg, however, has a sharply differing view. To him, Jack continually quoted the injunction in the *Diamond Sutra* to discard "such arbitrary conceptions of phenomena as one's own self, other selves, living beings and a Universal Self"—using it to deflate Allen's rash enthusiasms and even to belittle the importance of his own work. The fact that Jack identified with the Tathagata, the one who passes through the world of time, is further evidence to Ginsberg that Jack comprehended the phantom nature of reality. Gary admitted years later that had Jack undertaken the formal study of Zen, he would probably have been able to solve the initial Koans rapidly. Yet there was some blindness in Jack to the actual distance between himself and Gary. In the novel Jack wrote about Gary, *The Dharma Bums*, he states that Japhy and Ray (Gary and himself) have the same favorite Buddhist saint, Avalokitesvara, who shows mercy to those in special need. In reality, Gary's favorite was Manjusri, the Bodhisattva of transcendental wisdom that cuts through all delusion, including such errors as the belief in a divine spirit overseeing the universe.

Gary felt that "Jack made the moment everything—the present was where he wanted to be, and for people around him the present became the only thing that mattered." While he admired Jack's ability to be "right on top of things," he also saw "a real self-destructive streak in him." It was clear that "Jack wanted to get out of the world"—a fact all the more tragic to those like Gary who sensed that he was on the verge of great success. Snyder maintains there was "a palpable aura of fame and death" around Jack, the force field of an energy beyond his control that couldn't help charting a course of its own for him.

Although Jack would say, "I am Buddha," Gary was sure Jack knew better. In early October, Cowley wrote Jack that Viking would offer him a contract for *On the Road* if he could get releases signed by all the living "characters" who might have grounds for libel suits. But Jack still worried about how long it might take to get all his novels published, and his complaints about lack of recognition led to bouts of pessimism in which he'd fall back on the consolation that "we'll all be dead quick." [246] Gary worried that he had fallen for the romantic notion that creativity is tied to alienation, despair, and loneliness. Gary's own belief was that artists have, over the ages, generally been representatives of sanity in their culture.

In any case, when Gary criticized his excessive drinking, Jack would snap, "Enough of this shit! I'm gonna do what I wanna do!" What that meant was *die* to anyone who saw the way he drank and the places in which he drank, where alcoholism was a minor danger compared to the beatings you might take from your fellow drinkers. Jack claimed he drank for joy, but by this time joy was simply a wiping out of his misery when sober, and he sought no knowledge that would leave him even more self-conscious than he'd always been.

What he did want to learn from Gary was the lore of the frontier and specifically the skills of autonomy. After fitting Jack up with sleeping bag, knapsack, and a bag full of peanuts and raisins, Gary led him on a hike up the twelve thousand-foot ridge of Matterhorn Mountain in Yosemite. They were accompanied by a hilarious, double-talking Berkeley librarian named John Montgomery, who fascinated Jack with his scholarly non sequiturs. For Gary the climb was tame; the only things that interested him were the zero temperature at night—it was late October, the end of the season—and the autumn light on the bleak, snow-patchy landscape. Jack, by contrast, felt he was mountain climbing not only to greater heights of adventure but to an entirely new independent life in the West. Eating Gary's homemade chocolate pudding frozen in the snow, and making up haikus as subtle as the gray-violet sunset, this was one of the happiest times in Jack's life.

Montgomery returned to the car to drain the crankcase, then climbed to meet Gary and Jack the next morning, but was too tired to follow them to the top. Unlike Kerouac's dramatization of the episode in *The Dharma Bums,* it was no great terror that caused Jack to quit 100 feet short of the summit. Only mildly unsure of himself, he would have made it easily, Montgomery felt, had John been there to give him a little push. In the novel, however, Kerouac uses his alleged cowardice as a foil for Gary's courage. Indeed Gary climbed much of the mountain naked, and scrambling to the top he did let out a yodel of joyous defiance. But never that whole fall had Gary an inkling that Jack saw him as a hero.

Actually Gary was nearly as shy as Jack, and far less a ladykiller than the character Jack modeled after him. Yet most remarkable was Jack's appreciation of Gary's anarchist roots and radical leanings. Of course partly Jack was excited to contact the intransigent Northwest socialism of workers' movements like the Wobblies, whose exploits had been so gloriously chronicled by Dos Passos. But he also showed a friendly interest in Gary's own political opinions. Although then a rabid defender of McCarthy, Jack had a nose for the fact that Gary was living on the leading edge of revolutionary social change. In Gary's life-style Jack foresaw the "rucksack revolution" that would lead to millions of hippies abandoning industrial America a decade later. McCarthy wouldn't have had the imagination for such a prophecy, let alone Jack's relish to see it carried out. Though he was eventually to become frightened by the drastic program for such change, he was in 1955 one of its greatest partisans. What impressed him most about Gary, perhaps, was Gary's understanding that the creation of art is a political act. According to Snyder: "Anybody who really captures the essential thusness of a time and place has changed things. To revoke a reality, and to make a [new] reality, is to make something political happen—because what do people act in terms of except what they take to be real?" That was the same insight Jack and Holmes had shared in 1948, when they predicted that through their writing America would begin "picking up, changing, becoming sweeter, no more wars, sweet presidents."

Jack gave a reading of *Mexico City Blues* to the Berkeley Buddhist Church study group, and members of the Young Buddhist Association liked it so much they asked to print a few of his poems in their annual, *The Berkeley Bussei.* But there were limits to Jack's willingness to collaborate, as he always distrusted friendship even a little more than he needed it. The strong bonds that developed that fall between himself and Gary, and Phil also, can be attributed to the willingness of those two Westerners to meet the crotchety Canuck more than halfway.

Despite Jack's "charming sweetness," [247] there were times when he actually was the crude drunken bum, when he would lacerate even close friends with a cruelty too incisive to be an act. Nor did he need to be provoked. With the amazingly gentle and tolerant "big booboo" Whalen,[248] his moods would veer from bright-eyed conviviality to morbid mournfulness. Out of the blue he would start extolling the virtues of Gerard and predicting that he would soon join his brother. These paeans to death often preceded an attack on his listener. With people he didn't know well his shyness ran strongly to aggression; taking an instant dislike to certain people he'd say anything, even an outright lie, to get rid of them. Interestingly, he talked a lot with Phil about "the great intelligence in madness," citing Dostoyevsky's works, Melville's *Pierre,* and Hawthorne's *The Marble Faun.* He also spent hours rapping about "total honesty," as though that justified his fits of meanness, as though to suppress anger made one more culpable than to give hurt. And sometimes too he would make scurrilous remarks, or challenge people with insulting questions, just to see how they would react—to bring them out from behind their defenses and find out what they were really like.

Jack wasn't an easy companion even when sociable. It was pleasant enough to observe his stunning feats of memory—such as reconstructing a previous conversation practically word for word—but Phil would get annoyed watching him "take a trip through a person's character" as though he were selecting "artistically true" details for a scene in his writing. Often equating someone he'd just met with someone in Lowell, he was forever analyzing people's motivations and, in Whalen's view, he usually "missed it by 480 degrees." Once he had made up his mind what a person was like, no one could persuade him differently (though Jack might change his view on his own). Many times Phil was maddened by Jack's refusal to accept simple explanations; if Phil said he didn't want to go to a party because he preferred to stay home and read, for example, Jack would produce elaborate evidence to prove him a "sorehead." [249] He even suspected anyone agreeing with him; walking through Berkeley with his notebook he would point out sights that struck him and wouldn't believe—as was usually the case—that Phil had noticed them on his own.

If Jack had one pristine tenderness left it was toward the Cassady family. One of the reasons he had vowed never to return to California was that he didn't want "to cause pain on any side" by prolonging his romantic triangle with Carolyn and Neal.[250] And while he was hurt to discover that their new ranchhouse in Los Gatos had no spare bedroom for him, he was also pleased to make a discrete place for himself on the periphery of the household, putting his sleeping bag under a prune tree in the large back yard.

The evening of his arrival in Los Gatos was like a family reunion. After his favorite supper he autographed a copy of *New World Writing* for Carolyn, proudly marking out the "prose writ in yr. Russell St attic." Later, as they watched TV, Neal continually switched channels and provided a running commentary on every show and commercial, and soon Jack joined in the game. They had just begun to clean some marijuana when the driveway flared red with the Mars light of a police car. Carolyn answered the door while Jack hid the pot behind his back. It turned out that the police merely wanted to collect an additional $60 in traffic fines from Neal (he was currently driving with a suspended license). The jolt was sufficient to spoil the party for Carolyn, but Jack and Neal's glee redoubled at having fooled the cops.

The next day Neal went to fetch Allen and Peter, so they could all attend the speech of a progressive bishop that evening. During the day Jack avoided Carolyn by playing with the children, demonstrating dives into the pool and teaching them to compose haikus. That night after the speech the bishop came to the house, a scene that years later inspired Kerouac's script for the movie *Pull My Daisy*. The bishop brought along his mother and aunt, whom Allen teased by placing himself between them on the sofa as he questioned the bishop about sex. Meanwhile Jack sat on the floor with his bottle of wine, leaning against the bishop's leg and blustering over and over, "I love you!" Something different about Jack struck Carolyn— the more raucous he got, the more he kept his eyes closed. It occurred to her that he was hiding his shame, that he no longer wanted people to read what his eyes, so exceptionally expressive, had to say.

Later, Neal drove Allen and Peter back to Berkeley, having privately advised Jack to "mind your own business—my wife." [251] Once again Neal was thrusting him on Carolyn, since assuaging her loneliness was the only way to forestall a definite break with her—and finalities were about the only thing Neal did fear. For all practical purposes he and Carolyn were now separated, as he had set up housekeeping with Natalie in San Francisco. That night Jack and Carolyn soothed each other's grief with the total abandon known only to people who have sworn allegiance to their chains.

Neal seemed determined to break out of his, but only in order that his rebellion might lead to punishment, which was the strongest purchase he had on life. In November he talked Natalie into forging Carolyn's signature to sell some securities worth $10,000, and used the money in an intensive campaign to follow her betting system and recoup past losses at the track. As usual, he wound up listening to random tips and losing the whole wad. When Carolyn learned of it, she did everything possible to prevent the prosecution of either of them, but for Natalie the sting of conscience was more than she could bear. Convinced that she and Neal were bound for prison, she determined to kill herself. After one unsuccessful attempt Hinkle and others told Neal to get her admitted to a hospital, but Neal believed she'd be all right if he just watched her continuously for a few days. Near dawn on November 30, when he finally dozed, she went up the fire escape to the roof, broke the skylight and with a piece of broken glass cut her throat. Police were called, and Neal fled. Backing away from the officer who grabbed her bathrobe, Natalie fell to her death.

Badly shaken, Neal returned to Carolyn; and perhaps to help console him, Jack moved down to Los Gatos soon afterward. Earlier in November, Jack had made an important decision about his future. Whalen and Snyder had suggested that he might support himself by working two months a year as a fire lookout for the National Forest Service in Washington. The job paid well because it required a person to live in complete solitude on a mountaintop—a discipline too severe for most people, but a great opportunity for a writer. Jack said the job sounded "groovy." Snyder's secret motivation for encouraging him to apply was his desire to force Jack to follow through on a project, something he seemed to have great difficulty doing. Although Jack readily adopted new plans, he had little ability to judge the endurance they demanded, and as a result was always getting himself into places he didn't want to be. Since a lookout was literally stuck in his observation post until a crew came to bring him down, Gary knew the job would hold Jack, for once, to a commitment to other people. It would also teach him what it was really like to be alone for an extended period, allowing him, for better or worse, to live out his most cherished dream. Jack agreed to apply, and recommendations from Whalen and Snyder improved his chances of being accepted. Before Jack left for Neal's, Gary took him to the army-navy store in Oakland to buy all the necessary equipment. Jack sent Phil a farewell note, calling him and Gary "the two best men I ever met" and claiming that their acquaintance compensated for all the drawbacks that had frightened him away from California.

The rainy season in Los Gatos forced Jack to sleep on the couch in the living room, and that was the least of his miseries. There was little cheer for him in fireside chats, TV, and wine, as he contemplated the fact that he had no real home anywhere. Carolyn wanted him to stay for Christmas, but to do so he would have had to enter into complicity with Neal. Carrying on Natalie's system with fanatic loyalty, Neal asked Jack to bet $300 for him. Instead, in mid-December, Jack caught the Zipper to Los Angeles, and spent a night in Skid

Row. A Jewish hobo there taught him the only cure for his phlebitis that ever worked: standing on his head three minutes a day. By bus and hitches he reached Calexico, where he met a trucker who wanted help finding prostitutes in Mexicali. Jack obliged, and was rewarded with a ride and food all the way to Ohio; from there he caught another bus to Rocky Mount and arrived three days before Christmas. His mother was just leaving for New York to care for her dying stepmother. With his sister's family Jack celebrated Christmas Eve by watching the Midnight Mass at St. Patrick's Cathedral on television.

Jack's second letdown came shortly after Christmas, when Nin, Paul, and Lil Paul took a trip to Florida. The final blow was news that Cowley was headed for California to spend a few months at Stanford, where he had hoped to work with Jack on the manuscript of *On the Road!* But as always, Jack bounced back from adversity with a new book. *Visions of Gerard* was written in pencil on the kitchen table, at night, on benzedrine, by electric light because his sister forbade candles. The novel pleased even cynical Lucien with its candid impressions of death. It may not be the best of his novels, as Jack thought at the time, but there were more than sentimental reasons for it being his favorite.

7.

Begun in late December, 1955, and finished on January 16, 1956, *Visions of Gerard* took more than the twelve days Kerouac claimed to his bibliographer, Ann Charters. John Kingsland asserts that many of the scenes had been included—not in the same language, to be sure—in the original draft of *The Town and the City*, which he read in Edie Parker's apartment. Kerouac also told Charters that if he hadn't been left alone in Rocky Mount, he wouldn't have bothered writing *Visions of Gerard*. The paradox, he well knew, was that he couldn't help writing the novel, that in fact all his books were simply ingenious variations of that one book, the way all of Thomas Wolfe's novels were recastings of *Look Homeward, Angel.*

Kerouac's final boast to Charters was that the novel's style was "directly influenced" by *Henry V*. What that actually meant was that he had let Shakespeare's sound—from his current rereading of *Henry V* as well as from the extensive passages of other plays he had memorized—filter into his spontaneous prose. Kerouac talked to Charters in 1966, but even by 1956 he was a highly unreliable reporter of his own life, becoming unable to distinguish between fact and fancy; and if one takes almost any of his words at face value they will be less than half true. In one letter to Carolyn that spring, Jack claimed to be Shakespeare and Balzac reincarnated; in a later letter he apologized for such "crazy" utterances, explaining that they were the only means he had to say things that couldn't be said, at least not logically. Buddhism had shown him the way to advance by paradox, that is, by denying one's accomplishment and so increasing it. So that for him to say the language of *Visions of Gerard* was "wind-blown and Shakespearean" was to point out its sustained iambic rhythms and uncribbed metaphor—and to apologize, perhaps, for the occasional windiness of the prose, since this is one of his few truly overwritten books. However, the novel is remarkable for its use of Middle English alliterative stresses, and many lines are like haiku: "the gritty gravel under restless many little shoes—Another day of school."

The achievement lies in Kerouac's parody; everything he imitates becomes self-imitation. The sentence: "High above, in the stormy sky, a bird with little buffeted birdy bones bats ahead, beak to the nose of the wind—" uses alliteration much as Gerard Manley Hopkins in "The Windhover." It is, besides, apparently modeled on Williams' famous poem "To Waken an Old Lady."

When Kerouac tries to imitate Shakespeare it is neither true megalomania (the self-aggrandizing "angel tendencies" with which the navy credited him) nor plagiarism, but simply a second vision of himself—just as Shakespeare's strength was his all-inclusive "vision of life, in which he was swilled like a pearl in a pigsty." That and other things Kerouac says about Shakespeare in his article "Shakespeare and the Outsider" seem to apply to himself—e.g., "Shakespeare heard *sound* first then the words were there in his QUICK HEAD"; "he apparently flowed in his writing and wrote in an inspired hurry." Kerouac sees both himself and Shakespeare, and his vision doubles itself in the birefringent crystal of mind. But mind can keep doubling to infinity. Claiming to have imitated *Henry V*,° Kerouac doubles his ties with Shakespeare, and the connection is more important than stylistic similarities. He creates a "joint authorship," a conception of the artist as one who is multiplied by every mind that has a profound influence upon him.

Once written, *Visions of Gerard* becomes the cornerstone of *The Duluoz Legend*, asserting once for all that the coherence of those novels lies in vision rather than plot, characters, theme, or even, as in

---

° After all, the style of *Henry V* is not notably different from that of Shakespeare's other mature works. The specific similarities between that play and *Visions of Gerard* are almost all in content. The jovial pessimism of Shakespeare's drinkers is shared by Kerouac's backstage carousers. Pistol's loneliness and hard lot still plague a poor man like Emil Duluoz. The King heartens his soldiers as the father cheers the family—though Emil is a King and Prince Hal and Falstaff all rolled into one. And the central theme of *Henry V*—the constancy of the heart—was Kerouac's long before he read Shakespeare.

Proust, style. After finishing *Visions of Gerard*, Kerouac contemplated adding the word *vision* to the titles of most of his other novels, changing *Maggie Cassidy* to "Visions of Mary," *October in the Railroad Earth* to "Visions of the Railroad," etc. The thread of the *Legend* is the sequence of cosmic moments, which depend on a focus from within (the imaginative power) and from without (the reflections of the material universe). *Visions of Gerard* records the birth of such a double vision in the author while exposing its mechanism again and again in the text. The existence of that vision, so established, forces a new reading of all the writer's other works; in a very real sense it doubles his literary output.

Growing up in a French-Canadian colony (itself a hybrid culture) separated by choice from the American melting pot, Kerouac came by double vision early. It is but one step from learning that your native language is not the only language to grasping that language itself is but one means of understanding, that beyond the rational there is an irrational, and beyond the material a spiritual. This learning was reinforced by a strongly mystical Catholic education, itself immeasurably aided by Jack's kinship with a child saint, whose presence grew increasingly vital after his death. That Kerouac should reveal the dynamics of double vision in a book centered on his experience of Gerard was not only apt but virtually inevitable.

Kerouac gives the key to the novel in an aside, quoting cartoonist J. R. Williams that "the scene behind the scene is always more interesting than the show." Observing the American dream from the backstage of Little Canada, Kerouac was always seeing "behind the scene," as a result of which life rapidly took on the trappings of a fiction, a "mind movie." [252] He was simply given a subject and a means of seeing it much earlier than most children. Shortly after Gerard's death he began staging his own one-actor movies to Victrola music, some of which evolved into long serial sagas. At eight, following Gerard's artistic example (as well as his father's), Jack transformed those sagas into comic strips. Three years later he was writing "whole little novels" in nickel notebooks. By seventeen, he claimed, he had found his serious vocation in fiction. In *Visions of Gerard*, he traces the lineage of his writing unequivocally to his brother: "the whole reason why I ever wrote at all . . . because of Gerard, the idealism, Gerard the religious hero—" Yet the point is that Kerouac didn't become a conventional religious writer but an impressionistic painter with words. The praises of Gerard are sung with all sincerity, but what Gerard gave Jack was what he made of Gerard: the symbol of a process in himself.

Gerard's religious message was, despite the attentiveness of the nuns at his bedside, quite old-hat: "We're all in Heaven—but we don't know it!" Dostoyevsky had put almost the same words in the mouth of Father Zossima's saintly brother, in *The Brothers Ka-*

ramazov, and even there it was really a simple derivative from the Gospel notion that those who don't see and hear God on earth lack the proper eyes and ears. In fact, Kerouac intimates that the depth of his writing is due to the *loss* of Gerard: "I would deliver no more obloquies and curses at my damned earth, but obsecrations only, could I resolve to keep his fixed-in-memory face free of running off from me—For the first four years of my life, while he lived, I was not Ti Jean Duluoz, I was Gerard, the world was his face, the flower of his face. . . ." If by losing Gerard he has lost purity, he has also gained a key to his own identity and to the conditions of life, for the understanding of duality was not possible while his brother still seemed a part of himself.

In harmony with Eastern religion, Kerouac sees separateness as the cause of suffering. One cold windy February night Gerard is sent out to buy aspirins for his ailing mother and on the way to the drugstore learns the truth of the winter night, "that we are not made for this world," that a climate fine for icebergs and stones is deadly to beings like himself. And the flaw that makes him vulnerable is consciousness: "Gerard divines that all of this is pure division, a grief of separation, the cold is cold because there are two to know it, the cold and he who is en-colded. . . ." In heaven there will be neither division nor suffering, Gerard believes, but he still can't understand *why* there should be suffering on earth. That is the main question posed in *Visions of Gerard*, as in the Book of Job. While there may be no answer, Kerouac manages through his double vision to circumvent the problem.

The novel is hinged on the cycle of the seasons, and its primary metaphor is weather. We first see Gerard in the summertime, lounging in the grass watching the clouds drift past, "Tao phantoms that materialize and then travel and then go, dematerialized," the way human souls become "substantial fleshy people themselves, like your quite substantial redbrick smokestacks of the Lowell Mills. . . ." Kerouac moves on to a specific description of his father, "Emil Pop Duluoz," and Gerard, anticipating Gerard's death as the completion of the cycle: the disembodiment of the soul in death. And though the father's death is not portrayed in this novel, as in *The Town and the City*, it is amply foreshadowed.

It is not that life and death are the same, but rather that one is no truer than the other—no more than one season is truer than another, no more than the image in one's left eye is truer than the image in one's right eye. The two eyes neither confirm nor disprove each other, but their unified sight yields a valuable perspective. One of Kerouac's favorite Koans dealt with the relativity of vision: "Zen is the moonlit night when I'm walking down the lake and the moon follows me south, and you're walking up the lake and moon follows you north: which one does the True Moon follow?" The perfection of the whole lies in the infinite multiplicity of its pieces, each one balancing another.

Appropriately, in contrast to its idyllic beginning, much of the novel takes place in a winter of "cold and chapped sorrow," of clouds and fierce winds that force their way into the house, of an earth laid bare to snow. When Gerard dies it is again summer, and the snow has changed to an inexorable rain, which intrudes into the church at his funeral. But that there is always a dwelling in which to shelter from the weather—be it home, school, or church—is one of the dualities Kerouac celebrates. And that he does celebrate them is one of his major originalities.

Early in the novel, just after invoking Gerard's blessing upon the world's fertility, Kerouac presents a dialogue in which Gerard tells Ti Jean that "Heaven is all white," the unity of all color wavelengths, and that "all the children and their parents are together forever" there. When the narrator, Ti Jean, persists to know the color of God, Gerard answers, *"Blanc d'or rouge noir pi toute*—White of gold red black and everything." Emphasis is thus put on the divisions that compose the unity.

Color symbolism works throughout the book. The red of life contrasts with the black of death; the gold, white, and crystal of purity (God and Void alike) with the gray, yellow, and brown of mortality; the blue sky of truth with the green illusions of nature. We know these colors separately, but only together do they produce the light we call consciousness:

> He bundles me in the coat and hat, he'll show me how to play in the yard—Meanwhile smoke sorrows from red dusk roofs in winter New England and our shadows in the brown frozen grass are like remembrances of what must have happened a million aeons of aeons ago in the Same and blazing Nirvana-Samsara Blown-Out-Turned-On light.

With consciousness, man, who is himself a division of the cosmos, creates an infinity of further divisions, things to cling to or to worry over: "For it's not innocent blank nature made hills look sad and woe-y, it's men, with their awful minds. . . ." And though Gerard would never be one of that "seedy lot" of French-Canadians who hide wife and daughter in dirty rooms as they do herrings and gold rings in their cellar, he suffers the tremendous pains of rheumatic fever—a punishment for nothing other than being alive:

> The morning he was born somehow there was gray rain and damp overshoes and rubbers in a dreary closet and a brown sad light in the kitchen and angry smirch of bepestered life-faces, and somehow from somewhere out, or in the center, Counsel coming to him, saying "Dont do it—Dont be born"

but he was born, he wanted to do it and be born and ignored
the Counsel, the Ancient Counsel—

Now the pain of his sickness confirms his separation, because he sees
that the other members of the family sleep peacefully while he
thrashes in bed, awake alone.

Fortunately, limitless division resolves itself back to unity. Suffering to the point of despair, of accepting death, Gerard wonders,
"Throughout all that, throughout that snowy window and the cold
night and the big wind, and my leg and everything else in the house,
throughout all that there isn't something else?" And suddenly for his
vigil he is rewarded with a miracle, he becomes one with what is
tormenting him, he is visited with the multifarious sameness of a
swarm of snow: "And ecstasy unfolds inside his mind like a flower
and says Yes, and he sees millions of white dots. . . ." In another
instant the pain returns, just as readers will eventually return to their
own life "because it's not happening to themselves," but the point is
that a current has been created that can jump the gap between self
and world: "Unceasing compassion flows from Gerard to the world
even while he groans in the very middle of his extremity."

Although there may be "no reason for Man," there is value in the
repetition of his cycles—of Gerard's holding his head with the same
tilt as his father does, for example—because through those cycles
comes the ability to feel for others. Son becomes father. After one of
Emil's binges, the narrator remarks: "Dawns white with drunkenness
I've had myself with my boys and after that were boys—And there'll
be more—Brothers that were saints that died on me, that too's happened a million times in a million repetitudes and reincarnations in
Samsara's sorrow parade. . . ." Calling himself a liar, the narrator
reveals that fiction—pretending to be someone other than who or
what you are—is the basis of man's most precious quality, sympathy.
In a kind of play within the play, Ti Jean acts the part of his always
sorrowful Uncle Mike. Sitting alone on the back steps of the church
hall, he bawls, "A BWA! A BAW!" in perfect imitation until a
woman chases him away. Soon afterward Gerard dies, and wandering lonely among a kitchen full of mourning adults Ti Jean senses
that the play has never ended:

> . . . suddenly in my mind, as tho it was only a dream, a vision
> in the mind, which it is, I see the whole house and woe open
> up from within its every molecule and become instead of
> contours of walls and ceilings and absence-holes of doors and
> windows and there-yawps of voices and lamentings and
> wherewillgo-beings of personality and name . . . just suddenly
> a great swarming mass of roe-like fiery whitenesses, as if a
> curtain had opened, and innumerably revealed the scene be-
> hind the scene . . . phantoms finagling in the gloom, goopy

poor figures haranguing and failing with lack-hands in a fallen-angel world of shadows and glore, the central entire essence of which is dazzling radiant blissful ecstasy unending, the unbelievable Truth that cracks open in my head like an oyster and I see it, the house disappears in her Swarm of Snow, Gerard is dead and the soul is dead and the world is dead and dead is dead.

Joy is no less inevitable than sorrow; immortality follows from mortality the way the men playing poker backstage at the B. F. Keith's Theatre are an essential link in the card games Kerouac envisions taking place all over America. Kerouac's religion of the "real world" is as embracing as the mystical religion expounded by Gerard (and later rediscovered by Ti Jean). But like Gerard and Ti Jean, those two religions are a pair that counts as one. Kerouac insists that life defies logic. As Old Bull Baloon says, "It's a dream, lads, it's a dream."

The irony is that if life is a dream we have even less control over its outcome than a dreamer. Man's "free will" has baffled generations of philosophers. Kerouac would have us forget fate and give the dream and reality equal weight. "Death is the other side of the same coin, we call now, Life," he writes, and the coin is consciousness. Its value lies in vision, its treasury in the knowledge that if you miss one focus you inevitably achieve another.

When Gerard dies, Ti Jean gleefully runs to tell his father, thinking it good news; in later life he believes it really was good news, but not in the way he at first imagined. Looking back on his relatives who feared their own death and seeing how time has already consumed them, the mature narrator respects the simple gladness of the child. If life is hard on men, as Uncle Mike says, then death will at least leave a child "pure for heaven." Vision does not change life: "It ends like it ends." But there is no end to the ways man can see. When the birds no longer come to the dead boy's window, one neighbor suggests, "They're gone with him!" The narrator says, "Or, I'd say, 'It was himself.'" Kerouac's point is that it's both, it's as many as you want it to be.

Although men are separate from the world and from one another, they are capable of seeing in the same way: "it's all God—Urinating, alone, won't get you far—It happens, every day, in all the latrines of Samsara. . . ." After the coffin leaves the family's old house, workmen building a new house watch the funeral procession. Scoffingly they make various guesses about who is getting buried—an old priest, a housepainter, a whore. But they are all quieted by the sight of the small coffin, which can only be a child's. In a scene Shakespearean for its subtle, sidestage comment on the main action, Kerouac suggests that childhood's seeing the best in things is balanced by adulthood's seeing the worst.

The only real mistake is to avoid seeing, like fat Mr. Groscorp, who pulls down the shade so he can keep eating his pork chop as the hearse passes. He is like the businessmen who think "the money in their pocket is real" while the things it buys vanish like reflections on water.

Like Shakespeare, Kerouac mingles starkly contrasting characters and diverse settings, which push at each other with centrifugal and centripetal motion, like the ripples in a pond—not simply to heighten the dramatic tension, but to dramatize the cosmic moment. Such moments sometimes narrow down and widen again like the pulse of life, or like the expansion and contraction of breathing: "the audience is filing out for a soda in Paige's or Liggett's Drugstore or in Dana the Greek's and there will be dense dyed neon of oldtime city night in America, like old cartoons showing the boy newspaper seller with little cloth cap and scarf and knickers holding out a paper to two men, one in derby, one with elegant cane. . . ." The cosmic nature of motivation ties all people, all beings, together—from Ti Jean's sister screaming for joy "like a little kitty" to the priest working (like Mr. Groscorp!) for a good meal of pork scraps.

If wishing be the same as doing, as Christ said, then memory, imagination, and occurrence are all one. When Ti Jean was a year old he found himself in a gloomy shoe repair shop on a gray rainy day. As his mother took him outside, he saw a little old man in a strangely slanted gray hat walking away, and suddenly he felt that that man was "going towards some inexpressibly beautiful opening in the rain," toward some "pure land," at which Ti Jean himself could never arrive because he was being wheeled another way. On the rainy day of the funeral, four-year-old Ti Jean felt that Gerard was also being delivered to the Pure Land. In the climactic scene, Ti Jean listens to the priest chant *"Et pro omnibus"* ("and for all") and takes it to be the name of that land; and the word *aeternam* ("eternity") shows him the very location. The little man appears again, and then for a second time Ti Jean's world dissolves into motes of light. As if he has become Gerard, he sees "a swarm of angels in the church in the form of sudden myriad illuminated snowflakes of ecstasy. . . ." In joy he cries aloud, but people who don't see as far think he doesn't see at all; they think, "He doesn't understand." But not only has Ti Jean escaped into Gerard's world, which now, accommodating him too, is twice as large; but for Kerouac it is the simultaneous escape from beat to beatific.

No matter if there is still farther to go: "the simplest thing in the world, when properly looked at, is the original riddle." The little boys who sing blessings for Gerard's soul are singing for themselves as well. The church bell tolling the "drizzly news" of Gerard's death is heard somewhere as "beautiful music." The grave that swallows Gerard places him forever in his brother's heart. The gravedigger who shovels dirt on the coffin has closed one book and opened another, the one the narrator will someday write. Life can no more comprehend death than Ti Jean's disconsolate mother can fathom her younger son's contentment. "Ti Jean, you dont understand," she says paradoxically, underlining the fact that all such paradoxes are just illusions produced by a partial view. It remains for Kerouac to place his characters in perspective, far enough away so that all the lines finally join: "Sometime in the same night that's everywhere the same right now and forevermore amen." Dead or asleep, it is the same dream as life. Separation in Kerouac's world leads only to a more complete togetherness.

To Kerouac, man is blessed because whatever is, he can see or dream beyond it. The mind continually allows for something better, or at least different. Such are Gerard's visions as well as the narrator's visions of Gerard (a pun that is at the core of the book, as it was to a lesser extent in *Visions of Cody*). Through the faculty of vision what we call "evil" or "pain" is annihilated—as is good in the petty sense. The vision of consciousness alone is. It resolves all contradictions because it contains them all. In the prolificness of vision lies man's salvation, for what is flawed can always be exhausted, taken out of bounds, overtopped. That is the message in the highflown hip archaic language of *Visions of Gerard*, as it is the very technique with which the book was written.

BOOK THREE

1956–1969

Jack Kerouac in Lowell, 1967. *(Photo by Stanley Twardowicz.)*

ELEVEN
Clowns in a Circus of Power

1.

Drained and depressed by the benzedrine intensity of writing *Visions of Gerard*, Jack was called to New York a few days later for his step-grandmother's funeral. For two weeks he stayed at his aunt's house in Brooklyn, where he had lived a year while attending Horace Mann, and the grim reminder of his past glories left him even more vulnerable to the snubbing he received in the Village. Mardou kissed a new boyfriend in front of him; and though befriended by bop musicians Don Joseph, Tony Fruscella, and Bill Heine, as well as veteran hipster Stanley Gould, who scatted with him as of yore, Jack felt "old and futile among the enthusiastic fools of the future." But he was cheered to visit Lucien's family, which had recently been augmented by a second son, and there was the added pleasure of returning in triumph, as *The Paris Review* had just come out carrying "The Mexican Girl." To revive the high hopes of his youth he walked across the Brooklyn Bridge in a boyish muffcap. This time, however, it was with a pint of wine in hand, and even the "Brooklyn Bridge Blues" he wrote couldn't allay his guilt at having become a "bum." [253] As if in judgment of himself—like a Dimmesdale sneaking to the scaffold—Jack stretched out on a park bench to muse in the cold wind.

The strongest comfort Jack had was his native optimism, which had spoken to him during a night of meditation in the woods just before he left for New York, saying: "Everything's Allright Forever and Forever and Forever." So it was for the first time that Jack felt real joy at leaving New York, to return to the piny woods where his distant drummer could still be heard.

Viking Press was still stalling him by not sending a contract, but back in North Carolina he plunged into a new round of literary labors to prove to Cowley that he was "no sluggard." Besides typing many old pencil manuscripts such as *Tristessa* and the unfinished novel "Visions of Lucien," Jack added continuously to *Book of Dreams* and "Some of the Dharma" (his newest effort was to explain Buddhism without using Buddhist terms), and began a new "Book of Prayers." He was astonished around this time to receive a letter from

Whalen suggesting he do more writing. It dawned on him that probably no one other than Burroughs and Ginsberg realized he had already composed a body of mature work amounting to over a million words.

Jack had fallen out with both Ginsberg and Rexroth before he left San Francisco. At one of Rexroth's soirées, he and Whalen had been drinking; Kenneth, offended by Jack's using foul language in front of his children, and snarling about "unmannerly geniuses," asked them both to leave. Allen took Rexroth's side—or so Jack thought, for he wrote Whalen that he was convinced Allen was his "secret enemy." [254] As a result, Jack wasn't anxious to return to California.

In Rocky Mount he found a letter of acceptance from the National Forest Service. His job was to start in late June, and he planned to spend a couple of months beforehand in Mexico, then merely stop in San Francisco briefly to see Gary and Phil on his way up to Washington. On Matterhorn, Gary had given him a string of Buddhist prayer beads, which Jack took with him on his daily forest meditations. Now, coming by mail, Gary's gift of a potholder for outdoor cooking struck Jack as another gesture of sublime tenderness. He was equally moved by the fine quality of Gary's poems in the *Berkeley Bussei* and his recent translation of the "Cold Mountain" poem by the great Chinese bhikku Han Shan. It saddened Jack to learn that Gary would soon be going to Japan to live as a Zen monk. He didn't understand why Gary felt the need to do that, for Jack thought Buddhism could be fully enjoyed as a private literary kick. Jack pledged that if he got any money he'd follow Gary to Japan to climb mountains and womanize with him there.

But he discovered a new pal closer to home. Nearly eight, his nephew Paul was looking more like Gerard all the time, and preferred Jack's company to that of his own father, who was a straight and somewhat impersonal electronics technician. Jack would take Paul into the woods to study nature and compose poems. He gave Paul "religious" lectures too, instructing him to kill no creature. Such meddling didn't sit well with Paul, Sr., a skilled hunter, especially since Jack was always taking Paul's bird dogs along on his hikes through places where the dogs picked up ticks. The least Jack could do, complained Paul, was remove the ticks, but Jack protested that he had vowed to harm no living thing! Lil Paul especially liked the way Jack talked to him like an adult, even if he didn't always understand what Jack was saying; Jack also spoke freely with him about everything including the drugs he used, a subject his parents and Mémère avoided. By the same token, Jack prized the openness Paul permitted him. Sometimes in the middle of the night he would wake Paul up because he had something on his mind and could confide in no one else.

He showed great courtesy to the child too. Paul was amazed by how much reading his uncle did, and yet Jack would never push him away roughly. If he preferred not to be interrupted, he'd explain, "I need to be alone right now." In fact, Jack simply kept out of everyone's way when he wanted to write, secluding himself on the screened-in back porch for a whole day or two, emerging only for a bite of food and some wine or beer.

Perhaps the most engaging quality Paul found in his uncle was an indomitable cheerfulness. Jack was always bursting with new ideas, unusual facts, and a zest to be out seeing and doing new things. When their woodland routine dulled, he put up a basket for a season of hot games. He also continued to coach Paul at football, and frequently told him stories about Jim Thorpe, known as "the greatest football player of all time." In addition, Paul was fascinated watching Jack play the baseball game he'd invented, which comprised four stacks of specially made cards. He promised to teach Paul how to play the game when he got older, because the computations were extremely complicated, and a whole season might take years to play. At one time Jack had thought of marketing the game, but decided against it because, as he told Paul, "then it wouldn't be mine anymore." Instead, he wanted Paul to carry on the game as a family tradition, and promised to turn the cards over to him someday.

But Paul's parents were making Jack feel unwelcome. They harped on his drinking and his reluctance to take a regular job. Mémère's original agreement with Paul, Sr., was that her investment in his television business would cover Jack's room and board as well as her own, but Paul was the sort of man who couldn't abide another man's idle hands. Writing didn't seem like a "concrete" goal to him, and he refused to support anyone who was "taking life at a whim," [255] as he supposed Jack was. Mémère was heartbroken over the trouble between them, since her fondest wish was for a home that would tie the family together, a base Jack could always come back to. Considering him a little boy who was sure to get in trouble wherever he went, she regretted that he no longer had Neal to travel with. On the road alone, and out of control as he often was now, he was bound for disaster. To avert it, she agreed to move to California with him, because that seemed the place to which his restlessness always tended.

Anxious to become self-sufficient, Jack arranged with Viking Press to meet Cowley at Stanford, to make whatever revisions they wanted. Out of his own pocket he would pay for the trip, seeing it as the only means to break the deadlock that was steadily demoralizing him. The recent rock'n'roll craze seemed likely to make the book a best seller if they brought it out soon enough. He had already submitted releases signed by Allen and Neal, but now Viking worried that Justin Brierly also had grounds for libel. Jack wrote Cowley that it would be a simple matter to disguise Brierly past recognition. With money borrowed from his mother he hitchhiked out of Rocky Mount on March 17, 1956. The trip took a little longer than he expected, and by the time he arrived at Stanford in early April, Cowley had left, taking the manuscript back to New York. Despite the fact that Cowley's wife was pregnant, Jack felt slighted and never forgave him.

Gary was now living in a shack in a horse pasture high on a steep, eucalyptus-forested hillside in Mill Valley. The shack—which he dubbed the "Marin-An," punning on Marin County, and several Japanese and Chinese words that meant in sum "horse-grove hermitage"—was owned by a carpenter and Buddhist lay brother named Locke McCorkle. Handsome and voluble, McCorkle loved stimulating company and was more than willing to let Gary have guests. His big house below the cabin was the site of weekly parties. At Gary's invitation, Jack began a peaceful and productive season in the Marin-An.

Gary was finishing *Myths and Texts*, and his diligence conduced to similar work habits in Jack. Jack typed up *Mexico City Blues* on a series of scrolls, which he sent to Allen and Phil. (Allen's further efforts to get Jack published—specifically, his promotion of Jack's works to the avant-garde *Black Mountain Review*—had patched up their friendship; though now *Gary* was temporarily on the outs with Allen after a fight precipitated by a month of being stuck together on a recent hitchhiking trip to Reed College.) At Gary's suggestion, Jack wrote his first "sutra," *The Scripture of the Golden Eternity*. The piece has a tenuous relationship to Buddhism, for, as Snyder noted, it displays Kerouac's fundamental belief in God. All the same, it is a valuable statement of Kerouac's views on epistemology and the origin of language.

Kerouac sees creation as the act of naming, and naming as a process of tracking motion: "the Animate Divine." What we call consciousness, he suggests, is a continuous flow in and out, a "going and coming" like light in darkness, like man's perpetual journeying on the road. He defines enlightenment as living "in time and in time-less-ness," which is the moment, the point where motion appears to freeze long enough for us to perceive it. But those "stops" are as illusory as the still images when a stroboscope flashes in darkness. He conceives of the mind as a "beating light" that reveals the fluctuation, and hence falseness, of all it illuminates. The mind's mechanism is pretense, the universe it creates a fiction. Emptiness radiates an "exuberant fertility" of forms that limn its boundaries—or else what would it be empty of?—the way men give endless names to God to convey the single idea of namelessness. Kerouac compares the "timeless moment" to the emptiness of a treasure given away, of a puzzle put together, of an "infinite completion" that leaves nothing more to be done. The timeless moment, then, is consciousness filled to the point of such abundance that the saturation blocks out and blacks out consciousness. With all the gaps filled in, all field and no space for design, no more perception is possible—all that remains is a pure undisturbable unconsciousness, until the next pulse of consciousness turns the past moment to ghost. At least this is the experience Kerouac claims to have had realizing the "golden eternity" when he passed out in his backyard in North Carolina.

From this philosophy he draws the implication that the method of art must also be exuberance, a commemoration of the essential emptiness by describing the fullness of things that are not there. To attempt to make a definite statement is a mistake because "the thing is easily false." One can only suggest truth by a multiplicity of false-hoods. In effect, Kerouac is minimizing the value of literature, the way a Buddhist teacher insists that scripture is only a pointer to enlightenment, not the path itself. Accordingly, he instructs the reader: "When you've understood this scripture, throw it away. If you can't understand this scripture, throw it away." After he wrote *The Scripture of the Golden Eternity*, he showed it to Locke Mc-Corkle, saying, "While I was writing this, I thought I knew what it meant, but now I don't know anymore."

Kerouac's questioning of the value of literature was no affectation but the sincere doubt of a man who worried that he had "written too much" and wondered just how much genuine substance he still had to communicate.[256] But the "compulsion" to write continued, and in part his drinking was an effort to "cool down" the voices in his head that demanded to be heard.[257] Nevertheless, he surrendered to the impulse to record them in a piece of "automatic writing" called "Lucien Midnight"[258] (and later published as *Old Angel Midnight*). What Jack meant by automatic writing was not, like Yeats' wife, that in a trance he wrote words inspired by some commanding spirit, but simply that he wrote—and by his own admission this was the only instance of his doing so—without the slightest effort to censor or alter his expression.

Set on Good Friday, *Old Angel Midnight* is a confessional dialogue between the writer and his accusers. Appropriately, the chief inquisitorial voice belongs to Lucien Carr, for Lucien and Jack had a fond habit of deflating each other's professions. Still, many of the charges against the hypocrisy of writing, no matter their origin, were subjects of Kerouac's own introspection. He upbraids himself, as he had in letters to friends, for having imagined he would get rich as a writer: "Boy, says Old Angel, this amazing nonsensical rave of yours wherein I spose you'd think you'd in some lighter time find hand be-almin ya for the likes of what ya davote yaself to, pah. . . ." At the same time there is a challenge to write something really worthwhile:

> I want to hear the sounds thru the window you promised me
> when the Midnight bell on 7th St did toll bing bong & Bur-

roughs and Ginsberg were asleep & you lay on the couch in
that timeless moment in the little red bulb-light bus & saw
drapes of eternity parting for your hand to begin & so's you
could affect—and *ee*fect—the total turningabout & deep revival of world robe-flowing literature till it shd be something
a man'd put his eyes on & continually read for the sake of
reading & for the sake of the Tongue & not just these insipid
stories writ in insipid aridities & paranoias bloomin & why
yet the image—let's hear the Sound of the Universe, son, & no
more part twaddle. . . .

Like *Mexico City Blues*, *Old Angel Midnight* is animated by the
tension between the knowledge that reality is deceptive and the
hope that art can be truer: "Tie it all together, Jack, the mirror
doesnt show the real right." And while there are other accusers, like
Corso charging—as he did in real life—that Kerouac's writing was
nothing but gossip, the author is justified by numerous writers both
dead ("Wasnt it Dostopoffsy who gossipped so much") and living,
like poets Robert Creeley ("Real magination realizing rock roll rip
snortipatin oyster stew") and Bob Kaufman ("the wild up-building
reinsurgence & Golden Ultimate Effulgence you'll find in Train No.
Let's Go—to heaven—Bob Kaufman wants to come too . . .").

By Kerouac's own admission there is "no direction and no story"
to *Old Angel Midnight,* but it does have a clear and very intriguing
structure. It is to be a report of "the sounds of the entire world
coming thru this window," i.e., the writer's ear. Like Joyce he as-
sumes that his private idiom speaks for mankind: "FRIDAY AFTER-
NOON IN THE UNIVERSE, in all directions in & out . . . I know boy
what's I talkin about case I made the world. . . ." Besides the religious significance of Good Friday, the fact of its being Friday afternoon is important as the time when the discipline of the work week
dissolves into the weekend's wild joy. It is the point midway between rational logic and irrational cry, between worldly boredom
and secret glee, that Kerouac seeks:

. . . and at night ya raise the square white light from your
ghost beneath a rootdrinkin tree & Coyote wont hear ya but
you'll ward off the inexistency devils just to pass the time
away & meanwhile it's timeless to the ends of the last light-
year it might as well be gettin-late Friday afternoon where
we start so's old Sound can come home when worksa done &
drink his beer & tweak his children's eyes—

In its ambitious scope as well as verbal ingenuity *Old Angel
Midnight* may indeed be the closest thing to *Finnegans Wake* in
American literature. Kerouac makes no bones about his debt to
Joyce within the text. But the ultimate failure of the piece is due to
its being too successful an imitation, for it lacks the original concep-
tion that distinguishes the majority of his works.

Old Angel Midnight, like the haiku Jack composed that spring, filled the void left by the work he had planned to do in California. In late April, Cowley wrote to explain why he had been unable to wait for him and mentioning that he had compiled a list of recommendations for revising *On the Road.* But though Jack repeatedly requested the recommendations so that he could begin following them, he received nothing before leaving for Washington in early June.

2.

A sweet rapport developed between Gary and Jack working side by side those early spring days. After work they'd brew a pot of tea and talk and watch the hummingbirds, then go for a walk or to visit the McCorkles. Later, having returned to the shack to cook supper, they'd talk on into the night.

At the weekend parties Allen and Peter often took off all their clothes, stimulating others to do the same. For Allen it was part of his function as a poet to reveal himself to others so as to reveal them to themselves; naked, they ought no longer to fear one another and would be free to love. Whether the Californians needed any help in this matter is questionable, however, since they seemed quite at ease coupling like rabbits. Jack wrote Holmes that the sexual revolution they had foreseen in 1948 was "happening everywhere here." He couldn't bring himself to take part in it not so much because he was a Buddhist—for he claimed he had "abandoned Buddhism now as a formalism"—but because he felt like "a general malingering despondent bum." He did begin dating a young brunette who reminded him of Marilyn Monroe, but when she asked if he had a car he decided she was a hooker, though he later blamed their breakup on the fact that she'd been shocked seeing naked Peter giving naked Allen a massage. Hearing Chet Baker sing "Stella by Starlight," Jack cried to think of the good girls like Sammy's sister he'd left behind in Lowell.

He and Gary went to dinner at Alan Watts', and Jack and Watts got on fine, Jack liking his "sincerity." By contrast, Jack detested the "Berkeley hornrimmed liberal bourgeois" and "academic poseurs," whom he thought "the worst people in America" because they feigned tolerance while snidely ridiculing any idea that seemed too unconventional.

Jack spent a few days visiting Beverly Burford in Sausalito, and she found Jack as "thoughtful" as ever. Coming from her job in education, classily dressed, she'd meet Jack in his favorite North Beach bar, The Place; and on the sawdust floor, among blue-jeaned boozers, commence her "double life." Her current fun with Jack was more like sightseeing than the companionship they'd once shared—a measure of the distance he'd traveled from Denver, 1947.

Allen was one of the few fellow travelers who had stayed with Jack all the way, so it was no surprise their friendship deepened despite Jack's paranoia. Impressed by Allen's courage in reading sexually explicit poetry in public, Jack decided he was a "great saint" masquerading as a demon, and showed his support by cheering modestly from the rear of the hall. But there was no doubt Jack enjoyed being recognized too. At readings he carried his conspicuous bottle like a trademark, and if no one spotted "Care-a-wack" he'd start shouting directions to the people on the stage. In San Francisco, he basked in the fame of being introduced as a friend of Allen Ginsberg.

One person who was interested in Jack himself was poet Robert Creeley, who had studied with Charles Olson at Black Mountain College in North Carolina and was presently editing the last issue of the *Black Mountain Review*. Having heard Kerouac's praises sung by Robert Duncan in Mallorca, Creeley read the two published excerpts from *On the Road,* and was deeply affected by the reality Jack gave to previously ignored segments of American society. It was astonishing to Creeley that anyone could write about people so commonly condemned—or, like "the Mexican girl," scorned—without moralizing at all, and yet investing them unsentimentally with worth. Kerouac seemed to have the rare quality of respecting the *capacity* for virtue and idealism inherent in anyone, regardless of the degraded circumstances in which they lived. At Creeley's request, Allen set up a meeting with Jack in North Beach.

Allen had talked so much about Kerouac and Burroughs that they began to sound like one vast genius, and Creeley thought Jack the man who had killed his wife. To introduce them, Allen was to arrive at The Place, a North Beach bar, after he came off work at the Greyound baggage room at midnight. Waiting in the bar, Creeley noticed a handsome man seated against the back wall; he seemed to be part of a company but also peculiarly detached from it. The man's large head was "remarkably manifest," and the eyes most beautiful of all. His extraordinary physical presence fascinated Creeley as much as Picasso's had. When Allen came in, he asked Creeley, "Haven't you met Jack yet? He's sittin' right over there!"

Neither surly nor indifferent, Jack seemed merely to be waiting to see what other people would do. He, Allen, Creeley, and Al Sublette got drunk and smoked pot at Sublette's place, then Jack fell asleep on the bed. When supper was cooked Creeley was delegated to wake him, and he was literally frightened of the monumental responsibility, so intense was Jack's aura of specialness. The instant Creeley woke him, Jack's eyes struck him like darts.

During the next few days, Creeley saw a lot of Jack. While all the other writers were "rehearsing endlessly modes and concepts of writing," Jack never talked technically about his art and was more interested in getting to know Creeley's background. Tall, rugged, darkly romantic looking with only one eye, Creeley was a lonely and restless drinker attracted to good jazz and easily drawn into fistfights. Like Jack, his wildness was just another form of being sad; all the greater must have been Jack's surprise to learn that Creeley grew up in West Acton, Massachusetts, just a few miles from Lowell. Furthermore, they shared the "New England apprehension" that big-city people were out to "run a number on them." [259]

At McCorkle's, Creeley began to appreciate Jack's shy kindness. After one party, both the house and cabin were filled with guests who had crashed. Jack brought out sleeping bags for himself and Bob to sleep in the meadow. In the morning, Jack asked him, "Are you pure?" Bob's quick answer—"That's like asking water to be wet"— was something Jack never forgot. Creeley never forgot Jack's home-made cornmeal dodgers, or the "terrific" difference made by the ice cubes he put in their port wine as they relaxed like millionaires on McCorkle's porch.

The genius Creeley saw in *Mexico City Blues* was Kerouac's "ability to translate immediate sensation into immediately actual language," and at the cabin he observed Jack being at once writer and man. Jack always participated in what was going on. He could be responding to various people's remarks, flipping an egg, and yet able to move instantly on the impulse of things being done or said— not figuring how to get it down in writing, but virtually *writing it in his head,* so that the actual putting of words on paper was but a mechanical extension of the process. Often he'd grab his notebook and begin to do just that. One day at the cabin, two of Ed Dorn's kids were having a lovely conversation while a hummingbird poised in the glassless window, and Jack was able to capture the experience with "no impedance" (Creeley felt), just as it happened.

It seemed to Creeley that Jack was able to compose with the process of reflection as a pattern in the writing itself, and Creeley recalled Olson's dictum that "judgment is instant upon recognition." For both Kerouac and Olson, the literary perception of an event required no more of a lag than it normally takes to decide whether you like or dislike being in a certain situation. Kerouac could move in that pattern so easily that he couldn't see how rewriting could ever serve him, other than to attain a better balance or economy by slight deletions and additions. Such an accomplishment was so exceptional that Creeley couldn't understand why many people cited Jack's improvisation as evidence that his writing was "unserious." [260] But then Creeley had been sufficiently trained at Harvard to know that Jack's work fit into a tradition of oral composition, whose recent practitioners included Conrad and Henry James, who had dictated many of their greatest works to secretaries. And as for "spontaneous" composition, Creeley knew of numerous esteemed precedents—such as Stendhal, after fifty pages of *The Charterhouse of Parma* had been lost at the printer's, filling the gap with fifty new pages on the spot.

Philip Lamantia stayed at the cabin for a while too, bringing Jack his anthologies of the French Symbolists and a volume by the surrealist poet Eluard. The best Jack could say for them was, "They're OK!" To Creeley, he explained that the French writers he preferred to use as models were the novelists in "the great French narrative tradition" like Balzac and Hugo, who used language as it is formulated in the commonest situations. Poets like Mallarmé seemed effete to Jack because the experience they presented consisted almost exclusively of their own modes of mental apprehension. The thing that bothered him most about the Symbolists was their insistent abstraction. If they used a word like *bread*, for example, it was not to refer to an edible loaf but rather to suggest some paradoxical alternate meaning—so that when they said one thing, they really meant something else. Like Williams, Jack held to the motto "no ideas but in things," and he was always put off by writing used as an intellectual activity to trick the reader.

The honor of being a writer to him was in the creation of something *real*, an achievement he expected others to respect. Discussing what to do if they were ever suddenly arrested, he told Bob, "I'd just tell the police to go down to the public library and find my book, and that would identify me, and they'd open the cell, and out I would walk!" Creeley thought, "Good luck!" Yet it was touching to him that Jack believed the reality of a great work of art could not help but impress people with the "responsibility and dignity" of the artist.[261] It showed a faith in the sacred tie between an artist and his audience that had all but dissolved in this century. Indeed of all the writers then around, Jack appeared the "most professional" to Creeley, in the way he worked daily at the development of his art with "love and absolute commitment." For Jack, writing was never, as it was for many of the others, "some beautiful addition" to the hours they spent discussing it.

Lamantia's own poetry Jack liked a great deal for its "fire." And Lamantia himself he liked even more for containing that fire in his art, since in his personal life Philip was "the sweetest man in the world." [262] Jack was intrigued by Lamantia's reconversion to Catholicism and appreciated Philip's concern for the well-being of his (Jack's) soul, but Jack was still a long way from choosing to observe the Christian strictures that had caused him so much guilt.

Another poet with whom Jack grew close that spring was the youngest member of the Six Gallery team, twenty-four-year-old Michael McClure. Handsome as a movie star, McClure was shyly self-conscious and responded immediately to the same tension in Jack. Despite a trembly stiffness like that of a teenager crossing the high-school cafeteria, Jack still carried himself with a grace McClure admired. Never, outside of Phil Whalen, had McClure met anyone as sensitive as Jack, or as able to communicate that sensitivity with so much "biological clarity." The "perfection of Jack's senso-rium" [263] was such that he could reproduce his responses to the world in "hard, bright, sharp" terms that gave the reader the sensa-tion of being inside his skin. As precious as was Jack's warmth, Mc-Clure was equally grateful for the gift of his sensibility.

McClure had studied under Duncan, who had taught him that one poem can move in a stream through a series of other poems. In *Mexico City Blues*, McClure saw a variety of "themes becoming streams and joining together, rippling away, the whole thing erasing itself into Jack writing down what junkies are saying in the other end of the room, and then it melts down into what Jack imagines the junkies are saying." Kerouac's technique of "stacking" images, one to a line, helped liberate McClure from the notion that meaning in a poem had to come from some conscious logic. *Mexico City Blues* was that different from any poetry McClure had read before that it be-came a major influence on his own work, and he asked Jack to let him publish a chorus from it in his magazine *Ark II/Moby I*.

Toward the end of April, Gary's sister Thea came to the cabin with her fiancé. Jack and Thea fell in love instantly, she because of his overwhelming masculine presence and sweaty male smell, he because she looked so much like Gary and showed his unflinching spirit. A New Yorker, her fiancé was a bit off balance in the loose sand of West Coast relationships, and Gary thought to give him a tumble by asking if he knew any good positions for his wedding night. Thea had the spunk to begin demonstrating a few. Jack's at-traction to her came out in snide attacks on her fiancé. Thea really didn't want to go through with the marriage and would much have preferred to start seeing Jack, but her family convinced her to do the honorable thing. After the marriage, when she tried to tell Jack about her discontent, he insisted she make the best of the situation, saying, "Well, you're a *married woman!*"

Jack and Gary had further tender times together. Alone with Gary, Jack could lie quietly reading *The Tale of Genji*, and some-times their communication was as gentle as a poem pinned up for the other to read. Their guards down, their quirks became a further bond. At the barber college Jack kept his eyes closed, fearing the ugliness while congratulating himself on the economy of a fifty-cent haircut. Afterward, in the rain, Gary hunted for used levis and com-plained but finally gave in to Jack's desire for a poorboy of ruby port. That night Jack was amused in turn when Gary came back from his discussion group having discovered—from the saki being freely circu-lated—that it was all right for Buddhists to get drunk. On their final hike, Jack stopped in a liquor store for another poorboy, haggling to pay thirty-seven instead of forty cents, and was too cheap to satisfy his craving for a Hershey bar. Later, waking up back at the cabin, he found three Hershey bars and a bottle of red wine on the table.

Their final hike came after Gary's three-day farewell party at

524 · M E M O R Y B A B E

McCorkle's. Away from all the debauch, they felt clean again under the weight of rucksacks, their eyes on the clouds and the red wood sorrel blossoms along the creek bed through Tamalpais Canyon. So beautiful were the woods along the Troop 80 trail that Jack and Gary vowed never to live in houses again. Trail after trail led them finally to Potrero Meadow, where they unpacked, made tea, and slept in the sun. From there they proceeded to Laurel Dell to camp for the night. As the sea wind blew fog through the Douglas firs, Gary made his famous pea soup mixed with bacon and bacon grease. For the main course he boiled bulgur with dried vegetables and more bacon thrown in, and fried sausage patties and slices of puff-ball. Dried fruit, tea, and hand-rolled smokes by the campfire led into more of the thoughtful quiet talk they had shared all day.

Along the trail Gary had told Jack, "I advocate the overthrow of all governments by peace and quiet." He had explained his theory that "governments depend, for their existence, on fostering and exploiting ignorance and clinging; making a people think their happiness and security depend on some abstract power structure. . . ." The true revolution would occur, he felt, when people learned to stop buying things they didn't need. That night, camped near the radar station barracks, it was Gary's opinion that the world of military power was much more fragile than the determination of two lone men seeking truth.

About to leave the United States for two years, Gary mused on his own position in the burgeoning Beat movement. The severe training of Zen seemed designed to yield an "utter beatness to work up from." By reducing one's life to the barest essentials, one cleared a space for fresh creation. To the term *beat* he added the connotation of being beaten by the Zen master's stick. Such beatings occasionally served as the master's experiential reply to the disciple's abstract questions.[264] The discipline of Zen did not strike Gary as at odds with the hipster's preference for jazzlike spontaneity. He knew that every great bop musician had been run off plenty of stages for incompetence before learning the right way to blow wild.

On May 5, Jack and a number of Gary's other friends gathered at the dock to see him off. His girlfriend, Neuri, climbed back onto the ship for one last good-bye kiss, and as the bow swung away from the dock Gary helped her get back safely by tossing her into McCorkle's arms. In *The Dharma Bums*, Jack changed the incident to augment the heroic image of Gary, as if he were renouncing fleshly pleasures in favor of religious duty.

Gary and Jack were never to meet again.

To dispel their melancholy, Jack and Creeley went to The Cellar to hear a favorite jazz pianist, and began drumming on the tabletop. When their "fourth-dimensional counterpoint" started to drown out the music, they were asked to leave. Before Jack could help drunken

Creeley out the door, the bouncer hauled off and hit Bob full in the face, driving a tooth through his lip. Jack took him to get cleaned up at a hotel where he knew the French-Canadian owner and then to a friend. But the next time Jack came into San Francisco, Creeley, his lip suppurating, got in a fight with Ed Dorn. He had brought Jack to meet Dorn, a writer racked by the responsibility of raising three children. Thinking Creeley and Jack had come to hustle him for free food or to start something with his wife, Helene, Dorn tried to throw them out. When Creeley inadvisably resisted Jack had to tackle him and lie on top of him to shield him from Dorn's punches. Then a few minutes later, they went at it again. Angry at her husband, Helene ran out and Bob followed to pacify her. Ed and Jack talked for hours and by late morning were fast friends. The next day, when a cop challenged Creeley's friend Ron Loewinsohn for an ID, Bob called him a fascist and was arrested. Jack decided it was time to get Creeley out of North Beach. Meanwhile, Bob Donlin had collapsed from a binge, and in his hotel room had envisioned himself being led to paradise by three Bodhisattvas: Neal, Allen, and Jack. Jack shepherded both Donlin and Creeley to Mill Valley to recuperate.

In the cabin Jack nursed them with peppermint tea and honey. Then a whirlwind struck in the form of Neal, Bob Kaufman, and Kaufman's lady. A black, Jewish Haitian steeped in Catholicism and voodoo, Kaufman had been around the world in the merchant marine, liked jazz, and could talk a witty surrealistic jive in both French and English, as well as write poems that were precise takes on contemporary America. Having met in New York in the early fifties, Bob and Jack were already friends and respectful of each other's work. Now Kaufman brought peyote to be taken in milkshakes while listening to a record of the Mescalero Indians performing a peyote ritual.

When Locke played an Indian record that purported to mimic the sound of the Bombay Express, Neal began a pantomime spiced with verbal interpretation, running through the routines of the various workers on the train. Later Creeley witnessed Neal's extraordinary ability to extemporize as he went into "lovely, hokey evangelist preacher raps" that could "take you right out of your head and bring you back again." [265] One of the loveliest fantasies Creeley ever heard was Neal imagining what he would do if he won a million dollars at the race track. The old affectionate rapport between Jack and Neal returned fully as Jack listened in delight.

Like Jack, Neal gave Creeley emotional reassurance, but unlike Jack there was a hard edge to his tenderness that advised you not to "tangle with him unless you wanted to take the consequences." Although Neal didn't go around beating people up, Creeley felt he used the suggestion of his physical power to stay on top of a situation, while Bob and Jack normally retreated into the background and made their presence known through some solitary skill—as at parties, for instance, when instead of dancing like everyone else they would sit in a corner drumming on pots and pans.

Protective of Creeley's shyness, Jack came along when he was to give his first reading before other poets. After securing Creeley in his seat and providing a jug of wine, Jack calmed him by pointing out all their friends in the audience. Then he excused himself, saying, "Your poems are really sad—I don't like to listen to you be in so much pain. I'll be down at the bar." Creeley reciprocated by offering to help print *Visions of Neal* and *Doctor Sax* on his own small press in Mallorca, if no one else wanted them. And in the *Black Mountain Review*, of which Ginsberg had become coeditor, Creeley published *October in the Railroad Earth* and "The Essentials of Spontaneous Prose."

The "projective verse" theory Creeley had been preaching didn't particularly interest Jack, who thought Olson's intellectual proposals useless in practice; but the other San Francisco poets were continually questioning Creeley about Olson, a situation that made Kenneth Rexroth very uneasy. One night in early May, Jack had gone with Creeley to Rexroth's house, where his wife, Marthe, was home alone. Bob and Marthe collapsed in each other's arms. Jack told them if they wanted to "talk" he'd go in the other room and read, and he ended up spending the night on the couch there. He disapproved of their adultery, which led to Kenneth's nervous breakdown, but to Bob he expressed only sympathy over the difficulty of the situation. Creeley knew that he could trust Jack completely. When Marthe eventually told Kenneth she was leaving him to live with Bob, he turned against both Jack and Neal as if they had been accomplices.

At one of Rexroth's final gatherings, Jack got drunk and loud as usual, but this time Kenneth called him a punk and gave him the bum's rush. It was an act of exclusion that cut Jack more deeply than anyone realized.

To purify himself from all his binges Jack hiked again to Laurel Dell, intending to stay three days. But on the way he got lost several times, and though he tried to imitate Gary, taking off his clothes to cook supper, by morning he was so lonely he thumbed a ride back to Mill Valley.

3.

Physically Jack was in better shape than he'd been for years. Standing on his head three minutes a day had cured his phlebitis, and for exercise he'd had the fifteen-mile walk between Mill Valley and San

Francisco several times a week, in addition to his walks all over the city. On June 18, 1956, he began hitching north, and managed to get rides all the way to the Ranger Station in Marblemount, Washington, in the midst of Mount Baker National Forest. Training began on June 25. After a week learning to spot, report, and fight fires, he and his two months' worth of food were carried by horse and mule to the top of Desolation Peak, twelve miles from the Canadian border.

He went to the mountains with the intention of seeing a vision that would change his life. Writing to Gary he likened himself to Hui-Neng, who had fled to Vulture Mountain after being chosen Sixth Patriarch. Because Hui-Neng was an "aborigine," there was opposition to his rule and his life was in danger, but on the mountain he became so wise that he was able to convert his pursuers into disciples. Jack had resolved to bring no marijuana, benzedrine, or booze with him. That spring he had read with admiration the haiku of Japanese monks, whose ascetic life seemed responsible for their incredible ability to grasp the most delicate images of the objective world. Two months on Desolation, he hoped, would do the same for his own writing.

Before his arrival he had written the rangers that he hoped to make firewatching his life's work, but disenchantment set in from the start. Although he enjoyed the company of Gary's old woodsman friend Blackie Burns, he grew sullen under the teasing of the other rangers, who had it in for city slickers. The rangers had no idea of what was making Jack's temper flare. He had been hoping against hope to receive Cowley's list of requested changes in *On the Road* before going up on the mountain. The day he left Marblemount he sent Cowley a searing postcard, warning that unless Viking offered him a contract by October 1 he would withdraw the manuscript.

He'd bluffed himself into believing that on the mountain he would start the thousand-page epic novel, "The Beat Generation." The first couple of days in solitude his mood did improve, and in fact he kept a journal all summer. But he was soon bored and excruciatingly lonely, despite the radio communication he had with other lookouts. Meditation helped no more than playing his baseball card game or singing himself pop songs, which dissolved in the void of space beyond his ledge. Visions came aplenty—the most insistent being that "the earth was truly upsidedown"—but the only thing they showed him was the need to escape from "the bottomless horror of the world." To the end of his days he believed that suicide could not be justified before God, and so he never dared attempt it directly. But on Desolation he decided that any anesthetic short of death was not to be ignored. "Hope is a word like a snow-drift," he advised himself in *Desolation Angels,* the novel in which he recorded the lookout experience: "So shut up, live, travel, adventure, bless and dont be sorry. . . ." When he came down the mountain in early

September, he was dead certain he would never return to a hermit's life anywhere. But he also knew he needed the *illusion* that he could do anything he wished. The chief change wrought on Desolation was that he no longer balked at lying to himself.

With several hundred dollars in traveler's checks, he hitched down to Seattle for a Friday night of beer in bars and watching the fights on TV, but he went to his Skid Row hotel before any real fights started. The next night, more to his gentle lecherous taste, he watched a tantalizing old-time burlesque, had a Chinese dinner, and retired to his room dizzy from too much wine. After sleeping it off, he splurged on a bus ticket to San Francisco.

For a week Jack was caught in the explosion of a socio-literary movement. He and his friends were soon to be published in a number of places, including Grove Press's new *Evergreen Review*, which had been started by Barney Rosset and editor Don Allen, and was soon to become a platform for many of the fresh literary voices of the time. Ginsberg's *Howl* would be issued by City Lights in October. Soon Jack got word that Viking Press had definitely accepted *On the Road*. He was already a legend in San Francisco, and walking into The Cellar he was pleased to be recognized by Gui de Angulo, daughter of an anthropologist whose works he admired. There were readings almost every night. From Robert Merrill's reading Jack begged off because he was bored by the sound of labored refinement; he preferred to mingle with street poets and hipsters like Kaufman, Bernie Uronovitz, and Peter Du Peru. Even at the dinner given by kindly Ruth Witt-Diamant, director of the Poetry Center at San Francisco State College, Jack was put off when everyone laughed at his statement about riding *first-class* freight trains like the Zipper. Poet Richard Eberhart had just published an article on the San Francisco Poetry Renaissance, "West Coast Rhythms," in *The New York Times Book Review*, and *Life* was preparing a similar article. When a photographer from *Mademoiselle* came to take Jack's picture with Allen, Whalen, and Corso, Jack was so off balance he let Gregory muss his hair to look more vagabondish, then complained that he came out looking "nutty" [266]—though he never regretted the silver cross Gregory had made him wear outside his shirt.

That photo, which showed Jack looking utterly beaten, was cropped for the jacket of *On the Road* and subsequently used in countless newspaper stories. But the face in it was scarcely recognizable to old friends like John Holmes, who remembered a Kerouac so square-jawed and fierce-eyed with determination that at first sight of him John had thought, "This man can be anything he wants, and whatever he does, he'll do it big." Holmes had been right, but the latest and last thing Jack was doing big was his own destruction.

Jack's loneliness glutted on new friends galore. Bright, lively Robert LaVigne pleased Jack with his modesty and his perseverance in painting despite few sales. Robert Duncan's poetry drew Jack's respect, and Jack was grateful that so august a man—author, professor, and world traveler—had recommended his works to New Directions. Knowing how close Duncan and Creeley were, he was anxious to become Duncan's friend. But in person, Duncan's sophistication cowed him, the more so because Duncan was that one being with whom Jack had no common ground: the well-adjusted homosexual. When he met Duncan Jack attempted to unnerve him, using his physical attractiveness, as he often did against homosexuals, by staring into Robert's eyes. But the ploy failed because Jack was bleary-eyed drunk and Duncan cross-eyed—and Jack couldn't figure which eye to stare into! When Duncan immediately sized up his enormous sexual ambivalence and determined to avoid any involvement, Jack told him spitefully to "stick the rose up his ass." But Duncan's disappointment in the man didn't diminish his respect for Kerouac's works, whose "immediacy" reminded him of Saroyan.

Allen's lover, Peter Orlovsky, was one of the few people on the scene with whom Jack felt completely comfortable. Allen and Peter had undergone a trial separation for several months, during which Peter returned to New York to rescue his fifteen-year-old brother Lafcadio from the poverty and discord of the family home. Another Orlovsky brother, Julius, was already in a mental hospital, and Lafcadio had been having severe problems adjusting to junior high school. In the spring of 1956, when Allen and Peter resumed living together in Peter's apartment in a black housing project on Potrero Hill, they began caring for the wayward, mystically indrawn boy as if he were their child. Upon meeting Jack, Peter was astonished to hear him recall almost every detail of a conversation that had taken place the night before. In the spring they enjoyed many walks together, with Jack pointing out flowers and little things of beauty and stopping to talk to people and especially to children. Since Peter worked as an ambulance driver, Jack christened him "the saint." What impressed Peter most was the fact that Jack, with his endless storytelling, put so much energy into keeping the group together. When he came back from the mountain he seemed very expansive to Peter. He talked continually about wanting to find the cause of suffering so that he could "save" other people. Although Peter was a poet too, he had no dreams of publishing. Consequently, between him and Jack there was none of the ego conflict that increasingly held Jack and Allen at a distance.

Although poetic rivalries were rampant, they were healthy in the sense that each of the writers was driven to find an original territory for himself. As Michael McClure says: "We pressed against each other with *extraordinary* vigor. Our ambitions were so proportionless that we forced new territories of subject matter and music and metrics and prosody and consciousness into existence—because none of us gave. And at the same time there was a lot of mutual defense and a lot of real camaraderie." As always, Corso played Puck with his inferiority. The man with the least to lose—without money, home, or family—his provocations could scarcely bring him more contempt than he'd already received; he was always, in effect, taking shots in the dark for love. To be noticed by McClure, Gregory accused him of living like a "phony phony Disney." Charmed, McClure in turn insulted Jack's friends that they might learn from him, saying, "None of you know anything of *language*—with the exception of Jack." Indeed there were many instructive sessions that fall, when for hours a room full of poets did nothing but read their works and discuss the differences between one another and speculate on the possibilities of poetry. Rapidly Jack's isolation dissolved in the feeling of playing on a prizewinning team.

That team was enlisting new members across the nation. In September, Elvis Presley made his first appearance on *The Ed Sullivan Show*, and Jack and Gregory watched him with great excitement. Elvis had returned popular music to its black origin as had "the blues" during the twenties. The "rocking and rolling" that became rock'n'roll was initially a black idiom for sexual intercourse, a fact about which Elvis with his rolling pelvis left no doubt. Although many connoisseurs of the blues didn't cotton to their slick debasement on Elvis' gold records, Jack and his friends applauded the giant crack the singer was making in the wall of fifties' sexual and social hypocrisy. Respectable matrons who lightened their work listening to "Hound Dog" or "Blue Suede Shoes" or "Jailhouse Rock" would find it a little harder to pretend that "sinners" didn't have fun and feelings too. According to *Look* magazine Elvis was a "nightmare"; his challenge to conventional morals was so great that the average man felt "he can't be—but he is." [267] An index of the current hypocrisy was Ed Sullivan's flip-flop. At first Sullivan swore he would never have Presley on his show, but after Steve Allen had him on and Allen's ratings topped his, Sullivan immediately offered Presley more money than he'd ever paid any star. Hedging at the last moment, for fear of condemnation by the newspaper reviewers who poured a steady stream of invective on Presley, Sullivan directed the cameramen to film him only from the waist up.

Side-burned and surly, Presley swaggered like a young tough, and his association with violence was fixed in the press by the story of his fistfight in a Memphis gas station. That aspect of Presley repelled Jack, as much as Hollywood's portrayal of youthful unrest as "juvenile delinquency" in movies like *The Wild One* with Marlon Brando and *Rebel Without a Cause* with James Dean. In 1957, Mailer's essay "The White Negro" would increase the tension between the straight culture and the hip counterculture—as well as robbing Jack of the right to use the word *hipster* in his own spiritual sense—by equating the hipster with cold-blooded criminals, psychopaths, and even killers, as existential heroes of a ruthless world. The nation's fear of nonconformism (now pejoratively labeled "deviance"), bred by such irresponsible use of the arts and media, came crashing down on the collective head of the Beats.

After a big party Jack found himself on a street corner, singing and rapping with Allen, Gregory, Peter, Lafcadio, Lamantia, and LaVigne. Failing to recognize artistic license a neighbor called the cops, who had the opportunity to arrest at least half the major figures of the Beat Generation. Thanks to Jack's diplomacy, the cops let them go (and never found their joint). Jack instructed his "bhikkus" that henceforth they should "avoid the authorities." [268]

Jack's Buddhism had dwindled to a means of survival, and he openly proclaimed himself no longer a Buddhist. Yet he never disavowed the strains of Buddhism in his writing, for they registered an authentic phase of his mental development. When he failed to retrieve his manuscript of *The Scripture of the Golden Eternity*, which he had left at the Asian House, he accepted the loss as fitting since he'd instructed the reader to "throw it away."

Visiting Carolyn in Los Gatos, Jack dwelled again on his homelessness, and was lost in such a funk that he depressed her too. At his request, she drove him through the Santa Cruz Mountains to look for a campsite. Her repeated explanations that he would be breaking the law by building a fire in the woods merely sent him into deeper glooms, and he castigated the government bureaucracy that couldn't keep its fingers out of people's personal business. In any case, it turned out he just wanted to make love there, and though Carolyn wasn't in the mood she felt too sorry for him to refuse. That night with Neal home from work they all sat down to dinner and television; then Jack left the family cheer for his prune tree in the yard.

The next day he returned to his friends in San Francisco. He was growing ever fonder of Gregory, whose sad lyrics sounded as pure to him as Sinatra's voice, and who had a line that went over well with women. But when Gregory succeeded with one of Neal's, the two men came to loggerheads. To make peace, Jack insisted Neal take Gregory to the race track. On the way, Neal demonstrated his "check out" technique, interpreting the behavior of people he spotted. Although Gregory acknowledged Neal's perspicacity he distrusted the fast-talking that reminded him of "scammers" he'd met in prison. Realizing Gregory's suspicion Neal grew even more bugged. Gregory's losses at the track, after failing to follow Neal's system, convinced Neal of his "dago" stupidity.[269]

Resolving as he had in Lowell to make all his friends like one another, Jack brought Gregory with him on his second visit to the Cassadys, on his way to Mexico. Jack had his usual good time hiking with the children, but Gregory grew restive under Neal's channel-switching TV routine and had no interest in one of the few shows Neal did watch: Oral Roberts, the Baptist faith healer. As the bubble of tension pushed them all into corners, Gregory finally performed his jester's function of popping it—exclaiming, as Neal and Carolyn prated about the decency of a lady butcher on some quiz program: "Who wants to hear her, she kills pigs!" Sensing the ridiculousness of the horror they were about to feel, Neal and Carolyn relaxed enough to humor Gregory's antagonistic mood. Later Allen and Peter showed up with Gui de Angulo, and a new party began as Neal and Carolyn retired to bed.

Before leaving, Jack had a long talk with Carolyn about his plan to move his mother to California. Reviving his old fantasy of living next door to her and Neal, he said he could travel with an easy mind if he knew Carolyn was keeping an eye on Mémère. Although Carolyn had been disappointed too often to place faith in Jack's expectations, she wished her heart out for his happiness.

After riding the Zipper to L.A., he took a bus to Palm Springs to visit Bob Donlin. All set to spend two weeks loafing among millionaire golfers, Jack in his lumberjack shirt and khakis stood out like a sore thumb among polo shirts and bermuda shorts. Unable to bear the ostracism, he left after only one day. His bus to Arizona stopped for a moment beside a prison bus, and he waved to the young men aboard it. That night, looking for a place to sleep in the desert outside Tucson, Jack was surrounded by police who wanted to know what he was doing there—and how could he tell them that he was looking for the peace to do his work? For in this new America the words *work* and *peace* were as antithetical as *artist* and *solitude*. The only way to get rid of them was to show them his Forest Service papers and money. But even those credentials failed, a year later, to impress the moderators of television talk shows—the only place in America, it turned out, where a writer was welcome.

For now, Jack had two months of peaceful writing ahead in Mexico City. Between his arrival in late September and the arrival of Allen, Peter, Peter's brother Lafcadio, and Gregory about November 7, he spent most of his time on the rooftop above doddering Bill Garver, finishing *Tristessa* and beginning a new novel about his experiences on the mountain and later in San Francisco, called "The Angels in the World" (*Desolation Angels*). The latter novel was an experiment in writing fiction as "intensely wild and personal" as his journals, and he planned to hold it back for a few years until publication of his other novels had brought about some understanding of his work.

When he did go out it was usually to find Esperanza, to check on her latest adventures in order to get fresh material for *Tristessa*. His compassion, so notable in the book, was waning fast in real life, as he finally forced her into bed when she was too weak from morphine and goofballs to resist. Emaciated and deathly ill, she wisely sought help from Garver, knowing that Jack had never been and never could be of her world. And Jack learned a painful lesson about the perils of slumming, even as a serious observer, when in his search for her a gang of Mexican bandits stripped him of his money, sunglasses, and worst of all a notebook full of new poems.

He gave up his pretensions to asceticism as he returned gaily to his fifteen-year-old prostitutes, and he was honest enough to admit that Allen's "leching" after young boys was no worse a weakness.[270] It was even getting easier for Jack to practice (if not admit) his own bisexuality. When Allen and Peter picked up some young Mexican boys, he participated in a game of spin-the-bottle as well as what followed. At least with regard to the difference between love and lust he permitted himself no more illusions. Love would always re-main sacred to him—"a trance of angels" he called it in a letter to Peter—while what he received from Esperanza he knew to be no different from his three-minute sessions with the girls on Panama Street, so typical of his affairs with all women except for Edie and Carolyn: "a convenience of temporary exchange of gyzm and money and dresses and rent."

Allen, Peter, Lafcadio, and Gregory moved into the apartment next to Garver's, and the good times Jack shared with them were poignant with the end of privacy they all faced. *Howl* was beginning to sell, thanks in part to the sensation Allen had made going naked at a poetry reading in Venice on the way down. Ferlinghetti had asked to publish a collection of Gregory's poems, and Gregory had been invited to Washington, D.C., by the Poetry Consultant to the Li-brary of Congress, Randall Jarrell. Grove Press had accepted *The Subterraneans* for publication in the *Evergreen Review*. Not only were their nerves about to be jangled by exposure—being a breed apart from tweed-and-pipe writers, they would be put on display like Kafka's "hunger artist"—but they were already suffering the emotional toll of trafficking in products of the soul. Jack had no complaints about the $500 Grove offered, but he was upset that the book wouldn't have the dignity of a hardcover publication before serialization. Even more disturbing was Don Allen's request that he meld *Doctor Sax* with *Visions of Gerard* "to make a good book."

Walking around Mexico City, visiting the pyramids of Teoti-huacán and the Floating Gardens of Lake Xochimilco, meeting the old painters at Mexico City College, Jack and his friends were no longer just happy fools enjoying life; their "eyeball kicks" were now fraught with the responsibility of public artists expected to comment on their age. It was a responsibility Jack didn't want. They spent many hours discussing what to do with their lives, and all of them agreed that a period of travel away from America would be salutary. But Jack was already contemplating an escape from writing itself.

Seriously he spoke of his desire to become a jazz singer and drummer, a musical composer, and a painter. With housepaint mixed with glue he did murals on his rooftop; and in oils, carefully, he painted God and Gerard. In a few years he expected to be a "top-flight painter." He was also again talking of his cabin, this time to be built in the hills of Marin. More and more when the others went out, he stayed home to sleep.

Entering his most productive period, Gregory was writing a fine poem almost every day, and at twenty-six still looked forward to fame with a childish zest. Jack thoughtfully tried to give him some hints about writing prose, but Corso didn't want to hear them, insisting, "Everything is poesy." Actually he felt that if he let Jack teach him anything Jack would own that part of him. Of all the Beat group, Gregory was one of the least anxious to belong to a movement. Repulsed by the grubby apartment on Orizaba, he moved to a posh hotel and arranged to fly to Washington, D.C. The others shared expen es with a man driving to New York. With six people in the car the tiip was tiring, but they kept up their spirits by singing and telling stories. Orlovsky recalls that as they neared New York Jack grew increasingly enthusiastic about his literary future. In West Virginia, he felt good enough to take the wheel himself. Arriving in New York on a snowy Sunday morning in late November, he was thin, bearded, and sunken-eyed. But his Mexican lethargy having passed, he was ready to embark on any project Allen had in mind.

4.

On the second floor of a once elegant dark brick building kitty-corner from the White Horse tavern on Hudson Street in the Village, lived Lucien's former girlfriend Helen Elliott. When Allen called up to her, Helen and her roommate both peered out. The roommate, Helen Weaver, was startled to find four rugged, seedy desperadoes with full packs invading their apartment, but the other Helen assured her they were gentle. Upstairs, after introductions, Jack and Helen Weaver took a look at each other and fell in love. A classy beautiful slim brunette, she was his type and the first such woman whose eyes didn't pitch daggers at him. To her, he was Jack London.

As the women watched the begriming of every towel in the house, Jack pocketed their pooled resources and motherlike ran to the deli to buy bacon, eggs, and English muffins. After breakfast they all sat down for a long talk, and soon Jack and Helen were engrossed in intimate conversation. Emptying his rucksack he showed her piles of manuscripts, then proudly handed her a dog-eared copy of *The Town and the City*, saying it was "like Thomas Wolfe." The childlike way he wanted to impress her was endearing; but indeed, as an

English literature major from Oberlin who dreamed of being a writer herself, she was deeply impressed. In Scarsdale, where she had grown up, she had been so moved by *Look Homeward, Angel* that she'd made her whole family read it. But now she found herself playing devil's advocate and declaring that, however wonderful Wolfe, he lacked the discipline of Henry James. It was like waving a red flag, and she and Jack went after each other in a fierce argument about the "putter-inners" versus the "taker-outers" that ended only when everyone collapsed in sleep.

Later that day they all went for a walk in the Village. One person after another recognized either Jack or Allen, and there were endless clappings on the back, goings for drinks, and recitings of poems, which made the two Helens feel like they were with celebrities. From the first, Weaver had instinctively felt Jack was a real writer. Watching him and Allen gather followers, she was overwhelmed by their aura of destiny, as though one could see American history making way before them. And understanding each other so well, they had developed an incantatory style of talking that was enchanting. Moreover, there was great charm for a girl of Helen's proper background in the glamor of published authors who were also raffish rebels.

For a week the whole group slept at the Helens' apartment—Allen, Peter, and Lafcadio in a row of sleeping bags on the floor, and Jack in Helen Weaver's bed. When the former three left, there was no question that Jack would stay. She had never met a man like him, and he had never met a woman like her.

Beyond the very strong physical attraction between them there was her appreciation of his foreignness—not only his total untucked-shirttail departure from Scarsdale, but his European cultural richness. Fluent in French—she later became a well-known translator—Helen delighted in learning his Canuck patois. In him she also prized the combination of wistful child with seasoned bard, whose "incredible utterances" came from deeper sources than either. Above all, she responded to his sweetness and gentleness. "One of the gentlest men I ever met," she said of him more than twenty years later.

Jack was one of the first people she knew who was not ashamed to talk about spirituality. Her parents had gotten a whiff of the publicity about him and were naturally concerned about his involvement with their daughter. When she brought him home to meet them, Jack developed an immediate rapport with her father over a bottle of Jack Daniels. Puffing his White Owl cigar like an old burgher, Jack disarmed her mother just as easily by asking what they believed in. Since Helen's mother was a pillar of the Congregational Church, Jack soon engaged them in a big philosophical discussion. Although her parents thought him strange, they were mollified by his obviously sincere interest in religion.

Helen was also intrigued by the coexistence in Jack of monastic discipline and profligacy. Up all night drinking and talking with his friends, all of them feeding off one another's excitement, he would wear himself out. Then, home for several days in isolation with his mother and cats, he would dry out and read and work. Jack and Allen had the contempt for the body—the willingness to sacrifice themselves to their ideals—of dedicated revolutionaries. And yet there was the further contradiction of the athlete in Jack, who, as Helen Elliott recalls, still sought to eat "healthy foods."

It was clear to Helen Weaver that much of Jack's vital anger came out of his strong aversion to bourgeois culture, that his flame fed upon the mass of contemporary values he had rejected. His intensity appealed to her, but it was hard for her to stay around such an outpouring of energy and continue to work regularly as an editorial assistant. The only person in the household holding down a job, she was tempted to join the party, but in so doing would have run into conflict with Jack's desire that she support him.

He always promised that when he got rich he would repay her and all the other friends he'd lived off. At her apartment he set himself a schedule of writing five hours every day, from two or three in the afternoon until suppertime, and he always worked sober. He was typing up *Tristessa* and *Desolation Angels* and revising *On the Road.*

Cowley wanted Jack to condense the trip to New Orleans, to omit the bus trip from San Francisco to New York via the northwest, to condense the trip from Denver to San Francisco, and to omit Sal's visit with Doris (Edie) in Detroit. Cowley also insisted Jack delete a paragraph explicitly describing Neal's relations with the gay man who had taken them to Denver. After incorporating all of Cowley's requested changes, Jack laid aside the manuscript, which had been hackled by four years of editing. To restore the novel's freshness he typed up a final version directly from the 120-foot roll.

Yet there was an essential passivity about Jack that bothered Helen. Were he not financially successful at writing, she felt, he would have had no qualms about letting her continue to pay the bills. And his cheapness with the money he did have further irritated her. What killed their romance, however, was not what troubled her but what didn't trouble Jack.

Helen was a very careful woman, and she wanted a man who was careful too, as indeed Jack was *when he was sober*. She wanted the same sort of consideration from her lover that she expected—and received—from her friends. Jack would fail to show up for dinner and, despite his promise, fail to call; three days later he'd call, having gotten even drunker to work up his courage. If he was home he might be too nauseated from eating peyote to touch the dinner she'd cooked, or so drunk that he would nod out at the table or start singing French-Canadian children's songs to himself. She understood that his drinking was a cushion he put between himself and painful realities like the publishing world; one day he showed up for a meeting at Viking two hours late and having consumed a pint of liquor in the elevator. But it scared her to find him using that cushion against her too. He was always protecting himself from too great an intimacy with her, and one means of doing so was to set up a rivalry between her and his male friends. Women made Jack uncomfortable with the demands, spoken or unspoken, he felt were their right (and which he resented). Too clearly in his drunken stupor she read the words: "Don't pin your dreams on me!"

Lucien out of his own particular tragic sense of life was putting his wife Cessa through a similar ordeal. When he and Jack got drunk, all hell broke loose. They egged each other on to bigger binges and wilder stunts, putting each other through enormous physical suffering. One night when Cessa didn't want to let Lucien out he sneaked down the fire escape, leaping ten feet to the ground. Following him, Jack hit the sidewalk head first, and later showed up at Helen's in deplorable shape, expecting to be nursed and consoled. Helen saw this self-punishment as another side of Jack's rejection of bourgeois values. Like his asceticism, hurting his body served a funny puritan streak in him, funny because it contradicted the pleasure-loving, comfort-loving nature that was so pronounced in him. Since he conceived of the artist as one who must suffer, a suburban home with a fat income and regular meals seemed to spell death for the only part of himself he wanted to save. By the same token, when he'd be in physical pain—as he often was, after his phlebitis was cured, with frequent attacks of slow-healing boils—he'd be pleased that his spirit was being elevated like Job's.

What was unconscionable about Jack's behavior was that, drunk, he didn't care who he made suffer with him. Helen Elliott had a German shepherd that Jack would take out and run with, and soon he began getting her in trouble by teaching it to corner people. Supposed to come to dinner with the Helens at Lucien and Cessa's, Jack took the dog and disappeared. Several hours later he called in his gruff drunken voice to announce that the dog was holding "three stooges" hostage. Another time, he and Lucien both vanished with the dog. When they returned, Weaver began punching Jack and tore out a chunk of his hair. Lucien complimented him on having a girl with spirit, and from then on they both called her "Slugger."

Between his writing, wine, and friends there seemed no room in his life for her. The fact that at times he could be a healthy, normal, nurturing lover sharpened the sting of his refusal to accept the responsibilities of a mature relationship. The impulse to give himself to women and children kept forcing its way out through the anger with which he tried to stifle it. A lot of that anger toward women seemed to arise from the restrictions with which his mother had saddled him. As a result he was determined to prove to the world, and especially to the female, that he was free. Frequently the only outlets for his frustrated tenderness were animals; he would sometimes stop on the street to tongue-kiss a dog, and he developed a fanatical devotion to his "little kitties." *Ad infinitum* he talked about how his cats were his muses, how they sat on his chest, how he talked with them. In the next breath, taking a picture of his daughter, Janet, from his wallet, he'd ask for people's reassurance that she didn't look like him—and seem secretly pleased when they maintained she did.

But for a while it appeared he might surrender to love. Together they sang the songs from *My Fair Lady*. Singing "Chicago," he became Sinatra for her. His songs went a long way toward apology (since he was never quite capable of saying he was sorry), particularly when he sang another of his favorites from Sinatra:

> So let people wonder, let 'em laugh, let 'em frown
> You know I'll love you till the moon's upside down
> Don't you remember I was always your clown?
> So why try to change me now?

On the town there was always the possibility that Jack would get drunk and disappear indefinitely, so naturally Helen was happier when he stayed home. On weekends they'd sometimes stay in her room for an entire day, talking, singing, watching TV, and making love.

The stability of their relationship was aided by the presence of a live-in confidante. From Nebraska, Helen Elliott shared Jack's love of the American land, and they had many long conversations about the West and in particular "the great Missouri." As a compliment, he told her she had Missouri River mud running through her hair. Having spent her youth in jazz bars, she was astonished at how much more Jack knew on the subject than she. He acquainted her with many great musicians then in obscurity, such as Muddy Waters and Major Holly, and he'd sometimes launch into a detailed history of the evolution of jazz. He often discussed operas and symphonies with her too. The only thing that bothered her was that he moved through facts and ideas too fast. For example, he'd put on a record, and even if there were a room full of people would sit next to the record player, ignoring everyone, until he had picked up exactly what was new or good about the music. Once he had what he wanted to know, however, he would let no one detain him from moving on to new experiences. It wasn't rudeness, though people took it as such, but just the operation of what Helen called his "steel-trap mind." In fact what Elliott liked most about Jack was that he tried harder than almost anyone to live by the Golden Rule, and when not "under the influence" he was a true gentleman.

Jack's little courtesies, like lighting a match in the bathroom to kill the smell of defecation, showed how much he wanted to avoid imposing on others. But the chief pleasure of being around him, for her, derived from a deep nobility in his character. He was a diehard optimist, who consistently looked to the good in his life and in other people's lives. The essence of his beliefs was succinctly expressed, she felt on reading *The Dharma Bums,* in the line: "You can't fall off a mountain." For in the complexity of his melancholic romantic soul there was also a voice of great lucidity promising him that (in Elliott's words) "you don't have to die in order to live." His idealism generated a great deal of anguish in that it forced him to hold onto his talent and make a reputation, even while with the other hand he was ripping apart the image of "Jack Kerouac the great American writer," insisting with enormous humility and honesty that anyone who put himself in such a role was a "shuck," a fraud. And yet the value of that idealism was that it kept him from admitting to unhappiness. Whenever he was unhappy, he quickly changed his physical circumstances in any way necessary to avoid pain.

The negative side of his idealism was what Weaver called his "sins of omission." Believing in the perfection of each moment of life, he didn't project on what was going to happen, or on what he or others might need in the future. The very concept of need was alien to him, and to think of the things he did need made him uneasy. There was in Jack a desire to be independent from, and able to dispense with, every other person on earth. Years later he would lament to Elliott about the impossibility of fellating himself. Futilely he had tried various acrobatic positions, not only because he wanted to experience everything but because he wanted "total gratification" without the indebting services of a lover.

Jack told Elliott that he wanted to marry Helen Weaver. Loving her, he wanted to put their relationship "on the up and up." He did not want to "live in sin." [271] At the same time he told Elliott that he didn't want to marry anyone ever again. He claimed the wound from his second wife's infidelity was still raw, too raw to allow another woman access to his remaining pride. To Weaver he even admitted that he hadn't yet gotten a divorce from Joan for fear he would weaken and remarry. Joan's lawyers were once more on his trail, and he could scarcely face the prospect of another round of litigation, let alone multiple rounds with further wives. The question of divorce aside, there was still the insurmountable obstacle—which both Helens understood—that Jack Kerouac was permanently married to isolation.

5.

He planned to spend Christmas with his mother in his sister's new home in Orlando, Florida. Before he left, Allen took him to meet Salvador Dali, who charmed Jack by saying that "the sign of genius is gold." On the way south Jack stopped in Washington, D.C., to visit Corso at Randall Jarrell's. After writing an article complaining that American poetry had become staid and academic, Jarrell had gone to San Francisco and been pleasantly jarred. Recognizing Jack as another man destined to tumble American letters, he predicted Jack would become both rich and famous. Although Jack depleted the household of whiskey, and replaced it with a pile of his own spontaneously painted "surrealistic" paintings, Jarrell took him out to a fancy dinner in his Mercedes. Returning the hospitality, Jack traded his expensive vicuña coat (procured by Henri Cru) for Jarrell's World War II leather coat, a red sweater, and a cap.

Of course he was a little miffed that Gregory had stopped using cuss words to please Jarrell, who had a wife and children; and when Corso sided with Jarrell about the need to polish a poem, Jack took them both on. But it was a friendly argument, and Jack finally agreed with Corso that "when you write down something it's automatically spontaneous anyway—so if you change it while you're writing, it's a spontaneous changing." [272] In any case, he proved his point by writing a series of poems called "Washington D.C. Blues" on the spot.

Drunk on the bus to Florida, he awoke to find his sack full of manuscripts missing, and was literally on the verge of throwing himself in front of a train until the clerk in Raleigh explained that it had been shipped on ahead. Jack had borrowed $40 from Lord (against his $1,000 advance from Viking) to fill his relatives' Christmas with turkeys and whiskey and presents, but only his mother seemed to appreciate his generosity. His sense of martyrdom had him prophesying to friends that he was about to "lead schools" in exile. But his self-worth was running just as high, as he remarked the appropriateness of Helen's sending a box of Dutch Masters cigars to "old Rembrandt sentimental Dutchman me."

He spent twelve days and nights typing up most of the remaining pencil manuscripts from his last season in Mexico. Much of his renewed vigor was a response to his mother's joy. They planned a permanent move back to Long Island in the fall. She would then be eligible for social security payments, and soon after he expected to be able to support her with royalties from On the Road, which was to be released in September. To make Mémère more receptive to the idea of a new daughter-in-law, Jack bragged that Helen could speak their patois. Helen was included in all his plans for successful authorhood. He wrote her that every page he typed would help make them rich, buy logs for their future fireplace. Upon returning to New York, he promised, he would take her to meet John Holmes, as well as dining her at the best restaurants in New York—although he also suggested they might get away without paying! Wryly she noted how his fantasies always ran toward not picking up the bill, and there wasn't much comfort in his counsel that "women must be guided by men." But he melted her heart with a quote from Elvis: "Love me tender, love me true."

Back in New York, Jack signed his contract with Viking on January 11, 1957. New Directions was excerpting the Mexican episode from *On the Road* for their new anthology, and a Berkeley publisher named Mike Grieg planned to use "Neal and the Three Stooges" from *Visions of Cody* in his anthology *New Editions*. Mardou's threats of a libel suit had meanwhile forestalled publication of *The Subterraneans* in the *Evergreen Review*. The manuscript had been haunting her for years, Jack having circulated it so freely that people she knew were always coming across it and asking her about what really happened. He had even used one of her actual letters to him in the text. The anguish of being put on exhibition had clouded all her subsequent relations with him. When he came to coax her permission, he claimed the novel was being published in a West Coast literary magazine (a deception, although *Evergreen* was popular in California). She signed the release under the assumption that she was consigning the book to oblivion.

Jack went with Allen, Peter, and Gregory to Rutherford, New Jersey, to meet William Carlos Williams. The weary seventy-three-year-old doctor praised their writings, and when asked to impart some wisdom, pointed out the window with a smile and said, "There's a lot of bastards out there." 273 On the way back from Allen's father's house in Paterson, when Jack begrudged the dollar and a quarter for Gregory's bus fare, they got into a big argument. Gregory understood that Jack's parsimony was necessitated by the tight budget he had to live on to write prose, so time-consuming even for a speed typist. Similarly, Jack understood that Gregory's mooching was an integral part of his helter-skelter poetic life-style. But once again they found themselves competing beyond the professional arena. Gregory had spent the holidays at the Helens'.

Without Helen Weaver, Jack joined Allen and Peter at Holmes' house in Old Saybrook the weekend of January 19. Buoyed by a squib about himself and Allen in *The New York Times*, he talked enthusiastically about his upcoming trip to Tangier and Europe; they boozed, played football in the snow, and read into a tape recorder. Not only was Jack "burning as bright and pure" as John had ever seen him, but there seemed to be a new calm, thoughtful objectivity about him, as though he had finally attained the serenity of an itinerant monk—the one attribute all his studies had heretofore failed to engender. What John didn't know was that Jack, far from having renounced his desires, had merely had them temporarily satisfied.

Back at the Helens', Weaver's dissatisfaction with Jack's neglect had led to a mild flirtation with Gregory. She knew Jack would be jealous, but she was angry enough not to care. Although he was clearly in torment he wouldn't let her near enough to draw him out of it; he preferred merely to dull it with alcohol, and to drain her of comfort. He was also jealous of Allen's success and continually accusing Allen of stealing from him—and no one could tell him different about anything. He blunted every sensible answer Helen gave with Buddhist catch-phrases: "Nothing matters . . . everything is the same . . . it's all illusion." He seemed angry over something that had been denied or taken away from him—Gerard and his father, perhaps—his stubborn stinginess an effort to conserve whatever was left. Having children was to Jack man's cardinal mistake. It wasn't only that he didn't want the responsibility of raising them, but he saw them as an emotional burden that he wasn't equipped to bear. Children might sicken and die, and death or the prospect of it was something he never took easily. He reasoned that if you don't have children, you can't lose them. Although Helen Weaver was by no means certain she wanted to have children herself, she was shocked at Jack's nihilism in believing that it was a sin to bring them into the world.

But the thing she absolutely couldn't bear was his self-destructiveness. His celebration of life came from a place dark as the grave. The pain in his eyes was a terrifying abyss. About him was the unmistakable odor of death.

Jack ended the relationship in his own passive way. She was still intrigued by his life-style and even his crazy friends, like Henri Cru. Henri came to visit and immediately dragged Jack off to some "marvelous" Salvation Army headquarters; he terrified Elliott by talking of murdering anyone who offended him, and later subjected his blind date (Elliott's girlfriend) to bondage!

One evening Henri had them over to dinner. He had cooked an exquisite *coq au vin*, but Jack wouldn't touch his plate. All he wanted was the red wine, and as he guzzled it he babbled. He was in a world of his own. Looking at him, Helen realized that reaching him was hopeless, and wept.

She was seeing an analyst at the time and trying to sort out her own conflicts. Deciding she needed some distance, she asked Jack to leave. It was a tense scene—Jack terribly angry and hurt at being "kicked out," and Helen sad but forcing herself not to relent. He blamed the break-up on her analyst, assuming she had passively followed his advice, ignoring the possibility that she might have a mind of her own.

She wanted to see him again, but as friends. He wanted her to give as unstintingly as a mother. In his eyes, those things she denied him were not her right but her sin. He later wrote her that the psychoanalyst's advice should have made no difference to her, and suggested she would do a lot better by going to confession. Besides, he added, confession is free.

Months later, after Helen had moved to her own apartment, her bell rang in the middle of the night, and there was Jack standing unsteadily on the sidewalk. He called up to her: "Are you Helen that wove the web of Troy?" She smiled at the poetry, but didn't let him in.

Directly after leaving Helen, Jack checked into the Marlton Hotel. Later he was shortchanged, and with only $5 left called Allen. Allen suggested he call one of Gregory's girlfriends, Joyce Glassman. A short, pretty blonde working at Farrar Straus, twenty-one-year-old Joyce was just beginning her own career as a novelist. Jack asked her to meet him at Howard Johnson's. After buying him supper, she took him home.

From the start, Joyce saw that Jack wanted someone to care for him, and she rapidly recognized the blocks keeping him from marriage. He discussed his devotion to his mother, his feeling that he would die soon (rehearsing the dangers of his phlebitis), and his aversion to bringing children into the world. In fact, he ran through the whole routine—which he had perfected with Helen, Carolyn, and others—of staking out his private territory. Again he pulled out the picture of Janet, declaring, "Look, this is not my child!" He made a big deal about how Joyce was not his type: blond, Jewish, "soft," etc. All she had to do was watch him loping down the street seizing and dropping people like words in a casual conversation to know he could never be possessed by anyone. No one save a few mad geniuses like Allen and Neal could even match his pace. Accepting the fact that they would have no long-term relationship, she was free to enjoy the adventure of loving him, and he was free to let her be his "Ecstasy Pie." If at the bottom of her heart she wished for a future with him, she said nothing to endanger the sweet, innocent, and passionate romance he was willing to provide.

For it was fun to wander Manhattan with him, visiting exciting people, sitting at the feet of his vast memory as he recounted anecdotes of the myriad characters in his past. It was exotic to have a lover who was about to depart for Tangier and would return for the publication of his celebrated picaresque novel. Since she placed no conditions on their going to bed, he was willing to be her friend outside of bed, and they eventually became close companions. He always took an interest in and encouraged her writing. In his massive ambivalence, however, he was just as capable of using pages from the manuscript of her novel for stationery when writing to his friends.

6.

After borrowing $200 from Allen, Jack set sail February 15, 1957, on a Yugoslavian freighter. Two days out the ship ran into a fierce winter storm. Tossed and lost as in a nightmare among mountains of hissing water, Jack remembered the boys he'd sailed with who'd drowned, and all the thousands who'd drowned before and since, and prayed to his childhood God. Indeed he had a vision that "Everything is God—nothing ever happened except God!" But his terror wasn't nearly as extensive as he portrayed it in *Desolation Angels*. He passed the time studying Kierkegaard's *Fear and Trembling*, and laughing his way through a murder mystery given him by Cessa. A day later the ship cleared the weather, and for the remainder of the trip he enjoyed the company of a woman he imagined a communist spy. Only after he landed in Tangier did his disgust with traveling set in.

He had originally planned to spend the rest of the winter and spring in Tangier, and the whole summer in Europe. His $20-a-month room above Bill's at the Villa Muniria had a patio facing the sea, and for a few days he simply relaxed, reading the New Testament, Genet, and Van Wyck Brooks' biographies of American writers. He took long walks alone along the sea to watch the fishermen, and with Burroughs he strolled through the casbah and hiked into the hilly green Moroccan countryside, marveling at the biblical-seeming shepherds. Besides the twenty-eight-cent-a-litre Málaga wine, which tasted a lot better than cut-rate American brands, every sort of drug was cheaply available. Living on coffee, boiled eggs, and thirty-five-cent meals at a native restaurant, Jack could have endured indefinitely. Word came that for British rights to *On the Road* André Deutsch was about to pay him an advance of 150 pounds—over $400.

But his complaint about the $3 cost of Arab prostitutes was just the beginning. Soon he was griping about the bad food and sanitary conditions, just as he had in Mexico. The opium he smoked "bugged" him, and some hashish made him violently ill. It turned out the hash contained arsenic; someone else who'd used it went insane.[274]

Burroughs was beginning to frighten Jack. He was in the midst of writing the novel *Naked Lunch* (though that title, originally suggested by Jack for a different manuscript of Bill's, wasn't applied until later; the novel was currently called "Word Hoard"). Burroughs was attempting to rid himself of all his deepest horrors, discharging them onto paper in the form of scatological, homosexual, violent fantasies of a quasi-futuristic, technologically enslaved society: chilling funhouse-mirror images of fifties America, which enlarged and twisted into view the shameful things hidden by everyday decorum. Jack thought that for sexual honesty "Word Hoard" bested anything by Miller or Genet. Helping Bill type the manuscript, he would get terrible nightmares of pulling endless bolognas from his mouth. Yet the most terrifying thing was the transformation the book was working on Bill's character. Whenever he talked, it was through so many layers of impersonation—British lord doing sputtering mad scientist doing Mr. Hyde, and so forth—that Jack couldn't discern a trace of any real man he had once known. Hence, while immensely entertained—as Bill spat out bones in an elegant French restaurant, for example, or swung his machete parodying himself, as if chopping up some Arab boy—Jack also felt exceedingly lonely, Bill's company no more comforting than that of actors in a play one is watching. Impatiently Jack awaited the arrival of Allen and Peter, delayed in New York by legal action to get one of Peter's brothers out of an asylum.

Meanwhile Jack was further depressed by the editing Don Allen had done on *The Subterraneans*. Besides cutting out half the novel, Allen had removed his "breath" dashes, added numerous commas, and reduced all the sentences, including some two-page masterpieces, to a uniform short length. Jack felt disgraced to be represented in the "San Francisco Renaissance issue" of *Evergreen Review* with such a "castrated" work. Worse, since writing had by now become his one reason for being, he felt that to let his prose be cheapened for commerce would "disvalue" his very life.[275] As much as he needed the money and recognition, he cabled his agent to halt publication and to offer Grove another novel or group of pieces instead. Insult added to injury was a letter from Cowley rejecting *Desolation Angels* and *Doctor Sax* as likely prospects for Viking. Having already dismissed *Visions of Gerard* as too heavily freighted with Buddhism, Cowley now advised Jack that his other novels were too "wild," and politely asked if he knew what he was doing in his writing.

Thunderstruck by the prospect that he might have to return to his "original bumhood" in order to preserve the integrity of his work,[276] Jack wrote to James Laughlin at New Directions, the only publisher who seemed interested in his experimental prose: "I am in the strange position of being able to offer various levels of novels to various levels of publishers—not 'novels' per se, but all my books are as it were poetry sheeted in narrative steel, a new kind of narrative which does not concern itself with discipline or dryness but aims at the flow of feeling unimpeded and uninterrupted by the calls of a dead craft, for I believe that the 'novel form' is dead, and the new prose literature of any originality and value will be cast in just that form, cf. Genet, Céline, and the new work of William Burroughs. I'm looking for a writer's publisher. I would, I will no more have my prose cut up than would Paul Bowles or Hemingway or any other conscientious artist." Laughlin did not answer for eight months.

In March, Allen and Peter descended on Tangier eager for fresh adventures. A few days after their arrival, U.S. Customs in San Francisco confiscated 500 copies of *Howl* that had been shipped from

England, and within a week of the seizure *Howl* had become a *cause célèbre*. At first Allen and Peter were ebullient over the prospect of an obscenity trial, an event certain to reveal Allen a poet of national stature. But their enthusiasm merely deepened Jack's discontent. Soon, however, Allen rapidly underwent a "turning-about" similar to Jack's, which restored their empathy. Disturbed by the poverty and disease among the Arabs, Allen realized that *Howl* had little to communicate to the world's masses, and told Jack, "I gotta write something better, more serious." [277]

The three of them found an Arab teahouse where North Beach–like hipsters never stopped sucking on their pipes of tobacco mixed with marijuana—legal in Morocco—to achieve a constant high. But, as always in a foreign country, it was America Jack saw, and the possibilities for his homeland to become more open. What pleased him about Morocco was its liberty of life-style, big enough to embrace someone like Neal Cassady, whose prototype he saw in the hero of the teahouse, by day a dock worker and by night a turned-on checkers champion. One night at Bill's apartment, however, he met a new breed of hipsters from France that repelled him: so cool were they that Jack's zany, ad-libbed humor struck them as gauche, and ignoring him they carried on a conversation using scarcely more than a dozen words like "like," "you know," "wow crazy," "a wig man," and "a real gas." What bothered him about their coolness was that it was merely a posture hiding their inability to respond emotionally to anything. In less than a year, much to Jack's perturbation, *he* would be credited with begetting just such indifference in America.

His best time in Morocco was a solitary hike to a Berber village in the mountains. These were the original *fellaheen* (the very word is Arabic) who had impressed him in the pages of Spengler with their endurance. Here in real life he was even more respectful of their simplicity and humility. In his notebook he made pencil drawings of their huts, imagining himself retired there to paint for the rest of his life. One of the peasants gave him a machete with a gold-braided handle, which he treasured ever after. Characteristically, Jack's response to Islam was based not on any intellectual apprehension but on his love for these villagers. The glory of their religion, embodied in their stolid faces, moved him to observe the fast of Ramadan. A few months later he would tell Malcolm Cowley that Islam and Buddhism were the only two religions capable of lasting another fifty years.

Reading a magazine article by Rexroth about American Indians, Jack was suddenly homesick, longing especially for the peace he had known with Gary in California. He decided that the only way for him to work and meet his obligation to his mother was to move her to Berkeley, then get McCorkle to build him a cabin retreat in Marin. Simultaneously it flashed to him that his next novel should be about Gary. Already he had the title: *The Dharma Bums*. The novel would contrast the constructive selflessness of Avalokitesvara as practiced by Gary, with the destructive ego worries of most of the hipsters. The plot would climax with Natalie's suicide. Anxious to get to California to begin writing it, he relinquished his summer in Europe. On April 5 he started back, traveling fourth class on a packet to Marseilles.

Herded down into the forecastle Jack felt like a stowaway, sleeping on a burlap mattress and next day scrounging a ration of bean slop by pretending to belong to the French army. But his landing in Marseilles was an unexpectedly warm homecoming. The little shops reminded him of the French-Canadian neighborhood in Lowell, and the cobblestone streets and eighteenth-century tenements took him even farther back on a journey toward his ancestry. A bus carried him to Aix-en-Provence, whose rusty red rooftops, hazy blue hills, and gray-green fields had been painted by Cézanne. After a few vermouths, he visited the Cathedral of St. Sauveur and cried over the singing of a boys' choir. He tried to hitchhike north but no one stopped; most of the cars were too small to accommodate him and his eighty-pound pack. Whenever he tried to rest in a field, some peasant chased him out. Forced to hike five miles to Eguilles, he used the opportunity to do more actual pencil sketching. From there it was a bus to Arles, through Van Gogh's landscapes of yellow tulips in windowboxes and cypresses tossing in the mistral, and on to Avignon, dismally dull and provincial on a Sunday afternoon. A crooked gum machine in the Avignon railroad station convinced him that the French were a race of thieves. He rode all night to Paris, cold and cramped in the vestibule of a packed train.

But again the misery of getting there was redeemed by the magic of emerging from the Gare de Lyon into the great radiating boulevards crowded with centuries of architectural splendor. Later that day, at a café in Montparnasse, Jack ran into Gregory Corso, who had come to Paris to earn a living writing pornography for Olympia Press. As usual Gregory was broke, but for every dollar he wasn't making there were two women he was. But while living off a variety of Americans, Gregory loved a Parisienne named Nicole, with whom he couldn't speak. In gratitude for Jack's services as translator and to make up for his past betrayal, Gregory offered her to Jack, but she didn't go for the deal. That afternoon Jack had a good time with him in the Luxembourg Gardens, drinking cognac with a group of French girls and gay Irish cyclists. But in the evening his gloom returned when Gregory introduced him to his friends, more phony cool American hipsters and painters.

Gregory bought a whole pie, Jack accused him of being wasteful, and they started arguing over money again. Then shamed by Gregory's charge that he was a killjoy, Jack treated him to an expensive dinner, but was soon fretting over the extras Gregory ordered and later, drinking with him, spent most of his money. Although Gregory let Jack share his room, Jack couldn't sleep for the sound of Gregory's lovemaking with Nicole. But the real horror began the next night. Gregory's landlady wouldn't let Jack in, and since Queen Elizabeth was visiting, most of the hotels were full of tourists. Tromping across Paris, Jack couldn't find a single acquaintance who would even let him have a floor; he was refused by such people as Mason Hoffenberg, James Baldwin, and Bernard Frechtman, the translator of Genet, to whom he had carried part of the manuscript of *Naked Lunch*. As a result, Jack got bounced from hotel to hotel for several days until he landed in the grubby whorehouse of some friendly Turkish pimps.

He haunted churches—St. Tomas d'Aquin, Sacré Coeur, Notre Dame—but the most powerful religious experience he had was in the Louvre. There he saw the works of such favorite painters as Tiepolo, Guardi, Canaletto, Brueghel, Rubens, Rembrandt, Fragonard, Goya, and Van Gogh. The progress of Western painting from an imitation of nature to the rendering of perception, the way light strikes the eye, by the Impressionists seemed to parallel Jack's own literary development. He felt that he had learned to use words like Van Gogh's nervous brush strokes to "paint what I see, color and line, exactly FAST." Yet the marvels of technique stirred him less than Rembrandt's sacred visions in *Christ at Emmaus, Sainte Famille*, and, above all, *St. Matthew Being Inspired by the Angel*. Matthew's rough hands reminded Jack of his own, and the red-lipped angel seemed about to visit him too with words of a new Gospel. When Jack looked again, the angel's mouth moved.

Arriving in Newhaven, England, with seven shillings ($1), he was detained by the immigration officials until he showed them Rexroth's article in *The Nation,* mentioning Kerouac and Henry Miller together. It turned out Henry Miller had been stopped there for the same reason. In London, after borrowing five pounds from his English agent, Jack went to Soho to see the Teddy Boys. These sharply dressed young jazz buffs and pleasure seekers seemed much more authentic to him than the academically trained "Angry Young Men," who were supposed to voice England's middle-class rebellion. The following week, hip was a long way from his thoughts as he visited Dr. Johnson's house, ogled the El Grecos in the National Gallery, and in the British Museum researched the crest and the motto of his ancestral Breton family: "Love, Work, and Suffer." On Good Friday his spirits finally soared to hear the choir at St. Paul's perform his favorite *Passion According to St. Matthew* by Bach. Having collected his advance from his publisher André Deutsch and booked passage home on a luxury liner, he slipped back at the last moment to watch *Antony and Cleopatra* at the Old Vic.

On the S.S. *Nieuw Amsterdam* his mood was dampened by the tuxedoed waiters who glared at his jeans and flannel shirt, but it was nothing like the suffocating doom of his arrival in New York in late April, when he learned that Joan had another writ out for his arrest. His hatred for her was so intense that he half seriously contemplated murdering her with his gold-handled African machete. To guard his sanity, he determined to get to California with his mother as fast as possible.

Originally he had wanted Neal to move them, but Neal was tied down by his new promotion to conductor. Sending their furniture to Phil Whalen, Jack and Mémère left Orlando by bus on May 6. Bone-weary of traveling, Jack could scarcely have borne those three thousand miles of squished, sweaty confinement and endless, exhausting rest stops were it not for Mémère's cheerfulness—undiminished after sixty-two years of unbroken losses and setbacks. She kept him peppy with aspirins and Coke, and in New Orleans she joined him for wine in a bar, where much to his annoyance she flirted with an Italian oyster man! On the way to El Paso they took turns nipping from a pint of whiskey. After resting a day there he took her across the border to Juarez, and in the Catholic church she was amazed by the devotion of the Mexican *penitentes*. Later, arm in arm, they strolled the streets meeting Indians and patronizing a fortune teller. Mémère got a kick out of it all, and he got a kick out of her glee. A pint of bourbon and the gaiety of a bunch of sailors saw them through to L.A. It was California port all the way to Oakland, where he dragged her half asleep to the bus to Berkeley. After installing her in a hotel, he gabbed through the night with Whalen.

By this time almost all Jack's friends were united in their assertion that he ought to leave his mother, and even unflappable Whalen was a little curious about their relationship. Jack explained that he not only loved her but *liked* her, that they were "perfect friends," who got along as quietly and effortlessly as two birds. Unlike anyone else Jack knew, she always took delight in things just as they were, an attitude that was Jack's "best spiritual possession." He reconciled himself to her obsession with television because that too was leavened with her shy, sly humor. She was known to joke even about sex, though she didn't like the idea that Jack's writing was "dirty"—an issue he avoided by advising her not to read his books. Last but not least, Jack stressed the obligation he felt to care for her after she had worked so many years to sponsor his career. Still, their relationship had its bizarre aspects, not the least of which was his notion that his mother was God.[278]

7.

In a cottage at 1943 Berkeley Way, Jack embarked on his "new life." [279] The first step was a regimen of never drinking without eating, to keep from getting soused. He also made a point to keep his address secret from his former drinking buddies. As a further aid to his stability he sent for Joyce Glassman, though with no promise of any commitment. Joan he planned to ditch by having Allen postmark his letters to her from Casablanca. It soon turned out she only wanted his signature on a Mexican divorce so she could remarry. Even the *Evergreen* fiasco was remedied by Don Allen's decision to print *October in the Railroad Earth*, as is, in place of his cut version of *The Subterraneans*.

Virtually burdenless for the first time in several years, Jack set to work on a number of projects. Besides expanding *Book of Dreams*, "Lucien Midnight," and his collection of haiku, he chronicled his travels abroad in "A Dharma Bum in Europe," typed up selections from his notebooks to form a "Book of Sketches," and began a novel called "Avalokitesvara." To the charge of certain people that he was repeating himself he rejoined that any great artist hitting his stride is repeating a certain beauty he's spent years learning to create. Jack saw no point in shutting off the flow just when it was strongest. Also he felt he was still making advances, citing the new freedom he had gained from "Lucien Midnight" to work explosions of pure sound into his narratives. An even grander conception tantalized him: a massive work to be called "Visions of Myself," which would exhaust his autobiographical material and permit him to begin writing truly fictional novels like those of Balzac.

Jack's typing impressed Phil as a slur of margin bells and carriage-slammings, although Phil did see him stop to cross out passages or skip around in the notebooks he was transcribing. Often Jack read aloud a passage before he typed it; other times he'd start goofing at the typewriter and incorporate even typographical errors into the text—as Neal had—in the form of new riffs.

In this period Jack also completed a large number of paintings and drawings—a few portraits of Whalen, but most of religious subjects.

His discipline cracked rapidly under the stress of a spiritual crisis. Deeply torn by the war between his philosophical preference for Buddhism and his heartfelt need for a personal God, he attempted a variety of sophistries to reconcile the two. For example, though he couldn't fault the logic in the *Lankavatara Scripture* that "there's nothing in the world but the Mind itself," he posited that the sentence made as much sense if one substituted the word "God" for "Mind." In his daily life, this dilemma manifested in the conflict between his desire to teach the tranquility of the Dharma by personal example, and his need for "ecstasy of the mind all the time." As he wrote Gary, it was impossible for him to "live without exuberance." On the one hand he wanted to get his hut built in Marin and then to construct several others nearby to form a zendo, a commune for "dharma bums"; he even contemplated climbing Matterhorn again to find a cave where he, Gary, and their friends could spend summers living like the Tibetan monk Milarepa. On the other hand he could no longer face "the dreary inconvenience of camping out," and the only activities still worth the effort to him were writing, getting high, drinking, and fucking. He saw no reason to keep meditating, aside from the fact that his phlebitis made prolonged sitting too painful anyway. Moreover, since Buddhism proved the uselessness of trying to understand life with any sort of concepts or logic, he wondered why, barring sickness and hangovers, Buddhists didn't remain continuously drunk.

Jack liked the reassurance given by Catholicism, and reinforced by his mother's stories of Gerard, that people died and went to heaven. He found St. Theresa's shower of roses more comforting than the transcendental charity of the Bodhisattva. Her roses were real to him, like the flowers in his garden; they were a tangible proof, which he desperately sought, that "everything is really all right." Whalen recalls Jack retreating into the belief that, human misery and the atom bomb notwithstanding, people could still take refuge in God by becoming Catholics. Like Merton, Jack believed being a Catholic entailed striving for sainthood. Though he had no confidence that he could live a saintly life himself, and worried constantly about how to manage his writing in a holy fashion, he was also consoled by the many eccentric Catholic saints and felt there might be room for him with his drinking and sex. Driven as he literally was by the need to see God's face, Catholicism kept him from going to pieces faster than he did.

He was also kept alive by Mémère. It was her means of controlling him that was destructive. She would continually throw up to Jack the fact that Gerard would never have done the things Jack was doing, and on occasions of exceptionally bitter disappointment she would say, "It should've been you that died, not Gerard." The guilt she generated in him could then be relieved only by her coddling and flattering. She exacted a terrible price, constricting his maturity, but she paid him back in a currency he craved. At the same time as she infantilized him, she glorified him as a genius. It was a fool's game—getting knocked down in order to be picked up—but he was hardly the first to play it.

Jack's claim that he had first learned storytelling from his mother gained credence when Phil heard Mémère, her tongue loosened by whiskey, rattle on about "little Jackie" or her escapades with Leo in Montreal. She liked Phil, but as soon as Jack wanted to go to San Francisco she'd warn him that his other friends just wanted his money. If that didn't stop him, she'd say, "Jackie, why don't you stay home? I'll cook you a nice meal." Jack would reply, "Aw, Ma!" and do what he wanted anyway. Returning a few days later from a binge he'd get a good scolding in patois—since she didn't want anyone to know they were arguing—but before long they would again be making merry.

In San Francisco Jack's fame was growing by leaps and bounds. *New Editions 2* containing "Neal and the Three Stooges" was released in late June, and *New Directions 16* containing "A Billowy Trip in the World" from *On the Road* would be out in July. *Chronicle* reviewer William Hogan speculated that *On the Road* was getting more prepublication publicity than any work since *Finnegans Wake*. When the *Examiner* dispatched Luther Nichols to interview him, Jack was jumpy and defensive until Nichols began talking about his own experiences hitchhiking and sailing in the South Seas. Even after Jack "opened up like a flower," he preferred to talk about sports rather than books. Finally, after Luther convinced him of his sincere appreciation of the work, Jack spoke of his dream: a long shelf of books all written by himself, like the interlocking novels in the *Comédie Humaine*, that he could point to from his old-age rocker. That he would never live to calmly survey his harvest might have been gathered from another comment of his that "the things I write are what an editor usually throws away and what a psychiatrist finds most interesting." Luther asked Jack to go on KQED-TV, but he refused and took off to roam the city alone.

Jack could scarcely get his old kicks if he wanted them, because California was now so "hounded down by cops." In both San Francisco and Berkeley, he and Phil were interrogated for talking (and singing) on a street corner. Caught crossing against a red light in Berkeley, on his way to do some work for John Montgomery, Jack was fined two dollars. The ultimate insult was getting stopped for simply walking down Milvia Street at midnight. It occurred to Jack that in such a "police state" a Zen commune (such as he had envisioned building) would be outlawed from the start.[280] In June, soon after Customs authorities had cleared *Howl*, Ferlinghetti and his clerk Shig Murao were arrested by San Francisco police for selling the book at City Lights. This time Jack was terrified that he could no longer get away even with writing what he wanted.

What finally drove him out of California was not the police but the new cliques of look-alike pseudo-hipsters (soon to be dubbed "beatniks" by Herb Caen). Jack was incensed by these mealy-mouthed rebels who dissected Ginsberg and pronounced *Howl* "too dirty." [281] Those who envied Allen's fame were always after Jack, "that guy that *Howl* is dedicated to," and he received more challenges than an aging gunfighter. A young poet friend, Dave Whittaker, remembers someone bursting into The Place, arms flailing, to "get Kerouac." Pushed beyond the limits of pacifism, Jack kayoed the guy with one punch. At the same time he was sought out by establishment curiosity-seekers, like the editors from *Esquire*, who pretended to be interested in his manuscripts just for the privilege of baiting him over lunch.

Jack admired Rexroth for defending Ginsberg on the radio, and was pleased to receive a letter from him praising *On the Road*; their differences couldn't keep Rexroth from admitting that *On the Road* was "full of a new language." Rexroth felt that Jack, like Allen, was returning American literature to the mainstream of world literature, rejecting the elitism of a Delmore Schwartz or an Elizabeth Bishop in favor of literature that talked to the masses. Yet in person Rexroth made no pretense of being Jack's friend. For his part, Jack cared nothing for the power play Rexroth wanted to make out of Allen's cause.

Neal, the only man capable of keeping Jack in California, was no longer interested in anything but women, horses, and chess. Irritated that Neal owed him $10, Jack chased him down in San Francisco but retrieved only $2, though Neal offered one of his spare women for the night. Later Carolyn wrote Jack complaining of his bad influence on her husband.

In North Beach Jack met LuAnne, who was astounded by the quantity of whiskey he was consuming as well as by his diatribe against marijuana. The old beer-sipping Jack had never expounded on anything. Nevertheless, they arranged to meet again for an afternoon in Golden Gate Park. At the start, Jack was the same soft, loving guy she'd fallen for ten years earlier, but as he kept dragging her across the street to a bar for quarter-hourly refreshment, his personality hardened frighteningly. The drinking made him opinionated but it also gave him a sort of smooth veneer, which he wanted, to let the world roll off him. She had never seen him handle himself so well, at least as far as dealing with people and speaking his mind. But it hurt her immeasurably to see him "dropping all the things that used to make Jack up." She wanted to put her arms around him and tell him how she felt. Sensing that, he bluffed independence. Every time she'd start to sympathize with him, he'd slap her on the back and say things like, "Don't let anything bother you!" She had the sense of a man "holding you off with one arm and reaching out with the other." But unlike Neal, who talked to her honestly no matter how greatly he changed, Jack refused to let any feelings emerge. Jack's demeanor conveyed a message of "Forget your feelings."

Finally they sat on the grass together again; she lay back and he lay with her, holding her hand, but that was clearly the most he could handle. He started reminiscing about the afternoon they had spent in New Orleans picking out shapes in the clouds. "I don't see anything in the clouds anymore," he said.

Mémère was as anxious as Jack to leave California. She was afraid of the mountains falling on her and the fog depressed her, but mostly she just wanted to be near her daughter again. She and Jack arranged to take a bus back to Orlando in mid-July. The day before they left, he received a box of advance copies of *On the Road*. He barely had one out of the box when Neal, LuAnne, and Al Hinkle appeared in his doorway.

Jack kicked the box under the table, but as soon as Neal learned what was there he insisted on seeing a copy. Sitting at a round table while the others hunched around him flipping through the novel, Jack was in agony. He said, "You people are gonna hate me when you read it," and kept apologizing for whatever passage they happened to scan: "In this period I was mad at you . . . ," etc. But Neal grabbed a copy and led them all outside, reading random pages aloud and interpreting the story with crazy routines. Even then Jack couldn't grasp that they were all thrilled at his success. With their arms around him they tried to explain that it made no difference to them what he had *written* because they loved *him*. Softly and sadly Jack repeated, "Aw, you're not gonna like it."

Eventually they did go over to San Francisco for a little celebration, and after a few drinks Jack started to relax and just enjoy their being together again. In the following months Neal frequently discussed the book with LuAnne, and always he spoke of his pride in the fact that Jack had found him interesting enough to write about. No one could have given him a finer compliment. But to LuAnne it was apparent that their friendship had culminated in a tragedy of complete misunderstanding; as much as they cared for each other, each was convinced that the friendship was more on his side than the other's.

Florida was sweltering. What really bothered Jack about their new small house was that he had no separate air conditioner for his room and so had to leave the door open to keep from stifling. The privacy of his room was all-important to him, and he even stressed to his nephew, "You should always have a room of your own. It's a special place." But his temper was short from the heat and all the money he'd lost with two superfluous treks across the continent, and one day he caught himself yelling at young Paul for drinking his Cokes. Ashamed of his meanness, Jack determined to return to the peace and easy gratifications of Mexico City. He left on July 23.

Preparing to join him in San Francisco, Joyce got a letter directing her to Mexico. At his old apartment on Orizaba Jack learned that Garver had died a month earlier. Jack imagined he had committed suicide after running out of junk, since Garver had often spoken of his plan to overdose with "Blue Heavens" (sodium amythol) in such an emergency.[282] To compensate for the dejection caused by news of his death, and since Esperanza wasn't to be found, Jack checked into a fancy downtown hotel. His first night there the bed began heaving. He leaped under it, lit a huge joint, and prayed to Avalokitesvara, Gerard, his father, Jesus, and the Virgin Mary. The earthquake killed and injured many people. Its seemingly gratuitous visitation of suffering and sorrow left Jack too upset to finish *Desolation Angels* as he'd planned. Instead he stayed in his room for most of two weeks. When he went out, it was for prostitutes, and the next thing he knew his testicles were swollen and he was in unbearable pain. In mid-August 1957, writing Joyce to stay in New York, he headed home to his mother.

Although he worked sporadically on his novel about Burroughs, now called "Secret Mullings about Bill," all Jack's enthusiasms had vanished "like a finger snap." Climbing mountains, camping, meditating, painting and drawing, even making love (with his sore balls) seemed quite as onerous as writing. Staring at the wall of his room, the thought of "the Wise Man's silence under a tree" was enough to make him want to puke. His Buddhism, he wrote Gary, was "completely dead." Crushed under despair of every sort, he felt like seventy instead of thirty-five. He was ranting against everyone and knew that as the ultimate futility. Appalled by his own anti-Semitism in a letter to Gary, he remarked prophetically, "That's the end when I start picking on poor dumb Jews." [283]

All he wanted was to laugh and cry again, to feel Goethean passion, to travel Blake's road to wisdom through excess. But where to start? In California everyone but Whalen had seemed "changed, dreary, sad, lost." To Alan Ansen, who was in Tangier continuing the typing of *Naked Lunch,* Jack wrote that he was "sick of the Fellaheen scene." To Burroughs he wrote that he never wanted to be outside America again. Joining Gary in Japan seemed the happiest alternative, but he hadn't the money. Having reached a "dead wall," he had left only the instinct to live. It wouldn't be long before he once more talked of the desert.

In the eyes of Gregory Corso, Jack's Buddhism and all his subsequent shifts were the last resort of a national leader with no nation behind him, a failed conqueror who'd learned to entertain—which indeed is the best stratagem of the powerless. What, if not that, was the chief discovery of the Beat Generation? But Jack's mistake, in Corso's view, was that he took himself too seriously to settle for the role of clown, as Gregory had. As Corso explained to Allen in a letter of that period, Jack was a victim of his own high purpose:

> When you say "Jack and the Buddhists are really right" yes, but right about what? I'll tell you, they're right about living a clown in a circus of power, that's Nirvana, the ability to step out of a small magic box, and lo, into the arena, for all to see, and laugh; that's what Jack is actually looking for, humor. . . .
>
> I say Jack has humor, of course, but he denies it; and I understand, I think, fully why; his ego is such that, it is not he that sees the universe, it is the universe that sees him. When the universe fails to see Jack, then Jack will die. . . .

TWELVE

"The Obsessive Violence of Rimbaud" and "The Raveled Nerve-Ends of Huysmans"

1.

On September 5, 1957, *On the Road* was hailed by Gilbert Millstein in *The New York Times* as "an authentic work of art" and "a major novel." Calling it "the most beautifully executed, the clearest and most important utterance yet made by the generation Kerouac himself named years ago as 'beat,' and whose principal avatar he is," Millstein prophesied that *On the Road* would become the testament of the Beat Generation.

Three days later the Sunday *Times* carried David Dempsey's review of the novel, "In Pursuit of 'Kicks.'" It marked a turning of public opinion against Kerouac that was never reversed in his lifetime. While admitting that *On the Road* was "enormously readable and entertaining," Dempsey deplored its subject matter. There was no Beat Generation, Dempsey claimed, but only a "sideshow" of "freaks." He warned that Kerouac's characters flirted with depravity and that his road led nowhere. What especially offended Dempsey was that in the face of so much robbery, adultery, and dope-taking, Kerouac maintained "a morally neutral point of view." A week later, *Time* followed suit by accusing Kerouac of creating "a rationale for the fevered young who twitch around the nation's jukeboxes and brawl pointlessly in the midnight streets."

The majority of reviewers sensed the vastness of Kerouac's talent but lacked a means of approaching it, so great was the gap between his technique and that of previous American novelists. Thus a critic like Carlos Baker, sensitive to the nuanced social codes of Hemingway, was left "sad and blank" by *On the Road*'s "dizzy travelogue." *The Atlantic* found the work monotonously repetitious, and the *Chicago Tribune* thought it the "completely uncontrolled" product of an author who "slobbers words." *Time* compared Kerouac's writing to his recent attempts at painting with a mixture of house paint and glue. No one had the courage or the ingenuousness to say they simply didn't understand what the man was doing.

One cannot discount jealousy in the reviewers, who are often writers *manqué*. It doubtless seemed unfair that this bummish lothario (already known all over New York by hearsay as "a big stick-man" [284]), whose handsome face was plastered all over newspapers and magazines, should also be getting attention as a serious writer. But the unkindest cut came from Kerouac's former Columbia classmate Herb Gold. In *The Nation,* Gold concluded that the sum of information in *On the Road* was conveyed by the exclamation "Whoee." Using all the flash and color of his novelistic skill, Gold elaborated the notion that Kerouac's work was an apologia for criminals and a naïve paean to madness. He also introduced a thread that was later woven into full-scale attacks; among the castoffs for whom Kerouac served as "spokesman," Gold spotted not only "pushers and panhandlers" but also "male hustlers." Soon Kerouac as well as Ginsberg and Burroughs would be cited as champions of a moral decadence that undermined both local law and order and national security. This immense non sequitur reached its *reductio ad absurdum* in Norman Podhoretz's article "The Culture of Appeasement" in *Harper's,* October 1977, where he suggested that the promulgation of homosexual cowardice by writers like Ginsberg, Baldwin, and Vidal resulted in the scrapping of the B-1 bomber!

Little did Kerouac dream such storms were brewing as he throve in childish glee upon the attention of his beloved New York. He arrived there on the day of publication and spent the next five weeks in a swirl of publicity, parties, and available women. But there was always the other part of him that stood apart, that was frightened, that had to get terribly drunk just to face the prospect of such desperate fun—the part that *knew better.* For he was still the Jack Kerouac who had wondered aloud to Holmes, at the party where they had met in 1948: "What am I doing here? Is this the way I'm supposed to feel?" His feeling that order was under attack in modern life remained the most intense thing about him. No surprise, then, that he feared the chaos of publishing parties. He didn't even want to attend the original party given by Viking. When he finally went, very late, he was accompanied by Helen Elliott, who watched him being devoured by a swarm of frantic people who all wanted to take credit for his success. That he did go to such affairs was due to more than his vanity, considerable though it was. For though he worried ceaselessly about "selling his soul to the devil," the idea of taking on chaos for other people was as deep in Jack as the image of the crucifix.

But forcing himself to be the person others thought him—the gay reveler, the devil-may-care adventurer, *the lordly author*—was taking a toll on his personality perhaps heavier than the unlimited whiskey he could now afford. At a party at Joyce's, his old friend Ed String-ham found Jack plainly obnoxious. Sodden drunk, surrounded by parasitic Time-Life journalists, Jack was pontificating ex cathedra, reminding everyone that he was the one who knew about life be-cause he had been through it and no one else had. They all laughed behind his back. What he was saying was so banal and so self-reveal-ing of his insecurity, that it was cruel for Stringham to watch these slick people using it against him. Yet there was no way Ed could reach out to help him. Their old rapport was shattered by Jack's belligerent insistence that people give him "incense at the altar" or nothing at all.[285] When Ed tried to get him to stop reading from *Old Angel Midnight* because it sounded as though he were babbling, Jack exploded that his writing was above criticism.

Yet none was more painfully aware of his foolish spectacle than Jack himself. At rare intervals, when conscience glimmered through his drunken haze, he would try to get off the merry-go-round. Gilbert Millstein gave a party for him, but the star failed to show and only phoned, asking to speak to Holmes. Unable to face more glittering spectators, he asked John to meet him at Joyce's. When John found him, Jack was ashen from hangover and nerves, and to-tally bewildered as to who he was. After a couple of hours Joyce and John calmed him enough so that he could sleep.

With enough quarts of whiskey, however, even his perspective vanished. At a party upstate with Lucien and Cessa, he was doing his nonstop jivetalk rap *à la* Neal Cassady while a doctor was recom-mending their children get flu shots; Jack interrupted: "Don't tor-ture your children!" "Shut your big mouth!" Cessa snapped. Caught off guard in his new idiocy, her words hit him like a satori, a spiritual kick in the eye. There were other satoris, as when poet Howard Shulman tried to impress him by driving seventy miles an hour up Park Avenue at midnight and Jack shuddered to realize exactly what universal justice had in store for him.

From some inner necessity he burned always and ever more furi-ously in the same direction. In Lucien's Cherry Plains farmhouse with Joyce and Cessa, Jack choked, wolfing down the heart of the roast beef; later there was a war with whipped cream, and after the women went to bed he and Lucien stayed up in their shorts howl-ing like coyotes and gibbering Shakespeare. Finally, after Lucien dropped off, Jack played "thundering oratorios" until morning.[286] For a chance to rest he asked to be left alone there for a few days, but as Lucien was driving away there was Jack on the road waving frantically to be picked up.

The financial rewards giddied him as much as fame itself. *On the Road* made the bottom of the best-seller list for several weeks, then sales faltered because Viking wasn't prepared to resupply the book stores rapidly enough. Nevertheless, translation rights had been sold to German and Italian publishers, and the novel had been selected by the Book Find Club. Sterling Lord promised Jack several thousand dollars in royalties by the end of the year. *On the Road*'s smash convinced Grove to do an unabridged hardcover edition of *The Subterraneans*. Furthermore, Jack was now able to sell old stories and new Beat Generation pieces to such publications as *Esquire, Playboy, Pageant,* and the *World Telegram and Sun.* The biggest deal cooking was sale of movie rights to *On the Road.* Warner Brothers had already offered $110,000, but getting word that Paramount and Marlon Brando were also interested, Lord decided to hold out for $150,000. Visions of a trust fund dancing in his head, Jack planned to "bhikku around the world" for the rest of his life. Meanwhile, off-Broadway producer Leo Garin wanted a play from him, and as soon as he got back to Florida Jack wrote it in one night. "The Beat Generation" comprised three acts: the first set in Al Sublette's apartment with Neal, Al Hinkle, and Charley Mew; the second, a day at the races with Neal; and the third the night the Bishop came to Neal's house. Unfortunately Jack wasn't able to concentrate long enough to get beyond the first few pages of another childhood novel, "Memory Babe."

There were moments of real satisfaction too. Nelson Algren telegraphed his praise. In a letter, Charles Olson pronounced Jack a true poet. (And a few months later, Olson would tell his friend Nell Blaine that Kerouac was "the greatest writer in America.") Jack responded by sending Olson a copy of "The Essentials of Spontaneous Prose" and praising Olson's poem about his mother, "As the Dead Prey Upon Us." And amid all the hangers-on at parties, Jack met one man he recognized as a genius in his own right: photographer Robert Frank. Discussing their mutual admiration for Charlie Chaplin and W. C. Fields, he and Jack immediately struck up a friendship, and Jack talked of his love for the movie *The Long Voyage Home,* about seamen disoriented during the war. Having enjoyed *On the Road,* Frank expressed the desire to film one of Jack's stories. He also asked him to write a preface to his book of photographs, *The Americans,* and a few days later Jack delivered it.

The hardest job Jack had was correcting misapprehensions about the Beat Generation. According to Ginsberg, there was a nationwide misperception that "beat" meant "angry at the world" rather than "weeping at the world." Mailer's *Village Voice* columns and his essay "The White Negro," as well as various pieces by Anatole Broyard, contributed to this image of the hipster as a sharp, ruthless, sometimes knife-carrying antihero, who could survive by his wits in the underworld as well as in elegant society. Jack was disturbed that Holmes too dwelled on the violent crimes of hipsters in his essay "The Philosophy of the Beat Generation" in *Esquire.* In the articles "Lamb, No Lion" for *Pageant* and "Aftermath: The Philosophy of the Beat Generation" for *Esquire,* as well as *Saturday Review* and *New York Herald Tribune* interviews, Jack stressed that "beat" meant "beatific," that its children weren't "roughnecks" but respecters of life like St. Francis, that they sought not "a lot of frantic nowhere hysteria" but rather a "spontaneous affirmation," a "joy of heart." Jack's *Esquire* piece, written in early 1958, also contained the wistful speculation that the Beat Generation was already dead, killed by a society that traded every spiritual blossom for hard cash.

On John Wingate's *Nightbeat* TV interview show in late September, forty million viewers heard Jack say he was "waiting for God to show his face." Pressed for a definition of the Beat Generation, he stated that it was "basically a religious generation"; but the examples he gave of the new spirituality, ranging from Eisenhower to rock'n'roll (and really a digest of the social content of the previous ten years), left Wingate puzzled. What Wingate wanted was cleverness; what he got was a man speaking directly out of himself—"coming from center," as psychologists might say—and admitting his weaknesses and contradictions with breathtaking candor. When Wingate asked what Jack meant when he said he had been drunk for several days, for example, Jack responded with a list of the unpleasant tasks and frustrations that had kept him drinking. After the show, while Wingate was sufficiently disarmed to get drunk himself with Jack, his viewers went wild. Within an hour, Holmes received over a dozen phone calls from people who were dying to meet Jack, including women who were dying to go to bed with him. Some Connecticut nuns even requested the Franciscan Fathers perform a Mass for his spiritual and temporal welfare—and with good reason. Dredging up the truth cost all Jack's energy and guts. A nervous wreck, he was forced to cancel several other scheduled TV interviews.

Such assaults upon his identity increased his need for the comfort of women. Over the next few years he slept with dozens of "chicks," who were no more to him than girls he wanted to go to bed with. Having taken his pleasure he had no further interest in them, nor would he go out of his way to seduce them; they had to be aggressive toward him. Jack only courted and fell in love with women of substance, and he assumed such women would not feel slighted by his one-night stands. The women he loved were always more sister than sex object to him anyway. The last thing Jack wanted was to make Joyce cry, but it was unbearable for her to watch swarms of women coming on to him and him always ready to yield. He felt that he could do anything and even tell her about it. But she could no longer accept that; she wanted a more substantial relationship. Just before he returned to Florida, they tentatively split up.

Partly their separation had to do with his meeting Helen Weaver, ravishing at a party in a white "Lost Generation dress," and falling for her all over again. She seemed unburdened of her old anger at him, and they agreed to meet when he returned to New York in December. Soon after in the mail came another box of cigars.

Jack's attitude toward women was also souring for a reason beyond their control: his chronic alcoholic impotence. Increasingly he was unable to become sexually aroused without fellatio, and most of the women he knew were loath to provide it. Drinking made him feel virile, gave him strength to manage his life a little more boldly than he otherwise could have, and he refused to admit that the booze was interfering with something as essential as his sex life. He hated himself for being impotent, and he hated the fact that his life was becoming unmanageable. By his own logic, someone else must be to blame. When women refused to do his bidding he threatened them with masturbation, and most of the time he got to carry out the threat.

There had always been one woman besides his mother enshrined in Jack's heart: his first wife, Edie. In January, having read about his success, she called him at the Marlton Hotel and they began corresponding; he wrote her that she would always be "a great woman" and signed himself "Your eternal old man." That fall she was in New York and managed to connect with him and Lucien. Jack promised to take her to one of his publishing parties but, looking old and shot, he was abashed before her trim figure and glowing beauty. In no time both men got roaring drunk on Scotch and went completely out of control. Frightened, Edie watched Jack fall onto the curb outside a Village bar and commence crying. He no longer seemed to realize that she was there. She took a cab to her hotel and didn't hear from him again for some years.

Home in Florida in mid-October, Jack got as much rest as ten fifths of Schenley's in two and a half weeks would allow. He crabbed that Nin's family kept coming over to his house for dinner, and it peeved him even more that long-lost Kerouac relatives were calling and writing from all over the country. The resentment he loosed on those close to him was fed by the broadening stream of attacks on him, Allen, and the Beat Generation. An Associated Press article claimed *beat* had been supplanted by the *beep* of the Russian satellite Sputnik, and that both noises were equally irrelevant to the hard-working American. What hurt most was Jack's betrayal by former friends. Rexroth was on the radio in December calling him "an insignificant Tom Wolfe." The February 1958 *Playboy* carried Herb Gold's "The Beat Mystique," a further attack on the irresponsible thrill-seeking that Gold imagined the Beat ethos. Yet Jack's response was never malice. He began praying "to get Rexroth into heaven" and attempted a reconciliation in a long letter that Rexroth never answered. Still, he was deeply disturbed by the hatreds and jealousies he saw sweeping the country, of which he was merely a minor victim. When Corso complained of the blurb Jack had sent to City

Lights for Corso's book *Gasoline*, which praised Gregory as an Italian singer, Jack reprimanded him for the same "sneering" pettiness being used against them all.

One bright spot was the verdict acquitting Ferlinghetti of selling obscene books and acknowledging the literary seriousness of *Howl*. And Jack had good news from publishers: the distinguished French house Gallimard bought rights to *On the Road*, *Holiday* commissioned him to do an article about his mountaintop experience, and Paul Carroll at the *Chicago Review* took *Lucien Midnight* for a Beat issue. Ferlinghetti and Laughlin both asked for poems, inspiring him to compose a new series called "Orlando Blues." Best of all, Laughlin agreed to publish a volume of selections from *Visions of Cody*. A trade edition of the whole book was sure to run afoul of censorship, but a high-priced, limited edition of the less bawdy passages was safe enough. Albeit his wildest prose would finally reach readers, Jack wished the novel could be published full-length. He wrote Laughlin that "someday this book will be clutched underarm by young American writers like some kind of Bible," and lamented that it should have to be "emasculated" for the sake of current conventions. Jack was strongly tempted to withhold it until it could be published intact.

With money flowing into his pockets, Jack practiced his own peculiar hypocrisy. Allen and Peter wanted to return to the United States as soon as possible, because Peter's brother Lafcadio was having violent fights with their mother. Nevertheless, Jack continued to postpone repaying Allen the $225 he owed him. As always writing came before people, but now it seemed booze came before writing. Cowley asked for a childhood novel free from the fantasy of *Doctor Sax*, but "Memory Babe" couldn't write it because his memories were washing away in an 80-proof tide. The only subject able to ignite the fumy haze around him was Gary Snyder. Feeding a teletype roll into his typewriter in late November, Jack intended to write *The Dharma Bums* nonstop. It was miracle enough that despite interludes of alcoholic oblivion he managed to get through the novel by December 9.

Doubtless in part because of all the furor over the Beat Generation's alleged destructiveness, Kerouac changed his original design to use Natalie's suicide as the climax. Early in the novel he reports her tragedy with a journalistic brevity, then proceeds with mythologizing Gary as a modern American hero in the lineage of Thoreau and naturalist John Muir. Jack was proud that he had bridged the gap between beatness and "good oldfashioned early-Christian John the Baptist wilderness tough sensitivity" without touching hipness at all. Instead, the joy comes out of the spiritual freedom of "Zen lunacy," which he foresaw as the new direction in American culture. At the same time he felt he was realigning himself with the American fron-

tier tradition, for Gary's optimism, unlike Neal's theosophical variety, had the solid "ring of the woods." [287]

If only because it remained in print throughout the sixties and
seventies, while so many of Kerouac's books vanished (even out of
libraries, from which they were stolen), *The Dharma Bums* became,
along with *On the Road,* one of his two most influential works. The
"rucksack revolution" prophesied in the novel became a reality a
decade later, when millions of hippies criss-crossed the continent for
nothing but flowers in their hair and love. Plenty of those sacks were
stuffed with Kerouac's novels, and *The Dharma Bums* served many
as a survival manual.

It is nonetheless a profound work, which asks the "big questions"
almost from page one: "Wa? Where am I, what is the basketbally
game of eternity the girls are playing here by me in the old house of
my life, the house isn't on fire is it?" Despite the blurbs promising an
abundance of "orgiastic sexual sprees" and other fleshly pleasures to
be found in its pages, the whole message of the novel is antisensual-
ist. The struggle of the narrator, Ray Smith, to mortify his lust for
women and his other appetites is one of the book's main themes.
What he learns is Christ's lesson that the spirit can never completely
subdue the flesh. Looking forward to the solitude of his firewatch
shack on Desolation Peak, Smith is warned by one of the rangers:
"You're sayin that now but you'll change your tune soon enough.
They all talk brave."

Kerouac's resolution of the dilemma comes from the Apostle
Paul, whose epistle to the Corinthians Smith reads on Christmas
Eve. The line that strikes Smith as more beautiful than any of the
San Francisco Renaissance poetry is: "Meats for the belly, and the
belly for meats; but God shall bring to naught both it and them."
Like excessive indulgence in pleasure, the effort to attain perfect
abstinence distracts one from the true purpose of life, which is to
"bless" and "pray for all living creatures." The ways in which the
characters make life livable are far less important than the compassion that living makes possible. Once again Kerouac's message is
Scriptural: "Charity shall cover the multitude of sins." The point
where Christianity coincides with the Buddhist "Paramita of Dana"
("the perfection of charity") is the dharma or true meaning toward
which all Kerouac's heroic bums are headed. That quest is necessarily circular for him, who mistrusts absolutes. Hence every new life
upon which the narrator embarks soon dissolves in weariness, and he
leaves the world only to return to it from another direction. The
wisdom he learns on the mountain he expresses as "Blah," which is
to say that wisdom is unspeakable, that the value of life cannot be
inventoried but only lived. That insight was as desperately needed
amid the Madison Avenue hype of the fifties as it was painful for
America's conspicuous consumers to practice.

The style of *The Dharma Bums* marks a downshift from *The Subterraneans* or even from *Tristessa*. The sentences tend to be shorter and they are certainly less labyrinthine. Yet there are many marvelously long sentences in the novel that utilize an oral syntax simple enough for a child to follow, and yet admit a complexity of perceptions into a single flow of thought. The prose is further notable for its limber grace, swinging cadences, and mimetic sound effects:

> Then also as we went on climbing we began getting more casual and making funnier sillier talk and pretty soon we got to a bend in the trail where it was suddenly gladey and dark with shade and a tremendous cataracting stream was bashing and frothing over scummy rocks and tumbling on down, and over the stream was a perfect bridge formed by a fallen snag, we got on it and lay belly-down and dunked our heads down, hair wet, and drank deep as the water splashed in our faces, like sticking your head by the jet of a dam.

Kerouac felt that "the final exhilarated moments of the book" describing his life on the mountaintop represented his best writing. Actually, however, the novel's momentum dies rapidly after Japhy Ryder (Gary) leaves for Japan, and the enervated prose of the last few pages relies heavily on Buddhist dogma as well as notes from Kerouac's mountain journal to keep moving toward a conclusion. There is none of the soul-searching that occurred there in real life, as he eventually recounted in *Desolation Angels*. Perhaps most disturbing is the sense that Kerouac's own interest in the book is flagging, that he wants to get it over with in a hurry. As indeed he did, for he was engaged to read at the Village Vanguard in New York the week before Christmas—for $500. "Fame," he wrote Allen, "makes you stop writing."

2.

By the time he got back to New York his mood had darkened. Having heard that Brando considered *On the Road* too loose to be filmable, Jack wrote him describing the screenplay Jack could write and, incidentally, suggesting ways to re-do the whole cinema and theater of America "to bring it up to par with her Divine Poets." Brando never answered. Ferlinghetti rejected *Book of Blues* on the grounds that it wasn't poetry. Although Jack himself was aware of the prosaic tendencies of his poetry—and felt that he could say what he wanted more exactly in prose—he was always outraged to hear similar criticism coming from someone else. He reminded Ferlinghetti that poetry was more a quality than a form anyway, since, as an example, there were passages in *Walden* that could be arranged in lines to form exquisite free verse. But worse than anything else was his fear that his serious literary career had ended with the advent of commercial success—in short, that he was selling out.

That was just what reviewers hinted about his performance at the Village Vanguard. Allen had warned him that it was sure to be a drunken fiasco, and Jack went ahead with it expecting the prophecy to come true. He told himself that he needed the money, even though he'd written Helen Weaver a couple of months earlier that he preferred poetry to "nervous wealth." Painfully shy in his coat and tie, he read rapidly from the original notebooks of *Mexico City Blues* while most of the people either snickered or loudly ignored him. Each night the audience got smaller and he got drunker and more reluctant to force himself onstage. Max Gordon, the owner of the club, would find him crouched in the vestibule with the musicians' instruments, drenched in sweat and fingering Gary's Buddhist prayer beads to work up his courage. Many friends stopped coming because they could no longer bear to see him patronized like a freak on show. He did everything possible to show his sincerity, often reading Allen's or Gregory's poems instead of his own, and on Christmas Eve reading a prayer. What appreciation he got came mostly in the form of notes from society women offering him assignations. Even his sensitive listeners felt the aptness of one wag's comment: "Well, Kerouac has come off the road in high gear . . . I hope he has a good set of snow tires."

Watching Jack read, Steve Allen thought it would be interesting to have a jazz musician spontaneously scoring his lines as he read them; and Gilbert Millstein, who arranged the reading, offered Allen himself the job. Jack couldn't have been more thrilled, bragging to Lucien that he was working with a "millionaire." Their combination was successful primarily because Allen laced his piano licks around the words rather than competing with them, and despite the pressure Jack read very well by pretending he was reading to his friends. Allen liked the "soft, loose and rather musicianlike way" Jack spoke, Lee Konitz concurred that Jack "blew music," and Gilbert Millstein was surprised by the "childlike timbre" in his voice. Bob Thiele of Dot Records signed them to cut a record of their performance, and soon Jack had a contract to record more of his material with jazz impresario Norman Granz.

He met Mardou, who asked him where *The Subterraneans* was going to be published. At last he sprang upon her the surprise of its publication in hardback, answering sarcastically: "Grove Press! Isn't that what you wanted to hear?"

Divorced, Thea Snyder had been in New York for several months, and Jack was seeing her on and off. He told friends she was the perfect woman for him, that he liked the way she stood up to him, especially since fame brought him cartloads of fulsome agreement. Previously he had complained of her "bad timing" repeatedly keeping them apart. Now that they were both available he led her from party to party all over the city. She'd never seen anyone use drink or marijuana so desperately. Every few minutes, she recalls, he'd look around to "to see if he was still with us, and if he was, he'd try again"—take another drink or light another joint, until he was incoherent. He was clearly knocking himself out. Later, when she scolded him on that account, he bridled. Indicating the void of depression into which he felt himself slipping, he maintained that alcohol was his "self-medication," which he used "not to feel so much." He said it worked as "a filter to make the world safe for his sensitivity." The more concern she showed for him, the more he grew rude and distant. It occurred to her that he was playing "a destructive and childish game," that he was only interested in her as long as she backed away from him, for as soon as she began to care for him *he* backed away.

Inevitably he returned to Joyce, one of the few people who would let him in when he was drunk and stand calmly by while he stood on his head and twirled his railroad lantern to prove himself sober. She was certainly the only woman besides his mother who was content to fix him hamburgers or pea soup at any hour of the night, let him cry over Frank Sinatra records, and listen to his fantasies of going to Hollywood, starring in his own movie, and becoming Sinatra's best friend. Jack's ultimate vision of success was himself and Sinatra as drinking buddies singing songs to each other! That dream, like his plan to reunite with Gary (who was back in the States), was little more than a reaction to the madness currently boiling out of him.

He was no longer about to stop for anybody. Philip Lamantia was living in the Village with another free-spirited Catholic poet, Howard Hart, who was also a jazz drummer. Jack, Philip, Howard, and French horn player Dave Amram did the first "jazz-poetry reading" in New York at the Brata Gallery. With Hart, Jack drank Thunderbird, discussed Maritain and the intellectual superiority of European Catholicism, and listened to jazz. Jack introduced him to his buddy Elvin Jones, then jumped in a cab with Jones to go hear Allen Eager jamming in Harlem. With Lamantia, Jack orgied and discussed God and ecstasy. When Hart and Lamantia went for their daily Communion at Our Lady of Guadalupe, Jack sat through Mass with them. After sleeping on Hart's floor among girls, musicians, editors, and junkies, Jack would take off every morning at eight sharp. Before his return to Florida in early January, he mingled with theater people, shot heroin, burst into the New School to read to a "bunch of seminar squares," walked through the Bowery with poet

Jack Micheline, meeting bums ("Look!" cried Jack, pointing at a graybeard, "there's Walt Whitman!"), and confronted deadpan interviewer Mike Wallace with the news that "God" is the same as "Tangerine."

There was a special reason for his excitement. Nancy Wilson Ross's intelligent article about Zen in *Mademoiselle,* together with Alan Watts' best seller *The Wisdom of Insecurity* and the new popularity of D. T. Suzuki, convinced Jack that 1958 was "the year of the Dharma." Back in Florida he immediately retyped *The Dharma Bums,* and the minute Viking's editors started reading it they saw dollar signs. Hollywood too was ready to jump on the Beat bandwagon. Jerry Wald of Twentieth Century-Fox wrote to Jack about getting him to consult on a script of *On the Road,* and Brando asked Lord not to sell movie rights until he had a chance to bid.

Of course there were catches. Wald wanted to endow *On the Road* with the brutality of *The Wild Ones,* and he specifically requested that Dean get killed at the end in a car crash, to exploit the sensational publicity over the death of James Dean (who, curiously, shared Neal's birthday). Meanwhile Jack continued to be condemned for the violent image these exploiters wanted to give him and his work. Norman Podhoretz's article "The Know-Nothing Bohemians" in the spring issue of *Partisan Review* hurt him more deeply than any other single piece of criticism. Podhoretz, later editor of the Jewish community organ *Commentary,* was Columbia's fair-haired boy, who had won a Kellett Fellowship to Cambridge a few years after Jack had been banned from the campus. Reinforcing Gold's *argumentum ad hominum* that Jack was "the spokesman for a group of rebels," Podhoretz claimed Kerouac's motto was: "Kill the intellectuals who can talk coherently, kill the people who can sit still for five minutes at a time, kill those incomprehensible characters who are capable of getting seriously involved with a woman, a job, a cause." Since rumors of Jack's reputed anti-Semitism were already abroad, members of the New York Jewish literary establishment were terrified of him, as though any minute he might invade some editorial office, switch open his blade, and go for the real jugular of those who were going for his in print. The wife of one of the editors at *The New York Times* warned Lucien not to mention Kerouac in front of her husband, who had a bad heart, because just the name might give him a seizure.

In late February Grove released *The Subterraneans* like a clay duck to the skeet-shooting critics, who'd already tested their sights on Kerouac. A highly innovative work requiring careful explication, it offered a broad target to those adept at ridiculing anything different from acceptable mediocrity. *The New Republic* reported that "nowhere [in the novel] is there any sign that either the author or his characters know what they are talking about," and concluded that

"Kerouac is simply ignorant." In *The New York Times*, David Dempsey quipped that the story "seeps out here, like sludge from a leaky drain pipe." *Time* announced that Kerouac "is not Rimbaud but a kind of latrine laureate of Hobohemia," as well as "a cut-rate Thomas Wolfe." While *Time* made no attempt to hide its aversion to Kerouac's characters, calling them "ambisextrous and hipsterical" and linking their "madness" to drug use, *Newsweek* let the cat out of the bag of favorite American taboos, calling the novel "a tasteless account of a love affair between a white man and a Negro girl. . . ."

Excruciatingly sensitive to any suggestion of his inadequacy, especially as a writer, Jack was always hit hardest by the put-downs of people he respected. Vying for the privilege of flooring Kerouac, Rexroth reviewed *The Subterraneans* in the *San Francisco Chronicle* with masterly equivocation. Conceding that "it is not a bad book," Rexroth nevertheless finds that "it has all the essential ingredients of a bad book." And while he admits that Kerouac "does portray, in a really heartbreaking fashion, the terror and exaltation of a world he never made," Rexroth sees no contradiction in declaring: "The story is all about jazz and Negroes. Now there are two things Jack knows nothing about—jazz and Negroes."

After all the hue and cry—which might better have been reserved for, say, the escalation of the nuclear arms race—there came one still small voice, from Sweden, in the form of a twenty-two-page letter from Gregory Corso. Rereading *The Subterraneans* he realized how much Jack had loved Mardou, and hence how deeply his own involvement with her had hurt Jack. Literally weeping as he wrote, Gregory told Jack in detail about the horror of his youth: the orphanages, bedwetting until he was twelve, his lack of friends. Reading of the vast unhappiness and insecurity that compelled Gregory's misdeeds, Jack cried too.

He never needed friends more himself. He took to drinking so heavily that Mémère would yell at him, even in front of the family: "You're gonna kill yourself!" Always he replied, "Not me! I'll live forever!" If she tried to argue with him, he'd remind her that she liked to nip at the cognac or Southern Comfort hidden in her dresser. Because he was so lonely and bored in Florida, she agreed to move back to New York with him, although she hated living so far from Nin and her grandson. In late February, 1958, Jack left for New York to hunt for a house on Long Island.

Neal Cassady reached the end of his line in exactly the same month. Like Jack, he had been giving steadily of himself for over a decade, and neither could any longer stand the emotional drain. They both wanted to give up, to rush death, and yet both feared the spiritual consequences of suicide. In fact, Jack was leery of Neal because he felt he was actually capable of doing violence to himself. After Natalie's death Neal had often talked of suicide, planning to make it look like an accident so that Carolyn could collect compensation from the railroad as a kind of atonement for all his sins against her.

Neal proceeded to box himself into a trap from which there were only two exits: death or prison. To continue playing Natalie's racetrack system he had been borrowing heavily from loan companies and perhaps also loan sharks; it may be they had threatened to collect on the debt one way or another. He may also have been involved in some shady dealings in order to pay them off; in any case, he was acting as if he feared for his life. Time was also running out on his unfulfilled promise to marry his mistress Jacky Gibson, a bright career woman with a baby boy, who was madly in love with him. As he had with Natalie, Neal spent his weekdays living at her apartment in San Franciso, but she had come to want him as husband or not at all. Neal could no more leave her than he could divorce Carolyn.

One day in February Neal bragged to Al Hinkle that he had just "split a joint with a narc." When Hinkle asked if he were worried, Neal replied that there was no evidence because they'd smoked it up. Not long after, on the train, Neal agreed to procure marijuana for another man he knew to be a narcotics agent. At the last minute he blew the agent's $20 at the racetrack, and failed to deliver the goods. Now more than ever the Narcotics Division of the S.F.P.D. wanted him off the streets, because he was able to identify one of their undercover agents. Carolyn grew frightened by the changes in Neal's personality; with her, as never before, he was "hard, cocky, sharp, and cynical." At Jacky's, according to her, he would point from the window at the same two agents parked across the street every day; he knew they were agents because they had already arrested a friend of his on a narcotics charge, and he laughed that they were just waiting for a chance to nab him. Finally he let them drive him to work, and to show his "appreciation" gave them three "off-brand cigarettes." In early April, he was arrested for "dealing," but a grand jury couldn't find sufficient evidence to indict him.[288] The day after his release, he was rearrested on slightly altered charges, which resulted in a felony conviction. On Flag Day (June 14), he was sentenced to serve five years to life in San Quentin, to which he was transferred on July 4.

Jack reacted to Neal's incarceration with anger. His hero was not supposed to put himself in prison. If Neal were dumb enough to do such a thing, Jack told his friends, then he could "fend for himself." Jack may have felt guilty that *On the Road* had focused public attention on Neal, leading to his arrest, although Neal had been a conspicuous character in North Beach long before the novel was published. High all the time, he'd be in and out of every meeting place in one night, jerking and twitching, and countless times both Allen and Jack had told him to "cool it." [289] Certainly Jack did feel guilty about *his* involvement in New York's glamorous, arty society, a world meaningless to Neal; and his own sense of shame may have contributed to the blame he put on Neal for betraying their youthful ideals.

3.

In early March, Jack bought a high, rambling old house with front and back porches, much like the Martin house he had envisioned in *The Town and the City*. Its address was 34 Gilbert Street in Northport, Long Island, a town he had discovered by visiting Lafcadio Orlovsky, who lived there with his mother. Fifty miles from New York, Northport reminded Jack of a New England village with its white frame houses, ancient trees, "little hills . . . and ghosts." There was also a harbor on the Sound, whose fishing boats and sand dunes suggested Maine, and he liked its nearness to Whitman's birthplace in Huntington. Best of all was a pine for meditating under in the hedged privacy of his back yard.

Unable to move in until mid-April, he spent another six weeks sleeping either at Joyce's or on Howard Hart's floor. Invited to lecture at Brooklyn College, he was mobbed by two thousand students and gave Zen answers to their intellectual questions, at one point making sounds like a child by slapping his finger against his lips. During another appearance on *Nightbeat*, Jack responded to Wingate's question "What is a 'mainliner'?" by singing "Skyliner." In late March, at the Circle in the Square Theater, Hart and Lamantia were to give jazz-poetry readings accompanied by Dave Amram's rather classical French horn. To help draw a crowd, Jack agreed to serve as master of ceremonies, though he eventually read with them. In addition to *The Subterraneans*, he read Corso's and Orlovsky's poems. When people clapped, he told them to hold hands instead. Despite feeling used by Lamantia, who seemed to be showing off "five different kinds of poems" rather than baring his soul like Ginsberg, Jack finished the two-week engagement.

Fate was making up for its neglect of him with a vengeance. By late march *The Subterraneans* had sold twelve thousand copies and was on its way to becoming a paperback best seller. *On the Road* was still selling steadily, he was about to receive an advance on *The Dharma Bums*, and Grove accepted *Doctor Sax*. *Life* commissioned him and Robert Frank to do a photo-story about their upcoming trip to Florida. The spring issue of the *Chicago Review* was out with the 211th Chorus from *Mexico City Blues* as lead poem, as well as Jack's compendium of Beat poetics, "The Origins of Joy in Poetry." The meaning of *beat* was discussed on the TV show "Last Word," and

The Young Socialists' League grappled with "The Kerouac Craze."

There were fresh attacks, by Richard Wilbur in *The Nation* and by Rexroth in a TV interview. Purporting to describe the evening Jack and Phil Whalen had got a little tipsy on white port, Rexroth claimed Jack had frightened his children by pulling out a hypodermic needle and giving himself a shot. Jack typically sought not to get back at him but merely to end such a foolish and one-sided feud. At the Five Spot, where Rexroth was reading, Jack approached him and said, "Hello, Kenneth." Rexroth turned his back and walked away.

Weary of "being attacked and misrepresented by the very people who were supposed to understand and HELP" in the "fight to instil peace & tenderness in the world," Jack told Jerry Wald of Twentieth Century-Fox that he would permit no movie containing any "cruelty" to be made from his novels. Consequently, Wald decided to forget *On the Road* and instead asked him to submit an original screenplay.

Jack talked of spending a year in his rocking chair in Northport, mulling over his new childhood novel. Sufficiently rested, he would then begin a round-the-world pilgrimage with Allen and Gary. Allen wanted to go to Russia in the near future, but Jack advised him to wait two years—when, he expected, they would both be invited as distinguished American authors. While Allen intended the world to hear him as if he were "speaking across Red Square," Jack advised him to "ignore politics" and return to New York, where there were endless balls and "all the angels you want."

Jack couldn't see anything worth worrying about, even the night when he drunkenly collapsed in an alley and woke up the next morning stripped of most of his clothes. He just sauntered over to Grove Press for a loan and showed up later at Hart's apartment in a camel hair overcoat and shiny Thom McAn shoes. He asked Howard to "dig" his outfit, and Howard made appropriate noises. "No! Don't you notice the pockets?" Jack retorted. "Perfect for Thunderbird!" He pulled a bottle out of each.

More and more he said and did outrageous things as a means of breaking through people's shells, to learn what they really thought. There came to be a fine line between what was completely natural and spontaneous behavior and what was deliberately shocking or downright cruel, and in Jack's constant stupor he was virtually incapable of observing the distinctions. After *Life* lost interest in the photo-story about "the road to Florida," he and Frank took their idea to *Esquire*, where an editor questioned them about what they needed to complete the assigment. Making great show of his boredom, Jack unbuttoned his lumberjacket shirt, folded it into a pillow, and actually went to sleep on the floor—which may explain why *Esquire* later killed the article.

Besides Mardou *The Subterraneans* upset a lot of people who had unwittingly sat for portraits. Among them was a gay ex-marine boxer, who avenged himself by beating up Jack. In retaliation, Henri Cru clobbered the boxer. Out to vindicate himself, the boxer stalked the Village looking for Jack and spotted him, soused to the gills, with Stanley Gould outside the San Remo. Jack flagged a taxi, but the driver, seeing him staggering, refused to let him in. The boxer had two friends with him, and in desperation Jack called them all "faggots." Gould fled. The boxer knocked Jack to the pavement and punched him in the head over and over, slashing his face with a huge silver ring, while Jack stared into his unbelievably furious eyes and asked meekly, "What did I do to you?" and finally started laughing hopelessly like Cannastra. Jack made no effort at all to defend himself. As he later explained to Cru, when he got drunk he believed himself to be Jesus Christ, so like Jesus he would never strike back. The boxer left Jack with a broken nose and arm.

Bleeding profusely, he made his way to Hart's apartment and crawled into his usual sleeping place on the floor. Hart looked at the immense gash in Jack's forehead and thought immediately of the beating Thomas Wolfe had taken in Germany, which had hastened his death. Hart first called a Village doctor, who when he learned the patient's identity refused to come. Then Hart and Lamantia labored to rouse Jack, to take him to St. Vincent's hospital two blocks away, but he wouldn't budge. Hysterically Jack cried, "You've got to get my wounds cauterized!"—a phrase that had stuck in Jack's head after the first beating, when Joyce had taken him to the hospital. At last photographer Leroy MacLucas arrived and commanded him to get up, and surprisingly he obeyed. After Jack was cared for at the hospital he was interviewed by the police, but he declined to press charges. He did accept pills from the doctor to help him stop drinking. Years later he would write to Lamantia that he never felt completely right in the head after that beating.

On April 10 he left with Robert Frank to pick up Mémère in Orlando. Jack was amazed by Frank's ability to capture on film the "lorn American landscape so unspeakably indescribable," though the text he matched to Frank's photos was equally evocative. When it came time to stop for the night, Jack demurred at all the fancy hotels Frank picked out and finally assented only to the shabbiest. The next day in the car he napped in the back seat, and upon awakening said, like Dmitri Karamazov, "I'm all right now—I had my dream." The surprise for Frank came when he met Mémère and Nin: they were the only two women with whom he ever saw Jack totally respectful.

A few days later Frank delivered Mémère, Jack, and his two beloved cats Tyke and Timmy to their doorstep in Northport. Happily Jack set to work putting on the screens, determined to retire from debauchery to "the tender art of writing artistic literature," just as Holmes had. Through the spring and summer he secluded himself in the house, only rarely taking the Long Island Railroad into the city for reunions with Joyce and family dinners with Lucien, Cessa, and their three sons—and afterward, of course, bats on the town. By June, sick again with phlebitis, he was doing his best to avoid even Joyce.

Thanks to Lucien, whose stoical sense of duty was as inspiring as his household was comforting, Jack learned that "people are tough enough to handle suffering and birth by themselves and don't need no Buddha." He derived further tranquillity and stability from a synthesis of Buddhism and Catholicism. The Buddhists' Dharmakaya, the Body of the Truth, seemed to him identical in its emptiness with the Catholics' Holy Ghost. What the Buddhists meant by the "dreamlikeness" of reality Jack assumed to be no different from his belief that God was the electromagnetic-gravitational force holding the universe together. Somehow he also believed in a personal God, the Father of Jesus, who wanted people to suffer so they would deserve heaven.

"Memory Babe" had evolved into the story of the Christmas weekend in Lowell in 1935, though his work on it consisted mostly of pacing his back yard and singing. He was also doing another story for *Holiday* about his travels abroad. Meanwhile he clashed with another publisher over the mutilation of his work. Viking Press had made some 3,500 changes in the manuscript of *The Dharma Bums,* mostly commas to break up long sentences. When Jack restored the original sentence structure in the galleys, he was billed $500 in printers' fees. Although he eventually established his editor's responsibility for the late changes, the experience—along with their refusal to publish *Visions of Gerard*—influenced him to leave Viking. Through it all he never flagged in the assistance he gave his fellow writers. Earlier in the year he had typed up enormous amounts of material by Burroughs, Ginsberg, Cassady, Huncke, McClure, Creeley, and others for the summer issue of *Evergreen Review.* Hardly knowing Jack Micheline, he wrote a preface for his book of poetry, *River of Red Wine.* Jack encouraged Snyder to write a novel and made a special effort to sign him with Sterling Lord. He also suggested Gary and Phil coauthor an article on California Buddhism with him, for which *Holiday* had offered $1,500.

Late that spring MGM bought movie rights to *The Subterraneans* for $15,000. Jack agreed to sell movie rights to *On the Road* to a small company, Tri-Way Productions, for $25,000. Twenty-five hundred dollars was paid in advance, but he never received the balance. Tri-Way commissioned a screenplay by Gene Du Pont and lined up Mort Sahl for the role of Dean, Cliff Roberts as Sal, and Joyce Jamison as LuAnne before its bankroll went flat.

Jack was taking less money than he felt he deserved for these works, but after Neal's arrest he preferred to keep a low profile. He turned down numerous offers to appear on TV, including a special to be made with Benny Goodman. In early June, when Steve Allen pulled him out of the audience and onto the stage of *The Jack Paar Show*, he was again asked, "What is the Beat Generation?" His reply: "Nothin'! " As Jack lit a cigarette, Paar's writer said, "Oh, I use morphine myself," whereupon Jack snapped, "Ain't you tried H yet?" A few nights later the show presented a cruel parody of him, in a sloppy sweater, lighting cigarettes and repeating "Nothin'." Cheap-shot satire bothered him not nearly so much as the media's association of Beat with juvenile murders and perverse crimes of every sort. One of the most vicious pieces of yellow journalism was an Art Cohn column in the *San Francisco Examiner* entitled "Sick Little Bums." Singling out Kerouac as the "Double Llama" [sic] of beatdom, Cohn credited his "pathetic, self-pitying degenerate" followers with pranks like feeding strangers hamburgers laced with ground glass. In late June *Chronicle* columnist Herb Caen labeled the young rebels "beatniks"—because they were as "far-out" as Sputnik, the Russian satellite, though the Yiddish suffix "nik" is also a nasty diminutive. To dissociate himself from the alleged Beat crimes, as well as the beatniks, Jack did an interview with Lucien Carr that went out over the U.P.I. wires July 5.

In February Peter Orlovsky had returned to America to care for his brother Lafcadio, and Allen was due back in August. Allen's letters to Jack were full of suggestions for counterattacks against the establishment. After springing Julius Orlovsky (virtually catatonic) from the madhouse, they were to proceed to California to lead protests against Neal's imprisonment, and eventually instigate a revolution against Cold War politics. Jack was upset to see Allen so "politically-minded." [290] Despite America's mistakes, Jack was sure it was still one of the most compassionate nations.

Mémère read Allen's letters on the sly and was disgusted by the references to drugs and gay sex. And she was convinced Allen's stunts would get Jack arrested. In allegiance to her husband's deathbed wish that she protect Jack from Ginsberg and Burroughs, she wrote Allen warning that unless he let Jack alone she would sic the F.B.I. on him. Especially she objected to Allen's mentioning Jack's name in his "dirty books," for Jack received prominent tribute in the dedication to *Howl*. Jack wrote Allen that he more or less agreed with her, that he wanted to return to the simple introverted world of his childhood and once again content himself with daydreams. To Ed White he wrote that he was too old and tired of "kid shenanigans" to go on any more "silly roads" like his trips with Neal. Even the urging of Gary and Phil that he come to California for hikes and climbs failed to overcome his deathly fear that cops would catch him associating with drug users and toss him into jail. As for New York, he had been deterred from further carousing by an ominous scrawl in the john of the White Horse tavern: "Kerouac Go Home."

Far from oblivious to the world situation, Jack worried over the U.S. occupation of Lebanon and the growing threat of radioactive fallout from the testing of nuclear weapons. But like Thoreau, he felt all reform begins on an individual level, and for himself presently there seemed no better change than to tend his fruits and vegetables and American Beauty roses, read the *Diamond Sutra* in the sun, meditate under the pine, shoot baskets, listen to the radio, watch old movies on *The Late Show* (with a few sips of iced white port), and go out later to study the stars and scribble poems. He was too "listless" to continue with the novel, and in any case saw no reason to write without "a religious or personal heart reason." Besides, there was work enough ahead just in getting his non-Beat works like *Doctor Sax* and *Visions of Gerard* published. Once *The Dharma Bums* was released in October, he planned to get a shack in the eastern mountains and fulfill his promise to Avalokitesvara to meditate for a month, in gratitude for the movie sale of *On the Road*.

Teenagers and college students seemed to have a dowsing rod for his house. At first Mémère was able to repulse them, but then they got smart and went around her, sneaking into the back yard and entreating Jack to explain "beat" or simply sitting at his feet. If they were polite enough, Mémère sometimes broke down and invited them to supper, and everyone would get drunk together. Many just wanted to take Jack's money, and when he was drunk he'd leave it lying on bars and even let people pull it out of his pockets. The greedier started stealing his pencil notebooks, until he had to keep his room off-limits. There was also a stream of teenage girls whose curiosity he was happy to oblige. When Joyce came to the house for dinner, Mémère, seeing her as a real rival, refused to let her stay the night. Although Mémère's official decree as devout Catholic head of the household was that there would be no extramarital sex under her roof, she also had a Yankee shrewdness that told her she had to make a way for her son's relief or he'd go looking for women in the city, an infinitely worse threat. At times convenient for Jack she would go shopping or to church for a few hours, without ever acknowledging that she was letting him get laid. His own combination of embarrassment and common sense about sex was to a large extent an introjection of his mother's naïveté and practicality.

That mother-son relationship, around which so much of the Beat dilemma revolved for Kerouac, awaits competent analysis. Astute observers have testified to the Oedipal tie between them. Having lost every other man in her life, Mémère was determined to hang onto Jack even if she had to strangle him with kid gloves or "unknowingly" drive him crazy. She succeeded in keeping him a child who had to look up to giants like his brother and father, and for whom the rites of passage to manhood consisted of "marriage" to her. Frequently now he talked of the "sacred trust" he had been given to care for his "father's wife"—as he specifically referred to her—as if to make the relationship sound less dangerously intimate than it was. The very fact that he called her Mémère ("Granny") put her at an additional remove from the possibility of incest.

That he was sick was terribly apparent. When Joyce came to dinner he passed out with his head in his plate. He was getting fat; the Dexamils he took for stimulation to write (which didn't work) left him depressed and constipated, and his boils returned. The kids had got him drinking again, and his rawness to fresh disparagement—a satire on him in *Esquire* and a *Horizon* article by one of Trilling's protégés once more accusing the Beats of fomenting teenage murders and other atrocities—made death itself desirable. "Gone from the earth to a better land I know" he quoted from the song *Old Black Joe* in a letter to Allen in August.

In October the reviews of *The Dharma Bums* sank him deeper in despair. Other than Ginsberg in *The Village Voice*, critics showed virtually no understanding of the book as spiritual pilgrimage or social prophecy. Charles Poore in *The New York Times* called it "a sort of juvenile, machine-age parody on the great American migrations in the nineteenth century," which proved the Beats "a syndicate or union of writers rather than anything like a true generation." A few weeks later the *Times* carried an even more absurd, if somewhat less contemptuous, review by J. Donald Adams. Adams complained that Kerouac hadn't heeded Kipling's admonition that East and West could never meet, and deplored the representation of a "world of drugs, drunkenness and aimless wandering, spiked by frequent orgies of sex in the raw"—as though characters in novels, like those in the movies, ought to keep their pajamas on during love scenes. Most revealing as a measure of the originality of Kerouac's vision was Adams' aside regarding the novel's "absurdities [such] as its vision of millions of young Americans strapping on knapsacks. . . ." The *Saturday Review*'s poetry editor John Ciardi was reputedly insulted by an aspersion in *The Dharma Bums* to the effect that he didn't know how to use a condom. The *Saturday Review* carried one of the most unfair reviews ever given Kerouac. Its author, William Bittner, hinted—among reams of misinformation—that the novel consisted of "material . . . stashed away, after innumerable rejection slips, in 1952," thereby explaining what he saw as a "muddle of maturity with adolescent blithering." If Kerouac continued to write this way, Bittner prophesied, he would "end up as forgotten as Thomas Holley Chivers."

Typical of the illogic of reviewers was a matching pair of faulty premises from reasonable old England: while the *Spectator* complained that Kerouac's Zen was "docked of its humour," the *Times London Literary Supplement* felt Kerouac's humor undermined his Buddhism! By contrast, some of the most intelligent words on the novel came from a publication that had no stake in literary fortunes. Declared *The American Buddhist,* the organ of the Buddhist Churches of America: "As a book *The Dharma Bums* is an answer to the literature of disillusion, petulant sensualism and indignation against dry-heart bourgeois hypocrisy. . . . As an alternative to the packaged way of life it should be taken seriously by youth and taken as a threat by our policy makers on the east coast."

4.

Jack's appearance of strength—the physical strength, the ability to outlast *everybody* on five- and six-day binges—misled even his close friends. But when Corso returned to New York late that fall he thought Jack "a changed man." Jack's face was beet red and he was drinking more heavily, but that wasn't what struck Gregory most forcibly. In a bar at which Jack was being lionized Gregory found him in the bathroom, sitting on a closed toilet seat, absolutely taken with himself, grooving in some private seventh heaven—for the first time in his life seemingly *happy.* Gregory figured, "That's what he wanted, the man wanted acceptance." Of course he realized that Jack's drinking resulted in part from his deep feeling for the tragedy in life and from his being "full of shadows at night." Still, he couldn't understand why Jack later began to rail vehemently against fame. In the first place, Gregory felt any smart man ought to know that the rewards of serious writing are spiritual, and that "the person who creates a new society will have no place in that society himself." And, in practical terms, Gregory felt that Jack had little to bitch about, since he at least had the money with which to hide from his fame.

In reality, Jack's exhilaration was the flip side of his mental exhaustion. He was having a nervous breakdown. And in a strange way, as he himself saw, it was tied to what Ginsberg called "the Fall of America." For as it rejected Kerouac, so did America reject its own tender heart in favor of police-state paranoias and hypertensive, aggressive anger and the brutality of military solutions.

As a means of self-preservation Jack had turned down offers to read from all over the country, knowing his stage fright always led to worse drinking. (Contrary to popular opinion, some of the Beats were not natural performers and approached their public role with extreme trepidation—even Allen, in those early days, was so nervous before reading that he'd sometimes vomit.) Mémère always pushed Jack to do TV shows, however, because she felt they were essential to his career, i.e., they sold books. In mid-October, on the *Ben Hecht Show,* he was asked, "Why are you afraid to speak out your mind, what's wrong with this country, what is everybody afraid of?"

Bringing up Eisenhower, Secretary of State Dulles, and the Pope, Hecht waited for Jack to speak against them, but Jack insisted that he wanted to speak *for* things—like the crucifix, the Star of Israel, Mohammed, Buddha, Laotse, D. T. Suzuki, and Bach.

Originally he had declined an offer to speak at a forum sponsored by Brandeis University. With his royalties dwindling, he later reversed his decision, although the $100 honorarium only partly explained his acceptance. He was told that a friend of his, Zev Putterman, would be present at the forum, which was to discuss the question "Is there a Beat Generation?" The organizers pleaded with Jack, stressing their need for his authoritative voice, and cajoled him with courtesies like a limousine there and back. The forum was to take place on November 6. A few weeks beforehand, spooked by the prospect of well-dressed people watching him "with slitted eyes," Jack canceled out. Besieged by telegrams urging him not to disappoint the university, he relented, prepared the twenty-minute speech they had requested, and went.

In the Hunter College Playhouse he discovered that he was participating in a debate, and that the lineup was three against one. His opponents were Ashley Montagu, an elderly Princeton anthropologist and the most benign of the lot, James Wechsler, editor of the *New York Post*, with a radical chip on his shoulder, and Kingsley Amis, one of England's Angry Young Men.

Kerouac was to speak first. His address, "The Origins of the Beat Generation" (enlarged and considerably edited for publication in *Playboy*), remains the definitive statement on the subject. It traced the flowering of beatitude back to its roots in traditional American gumption and enthusiasm and glee. Beat was the bounce back from the bottom, the will to survive of his down-and-out grandfather, the wild parties thrown by his bankrupt father, the angelic music and irrepressible smile of melancholy Harpo. Disavowing his paternity of the cool, conformist beatniks on TV and the rich beatnik apes sporting "Brooks Brothers jean-type tailoring and sweater-type pull-ons," Jack saved his harshest denunciation for those who used the cover of "beat" to vent their own bitterness and hatred or, worse, to prey upon the buried malice in others. He concluded with a single word of affirmation: "Yair"—the slang of Dos Passos' tramps and workers for "yes."

Five minutes into Jack's speech, Dean Kauffman announced that his time was up. When Jack continued reading, he was repeatedly prodded by the sponsors to hurry up and stop hogging the others' time. It seemed to Ginsberg that under pretense of giving Jack a vehicle to express himself they had set him up to ridicule. The whole suit-and-tie lot were regarding him in his red-and-black checked shirt as some sort of monster, spurring him to milk the role. He stumbled on and off stage a dozen times, played the piano in the back, and insulted the photographers. Meanwhile, Amis propounded non sequiturs like, "There may be a Beat Generation, but I doubt it," and Wechsler explained why the Beat Generation was a "joke" beside the liberal causes he'd spent a lifetime championing. Since Jack had just finished abdicating the political leadership others ascribed to him, Wechsler's response couldn't have been less to the point. When Wechsler had finished chiding the Beats' "flight and irresponsibility," Jack pushed the dean aside, grabbed the mike, and called the party onstage "a bunch of communist shits." If they got what they wanted, "the Sovietization of America," Jack warned, there would no longer be such meetings as this. During the ensuing argument, Wechsler told Jack, "We're going to have to fight for peace." Jack came and sat beside him.

As Montagu sleepily requested compassion for these "children who were failed by their parents," Kerouac grabbed Wechsler's hat, put it on his own head, and slumped down in exactly the same position as Wechsler. It was the perfect Zen gesture to test a newsman's egotism. Instead of shrugging off the harmless insult, Wechsler got very angry and demanded Jack return the symbol of his power and poise, and naturally Jack went on cavorting with it.

Despite being slammed in the press, Jack was pleased with one release that said he had proved there *was* a Beat Generation.

He was actually getting a fair share of recognition. *The Dharma Bums* elicited a laudatory letter from Henry Miller and an invitation to visit D. T. Suzuki. Suzuki felt the Koan Jack had written was "too complicated" and reprimanded him for bragging about the length of his Samadhis. Although hurt, Jack was overcome by the venerableness of this shaggy-eyebrowed sage. When Jack asked to spend the rest of his life with him, Suzuki replied, "Sometime."

What Jack wanted, if not constant attention, was something equally hard to come by: the right to demand attention when he willed it. Taking Jack and Allen home from his upstate farm, Lucien pulled into a gas station behind a car containing two beautiful girls. Allen rushed up to them declaring, "I'm Allen Ginsberg!" and Jack announced, "I'm Jack Kerouac!" "*Who?*" asked the girls. Lucien had never seen two men more crestfallen.[291] But whereas Allen understood the absurdity of wanting to be famous, Jack now felt a professional slight when people failed to acknowledge his presence. One of the reasons he kept drinking so heavily was that it was the surest means he had of getting notice. Drunk he could bellow loud enough to shake walls, sober he might have been mistaken for a mute. On one of those rare sober days he entered the Cedar Tavern while Franz Kline was holding forth with Fielding Dawson and several other artists and writers. Outside it was pouring, and Jack stood there dripping and fuming for half an hour waiting to be greeted, until finally he slammed a glass on the table and they said, "Oh, Jack? Sit down."

At the Cedar Jack ran into Matsumi Kanemitsu, whom he had

met in 1948 at the New School, and who was now a famous painter. In everything but his desire to be a great writer Jack seemed a totally different man. During the next few years, Matsumi was to become one of Jack's closest friends. Weary of his ceaseless talk about being victimized—by Jews, publishers, critics, producers, other writers—Matsumi suggested: "Jack, just try thinking you're a simple merchant seaman who writes. I think of myself as a simple house-painter who sells paintings to make a living. Don't think you're gonna be a number-one man. I'd rather be a number-two man." Jack said he'd like to be a "number-two man" but couldn't help wanting to be best because he was "an all-American boy."

Part of Jack's conception of being number one was the privilege of taking any woman he wanted. In late October, at Robert Frank's, he met a recently widowed artist named Dody James Müller. A descendant of Jesse James, she was black-haired, beautiful, full of Texas pluck, and ready for anything. Joyce was present—ostensibly he had come to see *her*—but right off he began a flirtation with Dody, inviting her along to dinner. It was bad enough Joyce had to share Jack with a drinking buddy like Lucien, with whom she felt he was actually "in love." Seeing Dody gazing into Jack's "gorgeous blue eyes" and the reciprocal gleam they shone on her, Joyce asked Jack to step outside and told him she'd had it. He mocked her "no-blesse oblige." Calling him "a big bag of wind," she hit him and left.

With Dody as his lady Jack had a built-in place among the paint-ers' group, which included among others Willem de Kooning, Alfred Leslie, Larry Rivers, Hugo Weber, Robert Beauchamp, Jacques Beckwith, and Miles and Barbara Forst. Several were involved in the Hansa Gallery, an avant-garde cooperative run by Dick Bellamy. At openings there Jack and Dody made a striking couple—not that they were any less conspicuous elsewhere. At any party, Jack was apt to break into a Sinatra song in his sweet but sodden voice, or to try standing on his head (and now usually ending up tumbling over to his embarrassment). To a costume party he wore only a thirties boater but drew everyone's attention by getting on the bandstand and doing a drum solo while Dody played an imaginary instrument by his side. Upstaged by Beauchamp and his girl dancing in a night club, Jack lay flat, spread-eagled, in the middle of the dance floor. He thought of himself and Dody as another Scott and Zelda Fitz-gerald—indeed he contemplated touring Europe with her—and they were quite as legendary. There was the story about the night they went into a Puerto Rican grocery store and made friends with every-body there, and how Jack bought a whole case of beer and heaved it onto his shoulder and it went right over and after the crash they fled . . . or the time he ran across a playground to "make a touchdown" for her . . . or the time after leaving the Half Note they were getting into a cab and a mob of women surrounded it and dragged him out and threw him in the gutter and tore his clothes off although Dody battled them.[292]

The month of November Mémère spent in Florida with Nin. Babysitting the cats in Northport, Jack hoped it would be a time of quiet work. He bought a tape recorder for experimenting with voice rhythms, but mainly he used it to tape jazz and classical music from his Grundig radio—the two big instruments from now on a major feature of his workroom, along with the rolltop desk, typewriter, and gooseneck lamp with improvised tinfoil shade (for a high-intensity beam) perched above it. Creative projects were preempted by the chores of successful-authorhood. Besides his correspondence with a growing circle of friends, among whom he now counted Henry Miller, he answered hundreds of fan letters. He helped Allen gather material for two proposed anthologies, one of American Zen poetry, and the other of Beat writings for City Lights. He also had a monthly column to write for *Escapade*. Ahead stretched the continuous burden of seeing his works into print.

He was dickering with Don Allen for a good advance on *Doctor Sax*. He was consulting with Laughlin over the problem of finding a printer who would handle the obscene material in *Visions of Cody*, and trying to convince Laughlin to do the whole novel rather than just selections. He was advising Irving Rosenthal and Paul Carroll of *The Chicago Review*, whose Winter 1959 issue had been suppressed by the University of Chicago because of offensive material, such as excerpts from Burroughs' *Naked Lunch* and Kerouac's *Old Angel Midnight* (retitled because of Lucien's objection). Although Jack couldn't bring himself to join in the benefit reading that Allen, Peter, and Gregory were to give in Chicago, to defray the printing costs for a new magazine containing the banned works, he contributed a variety of services. He wrote a preface to *Naked Lunch* and when the preface turned out to be more about Kerouac than Burroughs, he directed Carroll to Alan Ansen. Having learned they were stuck for a title, Jack looked at a note on his writing desk—"Get a bigger table"—and cabled Carroll: "Call it *Big Table*."

As soon as word got out that Mémère was gone, so was Jack's chance to work. Carloads of young people arrived asking him to drag race, and were incredulous when he said he couldn't drive. Even Ginsberg visited now that Mémère wasn't there to chase him out (he'd had to hide in the bushes once when he and Lucien came to pick up Jack). Dody too luxuriated in the freedom to live with Jack, though they were harassed by cops who drove them off the beach.

In December the party moved back to the city, and Mémère made sure it stayed there. She had taken a violent dislike to Dody even before she met her. While Dody was staying at the house she had made some sculptures out of candle wax, and when Mémère saw them she assumed Dody was putting "gypsy hexes" on her son.

When Jack brought Dody to dinner in Northport, Mémère took one look at her and called her "the spic savage." Dody wanted to help with the cooking, but Mémère, revolted by her long hair, insisted she wear a hairnet. Dody refused, saying, "I'm going to make spaghetti out of it one day." Certain she was a witch, Mémère was scared of her, and after Dody did the dishes and swept the floor, Mémère cleaned the kitchen again to remove any trace of her "spells." Nevertheless, Mémère didn't dare throw her out. The next morning Dody found her in a vibrating armchair, her feet propped up, watching Sunday Mass on TV with a glass of cheap whiskey and No-Cal ginger ale in one hand and the other telling her rosary. This time Mémère lit into her about going barefoot in the house. What really shocked Dody, however, was the stream of poison-pen letters Mémère began sending her a few days later, demanding Dody stop trying to take her son away from her.

Robert Frank wanted to complete his in-progress trilogy of films with a movie based on *On the Road.* One of the other three was called *The Sin of Jesus.* Initially Jack was incensed at the idea of such a film, shouting at Frank, "Jesus never sinned! Do I write a book called *The Sin of Moses?* I don't insult other people's religions. Why do the Jews insult the Catholics all the time?" But, unlike his mother's, Jack's anti-Semitism was a way of setting people straight about his own beliefs, to strike before being struck. Once people accepted his peculiar religious orientation he would joke about it himself, later suggesting to Frank, for example, that the movie would be "funnier" if he had a black man play Jesus. By contrast, Mémère simply didn't want Jews in her house, considering them scarcely less dangerous than witches.

Frank's partner Al Leslie felt it would be too difficult to film all the locales in *On the Road,* so one day he and Robert drove with Dody to Jack's house to see what suitable script material he might have. After providing Al and Robert with a quart of enchiladas for nourishment, Jack and Dody went out together. Ordering Robert and Al to leave, Mémère vanished into her room. Robert went to a restaurant, but Al persisted in heating his enchiladas. After he'd finished eating them she pounced on him, screaming, "Hey you, Jewboy! You look for my whiskey? No whiskey for you, Jew!" As she locked her whiskey cabinet, he ran out to vomit on the front lawn. When Jack got back he complained to Al, "Why didn't you throw up on the lawn next door?"

But the day wasn't a total loss. Jack had "rewritten" his play *The Beat Generation* by improvising it aloud into his tape recorder, taking all the parts himself and bouncing off Symphony Sid's jazz from the radio. When Leslie heard the tape, he realized why he had had so much trouble imagining actors speaking the dialogue in Kerouac's novels. It struck Leslie that all the characters were really aspects of

Jack, and that no voice but Jack's own could bring them to life. It was decided to make a silent film of Act Three, the scene of the Bishop's visit to the Cassady household, with Jack providing dubbed-in lip synchronization for all the parts.

Production wouldn't start until after the holidays, and in the meantime Jack kept pouring out his incredible reserves of energy in parties that went on for days. Every so often, for a respite of quiet talk, he would call Bob Lax at the offices of the Catholic magazine *Jubilee,* to which he had donated several pieces. He and Bob spent a memorable Christmas Eve together in Northport, Jack reading him many of his unpublished works, and the two of them reading to each other favorite passages from *Finnegans Wake.* Overheated from wine, Jack then retired to his attic room to sleep, as was his wont, with the window open to a winter gale.

That peace was shattered on New Year's Eve, in a succession of parties that led him across the city with the cast and crew of the movie. In the wee hours they ended up at the Artists Club. They were all, in the words of photographer Fred McDarrah, "stoned out of their skulls." Jack fooled with a set of drums, although he looked as if he were about to throw up on them. As he was leaving, McDarrah went to snap his picture. Furiously Robert Frank lunged to stop him, to protect his friend, who could no longer protect himself, from being invaded by the camera. But McDarrah got the picture. A doll clutched in his hand, hair matted on his forehead, Jack looked more like a snarling, wounded beast—a veritable Mr. Hyde—than a man.

5.

Filming began on January 2, 1959, in Leslie's loft near the Bowery. Originally the movie was to be called *The Beat Generation,* but much to Jack's exasperation MGM had already copyrighted that title. For song lyrics Ginsberg brought in some of their poems, and Leslie took a fancy to the lay Ginsberg had coauthored with Jack in 1949, "Pull My Daisy." Set to music by Dave Amram it became the theme song, and the title *Pull My Daisy* was used for the film as well.

Their budget was $15,000. Leslie and Frank each put in $1,000 of their own, and the rest was drawn from the Dreyfus Fund via the agentry of Wall Street wizard and art critic Walter Gutman, who got involved simply because he was charmed by the sculptor Mary Frank, Robert's wife.

The plan was to shoot a minute of action each day. Several fixed positions were established for the camera, and for the first few days Leslie led the actors through their paces ahead of time; then, during the filming, he spoke their lines and they mouthed them back. Leslie

wanted to create characters by merging fiction and reality, the actors' parts with their real selves. The whole cast consisted of ama-
teurs—Ginsberg and Orlovsky as themselves, Larry Rivers as Neal,
Corso as Jack, Richard Bellamy as the Bishop, Dave Amram as a
cowboy—with the exception of actress Delphine Seyrig, who played
Carolyn. Seyrig lacked the ease of movement of the others, who
were so free Leslie soon gave up all effort to control them, but her
impassivity served as the perfect foil to their spontaneity. Looking
down on the action from a scaffold, Jack also perceived that the
film's virtue was its exact visual documentation of real life—this before the era of documentaries. Spotting the awkwardness of Gregory's attempts to act like him, Jack told him: "Be yourself." The
same artless impulse moved Frank to swing the camera according to
the natural eye movements of an observer in the room.

Jack and Leslie had never gotten on well since their first meeting
in the late forties in a Village bar, where Jack was using black slang
in a manner that seemed to Leslie like reverse discrimination, a sort
of glamorization of blacks as underdogs, which ignored their common humanity. Also Leslie enjoyed intellectual discussions, which
Jack abhorred. Even while others conversed about his beloved Céline, Jack ventured no more than three words: "Yeah, he's good." One
day during the filming there was a big scuffle in the hall. It turned
out Jack was bringing in a Bowery bum so filthy and full of sores that
even the bums who lived in the stairwell were protesting. Escorting
him into the loft, Jack announced, "My friend and I want to have a
drink and say hello!" When Leslie flew into a rage Jack began singing a song. Leslie banished him permanently from the set.

After six weeks of shooting Leslie made the first complete cut of
the film, which ran ninety minutes. In Northport Jack taped a pre-
liminary commentary that sounded like the Stage Manager in *Our
Town*. It was apparent at once that he wasn't capable of talking in
lip synchronization with the actors. After Leslie reduced the film to
twenty-nine minutes, Jack improvised a new narration at Jerry Newman's studio while watching the film and listening on earphones to
Amram play jazz. He hadn't slept in a day and a half but was keyed-
up, and the flow of his voice was too magical, like a singer singing, to
interrupt with directions. Instead, Leslie had Jack repeat his performance twice more, one of which was executed mostly in a Chinese accent. Jack also made an additional narration in French,
describing the story as if it were taking place in Lowell, for his own
and Frank's amusement. It was the universality of the story that he
was trying to get across. The emphasis in *Pull My Daisy* upon the
environment of a fifties New York tenement heightens the impact of
the basic human situations the film portrays.

Jack assumed Leslie would just use the tape he liked best, but
actually none of them was as good as his original dictation of the

story, unusable because of the radio music in the background. Leslie preferred to cut between the last three versions to change the pace and to extend the climax, which began, "Is baseball holy?" Disappointed that his rap hadn't been preserved intact, Jack was later embarrassed when *Esquire* film critic Dwight McDonald called the narration the best piece of spontaneous prose he had written. Undoubtedly he was pleased, though, when *Pull My Daisy* came to be honored around the world as part of the American "New Wave" and one of the first underground films. The ultimate compliment came from filmmaker and critic Jonas Mekas, who credited Kerouac's narration with an "immediacy, poetry and magic that is without precedent in American cinema." Yet according to Dave Amram the happiest moment for Jack came at the cast party, when he was surrounded and respected by his fellow artists, and, for the first time, able to share the joy of his creative accomplishment.

He found a way to share even spontaneous composition as he sat at the typewriter to take dictation from Allen, Peter, and Gregory for an article called "The Beat Nightlife of New York" for *Holiday* (later published as "New York Scenes" in *Lonesome Traveler*). *Holiday* editors Ted Patrick and John Knowles had become friends with Jack and continued to provide him with lucrative assignments. In March, Allen, Peter, and Gregory helped with a second article, "The Vanishing American Hobo." It was a way for Jack to let his friends earn some money. Gregory, still penniless, got $500 (which he blew at the racetrack), and Allen and Peter got $500 to pay their boat fare to India, to which they planned to escape from the current American madness.

The change for the worse in America was the subject of "The Vanishing American Hobo." It stands as a classic statement in the tradition of Emerson, Thoreau, Whitman, London, and Dos Passos, of the value to society of the peaceable nonconformist. It is also a lamentation over the loss of trust in one's fellow men—the trust that was so essential to the building of America—as well as a foreboding of a nation that prizes efficiency above the people who produce it. With dread Kerouac saw America becoming *Amerika*, Kafka's inhuman paradise, and in fact used that spelling ten years before it was adopted by Abbie Hoffman.

Another plum dropped in Jack's lap was the editorship of an Avon paperback Beat anthology, to be published tri-yearly. Meantime Viking was coaxing him to do a book on Europe—with vague promises to pay all his travel expenses—in the hopes that a nice cultural work would launder his reputation still further (*The Dharma Bums* had already won back some of the critics alienated by the hedonism they saw in *On the Road*). Allen, however, warned Jack against watering his genius for public consumption. Having talked with Lord, he was convinced that neither Jack's agent nor the editors at Viking understood what an important, innovative writer he was. To correct that situation, Allen recommended Jack get out *Doctor Sax, Book of Blues,* and the complete *Visions of Cody* at all costs.

Postponing the European trip, Jack planned to return to Mexico for the solitude to complete *Desolation Angels.* The second half, to be called "Beat Traveler," would chronicle his adventures between his departure from Mexico City in 1956 and his rise to fame in New York. He was again seeking a spot for his hermit's shack, to escape not only the hounds of publishing and his young hangers-on, but also the relatives in Lowell who were now claiming he had disgraced the family name.

First there was the problem of getting Mémère resituated in Florida, for she was terribly lonely away from Nin. She and Jack hatched the plan of building a duplex on their lots in Sanlando, Florida, so that they could live next door to Paul and Nin. He was to buy some adjoining woodland lots to insure privacy, and it would be a family homestead complete with joint patio for cookouts. Mémère even envisioned young Paul someday getting married and living next door to *his* mother there. However cheap with his friends, Jack had no objection to footing most of the cost of this project. He wrote Nin that the house in Northport, which he owned clear, was worth $14,-000, and that he had $3,000 in the bank, $8,000 in royalties coming in April, and the final installment of $12,000 from MGM for *The Subterraneans* due in June. Nor would he require Paul to pay him back, though he suggested that when Paul could afford it he might contribute to Mémère's living expenses.

Another reason Jack didn't hesitate to leave New York was that he had had a very distressing breakup with Dody in late February. While most authors are content with a philosophical understanding of their subjects, Jack was always moved to practice what he preached. One of the ways he saw to keep the American hobos from vanishing was to go to the Bowery and take care of them. His method was to gather three or four, if possible, and take them to the home of one of his friends for a meal and a good sleep. The trouble was that when he hung out with bums he got drunk with them. The chosen benefactor(tress) would have to accommodate not only a bunch of stinking, scabrous derelicts—any of whom was likely to die on the premises—but a fiercely unreasonable Jack Kerouac as well. Helen Elliott knew the way to deal with him. He would always submit to a forthright request to go away, though to protect the feelings of the bums he'd usually say, "Come on, she's cross today." Unlike Helen, Dody found it hard to say no to Jack and ended up with a studio heaped with bodies. Jack would tell her about what "wonderful angels" they were, and how terribly they had suffered, but she felt he was endangering her, not to mention risking his own life, as some of these angels were strong as an ox.

Jack had talked of wanting to marry her, but she balked at the idea of having to marry his family too. And she was exhausted from following him on five- or six-day, around-the-clock drinking binges—sometimes hitting every White Rose bar in the city—and didn't want to keep putting herself through such ordeals. They had reached a point where all he had to offer her was "his sweet self maybe one and a half days [a month] sober, plus Mémère." The "creatures" he dumped in her studio were the final straw. She told him, "Never darken my door again!" For a few weeks he kept coming around and appealing to her with his "hound dog act"—bewailing his fatness, his "disgusting" appearance, and the fact that nobody loved him any more—until she demonstrated that "never again" was just what she meant.

If women were in some sense replaceable to Jack, men were not, and it was an even harder blow when Gary stopped writing him after the publication of *The Dharma Bums*. Jack pleaded that he had written the book from a sincere desire to unify all the modern factions of Buddhism, and as an answer to cavilers like Gary's Japanese sponsor, who had declared that Gary knew nothing about Buddhism. Gary broke his silence to Jack only to describe a certain hell where writers have their tongues pulled out. People now came to Gary expecting him to behave like the hero of *The Dharma Bums*, and through no fault of his own he suddenly found himself disappointing them, not a pleasant experience to a conscientious man. Fortunately when he left for Japan again in the spring of 1959 he gained some perspective on the affair, and soon he and Jack were again corresponding and planning as before to rendezvous in Japan.

For a couple of years Neal was protected by his prison walls from having to play Dean Moriarty, but the reality of his life there was more horrible than any fiction Jack could create. That spring, the Beat Generation was the subject of a twelve-part series in the *New York Post* by Alfred Aronowitz. All Aronowitz's pejorative preconceptions had melted in the presence of Kerouac's openly broken heart. As a result, he conducted the first intelligent interviews with the Beat writers, and his articles were strikingly honest and nonjudgmental. Reading Aronowitz's story about Neal, Jack was frightened by the stark facts of his life in San Quentin: his armed-robber cellmate, his job sweeping the floor in the textile mill, the extreme discipline that forbade him even to take a piece of candy from his visitors. At the same time he was impressed by the fire still in Neal as he proselytized Aronowitz to Cayce and educated him about the cruelty and arbitrary enforcement of American drug laws. Neal added a fillip about his own lack of interest in *On the Road*, challenging Jack to show his true concern by sending him a typewriter with which to finish *The First Third*. After several weeks of paranoia about how his money might be misspent, Jack sent a check for $50 to

Allen (who was in California) to get Neal a *used* machine. Jack also applied for permission to correspond with Neal, but his petition, like Allen's, was denied.

Jack was suffering from insomnia. In New York he often stayed at Matsumi Kanemitsu's studio, where he liked to sleep in a big Gothic bed he called "the monk's bed." But every hour or so he'd wake up screaming, and one night he told Matsumi, "I don't need a bed, I need a beer." Matsumi rushed out to buy some, but even that provided scant relief.

On April 30, Grove Press released *Doctor Sax*. Reviews were so devastating Jack asked Matsumi to read them to him over the phone, as if muffled by a Japanese accent they wouldn't be so painful. One of the most perceptive remarks, though hardly meant flatteringly, came from Barnaby Conrad in the *Saturday Review*: "I can hardly bring myself to call it a novel." Since the word *postmodernism* hadn't yet been coined, Conrad contented himself with listing everything Kerouac's writing lacked—"charm and compassion and invention and taste"—and filled out the review with several complaints about Kerouac's "dirty words." This level of criticism was fully matched by David Dempsey in *The New York Times*, who railed against the fact that such an "unreadable" and "psychopathic" book had even been published; and by the *Atlantic* calling it "juvenile scrimshaw"; and by the *New York Herald Tribune* calling it "boring." Only *Time* thought it Kerouac's best book, but for the curious reason that it contained "no such adult concerns as marijuana, Zen Buddhism, or women."

The contest for the cleverest Kerouac put-down was won by Truman Capote, who declared on David Susskind's TV show that Jack's work wasn't "writing at all," it was "typing." The quip had an ironic sting since Jack had spent the winter and spring typing up several years' worth of pencil manuscripts, including "Book of Sketches" and *Maggie Cassidy*. The latter, accepted by Avon, was due out in July.

His editor at Avon, Tom Payne, was canny and ruthless and not about to risk an obscenity trial. Since Jack had taken a vow to see the rest of his works printed without editorial changes, Payne came to his house to discuss a troublesome passage in *Maggie Cassidy*. The postscript of Vinny's letter to Jack at the end of Chapter 38 contained five *fucks*. Dismissing them as insignificant, Payne insisted they would have to go, while Jack argued that the integrity of the book depended upon them because they showed an important side of Vinny's character. Jack grew increasingly vehement as he saw that Payne would go ahead with the deletion no matter what he said— that, in fact, the visit had been perfunctory. A few copies of the book containing the *fucks* had already been printed. Turning from Payne to autograph a copy for his friend Frank Feminella, who had come to visit that evening, Jack said, "You keep this; I want *you* to have it, and *you* remember," as though he were entrusting a witness to posterity.

6.

If there were too many *fucks* in Jack's books, there were getting to be too few in his life. Still unwilling to admit that excessive drinking caused his sexual dysfunction, he decided that the problem was his small penis. He developed a morbid fear of people ridiculing his genitals, and as a concomitant began exposing himself all over New York—trying to bring his worst fears to pass, perhaps, to see just how real they were. In Robert Frank's apartment he got into an argument about penis size with actor Robert Blossoms. With Mary Frank looking on, Jack laid his out on the kitchen table—as they used to do in the Pawtucketville Social Club—for measurement. Mary threw them out. At a fancy party with Paul Bowles, Jack exposed himself and invited everyone to do the same. Although the complexity of his behavior in later years defies simple solutions, at least part of his reversion to his parents' prejudice against blacks may have been due to his obsession with the idea that black men have larger penises.

In any case it was strange for Matsumi to hear the author of *On the Road* declare, prior to an opening party, "If there are Negroes there, I'm not going!" Matsumi was relieved, because the party was being given in his honor by some rich people on Park Avenue. But, consistently inconsistent, Jack showed up anyway, with his favorite drinking partner Hugo Weber. He worshiped Weber, who was everything he himself wanted to be: tall, slim, "aristocratic." Weber's aristocracy was mostly in Jack's mind, based on the fact— which impressed him no end—that Weber came from Basel, Switzerland. In reality, Weber was one of the sloppiest drunks on or off the Bowery. They arrived at Matsumi's party dead drunk, and Jack promptly locked himself in the bathroom and passed out.

After the party it was snowing so heavily there were no cabs operating, so Matsumi walked Jack and Hugo to their subway station. Along the way, the latter two decided to have a contest to see who could pee the longest. The loser had to buy more beer. Jack asked Matsumi to close his eyes so as not to see his penis. Near the Plaza Hotel a couple of policemen demanded to know what they were doing. Matsumi explained to the sergeant, who said: "This is indecent exposure!" As Matsumi began to apologize, up came Jack, his penis hanging out of his fly, yelling, "I don't like a bunch of peeping Toms!" Only through Matsumi's politic defense—no one else was on the street, it was just for fun—did they avoid getting arrested.

Not all Jack's pranks were as innocent. Peter's younger sister Marie was living with him and Allen at their East 2nd Street apartment. At four in the morning Jack burst into her room drunk, and did his bogeyman routine, scaring her out of her wits. When Allen screamed at him for disturbing the household, he fell to the floor laughing. Referring to Allen's new beard, Jack bellowed, "Ginsberg, you're a hairy loss!"

Barney Rosset, the publisher of Grove Press, had liked Jack well enough at a cocktail party with Gallimard in the fall of 1958, primarily because Mémère was present to keep an eye on his drinking. Again curiously like Jackson Pollock, Jack was terrified of his mother's censure and would sober up at the mention of her name. Indeed it became a favorite game at parties to tell him his mother was on the phone, just to watch the transformation in his face, voice, and posture. On the publication day of *Doctor Sax* Jack failed to show up at Grove because he was partying with Gutman and a couple of black dancers. But it wasn't Jack's irresponsibility that worried Rosset, it was Rosset's sense that Jack was capable of physical violence if things didn't go right. Though Rosset never saw him assault anyone, he was present once in a friend's loft when Jack, horribly red-faced, started jumping about and exclaiming angrily. Any minute it seemed he might leap out the window, carrying someone with him.

At Hugo Weber's studio, in a stupor and craving fresh air, Jack hung farther and farther out a window several stories above the street. Seeing him about to fall, painter Stan Twardowicz seized him just in time.

"Eighty-sixed" (excluded) from the Cedar Tavern for pissing in the sink, Jack would stand outside the locked door making supplicatory motions to be let in. Twardowicz smuggled him out some beer. At a showing of the Japanese movie *The Lower Depths* (one of his favorites) with Robert Frank, Jack was kicked out of the theater for slugging from a bottle of Thunderbird. Although he complained about the intolerance *in* an America that condemned such harmless pleasures, he never—much to Frank's amazement—lost his love for America itself, as a land of vast beauty and potential good. It was exactly this potential that America, and even many of Jack's contemporaries, failed to see in him. He was being ejected from dozens of New York bars, but what really hurt was to be rejected by people he thought of as friends. When shown the door by Lee Krassner, Jackson Pollock's widow, Jack said, "You don't understand, I'm *Jack Kerouac.*" Krassner roared, *"Ouuuutttt!!!"*

Toilet matters played a significant role in the way Jack was received. With the drunkard's loss of control and urgency of release, he could no longer hit the bowl. He told Matsumi he was going to write a book about him and when Matsumi asked why, he replied, "Because you let me use your toilet."

In May, John Holmes accompanied Jack to a private showing of *Pull My Daisy* at the Museum of Modern Art. They had lunch, then repaired to their respective agents, agreeing to meet at their old bar Glennon's later in the afternoon. Delayed, John arrived late at Glennon's and found Jack loud and argumentative, downing shot after shot of whiskey. John took him to the friend with whom he and Shirley were staying, and they tried unsuccessfully to get him to eat dinner.

He was starting to dissociate in a way John had never seen before; his mind was racing on ahead of itself. It was as though he were trying to say or do something that would show he was still in control, when everything he did unbalanced him further. Acutely aware of the mess he was making of himself in front of John's staid friend, Jack took a Mason jar from the kitchen and in full view filled it with the man's Scotch and put that in his pocket, laughing. As they were leaving for the theater, he suddenly turned around and kissed the man on the lips. In a way the gesture said "thank you," but Holmes also saw something alarming in it. It was a kind of mockery, like Allen's old attitude of "I'm going to *do* the thing that you can't stand most," but beyond even that halfway funny ego-baiting it was the clear message of a man on the way out, who was at a loss to say he didn't want to talk anymore.

That night, at the premiere of Jay Landesman's musical *The Nervous Set*, Jack had to sit by himself. He kept his camel's-hair overcoat buttoned up to the neck, and twenty rows forward John could hear his laughing. But he wasn't laughing at the play, which he thought an awful condescension to *lumpen* beatniks. He was thinking about his unproduced play *The Beat Generation* and his unsold movie rights to *On the Road* and wondering at the curious fact that his life was no longer his. After the show, searching for Jack to say good-bye, John saw the back of a camel's-hair overcoat getting into a cab with Elvin Jones.

There were fewer and fewer people with whom Jack could let down his guard—alcoholic or otherwise—and they were always people who ignored his fame. At Lucien's he had met a six-foot, mountaineering painter named Jacques Beckwith, who looked much like Sammy Sampas. Challenging Beckwith to Indian wrestle, Jack was delighted when Beckwith set him down. Jacques's stories of living in the woods cemented their friendship. One day Jacques got a call to join Jack in a bar. When he walked in, Jack said, "Kiss me." Since he looked so forlorn, Jacques kissed him, and soon found out what had happened: Jack had gone around the bar saying: "I'm Jack Kerouac! Don't you know me?"—and not one person did.

His head could be turned by anyone, and after a while it spun so fast it was no wonder his identity was in doubt. At Luvacci's in the Village with Gutman, Jack sat a group of autograph-seekers around him and commenced to play Socrates with his disciples.

The winter and spring of 1959 he gave numerous readings with Allen, Gregory, and many fine new poets like Ray Bremser, LeRoi Jones, Ted Joans, and Denise Levertov, at such places as the Artists Studio, the Seven Arts Coffee Gallery, the Gaslight Café, the Living Theatre, and Wesleyan University. As always, he read spectacularly, but with a new demand for instant attention that gave a cutting edge to his soulfulness. His baggy pants and checkered shirt with the tails hanging had come to be a kind of uniform, and he sometimes varied the act by wearing a shirt with a big hole in the sleeve and pushing his elbow out from time to time as he read. Not the least of the rewards of being "King of the Beats" was a host of willing female subjects. The dazzle of their adulation rapidly blinded him to his treason against the child Ti Jean he had spent so many years protecting. That treason, that *phoniness*—a word it had never before been possible to apply to Jack—was apparent to the stranger who yelled at one of his readings: "When he falls, man is he gonna fall!" He'd already fallen in so far as he was now capable of viciously abusing even people he respected. At a Living Theater reading, he ridiculed Frank O'Hara's nasal, lisping delivery, gibing, "You're ruining the sound of American poetry, O'Hara!" O'Hara let him hog the stage, but in parting admonished, "That's more than you could do, Jack. My silence is more golden than your blather."

And reasonably sober Jack was the first to know it. The next day he went to O'Hara's and typed an apology on his typewriter while he was out. At one of Robert Beauchamp's parties, some literary type was taunting him to defend his art, tongue-tying him with clever intellectual quips that Jack wasn't prepared to answer. Backed against the sink he finally exploded: "Well I'm not a Hollywood star!" So essentially quiet was Jack that he would sometimes go to extreme lengths to avoid talking to new people. When he met Anaïs Nin he put on a record of his own reading to let that speak for him, and when the phone rang he simply laid the receiver beside the phonograph. He knew too that many of the painters and writers thought of him as a child who wanted to hang around and tag after the adults. But there were things terribly wrong in his life over which he had no control. Stardom, like alcohol and the heroin he turned to now and again, was another drug.

Frequently he had alcoholic blackouts, which were agonizing for a man once so proud of his memory. To keep from missing anything he deliberately slowed himself down, which went against his grain. At the same time, scarcely eating and poisoning his system with alcohol, he was slowing down from lack of energy, which he hated more. Allen, balding, fuller-faced, was aging with grace and dignity, and Jack couldn't understand it. Frightened of losing his boyish good looks and sexual potency, Jack also had to contend with the fact that he was getting older with a mess of a life. Looking anywhere but to his drinking, he began for the first time to attack his mother. He complained bitterly against her control of his money—they had an arrangement whereby she had to cosign his checks—and called her "dull" and "dumb," saying she read the *Daily News* because she couldn't read *The New York Times*. But when anyone suggested he do something about his home situation, he'd start to brag about how "perfect," "wonderful," and "funny" she was.

Matsumi told Jack to forget all his problems, and to stop thinking of himself as a god, but Jack didn't want to listen. Jack equated life with happiness, and happiness with success and money.

"But you have a house," argued Matsumi. "I live in a ghetto in New York. You have a mother. You have two cats! You have a flower to take a piss on! Aren't you happy about it?"

"If you look at it that way, I should be a happy man," Jack admitted, but went on to say that he still wanted to conquer women and win literary honors and, on top of everything, become a saint.

"You're asking too much," Matsumi told him, but again Jack wasn't listening.

The alternative to not getting those things was to withdraw from the competition, which he was doing more and more. Beside the big numbers leading to death there were a variety of lesser methods: free-associating in a torrent that no one could keep up with, keeping his eyes closed or shielding his eyes with his hand, or when all else failed literally crawling into some hole. Once when Peter Orlovsky's girlfriend, poet Janine Pommy, was anxious to talk with Jack she found him under the kitchen table, passed out, and covered with watermelon seeds.

Art is withdrawal put into gear, and Jack was still getting some productivity out of his escapes. Ferlinghetti wanted to publish the complete *Old Angel Midnight*. Adding five thousand words to the text, Jack extended it in the direction of a "space prose" illustrating the endless void of universal illusion, which he now saw as the female principle, personified by the Hindus as Maya, Shakti, and Kali. His enthusiasm was dampened, however, by news that *Big Table* wouldn't release reprint rights to Ferlinghetti. Meanwhile, his monthly *Escapade* column was a cover for the creative work he wasn't doing, since he generally filled it with pieces he'd written years earlier, like the description of a Mexican bullfight, the essay "The Beginning of Bop," notes on his stay in Tangier, and excerpts from *Visions of Cody*.

Drugs too sometimes provided a breakthrough instead of just release. In October Jack took mescaline and had an immensely reassuring vision of the world as "One Flower," with everybody united peacefully in a constellation of saints whose flashing dance it was his duty to report, which he did in a five-thousand-word journal entry. Jealous of Anaïs Nin's LSD experience, he had importuned her for some as if she were a pusher. He was even more anxious to try the hallucinogen after Allen's initiation into its use at Stanford in June.

Since his second experience of "the Golden Eternity" in the fall of 1958, Jack's religious visions were coming more often, and whether or not drug-induced were taking on a hallucinatory character. He saw an image of Cardinal Giovanni Montini wearing papal dress and painted him thus, four years before Montini became Pope Paul VI. He always made clear, however, that his visions were secondary to those of Gerard.

To Frank Feminella, meeting Jack was like meeting the Pope. He was introduced through his fellow sociologist Victor Gioscia, a close friend of Jack's who lived in Northport. Feminella had traveled extensively and met many great men, including some Presidents, but no one had impressed him with "a sense of reality and of history" as much as Jack. They got into a discussion of the Gregorian chant, which Jack called a "jazz Mass." Jack explained that since the chant is unharmonized and unmeasured you sing it as you feel it, and that you have to be actually praying to get the rhythm right. As interesting as was Jack's insight into Catholicism, Feminella was even more impressed by his manner of practicing his religion. That evening Tom Payne was bringing over a notorious nymphomaniac for him; ahead of time Jack went into the bathroom and masturbated so he wouldn't come too quickly with her.

When Feminella told this story to his friend Father Joe Scheuer, a warm and unassuming Passionist priest, Scheuer declared: "That's real Christian charity!" and asked to meet Kerouac himself.

After Vic and Frank introduced the priest to Jack, Jack whipped out some Zen prayers he'd written. When those failed to rock Scheuer, Jack launched an attack against institutionalized religion, asserting that the Catholic Church wasn't interested in spirituality but merely in organization. Scheuer agreed with everything he said. As soon as Jack saw that Scheuer wasn't going to try to reconvert him, it was as if he'd lost twenty years and was again an embarrassed teenager at the rectory of St. Jean Baptiste, a fact all the stranger since Scheuer wasn't wearing priestly garb. Sensing in Jack the little boy awestruck at his own talent, full of adolescent petulance toward the world that would infringe on its development, Scheuer relaxed Jack by drinking wine with him and showing his eagerness to learn from him. Gradually Jack became the man of letters again, and they talked of America, and later of Bach. The evening ended on the front porch, with them identifying the stars and speculating about life after death.

On the way home, Father Scheuer said, "We visited a very holy man tonight."

Gioscia, a professor at Fordham University, was just beginning to break out of his own strictly Catholic background. Vic and Jack had met through the bookstore owner in Northport, and Vic with his Volkswagen quickly became Jack's wheelman. Although he towered above Jack in height, he was like a lamb among lions in the company of Jack's New York friends, and Jack was exceptionally kind and protective in helping him adapt. That is not to say that Jack in any sense corrupted him, but rather that he helped enlarge Vic's world to accommodate not only St. John of the Cross and Brother Antoninus—both favorites of Jack—but also hipsters and beaten people.

A man like Huncke, for example, always knew "what was going down." To survive on the street, his moves had to be as fast as the flashes of truth by which a mystic becomes one with God. Both the beat and the beatific get their revelations from intuition. Both are pushed beyond the limits of the physical and the rational by the horrors of suffering and death. In the case of the Beats, the urgency of vision was poignant with their sense that America had lost its soul. Their homeland was being sold to the colossus of industrial materialism. The holiness in America had been beaten and covered over. It could be ransomed, Jack believed, only by people who had learned to speak not *of* themselves but *from* themselves, who had learned to tap those deep sources that are the fount of all religion. This was why he wrote as he did, in the very same manner as St. John of the Cross had written for the salvation of *his* fellow men. "When God speaks," Jack told Gioscia, "just take it down."

Jack's mysticism was earthy and full of contradictions. He loved the story about St. Teresa walking through a thunderstorm and being struck by a vision just as she stumbled into a mud puddle. After quivering helplessly for several minutes, she got up and shook her fist at the heavens, crying, "Lord, if this is how you treat your friends, it's no wonder you have so few!" That sensibility was very close to Jack's own, for he too railed against God. It was clear to him that life was sacred and not his to take, and yet he wanted to be free of his immense passion. The root meaning of *passion* is to suffer, and he suffered in both senses—to be with things on their own terms, without judgment, and to be hurting. He was in constant pain not only about the condition of America but also of humankind and all life. As he wrote on a napkin for Gioscia: "Every little fishy in the sea worries me like the Children's Crusade."

To deal with the world's inexplicable wrongs Jack felt he had to live in a monastery, and so he made his house a monastery with his mother the Reverend Mother. Like disciples of St. Francis, they would carry basketfuls of cubed stale bread into the back yard to feed the birds, and their cats battened on lamb kidneys and liver pâté that she spent many hours a week making by hand. For Jack there was plenty of mortification too as he'd sit quietly sipping his morning port while she'd yap at him: "Jack-ie, you come home very late last night, you know, you were drunk again, and you know you left the door open, and I told you that I worry. . . ." And sometimes he'd start to argue with her, and then she'd cry, and he'd break down completely and beg her forgiveness.

He was able to resolve nothing because he was speaking directly from a genius whose locus was outside his personality—a genius that might be triangulated somewhere between Rivière du Loup, Hollywood, and heaven. He was a hillbilly scholar and a hokey saint, with Japanese mezzotints and works by El Greco, Rouault, Picasso, Van Gogh, Rousseau, and Gauguin sharing his bedroom walls with little pictures of the Virgin Mary and St. Joseph and the crucifix above the bed. He was determined to blast out from his very heart all the garbage of the age, the processed shit with which fifties America was stuffed like a Christmas turkey—even if much of the time he was flipping or weeping, really weeping—and to give his tortured and grappling nation a voice, even though the job would kill him; and knowing that, he had taken it on anyway, and there was no reforming him now.

Yet with Gioscia, with people he knew couldn't "take it," he was never anything but gentle.

When Jack talked about his visions with Vic, he avoided using Catholic terms, knowing that Vic's bitter quarrels with the Church would create a needless barrier to the experience. By the same token, when he shared his knowledge of Buddhism with Vic, it was never as a guru attempting to change the direction of his life, but always as a friend giving him new, peaceful space to grow in. Furthermore, Jack related Buddhism to the Western idealism in Plato, Meister Eckhart, and Emerson, with which Vic was familiar. Jack helped him see that there is but one experience of enlightenment, translatable into "dialects" as dissimilar as Catholicism and Zen. Jack's point was that words make no difference, because enlightenment exists solely as an experience adding dimension to the human spirit.

In fact Jack's greatest influence upon Gioscia was to switch him, gently, from the conceptual mode enforced by massive erudition to an experiential mode. Again, Jack did this not by talking about life intellectually but by celebrating it. A jazz pianist, Vic got a fresh musical education from Jack that had nothing to do with comprehension. Listening to the radio together, Jack would start snapping his fingers to the beat, or scatting the phrases, and every so often they'd yell to each other, "Hey! Get this!" Jack's hearing of a jazz piano was as good as any professional musician's. When some tired song would come on, one or the other would switch the channel without need to explain. Jack responded only to things he felt, and his method of learning about them was to give rein to his feelings. They'd often listen to records of the old-time blues singers, and there was a prison song from New Orleans that Jack would always wail along to; and at times he'd get so caught up in the experience of those black prisoners that he'd cry for twenty minutes. The reach of Jack's joy was equally extravagant. Not only did he love to read the Bible to Vic as poetry, but he'd sing it with jazz riffs. Jack read Ecclesiastes like a symphony by Mahler.

The connection Jack made between jazz and America opened up Vic's life. As a pianist Vic knew "you can't play the tune just like somebody else," but in his life-style he had learned to fit into traditional molds. Jack showed him that jazz was central to the nature of America, in that America had given room for human individuation on a scale never before experienced in history. Years later, Gioscia was to win numerous awards for teaching sociology with the style he had learned from Jack.

Curiously, what Jack got from Vic was a way back into the traditional structures from which he'd been banished. Jack was always deeply aware of his responsibility to teach, in the sense that it is beholden upon one to whom God's grace has been given to share it. And as he believed that his experiences had genuine religious value, it pained him that he couldn't communicate them to the Church, having been cut off on a number of counts, and irrevocably so because of his divorce from Joan. Part of his friendship with Vic was a flirtation with the Church, the tacit expression of a wish to be accepted back. When Gioscia invited Jack to be interviewed on the Fordham radio show *Dialogue*, he seized the opportunity to confront a Jesuit campus with his heresy.

Vic knew the chances he was taking. Jack was liable to expound about the Jesuits, whom he considered "wise men who had been corrupted by civilization," or come out with one of his quips like, "If Jesus ever started walking across the United States, he'd be arrested outside of Altoona, Pennsylvania." As it turned out, the broadcast proved even more "offensive." Jack discoursed to the effect that life was gentle and God was good and that people should relax and take it easy and that he was weary with suffering and hoped everyone loved everyone. He also talked a little about Buddhism and said there was no point in trying to distinguish between religions, because once you attained a "sense of the beyond," the way you got there was irrelevant.

Angry phone calls poured in. Both Gioscia and the priest who managed the show received sanctions. From His Eminence Francis Cardinal Spellman came word that it was forbidden on Fordham radio to say that it didn't matter whether one was a Buddhist or a Catholic.

7.

In June 1959, Jack sold the house on Gilbert Street. Nin's husband having objected to the duplex idea, the new plan was to build two separate houses on their lots. Mémère went to Florida to help Nin find a house to rent for all of them in the meantime. Jack waited in the house in Northport, since the buyers weren't moving in until August. As soon as the move was completed, he intended taking off for Mexico.

Alone, he was again prey to young people and locals. He developed a paranoia of people watching him, and was angry from lack of sleep and the inability to work. He was absolutely sure that everybody in the world wanted to rip him off or use him, and he had reason.

One night when he was drinking with the clammers in Gunther's bar, there was a bust. A stocky Sicilian named Leo slipped a half-ounce of pot into Jack's shirt pocket. Paralyzed, Jack said nothing until the cops left, but then he demanded, "What the hell did you do that for?"

"If I got caught, I'd get sent to jail," Leo said, "but if they find it on you, you can talk your way out of it."

Jack was so flattered he suggested they cross the street to the Galley for another round, and while they were crossing he took out his notebook to write down what Leo was saying.

Leo said, "Put that fucking notebook away, you're no writer."

"What d'ya mean I'm no writer?"

"You're no fuckin' author!"

"You can't talk to me like that!" Jack said. "I'm a marine!"

Leo punched him under the eye, knocking him flat on Main Street.

Jack asked, "What'd you do that for?"

"It's your fault," Leo said. "Nobody talks to me like that. Put that in your book!"

After that, Jack loved him. The only people he really hated were those who didn't react at all. If you'd swear at him or hit him you were in, because it meant you were relating to *him* and not the famous author.

Being used, Jack felt he had the right to use others. He took Leo to meet Allen, but when they knocked on his door Allen yelled, "Get lost!" Jack told Leo to break down the door, promising to take care of any trouble or expenses. As Leo did so, a boy jumped out of Allen's bed, and grabbing his clothes, ran out. Though Allen hollered about the "good thing" they had spoiled, in a few minutes Jack had him charmed as always.[293]

Stuck in his efforts to get started on the second half of *Desolation Angels*, Jack decided he would write about Lucien and Kammerer instead, since he already had the story down in his apprentice novel *And the Hippos Were Boiled in Their Tanks*. He talked all about the projected novel in front of Lucien and Cessa, terrifying her and profoundly disturbing him. It wasn't only what he wanted to write that was objectionable, but how he wanted to write it. Jack seemed to admire the killing as a heroic deed. Although at their behest he temporarily agreed not to do the book, he would keep bringing up the idea every few months, pushing Cessa to the brink of hysteria. She felt he was breaking up their marriage, while he resented her for taking Lucien away from *him*.

There was no second-guessing him, for he was now observing a complete fidelity to the moment, changing colors like a litmus as impressions flowed through him, simply registering everything and, like Whitman, unafraid to contradict himself. Hidebound anti-communist that he was, when Soviet Premier Khrushchev arrived in Washington in September, Jack protested the fact that "the man Khrushchev" was made to stand bald-headed in a hot sun while Eisenhower made a long welcoming speech.

Jack's compassion was still extraordinary, but nowadays he tended to save it for the broken-winged people he assembled around him. One of them was the brilliant composer Charles Mills, who had charmed Mémère with his perfect manners and Deep Southern flattery. Like Jack, Mills was a man with everything going for him, who, unable to accept success and fame, drowned his hopes in alcohol. At Mills' lowest, Jack sent him a heartening letter, which Mills hung on his wall, as well as a little money to keep him alive.

In July Jack reeled again from the barrage of critical attacks on *Maggie Cassidy*. Dempsey in *The New York Times* damned it with the same faint praise he had given *On the Road*, applauding the book's "poetry" while concluding that as a novel it was "patchy and half-hearted." In the *Saturday Review*, John Ciardi finally appeared in person to condemn the book as "one of our boy's earliest scrolls," using language strikingly similar to that of Bittner in his review of *The Dharma Bums*.

More than ever Jack's indignation turned against the source of life, the womb. Learning that Creeley's wife Bobbie was pregnant, he wrote a bleak letter rebuking them for "bringing another child into the void." But children surfaced the wildest contradictions in his nature. When Northport librarian Joan Roberts, who was buying his house, brought her children over, he found them things to use as toys and bent over backwards to keep them amused. The problem for him was that to accept children was to justify women, whom he would have preferred to deny.

Except when he was with a woman like Lois Sorrells. Twenty-four, Lois had gone to study in Berkeley and married there, but after her divorce had returned home to Northport, where her mother was dying of cancer. While in Berkeley, she had read *The Subterraneans* and fallen in love with Jack, who had clearly been hit in the face by life as she had and just as readily turned the other cheek. That summer she was introduced to Jack by Mona Kent, the soap-opera writer who had formerly owned his house. Caught meditating under his pine, he was "very sweet and very shy" in Lois's presence. But, with Mémère in Florida, he was also happily at liberty, and soon they were playing house in the barren rooms, dancing to Sinatra, and sleeping on a mattress on the floor. It was the perfect therapy for her. As Gioscia observed: "When you played with Jack you were in a treehouse, and you closed the curtains, and it was make-believe and it was absolutely safe. But it was quite real; it was high play."

Lois was something new for Jack: an intelligent, attractive, sexy woman who was intensely devoted to him, available, and made no demands other than that he love her, which he did. As she was working and living in New York, he began coming in on weekdays to visit her, and on weekends she would come to Northport. In a pique, Dody, whom Jack was seeing occasionally, nicknamed Lois "Olive Oil," after the skinny, long-necked cartoon girlfriend of sailor Popeye. Calling himself "Popeye," Jack turned "Olive Oil" into a term of endearment, using the nickname to touch a part of her that no one had touched before.

In late August Mémère wrote him that everything had "blown up" and that she was on her way back to Northport. Nin and Paul were having marital problems, and it may be they felt living with Jack and Mémère would aggravate matters. Scrambling for a place to live, Jack bought a house at 49 Earl Avenue in Northport because it had a finished basement he could use for a study.

It seemed like the start of a new peaceful season of work. His aim was still to complete *Desolation Angels,* and the companionship of Vic and Lois was helping him overcome his block. They'd all sit together in the basement, smoking a joint and sipping Taylor's Tawny Port (of which Jack had gallon jugs stashed all over the house to frustrate Mémère's temperance campaigns). On his thirty-dollar hi-fi Jack played Charlie Parker and Bach's *St. Matthew Passion* and *B-Minor Mass* until he was "hallucinating Parker and Bach, one in each ear." Sufficiently high, he would turn up the volume, go over to his desk, switch on the gooseneck lamp, and begin typing furiously on the teletype roll that fed into the machine. At intervals he would rip off a strip of several feet and throw it into the waste basket and then keep going, ripping, going, and ripping until "it hit." Explaining his method to Vic, he used the analogy of turning on a faucet and waiting until the water ran cold. "Once the water was cold, that was *it*"—he had what he wanted, the Voice that needed no editing had spoken through him.

When the weather got colder he found the basement too damp

and decided to build a workroom in the attic. Afraid of being cheated, he and Mémère worried endlessly about which carpenters to call, and finally hired a crew at an hourly rate. When the men arrived one afternoon, a few days into the job, Jack hopped in their truck and took them out on a two-day drinking binge—paying them wages all the while! Mémère had a fit. As much as he groused about being "disturbed," he was bored and bent on mischief. He started hitting Northport's bars again and brought home half a dozen clammers, who turned the house upside down. And in the city he'd be back on his day-and-night binges, leaving Lois by the wayside and finally checking into some cheap hotel to sleep it off. He was tormented by demons, and he chose to surrender to them, to go with what he had without question, because the more insanity he could tolerate the more he would be enlarged as a man and an artist.

On those binges he was sometimes crazy as a bedbug, having lost all ability to distinguish between fantasy and reality. Beforehand, knowing what was going to happen, like Dr. Jekyll he took precautions. If Vic was driving him into the city Jack would give him traveler's checks with which to pay the bar bills. If he came in alone, he would bring only a few dollars and borrow from Lois and other friends as he went along, always careful to keep vouchers for the exact amounts borrowed. As soon as he got home, he faithfully mailed out checks to those he owed.

But Jack's conservative streak kept running closer to hypocrisy. Having served five years in Sing Sing, Huncke was released that fall and needed money for a fresh start. He asked Jack for a loan of $25, and Jack refused. Here was Jack with a brand new attic study complete with tile floor, bath, and artificial fireplace (with a red light behind the real log to make him feel cozy), and he couldn't spare a hundredth of its cost to help the man who'd given him the word *beat*. When Allen got on Jack's back, Jack wrote a short check, stressing that he expected repayment as soon as possible. Then Mémère got out her envenomed stationery to harass Allen again for involving Jack with "bums," though her threats were getting milder since she saw Allen as a lesser evil compared to some of Jack's new drinking buddies.

Free of animosity, Huncke joined Jack, Allen, Lois, and several others for dinner in Chinatown, and later Jack led them to the Egyptian Gardens to watch the belly dancers. Drinking heavily, he was seized by the desire to touch the beautiful woman writhing her stomach before him. He walked onto the dance floor and knelt before her, his arms extended for an embrace. As she tried to escape he crawled after her, moaning "Yes!" while she screamed "No!"—until the bouncer carried him out. After that incident Huncke avoided Jack's company to keep from feeling pity.

It was terrifying to be "Jack Kerouac." In bars people expected him to give them money, and he'd placate them with promises, and sometimes they'd strong-arm him to exact fulfillment. One night he showed up at Lois's with a guy holding a knife to his back, and she had to buy his release. His attempts to escape that identity were fatuous and futile. He wanted to be a painter, a musician, an actor who played tough guys—anything but a writer. He'd sit in on drums at the Village Vanguard, for example, and then come off more embarrassed than before at the spectacle he'd made.

Gradually the old identity of Ti Jean began to fade from him, and unsure of who he was he would grasp at "Jack Kerouac" like the drowning man's straw. Trying to cash a check in a liquor store, he thrust *On the Road* at the cashier and pointed to the picture: "See, that's me!" When the woman at the door of the Village Vanguard refused to let Lois and him in for free, he pulled out his birth certificate and said, "Here's a paper that proves I'm Jack Kerouac."

For him to accept that identity was as suicidal as his drinking, because "Jack Kerouac" was out of his control, multiplied by thousands of fevered brains. In October he saw Louis Nye parody him on TV as "Jack Crackerjack," a maniac screaming, "Kill for the sake of killing!" The nightmare was taking on a disquieting reality as law enforcement agencies began to act on fear alone. San Francisco police watched The Place and The Bagel Shop day and night. Bob Kaufman was persecuted by an Italian policeman, who resented Kaufman's white wife. In October Kaufman was arrested simply for posting some "offensive" poems in a North Beach café window, and in the jail cell a policeman stomped on his sandaled foot. By June 1960, New York police had closed the Gaslight and several other cafés as "fire hazards."

The most bizarre turn was the move by the F.B.I. to suppress the Beat Generation. In 1961 J. Edgar Hoover stated publicly that beatniks were one of the three greatest threats to America. As early as 1959 Jack reported to Allen many episodes of getting drunk with ex-military officers, who were always telling him, "Why do you want to run around with those radicals, Kerouac? You're an American, not like your fucking Jewish friends." Reading his work in the Village, he recognized a person taping him as the homosexual bosun who had scared him into jumping ship in Norfolk in 1944. Later, in private, the man turned on his recorder again and exhorted Jack to talk about communist involvement in the Beat movement. "You know how the tape ends?" Jack told Stan Twardowicz. "I was fuckin' him in the mouth! That's the F.B.I. for you." And he didn't say it as a joke. He was frightened by the paranoia fragmenting the nation, and felt the sixties augured a "science fiction sinister new America that will destroy us all." Like a contagion, that paranoia affected Jack also through his mother, who would scan the street from behind her curtains, convinced that every man in a parked car was a federal agent.

No wonder, then, that Jack increasingly discountenanced Allen's crusade for political reforms. Another thing that antagonized Mémère and him was Allen's indiscretion in discussing Jack's personal life; on WBAI radio, for example, Allen announced that he had "had" Jack a few times. Yet, as Allen reminded him, Jack had often drunkenly screamed in public, "C'mon, I'll fuck you!" to Allen and other men. More importantly, Allen never failed to defend Jack to detractors. At a party, Norman Podhoretz took Allen aside and said (as Ginsberg recalls), "You're OK. If you'd only get rid of Kerouac and Burroughs, then you could have a career in New York as a writer." Allen looked at him as if he were the villain in a grade-B movie. It dawned on him that Podhoretz actually thought the Beat writers had gotten together for the purpose of "making it." Ginsberg began to curse Podhoretz's stupidity, and as Podhoretz prepared to meet Allen's imaginary blows, Norman Mailer rushed between them yelling, "Don't hit him!"

What Ginsberg saw that night frightened him immensely. It was "this enormous suppressed violence of their own which they were projecting into us." Dreading the outbreak of that same violence, Kerouac put on the protective coloration of a fanatical patriotism.

In the light of his severe alcoholism and frequent attacks of delirium tremens, Jack would have preferred to make no more public appearances. But when he was invited to read on *The Steve Allen Show*, Mémère told him he had to do it. Not only would he earn $2,000, but he would be viewed by thirty million potential book buyers. Against his better judgment Jack accepted, and made train reservations to Los Angeles. Then he went to the Northport clothing store to buy dress pants and a sports jacket. Wandering at sea among the resplendent racks, in his untucked flannel shirt and baggy pants, he was mistaken for a mental patient from nearby Pilgrim State Hospital by the proprietor, Ken Arndt. As Ken attempted to evict him, Jack asked, hurt, "Don't you know who I am?" After he was properly identified, Jack bought a pair of grey slacks and a grey tweed jacket. The slacks he wore on the show and never again, eventually giving them to Twardowicz to paint with. The jacket he wore on only a few subsequent occasions, the last being his funeral.

Of course he was excited about getting material for his long-envisioned novel about Hollywood. After the show he was to go up to San Francisco for a film festival in which *Pull My Daisy* was entered. Most alluring was the chance to see Neal, who would be paroled in six months. Equally excited, Neal scheduled Jack to address his class in comparative religion taught by Gavin Arthur.

He was due to appear on *Steve Allen* on November 16. Since he procrastinated leaving until the day before, he had to fly, although he was afraid of airplanes. Following Mémère's instructions, Gioscia drove him to the airport, bought his ticket, put his money in his pocket, and babied him until he got on the plane. Jack asked Vic to accompany him all the way to the gate. Usually in parting they would kiss, but Jack refrained this time to protect Vic from hostile glances. Instead, he took Vic's arm and put his forehead to it, saying, like Christ to John, "If I don't come back, take care Mémère."

8.

On the show, holding a copy of *On the Road* with the last page of *Visions of Cody* taped in, Jack actually read a medley of the conclusions of both books. After a good performance, he threw up offstage.

Whether watching rushes of *The Subterraneans* or dining with the stars or hiking by himself down Sunset Boulevard late at night, Jack found Hollywood unutterably drab and dreary, and he only enjoyed himself there after he met up with Al Leslie and a group of Leslie's friends. One day the whole bunch got silly on vodka and decided to visit Steve Allen. On the way they stopped at an army-navy store and bought a metal footlocker as a present for Allen. With Leslie bearing the locker, they paraded past the secretaries and into Allen's office. Profoundly embarrassed, Allen clapped his hands on his desk and lowered his head. Leslie dedicated the locker to Allen for his contribution to American society. Allen said nothing. Finally Leslie said "Fuck you!", and taking back his locker, walked out. Jack gave Allen the finger and followed Leslie. For months after, Jack anguished over that gratuitous insult but could never get up nerve to apologize.

In addition to the $2,000 he had made on TV, Jack picked up $12,000 from MGM, the balance due on their purchase of *The Subterraneans*. He sent every cent to his mother and lived off Leslie all the way to San Francisco. Moreover, Leslie had to take care of Jack as if he were a little child. In San Francisco, he stayed with Whalen in a communal residence called East-West House or Hyphen-House, at 1713 Buchanan.

At Hyphen-House Jack met a whole new group of writers and artists including Lew Welch, Jay Blaise, and Albert Saijo. A friend of Whalen's from Reed College days, tall and handsome, Welch had a high-voltage intellect and almost as much energy as Neal Cassady. What poetry he had written showed great originality, but as with Neal, tremendous problems in adjusting to society had stymied his production. Jay Blaise was a dark, handsome French-Canadian from Vermont, who had come to California to be an artist after being inspired by *On the Road*. Albert Saijo was a Japanese poet.

Hyphen-House was no placid colony of self-contained workers; it was a madhouse of Zen lunatics. At two in the morning, arguing about the mistakes of the American government, Jay would emphasize each of his points by flinging some object through one of the numerous panes of the latticed windows. Joanne Kyger, Gary Snyder's fiancée, made a point to Jay by hitting him in the face with a full half-gallon wine jug. Meanwhile, John Montgomery was always staggering in and out with superfluous pieces of furniture. The humor of Albert and others was wry and nutty, tending to subjects like the benefits of washing one's asshole after defecation.

Jay introduced Jack to a literate boxer named Bob Miller, who had once driven getaway cars. Their rapport was perfect, as Jack wanted to go cruising all the time and Bob just wanted to drive. One night they went to The Paddock to watch old fight films. Dressed in his "peasant costume"—mustard canvas pants, pullover sweater, and beret—Jack ordered drinks for two "Powell Street bimbos" at the other end of the bar. Failing to get their attention, he skipped over to them and merrily announced, "I'm Jack Kerouac!" They replied, "Yeah? Well, fuck you!" Downcast, he led Jay and Bob to another bar, where he saw two more bimbos. He told Jay, "From now on you be Jack Kerouac, and I'll be Jay Blaise." Buying the girls drinks Jack introduced himself, then said: "By the way, over there is Jack Kerouac." The girls took off like roadrunners for Jay, dancing attendance on him while Jack pleaded, "Hey! I'm Jay Blaise!" They told him, "Beat it, bum." [294]

A fifteen-year-old Chinese girl came to interview him and floored him with her first question: "How are you?" Afterward he just bellowed, "It's all true stories!" to each of her questions, and finally told Montgomery to field them.

He was growing daily more insecure, and when he discovered Helen Elliott was in town he wanted a romance with her. One night he asked to walk her home. Since she said she was too tired to walk, he said, "We'll run home!" and chased her all the way. In bed, he stopped short.

He and Al Leslie joined Robert Frank for interviews regarding *Pull My Daisy,* and as usual Jack was petrified and had to tank up first. In Leslie's view, Jack had such an apprehension of being used by strangers that he only wanted to deal with friends, and when he had to deal with strangers, he'd erect impenetrable walls and "Wagnerianize his fear to make it bearable for himself and others." At the interviews, ignoring the questions, he sang, did his Indian routine, and (a week later in New York) enlivened a radio tape by asking the interviewer, "Have you cleaned your asshole today?"

Arriving at a party in his honor at The Matador, Jack looked so sleazy and disheveled he was turned away at the door. Tuxedoed Leslie finally got him admitted, but no one at the party would talk to them. Finally David Niven appeared and toasted the guest of honor: "Strike another blow for freedom, Mr. Kerouac!"—after which the other guests grew suddenly hospitable.

The main cause of Jack's increasing anxiety was the approach of his speaking date at San Quentin. In a postcard Neal had already twitted him about his fame, saying he continually heard inmates in the yard mispronouncing the name Kerouac. Jack worried that Neal scorned him for making money off what for Neal had been plain good times. The day before they were to meet, *Pull My Daisy* was shown at the festival. The film got a terrible reception, primarily because that week *Life* came out with a horrendously slanted article on the Beats called "The Only Rebellion Around." Its author, Paul O'Neil, could have won an award for the number of cheap shots he got in per page. His ingenuity produced belittling epithets for half the major midcentury American writers; Kerouac's was "the only *avant-garde* writer ever hatched by the athletic department at Columbia University." At the festival there was also a perverse reaction against Jack and his friends for getting all that attention. They found themselves treated like a gang of "violent, macho bikers." So drunk he fell off the stage, Jack overslept the next morning and missed his date at San Quentin.

In the meantime, Neal had been getting cold feet too because he didn't like friends to see him in his present condition. Al Hinkle offered to drive Jack to the prison, but at the last minute Jack begged off going, knowing the meeting would be traumatic for both of them.

He quickly blotted out thoughts of Neal's gloom in another frantic cross-country drive, riding shotgun in Lew Welch's Jeep station wagon, while Albert Saijo meditated in the back. Lew's nonstop rap helped Jack retrieve the past. For Lew's sake they stopped in Las Vegas, but as ever Jack refrained from gambling. On Route 66 they pulled out a roadside cross marking a highway fatality. In St. Louis they stopped for a striptease. The best part of the trip was their oral composition of haiku and short poems about the road, which Jack took down in his notebook.

Their first stop in New York was East 2nd Street to present Allen with the cross. Later at Fred McDarrah's, despite the bright lights and clicking camera, they jointly composed a poem for the forthcoming illustrated anthology *The Beat Scene*. For a few more days they caroused together in the city. Visiting the First Zen Institute of America, Jack was too drunk to concentrate on the ceremony and spent the time writing little poems on Albert's program, such as: "Wait! Ho!/ Watch the candle burn," and comments, such as: "This is as dull as Old Angel Midnight."

In Northport Lew and Al stayed a few days at Jack's house, where Mémère cooked and cleaned for them, glad Jack again had polite friends. After another bout in the city bars in early December, Lew and Al left for California. As much as Al loved Jack's "great beauty and sweetness" of character, he was repelled by his equally great sadness. Jack drank as if he were performing an act of penance.

And for Lew, an outdoorsman, the city was anathema. He tried to convince Jack to escape the madness, and Jack agreed to join him on a camping expedition along the Rogue River in Oregon the next spring.

Released in October and generally ignored, *Mexico City Blues* was lambasted as Buddhist idolatry by Kenneth Rexroth in the November 29 *Times*. Writing to Gary, Jack reaffirmed his love for Rexroth's poetry, and wondered how Kenneth could have forgotten that he had once promoted Beat literature. It was especially hard for Jack to bear the burden of such hate now, since he again lacked his two chief Beat compatriots: Gregory had returned to Europe the previous summer, and Allen was to leave in January 1960 for a writers' conference in Chile, and would spend several months in South America.

Staying out of New York became essential to Jack's health, but he was never capable of leading just one life, and his best intentions merely paved the road back there. On New Year's Eve, 1959, he refused to join Lucien for their traditional rout *unless* Lucien paid his cabfare in from Northport. It cost Lucien $20 to get Jack and Lois to his party. Later in the evening Jack took off his shoes, expelling scads of crumpled greenbacks. He had no intention of cheating anyone, and eventually sent checks to all the people from whom he borrowed during his long debauch; he had simply needed an excuse to trick himself into it.

Home in Northport he told Lois he was "safe for one thousand years." He made a New Year's resolution to exert his own will and "not just follow everybody" as he had been doing, out of bewilderment, since the publication of *On the Road*. He evaded Ginger, who was in New York looking for him. Marriage to Lois seemed the only permanent solution to his instability, but he puzzled over the problem of how he could have a wife and still obtain the solitude necessary to work. He considered buying a cabin in the Berkshires or Adirondacks, a couple of hundred miles from New York, and having Lois join him by bus on weekends.

He succeeded in getting a $7,500 advance from Avon for *Tristessa*, as well as their assent to his demand for no editorial changes. He blasted Harcourt for selling reprint rights to *The Town and the City* without notifying him. At the same time he realized his tangle with the publishers was just a diversionary action, for he had already squeezed more money out of them than the majority of serious writers. In over two years he had completed not one creative work. The truth of that barrenness shook him one day when, bound for his attic, he told his mother, "I'm going to write letters now," and suddenly remembered how he used to say just, "I'm going to write now." To avoid answering all letters immediately, he devised a filing system—"Fan Letters," "Interesting Letters," and "Cream File."

His new resolve to finish *Desolation Angels* resulted in four more

false starts, totaling forty thousand words. He asked Lois to come to
the house on weekends in the hope that her comforting presence
downstairs would coax his writing, but as soon as she arrived he
couldn't resist whisking her up to the attic. His desperate need for
her was not the problem but rather the result of his deepening malaise over his infamous position in American letters. He might have
expected his literary techniques would be questioned but had never
dreamed his heart could be so thoroughly misunderstood. Especially
disturbing was a letter from some fan suggesting a new hero for Jack
to write about: a high school student who robbed from private
homes and later got elected vice president of his class. That such a
selfish character could be mistaken for Dean Moriarty cast doubt
upon not only Jack's ability to communicate, but, much more fear-
fully, upon the ability of America to receive what he had to say.

That lack in America was nowhere more apparent than in the
petty vendettas of her most learned scholars. In the *Saturday Review*
of February 6, John Ciardi continued to flog a half-dead Kerouac in
his "Epitaph for the Dead Beats." "The Beats like to claim the obsessive violence of Rimbaud as theirs," wrote Ciardi, "but too much of
what they do is much closer to the raveled nerve-ends of Huysmans.
For the Beats are sprung out of a generation that had it easy." One
wonders about the sanity of an age that assumed the critical function
is to make life hard, as much as one wonders whether critics like
Ciardi never realized the self-fulfilling power of their pronounce-
ments.

Lois was the one bright hope in Jack's darkening future. Since
she came from a very respectable family and was quiet and well-
mannered, Mémère had no arguments to use against her. Although
Mémère resented Lois and Jack retiring to the private world of his
attic, she saw that it was in her best interest to feign ignorance of
what went on there.

When they weren't dancing or making love, he often drew her
pictures of the Virgin Mary. They also read to each other. Discovering her a poet "a lot like Emily Dickinson," he recommended her
work to several publishers. He was intrigued by the serendipity of
her maiden name, Milemore (the last syllable pronounced like
"moor"), since he believed the name Kerouac derived from Celtic
words meaning "house on the moor." Much of the time they listened
to music and sang along. By now Jack had most of Sinatra's repertoire by heart, and he would endlessly repeat songs like "I've Got the
World on a String," "It Was Just One of Those Things," and "More
Than Glad to Be Unhappy." Listening to the pain in his voice, so
much like Sinatra's, Lois "felt a hole in her stomach." Yet the reality
of Jack's tragedy was softened by its beautiful expression, to a point
where she sometimes wondered whether they didn't love Sinatra
more than each other. Actually it was their extraordinary sympathy

for each other that permitted their relationship to outlast almost all his others. Although at times they wept together, they also buoyed each other with jokes like: "Shall we get lobotomies now or shall we wait?" Perhaps because Lois asked so little, he was more prone than in the past to practice the kindness he felt. Learning that she was at her father's house in a deep depression, he carried his tape recorder on his back four miles, in the middle of the night, so that she could cheer up listening to Handel's *Messiah*.

For a time they almost lived as husband and wife. When Lois slept over Jack would wake her gently, sometimes pretending to dust the room, and then cook her breakfast. He talked seriously of getting a rose-covered cottage for both of them, his mother, cat, and their pink refrigerator. Gradually she came to realize that his emphasis upon his promise to care for his mother was his way of admitting that *he* needed to be cared for (something he was not able to say outright). It was as if he were saying, "Don't anybody leave me." Perhaps the reason he kept a distance from most people was that up close it was easy to see his fatal weakness. Lois saw the King of the Beats costumed in the inside-out morality of a small-town Catholic mama's boy, and she saw the double-edged guilt from that disguise (which he wore rather than show his true individuality) destroying him.

That guilt also made him totally ineffectual as a man of the world. He wasn't capable of fending for himself, let alone a wife and family. With Lois he traveled to the Amish territory in Pennsylvania to look over a property with a cabin and a brook. On the bus he got drunk and started singing with some men in the back, and when he and Lois got off he discovered his pocket had been picked. With no money, they checked into a hotel and spent the evening riding up and down in the elevator because it was the only affordable place with music they could dance to. They lived off room-service meals until their credit was cut off, then wired Miles Forst for money to pay the bill, and went home.

In New York that April, Jack met Dody with her new lover Willem de Kooning. Exhausted and without Lois to restore his confidence, he pleaded to be taken back to her apartment, where she was going to cook a meal for de Kooning, Lucien, and Cessa. She let him come, and she and the men stayed up all night talking and drinking. After they slept a little, Bill went out for vodka, and they cured their hangovers with *huevos rancheros* and Bloody Mary's. The routine of talking, eating, drinking, and sleeping lasted over two days. On the third day Jack, Lucien, and Bill made a run to the liquor store together. Along the way, de Kooning complained about the repulsive silk-screen print in the window of a cleaners, and Lucien promptly kicked in the plate glass. Out ran the owner and his son, and Lucien and Jack tried to explain about the honor of being visited by "the world's greatest writer, the world's greatest painter, and the world's greatest journalist." De Kooning saved their necks with a $100 traveler's check. Back at Dody's, in great agitation, Jack called Sterling Lord to come and get him. At home in Northport he subsequently suffered two days of sweating, trembling, and breathlessness so severe he feared a heart attack.

After a few days of reform, staying in his room playing his baseball card game and taping from the radio, boredom made him "call for his dragon." [295] He couldn't stay out of the city, despite his dread of becoming unhinged by his own merciless thirst for oblivion. He was becoming a mean drunk. In the Cedar Tavern he took Kenneth Koch's stein of beer and poured it into Kenneth's upturned hat. He ridiculed Lafcadio Orlovsky, Peter's touchy, mentally deficient brother, whom previously he had helped care for. At a party at Robert Frank's he met Thomas Merton and was too drunk to exchange a few sensible words with this man who had once been his model.

Even at home he was drinking hard; and, what really worried Mémère, he had virtually stopped eating. In late April, he fell down in Penn Station and smashed his elbow. During a week-long drunk in May, he fell on his head on the Bowery. Afterward, with his face "redder than a red beet cooking hot," [296] he appeared at Peter's looking close to death. He told Peter he was distraught over an article in Hearst's *Journal American* (which in the 1940's had been Jack's favorite newspaper) calling himself, Allen, and Peter "black spots on America."

It is so characteristic of the man that he should have been vulnerable to defamation at the peak of his career. Spring of 1960 marked his professional *tour de force*. The New Directions limited edition of *Visions of Cody* was selling out. LeRoi Jones published his long poem "Rimbaud" in *Yugen* and brought out *The Scripture of the Golden Eternity* with his Totem Press. Avon issued *Tristessa* in June. McGraw-Hill had accepted a collection of his *Holiday* pieces called *Lonesome Traveler*, to be published in the fall. Ferlinghetti had agreed to do a selection from the *Book of Dreams* with City Lights. Jack's books were being translated into twenty languages, including Japanese. There was a new Hanover record of him reading blues and haiku with jazz responses from Al Cohn and Zoot Sims, and the movie of *The Subterraneans* would be released in July. Though Avon, under new ownership, had canceled his Beat anthology, he was (and would be) featured prominently in a variety of current and coming anthologies, among the most notable *The Beat Generation and the Angry Young Men*, Seymour Krim's *The Beats*, Don Allen's *The New American Poetry 1945–1960*, *The Beat Scene*, Thomas Parkinson's *A Casebook on the Beat*, and LeRoi Jones' *The Moderns*.

9.

In April Ferlinghetti had come to Northport to sort through Jack's manuscripts. The two men became good friends, finding that they had in common a French childhood, high-school athletics, seaman days during the war, a vagabondish propensity, and many favorite authors including Wolfe and Baudelaire. In June, learning that Jack was being pushed to the brink of madness by unwanted visitors, insomnia, nightmares, stomach cramps, the return of his phlebitis, and a general horror of confinement, Ferlinghetti offered him use of his cabin in Big Sur. Besides a convalescence in solitude, Jack would get a chance to work directly with Lawrence on *Book of Dreams.* Equally attractive was the possibility that the experience might lead to a new novel. Hastily accepting, Jack left New York by train on July 17, expecting to "sleep" in the woods until October.

He asked Ferlinghetti to keep his presence in California secret from everyone, but as soon as he hit town he went to North Beach, got drunk in Vesuvio's, and burst into the midst of a Saturday night crowd at City Lights Book Store. With William Morris, a young painter, Jack went on a two-day binge, picking up Whalen along the way and ending up at the Mars Hotel on Skid Row.

Monday he took a bus to Monterey, then a cab to Bixby Canyon, arriving late at night. It was the height of the foggy season, and even with his railroad lantern he barely negotiated the steep dirt road down the precipice to the cabin. Next day he found himself situated beside a cliff that reminded him of the "Mountain of Mien Mo" he'd been seeing lately in his nightmares, and to add to his terror the canyon was overspanned by a frail wisp of a bridge jutting through the sky. Below it there was tangible proof of the doom it presaged: a rusty auto that had careened off years before.

For a few days he occupied himself with building a dam in the creek, cutting wood, making the fire, cooking meals, washing, hiking, playing his baseball game, and reading *Dr. Jekyll and Mr. Hyde.* His sense of humor returned—he dubbed the local donkey "Alf the Sacred Burro" after Coleridge's "Alph the sacred river" in *Kubla Khan*—as did his wholesome boredom, which, when not derailed by revelry, had always led to fresh writing. Every evening he would navigate with his lantern to the rocky shore. There, dressed in a fisherman's hat, raincoat, and waterproof pants, he would write "the sounds of the sea" in a notebook protected by a plastic bag. His aim was to fulfill James Joyce's plan of recording in stream-of-consciousness syllables the rhythms of the ocean. The result was a long, playfully mimetic sound-poem, "Sea."

At last his creative block was broken, but he had paid a high cost in nerve. The sustained isolation of serious writing leaves a writer raw to the world, and the thundering waves of Big Sur overwhelmed

Jack's open heart with a sense of the annihilation he had long been coyly seeking. Now, suddenly, death was heavy on his mind, and he saw evidence of it everywhere. Daily he grew sick watching dry leaves being blown relentlessly into the ocean. Three weeks after his arrival he went down to the shore one afternoon, took a deep breath of sea air, and swooned with nausea. At that moment he decided to leave Big Sur. Although he rationalized the incident as "an overdose of iodine," he also knew that blast of desolation came from an emptiness in his life he could no longer ignore.

He packed his rucksack and set out to hitch the eighteen miles to Monterey. Painfully, with every new blister from the hot tar pavement, he learned that modern sanitized tourists did not pick up hitchhikers. Hours later, his feet burned and bleeding, he was finally driven to the bus station by a man in a small truck.

Braced by a good night's sleep in the Mars Hotel he went to see Ferlinghetti, who gave him a letter from his mother. Mémère described, in gruesome detail, the death of their cat Tykey. The news hit him as though he had just learned of his brother's death. He went out drinking with Phil Whalen and Les Thomson, another Hyphen-House boarder, until Phil and Les gave place to his true drinking buddy, Lew Welch. Accompanied by Lew and Lew's friend Paul Smith, a handsome blond teenage singer from Reno, Jack went on another long bat in San Francisco. Cashing $500 in traveler's checks Jack picked up all the tabs for his fast-growing entourage.

Wanting to meet Neal, who had been paroled in June, Lew drove Jack, Paul, and John Rapinic (of the Seven Arts Coffee Gallery) down to Los Gatos. On the way they emptied a couple of bottles of Scotch. When they arrived late in the evening, Neal was at work recapping tires. As Carolyn went to embrace Jack, he shoved her away with a rude remark. He was just as truculent with his friends, complaining that they only loved him for his traveler's checks; and then as if to prove it, he led them to one of the ritziest restaurants in town for a take-out dinner. While they waited for the food, he tried to seduce a waitress and to impress everyone there with the fact that he was the world famous author Jack Kerouac. Later they visited the tire shop, where Neal, begrimed and wearing goggles, looked like Vulcan in his forge. Since he was a convicted felon, the railroad had refused to rehire him, but he showed no bitterness. His reunion with Jack was less than joyful only because he was deeply embarrassed by Jack's sloppy drunkenness.

The group stayed over and Jack slept under the prune tree; sober in the morning he was his old gentle, loving self with Carolyn. But his eyes were tormented, she thought, like a character from Poe. He told her he had learned why Buddha forbade the use of alcohol. But when Lew Welch got up, he forgot his troubles with jokes and monkeyshines that went on until they left for the city.

Drinking steadily, Jack one night egged on Bob Miller to show him his getaway driver's technique, and they came down Gough toward Market covering half of each block in mid-air. Bob had some friends who wanted to meet Jack, but no sooner was he introduced than he pissed all over the bathroom, and the lady of the house ordered the "son of a bitch" out. Back at Hyphen-House, Jack painted a man on a cross and underneath the figure wrote "Duluoz." A group of African drummers living there gave the beat to a party that went on for several days. Miller, one of the few to go the distance with Jack, saw him take out his notebook every morning at sunrise to record the past day's events.

With Lew and his girlfriend Lenore Kandel, Jack went to visit Albert Saijo, who was recovering from tuberculosis in a sanitarium near Tulare. Jack worried to find Albert subdued and lacking his usual relish for funny tales, and in parting contrived a game to bring him back to life. Walking away, Jack would suddenly whirl round and wave again, or duck behind a tree and pop out waving; soon Albert was responding with even more extravagant gestures. They carried on these antics until they were so far apart that the sadness of saying good-bye was already forgotten.

Meanwhile, Neal had lost his job and needed to borrow $100 for his mortgage payment. Jack offered to *give* it to him. Since the weekend was coming up, he thought it would be a good idea to have Neal join him, Lew, and Paul at Ferlinghetti's cabin. Ferlinghetti decided to make a big party of it by coming down himself with his friend Victor Wong, and invited Whalen and the McClures too. Ferlinghetti's jeep followed Lew's down to Los Gatos. Later they were to rendezvous with McClure in Santa Cruz and to visit Henry Miller, who was there also at a friend's. Miller had written a laudatory preface for the paperback edition of *The Subterraneans,* and on the phone now he told Jack how anxious he was to meet him. In Los Gatos the group went out for pizza and drinks; and perhaps to avoid letting Miller see him in such bad condition, Jack encouraged everyone to keep drinking and making merry until past Miller's bedtime.

Jack insisted on visiting the Hinkles in San Jose. In their kitchen he read his poem "Sea" with magnificent sound effects, then praised Helen as one of the few women who always fed him. He was so drunk he knocked his reheated pizza on the floor. When he asked her to help him outside, she feared he was about to vomit, but he merely wanted her to hold him up while he peed.

After he returned to Neal's, the whole crew made directly for Big Sur.

The next day McClure and his wife and daughter arrived. There was a log-chopping contest (cool, dogged Ferlinghetti the winner) and a big steak feast. Jack undertook to open all the wine bottles, proudly demonstrating the special twist it had taken him years of mingling with bums to learn. They rapped, told stories, and read poetry. Jack was very taken with McClure's *Fuck Ode* and *Dark Brown,* and offered to help him get the latter poem published by Olympia Press in Paris. McClure also learned a valuable lesson from Jack about literary discussions. Several people were asking one another about what books they had read, and the conversation never got beyond the enumeration of titles. Jack castigated them for "mutual intellectual masturbation," and suggested they would learn more by each giving his personal impressions of a single book.

He struck up a friendship with Victor Wong. Son of one of the most politically influential families in Chinatown, Victor had rebelled against tradition by marrying outside his race, getting divorced, and becoming an artist. At times hostility from his own people was so great that he feared for his life, and from Caucasians he received only contempt and condescension. Knowing how highly Jack was respected by his peers, it astonished Victor that he should so warmly praise his drawings. Moreover Jack was the first Caucasian to show him "utter acceptance as a human person."

Jack also impressed Victor as much deeper than any of the others. Often he was silent, and his silences were quite different. Like an old man Jack would brood, and yet again like a child he would simply be quietly looking on. When he was that child, Jack seemed to be watching the world like a motion picture. At other times he seemed to be straining to hear a voice that never spoke to him. He hesitated to join conversations even though Lew and Neal frequently goaded him to talk, but occasionally he would say something that showed he had been paying attention. After Victor had been telling about his daughters, Jack said matter-of-factly, "I have a daughter too." But when Victor pressed him to describe her, his brows drew down and seemed to darken, signaling a definite end to the discussion.

That night, after a bonfire on the beach, Jack put almost everyone to sleep reading from *Dr. Jekyll and Mr. Hyde.* Enchanted by his monotone, Victor suddenly realized that Jack was no longer reading from the book, but improvising. Victor began to make up lines as wild as his, and they answered each other for hours in a magical harmony until the candle flickered out.

Sunday they all went to a nearby hot-springs bathhouse owned by Jack's friend, novelist Dennis Murphy. Everyone went in nude but Jack, who wore a bathing suit, and Neal, who didn't undress at all. Although in front of his women it was hard to get Neal to put clothes *on,* in public or before children he was as modest as Jack. Later they had dinner at a sumptuous restaurant, where Jack downed numerous Manhattans. The sweet vermouth on top of all the sweet white port he'd been drinking filled his blood with sugar, and he was in a highly nervous state. On the return trip he got into a violent argument with Lew over some minor point of literature. Finally Lew stopped the jeep just short of a blind curve and made Jack get out to kneel with him on the yellow line in a ceremony of appeasement. Victor Wong huddled in the back, knowing they'd all be wiped out by the first car to come around the bend. Miraculously they got back to the cabin. Everyone had to leave that evening except Paul Smith, who volunteered to stay with Jack. After a long night drinking, talking, and singing with Paul, Jack awoke with the D.T.'s.

Paul hitchhiked to McClure's. Left alone for a few days, Jack recovered his composure. On Friday, Paul returned with the McClures, and shortly after their arrival, Neal and his whole family barged into the cabin in a dazzling file of golden heads. As of old, Jack was humbled by the love of this good family, but it took only one joint—shared in private with Neal—to bring back his paranoia. He grew fiercely jealous of Paul's attention to Carolyn, though Neal himself was unconcerned and even arranged for her and Paul to be alone while he took Jack and the children into Monterey for more wine.

The next morning Jack's mood improved after Carolyn convinced him she had held off Paul's siege. The McClures returned and they all drove to see an artist, Ephraim Doner, in Carmel. Then Jack headed back to Los Gatos with the Cassadys, who were to attend a Western play for which Carolyn had designed the costumes. Carolyn hoped the event would revive the good memories Jack had of visiting her in the drama department at the University of Denver in 1947. Along the way they stopped at a restaurant, but once again Jack was drinking too heavily to want food. By the time they arrived at the theater in Old Town, he was singing with his eyes closed. He got very defensive when the actors wanted to meet him, and began bellowing, "What're you looking at me like that for? You think I'm somebody?" To settle him they told him to play some "old West" music on the piano. Instead he plunked a few chords of progressive jazz and got himself tossed out by arguing with the big "sheriff" who owned the place. Disregarding Carolyn's angry tears, he and Neal took off by themselves for San Francisco.

The main reason Jack was anxious to get away was that Neal had already promised to fix him up with his mistress, Jacky Gibson. After returning from prison, Neal had fallen into the same dilemma with her that had landed him there. Jacky insisted he divorce Carolyn and marry her. Neal figured that if she fell in love with Jack he could avoid losing her completely and at the same time quell her demands for a monogamous relationship. For a long while Neal had been praising Jack to her, and he had even instigated a correspondence between them. When they met that night at her apartment, Neal found he needn't have gone to such trouble. Jack and Jacky fell for each other instantly. She looked to him like a female Lucien Carr, and he actually began calling her Lucien. After Neal conveniently left, they stayed up all night talking and making love.

He never listened to what she said. In the middle of her life story she bridled at his complimenting "the lovely sound" of her voice. And as usual he was in love not with the woman but with the sorrow he imagined in her. The "sobbing break" he heard in her voice mesmerized him like the pool that captured Narcissus. Of course, the strongest bond between them was their mutual commitment to Neal, an allegiance so strong in Jack that the very next day he agreed to marry Jacky, even though he had decided before leaving North- port that he would never remarry—simply because married he would no longer be able to do whatever he felt like whenever he felt like it.

Jack's sacrifice included taking on a stepson he detested. Making love in the morning, he discovered four-year-old Eric staring at him. Worse, Jacky encouraged Eric to learn about sex by watching it firsthand. A bright child raised among hipsters, Eric would have given "precocious" a bad name, so there was ample cause for para- noiac Jack to imagine himself being hexed by a little warlock. He would have resented the boy under the best circumstances, however, because Eric was the son of Gerd Stern, the poet who had sup- posedly lost Neal's 23,000-word "Joan Anderson letter" off his house- boat in Sausalito. In front of both Jacky and Eric Jack sniped at Stern, telling Neal; "The guy not only lost your masterpiece, he knocked up your girl."

As their marriage plans became more concrete Jack grew more frightened. Their honeymoon in Mexico might have seemed dreamy enough until it was given official status through mention in gossip columns in both San Francisco dailies. At that point he began doing everything in his power to convince Jacky that marriage to him would be disastrous. He told her that he couldn't be a father to Eric, and that, besides, his own mother would be unbearably lonely with- out him. She suggested they kill two birds by shipping Eric to Mémère as a substitute (though Eric didn't concur in the plan). Jack then conceived a honeymoon on which they would be accompanied not only by Eric but by Neal's pal Jaimie, an ex-convict who offered to rob for them. Since she was still enthusiastic, he told her that Carolyn was the perfect woman for him, and that they were mated by a karmic destiny. She told him she would be perfectly satisfied if Carolyn divorced Neal to marry him. He made a mess of her apart- ment, killed her goldfish by pouring wine in their bowl, and called Paris on her telephone. As a result, her concern for his welfare in- creased steadily. Finally he told her she would have to let him keep Lois as his mistress. Jacky nearly rebelled at this condition, but her devotion to Neal outweighed even her hurt feelings.

Jack spent a week in her apartment, drinking in her armchair until it collapsed under him. Ferlinghetti, Whalen, and McClure visited him there, and they had many pleasant talks. If his speech was a bit slurred, his mind was still clear and witty. Yet his desperation was mounting as he felt trapped with a woman he had begun to actively dislike. He felt she was betraying Neal with her intense friendships with a number of men, and was especially outraged to find her on intimate terms with a suave, articulate black man who so cowed him that Jack dared not even speak to him.

To break out, Jack proposed a weekend with Lew and Lenore at Big Sur. On the way down he insisted they stop at Neal's to pick up some clothes. Doubtless he sensed that some resolution might occur if Carolyn and Jacky came face to face. Arriving at midnight, they threw Neal into a tizzy, and he began huffing and growling to show Jacky how jealous he was. To show Neal that he wanted to surrender his claim to Jacky, Jack began making passes at Carolyn! Lew was meanwhile making snide remarks about cream for the cats. The two women discomfited the men by calmly surveying their intrigues. Then, with a slug from his bottle and a hasty good-bye, Jack left Carolyn forever.

At the cabin he wanted solitude, but he couldn't refuse Jacky when she wanted to climb into his sleeping bag. He could never say no to women but only walk away from them, and the trouble in Bixby Canyon was that he couldn't walk farther than the ocean or the creek. The morning after they arrived he kept running down to the creek to sip water for a chance to be alone, but each time he returned to Jacky she scared him more with her own terror of abandonment. An ocean of guilt crushed him as she contemplated killing herself and her son, and he suffered the worst delirium tremens attack of his life.

As Lenore Kandel recalls, he tried to find a way out of the labyrinth of pain by dissecting everyone's motives on every possible level, and ended up losing a handle on his life. Since he had stopped trusting others, he had no standard by which to judge the reality of his thoughts, and he was tyrannized by his worst nightmares. Everyone was concerned about him; they cooked him a nice dinner and tried to get him to eat. During the day he had even had a vision of Jacky's good heart, knowing her to be "St. Carolyn by the Sea." But he was maddened by the lack of absolute proof that they were not communist spies trying to poison him or drive him mad. Not even Jacky's sensible rebuke—"You're so fucking abnormal!"—restored his perspective. There seemed no way out of his locked self short of suicide, from which he was still barred by the dread of mortal sin.

That night, shivering alone on his cot, he at last found someone he could give himself to. Again and again, just as his agony became unendurable, he was relieved by a vision of the Cross. Jack eventually explained the experience to Ferlinghetti with a quote from Pas-

618 · MEMORY BABE

cal. As the Jews had been saddened "for having misrecognized their Messiah," so was he being punished for the same error; that night he resolved to commit it no more.

The next day he asked Lew to drive him back to San Francisco. After a day's sleep on Skid Row he went to see Ferlinghetti, who counseled him to drink burgundy instead of sweet wine and to eat plenty of fruit and cheese. Lawrence shaved him, and Victor Wong helped him clean up and even gave him an old cashmere sweater. Jack joked that he was receiving the mantle of the dharma from the Seventh Patriarch, thereby becoming the Eighth Partriarch himself. His senses were again so sharp that when an Italian bartender denied service to Victor, he protested by walking out of the bar. But he was still at a loss as to what his next move should be, and asked Victor to take him to his father for advice.

Ensconced in the back of his little store in Chinatown, amid huge scrolls of ancient calligraphy, Mr. Wong received Jack with awesome solemnity. He didn't often meet with Caucasians, but he had great respect for artists, even a red-faced, rumpled one. After patiently hearing out Jack's troubles, he thought a long time. "You like to write, you like to drink," the old man said. "You should go to Japan, become a Zen monk, go up into the mountains, and write and drink all you want." Jack had no reply.

He stayed a couple of days with Ferlinghetti, who persuaded him to return to his mother's care. Speculating that Jack might be blocked because he was severed from his roots, Lawrence also suggested he return to live in Lowell.

The day before Lawrence was to drive him to the airport, Jack went drinking with Bob Kaufman and slept over in Kaufman's apartment. In the morning, Bob went into the kitchen to fix him breakfast, but when he returned with it Jack was already gone. On the wall was a scribbled poem:

> To Bob Kaufman—
> Though I have known you
> And slept with you
> And loved you,
> Yet I don't even know your name.

THIRTEEN
The Ghosts of Northport

1.

Late 1960 to early 1961 was a time of major decisions in Jack's life. He had been badly frightened by Neal's new friends, who seemed to comprise "hysterical" women like Jacky and "evil underworld" characters like Jaimie. Although he was deeply disappointed that Neal was wasting his "brilliant Jesuit mind" among such people, he preferred to stay out of California and out of Neal's life, for fear those people would push him to some violence. As he told Ed White, Neal's friends were bent on killing themselves "not like you and me, with a bottle or a *bom*, but literally jumping out windows and so on." [297]

In July, watching *The Subterraneans* movie with Gioscia, Jack had been furious to see his work travestied. Mardou was changed to a white girl and, most abhorrent to him, Leo Percepied became a murderous brawler. Jack grumbled that he hadn't even been paid a decent price for selling out, but clearly his anger was mostly against himself for having done so at all. That fall he told Matsumi that he felt like a whore for having written so many magazine pieces. He had already declined several big *Holiday* assignments and ceased writing his *Escapade* column too. Yet as much as he worried about being a phony, there was one person he still sought to fool. Mémère was so anxious for him to resume writing that he would sometimes start typing nonsense or just rattle his papers, to content her with the sounds of work.

He was also troubled by the problem of *how* to write. He was weary of spontaneous writing and wanted to change his style. But he was unenthusiastic about returning to either the elaborate, deliberative prose of "October in the Poolhall" in *Visions of Cody* or the unlettered simplicity of *The Dharma Bums*.

Once again he was seized by the desire to be anything other than a writer. He wished he had followed Ed White into architectural school. When Matsumi began working at the Actors Studio he asked for help in enrolling there.

Lee Strasberg was happy to meet him, but fifteen minutes into a rehearsal Jack was bored stiff and demanded, "Don't they give you any drinks in this place?" The only reason he stuck around was to meet Marlon Brando. Since Matsumi dissuaded him from asking Brando for an autograph, Jack simply told him how much he had admired him in *On the Waterfront* and asked him to go out for a drink. Brando declined. Learning that Marilyn Monroe was present, Jack declared, "I want to fuck her!" After they were introduced, he told her, "I like your legs!" and she walked away steaming. Later in the Cedar he told everyone about meeting her, at first gushing like a little kid and later dejectedly calling her a "trash broad."

In January 1961 Joan began new proceedings against him to obtain support for Janet. Divorced from her second husband and with a set of twins to care for, she was barely making ends meet in a tenement on the Lower East Side. It seemed high time Janet's prosperous dad showed some interest in her welfare. Convinced by Mémère that Joan wanted all his money, Jack flew into a near-psychotic rage, denouncing her and denying his fatherhood to everyone. He went so far as to assure his friends that Janet's father was "the Puerto Rican dishwasher Rosario" and that he would establish that fact with a blood test. Close friends like Lucien and Helen Elliott, who knew the score and had seen the girl's picture, refused to listen to his denials and pressured him to send her some money. Cornered, Jack would rejoin, "The mother'll spend it!" Fortunately Eugene Brooks handled the case with a good deal more tact.

This new assault on Jack's autonomy redoubled his hatred of women. Moreover, he now had the perfect excuse for not marrying Lois. Men had to protect themselves, he argued, because the law favored women. To Allen he joked that he was ready to become "queer." He joked with Gioscia that men or women didn't make much difference because he wanted blow jobs anyway. The jokes covered an increasing malaise over what his rejection of women spelled for the future. Certainly he was practicing bisexuality more openly than ever—Lois grew accustomed, for example, to finding him in Allen's bed on East 2nd Street. But he was also terrified that Allen might influence him to become homosexual. Nor was he comfortable with the indeterminate label "bisexual." Often he expressed anguish to Matsumi over the fact that he was sexually attracted to both men and women, and at times refused to acknowledge his relations with men, as though they represented a shameful weakness.[298]

All his sexual phobias and ambivalences were fed by his mother. She was continually warning him against homosexuality. Concerned that Matsumi was a bit too charming for a regular man, she told him to "leave Jackie alone." But she was equally outraged by Jack's heterosexual activity, and Matsumi once heard her reproach him: "I smell a woman! Go take a shower!" Now that she had him on the run—he was inviting Lois over less and less—she hounded him to death. She actually made a ritual of checking his underwear for "evidence." He was coming to prefer masturbation because it cost him the least trouble. But his mother forbade even that, and he was so intimidated he borrowed a towel from Matsumi to keep from staining her sheets.

Many of Jack's friends, failing to understand the incredibly tight corner he was in, bemoaned his political irresponsibility. In December 1960 Ferlinghetti went to Cuba, was favorably impressed by Castro's efforts to raise the standard of living there, and upon his return to the United States solicited Jack's participation in the Fair Play for Cuba Committee. Refusing, Jack snapped angrily, "I've got my own revolution right here in Northport—the American Revolution!" In any case, his political opinions were never reliable beyond the immediacy of his own response to some event. After watching TV news stories about Cuban firing squads he reviled Ferlinghetti for his support of Castro, and Lawrence concluded that he had been "brainwashed." [299] But though there was a grain of truth in Jack's assertion that "they [revolutionaries] invent new reasons every day" for killing people, Jack's insights were never of a kind that one could act on—or that he saw any need to act on. In the 1960 presidential race he preferred Kennedy over Nixon because he "was brought up with Massachusetts guys like that [the Kennedys]." Knowing that John Kennedy had played varsity football at Harvard, Jack felt he must have some of the championship drive and sportsmanship and glee that he wanted to see restored to America. Still he didn't believe it would help any for him to vote, and he didn't.

His mission was not to do but to absorb, and he continued to perform it with avidity despite the sickening of his body from alcoholism. He bought the Eleventh Edition of the *Encyclopedia Britannica* and set about to peruse the sum of universal knowledge up to 1909 in the prose of Oxford and Cambridge scholars. Frequently his solitary voyage took darker turns. In January 1961 he joined Allen in Newton Center, Massachusetts, to be administered the psychedelic drug psilocybin (derived from the *Psilocybe mexicana* mushroom) by Dr. Timothy Leary. Under its influence he relived his experience in the navy mental ward and became very depressed. Although he gained some insight into his dilemma—"Walking on water wasn't built in a day," he asserted—his final revelation was merely: "Everybody is full of shit." Nevertheless, according to Leary, his gift of gab enabled him to bluff his way through the rough spots of the trip. And he liked Leary, who also had been raised a Catholic in Massachusetts and had been a high-school athlete. When Leary asked him to write a report about his experience on psilocybin, he readily complied.

Jack was now seeing a great deal of Jerry Newman. Esoteric Records had made Newman a lot of money, but he was another of the brotherhood of self-willed failures. Like Jack, he was lushing himself to the grave, and using whatever drugs he could get to soar with the angels before he got there. His bathroom was a jungle of marijuana plants. When Jack arrived they would romp for days in fantasyland until they both passed out. Newman would provide Jack with the accompaniment of professional musicians and record his maudlin singing with the care he might have given Sinatra. They did endless takes of the same song—"Ain't We Got Fun?" and "Come Rain or Come Shine" were a couple of Jack's favorites—just for the kick of seeing how many different lyrics he could improvise.

Sometimes Jack would stagger into the apartment of Newman's neighbors, novelist David Markson and his wife Elaine, crying and slobbering and searching for some impossible way to get still higher. All their crazy adventures were perhaps best typified by the time Jack seized a skull David had brought back from Mexico. Insisting that the skull belonged to Edgar Allen Poe, he spent hours trying to get a lighted candle inside it—certain that once he did, the whole skull would glow. When at last the flame was inserted, a feeble luminescence flickered from the teeth.

In Northport Jack's house was filled with local kids, clammers, and assorted riffraff almost every night, sometimes until dawn, while Mémère lay awake listening and worrying. One day on Main Street Jack met painter Stan Twardowicz, who lived in Northport too. Jack expressed surprise that Stan had never bothered him. "I figured you didn't want to be disturbed," Stan explained, and after a short chat said, "I'm going to work." Retorted Jack: "Don't call it work—it's your whole life." Then Jack talked him into going for a drink.

In the bar he cosigned a $5 check already signed by his mother. During the next few hours they had boilermakers at every bar on Main Street, collecting a crowd of fishermen along the way. When Jack ran out of money Stan led the troop up to his studio. Swigging from a bottle of bourbon, Jack instigated arm wrestling and Indian wrestling. He was in his glory, laughing madly, looking at everybody like a voyeur. He challenged big Adolph Rothman, who took off his shirt for the contest. Rothman landed on a whiskey bottle, gouging an inch of flesh from his back. The sight of his spurting blood drove everyone crazier, and they poured whiskey and kerosene into the wound and jokingly stuffed toilet paper "up his gash." Jack got home that night covered with blood.

His friendship with Twardowicz was one of the most important of his last years. He liked the representational paintings of Stan's early period—somber, hauntingly distant views of himself and the world, including one ghostly red brick factory lost in a dimensionless gloom. But when he saw Stan's later abstract work, he said, typically, "You used to be a good painter. Why did you turn to that crap?" Nevertheless he was powerfully impressed by the depth of Stan's character. Born in 1917, Stan had lost his father in early childhood and had grown up in reform schools in Detroit. During the

Depression he had ridden the rails and husked corn for a living, and had later become a semi-pro boxer and baseball pitcher. Like Jack, he depended on art to bind together a life grown too large.

Jack invited Stan to his house and proudly showed him the orderly files of his writings, which included everything back to his childhood newspapers and cartoons. When Jack asked what music he wanted to hear, Stan replied, " 'Trane." Jack not only had tapes of almost all Coltrane's songs, he knew most of the solos by heart and could scat along perfectly. (No surprise, as Coltrane too had been criticized for being undisciplined and just making noises.) Soon he was calling Stan "Stasiu" and suggested Stan call him "Jasiu." Rather than ignoring people's ethnicity, Jack paid special attention to it, part of his manner of reaching out to people in their most private places. He asked Stan to teach him to dance the *kozatski*, and kidded, "All Polacks are sweet."

2.

About this time he suffered a relapse of phlebitis, and Mémère decided they should get out of Northport. In April 1961 they sold the house and moved to Orlando, where they bought a ranchhouse at 1309 Alfred Drive, two doors away from Paul and Nin. The area had once been mostly fields and woods, and Jack was disappointed to find new tract homes going up on all sides. As usual he was lonesome there almost immediately, although he welcomed the chance to soak up sun and get his mind off books by working in the yard and having cookouts. And in front of his house were two Georgia pines whose soughing he loved to listen to at night.

Despite the complete silence of reviewers regarding *Book of Dreams*, he felt like the great author in retirement to discover two graduate students in literature doing their theses on him. Granville H. Jones at Columbia was comparing Kerouac's works to those of Whitman and Melville. Jack thanked Jones profusely for restoring his faith in his own writing. While Jones' thesis comforted him with the prospect of academic recognition, he was flattered in a more personal way by the biographical study of him being prepared at Boston College by a French-Canadian woman from Beaulieu Street in Centralville. Bernice Lemire was well-acquainted with Jack's friends and neighbors. Her thesis, *Jack Kerouac: Early Influences*, the only biography undertaken in his lifetime, and the only one to which he directly contributed information, remains an essential piece of Kerouac scholarship.

His pride was tempered with the fear that he wouldn't live up to the expectations of such erudite admirers. Before he was fossilized in professional journals as "Kerouac the Younger" he sought to begin the *oeuvre* of "Kerouac the Elder." He wanted to express some of the harsher, bitterer truths he had learned on the other side of success, much as Melville, Whitman, and Wolfe had revealed their darkening vision in their final works. In late June, 1961, Jack flew to Mexico City and spent a month extending *Desolation Angels* with a fifty-thousand-word section called "Passing Through." He wasn't satisfied with it, however, and spent three years reworking it before he released the novel to his agent.

Desolation Angels is a vital work chronicling with fidelity large segments of American society and a variety of peculiarly American experiences at a crucial period, the late 1950's: life in a fire lookout's shack, an evening at the Seattle burlesque, the North Beach coffee-house-poetry reading coterie, the dreary circuit of bars, parties, and fruitless introductions that was and may always be fame in New York. There is not a sentence in the book that is not absolutely real to any American alive at that time—other than the lines that are merely nonsense for the sake of nonsense, and even those are true to the inane, campy, commercially manufactured hype that was then entering the American mainstream largely through the triumph of video. Furthermore, *Desolation Angels* is distinguished by a sympathy for its subjects unique in an era of detached, dry-hearted, professional observers. Attempting to characterize Sinatra's style, someone once said, "The little sonofagun sounds like he means it," and likewise it is the benchmark of Kerouac's prose that he always seems to care about the people and events he describes. Those accomplishments easily set *Desolation Angels* above most of the novels published in America in the sixties.

It is nevertheless a diffuse book, critically lacking a center. Its narrator is no longer as self-effacing as Sal Paradise, but neither is he comfortable on center stage. He lacks a Dean Moriarty whose depths he can plumb with impunity, and still unwilling to plumb his own he now intimates that the truth is simply a little farther down the road, a proposition whose falseness Kerouac himself had proved in *On the Road*. The story manages to cohere solely by the virtue of a single, original structural device. The narrator seeks to pinpoint the occurrence of moments on a cosmic grid, and he isolates them at the places where his life changed direction. Indeed, as he shows, it is by the intersection of such vectors that we are able to get our bearings and sensibly steer our path.

Early in the novel the narrator says: "It's that vicious *change* that hurts, as soon as something is cool and complete it falls apart and burns." To keep from being overwhelmed by changes we must track them, and for Kerouac this purpose is served by fiction: "Why else should we live but to discuss (at least) the horror and the terror of all this life, God how old we get and some of us go mad and everything changes viciously. . . ." Kerouac rings infinite changes on the notion of change. He refers to the biblical Fall, to the Dantesque concept of a "new life," to disillusionment, to the chemical change in old photos, to the end of frontier America, to nuclear fission, to the physical zigzagging of our course over the earth, and to the most mysterious and terrifying change of all: death. All these changes would create a chaos could we not link them to some meaningful series of "turnabouts" in our own life. From the framework of such links hangs the tale of *Desolation Angels*. The climax of the novel comprises the "complete turningabout" in the narrator's feelings about life, which is to say, his enlightenment.

The idea that the seeker must change inside before he will find wisdom is as old as Buddhism. The *Lankavatara Scripture* warns that disciples must undergo "a 'turning-about' in the deepest seat of consciousness." To the same end, the whole thrust of *Desolation Angels* is to show that change in the exterior world is really change in the mind. What is new is Kerouac's quintessentially American, optimistic belief that the will to change is itself sufficient to bring change about. Reminiscent of the Yankee adage that "words are deeds," Kerouac pursues the idea that stating a fact is fact enough. Duluoz has but to say "a new life for me" and he gets one. Thus writing promises even an escape from death: "I know it's inexcusable to interrupt a tale with such talk—but I've got to get it off my chest or I will die. . . ." There is, as well, a Job-like assumption inherent in the book that by asking unanswerable questions they are already answered. At the same time, Kerouac attempts to bring East and West together in the magic of language. As the Buddha passes through the world, the world passes through him. So, for Kerouac, should the writer pass through his material, making it part of himself as he is part of it.

These are the bones that make *Desolation Angels* such a powerful work. Unfortunately they are scarcely fleshed out, and the novel too often drifts into Kerouac's old dialectic between his need to believe that "nothing matters" [300] and his need for faith in a personal God, an argument by now blurred with years of alcoholic sentimentality. The greatness of this novel even in its failure is yet another testament—as if one were needed—to the rapid attrition of great artists in American society.

The tragedy for Jack Kerouac is that he felt at home nowhere else. Without his compatriots Jack was lost in Mexico, and to add to his depression he was staying in the damp, dusty apartment beneath Bill and Joan's old duplex on Cerrada de Medellin. When the Indian clerk in a liquor store said, "I love you!" he replied, "Ah, buy me a drink!" and let himself be picked up. For a few weeks they had one of the strangest romances on record. Guillermo led Jack to movies to see actors he considered beautiful, though Jack complained they were "fat tubs." He fed Jack secanols, lectured him about Santa Teresa de Ávila and San Juan de la Cruz, read him *The Subterraneans* in Spanish and English, and followed him plaintively to the door of a whorehouse. Jack was jolted back to his senses when a gang of Guillermo's hoodlum friends stole his knife, flashlight, and shaving cream right in front of him. They asked for his raincoat too, but he told them if he lost it his mother would kill him, and they laughed: "So you *are* afraid of something!" Later, when he went to a movie, they broke into his place and took not only the raincoat but his suitcase, containing such valuables as his baseball game and Buddhist prayer beads.

Jack had started the trip with the vague desire to proceed from Mexico to California, but by now he had a bad cough, and the robbery convinced him that he would be victimized again there too. Still, despite the high cost in a variety of currencies, the trip had been more fruitful than any since the one to Mill Valley in 1956. Besides nearly completing *Desolation Angels*, he had produced another collection of poems, "Cerrada Medellin Blues." In addition, he was taking back a supply of benzedrine and sleeping pills. He flew home in early August and nursed himself out of the dumps with six weeks of bennies, slowly-sipped brandy, and several novels by Dostoyevsky and Balzac.

His litigation with Joan dragged on, though he was happy that the judge agreed to strike out of her complaint a clause citing him as "King of the Beatniks." Desperate for money, Joan had sold her story to *Confidential*, a scandal sheet. The ghostwritten article was published in August under the title "My Ex-Husband Jack Kerouac Is An Ingrate." He was incensed, but the charges stung deeply enough for him to write a fresh round of letters defending himself to his friends, this time claiming a doctor had certified his abnormally low fertility rate. To his family the truth was so obvious that he scarcely protested at all. When thirteen-year-old Paul asked him if Janet was his daughter, he replied, "Might be, might not."

Paranoia was becoming his way of life. That fall there was a new TV program called *Route 66*, about two men traveling cross-country in a car. One of the actors, George Maharis, resembled Jack. Since the two producers of the show were Jewish, Mémère put extra malice into her argument that he was being cheated of "a million dollars"; and he bought it. Requesting his lawyer to sue for plagiarism, Jack somehow forgot that the originator of the idea was Bobby Troup, whose song "Route 66" had generated his own road enthusiasm.

In late September, Jack "exploded angrily" out of his rocking chair, fed a teletype roll into his typewriter, and driven by bennies wrote *Big Sur* in ten nights. The novel chronicles his six weeks in California in the summer of 1960, climaxing with his breakdown at

Ferlinghetti's cabin. Its tight organization results not only from the brief time span but from a refined selectivity. Whalen was impressed with the way Jack had "jumped through" the real events to pick out incidents for his plot, and he was surprised that most of the events Jack chose to narrate were the ones *he* would have ignored.

The book is structured like a medieval morality play, a form Kerouac may have gotten indirectly from the Faust legend. In the first chapter, Christ's word is preached by a Salvation Army crier to Jack Duluoz, waking from a hangover on Skid Row: "*Satan* is the cause of your alcoholism, *Satan* is the cause of your immorality, Satan is *everywhere* workin to destroy you unless you repent now. . . ." A typical sinner, Duluoz ignores the warning, setting up the book's principal conflict: the battle between good angels and evil angels for his soul.

Kerouac characterizes Duluoz's spiritual journey with metaphors common to both Christianity and Buddhism. When Duluoz advises himself, "Cross the bridge you woken bum and see what's on the other shore," he condenses an enormous body of Eastern and Western religious imagery. Both Christ and Buddha commanded their disciples to "wake up." Buddha specifically referred to attaining enlightenment as "crossing to the other shore." Christ didn't use the image, but it became a stock in trade of later Christian fablers—most notably, John Bunyan in *Pilgrim's Progress*. A few sentences later, Kerouac makes clear that his bias is with Christianity: "I'd just popped thru from hell into familiar old Heaven on Earth, yair, and Thank God. . . ."

The Buddhist allusions merely jive up the novel. Although Kerouac again compares his hero to a Bhikku and a Bodhisattva, the novel has nothing to do with how to live in this world as a Buddhist, which was a serious consideration in *The Dharma Bums* and *Desolation Angels*. In fact *Big Sur* is scarcely concerned with how to live as a good Christian either: its chief concern is how to survive as an alcoholic. Such theology as it has comes largely from Emerson's *Self-Reliance*. Kerouac states the novel's moral with a quote from Emerson: "Life is not an apology."

Nevertheless, the novel is preoccupied with sin. Several times Big Sur is equated with the Garden of Eden. Duluoz calls himself a "sick clown," and his sickness is "mortality." In a very traditional sense Kerouac conceives of Duluoz having earned death through participation in original sin. He refers to Duluoz confronting "the evil serpent of Big Sur," and stresses that man is doomed to do wrong despite his best intentions. For example, to avoid angering Monsanto (Ferlinghetti), Duluoz leaves the cover off the rat poison in the cabin, and later condemns himself for having killed a mouse, a creature he loved. Following Dostoyevsky, Kerouac believes in universal guilt: "I feel guilty for being a member of the human race."

His view of nature is thoroughly Christian, and as such is diametrically opposed to Emerson, who saw man as "part and parcel" of nature. Kerouac, like Christ, deems man a spirit burdened by the weakness of his flesh and surrounded by a vicious and alien kingdom: "I ran away from that seashore and never came back again without that secret knowledge: that it didn't want me there . . . the sea has its waves, the man has his fireside, period."

Big Sur continues Kerouac's examination of change, but here he is concerned almost exclusively with death. *Death* and *madness* are the key words in the novel, and the intimate relationship between the two conditions is its main theme. The narrator goes mad because he cannot understand death. Again, as in *Desolation Angels,* his voice merges with that of Job: "but why did the fish die? . . . Why would they do that? why? what kind of logic is that for fish to have?"

Kerouac boasted to friends that *Big Sur* was "honester" than his other novels, and it *is* in the sense that he comes clean about the ravages of his alcoholism. Yet he still disingenuously ignores the hopelessness of his situation. The book ends on a sanguine note that even a Pollyanna like Kerouac cannot bring off convincingly: "we'll drink dry wine instead of sweet and have quiet evenings . . . Something good will come out of all things yet—And it will be golden and eternal just like that—There's no need to say another word." We are to take it that the Christian faith restored by Duluoz's vision of the Cross has made all explanations superfluous. Indeed the book makes a big point of the futility of writing. Kerouac quotes Milarepa that one should not be "anxious to tell other people" about one's experiences. Cody (Neal) is praised because he embodies this truth: "becoming a writer holds no interest for him because life is so holy for him there's no need to do anything but live it, writing's just an afterthought or a scratch anyway at the surface. . . ." Even without the example of Kerouac's life before us, the "answers" in *Big Sur* are obviously pat. One cannot help finding more honesty in the despair of *Desolation Angels,* where Duluoz admits: "Every night I still ask the Lord, 'Why?' and havent heard a decent answer yet."

In so far as it avoids more issues than it grapples with, *Big Sur* is one of Kerouac's minor novels, and though there are a few passages of lyrical beauty, his prose is often tiresomely repetitious. Once so deft with motifs, he now resorts to larding almost every page with the words *death* and *madness* or some variation thereof.

What holds the reader's interest is a series of striking images. Few authors have painted death so ingeniously. The novel contains such pictures as a cat dying, a dead otter floating in seaweed, and upside-down goldfish. An instance of how Kerouac changes things is the way he increases the mystery of the fishes' death by omitting to mention that he poured wine into their bowl.

The most original and affecting images, however, are Duluoz's two collapsing seats. The book pivots neatly between Duluoz's two broken chairs. One is the armchair in Billie's (Jacky's) living room that collapses under him after he has been drinking in it all week. The other is the rocking right front seat in Dave Wain's (Lew Welch's) jeep, in which Duluoz also swigs at his bottle while riding shotgun. The images not only suggest the way life is crumbling from under Duluoz, but in their antithesis they hint that collapse is no simple thing. Duluoz's joy as he bounces along in Welch's jeep seat— which does not disintegrate as does the armchair—reveals a vitality in collapse that is seldom observed but very real. In the juxtaposition of those images there is more honesty, and a deeper insight into Kerouac's own life, than he was ever capable of simply stating.

3.

To celebrate the completion of the novel he bought a case of cognac. Two weeks later he woke up in a hospital, unable to remember how he got there. It had been less a celebration than an expiation. Once again he felt guilty for revealing the intimate details of his friends' lives. Neal no longer answered his letters, and Jack acknowledged to Ed White that the greatest friendship of his life was "washed up." But he felt an even greater guilt from the horror he had engendered in his mother and sister, who were frightened and revolted by reading his books. The one humiliation he couldn't bear was to be "without honor in me own house." As he had once quit football because he was getting nowhere, he wrote Ferlinghetti, he was now ready to quit literature.

For a break before retyping *Big Sur*, he went to New York on a month-long, drunken spree.

Allen was currently traveling in the Middle East, on his way to meet Snyder in India. Peter, having temporarily separated from Allen, was in Greece. Corso was in London. Burroughs was in New York, but failed to respond to Jack's messages.

An internationally celebrated author since the publication of *Naked Lunch* in Paris by Olympia Press, Burroughs had met Jack earlier in the year, but their friendship was seriously eroded. Seeing them together, Gioscia was reminded of two ships that had long ago passed in the night. Whereas Jack's personality was by now completely dominated by affects, Burroughs had grown wholly mental and seemed like "a vast computer running all the time, making arcane comparisons silently." [301] Although Burroughs had never unbent very far, he was uncustomarily formal with Jack. A further strain was put on their relationship by Jack's antipathy toward Bill's new writing technique. Burroughs was experimenting with cutups, segments of prose created by grafting the left half of one page onto the right half of a different page. The technique helped him to uncover the bases of language and to "decode" messages that might be programmed into ordinary syntax. Jack wanted Burroughs to continue writing in a style true to his original conception of him, as a mixture of elegant aristocrat and Hemingway tough guy. Of course Jack opposed change, period. He was always trying to reconstruct the past, but often now—as Huncke found him one day, his bloated face streaming tears—he failed even to salvage the memories.

Lucien was his one diehard companion in anachronistic dissipation. Together that November in New York, they revived not only the beery brotherhood of 1944, but the wassailing whoopee of the lairds of Scotland, from whom Jack insisted they were both descended. Jack also stayed with that other veteran tippler Hugo Weber, who found him a teenage girlfriend named Yseult. Although Lois had made no definite break with him she had started dating other men, since he had convinced her he could never trust any woman enough to remarry.

The violence so long suppressed in him emerged in cruelty to those he cared about, for he knew they alone would understand it. At Jerry Newman's studio Jack and Lucien tore each other's clothes off and wrestled until both were bloody. At Lucien's upstate farm Jack kicked over Lucien's chair, knocking him on his back, three times in a row. Few of Jack's friends tolerated as many affronts as Lucien. Miles Forst blew up when Jack demanded to sleep with his wife, Barbara. Barbara couldn't have been happier over the rupture, because, like Cessa Carr, she felt Jack was destroying her marriage. At parties, Jack and Miles would encourage each other's worst tendencies in bouts of one-upmanship that included tossing punchbowls and swinging from chandeliers.

As it became harder for Jack to distinguish between fantasy and reality, he began trying to live out all the roles he had imagined for himself. On Lucien's farm, asked to move a car, he made one last stab at driving like Neal Cassady and hit a tree. Eager again to be Thoreau, he made a trip to Vermont with expert woodsman and carpenter Jacques Beckwith to select land for a cabin. Equipped with his railroad lantern Jack was prepared for all hardships, but he nearly fell apart when he saw a hunter's car with a bleeding deer draped over the trunk. The farmer who was to sell him the land informed him that he intended to cut down all the pine trees first. Aghast at the prospect of such "slaughter" Jack turned tail for New York,[302] and later explained the fiasco to Lois by saying Jacques had taken advantage of him.

Looking for any way out, he got a dozen *Psilocybin mexicana* mushrooms from Tim Leary and ate them all in one afternoon. For a few hours he was euphoric, leading Leary out into the snowy Lower

East Side streets to pass a loaf of bread as if it were a football. But the drug succeeded too well in freeing him from his present torments. "Emptied" of his complex adult personality, he was more utterly lost than before. What the drug showed him, and what he didn't want to face, was that there was no "new life" ahead. When Leary later asked for permission to publish Jack's report about his experience on psilocybin, Jack refused, ranting about communist brainwash techniques.

He retyped *Big Sur* in Orlando in December and then returned to New York in mid-February 1962, for the disposition of Joan's suit against him.

On February 20, ten-year-old Janet Michelle Kerouac sat beside her mother in a bar in Brooklyn, eating a hamburger. The TV up in the corner showed John Glenn beginning his third orbit of the earth, but Janet wasn't watching it. Her eyes were fastened on the handsome, dark-haired, blue-eyed fellow across the table. He not only looked like her, with his long lower lip stuck out broodingly, he even talked like her. Every so often he'd say, "You're a lovely little girl, but you're not my daughter." Finally Jan replied, "Jack, I don't care if you're my father or not—I'll still love you."

After lunch, Jack and Jan went for blood tests, which showed that she was possibly his daughter (at that time it was impossible to obtain conclusive physical proof). He was so fascinated with the girl—as he later admitted to Holmes—that he came back to Joan's apartment with her. He asked Jan to lead him to the nearest liquor store, where he bought a bottle of Harvey's Bristol Cream, whose cork she saved for years. Back at the apartment he told stories to her twin sisters, seemingly afraid to talk to her. When he left, Jan watched the door, as if she knew he was about to come back any minute, and he did. He said, "Whoops! I forgot my survival hat!" They gave him his hunting cap, and then he said, "Well, see ya in January."

But in his final appearance before Judge Benjamin Fine, Jack still denied the girl was his. He submitted to the judge Joan's 1957 letter absolving him from further litigation if he agreed to divorce her. Setting the letter aside, Judge Fine winked and said, "I'd rather read *On the Road.*" A sensible man, he called Jack into his chambers and told him that, whatever his feelings about the mother, he shouldn't deny the girl a name. The judge promised that if Jack acknowledged her, he would only have to pay $52 a month, the minimum amount of child support. Jack accepted the deal, though he futilely tried to get into the court record the fact that he was recognizing *her name* rather than her. For months afterward, he griped that the $2,500 in legal fees from the case had plunged him into poverty.

Gregory, back in New York, found Jack "lightless to me—and unto himself." Visiting Ted Wilentz, they got into a drunken argument over Proust. Recalls Wilentz: "Knowledge and thought streamed from each of them in louder and louder tones as though they were doing combat with words," while Proust got "lost in an ego conflict."

In March Jack returned to Orlando. Dread of the stifling inland heat and humidity of summer had already decided him to move. With his $10,000 advance from Farrar, Straus, and Cudahy for *Big Sur,* he planned to move his mother to Cape Cod.

Domestic troubles between Nin and Paul had grown critical. Paul had an out-of-state mistress and would often spend six months away from home. At least part of the problem between him and Nin was that he had never felt accepted in the Kerouac family. When Mémère and Nin were together they would almost always speak French, which he didn't understand. He forbade them to teach young Paul French, but Jack taught him anyway on the sly. Moreover, Mémère and Jack continually reminded the boy that he was a Kerouac.

Paul had borrowed $5,000 from Jack to build an addition on his house, but he had used the money elsewhere and never repaid it. Although this gave Jack reason to resent him, Paul must have sensed that most of Jack's hostility arose because he was an outsider, for Jack never begrudged Nin anything. Hearing her say how much she'd like a piano, for example, he bought her one.

Once again, with his nephew, Jack showed what a good father he might have been. Every afternoon he would meet Paul at his junior high school and walk him home, telling him stories about his travels and promising to buy him any car he wanted when he was sixteen, so Paul could drive him around the country. The boy was on the school football team, and Jack attended his games as well as continuing to coach him. To spur him to run faster, he would run the 100-yard dash against him, and was still fast enough to beat him on occasion. When Paul made touchdowns and when he won ribbons at track, Jack couldn't have been prouder, boasting, "Comes from the family." As a reward, he promised someday to give Paul his African machete, one of his most precious possessions. Then, too, Jack always got along better with young people than with adults because they loved his comical capers. Paul's parents saw nothing funny when Jack would dress up like an Arab, with a towel for a turban, or go to sleep under the "Keep Off the Grass" sign on the school lawn.

In March, Jack was distraught at turning forty. Rapidly gaining weight, he worried that he could no longer "control" women "with a lothario air." All day long he would brush his hair to prevent balding. While he struggled to conserve his identity against physical change, he was overwhelmed by the inroads being made on his public self. The world was suddenly full of Kerouac impostors. From Vienna, he received a letter and snapshot from one. On Fifth Avenue, another walked into a men's clothing store, bought a $12 tie, and walked out with the tie around his hips. The prank made a New York gossip column and enraged Jack, who hadn't bought a tie in fifteen years. In April yet another impostor in San Diego made a speech in favor of the John Birch Society. Worse, Ferlinghetti believed it was really he who had made the speech. What appalled Jack was that Lawrence could think him capable of promoting any "violence group," whether right or left wing.

4.

He wrote Montgomery asking him to look around for a cabin property, preferably on a mountain, for his "final retreat." If John hadn't found anything by fall, Jack promised to join him for a search through northern California and Oregon, and possibly down to Arizona and New Mexico. For the summer he planned an extensive trip through Europe and Scandinavia. He especially wanted to stay in Cornwall, where he believed he would find the original Kerouac family. An uncle had once told him that Cornwall was their ancestral home. Recently Jack had learned that the Celtic name for the Cornish language was "Kernuak," and that there was a seaside castle in Cornwall called "Kernodjack." At his request, Montgomery researched some facts that contributed to his belief that his family had migrated from Cornwall to Brittany in the fifteenth-century Cornish Rebellion. Just beginning was the great genealogical passion that would consume Jack in his last years.

That spring he achieved a major victory with the acceptance of *Visions of Gerard* by Farrar, Straus, and Cudahy, and was especially pleased that Robert Giroux, now his editor again, promised to make no editorial changes in it. In some respect, however, getting that book published meant one less reason for him to stay alive—although, as he wrote Whalen, he was still hanging on for his mother's sake. With a premonition of approaching death he made out a will in which he left everything to his mother. If she were to die first, he requested that his estate be divided equally between his sister and her heirs, his two boyhood churches in Lowell, St. Louis de France and Ste. Jeanne d'Arc, and St. Joseph's Hospital, which had cared for his mother after he was born. He also put his literary archives in order. He bought a four-drawer steel cabinet and spent two months filing all his manuscripts and letters, to provide "a gold mine of information for scholars."

With the advent of the hot, sticky summer Jack grew restive. The nearest store was miles away and he was ready to collapse after hiking the first mile, but he didn't like the alternative of depending on his sister for rides. To insure his privacy he had provided his back yard with two separate fences, one around the perimeter and another around the patio; but the neighborhood was so full of children that sometimes he felt as though they had his house under siege, and he'd sit by the window neurotically counting them. Mémère worried for his life. To young Paul she acknowledged the tragedy, which she had helped bring on, that "Jackie doesn't have any more friends." In mid-May he lost one of his best. Prostrated by the death of Franz Kline, the hard-drinking painter whose loft had been a second home for him in New York, Jack stayed in his room drinking and sleeping for two weeks.

That summer the heat and the endless cognac and Irish whiskey drove him out of his mind at last. Since Paul, Sr., was out of town, Jack told Paul to take him for a ride in his father's Sprite. At fourteen Paul only had a learner s permit, but he was reassured by his uncle's bravado. As they passed the brick wall that separated the black neighborhood from the rest of Orlando, Jack blustered, "You ought to go burn a cross up there!" After they returned home he helped Paul build a cross with two-by-fours, and at night they drove back to the wall, covered the cross with cloth, and saturated it with kerosene. After erecting it on the wall and lighting it, Jack started yelling obscenities.[303]

In July he bought a round-trip ticket to Paris, then cashed it in and took a train to Maine to hunt for a seashore home for himself and Mémère. Finding nothing he proceeded to Cape Cod, where he got drunk in a jazz club, was knocked out by the black bouncers, and woke up rain-soaked, in a field. The next ten days he went on a binge in New York. He avoided interviews regarding *Big Sur*, due out in September, by declaring, "I'm interviewing myself anyway." If he was, it was the fastest-moving interview on record. He went to a gallery opening, saw Johnny the bartender at the West End, visited Jerry Newman and Jay Landesman, made a new friend from Georgia, Jim Benenson, argued with a Yugoslavian diplomat, picked up numerous women and fans who mooched drinks off him and robbed him of his sunglasses and notebooks, and was barred from the White Horse tavern. Waking up sick, short hundreds of dollars, and disappointed, he had a sudden realization that the world was laughing at him. He thought of his death, and imagined the bartenders and patrons of the White Horse talking about how well they had known and loved Kerouac—just as they already talked about Dylan Thomas.

On the train back to Florida he thought of his father's death and cried through the night. When he got home he learned that Lois's mother had died. Jack wanted to invite Lois to Orlando, buy a car, let her drive him back to New England to find a home, and then marry her. Naturally Mémère vetoed the plan, telling him, "You've got plenty of time to find a wife and you don't have to get married just for that." At last he persuaded her to let Lois come down "for a rest." He was so anxious to see her that he paid her round-trip fare.

Arriving two days late, she found him in his chair, wearing his sports jacket with a wilted flower in the lapel. Overcome by the agony of waiting for her, he was drinking, playing records, and babbling. The week she spent with him was a nightmare. He downed over a quart of whiskey a day. One night he brought someone home from a bar, and when Jack passed out the man tried to rape her. Lois ran into Mémère's room. Iron-fisted Mémère got rid of the rapist, counted some coins out of the box under her bed, and put Lois in a cab for the airport.

Certain that John Holmes was a gentleman, Mémère told Jack to see him about getting a house for them in New England. Meanwhile, she wrote John's wife Shirley to the effect that they had to help her save Jack "or he'll be a very sick Man." On September 9, after traveling by plane and train, Jack arrived at Holmes' house in Old Saybrook, Connecticut, carrying a fifth of bourbon. For a week John couldn't get him out of the house, and could scarcely even rouse him from the armchair where Jack sat playing jazz, reading John's shelf of Balzac, smoking Camels, killing a quart of cognac a day, and talking a mile a minute—deluging John with "his strange amalgam of spurious ideas, verbal illuminations, cornball politics, dead certain aesthetic feeling, huge relish for life, fatalistic physical strength." Jack claimed to be Christ, Satan, various holy men, an Indian chief, and a "universal genius." With sadness and awe, Holmes watched him incinerating in the flame Keats had called (referring to Shakespeare) "negative capability." Writing his own life, Kerouac more than most writers had sacrificed himself, in Holmes' words, to "the search for the role. The mile-deep final puzzle of identity that goes on in someone who can imagine *all* alternatives, *all* roles."

At dinnertime John had all he could do to get Jack to nibble a few bites of steak; mostly he supped on wine. The last three days he went unshaved and unbathed in his T-shirt and pajama bottoms. The last day John had to bring him a glass of brandy so he could get out of bed. Rebuking himself, Jack sobered up as much as he could and cleaned up. He had John take him out house-hunting, but a few hours later they were in a bar drinking beer, and by evening Jack was back on brandy. He said, "I want to go to Lowell." After Shirley found a cabbie who would take him the 150 miles, John fixed him a mason jar full of brandy and soda for the trip.

In the middle of the night, wearing a T-shirt and sneakers, Jack showed up on the doorstep of G.J. Apostolos. A husband and father, well-established in the real estate business, G.J. was no longer in a position to spend all night talking, especially when Jack wasn't talking so much as free-associating and spouting delicious-sounding gibberish. Then Jack frightened G.J.'s wife by trying to dance on the piano, and got thrown out. During Jack's ten-day rush around Lowell G.J. never had a meaningful conversation with him. Whenever they met, Jack would talk as if the old gang were still down in Falls Park waiting to throw snowballs at passing cars. An hour with him felt like a week and left G.J. exhausted. It seemed as though whatever had been chasing Jack all these years had finally almost caught him, and G.J. had a good idea what it was. In a rare pensive moment, Jack said, "Jesus! What have I done to my mother?" "Zagg, you didn't do anything to her," G.J. replied. "Perhaps you should ask, 'What has *she* done?' "

G.J. warned Scotty Beaulieu that Jack was "getting like Luxey Smith." Although red-faced when he showed up at Scotty's house Jack was as kind as ever. He did tricks for Scotty's twelve-year-old son and offered to write an article soliciting aid for his sick daughter. But again his mind was drifting. He said, "Scotty, you're one of the greatest baseball players ever to come out of Lowell." Scotty explained that he was now a printer, and Jack's voice went suddenly heavy as he recalled Leo's print shop. Visiting Sam Samaras, his Bartlett Junior High friend, Jack said, "Someday I'm going to write a book about all the guys we grew up with—that's how I want you to remember me."

He serenaded Mary Carney, who was engaged to be married, but she sent him away. From Cuckoo O'Connell's bar he called Stella Sampas, Sammy's sister, and told her he wanted to come over. Afraid he was an impostor, she dispatched her brother Tony to check him out. Tony had been a little kid when Jack knew Sammy; Jack didn't recognize him and thought he was a cabbie Stella had sent. Astonished to see Jack in the door of their old house in the Highlands, Stella asked what he was doing in Lowell. He answered, "I came here to marry you, Stella."

That night Stella told Tony to take care of him. Since Tony was going to play dice, he left Jack with his friend Manuel "Chiefy" Nobriga, bartender at the Sportsmen's Athletic Club. The dark, seedy SAC Club was dear to Jack because it had formerly been the Hi-Ball, where he used to hang out with G.J. and the gang in 1941. Now it had the added interest for him of being a hangout for local gangsters and bookies. After hours you could only get in by ringing a buzzer and showing your face through the glass in the door. Closing up the bar for the night Chiefy locked Jack in, so he could sleep on one of the couches. For the privilege of being locked in a bar Jack ever afterward called Chiefy "the Saint."

The SAC Club became Jack's court, where he reigned for a week as "King of the Beatniks," a title he now reveled in. His high jinks were described almost daily in the *Sun* column by Pertinax, a pseudonym for Stella's sister-in-law Mary Sampas. As soon as his presence was known a tide of curiosity seekers flooded the SAC Club to see him. Dressed in his plaid shirt and often a filthy raincoat, never without a whiskey and soda, he'd jump up and down, wave his arms, bite his nails, comb his hair, draw on napkins, and interrupt his monologue only to break into songs like "A Pretty Girl Is Like a Melody" and "Moon River." Words volleyed from his mouth without the control they used to have from his typewriter, where he'd only "blast" out a book after months or years of thinking about it.[304] Now it mattered not how or why a quotation from *Hamlet* segued into an imitation of Truman Capote or a boast about how many thousand dollars a day he could earn—just so the words didn't stop. When the crowd of hangers-on began to thin a little, he went out to other bars to round up fresh ones. Outside Chuck's on Moody Street, Jack held up traffic by sitting on the curb with his jug and reciting poetry to several hundred people. Another night he was introduced at the Hideaway by bandleader Bucky Auger, came onstage to dance the *kozatski*, and then spent an hour signing autographs. If he were playing Kerouac in a movie, observed Pertinax, he would win an Oscar.

Doubtless the adulation of his hometown helped him recover from the reviews of *Big Sur*. *Time* snidely dismissed the novel as the product of "a perpetual adolescent" who had just discovered death. The *Saturday Review* and *The New York Times* gave the novel slightly favorable reviews, but only because it pleased the reviewers to find that "the Beatnik" had finally cracked up. Herbert Gold in the *Saturday Review* was particularly spiteful and condescending, fitting every compliment with two barbs. After referring to Kerouac's thirteen previous published books as a "flood of trivia," Gold complained that Jack's pervasive literary allusions betrayed a lack of innocence! The irony was that in Lowell Jack was largely scorned, even by his hangers-on, for the same reasons that the literati hated him. By virtue of his genius he had been alienated from his working-class environment, but he had never lost faith in the proletariat (though he disliked the Marxian connotations of the word), and for years he had been trying to work his way back in. Yet his adoption of a millworker's clothes and manners didn't set well with the majority of townspeople, who were struggling to rise above that position. And the real barroom bums of Lowell were jealous of all the attention this "ordinary slob" [305] was getting just because he happened to be a writer; they weren't fooled by all that fancy lingo coming out of his mouth and knew he was just "talking ragtime," like any old drunk could do.

Still and all, Jack did make many devoted friends such as Huck Finneral, a cat burglar and actor, Paul Bourgeois, a drunken ne'er-do-well steeplejack, Charles Jarvis, a professor at Lowell Textile Institute, and James Curtis, a lawyer.

Jarvis and Curtis hosted a local radio show on which Jack con-

sented to be interviewed. There was a certain point in his drunkenness at which he was more perfectly in touch with his thoughts than
when sober, and still in complete control of their expression. This
was his condition at the interview with Curtis and Jarvis, a perfect
example of his new technique of interviewing the interviewers. Jarvis begins with the nervous slip, "This morning we have a milestone
in our program," and immediately Jack interrupts: "Ask me my
name!"

"What's your name?"

"Louis Milestone."

Curtis tries to mend the breach of etiquette with a jocular anec-
dote: "Last night I walked down Market Street and heard thunder
and looked to the right and there he was! Tell them about this
thunder, Jack."

But Jack won't let him get away with that.

"Louis Thunder is my name."

"I thought your name was Louis Milestone."

"Louis Milestone . . . Gallstone . . . Death."

Jack manipulates Jarvis to find out how much he knows about
literature, and exposes a few of Curtis' weak points in the history of
law; but his tone is never mean and he quickly turns to a joke any
remark that seems to offend. Only once in the interview is he so
angry and serious that he cows them into silence. Halting their conventional queries about his writing technique, he pounds on the
table and does literally thunder: "Once God moves the hand, you go
back and revise, it's a sin!"

Two other new friends Jack made in Lowell were Tony Sampas
and Billy Koumantzelis, Johnny's brother. As soon as he saw Billy,
a short, thickset professional boxer, he gibed, "You're Johnny's
brother? What happened to you, you ugly sonofabitch?" Later,
when Jack pissed on the front lawn and started swearing vilely in
front of Stella and some other women, Billy was mad enough to nail
him, but Tony intervened. After a stop at the SAC Club, they repaired to the apartment of one of the women, and Jack made a pass
at her. When she rebuffed him he called her a lesbian. Tony's
girlfriend walked out, Billy prepared to whack Jack, and again Tony
saved him.

What Jack loved immediately in Billy was his fundamental decency, a sense of right and wrong too staunch to be deflected by the
opportunity to use a famous man. Jack found that same noble disinterest in Tony too, as well as the secret grimness of a man who had
seen too much hurt to ever want to inflict any anywhere again. As a
member of the O.S.S. Tony had performed some of the deadliest
military operations in Italy during World War II. He also had a
Master's Degree in psychology from Marietta College and knew a
lot more about literature than Jack ever realized, for Jack was more

interested in his colorful life as one of the most important bookies in Lowell. Right away he wanted to learn all about the local mafia, boasting that he knew about rackets because he had been in "the Opera House" with Gallo and the Hawk. Tony laughed because actually Jack knew almost nothing of what was going on. It struck Tony as pathetic that he should be bragging about the $10,000 he'd made from *Big Sur*, while Tony in a far less valuable "profession" was raking in $1,500 a week. He loaned Jack money hand over fist, and as soon as Jack returned to Florida, he repaid it all.

The main thing Tony and Jack had in common, at that point, was that they both wanted to escape their frantic careers. Another Sampas brother, Nicky, had bought the Old 66 Café, one of the oldest bars in Lowell. Rechristened "Nicky's," the barroom had a high ceiling, gas lamps, and a long mahogany bar with rails. The only true relaxation for either Tony or Jack was the simple conversation they shared there after hours.

The most intense relationship Jack had in Lowell was with Paul Bourgeois. A short, dark, handsome, and immensely powerful Canuck, Bourgeois came from a broken home in Lowell and had spent twelve of his thirty-four years in prison. As a boy he had made many trips to Canada with his father, and his experiences there were now the source of his lively, if improbable, barroom tales. Bourgeois never walked across a barroom, he danced; and he'd set the whole room on its ear with his blood-curdling "Iroquois war whoops." Jack was completely taken in by Paul's claim to be the Chief of the Four Nations of the Iroquois. Around this claim Paul had woven an elaborate story, which included the "fact" that two of the tribes were named Kirouac and L'Evesque (Mémère's maiden name)! Jack accordingly began calling Paul his "cousin." As the tale went, the Four Nations had been pushed to Prince of Wales Land, near the North Pole, and now were starving because atomic submarines and underwater nuclear blasts were killing their fish and polar bears. As a result, Bourgeois had been dispatched to Washington to confer with the Secretary of State. Aglow with family pride, Jack repeated every detail in letters to his friends. When he began talking of writing a book about the affair, Paul knew the hoax had gone too far, and confessed, "I'm not an Indian chief, I'm a French thief from Lowell." But Jack conveniently didn't hear.

Bourgeois' vitality offered Jack a chance to get the spotlight off himself. He put on Paul's zoot suit and dressed Paul in his millworker's clothes, and in bars would point out Paul as "Jack Kerouac." At Charlie and Mary Sampas' he told Paul to read from *Mexico City Blues*, but when Paul started to murder the poetry Jack grabbed the book out of his hand and took over. If Paul got plenty of free drinks off him, he at least earned his keep by protecting him from the people angered by Jack's acid wit.

Promising to write a book about his new adventures, Jack left Lowell on September 24. He was driven to New York by Bourgeois and a Portuguese, Marty Gouveia. After Bourgeois spent a week terrorizing Jack's friends, he and Jack flew to Orlando. Mémère and Nin had only to look at Paul to know his story was "bunk," [306] but Jack installed him in the guest room anyway. They went through their usual bar routines, until one night at the house they got into an argument and Bourgeois threw him out the window. By the time Jack woke up the next day, Mémère had put Paul on a train for Lowell.

Alone Jack drank even more heavily, and his blackouts were now so frequent and severe that he would forget when he wrote to his friends and so send them duplicate letters. He was additionally depressed to learn that Neal and Carolyn were on the verge of divorce. In despair Mémère sent him back to Northport, where he bought her the most beautiful home of her life.

5.

On the snowy Christmas Eve of 1962 Jack, Mémère, and their caged cats arrived by train in Northport. Their new ranch house at 7 Judyann Court had two baths, a fireplace, and a completely finished basement. High above the center of town, it was surrounded by trees and Jack had enclosed the back yard with a six-foot cedar basketweave fence. He gave the address to only his most trusted friends.

Big Sur was selling less well than an average first novel, but for the present the steady influx of foreign royalties paid his high taxes and kept the wolf from the door. Before 1957 Jack had written all his books without expecting even to get them published; he now regretted the past several years of writing for money, and resolved never to do it again. He set to work on the novel he wanted to write, filling in the last major gap in *The Duluoz Legend* from his birth up to 1960. This novel would cover the years 1935 to 1946, which had been fictionalized in *The Town and the City*. Regardless of Lucien's wishes, this time Jack would relate the actual events, as well as examining more fully the impact of his father's death. Surveying the beauties and luxuries of his new home, which Leo Kerouac would never see, Jack couldn't help dwelling on how he had broken his father's heart by leaving football to become a writer. He was haunted by the feeling that success had come too late. Sick of his own former optimism in books like *The Dharma Bums* and even *Big Sur*, he vowed to let loose all the angry pessimism weighing in his soul. The novel would be called *Vanity of Duluoz*, the title of the first novel he had tried to write after leaving home in 1941.

The trouble was that his gloom and loneliness made writing as hard as pulling his own teeth, and for several months the work merely inched along. Nevertheless he took time out to write answers to twenty-four questions about himself sent by Holmes, who was doing a book on the current literary scene.

One morning Mémère heard the old signal of three taps followed by the hesitant words, "Mama-mère! It's *me*, Stasiu!" Stan Twardowicz had brought along an English teacher who wanted to meet Jack, and eventually she let them into his room, where he was pleading for a beer. Stan suggested coffee instead, but Jack, who was sweating bullets, insisted on the beer and drank it down quickly. When he'd almost finished his second, and his hands had stopped trembling, he was ready to talk. In a distinguished accent the English teacher rattled off the names of a dozen books he wanted to know if Jack had read. Jack was silent. The professor excused himself, but Stan stayed. "What the fuck did you bring this guy for?" Jack growled. Then with a laugh he repeated the professor's whole speech, even down to the titles of the books, imitating his "English" accent perfectly.

Frequently Jack would stop by Stan's studio and say, "I just wanna sit down and have a coupl'o' beers." He was the only person Stan would allow there when he was working. Jack would wander about quietly, staying away from Stan's corner, and sometimes he'd sit watching or start painting on his own—usually a Pietà. In his conservative way he'd use charcoal to sketch the design first, then add the oil colors. Yet he used the brusque, muscular strokes characteristic of abstract painters. And having been around abstract painters so long, he had learned to translate their paintings into a poetic shorthand. Of Stan's gayer ones, Jack said, "You paint with kissing colors," and of one from Stan's early "black period": "What the fuck is that, a rubber raft at midnight?" In such spontaneous responses Stan recognized that Jack had got what he meant to convey.

Sometimes architect Larry Smith would come over, and the three of them would talk for hours. Young and on the way up, Smith lamented Jack's lack of drive but he enjoyed relaxing with him from the pressures of his own career. If Jack was joined by his teenage followers, however, Smith would leave. No matter how hard Jack had to strain, he always tried to give them the handsome young hero of *On the Road*.

At the Twardowiczes' open house every weekend, Jack was able to meet neighbors more his own age. These were mostly married couples, the men professionals: fledgling journalist Mike McGrady, psychologist Robert Walters, teacher "Bill Crabtree." Matsumi Kanemitsu, a mutual friend, was often invited too. Jack would be at ease there, trading W. C. Fields stories, quoting Shakespearean sonnets, and talking his own peculiar brand of red-neck politics. Of the Civil

Rights movement he speculated that most of its white proponents were people "who would hire Negroes to wash their toilet bowls." He was not against integration—"I was integrated with Jews"—but felt the Jews had "flung the Negro at America so that we'd forget anti-Semitism." Despite the racial and religious mixture at Stan's parties no one ever got mad at Jack, because it was always clear that he was attacking people "out there," and that he felt nothing but loving good will toward people he knew. In fact, he developed a deep, romantic friendship with Stan's Jewish wife Anne. Adept at charming women-shy men, she coddled and protected Jack without ever competing with him, sat on his lap, and delighted in his playful flirtations. The only time Jack caused a ruckus was when the men played poker. Refusing to join in, he was frustrated by the loss of his audience and would start hollering to get their attention.

Many of these people were in turn treated to the extraordinary experience of visiting Jack's house. Nowadays, rather than his literary archives, he was more apt to show them the specially coded card file by which he could quickly locate any song on his hundreds of tape reels. Stan was entranced to see him seated on his bed surrounded by religious calendars and little holy pictures, with a rosary hanging from the suspended light so that the cross dangled just above his head. In the basement, Jack put on *The Messiah* full blast. Later, drinking together, Stan was puzzled by the immaculate condition of the bathroom after Jack had used it. The next time Jack excused himself, Stan trailed him. Jack went out to the back yard to urinate, to avoid soiling his mother's illusion of her spotless son.

The one thing you didn't have at Jack's house were intellectual discussions; Jack would fend them off with one-liners. Stan asked, "How can you like Céline? He's so anti-Semitic." Replied Jack, "What's wrong with that?" Learning of Stan's passion for Beckett, Jack scoffed, "I can never figure what the hell he's writing about." When Stan inquired about his interest in Buddhism, Jack asked, "What's the sound of one hand clapping?" and then slapped Stan's face with all his might.

Matsumi, a Japanese Jew, didn't mind the fact that Mémère would cook him roast pork and make him participate in her Catholic grace, but he was exasperated by her dinnertime conversation. She chattered endlessly about what Jack had done as a child, and repeated her favorite joke: "I sure had a hard time when I made Jack, and he's still giving me a hard time!" Seeming to forget Matsumi altogether, she recalled Gerard: "You remember the first time I went to Sears to buy Gerry's socks?"—so obviously flailing Jack with time-worn stories that Matsumi was reminded of *The Glass Menagerie*. Continuing with memories of her husband, she'd eventually progress to uncles and cousins of whom Matsumi hadn't the faintest knowledge. Her other chief topic was her hatred of Jews, Puerto Ricans, and blacks. Of black men she had an especial terror, which she used as an argument for Jack to stay home: she insisted that someday while he was gone they were going to break in and rape her.

She also tortured Jack by praising her other children. On Valentine's Day she showed him a box of chocolates Nin had sent her, to remind him of his neglect. Feeling low, he went into town with Matsumi to find her a present. After browsing through a few stores he darted into his favorite bar, Gunther's, and challenged Matsumi to pinball—the winner to buy the beers. When Matsumi kept beating him, Jack angrily challenged him to pool. As Jack started to lose he pouted like a little boy who couldn't have his own way, so Matsumi let him win.

Although Mémère bewailed his drinking, Jack showed Matsumi the bottle of Southern Comfort under her bed. The level was marked to reveal if he had taken any.

One day Matsumi came in wearing a yarmulke, and Mémère asked him to take it off. When she tried to persuade him to become a Catholic, he told her he would go to her church if she'd take him. She replied that it would be a sin for her to enter with a Jap. Besides, she complained, every time she went to church they asked her for money.

She told Matsumi, "I feel sorry for the Jew boys having their penis cut off." When he told this to Jack, Jack said, "Why don't you show it to my mother?" Matsumi did so, and she rushed out screaming about his "insult to a Christian woman."

He and Jack planned a joint book about cats, Matsumi to do the illustrations and Jack to provide a text of haiku. Soon Mémère was writing haiku herself. She told Matsumi that she wanted recognition too.

She told Jack she liked Matsumi because he was "exotic," and she became so jealous of his friendship with Jack that as soon as he came to visit she'd drag him into the kitchen to help her chop chicken livers for the cats! While they worked, she kept touching his knee and putting her arm around him. Jack warned him in deadly earnest: "Don't touch my mother."

At a party in the city, Matsumi saw Jack ready to attack a man who wouldn't stop using the word *motherfucker*. "What did I say?" the guy taunted, feigning ignorance, but Jack refused to repeat the word. At Matsumi's loft he recounted with great anguish an episode in which his mother had allegedly tried to make love to him. Matsumi told him, "If you want to fuck your mother, please do. Then you'll feel much better." Enraged, Jack smashed two of his vases and threatened to kill him if he ever suggested that again. Matsumi agreed to avoid the subject provided Jack stopped asking for advice about what to do with his mother. Telling Matsumi to leave him alone, Jack retreated to the "monk's bed" to cry, and later went out to get drunk.

Other friends were also beginning to challenge Jack's hypocrisy.

He was procrastinating writing the article *Playboy* wanted about the Beat Generation, and he offered to coauthor it with Gregory, who needed money for his upcoming marriage. At Jack's house they taped a discussion in which Gregory tried to force him to admit that his unconcern for the welfare of blacks belied the love for them he had vaunted in *On the Road,* in the passage beginning: "I walked with every muscle aching . . . wishing I were a Negro . . ." Blind to the contradiction, Jack kept asserting that his "poetic statements" were true to the moment he made them. Of the encounter he wrote bitterly to Allen that heroin was "going to Gregory's head." Actually Gregory saw Jack with remarkable acuity. He wrote Allen that Jack "needs help, a real good awakening or he is forever lost, just don't say aw good old Jack because you wont be helping him much that way."

In May Gary Snyder sent Jack the work of a Japanese college girl who had attempted to psychoanalyze him using material from *The Subterraneans.* Jack shot back to Gary a fierce tract of misogyny: women he sees as "Mara demons" who lure men into sex only to dominate and destroy them, and he excoriates both Snyder and Ginsberg for their fervent sexual activity, concluding that they are both deluded by the "Zen heresy" that Samsara is the same as Nirvana. Although Snyder sent a considerate reply, Jack never wrote him again.

Indeed mid-1963 marks the point where Kerouac broke off correspondence with almost all his Beat friends; significantly, he continued to correspond regularly with John Holmes, Ed White, and Lois Sorrells. His life in Northport had fallen into the not unpleasant rut of an almost square suburban tippler.

In the spring, Stan played softball with Larry Smith, Bob Walters, Mike McGrady, Bill Crabtree, and other weekend sportsmen. Since Jack's house was only half a block from the school field, they'd drag him out of bed and station him in the outfield still in his ragged red terrycloth slippers. When he missed a fly ball (which happened often), he'd do somersaults to show he really didn't care—making his embarrassment all the more obvious. They all knew of his football heroics twenty years earlier. Once, backpeddling for a fly, his slippers came off and he toppled and passed out. Fifteen minutes later he got up and said, "OK, I missed that one, but let's get on with the game," as if he didn't know he'd missed two innings.

His prodigious memory functioned sporadically. One night, after Jack had apparently passed out at Stan's house, someone joked, "Stan, you're getting a big fat ass." Stan retorted, "You can't drive a spike with a tack hammer!" Suddenly Jack sat up and asked him to repeat the quip. Stan did so, and Jack said, "I got it," then went back to sleep. A few years later, Stan read that line in *Satori in Paris.*

Physically Jack was still powerful, even if his waistline was several sizes larger. When he connected with a softball, he often belted a home run. But he suffered from D.T.'s and other alcoholic maladies oftener than before. Once again young people crashed over his fence at five in the morning, screaming, "Are you busy?" Sometimes he'd attempt to hide from them. He requested librarian Joan Roberts to deliver his books so he wouldn't have to appear in public, and when she knocked at his darkened front room, he answered the door with a flashlight. Other times he joined the kids of his own volition. Stan would find him shooting pool with them in Gunther's, though after enough whiskey he'd retire to a little table with his back against the space heater, to ease his chills.

Some long nights Jack lacked both the strength and the will to go home. Unable to get him into the car, Stan would walk him to his own house and put him to bed. Jack always wanted to go on talking. When he had the energy, Stan would talk back until Jack fell asleep. But many times Jack would keep waking every ten minutes and just go on talking to the empty room.

At times just getting him to the house was a project. Leaving Gunther's once, Jack was fascinated by a group of kids getting set to drag race. He yelled, "Hey, watch me, Stan!" and went to lie on the streetcar tracks in the middle of Main Street. There was no way for Stan to budge the 195 pounds of his dead weight. Opposition only made him more stubborn. One car started toward him and then swerved aside (and there wasn't much leeway with the parked cars starting to back out on either side). Thinking fast, Stan said, "Jack, I see you're back on the road again." Jack laughed and sat up, said, "Hey, that's pretty good," and got out of the way just as the race began.

One night Stan got a call from Mémère, who was worried about Jack's prolonged absence. After a fruitless night searching the bars, Stan found him the next morning passed out in the woods on the trail to Stan's house. Said Jack: "Stanley, you're the most compassionate man I ever met."

The clammers, by contrast, had their eyes on the pale blue airline satchel Jack carried on all his walks around town, which contained a fifth of Jack Daniels and a fifth of Canadian Club. By sipping his own hard stuff in the vestibule or bathroom of a bar he could stretch his money just buying beers, but the bartenders soon caught on to his trick and either confiscated the bottles or tossed him out. In the latter case, the clammers were always ready to take him joy-riding. One night, after Jack's supply was depleted, they bamboozled their way into a lighted house for further drinks. On the way home Jack was so drunk they had to push him out of the car. As he lay in a heap on the road one clammer said, "I like your books, but I don't like you."

He tried to write. He would hole up for two or three weeks, and neither Stan nor anyone else would get as much as a phone call or card from him. Afterwards he'd sometimes have a fresh scroll of typescript to show, or little articles that he'd boast about, like his "Address to the Italian Judge" (pertaining to the Milanese obscenity trial of *The Subterraneans*), which were mostly pitiful excuses for the time he'd wasted. Still capable of readying a book for publication, he looked forward to the release of *Visions of Gerard*. But he had to face the fact that the old pattern of distraction and retreat—going out to get material and coming home to write it down—no longer worked. The purpose that had bound together the fragments of his life was simply lost; and retracing his steps down the years gave no clue to its whereabouts.

6.

Divorced from Carolyn, Neal made a trip to New York with a new woman and a young man in August 1963. Jack found Neal "as sweet and gentle and polite and intelligent and interesting as ever," but his two friends devastated Mémère's kitchen, forcing Jack to evict them all. Returning to California, Neal told his friends how disappointed he was in Jack. He said all Jack did lately was sit in the house, letting his mother serve him and raving that the youth were ruining America.

In June Jack had written to Allen in Japan, pledging that he was with him "all the way," but requesting Allen get a shave and a haircut before coming to visit him. In December 1963, Allen and Peter reunited in New York—Allen bearded and both of them with long hair. Mémère wouldn't let either one in the house. Jack wrote Holmes that he was irritated with Allen's "long white robe Messiah shot." The Allen he loved was the lyrical poet weeping over the death of his mother in *Kaddish*—that was the direction he wanted Allen to pursue. Instead, Jack imagined that he had become a polemicist for Castro, and he was revolted by what he heard were Allen's latest projects: a TV program called *The Fall of America*, and an autobiographical movie featuring shots of his mother's asshole and a cross made of broken dolls.[307]

At Christmastime his daughter Jan got his phone number from Lucien Carr. When she called, Jack was drunk, and they talked for hours. He told her about the Kerouac family crest, referring to it as *your* and *our*. He also told her, "Remember, you're not a Canuck, you're a Bretonne." Later, realizing what he'd done, he got so angry that he scarcely spoke to Lucien for a year.

In February 1964, Gregory and his wife had a daughter. Meeting him, Jack began his usual diatribe: "Why did you bring something into this world just to die?" But when Gregory brought the little girl to Northport Jack melted, saying, "I bless this house for your child."

Despite his bluff to Gary that he could do without women, he longed for another love affair. His teenage girlfriend Yseult visited a few times in Northport, and he bragged to friends that she called him "Tristram," but she lacked the devotion of her namesake. He began calling his old girlfriends, often late at night, until he could no longer afford the phone bills. He asked Thea Snyder, remarried and living in California, to "run away" with him, claiming, "You have to do this! You're the only one who could rescue me!" He asked Joyce, also married, to join him at Lucien's and to bring her "little husband." When she got there she was frightened to find Jack and Lucien both very drunk, sticking lit cigarettes under each other's ears and baiting each other in diabolic ways. A few months later, after her husband was killed, she got another call from Jack. Disremembering that she had been married, he told her she was "the only one" for him because she had never asked him for fur coats and had been content with pea soup.

He met Mardou in the Village and bellyached that everywhere he went people "attacked" him. As she started to get into a taxi, he cried, "Mardou, you're always shutting me out!"

Thanksgiving of 1963, Jack had a warm reunion with Helen Weaver, and solved his sexual problem by eating oysters. But when they parted it was only as old friends.

He invited Stella Sampas to visit him in Northport but Mémère refused to let her in the house.

Since Stan was seriously involved with one of his art students, Anne Twardowicz turned to Jack for solace, as he turned increasingly to her. Eventually Anne became a combination of mother and mistress for Jack. One day when Stan wasn't home he pushed her against the wall, and she didn't resist. But he was impotent and she discouraged further intimacy between them, realizing that to take on Jack as a lover would only complicate her life still further.

The fact that he was no longer making it with women became a common joke, in which he himself participated. On crowded Main Street he yelled to Stan, "I was in New York, and guess what? I got laid . . . by a *girl!*" Amid numerous giggles Stan replied, "Jack, it's about time."

But it wasn't funny when he would appear at Allen and Peter's new Lower East Side apartment pleading for a blow job from them or anyone else present. He even humbled himself before Carl Solomon. "Come on, you're not fair, come on!" he would whine. "Nobody loves me! I'm too fat and old and red-faced! I'm lonesome!" But even when Allen and Peter did what he asked, he rarely got satisfaction. He was desperate to continue functioning sexually and didn't know where to turn. He only knew he should stay out of New

York, because every time he went there he got sick from drinking and often fell down in the street and had to "return staggering home in pieces."

Stan was nonplussed to find him putting a hand on his shoulder and demanding, "Open up! Show me what you got!" Finally Stan said, "You're not my type," and Jack never bothered him again. Knowing Bill Crabtree to be bisexual, Jack "courted" him with embarrassing persistence, harping on the fact that Bill resembled Seymour Wyse. Having lost a beloved first wife, Bill was searching for some meaning in life beyond one-night stands, and Jack certainly wasn't the answer. To mock Bill's indifference, Jack stood under his window and sang "On Top of Old Smokey."

In the spring of 1964, according to a letter Jack wrote Holmes, Mémère slapped Lois in the face and chased her out. By that time Jack was running with a gang of bisexual teenage boys.

The publication of *Visions of Gerard* in September 1963 helped him recoup his dignity. When people recognized him on the street and asked, "Aren't you Jack Kerouac?" he'd straighten up and say slowly in a basso profundo, "Yes . . . I . . . am." More than ever, it wasn't just a book but his very life on trial. In one of those eerie, vague moments when life merges with art, Jack bought a drawing of Gerard that had served as an illustration for the book and hung it on his living room wall.

The critics seemed to be striving for new lefthanded and underhanded ways of putting him down. Robert Phelps in the *New York Herald Tribune* found the book "so pridefully 'sincere'" that he couldn't "help question the value of sincerity itself," and he was even more distressed to find that this "slapdash, grossly sentimental" story had been the work of "a man with a subtle sense of human nature and a gift of language." Paradoxically, Phelps concluded that "in someone else's hands, it could have been moving." *Newsweek*, after bandying such words as "bore," "fraud," and "self-indulgent," attained some originality in the phrase "he casts his deficiencies about him like confetti." Complaining against Kerouac's "inflated" prose, Saul Maloff in *The New York Times* inflated his own prose with tautologies like "bathos of the most lachrymose kind." Even more unconscionably, Maloff accused Jack of "betraying" and "debasing" Gerard's suffering with his "garrulous hipster yawping."

At the same time, Jack read an article calling Norman Mailer a "radical moralist." He wondered what compassion Mailer could teach after having stabbed his wife, Jack's old girl Adele Morales. He wrote Holmes that he was sick enough to quit writing for good. But there was no real chance of that, as he still burned with the desire for recognition. Invited to dinner at Larry Smith's Jack showed up sober, with his hair combed and wearing a sports shirt. Sitting on the porch, overlooking Whitman's beloved Sound, he said softly and sadly, "I'm the only major writer in America today who never won a prize. *Never.*"

In March 1964, the students in Lowell House at Harvard asked Jack to give a reading. Although their undergraduate dormicory was named for a past Harvard President, Abbot Laurence Lowell, rather than Jack's hometown, he was beckoned by the fortuitous pun. Impressed above all by the fact that *Harvard had written to him*, a kind of personal bow to the Beat achievement, he packed his sports coat, flew to Boston, and was installed in the Preacher's Room by resident tutor Al Gelpi.

Gelpi made a hit with him even before Jack found out Al had written his doctoral thesis on Emily Dickinson. On a piece of "Preacher's Room" stationery Jack sketched a Pietà that Gelpi, a devout Catholic, recognized as unique. Behind Christ's body being taken down from the cross, Jack had collapsed time with a rising Easter sun.

That evening and the next day he was constantly drawing Crucifixions and Pietàs, frequently on bar napkins, as he confided his insecurity about the reading to Gelpi. His drinking heightened Al's own insecurity. Certain students were selected to have a private dinner with Jack before the reading. In the elegant Georgian dining room, growing more defensive in proportion to the exaggeratedly tasteful manners of everybody else, Jack hardly touched his food and continued to drink steadily. At the end of the dinner he was so glad to be free of the oppressive atmosphere that he leapt up—and keeled over with a thump, flat on the floor. Al said, "Gee, Jack, you're supposed to go in now and read." Jack sat up and said, "I'll be fine, fine."

As soon as he got into the Common Room he began to jump around, cracking anti-Semitic jokes with—and occasionally at—people in the audience. Sitting down, he yelled, "I want to read Emily Dickinson!" and Al fetched a volume. In the meantime the undergraduates were finding the scene funny and curious and having a lark. Somebody began passing him drinks through the window. At last the Dickinson arrived. Jack mumbled a few poems, then—furious at the students' continuing laughter—whanged the book at the wall. Next, he picked up *Visions of Gerard* and began to read with great tenderness. Some kid asked, "Why do you have no discipline?"

"Is that the way to talk to your professor?" Jack replied. "Try it if you can. If you can you'll pull the rug out from under everybody."

He pulled the rug out from under the reading by launching a tirade against the "communist threat" and Mao, and when he started making faces at the senior tutor who had invited him, the tutor passed a note up to Gelpi: "Get him out of here!" But for better or worse, Jack couldn't be coaxed from his chair. Gelpi wondered at the strangeness of the man, whose mouth could smile while his eyes seemed ready to cry, his gaze miles away from where he was at the moment.

The next day the Harvard *Crimson* satirized Jack as the visiting literary drunk and printed a photo that made him look like a pugnacious windbag. He was especially hurt by their calling him a "clown," and he kept brooding over it all the days he stayed, and overstayed.

While Al slept, Jack would find others with whom to drink and talk. In the morning he'd sleep a few hours, get up around nine, stand on his head a few minutes, and begin drinking beer and discussing music, poetry, and theology with Al while Al prepared for his tutorial sessions. In the midst of a joke or story, his eyes would suddenly mist, and in a choking voice he'd describe how neat and clean his mother kept his room in Northport, or explain that part of him was always with Gerard in heaven. One afternoon in the Oxford Grill he had been quietly scribbling Pietàs on napkins when he blurted out that the trip had been a disaster and that he would never give another reading. He took his full glass of beer and overturned it on the table.

Jack remained in the Preacher's Room until the senior tutor kicked him out. After a brief stay with Tony Sampas in Lowell, he returned to the ordered center of his life—the house on Judyann Court, which Mémère had already put up for sale in order to return to Florida.

7.

The Northport Public Library wanted to include Jack in a series of interviews with local artists. Despite Joan Roberts' persuasion, he refused to make another public spectacle of himself. Rather than wrestle with more unanswerable questions, he rounded up four of his teenage followers and spent a few days "storming" a castle in Centerport. It was a real European castle, imported stone by stone and then abandoned. But even the boys thought he was nuts when he told one who had just scaled a high wall: "You should join the army!" When the police came to clear them out, as Jack told it, he got them all away safely by "taking up the rear of a perfect guerilla sortie."

Stan was a strategist too. In mid-April he called Jack to his studio to see a new painting. But as soon as Jack saw Miklos Zsedely, assistant director of the library, seated beside a tape recorder, he bolted down the stairs, out across Main Street, and into Gunther's Bar. Stan told Zsedely to wait and ran after him.

Jack was hurt that Stan could pull such a trick, but Stan replied that since Jack wanted tributes to his memory, he should seize this chance to leave a permanent record of his opinions and methodology that could be "studied by scholars in fifty years." After six boiler-makers, Jack was ready to begin.

For the first half-hour, as Stan helped him to more beers, Jack delivered a serious monologue. But then while changing the tape Zsedely found that the machine hadn't been recording. Angrier (and drunker) than before, Jack introduced himself as "Lala G. Pa-poosnick" and vented much of his wit on "Mr. Funny Hungary" and his thick accent. It became a Zen non-interview. Twardowicz kept painting in the background, as well as providing fresh booze and jazz accompaniment, and cueing Jack's humor. At various times they were joined by Anne and a host of local characters.

When a fire siren blew and Twardowicz automatically said, "The church is on fire," Jack roared back, "Over my dead body!" Then followed a sequence of haikulike exchanges between them such as "combustion on the fire-pole," "no, it's made of aluminum," etc., which carried off into a discussion of what type of jar Stan was mixing his paints in. "Wheat-germ jar," said Jack, "that sounds like a town in Hungary . . . was it in Buddha, or was it Pesht?" Before Zsedely could react to Jack's remark about the "pink-dressed 'hoors' in the alleyways" of Budapest, Jack cried, "Get that sound!"—the swishing of paint being stirred.

To show he was still in control, Jack would later revert to Zsedely's chosen topics and frame his own questions, such as: "Well, what do you want me to say about Proust?" Zsedely would lamely try to answer what were to have been his own questions, thereby letting Jack gauge his ignorance:

KEROUAC: I understand that Proust, all the girls that Proust is writing about, were boys. Is that true?

ZSEDELY: I don't know. I wasn't there.

KEROUAC: Well, that's what they say. That's what Maurois says, but I think Maurois was a *crétin*.

Politically Jack made no startling revelations: "I'll tell you what I really am—a Republican!" Jack-like, he asserted that *if* he voted it would be for Goldwater, but he wasn't voting at all because he didn't want to "encourage Caesarism." The hottest thing he said was to call Ginsberg a "communist."

Talking about his work, a genuine pathos entered his voice: "I don't want to write anymore." A heaviness also crept in when he said he would soon move to Florida to take care of his mother: "And I've been doing that—that's all I'm doing. I could go off and get married and have children . . . not if I take care of her. . . . If she dies before me, you know what I'm gonna do? I'll end my life living in a hut in Tibet."

Perhaps most surprising was the openness with which he discussed his sexual experiences with men. The impression of his "ho-mosexuality" was so strong that when Jack said to Anne in a thick voice (so close to crying one might really call it a *cri de coeur*), "I kind of like you . . . I wish you weren't married to Stanley," she merely laughed and said, "I bet you'd wanna marry Stanley."

"Yeah," said Jack with no feeling whatever. He speculated about getting himself a "slave boy."

"You would have to drink to do it, right?" Anne asked.

Jack reared up: "You must think I'm the very devil!"

"The devil? You always say you're an angel?"

"I'm no Lucifer!"

"Who's the guy that stands over your shoulder?"

"The archangel Michael."

"Does he ever bang you over the head?"

"I guess so because I've never gone wrong."

They all laughed, but Jack repeated with all the solemnity he could muster: "I've never gone wrong."

Later he claimed to be the Holy Ghost, although "actually I'm not the Holy Ghost. Everything is the Holy Ghost including me and you. . . . If we're not ghosts, tell me what we are, Einstein?"

Fearing libel suits, the Northport Library severely edited the tapes, so that the voice left behind is even more of a "ghost."

Jack's Northport days were dwindling. Although Mémère claimed she wanted to be near Nin, she also sought to remove Jack from his present drinking nexus. This time, however, he insisted on moving to St. Petersburg, to put fifty miles between himself and the Blakes. He was mad at both Nin and Paul; since when he had gone down there in 1963 drunk and bellicose, to collect on his debt, Nin had called the sheriff to escort him back to the airport.

Spring turned to summer on the softball field. As though it were the last summer in Eden, Jack took stock of his life. In late April he wrote Ed White asking him to visit, anxious to "restore that spirit 'at used to join us." He told Ed that the determination to get back on his feet financially had started him writing again. And was he writing! All at once he was doing a travel article for *Holiday*, expanding *Old Angel Midnight*, revising *Desolation Angels*, and working full speed on *Vanity of Duluoz*, confident that he was producing the first decent sentences he'd written in ten years.

In late May Ed, his wife Ann, and Tom Livornese found Jack seated in his rocking chair with a typewriter on his lap. Stacked beside him were his favorite books: Boswell's *Life of Johnson*, *Tristram Shandy*, Blake, Pascal's *Pensées*, Spengler, and Melville. On his desk was a little Woolworth lamp his mother had given him; it said: "Genius at Work." He told them his strength was giving out, and that he had to sleep until noon each day. He wanted to get himself a little hideaway cabin out West after he had settled Mémère in Florida. Now he was thinking of the hills outside Denver, where there was enough timber and water to live year round, and friends would have to climb in or arrive by jeep! The cabin itself he commissioned Ed to design.

In New York they hit the plusher bars, where Jack drank just enough whiskey to get his glow; he had come to hate the taste, which he killed with ginger ale chasers. Gaily he talked of his dream to live like Frank Sinatra, chauffeured in a limousine and surrounded by bodyguards. Finally, in the cocktail lounge of Ed's hotel, as Ed dozed from the crème de menthe mixed with champagne, Tom played the piano while Ann and Jack sang old songs. He was literally overwhelmed to be again in the company of friends from his youth, instead of the hangers-on who kept bringing strangers "to meet the author, or, rather, to go witness the idiot."

In the summer Neal was again in New York, but he was now more a stranger to Jack than an old friend. Neal was the driver for a troupe of acidhead dropouts from society, proto-hippies known as the Merry Pranksters. The Pranksters were led by Ken Kesey, the Oregonian woodsman novelist who had migrated to California after reading *On the Road*. Jack had liked Kesey's first novel, *One Flew Over the Cuckoo's Nest*, but he must have felt some enmity to find Kesey becoming the anode for a new generation—a generation he considered "disrespectful" and "illiterate." Nor was Jack happy to see the changes in Neal wrought by his unlimited access to amphetamine and LSD. Not only was Neal starting to look like the balding, disheveled bum who had been his father, but his personality had hardened, and his eyes become frighteningly empty.

Having driven cross-country in a Day-Glo-painted bus named "Further," the Pranksters were now ensconced in a Park Avenue apartment. Kesey wanted to meet Kerouac, and despite Jack's feeling that Kesey was "nuts" and "too wild," he agreed to come to one of their parties. When he arrived they were all high on acid. The apartment was filled with high-powered recording and movie-making equipment, wires snaking everywhere, the smoky air reechoing with electronic cacophonies, and the whole scene even more hellish in the blinding glare of floodlights. Jack was further bewildered when one of the Pranksters tied an American flag around his neck. The couch was also covered with flags. Jack, who had spent a lifetime teaching friends how to fold the flag properly, was not about to sit on one. He picked one up and folded it to make a space for himself. Many of the Pranksters were mocking his obvious dejection, and Kesey tried to cheer him. When Jack didn't respond, Ken attempted a little flattery. He declared that Jack's place in history was secure. Jack's answer floored him: "I know."

If his place was secure, his identity still foundered. When Val Duncan came to interview him for *Newsday* in July, Jack traced his ancestors to Canada, Ireland, Cornwall, Wales, and Brittany. He also told him of his past lives as Tristan and a Tartar horseman. In letters to friends he had claimed such reincarnations as Buddha, Shakespeare, Balzac, the composer Buxtehude, and a queer English footpad named Robert Horton, who had been hanged. He would eventually tell Carolyn Cassady that he had been Christ, and he extended the Kerouac lineage to Scotland, England, Russia, and Persia. What it all boiled down to was an attempt to relate himself to mankind, from which he had always felt excluded.

And he was feeling ever more so. After their house was sold in August, Jack left Mémère for a couple of days to relax on Fire Island. Shambling from beach to beach in his torn T-shirt and baggy pants, with uncombed hair and a nose that had been punched once too often, he barged into groups of young people announcing that he was Jack Kerouac. They'd heard of Kerouac all right, but they were sure this wasn't the man. Finding a beautiful girl in a bikini reading *On the Road*, he asked, "Is the book any good?" But she wouldn't believe he'd written it, and when he kept bothering her she called for the police, who arrested him. At the station, learning he was a writer, they were afraid he would start a Civil Rights–type protest and let him go for $10.

Stan and Anne gave a going-away party for Jack and Mémère. Dressed to the nines, with his hair perfectly parted (the condition of his hair was now a gauge of his sobriety), Jack was careful not to drink too much. Mémère had a great time telling dirty stories with Anne, though later, learning Anne was Jewish, her face fell and she exlaimed, "But she's so *nice!*"

Jack was far more frantic at the party at his own house on August 26, the night before he and Mémère were supposed to entrain for Florida. He didn't want to leave, and he dreaded St. Petersburg, "the City of the Living Dead." All day he had been badgering Mémère. When she brought him a hamburger to calm him, he told her, "Mother, cut my throat!" Stan, Anne, Larry Smith, and Larry's wife Tsuneko tried to humor him, but Jack's agitation precipitated a fight between Larry and Tsuneko. Tsuneko ran out, Stan ran after her, and Jack spent much of the evening blustering into Smith's tape recorder. His central theme was disappointment—with his own life, not having stayed in the navy, for one thing, and with America. "Vietnam," he mused, "the Americans should get out of there. What are they doin' there? That's part of China—we're no Chinese. It's the ricebowl of China. . . . The Viet Cong are getting money from Americans."

After the company left he went out drinking and disappeared for two days. Mémère was hysterical until a search party discovered him sleeping in a field in Centerport. Anne made their new travel arrangements.

Before Jack left, Stan told him he was splitting up with Anne to live with his student, Lil.

"For that blond broad?" Jack groaned, practically in tears. "How can you do that to her, Stan?"

"It's not 'how can I do that to her,' it's what I have to do for me," said Stan, "and it's better for her too."

Jack made no further protest. He was too considerate to ask of others what he asked of himself—to be a saint. Where he wanted to live was a place in which he could care for himself as much as he cared for others, and it didn't exist on earth. Unable to forgive his own sins, unsatisfied with just the goodness of his heart, he would go on poisoning his body until it rotted around him, rotted, bloated, exploded, and fell away to let the pure Jack Kerouac, the saint, escape free at last—remembered only as a ghost.

FOURTEEN
Jack's Last Tape

1.

When Jack and Mémère arrived in St. Petersburg, their new house at 5155 10th Avenue North was still under construction, and they stayed temporarily in an unfurnished apartment. Restless without his work setup, Jack spent nights shooting pool at the Tic-Toc club.

He was so adamant about not gambling with his own money that he would bum quarters off people to put in the pool table. One night, thanking the handsome, bushy-haired young man who'd given him a quarter, he said, "I'm Jack Kerouac." The guy laughed out loud and played along as if it were a joke, asking Jack about Doctor Sax and Dean Moriarty. As Jack authoritatively answered question after question, Cliff Anderson stood entranced in the real-life presence of his hero. Cliff was a literature student at the University of South Florida, but that alone wouldn't have enabled him to so rapidly become Jack's best friend. He was also the leader of the poolhall gang, a "fast rapper" who could quote *Finnegans Wake* and coax a coed into bed with equal finesse. He never lacked the means to get high, and though he was no taller than Jack he was powerful and could handle himself in tough situations. In short, Cliff Anderson was Neal Cassady minus twenty years.

Returning home with Cliff the night of September 19, Jack saw his mother in the doorway, crying. She told him, "Your sister is dead." Tremendously shaken, Jack went back to the bars to get drunk. He couldn't bear to attend her funeral. For months afterward he wept almost daily. To comfort himself, he'd sit on the front porch and listen to the wind blowing through a huge Georgia pine, which spoke to him like the ghostly voices of Gerard and Ti Nin.

Nin's husband had left her several months earlier to live with his mistress in Virginia. She had sold their house and moved to an apartment, supporting herself and young Paul by managing the building. Anguish and overwork had reduced her to ninety pounds. Supposedly her husband had phoned to ask her for a divorce so he could remarry. In any event, a few minutes after the call she collapsed of a heart attack.

The last time Jack had seen her they had argued about the way she managed the money he was lending her. Her death doubtless burdened him with guilt, especially since she was now elevated to sainthood beside Gerard. Mémère claimed that Nin's ghost appeared to her the second night, saying she was about to ascend to heaven and asking Mémère to care for young Paul. Jack would tell people that Nin "was too good for this world." His rage turned against her husband; at first he simply blamed Paul for her heart attack, then later convinced himself that Paul had driven her to "suicide," and told this story to a number of close friends. For a few weeks after her death he was frightened enough to reduce his drinking, but the deep depression into which he and Mémère had been plunged eventually led to their both drinking more heavily. By early 1965 he would keep a green water bottle filled with Cutty Sark Scotch by his chair and sip from it all day, and when anyone mentioned his drinking he'd say, "This is my water."

He completely severed relations with Allen and Peter, warning friends not to give them his address. The countercultural youth movement against the Vietnam War was just beginning, and Allen was active in all its ramifications, including the campaign to legalize marijuana. Derisively Jack would tell his Florida friends, "Allen doesn't work anymore." He felt equally betrayed by Lucien, not only because of Janet's phone call, but because Lucien had begun living with Mardou. The only old friend for whom Jack seemed to retain genuine affection was Neal. In fact he had come to worship the image he had of Neal. He would tell Cliff not only that Neal was a better writer than himself, but that "I'm nothing compared to Neal—I just follow him around." Since Cliff had never met anyone with as much energy as Jack he was dying to meet Neal, and Jack promised that if Cliff drove him West he would introduce them. Yet Jack's devotion to Neal didn't entail any obligation in the real world. In the fall of 1965 Neal asked his permission to publish their correspondence, in order to continue supporting Carolyn and the children. In a one-sentence letter, Jack denied it.

While Neal sought an elusive future among the young, Jack escaped an alien world among his own disciples. In Cliff's 1950 Chevy, he rode to football and baseball games, fraternity parties, and every poolhall and honky-tonk on Nebraska Avenue in Tampa. Cliff introduced him to a slew of new friends: Ron Tichener, a football player; Ronny Lowe, an even brawnier rock 'n' roller; Paddy Mitchell, a titanic harmonica player; Carl Adkins, a philosophy student and aspiring novelist; Mike Baldwin, a blues singer; and Larry Vickers, another U.S.F. student. To some extent this young crowd was using Jack. According to Vickers they never lost sight of the fact that he could grant them immortality in his writing. In a less vulturish way they also sought Jack's approval, because he was more truly their father than the genetic fathers against whom they were rebelling.

Ben Brown, another student, wrote that most of the group imagined themselves living like Jack's characters. On the other hand, they provided Jack with the only companionship he had for over a year, and served as his needed protectors.

In minutes he could get a party or a barroom jumping, and just as quickly he could provoke a riot. He was now living his Jack London script to the hilt, embellishing it with touches of Dylan Thomas and Maxwell Bodenheim, about whom he used to collect stories in the Village. He'd tear into tough bars shouting at the top of his lungs: "I'm the world-famous author, Jack Kerouac!" If that didn't get a rise, he might bellow: "I'm the greatest pool player, the greatest drinker, and the greatest lover in the place!" That was just the beginning. Once he took a full pitcher of beer and flung it to the ceiling. Another time, seeing a girl with unusually big breasts, he made a beeline for her and seized one in each hand. At a New Year's Eve party, he told a fancy Parisienne that she spoke French like an Algerian. And if anyone had anything they didn't want noticed, Jack would be the first to point it out. Then he'd keep pricking them until the person blew his top or laughed or did something to acknowledge that his little shame was out in the open.

The curious thing is that he couldn't take such ribbing himself. Tired of hearing Jack burlesque his West Virginia drawl, Carl Adkins asked, "Is it true that Canucks are built close to the ground to make it easier for them to pick potatoes?" Jack snapped, "That's getting personal." Nor would he ever accept responsibility for the consequences of his capers. When he was arrested for pissing in the street he blamed Cliff, who was with him, for being "jail-prone."

There was still the other, studious Jack who'd hike to the library with his rucksack for a fresh load of books, the serious writer who was launched into pure ecstasy, not by cognac or Cutty Sark, but by the news that *Visions of Gerard* was being translated into French. Late in 1964, Coward-McCann accepted *Desolation Angels,* and Jack was even happier to learn that Seymour Krim was slated to write an introduction. Krim's piece turned out to be the first intelligent critical assessment of Jack's work in print since Warren Tallman's "Kerouac's Sound" in 1959. The only objection Jack raised was to Krim's comment about his familiarity with the homosexual subculture of New York. Jack wrote asking him to specify that Jack had developed a "non-participant acceptance of the homosexuality of (my) literary confreres."

Krim's introduction made a dent, if only a tiny one, in the wall excluding Kerouac from the ranks of seriously considered American writers. The book was released May 3, 1965. In *The New York Times,* Saul Maloff did his usual hatchet job, employing a goodly dose of *argumentum ad hominem:* "the characters are as fatuous in life as in art. . . ." In a second review in the *Times,* Charles Poore, who had praised *The Town and the City* in 1950, struggled to overcome his basic enjoyment of *Desolation Angels*. He could now hear Kerouac speaking with Saroyan's voice as well as Wolfe's, and he admired the "genuine attempt here to seize the color and sweep of human destiny." But like Maloff, Poore was repelled by the unsavory character of Beatdom, especially its role in spreading "narcotic experimentation," and so he was driven to pronounce the book "a nonclassic of a vanishing era." An even harder blow was the judgment by Nelson Algren in *Book Week* that "Kerouac's prose is not prose: it is a form of self-indulgence." *The New York Review of Books* gave the book lengthy and rather neutral consideration, though their bias showed in a Levine cartoon cruelly caricaturing Kerouac as a baggy-eyed, middle-aged adolescent. Only one voice joined Krim's in praising the vastness of Kerouac's accomplishment. Dan Wakefield in *The Atlantic* suggested *Desolation Angels* merited a Pulitzer Prize as "the book that is most representative of American life."

The adverse reviews helped Jack to an important professional decision. For years he had been agonizing over the question of whether he should attempt some critical defense of his works, a job that would have been exceptionally hard for him. It was now evident that even a clear explication like Krim's could not overcome the moral prejudice afflicting most of the critics. As he wrote Lois, he was grateful he had been spared "a great long lifetime in a briefcase proving my work and my work itself stopped dead at the level where I took to proving myself . . . I quit self promotion, I enter my page." Another major professional decision aided his peace of mind. He had given up the idea of changing his style. After attempting to write "careful 'Johnsonian' sentences," he realized that classical English prose "just doesnt EXPRESS the swirl of things as they are in this swirling age. . . ."

What so many of Kerouac's critics never understood was that he loathed that "swirl" as much as they. He loved the order of great poetry and denounced the current taste for Ian Fleming's James Bond spy novels, full of flashy gimmicks but lacking in any consistent sense of life. "The baby daydream of violent glamor" on TV disgusted him just as much, and as a protest (and compensation) he'd watch shows with the sound off while his hi-fi thundered the *Messiah*. It occurred to him that as the Beat thesis had been stated in the fifties, the sixties was manifesting its antithesis, and the synthesis wouldn't arrive until the late seventies.

Spring of 1965 he retired into the past reading Voltaire and Chauteaubriand while planning a trip to Europe to delve further into his ancestry. With $1,500 saved from his advance on *Desolation Angels* he flew to Paris on June 1, bound for Brittany, Cornwall, Amsterdam, and Germany. The first night he got drunk and picked up a prostitute who charged him $120. The next day, at the Bibliothèque Nationale, he was delighted by a reference in Moréri's *Grand Dictionnaire Historique*—"CARR, famille d'Ecoffe, cherchez KERR"—which seemed to prove that he and Lucien had descended from the same family. The librarians, smelling alcohol on his breath, were unwilling to entrust him with the rarer volumes necessary to trace the royal lineage of his family. They met all his inquiries with bureaucratic equivocation. The evasiveness of officials stymied him at two other libraries. The most painful snub, though, came from his own publisher, Gallimard, from whose offices he was excluded because of his intoxication. Yet he hardly expected better, since he knew the gamble of his crazy "routine" (as he called it to Al Gelpi)—that while it liberated some people, it merely aggravated others. The real purpose of his visit was a gesture, and it was accomplished simply by his being there. The point, as he vainly tried to communicate to librarians and secretaries, was that he was the first Kerouac to connect with his French roots in 210 years.

Considering his dislike of travel, this trip was unusually joyous. He stayed so drunk that even prostitutes disdained commerce with him, and he looked so shabby that in St. Louis de France (the namesake of his boyhood church) he was mistaken for a beggar. But there were always those who saw his madness for what it was: just an enormous want of love. A teenage Tunisian girl accompanied him to a performance of Mozart's *Requiem* in the church of St. Germain de Prés. A Jewish art dealer warmed his heart with friendly conversation in an otherwise frigid restaurant. A few days later, in Brest, a wealthy aristocrat of the Lebris family, a relation of the Kerouacs, invited Jack to his home and regaled him with expensive cognac and cultured wit.

But after a week he was homesick for Florida and his $1,500 had vanished, much of it down the gullets of barroom leeches. He flew directly back to Tampa. Since Cliff was in Mexico for a month, Jack rested. Seven consecutive nights in mid-July he hand-printed the story of his trip. The result was the novel *Satori in Paris.*

Satori in Paris purports to recount the adventures of a French-Canadian investigating his heritage. Actually it is the twentieth-century equivalent of *Sir Gawain and the Green Knight,* a great Middle English chivalric poem that Kerouac had read a year earlier. A Knight of the Round Table, Sir Gawain falls victim to his pride, but is spared death by the grace of Christ's sacrifice. The theme of the tale is "the complete incapacity of the greatest of Arthur's knights to help himself." The link between that theme and Kerouac's travelogue is in the consciousness of the beholder "Jack Kerouac," *

---

* In this novel, the narrator is called "Jack Kerouac" rather than "Jack Duluoz" to make use of Kerouac's etymological research and puns involving his own surname.

a generic pilgrim who believes (like Kerouac himself) that "the beauty of cultures lies not in exteriors & in stone work, but in *Caritas*, if any."

Caritas (translated as "charity" in the King James Bible) is the brotherly love Peter promised would "cover the multitude of sins." Early in *Satori in Paris* the narrator notes the importance of teaching *caritas* to children; indeed his whole quest is to teach it to the people he meets and, by writing about his adventures, to the reader too. The title of the novel, employing a Zen expression for enlightenment, merely emphasizes the universality of Kerouac's religious experience. The actual terms of his narrator's journey are profoundly Christian. Jack is seeking the Grail, which he never finds and never can find, but he finds kindness instead, and the perception of that is his satori. In a Breton bar where he has been befriended, he realizes, "*Ciborium,* I can't find that." Earlier, at the inn, he admitted that the apparently hostile innkeeper was really doing his best to be kind, which is the most one can ask of anyone. He imagines the innkeeper saying: "Well pay your room bill and go down rue Victor Hugo, on the corner is cognac, go get your valise and settle your affairs and come back here and find out if there's a room tonight, beyond that old buddy old Neal Cassady cant go no further."

The irony is that the narrator, whose professed goal is to distinguish himself by finding his relatives, ends up learning that he belongs to the brotherhood of man. As in *Big Sur*, Jack becomes Everyman: "This, in short, scared and humbled dumbhead loudmouth with-the-shits descendant of man." His genealogy can only be a hopeless farce because, he says, "Johnny Magee around the corner as anybody knows can, with any luck, find in Ireland that he's the descendant of the Morholt's King and so what? Johnny Anderson, Johnny Goldstein, Johnny Anybody, Lin Chin, Ti Pak, Ron Poodlewhorferer, Anybody." When Jack identifies with "the people," [308] he makes clear that he's not talking about any political body like the proletariat but rather mankind as it was known to John Donne: a sum of individuals each of whose lives is invaluable.

Kerouac's shift from Buddhism back to Christianity is most prominent in his insistence that life is *real.* At the beginning of the novel he states that he wishes "to teach something religious, of religious reverence, about real life, in this real world which literature should (and here does) reflect." In part this is an extension of his insight in *Big Sur* that heaven and earth are inalterably separate: "So I go into that bar so's not to miss my suitcase with its blessed belongings, as if like Joe E. Lewis the comedian I could try to take my things to Heaven with me. . . ." But in *Satori in Paris* there is a new optimism. If life is *not* a dream, there is then the possibility of reaching others—communicating with and helping them. The narrator marvels "that people actually understand what their tongues are babbling. And that eyes do shine to understand, and that responses are made which indicate a soul in all this matter and mess of tongues and teeth, mouths, cities of stone. . . ."

The response of kindness, especially, ties humanity together, and the narrator is a classic religious hero because he provokes that response in the people he meets. Always in need of someone to drive him around, to put him up, to give him a drink or even just to talk to him, Jack coaxes compassion from people, thereby improving their own lives. Sometimes his helplessness virtually forces others to help him, engendering a goodness that may not have existed before. Although he offers fertile ground for good Samaritans, his function is not specifically Christian. The wandering Buddhist monk is likewise considered a "field of merit" for the charity he nourishes. Nevertheless, Kerouac's moral *is* Christian. He believes kindness our prime concern on earth: "Poets of genius are just decorations on the wall if without the poetry of kindness and Caritas." And his genius, as always, is to see these old ideas embodied in modern sources like the W. C. Fields quote: "The situation is fraught with eminent peril."

Kerouac presents his philosophy with an equally original technique. His narrator develops a "set" of paranoia, whereby he always expects abuse and cruelty from strangers and is that much more happily surprised when someone shows him tenderness or generosity. It is this element of surprise that lends force to the numerous satoris. The novel is further enlivened by the hyperbole of Southern speech, which Kerouac had picked up in word games with his college kids—topping one another's most extravagant insults and threats with an exuberance that made malice serve friendship.

2.

After it opened in August 1965, The Wild Boar on Nebraska Avenue in Tampa became *the* hangout bar for the U.S.F. campus. Its star attraction was its owner, six-foot-four, 230-pound Gerry Wagner, a hyacinthine-haired, turned-on Mississippi Cajun speech professor who couldn't keep out of trouble with the university administration any more than he could keep from being a guru to his students. The Boar itself was a decrepit frame shack that literally began to sway when overcrowded, as it normally was. It was also the only bar in Tampa (and perhaps in Florida) where college students and their professors actually mingled. If that were not enough to make the local law suspicious, the Boar's largely "red-neck" clientèle included farmers, dope dealers, rodeo riders, drag queens, motorcycle gangs (most of whom didn't even have cycles), artists, revolutionaries, hippies, truck drivers, and musicians. In fact, cops, sheriffs, and assorted undercover men began hassling Wagner and his patrons from the first night—and according to Wagner it was probably some man with a badge who finally torched the place a year later. The line of hate was already sharply drawn between fanatic patriots and partisans of the New Left's new humanism, and Jack was caught in the middle. The night Cliff introduced him to the Boar, he was nabbed for sleeping in a car parked outside after closing. The police tried to charge him with drunken driving, until he established the fact that he couldn't drive.

By fall 1965, Jack was already tired of the students and tired of performing for them, but he was even sicker of Mémère and her increasingly vicious complaints. If he couldn't get Cliff to drive him the twenty miles from St. Pete to Tampa, he'd charm a cab driver into taking him and then have Gerry pay the bill. Every two weeks he would come for four or five days, staying over at Wagner's house but almost never sleeping. Nor did he eat. He would drink everyone under the table—mixing beer, whiskey, and wine—and run up a sixty-dollar tab which he always paid as soon as he got home.

At the Boar Jack confronted English professors on their own level. Anxious to get his goat, they'd say things like, "I can write better than you, Kerouac, I just can't get it down." But disarmed of their red pencils, the professors took a terrible beating as Jack lashed them with a torrent of learned references, proving that even in decline his memory was unmatched. Many of them were so humiliated they never returned. At this point he was driven to compete with everyone on any level. He'd tell the biggest brute, "I can beat you up, but I'd go to jail," and if challenged to fight would slip away with a gag: "All right—we'll have a duel with sledgehammers in nine feet of water." But he was also bent on proving his courage by taking idiotic risks. After hearing Cliff tell about a bar so rough that jokers left by ambulance, he went there alone and got his nose broken. He also flaunted his strength in "belly-busting" matches with the largest men, including Wagner. They would rush at each other from across the room, meeting stomach first, the winner knocking the other down. Jack was the permanent loser, as he soon developed a hernia (to which his cirrhosis of the liver also may have contributed). His worst obsession—because the most unfulfillable—was with proving his sexual prowess. He would proposition anyone. One night he proposed marriage to a John Wayne look-alike but usually he ended up with some tart whom he would take to a motel room specially furnished with a shelf of his books. None was ever known to return there a second time.

Through all the frenzy there were also gentle moments. In the quiet early morning hours at Gerry's lakeshore house, he and Jack would sit by the wood stove listening to jazz and sometimes performing a whole Shakespearean play. They would also have calm discussions of literature; and now with a friend, not defensive but merely sad, Jack would say, "In a hundred years they'll be teaching my stuff in freshman rhetoric." Exhaustion eventually sent Wagner to bed. In the morning he'd find Jack sitting beside a few more empty wine bottles, telling stories to his children.

One night when Cliff was at his house, Jack turned on the tape recorder and began drumming and plucking on Cliff's guitar as he sang a "talking blues" called *The Midnight Ghost.* Since Jack was off in his own world Cliff left, and Jack continued for over an hour. The song describes a ride on the Zipper freight train from San Francisco to Los Angeles, and he made poetry of the place names along the way, much as Neal used to do, and finally just invented names. It is a remarkable improvisation—the mood, pitch, and pace of his voice continually changing as he digressed to events in his life that still troubled or amused him.

In mid-November he headed north in Cliff's Chevy, with Paddy Mitchell in the back seat playing harmonica. Sometimes Jack would grab the harmonica and do everything from train whistles to flamenco—he could even sing flamenco, having practiced with Adkins. They visited Wolfe's university in Chapel Hill, North Carolina, and were invited to a cocktail party where Jack put on the professors by disagreeing with all their opinions. In Connecticut, when they stopped to see John Holmes, Jack's inferiority complex became even more apparent. Drinking only wine, he talked more coherently than in 1962, but when John played a Lenny Bruce record he began savagely attacking the "Jew bastards." Of Bruce, he said, "I hate him! He hates everything, he hates life!" Holmes argued that the latter objection was rational, whereas his blanket denunciation of the Jews was not, but Jack refused to see the distinction. A few weeks later he wrote John admitting that his bigotry was merely a "tactic" to shock people into revealing their true feelings. Indeed Jack would spend the rest of his life testing people, and the tests were by no means simple. Among other things he wanted to find out how much his friends loved him, which he gauged by the amount of inconvenience, embarrassment, and verbal garbage they would accept.

In Lowell, Jack gave Cliff and Pat a tour of the locations featured in his books. He saw many of his new friends, but his warmest reunion was with Tony, Stella, and the rest of the Sampases, who had become his surrogate family. So that he could spend time alone with Tony, he gave Cliff and Pat expense money to drive back to Florida with Paul Bourgeois.

Tony took him to Albany to meet some psychiatrists with whom he had gone to college. Although Jack thought most of them either squares or fascists, he was tolerant enough to try to reeducate them with his hip Zen Socratic method. Vexed by the pretentiousness of a self-made European Swami, he put the feel on the Swami's dhoti. The Swami charged Jack with ignorance, whereupon Jack challenged him to a contest of Buddhist knowledge. They successfully fielded each other's questions until Jack demanded, "Who was Buddha's charioteer?" The Swami couldn't answer and retired to the kitchen in humiliation. Jack had more fun with Dr. Roseman, whom he lectured about Harry Stack Sullivan. Impressed with Jack's learning, Roseman asked where he had gone to school. As recorded by Phil Singer, the conversation continued as follows:

KEROUAC: I pick up all I know from those Jewboys I hang around with in the city.

ROSEMAN: You shouldn't say that. It isn't nice.

KEROUAC (*pointing to Roseman's crippled leg*): What happened to your leg, Mr. Roseman?

ROSEMAN: Why are you so hostile?

KEROUAC: Man, I am everything. I am all peace. I am a catatonic Buddha. But in the navy they told me I had too many loose associations. What does that mean?

ROSEMAN: You needn't worry about that. Lots of people have it.

KEROUAC: Doctor, why is it that when I come now, it's not as much as it used to be?

ROSEMAN: Well, have you had an examination lately?

KEROUAC: Would you like to examine me?

ROSEMAN: You know, I think I understand you now. You're really frightened of your homosexual tendencies.

KEROUAC: I hate queers. I just don't go for men. When you snuggle up to them sometimes they have beards and their face is rough. But I could go for a nice six-year-old girl.

ROSEMAN: Then you really are afraid of women. You feel safe with a child.

KEROUAC: I'm afraid of men. I leave 'em alone.

ROSEMAN: Where do you live now? Are you married?

KEROUAC: I live with my mama.

ROSEMAN: That must be nice. Do you have any dreams?

KEROUAC: Like now?

ROSEMAN: No, I mean real dreams. You're not dreaming now?

KEROUAC *(leaping up)*: You mean I'm not dreaming all this? And you're really for real?

ROSEMAN *(puzzled)*: Yes.

KEROUAC: I am Buddha, I'm from 500 B.C.

ROSEMAN: People ought to concentrate on living now. They should think about their future too. But we shouldn't make too many plans.

KEROUAC: I have fifteen grand. That is my past and my future. What else do you have besides a cane?

ROSEMAN: It's a funny thing you should mention my cane. I've lost a lot of canes. Do you think that unconsciously I wish that I didn't have to have a cane? I never thought of it until you mentioned it.

KEROUAC: Well, what happened to your leg?

ROSEMAN: Polio.

KEROUAC: You've got that whipped now, haven't you?

ROSEMAN: Oh, I can walk on it without the cane.

KEROUAC: I mean, you medicine men, you have got polio whipped.

ROSEMAN: Wouldn't it be wonderful if we could eliminate all illness?

KEROUAC: Like peace and war and loose associations?

ROSEMAN: Oh, they're not illnesses. We don't believe any more in the myth of mental illness.

KEROUAC: Then you mean, my friend Ginsberg and I aren't crazy? And I can't be a manic-depressive? That makes me sad. I want to cry. I feel blue, Rosy. I'd rather have them take my whiskey away. I cannot be schizophrenic, I cannot have loose associations? You've taken away my bread.

ROSEMAN: Gee, you'd be great in group.

(TV comes on with a news announcement about fighting in Vietnam.)

ROSEMAN: War is terrible. Why do people have to fight?

KEROUAC: Have no fear. They will never drop de big bomb. They are fighting for you. They've got to protect those bamboo plantations, make those canes. Absentmindedness leads to great wars. Try to remember that.[309]

The only one of the group Jack really warmed to was Dr. Danny DeSole, a fiery Italian psychiatrist with a heart as large and as wounded as Jack's, the kind of doctor who walked through wards doling out his own money to poor patients. DeSole saw to it that Jack had sufficient dexedrine for future writing sessions, and he prescribed benadryl to help him drink less. On the ride back to Lowell, Jack tossed the benadryl out the window.

Tony also took Jack to visit Al Gelpi in Cambridge, where Jack had a fervent religious discussion with Al's brother Don, a Jesuit priest. At the height of the evening Jack went around the room telling each person which angel or saint he saw over his or her shoulder. Lastingly influenced by the meeting, Father Don recalled it in his book *Experiencing God.*

3.

From Boston Jack flew back to Florida, determined to move to New England. The year in Florida had allowed him to live cheaply while his royalties lagged. Nineteen sixty-four and 1965 had been his two leanest years since 1957, but 1966 would see the publication of *Satori in Paris* by Grove, the reissue of several of his books in paperback, and an increase in foreign translations. In addition, through the agentry of his Italian proponent Nanda Pivano, the publisher Mondadori was offering him $1,000 to come to Italy to promote the new Italian edition of *Big Sur,* volume 500 in the distinguished *La Medusa* series.

Waiting to sell the St. Petersburg house, Jack was too nervous to write and spent most of his time at the Boar. Earlier he had written to Twardowicz admitting that Stan was right about art being "work"; if he didn't call it that, Jack realized, people would never leave him alone to write. When the house was sold in March 1966, he traveled to Cape Cod and bought a house at 20 Bristol Avenue in Hyannis. There he felt sufficiently isolated from everyone to write in peace, and yet he was only an hour and a half by bus from Boston, where he planned to use the Harvard Library to do further research on his Cornish Celtic ancestors—with, of course, side trips to Lowell. Furthermore, Jack loved living by the Atlantic. Its cold gray sky was to him the essence of New England.

For a month after moving in Jack did nothing but sleep, drink at home, and tape jazz. He kept postponing his trip to Italy, as well as his trip to Boston. He was afraid of traveling alone, knowing he could no longer safeguard his health or even his life. Gradually he ventured out to the local bars, where the Florida scene repeated itself. For intellectual companionship and protection he was fortunate to have the black novelist Robert Boles. Boles was awed by Jack's honesty and moved by his pain, so great now that Jack would cry on and off all night long. One moment he would bemoan the fact that "it was all over" for him, the next he would leap through the house like Nijinsky to prove he was still young.

His long-distance phone calls multiplied. Desperate to see *Some of the Dharma* and the complete *Visions of Cody* published in his lifetime, he made a personal appeal to both Barney Rosset and Lawrence Ferlinghetti. He pleaded with Robert Frank to make a movie of *On the Road*. Most of his calls, however, were to friends he held in special regard: his nephew Paul, Scotty Beaulieu, Edie Parker, Ed White, Bob Burford, Carolyn Cassady, Holmes, Lucien, Allen, Helen Elliott, Helen Weaver, Lois Sorrells and her new husband Jacques Beckwith, Al Gelpi, and Stan Twardowicz. Their phones would often ring at three in the morning, and Jack's voice, slow, heavy, hopelessly drunken, would begin to ramble through a labyrinthine carnival of images and quips and profundities in which even his fellow geniuses would soon be lost. To the women he often uttered sexual crudities. There were long runs of drivel and babble, and even longer silences, but any moment his mind might flash as brilliantly as ever. Some listeners, like Helen Weaver, were so torn by the sound of a man longing for death that they eventually cut him off. Others, like Helen Elliott, vowed they would never hang up on Jack Kerouac, though they shivered for hours in a bathrobe in the predawn cold.

The nightmare intensified with two more arrests. Investigating a peace demonstration, he was taken for one of the protestors and handcuffed. Another night, with Tony Sampas after the bars closed, he failed to get the attention of a lovely woman and so began to shout down the street, "I protest all this beauty!" He and Tony spent four hours in the drunk tank.

Helping the summer pass pleasantly were visits from Tony, Dan DeSole, Dr. Roseman, Jack's cousin Harvey Kerouac and his family, and Youenn Guernic of Finistère, a wood carver and folk singer active in the Breton separatist movement. Around the Fourth of July, Mémère began complaining of pains in her arm, which the doctors couldn't explain. Then Jack got a worse scare when his doctor told him that unless he drastically cut down his drinking he would soon be dead. In August he began faithfully taking the pills DeSole had prescribed, and he sobered up enough to do a fair amount of work on *Vanity of Duluoz*.

Above all, he wanted to avoid the whole Beat world. He painted over the dial on his phone so visitors couldn't get or give out his phone number. When he called Allen it was to heap obloquy on him for "hanging around with all those hairy dirty Jew communist fairies"—i.e., the leaders of the antiwar movement, whom Jack charged with "inventing new reasons for spitefulness." (Jerry Rubin had especially offended him by exhorting his followers to kill their parents.) One night Allen asked him if Mémère was putting words in his mouth. Jack snapped, "I'm not going to throw my mother to the dogs of eternity, like you did." The bizarre thing was that at other times he had declared that Mémère was as "crazy" as Allen's mother. It struck Allen that Jack was testing the extent of Allen's ego, and he began insulting Mémère in the vilest terms imaginable. The game over, Jack burst out laughing.

That summer Allen, Peter, Lafcadio, and Allen's girlfriend Maretta Greer were driving from Boston to New York and called ahead to Jack asking if they could visit. He said yes. But when they got to Hyannis no one answered the door. Since they persisted in circling the house, Mémère finally came out and ordered them away, saying, "My Jackie's a good boy, you bad boys stay away."

Ann Charters, arriving to gather material for a bibliography of Kerouac's works, found further evidence of troubled currents beneath the placid surface of the household. Proud that a Ph.D. in English was taking the trouble to catalogue his publications, Jack worked diligently with her all day. But come evening he grew desperate to see her leaving and even threatened to masturbate unless she went to bed with him. As she left, Mémère showed her a gouge in the plaster made by the knife he had recently thrown at her.

Mondadori rescheduled the publicity tour of Italy, and sent a plane ticket in early September, but stage fright combined with worry over his deteriorating physical appearance caused Jack to start hitting the bars again.

He had developed the habit of sticking his head into Mémère's room whenever he got home, to let her know he had returned safely. Usually he would knock first, but on September 9 he didn't get in until six A.M. and simply staggered into her bedroom. She had just gotten out of bed and was completely nude. Clutching her breasts, she collapsed to the floor, and foam came from her mouth. Jack called the doctor, who found she had had a stroke and would have to be hospitalized. Later Jack phoned Stan Twardowicz to confess his guilt.

For nine days he waited in agony to learn the extent of Mémère's paralysis. Her right side had been unaffected, and at last she regained a modicum of feeling in her left side, although she lacked sufficient control to get out of bed on her own. Nevertheless she insisted on returning home, where Jack had to nurse her and manage the house too. He asked Mondadori for another postponement, but they would give him only until September 27 to arrive in Milan. Now more in need of the money than ever, he resolved to go. He called Stella Sampas to take care of Mémère.

By the time he reached London he was so drunk that the flight attendants carried him off the plane. He had the airline call Mondadori, where some presumptuous subordinate got on the phone and told Jack, "Don't make a fool of yourself!" That sentence plunged him into hysteria and stuck in his head like a thorn during his whole tour of Italy. He drank so heavily that when Mondadori's people met him in Milan they called a doctor to sedate him. Held down while the doctor injected him with morphine, Jack went out of his mind, and as soon as they locked him into his hotel room, he called Nanda begging her to "rescue" him, certain that he was about to be murdered.

Nanda objected to such cruelty, but those responsible replied disdainfully, "A serious man doesn't drink that way," and scoffed that Kerouac looked like an "old worker," not a writer. She found Jack in an armchair, in his lumberjack shirt and railroad boots. His suitcase had been lost, so he had no other clothes. She took him to her house. Lying on her couch looking out at the mountains, he regained a measure of calm. Since he begged her for a drink, she gave him champagne, figuring that would do him the least damage. On the terrace he autographed a few books for her, then realized she was watching him as a doctor does a critically ill patient. With terrible anguish in his eyes he told her, "You're disappointed."

Later, when she told him how much she loved Allen, he said, "You don't know that Allen is very wicked."

Emptying several bottles of champagne, he moaned that his mother needed him and that he would have to remarry to have someone to care for her. The next day, at the TV studio where Nanda was to interview him, he was too drunk to talk. Only by virtue of a thaumaturgic sound engineer, who spliced together Jack's barks and snarls, was a show produced. That night, at the party in his honor at Mondadori's house, Jack passed out, his head falling in his plate.

Since Jack had been reacting like a wounded lion to the sneering, dark-suited critics, Mondadori had him escorted to Rome with a Sicilian bodyguard. There, his live TV interview was a fiasco. They sat him in the center of the stage with spotlights hitting him from every side. Hunched over, with his hands folded in his lap, he looked around like a madman. He began to scream, "Shoot me! Shoot me!"—meaning, "Get the show over with!"—while they protested that they didn't want to kill him.

When Jack got home, he seriously accused Nanda of being a "Russian Jewish Communist spy."

4.

On November 18, 1966, Jack was wed to Stella Sampas. The ceremony was performed by a justice of the peace at Jack's house in

Hyannis. Having loved him since he first came to her house to visit Sammy, Stella had reached the end of the rainbow. Four years older than Jack, she looked, some people felt, old enough to be his mother. Yet he was proud of her real name Stavroula ("Of the Cross") Sampatacacus, as well as her Spartan descent. He also boasted that she was a virgin, who had saved herself for him.

Since most of the large Sampas family still lived in Lowell, he and Stella immediately went there to pick out a house. He had enough money in the bank to keep the one in Hyannis for rent income. His heart's desire was to buy the house on Beaulieu Street where Gerard had died, but it wasn't for sale. They ended up with a modern split-level at 271 Sanders Avenue in the Highlands, a quiet, manicured, upper-middle-class neighborhood. In mid-January 1967, they moved in. Mémère was installed on a bed in a central room on the first floor, from which her call bell could easily be heard. Jack and Stella had separate bedrooms upstairs.

Jack couldn't have bought the meticulous, devoted care Stella gave Mémère. Even Mémère grudgingly admitted her efficiency, though she had been against the marriage and was often sharp and antagonistic with Stella, for no one threatened her hold on Jack more than another motherly woman. Jack, however, soon felt the marriage was a mistake. Stella was possessive and would hide his clothes and shoes to keep him in the house, though he would go out anyway in his pajamas and bedroom slippers, which got him in as much trouble with the neighbors as peeing in the back yard. Not that he any longer cared about trouble, but she wanted him to write at regular hours, and to enforce her wish she'd send her seven brothers out to catch him when he disappeared. No longer a caged lion in a traveling circus, he had been fenced permanently into a zoo. As a compromise he agreed to do most of his drinking at Nicky's, the family bar, where he'd loudly and bluntly proclaim Stella's unattractiveness—his mildest attacks on her—and declare that he had married her against his will. His own brother-in-law Nicky would sometimes be driven to kick him out of the bar. And Jack didn't care about that either, just so he didn't have to go home.

Walking fast, hands a-pocket, his baseball-capped head downturned, musing, he was the loneliest figure in Lowell. His loneliness was painfully apparent even in the bars and all-night cafés he haunted. Jim O'Dea's son James, a policeman on the night beat, used to find him drooling drunk in Dana's Soda Fountain off Kearney Square. In Nicky's, Jack would sometimes sit silent for hours, from time to time ejaculating a remark no one understood. Other times he'd talk nonstop, but he wasn't talking *to* anyone, or he'd play Bunny Berigan's "I Can't Get Started" on the jukebox and mime the singing and trumpet playing, or fall on his knees and actually start to sing like Sinatra. Occasionally some newcomer would ask to have the bum tossed out, and then he would learn that that was "Nicky's brother-in-law." Ultimately Jack would pass out and topple onto the floor, and they'd carry him out.

Going weeks without a change of clothes or a bath, Jack stank like a goat. He would pee wherever the urge struck him. He would call dignified matrons "old bags" or tell them he wanted to "eat their cunt" [310]—and that put an end to Nicky taking him out to meet and impress his rich friends. He swore like a sailor even at the houses of his old friends, and if he met them anywhere he'd expect them to spend the next two days and nights with him. Consequently even buddies like G.J. would cross the street or duck out a back door to avoid him. Fortunately most of the cops knew and protected him, because he was thrown out of almost every bar and half the other public places in Lowell. After *Vanity of Duluoz* was published he went to Lowell High to look up his assistant coach, Fritz Drescher, to tell him he was in the book and that he'd bring him a copy; then he sat down in the school hall and wouldn't budge, forcing two gym coaches to haul him out. At Prince's Bookstore he couldn't find *Vanity of Duluoz* and began to yell about their not keeping his books in stock, until another old acquaintance Nick Zamanakis had to boot him out. At the Three Copper Men, Stella's cousin John Delamus kicked him out for scaring patrons by sitting on the dance floor. His fellow football player John Chiungos tossed him out of his bar, and John's brother Duke was so provoked by Jack's foul language that he decked him in Kay's bar. Even loving Billy "Koums" was taunted into punching him, and seeing the tears in Jack's eyes he regretted it ever afterward. In Lowell if you break the rules you pay the price. One rule is that you don't infringe on a man's moneymaking, another is that you don't offend common decency. At the Pawtucketville Social Club, when Jack swore and put his feet up on the table, he was carried out by Pete Houde (the Moon Man) and a few other of his old Phebe Avenue pals. The small minority of Lowell blacks had a different set of rules, from which whites were mostly exempt, but there was a line they wouldn't let a white man cross with impunity. In Omer's pool hall on the Sixty-Six Corner Jack crossed it many a night, spitting, "Shut up ya fucking niggers!" at the blacks who might try to throw him out for fencing with pool cues and sometimes tossing chairs through the window.

A little encouragement from any rowdy would turn Jack into a wild man, but he could also be gentled by a word from close friends like Tony, Billy, Chiefy, and a distinguished French-Canadian scholar and gallant, Joe Chaput. Though Jack often burst into his own house at three A.M., shouting and banging on the piano, he usually respected the sanctity of his friends' homes. At Billy's he became the children's favorite "uncle"; they would rush to sit on his lap to hear him tell stories or gather to watch him perform a skit like *Dr. Jekyll and Mr. Hyde.* Sometimes when Chiefy wasn't home Jack would have long, quiet talks with his wife; if he was out of control she would ask him to sit on the porch so as not to scare the kids, and he would docilely obey. He still performed extraordinary acts of kindness. Chiefy's son had asthma, and Jack brought him a harmonica to provide him with an enjoyable form of breathing exercise. Grateful to Manny Bello, who always welcomed him at the Celebrity Club, Jack proofread the rules for a golf game Manny marketed. Such examples could be listed for pages.

His sense of duty, moreover, was still acute. One of the reasons he had always avoided responsibilities was that he felt so tightly bound once he had accepted them, and he didn't want to take on more than he could handle. Contracted to write *Vanity of Duluoz* for Coward-McCann and pledged to support his family, Jack set about finishing the novel in March 1967.

Arranging a full mirror over his writing table so that he could study his face while he worked, as cartoonists often do, Jack wrote for an hour or two each day or as long as his strength and concentration held out. He typed on a teletype roll, but he could no longer compose rapidly. The results of each sitting—sometimes the length of several ordinary pages, sometimes a short paragraph—took organic form as chapters. Worried about the quality of the novel, he recorded most of it on tape and also had Tony read it aloud to him as it was written, to check the sound.

5.

Referring to *Vanity of Duluoz,* Allen Ginsberg asked, "How do you draw the line between complete honesty and disillusionment? or drunken soul?" Ginsberg admits he never solved the problem; but in the novel itself Kerouac, like an old Zen master, answers merely with a laugh.

Vanity of Duluoz is the masterwork of a master paradoxist. The prose is perhaps the most careless and yet the most graceful he ever wrote. The key word in the text is *funny,* and the novel is, in every sense, his "funniest" book. Its humor derives, above all, from self-parody. The narrator's cocky tone and bold mockery—even of the reader, by asking and then answering his own questions, for example, or by instructing the reader how to read—are devices straight out of *Tristram Shandy.* Like Sterne, Kerouac would make a fool out of himself and everyone else, to reveal how serious life is.

Vanity of Duluoz deals with the period when the characters who would later incarnate beatness and beatitude were just meeting one another, not yet demons or angels but (with the exception of the older Burroughs) just high-strung youths with a seemingly infinite potential. How that potential was expended, leaving the hardened

carcasses of their finite lives, is the book's main theme. It was in fact
the implied theme that unified even the most episodic of the Beat
novels, the silent note that thundered through Kerouac's lifelong
symphony. That he finally decided to blow it doesn't mean his conception of art had changed but merely that he had at last attained a
masterful indifference—and like mirror facing mirror, that attain-
ment of the peace beyond vanity becomes another of the book's
themes. Indeed the novel becomes at last its own theme. It is written
because America has changed, "everybody's begun to lie," and the
narrator, echoing Céline, feels compelled to respond: "I remember
very well many things. . . ."

   Vanity of Duluoz is not autobiography. There is a persona who is
speaking to his wife, telling her the troubled history of his life so that
she might better understand his present disillusion and drunken
crankiness. The frame is similar to that used by Melville in the
poems "Bridegroom Dick" and "To Ned," where the old seaman
remembers the "good times o' yore"—in the first addressing his "old
wifie," in the second addressing a companion of his youth. Long
before Melville, the genre of old-age reminiscence had been utilized
for viewing the past through the new eyes of wisdom, and the "voice
of experience" might be as young as Keats in the *Ode to Melancholy*.
Several Shakespearean sonnets deal with this theme, including 97,
containing one of Kerouac's favorite lines: "What freezings have I
felt, what dark days seen!" *Sere*, Kerouac's favorite word from Shakespeare, likewise sets the book's predominant color tone of reds and
browns.

   Although Kerouac laughs at much of his early writing, he is also
seriously reviewing his sources. His years of study of "the old
Dharma Masters like Hui-Neng" enable him to dismiss them in an
offhand remark. Wolfe's romantic view of America, which Kerouac
went down with like the captain of a sinking ship, becomes an important motif.

   The narrator begins by telling his wife that he's suffered from
"being too sensitive." His innocent belief in others, which has enabled him to learn from the best, has also allowed him to be hurt by
the worst, by people who even deny his existence. But he still believes that "lying is a sin," and this book is a vindication of his
literary method of personal honesty. The style, growing out of his
desire to "simplify matters," is one of "regular punctuation for the
illiterate generation"—not from bitterness, but to reach all those who
have failed to come up to his former ideals (as he has too, of course).
By "telling the truth still" he creates a continuity with his past.
Gently he reminds the reader that he is no "dumb ox," that he has
learned his share of craft; but the important thing is that he is "writing exactly what I remember" even if it is "according to the way
that I want to remember in order."

He is writing the way he lived, and he explains that what he means by "An Adventurous Education" (the novel's subtitle) is learning one's own way, doing "what you feel like all your life," the very thing the narrator's father told him was impossible. This is an education in sensibility, not subject matter. The presence of Kerouac the perfected writer hovering just above the narrator, who is struggling with his vanities, creates an instructive tension between process and its products, which are as empty as names. The only place to learn wisdom is the mind, and it's the learning, not what you call it—"an adventurous education, an educational adventuresomeness, name it"—that matters.

Beginning with his teenage ambitions to be a football star and brilliant scholar, the novel follows Jack Duluoz's career through high school and college to the point where he decides to become a great writer. In the key scene in the book he daydreams in the parlor of his parents' new house just before the start of his sophomore year at Columbia. The tone of the passage is easy and flippant, yet delicately lyrical and no more truly cynical than W. C. Fields: "I'm the world's heavyweight boxing champion, the greatest writer, the world's champ miler, Rose Bowl and (pro-bound with New York Giants football non pareil) now offered every job on every paper in New York, and what else? Tennis anyone?" Suddenly Jack realizes that if he goes out on the porch and sits staring at the stars, his life will play out to its destination just the same. There is no need to consciously strive for anything, since "in the intervening space between human breathings and the 'sigh of the happy stars' " there is nothing to strive for: "It just didn't matter what I did any time, anywhere, with anyone; life is funny like I said."

The worst effect of struggle is a spiritual corruption; it interrupts the flow of consciousness: "O God in the Heavens, what a fumbling, hand-hanging goof world it is, that people actually think they can gain anything from either this, or that, or thissa, or thatta, and in so doing, corrupt their sacred graves in the name of sacred-grave corruption." Since, like Solomon in Ecclesiastes, Kerouac has pronounced that "all is vanity," that judgment must pass onto all his books as well, including this very book about vanity. Such a disclaimer of high seriousness gives him an enormous freedom, not only to "write what I want" (and the book is symbolically written, like *Old Angel Midnight,* on Good Friday, the day of confession before the Easter Absolution), but also to play with his own disillusionment. That tautology about corrupting one's grave for the sake of grave corruption winks like the best dada. He mocks his own writing—as he did in *Mexico City Blues,* where he wondered why he should "rack" his hand "with labor of nada"—while turning in a virtuoso performance.

The function of vanities may be to foreshadow the future by

marking the direction of the flow, like twigs carried in a current, and it's the direction, not which are lost and which are saved, that's important. Here, as in his earlier books, Kerouac disdains the suspense of plot by continually pointing out what's going to happen; but now, as he collapses time, he collapses meaning too, literally telling the reader which parts of the book he should pay more attention to. Of the dream of multiple championships, he writes: "this is the key to the story, wifey dear." And later, when the narrator exchanges his illusions of football and college studies for those of writing and "thinking," he states: "this is where the book, the story, pivots," warning the reader to watch for "deep form"! At one point the narrator even tells *himself* how to write the story: "Allegro, the composer should write here."

The book's self-examination is a model for Kerouac's much grander study of the nature of art. Early in the novel the narrator equates the vanity of his private ambitions with the vanity of an artist's intentions. A man's life and a work of art both spend themselves in trying to realize the unrealizable. The irony lies in each man's—or artist's—thinking he can succeed where all others have failed. Reading Thomas Wolfe at Columbia makes Jack "want to prowl, and roam, and see the real America that was there and that 'had never been uttered.' " But although Wolfe himself never got much beyond surface description—"he's the kind of writer whose prose-poems you can just about only read once; and deeply and slowly, discovering, and having discovered, move away"—yet his works facilitate the flow of Jack's own life: "he just woke me up to America as a Poem instead of America as a place to struggle and sweat around in." The common assumption about vanities is that they are bad. On another level, Kerouac sees that vanities are essential to the growth of awareness. Art, as the most conscious form of vanity, is thus most indispensable of all.

In *Vanity of Duluoz* the cosmic moment is often superbly condensed in a phrase—"I see Lu Libble and Cliff Battles, and Rolfe Firney our coach too . . . dancing little Hitler dances on the sidelines"—showing that time serves "foreordainment" (predestination) the way words serve meaning. Kerouac here has at last fused his religious and artistic visions, and their union is faith in the mental process, in a life of nonresistance: "I believe in Jesus. Tell you why if you don't know already: Jacob wrestled with his angel because he defied his own Guardian Angel." That is to say, time can be lost but process is inescapable. For example, the narrator is on a ship carrying dynamite; as it docks in Liverpool it crashes against an old wooden pier, which gives way. Had that accident occurred twenty-five years later against the modern concrete pier, the ship and narrator would have been blown away and *Vanity of Duluoz* never been written. But as he is still alive and the book has been written, no such change is possible. Time is just the opening and closing of possibility along a fixed sequence.

While in Horace Mann prep school, Jack had kept a literary journal. At the time it proved useless, but during the composition of *Vanity of Duluoz* years later its awful stiltedness typified an era. In the first novel he tried to write, also called *Vanity of Duluoz,* he had failed in his attempt "to delineate all of Lowell as Joyce had done for Dublin." Twenty-five years later he "completed" *Vanity of Duluoz* and accomplished his original intention by virtue of the perspective only time could provide.

The main divisions of the novel into thirteen "books," each describing a "season" in his life, and the lesser divisions into chapters, each representing a session of writing, grow from Kerouac's conception of the work as the product of a unique flow of events. The implication is that this book (and each book) could not have been written any earlier or later than it was. For example, he quotes a bit of romantic description from his 1942 seaman's diary and adds on a cadenza of the vowel assonances that he spent years mastering, at the same time re-viewing the moment with cosmic vision: " 'Up we go, to northern seas. Ah there you'll find that shrouded Arctic.' (That wash of pronounced sea-talk, that parturient snowmad ice mountain plain, that bloody Ghengis Khan plain of seaweed talk broken only by uprisings of foam.)"

For a writer, each piece of writing will eventually be rewritten, if only in his head. Kerouac continues to alternate quotations from his seaman's diary with the spoofing, post-hip commentary of 1967:

> "Death hovers over my pencil. How do I feel? I feel nothing but dim acceptance." (O Eugene O'Neill!) ". . . as I was writing just now, I heard a hissing outside my porthole . . . and I thought: 'Torpedo!' I waited for one long second. Death! Death!" (Think of your death scenes and death trips, LSD users!) "I tell you," sez confident young Jack London in his bunk, "I tell you, it is NOT hard to face death"—no sirree. . . .

This structure of interlaced time periods emphasizes the coexistence of falsehood and truth: in other words, every thought is true to the moment of its conception and false ever afterward.

From accurate observation of the shore of Greenland the seaman's journal suddenly waxes poetic: " 'these cliffs are absolutely enchanted . . . like the dream cliffs of a child, or the place where resides the soul of Wagner's music. . . .' " Interrupting that old moment of vision, the 1967 Kerouac deflates its pomposity: "And so on. I don't want to bore the reader with all this stuff about Greenland." His perceptions of Greenland aren't as important as the continuity and progression of his visions. Each time he perceives something he

creates it anew, and each time he notes the change in his perceptions he creates the cosmos all over. In *Vanity of Duluoz* he works
his final variation on the cosmic moment, using it here as a metaphor
for the growth of consciousness from youth to old age.

Vanity of Duluoz contains many paraphrases and even direct
quotations from Kerouac's published books. In *On the Road,* for example, when Dean Moriarty and Sal Paradise discovered Mexico as
their spiritual home, he had written rather arrogantly: "The waves
are Chinese, but the earth is an Indian thing." Sixteen years later he
cannot take that line seriously; he turns it around and burlesques it
(as well as his pretension to Indian sagacity) with a Fieldsian whine:
"Yessir, boy, the earth is an Indian thing but the waves are Chinese.
Know what that means? Ask the guys who drew those old scrolls, or
ask the old Fishermen of Cathay, and what Indian ever dared to sail
to Europe or Hawaii from the salmon-tumbling streams of North
America? When I say Indian, I mean Ogallag." Likewise, the porten-
tous opening of *Old Angel Midnight,* "Friday afternoon in the universe," now sets the stage for "a dreary old Ka-*Ween*" to begin
gathering his dirty laundry for wash day! No less is Kerouac gathering up the dirty laundry of his career as a writer.

What needs cleansing is the writer's last and hardiest illusion
that something he wrote might somehow, somewhere, have slightly
mattered. The theme of *Vanity of Duluoz* is "nothing matters." It is
a dirge sung by the dead man himself, for to be completely honest
Kerouac must view life from his own grave, which alone can detach
him from the vanity of ego. In Browning's famous monologue, the
dying Bishop of St. Praxed's begins ordering his own tomb with that
same quote from Ecclesiastes about universal vanity; like the narrator of *Vanity of Duluoz,* the Bishop suspects "the world's a dream"
and asks, "Life, how and what is it?" But to his last breath the
Bishop clings with delighted sensuality to things of material value,
savoring the color and texture of the stones and jewels that will
surround him as he lies for centuries—so he imagines—listening to
the Mass and tasting "good strong thick stupefying incense smoke."
By contrast, the narrator of *Vanity of Duluoz* cares to preserve only
the direction of his life, not the individual points of change (as in
Desolation Angels) but the line drawn between them: "On our return trip to Boston Harbor . . . we were light as a cork and bobbed in
a huge October tempest, the likes of which I only saw fifteen years
later."

Vanity of Duluoz begins with the narrator a step from his grave
and ends with the death of his father and his setting out to experience life, both in spring. Furthermore, the cycle of reminiscences
moves from "a guy going home for supper" on an autumn night to a
prayer at dawn in spring. Like Shakespeare in the sonnets—whose
theme is the persistence, even to death, of the love that brings back

summer and revives the fire inside—Kerouac repeatedly waits past the end to find a new beginning, calling time's bluff, just as he calls death's bluff by accepting it as a given, then seeing what life has to offer. The meanings of human life may always be relative, but by bringing youth and old age as close together as possible—bound together in the book as in his consciousness—he can find just what, if any, differences exist. Two points exist only when a line is drawn between them, as places where space begins and ends; then, paradoxically, they are no longer separate but one entity. Similarly, human life exists as a continuum between birth and death.

Sometimes we bend the direction of that line ourselves, and sometimes other people change our direction, like Coach Lu Libble refusing to let Jack play football. But ultimately our direction can be determined only by reference to some point outside ourselves, and seeking one we discover our complete lostness. The narrator last heard his friend Big Slim "was punching cows in East Texas, probably not true." He wonders, "Where is he tonight? Where am I? Where are you?" Seeing the face of his dead cat Timmy in heaven the narrator asks how the cat could have died when for eons he wasn't even born: "If he wasn't born, how can he be dead?" The endless questioning of Kerouac's artistry has broken through to religion the way Pascal broke through from science. Quoting him, Kerouac writes: " 'There are perfections in Nature which demonstrate that she is the image of God'—Timmy sitting like a lion, Big Slim in his prime, Pop in his prime, me in my careless 1943 youth, you, all—'and imperfections'—our decay and going-down, all of us— 'to assure us that She is no more than His image.' I believe that."

Far from being the despairing cry of an embittered old man, most of *Vanity of Duluoz* reaffirms the faith of Kerouac's youth, when he wrote in his sea diary: "I could get killed walking across the street, if Supreme Reality's arranged it, so why not go to sea?" It is also a final blessing on youthful idealism, despite his vociferous differences with the Flower Children. As a young man at sea he had imagined that his father would love to share his adventures: "Everything is romantic when you're twenty-one in 1943." As an old man himself, worn and weary as his father, Kerouac has come to prize new values: "The war brought people closer together, no matter what you say about the rest of it." Children misunderstanding, then becoming, their parents is the human root of time collapse, and it assures that the best values, winnowed by time, will endure.

Certainly tragedy may strike, and in Kerouac's own case the tragedy was twofold. He was no longer physically capable of completing *The Duluoz Legend*. Even more demoralizing, his subject was the promise of America; and instead of fulfilling that promise, America had betrayed its ideals: "I didn't intend this to be a poetic paean of a book, in 1967 as I'm writing this what possible feeling can be left in me for an 'America' that has become such a potboiler of broken convictions . . . ?" His writing came through the frame of America, but what she offered him was a succession of windows, each getting darker: "I wrote seventeen novels after a youth of solitary practice amounting to over two million words, by the window with the star in it at night, the bedroom window, the cheap room window, the nut ward window, the porthole window, eventually the jail window."

The most effective cosmic moment of the book begins looking from the window of Jack's jail cell: "It's Saturday evening in August, in New York, a late sunset goldenly appears in a gap in the firmament between great dark cloudbanks so that the early lights of the city in the streets and on the watchers in the wallsides of high buildings suddenly shine quite feebly in the big light that was like the glow of a golden rose in the world. . . ." It moves to "mysterious new kindsa glory for everybody even over the soft tremblings of Times Square," thence over Brooklyn, over Staten Island "and her silly wretched statue to the rose night true sea," over Harlem, over "the Upper Italian East Side, and even over the millions of packed places where in my New York life I'd seen so many people who were preparing for the soft air and whatever celebrations and occasions that must, and do, arise in piddling earth in the vast night's camp." It becomes "like the last day of the world," when the truth of art becomes the stuff of life itself: "men can go about with a kind of jaundiced toolbag sorrow and black hats and coats to a card game like Cezanne's which is more sorrowful than sources of disenchanted soul itself." All day the windows were "darkened"—sorrow and gloom being necessary counterparts to joy, just as a window implies its opposite: blacking out. Yet in these "awful fogs" is "the central joyous center of the universe [where] there still hung on, clear as a bell ever, the pearl of Heaven flaming on high." The reactions of the prisoners to the sudden appearance of sunlight are so banal as to be a joke: "Yah, red out there, ugh," or, "What's that, no rain?" Words can't express what they're feeling any more than the narrator can explain his joy at having recreated the moment on paper: "Anyway, see? No time for poetry. And anyway, see? No time for poetry." Like a mantra pronounced until it is meaningless, Kerouac's words turn back to pure sound. His final point—the greatest modesty a writer or any artist can assume—is to suggest that life completely perceived is poetry, is art, and needs no labor of pen, brush, or anything else to make it so: "Of course there's someplace to go! Go mind your own business."

Unfortunately *Vanity of Duluoz* doesn't end there. It goes on to a bitter description of his father's death by cancer and of the funeral. Discarding the mask of his persona, Kerouac accuses Jehovah of "a mean heartless creation." He pleads that he can't give up drinking because of the pain sober thought causes him, and he petulantly charges Jesus with hypocrisy about claiming independence of material things: "How can you be redeemed when you have to pass food in and out of your body's bag day in day out, how can you be 'saved' in a situation so sottish and flesh-hagged as that?" Buddha he ridicules for dying in "an awful pool of dysentary"; and capping this fit of spite, he rants on: "Who's going to come out and say that the mind of nature is intrinsically insane and vicious forever?" In his own disgusted, dying voice, Kerouac admits that the source of his resentment is his mother's failure to recover from a stroke: "Do you blame it on society that a seventy-year-old woman lies in bed paralyzed as if a great stone was on her chest even after ten months of hopeful waiting and perfect care from her children?"

This isn't to say the ending is unrelated to the rest of the book. When he collapses the terminal points of birth and death with such word-play as "basket (almost said 'casket')" or reaches across space and time to "that horrible Mother Kali of ancient India," he is again making statements about the continuity of process—i.e., if we accept birth then we can't begrudge death; and by their universality, cruelty and suffering seem to be part of the flow as well. But the tone is uneven and often sharply discordant with the gentle amusement that characterized most of the book. Restoring equilibrium as best he can, Kerouac does append a little scene where, after his father is buried, his Uncle Vincent gives up trying to explain the misery of life and simply makes "a Breton Gallic shrug at the empty blue sky above." Again Kerouac affirms the nobility of silence; it is more honest than talk, and the only cure for vanity. But since he failed to keep that silence himself at a point where it was called for—his life going farther out of kilter even as his art approached an ideal serenity— there is nothing more for him to say but "Forget it, wifey. Go to sleep. Tomorrow's another day.

"*Hic calix!*

"Look that up in Latin, it means 'Here's the chalice,' and be sure there's wine in it."

Just as, addressing Carl Solomon, Kerouac once wrote, "This madhouse shot of yours is not exactly the immemorial *miel*," it might have been told him that neither was his drinking shot. But artistically the way he ended *Vanity of Duluoz* is beside the point, as much so as the farcical ending with which Twain muted the radical honesty of *Huckleberry Finn*. In *Vanity of Duluoz* Kerouac still has the power to see his own life in universal terms. He hasn't forgotten that living is the only solution to life, he doesn't delude himself that anything "ever came of it," and he has found some acceptance of death as just another of life's mysteries. In fact, in that Latin mystification of his worried wifey, there's the hint of his old grin, which might even break into a laugh . . . the last laugh:

"Funny halfbacks dont have to sell Pepsi-Cola."

They can write great books.

6.

Vanity of Duluoz was finished by mid-May, 1967. Jack's deadline to deliver the manuscript was June 10, but he was drinking so heavily he could barely retype the scroll onto regular pages. Nor could he resist celebrating with an enormous binge, in which he enlisted G.J., Mayor Ray Rourke, and several Lowell policemen. The whole mob ended up at his house at four in the morning. Officer Mahoney was sobbing on Jack's shoulder, telling him *he* had always wanted to be a writer. Jack's reply was "Stay away from it!"

After a brief stint of therapy at the Holy Ghost Hospital in Cambridge Mémère begged to come home, complaining it depressed her to live among invalids. Witnesses testify that physically she was now quite strong, and it may be that she didn't want to relinquish the hold on Jack her disability guaranteed.

As his despair increased so did his late night phone calls, and he was running up a $150 bill each month. The people he called would hear him fighting with Stella, who was always trying to get him to hang up. At one point she poured a bottle of cognac on his head, and he frequently threw chairs at her. Finally she tore the phone out of the wall. After a lifetime of being dominated by his mother, Jack couldn't stand being bossed by another woman. He'd complain to Joe Chaput, *"Il mouille des grecs"* ("It's raining Greeks"), and to other friends he carped that he was stuck with a bunch of Greek peasants. One of his small comforts was that the Kerouac family had reaccepted him into their bosom, and he received weekly visits from his cousins Harvey and Armand and their wives and even old Aunt Léontine, Uncle Joe's wife. They would gather around the piano to sing old French-Canadian songs, and Jack would fix them his special Canadian baked beans and other treats.

He went with bartender Peter Dizoglio to visit Mary Carney and got in a terrible fight with her because he wouldn't stop calling her "Maggie." Still obsessed with the sex he wasn't getting, he'd take prostitutes into the back of Nicky's, and he phoned groupies in Greenwich Village to come see him. He was drinking over a quart of Johnny Walker Red Label a day, washing it down with beer and Colt 45 malt liquor. The question became not only "How does this guy write?" but "How does he go on living?" [311] He told Chiefy that being a Catholic he was forced to take "the slow way out." Though he got into shouting matches with other drinkers, at the last minute he'd always back out of a fight, and if anyone got really mad he'd joke and buy them a drink. But there were times, like at Omer's, the black pool hall, when he grew impatient with the slow way and pressed for something quicker. And well he might, since his life, as he wrote in *Vanity of Duluoz,* had become one crisis after another.

In June Stan Twardowicz and Lil stopped to see him on their way to Maine, bringing along Bill Crabtree. Jack gave them the grand tour of his literary kingdom, including Lowell High School, St. Jean Baptiste Church, St. Joseph's School, the Moody Street Bridge, and the Stations of the Cross. They felt as if he were reliving his past, a sensation that grew even eerier when well past dark he knelt in turn at each Station of the Cross.

That night at Nicky's, Jack showed that he finally accepted "Blondie" by asking her to dance. But at the house he refused to let Stan and Lil sleep in the guest bedroom because they weren't married, claiming it would upset Mémère; he himself was so upset he kept coming out to shake their camper, yelling, "Come on out, Stan, damn it! Quit fucking the blonde!" It wasn't just that he wanted Stan's company, for Bill was glad to stay up with him all night. Knowing he would never see Jack again, Bill gave in to Jack's sexual request. When Stella finally burst into Jack's room she found them naked, sitting on the floor, and Jack popping pills by the fistful. Hysterical, she beat Jack with a hairbrush and confiscated the pills. The next day, hugging Stan and crying, Jack begged him to stay. They left him at Nicky's, where he darted in and out to wave until they were out of sight.

That summer Allen Ginsberg appeared with his biographer Jane Kramer. Mémère refused to let him in the house, but Jack was thankful for the company and led them on the customary circuit around Lowell. In Nicky's he explained to the locals why he liked Allen: "The fact that everyone should be loved as they already are, as Ginsberg says, strikes a note in my big 1930's blue Depression behind." [312] But seeing Allen peel off the $100 bills he'd just made at some reading Jack grew surly, and when Kramer turned on her tape recorder he exploded at Allen: "I see you're trying to steal my lines again!"

In Lowell to make a documentary about the French-Canadian community, a Montreal television crew sought Jack's assistance. He participated because he needed the money, but he couldn't stomach being directed how to behave in Nicky's or the Pawtucketville Social Club. Since they wanted Kerouac, he decided to give them Kerouac, and yelled "Fuck you!" every time the camera swung on him. His honesty evidently made a good impression, because he was asked to Montreal to appear on the Radio-Canada television program *Sel de la semaine.* There he gave the interviewer an even starker glimpse of his soul, saying: "What do I think of myself? I'm sick of myself! OK, I know I'm a good writer, a great writer . . . I'm not a brave man. But there's one thing I do, I write stories, and that's it." The last thing Jack expected was that the *Québecois* would ridicule the way he spoke French, as the Parisians had; but the Montreal studio audience had never heard anything like his quaint Pawtucketville phrasing. Much to his astonishment they laughed hardest when he said that the most beautiful words in *joual* (the French-Canadian dialect) were *ragoût d'boulettes:* "pork-ball stew."

At any rate, the trip to Montreal stimulated his interest in his French-Canadian ancestry, and that summer he asked Joe Chaput to drive him to Rivière du Loup so that he could examine the civic and parish records. A few hours out of Lowell they picked up a hippie with a backpack, who said, "Man, this is the life on the road!" When Chaput told him who was in the car, the boy almost had a fit. Slugging from his bottle of cognac (in honor of Canada), Jack was talking his head off. By the time they stopped in Maine he had taken a number of bennies and was primed to go all night. He made a big hit with the French people in the local bars.

The next day he was still bouncing, telling stories of how his ancestors used to drink caribou blood, but when they got to Rivière du Loup he went straight to the motel lounge for whiskey and soda. Although the speed had kept him from getting stupefied from the booze, he was already dragged by fatigue. Walking through the countryside he pointed to some bull oxen and said, "Sometimes I feel like that, and other times I feel like I'm ready to croak." He was depressed too by the poverty of Rivière du Loup. Most of the houses were tarpaper-brick blocks reminiscent of the old slums of Lowell. The most beautiful and imposing building, as in any French-Canadian town, was the brown brick (*real* brick), high-steepled Catholic church.

But for Joe's protection Jack would have been badly beaten in a bar when he began spouting off about how the Jews had corrupted the French language. Without bothering to look in the archives, he asked Joe to drive him on to Montreal. Halfway there he was in such bad condition that they were being turned away from motels. After a raucous night in Lévy, they headed back.

To help Jack through another financially dry period, Charles Jarvis tried to line up a teaching job for him at Lowell Tech. As a start he was to give a single lecture, but he so panicked at the thought of another public disgrace that he began drinking himself sick. At Stella's request, Jarvis released him from the date.

Despite his shyness Jack felt it was time he set the record straight on a number of personal as well as literary matters. Ted Berrigan's offer to interview him for the *Paris Review* seemed the perfect opportunity. Jack respected Berrigan as a poet and had had many good talks with him on the phone. When Ted showed up with two younger poets, Aram Saroyan and Duncan McNaughton, Stella thought another gang had come to invade the house and barred the door. To get her to let them in, Jack lied that they were paying him $1,000.

One of the first things he said to Berrigan was, "You should get your teeth fixed!" Normally when people said that Ted got angry, but Jack's charm made him grin. It was Jack's way of showing that he was comfortable with Berrigan, and it was also a gentle warning that nothing was going to be hidden. Using a minimum of questions and promptings, Berrigan simply let him go where he wanted to, and Jack gladly accepted that freedom and performed marvelously for them. Both Saroyan, who had expected to be amused by a potbellied drunken redneck, and McNaughton, who already admired Kerouac's work, were overcome by the genius and the reality of the man—more real, Saroyan felt, than anyone in their generation.

Dusk was gathering but there were no lights on in the living room. Jack's voice, changing all the time, seemed to issue from the darkness itself. He was delighted to be visited by William Saroyan's son, but he wasn't about to toady to Aram. Rather, knowing Aram was half-Jewish, he said, "Goy is joy!" With amazement and gratitude, Aram realized that Jack wasn't some big shot having a PR interview but an ordinary aging guy, disappointed and angry, who wanted to share himself with some younger men. He was showing them that anti-Semites and rednecks are human too, and to do so he made himself unbelievably vulnerable. For the first time he was willing to make a public statement about his bisexual experiences. As Stella quietly listened, Jack talked about having been "on a lot of couches with young men." Then he specified the code that had governed his behavior: "Blow jobs, yes! Assholes, no!" Over Jack's protests George Plimpton, editor of the *Paris Review*, deleted the whole sexual discussion from the printed interview.

As the three poets left, Jack told McNaughton to remember that Melville's greatest novel was not *Moby Dick* but *The Confidence Man*.

In November, Harvey and Doris Kerouac forced Stella to admit another visitor to the house: Janet Michelle Kerouac. Fifteen years old, an American Beauty rose from Jack's own garden, her small frame beginning to show the bulge of pregnancy, Jan was on the lam from the Bronx Youth House. Her past had included LSD at twelve, heroin at thirteen, prostitution, and stints in most of New York's most brutal institutions, including Bellevue. Bound for Mexico with her boyfriend, she had to see Jack one last time. She found him in his rocker, upending a quart of scotch as he watched *The Beverly Hillbillies* on TV. When he recovered his composure, he asked if she'd been getting his checks.

He sat on the couch, and she embarrassed him by sitting beside him. They compared hands. Then someone brought her boyfriend in, and seeing his hair in a bun Jack said, "Ahhh? Genghis Khan?" Gradually he warmed to her and began telling her about the art on the wall: the drawing of Gerard, his painting of the Pope, and Twardowicz's painting of underwear hanging on a line, dubbed "Mémère's Wash." Mémère herself, in her wheelchair, began to rave in French; Jan caught the name "Caroline." Stella told her they'd have to leave. On the way out Jack told her, "Sure, you can go to Mexico. Use my name. Write a book."

In the following months Jack often talked with Chiefy's wife about his pride in his daughter and his fear that she was damaging herself with drugs, but there were still few people to whom he even acknowledged her. His need for the solace of children, of hope for the future, was never stronger. There is a tape Chiefy made at Christmas 1967, that may tell more about Kerouac than all biographies. It records Jack teaching Christmas carols to Chiefy's little boy.

7.

Vanity of Duluoz was released on February 6, 1968. Beforehand, *Newsweek* dispatched a reporter and photographer to do a story on the senescent King of the Beats. It seemed a harmless assignment, but what they found left them profoundly disquieted. Though they no doubt didn't realize it, Jack, roly-poly and balding, had begun to look much like his father. And like his father he kept thrashing over the fact that he had been ruined by "aliens" (Jews). All this, more or less, they had expected. But they didn't expect to see a man with the "don't hit me" nerves of a has-been boxer. It was pathetically obvious that he dreaded their disapproval, and the only method of self-protection he had left was to show them that Jack Kerouac was crazy. He became a playful fuzzy bear for them; he talked in all his accents and led them to the frozen Merrimack River. While the photographer snapped, he rolled out onto the snow-covered stream like a child. But being a two-hundred-plus-pound child, he broke through and was drenched in the icy water. He caught pneumonia and was sick for two months. *Newsweek* never printed the story.

The reviews of *Vanity of Duluoz* hit him again.

In early February Carolyn Cassady called to tell Jack that Neal had been found dead in Mexico. Having wandered out of a party where he'd mixed booze and barbiturates, wearing only a T-shirt in a cold rain, Neal collapsed beside some railroad tracks; discovered too late, he died of "general congestion" in the hospital. On the phone

Jack refused to accept the fact of Neal's death. A few years earlier Ken Kesey had left his van parked over the edge of a cliff at Big Sur to make the police think he had been killed, and Jack suggested that Neal might have pulled a similar trick to enable Carolyn to collect welfare. Another reason he disputed the news may have been his fear of Carolyn's claim on him, since they had had a vague agreement to marry if Neal died first. Soon after her call, he wrote a letter to Cliff Anderson mourning Neal, a letter of such tenderness that Cliff carried it in his wallet for years.

For another year Jack continued to call Carolyn, to reminisce about "those old days of serious work, railroad, bubble baths, pizza, and wine," but he also grumbled endlessly about things like his mother stealing his whiskey. Early one morning, exhausted, she hung up and he never called again.

In January 1968, journalist Bruce Cook came to Lowell to interview Kerouac for his book *The Beat Generation.* Cook wanted Jack to admit paternity of the Flower Children. Jack didn't deny that the hippies were spiritual descendants of the Beats—how could he, when hippie bards like Bob Dylan and Ed Sanders acknowledged their debt to him?—but he made a very important distinction between the two groups. Whereas the Beats had struggled for years to make their psychic breakthroughs, the hippies sought instant consciousness-expansion with LSD. Distrusting the permanence of such painless enlightenment, Jack feared that all the Beat gains would become a cant, as insidiously demoralizing as the slick vaudeville Abbie Hoffman and his cohorts passed off for revolution.

Jack was no hawk. He encouraged his nephew to avoid being drafted into a combat force by joining the national guard. He didn't want to see any young men become casualties in Vietnam, but he felt it was equally criminal to treat those who were there as if they were lepers. When Jim Droney had antiwar activist Noam Chomsky on his Boston radio show, Jack called in during the program to rebuke Chomsky for dwelling on the politicians who were promoting the war. Nobody, he lamented, bothered to say a good word about the poor grunts who were fighting over there.

Furthermore, he felt that the violent antiwar demonstrations were merely providing an excuse for increased oppression within America. A lot of his antipathy to the Civil Rights movement arose similarly from his sense of the futility of pitting force against force. When the Black Panthers wrote him for a contribution he burned the letter, put the ashes in an envelope, and was about to mail it back to them—as a lesson—until Tony stopped him. The victims of police brutality, he wrote Allen, were not the demonstrators whose arrests were widely publicized—who could, and often did, make a career of disrupting society—but the anonymous slobs like himself who happened to trip some jittery cop's hair trigger. In May 1968, police apprehended Jack for carrying an open bottle of beer down the street and tossed him into a cold, filthy cell, where he caught strep throat.

Most of Jack's friends and relatives were scarcely more considerate of *his* welfare. In March 1968 Tony and Nick were going to Europe with their cousin John Delamus and a friend, Paul Lekas. For kicks they decided to take Jack along. As always, Jack was more than willing to collaborate in his dissolution, and was drunk through Lisbon, Madrid, Geneva, Munich, and Stuttgart. Although he provided the expected amusement, he also proved an impossible burden, dragging scummy whores into posh hotels and always disappearing just when the group was supposed to leave for their next destination. In a week and a half he blew $2,000. In Stuttgart the severity of the Germans cast him into a terrible funk. They all seemed to walk like storm troopers, and at the hotel they upbraided him for drinking too much. Late one night he was frozen in his tracks as a dozen police wagons wailed past. Later, sobbing that he now sympathized with the Jews, he locked himself in his hotel room. The others abandoned him there, and somehow he managed to get home on his own. All he remembered of the trip, aside from the way Germans walked, was the Portuguese prostitute he had paid ten dollars an hour for the privilege of staring into her eyes.

He felt victimized even in his home as he watched Stella tear up his address book to keep him from calling his friends. He decided to prove that he was still in control of his life by asserting his manhood. He made her pick up the pieces and write him a new book. He also exacted his marital due from her. She bled so badly that she had to be taken to the hospital. Jack was devastated and abased. When friends Jim Droney and Ray Rittick came to the house, he took them upstairs to show them the bloodstains. Then he dropped his pants, looked at himself in complete bewilderment, and in an apologetic voice said, "You wouldn't think a guy with this would be able to do all that, would you?"

That summer novelist Gregory McDonald came to interview him for the *Boston Globe*. He found Jack on the verge of cracking up, drinking an average of fourteen boilermakers an hour from morning until night. The house on Sanders Avenue was up for sale, as was his house in Hyannis. Bothered by the cold drafts that came in with Jack's many visitors, Mémère had demanded he take her back to Florida. He wanted to remain in Lowell but her wishes still came first, though as a concession she promised to take therapy down there. But Jack didn't have the money to move until he sold at least one of the houses. His book sales had gone into another slump, and no publisher would even do a paperback reprint of *Vanity of Duluoz*. Mémère was continually needling him about his incompetence. "You're here interviewing Jackie because he's so great?" she told

McDonald. "If Jackie's so great, why can't he sell the house? He says he doesn't have any money. All the people who know Jackie, all around the world, and yet nobody's helping *me!*" Retorted Jack, *"My mother* is a descendant of Napoleon."

McDonald was astonished that no one in the house or in the entire city seemed to see that Jack was in desperate need of help himself. Stella kept bringing him trays of food that he couldn't eat and turned over to McDonald. Showing his paintings, playing the piano and harmonica, jumping up and down, Jack performed for him like a trained seal. After McDonald did his best to show the love Jack seemed to be soliciting, they spent the day wandering through Lowell together. McDonald was in for one embarrassment after another—Jack stopping at every brick wall to pee, Jack blabbing the most inane anti-Semitism, almost as a challenge for McDonald to print it, Jack hugging him in the bars, punching him, coaxing him to wrestle in a blatant sexual comeon. But all this didn't bother McDonald. What sickened him like a gut punch was the sight of this great novelist, who was literally a precious natural resource, going to a premature grave with not one person making the slightest effort to stop him, and Jack himself doing everything possible to dramatize his situation, sacrificing whatever life was left him to make a visible statement about the undeserved plight of American writers. But nobody in town got it; everyone, however respectful to him, seemed also secretly pleased to have this buffoon as proof that it doesn't pay to be exceptional. And that humiliation, in his lonely desire to come down off his mountain, was somehow also exactly what Jack wanted.

He talked so long and so longingly of Gerard that McDonald was moved to inquire whether Jack had any satisfying relationships with living people. He had none to speak of. Finally McDonald asked, "Jack, have you ever felt one-on-one with anybody?" Without a second's thought, Jack answered, "Yeah, Cassady," and began to talk of Neal as he had talked of Gerard, describing their trips together but concentrating on Neal's eyes and the rare communication that had passed between them and his own. At the same time he kept apologizing for his obsession with Neal, as though their relationship also deeply frightened him. Yet he didn't want Neal to be dead; he spoke of his belief that Neal might be alive, but also talked of meeting him in his afterlife.

McDonald's article, "Off the Road . . . the Celtic Twilight of Jack Kerouac," was written in an attempt to give Jack's living statement the weight of print. It was McDonald's way of asking someone with some authority in Jack's life to reach out to him.

To get money for the move south, Jack sold the University of Texas his letters from Allen Ginsberg and Neal Cassady, and sold Columbia his letters from Burroughs. Before leaving Massachusetts he wanted to visit Charles Olson and John Updike, two local authors he admired. One August night, he started out with Tony and Nick and a couple of bottles. Their first stop was Gloucester, where Jack began shouting from the street below Olson's window. Olson recognized him and invited them up, laying down sheets of the *Boston Globe* Sunday magazine, which turned out to be the issue containing McDonald's interview, on the long staircase as a "red carpet." After Jack had crawled up on hands and knees Olson brought out a fifth of Cutty Sark, and they talked and drank until Jack fell asleep. They never made it to Ipswich to see Updike, who, coincidentally, had just finished giving an interview to the *Paris Review* in which he praised Kerouac for "emphasizing a certain flow, a certain ease."

With the approaching presidential election, William F. Buckley, Jr., invited Jack to appear on his television show *The Firing Line.* Jack had known Buckley slightly at Columbia, and Jack's stated politics had some rough similarity to Buckley's staunch conservatism, except of course that in practice Jack was absolutely apolitical. However much he admired Buckley's magnetic leadership, he didn't want to do the show, but once again Mémère pushed him to seize the publicity. With Joe Chaput at the wheel, and Nick and Billy Koums along for protection, Jack drove to New York.

A few miles out of Lowell he made them stop for Scotch and beer. Well-oiled by the time they reached the Columbia campus, he led them into the West End Bar. Next, angry because Sterling Lord didn't write for months at a time and was holding out for more money on reprint rights, Jack went to his office to dismiss him. Lord brought out a bottle and smoothed over their differences. Then at a club run by Billy Conn, another Lowellite, Jack had a few more. That night they slept at the Delmonico Hotel, where Burroughs was staying to write his coverage of the Democratic National Convention for *Esquire.* He and Jack had a warm reunion, though Bill spent most of his time questioning Billy Koums about professional boxing. Lucien arrived, and that called for more Scotch. By morning Jack was gulping it from a water glass.

Despite everyone's advice to cancel his appearance, he was hot to trot. Riding to the studio in a cab with Ginsberg, Nick and Billy were surprised to realize how much Allen really respected Jack. "In a hundred years, most of today's writers won't even be remembered," said Allen, "but they'll still be reading Jack."

In the elevator they bumped into Ed Sanders, who mistook Jack for a state trooper. On the phone Jack had always been friendly to him, and he had contributed to Sanders' magazine *Fuck You,* but now the tension of doing the show made him shrug off Ed's greeting with a real "Fuck you!" Although Jack disdained makeup, he stopped in the dressing room to see Truman Capote, who was being made up for another show. In his high nasal voice Capote said, "Hellowww, Jack." Jack replied, "Hello, you queer bastard!" Capote smiled and then broke into a laugh. "You've been saying bad things about me," Jack said, "but I have nothing against you. I'll still shake your hand." And they shook hands.

The interview was a nasty surprise, much like the Brandeis symposium, because at the last minute Jack found that he was to be set up with Sanders and a sociology professor, Lewis Yablansky. Keeping a cup of whiskey beside his chair, Jack reacted defensively, calling attention to Yablansky's Jewishness, denying that he was Sanders' "father," and showing his "thumbs down" disapproval when the camera turned on Ginsberg in the audience. But at points his wit was as sharp as ever, as when he quipped that a cop had given him "a ticket for decay," and that the war in Vietnam was a conspiracy by the North and South Vietnamese to acquire American jeeps. Most importantly, Jack affirmed that the hippies were part of the same "Dionysian movement" as the Beats, and stated his belief that "the hippies are good kids, they're better than the Beats." When Buckley questioned whether the Beat movement had ever been pure, Jack protested, "Yes, it was pure—my heart." By the midpoint of the show Buckley was so nonplussed he wanted to replace Jack with Allen, but Allen gallantly declined. Later, at ease in a bar, Jack was his old self and quite friendly to both Allen and Sanders.

That night Jack and Joe visited some jazz clubs in the Village. For old time's sake, Jack picked up a black hooker; but, as usual, nothing came of it.

He had purchased a concrete block house at 5169 10th Avenue North in St. Petersburg, a few doors from his previous house. In September, with Stella, Mémère, and the cats on mattresses in the back of Chaput's station wagon, and Jack riding shotgun with his bottle, Joe drove the Kerouacs to Florida. Helping unload his own furniture to save money, Jack cracked his shinbone. His hernia was also getting worse, and he only managed to hold his navel in with a Kennedy half dollar strapped over it.

As soon as Joe left, Jack began seeing Cliff again. Desperate to change the direction of his life, he went to Cliff's cabin in the woods and took a massive dose of LSD. For six weeks afterward, he stayed in bed sleeping off its effects.

Mémère soon quit therapy, this time because it was too painful, and to escape her gloomy dominion he again began hitting the Tampa bars. The Boar having burned down, he patronized its successor, The Collage, but he preferred a nearby redneck bar where there was a stabbing a night.

Frequently Jack called his nephew Paul, now living in Alaska, and made plans to live with him in a cabin in the wilderness, where he could continue in the footsteps of Jack London. In reality, he had trouble getting out of his chair. The phone bills were astronomical, but when Stella would holler at him to hang up, he'd make ripostes like, "We've got to keep the connection—you know how much trouble it is to get a phone in his igloo." Calling Helen Elliott, he said something she thought she'd never hear from Jack Kerouac: "Helen, *I'm so unhappy!*" Then out went the phone again.

In April 1969, he grew hysterical to learn that there were several years of back taxes owed on the house, which the former owner had deducted from the selling price. Jack had less than the $1,600 required to keep the house, so he called Lord for a loan, but Lord said he couldn't manage it. Crying so that he couldn't get his words out, Jack handed the phone to Stella. In the end she borrowed the money from her brother Nick and went to work as a seamstress to pay it back, until Lord was finally able to provide an advance.

Jack wasn't writing, and his loneliness was unbearable. But when Al and Helen Hinkle stopped to see him on their trip through Florida, he told them he just didn't like people anymore. Perplexed by the vast changes occurring among the young, he bemoaned the fact that they no longer played hopscotch or had neighborhood baseball games or even kept clean. Especially he was disappointed in Allen for helping promote this degeneration. When he began to rant against the communist conspiracy that had taken over the Beat movement, Hinkle had the impression of a man completely detached from reality, without a trace of the zest for life that used to be his most remarkable quality.

But at least when semi-sober his mind was still lucid; as late as May 1969 he wrote a letter to Ed White scintillating with his best wit. He had become dependent on dexedrine, however, and he was beginning to show signs of a real psychotic paranoia. He liked to sit in the back yard reading, with a cooler of beer, but he gave that up because he feared being watched by the nosy woman next door. Moreover, he became fanatically jealous of a seventy-five-year-old man who used to watch Stella hang clothes. The five-foot fence he put up merely caused a big row with the woman and failed to cure his jealousy. Soon he was suspicious whenever Stella as much as offered one of his men friends an extra cup of coffee.

Although Jack and Stella fought as much as ever, he told her that whatever happened during the day she must never go to bed without kissing him. At the same time as he'd complain that she wasn't doing her housework properly, he'd also demand that she sit with him and listen while he talked himself to sleep. If he saw her beginning to nod, he'd hit her with a pillow to keep her awake. They still had good times together. He called her "Stella by Starlight," and often they'd stay up late outside while he taught her about the stars. Knowing how much he liked to lie on his back watching them, she got him a cot with S & H green stamps. Nevertheless, by summer 1969 he was convinced that she was trying to poison him for his money, and unbeknownst to her he began proceedings to obtain a divorce. It is probable that he wasn't acting solely out of madness though, for at this point he would quite simply try anything to break out of the nightmare his life had become.

8.

The only escape, as always, was inside. Jack began secluding himself in his room to make tapes in which he talked to and sang along with the radio, played his harmonica, drummed, and sometimes just sang to himself. One such tape survives:

He puts on WBKL Tampa. "Night and Day" comes on. He picks certain lines to sing.

"Oh such a hunger burning burning inside me."

He scats.

"Ooo! Ooo! Ooo!"

"Come Dance With Me" comes on. Jack, excited: "Frank Sinatra! . . . He's great, isn't he? . . . Yessir!"

Sinatra: "Put on your Basie boots. . . ."

Jack: "Put on your happy boots!"

As the song ends, he hums a few bars of the *Marseillaise*.

"Cherish Is the Word," a pop tune, comes on. Over it, sounding like Bob Dylan, he improvises an Okie blues describing an imaginary trip hoboing through the West. It ends: "In Portland, Oregon, they raised up a bridge for me! Woo! (repeat) Had to go to 'Frisco down from there—meet all the cats, gonna come out on the street, Market Street, corner street. Beat Beat Beat Beat Beat Beat Beat Beat Beat! Had to go downtown to find all the girls and boys—they all look alike to me—except they were built different. So I started a prune orchard in San Jose."

"Here's to My Lady" comes on. Jack sings along, then comments: "Nobody can sing that but me 'n' Nat King Cole 'n' Sinatra."

"I Concentrate on You" comes on. Jack sings along.

Announcer begins: "When you drop unused and repairable household items into a Good Will bag. . . ."

Jack, angry, shouts: "Love your household items!"

"Do You Know the Way to San Jose?" comes on. He switches stations.

"Are You Lonesome Tonight?" comes on. Jack sings and improvises: "Are you lonesome tonight? You want to play with my spike? Because it never happened before." He says, "I remember this being sung on the old porches."

During another song he improvises lyrics in *joual*.

"Love Is a Many Splendored Thing" comes on. He sings along

and improvises: "High on a windy hill, William Holden and a Chinese gal are tryin'-a take a swim." Wicked chuckle. "Be sure if you're Tristessa's *français* that love will triumph." He scats, holds a note like Jerry Colonna. "Up and down your organ up in Chinatown!" *Marseillaise.*

Lullaby of Birdland comes on. Jack snaps his fingers and whistles, eventually doing a long improvised whistle solo.

Edie Gormé sings "The Sweetest Sounds." Jack: "Bring back Peggy King and let her sing! . . . The stupidest sounds I ever heard were never concocted in brew . . . I'll take Brue Moore."

"You Made Me Love You" comes on. Jack: "I want a girl just like the girl who married Harry James! You can have her! . . . 'Up against the monument, dearie!' . . . You made me hate you!"

Announcer begins: "Graduates average $2,000 more per year than people who haven't finished school. Invest yourself in your education—it'll pay off in the future—" Jack changes the station.

"The Sound of Music" comes on. Jack sings along and improvises: "The earth is alive with the sound of music . . . No wonder I'm sitting right here! There's nothing in my heart but shame—I think it was planted there by Spiro Agnew. I think I'll go home again." He turns up the volume on the crescendo.

"A Love Affair" comes on. Jack: "Our love affair will have to be the way I say and not what you say—or I'll roll you in a barrel in the river in the morning. . . . Who's that faggot that's banging on my piano? And all those faggots with their violin strings—why don't they play with themselves like an old bow up the hole? . . . Our love affair is concluded."

He shuts off the radio and says, "Now we go to Spain and we hear the flamenco harmonica!" He plays and sings flamenco: *"El caballo en la montaña . . . ver te ver te como te quiero ver . . . Federico García Lorca!"* He compliments himself: *"Bueno! Juan Luís!"* He sings "It Happened in Monterrey" accompanied by the sound of a flamenco dance. He says, *"Hombres que rezan,"* then translates: "Men who pray."

A new song on the radio. He improvises: "My life's been closed—the Lord's gonna send me down from heaven . . . a heart attack . . . I'll see my love—I'll go my way—because all that's from heaven can never be countermanded. . . . You can't go AWOL in heaven . . . I don't care about you, you fuck! . . . To have glorious harmony is to keep your cock in shape—that's right! . . . If a shark ever bit my cock off I'd yell, 'Ahhhh!' " Wicked chuckle.

"Yesterdays" comes on. Jack: "Yesterdays, golden times that were not there . . . yesterdays, things that never happened to Billie Holiday." He scats. "You've got to explore all the fields of the twelve-tone scale . . . days I knew were always my own days . . . I could go walking in the cowflap fields of time . . . I could always go run around in some sailor town . . . I could wander all over Liverpool, bring 500-pound bombs to Germany . . . I could wind up in old Germany with an old friend of mine."

Stella interrupts, asking, "What's that?"

Jack: "This's the mike. Hi, Mike! . . . I'm practicing to get on a horse."

Stella: "What horse?"

Jack: "I'm writing a book."

Stella: "I knew there's method to your madness . . . I knew it, Jackie."

9.

The one person Jack still managed to phone regularly was Edie Parker in Grosse Pointe. If he'd get a man instead, he'd start yelling, "Get out of my wife's bed, you bastard!" Jack told Edie that he was divorcing Stella and that he wanted her to visit him in St. Petersburg. Eventually he grew so anxious to see her that he telegraphed offering to pay her air fare.

Meanwhile he worked on a new novel. Unable to produce any substantial amount of new material, he made a mosaic from several of the unpublished pieces he had accumulated over the years. The central plot and characters came from the story he had written in 1951 about a North Carolina black boy named Pictorial Review Jackson. Incorporated into *Pic* (as he called the novel) were the story of the Prophet on Times Square, first drafted in 1941 for the Young Prometheans' study group, a chapter about a fudge factory deleted from *The Town and the City,* and the full story of the Ghost of the Susquehanna, much of which had been cut from *On the Road.* For the sake of unity he retold all these tales in the black Southern dialect of the narrator-protagonist. But the book coheres in an even more fundamental way as an allegory of Kerouac's whole life.

Almost every incident in *Pic* comments on something that happened to Jack, and does so from the fresh perspective of viewing himself as a member of another race. That Kerouac should cast himself as a black boy is not so surprising considering that the Canucks were *les nègres blancs.* The book is also one grand time collapse, as Jack follows himself from youth to old age within a few months of Pic's life. "Ain't never nobody loved me like I love myself, cept my mother and she's dead," Pic tells us at the start, and of course Jack's mother is presently as good as dead. One day Pic's brother John disappears. An outcast even among his own kind—"the darkest, blackest boy ever to come to that school"—Pic spends his time in solitude learning songs off the radio. One of his favorite kicks is drinking—Dr. Pepper! He likes to go to sleep watching the stars. His last protector, his grandfather (like Jack's father), sickens and dies. He's forced to live with in-laws who detest him. His cousin introduces him to Saturday night in the town. Although Pic is burdened with a "curse" (original sin) that he can't understand, some people sense his essential innocence. Having become a saxophone player, his brother returns to take him to New York, where jazz gives him new joy. He and his brother go out on the road. Broke and stranded, they take refuge in a church. Pic's singing charms a Jesuit, who gives them jobs. Finally they reach California and the comforts of a loving woman.

In the original ending, to which Stella objected, Pic and his brother were to meet Sal Paradise and Dean Moriarty. Black joins white, and the circle is complete.

In addition, *Pic* contains some very subtle parables of the Beat Generation. As just one example, when John takes Pic to New York, the children Pic has lived with are saddened. Says John: "Don't cry, chillun, 'case me and Pic come back tomorrow or next year and we all have a big fine time t'gether and go down the crick and fish, and eat candy, and th'ow the baseball, and tell tales t'each other, and climb up the tree and *hant* the folks below. . . ."

On September 4 Jack went to his lawyer to sign his new will, leaving his entire estate to his mother. The alternate beneficiary was his nephew Paul. Stella didn't know the contents of the will. As soon as Jack left the house Mémère called Stella into her room and told her, "Jack's going down to divorce you."

A few days later Jack went into the Cactus Bar in St. Petersburg, a rough black bar. He was accompanied by a wacky, disabled air force veteran with a steel plate in his head. When the vet put his arm around the young black band manager, the manager slugged him. Trying to protect the vet, Jack yelled, "He's no queer!" and tried to explain that the vet was just showing affection. The manager said, "So you want it too?" Finding himself surrounded by black men Jack realized he'd have to accept a beating or wind up stabbed or shot. Hence he didn't attempt to defend himself as the manager (an ex-boxer) bashed his head and cracked his ribs.[313] The police were called, and he was arrested.

Stella got a neighbor to drive her to the jail to bail him out. Jack's face was black and blue and bloodied, and his shirt was bloody too. When they got home, she advised him to clean up before he went in to Mémère. For ten minutes he sat in the corner just thinking. Out of the blue he said, "You know, Stella, *I love you!*" After he came out from seeing Mémère, he was even more discomfited. "I don't know what's the matter with me," he told Stella. "I've got a good home, a good wife. I'm not like those bums, like those drunks in the jail. You should hear them! But I'm not like those people, *am I?*"

Stella reassured him, "Jack, you're telling stories, that's your business. Don't be worried."

He had to sleep with a pillow under his stomach to ease the pain of his cracked ribs. By the end of September he was so sick he wrote Edie asking her not to come down as planned.

Under terrible stress and discomfort he completed a nationally syndicated article called "After Me, the Deluge." It was taken at the time to be a reactionary screed against the antiwar movement and hippies. Actually the tone was far more sad than angry. It was the lament of a great idealist who'd once seen America bound for glory and suddenly saw her fatally sidetracked. His complaint was basically that serious workers and artists like himself were no longer a focal point for the young.

The Miami *Herald* sent journalist Jack McClintock to do an interview to accompany the article. McClintock and two of his friends, Richard Hill and Al Ellis, began to visit Jack regularly. Stella welcomed them, as she always welcomed Cliff too, for the company they provided Jack.

Knowing he would die soon, Jack often asked Richard Hill questions about funeral homes and embalming, concerned that the undertaker treat his body with dignity. The last time Cliff saw him, October 18, Jack kept waving good-bye.

On Friday October 17, a neighbor hired some men to cut down the huge Georgia pine in front of her house. It happened to be the same tree through whose branches Jack used to listen to the wind "speak" to him after his sister had died. When he found out what was taking place he began to shake violently, and the vein in his forehead bulged so that Stella feared it would burst. He rushed out and began hysterically shouting that the neighbor was a "murderer," that she was "killing his brother." Tony Sampas, apprised of the crisis, was on the verge of flying down with Billy Koums, but gradually Jack seemed to be working out of it.

The night of Sunday October 19, he couldn't sleep and lay outside on his cot to watch the stars. The next morning after eating some tuna, he sat down in front of the TV, notebook in hand, to plan a new novel; it was to be titled after his father's old shop: "The Spotlight Print." Just getting out of bed Stella heard groans in the bathroom and found him on his knees, vomiting blood. He told her he didn't want to go to the hospital, but he cooperated when the ambulance attendants arrived. As they were leaving, he said, "Stella, I hurt," which shocked her because it was the first time she had ever heard him complain. Then he shocked her even more by saying, for the second time since they had married, "Stella, I love you."

Less than a day later, on the morning of October 21, after twenty-six blood transfusions, Jean Louis Kerouac died in St. Anthony's Hospital of hemorrhaging esophageal varices, the classic drunkard's death.

On Dizzy Gillespie's birthday.

Epilogue

With his custodian's key, Freddy Bertrand let G.J. and Scotty into the Pawtucketville Social Club, where they drank all night. (Holed up in his studio in Northport, Stan Twardowicz was also drinking himself unconscious.) Hurt that they had not been asked to be pallbearers, and loath to mix with the hippies anyhow, Jack's old friends decided they wouldn't attend his burial. But they did pay their respects in the Archambault Funeral Parlor. It was the same home where Gerard had been waked; coincidentally the little boy laid out in the room next to Jack's was named L'Evesque. The funeral parlor was so crowded you couldn't kneel in front of the casket. One half of the room was filled with beaded hippies, the other half with black-clad Greeks. The talk was so loud it sounded like a party, and the thick cloud of smoke reminded Scotty of Barrett's café the night he had gone with Jack for their first beer. Looking at Jack with his rosary and gray houndstooth jacket and red bow tie, G.J. asked Scotty, "Can you believe that this is our buddy Jack lying there . . . and *dead?*"

Allen thought Jack looked like a "serious mouthed painted-up buddha doll gone *away.*"

When Edie Parker and her sister Charlotte strode in, everyone became quiet and stared. One of the Sampases came up to ask who they were. Edie yelled, "I'm Mrs. Jack Kerouac!"

At St. Jean Baptiste Church Father Armand Spike Morissette said a short eulogy. He concluded: "Our hope and prayer is that Jack has found complete liberation . . . Jack is now sharing the Visions of Gerard."

As the coffin left the church, one of the local French-Canadians was heard to ask, "Who's that?"

"Jack Kerouac," someone answered.

"Who's Jack Kerouac?"

BOOKS BY JACK KEROUAC

Big Sur. New York: Farrar, Straus and Cudahy, 1962.

Book of Dreams. San Francisco: City Lights Books, 1961.

Desolation Angels. New York: Coward-McCann, 1965.

The Dharma Bums. New York: Viking Press, 1958.

Doctor Sax: Faust Part Three. New York: Grove Press, 1959.

Heaven & Other Poems. Bolinas, Cal.: Grey Fox Press, 1977.

Lonesome Traveler. New York: McGraw-Hill Book Company, 1960.

Maggie Cassidy. New York: Avon Books, 1959.

Mexico City Blues. New York: Grove Press, 1959.

On the Road. New York: Viking Press, 1957.

Pic. New York: Grove Press, 1971.

Pull My Daisy. New York: Grove Press, 1961.

Satori in Paris. New York: Grove Press, 1966.

Scattered Poems. San Francisco: City Lights Books, 1971.

The Scripture of the Golden Eternity. New York: Totem/Corinth, 1960.

The Subterraneans. New York: Grove Press, 1958.

The Town and the City. New York: Harcourt, Brace, 1950.

Tristessa. New York: Avon Books, 1960.

Two Early Stories. New York: Aloe Editions, 1973.

Vanity of Duluoz: An Adventurous Education. New York: Coward-McCann, 1968.

Visions of Cody. New York: McGraw-Hill Book Company, 1972.

Visions of Gerard. New York: Farrar, Straus and Company, 1963.

Sources and Notes

The bibliographical information in the sources below is based on the original editions of Jack Kerouac's work, while more readily available, current paperback editions are cited in the footnotes which refer to specific quotations in the text.

PROLOGUE

The Prologue is based on the author's interview with Quebec writer Victor-Lévy Beaulieu, April 1978, Beaulieu's book *Jack Kerouac: a chicken-essay*, Toronto, 1975, and the author's own experiences in Lowell.

ONE: THE TRADEMARK OF A BRETON

1.

Letters of JK: to John Clellon Holmes, July 11-12, 1950; to Lawrence Ferlinghetti, Oct. 6, 1962; to the *Albany Mirror*, Nov. 27, 1965; to Ed White, May 12, 1969.

JK's work: (a) Unpublished: the 1075-page original edited typescript of *The Town and the City* on deposit at the Northport Public Library, Northport, N.Y. (b) Published: *Doctor Sax*, N.Y., 1959; "The Origins of the Beat Generation," *Playboy*, Vol. 6 (June 1959).

Books and articles: Bernice Lemire, *Jack Kerouac: Early Influences* (unpublished doctoral thesis at Boston College), 1962; "Jack Kerouac at Northport," an interview with JK by Miklos Zsedely, April 1964, for the permanent collection of the Northport Public Library, Northport, N.Y. transcribed by Diana Scesny and published in three successive issues of *Athanor*, Winter/Spring 1971, Fall/Winter 1971, and Summer/Fall 1972 (much of the original interview was erased due to fear of libel suits, and one whole reel of tape was given away to Stanley Twardowicz, in whose studio the interview took place; Scesny's transcript on deposit at the Northport Public Library is slightly more complete than the version in *Athanor*); Father Armand Morissette, "A Catholic's View of Kerouac" (unpublished), 1977.

Author's interviews: with Fr. Armand Morissette, Aug. 1977 and Aug. 1978; with William Koumantzelis, Aug. 1977; with Elzear "Scoopy" Dionne, Aug. 1978; with Armand Gauthier, Aug. 1978; with Reginald Ouellette, Aug. 1978.

2.

Letters of JK: to Don Allen, Oct. 1, 1959 (printed in *Jack Kerouac: Heaven & Other Poems*, Bolinas, Calif., 1977).

JK's work: (a) Unpublished: typescript of *The Town and the City*. (b) Published: *Doctor Sax*; *Visions of Gerard*, N.Y., 1963; *Desolation Angels*, N.Y., 1965.

Books and journals: Lemire, *Jack Kerouac: Early Influences*; Victor-Lévy Beaulieu, *Jack Kerouac: a chicken-essay*, Toronto, 1975; notes from the conversation of JK taken down by Phil Singer, fall 1965 (unpublished).

Author's interviews: with Fr. Armand Morissette, Aug. 1977; with Roger Ouellette, Aug. 1978; with Annette Beauregard, Aug. 1978; with Elzear Dionne, Aug. 1978; with Armand Gauthier, Aug. 1978; with Armand Houde, Aug. 1978; with Hal Chase, Oct. 1978; with Paul Blake, Jr., Oct. 1978.

Lectures: Allen Ginsberg, "Literary History of the Beat Generation," Naropa Institute, Boulder, Colo., summer 1977 (available on tape from Vajradhatu Recordings, Boulder, Colo.).

1. Jack Kerouac, *Doctor Sax* (New York: Grove Press, Evergreen Black Cat ed., 1975), p. 18, p. 4, *et passim*; Jack Kerouac, *Visions of Gerard* (New York: McGraw-Hill, paperback ed., 1976), pp. 145-147, *et passim*.

2. Kerouac's childhood fantasy world is related by Allen Ginsberg in his "Literary History of the Beat Generation" lectures, summer 1977; and the relationship between that fantasy world and Kerouac's subsequent writings is detailed in Kerouac's letter to Don Allen, Oct. 1959, printed in *Jack Kerouac: Heaven & Other Poems*, Don Allen, ed., (Bolinas, Calif.: Grey Fox Press, 1977), p. 51.

3.

Letters of JK: to Bernice Lemire, June 15, 1961; Oct. 14, 1961; Dec. 9, 1961.

JK on tape: untranscribed reel from the Northport Public Library interview of JK, April 1964, in the possession of Stanley Twardowicz.

JK's work: *Doctor Sax*; "In the Ring," *The Atlantic*, Vol. 221 (March 1968).

Books: Lemire, *Jack Kerouac: Early Influences*.

Author's interviews: with Fr. Armand Morissette, Aug. 1977; with Leo Nadeau, May 1978; with Odysseus "Duke" Chiungos, May 1978; with Armand Houde, Aug. 1978; with Armand Gauthier, Aug. 1978; with Arthur Louis Eno, Aug. 1978; with Demosthenes "Sam" Samaras, Aug. 1978; with Beatrice Rouleau Jasmin, Oct. 1978.

3. Kerouac's knowledge of the sexual play behind the Grotto was reported by Fr. Armand Morissette in our interview, Aug. 1977; the euphemism "dingdongs" is Kerouac's, in *Doctor Sax* (p. 59) and *Visions of Gerard* (p. 48).

4.

JK's work: (a) Unpublished: typescript of *The Town and the City*. (b) Published: *Doctor Sax*; *Visions of Gerard*; "The Origins of the Beat Generation"; "In the Ring."

Articles: Henry "Scotty" Beaulieu, "My Boyhood Years with Jack Kerouac" (unpublished), 1973.

Author's interviews: with Leo Nadeau, May 1978; with Peter Houde, May 1978; with G.J. Apostolos, May 1978 and Aug. 1978; with Joseph Voyer, May 1978; with Elzear Dionne, Aug. 1978; with Stanley Bocko, Aug. 1978; with Armand Charbonneau, Aug. 1978; with Armand Houde, Aug. 1978.

5.

JK's work: *Doctor Sax*, *Maggie Cassidy*, N.Y., 1959.

Books and articles: Charles E. Jarvis, *Visions of Kerouac: The Life of Jack Kerouac*, Lowell, 1973; Henry Beaulieu, "My Boyhood Years with Jack Kerouac."

Author's interviews: with Joseph Voyer, May 1978; with Victor Sawyer, May 1978; with Peter Houde, May 1978; with Odysseus "Duke" Chiungos, May 1978;

with Wilfred Bertrand, May 1978; with Roland Salvas, May 1978; with Steve Tsotakos, May 1978; with G.J. Apostolos, May 1978 and Aug. 1978; with Victor Alberts, Aug. 1978; with Gerald Parent, Aug. 1978; with Roger Ouellette, Aug. 1978; with Fred "Fritz" Drescher, Aug. 1978; with Joseph Nolan (interviewed on my behalf by Elmer Rynne), Aug. 1978; with Elmer Rynne, Aug. 1978; with George O'Maera, Aug. 1978.
4. *Doctor Sax*, p. 34.

6.

JK's work: *Vanity of Duluoz*, N.Y., 1968.
JK on tape: untranscribed reel from the Northport Public Library interview.
Articles: Henry Beaulieu, "My Boyhood Years with Jack Kerouac"; Fr. Armand Morissette, "A Catholic's View of Kerouac" (unpublished), 1977; numerous sports clippings from the *Lowell Sun* provided by Mary McCarron Murphy and by librarian Robert McLeod of the Lowell Public Library.
Author's interviews: with Fr. Armand Morissette, Aug. 1977; with G.J. Apostolos, May 1978, and Aug. 1978; with Elzear Dionne, Aug. 1978; with Stanley Bocko, Aug. 1978; with Elmer Rynne, Aug. 1978; with Joseph Sullivan, Jr. (interviewed on my behalf by Elmer Rynne), Aug. 1978; with James Cudworth, Aug. 1978; with James O'Dea, Oct. 1978; with Albert "Skippy" Roberge, Aug. 1978; with Fred Drescher, Aug. 1978; with Joseph Sorota, Aug. 1978; with Julian Beaulieu, Aug. 1978; with Charles Ruiter, Aug. 1978.
5. Joseph Sullivan, Jr., interviewed on my behalf by Elmer Rynne, Aug. 1978.
6. Jack Kerouac, *Vanity of Duluoz* (New York: G.P. Putnam's Sons, Capricorn paperback ed., 1978), p. 19. Kerouac is quoting an unnamed sportswriter. As far as I was able to check, his reference to sports stories in *Vanity of Duluoz* is quite accurate to fact.
7. Interview with Elmer Rynne, Aug. 1978.

7.

Letters of JK: to Bernice Lemire, June 15, 1961.
JK's work: *Maggie Cassidy; Vanity of Duluoz.*
Books and articles: Lemire, *Jack Kerouac: Early Influences*; Henry Beaulieu, "My Boyhood Years with Jack Kerouac"; *The Review* (Lowell High School magazine), issues Nov. 1938, Dec. 1938, Feb. 1939, March 1939, and May 1939, provided by Lowell City Librarian Robert McLeod; a news clipping of JK's seventeenth birthday party, which identifies "Maggie Cassidy" as Mary Carney.
Author's interviews: with Albert Blazon, Aug. 1978; with Charles Ruiter, Aug. 1978; with Mary McCarron Murphy, Aug. 1978; with Ray "Red" McNulty, Aug. 1978; with Ray "Red" St. Louis, Aug. 1978; with G.J. Apostolos, May 1978, and Aug. 1978; with James O'Dea, Oct. 1978; with Odysseus Chiungos, May 1978; with Elmer Rynne, Aug 1978; with James Cudworth, Aug. 1978; with James Taylor, Aug. 1978.

8.

JK on tape: "The Midnight Ghost," an improvised talking blues song (from which the title of this chapter is taken), JK accompanying himself on guitar—tape courtesy of Tony Sampas.
JK's work (a) Unpublished: typescript of *The Town and the City*. (b) Published: *Maggie Cassidy; Vanity of Duluoz.*
Articles: Henry Beaulieu, "My Boyhood Years with Jack Kerouac."
Author's interviews: with Allan Temko, Oct. 1977, and June 1978; with Elmer

Rynne, Aug. 1978; with Steve Eastham, Aug. 1978; with G.J. Apostolos, May 1978, and Aug. 1978.

TWO: THE RUINS OF PEARL HARBOR

1.

JK's work (a) Unpublished: typescript of *The Town and the City*; "Character Key to the *Duluoz Legend*" (currently in the Kerouac archives, a copy of which was provided for me by Dr. Dan DeSole; it has, of course, been of indispensable aid throughout this biography). (b) Published: *Maggie Cassidy; Vanity of Duluoz;* "He went on the road, as Jack Kerouac says," *Life,* Vol. 52 (June 29, 1962).

Articles: Newspaper clippings pertaining to JK's athletic career from the *Lowell Sun* and other newspapers were provided by Lowell City Librarian Robert McLeod (the quote "the name of Kerouac was law in the dormitories" is taken from the article "Horace Mann Hero Home for Short Visit" in the *Lowell Sun,* Wednesday, November 22, 1939—the same article in which Kerouac spoke to the reporter of his desire to become a professional sports reporter); Walter Gutman, *The Gutman Letter* (Stearns & Co. newsletter), N.Y., Oct. 25, 1960 (pertaining to JK and Eddy Gilbert).

Author's interviews: with Allan Temko, Oct. 1977; with G.J. Apostolos, Aug. 1978.

8. In addition to his conversations with Julian Beaulieu, Kerouac referred to these suicidal tendencies in his article "He went on the road, as Jack Kerouac says," *Life,* Vol. 52 (June 29, 1962), p. 22; and he spelled them out in detail in the Northport Public Library draft of *The Town and the City,* pp. 97-99.

9. *Vanity of Duluoz,* p. 207.

2.

JK's work: *Maggie Cassidy; Vanity of Duluoz;* "Count Basie's Band Best in Land: Group Famous for 'Solid' Swing," *The Horace Mann Record,* Vol. 33 (February 16, 1940); "Glenn Miller Skipped School to Play Trombone, Now Is Nation's Most Popular Dance Band Leader," *The Horace Mann Record,* Vol. 33 (March 15, 1940) (coauthored by Morton Maxwell); "Music Notes," *The Horace Mann Record,* Vol. 33 (April 5, 1940); "Real Solid Drop-Beat Riffs and Kicks Are Plentiful in George Avakian's Unique Album of Chicago-Style Jazz," The Horace Mann Record, Vol. 33 (May 23, 1940) (coauthored by Albert Avakian); "The Brothers," *The Horace Mann Quarterly,* Vol. 22 (Fall 1939); "Une Veille de Noel," *The Horace Mann Quarterly,* Vol. 22 (Summer 1940).

Books: Frank Tirro, *Jazz: A History,* N.Y., 1977.

Author's interviews: with James O'Dea, Oct. 1978; with Cornelius Murphy, Oct. 1978.

3.

Letters of JK: to Bernice Lemire, Oct. 14, 1961; to Carolyn Cassady, spring 1955.

JK's work: (a) Unpublished: typescript of *The Town and the City.* (b) Published: *Maggie Cassidy; Vanity of Duluoz.*

Books: Bernice Lemire, *Jack Kerouac: Early Influences* (unpublished), 1962 (of especial use here was Lemire's interview with Mary Carney, since Ms. Carney has since refused information to all would-be interviewers); Henry Beaulieu, "My Boyhood Years with Jack Kerouac" (unpublished), 1973.

Author's interviews: with James Taylor, Aug. 1978; with Allan Temko, Oct. 1977, and June 1978; with Charlotte Parker, Oct. 1978; with Tony Sampas, May 1978, and Aug. 1978; with Cornelius Murphy, Oct. 1978; with George Constantinides, Oct. 1978; with James O'Dea, Oct. 1978; with William Koumantzelis, Aug. 1977; with G.J. Apostolos, May 1978, and Aug. 1978; with Roland Salvas, May 1978; with Leo Nadeau, May 1978; with Emil Descheneaux, Aug. 1978.

10. Jack Kerouac, *Maggie Cassidy* (New York: McGraw-Hill, paperback, 1978), pp. 178-189.

4.

Letters of JK: to Ed White, Nov. 9, 1949; March 2, 1951.

JK's work: *The Town and the City,* N.Y., 1950; *Vanity of Duluoz.*

Articles: Henry Beaulieu, "My Boyhood Years with Jack Kerouac"; "Lou Little Figures Kerouac Sure Fire on Columbia Eleven: Lowell Boy Well Liked by Famed Lions' Coach," sports clipping, n.d., from the *Lowell Sun,* provided by Lowell City Librarian Robert McLeod.

Author's interviews: with G.J. Apostolos, May 1978, and Aug. 1978; with Frankie Edith Parker Kerouac, Oct. 1978; with George Constantinides, Oct. 1978; with James O'Dea, Oct. 1978.

Lectures: Ginsberg, "Literary History of the Beat Generation."

5.

JK's work: (a) Unpublished: typescript of *The Town and the City.* (b) Published: *Vanity of Duluoz.*

Articles: Henry Beaulieu, "My Boyhood Years with Jack Kerouac."

Author's interviews: with G.J. Apostolos, May 1978, and Aug. 1978; with Tony Sampas, May 1978, and Aug. 1978; with George Murray, Aug. 1978; with Elmer Rynne, Aug. 1978; with George Constantinides, Oct. 1978; with James O'Dea, Oct. 1978; with Cornelius Murphy, Oct. 1978.

11. Cornelius Murphy and George Constantinides recalled these incidents and their views of Kerouac in my interviews with them, October 1978; these interpretations were also substantiated by other members and intimates of the group, such as George Murray and Tony Sampas.

12. Sammy's views of Kerouac and John Koumantzelis were reported to me by George Constantinides in our interview, October 1978.

13. The events at the "Friends of Sam" meetings, as well as Kerouac's story about the prophet, were recounted by George Murray in our interview, August 1978.

6.

Letters of JK: to Bernice Lemire, June 15, 1961.

JK's work: *Vanity of Duluoz.*

Articles: Fr. Armand Morissette, "A Catholic's View of Kerouac."

Author's interviews: with Fr. Armand Morissette, Aug. 1977, and May 1978; with James O'Dea, Oct. 1978; with Tony Sampas, May 1978; with Frankie Edith Parker Kerouac, Oct. 1978, and July 1979.

14. Father Morissette recalled this conversation with Kerouac in our interview, August 1977.

15. Ivan Bunin, *The Gentleman from San Francisco* (New York: Alfred A. Knopf, 1941), p. 280.

16. *Vanity of Duluoz,* pp. 86-89. Kerouac's desire to excel in all fields was confirmed by numerous interviewees.

7.

JK's work: (a) Unpublished: typescript of *The Town and the City*. (b) Published: *Vanity of Duluoz*.

Articles: Henry Beaulieu, "My Boyhood Years with Jack Kerouac."

Author's interviews: with G.J. Apostolos, May 1978, and Aug. 1978.

17. Jack Kerouac, *The Town and the City* (New York: Harcourt Brace Jovanovich, Harvest paperback ed., 1978), p. 266.

18. The visit by Scotty and G.J. was recalled in detail in Scotty's unpublished memoir, "My Boyhood Years with Jack Kerouac," in the possession of his son Henry Beaulieu, Jr. The visit by Sam is recounted in *Vanity of Duluoz*, pp. 100-102.

THREE: THE SOUND OF NEW YORK

1.

JK's work: *Vanity of Duluoz*.

Books: Jarvis, *Visions of Kerouac*.

Author's interviews: with James O'Dea, Oct. 1978; with Elmer Rynne, Aug. 1978; with George McGuane (interviewed on my behalf by Elmer Rynne), Aug. 1978; with Clare Mullen Foye, May 1978; with William Dabilis, Aug. 1978; with Joanne O'Dea, Oct. 1978; with G.J. Apostolos, May 1978, and Aug. 1978.

19. McGuane described his impressions of Kerouac to Elmer Rynne, who interviewed him on my behalf, August 1978.

20. The Arrows' opinion of Kerouac was summarized by Billy Dabilis in our interview, August 1978.

21. George Apostolos recalled these impressions in our first interview, May 1978.

2.

Letters of JK: to Seymour Krim, Feb. 13, 1965; to Charles G. Sampas, Oct. 4, 1969 (printed in "Sampas Scoopies"—see below).

JK on tape: party at JK's house, Aug. 26, 1964, recorded by Lawrence Smith—tape courtesy of Lawrence Smith and Stanley Twardowicz.

JK's work: *The Town and the City; Doctor Sax; Vanity of Duluoz*.

Articles: Ted Berrigan, "The Art of Fiction XLI: Jack Kerouac" (interview with JK), *Paris Review*, Vol. 11 (Summer 1968); Charles G. Sampas, "Sampas Scoopies," *Lowell Sun*, Oct. 23, 1969.

Author's interviews: with Cornelius Murphy, Oct. 1978; with George Murray, Aug. 1978; with William Dabilis, Aug. 1978; with Leo Nadeau, May 1978; with George Constantinides, Oct. 1978; with Mary Sampas, Aug. 1977; with Frankie Edith Parker Kerouac, Oct. 1978; with G.J. Apostolos, May 1978.

22. *Vanity of Duluoz*, p. 117.

23. Kerouac's use of the words "interview" and "material," as well as this interpretation of his behavior, comes from my interview with Billy Dabilis, Aug. 1978.

24. *Vanity of Duluoz*, p. 126 and p. 134.

25. *Vanity of Duluoz*, pp. 141-146.

26. This escapade and Sammy's revulsion toward it was described to me by George Constantinides and Cornelius Murphy in my respective interviews with them, both in October 1978.

27. Jack Kerouac quoted in Ted Berrigan, "The Art of Fiction XLI: Jack Kerouac," *Paris Review*, Vol. 11 (Summer 1968), p. 72.

3.

Letters of JK: to Allen Ginsberg, July 26, 1949.

JK on tape: party at JK's house, Aug. 26, 1964; untranscribed reel from the Northport Public Library interview.

JK's work: (a) Unpublished: typescript of *The Town and the City*. (b) Published: *The Town and the City; Vanity of Duluoz.*

Author's interviews: with Cornelius Murphy, Oct. 1978; with G.J. Apostolos, Aug. 1978; with Frankie Edith Parker Kerouac, Oct. 1978.

Lectures: Ginsberg, "Literary History of the Beat Generation."

28. *Vanity of Duluoz,* p. 157. Kerouac described these events in almost identical words to Larry Smith and friends, as recorded on Smith's private tape (August 1964).

29. *Vanity of Duluoz,* p. 163.

30. *Vanity of Duluoz,* p. 173.

31. *Vanity of Duluoz,* pp. 174-175.

32. *Vanity of Duluoz,* p. 181.

33. *Vanity of Duluoz,* p. 190 and p. 195.

4.

Letters of JK: to Ed White, November 9, 1949.

Other letters: Frankie Edith Parker to Charlotte Parker, Jan. 27, 1944.

JK's work: (a) Unpublished: typescript of *The Town and the City*; book review of James Farrell's *My Days of Anger*. (b) Published: *Vanity of Duluoz*; "The Origins of the Beat Generation."

Author's interviews: with Frankie Edith Parker Kerouac, Oct. 1978, and July 1979; with Charlotte Parker, Oct. 1978.

34. Frankie Edith Parker in our interview, Oct. 1978.

35. Northport Public Library draft of *The Town and the City*, p. 822.

36. Frankie Edith Parker Kerouac in our interview, Oct. 1978.

37. Jack Kerouac, "The Origins of the Beat Generation," in *A Casebook on the Beat*, ed. Thomas Parkinson (New York: Thomas Y. Crowell, 1961), p. 72.

38. Jack Kerouac in the book report he wrote for Charlotte Parker on James Farrell's *My Days of Anger* (described subsequently).

39. "Adorable": Charlotte Parker in our interview, Oct. 1978; "OK, we'll get married sometime," Frankie Edith Parker Kerouac quoting Kerouac in our interview, Oct. 1978; "like a love story in the ladies' magazines" and "fooling around": Kerouac in the Northport Public Library draft of *The Town and the City*, p. 923.

5.

Letters of JK: to Allen Ginsberg, Sept. 6, 1945.

Other letters: Gabrielle Kerouac to JK, Sept. 10, 1944; Gabrielle Kerouac to JK, Sept. 16, 1944.

JK on tape: untranscribed reel from the Northport Public Library interview.

JK's work: (a) Unpublished: typescript of *The Town and the City*. (b) Published: *Vanity of Duluoz.*

Articles: Berrigan, "The Art of Fiction XLI: Jack Kerouac."

Author's interview: with Frankie Edith Parker Kerouac, Oct. 1978, and July 1979; with Lucien Carr, July 1977, and May 1978; with John Kingsland, Sept. 1978.

Lectures: Ginsberg, "Literary History of the Beat Generation."

40. *Vanity of Duluoz,* p. 220.

41. Frankie Edith Parker Kerouac in our interview, Oct. 1978.
42. Kerouac and Ginsberg have both recorded their initial meeting, whose outward facts (except for the exact dialogue) seem rather clear-cut. In his 1967 *Paris Review* interview (p. 97), Kerouac, however, credits himself with a rather strong initial antagonism toward Ginsberg; while Ginsberg, in both his "Literary History of the Beat Generation" lectures at the Naropa Institute, and in our private interviews, argued that Kerouac was actually a good deal gentler and more receptive toward him.
43. Northport Public Library draft of *The Town and the City*, p. 899.

6.

Letters of JK: to Allen Ginsberg, 1944; to Seymour Krim, Feb. 13, 1965.
JK on tape: untranscribed reel from the Northport Public Library interview.
Books and articles: Barry Gifford and Lawrence Lee, *Jack's Book*, N.Y., 1978; John Tytell, "An Interview with William S. Burroughs," *The Beat Diary (the unspeakable visions of the individual*, vol. 5), California, Pa., 1977.
JK's work: (a) Unpublished: typescript of *The Town and the City*. (b) Published: *Vanity of Duluoz*.
Author's interviews: with William Burroughs, Aug. 1977; with Lucien Carr, July 1977; with Frankie Edith Parker Kerouac, Oct. 1978, and July 1979; with Charlotte Parker, Oct. 1978; with Herbert Huncke, Sept. 1978; with George Murray, Aug. 1978; with Cornelius Murphy, Oct. 1978; with James O'Dea, Oct. 1978; with G.J. Apostolos, May 1978, and Aug. 1978.
Lectures: Ginsberg, "Literary History of the Beat Generation."
44. *Vanity of Duluoz*, p. 206. In our interview (Aug. 1977), Burroughs told me that Kerouac's account of their initial meeting was substantially correct.
45. "Millionaire's son": Lucien Carr to me in our interview July 1977; "mischievous young punk": Kerouac in *Vanity of Duluoz*, p. 224.
46. Letter of Jack Kerouac to Allen Ginsberg, 1944.
47. James O'Dea in our interview, Oct. 1978.
48. Letter of Jack Kerouac to Seymour Krim, Feb. 13, 1965.
49. Frankie Edith Parker Kerouac in our interview, Oct. 1978.
50. Frankie Edith Parker Kerouac in our interview, Oct. 1978.

7.

Letters of JK: to Allen Ginsberg, Jan. 13, 1950 (in this letter Kerouac quotes Sebastian Sampas' voice recording, sent to Kerouac from Italy just prior to Sampas' death); Sept. 6, 1945; Dec. 22, 1954.
Other letters: Allen Ginsberg to JK, spring 1945; Caroline Kerouac to JK, July 12, 1944.
JK's work: *Vanity of Duluoz*.
Lectures: Ginsberg, "Literary History of the Beat Generation."

8.

Letters of JK: to Ed White, Jan. 16, 1950.
Other letters: Caroline Kerouac to JK, July 12, 1944.
JK's work: *Vanity of Duluoz*.
Articles: Henry A. Kingswell and Thomas Martin, "The Brief Detroit Sojourn of Jack Kerouac," *Detroit* magazine, *Detroit Free Press*, Dec. 29, 1974; numerous clippings relating to Lucien Carr's homicide were supplied by Norman Davis.
Author's interviews: with Lucien Carr, July 1977, and May 1978; with Frankie

Edith Parker Kerouac, Oct. 1978, and July 1979; with Tony Sampas, Aug. 1978.
51. Lucien Carr in our interview, July 1977.

FOUR: WOLFEANS AND BLACK PRIESTS

1.

Letters: Gabrielle Kerouac to Frankie Edith Parker Kerouac, Nov. 25, 1944; Sept. 10, 1944; Céline Young to Frankie Edith Parker Kerouac, Aug. 1, 1945.
Articles: Henry A. Kingswell and Thomas Martin, "The Brief Detroit Sojourn of Jack Kerouac."
Author's interviews: with Frankie Edith Parker Kerouac, Oct. 1978, and July 1979; with Charlotte Parker, Oct. 1978.
Lectures: Ginsberg, "Literary History of the Beat Generation."
52. Kerouac as quoted by Charlotte Parker in our interview, Oct. 1978.
53. Ginsberg, "Literary History of the Beat Generation."
54. The word *facts* is put in quotation marks to denote its specific significance in Burroughs' vocabulary; for Burroughs, a fact is a perception true only in the context of a specific level of reality.
55. *Vanity of Duluoz*, p. 267.

2.

Letters of JK: to Bernice Lemire, Aug. 11, 1961; to Seymour Krim, Feb. 13, 1965.
Other letters: Allen Ginsberg to JK, 1945, a copy of Ginsberg's prizewinning poem "The Last Voyage," on which JK has added the postscript: "Hitler died on May Day—And I planned *Galloway*."
JK on tape: untranscribed reel from the Northport Public Library interview.
JK's work: *The Town and the City; Vanity of Duluoz;* "The Origins of the Beat Generation."
Books and articles: Jane Kramer, *Paterfamilias: Allen Ginsberg in America*, London, 1970; Allen Young, *Allen Ginsberg: Gay Sunshine Interview*, Bolinas, Calif., 1974; Berrigan, "The Art of Fiction XLI: Jack Kerouac."
Author's interviews: with Frankie Edith Parker Kerouac, Oct. 1978, and July 1979; with Ed White, Oct. 1977; with Hal Chase, Oct. 1978; with Allen Ginsberg, Aug. 1977, and May 1978; with Herbert Huncke, Sept. 1978.
Lectures: Ginsberg, "Literary History of the Beat Generation."
56. *Vanity of Duluoz*, p. 270.
57. *Vanity of Duluoz*, p. 269.
58. Letter of Jack Kerouac to Seymour Krim, Feb. 13, 1965.
60. Ginsberg, "Literary History of the Beat Generation."
61. Kerouac quoted by Allen Ginsberg, "Literary History of the Beat Generation."
62. Allen Ginsberg, *Gay Sunshine Interview* (Bolinas, Calif.: Grey Fox Press, 1974), p. 4. This account also relies upon material from Ginsberg's "Literary History of the Beat Generation" lectures.

3.

Letters of JK: to Allen Ginsberg, Sept. 6, 1945; Aug. 23, 1945; to Ed White, Jan. 16, 1950.
Books: Kramer, *Paterfamilias*; Young, *Allen Ginsberg: Gay Sunshine Interview*.
Author's interviews: with Allen Ginsberg, Aug. 1977, and May 1978; with Hal Chase, Oct. 1978; with Ed White, Oct. 1977; with Don Allen, Oct. 1977;

with Thomas Livornese, Aug. 1978; with Frankie Edith Parker Kerouac, Oct. 1978.

Lectures: Ginsberg, "Literary History of the Beat Generation."

63. This phrase is the recollection of Allen Ginsberg in Jane Kramer, *Paterfamilias: Allen Ginsberg in America* (London: Victor Gollancz, 1970), p. 118.

64. Ginsberg, "Literary History of the Beat Generation."

65. Letter of Kerouac to Allen Ginsberg, Sept. 6, 1945.

4.

Letters: Neal Cassady to JK, July 3-4-16-17-23, 1949; Neal Cassady to Justin Brierly, 1945 (printed in *Mano-Mano/2*, Bowery Press, Denver, Colo., July 1971).

JK's work: *On the Road*, N.Y., 1957.

Books: Neal Cassady, *The First Third*, San Francisco, 1971.

Author's interviews: with Hal Chase, Oct. 1978; with Justin Brierly, Oct. 1977; with Thomas Livornese, Aug. 1978; with Ed White, Oct. 1977; with Frankie Edith Parker Kerouac, Oct. 1978, and July 1979.

66. Ed White and Justin Brierly both stated that Neal had been a hustler in Denver, in my respective interviews with them, both in Oct. 1977. Kerouac refers to Neal's experience as a hustler in *On the Road* (New York: New American Library, paperback edition, n.d.), p. 173.

67. The source of these quotations and the specifics of Kerouac's early theory of composition derive from my interview with Hal Chase, Oct. 1978.

68. Kerouac quoted by Hal Chase in our interview, Oct. 1978.

69. Hal Chase in our interview, Oct. 1978. This phrase also recurs in Ginsberg's letters of the period.

5.

Letters of JK: to Allen Ginsberg, Aug. 10, 1945; Aug. 23, 1945; July 17, 1945; Sept. 6, 1945; Nov. 13, 1945.

Other letters: Joan Vollmer Adams to Frankie Edith Parker Kerouac, Dec. 29, 1946; Céline Young to Frankie Edith Parker Kerouac, Aug. 1, 1945; Sept. 6, 1945; Frankie Edith Parker Kerouac to C. M. Parker (her mother), n.d.

JK's work: "New York Scenes," *Lonesome Traveler*, N.Y., 1960.

Articles: Berrigan, "The Art of Fiction XLI: Jack Kerouac."

Author's interviews: with Frankie Edith Parker Kerouac, Oct. 1978, and July 1979; with Ed White, Oct. 1977; with Hal Chase, Oct. 1978; with Carolyn Cassady, Dec. 1979.

Lectures: Ginsberg, "Literary History of the Beat Generation."

70. Letters of Kerouac to Ginsberg, Aug. 23, 1945, and Aug. 17, 1945.

71. These quotations are from Céline's account of the episode written directly afterward in a letter to Frankie Edith Parker Kerouac, Sept. 6, 1945.

72. Jack Kerouac, *Lonesome Traveler* (New York: Grove Press, Evergreen Black Cat paperback ed., 1970), p. 112.

73. Ginsberg. "Literary History of the Beat Generation."

74. This summary of Kerouac's sexuality is composed from a variety of sources. Especially helpful were my interviews with Helen Elliott (May 1978), Hal Chase (Oct. 1978), and Ted Berrigan (May 1978), with whom Kerouac had discussed his sexual experiences in great detail as part of the interview Berrigan did with him for the *Paris Review*—a section of the interview that was never printed. In a letter to Kerouac, Oct. 29, 1958, Ginsberg reminded Kerouac of his tendency to challenge men in public: "C'mon I'll fuck you." Manuel "Chiefy" Nobriga and several of the habitués of Nicky's Bar in Lowell told of Kerouac demanding to "blow" or "fuck" them, sometimes in

quite humorous terms; though other male interviewees related similar, very serious requests from Kerouac. Gore Vidal, in his interview with Barry Gifford and Lawrence Lee, describes Kerouac bragging in the San Remo Bar of having given Vidal a blow job, in *Jack's Book* (New York: St. Martin's Press, 1978), p. 183.

6.

Letters of JK: to Allen Ginsberg, Nov. 13. 1945.
Other letters: Frankie Edith Parker Kerouac to Allen Ginsberg, Jan. 17, 1945.
JK's work: (a) Unpublished: typescript of *The Town and the City*. (b) Published: *Vanity of Duluoz*.
Books: Arthur Rimbaud, *A Season in Hell & The Drunken Boat*, trans. Louise Varèse, N.Y., 1961.
Author's interviews: with Allen Ginsberg, Aug. 1977; with Hal Chase, Oct. 1978.
Lectures: Ginsberg, "Literary History of the Beat Generation."
75. The preceding quotations are from Ginsberg, "Literary History of the Beat Generation."
76. Northport Public Library draft of *The Town and the City*, p. 773.
77. Most of the preceding discussion of Leo Kerouac's views of Ginsberg come from the Northport Public Library draft of *The Town and the City*, p. 881.
78. Hal Chase in our interview, Oct. 1978.
79. Leo Kerouac quoted by Hal Chase in our interview, Oct. 1978.

7.

Letters of JK: to Carl Solomon, April 7, 1952; to Carolyn Cassady, summer 1954; to Lois Sorrells, Aug. 8, 1962; to Charles G. Sampas, Dec. 27, 1949 (printed in "Sampas Scoopies"—see below); to Ed White, July 21, 1958.
JK on tape: Diana Scesny's transcription of the Northport Public Library interview of JK, on deposit at the Northport Public Library, contains JK's account of reading *The Brothers Karamazov* in the Veterans Hospital (this account is not included in the selections printed in *Athanor*).
JK's work: (a) Unpublished: typescript of *The Town and the City*. (b) Published: *Vanity of Duluoz*.
Books and articles: Norman Mailer, *Advertisements for Myself*, N.Y., 1959; Charles G. Sampas, "Sampas Scoopies"; Berrigan, "The Art of Fiction XLI: Jack Kerouac."
Author's interviews: with Hal Chase, Oct. 1978; with John Kingsland, Sept. 1978; with Frankie Edith Parker Kerouac, Oct. 1978; with Thomas Livornese, Sept. 1978.
80. *Vanity of Duluoz*, p. 273.
81. *Vanity of Duluoz*, p. 274.
82. *Vanity of Duluoz*, pp. 278-279.
83. Kerouac quoted by Hal Chase in our interview, Oct. 1978.

8.

Letters of JK: to Carol Solomon, April 7, 1952.
Books: Tirro, *Jazz: A History*; Gifford and Lee, *Jack's Book*.
Author's interviews: with Ed White, Oct. 1977; with Thomas Livornese, Sept. 1978; with Allan Temko, Oct. 1977, and June 1978.
84. Kerouac quoted by Thomas Livornese in our interview, Sept. 1978.
85. Thomas Livornese in our interview, Sept. 1978.
86. Allan Temko in our interview, Oct. 1977.
87. This quote, like all of the preceding in this discussion of Temko's relationship

with Kerouac, come from my interviews with Temko, Oct. 1977, and June 1978.

88. Letter of Kerouac to Ed White, Nov. 9, 1949.

9.

JK's work: *On the Road.*

Books: Cassady, *The First Third*; Gifford and Lee, *Jack's Book.*

Author's interviews: with Thomas Livornese, Aug. 1978; with LuAnne Henderson, Oct. 1978; with Hal Chase, Oct. 1978; with Ed White, Oct. 1977; with Allan Temko, Oct. 1977, and June 1978; with Allen Ginsberg, Aug. 1977.

89. All quotations in the paragraph are from Thomas Livornese in our interview, Sept. 1978.

90. LuAnne Cassady in our interview, Oct. 1978.

91. The abnormally large size of Neal's penis has been attested by many witnesses, among them Ed White and Al Hinkle.

FIVE: METAMORPHOSIS

1.

Letters of JK: to Allen Ginsberg, July 17, 1945; Aug. 10, 1945; to Neal Cassady, May 7, 1948; to William Burroughs, July 14, 1947; to Ed White, July 15, 1947.

Other letters: Neal Cassady to JK, March 7, 1947; March 27, 1947; Allen Ginsberg to JK, summer 1947; spring 1947; Neal Cassady to JK, March 13, 1947; May 20, 1947; April 15, 1947; Jan. 7-8, 1948.

JK's work: (a) Unpublished: *"On the Road* Journal," 1948-1949, on deposit at the University of Texas, Austin. (b) Published: *On the Road;* "He went on the road, as Jack Kerouac says."

Books: Gifford and Lee, *Jack's Book.*

Author's interviews: with Ed White, Oct. 1977; with Hal Chase, Oct. 1978; with Beverly Burford, July 1978; with Thomas Livornese, Sept. 1978; with William Frankel, Oct. 1978.

Lectures: Ginsberg, "Literary History of the Beat Generation."

92. Letter of Kerouac to William Burroughs, July 14, 1947.

2.

Letters of JK: to Ed White, July 15, 1947; to William Burroughs, July 14, 1947.

JK's work: *On the Road.*

Author's interviews: with Ed White, Oct. 1977.

93. *On the Road*, p. 16.

3.

Letters of JK: to Ed White, July 8, 1948.

Other letters: Neal Cassady to JK, Aug. 22, 1947; Allen Ginsberg to JK, summer 1947.

JK's work: *On the Road.*

Books: Carolyn Cassady, *The Third Word* (unpublished, except for the in-progress excerpt *Heart Beat*, Berkeley, 1976), 1978.

Author's interviews: with Allan Temko, Oct. 1977, and June 1978; with Ed White, Oct. 1977; with Beverly Burford, July 1978; with Robert Burford, July 1978; with Carolyn Cassady, Oct. 1977, and June 1978; with Allen Ginsberg, Aug. 1977; with LuAnne Henderson, Oct. 1978.

94. Letter of Ginsberg to Kerouac, summer 1947.

712 · M E M O R Y B A B E

95. All quotes in the preceding three paragraphs come from Ginsberg's letter to Kerouac, summer 1947.

4.

Letters of JK: to Ed White, Aug. 16, 1947; Sept. 11, 1947.

Other letters: Allen Ginsberg to JK, summer 1947; Neal Cassady to JK, Aug. 31-Sept. 2-9, 1947; Sept. 20, 1947; Joan Vollmer Adams to Frankie Edith Parker Kerouac, Dec. 29, 1946.

JK's work: *On the Road.*

Books: Kramer, *Paterfamilias.*

Author's interviews: with Robert Creeley, July 1978; with Byron Hunt, June 1978; with Al Hinkle, Oct. 1977.

5.

Letters of JK: to Ed White, May 12, 1949; July 8, 1948; to Bernice Lemire, Aug. 11, 1961; to Ed White, Dec. 23, 1947.

Other letters: Neal Cassady to JK, Nov. 5. 1947; Sept. 20, 1947; Nov. 21, 1947; April 15, 1947; Dec. 25, 1947; Jan. 7-8, 1948; June 16, 1948; March 27, 1947; Allen Ginsberg to Neal Cassady, April 1948 (printed in *As Ever: The Collected Correspondence of Allen Ginsberg & Neal Cassady,* Berkeley, 1977).

JK's work: (a) Unpublished: *"On the Road* Journal," 1948-1949; (b) Published: "The Origins of the Beat Generation."

Books and articles: Carolyn Cassady, *The Third Word; Bird: The Legend of Charlie Parker,* ed. Robert Reisner, N.Y., 1962; Norman Mailer, "The White Negro," in *Advertisements for Myself.*

Author's interviews: with Hal Chase, Oct. 1978; with Ed White, Oct. 1977; with Thomas Livornese, Sept. 1978.

96. Interview with Robert Creeley, July 1978.

97. Letter of Neal Cassady to Kerouac, Jan. 7-8, 1948, and Kerouac in his *"On the Road* Journal," entry Dec. 1, 1948.

98. Kerouac, "The Origins of the Beat Generation," in *A Casebook on the Beat,* ed. Thomas Parkinson (New York: Thomas Y. Crowell, 1961), p. 73.

99. The title of one of Parker's subsequent songs.

6.

Letters of JK: to Neal Cassady, May 7, 1948; to Allen Ginsberg, April 1948.

Other letters: Allen Ginsberg to JK, fall 1947; Allen Ginsberg to Neal Cassady, May 1948 (printed in *As Ever);* Allen Ginsberg to JK, 1948; Allen Ginsberg to Neal Cassady, April 1948 (printed in *As Ever);* Allen Ginsberg to JK, 1948 (separate letter); Allen Ginsberg to JK, April 15, 1948 (at the end of this letter, Kerouac adds the postscript: "This was the time Allen went mad & wanted me to beat him up in the subway—after such a refined self-composed letter!").

JK's work: *On the Road.*

Books: Kramer, *Paterfamilias;* John Tytell, *Naked Angels: The Lives & Literature of the Beat Generation,* N.Y., 1976; Carolyn Cassady, *The Third Word.*

Author's interviews: with Hal Chase, Oct. 1978; with Elmer Rynne, Aug. 1978; with Thomas Livornese, Aug. 1978; with Ed Stringham, Sept. 1978; with Ed White, Oct. 1977; with John Clellon Holmes, Aug. 1978; with John Kingsland, Sept. 1978; with William Frankel, Oct. 1978.

Lectures: Ginsberg, "Literary History of the Beat Generation."

100. Letter of Kerouac to Neal Cassady, May 7, 1948.

101. Letter of Allen Ginsberg to Kerouac, fall 1947.

102. Letter of Allen Ginsberg to Kerouac, April 15, 1948; and John Tytell, *Naked Angels* (New York: McGraw-Hill, 1976), p. 88.
103. This phrase, usually capitalized, appears in letters of both Kerouac and Ginsberg of this period.
104. Ed Stringham in our interview, Sept. 1978.
105. Letter of Allen Ginsberg to Kerouac, 1948.

7.
106. William Frankel in our interview, Oct. 1978.
107. Robert Christianson in our interview, Aug. 1978.
108. William Frankel in our interview, Oct. 1978.

8.
Articles: Berrigan, "The Art of Fiction XLI: Jack Kerouac."
Author's interviews: with Howard Moss, Sept. 1978; with Ed Stringham, Sept. 1978; with Lucia Hacker Vernarelli, Sept. 1978; with Jorge Davila, Sept. 1978; with Robert Christianson, Aug. 1978; with Nathan Lerner, April 1978; with Chris Lerner, April 1978; with William Frankel, Oct. 1978.
109. Kerouac, "*On the Road* Journal," entry Dec. 1, 1948.
110. Ed Stringham in our interview, Sept. 1978.

9.
Letters of JK: to Neal Cassady, May 7, 1948; to Allen Ginsberg, May 18, 1948; July 1, 1948; Sept. 9, 1948; Sept. 18, 1948; fall, 1948; late 1948; to John Clellon Holmes, Oct. 12, 1955; to Brom Weber, Jan. 10, 1949; to Ed White, July 8, 1949.
Other letters: Allen Ginsberg to JK, May 1948; June 1948; Sept. 1948; Dec. 1948; Dec. 1948 (separate letter).
JK's work: "*On the Road* Journal" 1948-1949; typescript of *The Town and the City* (unpublished).
Books, articles, and journals: Bruce Cook, *The Beat Generation*, N.Y., 1971 (interview with Alan Harrington); Ann Charters, *Kerouac: A Biography*, San Francisco, 1973 (reminiscence of Allen Ginsberg by Herbert Gold); John Clellon Holmes, *Go*, N.Y., 1952; "The Great Rememberer," in *Nothing More to Declare*, N.Y., 1957; "Gone in October," *Playboy*, Vol. 20 (Feb. 1973); "Journal" (unpublished), entry Oct. 7, 1948; John Tytell, "An Interview with John Clellon Holmes," *The Beat Book* (*the unspeakable visions of the individual, vol. 4*), California, Pa., 1974.
Author's interviews and correspondence: from John Clellon Holmes, Sept. 2, 1977; from Alfred Kazin, July 17, 1978; with Allan Temko, Oct. 1977; with Ed Stringham, Sept. 1978; with William Frankel, Oct. 1978; with John Clellon Holmes, Aug. 1978; with Brom Weber, June 1978; with Helen Elliott, May 1978; with George Murray, Aug. 1978; with Matsumi Kanemitsu, Oct. 1978; with Cornelius Murphy, Oct. 1978.
111. Letter of Allen Ginsberg to Kerouac, Sept. 1948.
112. Kerouac, "On the Road *Journal*," entry Dec. 1, 1948.
113. Brom Weber in our interview, June 1978.
114. Weber quoted by Kerouac in Kerouac's letter to Weber, Jan. 10, 1949.
115. Letter of Kerouac to Brom Weber, Jan. 10, 1949.
116. Brom Weber in our interview, June 1978.
117. Cornelius Murphy in our interview, Oct. 1978.
118. Kerouac, "*On the Road* Journal," entries Dec. 5, Dec. 6, Dec. 9, and Dec. 10, 1948.

SIX: SLOW BOAT TO CHINA

1.

Letters of JK: to Ed White, Jan. 15, 1949; to Allen Ginsberg, May 18, 1952; to Ed White, Nov. 30, 1948; to Allen Ginsberg, Dec. 19, 1948; Dec. 15, 1948.
Other letters: Neal Cassady to JK, Oct. 7, 1948.
JK's work: "*On the Road* Journal," 1948-1949; typescript of *The Town and the City* (unpublished).
Journals: Holmes, "Journal," entry Oct. 7, 1948.
Author's interviews: with Ed White, Oct. 1977; with Thomas Livornese, Sept. 1978; with LuAnne Henderson, Oct. 1978; with John Clellon Holmes, Aug. 1978; with Ed Stringham, Sept. 1978.
119. Kerouac, "*On the Road* Journal," entries Dec. 14 and Dec. 1, 1948.
120. Kerouac, "*On the Road* Journal," entry Dec. 1, 1948.
121. Ibid.
122. Kerouac, "*On the Road* Journal," entry Dec. 9, 1948.
123. Ed Stringham in our interview, Sept. 1978; Allen Ginsberg takes issue with Stringham's use of the word "ritual," maintaining that he (Allen) "went to Royal Roost rarely."
124. Ed Stringham in our interview, Sept. 1978.
125. Letter of Kerouac to Ed White, Nov. 30, 1948.

2.

Letters of JK: to Ed White, Nov. 20, 1948; to Allen Ginsberg, Dec. 15, 1948; Dec. 19, 1948; to Brom Weber, Jan. 10, 1949.
Other letters: Neal Cassady to JK, June 16, 1948; July 5, 1948; July 23, 1948; Sept. 10-22, 1948; Oct. 7-15, Nov. 1, 1948; Allen Ginsberg to JK, late Sept. 1948.
Books and articles: Carolyn Cassady, *The Third Word*, 1978; Allen Ginsberg, "A Version of the Apocalypse" (unpublished), 1949 (?), on deposit at Columbia University.
Author's interviews: with William Burroughs, Aug. 1977; with Carolyn Cassady, Oct. 1977.
126. Letter of Neal Cassady to Kerouac, June 16, 1948.
127. Letter of Neal Cassady to Kerouac, Oct. 7, 1948.
128. Letter of Neal Cassady to Kerouac, Nov. 1, 1948. The term "blank period" in reference to Neal is used also by Kerouac and Ginsberg in their letters of this period.
129. Mémère quoted in letter of Kerouac to Ed White, Nov. 30, 1948.
130. Letter of Kerouac to Allen Ginsberg, Dec. 15, 1948.
131. All quotes in the preceding three paragraphs are from letter of Kerouac to Allen Ginsberg, Dec. 15, 1948.

3.

Letters of JK: to Ed White, Jan. 15, 1949; to Allen Ginsberg, Dec. 19, 1948.
Other letters: Neal Cassady to JK, Jan. 7, 1948.
JK's work: (a) Unpublished: "*On the Road* Journal," 1948-1949. (b) Published; *On the Road.*
Books: Kramer, *Paterfamilias;* Holmes, *Go.*
Author's interviews: with Al Hinkle, Oct. 1977; with LuAnne Henderson, Oct. 1978; with Ed Stringham, Sept. 1978; with Lucien Carr, May 1978.
Lectures: Ginsberg, "Literary History of the Beat Generation."
132. Letter of Neal Cassady to Kerouac, Jan. 7, 1948.

133. Kerouac, *"On the Road* Journal," entry Jan. 3, 1949.
134. LuAnne Henderson in our interview, Oct. 1978.

4.

Letters of JK: to Ed White, Jan. 15, 1949; to Brom Weber, Jan. 10, 1949; to John Clellon Holmes, May 1-2-3, 1950; Oct. 12, 1955; May 21, 1956; Sept. 18, 1965.
JK's work: (a) Unpublished: *"On the Road* Journal" 1948-1949. (b) Published: *On the Road; Visions of Cody,* N.Y., 1972; "The Origins of the Beat Generation."
Books and journals: Holmes, *Go;* "Journal," entry Oct. 7, 1948.
Author's interviews and correspondence: with Ed Stringham, Sept. 1978; with William Frankel, Oct. 1978; with Al Hinkle, Oct. 1977; from Alfred Kazin, July 17, 1978; with LuAnne Henderson, Oct. 1978.
135. Letter of Kerouac to Ed White, Jan. 15, 1949.
136. Ibid.
137. John Clellon Holmes, "Journal," entry Oct. 7, 1948.
138. *On the Road,* pp. 106-107.
139. Kerouac, *"On the Road* Journal," entry Jan. 10, 1949; and *On the Road,* p. 107.
140. Kerouac, *"On the Road* Journal," entries Jan. 10 and Jan. 12, 1949.
141. Letter of Kerouac to Ed White, Jan. 15, 1948, and Kerouac's *"On the Road* Journal," entry Jan. 10, 1949.
142. John Clellon Holmes, *Go* (Mamaroneck, N.Y.: Paul P. Appel, 1977), pp. 164-165. The character of Hart Kennedy in this novel is a very thinly disguised portrait of Neal Cassady, and much of Neal's actual dialogue, recorded in Holmes' journal of the period, found its way into Kennedy's speeches.

5.

Letters of JK: to Allen Ginsberg, Dec. 15, 1948; to Ed White, Jan. 15, 1949.
Other letters: William Burroughs to Allen Ginsberg, Jan. 30, 1949; Neal Cassady to JK, Aug. 31, Sept. 2-9, 1947; Joan Vollmer Adams to Frankie Edith Parker Kerouac, Dec. 29, 1946.
JK's work: (a) Unpublished: *"On the Road* Journal" 1948-1949. (b) Published: *On the Road; Visions of Cody.*
Author's interviews: with Al Hinkle, Oct. 1977; with LuAnne Henderson, Oct. 1978.
143. Letter of Kerouac to Allen Ginsberg, Dec. 15, 1948.

6.

Letters of JK: to Allen Ginsberg, July 11, 1949; to Ed White, Jan. 28, 1950.
JK's work: (a) Unpublished: *"On the Road* Journal" 1948-1949. (b) Published: *On the Road;* "The Great Western Bus Ride," *Esquire,* Vol. 73 (March, 1970).
Author's interviews: with LuAnne Henderson, Oct. 1978; with Robert Burford, July 1978; with Ed White, Oct. 1977.
144. Kerouac, *"On the Road* Journal," entries Feb. 20-21, undated entry between Feb. 21 and March 25, 1949, and entry March 25, 1949.

7.

Letters of JK: to Ed White, Jan. 16, 1950; March 29, 1949; late April, 1949.
Other letters: William Burroughs to Allen Ginsberg, April 16, 1949; Joan Vollmer Adams to Frankie Edith Parker Kerouac, Dec. 29, 1946.
JK's work: *"On the Road* Journal," 1948-1949.
Books: Holmes, *Go; A Buddhist Bible,* Dwight Goddard, ed., N.Y., 1938, 1966.

145. Letter of Kerouac to Ed White, March 29, 1949.

146. Kerouac, *"On the Road* Journal," entry April 1949.

147. Ginsberg quoted by Kerouac in letter of Kerouac to Ed White, April 1949.

148. Kerouac, *"On the Road* Journal," entry April 23, 1949.

149. Kerouac, *"On the Road* Journal," entry April 1949.

150. Ibid.

8.

Letters of JK: to Ed White, late April 1949; Nov. 9, 1949; May 12, 1949; Jan. 16, 1950.

JK's work: (a) Unpublished: *"On the Road* Journal," 1948-1949. (b) Published: *Vanity of Duluoz; Visions of Cody.*

Books: Holmes, *Go.*

Author's interviews: with Thomas Livornese, Sept. 1978; with Paul Blake, Jr., Oct. 1978; with Frankie Edith Parker Kerouac, Oct. 1978.

151. Kerouac, *"On the Road* Journal," entry April 23, 1949, and letter of Kerouac to Ed White, May 12, 1949.

9.

Letters of JK: to Ed White, May 12, 1949; late April, 1949; to John Clellon Holmes, June 24, 1949; to Allen Ginsberg, May 23, 1949; July 11, 1949; July 26, 1949; June 10, 1949.

Other letters: Allen Ginsberg to JK, July 13, 1949; June 15, 1949; June 17, 1949; Neal Cassady to JK, July 4-16-17-23, 1949.

JK's work: (a) Unpublished: *"On the Road* Journal," 1948-1949. (b) Published: *Visions of Cody.*

Books: Kramer, *Paterfamilias.*

Author's interviews: with Justin Brierly, Oct. 1977; with Ed White, Oct. 1977; with Brom Weber, June 1978; with Hal Chase, Oct. 1978.

152. Letter of Kerouac to Allen Ginsberg, July 26, 1949.

SEVEN: THE SPONSORS OF WASTE

1.

Letters of JK: to John Clellon Holmes, June 24, 1949; to Allen Ginsberg, July 11, 1949; July 26, 1949.

Other letters: Neal Cassady to JK, July 4-16-17-23, 1949; late July, 1949; Oct. 15, 1950; Nov. 28, 1951.

JK's work: *On the Road; Visions of Cody.*

Books and articles: Carolyn Cassady, *The Third Word,* 1978; Aram Saroyan, "The Driver: Reflections on Jack Kerouac" (unpublished), 1979; Kingswell and Martin, "The Brief Detroit Sojourn of Jack Kerouac."

Author's interviews: with LuAnne Henderson, Oct. 1978; with Frankie Edith Parker Kerouac, Oct. 1978, and July 1979.

Lectures: Ginsberg, "Literary History of the Beat Generation."

153. *On the Road,* p. 155.

2.

Letters of JK: to Ed White, Nov. 9, 1949; Jan. 16, 1950; to Allen Ginsberg, Jan. 13, 1950; to Ed White, March 5, 1950; Jan. 28, 1950.

JK's work: (a) Unpublished: "The Wire to the Crack of Doom; or, Blook's Way," coauthored by Allen Ginsberg, John Clellon Holmes, Tom Livornese, Ed

White, and Reva; typescript of *The Town and the City*. (b) Published: *On the Road; Visions of Cody.*

Books: Carolyn Cassady, *The Third Word;* Gifford and Lee, *Jack's Book.*

Author's interviews: with Ed White, Oct. 1977; with Thomas Livornese, Aug. 1978; with Allan Temko, June 1978; with Frankie Edith Parker Kerouac, Oct. 1978.

154. Letter of Kerouac to Ed White, Oct. 1949.
155. Letter of Kerouac to Ed White, Nov. 9, 1949.
156. Ibid.
157. Ibid.
158. Letter of Kerouac to Ed White, Jan. 16, 1950.
159. Letter of Kerouac to Ed White, Jan. 28, 1950.

3.

Letters of JK: to Ed White, Jan. 28, 1950; to Allen Ginsberg, late Feb., 1950; to Ed White, March 5, 1950.

Other letters: Allen Ginsberg to JK, spring 1950.

JK's work: *On the Road; Mexico City Blues,* N.Y., 1959; *The Town and the City.*

Articles and journals: Holmes, "Journal," entry Feb. 3, 1950; Hugh F. Downey, "Books," *Lowell Sun,* Feb. 26, 1950; James F. Droney, Elizabeth S. Drury, Joseph G. Principato, "Sun Spots," *Lowell Sun,* Feb. 26, 1950; James F. Droney, *"The Town and the City*—Lowell Author's First Novel Features Lowell Faces and Places," *Lowell Sun,* March 12, 1950; Raymond Foye, "A Lowellian Remembers Kerouac" (unpublished), 1977.

Author's interviews: with Allen Ginsberg, May 1978; with Ed Stringham, Sept. 1978; with Lawrence Lee, Aug. 1979; with Roland Salvas, May 1978; with Fr. Armand Morissette, May 1978; with James Droney, Aug. 1978; with Elmer Rynne, Aug. 1978; with Clare Mullen Foye, May 1978.

4.

Letters of JK: to Ed White, Jan. 28, 1950; to Beatrice Lemire, Aug. 11, 1961; to Ed White, Jan. 15, 1948; to John Clellon Holmes, May 1-2-3, 1950.

JK on tape: untranscribed reel from the Northport Public Library interview.

JK's work: (a) Unpublished: "Notebook," 1943-1944, in the possession of Frankie Edith Parker Kerouac. (b) Published: *The Town and the City; Vanity of Duluoz; Visions of Cody; Maggie Cassidy.*

Books and articles: Fyodor Dostoyevsky, *The Brothers Karamazov*, trans. Constance Garnett, N.Y., n.d.; William Saroyan, *The Human Comedy*, N.Y., 1943; Thomas Wolfe, *Of Time and the River*, 2 vols., N.Y., 1935; Tirro, *Jazz: A History*; Book of Job; Djuna Barnes, *Nightwood*, N.Y., 1937; Emily Dickinson, *Selected Poems & Letters*, ed. Robert N. Linscott, Garden City, N.Y., 1959; Johann Wolfgang von Goethe, *Faust: Part Two*, trans. Philip Wayne, Middlesex, England, 1959; Seymour Krim, "Introduction" to *Desolation Angels*, N.Y., 1965.

Author's interviews: with Kenneth Rexroth, Oct. 1978; with Allen Ginsberg, May 1978; with Raymond Foye, June 1978; with Robert Burford, July 1978; with Jan Kerouac, Oct. 1979; with Dan DeSole, May 1978; with Helen Parker, May 1978; with Frankie Edith Parker Kerouac, Oct. 1978.

Lectures: Ginsberg, "Literary History of the Beat Generation."

160. Letter of Kerouac to Ed White, Jan. 15, 1949.
161. Jack Kerouac, *The Town and the City* (New York: Harcourt Brace Jovanovich, Harvest paperback edition, 1978), p. 439.

5.

Letters of JK: to John Clellon Holmes, May 1-2-3, 1950; Dec. 9, 1952; to Ed White, April 12, 1950; April 26, 1950; (dedication in copy of *The Town and the City*), May 1950; to Allen Ginsberg, Feb. 1952; April 1950; to Ed White, May 12, 1950; to Allen Ginsberg, June 2, 1950; to Neal Cassady, Dec. 14, 1950; to Ed White, June 13, 1950.

Other letters: Allen Ginsberg to JK, 1950; Neal Cassady to JK, Sept. 22, 1950; July 22, 1950; Allen Ginsberg to Neal Cassady, Feb. or March 1951 (printed in *As Ever*); Frank Jeffries to Ed White, July 5, 1950; June 13, 1950.

JK on tape: untranscribed reel from the Northport Public Library interview.

JK's work: (a) Unpublished: typescript of *The Town and the City*. (b) Published: *On the Road*.

Books and articles: Carolyn Cassady, *The Third Word*; "Jack Kerouac at Northport," *Athanor*, Summer/Fall 1972.

Author's interviews: with Hal Chase, Oct. 1978; with Ed Stringham, Sept. 1978; with Joseph Chaput, May 1978; with Allen Ginsberg, May 1978; with Justin Brierly, Oct. 1977; with Robert Burford, July 1978; with Beverly Burford July 1978; with Al Hinkle, Oct. 1977; with Ed White, Oct. 1977; with Robert Beauchamp, Sept. 1978.

162. Hal Chase in our interview, Oct. 1978.

163. Kerouac on tape, untranscribed reel from the Northport Public Library interview of JK.

164. Letter of Kerouac to Ed White, April 12, 1950.

165. Letter of Kerouac to John Clellon Holmes, May 1-2-3, 1950.

166. Ed White in our interview, Oct. 1977.

6.

Letters of JK: to Ed White, July 5, 1950; to John Clellon Holmes, July 11-12, 1950; to Allen Ginsberg, June 1950; to Allen Ginsberg, June 27, 1950; to James Sampas, Aug. 1, 1950; to Ed White, Aug. 29, 1950; to Allen Ginsberg, Aug. 8, 1950; to John Clellon Holmes, Aug. 8, 1950; to Ed White, April 12, 1950; Sept. 6, 1950; Sept. 23, 1950; to Allen Ginsberg, Oct. 29, 1950.

Other letters: Allen Ginsberg to JK, summer 1950; Allen Ginsberg to Neal Cassady, Oct. 31, 1950 (printed in *As Ever*); Neal Cassady to JK, July 8, 1950; July 22, 1950; Allen Ginsberg to JK, July 8, 1950; Neal Cassady to JK, Sept. 22, 1950; Neal Cassady to JK, Nov. 5, 1950; Neal Cassady to Allen Ginsberg, Nov. 25, 1950 (printed in *As Ever*); Allen Ginsberg to Neal Cassady, November 18, 1950 (printed in *As Ever*); Neal Cassady to JK, Sept. 25, 1950; Oct. 22, 1950.

JK's work: *Visions of Cody*.

Books: Jane Kramer, *Paterfamilias*; Carolyn Cassady, *The Third Word*.

Author's interviews and correspondence: with Justin Brierly, Oct. 1977; from John Clellon Holmes, Sept. 2, 1977; with Helen Parker, May 1978.

Lectures: Ginsberg, "Literary History of the Beat Generation."

167. Jack Kerouac, *Visions of Cody* (New York: McGraw-Hill, paperback edition, 1974), p. 47.

7.

Letters of JK: to Ed White, Nov. 3, 1950.

Other letters: John Snow to Allen Ginsberg, n.d.; Allen Ginsberg to Neal Cassady, Oct. 31, 1950 (printed in *As Ever*); John Snow to Allen Ginsberg, June 25-26, 1950; Neal Cassady to JK, Nov. 5, 1950; Allen Ginsberg to Neal Cassady, Nov. 18, 1950 (printed in *As Ever*).

JK's work: *On the Road*.

Books and poems: Joan Haverty Kerouac Stuart, *Nobody's Wife* (unpublished), 1979; Dennis McNally, *Desolate Angel*, N.Y., 1979; Allen Ginsberg, "In Memoriam: *William Cannestra 1922-1950*," in *The Gates of Wrath: Rhymed Poems: 1948-1952*, Bolinas, Calif., 1972.

Author's interviews and correspondence: with William Frankel, Oct. 1978; with Howard Moss, Sept. 1978; with Lucia Hacker Vernarelli, Sept. 1978; with Nell Blaine, May 1978; from Nell Blaine, Jan. 17, 1978; with Joan Haverty Kerouac Stuart, June 1978, Aug. 1979, and Nov. 1979.

EIGHT: MORE DAY TO DAWN

1.

Letters of JK: to Ed White, Dec. 16, 1950; Dec. 29, 1950; March 2, 1951; to Allen Ginsberg, Jan. 11, 1951; to John Clellon Holmes, May 1-2-3, 1950; to Neal Cassady, n.d.

Other letters: Neal Cassady to JK, Dec. 3, 1950; Jan. 8, 1951; Dec. 30, 1950; Oct. 15, 1950; Sept. 10, 1950.

Books and articles: Allen Ginsberg, footnote in *As Ever*, Berkeley, 1977, p. 104; Stuart, *Nobody's Wife*; Neal Cassady, *The First Third*; Joan Kerouac, "My Ex-Husband, Jack Kerouac, Is an Ingrate," *Confidential*, Vol. 9 (Aug. 1961); Luther Nichols, "On the Road Back" (interview with JK), in "Books," *San Francisco Examiner*, Oct. 5, 1958; Berrigan, "The Art of Fiction XLI: Jack Kerouac"; Aaron Latham, review of *Visions of Cody*, *New York Times Book Review*, Jan. 28, 1973.

Author's interviews: with Joan Haverty Kerouac Stuart, June 1978; with Ed Stringham, Sept. 1978; with William Frankel, Oct. 1978; with Thomas Livornese, Sept. 1978; with Carolyn Cassady, Nov. 1979.

Lectures: Ginsberg, "Literary History of the Beat Generation."

168. Ed Stringham in our interview, Sept. 1978.
169. Letter of Kerouac to Ed White, Dec. 29, 1950.
170. Letter of Kerouac to Ed White, Dec. 29, 1950.

2.

Letters of JK: to Ed White, Dec. 29, 1950; to Allen Ginsberg, Jan. 11, 1951; to John Clellon Holmes, March 7, 1951; to Ed White, March 2, 1951; April 20, 1951.

Other letters: Neal Cassady to JK, Dec. 30, 1950; Feb. 13, 1951; Feb. 6, 1951; April 1, 1951.

JK's work: *Visions of Cody; On the Road.*

Books, articles, and journals: Stuart, *Nobody's Wife*; Carolyn Cassady, *The Third Word*; Joan Kerouac, "My Ex-Husband, Jack Kerouac, Is an Ingrate"; Jerome Beatty, "Trade Winds" (interview with JK), *Saturday Review*, Vol. 6 (Sept. 28, 1957); John Clellon Holmes, "Journal," entries April 9, 1951, and April 27, 1951.

Author's interviews: with Joan Haverty Kerouac Stuart, June 1978; with Carolyn Cassady, Jan. 1980; with Helen Parker, May 1978; with Helen Elliott, May 1978; with John Clellon Holmes, Aug. 1978; with Allen Ginsberg, May 1978; with Lucien Carr, July 1977.

171. Henri Cru quoted by Joan Haverty Kerouac Stuart in our interview Jan. 1980.
172. Letter of Kerouac to Ed White, March 2, 1951.
173. Kerouac quoted by John Clellon Holmes in Holmes' "Journal," entry April 27, 1951.

720 · M E M O R Y B A B E

3.

Letters of JK: to Philip Whalen, Feb. 7, 1956.

JK's work: *On the Road.*

Books: Walt Whitman, *Leaves of Grass,* N.Y., 1955; Jack London, *The Road,* N.Y., 1907, reprinted Salt Lake City, 1978; Wolfe, *Of Time and the River.*

Author's interviews: with Allen Ginsberg, Aug. 1977, and May 1978; with Fernanda Pivano, July 1978.

4.

Letters of JK: to John Clellon Holmes, June 3, 1952; to Allen Ginsberg, July 15, 1951; to John Clellon Holmes, July 14, 1951; to Allen Ginsberg, July 30, 1951; to Ed White, Sept. 1, 1951.

Other letters: Allen Ginsberg to Neal Cassady, May 7, 1951; Allen Ginsberg to JK, early July, 1951; Joan Vollmer Adams Burroughs to Allen Ginsberg, July 9, 1951; Neal Cassady to JK, June 20, 1951; July 2, 1951; Aug. 10, 1951.

JK's work: "The Origins of the Beat Generation"; *Visions of Cody.*

Books, articles, and journals: Ann Charters, *Kerouac: A Biography,* San Francisco, 1973; Cook, *The Beat Generation;* Tytell, *Naked Angels;* Joan Kerouac, "My Ex-Husband, Jack Kerouac, Is an Ingrate"; Donald Hall, "Robert Giroux: Looking for Masterpieces" (interview with Robert Giroux), *New York Times Book Review,* Jan. 6, 1980; Allen Ginsberg, "Introduction" to William S. Burroughs' *Junky,* Middlesex, England, 1977; Holmes, "Journal," entry April 27, 1951.

Author's interviews: with John Clellon Holmes, Aug. 1978; with Joan Haverty Kerouac Stuart, June 1978, and Jan. 1980; with Ed Stringham, Sept. 1978; with Paul Blake, Jr., Oct. 1978.

174. Letter of Kerouac to John Clellon Holmes, July 14, 1951.

5.

Letters of JK: to Ed White, Sept. 1, 1951; to Allen Ginsberg, fall 1951; to Ed White, Aug. 7, 1961; to Allen Ginsberg, May 18, 1952; March 1952; to Neal Cassady, May 1952; to John Clellon Holmes, March 12, 1952; to Carl Solomon, Dec. 27, 1951.

Other letters: Carolyn Cassady to JK, Sept. 7, 1951; Neal Cassady to JK, Sept. 7, 1951; Sept. 13, 1951; Allen Ginsberg to JK, Oct. 1951; Carl Solomon to JK, Dec. 13, 1952; Neal Cassady to JK, Nov. 28, 1951; Allen Ginsberg to Carolyn Cassady, late 1952 (printed in *As Ever*).

JK on tape: untranscribed reel from the Northport Public Library interview.

JK's work: *Visions of Cody; On the Road;* "The Origins of the Beat Generation"; "Piers of the Homeless Night," in *Lonesome Traveler,* N.Y., 1960.

Books and articles: Neal Cassady, *The First Third;* Tytell, *Naked Angels;* Jane Kramer, *Paterfamilias;* Carolyn Cassady, *Heart Beat,* Berkeley, 1976; Carolyn Gaiser, "Gregory Corso: A Poet, the Beat Way," in *A Casebook on the Beat,* ed. Thomas Parkinson, N.Y., 1961; James McKenzie, " 'I'm Poor Simple Human Bones': An Interview with Gregory Corso," *The Beat Diary (the unspeakable visions of the individual,* vol. 5), 1977; John Barth, "The Literature of Replenishment," *The Atlantic,* Vol. 245 (Jan. 1980); "Jack Kerouac at Northport."

Author's interviews: with Helen Parker, May 1978; with John Clellon Holmes, Aug. 1978; with Allen Ginsberg, May 1978; with John Kingsland, Sept. 1978; with Paul Blake, Jr., Oct. 1978; with Ed White, Oct. 1977; with Carl Solomon, May 1978; with Joan Haverty Kerouac Stuart, Jan. 1980; with Gregory Corso, Aug. 1977; with Carolyn Cassady, Oct. 1977; with Al Hinkle, Oct. 1977.

Lectures: Ginsberg, "Literary History of the Beat Generation."
175. Solomon referred to these insults in his letter to Kerouac, Dec. 13, 1951; and he mentioned Kerouac's threat in our interview, May 1978.
176. Gregory Corso in our interview, Oct. 1977.
177. Carolyn Cassady in our interview, Oct. 1977; and Carolyn Cassady, *Heart Beat* (Berkeley: Creative Arts, 1976), p. 21.

6.

Letters of JK: to Ed White, March 12, 1952; to Allen Ginsberg, March 12, 1952; to John Clellon Holmes, March 12, 1952; June 3, 1952; to Allen Ginsberg, May 18, 1952; to Carl Solomon, Dec. 27, 1951; to John Clellon Holmes, Oct. 12, 1952; to Allen Ginsberg, March 1952; May 10, 1952; March 15, 1952.
JK's work: *On the Road; Visions of Cody.*
Books: Carolyn Cassady, *Heart Beat.*
Author's interviews: with Carolyn Cassady, Oct. 1977, and Jan. 1980; with Joan Haverty Kerouac Stuart, Jan. 1980; with Robert Creeley, July 1978; with Philip Lamantia, Oct. 1977.
178. A common epithet for bop, according to Philip Lamantia in our interview, Oct. 1977.
179. Philip Lamantia in our interview, Oct. 1977.

7.

Letters of JK: to Allen Ginsberg, May 10, 1952; to Carl Solomon, Dec. 27, 1951; to Allen Ginsberg, March 15, 1952; to John Clellon Holmes, March 12, 1952; to Jay Laughlin, Feb. 24, 1952; to Allen Ginsberg, March 12, 1952; April 8, 1952; to William Smock, April 3, 1961 (printed in Jacqueline Starer, *Les Ecrivains Beat et le Voyage*, Paris, 1977); to Carl Solomon, April 7, 1952; to John Clellon Holmes, June 15-17-21, 1952; to Ed White, March 12, 1952; to Allen Ginsberg, Feb. 28, 1952.
Other letters: Carl Solomon to JK, Jan. 31, 1952; Feb. 6, 1952; Carl Solomon to Neal Cassady, Feb. 1952; Allen Ginsberg to JK, March 20, 1952; Allen Ginsberg to JK and Neal Cassady, Feb. 15, 1952 (printed in *As Ever*); Allen Ginsberg to JK, March 1952.
Articles: Jerome Beatty, "Trade Winds."
180. Letter of Kerouac to John Clellon Holmes, March 12, 1952.

8.

Letters of JK: to John Montgomery, May 9, 1961.
Other letters: Allen Ginsberg to Neal Cassady, July 3, 1952 (printed in *As Ever*).
JK's work: *Visions of Cody* (abridged version published in a small collector's edition), N.Y., 1959; *Visions of Cody.*
Books: Neal Cassady, *The First Third*; Allen Ginsberg, *The Visions of the Great Rememberer*, Amherst, Mass., 1974; Henry David Thoreau, *Walden*, N.Y., 1960.
Author's interviews: with Robert Creeley, July 1978.
181. *Visions of Cody*, p. 348.

NINE: THE FOOTSTEPS OF THE BARD

1.

Letters of JK: to Allen Ginsberg, March 1952; April 8, 1952; March 15, 1952; Feb. 28, 1952; to Ed White, March 12, 1952; to Allen Ginsberg, May 10, 1952; to

John Clellon Holmes, March 12, 1952; to Carolyn Cassady, June 3, 1952; to Neal and Carolyn Cassady, May 27, 1952; to William Smock, April 3, 1961 (printed in Jacqueline Starer, *Les Ecrivains Beat et le Voyage*, Paris, 1977); to Allen Ginsberg, May 18, 1952; May 17, 1952.

Other letters: Allen Ginsberg to JK, March 20, 1952; Allen Ginsberg to JK and Neal Cassady, March 1952; Allen Ginsberg to JK, March 1952; William Burroughs to Allen Ginsberg, May 15, 1952; Allen Ginsberg to Neal and Carolyn Cassady, May 1952 (printed in *As Ever*).

Books: Oswald Spengler, *The Decline of the West*, 2 vols., trans. Charles Atkinson, 1926, 1928; Carolyn Cassady, *The Third Word*; Carolyn Cassady, *Heart Beat*.

Author's interviews: with Joan Haverty Kerouac Stuart, Jan. 1980.

182. Letter of Kerouac to Allen Ginsberg, April 8, 1952.

183. Ibid.

184. Letter of Kerouac to Carolyn Cassady, May 27, 1952.

2.

Letters of JK: to Allen Ginsberg, May 18, 1952; to John Clellon Holmes, June 3, 1952; to Bernice Lemire, Aug. 11, 1961; to Allen Ginsberg, June 20, 1952.

JK on tape: JK reading from *Doctor Sax*, in the possession of Carolyn Cassady; JK reading from *Doctor Sax*, in the possession of Lois Sorrells Beckwith.

JK's work: *Doctor Sax*.

Books and articles: Johann Wolfgang von Goethe, *Faust: Parts One and Two*, trans. Philip Wayne, Middlesex, England, 1949, 1959; Ann Charters, *Kerouac: A Biography*; Tytell, *Naked Angels*; "Jack Kerouac at Northport"; Barth, "The Literature of Replenishment."

Author's interviews: with Stanley Twardowicz, May 1978; with Robert Beauchamp, Sept. 1978; with Lucien Carr, May 1978.

185. Letter of Kerouac to Allen Ginsberg, May 18, 1952.

186. Ibid.

187. Letter of Kerouac to Bernice Lemire, August 11, 1961.

188. *Doctor Sax*, p. 59.

189. Ibid., p. 73.

190. Letter of Kerouac to Allen Ginsberg, June 20, 1952.

3.

Letters of JK: to Neal and Carolyn Cassady, May 27, 1952; to Neal Cassady, June 20, 1952; to Allen Ginsberg, June 20, 1952; to Carolyn Cassady, June 3, 1952; to John Clellon Holmes, June 3, 1952; to Neal Cassady, late May, 1952; to John Clellon Holmes, June 15-17-21, 1952; to Carolyn Cassady, June 23, 1952; to Allen Ginsberg, Oct. 8, 1952; to John Clellon Holmes, May 21, 1952; to Allen Ginsberg, May 18, 1952; to Neal and Carolyn Cassady, July 3, 1952; to Allen Ginsberg, Nov. 8, 1952; to John Clellon Holmes, Oct. 12, 1952; to Allen Ginsberg, July 28, 1952.

Other letters: John Clellon Holmes to JK, June 9, 1952; Allen Ginsberg to Neal Cassady, July 3, 1952 (printed in *As Ever*); William Burroughs to Allen Ginsberg, Aug. 20, 1952; July 13, 1952; Neal Cassady to J. C. Clements (recommendation for JK), Aug. 23, 1952; Neal Cassady to JK, Aug. 22, 1952; Aug. 17, 1952; Sept. 2, 1952.

JK on tape: JK reading from *Doctor Sax*, in the possession of Carolyn Cassady.

JK's work: *Doctor Sax*; "October in the Railroad Earth," in *Lonesome Traveler*, N.Y., 1960.

Books, articles, and documents: Carolyn Cassady, *Heart Beat; The Third Word;*

Holmes, "Gone in October"; invalidation of the marriage of Frankie E. Parker and John L. Kerouac, by the Matrimonial Curia of the Archdiocese of Detroit, April 5, 1952.

Author's interviews: with LuAnne Henderson, Oct. 1978; with Helen Weaver, Aug. 1978; with Gregory Corso, Oct. 1977; with Carolyn Cassady, Oct. 1977, and Nov. 1979; with Al Hinkle, Oct. 1977; with Philip Whalen, Aug. 1977; with William Burroughs, Aug. 1977.

191. Letter of Kerouac to John Clellon Holmes, June 3, 1952.
192. Letter of John Clellon Holmes to Kerouac, June 9, 1952.
193. Letter of William Burroughs to Allen Ginsberg, Aug. 20, 1952.
194. Letter of Kerouac to Allen Ginsberg, May 18, 1952.
195. Gregory Corso in our interview, Oct. 1977.
196. Letter of Neal Cassady to Kerouac, Aug. 17, 1952.
197. Kerouac quoted by Carolyn Cassady in our interview, Oct. 1977.
198. Al Hinkle in our interview, Oct. 1977.

4.

Letters of JK: to John Clellon Holmes, Oct. 12, 1952; to Allen Ginsberg, Oct. 8, 1952; Nov. 8, 1952; to John Clellon Holmes, Dec. 9, 1952.

Other letters: Neal Cassady to Allen Ginsberg, Oct. 4, 1952 (printed in *As Ever*).

JK's work: "October in the Railroad Earth."

Books and articles: Charles E. Jarvis, *Visions of Kerouac*; John Clellon Holmes' annotation to "This Is the Beat Generation" entry in Richard K. Ardinger, *An Annotated Bibliography of Works by John Clellon Holmes*, Pocatello, Idaho, 1979; Spengler, *The Decline of the West*; John Clellon Holmes, "This Is the Beat Generation," in *Nothing More to Declare*, N.Y., 1967.

Author's interviews: with Carolyn Cassady, Oct. 1977, and Dec. 1979; with John Clellon Holmes, Aug. 1978; with Al Hinkle, Oct. 1977.

199. This particular dynamic was posited by Carolyn Cassady in our interview, Oct. 1977.
200. Letter of Kerouac to John Clellon Holmes, Oct. 12, 1952.
201. Ibid.
202. Ibid.
203. Ibid.
204. Carolyn Cassady in our interview, Dec. 1979.
205. Cassady quoted by Kerouac in letter of Kerouac to Allen Ginsberg, Nov. 8, 1952.
206. Letter of Kerouac to Allen Ginsberg, Nov. 8, 1952.

5.

Letters of JK: to Ed White, Aug. 31, 1953; to John Clellon Holmes, Dec. 9, 1952; to Carolyn Cassady, Feb. 11, 1953; to Neal and Carolyn Cassady, Jan. 10, 1953; to Carolyn Cassady, Dec. 1952; to Neal and Carolyn Cassady, Dec. 9, 1952; March 20, 1953; to Allen Ginsberg, Dec. 29, 1952; to Ed White, 1953; to Carolyn Cassady, March 1953; to John Clellon Holmes, March 9, 1953; to Carolyn Cassady, Jan. 1953; to Allen Ginsberg, Feb. 21, 1953.

Other letters: William Burroughs to Allen Ginsberg, July 13, 1952; Oct. 6, 1952; Nov. 1952; Nov. 5, 1952; Allen Ginsberg to Neal Cassady, Jan. 1953 (printed in *As Ever*); Malcolm Cowley to Ann Charters, Oct. 10, 1972; Phyllis Jackson to Malcolm Cowley, May 12, 1953; Allen Ginsberg to JK, Feb. 1953; Feb. 24, 1953.

JK's work: *October in the Railroad Earth.*

Books: Carolyn Cassady, *Heart Beat; The Third Word.*
Author's interviews: with Jorge Davila, Sept. 1978; with Cornelius Murphy, Oct.
  1978; with John Clellon Holmes, Aug. 1978.
207. Letter of Kerouac to Carolyn Cassady, Dec. 1952.
208. Jorge Davila in our interview, Sept. 1978; and a piece of Kerouac's writing (in
  the possession of Ed White) in which he plays with this quote from Eliot.

6.

Letters: Allen Ginsberg to JK, July 13, 1953.
JK's work: *Maggie Cassidy.*
Books and articles: Bernice Lemire, *Jack Kerouac: Early Influences*; Herman
  Melville, *The Confidence Man: His Masquerade*, N.Y., 1971; John Ciardi, "In
  Loving Memory of Myself," *Saturday Review*, July 25, 1959.
Author's interviews: with Allen Ginsberg, Aug. 1977, and May 1978.

7.

Letters of JK: to Phil Whalen, June 10, 1959; to Allen Ginsberg, May 7, 1953; to
  Dusty Moreland, April 1953; to Carolyn Cassady, Aug. 10, 1953; to Ed
  White, Aug. 6, 1953; to John Clellon Holmes, Feb. 19, 1954; to Neal and
  Carolyn Cassady, June 8, 1953; to Allen Ginsberg, July 14, 1953; Dec. 1953;
  to Ed White, Aug. 31, 1953; to Carolyn Cassady, Feb. 11, 1953.
Other letters: Phyllis Jackson to Malcolm Cowley, May 12, 1953; Allen Ginsberg to
  JK, May 13, 1953; July 1953; May 13, 1953; May 21, 1953; Neal Cassady to
  JK, May 6, 1953; Allen Ginsberg to Neal Cassady, June 23, 1953 (printed in
  As Ever); Sept. 4, 1953 (printed in *As Ever*); Neal Cassady to Allen Ginsberg,
  June 1953 (printed in *As Ever*); Allen Ginsberg to JK, July 13, 1953.
JK's work: *The Subterraneans*, N.Y., 1958; "Slobs of the Kitchen Sea," in *Lonesome
  Traveler*, N.Y., 1960.
Books: Carolyn Cassady, *The Third Word; Soundings-East: Kerouac Issue* (a com-
  plete transcription of the Salem State College Seminar on Jack Kerouac,
  April 1973, published as an issue of *Soundings-East*, Vol. 2, Salem, Mass.,
  Fall/Winter 1979); Gifford and Lee, *Jack's Book.*
Author's interviews and correspondence: with Al Hinkle, Oct. 1977; with Gregory
  Corso, Aug. 1977, and Oct. 1977; with Gerard Wagner, May 1978; with
  "Mardou Fox," May 1978; from "Mardou Fox," Nov. 15, 1980; with John
  Clellon Holmes, Aug. 1978; with Lucien Carr, July 1977, and May 1978;
  with Stanley Gould, May 1978.
Lectures: Ginsberg, "Literary History of the Beat Generation."
209. Letter of Kerouac to Ed White, Aug. 31, 1953.
210. Ibid.
211. Jack Kerouac, *The Subterraneans* (New York: Grove Press, Black Cat paperback edition, 1971), p. 76.
212. Ibid., p. 62.

8.

Letters of JK: to Ed White, Aug. 6, 1953.
Other letters: Allen Ginsberg to Neal Cassady, May 14, 1953 (printed in *As Ever*);
  Allen Ginsberg to JK, Dec. 1953.
JK's work: *The Subterraneans.*
Books and articles: *Soundings-East: Kerouac Issue*; Wilhelm Reich, *The Function of
  the Orgasm*, N.Y., 1973; Sophocles, *Oedipus the King*, trans. Bernard M. W.
  Knox, N.Y., 1959; Warren Tallman, "Kerouac's Sound," *Evergreen Review*,
  Vol. 4 (Jan/Feb. 1960).

Author's interviews: with John Clellon Holmes, Aug. 1978; with Robert Burford, July 1978.

213. *The Subterraneans*, p. 150.

214. Robert Burford in our interview, July 1978.

TEN: DOUBLE VISION

1.

Letters of JK: to William Smock, April 3, 1961 (printed in *Les Ecrivains Beat et le Voyage*, Paris, 1977); to Ed White, Aug. 6, 1953; to Malcolm Cowley, Nov. 21, 1953; to Carolyn Cassady, Dec. 3, 1953; to Allen Ginsberg and William Burroughs, Nov. 21, 1953; to Allen Ginsberg, June 1954; to Ed White, Aug. 31, 1953; to Don Allen, 1958 (printed in *Heaven & Other Poems*, Bolinas, Calif., 1977).

Other letters: Allen Ginsberg to Neal Cassady, Nov. 25, 1953 (printed in *As Ever*); Nov. 14, 1953 (printed in *As Ever*); Allen Ginsberg to JK, Oct. 8, 1953; Allen Ginsberg to Neal Cassady, Dec. 1953 (printed in *As Ever*).

JK's work: *The Subterraneans*; "Belief & Technique for Modern Prose: List of Essentials," *Evergreen Review*, Vol. 2 (Spring 1959); "Essentials of Spontaneous Prose," *Evergreen Review*, Vol. 2 (Summer 1958).

Books, articles, and documents: Gifford and Lee, *Jack's Book*; Berrigan, "The Art of Fiction XLI: Jack Kerouac"; Viking Press's editorial evaluations of *On the Road*, on deposit at the Newberry Library, Chicago (specific reference is made to evaluations by Helen Taylor for Malcolm Cowley, Oct. 22, 1953, and by Evelyn Levine, n.d.).

Author's interviews and correspondence: with "Mardou Fox," May 1978; with John Clellon Holmes, Aug. 1978; with Stanley Twardowicz May 1978, and Sept. 1978; with Harold Anton, May 1978; with Robert Beauchamp, Sept. 1978; with Robert Burford, July 1978; with John Kingsland, Sept. 1978; with Jorge Davila, Sept. 1978; with Robert Christianson, Aug. 1978; from Alan Ansen, fall 1977.

Lectures: Ginsberg, "Literary History of the Beat Generation."

215. "Mardou Fox" in our interview, May 1978.

216. *The Subterraneans*, p. 23.

217. Robert Beauchamp in our interview, Sept. 1978; and Stanley Twardowicz in our interview, May 1978.

218. John Kingsland in our interview, Sept. 1978, and Robert Christianson in our interview, Aug. 1978.

2.

Letters of JK: to Carolyn Cassady, Dec. 3, 1953; to Neal and Carolyn Cassady, Jan. 25, 1954; to John Clellon Holmes, Feb. 19, 1954; to Carolyn Cassady, July 2, 1954; to Allen Ginsberg, March 1954; to Carolyn Cassady, April 22, 1954; May 1954; to Allen Ginsberg, March 10, 1954; Aug. 24, 1954; to Don Allen, June 10, 1961 (printed in *Heaven & Other Poems*, Bolinas, Calif., 1977); Oct. 1, 1959 (printed in *Heaven & Other Poems*); fall 1959 (printed in *Heaven & Other Poems*); to Allen Ginsberg, June 1954.

Other letters: Neal Cassady to Allen Ginsberg, Nov. 29, 1953 (printed in *As Ever*); Allen Ginsberg to JK, Dec. 1953; Allen Ginsberg to Neal Cassady, Dec. 1953 (printed in *As Ever*); Nov. 1953 (printed in *As Ever*); Carolyn Cassady to JK, Dec. 6, 1953.

JK's work: "The Last Word," *Escapade*, Vol. 4 (Oct. 1959); *San Francisco Blues*

726 · M E M O R Y B A B E

(unpublished in its entirety, though the two poems reprinted here were originally published, respectively, in *the unspeakable visions of the individual*,
Vol. 10, California, Pa., 1980, and in *Palantir*, Lancashire, England [Dec.
1978]).

Books and articles: Carolyn Cassady, *The Third Word; A Buddhist Bible*, Dwight
Goddard, ed. Paul Garon, *Blues and the Poetic Spirit*, N.Y., 1979; Berrigan,
"The Art of Fiction XLI: Jack Kerouac."

Author's interviews: with Gary Snyder, June 1978; with Gregory Corso, Aug. 1977;
with Robert Creeley, July 1978.

Lectures: Ginsberg, "Literary History of the Beat Generation."

219. Letter of Allen Ginsberg to Kerouac, Dec. 1953.

220. "Hero of the snowy West": *On the Road*, p. 6. "Billy Graham in a suit": letter
of Kerouac to Allen Ginsberg, March 1954.

221. Letter of Kerouac to Don Allen, June 10, 1961, in *Heaven & Other Poems*,
Don Allen, ed., (Bolinas, Calif.: Grey Fox Press, 1977), p. 56; and letter of
Kerouac to Allen, fall 1959, p. 53.

3.

Letters of JK: to Carolyn and Neal Cassady, April 22, 1954; to Carolyn Cassady,
May 1954; to Allen Ginsberg, May 1954; June 1954; to Carolyn Cassady,
May 19, 1954; to Allen Ginsberg, Feb. 10, 1955; May 18, 1952; to Carolyn
Cassady, July 2, 1954; to Ed White, Aug. 15, 1954; to Allen Ginsberg, Oct.
26, 1954; to Neal Cassady, fall 1954; to Ed White, June 19, 1958; to Neal
Cassady, Sept. 1954.

Other letters: William Burroughs to JK, May 4, 1954; May 24, 1954; April 22, 1954;
Allen Ginsberg to JK, June 18, 1954; summer 1954; William Burroughs to JK,
Aug. 1954; Allen Ginsberg to JK, Sept. 7, 1954; William Burroughs to JK,
Sept. 3, 1954; Allen Ginsberg to JK, summer 1954.

JK's work: "Jack Kerouac Tells the Truth," a letter from JK, Oct. 6, 1958, to Robert
Lowry, containing an excerpt from *Some of the Dharma*, printed in *Robert
Lowry's Book U.S.A.*, No. 1 (Oct. 1958); "cityCityCITY," in *The Moderns: An
Anthology of New Writing in America*, ed. LeRoi Jones, N.Y., 1963; *Desola-
tion Angels;* "The Origins of the Beat Generation."

Books and articles: Dennis McNally, *Desolate Angel*; Carolyn Cassady, *The Third
Word*; Berrigan, "The Art of Fiction XLI: Jack Kerouac."

Author's interviews and correspondence: with Peter Schell, May 1978; with William Burroughs, Aug. 1977; with Jorge Davila, Sept. 1978; from Robert Lax,
July 27, 1978; with "Mardou Fox," May 1978; with Victor Gioscia, Oct.
1978; from Alan Ansen, fall 1977; with Robert Burford, July 1978; with Ed
White, Oct. 1977; with James Curtis, July 1977; with G.J. Apostolos, May
1978, and Aug. 1978.

222. Jorge Davila in our interview, Sept. 1978.

223. Letter of Kerouac to Allen Ginsberg, June 1954.

224. Letter of William Burroughs to Kerouac, April 22, 1954.

225. Letter of Kerouac to Allen Ginsberg, Oct, 26, 1954.

226. Robert Burford in our interview, July 1978.

227. Letter of Kerouac to Ed White, June 19, 1958.

228. Robert Burford in our interview, July 1978.

4.

Letters of JK: to Allen Ginsberg, Oct. 26, 1954; Nov. 24, 1954; Dec. 22, 1954; Dec.
7, 1954; to Lois Sorrells, Jan., 1960; to Allen Ginsberg, Jan. 18, 1955; Feb. 10,
1955; to Malcolm Cowley, Feb. 20, 1955; to Allen Ginsberg, March 4, 1955;

to William Burroughs, May 1955; to Allen Ginsberg, April 20, 1955; May 20, 1955; May 27-28, 1955; May 3, 1955; to Carolyn Cassady, April 15, 1955; spring 1955; to Allen Ginsberg, June 1955; to Malcolm Cowley, June 1, 1955; July 19, 1955; to Dwight D. Eisenhower (coauthored with a friend and never mailed), June 1955.

Other letters: Allen Ginsberg to JK, Sept. 7, 1954; summer 1954; Nov. 9, 1954; fall 1954; Lucien Carr to Allen Ginsberg, Nov. 27, 1954; Neal Cassady and Allen Ginsberg to JK, summer 1954; William Burroughs to JK, June 9, 1955; Dec. 7, 1954; Allen Ginsberg to JK, April 22, 1955; March 10, 1956.

JK's work: *Some of the Dharma* quoted in "Jack Kerouac Tells the Truth."

Books: Kramer, *Paterfamilias*; Malcolm Cowley, *The Literary Situation*, N.Y., 1954.

Author's interviews: with Gregory Corso, Aug. 1977; with Joan Haverty Kerouac Stuart, June 1978; with Paul Blake, Jr., Oct. 1978; with Lois Sorrells Beckwith, Sept. 1978.

229. Letter of Kerouac to Allen Ginsberg, Oct. 26, 1954.
230. Letter of Kerouac to Allen Ginsberg, Nov. 24, 1954.
231. Letter of Lucien Carr to Allen Ginsberg, Nov. 27, 1954.
232. Jack Kerouac, Dec. 19, 1954, entry in his unpublished book *Some of the Dharma*, quoted in "Jack Kerouac Tells the Truth."
233. Letter of Kerouac to Allen Ginsberg, March 4, 1955.
234. Lois Sorrells Beckwith in our interview, Sept. 1978, was the first person to explicitly point out this trait in Kerouac, so often obscured by the legendary, heroic figure he became in the media.
235. Letter of Kerouac to Carolyn Cassady, April 15, 1955.
236. Letter of William Burroughs to Kerouac, June 9, 1955.
237. Letter of Kerouac to Malcolm Cowley, July 19, 1955.

5.

Letters of JK: to Allen Ginsberg, July 14, 1955; Aug. 7, 1955; Sept. 1-5-6, 1955; to John Clellon Holmes, Aug. 20, 1955; to Malcolm Cowley, Aug. 19, 1955; Sept. 11, 1955; to Don Allen, June 10, 1961 (printed in *Heaven & Other Poems*); to Allen Ginsberg, Aug. 19, 1955; to Malcolm Cowley, Feb. 10, 1956; to Allen Ginsberg, June 27-28, 1955; to Carolyn Cassady, May 19, 1954; to Ed White, June 19, 1958.

JK's work: *Tristessa*, N.Y., 1960; *Mexico City Blues*.

Books: *A Buddhist Bible*, Dwight Goddard, ed.

Author's interviews: with Gregory Corso, Oct. 1977; with Philip Whalen, Aug. 1977; with Peter Orlovsky, Aug. 1977; with Janine Pommy Vega, Sept. 1978; with Allen Ginsberg, May 1978; with Gary Snyder, June 1978; with Michael McClure, July 1978.

Lectures: Ginsberg, "Literary History of the Beat Generation."

238. Letter of Kerouac to Allen Ginsberg, Aug. 7, 1955.
239. Jack Kerouac, *Tristessa* (New York: McGraw-Hill, paperback ed., 1978), p. 52 and p. 59.
240. Jack Kerouac, "217th Chorus," *Mexico City Blues* (New York: Grove Press, Evergreen paperback ed., 1981), p. 219.
241. *Mexico City Blues*, p. 230.
242. Ibid., p. 244.

6.

Letters of JK: to Allen Ginsberg, Sept. 1-5-6, 1955; to John Clellon Holmes, Oct. 12, 1955; to Allen Ginsberg, Peter Orlovsky, William Burroughs, and Alan Ansen, June 7, 1957; to Malcolm Cowley, Oct. 14, 1955; to Gary Snyder, March

8, 1956; to Carolyn Cassady, Sept. 11, 1955; to Allen Ginsberg, Nov. 30, 1955; to Phil Whalen, Nov. 22-23, 1955; Jan. 5, 1956; to Carolyn Cassady, Feb. 11, 1956; to Gary Snyder, Feb. 14, 1956; to Carolyn Cassady, Dec. 30. 1955; to Malcolm Cowley, Dec. 22, 1955; Feb. 10, 1956.

Other letters: Allen Ginsberg to JK, May 10, 1955; Allen Ginsberg to Richard Eberhart, May 18, 1956 (printed in *To Eberhart from Ginsberg*, Lincoln, Mass., 1976); Allen Ginsberg to JK, March 13, 1955; April 25, 1955.

JK's work: *The Dharma Bums*, N.Y., 1958; *Desolation Angels*.

Books, articles, and journals: Gifford and Lee, *Jack's Book*; Kramer, *Paterfamilias*; John Montgomery, *Kerouac West Coast: a Bohemian Pilot Detailed Navigational Instructions*, Palo Alto, Calif. 1976; Carolyn Cassady, *The Third Word*; "Jack Kerouac at Northport"; Gary Snyder, "Journal" (unpublished), entries Oct. 22, 1955, Dec. 2, 1955, and Nov. 3, 1955.

Author's interviews: with Al Hinkle, Oct. 1977; with Gary Snyder, June 1978; with Robert Creeley, July 1978; with Philip Whalen, Aug. 1977, and Jan. 1980; with Kenneth Rexroth, Oct. 1978; with Robert Donlin, Aug. 1977; with Allan Temko, Oct. 1977; with Thomas Parkinson, Jan. 1980; with John Montgomery, Oct. 1977; with Carolyn Cassady, Oct. 1977, Oct. 1979, and Jan. 1980.

243. Philip Whalen in our interview, Aug. 1977.
244. Allan Temko in our interview, Oct. 1977.
245. Ibid.
246. Kerouac quoted by Philip Whalen in our interview, Aug. 1977.
247. Gary Snyder in our interview, June 1978.
248. Jack Kerouac, *The Dharma Bums* (New York: New American Library, paperback ed., 1959), p. 11.
249. Kerouac quoted by Philip Whalen in our interview, Aug. 1977.
250. Letter of Kerouac to Carolyn Cassady, Sept. 11, 1955.
251. Letter of Neal Cassady to Kerouac added to letter of Allen Ginsberg to Kerouac, April 25, 1955.

7.

Letters of JK: to Gary Snyder, Dec. 30, 1955; to Carolyn Cassady, Feb. 11, 1956; to Gary Snyder, Jan. 17, 1956; to Philip Whalen, Jan. 5, 1956; to Carolyn Cassady, March 2, 1956; March 16, 1956; to Philip Whalen, March 6, 1956; to Don Allen, Oct. 1, 1959 (printed in *Heaven & Other Poems*).

JK's work: *Visions of Gerard; Doctor Sax*; "Shakespeare and the Outsider," *Show*, Vol. 4 (Feb. 1964); "The Last Word, *Escapade*, Vol. 5 (Oct. 1960)."

Books: Ann Charters, *A Bibliography of Works by Jack Kerouac: 1939-1975*, N.Y., 1975.

Author's interviews: with John Kingsland, Sept. 1978.
252. *Visions of Gerard*, p. 71.

ELEVEN: CLOWNS IN A CIRCUS OF POWER

1.

Letters of JK: to Philip Whalen, Feb. 7, 1956; to Carolyn Cassady, Feb. 11, 1956; to Philip Whalen, Jan. 19, 1956; to Malcolm Cowley, Feb. 10. 1956; to Philip Whalen, March 6, 1956; to Gary Snyder, Dec. 30. 1955; to Carolyn Cassady, March 2, 1956; to Gary Snyder, Feb. 14, 1956; to Philip Whalen, Jan. 5, 1956; to Gary Snyder, Jan. 17, 1956; March 8, 1956; to Carolyn Cassady, March 16, 1956, to Malcolm Cowley, March 16, 1956; Dec. 22, 1955; April

12, 1956; to Philip Whalen, Oct. 17, 1961; to John Clellon Holmes, May 21, 1956; to Lawrence Ferlinghetti, April 5, 1959; to John Montgomery, May 9, 1961; to Malcolm Cowley, April 19, 1956; May 19, 1956.

Other letters: Allen Ginsberg to JK, March 10, 1956.

JK's work: *The Dharma Bums; Scripture of the Golden Eternity*, N.Y., 1960; "Old Angel Midnight," in *Big Table*, Vol. 1 (Spring 1959).

Books: Charters, *A Bibliography of Works by Jack Kerouac: 1939-1975*; Gifford and Lee, *Jack's Book*.

Author's interviews: with Philip Whalen, Oct. 1977; with Paul Blake, Jr., Oct. 1978; with Tony Sampas, Aug. 1978; with Gary Snyder, June 1978; with Locke McCorkle, Oct. 1977; with Lucien Carr, May 1978.

Lectures: Ginsberg, "Literary History of the Beat Generation."

253. Letter of Kerouac to Philip Whalen, Feb. 7, 1956.
254. Letter of Kerouac to Philip Whalen, Jan. 5, 1956.
255. Paul Blake, Sr., quoted by Paul Blake, Jr., in our interview, Oct. 1978.
256. Letter of Kerouac to John Clellon Holmes, May 21, 1956.
257. Philip Whalen in our interview, Aug. 1977.
258. Letter of Kerouac to John Clellon Holmes, May 21, 1956.

2.

Letters of JK: to John Clellon Holmes, April 19, 1956; May 21, 1956; to Gary Snyder, May 31, 1956; to Malcolm Cowley, May 19, 1956; to Gary Snyder, March 8, 1956; to Lucien Carr, Feb. 24, 1956; to Malcolm Cowley, Dec. 22, 1955; to Thea Snyder, spring 1958.

Other letters: Gabrielle Kerouac to JK, April 10, 1956.

JK's work: "Old Angel Midnight"; *Desolation Angels; The Dharma Bums*.

Journals: Gary Snyder, "Journal," entries Nov. 30, 1955, April 8, 1956, April 19, 1956, April 25, 1956, May 15, 1956, May 1, 1956, May 6, 1956, and May 7, 1956.

Author's interviews: with Gary Snyder, June 1978; with Luther Nichols, June 1978; with Robert Creeley, July 1978; with Gerard Wagner, May 1978; with Michael McClure, July 1978; with John Clellon Holmes, Aug. 1978; with Thea Snyder Lowry, Oct. 1977; with Robert Donlin, Aug. 1977; with Bob Kaufman, Oct. 1977.

259. Robert Creeley in our interview, July 1978.
260. Ibid.
261. Kerouac quoted by Robert Creeley in our interview, July 1978.
262. Letter of Kerouac to John Clellon Holmes, May 21, 1956.
263. Michael McClure in our interview, July 1978.
264. Gary Snyder, "Journal," entry May 25, 1956.
265. Robert Creeley in our interview, July 1978.

3.

Letters of JK: to Lucien Carr, Feb. 24 1956; to Gary Snyder, May 31, 1956; March 8, 1956; to Philip Whalen, Feb. 7, 1956; to Malcolm Cowley, July 3, 1956; to John Montgomery, Nov. 6, 1956; to Philip Whalen, n.d.; to Allen Ginsberg, Sept. 26, 1956; to Philip Whalen, Oct. 1956; to Gary Snyder, Dec. 6, 1959; to Allen Ginsberg, Oct. 10, 1956; to Peter Orlovsky, Oct. 11, 1956; to Philip Whalen, Nov. 1956.

Other letters: Allen Ginsberg to Neal Cassady, Jan. 1957 (printed in *As Ever*).

JK's work: *The Dharma Bums; Desolation Angels;* "The Origins of the Beat Generation"; *Tristessa*.

Books and articles: Carolyn Cassady, *The Third Word*; Douglas T. Miller and Mar-

730 · M E M O R Y   B A B E

ion Nowak, *The Fifties: The Way We Really Were*, Garden City, N.Y., 1977; Richard Eberhart, "West Coast Rhythms," *New York Times Book Review*, Sept. 2, 1956; Mailer, "The White Negro"; Berrigan, "The Art of Fiction XLI: Jack Kerouac."

Author's interviews: with Philip Whalen, Aug. 1977; with Manuel "Chief" Nobriga, May 1978; with Allen Ginsberg, Aug. 1977; with Luther Nichols, June 1978; with Gregory Corso, Aug. 1977, and Oct. 1977; with John Clellon Holmes, Aug. 1978; with Robert Duncan, July 1978; with Peter Orlovsky, Aug. 1977; with Michael McClure, July 1977; with Rambling Jack Elliot, Oct. 1977; with Robert Donlin, Aug. 1977.

Lectures: Ginsberg, "Literary History of the Beat Generation."

266. Gregory Corso in our interview, Oct. 1977.

267. *Look* magazine, Aug. 7, 1956, pp. 82-84, quoted in Douglas T. Miller and Marion Nowak, *The Fifties: The Way We Really Were* (Garden City, N.Y.: Doubleday, 1977), p. 302.

268. Jack Kerouac, *Desolation Angels* (New York and London: Panther paperback ed., 1979), p. 202.

269. Ibid., p. 172.

270. Letter of Kerouac to Allen Ginsberg, Sept. 16, 1956.

4.

Letters of JK: to James Laughlin, Nov. 1957; to Allen Ginsberg, May 1957.

JK's work: *Desolation Angels; The Dharma Bums.*

Documents: Malcolm Cowley, "*On the Road* Chapter Analysis," on deposit at the Newberry Library, Chicago.

Author's interviews and correspondence: with Helen Weaver, Aug. 1978; from Helen Weaver, Sept. 5, 1980; with Helen Elliott, May 1978; with Jacques Beckwith, Sept. 1978; from John Clellon Holmes, Sept. 2, 1977.

271. Kerouac quoted by Helen Elliott in our interview, May 1978.

5.

Letters of JK: to Allen Ginsberg, Dec. 26 1956; to Gary Snyder, Dec. 29, 1956; to Philip Whalen, Dec. 31, 1956; to John Clellon Holmes, Jan. 10, 1957; to Helen Weaver, Dec. 26, 1956; Jan. 5, 1957; to Gary Snyder, Aug. 20, 1957; to Helen Weaver, Oct. 22, 1957; to John Clellon Holmes, June 23, 1957; to Ed White, April 28, 1957.

JK's work: *Desolation Angels.*

Books and journals: John Clellon Holmes, *Visitor: Jack Kerouac in Old Saybrook (the unspeakable visions of the individual,* vol. 11), California, Pa., 1980; Holmes, "Journal," entry Jan. 22, 1957 (printed in *Visitor: Jack Kerouac in Old Saybrook*).

Author's interviews and correspondence: with Gregory Corso, Oct. 1977; with Helen Weaver, Aug. 1978; from Helen Weaver, Sept. 5, 1980; with "Mardou Fox," May 1978; with Paul Blake, Jr., Oct. 1978; with Helen Elliott, May 1978; with Joyce Glassman Johnson, May 1978; with Lucien Carr, July 1977.

272. Gregory Corso in our interview, Oct. 1977.

273. *Desolation Angels*, pp. 294-295. Kerouac's account was corrected by Allen Ginsberg in our interview, Jan. 1981.

6.

Letters of JK: to Allen Ginsberg, Dec. 26, 1956; to Lucien Carr, Feb. 28, 1957; to Neal Cassady, March 25, 1957; to Gary Snyder, March 4, 1957; to Malcolm

Cowley, March 8, 1957; to Gary Snyder, May 25, 1957; to James Laughlin, March 8, 1957; to Malcolm Cowley, Feb. 4, 1957; May 19, 1956; to Gary Snyder, April 3, 1957; March 7, 1957; to Allen Ginsberg, May 1957; to Allen Ginsberg and William Burroughs, May 1957; to Philip Whalen, April 30, 1957; to Ed White, April 28, 1957; to Allen Ginsberg, May 6, 1957; to John Clellon Holmes, June 23, 1957.

Other letters: Gregory Corso to Allen Ginsberg, May 6, 1957.

JK's work: (a) Unpublished: original typescript scroll of "Big Trip to Europe," in the possession of Joan Roberts. (b) Published: *Desolation Angels;* "Big Trip to Europe," in *Lonesome Traveler,* N.Y., 1960.

Author's interviews: with William Burroughs, Aug. 1977; with Peter Orlovsky, Aug. 1977; with Paul Blake, Jr., Oct. 1978; with Malcolm Cowley, May 1978; with Gregory Corso, Aug. 1977, and Oct. 1977; with Philip Whalen, Aug. 1977.

274. Letter of Kerouac to Gary Snyder, March 4, 1957; and William Burroughs in our interview, Aug. 1977.

275. Letter of Kerouac to Gary Snyder, March 4, 1957; and letter of Kerouac to James Laughlin, March 8, 1957.

276. Letter of Kerouac to Gary Snyder, March 4, 1957.

277. *Desolation Angels*, pp. 321-322; and letter of Kerouac to Gary Snyder, April 3, 1957.

278. Letter of Kerouac to Philip Whalen, April 30, 1957; and Paul Blake, Jr., in our interview, Oct. 1978.

7.

Letters of JK: to Philip Whalen, April 30, 1957; to Allen Ginsberg and William Burroughs, May 1957; to John Clellon Holmes, June 23, 1957; to Gary Snyder, June 14, 1957; to Allen Ginsberg, Peter Orlovsky, William Burroughs, and Alan Ansen, June 7, 1957; to Gary Snyder, May 24, 1957; Aug. 20, 1957; to Allen Ginsberg, Peter Orlovsky, and Alan Ansen, July 21, 1957; to Allen Ginsberg, May 17, 1957; to Philip Whalen, Sept. 4, 1957; to Gary Snyder, Sept. 3, 1957; to Alan Ansen, Aug. 20, 1957.

Other letters: Gabrielle Kerouac to Philip Whalen, July 29, 1957; Gregory Corso to Allen Ginsberg, 1958.

JK's work: *Desolation Angels.*

Articles: William Hogan, "A Bookman's Notebook: San Francisco Scene: Avant Garde at Work," *San Francisco Chronicle,* Aug. 13, 1957; Luther Nichols, "The Book Corner: Writing Novels by the Foot," *San Francisco Examiner,* June 1957.

Author's interviews: with Joyce Glassman Johnson, May 1978; with Philip Whalen, Aug. 1977; with Victor Gioscia, Oct. 1978; with Luther Nichols, June 1978; with LuAnne Henderson, Oct. 1978; with Al Hinkle, Oct. 1977; with Paul Blake, Jr., Oct. 1978; with Gregory Corso, Aug. 1977; with William Burroughs, Aug. 1977.

279. *Desolation Angels*, p. 335.

280. Letter of Kerouac to Gary Snyder, June 14-24, 1957.

281. Letter of Kerouac to Alan Ansen, Allen Ginsberg, William Burroughs, and Peter Orlovsky, June 7, 1957.

282. Letter of Kerouac to Philip Whalen, Sept. 4, 1957.

283. Letter of Kerouac to Gary Snyder, Aug. 20, 1957.

TWELVE: "THE OBSESSIVE VIOLENCE OF RIMBAUD" AND
"THE RAVELED NERVE-ENDS OF HUYSMANS"

1.

Letters of JK: to Gary Snyder, Sept. 3, 1957; to Allen Ginsberg, Oct. 1, 1957; to Lucien and Francesca Carr, Oct. 22, 1957; to Neal Cassady, late Oct., 1957; to Philip Whalen, Oct. 1957; to Malcolm Cowley, Dec. 9, 1957; to Allen Ginsberg, Sept. 8, 1957; to Helen Weaver, Oct. 22, 1957; to Allen Ginsberg, Oct. 18, 1957; Jan. 1958; Dec. 10, 1957; to Lucien Carr, fall 1957; to Frankie Edith Parker Kerouac, Jan. 28, 1957; to John Clellon Holmes, April 13, 1958; to Philip Whalen, early 1958; to Allen Ginsberg, Nov. 30, 1957; to Lawrence Ferlinghetti, Nov. 12, 1957; to James Laughlin, Nov. 1957; to Allen Ginsberg, Jan. 8, 1958.

JK's work: *The Dharma Bums*; "Lamb, No Lion," *Pageant*, Vol. 8 (Feb. 1958); "Aftermath: The Philosophy of the Beat Generation," *Esquire*, Vol. 49 (March 1958).

Books and articles: Neeli Cherkovski, *Ferlinghetti*, Garden City, N.Y., 1979; Gilbert Millstein, "Books of the Times," *New York Times*, Sept. 5, 1957; David Dempsey, "In Pursuit of 'Kicks,'" *New York Times*, Sept. 8, 1957; "The Ganser Syndrome," *Time*, Sept. 16, 1957; reviews of *On the Road* in the *Saturday Review*, Sept. 7, 1957; in *The Atlantic*, Oct. 1957; in the *Chicago Tribune*, Oct. 6, 1957; Herbert Gold, "Hip, Cool, Beat—and Frantic," *The Nation*, Nov. 16, 1957; Norman Podhoretz, "The Culture of Appeasement," *Harper's*, Vol. 225 (Oct. 1977); "Trade Winds" (interview with JK), *Saturday Review*, Sept. 28, 1957; Maurice Dolbier, "Books and Authors: Beat Generation; Parade of Paperbacks" (interview with JK), *New York Herald Tribune*, Sept. 22, 1957; Ed Creagh, "Lowellian's 'Beat Generation' Finds Itself in the Middle of the 'Beep' Era," AP syndicated article, Oct. 8, 1957.

Author's interviews and correspondence: with Robert Beauchamp, Sept. 1978; with John Clellon Holmes, Aug. 1978; with Helen Elliott, May 1978; with Howard Hart, June 1978; with Lucien Carr, May 1978; with Ed Stringham, Sept. 1978; with Nell Blaine, May 1978; from George Butterick (curator of the Olson Archives, University of Connecticut, Storrs), March 16, 1978; with Robert Frank, May 1978; with Victor Gioscia, Oct. 1978; with Frankie Edith Parker Kerouac, Oct. 1978.

Lectures: Ginsberg, "Literary History of the Beat Generation."

284. Robert Beauchamp in our interview, Sept. 1978.
285. Ed Stringham in our interview, Sept. 1978.
286. Letter of Kerouac to Allen Ginsberg, Oct. 1, 1957.
287. Letter of Kerouac to Malcolm Cowley, Dec. 9, 1957.

2.

Letters of JK: to Gary Snyder, Nov. 5, 1957; Feb. 14, 1955; to Lawrence Ferlinghetti, Dec. 1957; to Helen Weaver, Oct. 22, 1957; to Allen Ginsberg, Dec. 10, 1957; Dec. 28, 1957; Jan. 8, 1958; to Gary Snyder, Jan. 5, 1958; to Neal Cassady, Oct. 1957; to Allen Ginsberg, March 22, 1958; to Thea Snyder, spring 1958; to Philip Whalen, Jan. 7, 1958; to Allen Ginsberg, Jan. 16, 1958; Jan. 21, 1958; to Lucien Carr, Jan. 16, 1958; to Ed White, Feb. 18, 1958; to Allen Ginsberg, Sept. 8, 1958; July 2, 1958.

Other letters: Gregory Corso to Allen Ginsberg, Aug. 29, 1958; Oct. 4-13, Nov. 7-12, 1958; Neal Cassady to JK, June 12, 1959.

Books and articles: Carolyn Cassady, *The Third Word*; Howard Smith, "Jack Kerouac: Off the Road, Into the Vanguard, and Out," in *The Village Voice*

Reader, N.Y., 1962; "Interview with Jack Kerouac: Lowell Author Gives His Version of the Generation" (transcript of Mike Wallace interview with JK), *Lowell Sun,* March 3, 1958; David Dempsey, "Diary of a Bohemian," *New York Times,* Feb. 23, 1958; "The Blazing & the Beat," *Time,* Feb. 24, 1958; "Bop-Beat Novel—Offbeat Tone," *Newsweek,* Feb. 1958; Kenneth Rexroth, "The Voice of the Beat Generation Has Some Square Delusions," in "This World," *San Francisco Chronicle,* Feb. 16, 1958.

Author's interviews and correspondence: with John Montgomery, Oct. 1977; with James Ryan Morris, June 1978; with Helen Weaver, Aug. 1978; with Max Gordon, May 1978; with Ed Stringham, Sept. 1978; with Howard Hart, June 1978; from Steve Allen, Sept. 29, 1977, with Lucien Carr, July 1977, and May 1978; with "Mardou Fox," May 1978; with Thea Snyder Lowry, Oct. 1977; with Joyce Glassman Johnson, May 1978; with Allen Ginsberg, May 1978; with Al Gelpi, Oct. 1977; with LuAnne Henderson, Oct. 1978; with Jacky Gibson Mercer, Oct. 1977; with Al Hinkle, Oct. 1977; with Helen Elliott, May 1978; with Carolyn Cassady, Feb. 1980.

288. Letter of Neal Cassady to Kerouac, June 12, 1959; and Carolyn Cassady in our interview, Feb. 1980.

289. Letter of Kerouac to Allen Ginsberg, July 2, 1958.

3.

Letters of JK: to Philip Whalen, March 4, 1958; to Gary Snyder, May 5, 1958; to John Clellon Holmes, April 13, 1958; March 14, 1958; to Allen Ginsberg, April 8, 1958; to Philip Whalen, late April, 1958; to Allen Ginsberg, Jan. 8, 1958; to Philip Whalen, early 1958; to Gary Snyder, Feb. 4, 1960; to Philip Whalen, April-May, 1958; to Allen Ginsberg (part of Peter Orlovsky to Allen Ginsberg letter), March 20-22, 1958; to Gary Snyder, Dec. 1, 1958; to James Laughlin, May 29, 1958; to Lucien Carr, Nov. 20, 1957; to John Clellon Holmes, late April, 1958; to Allen Ginsberg, Jan. 21, 1958; to Ed White, June 19, 1958; to Allen Ginsberg, Aug. 11, 1958; to Gary Snyder, June 19, 1958; to Allen Ginsberg, July 2, 1958; to Philip Whalen, May-June, 1958; to Allen Ginsberg, Nov. 19, 1958; to Philip Whalen, late Feb., 1958; to Don Allen, Feb. 18, 1958 (printed in *Heaven & Other Poems*); Feb. 11, 1958 (printed in *Heaven & Other Poems*); to Philip Whalen, June 1958; to John Clellon Holmes, July 21, 1958; to Philip Whalen, July 18, 1958; to Gary Snyder, July 21, 1958; to Allen Ginsberg, Aug. 28, 1958.

Other letters: Peter Orlovsky to Allen Ginsberg, March 20-22, 1958 (printed in Allen Ginsberg and Peter Orlovsky, *Straight Hearts' Delight: Love Poems and Selected Letters,* San Francisco, 1980); June 24, 1958 (printed in *Straight Hearts' Delight*); Sterling Lord to JK, July 22, 1958; Peter Orlovsky to Allen Ginsberg, June 3, 1958; Feb. 19, 1958; Gabrielle Kerouac to Allen Ginsberg, July 13, 1958.

JK's work: "On the Road to Florida," *Evergreen Review,* Vol. 14 (Jan. 1970).

Articles: "Jack Kerouac in Northport," *Athanor,* Summer/Fall 1982; Fernanda Pivano, *Yessir, Jack Kerouac,* Milano, 1969; Charles Poore, "Books of the Times," *New York Times,* Oct. 2, 1958; J. Donald Adams, "Speaking of Books," *New York Times,* Oct. 26, 1958; William Bittner, "The Yabyum Set," *Saturday Review,* Oct. 11, 1958; D. J. Enright, review of *The Dharma Bums,* in *The Spectator,* Sept. 18, 1959; Robert P. Jackson, review of *The Dharma Bums,* in *The American Buddhist,* Vol. 2 (Oct. 1958).

Author's interviews: with Peter Orlovsky, Oct. 1977; with Stanley Twardowicz, July 1977; with Joyce Glassman Johnson, May 1978; with Howard Hart, June 1978; with John Clellon Holmes, Aug. 1978; with David Amram, July 1978;

with Philip Lamantia, Oct. 1977; with Robert Frank, May 1978; with Dody James Müller, May 1978; with Ken Arndt, July 1977; with Victor Gioscia, Oct. 1978.

290. Letter of Kerouac to Gary Snyder, July 14, 1958.

4.

Letters of JK: to Allen Ginsberg, Oct. 5, 1958; Aug. 28, 1958; to John Montgomery, Nov. 1958; to Allen Ginsberg, Oct. 15, 1958; Dec. 16, 1958; to Philip Whalen, Nov. 4, 1958; to Gary Snyder, Feb. 23, 1959; to Allen Ginsberg, Nov. 19, 1958; to Philip Whalen, Jan. 10, 1959; to James Laughlin, May 29, 1958.

Other letters: Gregory Corso to Allen Ginsberg, March 20, 1960; Allen Ginsberg to JK, Oct. 20, 1958; Oct. 29, 1958.

JK on tape: untranscribed reel from the Northport Public Library interview.

JK's work: "The Origins of the Beat Generation."

Articles: Marc D. Schleifer, "The Beat Debated—Is It Or Is It Not?" in *The Village Voice Reader*, N.Y., 1962; Paul Carroll, "Call it *Big Table*," Chicago, March 1979.

Author's interviews and correspondence: with Gregory Corso, Aug. 1977, and Oct. 1977; with Al and Helen Hinkle, June 1978; with Allen Ginsberg, May 1978; with Ken Arndt, July 1977; with Dody James Müller, May 1978; with Lucien Carr, July 1977; with Matsumi Kanemitsu, Oct. 1978; with Robert Beauchamp, Sept. 1978; with Joyce Glassman Johnson, May 1978; with Walter Gutman, May 1978; with Fred McDarrah, Sept. 1978; from Alan Ansen, fall 1977; from Robert Lax, July 27, 1978; with Alfred Leslie, May 1978.

291. Lucien Carr in our interview, July 1977.

292. Dody James Müller in our interview, May 1978.

5.

Letters of JK: to Allen Ginsberg, Aug. 28, 1958; to John Clellon Holmes, April 28, 1959; July 21, 1958; to Gary Snyder, Feb. 23, 1959; to Carolyn Cassady, April 17, 1959; to Gary Snyder, June 14, 1957; to John Clellon Holmes, April 15, 1959; to Allen Ginsberg, Dec. 16, 1958; April 5, 1959; to Caroline Kerouac Blake, Jan. 29, 1959; Feb. 1959; to John Clellon Holmes, Feb. 21, 1959; to Allen Ginsberg, March 1959; to Philip Whalen, April 19, 1959; June 10, 1959; to Gary Snyder, May 25, 1959; to Allen Ginsberg, May 7, 1959; Nov. 19, 1958.

Other letters: Gregory Corso to Allen Ginsberg, May 15, 1959; Peter Orlovsky to Carolyn Cassady, Jan. 10, 1959 (printed in *As Ever*); Allen Ginsberg to JK, Oct. 29, 1958; Nov. 17, 1958; Gabrielle Kerouac to Caroline Kerouac Blake, Jan. 29, 1959.

JK's work: *Pull My Daisy*, N.Y., 1961.

Books and articles: David Amram, *Vibrations*, N.Y., 1968; Jonas Mekas, "Free Cinema and the New Wave," *The Emergence of Film*, Lewis Jacobs, ed., N.Y., 1969; Charters, *A Bibliography of Works by Jack Kerouac: 1939-1975*; McNally, *Desolate Angel*; Alfred Aronowitz, "The Beat Generation: Article III" (interview with Neal Cassady), *New York Post*, March 11, 1959; Barnaby Conrad, "Barefoot Boy With Dreams of Zen," *Saturday Review*, May 2, 1959; David Dempsey, "Beatnik Bogeyman on the Prowl," *The New York Times*, May 3, 1959; Phoebe Adams, review of *Doctor Sax*, in *The Atlantic*, Vol. 204 (July 1959); K. S. Lynn, review of *Doctor Sax*, in *New York Herald Tribune Book Review*, May 31, 1959; review of *Doctor Sax* in *Time*, May 18, 1959.

Author's interviews: with Alfred Leslie, May 1978; with Walter Gutman, May 1978; with Gregory Corso, Oct. 1977; with Robert Frank, April 1978; with Peter Orlovsky, Aug. 1977; with Dody James Müller, May 1978; with Helen Elliott, May 1978; with Joyce Glassman Johnson, May 1978; with Gary Snyder, June 1978; with Lois Sorrells Beckwith, Sept. 1978; with Matsumi Kanemitsu, Oct. 1978; with Frank Feminella, Sept. 1978; with Victor Gioscia, Oct. 1978.

6.

Letters of JK: to John Clellon Holmes, April 28, 1959; to Allen Ginsberg, June 20, 1960; to Don Allen, Dec. 4, 1958 (printed in *Heaven & Other Poems*); to Allen Ginsberg, May 7, 1959; May 19, 1959; to Jacques and Lois Beckwith, May 11, 1965; to Allen Ginsberg, July 28, 1958; to John Clellon Holmes, Feb. 21, 1959; to Allen Ginsberg, April 23, 1959; Oct. 19, 1959; Oct. 6, 1959; Oct. 23, 1958; Oct. 4, 1962; to Neal Cassady, 1960; to Allen Ginsberg, Aug. 19, 1959.

Other letters: Peter Orlovsky to Carolyn Cassady, Jan. 10, 1959 (printed in *As Ever*).

JK's work: "The Last Word," *Escapade*, Vol. 5 (Dec. 1959); "The Beginning of Bop," *Escapade*, Vol. 3 (April 1959); "The Last Word," *Escapade*, Vol. 5 (Aug. 1960); "The Last Word," *Escapade*, Vol. 6 (April 1961).

Books and articles: Anaïs Nin, *The Diary of Anaïs Nin: 1955-1966*, Vol. 6, N.Y., 1976; Al Aronowitz, "The Beat Generation: Article II" (interview with JK), *New York Post*, March 10, 1959; Val Duncan, "Kerouac Revisited," *Newsday*, July 18, 1964.

Author's interviews and correspondence: with Helen Elliott, May 1978; with Robert Frank, April 1978; with Matsumi Kanemitsu, Oct. 1978; with Lois Sorrells Beckwith, Sept. 1978; with Barney Rosset, Sept. 1978; with Stanley Twardowicz, Sept. 1978; with Ted Joans, Aug. 1979; with Robert Beauchamp, Sept. 1978; with Nadine Beauchamp, Sept. 1978; with John Clellon Holmes, Aug. 1978; with Nell Blaine, May 1978; with Albert "Pancho" Gonzales, Aug. 1978; with Walter Gutman, May 1978; with Victor Gioscia, Oct. 1978; with Ted Berrigan, May 1978; from Ted Wilentz, July 18, 1978; with Joyce Glassman Johnson, May 1978; with Dody James Müller, May 1978; with Janine Pommy Vega, Sept. 1978; with Frank Feminella, Sept. 1978; with Jacques Beckwith, Sept. 1978.

Lectures: Ginsberg, "Literary History of the Beat Generation."

7.

Letters of JK: to Caroline Kerouac Blake, May 1959; to Allen Ginsberg, Sept. 14, 1959; Nov. 2, 1959; Oct. 18, 1960; to Lois Sorrells, Jan. 1960; to Allen Ginsberg, Aug. 19, 1959; to Lois Sorrells, Sept. 1959; to Allen Ginsberg, Sept. 23, 1959; Dec. 24, 1959; Nov. 6, 1959; to John Clellon Holmes, Oct. 14, 1959; to Allen Ginsberg, Oct. 6, 1959; to Granville H. Jones, 1961; to Gary Snyder, Dec. 6, 1959; to John Clellon Holmes, Nov. 8, 1959; to Lois Sorrells, Sept. 22, 1959.

Other letters: Gabrielle Kerouac to Caroline Kerouac Blake, May 1959; Allen Ginsberg to JK, Nov. 1959; Gabrielle Kerouac to Allen Ginsberg, Nov. 2, 1959; Neal Cassady to JK, Oct. 27, 1959.

JK on tape: untranscribed reel from the Northport Public Library interview.

JK's work: "The Last Word," *Escapade*, Vol. 5 (June 1960); *Vanity of Duluoz; Big Sur*.

Articles: David Dempsey, "The Choice Jack Made," *New York Times*, July 19, 1959;

John Ciardi, "In Loving Memory of Myself," *Saturday Review*, July 15, 1959; Aronowitz, "The Beat Generation: Article II."

Author's interviews: with Victor Gioscia, Oct. 1978; with Leo Parla, July 1977; with Barbara Forst, Sept. 1978; with Lucien Carr, May 1978; with Robert Beauchamp, Sept. 1978; with Howard Hart, June 1978; with Jack Micheline, Oct. 1977, and Nov. 1979; with Robert Creeley, July 1978; with Bobbie Louise Hawkins, Aug. 1979; with Joan Roberts, July 1977; with Lois Sorrells Beckwith, Sept. 1978; with Dody James Müller, May 1978; with Paul Blake, Jr., Oct. 1978; with Herbert Huncke, Sept. 1978; with Jacques Beckwith, Sept. 1978; with Matsumi Kanemitsu, Oct. 1978; with Eileen Kaufman, Dec. 1979; with Allen Ginsberg, May 1978; with Ken Arndt, July 1977; with Al Hinkle, Oct. 1977.

293. Leo Parla in our interview, July 1977.

8.

Letters of JK: to John Clellon Holmes, Jan. 21, 1960; to Gary Snyder, Dec. 3-6, 1959 (written with Albert Saijo and Lew Welch); to Gary Snyder, Feb. 4, 1960; to Allen Ginsberg, June 20, 1960; to Phil Whalen, Dec. 6, 1959; to Allen Ginsberg, Dec. 24, 1959; Jan. 4, 1960; to Lois Sorrells, Jan. 1960; Jan. (Tuesday), 1960; to Ed White, Dec. 30, 1959; to Lucien Carr, Jan. 19, 1960; to Allen Ginsberg, Feb. 20, 1960; to Lawrence Ferlinghetti, April 25, 1960; to Lois Sorrells, April 1960; Feb. 19, 1960; to Carolyn Cassady, April 29, 1960; to Lawrence Ferlinghetti, July 2, 1960.

Other letters: Neal Cassady to JK, Oct. 27, 1959; Neal Cassady to Carolyn Cassady, Dec. 3, 1959; Lew Welch to Philip Whalen, April 17, 1958; Peter Orlovsky to Allen Ginsberg, Feb. 4, 1960; March 25, 1960 (printed in *Straight Hearts' Delight*); Peter Orlovsky to Allen Ginsberg, May 13, 1960 (printed in *Straight Hearts' Delight*); April 9, 1960; June 23, 1960 (printed in *Straight Hearts' Delight*).

JK's work: (a) Unpublished: notes made on Albert Saijo's program of the evening ceremony at The First Zen Institute of America, New York, N.Y., Nov. 1959, in the possession of Saijo; "An Introduction to Some Collected Poems of Lois Sorrells," May 7, 1963. (b) Published: "This is what it's called," coauthored by Albert Saijo and Lew Welch, in *The Beat Scene*, Elias Wilentz, ed., N.Y., 1960.

Articles: Albert Saijo, "A Recollection," in Jack Kerouac, Albert Saijo, and Lew Welch, *Trip Trap*, Bolinas, Calif., 1973; Lew Welch, "We Started for New York," in *Trip Trap*; Paul O'Neil, "The Only Rebellion Around," *Life*, Vol. 47 (Nov. 30, 1959); John Ciardi, "Epitaph for the Dead Beats," *Saturday Review*, Vol. 43 (Feb. 6, 1960).

Author's interviews: with Alfred Leslie, May 1978; with Helen Elliott, May 1978; with Jay Blaise, Oct. 1977; with Albert Saijo, Oct. 1977; with Robert Miller, Oct. 1978; with Joanne Kyger, Oct. 1977; with John Montgomery, Oct. 1977; with Robert Frank, April 1978; with Carolyn Cassady, June 1978; with Al Hinkle, Oct. 1977; with Lucien Carr, July 1977, and May 1978; with Lois Sorrells Beckwith, Sept. 1978; with Jacques Beckwith, Sept. 1978; with Dody James Müller, May 1978; with Victor Gioscia, Oct. 1978.

Tapes: discussion between Gregory Corso, Gerard Wagner, and Dan DeSole following JK's funeral—tape courtesy of Dr. Dan DeSole.

294. Robert Miller in our interview, Oct. 1978.

295. Letter of Kerouac to Lois Sorrells, Feb. 19, 1960.

296. Letter of Peter Orlovsky to Allen Ginsberg, May 13, 1960, printed in Allen

Ginsberg/ Peter Orlovsky, *Straight Hearts' Delight: Love Poems and Selected Letters 1947-1980* (San Francisco: Gay Sunshine Press, 1980), pp. 196-197.

9.

Letters of JK: to Lawrence Ferlinghetti, July 2, 1960; to Carolyn Cassady, April 29, 1960; to Lawrence Ferlinghetti, July 8, 1960; to Lois Sorrells, July 18, 1960; to Lawrence Ferlinghetti, July 21, 1960; Oct. 23, 1961; to Philip Whalen, April 12, 1960; to Neal Cassady, fall 1960; to Lois Sorrells, fall 1960; to Lawrence Ferlinghetti, May 3, 1966.

Other letters: Peter Orlovsky to Allen Ginsberg, April 5, 1960; April 9, 1960.

JK's work (a) Unpublished: "To Bob Kaufman" (poem written on Kaufman's North Beach hotel room wall, a copy of which was provided by Kaufman). (b) Published: *Big Sur.*

Books: Carolyn Cassady, *The Third Word*; Gifford and Lee, *Jack's Book.*

Author's interviews: with Lawrence Ferlinghetti, Oct. 1977, and June 1978; with Philip Whalen, Aug. 1977; with Victor Wong, June 1978, and Oct. 1979; with Robert Miller, Oct. 1978; with Al Hinkle, June 1978; with Helen Hinkle, June 1978; with Michael McClure, July 1978; with George Nelson, Dec. 1979; with Jacky Gibson Mercer, Oct. 1977; with Bob Kaufman, Oct. 1977.

THIRTEEN: THE GHOSTS OF NORTHPORT

1.

Letters of JK: to Ed White, Feb. 9, 1962; to Philip Whalen, Nov. 8, 1960; to Neal Cassady, fall 1960; to Ed White, Aug. 7, 1961; to Allen Ginsberg, March 2, 1961; to Philip Whalen, Feb. 2, 1961; to John Montgomery, early 1962; to Allen Ginsberg, March 1961; to Lawrence Ferlinghetti, Feb. 1, 1961; to Allen Ginsberg, Oct. 18, 1960; Sept. 22, 1960; to Philip Whalen, Feb. 23, 1961; to Neal Cassady, April 3, 1961; to John Montgomery, May 9, 1961; to Neal Cassady, April 3, 1961; to John Montgomery, May 9, 1961; to Stanley Twardowicz, Nov. 23, 1964; Nov. 5, 1964.

Other letters: Gabrielle Kerouac to Caroline Kerouac Blake, late Nov., 1960.

JK on tape: party at JK's house, Aug. 26, 1964.

Books and documents: Cherkovski, *Ferlinghetti; Soundings-East: Kerouac Issue;* Allen Ginsberg, "Friday Nite Cylocybin Mushroom" notes, taken down in hand, Jan. 13, 1961, on deposit in the Columbia Archives.

Author's interviews and correspondence: with Victor Gioscia, Oct. 1978; with Matsumi Kanemitsu, Oct. 1978; with Lois Sorrells Beckwith, Sept. 1978; with Paul Blake, Jr., Oct. 1978; with Helen Elliott, May 1978; with Lawrence Ferlinghetti, Oct. 1977, and June 1978; with Eileen Kaufman, Dec. 1979; with David Markson, Sept. 1978; from David Markson, May 5, 1980; with Joseph Scianni, Sept. 1978; with Stanley Twardowicz, July 1977, and Sept. 1978.

297. Letter of Kerouac to Ed White, Feb. 9, 1962.
298. Lois Sorrells Beckwith in our interview, Sept. 1978; and Matsumi Kanemitsu in our interview, Oct. 1978.
299. Marginal note of Lawrence Ferlinghetti on the letter of Kerouac to Ferlinghetti, Feb. 1, 1961.

2.

Letters of JK: to Lois Sorrells, May 31, 1961; to Allen Ginsberg, April 14, 1961; to

Bernice Lemire, June 15, 1961; to Granville H. Jones, 1961; to Lawrence Ferlinghetti, June 25, 1961; to Carolyn Cassady, Oct. 17, 1961; to Allen Ginsberg, July 18, 1961; to Carolyn Cassady, June 23, 1961; to Ed White, Feb. 9, 1962; to Allen Ginsberg, July 18, 1961; to John Clellon Holmes, Aug. 9, 1961; to Ed White, Aug. 7, 1961; to John Clellon Holmes, Dec. 29, 1961; to Philip Whalen, Oct. 17, 1961; to Gary Snyder, Nov.-Dec., 1961.

Other letters: Gabrielle Kerouac to Lawrence Ferlinghetti, July 28, 1961.

JK on tape: untranscribed reel from the Northport Public Library interview.

JK's work: *Desolation Angels; Big Sur.*

Books: Charters, *A Bibliography of Works by Jack Kerouac: 1939-1975.*

Author's interviews: with Bernice Lemire, Aug. 1978; with Paul Blake, Jr., Oct. 1978; with Philip Whalen, Aug. 1977.

300. *Desolation Angels,* p. 113.

3.

Letters of JK: to Ed White, Aug. 7, 1961; to Lawrence Ferlinghetti, Aug. 1961; to Gary Snyder, Nov.-Dec., 1961; to Lois Sorrells, Dec. 18, 1961; to Allen Ginsberg, Dec. 28, 1961; to John Montgomery, early 1962; to Ed White, Feb. 9, 1962; to John Clellon Holmes, Dec. 29, 1961; to John Montgomery, Feb. 1962; to Neal and Carolyn Cassady, Nov. 28, 1962; to John Clellon Holmes, April 17, 1962; to John Montgomery, May 26, 1962; to Neal Cassady, Nov. 28, 1962; to Lawrence Ferlinghetti, April 28, 1962; to Allen Ginsberg, April 30, 1962.

Other letters; Gregory Corso to Allen Ginsberg and Peter Orlovsky, Nov. 14, 1961; William Burroughs to JK, March 15, 1962; Gregory Corso to Allen Ginsberg, March 9, 1962; March 1962.

Books: Allen Ginsberg, *Journals: Early Fifties Early Sixties,* N.Y., 1977.

Author's interviews and correspondence: with Robert Miller, Oct. 1978; with Lucien Carr, May 1978; with Victor Gioscia, Oct. 1978; with Herbert Huncke, Sept. 1978; with Lois Sorrells Beckwith, Sept. 1978; with Jacques Beckwith, Sept. 1978; with Eileen Kaufman, Dec. 1979; with Tony Sampas, Aug. 1978; with Joan Haverty Kerouac Stuart, June 1978; with Jan Kerouac, June 1978, and June 1979; with Stanley Twardowicz, July 1977; from Ted Wilentz, July 18, 1978; with Paul Blake, Jr., Oct. 1978.

301. Victor Gioscia in our interview, Oct. 1978.

302. Kerouac quoted by Jacques Beckwith in our interview, Sept. 1978.

4.

Letters of JK: to John Montgomery c/o Philip Whalen, n.d.; to John Montgomery, early 1962; to Philip Whalen, June 19, 1962; to John Montgomery, May 26, 1962; to Ed White, Feb. 9, 1962; to John Montgomery, Feb. 1962; to Bernice Lemire, March 21, 1962; to John Clellon Holmes, June 8, 1962; to Philip Whalen, Jan. 14, 1963; to John Clellon Holmes, Aug. 8, 1962; to Lucien Carr, May 17, 1961; to Allen Ginsberg, April 30, 1962; to John Clellon Holmes, Oct. 9, 1962; to Ed White, April 4, 1962; to Carolyn Cassady, Oct. 21, 1962; to Neal and Carolyn Cassady, Nov. 28, 1962; to Lois Sorrells, Aug. 8, 1962; to Allen Ginsberg, Aug. 28, 1962; to Lois Sorrells, Aug. 17, 1962; to John Clellon Holmes, Sept. 3, 1962; to Allen Ginsberg, Oct. 4, 1962; to Lucien Carr, Oct. 22, 1962; to John Clellon Holmes, Nov. 22, 1962.

Other letters: Lawrence Ferlinghetti to *Time* magazine, Sept. 15, 1962.

Books, articles, and journals: Holmes, *Visitor: Jack Kerouac in Old Saybrook*; Jarvis, *Visions of Kerouac*; Beaulieu, "My Boyhood Years With Jack Kerouac"; Pertinax (Mary Sampas), "The Rambler: Conversation with Kerouac," *Lowell*

Sun, Sept. 20, 1962; "Lions & Cubs," *Time,* Sept. 14, 1962; Herbert Gold, "Squaring Off the Corners," *Saturday Review,* Sept. 22, 1962; William Wiegard, "A Turn in the Road for the King of the Beats," *New York Times,* Sept. 16, 1962; Pertinax (Mary Sampas), "The Rambler: Kerouac Leaves Lowell," *Lowell Sun,* Sept. 25, 1962; Holmes, "Journal," entries Sept. 12, 1962, Sept. 13, 1962, and Sept. 16, 1962 (printed in *Visitor: Jack Kerouac in Old Saybrook*).

Author's interviews: with John Clellon Holmes, Aug. 1978; with Paul Blake, Jr., Oct. 1978; with G.J. Apostolos, May 1978, and Aug. 1978; with James Curtis, Aug. 1977; with Tony Sampas, Aug. 1978; with Manuel "Chief" Nobriga, Aug. 1978; with Bernice Lemire, Aug. 1978; with Huck Finneral, Aug. 1978; with Paul Bourgeois, May 1978; with Leo Grenier, Aug. 1978; with Helen Elliott, May 1978; with William Koumantzelis, Aug. 1978; with Stanley Twardowicz, July 1977.

Tapes: Charles E. Jarvis and James Curtis, interview with JK for their Lowell radio show "Dialogues in Great Books," Sept. 1962, on deposit in the Special Collections of the Lowell University Library.

303. Paul Blake, Jr., in our interview, Oct. 1978.

304. Letter of Kerouac to John Clellon Holmes, June 8, 1962; and Kerouac on tape, Northport Public Library interview.

305. Actual quotation spoken to me by a drinker in a Lowell bar, who claimed to have known Kerouac (August 1978).

306. Letter of Kerouac to Lucien Carr, Oct. 22, 1962.

5.

Letters of JK: to Lois Sorrells, Dec. 1962; to Philip Whalen, Dec. 13, 1962; to Ed White, April 24, 1964; to Philip Whalen, Feb. 23, 1963; Feb. 2, 1961; to Neal and Carolyn Cassady, Nov. 28, 1962; to Philip Whalen, Jan. 14, 1963; June 19, 1962; to John Clellon Holmes, June 23, 1963; April 14, 1963; to Allen Ginsberg, June 29, 1963; to Gary Snyder, May 23, 1963; to Carolyn Cassady, Aug. 16, 1963.

Other letters: Gregory Corso to Allen Ginsberg, March 7, 1963.

JK on tape: untranscribed reel from the Northport Public Library interview.

Books: Jarvis, *Visions of Kerouac; Soundings-East: Kerouac Issue.*

Author's interviews: with Stanley Twardowicz, July 1977, May 1978, and Sept. 1978; with Lawrence Smith, July 1977; with Mike McGrady, Sept. 1978; with "Bill Crabtree," May 1978; with Matsumi Kanemitsu, Oct. 1978; with Joan Roberts, July 1977; with Leo Parla, July 1977; with Pete, the bartender of Gunther's, and assorted citizens of Northport.

6.

Letters of JK: to Carolyn Cassady, Aug. 16, 1963; to Allen Ginsberg, June 29, 1963; to John Clellon Holmes, Dec. 11, 1963; to Gary Snyder, May 23, 1963; to Carolyn Cassady, Jan. 7, 1962; to Allen Ginsberg, Dec. 28, 1961; to Ed White, April 24, 1964; to John Clellon Holmes, Sept. 22, 1966; Oct. 5, 1963; to Ed White, May 27, 1964.

Other letters: Allen Ginsberg to JK, Oct. 1963; Peter Orlovsky to Allen Ginsberg, Nov. 14, 1963.

JK on tape: party at JK's house, Aug. 26, 1964; untranscribed reel from the Northport Public Library interview.

JK's work: "Jack Kerouac Takes a Fresh Look at Jack Kerouac: The First Word," *Escapade,* Vol. 12 (Jan. 1967).

Books and articles: Young, *Allen Ginsberg: Gay Sunshine Interview*; Robert Phelps, review of *Visions of Gerard,* in *New York Herald Tribune,* Sept. 8, 1963; review of *Visions of Gerard,* in *Newsweek,* Sept. 9 1963; Saul Maloff, "A Yawping at the Grave," *New York Times Book Review,* Sept. 8, 1963.

Author's interviews: with George Nelson, Dec. 1979; with Stanley Twardowicz, July 1977, May 1978, and Sept. 1978; with Jan Kerouac, June 1978; with Lucien Carr, May 1978; with Gregory Corso, Oct. 1977; with Matsumi Kanemitsu, Oct. 1978; with Lois Sorrells Beckwith, Sept. 1978; with Thea Snyder Lowry, Oct. 1977; with Joyce Glassman Johnson, May 1978; with "Mardou Fox," May 1978; with Helen Elliott, May 1978; with Helen Weaver, Aug. 1978; with "Bill Crabtree," May 1978; with Allen Ginsberg, Aug. 1977; with Carl Solomon, May 1978; with Lawrence Smith, July 1977; with Al Gelpi, Oct. 1977; with Tony Sampas, Aug. 1978.

Lectures: Ginsberg, "Literary History of the Beat Generation."

307. Kerouac on tape, untranscribed reel from the Northport Public Library interview.

7.

Letters of JK: to Philip Whalen, Nov. 18, 1963; to Ed White, April 24, 1964; May 27, 1964; to John Clellon Holmes, July 21, 1965; to Phil Whalen, Jan. 10, 1965; to Carolyn Cassady, Aug. 16, 1963; to Philip Whalen, May 9, 1963; to Stanley Twardowicz, Oct. 5, 1964.

JK on tape: untranscribed reel from the Northport Public Library interview; party at JK's house, Aug. 26, 1964.

JK's work: *Vanity of Duluoz.*

Books and articles: *Soundings East: Kerouac Issue;* "Jack Kerouac at Northport"; Val Duncan, "Kerouac Revisited" (interview with JK), *Newsday,* July 18, 1964; Mike McGrady, "Beat Even in Northport," *Newsday,* April 19, 1973.

Author's interviews: with Joan Roberts, July 1977; with Richard Barnetz, Sept. 1978; with Stanley Twardowicz, July 1977, May 1978, and Sept. 1978; with Ed White, Oct. 1977; with Thomas Livornese, Sept. 1978; with Tony Sampas, Aug. 1978; with Matsumi Kanemitsu, Oct. 1978; with Herbert Huncke, Sept. 1978; with Allen Ginsberg, May 1978; with Helen Elliott, May 1978; with Mike McGrady, Sept. 1978.

FOURTEEN: JACK'S LAST TAPE

1.

Letters of JK: to Ed White, Oct. 16, 1964; to Philip Whalen, Jan. 10, 1965; to John Clellon Holmes, Oct. 16, 1964; to Lois and Jacques Beckwith, June 29, 1965; July 21, 1965; to Neal Cassady, Dec. 4, 1965; to Stanley Twardowicz, Oct. 5, 1964; to Stanley and Anne Twardowicz, Nov. 5, 1964; to Seymour Krim, Feb. 13, 1965; to Jacques and Lois Beckwith, May 11, 1965; to John Clellon Holmes, July 21, 1965; to Lucien Carr, June 2, 1965; to Al Gelpi, April 5, 1964; to Philip Whalen, Nov. 18, 1963; to Al Gelpi, June 22, 1965.

Other letters: Gabrielle Kerouac to Stanley and Anne Twardowicz, Oct. 13, 1964; Neal Cassady to JK (included in Allen Ginsberg to JK), Oct. 1, 1965; Gabrielle Kerouac to Stanley and Anne Twardowicz, Jan. 20, 1965.

JK's work: *Satori in Paris,* N.Y., 1966.

Books and articles: *The Norton Anthology of English Literature,* Vol. 1, N.Y., 1968; Larry Vickers, memoir of JK published in *Father Joe's Handy Homilies,* June 1970; Carl Adkins, "Jack Kerouac: Off the Road for Good," *The Kerouac Companion* (unpublished), John Montgomery, ed., 1977; Ben Brown, "The

Last of the Great Hang-Out Bars," *The Bay Area Chronicle*, Tampa, April 1976; Saul Maloff, "A Line Must Be Drawn," *New York Times Book Review*, May 2, 1965; Charles Poore, "Books of the Times: An Elegy for the Beat Syndicate of Writers," *New York Times*, May 4, 1965; Nelson Algren, "His Ice-Cream Cone Runneth Over," *Book Week*, May 16, 1965; Robert Mazzocco, "Our Gang," *The New York Review of Books*, May 20, 1965; Dan Wakefield, "Jack Kerouac Comes Home," *The Atlantic*, Vol. 216 (July 1965).

Author's interviews: with Stanley Twardowicz, May 1978; with Cliff Anderson, May 1978; with Bill Alexander, Aug. 1979; with Paul Blake, Jr., Oct. 1978; with Carolyn Cassady, Sept. 1977; with Wilfred Bertrand, May 1978; with Helen Elliott, May 1978; with Gerard Wagner, May 1978; with Matsumi Kanemitsu, Oct. 1978; with Howard Hart, June 1978.

Tapes: Stella Sampas Kerouac, interviewed by Dr. Dan DeSole, Nov. 1969—tape courtesy of Dr. Dan DeSole.

308. Jack Kerouac, *Satori in Paris* (New York: Grove Press, Black Cat paperback ed., 1966), p. 111.

2.

Letters of JK: to John Clellon Holmes, Feb. 18, 1966; Sept. 18, 1965; Dec. 23, 1965; to Dr. Dan DeSole, March 31, 1969; to Al Gelpi, Jan. 14, 1966.

JK on tape: "The Midnight Ghost."

Books, articles, journals, and notes: Holmes, *Visitor: Jack Kerouac in Old Saybrook*; Vickers, memoir of JK; Brown, "The Last of the Great Hang-Out Bars"; Adkins, "Jack Kerouac: Off the Road for Good"; Holmes, "Journal," entry Nov. 15, 1965 (printed in *Visitor: Jack Kerouac in Old Saybrook*); notes of JK in conversation with several friends of Tony Sampas, Nov. 1965, taken down by Philip Singer.

Author's interviews and correspondence: with Cliff Anderson, May 1978; with Bill Alexander, Aug. 1979; with Gerard Wagner, May 1978; with Dr. Dan DeSole, May 1978, and July 1978; with Paul Blake, Jr., Oct. 1978; from Dianne Randall, Oct. 26, 1979; with Howard Hart, June 1978; with John Clellon Holmes, Aug. 1978; with Phil Singer, June 1978; with Tony Sampas, May 1978; with Al Gelpi, Oct. 1977.

309. The preceding conversation was taken down at the time by Tony Sampas' friend Phil Singer. A copy of Singer's notes was provided by Dan DeSole.

3.

Letters of JK: to John Clellon Holmes, Aug. 3, 1966; to Stanley Twardowicz, Aug. 12, 1965; to Ed White, Oct. 2, 1965; to Seymour Krim, April 20, 1965; to John Clellon Holmes, May 12, 1966; to Al Gelpi, May 18, 1966; to Ed White, April 28, 1966; to John Clellon Holmes, Feb. 18, 1966; March 21, 1966; to Stanley Twardowicz, Jan. 17, 1965; to Stanley and Anne Twardowicz, May 22, 1965; to Dr. Dan SeSole, May 12, 1966; Aug. 25, 1966; to Cliff Anderson, Sept. 18, 1966; to Dr. Dan DeSole, Sept. 18, 1966.

Books and articles: Charters, *Kerouac: A Biography*; Joe David Bellamy, "Jack Kerouac's Last Years: An Interview with Robert Boles," *Falcon*, Summer 1970; Beaulieu, "My Boyhood Years with Jack Kerouac."

Author's interviews: with Fernanda Pivano, July 1978; with Helen Weaver, Aug. 1978; with Helen Elliott, May 1978; with Tony Sampas, Aug. 1978; with Cliff Anderson, May 1978; with Dr. Dan DeSole, May 1978; with Peter Orlovsky, Aug. 1977; with Allen Ginsberg, May 1978; with Robert Creeley, July 1978; with Robert Miller, Oct. 1978.

Lectures: Ginsberg, "Literary History of the Beat Generation."

742 · M E M O R Y B A B E

4.

Letters of JK: to Stanley Twardowicz, Dec. 18, 1966; to John Clellon Holmes, May 22, 1967; Jan. 27, 1967; March 30, 1967.

Articles: Frank Falacci, "Lowell Girl Wed to Jack Kerouac," *Boston Sunday Herald*, Nov. 20, 1966; Bellamy, "Jack Kerouac's Last Years"; Foye, "A Lowellian Remembers Kerouac"; Berrigan, "The Art of Fiction XLI: Jack Kerouac."

Author's interviews: with Gregory McDonald, May 1978; with Helen Elliott, May 1978; with Paul Blake, Jr., Oct. 1978; with Dr. Dan DeSole, May 1978, and July 1978; with Manuel "Chief" Nobriga, Aug. 1978; with Joseph Chaput, May 1978, and Aug. 1978; with Officer John Mahoney, Aug. 1978; with Raymond Foye, June 1978; with James O'Dea, Oct. 1978; with Albert "Pancho" Gonzales, Aug. 1978; with William Koumantzelis, Aug. 1977, May 1978, and Aug. 1978; with George Poirier, Aug. 1978; with Manny Bello, Aug. 1978; with Peter Dizoglio, Aug. 1978; with Phyllis Nobriga, Aug. 1978; with Tony Sampas, Aug. 1978; with numerous Lowell bartenders, barmaids, and their clientele, May 1978, and Aug. 1978.

Lectures: Ginsberg, "Literary History of the Beat Generation."

310. Manny Bello in our interview, Aug. 1978; and an unidentified former bartender at Nicky's in our interview, May 1978.

5.

Letters of JK: to John Clellon Holmes, May 22, 1967; to Allen Ginsberg, Aug. 19, 1955.

JK's work: *Vanity of Duluoz.*

Lectures: Ginsberg, "Literary History of the Beat Generation."

6.

Letters of JK: to John Clellon Holmes, May 22, 1967; to G.J. Apostolos, May 26, 1967; to Charles E. Jarvis, July 21, 1967.

JK on tape: JK at a Christmas party at the house of Manuel Nobriga, recorded by Manuel Nobriga.

Books and articles: Jarvis, *Visions of Kerouac*; Cook, *The Beat Generation*; Beaulieu, *Jack Kerouac: a chicken-essay.*

Author's interviews: with Officer John Mahoney, Aug. 1978; with Gregory McDonald, May 1978; with Helen Elliott, May 1978; with Doris Kerouac, May 1978; with Joseph Chaput, May 1978, and Aug. 1978; with Peter Dizoglio, Aug. 1978; with Albert "Pancho" Gonzales, Aug. 1978; with Stanley Twardowicz, July 1977, and Sept. 1978; with Allen Ginsberg, May 1978; with Tony Sampas Aug. 1978; with Paul Dunnigan, Aug. 1978; with Victor-Lévy Beaulieu, April 1978; with Charles E. Jarvis, May 1978; with Ted Berrigan, May 1978; with Aram Saroyan, Oct. 1977, and Sept. 1979; with Duncan McNaughton, Oct. 1977; with Jan Kerouac, June 1978, and June 1979; with Manuel "Chief" Nobriga, Aug. 1978; with Phyllis Nobriga, Aug. 1978; with numerous patrons of the bars of Lowell, May 1978, and Aug. 1978.

Other tapes: Stella Sampas Kerouac, interviewed by Dr. Dan DeSole.

311. Albert "Pancho" Gonzales in our interview, Aug. 1978; and Peter Dizoglio in our interview, May 1978.

312. At the request of one of his drinking buddies, Kerouac wrote this pronouncement on a scrap of paper, which is still in that individual's possession.

7.

Letters of JK: to Ed White, April 21, 1968; to Carolyn Cassady, n.d.; to Allen

Ginsberg, June 4, 1968; to John Clellon Holmes, April 1, 1969; March 1, 1969; to Joseph Chaput, Nov. 15, 1968; to Ed White, May 12, 1969; to Dr. Dan DeSole, March 31, 1969.
Other letters: Stella Kerouac to Dan and Gloria DeSole, Aug. 15, 1968; Stella Kerouac to Dr. Dan DeSole, n.d.
JK on tape: untranscribed reel from the Northport Public Library interview.
Books and articles: Cook, *The Beat Generation*; Gifford and Lee, *Jack's Book*; "Sanity of Kerouac" (review of *Vanity of Duluoz*), *Time*, Feb. 23, 1968; Thomas Lask, "Books of the Times: Road to Nowhere" (review of *Vanity of Duluoz*), *New York Times*, Feb. 17, 1968; Gregory McDonald, "Off the Road . . . the Celtic Twilight of Jack Kerouac," *Boston Sunday Globe*, Aug. 11, 1968; Gregory McDonald, "Rap-up; 'I knew Jack Kerouac'," *Boston Sunday Globe*, Oct. 26, 1969; Peter Anastas, "Reflections of Kerouac lover: Of the time the author of *On the Road* came to Gloucester," *North Shore '74* (weekend magazine supplement of Essex County Newspapers, Inc.), Oct. 5, 1974; Berrigan, "The Art of Fiction XLI: Jack Kerouac"; Jack McClintock, "Jack Kerouac is Alive and Not-So-Well in St. Petersburg," *Miami Tropic*, Oct. 12, 1969.
Author's interviews and correspondence: with Gregory McDonald, May 1978; with Carolyn Cassady, Oct. 1977, and June 1978; from Carolyn Cassady, Nov. 1977; with Paul Blake, Jr., Oct. 1978; with James Droney, Aug. 1978; with John Delamus, May 1978; with Tony Sampas, Aug. 1978; with John Sampas, May 1978; with Dr. Dan DeSole, May 1978; from George Butterick, March 16, 1978; with Joseph Chaput, May 1978; with Doris Kerouac, May 1978; with William Koumantzelis, Aug. 1977, and Aug. 1978; with Allen Ginsberg, May 1978; with Helen Elliott, May 1978; with Bill Alexander, Aug. 1979; with Al Hinkle, Oct. 1977; with James Curtis, Aug. 1977.
Other tapes: Stella Sampas Kerouac, interviewed by Dr. Dan DeSole.

8.
JK on tape: JK singing with radio, in his room, in St. Petersburg, Florida, 1969, recorded by JK—tape courtesy of Dr. Dan DeSole.

9.
Letters of JK: to Frankie Edith Parker Kerouac, Sept. 20, 1969; Sept. 8, 1969; Sept. 21, 1969.
JK's work: *Pic*, N.Y., 1971; "Man, Am I the Grandaddy-o of the Hippies," (syndicated nationally under the title "After Me, the Deluge"), *Miami Tropic*, Oct. 12, 1969.
Books, articles, and documents: Gifford and Lee, *Jack's Book*; Richard Hill, "Jack Kerouac: Sad in the Sixties," *Knight*, Vol. 8 (Sept., 1970); McClintock, "Jack Kerouac is Alive and Not-So-Well"; "The Last Will and Testament of Jean Kerouac, A/K/A Jack Kerouac," Sept. 4, 1969, filed in St. Petersburg, Fla.
Author's interviews: with "Jaki," July 1979; with Frankie Edith Parker Kerouac, Oct. 1978; with Cliff Anderson, May 1978; with Tony Sampas, Aug. 1978; with William Koumantzelis, Aug. 1978.
Tapes: Stella Sampas Kerouac, interviewed by Dr. Dan DeSole.
313. Kerouac's logic in not defending himself was related in his letter to Frankie Edith Parker, Sept. 8, 1969.

EPILOGUE
Letters: Allen Ginsberg to Ed White, Dec. 10, 1969.
Articles: Beaulieu, "My Boyhood Years with Jack Kerouac"; "Jack Kerouac

Eulogized as Exponent of Beatitudes," *Lowell Sun,* Oct. 26, 1969; Eric Ehrmann and Stephen Davis, "There Is Really Nothing Inside," *Rolling Stone,* Nov. 29, 1969.

Author's interviews: with Frankie Edith Parker Kerouac, Oct. 1978; with Charlotte Parker, Oct. 1978; with William Koumantzelis, Aug. 1977; with Fr. Armand Morissette, May 1978.

INDEX

abstract expressionism, 423-24
    See also indiv. painters
Ace Books, 354, 357, 367, 368, 369,
    370, 391, 428, 440
Adamakis, Pete, 59, 60, 61, 77
Adams, J. Donald, 576
Adams, Joan Vollmer, 107, 109, 110,
    135, 153, 199, 258, 355, 368,
    442
Adams, John, 77
Adams, Walter, 296
Aeschylus, 76, 134
Algren, Nelson, 344, 559
Allen, Don, 528, 543, 545, 548, 550
Allen, Steve, 53, 565, 603
Ameche, Don, 56
Amis, Kingsley, 578
Amram, David, 566
Anderson, Cliff, 656
Anderson, Sherwood, 211
Andrews Sisters, 85
Angulo, Gui de, 528
Ansen, Alan, 219, 247-48, 356, 400,
    456, 464, 555
Anslinger, Harry J., 121
anti-Semitism, 105, 118, 156, 415,
    555, 582, 642
Anton, Harold, 455
Apollo Theater, 60, 65
Apostolos, George J., 34, 35, 39, 40,
    41-42, 43, 44, 45, 49, 51-52,
    54, 55, 57, 64, 72, 73, 74, 76,
    78-81, 91-92, 96, 97, 99, 101,
    123-24, 282, 431, 468, 635, 698
Archambault Funeral Home, 26
Army football team, 76, 101, 102
Arnold, Matthew, "Dover Beach," 485
Aronowitz, Al, 587

"Arrows" (children's gang), 94
Artaud, Antonin, 284
Arthur, Gavin, 603
Associated Press, 245
Atkinson, Charles, 87
Atlantic, The, 556
Auden, W. H., 219
Avakian, Albert, 66, 488
Avakian, George, 66
Avon Books, 588, 607

Baker, Carlos, 556
Baker Jenny, 493
Baldwin, James, 468
Balzac, Honoré de, 136, 501
    Comédie Humaine, La, 552
Bantam Books, 428
Barnes, Djuna, 455
    Nightwood, 408
Barth, John, 393
Baruch, André, 42
Basie, Count, 65-66
Battles, Cliff, 76
Baudelaire, Charles, 120, 155, 442
Baudelaireans. *See* Black Priests
Bauer, Harry, 77
Bean, Jacob, 213
"Beansey," 72, 73
beat, "beatness," 70, 109
    "beatific" as origin of, 468
Beat Generation, 194, 252, 423,
    559-60, 574, 602
    literature of, 293
    See also indiv. members
Beat Scene, The (anthology), 606
Beauchamp, Robert, 580

Beaulieu, Joseph Henry ("Scotty"), 34, 39, 40, 41, 42, 43, 44, 46, 49, 51, 57, 64, 73, 78-79, 81, 91-92, 431, 636, 698

Beaulieu, Julian, 49

bebop, 112, 125, 365

  See also indiv. performers

Beckett, Samuel, 376

Beckwith, Jacques, 591

Beebe, Lucius, 281

Beethoven, Ludwig van, 134

  Fifth Symphony, 102

Beiderbecke, Bix, 66

Beland, Pauline, 97

Belson, Jordan, 469

Benjamin, Herb, 246

Berigan, Bunny, 91

Berle, Milton, 373

Bernier, Pierre François, 22

Bernier, Clémentine. *See* Kirouack, Clémentine Bernier

Berrigan, Ted, 682

Bertrand, Freddy, 34, 41, 42, 49, 51, 64, 73, 74, 78, 81

Billerica News, 37, 45

Birdland, 207, 251

Biron, Louis, 23, 24

Bismarck (German battleship), 107

Black Mountain Review, 520

Black Priests, 156

Blaine, Nell, 219, 559

Blaise, Jay, 604

Blake, William, 68, 134, 245, 283, 353, 400, 406, 443

  Marriage of Heaven and Hell, The, 353

  "Sick Rose, The," 347, 403

  "Tyger, The," 347

Blazon, Albert, 51

Bleistein (fictional name for Ginsberg), 144

Blossoms, Robert, 589

Blumenkrantz, Shel, 63

Bobbs-Merrill, 369

Boccaccio, Giovanni, *Decameron, The*, 283

Bogart, Humphrey, 112

Boles, Robert, 668

Bolkonsky, Andrey, 58

Bonaparte, Napoleon, 22

bop. *See* Bebop

Boston College, 48, 56, 60, 74, 76

Bourgeois, Paul, 632, 639

Bow, Clara, 69

Bowles, Paul, 589

Brandeis University, 578

Brando, Marlon, 559, 620

Brierly, Justin, 145, 185, 280, 300, 327, 416

Brodie, Iris, 454

Brooklyn Bridge, 67, 77, 101

Brooks, Eugene, 388, 471, 620

Brown University football team, 101

Broyard, Anatole, 559

Bruce, Lenny, 664

Buckley, William F., Jr., 67, 77, 690-91

Buddha, 22, 457-58

  as influence on Kerouac, 26, 451, 457-59, 490, 494-95, 531

Bunin, Ivan, *Gentleman from San Francisco, The*, 87

Bunyan, John, *Pilgrim's Progress*, 272

Burford, Beverly, 183, 191, 222, 276, 321, 416, 456, 463, 519

Burford, Bob, 191, 256, 262, 464, 467, 468

Burnett, David, 474

Burroughs, William S., 118-20, 121, 151, 212, 324, 326, 389, 390, 414, 425, 428-29, 473-74

  And the Hippos Were Boiled in Their Tanks, or I Wish I Were You (with Kerouac), 143, 162, 166, 370-71, 599

  "Burroughs on Earth," 469-70

  changes in, 629

  and Ginsberg, as lovers, 466-67

  Junkie, 353-54, 370, 428, 465, 467

  Kerouac and, 118-19, 120, 126, 134-35, 136-37, 138, 389,

390-91, 414, 419, 422, 427, 429, 444, 465-66, 475, 544
Kerouac's "education" by, 134-35, 136
lifestyle of, 199, 258, 268
literary technique of, 156
murder of Joan Adams by, 355
Naked Lunch, 473, 544
problems of, 425
psychoanalysis of, 138
"Twilight's Last Gleaming," 119
underworld connections of, 136, 148, 153, 256
Yage Letters, The, 444
Byron (Gordon, George), 58, 71, 72

Caen, Herb, 574
Calloway, Cab, 42
Canadian Shore Patrol, 101
Cannastra, Bill, 214, 218, 220, 251, 330-32, 350, 427
Capote, Truman, 423, 588, 690-91
Carlyle, Thomas, 352, 381
Carnegie Hall, 67
Carney, Mary, 52-53, 54-55, 56, 64, 69-70, 270, 420, 426, 431, 468, 636
Carr, Lucien, 114-15, 117, 425, 470, 599, 630
    career of, 185, 226, 246, 320, 369, 370, 558
    imprisonment of, 132
    Kerouac and, 114-15, 120-26, 127-28, 129, 410, 427, 442, 443, 464
    manslaughter of Kammerer by, 127-28
    release of, 172
Carrufel (high school football player), 41, 61, 102
Cassady, Carolyn Robinson, 191, 192, 195, 202, 242-43, 287-88, 354, 359, 367
    children of, 356, 360, 411-12, 417, 418, 460
    divorce of, from Cassady, 322, 646

Kerouac's relationship with, 195, 360, 361-64, 411, 417, 425, 426, 429, 440, 617
    marriage of, to Cassady, 212
Cassady, LuAnne, 172-73, 243, 553
    Kerouac's relationship with, 176, 247, 251, 254, 259, 269
Cassady, Neal, 146, 177, 242-43, 439, 440, 469, 612
    accident of, 440
    death of, 686
    degeneration of, 553, 568
    divorce of, from Carolyn, 322, 646
    drug use by, 653
    family abandoned by, 288
    First Third, The, 329
    Ginsberg and, 173, 192, 193, 248
    "Great Sex Letter, The," 183
    Holmes and, 249
    "Joan Anderson" letter, 336-38
    Kerouac and, 174, 176, 178, 179, 185-86, 197, 202, 238, 239, 245, 250, 251, 259, 260-61, 287, 289-90, 292, 322, 329, 337, 354, 367, 411-12, 417, 418, 422, 425, 426, 429, 452-53, 457, 460, 466, 473, 497, 525, 531, 612, 615, 629, 657
    lifestyle of, 290-91
    LuAnne and, 172-73, 177
    marriage of, to Carolyn Robinson, 212
    in New York, 172-73, 177
    "novelette" letter of, 336
    personality of, 174-75, 239
    in prison, 569, 586
    problems of, 203, 286-87, 289-90, 292, 328, 330, 341, 466, 469
    sexual prowess of, 173-75
    sexual sadism of, 363
    sex life of, 191, 192
    "soul" of, 337
    as writer, 186, 202, 203, 239-40
Catholic Church:

influence of, on French Canadians, 15, 24-25

influence of, on Kerouac, 49, 52, 54, 86, 205, 464, 490

Catholic Youth Organization programs, 94-95

Cayce, Edgar, 457, 466

Céline, Louis-Ferdinand, 134, 143, 205, 211, 491, 545

   Death on the Installment Plan, 283, 376-77

Chamberlain, Neville, 58

Chandler, Billy, 34, 35, 79

Chaput, Joe, 672, 684, 690

Charters, Anne, 500

Chase, Ginger, 427, 444, 467

Chase, Hal, 135, 170, 190, 209, 283, 319, 419, 444

   Kerouac's admiration of, 137, 144-48, 442

   Kerouac's alienation of, 153, 204, 276

S.S. *Chatham*, 100

"Chesterfield Hour, The," 85

Chicago Review, The, 581

Chiungos, Duke, 43, 54

Chomsky, Noam, 687

CIA, 71

Ciardi, John, 429, 599, 608

Citizen Kane, 92

City Lights Bookstore, 469, 552

Civilian Conservation Corps, 76

Clayton, Buck, 65

Cleophus, 298

C.M.A.C. (sports club), 28, 74

Cocteau, Jean:

   Blood of the Poet, The, 134

   Opium, 134

Coffey, Peggy, 53, 54, 55, 56, 85-86, 87, 94, 97

Cohn, Art, 574

Colbert, Stanley, 453

Coleridge, Samuel Taylor, 405

Columbia College, 54, 56, 75-76, 87, 88, 89, 90, 96, 101, 102, 139

football team, 56, 61, 64, 75, 76, 77-78, 87, 88, 89-90, 101, 102

Communists, Communist Party, 115, 463

Condon, Eddie, 121

Connors, Charlie, 24

Conrad, Joseph, 108

Constantinides, George, 71, 82-83, 102

Cook, Bruce, 687

Corso, Gregory, 358, 415-16, 441, 444-45, 455, 460, 464, 470, 475, 477, 531, 533, 534, 541, 547, 568, 577, 631, 646

   analysis of Kerouac by, 555, 644

   Gasoline, 561

   Ginsberg and, 415

   This Hungup Age, 475

   Vestal Lady on Brattle, The, 475

Costello, Tom, 93

Cotton Club, 112

Courier-Citizen, 49, 55

Coward-McCann, 658

Cowley, Malcolm, 427, 440, 441, 453, 465, 472, 474, 475-76, 480, 510

   Literary Situation, The, 465, 467

Crabtree, Bill, 648, 683

Crane, Hart, 353

   Collected Poems, 134

Crawford, Joan, 364

Creeley, Robert, 460, 520-22, 599

Crisp, Quentin, 397

Crosby, Bing, 50

Crosby, Bob, 73

Cru, Henri, 88-89, 108, 112, 187, 198, 288, 340, 353, 357-58, 359, 360, 464, 475, 572

Cudworth, Jim, 45, 55, 133

Curtis, James, 637

Dabilis, Billy, 94, 95, 97-99

Dali, Salvador, 539-40

Daly, Jack, 289

Darwin, Charles, 434

Dastou, George, 72, 73, 74, 84, 468

Dastous, Edmund, 37
Davila, Jorge, 426-27, 456, 464
Davis, Miles, 207
Dawson, Fielding, 579
Dean, Daffy, 41
Dean, Dizzy, 41
"Deep Purple," 51
de Kooning, Willem, 219, 423, 454,
    609
de Maupassant, Guy, 72
Dempsey, David, 428, 556, 588, 599
Dempsey, Jack, 59
Denby, Edwin, 219
Depression, 70, 77, 455
Descheneaux, Emil, 75
DesJardins (store owner), 34-35
De Sole, Danny, 667
de Tocqueville, Alexis, 97
Deutsch, André, 544, 548
Diamond, David, 228
Dickens, Charles, 373
Dickinson, Emily, 51, 68, 353, 412
Dinneen, Miss (English teacher), 32
Dionne, "Scoopy," 23, 31, 37, 44-45
"Dirty Marilyn," 73-74
Dodd, Mead, 474
Doner, Ephraim, 615
Donlin, Bob, 493, 525, 532
Donohue, Eddie, 48
S.S. Dorchester, 99-100, 101
Dorn, Ed, 525
Dorsey, Jimmy, 85
Dorsey, Tommy, 53, 85
Dos Passos, John, 87, 496
    Manhattan Transfer, 79
    U.S.A., 79, 344, 345, 382
Dostoyevsky, Fyodor, 354
    Brothers Karamazov, The, 148,
        355, 502-03
    Friend of the Family, The, 352
    Idiot, The, 126
    Notes from the Underground, 92,
        372, 453
Dodd & Ostreicher, 28
Downey, Hugh, 301
Doyle, Arthur Conan, 63

Dreiser, Theodore, American
    Tragedy, An, 469
Drescher, "Fritz," 43, 47, 48, 672
Droney, James, 301, 688
Ducasse (fictional name of Kerouac),
    144
Duke University, 49
Duncan, Robert, 385, 460, 469
Duncan, Val, 653
Du Peru, Peter, 469, 528
Durgin, Russell, 213
Dutton (Apostolos's roommate), 96
Dutton, E.P., 468, 472

Eager, Allen, 470
Eastham, Steve, 57
Eberhart, Richard, 528
Eberle, Bob, 42, 73
Eberle, Ray, 42, 73
Eckstine, Billy, 112
Edison, Harry "Sweets," 65
Einstein, Albert, 403, 447
Eisenhower, Dwight D., 475
Eisner, Joan, 342
Ellington, Duke, 66
Elliott, Helen, 342, 534, 605
Elliott, Rambling Jack, 456, 464
Ellis, Al, 697
Encyclopedia Britannica, 50, 94, 367
Eno, Arthur Louis, 31-32
Epstein, Jason, 354
Escapade, 581
Esoteric Records, 356, 621
Esquire, 552-53, 559
L'Etoile, 23, 24, 48
Evans, Herschel, 65
Evergreen Review, 528, 533, 541, 544,
    550, 573
Everitt, Rae, 225, 236, 349, 352, 359,
    368, 369
Eyre and Spottiswoode, 300

Fair Play for Cuba Committee, 621
Fantasia, 112

Farrar, Straus, and Cudahy, 633

Farrell, James T., 112, 344

Faulkner, William, 353, 427, 445

Faye, Alice, 60

Feminella, Frank, 588, 594

Ferlinghetti, Lawrence, 469, 493, 533, 564, 510-11, 552, 612

Ferron, Marie-Rose, 26

Fields, W. C., 28, 373, 380, 397, 400, 407, 426, 559

Firing Line, 690-91

Fitzgerald, F. Scott, 63

Fitzgerald, Jack, 102, 113, 152, 165, 235, 293, 298, 463-64

"Five Aces," 74

Flaubert, Gustave, *Madame Bovary*, 353

Flower Children, 687

Flynn, Errol, 60

Focus, 24

Forst, Miles, 609

Fouché, Eddie, 74

Fournier, Michel, Jr., 34, 38, 209

Fournier, Michel, Sr., 71

Fox, Mardou, 441-46, 452, 464, 541, 565

Fox and Hound, 80

Franco, Bea, 200, 235

Franco-American Orphanage, 26, 123

Frank, Robert, 559, 572, 582, 605

Frankel, Bill, 213, 218

Freilicher, Jane, 219

French Canadians, as "white Negroes," 15-16

Freud, Sigmund, 134

Fuck You, 690

Furey, Ralph, 57, 62, 75, 76

Gabin, Jean, 60, 77, 112

Gabler, Hedda, 58

Gaddis, William, 445

Gaillard, Slim, 261, 347

Gallimard (French publisher), 562

Galsworthy, John, *Forsyte Saga, The*, 107

Garbo, Greta, 58

Garfield, John, 113

Garfinkel, Merrill, 63

Garin, Leo, 559

Garon, Paul, *Blues and the Poetic Spirit*, 461

Garver, Bill, 153, 425, 476, 554

Gauguin, Paul, 59

Gauthier, Armand, 28, 30

Gelpi, Al, 649, 667

Gelpi, Don, *Experiencing God*, 667

Genet, Jean, 419, 491, 544, 545

U.S.S. *George Weems*, 107-8, 109

Gershwin, George, 59

Gershwin, Ira, 59

Gide, André, 211

Gibson, Jacky, 615

Gilbert, Eddy, 63

Gillespie, Dizzy, 65, 112, 124, 697

Gilmore, (math professor), 60

Ginsberg, Allen, 74, 115-17, 133, 245-46, 293, 425, 443, 460, 569-70, 698

    arrest of, 268

    Blakean poems of, 245

    Bleistein as fictional name of, 144

    Book of Doldrums, 210, 211

    Buddhism, interest in, 450-51

    Burroughs's analysis of, 138

    Burroughs and, as lovers, 466-67

    Cassady and, 173, 192, 248

    at Columbia, 140-41

    in Columbia Psychiatric Institute, 284

    Corso and, 358

    creative relationship to Kerouac and Cassady of, 193

    Denver Doldrums, 193

    Doctor Sax: reaction to, 422

    Empty Mirror, 369

    film interest of, 469-70

    heterosexual experiences of, 328

    Holmes and, 223

    as homosexual, 117, 140, 141, 156, 242, 248, 415, 442, 466-67

    Howl, 475, 480, 492, 533, 552

Kerouac and, 134, 137-38, 140, 142, 156-58, 185, 210-12, 241, 242, 250, 370, 422, 440, 442, 444, 465, 472, 473-74, 475, 491, 514, 516, 520, 546, 657, 690

as Kerouac's agent, 440-41

Kerouac's parents and, 158-59

loneliness of, 212-13, 245

"masterpiece" letter of, 465

mystique of, 209-10

On the Road and, 349

paranoia attacks of, 233

political ideas of, 574, 603

problems of, 227, 230, 245-46

recognition of, 492

as reporter, 352

respectability of, 428, 593

"River Street Blues," 370

Town and the City, The, and, 302

underworld connections of, 148

"Wire to the Crack of Doom," 293-94

Ginsberg, Louis, 116, 140, 141, 246

Gioscia, Victor, 465, 594, 596-97

Giroux, Robert, 250, 267, 281, 294, 319, 332, 349, 414, 465, 472, 474, 633

Glassman, Johnny, 77

Glassman, Joyce, 543, 558, 560, 566

Globus, Rudo, 63

Gnosticism, 139

Goddard, Dwight, *Buddhist Bible, A,* 457-59

Goethe, Johann Wolfgang von, 50, 75, 134, 392

Faust, 94, 392-93

Gold, Herbert, 561, 636

Goodman, Paul, 218

Gordon, Max, 565

Gordon, Peter, 62-63, 64, 69

Gorky, Maxim, 353

Gould, Stanley, 441, 442, 443, 464, 475

Governali, Paul, 90

Grande Illusion, La, 397

Granz, Norman, 565

Gray, Thomas, "Elegy Written in a Country Churchyard," 88

Green Lantern, The, 33

Grieg, Mike, 541

Grosz, George, 114

group analysis, charades as form of, 138

Grove Press, 528, 559, 565, 570, 571, 588, 590, 667

Guthrie, Woody, 456

Hall, Leonard, 469

Hammond, John, 217

Handel, Georg Friedrich, 77

Hansen, Diana, 292

Harcourt, Brace, 232, 267, 349, 368, 415, 474

Hardy, Thomas, 71

Harrington, Alan, 223, 260

Harris, Bill, 167

Hart, Howard, 566

Harvard Classics, 50

Harvard University Press, 474

Haverty, Joan. *See* Kerouac, Joan Haverty

Hawkes (Columbia dean), 76

Hawkins, Coleman, 125

Hawthorne, Nathaniel, 353

Marble Faun, The, 497

Scarlet Letter, The, 403

Hemingway, Ernest, 63, 71, 91, 168, 373, 556

"Clean, Well-Lighted Place, A," 68

For Whom the Bell Tolls, 407

"Gambler, the Nun, and the Radio, The," 68, 483

Kerouac meeting with, 112

To Have and to Have Not, 382

Henry, O., 68

Henry, Pat, 370

Herald Tribune, 61

Hewitt, Ralph, 48

Hill, Richard, 697

Hinkle, Al, 198, 242, 243, 247, 252, 256, 258, 259, 322, 359, 418, 421, 440, 468, 554, 559, 606, 692

Hinkle, Helen, 258, 259, 288, 322, 613

"hipster," 206

    See also individuals

Hitler, Adolf, 58, 87, 118

Hoffenberg, Mason, 441, 548

Hogan, William, 552

Hohnsheen, John, 213

Hollander, John, 133

Holliday, Billie, 111, 365, 372, 373, 412

Holly, Major, 538

Holmes, John Clellon, 223, 249, 282, 293, 298, 347, 348-49, 356, 399, 442, 558, 591

    "Afternoon of a Tenor Man, The," 412

    Go, 342, 369, 370, 419, 428

    Kerouac and, 223-24, 225, 236, 238, 412-14, 419, 428-29, 434, 464, 635, 664

    Nothing More to Declare, 224, 252

    on *Subterraneans*, 446

    "This is the Beat Generation," 423

Holmes, Marion, 321, 350, 412

Holmes, Sherlock, 77, 347, 373

Homer:

    Iliad, 76

    Odyssey, 76

homosexuals, homosexuality. *See* individuals

Hopkins, Gerard Manley, "Windhover, The," 501

Hopkins, Miriam, 60

Horace, 76

Horace Mann Preparatory School, 56, 57, 58, 59, 61-62, 64, 65, 66, 68, 70, 77, 78, 131, 415, 677

    reunion, 184

Horace Mann Quarterly, 66

Horace Mann Record, 66

Horton, Robert, 22

Houde, Mike, 33, 34, 35, 40

Houde, Ninip, 35, 394

Houde, Pete, 33, 34, 35, 40

Hubbard, William Holmes ("Big Slim"), 104-5, 106, 107

Hugo, Victor, 50

    Les Miserables, 58

Huncke, Herbert, 136, 149, 283, 284, 425, 601

Huxley, Aldous, 134

Ibsen, Henrik, *Hedda Gabler*, 58

L'Impartial, 23

Ireland, as Kerouac's ancestral home, 108

Isolde, 21

Ives, Burl, 112

IWW, 496

Jackson, Chubby, 167, 206

Jackson, Natalie, 469, 491, 498-99

Jackson, Phyllis, 419, 427, 428

Jackson, Sheila, 469

Jackson, Willie, 275

Jackson, Willis, 206

James, Harry, 66

James, Henry, 535

    Ambassadors, The, 353

    Daisy Miller, 264

Jarrell, Randall, 540

Jarvis, Charles, 637, 684

jazz, 298, 360

    See also indiv. performers

Jeannie (girlfriend), 97

Jeffries, Frank "Buck," 262, 280, 321

Jennison, Keith, 474

Jesus, 26, 54, 68, 86

    as image, 68, 373

Jews, 62, 474

    See also Anti-Semitism

Job: Book of, 94

Johnson, Samuel, 56, 106

"Jolly Fourteen" (club), 28, 34

Jones, Granville H., 623

Jones, Jo, 66

Jouvet, Louis, 60, 77

Joyce, James, 33, 108, 365-66, 376, 380

   Finnegans Wake, 134, 365, 377-78, 423, 552

   Portrait of the Artist as a Young Man, 79, 87

   Ulysses, 93, 74, 365, 376, 441

Jubilee, 583

Kafka, Franz, 205

   Castle, The, 134, 408

Kallman, Chester, 219

Kammerer, David, 117, 127-28, 129

Kandel, Lenore, 613

Kanemitsu, Matsumi, 232, 579, 588, 641, 642, 643

Karenina, Anna, 58

Kaufman, Bob, 460, 525, 618

Kazin, Alfred, 226, 232, 247, 250, 253

Keady (Lowell High School coach), 43, 47, 48

Keady, "Baron," (assistant coach), 48

Keats, John, 270

Keck, Bill, 441

Kennedy, Joe, 67, 77

Kennedy, John F., 71

Kennedy, Joseph P., 97

Kent, Mona, 600

Kéroack, Caroline ("Ti Nin")(sister), 23, 27, 35, 36, 38, 55, 360, 414, 416

   children of, 351, 514-15

   death of, 656

   divorce of, 146

   as Kerouac's playmate, 29, 30

   as Kerouac's teacher, 62

   marriage of, 35, 58

   second marriage of, 276, 280, 632

Kéroack, Francis Gerard (brother), 23, 698

   as cartoonist, 35

   death of, 24, 27, 29, 36, 506, 551

   illness of, 24, 25

   influence of, on Kerouac, 25, 26, 27, 29, 30, 31, 35, 38, 44, 376-77, 395

   as "saint," 25-26

Kéroack, Gabrielle Lévesque (mother), 23, 33, 93, 414, 420

   anti-Semitism of, 582

   appearance of, 23

   as breadwinner, 34, 36, 38

   Catholicism of, 24, 117

   children of, 22-24

   courage of, 25

   drinking habits of, 643

   friends of, 28, 34, 159

   marital fights of, 24, 27, 28, 29, 80

   marriage of, 23, 106

   as Mémère, 352

   as mother, 27, 36, 37, 38, 42, 56-57, 96

   musical talent of, 106

   nagging of, 551-52

   Oedipal relationship of, with Kerouac, 27, 29, 37, 39, 56-57, 59-69, 118, 415, 416, 535, 539, 549, 551, 575, 620

   relationship of, to Kerouac's wives, 109, 132, 338, 339-40, 671, 677

   relationship of, to Kerouac's women, 581-82, 643

   self-reliance of, 36

   stroke suffered by, 669

   traditional values of, 37-38, 39, 45, 70, 75, 81, 91, 109

Kéroack, Joseph Alcide Léon (Leo) (father), 22, 47-48, 93, 120, 420, 431

   anticlericalism of, 24

   appearance of, 23, 28, 109-10

   as athlete, 23

   as athletic promoter, 30

   childlike qualities of, 28

   courage of, 25

   death of, 163

   drinking habits and problems of, 28, 37, 107

   education of, 23

as father, 27, 47, 56, 61, 77,
        96-101, 102, 163
financial problems of, 28, 30, 32,
        33, 36-37, 44-45, 50, 56-57, 58
friends of, 28, 34, 159
gambling habits and problems of,
        28, 30, 32, 33, 36, 106
as insurance salesman, 23
marital fights of, 24, 27, 28, 29, 88
marriage of, 23
personality of, 49
as printer, 23, 24, 29, 30, 31, 36,
        45, 56-57, 60, 69, 87-88, 92,
        93, 106
spelling of name changed by, 23
temper of, 32-33, 43, 47, 90
traditional values of, 45, 70, 75,
        81, 91, 102
weakness of, 28, 29, 31, 37, 58, 74
as writer/translator, 23, 24, 373
Kerouac, Frankie Edith Parker
        (Edie)(first wife), 89, 90, 102-3,
        107, 109-14, 122-23, 126, 127,
        129, 131, 132, 135, 138, 151,
        152, 165, 199, 285, 291, 415,
        561, 694, 695, 698
    abortion of, 126
    divorce of, from Kerouac, 292
    grandmother of, 89, 103, 107, 111,
        114
    marriage of, to Kerouac, 129, 132,
        138
    separation of, from Kerouac, 152,
        165, 262, 285, 292
Kerouac, Janet Michelle (daughter),
        370, 631, 646, 685
Kerouac, Jean Louis (Jack):
    abortion of son, 126
    abstract artists and, 454, 580
    adolescence of, 32-36, 37, 51-57,
        70-75
    alienation from family of, 476
    alienation from friends of, 425, 513
    America as symbol for, 68, 72,
        76-77, 92, 130, 189, 269
    anger of, 40, 41

    as anti-Communist, 463, 599
    anti-Semitism of, 415, 555, 582
    antisocial behavior of, 672
    as artist, 29, 32, 33, 34, 35, 59,
        130, 132, 134, 367, 534, 554
    as athlete, 34, 35, 38, 40, 41-43,
        45, 46-50, 51, 59, 60-62, 74,
        75, 76, 77-79, 83, 87, 88,
        89-90, 101, 102, 103, 113
    attacks by friends on, 561, 571
    aversion to public appearances of,
        603
    and "beats," 194, 602, 644, 448
    birth of, 21, 23, 24
    bop as influence on, 124-25, 134.
        See also indiv. performers
    boredom, feelings of, 96
    Buddhism as influence on, 22, 26,
        457-59, 490, 494-95, 531
    Burroughs and, 118-19, 120, 126,
        134-35, 136-37, 138, 389,
        390-91, 414, 419, 422, 427,
        429, 444, 465-66, 475, 544
    career peak of, 610
    career problems of, 619
    Carr and, 114-15, 120-26, 127-28,
        129, 410, 427, 442, 443, 464
    and Cassady, Carolyn Robinson,
        195, 360, 361-64, 411, 417,
        425, 426, 429, 440, 617
    and Cassady, LuAnne, 176, 247,
        251, 254, 259, 269
    and Cassady, Neal, 174, 176, 178,
        179, 185-86, 197, 202, 238,
        239, 245, 250, 251, 259,
        260-61, 287, 289-90, 292, 322,
        329, 337, 354, 367, 411-12,
        417, 418, 422, 425, 426, 429,
        452-53, 457, 460, 466, 473,
        497, 525, 531, 612, 615, 629,
        657
    Catholicism as influence on, 30,
        49, 53, 54, 86, 205, 464, 490
    childhood of, 25, 26-27, 28-32
    childlike qualities of, 89

class feelings of, 37, 62, 63-64, 67, 74-75, 137
cleanliness fetish of, 113, 538
clothing problems of, 275
color symbolism of, 271, 315, 401, 403, 434, 438, 478
at Columbia University, 75-78, 88, 89-90, 92, 101, 102-3, 123-24, 139, 140, 166, 295
communal farm, plans for, 269, 276
compassion of, selective use of, 599
as "Count Condu," 33-34, 35, 397, 399-400
creativity of, 59
cruelty of, 571, 630
death of, 697
death thoughts and premonitions of, 97, 99, 162, 633
depression of, 27, 29-30, 125, 137, 555, 605-06
desire for commercial success of, 419
desire for fame of, 579
dilemma of, 70
domesticity of, 126
dream interpretation, preoccupation with, 126
drinking habits and problems of, 78, 87, 88, 91, 96-97, 100, 101-2, 106, 107, 112, 115, 125, 126, 132, 171,225, 493, 536, 537, 553, 558, 561, 562, 579, 589, 592, 601, 610, 615, 640, 687
drug habits and problems of, 67, 102, 121, 125, 134, 135, 136, 148, 160, 324, 325, 366, 544, 593, 621, 626, 631
early writing, 32, 51, 66, 67-68, 70-71, 77, 84-85, 90-91, 92, 110. *See also* Writings section
eating habits, 111
emotional dependence of, 168, 421
energy of, 59, 94-95, 97, 111

English as second language for, 32, 47
failure, feelings of, 58, 70
family relationships of, 249, 682
family roots of, 21-22, 184
fantasy life of, 33-34, 35-36, 38-39, 97, 106, 107
fearfulness of, 27, 29, 30, 33, 35, 38, 39, 77
fear of madness of, 212
fear of sucide of, 473
feelings about self of, 209
film as influence on, 60, 77, 112, 128
film ideas of, 470
financial pettiness of, 541, 562, 601
financial problems of, 684, 692
Firing Line interview of, 690-91
and Fox, Mardou, 441-45, 452, 464, 541, 565
as French-Canadian and Breton, 21, 53, 59, 60, 99
French influence on, 112, 155, 325. *See also* specific authors
friends of, 208. *See also* indiv. friends
friends' attacks on, 561, 571
and friends, as misfit generation, 149
frontier philosophy of, 495
in Fruehauf factory war job, 131
funeral of, 698
future, concern with, 148
gambling of, 606
Ginsberg and, 134, 137-38, 140, 142, 156-58, 185, 210-12, 241, 242, 250, 370, 422, 440-41, 442, 444, 465, 472, 473-74, 475, 491, 514, 516, 520, 546, 657, 690
goals of, 335
Greenwich Village life of, 475
guilt feelings of, 58, 70, 137
Harvard reading by, 649
hate of deception by, 275
as hero worshipper, 31-32

heterosexual behavior of, 34, 53, 67, 68, 69, 72, 73-74, 85-86, 87, 107, 110, 114, 122, 124. *See also* indiv. women
as hipster, 207-08
Hollywood dreams of, 274
and Holmes, 223-24, 225, 236, 238,412-14, 419, 428-29, 434, 464, 635, 664
home as monastery for, 595
homosexual behavior of, 34, 102, 117, 122, 129, 142, 154-55, 220, 456, 493. *See also* indiv. men
at Horace Mann Preparatory School, 56, 57, 58, 59, 61-62, 64, 65, 66, 68, 70, 77, 78, 131, 184, 415, 677
humor of, 81, 88, 105
idealism of, 119, 137, 253
ideas on fame of, 166
identity problems of, 601-02
inferiority complex of, 51, 52, 62, 131
insecurity feelings of, 21, 33, 35, 37, 38, 46
insomnia of, 97-98
integrity of, 45, 119
intelligence of, 31, 32, 33, 44, 45, 50, 85, 104, 131-32
introvertedness of, 29, 31, 37, 38-39, 43-44, 46, 51, 84, 92, 134
jazz as influence on, 41, 42, 63, 65-66, 67, 68, 91, 101, 111-12, 121-22, 124-25. *See also* indiv. performers
job ideas of, 237
journals of, 59, 70, 77, 92, 100, 131, 677
in Kammerer murder, 128-29
lack of consideration by, 537-39
lack of help for, 689
last will and testament, 696
legal problems of, 415
literary influences on, 63, 67, 68, 71, 72, 76, 86, 87, 91, 103, 107, 120, 134, 135. *See also* indiv. authors
literary style of, 67, 68, 84, 87, 103, 125. *See also* Writings: analysis
literary themes of, 68. *See also* Writings: analysis
literary theory of truth of, 279
loneliness of, 221, 263, 264, 671
longing for love of, 660
loss of compassion of, 532
loss of friends of, 634
Lowell, feelings about, 209
Lowell, publishing reception in, 302
Lowell, trips with Edie to, 122-23
marriage, ideas of, 222, 235, 327, 539
marriages. *See* Kerouac, Frankie Edith; Kerouac, Joan Haverty; Kerouac, Stella Sampas
materialism of, 270
megalomania of, 472
memory feats and strength of, 39, 663
memory lapses of, 644
misspelling and mispronouncing of name, 21, 101
moodiness of, 98-99
money problems of, 169, 415
money uses of, 276
mortality fears of, 161
movie rights of, 573
music influence on, 41, 42, 85, 94, 111, 112, 124-25, 134, 165, 185, 207, 217, 336, 364-65, 596. *See also* indiv. composers and performers
mysticism of, 26-27. *See also* Buddhism and Catholicism subheads under this entry
National Forest Service jobs of, 514, 527-28
National Institute of Arts and Letters grant of, 474, 479

nausea attacks of, 232

need for attention of, 463, 568

nervous breakdown of, 577-78

New Criticism, precepts of, 230

at New School for Social Research, 226, 227, 232, 241, 256, 262, 263, 269, 295

New York's attraction for, 77, 84, 610

nightmares of, 278, 297

nihilism and, 149

Oedipal relationship with mother, 27, 29, 37, 39, 56-57, 59-69, 118, 415, 416, 535, 539, 549, 551, 575, 620

pacifism of, 100, 105

"panoramic awareness" of self, of, 157

paranoia of, 172, 232, 277, 411, 574, 602, 626, 692

parsimony of, 541, 601

as partygiver and partygoer, 112, 115, 293

patriotism of, 131, 463, 580, 603

philosophy of, 263, 275-76

phlebitis attacks of, 161, 352, 355, 425, 463, 465, 474, 623

physical appearance of, 192, 526

physical changes in, 632, 691

physical condition of, 645-46

poetry group, 529-30

poetry as jazz for, 460-62, 565

poetry readings of, 292, 565. *See also* Writings

political aspirations of, 299

political concerns of, 328, 463

political ideas of, 621

poverty of, 28, 31, 36-38, 45, 56, 58, 59, 62, 70, 95, 110, 114, 119, 120, 137, 138, 353

pranks of, 589-90

publicity fears of, 273-74, 603

public opinion against, 556

railroad work of, 416, 417, 439, 462

reaction to lawbreaking of, 269

reading habits, 31, 33, 50, 59, 60, 77, 94, 99, 107, 127, 131, 139

as rebel against Establishment, 37, 102, 103, 104, 111, 114, 130

recognition for, 579

redemption search of, 164

refusal to grow up of, 37

relationship with brother, 25, 26, 27, 29, 30, 31, 35, 38, 44, 376-77, 395

relationship with father, 27, 47, 56, 61, 77, 96-101, 102, 163

relationship with mother. *See* Oedipal relationship subheading

relationship with women, 67, 68, 69, 72, 91, 102, 108, 109, 164, 169, 205, 209, 225, 235, 254-55, 560-61, 599, 620, 647. *See also* indiv. women.

and religion, 154, 254, 263, 277, 278-79, 326, 465, 473, 533, 573, 594-96

repressed hostility of, 456

rhythmic prose of, 306-07

self-analysis of, 120, 160

self-confidence, damage to, 26

self-destructiveness of, 528, 568

self-love of, 21

sense of mission of, 188-89

sexual experience as adolescent, 34, 53, 85, 86, 87

sexual experience as adult, 107, 110, 111, 122

sexual experience as child, 27, 30

sexual problems of, 150, 152, 162, 221, 456, 533, 589, 647. *See also* indiv. sex partners

as "The Shadow," 33-34, 35, 52, 96, 111, 115, 125

"Shrouded Stranger" image of, 278, 280

shyness of, 38, 44, 53, 74, 85, 105

significance of confession to, 278

as the "Silver Tin Can," 35-36

social awkwardness of, 51, 52, 62, 111, 113

speech patterns of, 95, 105, 109

split values of, 53-54, 55-56, 70

spontaneous writing of, 207-08

suicidal thoughts of, 58

teachers as influence on, 32, 50-51, 60

television interviews, 683, 690-91

testing people, 664

thirst for praise of, 225

toilet habits of, 590

traditional values of, 117-18, 120, 139

at 20th Century-Fox, 341

typing habits of, 33, 110

unpleasantness of, 497

upbeat mood of, 475

vacillation period of, 254-55

and Vietnam War, 687

Village Vanguard reading, 565

violent nature of, 421, 630

visions of, 26-27

visual sense of, 148

warmth of, 115, 116, 135

West, as concept for, 144

Western "fever" of, 183-84

word games of, 111, 126

word sketches of, 357, 359

in World War II, 99-101, 103-6, 107, 131, 133-34, 137

as writer, 46, 63, 70, 79, 81, 83, 84, 87, 92, 93, 102, 107, 108, 109, 117, 118, 130, 134-35, 136, 137, 138-39, 142-43, 659

writer's blocks of, 132, 185, 576, 593, 598, 607, 646

writing methods, 147, 191, 196, 306, 453-54

writing plans of, 264, 353, 479

writing volume of, 208

as "Zagg," 41, 55, 78, 80, 123

Writings

"Address to the Italian Judge," 646

"Aftermath." *See* "Philosophy of the Beat Beneration, The"

"After Me, the Deluge," 697

"And the Hippos Were Boiled in Their Tanks, or I Wish I Were You" (with Burroughs), 143, 162, 166, 370-71, 599

Atop an Underwood, 90-91

Beat Generation, The, 559, 582, 591, 687

"Beat Night Life of New York," 585

"Beat Traveler," 586

"Beginning of Bop, The," 593

Berkeley Blues, 492

Big Sur, 631, 640, 661, 667
   analysis of, 626-29
   reviews of, 637

"Blook's Way," 293-94

Book of Blues, 460, 564, 586

Book of Dreams, 463, 513, 550, 623

"Book of Memory," 468

"Book of Prayers," 513

"Book of Sketches, A," 550, 588

"Bowery Blues," 472

"Brakeman on the Railroad," 479

"Brooklyn Bridge Blues," 513

"Brothers, The," 67-68

"Buddha Tells Us,' 472

"Cerrada Medellin Blues," 626

"cityCityCITY," 463, 466, 472

"Confession of Three Murders," 229

"Cop on the Beat, The," 32

Daisy Miller, 264

Desolation Angels, 527, 564, 586, 598, 599, 600, 626, 627, 628, 542, 659
   analysis of, 624-25
   publication of, 650

"Dharma Bum in Europe, A," 550

Dharma Bums, The, 496, 547, 570, 573, 575, 577, 579, 585, 587, 599, 619, 627, 640
   analysis of, 562-64
   publication of, 567
   reviews of, 576

Doctor Sax: The Myth of the Rainy Night, 26, 36, 234, 245, 263, 266, 297-98, 324, 391-410, 562,

563, 564, 567, 573, 576, 577, 579, 585, 587, 588, 599, 619, 627, 640
analysis of, 391-410
publication of, 570
reviews of, 588
Duluoz Legend, The (working title), 106, 109, 234, 420, 640, 679. *See also Vanity of Duluoz, The*
early writing, 32, 51, 66, 67-68, 70-71, 77, 84-85, 90-91, 92, 110
Escapade monthly column, 581
"Essentials of Spontaneous Prose, The," 453-54, 559
French novelette, 425
"Galloway" concept and working title, 139. *See also Town and the City, The*
"Go, Go, Go," 370
"Good Heart, A," 330
"hip generation" novel (beginning), 420
"History of Bop, The," 428
"Horn," 353
"Jazz of the Beat Generation," 465, 473
"Joan Crawford in the Fog," 364
"Lamb, No Lion," 559-60
Lonesome Traveler, 585, 610
"Long Night of Life, The," 471
"Love is Sixteen, Mary Cassidy," 426
"Lucien Midnight," 550, 562
"MacDougal Street Blues," 475
Maggie Cassidy, 588
analysis of, 429-39
review of, 599
"Memory Babe," 21, 559
evolution of, 573
"Mexican Girl, The," 474
Mexico City Blues, 516, 565, 570, 607, 639, 675
analysis of, 480-90
as religious poem, 490
"New York Scenes," 585
October in the Railroad Earth, 423-25

publication of, in *Evergreen Review,* 550
Old Angel Midnight, 593, 652, 675, 678
analysis of, 517-19
On the Road, 158, 175, 176, 190, 234, 245, 262, 265, 266, 269, 273, 324, 343, 368, 371, 495, 528, 554, 558, 559, 562, 563, 564, 567, 569, 570, 571, 573, 575, 582, 585, 587, 589, 591, 599, 604, 607, 624, 631, 641, 644, 653, 654, 668, 678, 695
analysis of, 343-48
book club sales of, 559
friends' criticism of, 415, 554
movie sale of, 559
publicity appearances for, 557
reviews of, 556
revision of, 352, 353, 356, 441
"Shrouded Stranger" in, 280
translations of, 559
"Origins of Joy in Poetry, The," 570
"Origins of the Beat Generation, The," 578
"Philosophy of the Beat Generation, The," 559-60
Pic, 695-96
Pull My Daisy:
film, 498, 583, 591, 603, 605
poem, 321, 583
reviews of, 585
script, 498
song, 583
"Rimbaud," 610
San Francisco Blues, 460
Satori in Paris, 667
analysis of, 660-62
Scripture of the Golden Eternity, The, 516-17, 610
Sea Is My Brother, The, 103, 104, 107, 139
"Shrouded Stranger" image, 278
in *On the Road,* 280
"Some of the Dharma," 463, 513, 668
Subterraneans, The, 533, 545, 559,

567, 568, 570, 571, 573, 586,
599, 604, 610, 613, 619, 646
analysis of, 445-51
reviews of, 567-68
"Trembling and Chaste," 477
Town and the City, The, 56, 110, 139,
162, 164, 184, 202, 205, 211,
230, 267, 281, 282, 294, 296,
570, 640, 659, 695
analysis of, 302-05, 308-19
British reception of, 320
commercial failure of, 319
criticism of, 229
friends depicted in, 302-03
friends' response to, 302
movie prospects for, 320
publicity for, 300
reviews of, 302
Tristessa, 532, 607, 610
analysis of, 477-79
"Vanishing American Hobo, The," 585
Vanity of Duluoz, The, 50, 58, 76,
139, 162, 672, 673, 674, 676,
677, 678, 679, 680, 681, 682,
683, 686
analysis of, 673-82
"Visions of Bill," 472
Visions of Cody, 291, 352, 562, 585,
593, 604, 610, 619, 668
analysis of, 370-87
friends' appraisal of, 414
rhythm in, 307
Visions of Gerard, 26, 501, 573, 575,
633, 649, 658
analysis of, 500-508
as cornerstore of *Duluoz Legend,*
601
reviews of, 648
"Visions of Lucien," 513
"Wake Up" ("Buddha Tells Us, The")
472
"Wine in the Railroad Earth." *See
October in the Railroad Earth*

Kerouac, Joan Haverty (second wife),
331, 332

financial demands of, 415, 620
marriage of, 333
mother-in-law problems of, 338,
339-40
nonsupport from Kerouac, 415,
471
pregnancy of, and birth of
daughter, 357, 370
Kerouac, Stella Sampas (third wife),
82, 423, 436, 636, 669-71
marriage of, to Kerouac, 670,
682-84, 688, 692, 693-98
Kesey, Ken, 653
Kierkegaard, Søren, *Fear and
Trembling,* 544
King, Wayne, 42
Kingsland, John, 117, 128, 142, 150,
454, 455-56
Kinsky, Leonid, 105
Kirouack, Clémentine Bernier
(grandmother), 22
Kirouack, Jean-Baptiste (grandfather),
22-23, 53
Kirouack, Joseph (uncle), 22, 27
Kirouack, Joseph Alcide Léon. *see*
Kéroack, Joseph Alcide Léon
Kline, Franz, 219, 423, 454-55, 579,
634
Knopf (Alfred), 467, 470, 471
Koestler, Arthur, 134
Konitz, Lee, 565
Korean War, 328-29
Korzybski, Alfred, *Science and Sanity,*
134
Kouchalakos, Pete, 47, 50
Koumantzelis, Billy, 317, 638, 690
Koumantzelis, John, 71, 83-84, 118
Koumantzelis, Nick, 690
Kramer, Jane, 683
Krassner, Lee, 590
Krim, Seymour, 658
Krupa, Gene, 41, 52, 91, 94

Lamantia, Philip, 366, 460, 469, 522,
566

Lamarr, Hedy, 56
Lamoureaux, Leon, 55
Lancaster, Bill, 140
Landesman, Jay, 321
Laughlin, James, 354, 545
Laurier Club (semipro team), 48, 83
Lautréamont (Ducasse, Isidore
    Lucien), 134
Lautrec, Henri de Toulouse, 60
LaVigne, Robert, 469, 528-29
Lawrence, D. H., 33, 353
    Rainbow, The, 353
Lawrence, Seymour, 471
Lax, Robert, 464, 583
Leadbelly (Ledbetter, Huddie), 112
Leahy, Frank, 48, 49, 50, 56, 74, 76
Leary, Timothy, 621, 630, 652
Lebris de Kerouac, François Louis
    Alexandre, 22
Lebris de Kerouac family, 21-22
Lee, William. See Burroughs, William
Lemire, Bernice, 623
Leslie, Al, 456, 582, 584, 604
Lévesque, Gabrielle. *See* Kéroack,
    Gabrielle Levesque
Lévesque, Josephine Jean
    (grandmother), 23
Lévesque, Louis (grandfather), 23
Lévesque family, 22, 53
Levine, Evelyn, 476
Lewis, Seward. *See* Kerouac, Jack
Liberty, 51
Lieberman, Billy, 213
Lion's Den, 76
Lipman, Mort, 102
Little, Brown, 463
Little, Lou, 49, 50, 56, 61, 62, 74, 75,
    76, 77-78, 88, 89, 101, 102
Livornese, Tom, 167, 207, 241, 275,
    293
Loewinsohn, Ron, 525
London, Jack, 71, 85, 99, 344-45
    "To Build a Fire," 434
Lord, Sterling, 462, 467-68, 472, 474,
    559, 690
Louÿs, Pierre, 135

Lowe, Jacques, 468
Lowell Public LIbrary, 50, 87, 94
Lowell Recreation Department
    W.P.A. baseball league, 41-42
Lowell Sun, 64, 81, 93, 94
Lowell Textile Institute, 96
Lower Depths, The (film), 60
Lull & Hartford, 48, 57
Lunceford, Jimmy, 66
Lupiano, Vincent, 333

McCarron, Mary, 51
McCarthy, Joseph R., 463, 464
MacClaine, Chris, 469
McClintock, Jack, 697
McClure, Michael, 460, 522, 529-30,
    613-14
McCorkle, Locke, 516
McCrea, Joel, 77
McDarrah, Fred, 583, 606
McDonald, Dwight, 585
McDonald, Gregory, 688-89
MacDonald, John, 33, 71, 82, 83, 93,
    123
McGuane, George, 93
McIlhennan, Hugh, 90
McKnight, Dean, 140
McLaughlin, James, 371
McNaughton, Duncan, 685
McNulty, Ray, 51, 52, 99
Mailer, Norman, 602, 648
    "White Negro, The," 206, 559
Maloff, Saul, 648, 658
Mann, Thomas, 211
    Magic Mountain, The, 126
Mansfield, Miss (librarian), 32, 71, 87
Markson, David, 622
Markson, Elaine, 622
Marlowe, Christopher, 185
Marmer, Mike, 94
Martinelli, Sherry, 455
Marx Brothers, 402, 407, 408
Mature, Victor, 73
Maxey, Bill, 110
Maxwell, Morty, 63, 66, 67

Mazur, Henry, 44, 102
MCA Management, 349, 357, 368, 369, 419
Melville, Herman, 72, 103, 108, 390, 406, 412
  Billy Bud, 107, 395
  Confidence Man, The, 437-38, 655
  Encantadas, The, 353
  Moby Dick, 408, 655
  Pierre, 497
Merrill, Robert, 528
Merry Pranksters, 653
Merton, Thomas, 464, 551
Metropolitan Life Insurance Company, 23
Mew, Charley, 364, 559
Michaux, Henri, 284
Micheline, Jack, 567
Mill, John Stuart, 76
Miller, Bob, 605, 613
Miller, Glenn, 53, 66, 77, 85
  "Moonlight Serenade," 51
  "Sunrise Serenade," 51
Miller, Henry, 548, 579, 613
Millstein, Gilbert, 423, 428, 556, 558, 565
Minton's (nightclub), 65
Mississippi Gene, 105
Molière (Poquelin, Jean Baptiste), 75
Monacchio, Tony, 221
Monk, Thelonius, 66, 121
Monroe, Marilyn, 620
Montagu, Ashley, 578
Montaigne, Leon, 46
Montcalm, Louis Joseph de, 22
Montgomery, Jack, 495-96
Montgomery, John, 552
Moore, Brue, 464
Moore, Douglas, 207
Morales, Adele, 234, 648
Morisette, Armand ("Father Spike"), 45-46, 86, 203, 302, 698
Morisette, Bob ("Iddyboy"), 40-41, 42, 282, 434
Morisette, Charlie, 37, 55, 106
Morley, Frank, 300, 338

Morold, 21
Morris, William, Agency, 332
Morton, Jelly Roll, 454
Moss, Howard, 214, 218
Müller, Dody James, 580, 582, 586
Murao, Shig, 552
Murphy, Cornelius "Connie," 71, 82, 83, 84, 85, 97, 101, 143, 232, 264, 427
Murphy, Dennis, 614
Murray, George, 82, 84, 85, 97, 232, 264

Nadeau, Leo, 33, 75, 99
Natanson, Leo, 213
Natanson, Phoebe, 213
Nation, The, 557
National Institute of Arts and Letters, 474, 479
Neurotica, 321
New American Reader, The, 474
New Directions, 369, 370
New Editions, 541, 552
Newman, Jerry, 124-25, 144, 339, 356, 412, 470, 621
New School for Social Research, 226, 227, 232, 241, 250, 262, 263, 269, 275
New Story magazine, 464, 467
Newsweek, 686
New World Writing, 453, 463, 465, 472-73
New York Public Library, 60
New York Times, The, 423, 428, 541, 556
Nichols, Luther, 552
Nick's (jazz club), 67
Nietzsche, Friedrich Wilhelm, 134, 434
Nin, Anaïs, 592
"920 club, The" (radio program), 41, 42, 73
Niven, David, 80, 605
Nosferatu, 397
Notre Dame University, 56

Noval, Ernie, 42

O'Connell, Helen, 42
O'Connell (priest), 45
O'Dea, Jim, 45, 53,71, 82-83, 84, 85,
    86, 87, 93, 99, 100, 104, 121-22
Oedipus Rex, 449, 450
O'Hara, Frank, 592
Old Glory (sea cook), 99-100, 101
Olson, Charles, 460, 589-90
    "As the Dead Prey Upon Us," 559
Olsted, Bob, 64, 67
Omar (halfwit), 34
O'Neil, Paul, 606
O'Neill, Eugene, 232
Orlovsky, Julius, 529
Orlovsky, Lafcadio, 529, 531, 533, 570
Orlovsky, Peter, 469, 519, 529, 574
Ouellette, Roger, 44
Owl Print Shop, 45

Paramount Theater, 66
Paris Review, 474, 684, 685, 690
Parker, Charlie "Bird," 66, 112, 205,
    207, 381, 386, 412, 442, 461,
    488, 489, 490
Parker, Charlotte, 111, 131, 698
Parker, Frankie Edith. *See* Kerouac,
    Frankie Edith Parker
Parkinson, Thomas, 494
Pavano, Nanda, 667, 670
Pawtucketville Social Club, 36, 71
Payne, Tom, 588
Penn, William, *Maxims*, 50
Perse, St.-John, *Anabase*, 353
Phelps, Robert, 648
Phi Gamma Delta, 77
Phillips, Flip, 167
Pioneer Club, 81
Pippin, Gene, 185, 213, 469
Pius VI, 22
Plato, 76
Plimpton, George, 685
Plomteau (train conductor), 440

Podhoretz, Norman, 602
    Culture of Appeasement, The, 557
Poe, Edgar Allan, "Ulalume," 384
Pollock, Jackson, 219, 423, 454, 455
Poore, Charles, 658
Pope, Alexander, 135
Porter, Arabelle, 453
Porter, Cole, "Begin the Beguine," 85
Pound, Ezra, 432, 455
    Cantos, 475
Powell, Mel, 102
Pozo, Chano, 366
S.S. *President Harding*, 357-58, 360
Presley, Elvis, 530
Prometheus, 86
Proust, Marcel, 211, 363, 417, 424,
    426, 502
    Cities of the Plain, 353
Purcell, Duncan, 113, 126, 277
Pure Land (symbol and image), 26,
    69, 478, 491
Puritans, 15
Putterman, Zev, 578
Pyne, Joe, 50-51, 60

Quinn, Billy, 60, 61

Rabelais, François, *Crazy Book, The*,
    283
Random House, 320
Rapinic, John, 612
Rathbone Basil, 77
realism (literary style), 266
Red Sox, 46
Reel, Pat, 100
Rembrandt (van Rijn), 548
Review, The (Lowell High School
    magazine), 54
Rex Ballroom 5, 152
Rexroth, Kenneth, 465, 469, 472, 491,
    514, 526, 553, 561
Rexroth, Marthe, 525
Rhodes, David, 67
Rich, Buddy, 41

Rimbaud, Arthur, 120, 126, 155, 432, 433

   Collected Poems, 134

Rittick, Ray, 688

Rivers, Larry, 219

Roberge, "Skippy," 46

S.S. *Robert Treat Paine*, 133

Romains, Jules, 59

"Roncho the Modmo," 104

Rondeau, Bob, 40, 42

Roosevelt, Eleanor, 105

Roosevelt, Franklin D., 105, 380

Roseman (doctor), 665-66, 668

Rosenberg, Anton, 441

Rosenberg (Navy psychiatrist), 106

Rosset, Barney, 528, 590, 668

Rouleau, Beatrice, 30-31, 88

"Round Table" (Algonquin), 84

Royal Roost (jazz club), 207

Rubin, Jerry, 668-69

Ruiter, Charlie, 50, 51

Russell, Vicki, 135, 205

Rutgers University, 76

Rynne, Elmer, 47-48, 57, 302

SAC Club, 636

Saijo, Albert, 604, 613

St. Benedict's Preparatory School, 76

St. John's Preparatory School, 61

St. Louis, Ray, 51, 52

St. Louis Browns, 46

Sakallarios, Tommy, 94

Salvas, Roland "Salvey," 34, 42, 54, 64, 73, 74, 78, 81, 302

Samaras, Demosthenes "Sam," 32

Sampas, Charlie, 81-82, 87, 164

   mother of, 81

Sampas, Nicky, 639

Sampas, Sebastian "Sam," 32, 71-72, 73, 78-79, 81-84, 85-86, 87, 92, 93, 94, 97, 101-2, 105, 442

   death of, 142

   "Friends of Sam," 84-86

Sampas, Stella. *See* Kerouac, Stella Sampas

Sampas, Tony, 637, 638, 667

Sandburg, Carl, 319, 353, 394

Sanders, Ed, 690

San Francisco Examiner, 552

Sargent, Frank, 49

Saroyan, Aram, 685

   "The Driver: Reflections on Jack Kerouac," 290

Saroyan, William, 72, 81, 91, 212, 303, 467, 529

   Human Comedy, The, 127

Sartre, Jean-Paul, 467

Saturday Review, 467

Savoy (nightclub), 65

Scheuer, Joe, 594

Schoenberg, Arnold, 134

"Scribbler's Club," 32, 71

Scribner's (Charles), 369

Sentinelists, 26

sex, in Kerouac's group, 150-51, 154, 475.

   See also individuals

sexual revolution, 137, 519

Shadow, The, 33, 34-35, 80, 96, 392, 407

Shakespeare, William, 33, 73, 85, 92, 120, 131, 135, 283, 363, 371, 372, 373, 289, 417, 459, 465, 481, 501

   As You Like It, 407

   Hamlet, 101, 479

   Henry V, 501, 501 n

   King Lear, 101, 477

   Macbeth, 101

   "Seven Ages of Man," 272

Shaw, Artie, 66, 85, 300

Shearing, George, 251, 347

Shedd Park (Boston), 57

Shelley Percy Bysshe, 71

   Adonais, 86

Sheresky, Dick, 63, 67, 88

Sheresky, Jacky, 66

Shore, Dinah, 101

Shostakovich, Dmitri, 134

   Fifth Symphony, 103

"Silent Madonna," 454

Simpson, Louis, 354, 369
Sinatra, Frank, 42, 66, 77, 85, 538
Singer, Phil, 665
Sloan, James Park, 391
Smart, Christopher, 475
Smith, Grover, 133
Smith, Larry, 641, 648, 654
Smith, Luxey, 39-40
Smith, Paul, 615
Smith, Tsuneko, 654
Snyder, Gary, 459, 460, 491, 492,
    495-96, 519, 523, 587, 644
  Myths and Texts, 516
Snyder, Thea, 523, 565
Snyder, Tooey, 315
Socinus, 276
Solomon, Carl, 166, 284, 354, 357,
    361, 367-69, 391, 414, 416
Sorota, Joe, 48, 49
Sorrells, Lois, 599, 648
Spanier, Muggsy, 65
Spender, Stephen, *World Within
    World*, 356
Spengler, Oswald, 203-04, 276, 363
    392, 423, 546
  Decline of the West, The, 87, 134,
    376, 383, 390, 405, 501
Spiegel, Adam, 90
Spillane, Mickey, 368
Spotlight, 24, 373
Stanwyck, Barbara, 77
Stalin, Josef, 87
Stalin-Hitler Pact, 87
Stein, Bob, 350
Stein, Gertrude, 373
Steinbeck, John, 373
Stendhal (Beyle, Marie Henri), 143
  Red and the Black, The, 481
Stern, Gerd, 441, 469, 616
Sterne, Laurence, *Tristram Shandy*,
    447
Stewart, Slam, 112
Stollmack, Burt, 63, 69, 88
Stone, Irving, *Lust for Life*, 59
Stravinsky, Igor, 134
Stringham, Ed, 223, 245, 349, 558

Sublette, Al, 364-65, 416, 460, 469,
    520, 559
subterraneans, 441
  See also Kerouac, Jack,
    Subterraneans, The
Sullivan, Bill, 76
Sullivan, Raymond, 51
Sullivan Printers, 45, 56, 60, 76
Suzuki, D. T., 579
Sweeten, Bill, 111
Symphony Sid, 207, 292

Tallman, Warren, 658
  "Kerouac's Sound," 447
Tamiroff, Akim, 105
Tatum, Art, 112, 167
Taylor, Jimmy, 69
Teddy Boys, 548
Tellinghast, Charles, 67
Temko, Allan, 69, 168, 191, 294, 297,
    300, 494
Tercero, Dave, 391, 425
Tercero, Esperanza, 476-77
Terkel, Studs, 387
Thiele, Bob, 565
Thomas, Jimmy, 77
Thompson, Lucky, 206
Thoreau, Henry David, 71, 75, 211,
    274, 383, 387, 421, 459
  Walden, 387, 451, 565
Tierney, Gene, 59
Times Square, 77, 84
Tolstoy, Leo:
  Anna Karenina, 58
  War and Peace, 58, 390
Tome (Maryland preparatory school),
    61
Tomson, Bill, 288
Tormé, Mel, 207
Trilling, Diana, 284
Trilling, Lionel, 143, 284
Tristan, 21, 58
Tristano, Lenny, 167
Trojan War, 60
truth, literary theory of, 279

Tschaikowsky, Peter Ilich, 108
Tully, Ed, 71, 82, 83
Twain, Mark, 344, 373
　Huckleberry Finn, 408
Twardowicz, Anne, 647
Twardowicz, Stanley, 21, 590, 622, 641, 683
Twist, Oliver, 106

Uhl, Ed, 290
Union Pacific, 77
U.S. Merchant Marine, 99-101, 104, 107, 440
U.S. Navy, Naval Air Force, 93, 103-6
U.S.O. Clubs, 101, 108
Updike, John, 689-90
Uronovitz, Bernie, 528

Valjean, Jean, 58
Van Doren, Mark, 138, 211, 267, 284, 358, 464-65
Van Gogh, Vincent, 59, 548
Van Metre, Peter, 441
Vaughan, Sarah, 207
Vendée, 22
Vico, Giovanni Battista, 134
Vidal, Gore, 391, 444, 453, 557
Viking Press, 440, 441, 453, 472, 474, 495, 528, 540, 541, 558
Village Vanguard, 565
Vivaldi, Antonio, 426
Virginia City, 60
Voltaire (Arouet, François Marie), 75
von Hartz, Francesca, 369
von Stroheim, Erich, 397

Wagner, Gerry, 662
Wakefield, Dick, 91
Waters, Muddy, 538
Watts, Alan, 519
Weaver, Helen, 534, 560
Weaver, Raymond, 139

Weber, Brom, 226, 228, 229, 231, 232, 243, 282
Weber, Hugo, 589
Wechsler, James, 578
Welch, Denton, 322
Welch, Lew, 604, 612
Welles, Orson, 92
Wells, Dickie, 65
Wells, H. G., 134
　Outline of History, The, 50, 94
West End Bar, 77, 103, 113
Whalen, Philip, 460, 491, 514, 549, 604
Whitaker, Dave, 552
White, Ed, 79, 170, 191, 256, 262, 267, 278, 293, 294, 295, 321, 323, 356, 416, 427, 442, 443, 446-47, 453, 456, 464, 629, 652
Whitman, Walt, 67, 68, 70, 72, 390
　"Song of the Open Road," 344
　Specimen Days, 353
Wickstrom, George, 456
Wilbur, Richard, 571
Wilentz, Ted, 631
Will, Len, 90
S.S. *William Caruth*, 440, 441
Williams, Tennessee, 467
Williams, Vicki, 77
Williams, William Carlos, 369, 453-54, 474, 541
　"To Waken an Old Lady," 501
Wilson, Edmund, 472
Wingate, John, 560
Witt-Diamant, Ruth, 528
Wizard of Oz, The, 408
Wobblies, 496
Wolf, Donald, 66
Wolfe, James, 22
Wolfe, Thomas, 67, 72, 76, 77, 87, 91, 102, 126, 146, 155, 164, 211, 232, 275, 304, 352, 421, 424, 431, 534
　Look Homeward, Angel, 535
　Of Time and the River, 84, 101, 345, 437
　You Can't Go Home Again, 126

Wolfean, definition of, 155

Wong, Victor, 613, 614

Woollcott, Alexander, 84

World's Fair, 67, 75, 91

World-Telegram, 64

World War II, 58, 95, 97, 99-100, 103-9, 114
   Pearl Harbor invasion, 92

W.P.A. 46, 57, 81

W.P.A. baseball league, 41-42, 46, 92

Wright, Richard, 467

Wyn, A. A., 354, 368, 369, 370, 389, 429, 440, 452

Wyse, Seymour, 65, 66, 112, 124-25, 339, 350, 353, 381, 412

Yablansky, Lewis, 691

Yale University, 67

Yeats, William Butler, 353, 373, 377, 382
   Vision, A, 134

YMCA, 94, 95

Yokeley, Sara, 300, 320-21

Young Buddhist Association, 496-97

Young, Céline, 114

Young, Lester "Prez," 65, 66, 112, 380, 381, 426

Ziegfeld Follies, 59

Zoukis, Chris, 50

Zsedely, Miklos, 650-51